The SCRIBNER ENCYCLOPEDIA *of*
AMERICAN LIVES

THE SCRIBNER ENCYCLOPEDIA OF AMERICAN LIVES

The *Scribner Encyclopedia of American Lives* presents original scholarly biographies of notable Americans.

The series consists of two branches. Chronologically organized, one branch includes volumes on figures who have died since 1981. Each concise summary of achievements ranges from 1,000 to 6,000 words and usually includes a photo of the individual. Also detailed, wherever possible, are family background; education; names of spouses with marriage and divorce dates; addresses of residences; and cause of death and place of burial. Volumes include:

Volume 1: 1981–1985
Volume 2: 1986–1990
Volume 3: 1991–1993
Volume 4: 1994–1996
Volume 5: 1997–1999
Volume 6: 2000–2002

The second branch is the *Scribner Encyclopedia of American Lives: Thematic Series*. These subject-oriented sets extend the coverage of the original series to high-interest fields of endeavor or periods in history. In order to appropriately document the selected subject, profiles cover both living and deceased individuals. Volumes include:

Sports Figures
The 1960s

A cumulative index for both branches appears in thematic volumes after Sports Figures and in chronological volumes after Volume 5.

The SCRIBNER ENCYCLOPEDIA *of*

AMERICAN LIVES

VOLUME SIX

2000-2002

KENNETH T. JACKSON
EDITOR IN CHIEF

KAREN MARKOE
GENERAL EDITOR

ARNOLD MARKOE
EXECUTIVE EDITOR

CHARLES SCRIBNER'S SONS®

New York • Detroit • San Diego • San Francisco • Cleveland • New Haven, Conn. • Waterville, Maine • London • Munich

THOMSON

GALE

The Scribner Encyclopedia of American Lives, Volume Six

Kenneth T. Jackson, editor in chief

For permission to use material from this product, submit your request via Web at http://www.gale-edit.com/permissions, or you may download our Permissions Request form and submit your request by fax or mail to:

Permissions Department
The Gale Group, Inc.
27500 Drake Rd.
Farmington Hills, MI 48331-3535
Permissions Hotline:
248-699-8006 or 800-877-4253, ext. 8006
Fax: 248-699-8074 or 800-762-4058

Library of Congress Cataloging-in-Publication Data

The Scribner encyclopedia of American lives / Kenneth T. Jackson, editor in chief ; Karen Markoe, general editor ; Arnold Markoe, executive editor.
    p.   cm.
    Includes bibliographical references and index.
    ISBN 0-684-80492-1 (v. 1: alk. paper)
    ISBN 0-684-31292-1 (v. 6: alk. paper)
    Contents: v. 1. 1981–1985
    United States—Biography—Dictionaries. I. Jackson, Kenneth T.
II. Markoe, Karen. III. Markoe, Arnold.
CT213.S37   1998
920.073—dc21   98-33793
                                                       CIP

Printed in the United States of America
1 3 5 7 9 11 13 15 17 19 20 18 16 14 12 10 8 6 4 2

The paper in this publication meets the minimum requirements of the American National Standard for Information Services—Permanence of Paper for Printed Library Materials, ANSI Z39.48–1992.

EDITORIAL *and* PRODUCTION STAFF

Project Editor
NEIL SCHLAGER

Associate Editor
VANESSA TORRADO-CAPUTO

Copy Editors, Researchers
JANET BALE   TERESA BARENSFELD   CYNTHIA GIUDICI   HARRABETH HAIDUSEK
JUDSON KNIGHT   HENRY KRAWITZ   JOSH LAUER   TARA MANTEL
MARCIA MERRYMAN MEANS   MADELINE PERRI   SUSAN SCHARPF

Proofreaders
DENISE EVANS   KYUNG LIM KALASKY

Editorial Assistant
KELLY BAISELEY

Imaging
LEZLIE LIGHT   MICHAEL LOGUSZ   DEAN DAUPHINAIS   DAN NEWELL
MARY GRIMES   LEITHA ETHERIDGE-SIMS   DAVE OBLENDER

Designer
BRADY MCNAMARA

Compositor
IMPRESSIONS BOOK AND JOURNAL SERVICES, INC.

Project Manager
SARAH FEEHAN

Editorial Director
JOHN FITZPATRICK

Publisher
FRANK MENCHACA

PREFACE

This sixth volume of the *Scribner Encyclopedia of American Lives (SEAL)* contains the biographies of 334 persons who left their imprint on history and who died between 1 January 2000 and 31 December 2002. With its publication, the number of subjects in the *SEAL* series increases to 2,296. Future volumes will cover persons who died in subsequent three-year periods. Wherever possible, each biography includes the names and occupations of parents, the number of siblings, the names of spouses and dates of marriages, the number of children, places of residence, cause of death, and place of burial. The authors of the essays have also endeavored to discuss the formative influences on the subjects and the lasting significance of their achievements.

The 217 contributors to this volume are biographers, journalists, academics, and others with a passion for history who possess well-honed skills in research and writing. Many have written entries for earlier volumes in the *SEAL* series. These authors have been resourceful in completing their biographies, often conducting original research and interviewing family members and professional associates of their subjects to gain previously unrecorded insights.

The *Scribner Encyclopedia of American Lives* has several distinguishing characteristics. First, almost every entry in this volume is accompanied by a photograph of the subject. Second, each biography alerts readers to the significance of the subject's life at a glance by encapsulating his or her most important achievements in the first paragraph. Third, a cumulative index listing the subjects by occupation is printed in the back matter of every volume. Fourth, all the authors are identified at the end of the book along with their institutional or occupational affiliations and a listing of the articles for which they are responsible.

The process of selecting a few hundred subjects from the many millions of Americans who died between 2000 and 2002 necessarily involved many specialists who helped us decide which persons will likely have the most enduring legacies. The final list, however, is solely the responsibility of the editors, who weighed the relative significance of politicians and poets, chemists and criminals, business leaders and baseball players, and actors and authors. The subjects represent diverse races and ethnic backgrounds, some born to privilege, others to poverty. Many were famous during their lifetimes, a few were infamous, and some were quietly important, but all the persons included in this book lived extraordinary lives, winning fame on the battlefield or in the laboratory, writing great books, governing cities or states, creating new business concepts, or entertaining the multitude.

The subjects in this volume are drawn from many professions, including the writers Eudora Welty, Gwendolyn Brooks, and Stephen Ambrose; politicians Mike Mansfield, John V. Lindsay, Carl Albert, and Paul Wellstone; sports figures Ted Williams, Dale Earnhardt, and Johnny Unitas; performing artists Isaac Stern, Chet Atkins, and Perry Como; actors Walter Matthau, Anthony Quinn, and Carroll O'Connor; military leaders Elmo R. Zumwalt and Benjamin O. Davis, Jr.; and media moguls Katharine Graham, Walter Annenberg, and Roone Arledge. Others memorialized herein include Charles Schulz, the cartoonist who created *Peanuts;* Ann Landers, whose practical advice column reached tens of millions of readers every day; Stephen Jay Gould, who combined brilliance as a paleontologist and evolutionary biologist with an extraordinary ability to write for ordinary citizens; Byron White, who went from All-America football player in college to the United States Supreme Court; Anne Morrow Lindbergh, who married the most famous person in the world and then endured tragedy before becoming an accomplished author in her own right; Steve Allen, who created the format for popular late-night talk shows; and Milton Berle, who was perhaps the most important figure in television at its transformative time in American history.

This volume of *SEAL* encompasses those who died on 11 September 2001, the day when terrorists took over and crashed four giant commercial airliners in a coordinated attack on New York City and Washington, D.C. More than three thousand persons, all but nineteen of them innocent, died in the carnage that morning. Three of the victims are included in this volume: David Alger, the chief executive officer of Fred Alger Management, who was in his office in the north tower at the time of impact; Father Mychal Judge, the beloved chaplain of the New York Fire Department (FDNY) who was officially listed as victim no. 1 in the tragedy; and First Deputy Fire Commissioner William Feehan, a legend among his fellow firefighters, the first man in the history of the FDNY to hold every rank in the department, and the highest ranking firefighter ever to die in the line of duty in the United States. This volume is dedicated to all those who perished in the worst terrorist event in American history.

As is the case in any large-scale research effort, *SEAL* depends upon the hard work and cooperation of hundreds of persons. We especially acknowledge Neil Schlager and Vanessa Torrado-Caputo at Schlager Group for their effective oversight of the administration and copy editing. As always, we recognize Richard H. Gentile for invaluable help of every kind, including pulling together the first master list of potential biographies and offering many suggestions to improve the occupations index. Similarly, William Gargan for literary and Peter Brancazio for scientific subjects provided thoughtful and extensive counsel. Finally, we wish to acknowledge the exceptional support of Charles Scribner's Sons, especially publisher Frank Menchaca, editorial director John Fitzpatrick, and associate editor Sara Feehan. We thank them all.

Kenneth T. Jackson, Editor in Chief
Karen E. Markoe, General Editor
Arnold Markoe, Executive Editor

CONTENTS

PREFACE   *vii*

BIOGRAPHIES, A–Z   *1*

DIRECTORY OF CONTRIBUTORS   *589*

OCCUPATIONS INDEX, VOLUMES 1–6 and
    THEMATIC VOLUMES   *597*

ALPHABETICAL LIST OF SUBJECTS, VOLUMES 1–6 and
    THEMATIC VOLUMES   *681*

The SCRIBNER ENCYCLOPEDIA *of*

AMERICAN LIVES

A

AALIYAH (*b.* 16 January 1979 in Brooklyn, New York City; *d.* 25 August 2001 in Abaco, Bahamas), sultry, mysterious, rhythm-and-blues pop singer who helped usher in the stuttering production style of hip-hop and urban soul of the late 1990s.

Aaliyah was born Aaliyah Dana Haughton and was one of two children born to Michael Haughton and Diane (Hankerson) Haughton. She was known simply as "Aaliyah," meaning "highest, most exalted one" in Arabic. When Aaliyah was two years old, the family moved from New York City to Detroit. Aaliyah began singing in church after watching her mother, an amateur singer. She made her acting debut in 1986 as an orphan in the Gesu Catholic School production of *Annie* and then had a supporting role in their production of *Hello, Dolly!* In 1989 she won an appearance on the television show *Star Search,* performing the song "My Funny Valentine," which she dedicated to her mother.

In 1991 Aaliyah's uncle, Barry Hankerson, introduced her to his wife, the soul singer Gladys Knight, who asked Aaliyah to perform a five-day stint with her in Las Vegas, Nevada. Knight took Aaliyah under her wing and coached her on how to make the most of her time on stage. Aaliyah stated that Knight taught her "how to work the audience and make them have fun." Two years later, Aaliyah entered the Detroit High School for the Fine and Performing Arts. In 1994 Hankerson introduced Aaliyah to R. Kelly (Robert Kelly), a singer-producer on his Blackground records label. Aaliyah signed a record contract, and Kelly began to produce her debut album, *Age Ain't Nothin' But a Number,* which was released in June 1994. It spawned two Top Ten singles—"Back and Forth" and "At Your Best (You Are Love)."

On 31 August 1994, fifteen-year-old Aaliyah and twenty-seven-year-old Kelly secretly married; however, Aaliyah's parents had a Michigan judge annul the union five months later. By that fall Aaliyah's debut album had sold more than one million copies. She returned to high school and majored in dance. Aaliyah also began working on her sophomore album with the innovative producer Timbaland (Tim Mosely), who was known for using the syncopated, fractured, rhythm tracks that became the standard for urban pop of the late 1990s.

In August 1996 Aaliyah released her second album, *One in a Million.* She had another Top Ten hit with the first track, "If Your Girl Only Knew." By that time, Aaliyah was gaining a reputation for her smooth, passionate singing, as well as for sultry, streetwise videos that became a staple on the cable television channel MTV. By June 1997, the same month she graduated from the Detroit High School for the Fine and Performing Arts, her second album had sold over two million copies. That year Aaliyah also recorded a song for the soundtrack to the film *Anastasia,* and the next year she recorded one for the Eddie Murphy comedy *Dr. Doo-*

little. She made a cameo appearance in that film, and her song "Are You That Somebody?" became a number-one rhythm-and-blues (R&B) hit.

Aaliyah began work on her third album with the producers Timbaland, Missy Elliott, and Slick Rick, but stopped when she got the opportunity to star in the film *Romeo Must Die,* hiring an acting and vocal coach to train for her role. In 1999 she contributed songs to movie soundtracks for the drama *Music of the Heart* and the comedy *Next Friday.* When *Romeo Must Die* was released in March of 2000, Aaliyah received glowing reviews for her intense performance. She also contributed four new songs to the soundtrack. One song, "Try Again," set a record as the first song to hit number one on the *Billboard* Hot 100 without a commercial release. That September the video for that song won two MTV Music Video Awards, for best female video and best video from a film. Aaliyah also became romantically involved with the Roc-A-Fella Records founder Damon Dash.

In February 2001 Aaliyah earned a Grammy nomination for best female R&B vocal performance for "Try Again." Soon after, she went to Australia to begin work on her next film, based on the Anne Rice novel *Queen of the Damned.* Aaliyah finished shooting the film in the spring, then resumed recording her next album, titled *Aaliyah.* Once again, she worked with the producer Timbaland. The album was released on 17 July 2001, and the first single, "We Need a Resolution," hit the Top Forty.

Aaliyah worked during the month of August 2001 shooting videos for her album so that she could spend the fall shooting a new film. She finished a video for the song "More Than a Woman" in California, then flew to Abaco Island in the Bahamas to shoot one for "Rock the Boat." On 25 August 2001, after the shoot was completed, Aaliyah chartered a private plane to take her and her entourage to Miami. The plane crashed on takeoff at Marsh Harbor International Airport, killing Aaliyah and the eight other passengers.

The hip-hop community was devastated by the news. Tributes were presented to Aaliyah at the Soul Train Awards and MTV's 2001 Video Music Awards. Aaliyah's funeral was held in Saint Ignatius Loyola Catholic Church on New York City's Upper East Side. Thousands of fans cheered in tribute as a horse-drawn glass carriage brought the casket to the church. Aaliyah was interred at a mausoleum in the Ferncliff Cemetery in Westchester County, New York.

By September, Aaliyah's self-titled album topped the *Billboard* 200 albums chart and went on to sell almost three million copies. The completed video for "Rock the Boat" was released at the end of the month. In October her brother, Rashaad, helped complete Aaliyah's performance

Aaliyah, 2001. AP/WIDE WORLD PHOTOS

in the film *Queen of the Damned* by adding vocal touch-ups. The film was released in February 2002, just as Aaliyah was nominated for two Grammy Awards for best female R&B vocal performance and best R&B album. Her single "More Than a Woman" became a Top Twenty hit.

In December 2002 a new album, called *I Care 4 U,* was released, containing some of Aaliyah's biggest hits, as well as six previously unreleased tracks. It spawned the Top Forty hit "Miss You." A video tribute was compiled for the song using artists prominent in the hip-hop community. Aaliyah's family donated a portion of the proceeds from *I Care 4 U* to the Aaliyah Memorial Foundation, which benefits the Revlon/UCLA Women's Cancer Research Program and the Memorial Sloan Kettering Cancer Center in Manhattan.

During her brief career, Aaliyah sold more than ten million albums and helped create a style of hip-hop music that combined sultry R&B vocals with syncopated, stuttering rhythms. She brought a subtle, sexy self-assurance to her music and her acting performances. Aaliyah's sensual, funky music took hip-hop off the streets and brought it closer to the heart.

★

Articles with information about Aaliyah and her career appeared in *Vibe* (Aug. 2001), *Jet* (Oct. 2001), *Ebony* (Nov. 2001), the *Chicago Sun Times* (5 June 2002), the *New York Post* (1 Dec. 2002), and *Rolling Stone* (Dec. 2002). Obituaries are in the *New York Times* and *USA Today* (both 27 Aug. 2001).

TIM MARTIN CROUSE

ABBOTT, Jack Henry (*b.* 21 January 1944 in Oscoda, Michigan; *d.* 10 February 2002 in Alden, New York), author who spent nearly his entire adult life in prison and whose correspondence with the author Norman Mailer was published under the title *In the Belly of the Beast: Letters From Prison* (1981).

Jack Henry Abbott being escorted by federal marshals in New Orleans, Louisiana, September 1981. AP/WIDE WORLD PHOTOS

Abbott, whose given first name was Rufus, was the son of a prostitute. He spent most of his early years in numerous foster homes and had his first encounter with the criminal justice system when he was sent to the Utah State Industrial School for Boys at the age of twelve. Abbott was released after he turned eighteen as an adult, but within six months was arrested for writing a fraudulent check and sent to the Utah State Penitentiary in Salt Lake City in 1963. Three years later, during a prison brawl, he stabbed another prisoner to death, and his sentence was extended.

Abbott would have been merely another prisoner if not for his letter in 1977 to the author Norman Mailer, then writing *The Executioner's Song*. The book focused on the Utah death-row inmate Gary Gilmore, who had received considerable media attention by requesting the death penalty. Abbott told Mailer that, as a career prisoner himself, he could offer insights regarding the effect prison had on the human psyche. Abbott and Mailer soon began a correspondence, and Mailer visited Abbott in prison. Fascinated and impressed by Abbott's obvious intelligence, his revolutionary politics, and his visceral descriptions of the prisoners' violent lives, Mailer used his literary renown to get excerpts from Abbott's letters published in the prestigious *New York Review of Books* in 1980. In 1981 Random House published Abbott's reflections on prison life as *In the Belly of the Beast: Letters from Prison*.

Mailer then led an effort to help Abbott receive early parole. He wrote a letter to the Utah Board of Pardons supporting Abbott's release, and promised that he would take him under his wing in New York City. By the time Abbott was paroled in June 1981 and had arrived in New York to stay at a halfway house in the Bowery, his book was on its way to becoming a best-seller. Terrence Des Pres in the *New York Times Book Review* called *In the Belly of the Beast* "awesome, brilliant, perversely ingenuous," and noted that "as an articulation of penal nightmare it is completely compelling."

True to his word, Mailer hired Abbott as his personal secretary. The combination of his writing talent, his association with Mailer, and his dark and troubled past made Abbott a darling of the New York literary set. Compared by critics to such prison authors as the Marquis de Sade, Jean Genet, and Eldridge Cleaver, Abbott became an object of media attention. He appeared on *Good Morning America* and was the subject of numerous magazine articles, including those in *People* and *Rolling Stone*.

Abbott was required to stay eight weeks in the halfway house before he could officially begin parole and live alone. In July 1981, about six weeks after he arrived in New York, Abbott and two female companions went to a twenty-four-hour restaurant called Binibon. When he was not allowed to use the restaurant's employee restroom, Abbott got into an argument with Richard Adan, an aspiring actor who was working there as a waiter. When the two stepped outside the restaurant, Abbott fatally stabbed Adan and then fled—but not before taunting the dying man, according to a witness.

Soon after the stabbing, Abbott kept a dinner appointment and returned to the halfway house for money. He then left New York, but was apprehended two months later in Morgan City, Louisiana. Abbott was both remorseful, calling the homicide a "tragic misunderstanding" during his murder trial in New York, and remorseless, saying that the victim's life "was not worth a dime" during the civil trial brought later by Adan's widow. Abbott was convicted of manslaughter and sentenced to fifteen years to life in prison. Mailer's only public response to the incident was the comment, "Tragic." However, the writer Jerzy Kosinski, who had also supported Abbott, noted, "I feel guilty in a way." The media criticized the "liberal naïveté" of Mailer and others who had supported Abbott as their own "pet convict," and called Abbott "brilliant" but "dysfunctional," noting that his statements at the murder trial proved that he refused to accept responsibility for his actions.

Serving time at Attica Correctional Facility in upstate New York, Abbott wrote another book, *My Return* (1987), with Naomi Zack. In addition to numerous essays and letters, the book included Abbott's version of Adan's murder in the form of a play. *My Return* did not receive the support that Abbott's first effort had garnered, with one reviewer calling it "pretentious and boring."

In 1990 Adan's widow, who had filed a wrongful death suit against Abbott, was awarded $7.5 million as the result of the civil trial. The award included the $100,000 that Abbott had earned for writing *In the Belly of the Beast*. Abbott represented himself during the trial.

Despite the fact that, as a high-profile prisoner who could be targeted by others, he had been placed in "protective custody," Abbott was attacked in March 2002. So bad were his wounds that he required surgery, and spent three days in the Erie County Medical Center. The attack had come only twelve days after Abbott's lawyer filed court papers on two Attica corrections officers, claiming that the guards harassed him and denied him privileges. Although Abbott maintained that the attack was a result of the court filing, his lawsuit was dismissed. He appealed the judgment and filed another lawsuit, claiming that the State of New York and the prison had failed to protect him adequately.

In June 2000 Abbott was moved to Wende Correctional Facility in Alden, New York, and taken out of protective custody. On 10 February 2002 he hanged himself in his cell using a bed sheet and a shoelace. Although his lawyer and his sister, Francis Amador, questioned whether Abbott's death was truly a suicide, the noted coroner Cyril Wecht, working independently in Pittsburgh, confirmed the original autopsy report. Abbott's body was cremated and his ashes flown to his sister in Seattle.

Attaining literary fame and a moment of freedom in the early 1980s, Abbott was a self-taught intellectual who read voraciously and could talk politics, philosophy, and religion. He was also a talented writer, whose insightful, literary look into prison life won wide acclaim. Noting that he "never knew a man who had a worse life," Mailer, in a statement after Abbott's suicide, said, "His life was tragic from beginning to end." Abbott, Mailer said, "left a bomb crater of lost possibilities for many," not only for "one young man full of promise" on whom he "brought a deadly tragedy," but also for himself. Adan's widow, on the other hand, was less nuanced in her appraisal. Informed of Abbott's death, she said, "I am happy he will not kill again."

★

Both of Abbott's books—*In the Belly of the Beast: Letters from Prison* (1981) and *My Return* (1987), with Naomi Zack—are autobiographical in nature. Obituaries are in the *Los Angeles Times* and *New York Times* (both 11 Feb. 2002), and *Washington Post* (12 Feb. 2002).

DAVID PETECHUK

ABEL, Sidney Gerald ("Sid") (*b.* 22 February 1918 in Melville, Saskatchewan, Canada; *d.* 8 February 2000 in Farmington Hills, Michigan), National Hockey League Hall of Fame player, coach, and broadcaster for more than thirty-two years with the Detroit Red Wings.

Abel was one of six children born to Daniel Abel, a farmer who also owned a moving business, and Etta Abel. As was typical of many small prairie towns, the winter activities in Abel's hometown of Melville, Saskatchewan, revolved around the local ice-skating rink. Young Abel took advantage of every opportunity to play hockey. His tenacious approach to the game greatly impressed "Goldie" Smith, the town's postmaster, who was also a scout for the Detroit Red Wings.

Advancing through the local minor-league system, Abel in 1936 graduated to the Saskatoon Wesleys Junior "A" team, the alumni of which include Hall of Fame icons Chuck Rayner, "Snuffy" Smith, and Doug Bentley. This sextet was sufficiently stacked with talent to take them to the Memorial Cup playoffs.

Goldie Smith was so taken by Abel's burgeoning talents that he arranged for him to attend Detroit's training camp in the fall of 1937. At that time, however, the nineteen-year-old carried only 155 pounds on a five-foot, eleven-inch frame, and manager Jack Adams doubted that he could stand the rigors of major league play. Refusing the offer to apprentice on the Michigan-Ontario circuit, Abel instead joined the Flin Flon, Manitoba, Bombers Senior team. There, he helped his squad to a berth in the all-Canadian Allan Cup playoffs.

Sid Abel. ASSOCIATED FEATURES, INC.

The next fall, Abel attended the Red Wings' training camp once more. This time he was offered his first professional hockey contract. Although he was assigned to the Red Wings' development team in Pittsburgh, he was recalled to the parent club for fifteen games during the 1938–1939 campaign. He scored his first goal with the National Hockey League (NHL) on 24 November and added another tally as a fill-in during the Stanley Cup semifinals.

Abel began the next season with Detroit, but a broken shoulder sidelined him for several weeks. When he was fit for action again, he was sent to the Indianapolis Capitals for the duration of that season. But at the start of the 1940–1941 season, his grit and determination paid off. Improving at both left wing and center-ice, he became a permanent fixture on this steadily improving sextet. He was a natural leader, and at the start of the 1942–1943 season, he was elected team captain.

World War II put a crimp in Abel's movement up the ladder of prominence in the world of ice hockey, and before the start of the 1943–1944 season, he joined the Royal Canadian Air Force (RCAF). During his absence from the world's premier circuit, he married Gloria Morandy, a secretary in manager Jack Adams's office. In the air force, he earned the rank of lance corporal and was able to compete

against quality players while skating as a member of teams such as the Montreal RCAF and the Wembley Lions in England.

When Abel returned to the world of professional ice hockey in the fall of 1945, he found that the game had changed considerably. The addition of the center-ice red line, meant to lessen offside situations, accelerated the pace of play. Never a fast skater, the twenty-eight-year-old found it difficult to keep up with his younger wingers. Lesser men would have given up in frustration; instead, he practiced skating for hours to adapt to the modern game. His determination paid off. When the statistics were tallied in the spring of 1947, he had fired nineteen goals, added twenty-nine assists for a total of forty-eight points, and was fourth in team scoring.

During the following campaign, coach Tommy Ivan tried an experiment whose results were to alter the equilibrium of the NHL, change the fortunes of the Red Wings in general, and enhance Abel's reputation for years to come. Abel was paired with the tenacious Ted "Scarface" Lindsay and a budding right-winger, Gordon "Gordie" Howe. Soon "they fit together like three coats of paint" and became known as the "Production Line." Within three years this triumvirate finished first, second, and third in league scoring. At the conclusion of the subsequent two seasons, all three were listed among the NHL's top ten scorers.

These were Abel's finest seasons. In 1949 and 1950 he was voted to the first NHL All-Star team at center. The only player to earn such honors at two separate positions, he had been selected in 1942 as a left-winger. In 1949 he also received the most prestigious individual award offered in the NHL—the Hart Trophy, presented to the player adjudged "the most valuable player to his team." As author Ron McAllister wrote, "his record will reveal him as the greatest competitor the Red Wings have ever had!" Meanwhile, Abel also added three Stanley Cup rings to his souvenir collection in 1943, 1950, and 1952, his final year with the Red Wings.

Abel's nickname, "Old Boot Nose," is credited to an incident involving Maurice "Rocket" Richard. One night at the Montreal Forum, Abel's line mate, Howe, bumped Richard, then slugged the startled Canadiens' superstar on the nose. Abel skated over to the fallen Richard, looked down, and snarled, "How do you like that, you Frenchman?" Richard's answer was a punch of his own, directly on Abel's proboscis. The blow broke Abel's nose and bent it to one side. Its profile resembled a boot; hence the long-lasting agnomen.

In 1952–1953 Abel became player-coach of the hapless Chicago Blackhawks, participating in half of the club's seventy games. For the first time in nine seasons, the Windy City sextet reached post-season play. However, the club's revival was short-lived, and the Hawks slipped to last place the following season, a fact that cost Abel his job. After spending the next five and half years as a radio-television color commentator for the Red Wings' home games, Abel replaced the ailing Jimmy Skinner as coach in January 1958, midway through the season. In 1962 he added the role of team general manager to his duties. He relinquished the bench-boss reins in 1968, and in 1971 a dispute over the coaching abilities of his successor, Ned Harkness, resulted in the severing of his ties with the Motor City contingent after thirty years with the organization.

In a stopgap move, Abel agreed to become a scout for the Los Angeles Kings, with a possible view to taking over later in the front office. Soon afterward, the Blues, a fledgling St. Louis franchise, welcomed Abel as head coach to start the 1971–1972 season. He was "bumped upstairs" to the front office after only a month behind the bench. In May 1975 the Kansas City Scouts, an expansion team, announced his appointment as manager. Abel remained with the Missouri franchise for only one season before relinquishing his last NHL executive position at age sixty. He continued his business interests in Detroit, his adopted hometown, and returned to broadcasting once more. He was elected to the Hockey Hall of Fame in 1969.

Abel spent his retirement years in Farmington Hills, Michigan, and died of heart failure at age eighty-two.

Abel left behind a legacy of the unusual. In 1967 his only son, Gerry, made his debut with the Red Wings, with his famous father as his coach. Abel, who also had a daughter, found himself in a similar situation as general manager of the Blues, when his son-in-law, Bob Johnson, became part of a rotating three-goalie system for the St. Louis team. He lived to see his grandson, Brent Johnson, don the pads for the same club.

★

Biographical information on Abel can be found in Ron McAllister, *More Hockey Stories* (1952); Tim Moriarty, *Hockey's Hall Of Fame* (1974); and W. A. Hewitson, *Hockey's Heritage* (1982). A memorial tribute featuring Howe's memories of Abel is in *USA Today* (9 Feb. 2000). An obituary is in the *New York Times* (10 Feb. 2000).

GLEN R. GOODHAND

ABRAM, Morris Berthold (*b.* 19 June 1918 in Fitzgerald, Georgia; *d.* 16 March 2000 in Geneva, Switzerland), lawyer, social justice and civil rights advocate, and president of Brandeis University.

Abram was one of four children of Sam Abram, a Romanian immigrant harness maker, and Irene (Cohen) Abram, a homemaker who was the daughter of a physician and granddaughter of a pioneering Reform rabbi. His small-town southern childhood left Abram with an acute awareness of his Jewishness in contrast to the surrounding society. A tall, good-looking, courtly man with a gentle southern accent, Abram earned an A.B. (summa cum laude) from the University of Georgia in 1938, winning a Rhodes scholarship to Oxford University in England, the fulfillment of which was delayed by Britain's entry into World War II. In the interim he earned a J.D. at the University of Chicago, graduating in 1940. During the war Abram served as a public relations officer in the Army Air Forces.

Abram was able to pursue his Rhodes scholarship after the war, receiving a B.A. in 1948 and an M.A. in 1953. During Abram's time at Oxford, a professor arranged for him to serve on the prosecutor's staff for the International Military Tribunal at Nuremberg. Stunned by what he learned about the Holocaust through these war-crimes trials, Abram spent much of his life serving Jewish causes. He was president of the American Jewish Committee (1963–1968), chairman of the National Conference on Soviet Jewry (1983–1988), and chairman of the Conference of Presidents of Major Jewish Organizations (1986–1989). "Everything I have ever done on behalf of Jewish interests," Abram once said, "is part of a quilt to try to create tolerance for all of us."

When he returned to Georgia, Abram took up the practice of law. In 1953 he sought the Democratic nomination to the U.S. House of Congress, running on a liberal platform that emphasized the need to desegregate schools. He received a majority of the votes but was defeated because of the Georgia unit rule, which gave disproportionate power to sparsely populated rural white counties over far more populous urban counties with large black populations. Ironically, Abram had been battling the unit rule since 1949. It took him fourteen years to defeat the unit rule; in 1963 the U.S. Supreme Court finally declared it unconstitutional, ruling that "within a given constituency there can be room for but one constitutional rule—one voter, one vote." The famed "one man, one vote" case was argued by Robert F. Kennedy (the brother of President John F. Kennedy and himself later a senator), whom Abram had briefed. Abram considered that triumph one of the greatest of his life.

Abram achieved numerous other major civil rights victories. He helped start the first large middle-income housing project in Atlanta that was open to blacks. He also defended civil rights workers in Georgia, winning decisions that overturned the state's insurrection and illegal assembly legislation, which had been used against civil rights protesters. In 1963 Abram moved to New York to join the law firm of Paul, Weiss, Rifkind, Wharton, and Garrison. In addition to practicing law, he was appointed to a variety of public service positions under five presidents. He was the first general counsel to the Peace Corps under John F.

Kennedy, U.S. Representative to the United Nations Commission on Human Rights under President Lyndon B. Johnson, chairman of the President's Commission for the Study of Ethical Problems in Medicine and Biomedical and Behavioral Research under President Jimmy Carter, vice chairman of the United States Commission on Civil Rights under President Ronald Reagan, and United States Permanent Representative to the United Nations in Geneva under President George H. W. Bush.

In 1968 Abram was named president of Brandeis University; he took office during a period of widespread student unrest and rebellion. During his tenure many students and faculty members demanded that he openly oppose the war in Vietnam and create housing for the poor. Abram insisted that "the university as an institution should stay out of politics. . . . Only a university without ideology could be a place of learning." He angered many by dismissing as frivolous a proposal for a black studies program. He did not call the police when a group of black students occupied a campus building, earning praise for his restraint, but he lost favor when he tried to punish those responsible.

Abram resigned his position in 1970 and returned to his law practice. Ironically, during the next nine years he served as president of the United Negro College Fund, which raises money for predominantly black colleges. Abram opposed affirmative action, group entitlement, and "those who seek equality of result." Because of Abram's opposition to affirmative action, President Reagan appointed him to the United States Commission on Civil Rights in 1983. The nomination was protested by prominent figures in the black community who considered Abram "not committed to equal opportunity," an allegation he found painful.

In 1973 Abram was diagnosed with acute myelocytic leukemia and was told that he had only a few months to live. He survived, chronicling his agonizing struggle in an autobiography, *The Day Is Short* (1982). In 1975, while he was still ill with leukemia, Abram headed the Moreland Act Commission's investigation of the nursing home industry in New York State. The commission's recommendations produced tougher standards and the closing of sixty-eight nursing homes that failed to meet fire-safety codes. After serving as permanent representative to the United Nations (1989–1993), Abram remained in Geneva. In 1993, joining with the businessman and philanthropist Edgar M. Bronfman, he founded U.N. Watch, an affiliate of the World Jewish Congress. The organization monitored and attempted to combat anti-Semitism in the United Nations.

On 4 January 1943 Abram married Jane Isabella Maguire, a Methodist who converted to Judaism at the time of their marriage. They had three sons and two daughters. The marriage ended in divorce in 1974. Abram's second marriage, on 25 January 1976 to Carlyn Feldman Fisher, ended in divorce in 1987. His third wife, Bruna Molina, whom

he had married in 1990, survived him. He had no children with either his second or third wives.

Abram died at age eighty-one from a sudden viral infection and was buried in Hyannis, Massachusetts. He had spent his career fighting the forces of the far right during the battle for desegregation and the forces of the far left during his tenure at Brandeis and at the United Nations. He perceived that "the extremes of right and left wear the same masks, though they think ill of each other's."

★

Abram's forthright autobiography, *The Day Is Short* (1982), focuses on his battles as a university president and cancer patient. The transcripts of interviews with Abram done for the Lyndon Baines Johnson Library Oral History Collection in Austin, Texas, provide a sense of his personality. An obituary is in the *New York Times* (17 Mar. 2000).

NATALIE B. JALENAK

ADLER, Lawrence Cecil ("Larry") (*b.* 10 February 1914 in Baltimore, Maryland; *d.* 7 August 2001 in London, England), world's most famous harmonica player, whose musical virtuosity and sensitivity raised the instrument to concert status.

Adler was the older of two sons of Louis Adler, a plumber, whose family name was originally Zelakovitch, and Sophie (Hack) Adler, a homemaker. Both parents were Russian Jews. He attended public schools in Baltimore but never went to high school. Adler entered a singing contest when he was five and began playing the harmonica—which he always called the "mouth organ"—at age nine, when he participated in his first competition. He enrolled in Baltimore's Peabody Conservatory of Music to study piano, but was soon expelled for being "incorrigible, untalented and entirely lacking in ear." About this same time, he entered a harmonica contest—which he won—becoming the Maryland state champion. At age fourteen he ran away to New York City to audition for Borrah Minevitch and His Harmonica Rascals. Their verdict: "Kid, you stink."

Undaunted, Adler stayed in New York City, soon signing a contract with Paramount, and by 1929 he was playing in a Gus Edwards act. Edwards became Adler's manager, and in 1931 he got Adler a job in Florenz Ziegfeld's *Smiles*, starring Fred and Adele Astaire. He even had a duet with Fred Astaire, which inspired Adler's later collaboration with the dancer Paul Draper.

In 1933 Adler traveled to California, where he played Ravel's *Bolero*—badly—at Grauman's Chinese Theater in Hollywood. Fortunately, his excited arm waving at the conductor during the performance so entranced the audience that he became an instant success. (In 1935 Adler met

7

Ravel, whose piece he had by now recorded, and in 1940 he was given exclusive rights to perform it.) Shortly thereafter Adler played in the movie *Many Happy Returns* (1934), whose score was conducted by Guy Lombardo. Adler disliked Lombardo, insisting that Duke Ellington back his solo of "Sophisticated Lady," instead. He got his way. In 1982, when Ellington introduced Adler to the singer Billie Holiday (who had just heard Adler play), she remarked, "Man, you don't play that . . . thing, you *sing* it."

In 1934 the British impresario Charles Cochran hired Adler to appear in a London revue called *Streamline*. Enormously successful, Adler was soon in demand all over Britain; in fact, these prewar years were golden. He played in the movies *The Singing Marine* (1936) and *The Big Broadcast of 1937* (1937), and supervised the music for the film *St. Martin's Lane* (also known under the title *Sidewalks of London*) in 1937. On 16 April 1938 he married Eileen Walser, a model, with whom he had three children. Adler toured South Africa and Australia, returning to the United States in 1939, where he teamed up with Paul Draper for several years. In 1940 he performed at President Franklin D. Roosevelt's White House.

Beginning in 1943 Adler toured overseas with Jack Benny for the United Service Organizations (USO) and played in the movies *Music for Millions* (1944) and *The Birds and the Bees* (1947). By 1946 accusations that Adler was a communist surfaced. He had traveled to Washington, D.C., with the Committee for the First Amendment to protest against the House Committee on Un-American Activities, and by 1948 Adler and Draper were said to be "selling Red propaganda from the stage." Their names appeared in *Red Channels,* the "Blacklister's Bible." It was anathema.

Also in 1948, Hester McCullough of Greenwich, Connecticut, the wife of a *Time* magazine photo editor, accused Adler and Draper of communist leanings, blocking them from performing in Greenwich. They sued. The press, including the columnist Walter Winchell, then took up the cry against them. Although Adler adamantly opposed having to state his political beliefs publicly, he did sign an affidavit during the McCullough proceedings stating that he was not and had never been a communist. But it was too late. The trial failed to clear him and he could not find work, so in 1949 Adler and his family moved to England for good.

Fortunately for Adler, his reputation as a musician was already solidly established abroad. Even before the war, composers who had heard him play created pieces specifically for the harmonica, including Darius Milhaud's *Suite for Mouth Organ and Orchestra* (1943), which Adler premiered in 1947. In 1952 Ralph Vaughan Williams wrote *Romance for Mouth Organ, Piano, and Strings,* which Adler first played in Dorking, England, in 1952, and in 1953 Arthur Benjamin and Malcolm Arnold both wrote har-

Larry Adler, ca. 1975. HULTON-DEUTSCH COLLECTION/CORBIS

monica concerti. Adler also played pieces originally composed for other instruments, often performing the works of Bach, Rachmaninoff, and Debussy, as well as Cole Porter and George Gershwin. In fact, Ira Gershwin gave Adler his brother's *Lullaby Time,* which had never been published or performed, and Adler premiered the piece at the Edinburgh Festival in 1963.

Adler continued to give concerts all over Europe, gradually returning to play in the United States. He performed with celebrated conductors such as Georg Solti, Pierre Monteux, Adrian Boult, and Eugene Ormandy. Until his late twenties Adler had played music mostly by ear. After studying composition with Ernst Toch for about a year, he was able to compose scores for such films as *Genevieve* (1953), *The Hellions* (1961), *The Hook* and *The Great Chase* (1963), *King and Country* (1964), and *A High Wind in Jamaica* (1965).

A slim, dark-complexioned man, Adler was witty and articulate. As well as composing, he wrote dispatches for the *Chicago Sun* during World War II, two books, *How I Play* (1937) and *Jokes and How to Tell Them* (1963), two autobiographies (1984 and 1994), and restaurant reviews for several magazines.

In 1961 Adler and Walser divorced. He married Sally Cline in 1969, with whom he had a fourth child before divorcing in 1977. Right up to his death, he continued to tour and perform; among other activities, he recorded a piece for a Sting album in 1993 and hosted a BBC radio program called "Larry Adler's Century" in 1998. Adler died of pneumonia at age eighty-seven at St. Thomas's Hospital in London.

Adler was fully aware of the harmonic and rhythmic limitations of his instrument, yet he confessed, "I love to play it." His musicianship was so extraordinary that, as Richard Severo of the *New York Times* wrote, "He brought dignity to the harmonica, which was previously regarded as . . . a toy," introducing the instrument in concert halls for the first time. Adler regretted the dearth of harmonica players, ruefully concluding, "I'm resigned to being a freak. I'll be a footnote in musical history." Yet the pieces written for him, as well as his own compositions and recordings, now an incontrovertible part of the Western musical heritage, surely belie that stark assessment.

★

Adler wrote two autobiographies, *It Ain't Necessarily So* (1984) and *Me and My Big Mouth* (1994), which remain the best sources about his life and career. The former is especially useful in describing his struggles with the House Committee on Un-American Activities in the 1940s. Margaret Case Harriman, "Big-Time Urchin," the *New Yorker* (18 July 1942), is an excellent, although dated, portrait of Adler based on her interview with him. A second, shorter article about a reunion with Paul Draper is "Reunion," the *New Yorker* (23 June 1975). Adler was featured in an article by Leonard Feather in the arts section of the *Los Angeles Times* (17 Oct. 1982). Except for "Fiery Footnote," *Newsweek* (30 May 1966), only brief references to Adler appear in the standard news magazines. Obituaries are in the *Chicago Sun-Times, Daily Variety, New York Times, Times* (London), and *Washington Post* (all 8 Aug. 2001); *Irish Times* (11 Aug. 2001); and *San Diego Union-Tribune* (12 Aug. 2001).

SANDRA SHAFFER VANDOREN

ADLER, Mortimer J(erome) (*b.* 28 December 1902 in New York City; *d.* 28 June 2001 in San Mateo, California), philosopher who helped create the Great Books program (1952), reorganized the *Encyclopaedia Britannica* (1974), and authored *The Paideia Proposal* (1982) for education.

Adler was the son of Orthodox Jewish immigrants Ignatz Adler, a jewelry salesman, and Clarissa (Manheim) Adler, a schoolteacher. A gifted child, Adler became bored with school and left DeWitt Clinton High School at the age of fifteen to become a copy boy for the *New York Sun.* Inspired by reading John Stuart Mill's *Autobiography,* Adler matriculated at the age of sixteen at Columbia University, hoping to emulate Mill as a philosopher. A brilliant student, Adler

Mortimer J. Adler, 1977. BETTMANN/CORBIS

failed to receive his bachelor's degree because he refused to take a required swimming course. He was, nonetheless, accepted into graduate school at Columbia, where he earned a Ph.D. in social psychology in 1928. (Six decades later, in 1983, Columbia waived the swimming requirement and awarded Adler his bachelor's degree. Also in that year, DeWitt Clinton High School gave him his diploma.)

At Columbia, Adler developed what would be a lifelong devotion to Aristotle's philosophy and the "great books." While still a student, he worked with his mentor, John Erskine, to create the first Great Books courses in America. For Adler, the great books were a way of entering the ongoing discussion that underlay the history of Western civilization. The great books recorded the responses of generations of thinkers over the course of 3,000 years to the key questions that perennially perplexed humankind. A great book, according to Adler, not only had a profound impact when it was first written but still speaks to people today. Therefore, it can serve as a vehicle for discussing important social, intellectual, and ethical questions.

During the late 1920s, Adler worked as a part-time lecturer at Columbia University, City College, and the People's Institute in New York City, teaching courses in philosophy and law. In 1930 Robert Maynard Hutchins hired Adler at the University of Chicago, where he taught philosophy of

9

law. Adler and Hutchins tried during the 1930s to remake undergraduate education at Chicago into a Great Books program, and Adler helped found Saint John's College in Annapolis, Maryland, which was dedicated to teaching the great books.

In 1940 Adler published his first best-seller, *How to Read a Book,* which promoted the great books for popular audiences. In 1946 Adler and Hutchins launched a program of great books seminars for adults that flourished during the 1950s. Adler also edited a fifty-four-volume set of 443 great books published by Encyclopaedia Britannica, a project for which he produced an index of 102 great ideas that he called a "syntopicon" (1952). Also in 1952, Adler left the University of Chicago and founded the Institute for Philosophical Research in San Francisco. He later founded the Aspen Institute in Colorado. In 1974, as chair of the board of editors of *Encyclopaedia Britannica,* Adler oversaw the first reorganization of the *Britannica* in over 200 years and added to it an outline of human knowledge that he called the Propaedia (1974).

During the 1980s Adler became concerned that educational discussion in America was becoming too politicized and polarized. He organized the Paideia Project, which brought together educators of various philosophies in an attempt to bridge the gaps among competing theories of education. Adler hoped to reach a consensus on reforming America's public schools, which would include Great Books seminars in elementary and high schools. The Paideia Project produced a series of books, conferences, and outreach programs to help schools institute the group's proposals. Adler's book *The Paideia Proposal* (1982) was highly praised, and Adler became a leading commentator on educational issues. From the 1970s into the 1990s, Adler published a series of popular books on philosophy, including *Aristotle for Everybody* (1978) and *Ten Philosophical Mistakes* (1985), that made him the best-selling philosopher in American history.

Adler married his first wife, Helen Leavenworth Boynton, on 2 May 1927. They had two sons and divorced in 1961. A second marriage, to Caroline Sage Pring in 1963, also produced two sons.

Adler died at the age of ninety-eight at his home in San Mateo, California, after a career that encompassed many of the philosophical and political movements of the twentieth century. His body was cremated in California, and his ashes were interred in Chicago.

Best known as an exponent of Aristotle, Adler's interpretation of Aristotle changed as he moved from one intellectual position to another. Adler was always controversial and thrived on intellectual combat. During the 1920s at Columbia, while most of his classmates became adherents of John Dewey's pragmatist philosophy and progressive educational theories, Adler developed an affinity for positivism and an aversion to pragmatism, progressivism, and Dewey. His an-

tagonism to Dewey was so strong that the normally mild-mannered, tolerant Dewey eventually banned Adler from speaking in his classes.

During the 1930s at Chicago, where positivism and liberalism prevailed in the social sciences and humanities, Adler converted to the scholasticism of Thomas Aquinas and developed a reputation as the Jewish philosopher who taught Catholic theology to predominantly Protestant students. He was at the center of intense struggles over what should be the theory and practice of the university. Denouncing the empirical sciences, democracy, and modern society in favor of metaphysics, elitism, and the European High Middle Ages, Adler promoted hierarchical conceptions of education and society, in which elite students should learn to think and rule and ordinary students should learn to defer and obey.

The horrors of Nazism and the coming of World War II prompted what Adler called his "conversion to democracy." From this point on in his life, Adler's social and intellectual views became increasingly liberal. In the late 1940s he began a bitter dispute with the conservative philosopher Leo Strauss over whether the classics should be taught didactically as a body of eternal truths, as Strauss believed, or dialectically as a set of perennial questions, as Adler maintained. In a democratic education, Adler contended, discussion should begin with the great books, not end with them. Adler continued this debate over the next fifty years with Strauss's disciples Allan Bloom and William Bennett.

During the 1950s and 1960s Adler argued that if capitalism were to be truly democratic, everyone must become a capitalist, and in *The Capitalist Manifesto* (1958), he advocated a radical redistribution of property to the propertyless. Finally, in the 1970s Adler declared himself a socialist, arguing thereafter in books such as *Haves without Have-nots* (1991) that political democracy and intellectual freedom cannot be fully realized without the economic equality of socialism. Emulating the progression of his childhood idol, John Stuart Mill, from classicism to liberalism to socialism, Adler dedicated himself to working thenceforth for "a future in which the ideals of democracy and socialism will be more fully realized." *The Paideia Proposal* was an attempt to use education as a means toward those ends. In the book, Adler also made peace with the memory of his longtime nemesis, Dewey, extolling him and incorporating many of his educational ideas.

★

Adler wrote an autobiography, *Philosopher at Large,* in 1977 in the belief that his career was coming to a close. In fact, his publishing and popularity were just beginning to take off, so he updated his life in 1992 with *A Second Look in the Rearview Mirror.* Mary Ann Dzuback, "Hutchins, Adler, and the University of

Chicago: A Critical Juncture," *American Journal of Education* 99, no. 1 (Nov. 1990), deals with Adler's eventful years at the University of Chicago during the 1930s. An obituary is in the *New York Times* (29 June 2001).

BURTON WELTMAN

ALBERT, Carl Bert (*b.* 10 May 1908 in McAlester, Oklahoma; *d.* 4 February 2000 in McAlester, Oklahoma), Democratic U.S. congressman from Oklahoma from 1947 to 1977 who served as Speaker of the House of Representatives from 1971 to 1977 and was first in the line of presidential succession twice.

Born in an unpainted coal company house, Albert, the oldest of five children, was the son of a coal miner and cotton farmer. Neither of his parents, Ernest Homer and Leona Ann (Scott) Albert, had attended more than four years of school. As Albert recalled, "We had everything but money." The family moved to Bug Tussle, Oklahoma, a rural school district about ten miles northeast of McAlester. Beginning in 1914, Albert went to school in a two-room schoolhouse and discovered that he preferred learning to chopping and picking cotton.

The young Albert focused his full attention and intellect on his studies and realized that telling his teachers what they wanted to hear paid dividends. Although he later questioned the intellectual honesty of this tactic, he recognized that it served him well all his life. During his first year in school, the district's congressman visited Bug Tussle and predicted that "a boy in this class might someday be . . . congressman." Albert recalled, "I knew . . . I was that boy."

The collapse of the cotton market and the distance to McAlester forced Albert to interrupt his education after completing the eighth grade, but in 1923 he was able to enroll in high school. Not allowed to take Latin as a freshman because of his country-school education, Albert chose a public-speaking class that opened avenues that led beyond Bug Tussle. As valedictorian and student body president, Albert graduated in 1927 from McAlester High, where he earned honors in oratory and a trip to Europe. The school yearbook characterized the five-foot, four-and-a-half-inch senior as "a little giant."

That fall Albert enrolled at the University of Oklahoma in Norman. There he supplemented his income from part-time work with money he won in oratorical competitions. In 1931 he earned a degree in government, a commission in the U.S. Army reserve, a Phi Beta Kappa key, and a Rhodes scholarship. At Oxford University in England he completed an LL.B. in 1933 and a B.C.L. the next year. When Albert returned to the United States, the economic depression limited his opportunities, but after admission to the bar in 1935 he worked as a legal assistant with the

Carl B. Albert. AP/WIDE WORLD PHOTOS

Federal Housing Administration in Oklahoma City. Two years later he became counsel for a privately owned oil company, where he learned the oil-lease business.

Specializing in title examination, Albert moved to Illinois, where he practiced law until his number was drawn in the draft. His commission in the reserves having expired, Albert was inducted as a private on 16 June 1941 and participated in the Louisiana maneuvers that summer. When Congress extended the enlistment of draftees, men twenty-eight and older were discharged. The thirty-three-year-old Albert resumed his legal practice until the Japanese attack on Pearl Harbor, which drew the United States into World War II, prompted him to apply for a commission in the U.S. Army Air Forces. On 20 March 1942 he was assigned as a second lieutenant in the Judge Advocate General's (JAG) Corps in Washington, D.C., where he met Mary Harmon, a twenty-two-year-old South Carolinian. They married on 20 August 1942 in Columbia, South Carolina; the couple had two children. Transferred to the Pacific theater of war, Albert rose to the rank of lieutenant colonel. As a JAG officer, he tried cases, primarily assault, theft, murder, and rape, and was awarded a Bronze Star for Meritorious Service for prosecuting officers and enlisted personnel engaged in selling U.S. government property on the black market.

Discharged in 1946, Albert returned to McAlester to practice law and to seek the vacant seat in Oklahoma's third congressional district. In a hard-fought campaign, Albert finished second in the Democratic primary, forcing a runoff he narrowly won. The general election in the heavily Democratic district was no contest. Albert entered Congress in 1947 in a freshman class that included John F. Kennedy and Richard M. Nixon. His committee assignment, which was not challenging, gave him time to observe the operations of the chamber and to become familiar with its members. Albert mastered the rules and procedures of the House and cultivated its 434 other members. Before the end of his first term, he had joined Speaker Sam Rayburn's "Board of Education," an informal group that met after adjournment to discuss business over drinks. He was equally diligent in serving his constituents. Although Albert was always more progressive than the voters of his district, he never lost their loyalty. His support of the economic reforms of the administrations of Franklin D. Roosevelt (the "New Deal") and Harry S. Truman, and his knowledge of the traditions of the House prompted Rayburn to appoint Albert as Democratic House whip in 1955. Discussing the reason for selecting Albert, Rayburn claimed, "I can tell big timber from small brush."

As whip, Albert employed persuasion rather than coercion to secure support for important legislation. He viewed Democratic cooperation with the administration of the Republican president Dwight D. Eisenhower as more responsible than the adversarial relationship that characterized subsequent divided governments. When Rayburn died in 1961 and John McCormack became Speaker, Albert faced a challenge for the position of majority leader from Richard Bolling, a Missouri representative with strong support outside the House. Albert called every member of the chamber and secured enough votes to assure his election before Congress convened.

Albert considered his years as majority leader the most productive of his career. During the time that Albert worked with two Democratic administrations, Congress passed legislation that realized most of the goals of the New Deal, revived the nation's lackluster economy, placed the power of the federal government behind efforts to secure equal rights for African Americans, and made a major assault on lingering pockets of poverty. In 1965 Albert said, "The Eighty-ninth Congress . . . accomplished more in more areas than any other session in the nation's history."

Like every voting member of the House, Albert approved the Gulf of Tonkin Resolution, which gave President Lyndon B. Johnson a wide latitude in responding to alleged Communist aggression in Southeast Asia. His support remained constant as the U.S. role in Vietnam expanded, and domestic opposition to the war grew. His presidency in shambles, Johnson asked Albert to chair the Democratic National Convention in Chicago in August 1968, where unruly demonstrators refused to be gaveled to order. Albert contrasted the "businesslike efficiency of the Republicans' earlier convention in Miami," at which police maintained order by killing three rioters, with the Democrats' "open convention, [which] chose a strong candidate, and gave him our best possible sendoff." Most Americans, however, retained vivid memories of the disorder inside and outside the Chicago convention hall.

Richard Nixon's election to the presidency in 1968 began the most trying period of Albert's career. In 1971, when Speaker of the House John McCormack retired, Albert's bid for the position met only token opposition. The new Speaker, the forty-sixth, had known President Nixon since they were freshman congressmen and harbored suspicions about the "new Nixon," but he hoped to establish amicable relations with the White House. That hope faded when the president began dismantling programs established in the Johnson administration by vetoing bills and impounding funds. Powerless to override presidential vetoes, some congressmen vented their frustration on Albert.

Even as he reduced the level of U.S. forces in Vietnam, Nixon intensified military pressure on Hanoi. Albert supported the administration's effort to preserve South Vietnam's U.S.-backed government despite his growing doubts. As Speaker, he led the House in rejecting measures to compel U.S. withdrawal from Vietnam until the 1973 Paris agreement to remove U.S. ground forces. When the administration continued to wage a secret air war over Southeast Asia, Albert and his chamber joined the Senate in denying the administration further funding. Later in 1973 Albert endorsed the War Powers Act, which required the president to secure congressional approval for the commitment of U.S. forces to combat for more than sixty days.

As majority leader and Speaker, Albert supported sweeping changes in House rules and structure. He urged Speaker McCormack to revive the Democratic Caucus and to end procedures that enabled members to conceal their voting records. He endorsed reforms that stripped committee chairs of their dictatorial power, broke the stranglehold of the Rules Committee, and concentrated greater power in the House leadership. Albert's reluctance to wield that power to challenge presidential vetoes and vigorously push a Democratic agenda antagonized his party's more zealous members.

Albert's restraint as Speaker was apparent when the abuse of power in the Nixon administration created crises in the executive branch. When Vice President Spiro Agnew pleaded no contest to charges of accepting bribes and resigned, Albert rejected the opportunity to take partisan advantage of the situation. After he told Nixon that the House minority leader Gerald Ford would be easily confirmed as vice president, the president nominated Ford, who quickly secured congressional approval. When evidence of Nixon's attempt to obstruct the investigation of a break-in at the Watergate office of the Democratic Party's National Committee raised the specter of impeachment, Albert rejected advice to stack a special committee with the president's opponents; instead, he chose the Judiciary Committee to conduct hearings. Before the House could consider its findings, Nixon resigned, and Albert expedited the confirmation of New York Governor Nelson Rockefeller to fill the vice presidency vacated when Gerald R. Ford became president.

Ford proved to be as tenacious as Nixon in opposing what he considered congressional budgetary irresponsibility, provoking liberal Democrats to demand a more adversarial response. Albert, more comfortable seeking compromise, felt the sting of their criticism. After a heart attack in 1966, subsequent health problems, and growing weariness, the sixty-eight-year-old speaker, who had promised to retire at seventy, decided not to seek reelection for a sixteenth term in 1976. Retiring to Bug Tussle, Albert maintained an office in the federal building in McAlester until 1998. Despite frail health, he taught college classes, spoke frequently, and wrote his autobiography, *Little Giant: The Life and Times of Speaker Carl Albert* (1990). Albert died in the McAlester Regional Health Center at the age of ninety-one and was buried at Oak Hill Cemetery in McAlester.

During his thirty-year congressional career, Albert accepted the House's traditions and mastered its rules. Operating quietly, he was willing to share or forgo credit for legislative accomplishments and preferred compromise to confrontation. Consequently, he never attracted the attention his more outspoken colleagues received, but during the turbulence in the executive department in 1973 and 1974, his low-key leadership and refusal to take partisan advantage facilitated what could have been a difficult transition.

★

Albert's papers are held at the Carl Albert Congressional Research and Study Center of the University of Oklahoma in Norman. His autobiography, written with Danney Goble, *Little Giant: The Life and Times of Speaker Carl Albert* (1990), surveys most of the major developments of his career, but is neither probing nor candid. He contributed a chapter, "The Speakership in My Time," to Ronald M. Peters, Jr., ed., *The Speaker: Leadership in the U.S. House of Representatives* (1994). He also wrote two autobiographical articles in the *Chronicles of Oklahoma*: "Recollections of My Early Life" (spring 1974) and "We Had Everything But Money," with Danney Goble (summer 1988). Two articles drawn

from his papers consider his record on Indian policy. W. Dale Mason, "The Carl Albert Collection: Resources Relating to Indian Policy, 1963–1968," *Chronicles of Oklahoma* (winter 1993–1993), is positive, but Dean J. Kotlowski, "Limited Vision: Carl Albert, the Choctaws, and Native American Self-Determination," *American Indian Culture and Research Journal* (2002), is critical. Obituaries are in the *Daily Oklahoman, New York Times, Tulsa World,* and *Washington Post* (all 6 Feb. 2000).

BRAD AGNEW

ALBERT, Frank Culling ("Frankie") (*b.* 27 January 1920 in Chicago, Illinois; *d.* 4 September 2002 in Menlo Park, California), Stanford football player who was the first modern-day T-formation college quarterback and who continued his wizardry in the professional game with the San Francisco 49ers.

Albert was one of two sons born to Nevin Culling Albert, an insurance company accountant, and Blanche (Marshman) Albert, a homemaker. The family moved to California when he was just a few weeks old. A gifted athlete who weighed only 130 pounds when he reported for his first high school football season at Glendale High, Albert was a standout in football in his only varsity season and a track star throughout his entire high school career. He was named Southern California's Prep Athlete of the Year in 1937. Still small at five feet, nine inches and 160 pounds, Albert matriculated at Stanford University in the fall of 1938. A student-athlete at a major university in those days had only three years of varsity competition. After playing a freshmen football schedule in 1938, the little left-hander moved up to varsity in 1939. Under Coach Claude ("Tiny") Thornhill, Albert was an obscure, fourth-string tailback in the single-wing formation then used almost exclusively at all levels of football. The Indians, as Stanford's teams were then known, won only one game, scored just seven touchdowns for the season (Albert had a hand in all seven), and saw their coach fired at the end of the season.

Things would immediately improve. Clark Shaughnessy, with the "new" T-formation, came to Palo Alto as head coach in 1940. He installed the same man-in-motion T that he had taught the professional Chicago Bears, who would astound the football world with a 73–0 victory in the 1940 National Football League (NFL) championship game. No one knew what to expect at Stanford. Opening the season with the Dons of the University of San Francisco, Stanford and Albert completely baffled their opponents. Said Albert, "They had no idea what to do with Pete Kmetovic [the left halfback who went in motion on most plays]. They never covered him." The Indians befuddled the remainder of their opponents and finished the season undefeated and hosts of the Rose Bowl on 1 January 1941 against a favored University of Nebraska team. Albert led his team to a 21–13

Frankie Albert, 1956. BETTMANN/CORBIS

could keep the Browns from winning the league championship in each of the AAFC's four seasons. Nevertheless, Albert was a star. In 1948 he and the quarterback Otto Graham of the Browns shared AAFC Most Valuable Player honors. Albert also was *SPORT* magazine's Pro Player of the Year. In the AAFC's four-year history, Albert threw more touchdown passes (eighty-eight) than Graham (eighty-six). He was a fine punter and dangerous runner, in addition to being the game's slickest ball handler. When the 49ers (along with the Browns, Baltimore Colts, and New York Yankees) joined the NFL in 1950, Albert and the 49ers had a fan-pleasing team but could not win a championship. Their games with the Los Angeles Rams regularly drew more than 100,000 spectators.

After the 1952 season, Albert, nearing age thirty-three, retired, or so he thought. Getting started in the automobile business, Albert could not resist additional "startup money" in the form of a year's salary to quarterback the Calgary Stampeders of the Canadian Football League (CFL). He returned to the San Francisco Bay Area in 1954 to broadcast 49ers games. The next year he was an assistant coach with his old team. In 1956 he became the NFL's youngest (thirty-six years old) head coach when he took over the 49ers. He retired from coaching in 1958 with a 19–16–1 record. He was inducted into the College Football Hall of Fame in 1956. Albert continued to own auto dealerships in the Bay Area and at times lived in Pebble Beach, Menlo Park, and Palm Desert, California. After contracting Alzheimer's disease in his later years, he moved back to Palo Alto and died from complications of the disease at a Menlo Park nursing facility. An impressive memorial service was held for him at Stanford. His body was cremated.

Albert's career statistics are modest compared with twenty-first-century players, but in his day he was among the game's elite. In an eight-year professional career—he lost four seasons to military service—he completed 935 passes in 1,789 attempts for 12,363 yards and 127 touchdowns. He was a shifty runner when the situation dictated—he rushed for twenty-nine touchdowns and was an excellent punter, with 42.6 yards per kick. His quick thinking and heady decision making are what set him apart, however. Dud DeGroot, who was frequently an opposing coach, said, "With Frankie Albert, it is like having a coach on the field—and that's giving the benefit of the doubt to the coaches." His college coach, Shaughnessy, said, "If Albert had not succeeded as a T [formation] quarterback, I may have abandoned the T." Without the T-formation that Albert helped to initiate, the face of football would have been vastly different.

★

There is no biography of Albert, but his career is discussed in Dan McGuire, *San Francisco 49ers* (1960); Murray Olderman, *The*

victory, throwing a forty-yard touchdown pass to Kmetovic and generally pestering the Cornhuskers all game long. The Nebraska coach, Biff Jones, said, "Tell Shaughnessy I'll buy him a hundred-twenty acres of fine corn, if he'll tell me where we can find a Frankie Albert."

Albert was a unanimous choice for All-American and finished fourth in the Heisman Trophy voting. The next season, Stanford went 6–3–0, and Albert repeated as a consensus All-American and was third in the Heisman balloting. He also was named Helms Football Foundation California Athlete of the Year. Albert was drafted on the first round by the Chicago Bears, but before he could report to the NFL team he enlisted in the navy. He served four years as a deck officer on an aircraft carrier in the Pacific during World War II. Before "shipping out," Albert starred in the 1942 Columbia Pictures film *The Spirit of Stanford*, for which he earned $6,000.

On 21 July 1942 Albert and his high school sweetheart, Martha Jean ("Marty") Barringer, who had followed him to Stanford, were married. They had three daughters. After his discharge in the fall of 1945, Albert played in the minor Pacific Coast League. Then, in 1946, he joined the upstart San Francisco 49ers of the newly formed All-America Football Conference (AAFC). The 49ers waged a spirited battle with the Cleveland Browns for AAFC supremacy but never

Pro Quarterback (1966); and Beau Riffenburgh and David Boss, *Great Ones: NFL Quarterbacks from Baugh to Montana* (1989). An obituary is in the *New York Times* (9 Sept. 2002).

JIM CAMPBELL

ALGER, David Dewey (*b.* 15 December 1943 in San Diego, California; *d.* 11 September 2001 in Manhattan, New York City), chairman and chief executive officer of Fred Alger Management Company, a New York investment management firm whose aggressive growth style yielded tremendous returns during the 1990s.

Alger came from a celebrated American family that could trace its roots in the United States to the seventeenth century. His paternal great-grandfather, Russell Alger, despite being orphaned as a boy, became a Civil War hero, created a fortune in the timber industry, served as President William J. McKinley's secretary of war during the Spanish-American War, and died while serving as U.S. senator from Michigan. Alger's grandfather, Frederick Alger, was a leader of Michigan's Republican Party, and expanded his father's holdings to include ownership interests in the Packard Motor Car Company and numerous banks.

Alger's father, Frederick Moulton Alger, Jr., served as the U.S. ambassador to Belgium under President Dwight D. Eisenhower, but ultimately his lack of enthusiasm for hard work, his penchant for the good life, and his alcoholism would consume much of the family fortune. Alger's mother, Suzette deMarigny (Dewey) Alger, came from an equally prominent family: her father, Charles Dewey, served in the Coolidge Administration and was a U.S. representative from Illinois.

Alger was the third of three children and, despite being his mother's favorite, saw little of his parents as a young child. He was essentially raised by his nanny, Mary McCrone. When he was nine years old, the family moved to Belgium, becoming the first to occupy the embassy's new residence. The embassy grounds became Alger's play area. He adapted well to his new surroundings and grew closer to his mother. He learned French so he could attend Belgian schools, and he found life in Europe exciting.

Like his older brother Fred, Alger attended Milton Academy, a prestigious preparatory school in Milton, Massachusetts. He found the readjustment to life in the United States difficult at first, but did well academically and excelled at track and football. After high school, Alger, as had his father and older brother, attended Harvard College in Cambridge, Massachusetts, graduating in 1966 with a B.A. in American history. Faced with the choice of entering military service during the Vietnam War or going to graduate school, Alger decided to attend the University of Michigan and earn his M.B.A. He found business school more chal-

lenging than college and struggled at first, but he eventually graduated in 1968 near the top of his class.

By the time Alger was at business school, his brother Fred, nine years older than he, was already a well-known money manager on Wall Street, with his own firm. Fred was an early advocate of the growth style of investing: in contrast to value investors, who search for companies with stocks trading below their liquidation or book value, he invested his clients' money in companies that had potential to increase their earnings quickly and dramatically. This strategy led to tremendous gains in some years and big losses when the stock market fell, and Fred's reputation went up and down with the market.

When Alger was in college, he had contemplated a career in law, but after making a quick windfall based on one of his brother's stock tips, he decided that he would follow him into finance. Though Alger and his brother were not close as children, Fred—driven hard by his desire to earn back the family fortune, and by a competitive urge to outperform his peers—took on a mentoring role in Alger's life after the death of their parents. He advised Alger to begin his career as an equity analyst at Irving Trust Company, where Alger followed various stock sectors, including the oil and retail industries. He quickly showed a knack for finding fast-growing stocks.

In January 1971 Fred was looking to build the research department at Fred Alger Management Company, and hired Alger. While neither was particularly interested in working with the other, Alger's analytical skills filled a need in the company. Known for being difficult, Fred was particularly hard on Alger, and often yelled at him in front of his coworkers. Alger, at least in retrospect, took it in stride, and said that he owed his "entire outlook on the stock market to Fred." He brought his knowledge of technology to the firm. Before long he gained Fred's trust, and in 1974 Alger began to manage the company's mutual fund portfolios, including the Spectra Fund.

While at business school, Alger had met his first wife, Roxana Barry, with whom he had a daughter. Two years later they separated and subsequently divorced. In 1975 Alger met Josefina Romanach, an executive at Chase Manhattan Bank and the daughter of a prominent Cuban architect. They married on 30 October 1976 and had one daughter.

Alger stepped out of his brother's shadow in 1989, when he directed the Alger Small Capitalization Fund to a gain of over 64 percent, leading the entire mutual fund industry. As a result, Alger was commissioned to write *Raging Bull: How to Invest in the Growth Stocks of the 90s*. Published in 1991, *Raging Bull* explained the Alger aggressive-growth investing style, and correctly predicted the gains in technology and health-care stocks that were to come in the years that followed. Alger strongly advocated the principle that "active management" could provide better investment performance than simply replicating market indices.

In 1995 Fred, in the midst of a bitter divorce and seeking to avoid estate taxes that would hurt the firm in the future, decided to retire from day-to-day management. He moved to Switzerland, leaving Alger to run the firm. Alger quickly became the face of the company, appearing regularly on television and becoming a favorite of investors who profited from his advice during the bull market of the late 1990s. At the point that Alger took over as chief executive officer, the firm managed $3 billion in assets for its clients. Six years later, at the time of his death, the firm, based in the North Tower of the World Trade Center (WTC) in Manhattan, had over $15 billion in assets under management, and 220 employees. *Money* magazine named Alger one of their top ten mutual fund managers of the 1990s, and his fifteen-year average investment return of 19.6 percent through August 2001 bettered the Standard and Poor's index of 500 large companies by 4.8 percent.

In March 2000 the stock market began to fall from record levels, and Alger's funds suffered greatly as a result. The seventeen mutual funds that he managed or co-managed, many of which invested largely in technology and biotechnology shares, lost up to 40 percent of their value in the last year of his life.

Alger was most likely at his desk or addressing his analysts at 8:46 A.M. on the morning of 11 September 2001, when American Airlines Flight 11—piloted by hijackers intent on destroying the WTC—crashed into his ninety-third floor office. Another hijacked plane struck the South Tower, and both towers later collapsed. Of the fifty-five Fred Alger Management employees who worked in the North Tower, all thirty-five present that day were killed.

Upon acknowledging the tragic loss of his brother and most of his other portfolio managers and analysts, Fred Alger announced that he would return to the United States and resume day-to-day management of the firm. Fred's son-in-law, Dan Chung, who had been a portfolio manager for the firm, replaced Alger as chief investment officer.

While Alger was known to be emotional and to have temper tantrums when the market was not going his way, his hard work and competitiveness earned the respect of his employees. A number of his analysts, including Tom Marsico, Warren Lammert, and Helen Young Hayes, went on to become celebrated fund managers elsewhere. Although he liked to make money, he was motivated mostly by a desire to win.

★

There is no biography of Alger. For information about the fate of Fred Alger Management after David Alger's death, see Riva D. Atlas with Geraldine Fabrikant, "After Havoc, Reviving a Legacy," *New York Times* (29 Sept. 2001), and Bridget O'Brian, "Surviving the Chills of 2003, Remembering the Fires of 2001," *Wall Street Journal* (31 Mar. 2003). An obituary is in the *New York Times* (25 Sept. 2001).

RICHARD L. DAVIDMAN

ALLEN, Stephen Valentine Patrick William ("Steve")

(*b.* 26 December 1921 in New York City; *d.* 30 October 2000 in Encino, California), comic entertainer, pianist, composer, and author who worked in radio, film, and television.

Allen was born in the proverbial show business trunk. His parents, Carroll and Isabelle (Donohue) Allen, were a vaudeville comedy team who performed as Billy Allen and Belle Montrose. His father's death before Allen's second birthday forced his mother to leave him in the care of his maternal grandparents in Chicago while she toured most of the year as a solo act. Allen, who suffered from severe asthma, described himself as a "pampered, sickly beanpole" of a child, living a sad boyhood in a succession of tenement apartments and rooming houses with his poverty-stricken relatives. He also credited his spontaneous wit to the "sarcastic, volatile . . . and always funny" tone of conversation maintained by the Donahues.

Allen's education was interrupted by more than a dozen

Steve Allen, 1962. AP/WIDE WORLD PHOTOS

changes in schools, but he nevertheless remained an avid reader and managed to master the piano after just three years of lessons, beginning at age seven. His asthma led his mother to move with him to Phoenix, Arizona, where he graduated from Union High School in 1940. Hoping to become a journalist, in 1941 Allen enrolled at Drake University in Des Moines, Iowa, but his condition forced him to return to Phoenix in less than a year. After another aborted attempt at furthering his education at Arizona State Teachers College in 1942, he gave up on formal education and set his sights on taking up the family trade of show business.

Still shy about his appearance, Allen found work at the Phoenix radio station KOY. He learned the radio business on the job, working as an all-purpose announcer, writer, and musician. He began to write comedy material, which he performed on the air with another announcer, Wendell Noble. When the latter was offered a job at a Los Angeles station in 1944, he helped Allen find work there as well. With so many radio performers serving in the armed forces during World War II, the stage was set for Allen's meteoric rise as a broadcasting personality in Los Angeles. (Allen was exempted from military service, owing to recurrent attacks of asthma.) Starting out in 1944 as an announcer at KFAC, he was courted away in less than a year to become program manager at the rival station KMTR. By 1945 he was performing with Noble on a regular basis on "Smile Time," a West Coast regional network program on the Mutual Broadcasting System.

Moving to KNX, a Columbia Broadcasting System (CBS) station, Allen launched a late-night radio program in 1948 in which the roots of his television work can be found. Although he was hired as a disc jockey, he played few records, preferring instead to talk about whatever crossed his mind, from world events to something he had seen on the street that day. He sat at a piano during the show, accompanying his own chatter with whimsical chords and runs, occasionally breaking out into song, some of which he improvised on the spot. "These were both forms of jazz, one verbal, one musical," he told an interviewer, "though at the time I just thought I was having fun."

During a typical show he answered letters, interviewed stars, ventured out into the studio audience and the street with a microphone, and experimented with a variety of segments, or "shticks," as he liked to call them. He introduced many of these elements to television, where they survive as generic features of late-night TV talk programs more than a half century later. Hoping to test the viability of Allen's offbeat personality with a national audience, CBS managers gave the show a thirteen-week trial on the radio network in 1950, with an eye toward determining Allen's potential for their emerging television operation.

Allen has been called the "Renaissance man" of American entertainment, and many of his talents were already beginning to flourish at this early point in his career. The first of his fifty-three books, *Windfall,* a volume of verse, was published in 1946. It was followed by novels, short stories, autobiographies, and nonfiction works on subjects ranging from the condition of migrant farm workers (*The Ground Is Our Table,* 1966) and corporate ethics (*Ripoff: A Look at Corruption in America,* 1979) to the "dumbing down" of America (*Dumbth and Eighty-one Ways to Make Americans Smarters,* 1989) and the moral decline of popular culture (*Vulgarians at the Gate. Trash TV and Raunch Radio: Raising the Standards of Popular Culture,* 2001). *Beloved Son: A Story of the Jesus Cults* (1982) was written after his son, Brian, joined the "Love Family" cult.

Allen also broke in as a songwriter in the late 1940s when Hoagy Carmichael and Nat King Cole recorded his composition "An Old Piano Plays the Blues." Eventually, his name would appear in the *Guinness Book of World Records* as the world's "Most Prolific Songwriter" (he wrote more than seven thousand songs). His best-known tune probably is the theme song "This Could Be the Start of Something Big." He began to publish a regular music column in *Song Hits* magazine and later wrote on jazz for *Downbeat.* As a musician and composer, Allen recorded or produced more than seventy albums and CDs.

In 1949 Allen earned his first film credits, helping compile the documentary *Down Memory Lane,* whose subject was the silent-era comedy director Mack Sennett. It also was the first of more than twenty documentaries for which he served as narrator, ranging from the history of professional wrestling to biographies of the satirical 1960s-era comedian Lenny Bruce and the actress Marilyn Monroe. He made his acting debut in 1950 in a minor role in the musical *I'll Get By.* He eventually appeared in scores of movies and television programs, often playing himself. His only starring vehicle was *The Benny Goodman Story* (1955), in which he portrayed the big-band leader.

It was television, however, that made Allen a household name. Impressed with the results of his national radio trial, CBS programmers summoned him to New York City in the fall of 1950 to adapt his radio show for the new medium. The first *Steve Allen Show,* a live local daily series broadcast from Manhattan, was cancelled after four months because of uncertainties about Allen's unorthodox style. Another prime-time network summer replacement series that aired in 1952 met with a similar reaction from management.

Although his quirky series had not caught hold on television, Allen did. He made network appearances as a substitute for vacationing hosts on two CBS "amateur night" vehicles, *Songs for Sale,* on which unknown songwriters competed with each other, and Arthur Godfrey's *Talent Scouts,* one of the most popular television series of the period. His skill at the role led to his own show, *Talent Patrol,* an American Broadcasting Company (ABC) knockoff of the Godfrey series. Over the years Allen would either host or appear as a panelist on a dozen network game shows, including his three-year stint as emcee of the top-rated *I've Got a Secret* (1964–1967).

If Allen's brand of personal comedy had been too unorthodox for CBS executives, it was better suited to the plans of Pat Weaver, president of the National Broadcasting Company's (NBC) television network. Weaver had created the early-morning *Today Show* in 1951 and was planning a late-night complement whose content would reflect the more whimsical concerns of the midnight hour. Allen always insisted that while Weaver may have coined the title, he (Allen) was the one who had shaped and developed the series: "We got on the air and basically I did what I had done earlier on radio. . . . Guess how many writers I had when the show started. Zero. . . . With me, it was an ad-lib operation."

The *Tonight Show,* starring Allen, premiered as a local program in New York City in June 1953, and just thirteen months later it was elevated to an NBC network show and has been running ever since. Many of the segments created by Allen—including "Stump the Band," "The Question Man" (which the later host Johnny Carson dressed up as "Karnak the Magnificent"), and the reading of comment cards filled out by the studio audience—remain intact on this and other late-night programs. The same can be said for the host's use of the announcer and bandleader as comic foils. Unlike his successors, Allen created a guest list notable for the jazz musicians, writers, and "fringe" performers who appeared alongside major celebrities.

In 1957 NBC persuaded Allen to give up the *Tonight Show* and take on an assignment that at the time seemed more crucial to the network. He was asked to create and host an hour-long comedy-variety show that would go head to head in prime time with CBS's *Ed Sullivan Show,* one of the most popular programs in the history of the medium. The Sunday-evening *Steve Allen Show* probably was the most fully realized work of his career. Given considerable resources and creative freedom, he assembled a cast of little-known comedians—including Don Knotts, Tom Poston, Louis Nye, and Dayton Allen—using them in fresh, intelligent sketch material that pushed prime-time TV comedy-variety beyond the pie-in-the-face slapstick that had predominated. Rare television appearances by the writer Jack Kerouac (who read his poetry to Allen's piano accompaniment) and Lenny Bruce were just two highlights. Dozens of jazz greats, including Charles Mingus and John Coltrane, gave memorable performances. Elvis Presley made his first prime-time network appearance on the show, forcing the conservative Sullivan to book him soon thereafter.

The move from a late-night to a prime-time slot proved to be a mixed blessing, halting the momentum of Allen's television career. Had he remained as host of the *Tonight Show,* he might well have occupied that position for decades. The prime-time show, as good it was artistically, managed to beat Sullivan in the ratings on only two occasions during its three-year run and was canceled in the 1960s, leaving the star without a network show. Relocating to Los Angeles, Allen made a deal with the Westinghouse Broadcasting Company to produce a similar ninety-minute daily program to be syndicated to stations around the country. During most of the 1960s the original creator of the *Tonight Show* was forced to compete with the latter program without the full audience coverage or promotional benefits of a national network behind him.

Allen's personal life was marked by a period of change that accompanied his television stardom during the 1950s. On 23 August 1943 he married Dorothy Goodman, whom he had met at Arizona State Teachers College and with whom he had three sons. The move to New York City put a great strain on the marriage, which ended in divorce in 1952. That same year Allen met the actress Jayne Meadows. They were married on 31 July 1954 and had one son. He has credited her with directing him to books, film, and intellectual ideas generally, which infused his work with a broader perspective and endowed it with greater social awareness.

Meadows collaborated with Allen on *Meeting of Minds,* a concept he said they first came up with in 1961 but were unable to produce until 1977. Aired on the Public Broadcasting System, the series featured Allen (playing himself) as the host of a talk show whose panel of guests consisted of a different group of historical figures each week. For example, on one episode the Egyptian queen Cleopatra (played by Meadows) appeared alongside the eighteenth-century political theorist Thomas Paine, Saint Thomas Aquinas, and President Theodore Roosevelt. The series won Allen his second Peabody Award. He also received the Emmy, Sylvania, and Television Critics Circle awards for various efforts. At age seventy-eight Allen was busier than ever, working on new books, songs, and television projects and running his company, Meadowlane Enterprises. He suffered a heart attack while driving to visit one of his sons, at whose home he died. He is buried at the Forest Lawn cemetery in the Hollywood Hills section of Los Angeles.

Allen's career defies easy categorization. At his best he used national television as a medium for personal creative expression, which remains a rare accomplishment. Especially in his later years, some critics found his attempts to bring his idea of American culture—with their predigested versions of philosophers and ideas—rather pretentious and middlebrow. For many Americans who grew up watching television in the 1950s and 1960s, he is likely to be remembered for the wit, intelligence, and occasional outrageousness that was generally unavailable on the tube.

★

Two of Allen's books, *Mark It and Strike It: An Autobiography* (1960) and *Hi-Ho, Steverino! My Adventures in the Wonderful Wacky World of TV* (1992), can be considered a two-volume autobiography. Allen gave taped interviews to two oral history archives: the Southern Methodist University Oral History Project on the Performing Arts (with Ronald Davis, 18 Nov. 1975), and the Center for the Study of Popular Television, S. I. Newhouse School of Public Communications, Syracuse University (with David Marc, 18 Sept. 1996). Obituaries are in most major newspapers, including the *New York Times, Chicago Tribune, Los Angeles Times, Washington Post,* and *Times* (London) (all 1 Nov. 2000).

DAVID MARC

AMBROSE, Stephen Edward (*b*. 10 January 1936 in Decatur, Illinois; *d*. 13 October 2002 in Bay Saint Louis, Mississippi), historian whose engaging prose in more than thirty books on U.S. history attracted a national audience and celebrated the heroes of World War II and the American West.

Ambrose was the second of three sons of Stephen Hedges Ambrose, a doctor, and Rosepha (Trippe) Ambrose, a homemaker. The family lived in Lovington, Illinois, where his father practiced medicine. After the Japanese attacked Pearl Harbor, Hawaii, in December 1941, the elder Ambrose joined the U.S. Navy. When he was assigned to the Pacific theater, the family moved to Whitewater, Wisconsin, where he practiced medicine after the end of World War II. A 1953 graduate of Whitewater High School, young Stephen became an Eagle Scout, the captain of the football team, the prom king, and a regular patron of the town library. He said, "I was either playing sports, or in that Carnegie library reading."

At the University of Wisconsin in Madison, Ambrose registered as a premedicine major and played varsity football. As a sophomore, he enrolled in Professor William B. Hesseltine's American biographies class to fulfill a history requirement. Ten minutes into the first lecture, he decided to abandon medicine and take up the study of history. In 1957 Ambrose earned a B.A. in history and married Judith Dorlester, with whom he would have two children. That autumn he began graduate work at Louisiana State University in Baton Rouge under T. Harry Williams, a Wisconsin historian who had studied under Hesseltine. Both scholars emphasized narrative history. After completing an M.A. in 1958, Ambrose returned to the University of Wisconsin, where Hesseltine directed his dissertation on Emory Upton, a U.S. Civil War officer who championed tactical revision after the war. In 1960, before completing his dissertation, Ambrose accepted a teaching position at Louisiana State University in New Orleans (later the University of New Orleans). He completed his Ph.D. in 1963, the year after his master's thesis on the Civil War general Henry Halleck was published.

Although Ambrose's study of Halleck sold fewer than 1,000 copies, one was purchased by the former president Dwight D. Eisenhower, who was looking for someone to edit his papers. In 1964 the twenty-eight-year-old historian received a call from Eisenhower that altered his career. A self-proclaimed New Left historian, Ambrose opposed U.S. involvement in the Vietnam War, emphasized America's flaws in his lectures, and had joined the Socialist Party as a student. Although with these views he found little to admire in the Eisenhower administration, Ambrose agreed to meet with him to discuss the assignment. Thus began an association that gave Ambrose access to Eisenhower, his papers, and his military and civilian associates. Until Eisenhower's death in 1969, Ambrose met regularly with him and taped hundreds of hours of interviews. He was the associate editor of the first five volumes of the *Papers of Dwight David Eisenhower* (1967); wrote several monographs focusing on aspects of the general's military career, in addition to a two-volume biography; coauthored a biography of Eisenhower's brother Milton; and laid the foundation for a series of books on the European theater in World War II. Ironically, Ambrose, whose career focused heavily on the conduct of war, never served in the military.

In 1964 Ambrose moved to the Johns Hopkins University in Baltimore, where he completed a history of the U.S. Military Academy at West Point. In 1966 Ambrose's wife, who had bipolar disorder, committed suicide. The next year he married Moira Buckley, a divorcée with three young children. Ambrose left Johns Hopkins in 1969 and, after a year as a visiting professor at the Naval War College at Newport, Rhode Island, was named the Dwight D. Eisenhower Professor of War and Peace at Kansas State University in Manhattan.

The passage of time and his association with Eisenhower had moderated the radical tendencies Ambrose had displayed early in his career. He retired the fringed buckskin jacket he had worn to class, cut his ponytail, and abandoned his New Left outlook for a more conservative orientation. Ultimately labeled a "super-patriot," he shifted his focus from America's flaws to its virtues. This new perspective was apparent in his biography of Eisenhower, a president considered ineffective by many historians. Emphasizing his positive contributions, Ambrose rated Eisenhower just below the top rank of presidents. However, Ambrose's political metamorphosis was incomplete in 1970 when he moved to Kansas State. Within a month of his arrival, Ambrose heckled President Richard M. Nixon and walked out of a speech he made in Manhattan. Although the university president resisted political pressure to fire Ambrose, he informed the historian, "I'd be a lot happier if you left."

After spending a single academic year at Kansas State, Ambrose returned to Louisiana State University and stayed there for the remainder of his academic career. In 1982 he became the Alumni Distinguished Professor of History and, seven years later, the Boyd Professor of History. In 1983 he founded the university's Eisenhower Center for American Studies to sponsor conferences and collect documents and oral histories about World War II. As the center's director, he collected more than 4,000 first-hand accounts of the war. During sabbaticals and leaves he served as a visiting professor at University College, Dublin, Ireland; the University of California, Berkeley; and the Army War College, Carlisle Barracks, Pennsylvania. He was also a senior fellow at the Rutgers Center for Historical Analysis in New Brunswick, New Jersey. Ambrose spent most summers researching, camping, and, beginning in 1981, conducting guided tours of European battlefields. Throughout most of Ambrose's academic career, he taught nine hours per semester in addition to his research and writing.

In the early 1980s Ambrose's editor urged him to write a biography of Nixon. When he objected, she asked, "Where else are you going to find a bigger challenge than to do a good job on the life of a man that you don't like?" Although Nixon refused to grant Ambrose an interview and dismissed him as "just another left wing historian," the three-volume biography, published between 1987 and 1991, was evenhanded. The decade Ambrose devoted to Nixon apparently completed his transformation to what he himself described as an "unabashed triumphalist"—an historian who celebrates the nation's history, ignoring its warts. In Nixon, Ambrose found much to admire and concluded, "When Dick Nixon resigned, we lost more than we gained." Like the Eisenhower biography, the Nixon volumes were well received by reviewers, but a few critics did suggest that the author's ability to describe was not matched by his power to analyze.

Despite this criticism, Ambrose's publications placed him in the front ranks of the historical establishment. In 1994, just before the fiftieth anniversary of the Allied landings in Normandy, France, his *D-Day June 6, 1944: The Climactic Battle of World War II* topped the best-seller list. President William J. ("Bill") Clinton asked him to write remarks he would deliver at the commemoration of the invasion, and the National Broadcasting Company (NBC) hired him to provide commentary on the event. In 1996 Ambrose's *Undaunted Courage: Meriwether Lewis, Thomas Jefferson, and the Opening of the American West* became a runaway best-seller. Other books, many on World War II, followed in rapid succession. After thirty-five years as a productive but obscure scholar, Ambrose was suddenly the most widely read historian of the late twentieth century, a frequent commentator and guest celebrity on television, and a highly paid speaker. In 1995 he retired from the University of New Orleans to write and pursue other interests, including an unsuccessful effort to draft the retired general Colin Powell to oppose President Clinton in the 1996 presidential election.

In the next seven years Ambrose wrote or revised almost two books per year. Many topped the best-seller lists; most revisited the European theater in World War II from the perspective of the fighting men; and others chronicled the construction of the transcontinental railroad and considered the history and significance of the Mississippi River. Ambrose was showered with awards from a variety of organizations, including the U.S. Department of Defense. A 2001 television miniseries based on his *Band of Brothers: E Company, 506th Regiment, 101st Airborne, from Normandy to Hitler's Eagle's Nest* (1992) won six Emmys, a Golden Globe, and a Peabody Award. The miniseries was produced by the actor Tom Hanks and directed by Steven Spielberg. Ambrose had worked with both men earlier as the chief historical consultant on *Saving Private Ryan,* a 1998 film acclaimed for its realistic depiction of the Normandy invasion. Ambrose also served as a commentator for Ken Burns's Public Broadcasting System (PBS) documentary *Lewis and Clark: The Journey of the Corps of Discovery* (1997).

Ambrose worked to found a museum honoring both Andrew Higgins, who designed the amphibious landing craft used on D day, and the men who spearheaded the amphibious landings in World War II. Eisenhower believed Higgins's boats "won the war for us." In the mid-1980s Ambrose launched a campaign to establish the National D-Day Museum and kept the project alive with large personal contributions. The museum, which opened on 6 June 2000 near the French Quarter of New Orleans, attracted 300,000 visitors in its first ten months of operation.

On 4 January 2002 an article in the *Weekly Standard* compared Ambrose's *Wild Blue: The Men and Boys Who Flew the B-24s over Germany* (2001) with a similar work by another author, and suggested Ambrose had copied passages with scant revision. Ambrose acknowledged the similarity, apologized, and blamed the problem on "sloppiness," but denied that it constituted plagiarism. The ensuing weeks produced more accusations concerning lifted passages in other books. One journalist detected "a pattern that can be traced all the way back to his University of Wisconsin doctoral thesis from 1963." With criticism mounting, Ambrose claimed the passages he neglected to enclose in quotation marks constituted only "10 pages out of a total work of some 15,000 pages in print." He and his supporters suggested the criticism was motivated in part by professional jealousy.

In April 2002, before the controversy faded, Ambrose learned he had lung cancer. He curtailed his public appearances, discontinued work on a manuscript on the Pacific theater, and concentrated on writing a memoir to "correct all the mistakes" he had made as a young professor. He still found much to criticize in the unfulfilled promise of the nation, but he believed the accomplishments of the past justified Americans' optimism in their country's future. Ambrose died of lung cancer at the Hancock Medical Center at the age of sixty-six, one month before the publication of *To America: Personal Reflections of an Historian* (2002). He is buried in the Garden of Memory Cemetery in Bay Saint Louis.

An academic maverick, Ambrose chose to focus on war (in spite of the fact that, in his words "My experiences with the military have been as an observer"), while others in the historical community fixed their attention on social and intellectual currents. By working longer and harder than most of his contemporaries, Ambrose established a reputation for balanced and skillful narrative, despite occasional criticism of his failure to provide fresh insight. The popular acclaim he achieved late in his career provoked the same questions about scholarship faced by many historians whose books attract a mass audience, but his books continued to top the best-seller lists, and his celebrity status grew. The charges of plagiarism raised in the last year of Ambrose's life were different, however. His initial acknowledgment of "sloppy" scholarship was replaced by rationalizations that resonated beyond the scholarly community. Ambrose's death may have saved him from further embarrassment, but his name will continue to remind Americans both of the "greatest generation" of fighting men and of the author who lifted the words of others in chronicling their deeds.

★

Ambrose's last book, *To America: Personal Reflections of an Historian* (2002), is autobiographical, describing his evolution as an historian and providing insight regarding his books. *Contemporary Literary Criticism,* vol. 145 (2001), features a biographical sketch of Ambrose, a list of his principal works, and extensive reviews of many of them. The charges of plagiarism are summarized in Paul Gray, "Other People's Words," *Smithsonian* 32, no. 12 (Mar. 2002); and Michael Nelson, "The Good, the Bad, and the Phony: Six Famous Historians and Their Critics," *Virginia Quarterly Review* 78, no. 3 (summer 2002). Obituaries are in the *New Orleans Times-Picayune, New York Times, Washington Post,* and (Madison) *Wisconsin State Journal* (all 14 Oct. 2002).

BRAD AGNEW

ANNENBERG, Walter Hubert (*b.* 13 March 1908 in Milwaukee, Wisconsin; *d.* 1 October 2002 in Wynnewood, Pennsylvania), billionaire publisher, philanthropist, art collector, and U.S. ambassador to the United Kingdom, who founded both *Seventeen* magazine and *TV Guide* as part of his media empire, Triangle Publications.

Annenberg was the sixth of nine children, and the only son, born to Moses ("Moe") Louis Annenberg, an East Prussian Jew who had immigrated to Chicago with his family in 1885, and Sadie Cecelia (Friedman) Annenberg, the daughter of German-Jewish immigrants. Moses was a dogged self-made millionaire who rose from poverty to make a fortune in the Chicago and Milwaukee newspaper business under the legendary publisher William Randolph Hearst, with a veritable monopoly on horseracing publications.

As the family's only son, Annenberg, whom his parents affectionately called "Boy" his entire life, was a favored child who stood to inherit his father's vast business interests. Born with a deformed right ear, Annenberg was deaf on that side and later developed a stutter that he struggled his whole life to master. Shy and self-conscious as a result, he initially exhibited little of his father's strength and competitive spirit. Annenberg's early education, from age six to twelve, was at the German-American Academy in Milwaukee, an exclusive private school. In 1920 the family relocated to New York and established residences at a Long Island estate and in the city. Annenberg attended a small private school in Manhattan while undertaking intensive speech therapy.

In 1922 he was enrolled at the Peddie School, a private institution near Princeton, in Hightstown, New Jersey. There he thrived socially but was an average student. At Peddie, Annenberg took an interest in the stock market and began to amass significant earnings. Before graduating in June 1927, he gave the school $17,000 for a new cinder track, his first charitable bequest and the first of many large donations to Peddie. The next fall Annenberg entered the University of Pennsylvania to study at the Wharton School of Finance and Commerce. Bored with classes and performing poorly, he dropped out in the spring of 1928, turning his full attention to stock trading instead. Annenberg continued to turn spectacular profits in the market until its crash in October 1929, which abruptly transformed his $3 million paper earnings into a $350,000 debt. Moses paid his son's tab but scolded him for trading on margin, a lesson that Annenberg never forgot.

At age twenty-one, a college dropout and chastened stock-market loser, Annenberg went to work at the New York headquarters of the Cecelia Company, the holding corporation for his father's far-flung business operations. During most of the 1930s he was occupied with titular low-level roles and, with few demands, spent much of his time mingling with Hollywood starlets and playing the part of the dapper playboy in the nightclubs and café society of New York, Chicago, southern California, and Miami. In 1934 Moses purchased the *Miami Tribune,* giving Walter an opportunity to cut his teeth in journalism as business manager and an occasional columnist at the paper. He also purchased the *Philadelphia Inquirer,* the 107-year-old bastion of Pennsylvania Republicanism, in 1936 and sold the

Walter H. Annenberg testifying before the Senate Foreign Relations Committee, March 1969. BETTMANN/ CORBIS

Miami Tribune the next year. Walter accompanied his father to Philadelphia to assist him at the paper.

On 26 June 1938 Annenberg married Bernice Veronica ("Ronny") Dunkelman, the daughter of a wealthy Toronto-based merchant. They purchased a Georgian mansion on fourteen acres in Wynnewood, Pennsylvania, a Philadelphia suburb in the city's exclusive Main Line corridor. The estate, called Inwood, would remain Annenberg's primary Philadelphia residence throughout his life. He had two children with Ronny. They divorced in 1950, and in 1951 he married Leonore ("Lee") Rosensteil, the ex-wife of the liquor magnate Lewis Rosensteil. Annenberg's second marriage was a happy one that lasted more than fifty years. He and Leonore had no children.

The Annenberg empire was shaken in August 1939 when Moses and Walter Annenberg and several associates were indicted for tax fraud by a federal grand jury in Chicago. Moses had a long history of dubious business dealings, from his participation in the Chicago newspaper wars at the turn of the century to his operation of a news wire for horseracing bookies. It was his strident criticism, in the *Philadelphia Inquirer,* of President Franklin D. Roosevelt and local Democrats, rather than his connection to unsavory elements of the publishing and gambling underworld, however, that ultimately brought his downfall at the hands of federal investigators. In April 1940 Moses pleaded guilty to one charge of tax evasion under the condition that all charges against his son be dropped. Moses was ordered to pay $9.5 million in back taxes and sentenced to three years in jail. He served two years before his release in June 1942

due to failing health and died of a brain tumor a month later.

The ordeal had a profound influence on Annenberg, who agonized over his father's personal sacrifice and public humiliation. The rest of his life was devoted in large part to honoring his father's memory and restoring the family's tarnished reputation. The second great tragedy of Annenberg's life occurred in August 1962, when his son died from an overdose of sleeping pills. A gifted but introverted child with an artistic temperament, he had attended Harvard University until deteriorating mental health, diagnosed as schizophrenia, forced him into a psychiatric facility in Bucks County, Pennsylvania, where he took his own life.

Upon Moses's death in 1942, Annenberg took over as editor and publisher of the *Philadelphia Inquirer* and the family's other publications, including the *Daily Racing Form,* the *New York Morning Telegraph,* and *Click* magazine. To the surprise of nearly everyone, he soon emerged as an able leader and prescient businessman. He renamed the family company Triangle Publications and, in 1944, conceived and founded *Seventeen* magazine, which was an immediate success. By 1946 he had paid off his father's tax penalty, returned the *Philadelphia Inquirer* to solvency, and added to the family holdings with the purchase of WFIL, a Philadelphia radio station. In 1948 he established WFIL-TV, only the thirteenth television station in the nation, and launched the innovative educational program *University of the Air* and the dance show *Bandstand,* which became the long-running teen favorite *American Bandstand.*

Over the next several years, Annenberg purchased additional television stations in Binghamton, New York, and Altoona and Lancaster, Pennsylvania. His appreciation of television as the medium of the future was apparent in 1953, when he founded *TV Guide,* a consolidation of several metropolitan television-listing periodicals that he had purchased the year before. *TV Guide* was the first national publication of its type and soon became the best-selling periodical in America, making Annenberg a fortune. In 1957 he purchased the *Philadelphia Daily News,* putting him in control of two of the city's three major papers.

Although Annenberg initially had distinguished himself as an evenhanded and civic-minded editor of the *Philadelphia Inquirer*—even endorsing two Democratic candidates for the city's leadership in 1951, despite his own Republican sentiments—he eventually skewed the paper's journalism to serve his own opinions and grievances. Unlike his father, who lambasted his enemies, Annenberg simply ensured that the names of those who offended him never appeared in his papers. At one time his list of unmentionables included a University of Pennsylvania president and the entire Philadelphia Phillies baseball team. Annenberg also was not above burying or killing stories that personally displeased him or engaging in mudslinging if he felt slighted. In 1969 he sold both the *Philadelphia Inquirer* and the *Philadelphia Daily News* to Knight Newspapers for $55 million.

A staunch Republican throughout his life, Annenberg befriended presidents Dwight D. Eisenhower, Gerald Ford, Ronald Reagan, and George H. W. Bush and was an early supporter and close friend of Richard M. Nixon. Upon assuming the presidency in January 1969, Nixon appointed Annenberg U.S. ambassador to the United Kingdom, one of the most coveted foreign diplomatic posts. Reluctant at first, Annenberg accepted at Nixon's insistence and was sworn in on 14 April 1969. Critics of the nomination suggested that Annenberg had purchased the ambassadorship and, during Senate confirmation hearings, his father's criminality was dredged up in an attempt to discredit him.

Upon his arrival in London, Annenberg was coolly received by British society and ridiculed for his curiously stilted locution when speaking to Queen Elizabeth II during his formal introduction. His debut speech, a harsh attack on student antiwar protesters in the United States, attracted further opprobrium. Nevertheless, Annenberg eventually earned acceptance through his perseverance and generous contributions to British cultural institutions as well as through his wife's good graces, establishing friendships with the royal family and the Queen Mother. He resigned from the position in October 1974, three months after the Watergate scandal forced Nixon out of office.

During the early 1970s Annenberg began to sell off parts of his corporate holdings, including all of his broadcasting properties, which netted some $87 million. In 1988 he sold the remainder of Triangle Publications to the Australian media mogul Rupert Murdoch for $3.2 billion. While dismantling his media empire, Annenberg turned to philanthropy on an unprecedented scale. Since his first bequest to Peddie, Annenberg had given hundreds of millions to educational institutions, including the Annenberg School for Communication at the University of Pennsylvania, which he endowed in 1962, and a second school of communication at the University of Southern California a decade later. In 1981 he donated $150 million to the Corporation for Public Broadcasting.

Using profits from the sale of Triangle, in 1989 he established the M. L. Annenberg Foundation, which accrued more than $3 billion and funded numerous cultural and educational programs in memory of his father. Annenberg donated $50 million to the United Negro College Fund in 1991 and gave a $500 million aid package to rural and urban public schools nationwide in 1993. He also had given to humanitarian causes during his life, donating $1 million to Israel as part of an emergency relief fund after the Six-Day War in 1967, and on several occasions he gave modest but meaningful unpublicized gifts to individuals, including employees who had suffered sudden misfortunes.

During the 1950s Annenberg developed a passion for collecting art. Over the next several decades he amassed one of the world's finest private collections of impressionist and post-impressionist masterworks, including pieces by Vincent van Gogh, Georges Seurat, Henri Toulouse-Lautrec, Paul Gauguin, Paul Cézanne, Edgar Degas, Auguste Rodin, Pierre Renoir, Claude Monet, Henri Matisse, Jean Arp, Alberto Giacometti, and Pablo Picasso. He housed the collection in his magnificent 240-acre Sunnylands estate in Rancho Mirage, California, near Palm Springs, where he spent much of his time. In 1991 he donated his collection, then valued at $1 billion, to the Metropolitan Museum of Art in New York City. In 1993 he purchased van Gogh's *Wheat Fields with Cypresses* for $57 million and also gave it to the Metropolitan Museum of Art. In 2002 *Forbes* magazine rated Annenberg the thirty-fourth wealthiest American.

Annenberg was knighted by Queen Elizabeth in 1976 and received the Presidential Medal of Freedom from President Reagan in 1986. He died at age ninety-four from complications of pneumonia at Inwood, his home in Wynnewood, Pennsylvania. He is buried at his Sunnylands estate in California.

During the 1940s Annenberg emerged from his father's shadow and a cloud of disrepute to build one of the most profitable media corporations in the United States. He was a smart businessman who intuitively grasped the importance of demographics and understood the potential of television, as revealed by his two greatest publishing ventures, *Seventeen* and *TV Guide.* Although he failed to win respectability through his uneven editorial leadership, he managed to redeem himself against great odds as a dignified and dedicated ambassador. His philanthropic generosity made him one of the most admired benefactors in American history, and his bequests to museums, schools, and charitable organizations were on a level rarely seen.

★

John Cooney, *The Annenbergs* (1982), and Christopher Ogden, *Legacy: A Biography of Moses and Walter Annenberg* (1999), are informative, comprehensive studies of Annenberg and his father. Gaeton Fonzi, *Annenberg: A Biography of Power* (1970), provides a useful but generally unflattering portrait of Annenberg from the perspective of a Philadelphia journalist. Obituaries are in the *New York Times, Washington Post,* and *Philadelphia Inquirer* (all 2 Oct. 2002).

JOSH LAUER

ARLEDGE, Roone Pinckney, Jr. (*b.* 9 July 1931 in Queens, New York City; *d.* 6 December 2002 in Manhattan, New York City), television producer and executive best known for his work at the American Broadcasting Company (ABC), where his innovative programming changed the way Americans watched sports and understood the news.

Arledge was the son of Roone Pinckney Arledge, a lawyer, and Gertrude (Stritmater) Arledge, a homemaker. Growing up in the Forest Hills neighborhood of Queens, he enjoyed an affluent childhood, which from every indication was happy and uneventful. He credited his mother for his personal reserve and attention to detail, and his father for his passionate curiosity and love of the news. Arledge grew up during the golden era of the radio, listening to President Franklin D. Roosevelt's "fireside chats" and the nightly reports of World War II. The stars of his youth were foreign correspondents such as Edward R. Murrow, Eric Sevareid, Howard K. Smith, and Charles Collingwood. He saw his first television when he was eight years old, at the 1939 World's Fair in New York City, not far from where his family lived. It was an early glimpse of the medium that would dominate Arledge's future career.

After earning a B.B.A. from Columbia University in New York City in 1952, Arledge briefly attended Columbia's School of International Affairs, served a stint in the U.S. Army (where he produced radio programs at the Aberdeen proving ground in Maryland), and then went to work in the fledgling television industry for the National Broadcasting Company (NBC). He rose rapidly from an entry-level position to jobs with increasing responsibility, and by the end of the 1950s he was producing *Hi, Mom,* an Emmy Award–winning show starring Shari Lewis and her puppets. Talented and young—and looking even younger, with his shock of red hair, freckles, and Huckleberry Finn

Roone Arledge. AP/WIDE WORLD PHOTOS

looks—Arledge aspired to greater programs. He angled to produce a show called *For Men Only,* "based on an amalgam of the men's magazines that were so popular at the time—*Playboy, True, Sport, Field & Stream,* and so on," as he later noted in his autobiography. NBC passed on the series, and a short time later, Arledge passed on NBC.

Timing was important in the television industry, and Arledge's was exquisite. In 1960 he accepted an ill-defined job in the sports department at the weakest of the three major networks. Indeed, the American Broadcasting Company (ABC) had 20 percent fewer stations than either NBC or the Columbia Broadcasting System (CBS), and many of its affiliates resided in the netherworld of the ultra high-frequency (UHF) channels. (In the era before cable, mainstream channels, numbered 2 through 13, were on very high frequency, or VHF; to access the relatively obscure UHF channels, with numbers higher than 14, viewers used a separate dial.) But the ABC sports department had just landed the *Friday Night Fights* series, and with it the television advertising of the Gillette Safety Razor Company. With that money, Ed Scherick, ABC's sports programmer, began to purchase the rights to televise other sports, including National Collegiate Athletic Association (NCAA) football.

Not long after starting at ABC, Arledge began to formulate a new way of televising sports. His idea was as revolutionary as it was simple. It was based on the notion that television sports should be for all viewers, not simply sports fans; in fact, it should be for people who were not particularly interested in sports. Arledge reasoned, "Sports were life condensed, all its drama, struggle, heartbreak, and triumph embodied in actual contests." The outcome of the contest was far less important than the process, and sports, far from inhabiting a realm all their own, were merely a form of entertainment. It was the drama of live entertainment, with its unpredictable happenings and evolving plot twists—not sports—that captured Arledge's interest.

How to realize that ideal became his quest. Ford Frick, the baseball commissioner, believed, "The view a fan gets at home should not be any better than that of the fan in the worst seat in the ball park," and he insisted that baseball be broadcast accordingly. Arledge believed the exact opposite, insisting that the television viewer should have the very best seat. He recalled the games he had seen with his father—the hot dog and peanut vendors, the mad scrambles for foul balls and home runs, and the other joys of the ballpark. "That was the game," he remembered, "as much as a home run or a diving catch. They were all part of a piece."

Arledge's philosophy in producing NCAA football games for ABC became "taking the fan to the game, not the game to the fan." He accomplished this through technology. Using directional and remote microphones, handheld and "isolated" cameras, split-screen and slow-motion replays, along with other innovations, Arledge's team was able to give the viewer the full game experience, from the action on the field and the coach on the sideline to the activities of the cheerleaders, marching bands, and spectators. Arledge's philosophy, including his "up close and personal" approach and emphasis on personal narration, became the heart of ABC Sports, and eventually sports programming at the other networks.

Arledge also expanded his philosophy into other sports programming. During the 1960s ABC acquired the rights to college and professional football, golf tournaments, horse races, All-Star games, the summer and winter Olympic Games, and a wide range of other activities. To provide sports coverage that was not subject to the vagaries of schedules or weather conditions, Arledge launched *Wide World of Sports,* an anthology program that emphasized exotic locales, interesting personalities, and the drama of contests—"the thrill of victory, the agony of defeat"—as much as the actual sports. Most of the shows were pre-recorded and pre-edited, and could fit nicely into any time slot. Between 1961 and 1966 *Wide World of Sports* presented eighty-seven different sports to American viewers. In 1970 Arledge also took sports to prime time with the introduction of *Monday Night Football.* The formula was the same—more technology,

more well-known announcers, more drama. The program was the longest-running show on prime-time television.

In 1968 Arledge became the head of ABC Sports. His inspired coverage of the crisis at the 1972 Munich Olympic Games, when Palestinian terrorists held a group of Israeli athletes hostage before killing them, demonstrated that his approach to sports merged effortlessly with hard news. In 1977 he was named the head of the news division as well as the sports division. At the time, ABC News was struggling. Using essentially the same formula he had pioneered in sports, Arledge made ABC the "up close and personal" news network. He created new programs, including *20/20, Prime Time Live,* and *This Week.* Perhaps his most important addition was *Nightline,* which debuted in 1979 and established the model for a host of nightly news shows.

Although the changes Arledge brought to ABC News proved as spectacular and successful as those he had effected with ABC Sports, they were not without controversy. Critics charged that his news shows emphasized glitz over content, and dramatic narrative over in-depth analysis. They also accused Arledge of turning news commentators into highly paid celebrities, pointing to the salaries of Peter Jennings, Barbara Walters, and Diane Sawyer. Arledge seldom answered his critics; however, he was deeply proud of the news coverage provided by shows such as *Nightline,* and never denied that he was in the entertainment business.

The string of successes that characterized Arledge's career did not always mark his personal life. He was married three times. His first marriage was on 27 December 1953, to Joan Heise; they had four children, but divorced in 1971. His second marriage was in 1976, to Ann Fowler; they had no children and divorced in 1984. On 21 May 1994 he married Gigi Shaw. Arledge retired from ABC in 1998 and was diagnosed with prostate cancer. He died from the disease four years later. His remains were cremated, and the ashes were given to his family.

Those who knew Arledge recalled that he could be both charming and irritating. "He was impossible, he was exasperating," noted Barbara Walters. "If you wanted to reach him, it was very hard. But no one ever had a greater 'vision thing' than Roone." The true measure of his impact was the large number of television producers, executives, and personalities who learned from and were indebted to him. His television—the marriage of storytelling with hard reporting—became the standard.

★

The best source on Arledge is his autobiography, *Roone: A Memoir* (2003). See also Bert Randolph Sugar, *"The Thrill of Victory": The Inside Story of ABC Sports* (1978); *ABC Sports: The First Twenty-Five Years* (1985); Randy Roberts and James S. Olsen, *Winning Is the Only Thing: Sports in America Since 1945* (1989); and Marc Gunther, *The House That Roone Built: The Inside Story of ABC News* (1994). An obituary is in the *New York Times* (6 Dec. 2002).

RANDY ROBERTS

ASH, Mary Kathlyn ("Mary Kay") (*b.* 12 May 1918 in Hot Wells, Texas; *d.* 22 November 2001 in Dallas, Texas), energetic, charismatic saleswoman whose direct-sales cosmetic company offered saleswomen, or "beauty consultants," the opportunity for personal flexibility and financial independence.

Born Mary Kathlyn Wagner, Mary Kay was the youngest child of Edward Alexander Wagner and Lula Vember (Hastings) Wagner, who ran a hotel in the tiny resort town of Hot Wells. After her father was hospitalized for tuberculosis, Mary Kay and her mother moved to Houston. When her invalid father returned home, the seven-year-old took on responsibility for her father and the household, while her mother worked long hours in a Houston restaurant to support the family. Mary Kay's mother kept in close touch by telephone during the day, giving instructions for household chores, but more importantly, encouraging her daughter with heartfelt exhortations of "You can do it!" Even as a young girl, Mary Kay took on challenges and competed against herself to be the best and to please her mother. In school, she achieved academically, winning prizes for public speaking and debate. Family finances precluded going to college, and after graduating with honors from Reagan High School in Houston, she married J. Ben Rogers, a popular singer on local radio, at age seventeen. The couple had one daughter, Marylyn, and two sons, Ben and Richard.

Mary Kay's first experience with sales occurred when she agreed to sell sets of child-rearing books in order to earn a free set for herself. By enthusiastically and persuasively approaching neighbors and fellow church members, Mary Kay did unexpectedly well, but learned an even more valuable lesson. When customers became irritated with her for selling them things they rarely used, Ash recognized the importance of teaching customers to use the product, so that whatever it might be, it became a valued item in the consumer's life.

After Rogers lost his day job as a gas-station attendant, Mary Kay and her husband worked together demonstrating and selling cookware at home parties. In 1938 she joined Stanley Home Products, a direct-sales, household-cleaning–products manufacturer. She was immediately caught up in the company's promotional campaigns, whereby successful salespeople were crowned "queen of sales" and rewarded with luxurious prizes. Understanding first hand that most people will work hardest for recognition and personal attention, Mary Kay began to compete in the Stanley sales contests. With her children helping her

Mary Kay Ash. MARY KAY INC.

fill orders while Rogers was away during World War II, Mary Kay sold competitively to support her young family as she attempted to begin a premedicine program at the University of Houston.

Mary Kay's frenetic activity as a saleswoman, college student, and homemaker came to an abrupt halt when Rogers returned home in 1945 and asked for a divorce. Burdened with marital troubles, Mary Kay was terrified that she would be permanently disabled by what had been diagnosed as rheumatoid arthritis. In response to these situations, she dropped out of college and pushed herself even more energetically into sales. Mary Kay succeeded at Stanley Home Products, eventually becoming a manager. She left Stanley for the Dallas-based World Gift Company in 1953, where she was named the national training director for direct sales.

As was the case during her years at Stanley, Mary Kay often trained young men, only to see them quickly surpass her in income and corporate responsibility. Derided for "thinking like a woman" and demeaned by being passed over for promotion, Mary Kay, who had married George Hallenbeck in 1963, decided to retire from sales and to write a "how-to" book for women in business. In the process of listing positive and negative features of businesses, Mary Kay realized that she was defining an ideal company, one that she and her husband could run successfully. Using her savings of $5,000, Mary Kay founded her company and bought the formula and production operations for locally produced skin care creams that she had personally used.

With Hallenbeck taking responsibility for the financial and administrative aspects of the business and Mary Kay running marketing and sales, the new company, Beauty by Mary Kay, was set to open in a Dallas storefront in September 1963. One month before opening, Hallenbeck died of a massive heart attack. Mary Kay was advised to cut her losses, but her children rallied around, offering her their savings. Her youngest child, Richard, offered to take administrative responsibility for the fledgling company, and eventually Mary Kay's other son and daughter also joined the business.

Mary Kay, Incorporated, opened with nine saleswomen, or "consultants," who gave facials to demonstrate the company's skin-care products. Mary Kay's sales philosophy required that each customer be treated individually in a relaxed environment. Saleswomen, who bought the company's products with cash or credit cards, could sell not only within specified districts but wherever they found willing customers. As salespeople brought additional consultants into the business, the recruiter received a percentage of the new consultant's sales, building networks of women who competed and supported each other. At the end of her first year in business, Mary Kay had generated nearly $198,000 in wholesale sales. By 1965 the figure was $800,000, and the sales force numbered 3,000. In 1968 the company went public, and in 1976 it was listed on the New York Stock Exchange.

Annual Mary Kay conventions celebrating sales success brought women together to be rewarded with jeweled bumblebee pins and the ultimate prize of a pink Cadillac. Recognition for a job well done, a form of emotional currency, was as important to Mary Kay, Inc., as it was to its founder. Pink, the Mary Kay signature color, connected the consultants and consumers to the company and to its products. Mary Kay opened her pink mansion in Dallas for visiting consultants and led the celebrations honoring them. She also established the Mary Kay Charitable Foundation to support cancer research and provide funds to educate and prevent domestic violence.

On 6 January 1966 Mary Kay married Melville J. Ash. In 1979 Ash was diagnosed with cancer, and he died a few months later, in 1980.

In 1984 *Fortune* magazine recognized Mary Kay, Inc., as one of the best companies in the United States to work for, and one of the ten best for women; the company received the same recognition in 1993 and 1998. In 1985 the company returned to family ownership and continued to grow both in the United States and overseas. In 1987 Mary Kay formally retired from active participation as chair, assuming the title of chairman emeritus. She continued for

another decade as a motivating force, with her speeches a highlight of the annual sales extravaganzas. Sales at Mary Kay, Inc., exceeded $1 billion beginning in 1991.

In 1996 Mary Kay suffered a stroke, and remained in frail health. After her death at age eighty-three, a memorial service was held at the Park Cities Baptist Church in Dallas.

Through her company, Ash offered unique opportunities for women, many of them with families, to work for themselves outside their homes with flexible hours and without the constraints of an office or a time clock. As famous for her cloud of blonde hair and her energy, enthusiasm, and egalitarianism as she was for her success in sales, Ash offered her saleswomen education, encouragement, vision, and the possibility for financial independence.

★

Ash's autobiography, *Mary Kay* (1981), was published again under the title *Miracles Happen* (2003). She discussed her business philosophy in *Mary Kay on People Management* (1984) and *Mary Kay—You Can Have It All: Lifetime Wisdom from America's Foremost Woman Entrepreneur* (1995). See also Jim Underwood, *More Than a Pink Cadillac* (2003). A profile of Ash is in Gene Landrum, *Profiles of Female Genius: Thirteen Creative Women Who Changed the World* (1994), and in Alan Farnham, "Mary Kay's Lessons in Leadership," *Fortune* (20 Sept. 1993). Obituaries are in the *Dallas Morning News* and *New York Times* (both 23 Nov. 2001).

WENDY HALL MALONEY

ATHERTON, Alfred Leroy, Jr. ("Roy") (*b.* 22 November 1921 in Pittsburgh, Pennsylvania; *d.* 30 October 2002 in Washington, D.C.), career diplomat in the United States Foreign Service who figured prominently in the negotiations that resulted in the Camp David Accords and who played a fundamental role in establishing positive relations between Egypt and the United States.

Atherton was born to Alfred Leroy Atherton, Sr., and Joan (Reed) Atherton. His youth seems to have been privileged; his ancestors were among the first to settle in Allegheny County when Pennsylvania was founded, and the Athertons remained among the social elite when Roy was born. He graduated with a B.S. from Harvard University in 1944 and joined the army. During his service, which lasted until 1946, he became a lieutenant in the field artillery in Europe and received the Silver Star for heroism. He earned an M.A. from Harvard in 1947. As his career in the Foreign Service took shape, he studied economics at the University of California, Berkeley, from 1961 to 1962.

On 26 May 1946 Atherton married Betty Wylie Kittredge, with whom he had three children. In 1947 he joined the Foreign Service and was posted to Stuttgart, West Germany, where he served as vice-consul. In 1950 he was sent to Bonn, where he remained until 1952.

In 1953 Atherton became the American embassy's second secretary in Damascus, Syria, an assignment that would mark the beginning of his rise to prominence in the State Department, as well as the start of his specialization in Near Eastern and South Asian affairs. He remained in Damascus until 1956, and from 1957 to 1958 he served as the American consul in Aleppo, Syria. In these posts, Atherton was developing the expertise that would put him at the heart of history-making events.

From 1959 to 1961 Atherton served in the State Department's Bureau of Near Eastern and South Asian Affairs, and from 1962 to 1965 as the American consul in Calcutta, India. He then served from 1965 to 1966 as deputy director of the State Department's Office of Near Eastern Affairs. It was his appointment in 1966 as director of relations with Arab States North that began his extraordinary seventeen years at the center of events in the Middle East.

In 1967 Arab states around Israel, led by Egypt, threatened war. Israel had already fought two wars against its neighbors, winning both. In 1967, supplied with the latest Soviet tanks, Egypt, Syria, and a reluctant Jordan arrayed troops along their borders with Israel. Egypt blockaded Israel's seaports in an attempt to cripple the Israeli economy. Historians disagree as to which side started shooting first, but on 5 June air and tank battles erupted along Israel's borders.

Atherton was pressed into service as a negotiator to get the combatants to agree to a cease-fire. Tall, balding, and unflappable, with an easy smile and a good sense of humor, he earned admirers on all sides. On 10 June the combatants agreed to a cease-fire, with Israel having driven Arab forces out of the Sinai Peninsula, the Gaza Strip, the West Bank of the Jordan River, and the Golan Heights. Negotiations with Syria had been particularly sticky, with the Syrian government insisting on micromanagement of cease-fire details, down to exactly where individual trucks would be stationed.

From 1967 to 1969 Atherton was the State Department's director of Arab-Israeli affairs. From 1970 to 1978 he was a member of the Bureau of Near East and South Asian Affairs, a role in which he had to deal with increasing frustration over Israel's refusal to return lands captured in the Six-Day War of 1967.

On 6 October 1973 Syria and Egypt launched a surprise attack on Israel, whose forces were celebrating the Jewish holiday of Yom Kippur. Iraq and Jordan joined Syria in an attack on northern Israel, while Egypt crossed the Suez Canal and sent tanks deep into the Sinai. Soon, Israel turned the tide of battle, while Atherton and other diplomats tried to put an end to the hostilities.

Atherton's outstanding performance during the Yom Kippur War earned him enough admiration to weather a

Alfred L. Atherton, Jr., January 1982. AP/WIDE WORLD PHOTOS

storm in 1976. He had become a shuttle diplomat, flying from nation to nation to carry on negotiations among parties who would otherwise not talk to one another. Eventually, Secretary of State Henry Kissinger became involved in the shuttles, and in 1976 details of Kissinger's confidential talks with Arab leaders were leaked to the American press. Atherton said that he was responsible for the leak, but some journalists maintained that he was taking the fall for Kissinger, who seemed the likelier source of the leak.

On 16 November 1977 Anwar Sadat, Egypt's leader, told his government that he intended to go to Israel to promote peace. Almost immediately, Atherton was in the thick of the negotiations between Egypt and Israel, and was appointed "ambassador at large" by the American government in order to focus on the peace negotiations. It was a dangerous assignment, making him a target for assassination; it was also the apex of his career.

Negotiators from both sides of the peace talks credit Atherton with soothing angry participants, making all concerned feel that peace could actually be achieved, and repeatedly persuading negotiators to continue when they were ready to quit. His efforts eventually helped to create the Camp David Accords, signed by Sadat, Prime Minister Menachem Begin of Israel, and President Jimmy Carter at the presidential retreat in Maryland on 17 September 1978. The accords returned the Sinai Peninsula to Egypt and resulted in a peace between the nations that lasted for decades. Atherton is credited by the participants with writing between one-third and two-thirds of the accords document.

From 1979 to 1983 Atherton was ambassador to Egypt, living in Villa Alaili on Taha Hussein Street in Zamalek, where he used his deft personal touch to improve relations between America and Egypt. He oversaw the expansion of the mission in Egypt into one of the largest America had in the world, with 872 American and over 500 Egyptian staffers. He also oversaw the distribution of billions of dollars in foreign aid that helped Egypt improve its economy. By the time he left, Egypt had become one of America's closest allies.

As director general of the Foreign Service from 1983 to 1985, Atherton took a special interest in training Foreign Service officers. After his retirement in 1985, he continued in an unofficial capacity to help with the training. He also remained an adviser to each successive president until his death at Sibley Memorial Hospital after surgery for cancer.

In the 1970s Atherton became the model for subsequent U.S. Foreign Service officers. His easy manner belied a remarkable memory for details, but his ability to earn trust from unfriendly foreign leaders was his most important asset. Repeatedly, he found ways to persuade people who hated each other to agree to talk about making peace with one another. This eventually helped in the triumph of peace between Egypt and Israel.

★

The best accounts of Atherton's activities during the long negotiations between Egypt and Israel are in the memoirs of the participants on the Egyptian and Israeli sides. Most notable among these are Boutros Boutros-Ghali, *Egypt's Road to Jerusalem: A Diplomat's Story of the Struggle for Peace in the Middle East* (1997), and Moshe Dayan, *Breakthrough: A Personal Account of the Egypt–Israel Peace Negotiations* (1981). Obituaries are in the *Washington Post* (31 Oct. 2002) and *Washington Report on Middle East Affairs* (Jan./Feb. 2003).

KIRK H. BEETZ

ATKINS, Chester Burton ("Chet") (*b.* 20 June 1924 near Luttrell, Tennessee; *d.* 30 June 2001 in Nashville, Tennessee), musician and record producer whose finger-picking style of guitar playing inspired performers in various genres, and whose role in creating the "Nashville sound" helped broaden the national appeal of country music.

Born on a fifty-acre farm in the foothills of the Clinch Mountains, Atkins was one of three children of James Arley Atkins, a piano tuner, music teacher, and evangelical

Chet Atkins, 1987. AP/WIDE WORLD PHOTOS

singer, and Ida (Sharp) Atkins, a homemaker. Atkins's father was often away from the farm, traveling with evangelical troupes, and eventually left the family for good. His mother married Willie Strevel in 1932. Although Atkins grew up in rural poverty during the depression, he was surrounded by a rich heritage of local folk music. His older half-brother, Jim Atkins, became an early professional role model; his guitar playing on radio stations and also with Les Paul and the Fred Waring orchestra inspired Atkins's interest in the instrument. As a child, Atkins played an old ukulele, and when he was nine years old he traded two guns to his stepfather for his first guitar. However, the first instrument he played for an audience was the fiddle, and soon he was earning a few dollars, as well as applause, performing with his brother and stepfather at local roadhouses.

When Atkins was eleven he went to live with his father in Georgia, where it was hoped the climate would improve his asthma. He began to experiment with finger picking on the guitar, developing the style that would characterize his musicianship. Atkins moved between Georgia and Tennessee, and his schooling was fragmented; he eventually dropped out of high school before his senior year. A shy teenager, Atkins bought a two-tube radio that opened new vistas, allowing him to hear Jim play on the *National Barn Dance,* as well as the music of the guitarists Les Paul and Merle Travis, who influenced his technique. Work as a laborer for the National Youth Administration in 1941 provided Atkins with money to electrify his guitar and purchase an amplifier. He had come to understand the underlying links among various styles of music: the hillbilly songs of his heritage, the blues and church songs of the African Americans he met in Georgia, and the jazz tunes he heard on the radio. At age sixteen he first performed on radio programs in Columbus, Georgia, with a preacher friend of his father.

Atkins made his way to Knoxville, Tennessee, to find work in radio. During 1942 at WNOX, he played fiddle for Archie Campbell and Bill Carlisle and accompanied them on personal appearances. When Atkins's finger-picking style of guitar playing was noticed by the station director, Lowell Blanchard, he was offered a spot playing solos on *Midday Merry-Go-Round* and was encouraged to expand his repertoire to include pop, jazz, and country songs. He joined the Dixieland Swingsters, the station's staff band, as a rhythm guitarist and by 1943 he was doing personal appearances, playing with Kitty Wells and Eddie Hill, as well as working several daily shows on the air. But after three years at WNOX, Atkins was encouraged to move on, particularly if he wanted to appear on the Grand Ole Opry in Nashville, a venue representing the height of musical aspiration for a young man raised on hillbilly music.

Moving to Cincinnati in 1945, Atkins worked at WLW, where he was friendly with his fellow performers Homer and Jethro and the singing Johnson Twins. Still painfully shy and introverted, he courted Leona Johnson. Although Atkins spent less than a year at the station, his playing began to reach national audiences on network broadcasts, and he met and played for Merle Travis, one of his early idols, who later told him, "I can't play the guitar. Not like you can, Chester." Nevertheless, Atkins was fired in December 1945. After a brief stay at WPTF in Raleigh, North Carolina, he went to Chicago, where he met Red Foley, the star of WLS's *National Barn Dance.* Foley took Atkins to Nashville and the Grand Ole Opry as part of his troupe, but after six months Atkins's featured spot was dropped by the network. Atkins returned to Cincinnati to marry Johnson on 3 July 1946. During the next two years he moved to WRVA in Richmond, Virginia, KWTO in Springfield, Missouri, and KOA in Denver.

In 1947 Steve Sholes, an executive with Radio Corporation of America (RCA) Victor, invited Atkins to record some country songs for the label. The sessions showcased Atkins's ability as a soloist, writer, and sideman, but none of the recordings was a hit. He returned to Knoxville and teamed up with his old friends Homer and Jethro, playing again on WNOX and taking the act on the road. Atkins and his wife had their only child, a daughter, in 1947, and again he found work at KWTO in Springfield with his new ensemble. Sholes and RCA still had faith in Atkins's talent, and his record "Galloping on the Guitar" (1949), with backing by Homer and Jethro, was popular on country radio stations. Another RCA instrumental recording, "Main Street Breakdown," with Homer and Jethro and Anita Carter, was a modest success late in the year. Meanwhile, he had teamed with the Carter sisters and Mother Maybelle; their shows on KWTO were transcribed for syndication. In 1950 they were invited to go to Nashville to appear regularly on the Grand Ole Opry.

Upon his return to Nashville, Atkins worked with Fred Rose, the most influential local music publisher and record producer at the time, doing session work for several leading stars, including Hank Williams and the Louvin Brothers. Over the next several years he became a popular session guitarist, accompanying country stars such as Faron Young, Webb Pierce, Porter Wagoner, and Kitty Wells on many of their hit records. Teaming with Boudleaux Bryant in 1953, he cowrote "How's the World Treating You" for Eddy Arnold and "Country Gentleman," which would become his signature tune. At the same time, Atkins recorded his own hit singles, including the successful instrumental version of "Mr. Sandman" (1955). In 1952 Atkins began to record long-playing (LP) albums for RCA, and in the following decades the label released more than 100 albums by the guitarist.

In 1954 RCA decided to set up a recording studio in Nashville, and at Sholes's suggestion Atkins was made the studio manager. Two years later Sholes brought Elvis Presley to Atkins's studio to record his first RCA sides, and Atkins played rhythm guitar on several of Presley's songs, including the singer's first national hit, "Heartbreak Hotel" (1956). Atkins also contributed to rock and roll by promoting the Everly Brothers as songwriters and performers, and by leading their studio sessions and playing on most of their hit records. By early 1957 Atkins was RCA's manager of operations in Nashville, and he helped convince the label to build Studio B, the first permanent record company office on Music Row, marking the beginning of Nashville's prominence as a recording center. In the late 1950s and early 1960s Atkins produced records for such artists as Don Gibson, Eddy Arnold, Hank Snow, Jim Reeves, Skeeter Davis, Hank Locklin, Bobby Bare, and Floyd Cramer. Atkins's careful production, combining country songs with sophisticated arrangements including strings and choral voices, became known as the "Nashville sound," enabling country music to cross over to the national pop scene.

By the 1960s Atkins was producing more than two dozen acts for RCA while establishing his reputation as one of the best-known guitarists in the world. At the studio, he signed and produced Charley Pride, Jerry Reed, Waylon Jennings, Willie Nelson, Jessi Colter, and Charlie Rich, among others. He was also responsible for bringing the singer Dolly Parton to the label. RCA released no fewer than thirty-nine Atkins albums during the decade. In 1965 he recorded "Yakety Axe," a major country instrumental hit that crossed over to the pop charts, and in 1967 he won his first Grammy Award, with *Chet Atkins Picks the Best* named as the best instrumental performance. When Sholes died in 1968, Atkins was named as the vice president for RCA's country music division.

During the 1970s Atkins was awarded five Grammys and performed in concerts around the world. His executive duties continued at RCA, and he fostered a new generation of Nashville producers, including Felton Jarvis and Bob Ferguson, as well as performers such as Tom T. Hall, Ronnie Milsap, and Steve Wariner. In 1973 Atkins became the youngest living member of the Country Music Hall of Fame, but as an artist he worked in a variety of musical genres, collaborating with guitarists such as Les Paul, Lenny Breau, Django Reinhardt, and Paul McCartney. Atkins had endorsed a line of guitars for Gretsch since the mid-1950s, but ended this relationship in 1977 and began designing guitars for Gibson.

In 1981 Atkins retired from RCA, and the next year he began to record for Columbia. For the rest of his recording career, Atkins diversified his repertoire further in pop and jazz, teaming with the guitarists Earl Klugh and George Benson. However, he frequently returned to his country roots, as in duet albums with his old friend Jerry Reed and with Mark Knopfler of Dire Straits. The latter collaboration, *Neck and Neck* (1990), earned Grammys for best country vocal collaboration and for best country instrumental performance. In 1993 the National Academy of Recording Arts and Sciences honored Atkins with its Lifetime Achievement Award for "his peerless finger-style guitar technique, his extensive creative legacy . . . and his influential work on both sides of the recording console as a primary architect of the Nashville sound." In 1997 he won his fourteenth Grammy, and in 2002 he was named to the Rock and Roll Hall of Fame.

During the 1970s Atkins battled colon cancer, and in 1997 he underwent surgery for a brain tumor. Nevertheless, he continued to perform until a series of strokes forced his retirement. He died at his home from complications of cancer and is buried in Harpeth Hills Cemetery in Nashville. As a professional musician for a half century, Atkins perfected his own finger-picking guitar style. Although he remained faithful to his country roots, he displayed mastery of pop, jazz, and classical music. Atkins became one of the most recognized and important guitarists in the world, and served as an inspiration to younger generations of noted players. At the same time, Atkins's role as a producer and talent scout rivaled his significance as a performer. As a principal architect of the Nashville sound, he brought country music "uptown," securing its place in the history of American popular music. Atkins helped to make Nashville as much of a center for songwriters and musicians in the last half of the twentieth century as New York City's Tin Pan Alley had been at the beginning.

★

An archive of materials by and about Atkins is held by the Country Music Hall of Fame in Nashville. Atkins's book with Bill Neely, *Country Gentleman* (1974), is the most useful biographical resource documenting the artist's career to the 1970s. Paul Hemphill, *The Nashville Sound: Bright Lights and Country Music* (1970), provides important background on the changes in country music beginning in the late 1950s. Paul Kingsbury, *Chet Atkins: The RCA Years* (1992), adds the perspective of the Country Music Foundation on his significance as an instrumentalist and a producer. Steve Waksman, *Instruments of Desire: The Electric Guitar and the Shaping of Musical Experience* (1999), devotes a chapter to Atkins's role in making the guitar a musical icon through his playing style and technical innovations. Atkins provided additional biographical insights in articles in *Guitar Player* (Feb. 1972) and the *Journal of Country Music* (1989). See also Chet Flippo, "King Picker," *Rolling Stone* (12 Feb. 1976). Obituaries are in the Memphis *Commercial Appeal* (1 July 2001), and the *New York Times* and *Washington Post* (both 2 July 2001).

JAMES F. SMITH

B

BALABAN, Elmer (*b.* 1 May 1909 in Chicago, Illinois; *d.* 2 November 2001 in Chicago, Illinois), businessman who built a chain of palatial theaters in the Midwest and a media empire in radio and television, and who pioneered cable and pay-per-view television.

Balaban was the youngest child in a family of seven boys and one girl. His parents, Israel Balaban and Goldie (Katz) Balaban, Jewish immigrants from Russia, owned a grocery store on Maxwell Street in Chicago. Noted for their generosity, they often allowed customers to make purchases on credit. In 1912 his mother took the older children to a motion picture theater, and, pointing out the fact that people paid to see a movie *before* they saw what they were purchasing, she told the oldest son, Barney, that the theater business should be his future career.

That year, Barney and his brothers Abe, John, Max, and Dave, along with their maternal grandfather, Sam Katz, bought the 100-seat Kelzie Theater, with a sheet for a screen, and began their careers as theater owners, impresarios, and motion picture executives. They would eventually build the 700-seat Circle Theater in Chicago in 1915 and the 2,000-seat Central Park Theater in 1917. In time their company, known as the B & K chain, would own more than 125 theaters throughout the Midwest. Meanwhile, Elmer attended the Latin School of Chicago and Culver Military Academy. His family sent him to the Wharton School of Business at the University of Pennsylvania in Philadelphia to prepare him for work in the theater business, and, upon graduation he joined his brothers in the B & K chain. In 1936 B & K merged with Paramount Pictures, and Barney became its chief executive officer, with John its executive in charge of motion picture production.

In 1932 Elmer left the family theater chain to become a partner with his brother Harry in a chain of their own, H & E Balaban. They specialized in building palatial theaters, forty in all. These included the impressive 4,000-seat Esquire Theater on East Oak Street in Chicago, the first movie house with balconies and a wide screen. Designed by William and Hal Periera, it was built in 1938 and hosted the Chicago premiere of *Gone with the Wind* the following year. In 1986 it was named a city landmark, but while it retained its historic exterior, its interior had been divided into six modern theaters. Balaban married his wife, Eleanor, with whom he would have a daughter and a son, in 1933. His son, Bob, went on to become a character actor and motion picture director and producer, perhaps most famous for his role as the cartographer-turned-translator in *Close Encounters of the Third Kind* (1977).

The H & E Balaban theaters featured stage shows as well as motion pictures and were centers of entertainment into the 1950s, when television began to draw away audiences. In 1955 Elmer began buying a total of forty-seven radio and television stations in the Midwest and South, including Dallas and St. Louis. He pioneered pay-per-view

Elmer Balaban, 1949. MICHAEL ROUGIER/TIME LIFE PICTURES/GETTY IMAGES

Magidson, and helped his son, Bob, establish and run the Chicagofilms production company.

In the 1990s Balaban tinkered with inventions and helped his son develop ideas for motion pictures, including *Gosford Park* (2001). Among his creations was a candy he called "Elmer's Fudge," for Balaban's Fine Foods, that he was working on at the time he died of heart failure in Chicago's Northwestern Memorial Hospital. During his years running the H & E Balaban theaters, Balaban stubbornly resisted selling popcorn, offering only candy. He admitted in 1993, however, that modern theaters probably could not survive without selling popcorn. Balaban and his family brought creative entrepreneurship to motion pictures when the industry was young. Their luxurious theaters helped establish the standards by which movie houses are still judged, with comfort and service as high priorities. Balaban helped show that theaters could be built that would satisfy the needs not only of motion pictures but of theatrical productions as well by staging plays, musicals, and concerts in his establishments. When television made inroads into his audiences, he proved to be a visionary who helped establish cable television in the United States.

★

There is no biography of Balaban. Obituaries are in the *Chicago Sun-Times* and *Chicago Tribune* (both 4 Nov. 2001), the *New York Times* (9 Nov. 2001), the *Los Angeles Times* (10 Nov. 2001), and *Variety* (12–18 Nov. 2001).

KIRK H. BEETZ

BARNOUW, Erik (*b.* 23 June 1908 in The Hague, Netherlands; *d.* 19 July 2001 in Fair Haven, Vermont), preeminent historian of mass media in the twentieth century and professor of film, radio, and television at Columbia University.

The first eleven years of Barnouw's life were spent in The Hague, where his father, Adriaan Barnouw, taught Dutch history and literature at the high school level. His mother, Ann Eliza (Midgley) Barnouw, an Englishwoman, gave lessons in English and taught Shakespeare to supplement the family income. The couple had four children.

In September 1919 Barnouw's mother and the children joined his father in the United States, where he had been offered a Queen Wilhelmina lectureship at Columbia University in New York City. Barnouw entered the prestigious Horace Mann School for Boys. He excelled at his studies and was also a first-rate soccer player. In 1925 Barnouw enrolled at Princeton University in Princeton, New Jersey, on a scholarship. Deeply interested in theater, Barnouw wrote a satire about student life entitled *Open Collars,* and its production in 1927 catapulted him into the campus elite. Princeton University Press published the script in 1928, the same year Barnouw was naturalized as a U.S. citizen.

television with coin boxes attached to televisions. To see a first-run motion picture, a subscriber had to put quarters into the box. The quarters were periodically collected. This proved to be an objectionable intrusion into the lives of many people, but Balaban soon was on his way to helping pioneer an alternative system, cable television. In the 1960s he purchased a small cable company in the northern Midwest, and expanded his holdings to cover much of the midwestern and western United States.

In 1964 Barney Balaban retired as chief executive officer for Paramount Pictures, and the company offered his job to Elmer, whose astuteness in the ways of business would have been helpful to a studio experiencing tough economic times. He turned the job down, however, saying that he did not want to move out of Chicago. He loved his hometown and, according to his son, did not care much for the actual show business part of his career or, indeed, for anything "showy." By contrast, he was a quiet man who stayed out of the limelight most of his life and reportedly read two books a week right up to his death. In the 1980s Balaban semi-retired, still managing his investments and helping with fundraising for the Sloan Kettering Memorial Hospital in New York City. He established and helped manage Balaban's Fine Foods, with the help of his daughter, Nancy

After graduating in 1929 with an A.B. in English, Barnouw accepted a one-year traveling fellowship in Europe. He returned to the United States at the dawn of the Great Depression, only to find that his once-bright job prospects in theater or magazine writing had dimmed. By chance Barnouw ran into an acquaintance whose husband was in the advertising business. From this point on his career path changed direction. His employment at two prominent advertising agencies during the 1930s—with Erwin, Wasey and Company from 1931 to 1935 and with Arthur Kudner, Inc., from 1935 to 1937—coincided with the ascension of network radio as the dominant form of American entertainment. Barnouw wrote and produced popular programs for various national clients, including Camel cigarettes and Chiclets chewing gum.

In 1937 Barnouw accepted an offer from Columbia University to teach a new course on the medium of radio. His notes from his first year as a classroom teacher were collected and published as a textbook entitled *Handbook of Radio Writing* (1939). Instructors of the many radio writing courses springing up around the country quickly adopted the book, and his publishing success brought Barnouw many commissions to write scripts. The most thrilling of these offers was an invitation from the great dramatist Norman Corwin at the Columbia Broadcasting System (CBS) to join his staff as writer and editor for his radio series *Pursuit of Happiness,* a position Barnouw held from 1937 to 1940.

Barnouw was of average height and build, with a winsome smile and full head of dark, wavy hair. A 1939 *Time* magazine review of Barnouw's handbook noted that the author "might have become a matinee idol had he not chosen backstage radio." That same year Barnouw married Dorothy Maybelle Beach. They had three children.

In 1942 Barnouw replaced a script editor who had left the National Broadcasting Company (NBC) because of a navy commission, but he continued to teach evening courses at Columbia University. In 1944 the Pentagon recruited Barnouw to be the educational director of the Armed Forces Radio Service for the remainder of World War II.

After the war Barnouw became president of the Radio Writers Guild and founded the Center for Mass Communication at Columbia University. A prolific scholar, he remained on the Columbia faculty until his retirement as a professor of dramatic arts in 1973. During his tenure at Columbia, Barnouw was the recipient of numerous honors, including a Fulbright grant, a Guggenheim Fellowship, and a John D. Rockefeller III Fund Fellowship.

Barnouw is most widely known for his three-volume study *A History of Broadcasting in the United States*, which was published by Oxford University Press. *A Tower in Babel* (1966) chronicles the development of radio until 1933; *The Golden Web* (1968) covers radio through the early 1950s;

Erik Barnouw. AP/WIDE WORLD PHOTOS

and *The Image Empire* (1970) documents the rise of television. These works soon became required reading in university media and communication programs. Barnouw's trilogy also legitimized the field of media studies. With the award in 1971 of the prestigious Bancroft Prize in American History for *The Image Empire,* media history became a field all its own. In recognition of his significance, the Organization of American Historians presents an annual Erik Barnouw Award. His book *The Sponsor: Notes on a Modern Potentate* (1978), which offers a historical critique of broadcast advertising, is also regarded as a landmark in the study of popular culture.

In January 1968 Barnouw read a news report about a film shot by Japanese cameramen in Hiroshima and Nagasaki in 1945 that was being returned to Japan by the U.S. government, which had impounded it at the time. Barnouw gained access to the footage and was engrossed with the idea of creating a documentary to reveal the horrific reality that had been preserved on celluloid. The result was the documentary *Hiroshima-Nagasaki, August 1945,* which was released in 1970, with a preview screening at the Museum of Modern Art. Film scholars consider it among the most significant documentaries about war ever produced.

His fascination with documentary film led Barnouw and his wife to undertake a world tour in order to examine this universal medium from foreign perspectives. He also wrote *Documentary: A History of the Non-fiction Film,* which became a standard reference in the field upon its publication in 1974. With his recognition as a leading promoter of the documentary concept, Barnouw became a "gurulike" figure to a growing movement of independent documentary producers, scholars, and archivists worldwide. He was especially devoted to the "Robert Flaherty Seminars," named in honor of the pioneering documentarian, the maker of *Nanook of the North* and *Man of Aran.*

Barnouw's post-Columbia years could hardly be considered retirement. In 1976 he was a Woodrow Wilson Fellow at the Smithsonian Institution. From 1978 to 1981 Barnouw contributed to the preservation of America's media heritage as chief of the newly formed Motion Picture, Broadcasting, and Recorded Sound Division of the Library of Congress. From 1983 to 1989 Barnouw served as editor in chief of the *International Encyclopedia of Communications.* Following the death of his first wife in 1987, Barnouw married Elizabeth Prince Allen on 28 April 1989. Barnouw's autobiography, *Media Marathon: A Twentieth-Century Memoir* (1996), earned high praise for its elegant prose and humanistic tone—signature characteristics of his writing.

On the occasion of Barnouw's ninetieth birthday, the film journal *Wide Angle* published a special issue in his honor. Scholars and practitioners in the field who were inspired, influenced, encouraged, and touched by Barnouw's life and work were invited to submit tributes, which testify to his legendary status and confirm his generous spirit and wit.

Barnouw died of prostate cancer at his Vermont home. He was born in the era of the nickelodeon, but the news of his passing spread quickly throughout the world thanks to the Internet. Barnouw's life spanned the history of modern communications he had so magnificently chronicled.

★

The Erik Barnouw Papers (1920–1983) are housed at the Rare Book and Manuscript Library at Columbia University; the collection of thirty-eight boxes consists of scripts, manuscripts, correspondence, and reports. Barnouw's personal and professional history is recounted in his autobiography, *Media Marathon: A Twentieth-Century Memoir* (1996). *Film & History* XXI, nos. 2 and 3 (May/Sept. 1991), is a special double-issue honoring Barnouw and includes biographical information. "A Festschrift in Honor of Erik Barnouw," *Wide Angle* 20, no. 2 (1998), is a special issue honoring Barnouw and provides a compilation of reflections about his life and work, as well as a bibliography of his books and monographs. The obituary "Erik Barnouw, 93, Columbia Professor and Legendary Media Historian," *Columbia News* (25 July 2001), summarizes his career at the university. Other obituaries are in the *Los Angeles Times* and *Washington Post* (both 21 July 2001); the *New York Times* (26 July 2001); and *The Hindu* (5 Sept. 2001).

MARY ANN WATSON

BASKIN, Leonard (*b.* 15 August 1922 in New Brunswick, New Jersey; *d.* 3 June 2000 in Northampton, Massachusetts), sculptor, printmaker, and teacher of art whose sizeable body of work, defying contemporary artistic trends, remained resolutely figural and concerned with humanistic themes, especially that of mortality.

Baskin was the second of three children of a scholarly Polish-born Orthodox rabbi, Samuel Baskin, and May (Guss) Baskin. The family moved to Brooklyn, New York City, when Baskin was a child, and with his older brother he was enrolled in a yeshiva. The rigorous education he received there from 1929 to 1937 established his lifelong love of books and learning. From the age of fourteen, when he saw a demonstration of plasticine modeling at a crafts show, Baskin was determined to become a sculptor, and in 1937 he started night classes with the sculptor Maurice Glickman at the Educational Alliance. In 1939, after finishing his secondary education at a public high school, he began courses at the New York University School of Architecture and Applied Arts, and in 1940 he received an honorable mention for sculpture in a Prix de Rome competition.

Baskin won a scholarship to Yale University's School of

Leonard Baskin. AP/WIDE WORLD PHOTOS

Fine Arts in New Haven, Connecticut, in 1941; two years later, however, he was expelled for "incorrigible insubordination." While at Yale—inspired by the example of the English artist and poet William Blake—he became interested in printing and taught himself to operate a printing press. At the end of World War II, after serving in the U.S. Navy and the Merchant Marine from 1943 to 1946, Baskin studied under the GI Bill at the New School for Social Research, from which he received a B.A. in 1949. In the meantime, on 26 November 1946 he married the writer Esther Tane, a friend of his sister. The couple had one son. In 1947 he was awarded a Tiffany Foundation Fellowship in sculpture.

Searching for new means of expression, Baskin turned to printmaking, and in 1949 showed a series of woodcuts in a group exhibition at the Philadelphia Art Alliance. A year later he resumed his study of sculpture at the Académie de la Grande Chaumière in Paris, with the Russian-French sculptor Ossip Zadkine, and then in 1951 at the Accademia di Belle Arti in Florence. Another trip to Europe, on a Guggenheim Fellowship for printmaking, followed in 1953. Chance encounters with Egyptian and Mesopotamian art, late-Gothic sculpture, and the work of the French sculptor Auguste Rodin and of the German expressionist wood carver Ernst Barlach, however, had far greater influence on Baskin's style than formal studio classes.

On his return to the United States in 1951, Baskin moved to Worcester, Massachusetts, where he taught graphic arts at the Worcester Art Museum and founded a printing operation called the Gehenna Press. The name is an erudite punning allusion to a line in John Milton's *Paradise Lost* (1674), Book 1: "And black Gehenna call'd, the Type of Hell." When in 1953 Baskin began to teach graphic arts and sculpture at Smith College, the press moved with him to Northampton, Massachusetts. Over the years, it established a reputation for superbly printed illustrated books, among them volumes of Baskin's drawings for Richmond Lattimore's translation of Homer's *Iliad* (1962) and for *A Primer of Birds* (1981), by the poet Ted Hughes.

From 1952 on, Baskin's prints, and later his sculptures, were shown regularly in Boston and New York City galleries. His first major museum show was *New Images of Man* at New York City's Museum of Modern Art in 1959, which included several of his works in wood and bronze, as well as the massive limestone *Great Dead Man* (1956). The latter was one of the austere *Dead Men* effigies he carved in the 1950s, influenced by photographs of casts of dead bodies found in the ruins of Pompeii, Italy. Recognition abroad, which began in 1953 with an award from the International Society of Wood Engravers in Zurich, continued with his inclusion in the 1961 São Paulo Bienal and the 1968 Venice Biennale.

Both in his prints and carvings, a characteristic Baskin figure is a male nude, often obese, with a huge head and spindly legs—a menacing, ugly, "ghoulish" (the artist's own word) symbol of the debauched spiritual condition of humankind. There is compassion, on the other hand, in the series of wrapped figures, such as *John Donne in His Winding Cloth* (1955), or the draped, sorrowing bronze figure commissioned in 1990 for the University of Michigan (Ann Arbor) Holocaust Memorial. An expression of hope for humanity is found in *Altar* (1977), one of Baskin's major pieces, in the Jewish Museum, New York City. With its figures of Abraham, Isaac, and the ram, carved in linden wood, it is a complex, majestic working out of the theme of redemption. Other later, life-affirming works included illustrated children's books, among them *Hosie's Alphabet* (1972), which was nominated for a 1973 Caldecott Medal, and *Iconologia* (1988), Baskin's essays on artists he particularly revered, accompanied by portrait studies reproduced from his drawings, etchings, lithographs, and sculptures.

Women's figures were conspicuously absent from Baskin's earlier oeuvre. However, after his second marriage in 1967, he introduced the female form in such works as *Lisa* (1971), a tender profile portrait in bronze relief. Although he once stated that the human figure "contains all and can express all," Baskin did many representations—some with symbolic undertones, some purely representational—of animals, insects, and especially birds. Works of note include the walnut carving *Man with Dead Bird* (1964), and the prints and drawings executed between 1971 and 1983 and reproduced in *The Raptors and Other Birds* (1985). Most of this "ornithology of evil," as Baskin termed it, consists of anthropomorphized compositions of birds of prey, alluding to the greed and rapacity of the twentieth century; in contrast are several serenely lyrical, delicate watercolors of more benign species.

In the mid-1950s, shortly before the birth of their son, Baskin's wife was stricken with multiple sclerosis. Baskin and Tane divorced in 1967, and the artist married his student Lisa Unger, although Tane continued to live with Baskin and Unger until her death in 1970. In 1968 Baskin and Unger's son was born, followed by a daughter in 1970. Baskin resigned from Smith College in 1974 and moved with his family to Lurley, in Devon, England, but maintained a home and studio on Little Deer Isle, Maine. Returning to the United States in 1983, he served as a visiting professor of art at Hampshire College in Amherst, Massachusetts, from 1984 to 1994. Six years later he died at age seventy-seven of kidney disease.

With his uncompromising professional standards, Baskin was a demanding yet encouraging teacher, highly respected by his students. He received the American Institute of Graphic Arts Special Medal of Merit in 1965, and was elected to the American Academy of Arts and Letters in 1993. Baskin's diverse works—examples of which are owned by museums and galleries throughout the United States—confront evil and death but at the same time affirm the potential dignity of human life.

★

There is no full-length biography of Baskin. However, for information about his life see Irma B. Jaffe, *The Sculpture of Leonard Baskin* (1980), which is based on extensive interviews with the artist in 1977. Alan Fern and Judith O'Sullivan, *The Complete Prints of Leonard Baskin: A Catalogue Raisonné, 1948–1983* (1984), has an introduction by Ted Hughes, and includes a biographical note, a listing of Baskin's honors and awards, and extensive listings of books he illustrated or designed and articles about him. Further details about Baskin's life are in Selden Rodman, *Conversations with Artists* (1957), which contains an interview; Claude Marks, *World Artists, 1950–1980: An H. W. Wilson Biographical Dictionary* (1984); and Brian O'Doherty, "Leonard Baskin," *Art in America* 50 (summer 1962), which gives an idea of Baskin's concerns, expressed with his characteristically acid wit. Information about the Gehenna Press may be found in Lisa Unger Baskin, et al., eds., *The Gehenna Press: The Work of Fifty Years, 1942–1992* (1992), which contains a catalogue of an exhibition curated by Lisa Unger Baskin, an assessment of the work of the press by Colin Franklin, a bibliography of the books of the Gehenna Press, and notes on the books by Baskin. An obituary is in the *New York Times* (6 June 2000).

ELEANOR WEDGE

Byron De La Beckwith, January 1963. ASSOCIATED PRESS

BECKWITH, Byron De La, Jr. ("Delay") (*b.* 9 November 1920 in Sacramento, California; *d.* 21 January 2001 in Jackson, Mississippi), salesman and white supremacist best known as the murderer of the civil rights worker Medgar Evers in June 1963.

Beckwith was an only child. His father, Byron De La Beckwith, Sr., was a postmaster, farmer, and businessman, as well as an alcoholic who gambled away his inheritance. He loved guns and saw to it that Beckwith was carrying firearms such as revolvers and rifles as soon as the child could hold them. Beckwith lived in Colusa until his father died of pneumonia in August 1926. His mother, Susan (Southworth Yerger) Beckwith, a homemaker, then took him to her family's home in Greenwood, Mississippi. When she was tired of young Beckwith's boisterous behavior, she would lock him in a closet for hours at a time. Beckwith said he learned that if he stood quietly and smiled steadily, eventually the door would be opened for him. The men in the family home beat him severely for even the slightest breaches of etiquette. When he was twelve, his mother died of cancer.

A poor student, Beckwith was more interested in joking around than studying, and he attended various schools, usually failing academically. There was the Webb School in Bell Buckle, Tennessee, for his freshman year, then Columbia Military Academy in Columbia, Tennessee, then public schools. He eventually graduated from high school in 1940, at the age of twenty. He lasted less than a semester at Mississippi State College before his failing grades made him depart. In January 1942 Beckwith joined the U.S. Marine Corps, serving with distinction in World War II. During the campaign in the Solomon Islands, he manned the forward machine gun on a landing craft, returning fire while exposed to a withering hail of bullets. Beckwith was severely injured in one leg and spent most of the rest of the war in hospitals, and he was awarded a Purple Heart for his service.

During his recuperation, he married Mary Louise Williams, a big, hard-drinking, hard-talking woman: they had one son. Beckwith worked at a variety of jobs during the 1950s but was most effective as a salesman, because his bright smile and soft-spoken manner appealed to people. In 1954 he joined the White Citizens' Council, a group that advocated racial segregation. During the 1950s and 1960s both Beckwith and his wife proved to be violent alcoholics. They divorced and remarried several times in the early 1960s. In October 1962 they even divorced and remarried in the same month, with the new marriage dependent on Beckwith seeing a psychiatrist. The psychiatrist seems to have diagnosed Beckwith as a paranoid schizophrenic. The couple divorced for the final time in 1965.

Beckwith hated African Americans, Jews, and Roman Catholics. Among the many people he despised was Medgar Evers, a field secretary for the National Association for the Advancement of Colored People (NAACP) in Mississippi. On 11 June 1963 Beckwith drove to Jackson, Mississippi, and cruised his distinctive white automobile through Evers's neighborhood. Beckwith then parked the car and went to a vacant lot opposite Evers's home, where his wife and three small children were while he was out picking up "Jim Crow Must Go" T-shirts. Beckwith had affixed a sniper's scope to his Enfield hunting rifle and waited behind overgrown honeysuckle. Soon after midnight, on 12 June 1963, Evers came home, stepped out of his car, and pulled out the load of shirts. Beckwith shot him in the back, then dropped his rifle and fled; his rifle and the fingerprints on the scope would tie him to the crime. Evers crawled to his front door but died shortly thereafter.

Although there were other racial murders in Mississippi that had not been prosecuted, the Jackson police and the district attorney, William Waller (who was later elected governor), were determined to find Evers's killer. They charged Beckwith with the killing, and his first trial began on 27 January 1964. A spy had given the defense the prosecution's strategy, allowing them to be prepared to sidetrack Waller's questioning of witnesses. Even so, a jury of twelve white men split six to six, creating a hung jury. It was a landmark moment, as observers had expected a quick acquittal, not a long, angry debate among jurors. Waller refiled the charges, and jury selection for the second trial began on 6 April 1964. Unknown until the late 1980s, save to the conspirators, the jury selection process had been stacked to favor racist whites. But again the trial ended in a hung jury, this time eight to four for acquittal.

In 1967 Beckwith ran for lieutenant governor of Mississippi, finishing fifth out of six candidates in the Democratic primary. In 1970 an informant for the Federal Bureau of Investigation (FBI) discovered a plot to blow up A. I. ("B") Botnick, the leader of the Anti-Defamation League in New Orleans. Beckwith's role in the plot was to deliver and arm a bomb to blow up Botnick's home. The FBI and local police laid a trap for Beckwith and caught him with the bomb in his car, along with numerous firearms and much ammunition. In January 1974 Beckwith's trial began in federal court in New Orleans. In spite of the mountain of evidence against him, he was acquitted on all counts, angering even the judge.

The newly elected district attorney, Harry Connick, then charged Beckwith with illegal possession of explosives under state law and won a conviction. The judge gave Beckwith the maximum sentence of five years in the Louisiana State Penitentiary in Angola. Beckwith served three years, with time off for good behavior. After his release from prison, Beckwith moved into an isolated house near Greenwood, his childhood home. In June 1983 he married Thelma Lindsay Neff, a retired nurse and divorcée ten years older than he, and moved to her home in Signal Mountain, Tennessee.

During the 1980s Evers's widow and others asked that the murder be reinvestigated, and Assistant District Attorney Bobby DeLaughter of Hinds County, Mississippi, took an interest in the case and uncovered new evidence. Jury selection for the third murder trial began on 18 January 1994. Much of the prosecution's case was argued by the district attorney, Ed Peters, who was brilliant in questioning witnesses. On 5 February 1994 Beckwith was found guilty of murder and sent to a state penitentiary to serve a life sentence.

Beckwith, who was known by the nickname "Delay" (pronounced "dee-lay"), had a history of heart ailments. He was taken in January 2001 from prison to the University of Mississippi Medical Center in Jackson, where he died of heart failure. Confederate flags seemed to bedeck everything at his funeral service. He is buried in Chattanooga Memorial Park Cemetery in Tennessee.

Beckwith had a blighted life. He conducted himself bravely in World War II but chose cowardice in his attacks on those he detested because of their race or religion. By murdering Evers, he gave the U.S. civil rights movement a prominent martyr, but there was only evil in the deed.

★

Two books chronicling the murder of Evers and Beckwith's trials are Adam Nossiter, *Of Long Memory: Mississippi and the Murder of Medgar Evers* (1994), and Maryanne Vollers, *Ghosts of Mississippi: The Murder of Medgar Evers, the Trials of Byron De La Beckwith, and the Haunting of the New South* (1995). Bobby DeLaughter, *Never Too Late: A Prosecutor's Story of Justice in the Medgar Evers Case* (2001), provides details about Evers's murder and the process that brought Beckwith to justice. An obituary is in the *New York Times* (23 Jan. 2001).

KIRK H. BEETZ

BENSON, Mildred Augustine Wirt ("Millie") (*b.* 10 July 1905 in Ladora, Iowa; *d.* 28 May 2002 in Toledo, Ohio), author of more than 130 children's books, including twenty-three of the first thirty Nancy Drew mysteries.

Benson was the younger of two children of J. L. Augustine, a doctor, and Lillian (Mattison) Augustine, a homemaker.

At age twelve she sold her first short story to *St. Nicholas* children's magazine. Other story sales followed, primarily to denominational publications. After graduating from high school in Ladora, Benson enrolled in 1922 at the University of Iowa, where she became the first woman to receive a B.A. in journalism at the university in 1925. She then worked for a year as a general reporter and society editor at the *Clinton (Iowa) Herald*.

In 1926 Benson traveled to New York City in search of a writing job. While there, she met with Edward Stratemeyer, whose Stratemeyer Syndicate was responsible for the vast majority of contemporary children's book series, including the Bobbsey Twins, Honey Bunch, Tom Swift, and the Hardy Boys. Most of the books were written by ghostwriters, who waived rights and royalties in return for up-front fees. Benson returned to her parents' home in Iowa, and shortly thereafter was assigned to write a book for Stratemeyer's Ruth Fielding series; *Ruth Fielding and Her Great Scenario* (1927) was published under the pen name Alice B. Emerson. Benson then returned to the University of Iowa to pursue an M.A. in journalism. While working on her degree, she wrote two more Ruth Fielding books.

In 1927 Benson became the first person to receive an M.A. in journalism at the University of Iowa and started work at the *Iowa City Press-Citizen*, where she met Asa Wirt, an Associated Press correspondent. They married on 4 March 1928 and had one daughter. When Wirt got a job at the *Cleveland Plain Dealer*, they moved to Ohio. Benson wrote several more Ruth Fielding books, and in 1929 she began another assignment for Stratemeyer. He was planning a mystery series about a girl detective, Nancy Drew, and Benson was asked to write the first book. "The plots provided me were brief, yet certain hackneyed names and situations could not be bypassed," she later wrote. "Therefore I concentrated upon Nancy, trying to make her a departure from the stereotyped heroine commonly encountered in series books of the day."

Stratemeyer, Benson later recalled, was not pleased with the *Secret of the Old Clock* (1930), the first Nancy Drew book, and felt the heroine was "much too flip." Still, he submitted it to the publishers Grosset and Dunlap. They were enthusiastic and requested two more books. Benson quickly completed the *Hidden Staircase* and the *Bungalow Mystery* (both 1930). She was paid $125 each for the three, which were published under the pen name of Carolyn Keene.

The character of Nancy Drew struck a chord with girls. She was the only child of a widowed lawyer who trusted his level-headed daughter completely and gave her permission to do almost anything. The only other significant adult in Drew's life, the housekeeper, Hannah Gruen, was hardly in a position to forbid her to undertake any dangerous task

Mildred Wirt Benson, December 2001. AP/WIDE WORLD PHOTOS

the intrepid sixteen-year-old (or eighteen-year-old, depending on the book) chose to pursue. Nancy Drew was pretty, smart, and courageous, and she could master any skill in an unbelievably short period of time. "I made her as girls wished they were, not as they were," Benson told *Newsday* many years later.

Stratemeyer died suddenly on 10 May 1930. The Nancy Drew series was the last he created, and it went on to be the most successful Stratemeyer series ever. His daughters, Harriet Stratemeyer Adams and Edna Stratemeyer, took over the running of the syndicate. Benson continued to write the Nancy Drew mysteries, but the outlines, written primarily by Adams, became considerably more detailed than those from Stratemeyer had been, and the editing on the manuscripts was more extensive.

In 1932, at the height of the Great Depression, Benson was told that her fee would be reduced from $125 a book to $75. She declined to write the Nancy Drew books for that amount, so Walter Karig wrote volumes eight, nine, and ten. By then, Benson was working on several book series of her own, including the Ruth Darrow Flying series and the Madge Sterling series. She produced most of her books in a few weeks; in 1936, the year her daughter was born, she also wrote ten books. In 1934 she returned to writing the Nancy Drew series, eventually writing twenty-three of the first thirty volumes (for fees ranging from $125 to $250 per book). For the Stratemeyer Syndicate, she also wrote twelve Dana Girls mysteries, twelve Kay Tracey mysteries, and five Honey Bunch books. On her own, she wrote under the names of Frank Bell, Joan Clark, Don Palmer, and Dorothy West. Her favorite series was the Penny Parker mysteries, which she began in 1939 and wrote under her own name. Her last Nancy Drew book was *The Clue of the Velvet Mask* (1953). By then, Adams's editing had become so extensive that the last few books contained significant rewriting.

In 1944 Benson began working as a courthouse reporter for the *Toledo Times.* The following year her husband was paralyzed by a stroke. She nursed him, held down her job at the *Times,* and continued to write books. Her husband died in 1947, and on 25 June 1950 she married George A. Benson, the editor of the *Toledo Times.* She continued to write for several book series. She also wrote three nonseries children's books: *Pirate Brig* (1950); *Dangerous Deadline* (1957), which won the 1957 *Boys' Life*–Dodd, Mead Prize Competition for Children's Fiction; and *Quarry Ghost* (1959), her last book. George Benson died in 1959. After Benson stopped writing books, she pursued numerous other activities—archeology, piloting airplanes, and golfing—and traveled extensively.

In 1959 the Stratemeyer Syndicate began updating the early Nancy Drew books. Some of the changes were welcome; racial and ethnic stereotyping was removed. But many of the telling details that made the books special were removed as well. In the 1960s, articles began identifying Harriet Stratemeyer Adams as Carolyn Keene. The claim was not totally false; Adams was responsible for keeping the Nancy Drew series alive after Benson stopped writing for it, and many scholars feel she wrote at least some of the later books. But it was Benson who had originally brought the character to life and had set the parameters for the extremely successful series.

Benson, while never making a secret of her authorship of the early Nancy Drew mysteries, did not go out of her way to publicly contradict Adams. She continued to work full-time as a reporter and columnist, switching to the *Toledo Blade* in 1975 after the demise of the *Times.* But in 1980, after Adams decided to switch publishers, Grosset and Dunlap sued the Stratemeyer Syndicate. Benson was called on by Grosset and Dunlap to testify that she was the original Carolyn Keene. Adams was unable to contradict Benson's testimony, which was backed up by her signed contracts with the Stratemeyer Syndicate.

After the trial, Benson was widely recognized as the creator of Nancy Drew. Although she appreciated the recognition, she found it tedious to answer countless questions about the series and remained more focused on her job at the *Blade,* where in her later years she wrote the column "On the Go with Millie Benson." She also won many journalism and writing awards, including the Agatha Award for lifetime achievement in 2000 and an Edgar Allan Poe special award in 2001. She was diagnosed with lung cancer in 1997, but she was back at her desk the next day. It was not until January 2002, at the age of ninety-six, that she reluctantly retired. Even after her retirement she continued to write a monthly column, "Millie Benson's Notebook." After suffering several strokes, Benson was at her desk at the *Blade* working on her column on the day that she died. She is buried in Toledo Memorial Park in Sylvania, Ohio.

Benson was a prolific writer with a knack for action and suspense. She is best remembered for creating Nancy Drew, a character beloved by generations of American girls for giving them a glimpse of what might be possible for them. "I'm not proud of any of the writing," Benson wrote of the Nancy Drew series, "but I think I did come through with a different concept, now accepted as common."

★

Benson's papers are held in the Iowa Women's Archives, University of Iowa Libraries, in Iowa City, Iowa; the Stratemeyer Syndicate papers are held by the New York Public Library in New York City. For information on Benson and the Nancy Drew series, see Karen Plunkett-Powell, *The Nancy Drew Scrapbook* (1993); Carolyn Stewart Dyer and Nancy Tillman Romalov, eds., *Rediscovering Nancy Drew* (1995); and Carole Kismaric and Marvin Heiferman, *The Mysterious Case of Nancy Drew and the Hardy Boys* (1998). Two essays provide good biographical information: Mildred Wirt Benson, "The Ghost of Ladora," *Books at Iowa* 19 (Nov. 1973): 24–29; and Geoffrey S. Lapin, "The Ghost of Nancy Drew," *Books at Iowa* 50 (Apr. 1989): 8–27. Other sources of information about the Nancy Drew books are Anita Susan Grossman, "The Ghost of Nancy Drew: The Story Behind the Teenage Sleuth," *San Francisco Chronicle* (21 Oct. 1988), and Lauren Terrazzano, "Nancy Drew, Heroine," *Newsday* (18 Nov. 1998). Obituaries are in the *Toledo Blade* (29 May 2002) and *New York Times* (30 May 2002).

LYNN HOOGENBOOM

BERLE, Milton (*b.* 12 July 1908 in Harlem, New York City; *d.* 27 March 2002 in Beverley Hills, California), comedian who had a long and varied career in show business, known as "Uncle Miltie" and "Mr. Television" to millions of fans.

Born Mendel Berlinger, Berle was one of five children of Moses Berlinger, a painter and decorator, and Sarah (Glantz) Berlinger, a department-store detective and theatrical manager. Berle grew up in Harlem, across the street from another future comedian, George Jessel, and attended schools in New York City. At age five he won an amateur look-alike contest by impersonating the silent movie star Charlie Chaplin. Prodded by an ambitious, stagestruck, possessive mother, Berle appeared in such early silent films as *Tillie's Punctured Romance* (1914), in which he was draped over Marie Dressler's knees, and *The Perils of Pauline* (1914), in which he was thrown from a train. During World War I Berle went on the road to entertain the troops.

After bit parts in nearly fifty films (most of them made in New York City), Berle moved on to the legitimate stage in a 1920 Schubert Brothers production of *Floradora*. Still just a twelve-year-old novice, the young Berle received a dual initiation in sex (with a showgirl) and in Broadway theater. He teamed up with Elizabeth Kennedy in a "kiddie act" that opened at the Palace Theater on 2 May 1921 and lasted for two years. Since child stars had to avoid the scrutiny of the Gerry Society, a watchdog agency established to prevent the exploitation of child labor, his mother, Sarah (now calling herself Sandra), circumvented the agency by securing various jobs for her talented son as an actor and singer and moving to Philadelphia to avoid prosecution.

More derivative than creative, Berle developed a series of impersonations of such stars as Al Jolson and Eddie Cantor. With energy, chutzpah, and talent, Berle plugged away at the comedy game. He encountered many hurdles, including the first of several encounters with anti-Semitism. In 1925, when the famed comic Frank Fay referred to him as a "dirty little Jew" and a "kike," Berle lashed out at the bigoted star and smashed his face. Working the vaudeville circuit enabled the young entertainer to hone his skills and learn his craft. When Jack Haley (the future Tin Man in *The Wizard of Oz*) canceled a stint at the Palace Theater, Berle stepped in and achieved stardom during a ten-week run. Soon on the road again, he appeared in nightclubs and theaters and eventually on radio, also performing in an experimental television telecast in 1929.

Recurrent stints on Broadway, beginning in 1932 with the *Earl Carroll Vanities*, led to a hefty weekly salary of $1,500 and billing with the comedians Bing Crosby and Bob Hope and the pianist Eddie Duchin at various benefits and engagements. Vaudeville, radio, movies, and nightclubs beckoned to Berle, who even coauthored a musical parody, sprinkled with Jewish humor, entitled "Sam, You Made the Pants Too Long." Berle's identity as a fast-talking ad-libber who would do anything for a laugh developed through trial and error over many years. The comic, however, took union membership seriously, picketing with striking stagehands at the Roxy Theater when he was supposed to be on stage.

During the 1930s Berle toured in the Harold Arlen–Yip Harburg musical review *Life Begins at 8:40;* hosted a radio show sponsored by Gillette; and, accompanied by his predatory mother, went Hollywood again as a featured actor in

Milton Berle. GETTY IMAGES

New Faces of 1937. In the early 1940s he appeared in several mediocre films, including *Sun Valley Serenade* (1941) and *Margin for Error* (1943). He also toured military hospitals for six straight months during World War II.

Trying to look less Jewish, Berle "bleached" his act and bobbed his nose. As he explained, "I cut off my nose to spite my race." The new nose morphed into "a thing of beauty and a goy forever," but Berle could never shed his ethnicity. While working at a Chicago club, he attacked a thick-necked heckler for calling him a "Jew bastard" and "kike." Unable to laugh it off through improvisatory shtick, the comic silenced the heckler with his fists.

Eventually Berle learned to channel his rage into aggressive humor. He told one vocal critic, "You've been heckling me for twenty years. I never forget a suit." To a bleached blonde in the audience he remarked, "You look like Judy Holliday, and the guy next to you looks like 'Death Takes a Holiday!'" When the journalist Walter Winchell dubbed him "The Thief of Bad Gags," Berle wore this rubric as a badge of honor and often engaged in self-deprecatory wit aimed at his alleged "borrowing" from other comics, saying, "I laughed so hard—I almost dropped my pencil." Imitation may suggest the highest form of flattery, but Berle's purloined performances sparked anger among his peers. Bert Lahr, a great comedic clown best remembered for his role as the Cowardly Lion in *The Wizard of Oz,* absolutely loathed Berle and blocked his entry into the Lambs' fraternity, a service organization whose members were mainly entertainers.

Superstardom eluded Berle until 1948, when he was given a budget of $10,000–$15,000 per television show, with which he hired the vocalist Pearl Bailey, Señor Wences (a pseudo-Hispanic comic with Jewish roots, who excelled as a ventriloquist), and circus performers. Berle originally was slated to alternate with Jack Carter and Henny Youngman as hosts of the *Texaco Star Theater,* a variety show, but the National Broadcasting Company (NBC) executives reversed course and tabbed Berle as the "Top Banana." For the premier show on 21 September 1948, television welcomed Berle's ethnic *landsleit* (fellow tribesmen) Smith and Dale and Phil Silvers (who eventually would knock his benefactor out of prime time in 1956 with his own show). In two months ratings vaulted skyward, and Berle "owned" Tuesday nights for the next five years. Glued to their sets until the show ended at 9 P.M., viewers then rushed to their bathrooms, reducing water levels to danger point in Detroit. Nightclubs were closed on Tuesday nights in deference to the show.

Berle's success led to a rise in the sale of television sets throughout the United States, from 136,000 in 1947 to 700,000 in 1948. Even the hotly contested 1948 presidential election could not preempt this Berle-watching ritual. Suddenly a national star with front-page coverage on *Newsweek* (16 May 1949), Berle's reputation crested thanks to rapid-fire gags, a phenomenal memory bag of jokes (ten thousand, according to his count), broad clowning, versatility, and hard work. Shamelessly, he disrupted the acts of his guests. Wearing a whistle, he demanded attention as "Whistler's Mother" led the live audience in a chorus of laughter. Berle also dressed as Howdy Doody (the popular country bumpkin character from the children's television show of the same name) and sang with Elvis Presley in an Elvis wig as he wiggled his pelvis.

A product of the Borscht Belt (the popular resorts in the Catskill Mountains of New York) coupled with vaudeville, Berle was always married to the premise "anything for a laugh!" Thus, the need for "makeup" invited a belt in the face from an oversized powder puff. He "who got slapped" with cream pies or squirted with seltzer elicited peals, if not pearls, of laughter. Guests pulled at Berle's hair as he mugged for the camera. Anything could and did happen on this often ad-libbed show. The comedian Red Buttons lost his clothes—including his undergarments—in a stunt that went awry, as did the "Brazilian bombshell" singer Carmen Miranda. Significantly, Berle opened doors for performers of color and ethnicity.

Despite mainstream popularity, Berle never lost his Jew-

ish flavor. In one of many cross-dressing capers—this time as a contessa—unable to fix his hair, he bellowed, "My *shytel* [a wig worn by Orthodox or balding Jewish women] is falling!" Another sketch found him encased in a heavy sailor suit, about which he complained, "I'm *shvitzing* [sweating] in here!" Berle favored outlandish costumes to impersonate figures of history as well as characters from fiction: a caveman with a club and missing teeth, George Washington crossing the Delaware in a bathtub instead of a boat, Cleopatra in drag, Carmen Miranda going bananas, Superman in tights, and Sherlock Holmes in robes. To generations bred in the depression and tempered by war, Berle provided a cathartic release through his high-octane brand of Jewish humor. He morphed into a crazy uncle who urged the kiddies—his countless nieces and nephews—to be good. While climbing the career ladder to success, Berle raised millions of dollars for the Damon Runyan Cancer Memorial Fund and other charities by appearing as a featured performer at numerous benefits.

Perhaps, as the author Lawrence Epstein has argued, "Berle proved too Jewish for America." His early popularity was grounded in an urban Jewish base. As television moved westward, Middle America preferred the blander kind of humor practiced by Herb Shriner, George Gobel, Johnny Carson, and (later) David Letterman. The renowned theater critic Frank Rich has several explanations for Berle's spectacular rise and precipitous fall. When people crowded into an affluent neighbor's home to watch "Uncle Miltie," the contagion of "group hysteria" made Berle seem funnier. That comic effect dissipated as viewers purchased their own sets. Competitive variety shows, such as those featuring Ed Sullivan and Sid Caesar, and situation comedies did not help. Certainly Berle's in-your-face persona alienated gentile viewers, who preferred the avuncular parent of *Father Knows Best.* Rich also concluded that Berle fell victim to a medium that confers instant stardom and rapid oblivion in our throwaway culture. The remarkable thing is that Berle kept at it. He was not content with the lifetime contract (actually thirty years, at $200,000 per year) that NBC tendered in 1951. After his last show for NBC was cancelled in 1959, Berle attempted a comeback with *Jackpot Bowling* (1961) and another (after renegotiating his NBC contract) on the American Broadcasting Company (ABC) in 1967.

When opportunity knocked, Berle continued to perform: in Las Vegas, on Broadway, in films, and as master of ceremonies at celebrity roasts. Interviewed for a documentary on Jewish humor, Berle offered the following joke:

A handsome, elegantly dressed man in his late sixties sits at a dining room table in the Borscht Belt. A woman on the prowl, bejeweled and *farputzt* (with lots of makeup) approaches.

"Hello," she starts. "Have we met before?"

"Not likely," he replies politely. "I've been away for thirty years."

"Traveling?"

"No. I was in the joint, the can."

"You mean the toilet?"

"No. That's an expression for prison."

"Oh. What did you do?"

"I murdered my wife."

"Oh," she responds happily. "So, you're single?"

A sick joke, to be sure, but Berle told it with impeccable timing, crystal-clear diction, and a twinkle in his eye that framed the punch line perfectly.

Berle had many affairs before matrimony claimed him. His first wife was Beryl Wallace. After they divorced, he married a beautiful showgirl, Joyce Matthews, on 4 December 1941. Her passion for shopping unnerved his parents, especially his possessive mother. Divorce ended the marriage in 1947, but remarriage brought them together again for a year in 1949. When queried concerning this bizarre behavior, Berle justified the "double jeopardy" by claiming that Joyce reminded him of his first wife. After playing the field with Marilyn Monroe and other sirens, in 1953 Berle settled into a long third marriage with the movie-studio publicist Ruth Cosgrove, which lasted until her death in 1989. In 1992, at the age of eighty-two, Berle found another bride in fashion designer Lorna Adams. He had three children from these marriages. Berle died in his sleep of colon cancer at age ninety-three and is buried at Hillside Memorial Park in Culver City, California.

Almost to the end of his long, active life, Berle craved an audience and welcomed approval of his many gifts, which spanned serious drama to low comedy. At age eighty-seven, he earned an Emmy nomination for his poignant portrayal of a man suffering from Alzheimer's disease in an episode of *Beverly Hills 90210*. Frank Rich provided the most fitting summation, "Berle was to television what an electric cord is to a socket: sheer energy the moment someone plugged him in." If heaven exists, no doubt Berle is *shpritzing* others, stealing jokes from fellow comedians, flicking ashes from Cuban cigars, and upstaging God with a standard Berlesque "saver"—just kidding.

★

Berle's autobiographies are *Out of My Trunk* (1950) and *Milton Berle: An Autobiography* (1974), written with Haskel Frankel. For Berle's personal recollections of his life and career, see *B.S. I Love You: Sixty Funny Years with the Famous and the Infamous* (1988). For Berle's comedic repertoire, see Milt Rosen, ed., *Milton Berle's Private Joke File: Over 10,000 of His Best Gags, Anecdotes, and One-Liners* (1989). For general appreciations of Berle's comedic gifts, see Steve Allen, *The Funny Men* (1956), and Lawrence J. Epstein, *The Haunted Smile: The Story of Jewish Comedians in America* (2001). For more information about Berle's career, see Frank Rich,

"TV Guy," *New York Times Magazine* (29 Dec. 2002). An obituary is in the *New York Times* (28 Mar. 2002).

JOSEPH DORINSON

BERRIGAN, Philip Francis (*b.* 5 October 1923 in Two Harbors, Minnesota; *d.* 6 December 2002 in Baltimore, Maryland), Roman Catholic priest and pacifist opponent of war and militarism who led raids on draft board offices to protest the Vietnam War.

Berrigan and his brother Daniel were the two youngest of six sons born to Thomas Berrigan, an itinerant railroad engine fireman, laborer in the iron-ore industry, and migrant wheat harvester, and Freda (Fromhart) Berrigan, a German-born housewife. Thomas Berrigan's inspirations for societal reform were those who sacrificed themselves for conscience, a way of life followed years later by Daniel and Philip.

Berrigan attended Catholic schools and later said of his experience, "I learn[ed] by rote, swallowing propaganda, and in examinations regurgitat[ed] nonsense and half-truths." Exceptionally athletic and powerfully built, he graduated from Saint John the Baptist High School, where he played baseball and basketball. He then enrolled at Saint Michael's, a small college in Toronto, and was drafted into the U.S. Army in 1943.

"[I was] excited to be following my [elder] brothers into battle, anxious to slaughter infidels and to return home bearing the standard of peace and justice," Berrigan later recalled. Berrigan served in England in the artillery, later becoming a second lieutenant, and witnessed the destruction caused by German bombing raids. In France, he was appalled at the harsh treatment black GIs received at the hands of some white American troops, and in Germany, he was stunned at the devastation war had inflicted on civilians.

Discharged, Berrigan entered the College of the Holy Cross in Worcester, Massachusetts, graduating in 1949. But World War II had affected him deeply, and he began wrestling with the Catholic "just war" doctrine and the moral dilemmas of means and ends. (The just war doctrine is a Catholic attempt to establish guidelines that distinguish between permissible and impermissible wars.) He shared these concerns with his brother Daniel, then studying theology at a Jesuit seminary.

Berrigan joined the Society of Saint Joseph in Newburgh, New York, in 1950. The Josephites, as they are commonly called, ministered to African-American Catholics. Following his ordination in 1955, Berrigan was appointed assistant pastor at Our Lady of Perpetual Help in Washington, D.C.'s Anacostia district, which was populated by

Philip Berrigan, 1980. AP/WIDE WORLD PHOTOS

poor African Americans living in bleak housing projects. He publicly condemned the prevailing silence and moral indifference of whites to the plight of his congregants, actions that led to his transfer to Saint Augustine's, an all-black, all-male Josephite high school in New Orleans.

At Saint Augustine's, Berrigan taught English and religion from 1956 to 1963 and became the first Catholic priest to join the civil rights "freedom riders," individuals who traveled to southern states during the 1960s to work against racial segregation. He reached a personal turning point during the Cuban Missile Crisis of 1962, as he became increasingly concerned about the urban ills he saw in American cities. "[O]ther people were deciding whether I would live or die," he said. "I felt betrayed, and not just about the urban crisis, but for all that was behind the threat."

Transferred again in 1963, Berrigan taught English at the Josephites' lower seminary of the Epiphany Apostolic College seminary in Newburgh, where he identified with poor black renters living in slum housing. But what upset many local conservatives was his participation in an inter-faith silent vigil against the Vietnam War in New York City in March 1965. He carried the antiwar message back to Newburgh, where he was excoriated by the war's supporters, and again was transferred in 1966 to Baltimore's Saint Peter Claver, a poor black parish, with a warning to hold his tongue—something he never would do.

By now the war in Southeast Asia consumed him, and Berrigan believed that nonviolent civil disobedience was the best way to protest what he perceived to be the war's brutality and senselessness. Early on the morning of 27 October 1967, he and three companions—dubbed the "Baltimore Four"—entered the city's customs house and poured blood on draft files, an act for which he received a six-year prison sentence. And on 17 May 1968 he, his brother Daniel, and seven other Catholic men and women seized draft files in Catonsville, Maryland, doused them with homemade napalm, and then set them on fire. "Better to burn paper than babies," said Daniel famously. Philip stated his own credo in 1996, quoting Thoreau: "Dissent without [nonviolent] resistance is consent." Baltimore and Catonsville ignited dozens of subsequent draft-board raids throughout the country. For Catonsville, Berrigan received another sentence to run concurrent with the jail time received from the Baltimore raid. He was eventually paroled after serving three years out of his six-year term.

Some Catholic pacifists were ambiguous about the raids, among them Thomas Merton, the widely respected monk, who called the action "in essence, nonviolent," though "not a necessary teaching of the Church." Still, Merton was more shaken when a Catholic bishop described the Vietnam War "as an act of Christian love."

Berrigan was back in court a few years later, indicted on 12 January 1971 and tried in Harrisburg, Pennsylvania, with other members of the Catholic Left for allegedly scheming to kidnap National Security Adviser Henry Kissinger and blow up heating pipes under government buildings in Washington, D.C. The charge was later reduced to conspiracy to destroy draft records. The jury could not reach a verdict, and a mistrial was declared.

In 1969 Berrigan secretly exchanged unofficial wedding vows with a nun, Elizabeth ("Liz") McAlister. After publicly revealing their marriage in 1973—a revelation that dismayed many Catholic followers—both were excommunicated. They were wed officially on 28 May 1973.

Also in 1973, Berrigan and his wife founded a war-resister community, Jonah House, in Baltimore. This small but determined group led in time to the Plowshares movement, the name drawn from the biblical call to "beat swords into plowshares." Insisting that nuclear first-strike strategies were a crime, their aim was to disrupt the American military machine. For the next two decades, they hammered and poured blood on MX missiles, Trident submarines, and B-52 bombers, often walking into restricted facilities with astonishing ease. Plowshares members were always willing to accept draconian punishment for these acts—their prison sentences sometimes reached as high as eighteen years—to dramatize their opposition to war, though the mass media was increasingly disinclined to report their actions or their trials. With the Vietnam War and its accompanying mass protests concluded, the media turned away from issues of war and peace to focus on other matters, and largely ignored the actions of the Plowshares members.

Berrigan and Liz participated in many more such actions, and by the time of his death he had served eleven years in prison. His autobiography, *Fighting the Lamb's War* (1996), summed up his "faith that passeth understanding"—a life of Christian faith and civil disobedience.

On 8 October 2002 Berrigan was diagnosed with cancer of the liver and kidney, and he died two months later at home in Baltimore, surrounded by family—including his three children and three surviving brothers—as well as members of his Jonah House community. Funeral services were held in his old church, Saint Peter Claver, and he was buried in its cemetery.

Berrigan dictated a statement on his deathbed defining the life he had willingly chosen. "I die with the conviction, held since 1968 and Catonsville, that nuclear weapons are the scourge of the Earth; to mine for them, manufacture them, deploy them, use them, is a curse against God, the human family, and the Earth itself."

★

The papers of Daniel and Philip Berrigan are housed at Cornell and DePaul universities. Berrigan's *Prison Journals of a Priest Revolutionary* (1970), compiled and edited by Vincent McGee, is a defense of draft-board raids and a portrait of life in prison; *The Time's Discipline: The Beatitudes and Nuclear Resistance* (1989), written with his wife, Elizabeth McAlister, tells the story of Jonah House and its antiwar actions; and *Fighting the Lamb's War: Skirmishes with the American Empire* (1996), written with Fred A. Wilcox, is a memoir of Berrigan's work and beliefs. Murray Polner and Jim O'Grady, *Disarmed and Dangerous: The Radical Life and Times of Daniel and Philip Berrigan* (1997), traces the brothers' path from conventional Roman Catholic priests to "holy outlaws." A memorial tribute by people who knew Berrigan best is in the Jonah House publication *Year One*, no. 1 (winter 2003): 1–12. An obituary is in the *New York Times* (8 Dec. 2002).

MURRAY POLNER

BIGGERS, John Thomas (*b.* 13 April 1924 in Gastonia, North Carolina; *d.* 25 January 2001 in Houston, Texas), painter, sculptor, and printmaker known for his depictions of African-American life.

Biggers was born in a house that his father had built. He was the seventh and youngest child of Paul Biggers and Cora (Finger) Biggers. His father owned a shoe store, and was also a Baptist minister and the principal of the local school for African Americans. Biggers's mother was a homemaker who oversaw the family farm and took in laundry to earn extra income. Biggers showed an early interest in art; some of his first drawings were of images he studied in his father's Bible. As a youth, Biggers developed a keen eye for his surroundings, which later provided his greatest source of artistic inspiration.

After his father died in 1937, Biggers's mother took a job at an orphanage in Oxford, North Carolina. Biggers attended school at Lincoln Academy, in nearby Kings Mountain. To pay for his tuition, he worked as a janitor. Among his duties were maintaining the boiler room, during which time he practiced drawing. Biggers graduated from Lincoln Academy in 1941 and enrolled at Hampton Institute (later Hampton University), a historically African-American college in Virginia. While at Hampton, Biggers met Hazel Hales, an accounting major. They married in 1948, and had no children.

Biggers intended to become a plumber. He had even included one of his boiler-room drawings, possibly made because he had to demonstrate that he could draw according to mechanical specifications, in his college application. However, Biggers took art classes at Hampton with Viktor Lowenfeld, a Jewish refugee from Germany, and the professor became Biggers's mentor. Lowenfeld also arranged the first public showing of Biggers's work. In 1943 his mural *Dying Soldier* was included in the exhibition *Young Negro Art,* which Lowenfeld had organized for the Museum of Modern Art (MoMA) in New York City. Although the mural was singled out for criticism, Biggers nevertheless continued to paint and to develop his artistic vision.

Shortly after the MoMA exhibition, in 1943, Biggers was drafted into the U.S. Navy. When World War II ended in 1945, Biggers returned to school at Pennsylvania State University in Philadelphia, where Lowenfeld now taught. During this time, the transportation union in Chicago purchased two of his murals, one of which was the controversial *Dying Soldier.* Biggers completed three more murals during his years at Penn State. He graduated in 1948, having earned both a B.S. and M.Ed. in art education. He received a D.Ed. in art education from Penn State in 1954.

After graduating, Biggers taught briefly at Penn State and then at Alabama State College. In 1949 he joined the faculty of Texas State University (later Texas Southern University), an African-American college founded in Houston only two years earlier. There one of Biggers's tasks was to create an art department. He taught art at Texas Southern for more than thirty years, serving as the head of the art department from 1949 to 1983. Biggers adopted a teaching style similar to Lowenfeld's, encouraging students to find artistic inspiration in their personal backgrounds and experiences. Biggers's own work, such as *Victim of the City Streets* (1946), continued to be filled with biting social commentary, as well as the celebration of African-American everyday life, depicted in such paintings as *Gleaners* (1943).

Biggers won his first prize in 1950 at the annual exhibition of the Museum of Fine Arts, Houston, for his painting *The Cradle*. He won another award in a competition sponsored by the Dallas Museum of Art. But in the racially segregated South of the 1950s, no one had expected an African-American artist to even enter such contests, let alone to win first prize. Neither museum rescinded its award, but both prevented Biggers from attending the ceremonies at which they were bestowed.

In 1957, with funding from a United Nations Educational, Scientific, and Cultural Organization (UNESCO) fellowship, Biggers and his wife made a six-month trip to West Africa. The trip transformed Biggers's art. Thereafter, he incorporated African design motifs, such as drums, masks, and scenes of African life, into his work. *Ananse: The Web of Life in Africa* (1962) chronicles Biggers's trip and includes more than eighty drawings he made of African life. The publication of *Ananse* coincided with the resurgence of the U.S. civil rights movement, which, in addition to demanding political rights and social justice for African Americans, awakened a greater awareness of their African heritage.

For the next two decades, Biggers painted many murals on the Texas Southern campus as well as at other sites throughout Houston. During this time, he also served as a visiting professor at the University of Wisconsin (1965–1966), and published *Black Art in Houston* (1978). Biggers returned to Africa three times. In 1988 the Art League of Houston named Biggers Texas Artist of the Year. His work was featured in the 1989 exhibition *Black Art, Ancestral Legacy: The African Impulse in African American Art,* which opened at the Dallas Museum of Art and traveled to Atlanta; Milwaukee, Wisconsin; and Richmond, Virginia. In 1995 Biggers was the subject of a traveling solo retrospective, *The Art of John Biggers: View from the Upper Room,* which was sponsored by the Museum of Fine Arts, Houston. The show featured 120 paintings, drawings, murals, and sculptures. Biggers also found time to create several murals for Hampton University, where he had begun his study of art almost fifty years before.

Some critics characterized Biggers as the "black Grant Wood," after the American painter of the 1930s known for his realistic style. The comparison obscures the originality of Biggers's vision and makes his work appear more derivative than it actually was. By incorporating everyday elements in his work, ranging from images of the shotgun houses of his youth to powerful African motifs, Biggers created an art that was bright, vibrant, and filled with motion and life. Over time, he also moved from the social-narrative realist style popular among the muralists during the 1930s to a more modern and abstract style, which nonetheless relied heavily on such concrete symbols as earth, fire, air, and water. In his later work, Biggers's "sacred geometry" prompted him to include groups of three, four, or seven objects in many of his paintings.

Biggers died suddenly at age seventy-six of a heart attack at his home, and is buried in Fayetteville, North Carolina. As a muralist, he demonstrated his talents as a storyteller, much in keeping with the African and African-American oral and narrative traditions. Biggers created compelling narratives that depicted African and African-American life and heritage and, on occasion, reflected on the experience of other cultures such as Native American and Asian. Finally, Biggers's art contains autobiographical elements, reflecting his own journey through life.

★

The best source of information about Biggers's life is Alvia J. Warlaw, *The Art of John Biggers: View from the Upper Room* (1995). Biggers's book, *Ananse: The Web of Life in Africa* (1962), contains insight and information about his trip to Africa and his awakening consciousness of his African heritage. Other biographical information may be found in Leann Davis Alspaugh, *The Storyteller: The Work of Dr. John T. Biggers* (1992), and Romare Bearden and Harry Henderson, *A History of African-American Artists: From 1792 to the Present* (1993). Obituaries are in the *Houston Chronicle* (27 Jan. 2001) and *New York Times* (30 Jan. 2001).

MEG GREENE MALVASI

BLACK, Charles Lund, Jr. (*b.* 22 September 1915 in Austin, Texas; *d.* 5 May 2001 in Manhattan, New York City), one of the most important scholars on constitutional law in the United States, who was instrumental in writing the legal brief attacking segregation in the landmark U.S. Supreme Court case *Brown* v. *Board of Education.*

Black was one of three children born to Charles L. Black, Sr., a successful appellate lawyer, and Alzada (Bowman) Black, a homemaker. Black was competitive and precocious as a child. These traits were evident when, after his mother admitted to him that there was no Santa Claus, he responded, "I suppose you'll soon be telling me the same thing about Jesus Christ." In 1931, after graduating from Austin High School at age sixteen, Black enrolled at the University of Texas at Austin. Rejecting his father's wish that he study law, Black instead chose to study Greek classics.

During that year an event occurred that would help shape Black's opposition to segregation and his support of civil rights in America. On 12 October 1931 Black paid a fee of seventy-five cents to attend a dance at Austin's Driskill

Hotel, in the hope of meeting girls. The jazz great Louis Armstrong performed in the hotel that night. Black, who at the time was ignorant of jazz music and who had grown up in the segregated South, was mesmerized by the genius of Armstrong and opened his eyes to racism. He later wrote, "Blacks, the saying went, were 'all right in their place.' What was the 'place' of such a man and of the people from which he sprung?" Black later recounted his encounter with Armstrong in the Ken Burns film documentary *Jazz* (2000).

Lacking direction in college, Black impressed his professors at the University of Texas. He showed great promise in language and literature; was fluent in Italian, French, and Spanish; and even attended the University of Mexico. After graduating with a B.A. in 1935, Black planned to enter Harvard to pursue a master's degree but either did not enroll or dropped out. Instead, he traveled to Europe and followed the Ballet Russe on tour in the United States, becoming infatuated with the prima ballerina. Black later admitted to having had a small, nondancing part in one performance. Afterward, Black enrolled at Yale, where he earned an M.A. in 1938 in Old and Middle English. He was on his way to earning a Ph.D. at Yale when, in 1940, despite his earlier objections to studying law, Black started pursuing his law degree at Yale Law School. Receiving his LL.B. in 1943, Black led his class with record-high marks. He served in the Army Air Forces as a teacher and practiced law after World War II with the Wall Street firm Davis, Polk, Wardell, Sunderland, and Kiendl. After only a year at the law firm, Black joined the law faculty at Columbia University in 1947 to teach constitutional law.

During his tenure at Columbia, Black joined the future Supreme Court Justice Thurgood Marshall and the National Association for the Advancement of Colored People (NAACP) Legal Defense and Education Fund as a legal adviser. He was instrumental in writing the brief for the 1954 landmark segregation case *Brown* v. *Board of Education,* which eliminated racial segregation at all levels of the public school system. Afterward, Black continued to work with the NAACP, collaborating on briefs and working on many segregation cases. On 11 April 1954 Black married Barbara Ann Aronstein, who was a former student of his at Columbia Law School and whom he credited with helping him produce serious scholarship. The couple had two sons and a daughter.

In 1956 Black left Columbia University to become the Henry R. Luce Professor of Jurisprudence at Yale Law School. In 1975 he became the Sterling Professor of Law, the highest teaching post at Yale, until his retirement in 1986. Among Black's students were some of America's future leaders, including Senator Hillary Rodham Clinton of New York. Black was so beloved by his students that following his retirement, the student body serenaded him with "The Battle Hymn of the Republic" and devoted an entire issue of the *Yale Law Review* to him.

Aside from academic success, Black also led a renaissance life. A successful poet with three volumes of his poetry published, Black also became a trumpeter, harmonica player, painter, long-distance jogger, and student of Iceland and modern Icelandic. An avid jazz fan, Black staged an annual event called the "Armstrong Evening," in which, at the Yale Law School faculty lounge, Black would play a collection of well-preserved 78s of Armstrong's works. Black even found diversion in acting. When the director of a Yale Repertory production of *Julius Caesar* asked Black to shed his Texas accent for the role of Cicero, Black's logic and wit took over, and he replied, "What makes you think Cicero talked like a Yankee?"

After retiring from Yale in 1986, Black returned to Columbia University, following his wife, who had become the dean of the law school there. Black taught as an adjunct professor until 1999 and passed away at the age of eighty-five at his Manhattan home from respiratory failure after a prolonged illness. He is buried in Philadelphia, Pennsylvania.

Sought out by many in the legal profession for his opinions, Black was an authority on constitutional law, capital punishment, segregation, admiralty law, and the issue of presidential impeachment. As the author of more than twenty books as well as numerous law journal and magazine articles, Black produced works considered classics in legal scholarship. *The Law of Admiralty* (1957), which Black coauthored with Grant Gilmore, remains a definitive text on the subject. During the 1972 Watergate crisis, a political scandal involving a break-in at the Democratic Party headquarters in Washington, D.C., Black authored *Impeachment: A Handbook* (1974). (The instigators of the break-in were traced to the White House, and President Richard M. Nixon eventually resigned in the face of the controversy.) This title was reissued in 1998 to coincide with the impeachment crisis of President Bill Clinton. Despite Black's identification as a liberal Democrat, the book was scholarly and provided no judgment on either Nixon or Clinton. Black's stance against capital punishment led him to pen another classic work, *Capital Punishment: The Inevitability of Caprice and Mistake* (1974).

★

Black wrote a collection of essays on his legal philosophy, published as *The Humane Imagination* (1986). There is no biography of Black, but tributes from friends, family, peers, and former students appear in issues of the *Columbia Law Review* (May 2002) and *Yale Law Review* (July 1986 and June 2002). Obituaries are in the *New York Times* (8 May 2001), *Chicago Tribune* (9 May 2001), *Los Angeles Times* (11 May 2001), and *Washington Post* (12 May 2001).

STEVEN WISE

BLACK, Joseph, Jr. ("Joe")   (*b.* 8 February 1924 in Plainfield, New Jersey; *d.* 17 May 2002 in Scottsdale, Arizona), relief ace for the Brooklyn Dodgers who in 1952 enjoyed one of the greatest rookie baseball seasons of all time and became the first African-American pitcher to win a World Series game.

Black was one of five children born to Joseph Black, an auto mechanic, and Martha (Watkins) Black. He grew up in an integrated neighborhood, playing makeshift baseball games in the street with tennis balls and broken sticks. With his father often out of work, the family became impoverished during the Great Depression, and Black sold newspapers to earn extra money. An extraordinarily gifted athlete, he dreamed of becoming a Major League Baseball player like his hero, Hank Greenberg of the Detroit Tigers. But baseball was still segregated during Black's youth, a fact of which he was ignorant until a baseball scout told him that only whites could play in the major leagues. "I ran all the way home and went up in the attic and got my scrapbook," Black later said. "And he was right. There wasn't a face of color there. I tore them all up except Greenberg and just laid in the bed and cried."

His dream deferred, Black graduated from Plainfield High School in 1942 and enrolled at Morgan State College in Baltimore, where he starred in football and track and field. For Black, higher education was an eye-opening experience. "Until I got to college I thought all colored people did was pick cotton and sing [spirituals]," he recalled. "The professors made you feel like you were someone. . . . From that point on, I never let anyone make me feel like I was less than they were." To earn money for tuition, Black spent his summers playing baseball for the Baltimore Elite Giants, a local team that was a power in the Negro National League. He started as a shortstop, but with a fastball that he estimated at ninety-eight miles per hour, he soon became a pitcher. Also during this period, Black enlisted in the U.S. Army in July 1943 and was discharged in 1946.

Black was a good, but not great, pitcher in the Negro Leagues, posting a known record of forty-five wins and thirty-seven losses over eight seasons. His most notable achievement was starting in the 1950 East-West all-star game. Later that year, he earned his B.S. from Morgan State and decided to quit baseball and accept a job as a schoolteacher in Maryland.

However, Jackie Robinson had recently integrated the major leagues, and Black learned that the Elite Giants had sold his rights to the Brooklyn Dodgers, the major league team for which Robinson played. At the time, major league teams often acquired African-American players in pairs to avoid the possibility that a white player would have to room with one. Thus, as Black recalled, the Dodgers signed him "not because I was good, but because I was the best friend of a guy who was good"—the second baseman Jim Gilliam.

Black spent the 1951 season in the newly integrated minor leagues, posting an 11–12 record while dividing his time between the Dodgers' top two farm clubs. He was considered a mediocre prospect, but during the ensuing winter he dominated the Cuban Winter League, leading the league with fifteen wins and a 2.42 earned run average (ERA). Black's manager in Cuba, Billy Herman, was also a coach with Brooklyn, and it was largely on Herman's recommendation that Black made the Brooklyn team in the spring of 1952.

Placed in the Dodgers bullpen, in 1952 Black became the unlikely stalwart of a piecemeal pitching staff and helped carry the team to the pennant. He had a 15–4 record, with fifteen saves and a league-best 2.15 ERA in 142 innings pitched. It was a season the likes of which had seldom been seen in baseball history: as a writer for the *New York Journal–American* wrote of Black, "his greatness defies accurate description." Black was named National League (NL) Rookie of the Year and narrowly missed being elected Most Valuable Player, finishing third in an extremely close vote.

Although Black had pitched in relief all season long, Brooklyn manager Charlie Dressen started him in three of the seven World Series games against the New York Yankees. As one writer put it, "If Joe Black wins two games, the Dodgers have a chance." He performed superbly in the opening contest, pitching a complete game to beat the Yankees 6–2. Black became the third African-American pitcher in World Series history, but he was the first to win a game. It turned out to be his only victory, however, as he lost narrow decisions in the fourth and seventh games, and the Dodgers lost the series.

In spring training the next year, Dressen encouraged Black to learn new pitches in addition to his fastball and curve ball. The effort to learn such pitches caused problems with Black's pitching mechanics, and he lost his status as baseball's most dominating hurler even more suddenly than he had gained it. After posting an awful 5.33 ERA in 1953, Black spent almost the entire 1954 season in the minor leagues, posting a solid 12–10 record with a 3.60 ERA. He rejoined the Dodgers in 1955, but shortly after the season started was sold to the Cincinnati Reds to make room on the Brooklyn roster for Sandy Koufax. After three seasons of unspectacular pitching for Cincinnati and the Washington Senators, Black quit baseball in 1957 to become an elementary school teacher in his hometown of Plainfield.

While teaching, Black simultaneously attended Rutgers and Seton Hall universities, where he undertook postgraduate work in educational and vocational guidance. In 1962 he became an executive with the Greyhound Corporation, devising ways to market the company in African-American communities. He spent twenty-six years with Greyhound,

Joe Black (*right*), with Brooklyn teammate Roy Campanella, 1952. AP/WIDE WORLD PHOTOS

becoming vice president of special markets in 1967. By 1971 he was making $38,000 a year, more than he had ever made in baseball.

Black dedicated much of his post-baseball life to winning public recognition for the accomplishments of his friend and onetime roommate Jackie Robinson. In 1972, with Robinson ailing from severe diabetes complications, Black began pressuring Major League Baseball to do something to honor the twenty-fifth anniversary of Robinson's 1947 breakthrough. As a result of Black's persistence, baseball officials invited the ailing Robinson to throw out the first pitch at the 1972 World Series. Scarcely one week later, Black served as a pallbearer at Robinson's funeral.

From the 1960s through the 1990s, Black involved himself in numerous social and charitable causes, becoming one of baseball's most eloquent and outspoken statesmen. In the early 1970s he served on the U.S. Task Force on Youth Motivation, in which he stressed the need for education to young people. He also worked as a consultant to baseball commissioners, counseling players about preparing themselves for post-baseball careers. In addition, Black served on the board of directors of the Baseball Assistance Team, which provides financial assistance to indigent ex-players. Along with the former Negro League player Sam Jethroe, Black was instrumental in gaining pensions from Major League Baseball for ex–Negro Leaguers.

Black was married five times and had two children. In 1992 he enrolled in law school at Arizona State University, where he was a classmate of his daughter. In his later years he also worked in community relations for the Arizona Diamondbacks, a Phoenix baseball team that joined the major leagues in 1998. He died of prostate cancer at the Life Care Center of Scottsdale, Arizona, and was cremated.

Thanks to his spectacular pitching during the 1952 season, Black remains one of the most renowned "one-year wonders" in baseball history. "His legacy is the thought that unheralded players can rise to the heights, that . . . an ordinary athlete could wind up pitching Game One of the World Series," said Vin Scully, the Dodgers broadcaster who announced Black's games. But Black's most important legacy was that he dedicated his life to improving educational and social opportunities for African Americans and young people. "Baseball was just a part of my life; that's all it was," Black said in 1992. "It wasn't my life."

★

The file on Black in the archives of the National Baseball Hall of Fame Library in Cooperstown, New York, contains many newspaper clippings and other items. Black wrote a self-published and difficult-to-find autobiography, *Ain't Nobody Better Than You* (1983). The seminal work about the Brooklyn Dodgers, Roger Kahn, *The Boys of Summer* (1972), contains a chapter about Black. Dick Clark and Larry Lester, eds., *The Negro Leagues Book* (1994), is the definitive source for Negro League statistics and information. Important articles are in the *Afro-American* (19 Apr. 1952), *Black Sports* (Nov. 1973), and *Sports Collector's Digest* (9 Apr. 1993). An obituary is in the *New York Times* (18 May 2002).

ERIC ENDERS

BLASS, William Ralph ("Bill") (*b.* 22 June 1922 in Fort Wayne, Indiana; *d.* 12 June 2002 in New Preston, Connecticut), world-famous fashion designer who created an enduring American style in the second half of the twentieth century.

Blass was the only son of Ethyl Keyser Blass, a dressmaker, and Ralph Aldrich Blass, a traveling hardware salesman who committed suicide when Blass was five years old. Although he played football, worked on the school newspaper, and studied art while attending Fort Wayne's South Side High School, he was most fascinated by the world of fashion. Blass won second prize in a design contest sponsored by the *Chicago Tribune*. "Something about glamour interested me," Blass told *People* magazine in a 1999 interview. "All my schoolbooks had drawings of women on terraces with a cocktail and a cigarette."

After graduating from high school in 1939, Blass moved to New York City to study fashion design, selling some of his designs to Manhattan designers. In 1943, during World War II, Blass enlisted in the army and was assigned to a specialized counterintelligence unit, the 603rd Camouflage Battalion. As a member of a secret unit, Blass landed in France about a month after D day (6 June 1944), when the Allies began their invasion of France; he was involved in the Battle of the Bulge and the crossing of the Rhine. Mean-

while, he continued sketching clothing and drew his first sketch for his company logo, a pair of mirrored *B*'s.

After serving for three and a half years in the military, Blass returned to New York, designing for such firms as Anne Klein and Anna Miller and Co., where he became the head designer. In 1959, when Miller retired, her business merged with that of her brother, Maurice Rentner, who at the time ran a well-respected fashion house. Blass continued working with the Seventh Avenue company and within two years was named vice president. As his designs gradually became recognizably his, Blass's influence in the fashion design world grew. In 1960, when Rentner died, the Blass label became a reality: "Bill Blass for Maurice Rentner." Blass purchased the Rentner firm in 1970 and in 1973 renamed the company Bill Blass Ltd. Blass sold the company in 1999 for a reported $50 million.

Blass's signature designs set new standards for casual American fashion. After establishing his reputation in women's design, Blass launched his line of men's fashion wear in 1967. By allowing his name to be attached to a variety of products, Blass became familiar to more people. Known for their chic casual look, his designs expanded to include swimwear, children's clothing, shoes, perfume, bed linens, jewelry, and furs. Items from chocolate to the interior of the Lincoln Continental sported the Bill Blass label. For several years he even signed an annual Bill Blass Lincoln limousine.

The Blass label was most noted for high-quality and high-priced clothing with a sophisticated and worldly look. His expensive, beautifully cut, tailored women's wear featured inventive combinations of patterns and textures and attracted many famous customers in upper-class social circles, including Pat Buckley, Gloria Vanderbilt, Brooke Astor, Nancy Kissinger, Happy Rockefeller, Candace Bergen, Barbra Streisand, Barbara Walters, Jacqueline Kennedy Onassis, Nancy Reagan, and Barbara Bush.

Blass received many industry and public service awards, served as a trustee of the New York Public Library, and became known for his philanthropy. He was a three-time winner of the Coty American Fashion Critics Award and in 1968 was given the first Coty Award for men's wear. In 1973 he was one of five American designers invited to a fashion show at the Palace of Versailles; this signified that American design was internationally recognized at last. Blass was awarded an honorary doctorate from the Rhode Island School of Design in 1977, and in 1987 he received the lifetime achievement award from the Council of Fashion Designers of America. President Ronald W. Reagan appointed him to the President's Committee on the Arts and Humanities, and in 1999 Blass received the first lifetime achievement award from the Fashion Institute of Technology.

Bill Blass, 1961. BETTMANN/CORBIS

In 1994 Blass donated $10 million to the New York Public Library to establish a public reading room in his name. Blass received the first Perignon Award for humanitarian leadership beyond fashion. An early supporter of programs concerned with acquired immune deficiency syndrome (AIDS), he was a prime mover in organizing AIDS-related benefits in New York. He also was a major donor to the Gay Men's Health Crisis at a time when many well-known people were silent about AIDS. Blass traveled extensively, making personal appearances in stores and lending his clothes and his presence to benefits for charities across the country. He appeared on many best-dressed lists.

Blass's life epitomized the modern American gentleman: charming, witty, and handsome. The Blass name represents an enduring symbol of American taste and began a trend that other designers followed. A bronze marker bearing his name is located in the Fashion Walk of Fame on Seventh Avenue in New York City. He completed his memoir, *Bare Blass*, shortly before his death of throat cancer at age seventy-nine. Blass, who rarely appeared without a cigarette, stated, "The secret of living is not staying too long. I have learned when to leave the party."

★

Blass's autobiography, written with Cathy Horyn, is *Bare Blass* (2002). See also Helen O'Hagen, Kathleen Rowold, and Michael Vollbracht, *Bill Blass: An American Designer* (2002). For information about his legacy as a designer, see Ruth La Ferla, "The Bill Blass Legacy: Simplicity with a Kick," *New York Times* (14 June 2002). Obituaries are in the *New York Times* and *Los Angeles Times* (both 13 June 2002).

REBECCA J. TIMMONS

BLOCH, Konrad Emil (*b.* 21 January 1912 in Neisse, Germany [later Nysa, Poland]; *d.* 15 October 2000 in Burlington, Massachusetts), biochemist who, with Feodor Lynen, won the 1964 Nobel Prize in physiology or medicine for research on how cholesterol is produced in the body.

Bloch was the son of Frederich ("Fritz") and Hedwig (Striemer) Bloch, and descended from a family of physicians and lawyers. After attending elementary school and the Real gymnasium in Neisse in Upper Silesia in what was then Germany, he went to Munich in 1930 and enrolled at the Technische Hochschule (technical university). He had intended to study metallurgy, but found the courses tedious. In his second year, an organic chemistry course taught by Hans Fischer, who received a Nobel Prize for his work on the heme structure in hemoglobin, piqued Bloch's interest in chemistry. He received the degree of Diplom-Ingenieur in chemistry in 1934. By this time the dictator

Konrad E. Bloch, 1964. BETTMANN/CORBIS

Adolf Hitler had come to power, and because of his Jewish background, Bloch was forced to leave Germany in order to find work.

Bloch spent two years at the Swiss Research Institute in Davos, Switzerland, where he studied the chemistry of phospholipids found in tuberculosis bacteria. When this job ended in 1936, he sought a position in the United States, receiving one at Yale University. It turned out that this position was not funded, but it did earn him a visa, and once in the United States he enrolled in a doctoral program in biochemistry at Columbia University in New York City, receiving his Ph.D. in 1938 and then joining the faculty there. At Columbia he worked with Rudolf Schoenheimer and David Rittenberg, who were studying the biochemistry of cholesterol and were pioneering the use of radioisotopes to trace molecular changes in living tissue. In his Nobel banquet speech, Bloch singled out Schoenheimer for special mention as the major influence on his career.

In 1941 Bloch married Lore Teutsch, whom he had met in Munich. They had a son and a daughter. Bloch became a naturalized U.S. citizen in 1944. Two years later he moved to the University of Chicago as an assistant professor of biochemistry, eventually becoming a full professor there in 1950. At Chicago he continued his research on cholesterol and also investigated the synthesis of glutathione, a molecule consisting of three amino acids. He hoped that working out how this molecule was put together would reveal something about the synthesis of proteins, in which there are many more amino acids. This hope proved unfounded, but the work on glutathione was nonetheless useful, as this molecule was later found to play a significant role in cell transport and in enzyme activity.

Bloch left Chicago in 1954 to become the Higgins Professor of Biochemistry at Harvard University in Cambridge, Massachusetts; he held this position until he retired in 1982. From 1979 to 1984 he was also a professor of science at the Harvard School of Public Health. At Harvard he again worked on cholesterol, ultimately discovering what building blocks are involved and how the molecule is constructed. This was a huge project because cholesterol is a large, complex molecule with twenty-seven carbon atoms. In early work, Bloch found that acetate, the salt of acetic acid, was the source of all of cholesterol's carbon atoms. Along with his friend Feodor Lynen of the University of Munich, Bloch also discovered that the acetate molecules first form a chainlike molecule called squalene, which is then folded on itself, and through a series of reactions, four rings of cholesterol form. In all, there are thirty-six reactions in the synthesis of cholesterol. Bloch also studied some of the enzymes that control these reactions. In addition, he found that cholesterol is an essential component of all the body's cells and that all the steroid hormones manufactured in the body are made from cholesterol.

After receiving the Nobel Prize in physiology or medicine in 1964, Bloch continued to study cholesterol synthesis and the metabolism of fatty acids. This led to an interest in the evolution of these molecules. After his retirement, Bloch searched for a project suitable for "a scientist on a permanent sabbatical" and decided to write a book on topics in biochemistry that he found particularly intriguing. The result was *Blondes in Venetian Paintings, the Nine-Banded Armadillo, and Other Essays in Biochemistry,* published in 1994. The title indicates his broad interests, including tracking down the hair dyes used in the Renaissance, which might explain why there are so many blondes in Italian paintings centuries before the use of hydrogen peroxide to bleach hair.

Over the years Bloch received a number of awards and honors in addition to the Nobel Prize. He was the recipient of three Guggenheim Fellowships, the U.S. National Medal of Science, and the Fritzsche Award of the American Chemical Society. Bloch was elected to the National Academy of Sciences in 1956 and served as an editor of the *Journal of Biological Chemistry.* He died at the age of eighty-eight of congestive heart failure at the Lahey Clinic in Burlington.

Bloch's work was a major contribution to cholesterol research, leading to discoveries in a number of different directions. Cholesterol is essential to stabilizing the structure of cell membranes and is the basic molecule from which are produced all of the steroid hormones, including the sex hormones. It is both found in food and manufactured in the body, and how the levels of the two sources are controlled has an important impact on health, since high levels of cholesterol in the blood increase the risk of blood-vessel disease, which can lead to heart disease and stroke. Ways to block the body's synthesis of cholesterol have been discovered and have led to drugs that lower blood-cholesterol levels and thus reduce this risk. Knowing all the steps in cholesterol synthesis was essential to this work.

★

Bloch wrote an autobiographical piece as the preface to his book, *Blondes in Venetian Paintings, the Nine-Banded Armadillo, and Other Essays in Biochemistry* (1994), and an autobiographical essay, "Summing Up," *Annual Review of Biochemistry* 56 (1987): 1–19. Obituaries are in the *New York Times* (18 Oct. 2000) and *Nature* (15 Feb. 2001).

MAURA FLANNERY

BLOCK, Herbert Lawrence ("Herblock") (*b.* 13 October 1909 in Chicago, Illinois; *d.* 7 October 2001 in Washington, D.C.), popular and influential liberal political cartoonist.

Block was the youngest of three sons of David Julian Block, a chemist and electrical engineer, and Theresa ("Tessie") B. (Lupe) Block. His father was Jewish and his mother Catholic, and he and his brothers were nonreligious. The first caricature he recalled drawing was of Kaiser Wilhelm II of Germany, on a Chicago sidewalk during World War I. His father encouraged his drawing and enrolled him in Saturday classes at the Art Institute of Chicago. Some of his cartoons and columns, submitted to his high school monthly magazine, were reprinted in the *Chicago Daily News.* Because pseudonyms were then common for cartoonists, his father suggested combining his first and last names into "Herblock," which stuck for life. Herblock attended Lake Forest College but left after two years to join the *Chicago Daily News,* which ran his first daily cartoon on 24 April 1929. In 1933 the Newspaper Enterprise Association (NEA) hired him as editorial cartoonist, distributing his work to seven hundred papers. His liberal, internationalist viewpoint fell out of step with the syndicate, however, as it turned conservative and isolationist. Following the 1941 Japanese attack on Pearl Harbor in Hawaii, which drew the United States into World War II, the NEA shrank the size of his cartoons, ostensibly to save paper. Once he won his first Pulitzer Prize in 1942, however, his cartoons returned to full size.

Drafted in 1943, Herblock drew cartoons for the army.

Herbert L. Block. THE LIBRARY OF CONGRESS

Because his artwork went to bases with only mimeograph machines for reproduction, he learned to simplify his drawings. His cartoons became more notable for their wit and perceptiveness than for graphic style. After the war the *Washington Post* recruited him. He liked the idea of working out of the national capital, where he could see his subjects firsthand and knew that they would see his work.

The cartoonist's friendship with the editorial writer Alan Barth, an avid civil libertarian, fortified his opposition to the aggressive tactics of congressional anticommunist investigations. On 16 May 1948 he drew members of the House Un-American Activities Committee as Puritans building a fire under the Statue of Liberty, with the caption "We've got to burn the evil spirits out of her." This was his first depiction of Richard Nixon, then a congressman from California, and it marked the beginning of the two men's long mutual animosity. Herblock condemned politicians such as Nixon and the Wisconsin senator Joseph R. McCarthy for fanning public fears to partisan advantage. In a 29 March 1950 cartoon he coined the term "McCarthyism," using it as the label on a tar bucket that represented character assassination, mudslinging, and guilt by association.

The *Washington Post* endorsed the Republican presidential candidate Dwight D. Eisenhower in 1952, trusting that he could restrain McCarthy's zealotry. Offended by Eisenhower's selection of Nixon for vice president, Herblock roasted the Republican ticket. When these drawings embarrassed his publisher, the cartoonist suggested not running them in the *Post* until after the election, but syndicated copies in other papers made it appear as though the *Post* had censored him. His publishers never repeated that mistake.

After his second Pulitzer Prize in 1954, Herblock's cartoons became synonymous with the *Washington Post*. The prestige he brought to the paper ensured his autonomy. He considered a cartoon a signed expression of his personal opinion, in contrast to an editorial, which expressed his paper's policies. Scouring the headlines for ideas, he worked out of an office piled high with newspapers, magazines, photographs, catalogs, and art equipment. He avoided editorial conferences, and instead of showing his preliminary sketches to the editorial page editor, he would walk through the newsroom each afternoon to get reactions from like-minded journalists.

Herblock recovered from a 1959 heart attack in time to employ his pen against Nixon's presidential bid. His relentlessly negative images of Nixon, with an ominous five o'clock shadow, caused the vice president to cancel home delivery of the *Post* to shield his young daughters. As a presidential candidate, Nixon said he needed to "erase the Herblock image." By contrast, the cartoonist sketched the Democratic candidate, Senator John F. Kennedy, as a heroic figure.

Kennedy's election trimmed Herblock's invective, but Lyndon B. Johnson, who became president upon Kennedy's assassination, rekindled his ire. Although he supported Johnson's Great Society and its attendant War on Poverty, he disliked the Texan's overbearing nature and the drain on domestic resources posed by the Vietnam War. Editorially, the *Post* marched in step with Johnson's war policies, and Herblock curbed his criticism until January 1968, when the Tet Offensive turned the tide of the war in favor of the North Vietnamese. After Tet, his cartoons ridiculed American claims of imminent military victory.

Although he was dismayed over Nixon's election as president in 1968, Herblock drew a barbershop with the sign "This shop gives every new President of the United States a free shave." Even clean-shaven, his portraits of Nixon remained distrustful. In response to readers who complained that he owed the office of president more respect, he replied that he respected the office enough to hold anyone who occupied it to high standards. Nixon's manner and politics infuriated him, but his "little black ink bottle" and reserved space on the editorial page gave him ample opportunity to retaliate.

On 20 June 1972 police arrested five burglars at Democratic Party offices in Washington, D.C.'s Watergate Hotel. Herblock instinctively linked the break-in to the president. His cartoon on 23 June showed footsteps labeled with various scandals, including the Watergate bugging, leading directly to the White House: "Strange—they all seem to have some connection with this place." Herblock shared in the *Post's* Pulitzer Prize for Watergate coverage in 1973. Another Pulitzer followed in 1979. He received numerous awards and honors and was honored with a retrospective showing of his work at the Library of Congress.

Herblock taunted presidents Gerald R. Ford, Jimmy Carter, Ronald Reagan, and George H. W. Bush alike. He treated Bill Clinton more gingerly, but his last cartoon, published on 26 August 2001, ripped into George W. Bush's diplomacy as the "speak-loudly-and-poke-'em-with-a-big-stick policy." He never married, nor did he ever retire. He worked until he died of pneumonia at age ninety-one and left an estate of $50 million, mostly in *Washington Post* stock, to the Herb Block Foundation to support the social, economic, and political reforms his cartoons had espoused.

An inspiration to generations of editorial cartoonists, Herblock produced images that at a glance carried more impact than any editorial. The columnist Mary McGrory described his pen as a terrible swift sword. "That so mild a man could flatten so many with so few strokes of ink and crayon is one of the wonders of the age," she wrote on Herblock's fiftieth anniversary with the *Post*. "Who else could have helped us through the manifold hypocrisies and treacheries of the McCarthy-Nixon years?"

★

Herblock's papers and drawings are in the Library of Congress. In addition to his memoirs, *Herblock: A Cartoonist's Life* (1993) and *Bella and Me: Life in Service of a Cat* (1995), Herblock collected his cartoons and commentary in *The Herblock Book* (1952), *Herblock's Here and Now* (1955), *Herblock's Special for Today* (1958), *Straight Herblock* (1964), *The Herblock Gallery* (1968), *Herblock's State of the Union* (1972), *Herblock Special Report* (1974), *Herblock on All Fronts* (1980), *Herblock Through the Looking Glass* (1984), and *Herblock at Large* (1987). Other useful sources are Chalmers Roberts, *The Washington Post: The First 100 Years* (1977); Katharine Graham, *Personal History* (1997); and the Library of Congress catalog *Herblock's History* (2000). See also the *Washington Post* tribute "Herblock's Half-Century" (31 Dec. 1995). An obituary is in the *New York Times* (9 Oct. 2001), and obituaries and memorial tributes are in the *Washington Post* (8–9 Oct. 2001).

DONALD A. RITCHIE

BOLAND, Edward Patrick (*b.* 1 October 1911 in Springfield, Massachusetts; *d.* 4 November 2001 in Springfield, Massachusetts), eighteen-term Massachusetts congressman who authored the Boland amendments restricting funding for the contra rebels in Nicaragua, which, when circumvented, led to the Iran-Contra scandal during President Ronald Reagan's administration.

Boland was the youngest of four boys born to Irish Catholic immigrants Michael Boland, a railroad worker, and Johanna (Cavanaugh) Boland, a homemaker. He grew up in the poor, blue-collar Hungry Hill section of the western Massachusetts city of Springfield. After graduating from Central High School in 1928, he attended the Bay Path Institute, a business school in nearby Longmeadow, Massachusetts, in 1929. Boland also attended Boston College Law School, but he left school in 1941 without earning a degree. Boston College awarded him an honorary LL.D. in 1979.

Imbued with the working-class Democratic culture of Springfield, Boland first ran for political office in 1934 at age twenty-three, winning a seat in the Massachusetts House of Representatives, where he served until 1940. His political organization consisted of teenagers from the sandlot baseball team he had organized as playground director for Springfield. Boland was elected register of deeds in Hampden County in western Massachusetts in 1940. He enlisted in the U.S. Army in 1942 and served in the Pacific during World War II; he left the army in 1946, having achieved the rank of captain. In 1946 he was reelected register of deeds, but he left in 1949 to become Governor Paul A. Dever's military aide.

In 1952 Boland ran for the congressional seat from the Second Massachusetts District. Winning the election, despite the Dwight Eisenhower–led Republican landslide, Boland held this seat until he retired in 1989 and never lost an election. He had such overwhelming support, often winning with over 70 percent of the votes, that Republicans ran only token opponents. Boland usually spent as little as $50.00 on his reelection campaigns and ran unopposed in seven of his eighteen campaigns.

For twenty-four years Boland shared an apartment with fellow representative Thomas P. "Tip" O'Neill in Washington, D.C. The two were known as the "odd couple": Boland was "neat, trim and reserved" with black hair, while the burly O'Neill was brash and outspoken. A bachelor, Boland furnished the apartment with only his toaster and coffee pot. He said that "in 24 years, we never had an argument there and we never had a meal." For his part, O'Neill said of the living arrangement: "The only four items ever seen in that fridge were orange juice, diet soda, beer, and cigars."

Edward P. Boland, 1987. BETTMANN/CORBIS

In 1960 Boland managed John F. Kennedy's presidential campaign in Ohio. A lifetime Kennedy family ally and supporter, he also nominated Edward M. Kennedy for the Senate at the Massachusetts Democratic convention in 1962. He marched with the Reverend Dr. Martin Luther King, Jr., in the momentous 1965 civil rights march in Selma, Alabama. On 9 August 1973 Boland married Mary K. Egan, a lawyer and president of the Springfield City Council who was considerably younger. They had two sons and two daughters. Boland kept his workweek Washington apartment with O'Neill.

Twice in his career, in 1970 and again in 1978, Boland missed opportunities to assume leadership positions in the House. In 1970 neither he nor roommate O'Neill could decide whether or not to run for Speaker, so neither did. In 1978 Boland did not actively seek the chairmanship of the Appropriations Committee, but was disappointed when O'Neill did not put forward his appointment.

Boland became the powerful number-two Democrat in the House as chair of the Select Committee on Appropriations from 1977 to 1983; the committee played a key role in government spending decisions. He also chaired the Independent Agencies Subcommittee, which oversaw the Department of Housing and Urban Development (HUD),

where he promoted President Lyndon B. Johnson's "Great Society" programs for public housing. Boland initially supported the Vietnam War, but he eventually opposed military involvement and in 1973 voted to override President Richard M. Nixon's veto of the War Powers Act.

When O'Neill became Speaker of the House in 1977, he appointed Boland as the first chairman of the Select Committee on Intelligence, which Boland chaired until 1984. Oversight of the Central Intelligence Agency (CIA) was one charge of the committee. Boland worked for bipartisan consensus in intelligence matters at a time when the intelligence community's reputation was plagued by accusations of CIA involvement in assassinations abroad and spying on American citizens at home. Boland became concerned with President Reagan's covert support of the rebels in Nicaragua, known as "contras," who were trying to overthrow the Marxist Sandinista regime. Although an anticommunist, Boland believed that the United States should not "be involved in the process of overthrowing . . . or destabilizing governments." In 1982 the first Boland amendment, unanimously passed by the House of Representatives, made aid to the contras dependent on the rebels not using those funds to overthrow the Nicaraguan government. A second Boland amendment, passed in 1983, capped aid to the contras at $24 million. There were five amendments altogether, which expired in June 1986. Boland eventually served on the House Select Committee to Investigate Covert Arms Transactions with Iran. He believed that the spending restrictions should apply to the National Security Council and that President Reagan knew that members of his administration were violating the funding restrictions. The 1987 hearings exposed what became known as the Iran-Contra scandal. Ex-Marine Lieutenant Colonel Oliver L. North and others in the Reagan administration were indicted for selling arms to Iran and secretly using the profits to fund the contras in order to evade the Boland amendments.

Boland's Appropriations Committee also funded the National Aeronautics and Space Agency (NASA). Since the Basketball Hall of Fame is in Springfield, he arranged to send a basketball on the ill-fated 1986 flight of the Space Shuttle *Challenger,* which exploded shortly after take-off in January of that year. He was proud to have dramatically increased support for the National Science Foundation as well.

In 1985 Boland received the Pynchon Medal for distinguished public service, and in 1989 the Massachusetts State Council of the Knights of Columbus gave him the Lantern Award. He retired from Congress in 1988 to spend more time with his family. In June 1989 the House of Representatives dedicated room H-405 as the Edward P. Boland Room, for "the gentleman from Massachusetts, the founder . . . of the Intelligence Committee," in a ceremony attended by congressional as well as intelligence community members. The room is open only to those with security clearance. The city of Springfield named a street Boland's Way.

Boland was a moderate liberal Democrat admired for his integrity and known as a quiet, self-effacing man. He rarely gave interviews and avoided the spotlight until the Iran-Contra scandal. He described his notoriety by saying it "gives me visibility I don't cherish and don't seek." Boland was able to keep secrets, which is why he lasted so long as chair of the Intelligence Committee. His congressional tenure was characterized by dedication to constituents' needs. As a powerful Democrat and friend of O'Neill and President Kennedy, Boland was able to obtain federal grants for Springfield, helping it to diversify an economy long focused on manufacturing.

In October 2001 Boland fractured his hip and was hospitalized. He died at Mercy Medical Center in Springfield of cardiovascular complications at age ninety. After a funeral on 9 November 2001 at Saint Michael's Cathedral, he was buried at Saint Michael's Cemetery in Springfield.

★

Boland's congressional papers, from 1952 to 1988, are held at the John J. Burns Library at Boston College. A profile of Boland is in *Politics in America: Members of Congress in Washington and at Home,* ed. by Alan Ehrenhalt (1986). Obituaries are in the *Springfield Union News* (5 Nov. 2001) and the *New York Times, Washington Post,* and *Boston Globe* (all 6 Nov. 2001).

JANE BRODSKY FITZPATRICK

BONANNO, Joseph ("Joe Bananas") (*b.* 18 January 1905 in Castellammare del Golfo, Sicily, Italy; *d.* 11 May 2002 in Tucson, Arizona), businessman, criminal entrepreneur, and American underworld leader.

Bonanno was the only child of Salvatore and Catherine (Bonventre) Bonanno. The extended family enjoyed considerable Sicilian respect for upholding what Bonanno called "the tradition" of patriarchal clannish loyalties, private justice, and a suspicion of outside value systems. Apparently fleeing prosecution in 1908, Salvatore Bonanno moved his immediate family to Brooklyn, New York City, where he operated a pasta factory and a tavern and where he enjoyed considerable respect within the Sicilian-American community. With his wife and son, he returned to Italy around 1912. After the deaths of both of his parents, Bonanno lived with relatives who reinforced a sense of family pride. As a teenager, the tall, handsome, self-confident Bonanno entered the Joeni Trabia Nautical Institute in Palermo. By 1924 the government of the Italian dictator Benito Mussolini was engaged in a campaign to crush the

Joseph Bonanno arriving at courthouse to surrender to federal authorities, May 1966. BETTMANN/CORBIS

feudal "Mafia" culture in Sicily, and college officials suspended Bonanno for anti-Fascist activities. Leaving Sicily, he booked passage with a cousin for Havana, Cuba. The two young men then boarded a small fishing boat, which took them to Florida. From there, Bonanno joined relatives in Brooklyn.

In 1925 Bonanno helped to expand his uncle's bakery operations and participated in the lucrative production and distribution of illegal whiskey. Bonanno never considered bootlegging during the Prohibition years of the 1920s and early 1930s "wrong." Nor did he shy away from the use of private force to settle scores with competing liquor operators. Bonanno served as an enforcer for Salvatore Maranzano, an older immigrant from Castellammare, in the internecine struggles over liquor and gambling turf in New York City. Maranzano functioned as a father figure to Bonanno, and the two regularly philosophized about "the tradition" and its erosion in the new polyglot, money-conscious American culture. Bonanno proved a faithful supporter of Maranzano in the "Castellammarese War" of 1930–1931 against Joseph Masseria, another Sicilian underworld figure.

In 1931 both Maranzano and Masseria were killed, and younger, more Americanized underworld entrepreneurs replaced them. Later, Bonanno claimed that he inherited much of the illegal liquor and gambling interests of Maranzano, becoming at age twenty-six the youngest "father" of one of the five organized crime "families" in New York. While the press exaggerated the centralization and Sicilian control within the underworld, there were ties of kinship and friendships between organized crime figures from various sections of the country.

For close to thirty years, Bonanno prospered. His marriage to Fay Labruzzo, on 15 November 1931, was a happy one, and they had two sons and a daughter. He became a naturalized U.S. citizen in 1945. Shunning the flashy lifestyle of other underworld figures, he cultivated business and community connections. Bonanno thought of himself as "a venture capitalist." He held interests in at least two firms in the ladies garment industry and owned a motel, a laundry, a Wisconsin cheese company, an upstate New York dairy farm, various real estate investments, and a funeral home. He had gambling interests, but denied ever being personally involved in narcotics or prostitution. He owned homes in Long Island, upstate New York, and Tucson.

In 1957 Bonanno's world began to unravel. That year, troopers raided a mysterious "national convention" of Italian-American underworld figures in Apalachin, New York. The raid fed endless speculation about the structure of organized crime. When Bonanno, who had not been at Apalachin, refused to testify about the gathering, a New York grand jury indicted him for obstruction of justice. A heart attack spared him a trial, and after a federal court overturned the conviction of others who had attended the meeting, Bonanno's indictment was dismissed. In 1963 a relatively minor criminal named Joseph Valachi maintained before a congressional committee that a highly structured Italian-American cartel known as La Cosa Nostra controlled the underworld and that Bonanno, representing one of New York City's five ruling "families," served on its governing "Commission." In October 1964, after being summoned before yet another grand jury, Bonanno disappeared for nineteen months. Whether underworld rivals had kidnapped him, as Bonanno asserted, or he had arranged his own disappearance was unclear. Even after he claimed his captors had released him, however, Bonanno waited for sixteen months before returning for questioning. The grand jury indicted him, but dropped the charges in 1971.

Whatever the truth about Bonanno's disappearance in the mid-1960s, his absence clearly factored into a complicated power struggle within the New York City underworld, presumably centering on the succession within Bonanno's own organized crime family. Much to the proud Bonanno's discomfort, the press referred to these shootings as the Banana Wars and generally disparaged the competency in these skirmishes of Bonanno's oldest son, Salvatore ("Bill"). Bonanno refused to speak to his son for a year

after the publication of Gay Talese's best-selling *Honor Thy Father* (1971), an account of the Bonanno family and the Banana Wars, written with Salvatore's assistance.

Around 1968 Bonanno withdrew to his Arizona home. There he continued his contributions to Catholic charities. He extended loans to businesses in which his sons were active, only to serve an eight-month prison sentence in 1984 for money laundering. Angered by friends in Tucson who seemed to have abandoned him, he also nursed grudges against reporters and law enforcement officials who he concluded were harassing him. In this context, he authored *A Man of Honor: The Autobiography of Joseph Bonanno* (1983). While Bonanno sketched a more decentralized structure for organized crime than law enforcement officials embraced, U.S. Attorney Rudolph Giuliani seized on Bonanno's account of the "Commission" to subpoena the aging underworld figure. When Bonanno refused to testify before the New York grand jury, he was imprisoned for fourteen months in 1985 and 1986. Bonanno died of heart failure at age ninety-seven and is buried alongside his wife, who died in 1980, in Tucson's Holy Hope Cemetery and Mausoleum.

Bonanno represented an older, decentralized Sicilian folkway of clannish honor and private justice. Seeking power and respect, he engaged in both legitimate and illegitimate business ventures throughout the United States. In the process, he watched with dismay as his Sicilian tradition gave way to a newer, interethnic, and more mercenary American gangsterism.

★

Two indispensable books are Bonanno's own *A Man of Honor: The Autobiography of Joseph Bonanno* (1983), with Sergio Lalli, and Gay Talese, *Honor Thy Father* (1971), a multigenerational study of the Bonanno family. For conflicting perspectives on the alleged Mafia control of organized crime in the United States, see Peter Maas, *The Valachi Papers* (1968), and Dwight C. Smith, Jr., *The Mafia Mystique* (1975). An obituary is in the *New York Times* (12 May 2002).

WILLIAM HOWARD MOORE

BOREMAN, Linda. *See* Lovelace, Linda Susan.

BORGE, Victor (*b.* 3 January 1909 in Copenhagen, Denmark; *d.* 23 December 2000 in Greenwich, Connecticut), entertainer who combined sophisticated verbal humor and broad physical comedy with classical piano.

Borge was born Borge Rosenbaum, the younger of two sons of Bernhard and Frederikke (Lichtinger) Rosenbaum. His father played viola in the Royal Danish Philharmonic, and his mother was a pianist. Borge played the piano by age three. He won a scholarship to the Copenhagen Music

Conservatory at age nine and made his concert debut when he was thirteen. Borge continued as a concert pianist until 1934.

Borge could not resist his comic impulse, and he gradually developed a nightclub act that was a mixture of comedy and music. He blended bits of serious piano playing with droll asides, slapstick, and satirical comments on world events. This became an act that thrived for more than sixty years. In the 1930s Borge worked as a comedian, actor, composer, pianist, writer, and director on stage, screen, and radio. He also married for the first time, to an American, Elsie Chilton, on 24 December 1932. By 1940 Borge was one of the best-known entertainment figures in Scandinavia.

In April 1940 the German army invaded Denmark. Borge, being Jewish and having frequently skewered the Nazis in his act, had to leave the country. He and his wife managed to escape through Finland to the United States, arriving on 28 August 1940. At the time Borge spoke no English; he eventually learned by watching countless movies. He changed his name to Victor Borge, translated his routines from Danish to English, and memorized them phonetically for his act. With time, he was able to get work in smaller nightclubs.

The entertainer Rudy Vallee saw one of Borge's performances and hired him to do audience warm-ups for his radio program. Then Borge auditioned for the singer and actor Bing Crosby's Kraft Music Hall and was hired for a guest spot. He was so successful that he became a regular on the show for more than a year. From that point on, Borge performed regularly on radio. *The Victor Borge Show* ran from 8 March to 9 July 1943 on the National Broadcasting Company (NBC) Blue network; from 3 July to 25 September 1945 on NBC; again on NBC from 9 August 1946 to 30 June 1947; and from 1 January to 1 June 1951 on the American Broadcasting Company (ABC) and the Mutual networks. Borge debuted at Carnegie Hall in 1945. Around that time Borge and his wife adopted twins; Borge became a naturalized American citizen in 1948.

After Borge and his first wife divorced in 1951, he married Sarabel Sanna Scraper Roach on 17 March 1953. Borge became father to his new wife's daughter by a previous marriage, and later he and Sanna had a son and a daughter. The Borges remained married until Sanna's death in September 2000.

For the rest of his career Borge toured top nightclubs and concert halls across the globe. He performed often as a soloist or guest conductor with symphony orchestras. He even made rare appearances in American film (*Higher and Higher* in 1944 and *The King of Comedy* in 1983). In 1953 Borge opened *Comedy in Music* at the Golden Theater. The show ran 849 consecutive performances, which at his death still held the record for the longest-running one-person Broadway show. He brought the show back in 1964 (with

Victor Borge, 1943. AP/WIDE WORLD PHOTOS

the pianist Leonid Hambro) and in 1977 (with the opera singer Marylyn Mulvey).

Although his 1951 television series ended with its first season, Borge did well on television as a guest star and in his own specials into the 1990s. He also wrote three books: *My Favorite Intermissions* (1971), *My Favorite Comedies in Music* (1980), and *Smilet er den korteste afstand* (A Smile Is the Shortest Distance, 1997). By releasing some of his best concerts on compact disc, video, and the Public Broadcasting System (PBS) in addition to performing live, Borge maintained a solid career to his death at age ninety-one.

Borge's most famous routines were "Phonetic Punctuation" and "Inflationary Language." In the former he read dialogues, making comical sounds to stand for the punctuation marks. In "Inflationary Language" he recited passages and changed them by increasing any number that occurred (or its homonym) to the next higher number ("Any two for elevennis?"). Borge wrote much of his material himself. He deliberately allowed room in his act for improvisation and retained ad-libbed bits that audiences liked.

Borge's hobbies included flying, yachting, and gourmet cooking. He also raised and marketed Rock Cornish game hens for many years. Active in charities, he cofounded a scholarship fund in gratitude to Scandinavians who rescued European Jews during World War II. This fund helps

Scandinavian students and health-care professionals come to the United States to study.

Borge received seven honorary degrees. He was knighted by five Scandinavian nations and honored by the U.S. Congress and the United Nations. In 1999 Borge was honored by the Kennedy Center for the Performing Arts.

Borge died of heart failure at his home in Greenwich, Connecticut, and was buried there at Putnam Cemetery. Critics debate how great a pianist and conductor Borge— known as the "Unmelancholy Dane," the "Clown Prince of Denmark," the "Great Dane," and the "comedian of the keyboard"—was. Even he acknowledged that he was a very good pianist but not a great one. But there is no such debate over his status as a comedian. Borge was not the only musical comedian of his time, but he was certainly the greatest. With witty quips, sight gags, amusing wordplay, and beautiful music, he created an act that pleased both sophisticated and simple tastes and gracefully stood the test of time.

★

For profiles from the peak of Borge's career, see profiles by G. T. Hellman in the *New Yorker* (7 May 1955) and H. Goldberg in *Cosmopolitan* (Oct. 1954). For a look at Borge near the end of his career, see Ralph Blumenthal's article in the *New York Times* (21 January 1999). A rare look at Borge as a musician is in *Etude* 73 (Feb. 1955). An obituary is in the *New York Times* (25 Dec. 2000).

PATRICIA L. MARKLEY

BOUDREAU, Louis ("Lou") (*b.* 17 July 1917 in Harvey, Illinois; *d.* 10 August 2001 in Olympia Fields, Illinois), Hall of Fame shortstop who became the youngest manager in modern baseball history in 1942 and led the Cleveland Indians to an American League (AL) pennant and a World Series championship in 1948.

Boudreau was the younger of two sons of Louis Boudreau, a machinist, and Birdie (King) Henry, a homemaker. He grew up in Harvey, Illinois, an industrial city eighteen miles south of downtown Chicago. Boudreau's father, a former semiprofessional baseball player, pitched and hit balls to his son each day after work and regularly took him to Chicago Cubs games. Originally a catcher on his grammar school team, young Lou, who batted and threw right-handed, moved to third base in order to learn the position his father had played.

At Thornton Township High School in Harvey, which did not field a baseball team during his years of attendance, Boudreau made his mark in basketball. As a five-foot, ten-inch playmaking guard, he led his team to the state championship in 1933 and to the finals in 1934 and 1935. He was named to the state tournament all-star team all three

Lou Boudreau, 1942. AP/WIDE WORLD PHOTOS

years. After graduation in 1935, Boudreau won a scholarship to the University of Illinois in Champaign, where he majored in physical education and helped propel the "Fighting Illini" basketball and baseball teams to Big Ten Conference titles in 1937. But in 1938 Boudreau was suspended from the basketball team after Big Ten officials discovered he had verbally agreed to sign a professional baseball contract with the Cleveland Indians after his college graduation, in exchange for payments of $500 to each of his parents (who had divorced) and an additional $100 per month to his mother. Although he had not received any money himself and the Indians later renounced all claims to his services, Boudreau was eventually declared ineligible for intercollegiate basketball and baseball. After completing his junior year at Illinois, he accepted an invitation from the Indians to play for their Cedar Rapids, Iowa, farm team in the Class B Three-I League. Boudreau married Della DeRuiter, his high school sweetheart, on 5 June 1938. They had four children.

Boudreau compiled a respectable .290 batting average in sixty games at Cedar Rapids and went hitless in one at-bat after being called up to Cleveland for the last month of the 1938 season. In 1939 he followed the advice of Indians manager Oscar Vitt and moved to shortstop from third base, where another budding star, Ken Keltner, stood in his way. Farmed out to Buffalo of the International League,

Boudreau adapted to his new position and hit for a .331 average, with seventeen home runs and fifty-seven runs batted in (RBI). This strong effort earned him a second late-season stint with the Indians, in which he batted .258 in fifty-three games. Boudreau finished his course work at the University of Illinois during the off-season and received his B.S. degree in 1940.

Boudreau cracked Cleveland's starting lineup in 1940 and, over the next decade, established himself as the preeminent shortstop in baseball. Despite having flat feet, arthritic ankles that had to be heavily taped before each game, and an average throwing arm, he became an outstanding fielder. A natural athlete, Boudreau used his basketball quickness to reach ground balls, and a glove without a pocket allowed him to get his throws off more easily. He led AL shortstops in putouts four times, in assists twice, in double plays five times, and in fielding percentage eight times.

As a hitter, Boudreau was considered a clutch performer on a level just below that of the contemporary superstars Joe DiMaggio and Ted Williams. Even though his painful slowness afoot generally deprived him of infield hits, he averaged over .300 four times, won the AL batting title in 1944 (.327), and was runner-up to Williams in 1948 (.355). Boudreau also drove in 100 or more runs twice, led the AL in doubles three times, and set a record by hitting four consecutive doubles in a game in 1948. All of this was accomplished with an unorthodox, crouching batting stance that one sportswriter likened to "a man leaning over a fence to read a neighbor's paper while in the act of beating a carpet."

After only two full major league seasons, Boudreau, who had captained all his athletic teams in high school and college, emerged as the Indians' team leader on the field. In the fall of 1941, the confident twenty-four-year-old applied for the job of manager when the incumbent, Roger Peckinpaugh, moved up to the front office. Although Indians president Alva Bradley at first opposed Boudreau's candidacy, board members eventually convinced Bradley that the appointment of a youthful manager would spark fan interest.

Boudreau, who was rejected by the U.S. Army because of his arthritic ankles, continued to enhance his credentials as a player during World War II, but the Indians were consistent also-rans in the AL pennant race. Military service deprived the "boy manager" of his best pitcher, Bob Feller, and a host of promising young players, and his teams finished fourth (1942), a distant third (1943), and fifth twice (1944 and 1945). But even when the war veterans returned in 1946, the Indians ended up in sixth place, thirty-six games behind the pennant-winning Boston Red Sox. As a manager, Boudreau's most notable contribution to baseball up to this time was the extreme defense he deployed in

1946 in an attempt to thwart Ted Williams, the most feared left-handed pull hitter in baseball. The "Boudreau Shift," which stationed all four infielders on the right side of the diamond, two outfielders in right field, and the third outfielder in short left-center, initially flummoxed the stubborn Williams and lowered his production somewhat. But the slugger got a measure of revenge in September when he poked a line drive into the open space in the outfield for an inside-the-park home run to beat the Indians, 1–0, and clinch the AL pennant for the Red Sox.

After the 1947 season, in which the Indians only improved to fourth (seventeen games out of first place), the team's new owner, Bill Veeck, sought to replace Boudreau as manager. At the World Series in New York, Veeck told reporters he was contemplating trading the shortstop to the St. Louis Browns. This news was greeted with howls of protest in Cleveland and an unusually large outpouring of public support for Boudreau. Forced to return home and mend relations with angry fans, a chastened Veeck ultimately signed his popular player-manager to a contract extension.

In 1948 Boudreau rewarded his supporters and Veeck by having his finest season as a player and manager, guiding the Indians to their first pennant and World Series championship in twenty-eight years. Voted AL Most Valuable Player, he recorded career highs in batting average (.355), hits (199), home runs (18), and RBI (106); led league shortstops in fielding for the eighth time; and went a perfect four-for-four (two home runs, two singles, and a walk) in the Indians one-game playoff victory (8–3) over the Red Sox after the two teams ended the season tied for first place.

Generally regarded as an inspirational leader among managers, Boudreau also displayed considerable ability as a decision maker in 1948. His move of Larry Doby, who had starred at second base in the Negro National League before joining the Indians in 1947, to the outfield strengthened the Indians lineup. Doby batted .301, with 14 homers and 66 RBI during the regular season, and led all Cleveland hitters (.318) in the World Series won by the Indians over the Boston Braves in six games. And, in support of his ace, Feller, who had a difficult season, Boudreau skillfully utilized the pitching talents of Bob Lemon, Gene Bearden, and Leroy ("Satchel") Paige during Cleveland's successful drive for the AL pennant. Lemon, an infielder and outfielder whom Boudreau and his coaching staff had converted into a pitcher in 1946, became the AL leader in innings pitched, complete games, and shutouts. Bearden, an unheralded rookie knuckleballer, topped the AL in earned run average (ERA) and won the playoff game with Boston (on one day's rest). Paige, the aging Negro Leagues legend whom Veeck signed at mid-season, was nearly flawless as a reliever and occasional starter.

Boudreau was signed to another two-year contract and given a raise by Veeck early in 1949. Showing signs of wear, he reduced the number of games he played at shortstop in 1949 and 1950, and his batting average slipped to .283 and .269, respectively. After the Indians dropped to third and then fourth in the standings, Ellis Ryan, who had purchased the team from Veeck in 1949, and his general manager, Hank Greenberg, felt the time was right to replace Boudreau as manager.

Released by the Indians, Boudreau signed with the Red Sox in 1951. After hitting .267 as a backup infielder, he became the team's manager in 1952. The loss of Ted Williams to military service in the Korean War for the better part of two years, and his own failed attempt to reshape the team by replacing older players with young prospects, made for an unhappy three-year experience for Boudreau in Boston. His Red Sox were never pennant contenders, finishing fourth in 1952, sixth in 1953, and a distant fourth (forty-two games behind the pennant-winning Indians) in 1954. Boudreau had ended his playing career in May 1952, after a pitch broke a bone in his left hand.

Fired by Boston after the 1954 season, Boudreau moved on to manage in Kansas City, where the former Philadelphia Athletics had taken up residence in 1955. An eighth (last) place team the previous two years, the Athletics moved up to sixth under their new field general in their new city in 1955, but reverted to their old ways in 1956 and 1957, finishing eighth and seventh, respectively. Returning to Harvey following his dismissal in Kansas City, Boudreau was recruited by the veteran Chicago announcer Jack Brickhouse to contribute color commentary for Cubs games on WGN radio and television. His broadcasting career was interrupted briefly in 1960, when the Cubs owner Philip K. Wrigley asked him to return to managing seventeen games into the season. After the team went 54–83 and finished seventh (of eight) in the National League, Boudreau returned to the broadcast booth and remained there until 1988. One of the earliest former ballplayers in the field of sports broadcasting, he also covered college basketball and football as well as professional hockey during his long career.

Elected to the National Baseball Hall of Fame in 1970, Boudreau had a lifetime batting average of .295 and a career fielding percentage of .973. As a manager his record was 1,162–1,224 (.487). Boudreau's number "5" was retired by the Indians in 1970 and by the University of Illinois in 1992. A street adjacent to Cleveland's Municipal Stadium is named for him. He died of heart failure from complications of diabetes and was buried in Pleasant Hill Cemetery in Frankfort, Illinois.

Although not quite in a class with Williams, DiMaggio, or Stan Musial, Boudreau was a genuine baseball star of the 1940s. In a remarkable career, he overcame physical limitations to become a great shortstop and played his best while also carrying out the responsibilities of the demanding job of team manager. His 1948 season, a tour de force, was one of the greatest in major league history.

★

The National Baseball Hall of Fame Library in Cooperstown, New York, has a substantial file on Boudreau. He wrote two autobiographies with sportswriters: *Player-Manager* (1949), with Ed Fitzgerald, which thoroughly covers his life and baseball career through 1948; and *Lou Boudreau: Covering All the Bases* (1993), with Russell Schneider, which is useful for his later years. Boudreau also authored an instructional book, *Good Infield Play* (1948). Franklin A. Lewis, *The Cleveland Indians* (1949), and Peter Golenbock, *Fenway: An Unexpurgated History of the Boston Red Sox* (1992), are solid histories that ably discuss Boudreau's contributions to his teams. David Kaiser, *Epic Season: The 1948 American League Pennant Race* (1998), and Russell Schneider, *The Boys of Summer of '48* (1998), are detailed accounts of Boudreau's career year. Notable contemporary articles are Kyle Crichton, "Lou Is Cleveland's Business," *Collier's* (15 May 1948), and Stanley Frank, "They're Just Wild About Boudreau," *Saturday Evening Post* (4 Sept. 1948). Obituaries are in the *Chicago Sun-Times, Cleveland Plain-Dealer,* and *New York Times* (all 11 Aug. 2001).

RICHARD H. GENTILE

BROOKS, Gwendolyn Elizabeth (*b.* 7 June 1917 in Topeka, Kansas; *d.* 3 December 2000 in Chicago, Illinois), Pulitzer Prize–winning poet and advocate of economic and artistic self-sufficiency among African-American writers and artists.

Brooks was the first of two children of David Anderson Brooks and Keziah Corinne (Wims) Brooks. Her father had hoped to be a doctor but could afford only one year of college; her mother had hoped to be a concert pianist but could not even afford to finish Emporia Normal School. Thus, when they moved with their baby daughter to Bronzeville, as the integrated neighborhood on the South Side of Chicago was called in those years, they still aspired to be members of the professional class.

It was not to be. David Brooks could get work only as a porter, a job that paid less and less as the Great Depression neared; conditions forced him to take a second job as a house painter. The family's efforts to raise their daughter in an "appropriate" manner only further alienated her from schoolmates, who saw her shyness as snobbery and looked down on her because of her dark skin and frizzy hair. As she reached high school age, Brooks's problems with socialization mounted. She first attended Hyde Park High School, the leading all-white school, and then transferred to the all-black Wendell Phillips High School; neither one offered her the combination of academic challenge and social ease she needed. Finally, she transferred to Englewood

High School, which was integrated and where she made friends who would stay with her for life.

After her graduation Brooks, with continuing financial support from her parents, attended Wilson Junior College, from which she graduated in 1936. She applied for employment at the *Chicago Defender,* the African-American newspaper to which she had been contributing poems for five years, but her application was rejected. She did join the Youth Council of the National Association for the Advancement of Colored People (NAACP), taking an active role in meetings, marches, and dances. At one such event she met Henry Blakely, Jr. Seeing him for the first time, she blurted out, "There is the man I'm going to marry."

Brooks and Blakely married on 17 September 1939. Although they were both aspiring poets, the pressures of economic necessity drove Blakely to a succession of jobs—for a black insurance company, a delivery service, an auto repair business, and finally a trucking company. As Brooks would write in her autobiography, "It is hard on the man's ego to be married to a [successful] woman." The couple separated in 1969 but reconciled in the mid-1970s, when Blakely finally began publishing his own work. Meanwhile, pregnancy and child rearing (they had a son in 1940 and a daughter in 1951) kept Brooks at home for two decades. As she wrote to her first editor, she managed to write while "scrubbing, sweeping, washing, ironing, cooking, dropping the mop, broom, soap, iron, or carrot grater to write down a line."

Success came with surprising speed. Brooks won awards from the Midwest Writers Conference in 1943, 1944, and 1945 and published two works in *Poetry* magazine in August 1945. That same month, Harper and Brothers published *A Street in Bronzeville,* the first of what would eventually be twenty books of poems. Her next volume, *Annie Allen,* was published in August 1949 and won the Pulitzer Prize. Brooks gained many speaking engagements as a result of the award but little hard cash; her royalty checks for 1950 amounted to a paltry $169. Furthermore, the family's housing woes—first memorialized in "kitchenette" (her 1944 prize-winning poem)—continued to plague them. Hoping for the greater sales that prose offered, Brooks adapted an earlier poem sequence into a "novel," *Maud Martha,* published in 1953. With the $500 advance and a loan from her parents, she was finally able to purchase a house.

Nevertheless, money remained a major issue. Brooks's advances for *Bronzeville Boys and Girls* (1956) and *The Bean Eaters* (1960) were a meager $100 each, forcing her to write book reviews to cover the mortgage. By 1962 her finances had finally started to improve. Her publisher agreed to bring out her *Selected Poems* (1963), which would win major cash prizes, and she was hired to teach literature and creative writing, first at the University of Chicago and then at Columbia College. She also was invited to contribute a

Gwendolyn Brooks, 1968. AP/WIDE WORLD PHOTOS

single poem to a Christmas issue of *Country Beautiful* magazine for the gratifying sum of $450 and was named by *Poetry* as one of the featured speakers at their annual Poetry Day, with an honorarium of $500.

Although none of her books had ever sold more than five thousand copies, Brooks's reputation as a writer was growing. In the spring of 1967 she experienced a personal, political, and artistic transformation when she attended the Second Black Writers' Conference at Fisk University in Nashville, Tennessee. Although Hoyt Fuller had been publishing *Negro Digest* in Chicago since 1961 (it became *Black World* in 1970), and she had participated in their 1965 symposium on the "Negro writer" in a segregated society, this conference signaled Brooks's first wholehearted acceptance of the ideology of the short-lived but widely influential Black Arts movement. (As the novelist and poet Ishmael Reed has stated, "There would be no multiculturalism movement without Black Arts.") In 1950 Brooks had written a short essay for *Phylon,* an Atlanta University journal, that toed the conservative line: "The Negro poet's most pressing duty, at present, is to polish his technique." Now, at Fisk, her position was visibly different: "Every poet of African extraction must understand that his product will be either italicized or seasoned by the fact and significance of his heritage." The "Negro" poet who focuses on technique rather than content had given way to the "African" poet who boasts of a rich racial and cultural heritage.

Upon her return to Chicago, Brooks wrote two odes reflecting this transition. The first, delivered on 15 August, celebrated the installation of a now famous piece of public art. Brooks described "The Chicago Picasso" as a symbol of generic, abstract "Art"—monumental, certainly, but "cold." In contrast, Brooks's second ode, on 27 August, celebrated "The Wall," a Black Arts mural: "Black / boy-men on roofs fist out 'Black power!'" Afterward, she and her fellow poets gathered in a neighborhood bar and recited their poems for an hour to appreciative patrons. As Brooks said in a 1972 interview, her aim was "to write poems that will somehow successfully 'call' . . . all black people: black people in taverns . . . in gutters, school, offices, factories, prisons."

The transformation was signaled with Brooks's publication of *In the Mecca,* a long poem that drew on her experience as a young woman just out of junior college. The poem depicts a mother's desperate search for her missing daughter, whose body is revealed in the last stanza under the bed of the murderer, "in dust with roaches." Yet it is a world in which a thousand or more people live and make plans and commit to a better future. Brooks sums up the paradox of her volume in its last poem: "The time / cracks into furious flower. . . . Nevertheless, live."

Brooks's own life "cracked into furious flower" during this period as well. In 1968 she announced that she would publish only with African-American presses such as Broadside and Third World Press. Illinois had named her poet laureate in 1968, and with money coming in more regularly, she seized the opportunity to endow a series of poet laureate awards (her husband would receive one in 1987). At the end of 1969 a "Living Anthology" of performers and artists packed the Afro-Arts Theater to salute her life and accomplishments. In the summer of 1971 she went to Africa for the first of several trips; to Montgomery, Alabama, to prepare a long poem for *Ebony* magazine; and then on to New York, where she had been named distinguished professor of the arts at City College of New York. A mild heart attack at the end of the first semester cut her busy schedule short. In the seventies Brooks published the first of two autobiographical volumes, *Report from Part One* (1972), as well as further works in support of African-American poetry, such as *A Capsule Course in Black Poetry Writing* (1975).

Brooks remained active well into her seventies; she published seven volumes of poetry between 1981 and 1991, served as poetry consultant to the Library of Congress from 1985 to 1986, and was named to the National Women's Hall of Fame in 1988. In 1994 she was named a Jefferson lecturer, the federal government's highest humanities award; a year later, an Illinois elementary school was named in her honor, as was the Center for African-American Literature at West-

ern Illinois University. She received more than fifty honorary degrees. Her health started to fail in the late 1990s. Blakely died in 1996, and Brooks was diagnosed with stomach cancer, which caused her death at the age of eighty-three.

Brooks blazed a double trail, both as a female poet and as an African-American one. She transformed her life and the lives of those around her, victims of racism and economic uncertainty, into an art that wove their voices into a tapestry of beauty and power. Her fusion of the high and the low—the literary metaphor and the vulgar catchphrase—offered her readers astounding vistas: "gargantuan gardens careful in the sun . . . summer sailboats / like cartoon ghosts or Klansmen." She was one of the great American poets of the twentieth century.

★

Brooks published an autobiography in two parts, *Report from Part One* (1972) and *Report from Part Two* (1995). Books about her include Haki R. Madhubuti, ed., *Say That the River Turns: The Impact of Gwendolyn Brooks* (1987); D. H. Melhem, *Gwendolyn Brooks: Poetry and the Heroic Voice* (1987); Maria K. Mootry and Gary Smith, eds., *A Life Distilled: Gwendolyn Brooks, Her Poetry and Fiction* (1987); and George Kent, *Gwendolyn Brooks: A Life* (1988). An obituary is in the *New York Times* (5 Dec. 2000).

HARTLEY S. SPATT

BROUN, Heywood Hale ("Woodie") (*b.* 10 March 1918 in New York City; *d.* 5 September 2001 in Kingston, New York), sportswriter, actor, television commentator, and memoirist known for his witty, irreverent, quotable style and engaging on-screen manner.

Broun was the only child of Heywood Campbell Broun, the well-known sportswriter and columnist and one of the founders and longtime president of the American Newspaper Guild, and his first wife, Ruth Hale, a newspaper writer and dedicated feminist. As the son of freethinking, permissive, unconventional parents—who encouraged him to address them by their first names and who debated matters of conduct with him rather than setting limits—Broun had an unusual childhood. Raised as a "miniature adult," he was, according to his contemporary, the writer Ring Lardner, Jr., "eerie, a little kid talking like some kind of old man." Asked by a guest at one of the many parties his parents gave in their Manhattan brownstone, "And whose little boy are you?" the precocious child's answer was, "You know goddamn well whose little boy I am." Hence the title of his memoir, written at the age of sixty-five, in 1983. *Whose Little Boy Are You? A Memoir of the Broun Family* ponders this question and describes Broun's far from idyllic childhood with a rueful humor that softens his confusions

Heywood Hale Broun, July 1950. AP/WIDE WORLD PHOTOS

and frequent sense of abandonment, avoiding overt anger or self-pity. It is an honest, felicitously written attempt to come to terms with the long-standing anxieties caused by his parents' insecurities and marital unhappiness.

Broun was a sickly child, sent away for his health first to California, with a nurse, and between 1930 and 1932 to the Arizona Desert School for Boys in Tucson. This was one of several progressive boarding schools—including the Horace Mann School for boys in Riverdale, New York— to which Broun was dispatched. In the summer of 1934, after his parents' divorce, his mother gave him the money to travel in Europe, from which he returned just before her sudden death. Shortly after, he entered Swarthmore College, where he majored in English, was elected to Phi Beta Kappa, and from which he graduated in 1940, despite his father's pressing him to drop out and become a reporter. To this end, in 1938 the elder Broun employed his son on the *Connecticut Nutmeg,* a short-lived publication he ran. There Broun learned how to put out a newspaper. "My father wanted me to be a newspaperman," he once commented. "Then, he'd be a better newspaperman than I was and that would end our long unconscious war."

In the end, although he wanted to become a college teacher of English, he gave in, and in the fall of 1940 joined the New York liberal tabloid *PM* as a sportswriter. In 1941, two years after his father's death, Broun paid him homage by compiling *The Collected Edition of Heywood Broun,* an anthology of writings the father considered his best. The preface, with its easy, fluid style, conveys admiration (but not adulation) of his father's achievements and gives promise of the writer the younger Broun would become.

After service in World War II as a field artillery sergeant stationed in Europe, Broun returned to *PM* to write a sports column; when the paper folded, he moved to its successor, the *New York Star.* When that journal went under in 1949, Broun, who had always been interested in dramatics, turned to a new career. In college he had simultaneously managed the Swarthmore football team and was secretary of the drama club, prompting a classmate to speculate whether Broun would eventually "run with the athletes or the aesthetes." It was now the aesthetes' turn.

In 1949 Broun made his Broadway acting debut in *Love Me Long,* and he went on to play minor roles with moderate success in some thirteen other Broadway shows. As he quipped, "If I had a good part, it was a bad show. If it was a good show, I had a bad part." He also appeared in Hollywood films and television shows such as *The Doctors* and the *U.S. Steel Hour.* Previously a member of the Newspaper Guild, he joined Actors' Equity, the Screen Actors Guild, and the American Federation of Television and Radio Artists. In 1965 he wrote *A Studied Madness,* an informal, chatty, open-eyed account of show business and his years in it.

Broun accepted an offer from the Columbia Broadcasting System (CBS) in 1965 to do television sports commentaries, and for the next nineteen years he was a familiar figure with his signature droopy brown moustache and bright tartan jacket (befitting a man of proud Scots descent on both sides of his family). His equally colorful reports on sports from baseball, golf, and thoroughbred racing (for which he had a particular fondness) to curling and marbles tournaments mingle cynicism, gentle affection, and an addiction to erudite literary allusions—always avoiding the sentimental, reverent tones often characteristic of sportswriting. Another of his memoirs, *Tumultuous Merriment* (1979), tells of this phase of his life. Its title, one of Broun's literary borrowings, is taken from Samuel Johnson's definition of *sport* in his *Dictionary of the English Language.* Broun also appeared as critic at large for the *CBS Sunday Morning* show and as a syndicated book-show host for WOR-TV programs.

In 1949 Broun married Jane Lloyd-Jones, a stage actress, who died in 1991. For many years they maintained homes in New York City and in Woodstock, New York. Their only child, the novelist Heywood Orren ("Hob") Broun, born in 1950, died at the age of thirty-seven following spinal surgery. In the 1990s, semiretired and having lost both wife and son within four years, Broun kept active as a speaker at schools, libraries, and fundraisers for literacy programs. In the spring of 2001 he fell and broke a hip. A few months later he died of complications in Kingston Hospital, near his Woodstock home. The funeral services were private.

Although Broun had some regret that he was not an athlete himself, he obviously enjoyed what he did for a living, just as his genial style and humor were enjoyed by his readers and viewers. Reflecting on his varied careers, he concluded that he was "either a Little League Renaissance man or simply a person who can't make up his mind." That, according to a fellow sportswriter, Robert Lipsyte of the *New York Times*, was "to our advantage."

★

In addition to the three memoirs mentioned above, biographical details of Broun can be gleaned from his father's newspaper columns devoted to humorous musings on the behavior of "H.3rd," as he referred to his small son; and from the elder Broun's seemingly prescient novel *The Boy Grew Older* (1922), on the growth of a loving relationship between a sportswriter father and his son who must choose between newspaper work and becoming a singer. An obituary is in the *New York Times* (8 Sept. 2001).

ELEANOR F. WEDGE

BROWN, Claude (*b.* 23 February 1937 in Manhattan, New York City; *d.* 2 February 2002 in Manhattan, New York City), author and lecturer on urban African-American life who was best known for writing *Manchild in the Promised Land* (1965).

Brown was born in the Harlem area of Manhattan. His father, Henry Lee Brown, a railroad worker, had migrated from South Carolina to New York City. His mother, Ossie (Brock) Brown, was a domestic worker. Brown grew up in a tenement on 146th Street and Eighth Avenue with his younger brother and two older sisters. At age eight he was expelled from school and spent a year in South Carolina with his grandparents, who were unable to curb his wild side. By age thirteen Brown had been hit by a bus, chain-whipped, thrown into a river, and shot in the stomach during a burglary while an active member of the Forty Thieves division of the Buccaneers Gang.

Brown's childhood was also characterized by a search for a father figure; his own father violently abused Brown and his brothers while escaping his own depressing reality through religion and alcohol. Brown's mother worried about her sons, but was exhausted with the effort of raising them. In the end, Brown grew up on the streets, where he learned to rely on his instincts, common sense, and fists for survival.

Brown experienced three separate stints at reform schools, starting in 1948 at Wiltwyck School in Ulster

Claude Brown, 1986. AP/WIDE WORLD PHOTOS

County, New York, and continuing at Warwick School for Boys in Orange County, New York, where he was released and then reincarcerated until 1953. Brown sold and used marijuana and hard drugs but was not an addict; he had almost died from a violent reaction to his first experience with heroin, and thus knew firsthand the extreme dangers of drug dependency.

While in reform school, Brown learned history, art, and music from responsible adult role models such as Ernest Papanek, the psychologist at Wiltwyck. With this education, Brown was able to break the ghetto's hold over his life and spirit. He began attending night classes at Washington Irving High School in New York City, supporting himself by working as a busboy and deliveryman and at other odd jobs.

After graduating from high school, Brown enrolled at Howard University, a predominantly African-American college in Washington, D.C. In 1959, Brown's first year at Howard, Papanek encouraged him to write an essay on Harlem life for *Dissent* magazine. Based on this essay, Brown was given a $2,000 advance by an editor at Macmillan to develop a book about his experiences growing up in Harlem. Brown took two years to develop a 1,537-page manuscript, which became *Manchild in the Promised Land* (1965). Brown dedicated his work to Eleanor Roosevelt, the former first lady and a cofounder of Wiltwyck, who had invited Brown to dinner at her house.

Brown married Helen Jones, a telephone operator, on 9 September 1961. They had one child and later divorced. He also had one child with his longtime partner and companion, Laura Higgins.

Brown graduated with a B.A. from Howard in 1965, the same year *Manchild* was published to widespread acclaim due to its nonideological, brutally honest, obscene yet tender voice. The book introduced mainstream audiences to the shocking reality of drugs and violence in the Harlem ghetto during the 1940s and 1950s. Brown was able to capture the day-to-day life of African-American transplants from the South, including their Coptic and Muslim religious traditions, jazz music, and unyielding poverty. Brown's voice was authentic and direct; *Manchild* was laced with profanity and urban street slang.

Published at the height of the U.S. civil rights movement, *Manchild* became an instant best-seller, providing readers with a definitive depiction of contemporary life in an African-American ghetto, but without self-pity, outrage, or sermonizing rhetoric. *Manchild* was written as a fictional autobiography, with Sonny, the protagonist, standing in for Brown. Sonny learns that personal resurrection comes not only from character and clarity of mind but also from the institutions and people who surround him; he is able to avoid the self-destructive habits of his friends.

In 1976 Brown published his second book, *The Children of Ham,* which revolves around a group of Harlem teenagers in the 1970s. The teens band together to form retreats from the heroin ravaging their streets, encouraging one another to stay away from drugs, complete their education, and survive. *The Children of Ham* did not receive the same critical acclaim as *Manchild in the Promised Land*. However, Brown continued writing about urban life and, in later years, worked on a third book comparing his own childhood experiences to those of children growing up in Harlem in the 1980s during the crack cocaine epidemic. Brown never finished this book, but he did publish articles on the subject for the *New York Times Magazine* (1984) and *Los Angeles Times* (1988).

Brown studied law at Stanford University in California and Rutgers University in New Jersey but did not earn degrees from either institution. However, the lecture circuit proved more lucrative, and the $60,000 he earned from this each year enabled him to teach, speak, and write as he pleased. He also served as an activist for the juvenile justice system. Brown was described by friends and colleagues as a caring, well-spoken, urbane, and reflective man. He moved to Newark, New Jersey, briefly during the 1970s,

but returned to Harlem, which he always considered home. Brown died at age sixty-four of lung cancer.

Brown's *Manchild in the Promised Land* is recognized as a classic autobiography. Critics rank it as equal to the great African-American autobiographies by Frederick Douglass, *Narrative of the Life of Frederick Douglass, an American Slave* (1845); Langston Hughes, *The Big Sea: An Autobiography* (1940); Richard Wright, *Black Boy, a Record of Childhood and Youth* (1945); and Malcolm X with Alex Haley, *The Autobiography of Malcolm X* (1965). At the end of the twentieth century, more than four million copies of *Manchild* had been sold, and it had been translated into fourteen languages. Brown's honest, unflinching depiction of his formative experiences in Harlem became required reading in many U.S. high school and college courses, ensuring that his message of hope in the face of crushing despair would continue to be heard.

★

For reviews of *Manchild in the Promised Land* (1965), which include biographical details about Brown's life, see Eliot Fremont-Smith, "Coming of Age in Harlem: A Report from Hell," *New York Times* (14 Aug. 1965); Martin Tucker, "The Miracle of a Redeemed Harlem Childhood," *Commonweal* 82, no. 22 (24 Sept. 1965): 700–702; Guy Daniels, "Claude Brown's World," *New Republic* (25 Sept. 1965); William Mathes, "A Negro Pepys," *Antioch Review* (fall 1965): 456–462; and Daniel Aaron, "Out of the Closet," *New Statesman* 72, no. 1,847 (5 Aug. 1966): 204. Reviews of *The Children of Ham* (1976) include Ishmael Reed, "The First Black Wasp," *Washington Post Book World* (11 Apr. 1976); Arnold Rampersad, *"The Children of Ham,"* *New Republic* (8 May 1976); and George Davis, "How to Survive in Harlem," *New York Times Book Review* (15 Aug. 1976). Tributes following Brown's death include Haki R. Madhubuti, *Black Issues in Higher Education* 19, no. 1 (28 Feb. 2002): 26; Irving Louis Horowitz, "Seeing Through a Manchild's Eyes," *Chronicle of Higher Education* 48, no. 31 (12 Apr. 2002): 5; and Herb Boyd, *Black Issues Book Review* 4, no. 3 (May/June 2002): 80. Obituaries are in the *New York Times* (6 Feb. 2002) and *Washington Post* (7 Feb. 2002).

LEE McQUEEN

BROWN, Dee Alexander (*b.* 28 February 1908 in Alberta, Louisiana; *d.* 12 December 2002 in Little Rock, Arkansas), western historian, novelist, and librarian who wrote more than thirty books about the West, including the widely acclaimed *Bury My Heart at Wounded Knee: An Indian History of the American West* (1970).

Brown (who from early years did not use his given name, Dorris, preferring Dee) was one of two children born to Daniel Alexander and Lula (Cranford) Brown. He was four years old when his father, a timberman, was killed while

Dee Brown. MR. DEE BROWN.

working for a lumber company. The following year the family moved to the town of Stephens in Ouachita County, Arkansas, to be near relatives. Brown's mother began working at a dry goods store, and Brown and his sister were raised primarily by his maternal grandmother, a former schoolteacher. Through her influence Brown developed a love of the printed word, and began reading novels by such celebrated writers as Robert Louis Stevenson and Mark Twain at an early age.

Brown's mother was appointed postmistress of Stephens in 1920; in 1924 she moved the family to Little Rock, seeking better schools for her children. At age seventeen Brown submitted a short adventure story to *Blue Book* magazine, for which he received $100. This early success and the opportunity to enroll in a printing class helped to shape his career. After his graduation from Little Rock High School in 1927, Brown worked briefly as a printer and reporter for the *Daily Times* in Harrison, Arkansas, but soon realized he needed more education. In 1928 Brown and his sister enrolled in Arkansas State Teachers College (later the University of Central Arkansas), in Conway. To fund their college education, their mother moved to Conway and opened a boarding house for students. Brown's mentor, Dean McBrien, was a history professor at Arkansas State and an enthusiastic student of the West. McBrien taught Brown to think of history as "incisive biographies," documented and authenticated.

Following his graduation from teachers college in 1931, Brown enrolled at George Washington University in Washington, D.C., where he earned a B.L.S. in 1937. Jobs were scarce at this time because of the Great Depression, but Brown was appointed to a minor library position with the U.S. Department of Agriculture, where he worked from 1934 to 1939. On 1 August 1934 he married Sara Baird Stroud, with whom he had two children. In 1940 Brown became a librarian at the Beltsville Research Center in Maryland.

During World War II Brown served in the U.S. Army (1942–1945), and afterward he worked as a librarian in the technical information branch at the Aberdeen Proving Grounds in Maryland. His final career move was to the University of Illinois at Urbana-Champaign, where he worked as the librarian of agriculture from 1948 to 1972, and as a professor of library science from 1962 to 1975, at which point he returned to Little Rock, where he lived for the remainder of his life. In 1952 he earned an M.S. from the University of Illinois.

Brown's first book, a novel satirizing "the burgeoning bureaucracy of New Deal Washington," was accepted by McCrae-Smith publishers. However, when the Japanese bombed Pearl Harbor, Hawaii, in December 1941, and the United States entered World War II, the manuscript's publication was quickly aborted as being too unpatriotic. At his editor's urging, Brown immediately wrote *Wave High the Banner, a Novel Based on the Life of Davy Crockett* (1942). Brown was fascinated by the drama of the development of the U.S. West, and was stunned by the costs and sacrifices accompanying the westward expansion of the nineteenth century. In the army Brown had met Martin Schmitt, a former librarian and fellow western fanatic. They collected historical photographs and made them the focus of three books, *The Fighting Indians of the West* (1948), *Trail Driving Days* (1952), and *The Settlers' West* (1955). Brown later compiled the books as *The American West* (1994).

Brown's subsequent books focused on additional specific topics of western development. *The Gentle Tamers: Women of the Old Wild West* (1958), a carefully researched nonfiction book aimed at correcting the "sunbonnet myth" of western women—the idea that women did not contribute to the development of the West, instead sitting quietly in wagons while their husbands determined their destinations—was popular with the general public. *The Galvanized Yankees* (1963), one of several books set during the U.S. Civil War, tells the story of 6,000 Confederate soldiers who, in lieu of prison sentences, enlisted in 1865 and 1866 in the U.S. Volunteers for the Frontier as Indian fighters. *Hear That Lonesome Whistle Blow: Railroads in the West* (1977) delineates the heroism of the builders and the treachery of the railroad companies.

Brown was quiet and unassuming and shunned the

limelight. However, the most thoroughly researched of his books, *Bury My Heart at Wounded Knee: An Indian History of the American West* (1970), brought him to national prominence. On the best-seller list for a year, *Bury My Heart at Wounded Knee* sold more than one million hard copies and was translated into fifteen languages. Brown's book challenged the doctrine of Manifest Destiny, the inevitability of the U.S. government expanding its holdings to the Pacific, which nineteenth-century white men promised would "lift up" Native Americans. Instead, Brown presented the mass destruction that facilitated white imperialism from the point of view of the Indian tribes.

The title of the book refers to the 1890 massacre at Wounded Knee, South Dakota, where 300 Sioux men, women, and children seeking asylum were killed by U.S. troops, in a battle that marked the end of the Indian wars and essentially closed the frontier. According to Lyman B. Hagen, in his biography of Brown, the author told the story in "straight factual reportorial narrative counterpointing the eloquent and poignant speeches of the Indian leaders." For the most part, Brown found these speeches in treaty proceedings in government records. In a 1971 article for the *New York Review of Books*, Peter Farb said that *Bury My Heart at Wounded Knee* "dispels any illusions . . . that the Indian wars were civilization's mission or Manifest Destiny." In 1984 the book earned Brown the Saddleman Award from the Western Writers of America.

In addition to his nonfiction works, Brown wrote novels that grew directly from intensive research and addressed issues of western history. His most successful and popular novel was *Creek Mary's Blood* (1980), which is based on a historical Creek Mary who led male warriors into battle in an attempt to save her people from extinction. Brown's last published book was *The Way to Bright Star* (1998), a coming-of-age novel set during the Civil War. Brown died at age ninety-four of heart failure at his home in Little Rock. His body was cremated.

Brown's uncanny ability to go beyond sympathy to absorb time, place, and human presence lends immediacy to his historical fiction and nonfiction. His compassion for the plight of the Native Americans is tempered by his straightforward reporting and conscientious examination of historical documents. From 1942 to 1998 Brown wrote about most of the major historical events that shaped the West. His eclectic range of subjects constituted universal moral and sociological themes endemic to any era. In *The Westerners* (1974), Brown wrote, "Only a Homer [the ancient Greek poet] could encompass the American West and sing its essence." Although Brown did not always reach Homeric heights, he invariably told the historical truth.

★

Brown's autobiography is *When the Century Was Young* (1993). The most sustained biographical and critical description of Brown and his works is Lyman B. Hagen, *Dee Brown* (1990), part of

Boise State University Western Writers Series. However, the date of publication predates a half dozen of Brown's writings. A less extensive, but more recent, piece on Brown is in Mary Ellen Snodgrass, *Encyclopedia of Frontier Literature* (1997). Obituaries are in the *Arkansas Democrat-Gazette* and *New York Times* (both 14 Dec. 2002).

MARY BOYLES

BROWN, J(ohn) Carter (*b.* 8 October 1934 in Providence, Rhode Island; *d.* 17 June 2002 in Boston, Massachusetts), director of the National Gallery of Art in Washington, D.C., who is credited with reshaping art museums in the second half of the twentieth century and with increasing federal support for the arts.

An unlikely hero in the cause of bringing high art to the masses, Brown was an aristocrat who was born, as one of three children, into one of America's oldest families. Roger Williams, the religious dissenter who founded the Rhode Island colony in the early seventeenth century, was an ancestor. Chad Brown, the first of the family to settle in America, arrived in 1638. Brown University in Rhode Island is named for another forebear, the manufacturer and philanthropist Nicholas Brown, and Brown's father, John Nicholas Brown, was called "the world's richest baby" when he was born into a fortune valued at $10 million in 1900. He spent his life collecting art and exploring ancient Byzantium. Among his other philanthropies, he established the Byzantine Institute of America to sponsor the uncovering and preservation of the ancient mosaics of Istanbul, and he was assistant secretary of the navy under President Harry S. Truman.

Brown's mother, Anne (Kinsolving) Brown, was a violinist with the Baltimore symphony orchestra and music critic for the *Baltimore News*. The family lived in an eighteenth-century house surrounded by art, antiques, and music. Brown, who attended various boarding schools and traveled frequently, was visiting his parents in Washington, D.C., at age fourteen when he swore that he would one day run the National Gallery. Brown graduated first in his class from Groton School in 1951 and then from Harvard University summa cum laude in 1956 and from Harvard Business School in 1958 with an M.B.A., the last of which he said would help prepare him for a career in arts administration. At Harvard he decorated his student lodgings with a watercolor by the French postimpressionist Paul Cézanne and a drawing by the French artist Henri Matisse. After graduating, he continued his studies at museums in Florence, Paris, and the Netherlands. He was taking classes at the Institute of Fine Arts in New York City when John Walker, then the director of the National Gallery, hired

J. Carter Brown, ca. 1991. CATHERINE KARNOW/CORBIS

him as his assistant in 1961. Brown became assistant director in 1964. In 1969 he was planning what is now the National Gallery's East Building when Paul Mellon, the gallery's top patron, asked him if he would replace Walker in 1969, when the latter retired.

Brown's impact was immediate. The National Gallery, founded in 1941, had at first been a poorly endowed and little-noticed museum. Its first collection consisted of 125 paintings from the founder Andrew Mellon's collection. Brown added more than twenty thousand works to its holdings, including the entire twentieth-century collection. The first show sponsored under his tenure featured African sculpture, a departure from the gallery's more conservative traditional offerings. The East Building, designed by the Chinese-American architect I. M. Pei, encouraged innovation in gallery design that was later echoed in the designs of the Getty Museum in California and the Guggenheim in Bilbao, Spain.

A proud patrician, Brown worked well with lawmakers, in particular, the National Gallery's most important funding source, the U.S. Congress. He swiftly persuaded Capitol Hill to increase spending on the gallery, from $3.2 million annually when he took over to $52 million when he left in 1992, and he also encouraged the passage of an act indemnifying art on loan from abroad. That relieved American museums from increasing insurance costs, making possible the blockbuster exhibits that drew record attendance. Attendance swelled during Brown's tenure—from

1.3 million visitors a year to nearly 7 million—not only because he put on good shows but also because he created the funding and regulatory framework that made those shows possible.

Brown helped transform Washington from a cultural backwater into a city with an art collection that could rival New York, Paris, and Saint Petersburg. Memorable shows under his tenure included "Treasures of Tutankhamen" (1976), "Rodin Rediscovered" (1981), "Impressionism to Early Modern Painting from the USSR" (1986), and "Circa 1992: The Art of Exploration" (1992), in which he gathered some six hundred works from five continents to mark the 500th anniversary of Christopher Columbus's voyage to America.

His influence on Washington's artistic expression went beyond the walls of the National Gallery. Brown was a pivotal figure behind the selection of the design of the Vietnam Veterans Memorial by Maya Lin, a simple wall inscribed with the names of each American soldier killed in that war. He weathered criticism from those who judged Lin's design as poorly befitting a war memorial and lived to see the Vietnam wall become perhaps the nation's most beloved war monument. The national arts commission he headed also oversaw the Korean War and Franklin D. Roosevelt memorials in Washington.

After the Columbus exhibition, Brown unexpectedly announced his retirement from the National Gallery at the age of fifty-seven. His final exhibition, which coincided with the Centennial Olympic Games in Atlanta in 1996, was "Rings: Five Passions in World Art," which brought together works from forty-four countries. After his retirement he also founded Ovation, a cable television network devoted to fine arts.

The last project in which Brown played a significant role was the national World War II memorial, under construction in Washington during the early years of the twenty-first century. The project attracted controversy because of fears that it would disrupt the continuity of the Capitol Mall. Shortly before his death, Brown told the *Washingtonian* magazine that time would prove the detractors wrong. "We're a spoiled nation of whiners and complainers—meism types," he said. "World War II should be our paradigm. We lost that war for two years," but the eventual success, he said, shows "you could get almost anything done if everybody puts every fiber of their being into a single cause."

Brown was married twice, first, in 1971 to Constance Mellon, a relative of Paul Mellon's; they divorced in 1973. He then married Pamela Braga Drexel in 1976 in a service performed at Westminster Abbey in London; they divorced in 1991. He fathered a son and daughter with Drexel. He was engaged to Anne Hawley, director of the Isabella

Stewart Gardner Museum in Boston, at the time of his death at age sixty-seven from a rare form of blood cancer.

★

Information on Brown is in books on National Gallery exhibits, among them Charles S. Moffett, *The New Painting, Impressionism, 1874–1886: An Exhibition Organized by the Fine Arts Museums of San Francisco with the National Gallery of Art, Washington* (1986), and Jack Cowart and Dominique Fourcade, *Henri Matisse: The Early Years in Nice, 1916–1930* (1986). Obituaries are in the *New York Times* and *Washington Post* (both 19 June 2002).

ALAN BJERGA

BROWN, Lester Raymond ("Les")   (*b.* 14 March 1912 in Reinerton, Pennsylvania; *d.* 4 January 2001 in Los Angeles, California), dance band leader and arranger.

Raised in the town of Lykens in the coal-mining region of Pennsylvania, Brown was the eldest of four children—three sons and a daughter—born to Raymond Winfield Brown, a baker and town bandmaster, and Hattie Mae (Nye) Brown. By age seven he could play the soprano saxophone and the piano, and at ten he played the horn in his dad's John Philip Sousa–style parade and concert band. From his father, he also learned how to write arrangements. At age fourteen Brown formed his own seven-piece group, the Royal Serenaders, for school dances. In 1926, after a year of high school, he enrolled at the Patrick Conway Military School in Ithaca, New York, where he studied musical theory and composition, mastered the classical E-flat clarinet and bassoon, and in 1927 organized and arranged for a new twelve-piece band, the Rainbow Men.

In the summer of 1932 Brown took the Rainbow Men on a concert tour. Near Boston a member of the Duke Blue Devils, the best-known college band, heard the group and persuaded Brown to attend Duke University and join the Blue Devils. Lured by the free room and board in exchange for playing nightly student union concerts, as well as gigs for pay, Brown enrolled at Duke, where he earned a B.A. in 1936. His father usually paid his tuition, but the Great Depression took its toll, forcing Brown to sell his bassoon.

Playing clarinet and saxophone and composing arrangements influenced by the saxophonist Benny Carter and the Casa Loma Orchestra's Gene Gifford, Brown rose to leadership of the twelve-piece Blue Devils after two years. (Late in life he endowed a faculty chair in music at Duke.) In 1936 the band made its first recording, for Decca. Following graduation that June, Brown took the band—a cooperative organization in which all players were partners—for a summer residency at Budd Lake, New Jersey. There he met a local fan, Georgia Claire ("Cluny") DeWolfe, whom he married on 14 September 1938. They had two children.

The band played one-night stands and recorded for another year but disbanded in September 1937 so that most of its members could complete their college degrees. Compared with the major bands of the early swing era, the band's style was stiff, a reflection of the leader's insistence on perfection. Also, his focus was on arrangements rather than jazz soloists. Brown moved to New York City, where he wrote arrangements for prominent dance bands and learned much about arranging from his roommate, Glenn Osser.

Prompted by Eli Oberstein of RCA Victor Records, in mid-1938 Brown organized a new twelve-piece band for a four-month stand at the Edison Hotel on New York's Times Square, broadcasting nationwide nightly through the National Broadcasting Company. He hired the impresario Joe Glaser as his agent (an association that lasted twenty-five years) and obtained a recording contract on Victor's less-expensive Bluebird label.

Brown preferred smooth arrangements to hot soloists and in 1939 loaned his superb rhythm guitarist, Allan Reuss, to the bandleader Glenn Miller for recordings that included Miller's theme song, "Moonlight Serenade." The addition of a third trombonist—Brown's brother Warren, two years younger than he—gave the enlarged band a distinctive sound, and the seventeen-year-old vocalist Doris Day greatly enhanced its popularity during the period 1940–1941, until she left to have a baby. The band's first hit was a novelty tune, "Joltin' Joe DiMaggio," in August 1941, commemorating the New York Yankees baseball player's incredible fifty-six-game hitting streak that season. It was written by Ben Homer, a permanent arranger who restyled the band's sound.

The band had matured remarkably from "an ungainly cocoon into a quite beautiful butterfly," in the words of the jazz critic Gunther Schuller. Its broad repertoire included not only pretty ballads but also straight-ahead swing numbers, as well as classical music themes adapted to swing, notably Homer's 1941 "Bizet Has His Day" (based on Georges Bizet's *L'Arlesienne Suite*). Novelty vocals became the specialty of Butch Stone, a baritone saxophonist who joined the band that fall and stayed for nearly half a century. Brown himself, content merely to conduct the band in his friendly and effective way, gave up his soloing on clarinet to the superb Abe Most. Attempts to add hot jazz players were frustrated by the wartime draft, which soon took the trumpeter Billy Butterfield and the drummer Shelly Manne.

A month-long December 1941 engagement at Chicago's Black Hawk Restaurant was extended by popular demand to four months, finally bringing financial stability to the band. During its subsequent stand at the Hollywood Palladium, the radio announcer ad-libbed his introduction as "The Band of Renown," an alliteration the leader formally

Les Brown, 1987. AP/WIDE WORLD PHOTOS

recorded before thousands of dancers for release on two long-play records, an early onsite innovation that captured the spirit of the band at its peak. At the same dance emporium that year, thirteen-year-old Les, Jr., made his professional debut playing a clarinet duet with his dad.

Brown served as musical director for the entertainer Bob Hope's radio program (1947–1966) and performed with Hope on eighteen Christmas tours starting in 1950. They entertained American troops in Korea and Vietnam and at military bases and on warships at home and abroad. The band played on Hope's first television show and on his many specials into the 1990s, when Hope retired. In all, they appeared some eight hundred times with Hope. The band also provided the music for the comedian Steve Allen's television program for two years and for the singer Dean Martin's for eight and performed at the inaugural balls of presidents Richard M. Nixon and Ronald W. Reagan.

In the mid-1950s Brown headed the Dance Orchestra Leaders of America in a futile attempt to revive the big bands to mass popularity. A cofounder of the National Academy of Recording Arts and Sciences in 1957, he became president of its Los Angeles chapter and was a catalyst for bringing its Grammy Awards ceremonies to television in 1972. Still playing some sixty annual performances in the 1990s, Brown shared band leadership responsibilities with his son. His wife died in 1996, and two years later he married a similarly widowed family friend, Evelyn Hutter Partridge. He retired in October 2000 due to lung cancer, which claimed his life at age eighty-eight. Les, Jr., took over the Band of Renown.

Brown stood five feet, seven inches tall and retained lifelong boyish looks. Although he was characterized in his early career for his precise musical standards and his lack of "intimacy" with audiences, his gentlemanly treatment of his musicians engendered so much warmth and respect that many of them refused better offers from other bandleaders. There was no better testament to his relations with the men who played in his band than the fact that the drummer Buddy Rich, renowned for his inability to get along with his bandleaders, in 1953 noted that Brown was the one with whom he never fought.

★

Analyses of Brown and his music may be found in George T. Simon, *The Big Bands* (1967) and *Simon Says: The Sights and Sounds of the Swing Era 1935–1955* (1971), and Gunther Schuller, *The Swing Era: The Development of Jazz, 1930–1945* (1989). His contributions to arranging are discussed in Gene Lees, *Arranging the Score: Portraits of the Great Arrangers* (2000). An obituary is in the *New York Times* (6 Jan. 2001).

CLARK G. REYNOLDS

adopted, naming his group "Les Brown and His Band of Renown." While in California the group appeared in the first of several motion picture musicals, *Seven Days Leave* (1942), as well as numerous film shorts. The arranger-trumpeter Frank Comstock joined in 1943, soon becoming the band's major arranger; he reshaped the riff tune "Leap Frog" into the band's theme song.

Brown persuaded Day to return in 1943. The next year they and the co-composers Homer and Bud Green fashioned the band's most popular tune ever, "Sentimental Journey," which became a timely allusion to returning soldiers upon its issue early in 1945. The band's second-greatest hit was Skip Martin's up-tempo instrumental version of Irving Berlin's "I've Got My Love to Keep Me Warm," released in 1948 (though recorded two years earlier). During the war Brown added a fourth (bass) trombone, his brother Clyde ("Stumpy") Brown, eleven years his junior, who stayed into the twenty-first century. Day left in 1946 when the group briefly disbanded.

Based thereafter in Los Angeles, Brown revamped and expanded his brass and reed sections. During the band's September 1953 gig at the Palladium, several numbers were

BUCK, John Francis ("Jack")   (*b.* 21 August 1924 in Holyoke, Massachusetts; *d.* 18 June 2002 in St. Louis, Missouri), sportscaster whose skills as a baseball and football announcer brought him national renown and endeared him to millions in the St. Louis area who listened to him on radio station KMOX.

Buck was the third of seven children born to Earle Buck, a railroad accountant, and Kathleen (Fox) Buck, a seamstress. In his autobiography, Buck recalled that baseball consumed his boyhood. When he was not playing the game or talking about it with his friends, he was following the Boston Red Sox on the radio and dreaming that one day he would become a sports announcer. Buck also remembered his family's constant struggles during the depression, his father's frequent absences from home on business, and all the odd jobs he and his siblings held.

Shortly after the family moved to Cleveland in 1939, Buck's father, only forty-nine, died of uremia. Buck considered dropping out of high school and going to work, but a teacher persuaded him to continue. He graduated in January 1942 and took a job on a Great Lakes ore boat. Seventeen

Jack Buck, 1971. BETTMANN/CORBIS

months later, he was drafted into the U.S. Army and eventually saw service with the Ninth Infantry Division in Germany. Shrapnel wounds in March 1945 earned him a Purple Heart. After the war he used the GI Bill to enroll at Ohio State University in Columbus, majoring in radio speech. He married Alyce Larson in 1948. They had six children and divorced in 1969. He married Carole Lintzenich in March of that year; they had two children.

Buck worked at WOSU, the Ohio State radio station, and then, before graduating in December 1949, at WCOL, a commercial station, where he did a nightly sports news show and some Ohio State basketball games. In 1950 he became the radio voice of the Columbus Redbirds, the Triple A farm team of the St. Louis Cardinals, and called Ohio State football games in the fall, including the famous "Snow Bowl" against Michigan. Broadcasting a full season of baseball games gave Buck time to polish his skills and develop the unhurried style, embellished by stories, that became his trademark.

When WCOL switched to an all-music format in 1952, the new owners fired Buck, but a day later he secured his first television job at WBNS, the Columbia Broadcasting System (CBS) affiliate in Columbus, again doing the sports news each night. The following year he moved to Rochester, New York, to broadcast the games of the Rochester Redwings, a Triple A baseball team that Anheuser-Busch and the Cardinals soon purchased. In 1954 he auditioned successfully for an opening on the St. Louis broadcasting team to work with Harry Caray.

Except for two interruptions, Buck's career with the Cardinals lasted forty-seven years. He was fired in December 1959 when the team reshuffled its broadcasting staff, but was rehired a year later. When Caray was dismissed after the 1969 season, Buck became the team's lead broadcaster. He relinquished this spot in 1975 to host *Grandstand,* a National Broadcasting Company (NBC) Sunday afternoon television show, but when it was cancelled after a few months, he resumed his job with the Cardinals. In 1995 he began to reduce his workload by broadcasting only home games, but he stayed behind the Cardinals microphone until late in the 2001 season, leaving only when he was diagnosed with lung cancer.

After being discharged in 1959, Buck signed on as a full-time employee of KMOX. He broadcast St. Louis Hawks basketball games and helped the station inaugurate its "At Your Service" program, a combination of news and talk sometimes called the nation's first talk radio show. He also began to expand his contacts in the St. Louis business and civic communities, eventually becoming the city's favorite master of ceremonies. One year, Buck recalled, he made 385 appearances. In 1960 the American Broadcasting Company (ABC) hired him to telecast baseball nationally, plus bowling, college basketball, and the first season of the American Football League.

In 1963 CBS hired Buck to telecast National Football League games. He was in the booth during 1967's famous subzero "Ice Bowl" in Green Bay, Wisconsin, as well as Super Bowl IV in 1970. He rebuffed ABC's invitation to do the play-by-play on a new venture called *Monday Night Football,* but in 1978 he teamed with Hank Stram to do Monday night games and the Super Bowl on CBS radio. This partnership lasted sixteen years. In 1990 Buck returned to CBS television to handle major league baseball games with Tim McCarver, an assignment that lasted three seasons.

Buck's signature phrase was "That's a winner," a line he began using in the 1980s after each Cardinals victory. He is also remembered for exhorting St. Louis fans to "Go, crazy, folks, go crazy," after Ozzie Smith's home run that won Game Five of the 1985 National League Championship Series and for his call, "I don't believe what I just saw," on national television after Kirk Gibson hit a home run to end Game One of the 1988 World Series. He was much honored for his work, receiving both the Ford C. Frick Award at the National Baseball Hall of Fame in 1987 and the Pete Rozelle Award from the Pro Football Hall of Fame in 1996. St. Louisans appreciated him as a treasured civic institution.

Buck spent the last six months of his life in the hospital, suffering from several staph infections, pneumonia, and advanced Parkinson's disease, and he endured several surgeries. The Cardinals honored him with a public memorial service at Busch Stadium, and he was buried in the Jefferson Barracks National Cemetery in St. Louis.

★

Other than his autobiography, *Jack Buck: That's a Winner!* (1997), with Rob Rains, Buck's life is remembered in two books: Rich Wolfe, *Remembering Jack Buck* (2002), and Carole Buck, *Jack Buck: Forever a Winner* (2003). Obituaries are in the *New York Times* and *St. Louis Post-Dispatch* (both 19 June 2002).

STEVEN P. GIETSCHIER

BUDGE, John Donald ("Don") (*b.* 13 June 1915 in Oakland, California; *d.* 26 January 2000 in Scranton, Pennsylvania), tennis star of the 1930s who in 1938 became the sport's first Grand Slam winner.

Budge was one of three children born to the Scottish immigrants John Budge and Pearl (Kincaid) Budge. His father, a member of the Glasgow, Scotland, Rangers soccer team, migrated to California due to respiratory problems and supported his family by managing a laundry business. His mother was a homemaker. During his school days in Oakland, Budge and his older brother Lloyd were active in

many sports, but Budge preferred baseball, football, and basketball. He did not really consider tennis until June 1930, when he was almost fifteen years old. One night at a family dinner, Lloyd—himself a tennis player—jokingly suggested that Budge enter the California state boys' tennis tournament. Budge did not consider his brother's challenge a laughing matter: he trained diligently for two weeks and proceeded to win his first tennis tournament.

Following this initial success, Budge devoted himself to the sport. In 1933 he won both the California junior and senior championships, then participated in the National Junior Championships at Culver, Indiana, where he won the national junior title by defeating Gene Marko, who would later be his Davis Cup teammate.

Budge traveled to the East Coast in 1934, making his debut at the Seabright Lawn Tennis and Cricket Club in New Jersey. Budge, who had learned the game on the hard courts of California, initially struggled on clay surfaces. However, the trip east provided him with the opportunity to observe and work with such outstanding tennis players as Ellsworth Vines and Fred Perry. Under the tutelage of Lloyd and the coach Tom Stow, the six-foot, one-inch, 155-pound redhead added an attack game to his power serve and dominant backhand. Budge also developed a reputation as an intense but gentlemanly player who refused to dispute the decisions made by line judges.

Budge was runner-up to Perry in the 1936 All-England (Wimbledon) and U.S. championships, titles he won the following year when Perry turned professional and was no longer eligible to compete in them. Following graduation from Oakland's University High School in 1937, Budge entered the University of California, Berkeley. He left the university in the spring of 1938 in order to devote his attention to tennis.

Budge was the world's number-one-ranked tennis player in 1937. In addition to his victories at Wimbledon and at the U.S. championships in Forest Hills in New York City, he led the United States to a Davis Cup championship over Germany. Down two sets to Gottfried von Cramm, Budge rallied to win the final three sets and the match. Although the contest lacked the racial dimension of victories by Jesse Owens and Joe Louis over German opponents, Budge recalled that the support of the German dictator Adolf Hitler for von Cramm and the gathering tensions in Europe made this victory one of his most memorable. Budge's heroics resulted in his selection for the James E. Sullivan Memorial Trophy as the outstanding U.S. amateur athlete of 1937.

In order to help the United States defend the Davis Cup, Budge declined lucrative offers to turn professional. Retaining his amateur status in 1938, he enjoyed his finest year in tennis when, in addition to helping his country retain the Davis Cup, he became the first tennis player to

Don Budge. CORBIS

win the sport's Grand Slam—that is, the Australian, French, Wimbledon, and U.S. championships all in the same calendar year.

On 10 November 1938 Budge turned professional with the blessing of the U.S. Lawn Tennis Association. He made his professional debut at New York City's Madison Square Garden on 3 January 1939, defeating Ellsworth Vines. He enjoyed a successful professional career from 1939 to 1942, with victories over such outstanding players as Perry, Bill Tilden, and Bobby Riggs. In 1940 and 1942 he won the U.S. professional championships, but with the advent of World War II, he enlisted in the U.S. Army Air Corps. On 26 May 1941 Budge married Deirdre Counselman, with whom he had two sons.

After his military discharge in 1945, Budge rejoined the professional tennis circuit, but due to a shoulder injury he suffered during his military service, his play was less dominant than before the war. He did, however, reach the U.S. professional finals in 1946, 1947, 1949, and 1953.

As his tennis career declined, Budge operated a laundry business in New York City, worked as a teaching professional and tennis consultant for sporting-goods manufacturers, and did promotional work for Prince Manufacturing Company. He also wrote *Budge on Tennis* (1939) and *Don Budge: A Tennis Memoir* (1969). In 1964 he was elected to the International Tennis Hall of Fame. Following a divorce from his first wife, he married Loriel McPherson in June 1967.

Budge was injured in a traffic accident in northeastern Pennsylvania on 14 December 1999. Hospitalized in Poughkeepsie, New York, for three weeks, he was transferred to a nursing home in Scranton, Pennsylvania, where he died and was buried. Tilden, a legendary tennis great in his own right, once described Budge as "the finest player 365 days a year who ever lived."

★

Budge described his playing style and life in two books, *Budge on Tennis* (1939) and *Don Budge: A Tennis Memoir* (1969). For biographical sketches, see Allison Danzig and Peter Schwed, eds., *The Fireside Book of Tennis* (1972), and Ellsworth Vines and Gene Vier, *Tennis Myth and Method* (1978). An obituary is in the *New York Times* (27 Jan. 2000).

RON BRILEY

BUNDY, William Putnam   (*b.* 24 September 1917 in Washington, D.C.; *d.* 6 October 2000 in Princeton, New Jersey), official with the Central Intelligence Agency (CIA), Defense Department, and State Department who was influential in planning the Vietnam War.

Bundy was one of five children and was born into an influential Boston family. His father, Harvey Hollister Bundy, had served as a clerk for the U.S. Supreme Court justice Oliver Wendell Holmes, later worked as an attorney,

William P. Bundy testifying before the Senate Judiciary Committee, July 1971. BETTMANN/CORBIS

and served in key positions with the administrations of presidents Herbert Hoover and Franklin D. Roosevelt. Bundy's mother, Katharine Lawrence (Putnam) Bundy, was herself from a prominent New England clan and was a homemaker. His brother, McGeorge, eighteen months his junior, would become perhaps the most well-known member of the family through his service in the administrations of presidents John F. Kennedy and Lyndon B. Johnson.

Bundy grew up in Boston, where his parents' family and social connections ensured a privileged childhood; his friends included Kennedy and the future *Washington Post* editor Benjamin Bradlee. From 1930 to 1935 Bundy attended Groton, a prestigious Massachusetts private school. Like his father and older brother Harvey, Jr., before him, he attended Yale University in New Haven, Connecticut, where he enrolled in the fall of 1935.

At Yale, Bundy excelled academically, and he was also inducted into the university's most exclusive society, Skull and Bones. During his senior year, with war in Europe looming, he decided to enroll in an army correspondence course in cryptology. Upon graduating with a B.A. in 1939, Bundy began work on an M.A. in history at Harvard University in Cambridge, Massachusetts.

In the summer of 1940, while working in Washington, D.C., for Archibald MacLeish at the Office of Facts and Figures, Bundy met Dean Acheson, who would later become secretary of state under President Harry S. Truman. He also met, and fell in love with, Acheson's daughter, Mary. Returning to school in the fall, he switched fields and entered Harvard Law School.

Bundy was drafted into the U.S. Army in the summer of 1941. He completed basic training, and his scores on the army's aptitude test were so high that he was selected to work for the Signal Intelligence Corps at Fort Monmouth, New Jersey. He and Mary Acheson became engaged in December 1942 and, with Bundy about to depart for England, married the following month. They had three children.

In the spring of 1943, just before being sent to Britain, Bundy became privy to one of the Allies' most sensitive secrets, the Ultra Project. Ultra, whose existence even most field commanders were ignorant of, was the code name for British efforts to crack the Germans' encrypted military communications. Bundy was stationed at Bletchley Park, Ultra's headquarters north of London, as the U.S. team's commanding officer.

After the war, Bundy returned to Harvard, graduating from law school in June 1947. He turned down an offer to clerk for the Supreme Court justice Felix Frankfurter and instead joined Acheson's firm, Covington and Burling, in Washington, D.C. However, bored with corporate law, he left the firm after three years to become an analyst for the Central Intelligence Agency (CIA) Office of National Estimates. Before he left, however, Bundy contributed to the legal defense fund of the brother of one of the senior partners, Donald Hiss. Although he did not realize it at the time, this tenuous connection to Alger Hiss, the alleged communist spy, would nearly ruin Bundy's career at its outset.

Bundy spent three productive, but relatively uneventful, years working as a geopolitical forecaster at the CIA before his link to Hiss began to cause problems. In the summer of 1953 he earned a promotion that gave him access to closely held nuclear secrets. He was therefore required to undergo another background check, but this time the Federal Bureau of Investigation (FBI), rather than the CIA, did the investigating. The FBI quickly leaked news of Bundy's connection with Hiss to the office of Senator Joseph McCarthy, then at the peak of his influence as the driving force behind a government effort to root out communists in American society. McCarthy sought to use Bundy as a means to tackle the CIA itself, one of the few federal institutions that remained beyond his grasp.

Although the CIA refused to let McCarthy interrogate him, Bundy did not know his fate for almost a year. After he failed a loyalty board hearing in February 1954, the CIA arranged for another board, whose members were beholden to the White House, to review his case. The second board overturned the verdict of the first, and Bundy finally received a higher security clearance. In 1956 he rose to the position of deputy assistant director of intelligence, and continued to serve the CIA with distinction until 1960.

Despite the fact that he came from a distinguished Republican family, Bundy, like his father-in-law, was an ardent Democrat. He was thrilled with Kennedy's victory in the 1960 presidential election. With his personal connection to the president-elect and his obvious foreign policy expertise and experience, Bundy hoped to be offered an influential post in the Kennedy administration, but that offer was made instead to his brother McGeorge, who became National Security Adviser. Bundy did, however, join the Kennedy team as deputy assistant secretary of defense.

Bundy's work at the Pentagon so impressed Secretary of Defense Robert S. McNamara that in the fall of 1963, he was promoted to one of the Pentagon's key posts, assistant secretary of defense for international security affairs. His nomination was confirmed by the Senate on 22 November 1963, thirty-four minutes before Kennedy's assassination.

Bundy did not remain under Pentagon auspices for very long. The new president, Lyndon B. Johnson, was looking for someone to prevent the simmering Vietnam conflict from erupting during an election year, and Bundy seemed the perfect choice. In February 1964 he moved to the State Department to become assistant secretary of state for Far Eastern affairs, making him one of the Johnson administration's most influential policymakers on Vietnam.

Unlike most of his colleagues, Bundy already had direct experience with Vietnam, and had always been something of a hawk. While working with the CIA in 1956, Bundy had recommended that the United States provide assistance to the anticommunist government of the South Vietnamese president Ngo Dinh Diem. This decision tied the United States irrevocably to the defense of South Vietnam. In the fall of 1961, he had advised Kennedy that sending U.S. troops to fight alongside the South Vietnamese would defeat the communists.

By 1964, however, Bundy was increasingly unsure about the war in Vietnam. As he looked into the problem more closely, he found himself confronted with tough questions: Could the United States save South Vietnam from communism? Was it worth it? Thus began a difficult period for Bundy, in which he planned for war but quietly advocated withdrawal. In the summer of 1964, he helped draft what would become the infamous Tonkin Gulf Resolution, giving Johnson a blank check to escalate the war, but a few months later, he also wrote two important memos, which argued that the United States should adopt a strategy of "fighting one's way to the negotiating table."

Such a plan could only work if the United States seized the political and military initiative and, by doing so, convinced the communists that it was futile to continue fighting. Neither, of course, came to pass, and the United States remained in Vietnam for another nine years. Nevertheless, this strategy shaped the recommendations of the Vietnam Working Group, a top-secret committee Bundy chaired in November 1964. When President Johnson accepted the group's report, this helped establish U.S. policy in Southeast Asia. This was Bundy's most important contribution to the escalation of the Vietnam War.

Once it was clear, by the spring of 1965, that Johnson would not risk losing South Vietnam, Bundy suppressed his doubts and stayed on. His deep commitments to loyalty and duty prevented him from speaking out or resigning quietly, as did several of his colleagues. Although he continued to play an important role in making Vietnam policy until the end of the Johnson administration in January 1969, Bundy would never again hold as much influence as he did in 1964 and 1965.

In 1971, after two years at the Massachusetts Institute of Technology in Cambridge as a senior fellow, Bundy became editor of the influential journal *Foreign Affairs*. He retired in 1984, taught part-time at Princeton University in New Jersey, and in 1998 published an exhaustive study on the foreign policy of Richard Nixon and Henry Kissinger, *A Tangled Web: The Making of Foreign Policy in the Nixon Presidency*. He died of heart trouble at his home.

An archetypal anticommunist liberal, Bundy's own unresolved struggle with Vietnam exemplified both the breakdown of the nation's cold war consensus and the breaking of the eastern establishment's grip on U.S. foreign policy. During the periods of Roosevelt's New Deal and Johnson's Great Society, he witnessed the triumphs of liberalism; during McCarthyism and Vietnam, he suffered through its turmoil. His career path followed the cresting wave of liberalism and the rise of conservatism. Although Bundy served the nation with honor and distinction in World War II and the early cold war, he will always be remembered for the mistakes he made in the Vietnam War.

★

Bundy wrote a memoir concerning his role in the Vietnam War; although it remains unpublished, copies are in Yale University's Manuscripts and Archives and in the Lyndon B. Johnson Library in Austin, Texas. Both the Johnson library and the John F. Kennedy Library in Boston house innumerable documents on Bundy's years at the Pentagon and the State Department. The single best source on Bundy's life is Kai Bird, *The Color of Truth:* *McGeorge Bundy and William Bundy, Brothers in Arms* (1998). Other information on Bundy and the Vietnam War is in David Halberstam, *The Best and the Brightest* (1972); Fredrik Logevall, *Choosing War: The Lost Chance for Peace and the Escalation of War in Vietnam* (1999); and David Kaiser, *American Tragedy: Kennedy, Johnson, and the Origins of the Vietnam War* (2000). Obituaries are in the *New York Times* and *Washington Post* (both 7 Oct. 2000).

ANDREW PRESTON

C

CALLAWAY, Ely Reeves, Jr. (*b.* 3 June 1919 in La Grange, Georgia; *d.* 5 July 2001 in Rancho Santa Fe, California), successful business executive best known as the founder of the Callaway Golf Company, which in the 1990s produced an innovative line of drivers that transformed the game of golf.

Callaway was the only son of Ely Reeves Callaway, who worked in the family textile business. The family was wealthy, and Callaway and his three older sisters enjoyed a genteel southern upbringing. At age ten Callaway began what became a succession of business triumphs, investing $150 he earned from magazine sales in a peach orchard; he sold his first harvest for $750. That same year Callaway took up the game of golf. Distantly related to the legendary golfer Bobby Jones, Callaway became a four-time champion (1936–1939) at the Highland Country Club in La Grange.

Callaway attended Emory University in Atlanta, graduating in 1940 with a B.A. in American history. He immediately joined the U.S. Army and began to lay the foundation for his business career. Callaway was assigned to the Quartermaster Corps and eventually became the army's chief procurement officer for cotton goods during World War II. In 1945 he returned to Atlanta to work for the giant textile company Deering-Milliken as the head of its wool fabric division. He moved to Textron and New York City in 1956, and after his division was purchased by Burlington Industries, he oversaw the development of Viracle, a new

fabric that blended polyester and worsted wool. In 1968, at age forty-eight, Callaway was named as Burlington president. He resigned in 1973, when he was passed over for the position of chief executive officer.

In 1968, while still with Burlington, Callaway had purchased 150 acres in Temecula, California, 500 miles south of Napa, with the intention of creating an innovative vineyard. It was an improbable location, but after careful study and the decision to take a calculated risk, he planted vines and set out to sell "the difference [from Napa wines], not the sameness." After leaving Burlington, Callaway was able to give the vineyard his full attention. In 1976 the legendary salesman arranged to have one of his Rieslings selected for a gala luncheon at the Waldorf-Astoria hotel in New York City, at which Queen Elizabeth II complimented his wine, thereby boosting its reputation. Five years later he sold Callaway Vineyard and Winery to Hiram Walker for $14 million, realizing a $9 million profit.

Not yet ready for retirement, in 1982 Callaway purchased Hickory Stick, a golf company with three employees that made unusual putters and wedges with a wood shaft and a metal core, which he had admired in a local golf shop. Hickory Stick eventually became the Callaway Golf Company based in Carlsbad, California. In less than two decades the company had annual net sales of $800 million, and by 1996 it had become the world's largest manufacturer of golf clubs. Callaway's and the company's mantra was to

Ely Callaway, 1968. AP/WIDE WORLD PHOTOS

always develop products that were "demonstrably superior and pleasingly different."

In 1988 Callaway Golf introduced its patented S2H2 design (short straight hollow hosel) in its irons. The following year the company produced S2H2 metal woods, and by the end of 1989 they were the number-one driver on the senior Professional Golfers' Association (PGA) tour. But the company's breakthrough product came in 1991, with the introduction of the "Big Bertha" driver (named after the long-range German World War I cannon). With its larger head, Big Bertha made the outings of weekend "hackers" more rewarding and the drives of skilled golfers considerably longer. "I knew if a seventy-two-year-old man could hit this driver off the ground," Callaway said at the time, "that anybody could hit it off the tee." By the end of the 1990s, when Eldrick ("Tiger") Woods entered the ranks of PGA competition, the Callaway metal-wood club revolution was nearly complete, with few PGA tour players using the traditional persimmon wood driver. Callaway Golf's competitors had quickly produced similarly designed metal woods to stay afloat financially. Talk of "Tiger-proofing" golf courses (extending their length because of Woods's prodigious drives) was a misnomer; the courses were being "Callaway proofed."

By lengthening golfers' drives, Callaway in effect had shortened golf courses, making par (the expected number of strokes needed by a skilled player to complete a hole) easier to achieve. Amateur golfers rejoiced, but the United States Golf Association (USGA), golf's governing body, demurred. In 2000 Callaway defiantly introduced his "hottest" driver, the ERC (Callaway's initials) II, to the U.S. market. The USGA ruled that the ERC was "nonconforming": its thin titanium face (the hitting area) produced a "spring-like effect" upon contact that violated Rule 4 of the established Rules of Golf. Callaway argued that the USGA was penalizing the average golfer in a misguided effort to control how the game is played by elite golfers on the PGA tour. Furthermore, Callaway noted, the Royal and Ancient Golf Club of Saint Andrews (R&A), the organization that sets the rules of golf in every country except the United States and Mexico, refused to ban the ERC II; Callaway drivers were being used in R&A sanctioned tournaments around the globe.

In May 2001 Callaway retired as chief executive officer of Callaway Golf after being diagnosed with pancreatic cancer. He stayed on as company chairman, maintaining his lifelong focus on his business ventures. Callaway was married four times, and had three children with his first wife. He died at age eighty-two at his home in Rancho Santa Fe, and was survived by his fourth wife, Lucinda Villa.

Callaway's life followed a trajectory of successful entrepreneurial initiatives. He repeated a winning strategy of sales, investment, innovation, and reinvestment as a corporate manager in the textile industry, as an independent producer of fine white wines, and, finally, as the manufacturer of a revolutionary line of golf clubs that altered both the game of golf and the business of making and marketing golf equipment. The golf president for Nike, Bob Wood, said of Callaway, "It is a rare business leader who creates both a successful company and a strong, enduring culture."

★

For details on Callaway's life and his running of the Callaway Golf Company, see articles in *Golf Week* (28 Apr. 2001): 20–21, and *Golf World* (13 July 2001): 16–22. Obituaries are in the *Los Angeles Times* and *New York Times* (both 6 July 2001).

MARTIN J. SHERWIN

CANBY, Vincent (*b.* 27 July 1924 in Chicago, Illinois; *d.* 15 October 2000 in Manhattan, New York City), influential film critic (1965–1993) and theater critic (1993–2000) for the *New York Times*.

Canby was the son of Lloyd Canby and Katharine Anne (Vincent) Canby. He spent his childhood in Lake Forest, Illinois, followed by high school at the Christchurch School, a private school in Christchurch, Virginia, about fifty-five miles east of Richmond.

Vincent Canby, 1977. CORBIS

During World War II, Canby served as a naval officer aboard a landing carrier in the Pacific. Following the war, Canby lived for three years in Paris, where one of his jobs was to write summaries of French scripts for an American movie company. During this period, he received an assignment to write a review of the famous restaurant Maxim's. After Canby showed the magazine's letter to the restaurant management, he and a friend ate free there for a week.

When Canby returned to the United States, he attended Dartmouth College, graduating with a B.A. in English literature in 1947. Canby held several positions from 1948 to 1965. In 1948 he worked at the *Chicago Journal of Commerce* as a general reporter, assistant to the drama critic and the foreign trade editor, and as a transcriber of stock tables. In 1950 he moved to New York City, where he was employed in public relations. In 1951 Canby worked at the *Motion Picture Herald–Motion Picture Daily,* where he remained for eight years. In 1959 he moved to *Variety,* where he reviewed films and the theater.

Canby's career at the *New York Times* began on 13 December 1965 as a member of the cultural arts department. Soon he was writing feature articles on entertainers for the daily and Sunday papers, thus beginning a twenty-eight-year career reviewing films. In 1993 he became the Sunday theater critic and in 1994 the chief theater critic, a job he held for two years. In 1996 Canby moved back to the position of Sunday theater critic.

On his vacations Canby wrote fiction and plays. Among his works are the novels *Living Quarters* (1975) and *Unnatural Scenery* (1979) and the plays *End of the War* (1978), *After All* (1981), and *The Old Flag* (1984). *End of the War* was produced in 1978 by the Ensemble Studio Theater; *After All* was produced in 1981 by the Manhattan Theater Club.

Canby's film reviews reflected an era that spanned the French New Wave, the rise of American independent cinema, the big-budget Hollywood blockbuster, and the advent of videocassettes and multiplex theaters. He supported the work of a diverse group of filmmakers such as Spike Lee, Jane Campion, Mike Leigh, Rainer Werner Fassbinder, Woody Allen, Ismail Merchant, and James Ivory, and the actors in their films.

Canby's reviews also added insight. When he reviewed the director Steven Spielberg's *E. T. The Extra-Terrestrial,* Canby said the film "freely recycles elements from all sorts of earlier children's works, including *Peter Pan* and *The Wizard of Oz.*" He added, "Dorothy has become E. T., Kansas is outer space, and Oz is a modern, middle-class real-estate development in California."

As a theater critic Canby displayed the same wide range of taste, praising the plays of Horton Foote, David Mamet, and Sam Shepard, while deploring the overamplification of the voices of singers and actors and criticizing other magnified stage effects. He also opposed the tendency to make theater more like film.

Canby reflected on and wrote about his profession. In 1979 he stated that the difference between a critic and a member of the public who attends movies is that the member of the public wishes to sit back and be entertained, while the critic cannot sit back and be entertained but must take an active part because that is his or her job. Canby went on to say that although critics pretend they are the same as the public, they are not. Critics do not stand in line for tickets, pay for them, or sit in bad seats. Canby felt these differences helped to explain the gaps that exist between critics' opinions of films and those of the ticket-buying public.

A diary of nine days in Canby's 1975 schedule reveals the intensity with which he viewed, wrote, and thought about films. He saw abstract films at the Whitney Museum of American Art in New York City and attended a D. W. Griffith program at the Museum of Modern Art, wrote an *Arts and Leisure* column, and watched the films *Galileo* and *Macon County.* He watched a documentary about the filmmaker Nicholas Ray and read *The Art of the Moving Picture* by Vachel Lindsay. He read the autobiography *Billy Bitzer,*

His Story, and *Biograph Bulletins, 1908–1912,* a publication issued by Biograph to promote interest in the studio's films.

For all his dedication to his profession, Canby also exhibited a sense of humor. He compared attending a multiplex to a visit to the Department of Motor Vehicles, when you do not know which line you are in.

As a theater critic, Canby was enthusiastic about all forms of productions, from works by new playwrights to Broadway extravaganzas. His reviews could be quite intense. His 1998 review of *Electra* stated, "Though you may come out of the theater quibbling about various aspects of the production (as I did), you may also be surprised to find that it haunts your consciousness for days afterwards."

Although Canby never married, he acknowledged a long-time relationship with the writer and film critic Penelope Gilliatt. They had no children. Canby died of cancer at the Columbia-Presbyterian Medical Center in Manhattan.

★

Information about Canby's life and career can be found in Stuart Klawans, "Romancing the Screen," *Nation* (27 Nov. 2000), and Doreen Carvajal, "Recalling the Civilized Voice of a Critic: Vincent Canby," *New York Times* (30 Nov. 2000). Obituaries are in the *Chicago Tribune* and *New York Times* (both 16 Oct. 2000); the *Los Angeles Times* (17 Oct. 2000); and the *Washington Post* (19 Oct. 2000).

SHEILA BECK

CANNON, Howard Walter (*b.* 26 January 1912 in Saint George, Utah; *d.* 5 March 2002 in Las Vegas, Nevada), Democratic senator from Nevada who served for four terms and was unseated after his alleged involvement in a bribery case.

Cannon, the eldest of three children of Walter Cannon, a cattle rancher, and Leah (Sullivan) Cannon, a homemaker, grew up in Utah. He received a B.A. in education from Arizona State Teachers College at Flagstaff in 1933, and an LL.B. from the University of Arizona Law School in Tucson in 1937. While attending law school, Cannon earned his pilot's license. He was admitted to the Arizona bar in 1937 and moved back to Utah the following year, after being admitted to that state bar in 1938. He served as a reference attorney for the Utah state senate in 1939 and was elected as the county attorney of Washington County, Utah, in 1940.

Cannon joined the U.S. Army in 1941 and served as a combat engineer. He transferred to the U.S. Army Air Forces in 1942. As the pilot of a transport plane, he was shot down over the Netherlands in 1944. With the assistance of the Dutch underground, Cannon and his copilot, Frank Krebs (who later became his Senate aide), hid behind German lines for the next six weeks. At one point he

Howard W. Cannon, June 1963. AP/WIDE WORLD PHOTOS

had to dress as a Dutch farmer, wearing bandages around his neck so he could pretend to be unable to speak. Finally, U.S. forces liberated the area. He was awarded the Distinguished Flying Cross, Silver Star, Legion of Merit, Purple Heart, and three Air Medal awards. He left the air force in 1946 as a lieutenant colonel, but remained in the air force reserve, eventually attaining the rank of major general.

Returning to civilian life, Cannon began practicing law in Las Vegas. On 21 December 1945 he had married Dorothy Pace; they had two children. In 1949 Cannon was elected as the city attorney for Las Vegas. He was reelected for three more terms, although there were questions about his role in a garbage contract, as well as in the secret wedding of Howard Hughes, the eccentric industrialist who became a recluse in Las Vegas. In 1956 Cannon ran unsuccessfully for a seat in the U.S. House of Representatives. Two years later he narrowly won the Democratic nomination for one of Nevada's U.S. Senate seats and defeated the Republican incumbent, George W. Malone.

Cannon withstood a tough campaign for reelection in 1964. His opponent, Paul Laxalt (later to join him in the Senate), tried to link Cannon to Bobby Baker, the Senate secretary who was convicted of influence peddling. In addition, Cannon's vote of cloture to end the Senate filibuster against passage of the 1964 Civil Rights Act had won him more enmity than support in Nevada. President Lyndon B.

Johnson went to Nevada to speak on Cannon's behalf. In the final count, his margin of victory over Laxalt was a mere thirty-four votes out of more than 134,000 cast, and there were accusations of fraud on both sides.

Cannon was easily reelected in 1970 and 1976, and became a senior senator, the chair of the Commerce, Science, and Transportation Committee, and a ranking member of both the Armed Services Committee and the Rules and Administration Committee. He also served on two Joint Committees on Inaugural Arrangements and the Joint Committee on Printing. Having been a chief sponsor of bills providing hundreds of millions of dollars for airport construction projects, Cannon reached what he and others considered the pinnacle of his career in 1978, with the passage of the Airline Deregulation Act, which, as the chair of the Commerce Committee, he helped to write.

Throughout his career in Washington, Cannon had been dogged by accusations of corrupt involvement with Nevada's gambling industry, but nothing stuck until 1979. On 10 January 1979 the Teamsters president, Roy Lee Williams, and the insurance executive Allen Dorfman visited Cannon's office in Las Vegas. The Teamsters owned land that Cannon was interested in purchasing. President James E. ("Jimmy") Carter had proposed a bill that would deregulate interstate trucking, a move the Teamsters opposed because regulated trucking brought them higher fees and kept out nonunion truckers. It was alleged that at this time Cannon agreed to keep the bill bottled up in his committee in exchange for a favorable price for the land.

Jackie Presser, an international vice president of the Teamsters Union who had been informing on the Teamsters and organized crime, persuaded the Federal Bureau of Investigation (FBI) to set their sights on Dorfman, who was believed to be a hidden owner of several Las Vegas casinos. The FBI set up a wiretapping operation called Operation Pendorf (*Pen*etrate *Dorf*man), which led them to suspect Cannon. The land in question was eventually sold to someone else. A trucking deregulation bill was passed in 1980, and Cannon went on to claim the bill, along with deregulation of the airlines, as his two major political accomplishments.

Also in 1980, the U.S. Department of Justice indicted Williams, Dorfman, and two others. Cannon was not charged in the case. The justice department said the only direct evidence against Cannon was an ambiguous telephone call, but some blamed political pressure for Cannon's exclusion from the indictment. At the November 1982 trial, Cannon denied that he had been offered a bribe and said he did not know Williams "from a bale of hay." Two witnesses, however, stated that the land offer had been made, and the codefendants were convicted of attempted bribery.

In the 1982 midterm elections, the Republican Jacob

("Chic") Hecht, a former aide to President Ronald W. Reagan, ran against Cannon for his U.S. Senate seat. Hecht made the bribery case an issue and accused Cannon of being a "tax-and-spend Democrat." Once again, Cannon was involved in a close election; this time he lost by about 5,800 votes out of 235,000 cast. After leaving the Senate in 1983, Cannon withdrew from public life but remained living in Virginia while providing consulting work for aircraft companies such as Northrop Grumman.

Cannon and his wife retired to Las Vegas in 1993. In his later years, Cannon suffered from Alzheimer's disease. He died of congestive heart failure at age ninety and is buried at Arlington National Cemetery in Virginia. Cannon showed admirable courage in World War II and in risking his reelection by supporting the Civil Rights Act. The airline and trucking deregulation bills he supported changed those industries. His senatorial career was undistinguished, however, and he probably will be remembered best for his role in the bribery case.

★

Cannon donated his papers to the Lied Library at the University of Nevada, Las Vegas. Information on Cannon's life and career is in *Biographical Directory of the United States Congress, 1774–1989.* His role in the Williams case is discussed in James Neff, *Mobbed Up: Jackie Presser's High-Wire Life in the Teamsters, the Mafia, and the F.B.I.* (1989), and Sally Denton and Roger Morris, *The Money and the Power: The Making of Las Vegas and Its Hold on America, 1947–2000* (2001). His civil rights record is discussed in A. Constandina Titus, "Howard Cannon, the Senate and Civil Rights Legislation, 1959–1968," *Nevada Historical Society Quarterly* 33 (winter 1990): 13–29. Obituaries are in the *New York Times* and *Washington Post* (both 7 Mar. 2002).

ARTHUR D. HLAVATY

CANTWELL, Mary Lee (*b.* 10 May 1930 in Providence, Rhode Island; *d.* 1 February 2000 in New York City), editor and writer who, in addition to her work for *Mademoiselle, Vogue,* and the *New York Times,* published a memorable series of memoirs.

Cantwell was the eldest daughter of I. Leo Cantwell, a production manager for the U.S. Rubber Company, and Mary Gertrude (Lonergan) Cantwell, a third-grade schoolteacher. Cantwell's ancestors had arrived in Bristol in 1852, but Cantwell was born in Providence, a grave injustice in her eyes as she would never be able to call herself a true Bristolian.

Cantwell grew up with her sister, Diana, at 232 Hope Street, the home of her maternal grandparents. In *American Girl,* she wrote of afternoons spent in her grandmother's sitting room, eavesdropping on "Ganny" and her friends, who would bring with them gossip and bits of Bristol history. Early on she realized that in Bristol, "Catholics came out of the second drawer." The Cantwell family lived on the Protestant side of town, "the country of the blue-eyed," and her first years of school were spent at the Lee School, a private institution at which she was the only Catholic. There she learned that, because of her religion, she, "the best speller and reader in the whole place, was the only girl there ineligible to sit upon the English throne." During this time, she suffered from polio but was spared any lasting effects.

Cantwell's father later enrolled her in the Walley School with the children of the mill workers, a population comprised of the local Irish, Italian, and Portuguese immigrants—all Catholics. She was a good student but not a popular one, and she was often criticized and ostracized by schoolmates. When she would return home crying after being called a showoff, or mocked for writing too many book reports, her father would admonish her: "Don't change, don't you dare change. . . . Someday you'll live in a place where there are lots of people like you."

As she progressed through Guiteras Junior High School and moved on to Colt Memorial High School, from which she graduated in 1949, Cantwell gained popularity and a sense of place among her peers. Her quote in the high school yearbook, *The Green and White,* for which she was a literary editor, was from the editor and poet Louis Untermeyer: "A glow, a heartbeat, and a bright acceptance of all the rich exuberance of life."

After earning a B.A. in English in 1953 from Connecticut College, she followed the advice of her father and moved to New York City. Her first job was as secretary to the press editor of *Mademoiselle* magazine. On 19 December of that year she married Robert Lescher; they had two daughters.

By 1958 Cantwell had worked her way up to the position of copywriter at *Mademoiselle.* From 1958 to 1959 she worked as a feature writer at *Vogue,* a position in which she languished as a writer and that she eventually walked out on. During the next three years, she entered a period of mental crisis that culminated in severe post-partum depression after the birth of her first daughter. In 1962 she returned to work, resuming her position as copywriter for *Mademoiselle* on a part-time basis. The magazine quickly promoted her to chief copywriter, a position she held until 1967. During this period her marriage began to break down. In 1968 she became the managing and features editor, and this gave her the opportunity to travel. As she later recalled in *Manhattan, When I Was Young* (1995), she traveled as much to avoid her fading marriage—and herself—as she did because her work required it.

After her divorce in 1971, Cantwell began a prolonged affair with the poet James Dickey, which ended with his leaving her for a younger woman. She continued at *Mademoiselle,* becoming the senior features editor in 1978 and remaining in that position until she left in 1980 to work for the *New York Times.*

While at the *Times,* Cantwell was a member of the editorial board, writing editorials, essays, book reviews, and a regular column called "Hers." In 1983 she received the Connecticut College Medal, and in 1986 she was awarded the Walker Stone Award from the Scripps Howard Foundation.

Cantwell worked as a freelance writer in the 1990s while maintaining her association with the *New York Times.* During that decade she published three memoirs: *American Girl* (1992), in which she describes her life from birth through the early 1950s; *Manhattan, When I Was Young* (1995), covering the period from the 1950s to 1980; and *Speaking with Strangers: A Memoir* (1998), which tells the story of her life through the end of the 1990s. Cantwell died of cancer at New York University hospital and was survived by her daughters and a granddaughter.

Throughout her life as a writer, from her earliest work for *Mademoiselle* through her memoirs, Cantwell was able to capture the mood of the times. Always underlying her writing was a subtle strain of nostalgia for a small-town life that had passed, not only for her but for America as well.

★

The best source on Cantwell's life is her own trilogy of memoirs: *American Girl: Scenes from a Small Town Childhood* (1992); *Manhattan, When I Was Young* (1995); and *Speaking with Strangers: A Memoir* (1998). These were later published together as *Manhattan Memoir* (2000). An obituary is in the *New York Times* (2 Feb. 2000).

ANNMARIE SINGH

CASE, Everett Needham (*b.* 9 April 1901 in Plainfield, New Jersey; *d.* 18 July 2000 in Cooperstown, New York), business executive and president of Colgate University (1942–1962) who helped form the core curriculum used by numerous institutions of higher learning.

Case was one of two sons of J. Herbert Case, chairman of the Federal Reserve Bank of New York, and Alice Needham Case, a homemaker. After attending public schools as well as the Hotchkiss School, Case graduated from Princeton University in 1922. Awarded a Rhodes Scholarship, he then received a master's degree in modern history at Cambridge University in 1924. From 1924 to 1927 he undertook graduate work in history at Harvard University but left to enter business without completing his dissertation.

Case first worked for Owen D. Young, chairman of the board of General Electric (GE) and founder of the Radio Corporation of America. Case became assistant secretary of

Everett N. Case. AP/WIDE WORLD PHOTOS

GE in 1929 and served until 1933. From 1928 to 1936 he was acting secretary of the National Broadcasting Company's council, and from 1930 to 1936 he was a director of the National Advisory Council of the Committee on Scientific Aids to Learning. On 27 June 1931 Case married Young's daughter Josephine; they had four children.

During 1932 and 1933 Case served as executive secretary of the Central Banking and Industrial Commission in Washington, D.C. From 1939 to 1941 he was assistant dean of the Harvard School of Business and taught there as well. Case was a member of the American Council of Foreign Relations, and he was a delegate to the Institute of Pacific Relations meeting in Shanghai, China, in 1931. Case also served as director of the Princeton-Yenching Foundation.

On 24 September 1942 Case became the ninth president of Colgate University in Hamilton, New York. Like all his predecessors, he was a lifelong Baptist. As an incoming president during wartime, Case acknowledged the need for technological skills to win the conflict but urged Colgate and other schools to emphasize the social sciences to prepare the nation for the postwar era. He warned that American colleges had done a poor job after the last global conflict. Case helped Colgate introduce a campus-wide course in American culture so that students could comprehend a vision larger than one based purely on national or chau-

vinistic sentiment. Case enabled Colgate to last through years of low enrollment during the war by securing training programs for U.S. Navy personnel. That experience led him to recommend years later that college graduates join the reserves for six to nine months. Notwithstanding this call for military training, Case later warned against the proliferation of what hc called "shadow faculties" composed of essentially nonteaching academicians involved in lucrative government research projects.

In the postwar era, however, Case was among the scholars to whom Washington turned in its effort to confront the emerging cold war. His trip to Shanghai years earlier had instilled in him what would become a lifelong fascination with China, and following the takeover of that country by communists in 1949, Secretary of State Dean Acheson appointed him a consultant on Far Eastern policy. In this capacity, Case advised the U.S. State Department in its searching review of U.S. China policy and assisted American nationals in leaving China.

Turning his attention to peacetime concerns, Case worked to enlarge Colgate's famous core curriculum, which had become a model for other institutions since its inception in 1924. According to the core curriculum philosophy of education, students should learn the basics of English, mathematics, history, and other foundational subjects before moving on to studies in career-oriented specialties. Thanks in part to Case's contributions, the core curriculum program permeated American education in the second half of the twentieth century.

Among Case's other achievements during his twenty-year tenure as Colgate president were the raising of faculty salaries, increases in fringe benefits for professors, enhancement of provisions for faculty research, and the addition of six major buildings on the campus. Colgate awarded him an honorary doctorate in 1957, one of thirteen such degrees he received. In 1962 the college named its library after him.

After leaving Colgate in 1962, Case became president and chief executive officer of the Alfred P. Sloan Foundation. In the meantime he had become a director of the Federal Reserve Bank in New York in 1961 and from 1965 to 1969 served as its chairman, as his father had three decades earlier. He also served as president of the American Council of Education; chairman of National Educational Television, a precursor to the modern Public Broadcasting Service; and board member of International Business Machines World Trade, the Committee for Economic Development, and the Fund for Financial Aid to Education. He was a trustee of Princeton, a member of the Harvard Overseers Committee, and a board member of the Sloan-Kettering Foundation.

In 1982 Case and his wife published a biography of her father, *Owen D. Young and American Enterprise*. Mrs. Case died in 1990. Case spent his later years living in the Clara

Welch Thanksgiving Home, a nursing home that had been established as a hospital by James Fenimore Cooper's daughter Susan in 1830. He died there in his sleep just nine months before his hundredth birthday. He is buried in Van Hornesville, New York.

Case was a sports fan, and greatly encouraged Colgate's football team. He often played softball and was a poet, pianist, and composer. Friends and colleagues at Colgate remembered that every Christmas for many years, Case would compose a special carol to commemorate that year's holiday season. His lasting influence on Colgate was the creation of a development office, his reorganization of the core curriculum, and his stewardship during times of hardship.

★

The papers of Everett Needham Case and Josephine Young Case are housed at Colgate University, Hamilton, New York. Colgate's library also has *The Inauguration of Everett Needham Case as the Ninth President of Colgate University: Founder's Day, September the Twenty-Fourth, Nineteen Hundred Forty-two, Hamilton, New York* (1942). See also Howard D. Williams, *A History of Colgate University, 1819–1969* (1969). For a short profile of Case just a few months before his death, see the *Colgate Scene* 28, no. 5 (Mar. 2000). An obituary is in the *New York Times* (21 July 2000).

GRAHAM GAO RUSSELL HODGES

CASEY, Robert Patrick ("Spike") (*b.* 9 January 1932 in New York City; *d.* 30 May 2000 in Scranton, Pennsylvania), two-term governor of Pennsylvania (1987–1995) whose anti-abortion views caused him to be denied the opportunity to speak at the Democratic National Convention in 1992.

Casey was the elder of two boys of Alphonsus Liguori Casey, a lawyer devoted to the causes of the working class, and Marie (Cummings) Casey, a homemaker. In his autobiography, *Fighting for Life,* Casey wrote of his parents' generosity and civility and attributed to them his own sense of obligation to others. Casey was born when his father was attending Fordham Law School in the Jackson Heights neighborhood of Queens in New York City. When his father finished law school, the Casey family returned to Scranton, Pennsylvania, where his father opened a law practice. There, Casey was raised as part of an extended family, living with his aunt and his cousins. He lived in or near his childhood home throughout his adult life.

After graduating from the Jesuit high school Scranton Preparatory School in 1948, Casey attended the College of Holy Cross in Worcester, Massachusetts. A basketball powerhouse, the college awarded "Spike" Casey one of its six basketball scholarships. Casey's years at Holy Cross were marked by study and a personal relationship with Ellen

Robert P. Casey, September 1988. AP/WIDE WORLD PHOTOS

Theresa Harding, whom he had met in high school. After serving as senior class president, Casey graduated cum laude with a B.A. in English in 1953. Casey and Harding married on 27 June 1953. They had eight children, one of whom, Robert P. Casey, Jr., served two terms as Pennsylvania auditor general from 1969 to 1977.

Casey began his political career in 1962 at the age of thirty, when he was elected to the Pennsylvania State Senate, having returned to Scranton after receiving his J.D. in 1956 from George Washington University. His first cause was the passage of a law that required mandatory testing of all newborns for PKU (phenylketonuria), a birth defect that, if undetected, leads to mental retardation. Later, Casey helped set up Pennsylvania's first state scholarship programs.

Encouraged by his successes in the state senate, Casey set out on what he later acknowledged was a premature bid for the Pennsylvania governorship. In 1966 he lost the primary to Milton J. Shapp, who in turn lost the general election to Lieutenant Governor Raymond P. Shafer. Casey ran a second primary race against Shapp in 1970 and lost again. He served as a delegate to the state constitutional convention in 1968 and shortly thereafter was elected Pennsylvania auditor general. Reelected in 1972 and serving until 1977, Casey aggressively managed the auditor's office and earned a reputation as an honest politician.

The 1978 Pennsylvania gubernatorial primary resulted in another loss for Casey. Another Bob Casey, a Pittsburgh school teacher, entered the Democratic primary for lieutenant governor, and the ensuing confusion on the ballot helped Casey lose to Pittsburgh mayor Pete Flaherty. After the election, Casey resumed his law career, becoming first a partner and then a senior partner in the Philadelphia-based firm of Dillworth, Paxson, Kalish, and Kaufman. Remaining active in local politics, Casey decided on yet another run for governor in 1986. Although he was decried as "the three-time loss from Holy Cross," Casey finally won the Democratic primary to run against the Republican nominee William W. Scranton, son of a former Pennsylvania governor. With the help of a little-known campaign operator from Louisiana named James Carville, who Casey described as having the eyes of a gunfighter, he surprised the political establishment by defeating the better-known and better-financed Scranton in an upset victory. Carville would later go on to help the Arkansas governor William Jefferson ("Bill") Clinton win the presidency in 1992.

Casey was sworn in as governor in January 1987. His first term got off to a rocky start, as he took on property-tax reform and met with defeat. He suffered a heart attack in 1987 and underwent heart bypass surgery. Despite these setbacks, Casey supported environmental, economic, and educational initiatives during his first term. In 1988 the Casey administration established Pennvest, a twenty-five-year, $2.5-billion program to provide improvements in water and sewer infrastructure in rural areas. A mandatory trash-recycling law, a children's health-insurance program, and increased funding for public education were among the Casey administration's key accomplishments. Casey was particularly proud of his economic development assistance to areas of Pennsylvania hard hit by industrial decline. To symbolize his commitment, Casey and his staff would spend several days in towns throughout the state listening to the concerns and expectations of citizens.

The most controversial legislation signed by Casey was the Pennsylvania Abortion Control Act, which became law in 1989. Abortion, he argued, failed to bring dignity to women and allowed society to "abandon the most defenseless and innocent members of the human family." Portions of the law, including parental consent and a 24-hour waiting period, were upheld by the U.S. Supreme Court in the 1992 decision *Planned Parenthood of Southeastern Pennsylvania* v. *Casey*. Casey's antiabortion position and his refusal to endorse Bill Clinton for the presidency resulted in his not being allowed to speak at the 1992 Democratic National Convention.

In his second term as governor, Casey was diagnosed with Appalachian familial amyloidosis, a rare and progressive genetic disease affecting the liver and heart. Casey consulted with the famed University of Pittsburgh surgeon Dr. Thomas Starzl, who recommended that Casey undergo heart and liver transplantation. Casey's condition deteriorated rapidly, and on 14 June 1993 Starzl transplanted a heart and liver. Surgery allowed Casey to serve out his term in office and was so successful that he briefly considered challenging President Clinton for the Democratic presidential nomination in 1995.

Although prostate cancer was diagnosed in Casey in 1997, he lived for seven years after his transplant surgery before succumbing to an infection. He died at Mercy Hospital in Scranton and is buried in Saint Catherine's Cemetery in Moscow, Pennsylvania. Described by the *New York Times* as a folk hero and as a living miracle for his comeback after surgery, Casey was an antiabortion Democrat who identified with the afflicted, the vulnerable, and the powerless. He once wrote that the most important quality a person can bring to political office is a passion for justice and a sense of outrage in the face of injustice. Casey was the recipient of numerous awards, including honorary degrees from the Catholic University of America and the University of Notre Dame.

★

Casey's official records are available from the Pennsylvania Records of the Office of the Governor. In his autobiography, *Fighting for Life* (1996), Casey recounts his political struggles and his personal battle with a deadly disease and sets out his philosophical views about public policy and service. Obituaries are in the *Philadelphia Inquirer* (31 May 2000); the *Pittsburgh Post Gazette* and *New York Times* (both 1 June 2000); and *New Republic* (3 July 2000).

ELOISE F. MALONE

CASHIN, Bonnie Jeanne (*b.* 28 September 1908 in Fresno, California; *d.* 3 February 2000 in Manhattan, New York City), costume designer for Twentieth Century–Fox (1943–1949) who later became most noted for originating Coach leather accessories (1962–1972) and designing women's clothing for Sills and Co. (1953–1977).

Cashin labeled herself a "practical dreamer," a fusion of her mother's practicality and her father's unbridled creativity. She grew up in a financially unstable but creative and intellectual environment. The unprofitable ventures of her father, Carl, who was at times an artist, photographer, inventor, and owner of a nickelodeon, were countered by the sound business sense of her mother, Eunice, the owner and operator of a custom dressmaking shop. Owing to financial concerns, the family, including Cashin's younger brother, moved so frequently within California that Cashin considered herself a "nomad by nature." The proximity of South American and Asian cultures mixed with western folklore led to Cashin's lifelong fascination with clothing as a means of storytelling and expressing identity.

Growing up as her mother's apprentice, Cashin had exceptional training in the construction of clothing and was encouraged to sketch clothing with a story line attached. By the time she graduated from Hollywood High School in 1925, she was illustrating a local fashion column and designing chorus girl costumes for Fanchon and Marco, a dance company contracted to provide all on-stage entertainment during the showing of Fox films. She married Robert Sterner, a Disney animator best known for his work on the movie classic *Fantasia* (1940). The marriage ended in 1942, but the couple had been estranged as early as 1934, when Cashin moved with her mother to New York to become the designer for the Roxy Theater's chorus line, the Roxyettes, the precursors and later rivals of the Rockettes. The couple had no children, and Cashin never remarried.

Cashin's fashion career began in 1937, when the *Harper's Bazaar* editor Carmel Snow discovered her work and arranged for her to become chief designer for the coat and suit manufacturer Adler and Adler. Cashin's name was not on the label, but she gained enough recognition to be appointed a designer of civilian defense uniforms for World War II. In the fall of 1942 Cashin returned to California, and in 1943 she began working at Twentieth Century–Fox under the wardrobe director Charles LeMaire.

Between 1943 and 1949 Cashin costumed more than sixty films, including *Laura* (1944), *Anna and the King of Siam* (1946), and *A Tree Grows in Brooklyn* (1946). Designing for the lavish productions that typified Hollywood's golden age, Cashin created historical, fantasy, and contemporary wardrobes, all with an eye to enhancing the story. Her experience designing for on-screen characters and off-screen style icons stood her in good stead when she returned to Adler and Adler in 1949. She received the 1950 Neiman Marcus Award and the Coty Fashion Critic's Award for her first collection. Displeased, however, with her manufacturer's control over her creativity, she decided to challenge the setup of the fashion industry. Working with multiple manufacturers, she designed a range of clothing at different price points, thereby specializing in complete wardrobes for a client she described as "my-kind-of-a-girl-for-a-certain-kind-of-living." She became known as an originator of American sportswear, but she disliked the term and described her objective as designing informal, sophisticated, and enduring clothing for all occasions of modern living.

In 1953 Cashin teamed with the leather importer and craftsman Philip Sills and pioneered the use of leather for high fashion. Designing for her own globe-trotting lifestyle, she developed modular, "layered" outfits for Sills and Co. that were inspired by traditional Chinese dress. The objective was to create a flexible wardrobe for living, given that seasonal changes were only an airplane trip away. She favored ponchos, tunics, No coats, and kimonos, which al-

Bonnie Cashin, ca. 1950. BETTMANN/CORBIS

lowed for ease of movement and manufacture. Approaching dress as a form of collage or kinetic art, she sculpted her designs from organic materials, including leather, tweeds, cashmere, mohair, and wool jersey. In 1962 Cashin became the first designer of Coach handbags and initiated the use of hardware on clothing and accessories, including the brass turn-screw closure that became Coach's hallmark. Unlike the contemporary rigid, hand-held bags, her vividly colored "Cashin-Carries" for Coach packed flat and featured wide straps, attached coin purses, industrial zippers, and sturdy brass toggles, the last inspired by the hardware used to secure the top on her convertible sports car.

Without licensing her name, Cashin designed cashmere separates, canvas totes, at-home gowns and robes, raincoats, umbrellas, and furs. She also ran the Knittery, a consortium of British mills that produced one-of-a-kind sweaters knit to shape rather than cut and sewn. Among many other industry awards, she received the Coty Award five times and entered the Coty Hall of Fame in 1972.

At once a maverick designer and a "mother" of American ready-to-wear clothing, Cashin was at the vanguard of fashion design for more than forty years. Working until 1985, she retired to focus on painting and philanthropy. One of her greatest concerns was the "care and feeding" of the designer, and she devoted herself to encouraging a higher level of creativity in a vastly mechanized society.

With her longtime partner, Curtis B. Kellar, she developed the Innovative Design Fund to sponsor the fabrication of design prototypes, and at the California Institute of Technology she established the James Michelin Distinguished Lecture Series.

Cashin died from complications during heart surgery. Her ashes were placed at Saint Thomas Church on Fifth Avenue in Manhattan. During the last year of her life she helped plan the exhibition *Bonnie Cashin: Practical Dreamer,* at New York's Fashion Institute of Technology. Additional retrospectives were shown in Tokyo in 2001 and Minneapolis, Minnesota, in 2003.

Cashin's instantly recognizable clothing concepts remain valid in the twenty-first century and serve as testaments to the timelessness of innovative design.

★

The Bonnie Cashin Collection is housed in the Department of Special Collections, Charles E. Young Research Library, University of California, Los Angeles. For further reference, see Stephanie Day Iverson, "'Early' Bonnie Cashin: Before Bonnie Cashin Designs, Inc.," *Studies in the Decorative Arts* 8, no. 1: 108–124; Pat Kirkham, ed., *Women Designers in the USA, 1900–2000: Diversity and Difference* (2000); and Valerie Steele, *Women of Fashion: Twentieth Century Designers* (1991). An obituary is in the *New York Times* (5 Feb. 2000).

STEPHANIE DAY IVERSON

CHAPMAN, Leonard Fielding, Jr. (*b.* 3 November 1913 in Key West, Florida; *d.* 6 January 2000 in Fairfax, Virginia), commandant of the U.S. Marine Corps (1968–1971) who introduced modern management techniques, guided the corps through its withdrawal from Vietnam, and maintained traditional Marine Corps standards during a period of rapid social change.

Chapman was the son of Leonard Fielding Chapman, Sr., a Methodist minister, Florida state legislator, superintendent of the Florida correctional system, and businessman, and Clare Singleton, a homemaker. Chapman grew up in DeLand, near Orlando, and graduated from DeLand High School in 1931 before entering the University of Florida in Gainesville. He participated in the university's mandatory Reserve Officer Training Corps and received a commission as a second lieutenant in the U.S. Army Field Artillery Reserve upon graduation in 1935. He resigned from the army to accept a regular commission as a second lieutenant in the Marine Corps on 8 July 1935, though he later admitted he had "never seen a marine in my life." Years later, a friend described Chapman, who stood six feet tall with a ramrod posture and hazel eyes, as a "poster marine."

Chapman completed Basic School at the marine barracks in Philadelphia in 1936 and was assigned to the marine barracks at Quantico, Virginia. After completing Field Artillery School at Fort Sill, Oklahoma, he was stationed at the Marine Corps base in San Diego and promoted to first lieutenant in September 1938. In July 1940 he became the commanding officer of the marine detachment on the cruiser USS *Astoria,* and he made the rank of captain in April 1941. Following the U.S. declaration of war against Japan in December 1941, Chapman took part in the Battles of Coral Sea and Midway and earned the Navy Commendation Ribbon with Combat "V." After his promotion to major in May 1942, he became an artillery instructor at Quantico. In 1943 he achieved the rank of lieutenant colonel and became the executive officer of the artillery section of the Marine Corps Schools. In July 1944 he returned to combat with the First Marine Division and earned the Legion of Merit with combat "V" for meritorious service in the battle for the Pacific island of Peleliu. He earned the Bronze Star Medal with combat "V" as a battalion commander at Okinawa, Japan, during April and May 1945.

After World War II Chapman gained experience in military planning in Honolulu, Hawaii, and Washington, D.C. In 1949 he returned to Quantico to lead training units and to complete advanced amphibious warfare training. In July 1950 he was promoted to colonel. Chapman became a regimental commander in the Third Marine Division in July 1952, and in August 1954 he became the commanding officer of the marine barracks at Yokosuka, Japan. In July 1956 he returned to Washington, D.C., to serve as commanding officer at the marine barracks and director of the Marine Corps Institute. Chapman's tour of "sea duty" early in his career likely contributed to his insistence on "spit and polish," which went on public display when Chapman initiated the Friday-night retreat parades, known as the "Silent Drill" platoon, that became a tourist attraction in the nation's capitol. On 1 July 1958 Chapman was promoted to brigadier general and assigned to Camp Lejeune, North Carolina, as commanding general, force troops, Fleet Marine Force, Atlantic.

Chapman spent the final ten years of his career focused upon logistic plans, policies, and programs. In November 1961 he became the assistant chief of staff for logistics, receiving his second Legion of Merit in December 1961 for his introduction of modern management techniques that included the increased use of computers for control and communication. Chapman also formulated a substantial portion of the principles of amphibious warfare that became Marine Corps doctrine.

In January 1964 Chapman was promoted to the rank of lieutenant general and named Marine Corps chief of staff. The Armed Forces Management Association bestowed upon him its 1967 Merit Award for "outstanding accomplishment in professional management." President Lyndon

Leonard F. Chapman, Jr., 1969. BETTMANN/CORBIS

B. Johnson nominated Chapman to become the twenty-fourth commandant of the Marine Corps in April 1967. Chapman, a "dark horse" candidate, was viewed by contending factions within the corps as an acceptable compromise. His elevation to the marines' top post was significant for two reasons. First, it validated the importance of modern management techniques. Second, Chapman, an artillery officer, was the first noninfantry officer to guide the corps. In preparation for leading the marines, Chapman served as the assistant commandant in the six months prior to becoming commandant.

When he became commandant on 1 January 1968, there were over 300,000 marines, the largest active duty force since World War II, with nearly one-third serving in Vietnam. In 1969 President Richard M. Nixon ordered the gradual withdrawal of U.S. forces from Vietnam. Chapman removed the bulk of marines, leaving only a small force for air support, pacification, and embassy security. (He brought the last combat marine out of Vietnam in 1971.) Racial tension and drug abuse, two major problems in U.S. society during the 1960s and early 1970s, challenged the cohesion and readiness of the corps. After a near riot along racial lines erupted at Camp Lejeune in the summer of 1969, Chapman issued a directive that committed the corps to racial equality, including the recruitment of more minority officers, a review of all recent promotions, and permission to use the clenched-fist salute for black power and to wear "Afro" or natural haircuts. Chapman's attempt to foster racial harmony met with criticism from some marines who thought that nonmilitary cultural expressions had no place in the corps, while some black marines felt the directives,

which included wearing an Afro haircut up to the regulation length of three inches, were insignificant compromises. Chapman's insistence upon strict military discipline led to a no-tolerance policy on drug use.

After thirty-six years of service, Chapman retired as a four-star general on 31 December 1971 and received the Distinguished Service Medal from President Nixon. Chapman headed the U.S. Immigration and Naturalization Service from 1973 to 1977, during which period he lobbied for a significant increase in budget and personnel to cope with the tremendous increase in illegal immigration, which he referred to as the "silent invasion." On 25 June 1980 he founded the Marine Corps Command and Staff College Foundation to enhance leadership among commissioned and noncommissioned officers; he served as foundation president for fourteen years. His wife, Emily Walton (Ford) Chapman, died in 1992. They had two sons, both of whom also served as marines. Chapman died of cancer and is buried at Arlington National Cemetery in Arlington, Virginia.

Chapman introduced modern management techniques to the Marine Corps, a branch generally known for colorful leaders. His leadership style meshed with that of Secretary of Defense Robert McNamara and his "whiz kids," who emphasized control and efficiency. Chapman commanded the largest Marine Corps since World War II and led the corps' withdrawal from Vietnam. When the military draft ended in 1973, other branches of the military used reforms and other inducements to attract and retain an all-volunteer force. Chapman, however, faced the impending volunteer military with an insistence upon "spit and polish," and an adherence to traditional marine values and standards.

★

A biographical file on Chapman is at the U.S. Marine Corps History and Museums Division in Washington, D.C. A detailed chronology of his career prior to becoming commandant is in Chapman's testimony for the Senate Committee on Armed Forces, "Nominations of Lt. Gen. Leonard F. Chapman, Jr., and Charles A. Bowsher: Hearing before the Committee on Armed Forces," 90th Cong., 1st Sess., 12 Dec. 1967. Other useful sources published at the time of his nomination include "A 'Poster Marine' Will Command the Corps," *New York Times* (5 Dec. 1967), and an entry in *Current Biography* (1968). Chapman's views on illegal immigration are found in Chapman, "'Silent Invasion' That Takes Millions of American Jobs," *U.S. News and World Report* (9 Dec. 1974). Obituaries are in the *New York Times* (11 Jan. 2000) and *Marine Corps Gazette* (Mar. 2000).

PAUL A. FRISCH

CLAIBORNE, Craig Raymond (*b.* 4 September 1920 in Sunflower, Mississippi; *d.* 22 January 2000 in Manhattan, New York City), epicure, cookbook author, and restaurant reviewer for the *New York Times,* who introduced the four-star rating system to restaurant reviewing in the United States.

Claiborne was the youngest of three children born to Lewis Edmond Claiborne, a cotton grower, businessman, and sometime local bank officer, and Mary Kathleen (Craig) Claiborne. Originally a homemaker, his mother became proprietor of Miss Kathleen's Boardinghouse after the failure of her husband's business ventures in the early 1920s. Claiborne often credited his mother and the black cooks she employed in her Indianola, Mississippi, boardinghouse for his lifelong interest in good food. Despite the family's change in circumstances, his mother insisted that they were blue bloods and "to the manor born" through her family.

Claiborne remembered his childhood as traumatic and emotionally devastating, although, shy and cherubic, he was pampered by all. He was never interested in sports and instead spent his time in the kitchen with the women. Due to the family's strained circumstances, he shared a bed with his father, for whom he came in time to develop a strong homoerotic attachment.

In 1937 Claiborne briefly followed his brother, Luke, into the pre-medicine program at Mississippi State University in Starkville, but he transferred in the following year to the University of Missouri in St. Louis, where he earned a B.A. in journalism in 1942. For want of a better plan and imbued with post–Pearl Harbor patriotism, he joined the U.S. Navy as a yeoman third class in communications—a "male secretary in uniform," as he later put it.

Although he claimed to "dislike the idea of being known as a third class anything," Claiborne sailed aboard the USS

Craig Claiborne, 1990. AP/WIDE WORLD PHOTOS

Augusta to North Africa, where he served as part of Operation Torch, the Allied invasion of North Africa, although he never was close to any of the fighting. He was most impressed by the food he found in Casablanca, Morocco—couscous, harissa, wine, and French cream pastries.

Claiborne returned to the United States for officer's training at the University of Notre Dame in Indiana in 1944, then proceeded to England, where he received an assignment as an ensign on a submarine chaser. He subsequently participated in the invasions of Sicily and Italy. As the war wound down, he was sent on to the Pacific, where he was present for the invasion of Okinawa (although again not part of any combat) and found himself in Japanese waters as the war ended. A hilarious description of his assignment to bring a ship back to Honolulu Harbor can be found in his memoir, *A Feast Made for Laughter* (1982).

Released from service in 1946 and sensing that his "sexual needs would be poorly served in the Mississippi Delta," Claiborne moved to Chicago, where he worked in advertising and public relations for the *Chicago Daily News* and for the American Broadcasting Company. He endured this for several years, but became increasingly restless, and finally took his savings and sailed to France in 1949. Intending to indulge his passionate Francophilia, he learned all he could about French food and wine before his money ran out and he returned to Chicago.

A year later, his debts paid off and boredom looming, Claiborne gave up his public relations job at the Merchandise Mart and joined the navy again—this time for the Korean Conflict. He left for the Pacific aboard the USS *Alfred Naifeh*. With time to reflect during his second stint in the service, he determined to find a career that married his two passions, food and writing.

Discharged once again in 1953, Claiborne used his savings and the GI Bill to attend L'Ecole Hôtelière de la Societé Suisse Hôteliers near Lausanne, Switzerland. He chose the school, which he attended for eighteen months, at the urging of his mother, who suggested it in lieu of the Cordon Bleu in Paris. This proved a happy choice, as the school trained him in the art of service as well as in cooking, and these qualifications served him well when he later became the restaurant critic for the *New York Times*. In 1954 Claiborne moved to New York City and found work with *Gourmet* magazine as a receptionist and freelance writer. He left *Gourmet* with the editor Ann Seranne and served as publicist for her consulting firm, where he mainly promoted Fluffo, a buttery yellow version of vegetable shortening.

When the *New York Times* hired Claiborne in 1957, he was the only male food editor and restaurant critic writing for a major newspaper in the country. He established a routine of dining incognito several times with friends at a restaurant and paying his own check (later to be reimbursed by the *Times*), a new approach in the field. He developed a system of four-star ratings, but at first did not find much to rate highly. It is said that he raised the bar for chefs and restaurant owners and introduced Americans to fine dining and an international palate.

Le Pavilion, owned by the French chef Henri Soulé, was the first New York City restaurant Claiborne championed. He and its chef, Pierre Franey, later embarked on a longtime friendship as well as a culinary partnership. Claiborne went on to become an early advocate of many chefs destined for fame, among them Jean Troisgros, Alain Ducasse, Paul Bocuse, Wolfgang Puck, and Paul Prudhomme. He also endorsed cookbook authors such as Madhur Jaffrey, Diane Kennedy, and Marcella Hazan.

Claiborne felt that he had found his true vocation, and—with the exception of a period between 1972 and 1974, when he and Franey operated a short-lived culinary newsletter, *The Craig Claiborne Journal*—stayed with the *New York Times* until his retirement in 1988. In addition to the thousands of articles and reviews he wrote for the *Times* over three decades, Claiborne published more than twenty cookbooks. These works included *The New York Times Cookbook* (1961), which sold more than three million copies; *The New York Times International Cookbook* (1971); *The Chinese Cookbook*, with Virginia Lee (1972); *Craig Claiborne's Southern Cooking* (1987); and half a dozen volumes with his longtime friend and professional collaborator, Franey.

In 1982 Claiborne published his autobiography, *A Feast Made for Laughter,* in which he frankly discussed his homosexuality and his complicated relationships with his parents. The book also included many of his favorite recipes, such as "My Mother's Chicken Spaghetti." He also produced numerous videotapes, among them *The Master Cooking Class* and *Craig Claiborne's New York Times Video Cookbook* (both 1985).

Claiborne's culinary writings for the *Times* made him a powerful man, and his cookbooks made him wealthy. He enjoyed living in East Hampton and Manhattan, traveled extensively, collaborated generously with the Culinary Institute of America in Hyde Park, New York, and often contributed his home and his cooking skills to benefit worthy causes. He gained a measure of gastronomic notoriety in 1975 when he bid $300 in a Public Broadcasting Service auction for an American Express offer of dinner for two anywhere in the world. Claiborne chose Chez Denis in Paris, and took Franey with him for a thirty-one–course meal that cost $4,000.

Among the many awards Claiborne received were induction into the Culinary Institute of America Hall of Fame, as well as the Ritz Carlton Lifetime Achievement Award (1993) and the Philadelphia Courvoisier Toque Award (1994). He died of pneumonia at Saint Luke's Roosevelt Hospital in Manhattan. Claiborne left the bulk of his estate, including his books and home, to the Culinary Institute of America. His body was cremated, and his ashes were sown at sea.

Claiborne's career as a cookbook writer and restaurant reviewer commenced at a time when Americans were not particularly food-conscious nor prone to dine out frequently He raised the standards for chefs and restaurant owners by knowing how food should be cooked and served, and he introduced Americans to fine dining and to an international palate.

★

The Culinary Institute of America Library in Hyde Park, New York, holds the most comprehensive collection of Claiborne's publications. The best source on Claiborne himself is his autobiography, *A Feast Made for Laughter* (1982). In addition, his videos give a sense of his quiet humor. See also Betty Harper Fussell and M. F. K. Fisher, *Masters of American Cookery* (1983). Obituaries are in the *New York Times* and *Washington Post* (both 24 Jan. 2000).

PAMELA ARMSTRONG LAKIN

CLEAGE, Albert Buford, Jr. (*b.* 13 June 1911 in Indianapolis, Indiana; *d.* 22 February 2000 in Calhoun Falls, South Carolina), black nationalist minister and founder of the Shrine of the Black Madonna.

Cleage was one of seven children, and the oldest of four sons, born to Albert Buford Cleage, Sr., a physician, and Pearl (Reed) Cleage. In his early years, the family moved to Kalamazoo, Michigan, and in 1930, when Cleage was nineteen, to Detroit. His father went on to establish Dunbar Hospital, the first African-American hospital in that city. After studying for a time at Fisk University, Cleage earned a B.A. in sociology from Wayne State University in Detroit in 1937. He then attended the Graduate School of Theology at Oberlin College, where he obtained a B.Div. and was ordained a minister in the Congregational church (later the United Church of Christ) in the summer of 1943. That same summer, he married Doris Graham, a teacher. They would later have two daughters, one of whom, Pearl, became a successful novelist.

Prior to his ordination, Cleage served as pastor of Chandler Memorial Congregational Church in Lexington, Kentucky (1942–1943), and then went on to the Church for the Fellowship of All Peoples in San Francisco. Cleage continued at the latter church, an interracial congregation, through 1944 but ultimately dismissed as a failure the church's attempt to integrate the races and sow unity.

Albert B. Cleage, 1967. AP/WIDE WORLD PHOTOS

After two years without a pulpit, and after studying at a film school in the Los Angeles area, Cleage went to Saint John's Congregational Church in Springfield, Massachusetts, in 1946. At Saint John's, the oldest African-American congregation in New England, Cleage became an outspoken activist who was heavily involved in the community. At the same time, his brash and sometimes imperious manner won him a number of foes among his parishioners. In 1951 Cleage moved back to Detroit, where he served as pastor of Saint Mark's Community Church through 1953. Although his father and uncle had helped start the church years earlier, Cleage led a group of dissidents to break from it and form Central Congregational Church, which met in a large house and later in Crosman School for five years. Cleage and his wife divorced in 1955, and she married his brother Henry shortly afterward.

The 1950s and early 1960s saw the rise of two very different groups within the black community. On the one hand was the civil rights movement, whose most visible figure was the Reverend Martin Luther King, Jr. In contrast to civil rights leaders, who called for nonviolent social change and who urged African Americans to work within the legal system, there was a rising tide of black nationalism whose most visible spokesperson was Malcolm X. Cleage began the 1960s in the same camp as King, but by mid-decade he had come to believe that, rather than striving for integration, blacks should protect their culture and history and ultimately their destiny. From this beginning, Cleage began to develop his concept of black Christianity, centered around the idea of Jesus as a black revolutionary.

In 1962 Cleage joined King on a march through Detroit, but during that period he also befriended Malcolm X. That same year, he ran unsuccessfully for governor of Michigan on the Freedom ticket. The turning point in Cleage's career came one Sunday in the spring of 1967, when he preached a sermon that called for a new black nationalist theology. On that same Sunday, an eighteen-foot-tall mural depicting a black Madonna and child—painted by Glanton Dowdell, who later helped start the Detroit branch of the Black Panthers—went on display at Central Congregational Church. The church was subsequently renamed the Shrine of the Black Madonna.

This new theology, which Cleage espoused in a collection of sermons published as *The Black Messiah* (1968), proved highly relevant to the time and place in which it was introduced. In contrast to black Muslims on the one hand and adherents of the theology and ideology taught by the civil rights movement on the other, Cleage offered a radical brand of black Christianity. Reacting to black Muslims' critique of Christianity, Cleage worked to make the Christian faith more truly a part of black culture, rather than merely an offshoot of a "white" religion. Race riots in

Detroit in 1967, which killed forty-three people, caused the congregation to swell and brought national attention to Cleage and his church. By the late 1960s the single church in Detroit had evolved into an entire denomination, the Pan African Orthodox Christian Church, located at 7625 Linwood Street, and Cleage thenceforth became known as a bishop. Nevertheless, the Shrine of the Black Madonna remained the heart of the denomination. Under Cleage's leadership, the Shrine of the Black Madonna became increasingly active in outreach programs and projects for economic self-sufficiency. He helped set up a neighborhood supermarket with reasonable prices and established a church-owned bookstore to promote the works of African-American authors.

In 1970 Cleage took the name Jaramogi Abebe Agyeman, meaning "liberator of people, defender, and blessed man" in Swahili. His *Black Christian Nationalism* (1972) further developed the principles of black Christian theology. In 1973 Cleage established Black Slate, Incorporated, which helped African Americans attain positions of responsibility in education, city and neighborhood leadership, the judiciary, and state government. The group helped Coleman A. Young become the first black mayor of Detroit. Among the other success stories of the Black Slate was Barbara-Rose Collins, who, through the group's backing, was elected to the Detroit school board. She went on to the city council and by the 1990s was representing Michigan's Thirteenth Congressional District in Washington. The Pan African Orthodox Christian Church established branches in Atlanta in 1975 and Houston in 1977, but its focal point remained Detroit. During the late 1980s and early 1990s Cleage lived in Houston, but he moved back to Detroit in the mid-1990s and then to South Carolina for the remainder of his life.

As part of a move toward self-sufficiency, in 1999 the Shrine of the Black Madonna established a farm called Beulah Land in Calhoun Falls, South Carolina. Cleage's aim was to create an agricultural complex wholly run by blacks, which would provide disaster relief and training. Beulah Land would also give inner-city youth a place to spend a summer vacation away from the dangers and temptations of urban life and would raise food for people in need. While on a visit to Beulah Land, Cleage died at age eighty-eight. A memorial service was held at the church in Detroit on 23 February 2000, and he was buried there three days later.

★

For information on Cleage, see Hiley H. Ward, *Prophet of the Black Nation* (1969), and James Haskins, *Profiles in Black Power* (1972). An obituary is in the *New York Times* (27 Feb. 2000).

KIM LAIRD

CLOONEY, Rosemary (*b.* 23 May 1928 in Maysville, Kentucky; *d.* 29 June 2002 in Beverly Hills, California), popular singer of the 1950s who revitalized her career in the 1970s to become an enduring interpreter of American popular standards.

Clooney was the eldest of three children of Andrew Clooney, who worked sporadically as a housepainter, and Frances (Guilfoyle) Clooney, who worked for a chain of dress shops. Her parents separated frequently, and she and her siblings, Betty and Nick, were raised mainly by their grandparents. When Rosemary was thirteen years old, her mother left for good, taking Nick to California. The girls remained with their father in Cincinnati, Ohio.

When their alcoholic father went on an extended drinking binge, his two teenaged daughters found a job singing at radio station WLW to pay for groceries and rent. They were unable to read music but had sung enough in their home to find natural harmonies. The sisters sang at the station and in the Cincinnati area for a couple of years while Rosemary attended Our Lady of Mercy Academy.

In 1945 the pair attracted the attention of the bandleader Tony Pastor, who invited them to tour with him. During the sisters' three years on the road with Pastor, Rosemary was increasingly singled out by audiences and critics. In 1948 Betty went home to Cincinnati. Rosemary stayed with Pastor for a year before moving to New York City to look for work as a solo artist.

She signed a contract with Columbia Records and was put under the supervision of Mitch Miller. In June 1951 Miller assigned Clooney—against her judgment—to record "Come on-a My House," a novelty number based on an Armenian folk tune. It proved to be her breakthrough recording. She quickly became a star, working on the radio with Bing Crosby and moving to Hollywood to make films for Paramount Pictures.

Clooney made four films, most memorably *White Christmas* (1954) with Crosby, and recorded vigorously. Her slender figure, blond hair, and girl-next-door image, combined with the sincerity with which she put across such songs as "Tenderly" and "Hey, There," brought her popularity with the public and the press. She later suggested that she felt driven to succeed, perhaps because of her uncertain childhood. Nevertheless, she enjoyed the acclaim she received from such tributes as a cover story in *Time* magazine in February 1953.

While at Paramount, Clooney dated the dancer Dante DiPaolo but instead married the older, "serious" actor Jose Ferrer. The two had met in 1951 while Ferrer was still married to another woman. He obtained a divorce and married Clooney on 13 July 1953.

Clooney wanted an "old-fashioned" Catholic marriage, and she and Ferrer had five children between 1955 and

Rosemary Clooney, 1950. AP/WIDE WORLD PHOTOS

1960. Her frequent pregnancies ended her film career, but she continued to record and hosted two musical television shows, the syndicated *Rosemary Clooney Show* (1956–1957) and the National Broadcasting Company program *Lux Music Hall* (1957–1958).

By the early 1960s, however, Clooney's life was beginning to unravel. She became increasingly disillusioned with Ferrer's frequent infidelities, and her own affair with the conductor/arranger Nelson Riddle ended unhappily. She and Ferrer separated, reunited, and then separated again, finally divorcing in 1967. A troubled affair with a drummer in her band added to her woes.

Clooney later recalled sadly, "The whole country had a nervous breakdown in 1968." Her depression over her romantic life and an addiction to tranquilizers and sleeping pills were exacerbated in that year when she was a close witness to the assassination of her hero Robert F. Kennedy, for whom she had campaigned.

Clooney became paranoid and lost her ability to tell the real from the unreal, maintaining that Kennedy had not been killed. Alienated from friends, colleagues, and audiences, she walked off stage one evening in the middle of a performance in Las Vegas. She was soon institutionalized.

After months of intensive therapy, Clooney rejoined her children and tried to reconstitute her career. "For a singer who'd called her audience 'stupid' and stormed off the stage, the road back was bound to be long and painful," she later wrote. Her employability was further damaged by the overall American music scene. "Girl singers" such as Clooney, who had come into popularity in the late 1940s and early 1950s, were by the late 1960s passé; popular music taste had by and large shifted to rock bands. Nevertheless, Clooney worked at minor hotels and other small venues and gratefully accepted chances to work on her brother Nick's radio show in Cincinnati, as well as the television talk show of her old friend Merv Griffin.

Clooney's personal life began to look up again in 1973, when she encountered DiPaolo at a Beverly Hills stoplight. DiPaolo moved in with Clooney and took care of the singer on the road. Clooney slowly made a comeback, helped along by former colleagues such as Crosby, who invited her to participate in a gala concert in 1974. She and Crosby toured frequently until his death in 1977.

In the fall of 1977 Clooney and three other middle-aged female performers—the singers Margaret Whiting and Helen O'Connell and the comedienne Rose Marie—capitalized on the era's nostalgia boom by touring the country as "Four Girls Four." Clooney began recording again during this period, signing a contract with Concord Jazz Records. By 1983 she was ready to strike out on her own again.

In the last two decades of her life, Clooney became a national favorite once more, recording regularly and playing such prestigious venues as Carnegie Hall and Rockefeller Center's Rainbow and Stars cabaret room. Although she had gained weight during her troubled years, she later said that she had made her peace with her changed appearance. She held her own vocally as she aged, perhaps because she was finally comfortable with her singing and her life. "I no longer have that burning ambition to reach the top of anything," she wrote. "My burning ambition now is to do as well as I can."

In 1997 Clooney married DiPaolo in her hometown of Maysville, Kentucky. She received a lifetime achievement Grammy Award a few months before her death from lung cancer. She is buried in Saint Patrick's Cemetery in Maysville.

Over the years, Clooney transformed herself from the girl next door into an icon of survival. Her nephew, the actor George Clooney, often cited her career as a cautionary tale for celebrities who were inclined to take their fame for granted. All the while, she moved audiences with her simple, heartfelt interpretations of songs by such masters as George Gershwin, Duke Ellington, and Cole Porter. Cabaret analyst Deborah Grace Winer called the singer the "Walter Cronkite of music," praising both Clooney and Cronkite for the truthfulness with which they addressed the American public in their work. "And if the truth should be difficult or painful," wrote Winer, "the fact that they're the ones telling you makes it easier to bear."

★

Clooney wrote two autobiographies, *This for Remembrance* with Raymond Strait (1977) and *Girl Singer* with Joan Barthel (1999). Deborah Grace Winer features Clooney prominently in *The Night and the Music: Rosemary Clooney, Barbara Cook, and Julie Wilson Inside the Cabaret World* (1996). Obituaries are in the *New York Times* (1 July 2002) and *People* (15 July 2002).

TINKY "DAKOTA" WEISBLAT

COBURN, James (*b.* 31 August 1928 in Laurel, Nebraska; *d.* 18 November 2002 in Los Angeles, California), actor renowned for the blend of strength, charisma, and style that he brought to film appearances in genres that included westerns, comedies, and domestic dramas.

The grandson of the Academy Award–winning character actor Charles Coburn, Coburn was the only child of James Harrison Coburn II, an auto mechanic, and Mylet Johnson, a schoolteacher. During the Great Depression, his father's garage business failed, and his family moved to the Los Angeles neighborhood of Compton, where Coburn grew up.

James Coburn accepting his Academy Award for *Affliction*, 21 March 1999. AP/WIDE WORLD PHOTOS

Coburn first developed an interest in acting while attending Los Angeles City College from 1952 to 1954. His first professional notices were for a role in a theatrical adaptation of Herman Melville's *Billy Budd* at the La Jolla Playhouse, a production that also starred Vincent Price. Coburn briefly considered attending the University of California, Los Angeles, but instead moved to New York City, where he studied acting with Stella Adler and worked in commercials and live television.

By the late 1950s Coburn was appearing regularly in well-known television westerns, such as *Bonanza, Wagon Train,* and *The Rifleman,* and landed a recurring role in *Bronco.* He also starred in two short-lived, action-oriented television series, *Klondike* and *Acapulco,* which ran in 1960 and 1961, and made his film debut in Budd Boetticher's 1959 western, *Ride Lonesome,* starring Randolph Scott.

On 11 November 1959 Coburn married Beverly Kelly, with whom he had a son. Coburn also became parent to Kelly's daughter from a previous marriage.

Coburn's breakthrough role came as Britt, the expert knife-thrower, in John Sturges's *The Magnificent Seven* (1960), which also starred Yul Brynner, Eli Wallach, and Steve McQueen. The film was a remake of Akira Kurosawa's *The Seven Samurai* (1954), which Coburn had watched fifteen times while studying acting in New York.

Coburn's repertoire expanded with strong character roles, including Corporal Frank Henshaw, a mechanic forced to assume command of a patrol in Don Siegel's *Hell Is for Heroes* (1962); the wicked pursuer Tex Panthollow in Stanley Donen's *Charade* (1963); and Louis Sedgwick, an Australian who escapes to Spain in *The Great Escape* (1963). After demonstrating his comic talent in *The Americanization of Emily* (1964) and also with *Major Dundee* (1965), the first of several films made with the director Sam Peckinpah, Coburn finally became a box-office success as a leading man.

He was especially successful as a leading man in his roles as Derek Flint, the sly American answer to James Bond, in *Our Man Flint* (1966) and *In Like Flint* (1967). In these films Coburn blended action-adventure heroics and flippant comedy. In 1968 he appeared in additional offbeat comedies, including *Duffy,* one of his personal favorites, and *The President's Analyst,* a cult classic about an insidious conspiracy, which he also produced. Victoria Horwell wrote of his performances in this era, "Coburn was a bridge between cool, in the Sinatra swinger sense and the counter culture cool." Coburn also starred in the film adaptation of Terry Southern's *Candy* (1968).

Although his style fell between the casting cracks—he was neither a neurosis-driven Jack Nicholson nor a stoic Clint Eastwood—Coburn worked steadily in the 1970s in such films as Sergio Leone's *A Fistful of Dynamite* (1972), and *Harry in Your Pocket* and *The Last of Sheila* (both

1973). One of his strongest roles was that of Pat Garrett in Peckinpah's *Pat Garrett and Billy the Kid* (1973), in which Coburn personified the struggle for friendship in a world of moral ambiguity—a common theme in Peckinpah's finest films.

During the early 1970s Coburn collaborated with Sterling Silliphant, as well as his martial arts teacher, Bruce Lee, on a project originally called *The Silent Flute,* which they touted to Warner Bros. as the "definitive martial arts movie." The studio cancelled the project, which reemerged in 1979 as *Circle of Iron* with Coburn and David Carradine in the lead roles, but it retained little of its earlier conception. In the meantime Lee had died, and Coburn, along with McQueen, served as a pallbearer at his 1973 funeral.

During the mid-1970s Coburn starred in such films as *Hard Times* (1975) and Peckinpah's *Cross of Iron* (1977). Coburn was diagnosed with rheumatoid arthritis in 1979, the same year he divorced his first wife, and his career slowed in the 1980s as his condition worsened. "I absolutely couldn't work," he said later. "I'd do things like little cameo things where I didn't have to move very much. I could just talk." He also took larger television roles and did voiceovers for documentaries. Later Coburn told the Associated Press that he had "healed" himself during the 1990s under a holistic treatment that included sulfur-based pills, a program for which he became the most visible advocate.

On 22 October 1993 Coburn married Paula Murad, a newscaster. By then he had returned to work, appearing in Robert Altman's *The Player* (1992), *Sister Act II* (1993), and the 1994 Mel Gibson vehicle *Maverick.* However, it was in his role as Glen Whitehouse, the abusive father in Paul Schrader's *Affliction* (1997), that Coburn demonstrated the kind of actor he might have been. Schrader requested Coburn for the part, he said, because Coburn was "physically large and represented another generation of Hollywood manhood." Accepting the Academy Award as best supporting actor for the role in 1998, Coburn said, "I finally got one right, I guess. See, some of them you do for money, some of them you do for love. This is a love child."

His career rejuvenated, Coburn worked on a dozen more films, including Paul Abascal's *Payback* with Mel Gibson (1999) and *Monsters, Inc.* (2001), for which he provided the voice of Henry J. Waternoose III, the company president. In 2002 he appeared in Alan Jacobs's *American Gun* (2002), a film making the rounds on the film-festival circuit at the time of his death. He died of a massive heart attack while listening to music with his wife at their Beverly Hills home. His body was cremated, and his ashes given to his family.

The critic Pauline Kael once suggested that, in appearance, Coburn might have been the product of a liaison between two characters from the world of opera, Lieutenant Pinkerton from Gilbert and Sullivan's *Mikado* and Madame

Butterfly from Puccini's work of the same name. A deeply spiritual man, Coburn spent his life exploring metaphysics, including the writings of G. I. Gurdjieff and Peter Ouspensky, and various spiritual disciplines, including Zen Buddhism, Sufism, and yoga.

Coburn appeared in 135 films during his career. His "Flint" films were unique in their self-referential irony to the genre itself and provided a template for the comedic mixing of high and low culture so apparent in contemporary cinema. Additionally, Coburn was one in the historic tradition of the American nonconformist involved in a spiritual quest. That this search was mostly unknown to the public is a testament to its personal quality and the hidden complexity of Coburn's character.

★

Information on Coburn is in David Weddle, *If They Move— Kill 'Em: The Life and Times of Sam Peckinpah* (1994). An essay by Steven Gaydos on Coburn's role in *Cross of Iron* is in Jerry Roberts and Steven Gaydos, eds., *Movie Talk from the Front Lines: Filmmakers Discuss Their Works with the Los Angeles Films Critics Association* (1995). See also James Pritivera, M.D., "James Coburn: Movie 'Tough Guy' Takes on Bone/Joint Health Concerns," *Journal of Longevity* 8, no. 9 (Sept. 2002). Obituaries are in the *Los Angeles Times* (19 Nov. 2002) and *New York Times* (20 Nov. 2002).

ROBERT VELLANI

COCA, Imogene (*b.* 18 November 1908 in Philadelphia, Pennsylvania; *d.* 2 June 2001 in Westport, Connecticut), versatile, rubber-faced actress and comedian best remembered for her partnership with the comedian Sid Caesar on *Your Show of Shows,* the landmark television variety program of the early 1950s.

Born Imogene Fernandez de Coca, Coca was the daughter of Jose Fernandez de Coca, a violinist and vaudeville band leader, and Sadie (Brady) Coca, a dancer. As an only child, Coca spent her early years in the theaters where her parents worked, mingling with actors, acrobats, and dancers. After attending school in Atlantic City, New Jersey, for several years, she began performing in vaudeville at the age of eleven. By the age of fifteen, she was appearing at Jimmy Durante's Silver Slipper Club in New York City. At seventeen, she made her Broadway debut in the chorus line of *When You Smile.*

For a number of years, she moved from show to show, finally getting her big break when she joined the cast of Leonard Sillman's musical revue *New Faces of 1934.* During one performance, when the heat failed in the theater, Coca donned an oversized overcoat to keep out the chill. Wearing the coat, she was sent onto the stage to distract the audience, which roared with laughter when Coca began

Imogene Coca, May 1966. AP/WIDE WORLD PHOTOS

people who would later come together for *Your Show of Shows:* not only Coca and Caesar, but the writers Mel Tolkin and Lucille Kallen and the choreographer James Starbuck. Featuring witty sketches, solo turns by the stars, and bright musical interludes, the *Admiral Broadway Revue* ran for nineteen weeks. Coca repeated many of the routines she had performed at Tamiment, all displaying her gift for combining buffoonery with warm human touches.

After the *Admiral Broadway Revue* was cancelled, Liebman was asked to create a new show that would again join sophisticated comedy with musical numbers. He used many of the same people as on the earlier show, in particular Caesar and Coca, and added such talented performers as Carl Reiner, Howie Morris, and later the writer Mel Brooks. The result was *Your Show of Shows,* a live, weekly, ninety-minute comedy and music revue that broke new ground for television. The program premiered on 25 February 1950 to enthusiastic reviews.

For each segment, Liebman assembled a troupe of artists from opera, musical theater, and dance, yet the comedy of Caesar and Coca dominated the weekly proceedings. Masters of pantomime, mimicry, and slapstick, they exhibited a remarkable rapport that carried them triumphantly through sketches, solo turns, and production numbers. Whether playing the embattled couple Doris and Charlie Hickenlooper or two strangers exchanging clichés, Caesar and Coca became a single entity in front of the television cameras.

Their special talents became even more notable when they starred in a series of satirical sketches spoofing the film world of the 1950s. Week after week, *Your Show of Shows* offered on-target parodies of then-popular movies such as *A Streetcar Named Desire* and *A Place in the Sun,* foreign films such as *The Bicycle Thief,* and even silent films of the past. Other sketches poked fun at basic genres, including the gangster film, the film musical, or the western. Coca was delightful in all these spoofs, bringing her impish charm to even the most outlandish characters.

She was equally memorable in her solo turns. Using her expressive features, she triumphed in a variety of guises, ranging from a smirking chanteuse to a manic fashion model flaunting a series of ludicrous hats. Drawing on her training as a dancer, she also appeared in addled—and hilarious—versions of classical ballets. Perhaps her most memorable creation, however, was a sweet and plaintive tramp who sang and danced. On the final show of the series, which aired on 5 June 1954, Coca won tears and laughter when she cavorted in her shabby tramp costume to the song "Wrap Your Trouble in Dreams."

In 1955 Coca's husband, who had become a record company executive in later years, died. She married the actor King Donovan in 1960.

After *Your Show of Shows* ended, Coca tried her hand

to parody a stripper. Sillman subsequently put the routine into the show, and although the revue failed, Coca was acclaimed as a rising comedian. Her next musical, *Fools Rush In,* also flopped, but on the day after its brief run ended in 1935, she married the actor Robert Burton.

During the 1930s and 1940s Coca continued to hone her comedy routines, using her tiny frame and flexible features to poke fun at every human emotion, from sheer joy to unbridled lust. By the late 1930s she had joined the performers at Tamiment, a summer camp in Pennsylvania where, under the guidance of the producer-director Max Liebman, the troupe presented sophisticated, New York–style musical revues. In the fall of 1939 Liebman brought the players, including Coca, Alfred Drake, and Danny Kaye, to New York City for a brief run in the *Straw Hat Revue.* In Florida, while preparing a show called *Tars and Spars* for the U.S. Coast Guard, Liebman discovered Sid Caesar, a talented young comedian whose act he began to develop.

By the summer of 1948 Liebman was discussing the creation of a "first" for television: a live, Broadway-style music and comedy revue, to be presented weekly by the National Broadcasting Company (NBC). The show, which premiered on 28 January 1949, was called the *Admiral Broadway Revue,* and its credits included many of the gifted

at new programs, but they failed to find an audience. The *Imogene Coca Show,* which ran for a single season starting in September 1954, could not settle on a workable format, and *Grindl,* which premiered in September 1963 with Coca as a maid, also lacked staying power. She played a Stone Age woman named Shad in an offbeat situation comedy called *It's About Time,* but again, it survived for only one season in 1966.

Occasionally Coca returned to the stage, most notably as a crackpot train passenger in the 1978 musical *On the Twentieth Century.* She was also a guest star on many television programs, including several reunions with Caesar, and took featured roles in a few movies, among them *Under the Yum Yum Tree* (1963) and *National Lampoon's Vacation* (1983). Her second husband died in 1987. Fourteen years later, Coca died of natural causes at her home, leaving no survivors. Her body was cremated and her ashes scattered.

Wistful tramp or sexy wanton, leering stripper or balmy ballerina, Coca was gifted with the ability to blend her uproarious clowning with more than a touch of poignancy. She was, indisputably, one of the treasures of television's golden era.

★

Information on Coca can be found in Ted Sennett, *Your Show of Shows* (1977; expanded edition 2002); Will Holtzman, *Seesaw: A Dual Biography of Anne Bancroft and Mel Brooks* (1979); and Sid Caesar, *Where Have I Been? An Autobiography* (1982). Obituaries are in the *New York Times* (3 June 2001) and *Variety* (11 June 2001).

TED SENNETT

COCKE, John (*b.* 30 May 1925 in Charlotte, North Carolina; *d.* 16 July 2002 in Valhalla, New York), innovator in computer design who gained renown as the creator of RISC computer architecture.

Cocke could have lived his whole life without ever picking up a paycheck. The son of Mary and Norman Cocke, the president of the Duke Power Company, Cocke was a child of privilege. He attended Duke University, where his father was a trustee, and earned a B.S. in mechanical engineering in 1946. He served in the U.S. Navy from 1952 to 1954 and then went back to Duke to study mathematics, gaining a Ph.D. in 1956. Cocke's first job after gaining his degree would be his only one, as he took a position with International Business Machines (IBM) immediately after completion of his doctorate and stayed with the company for thirty-five years.

Cocke soon became known throughout IBM as a "wild duck." He spent hours roaming the hallways and labs, amazing colleagues with his knowledge of the most esoteric

field. A chain smoker, he could be followed by the trail of cigarette butts he left in other people's offices; the ones still smoldering showed where he had been most recently. A bachelor until the age of sixty-four, Cocke was known to wear the same clothes for as long as a week and to leave stock certificates and paychecks on windowsills and in trash cans. "I guess I was relatively absentminded," Cocke admitted, adding that he was simply "more interested in science than in normal ways of life." In the buttoned-down world of IBM, where a striped tie marked a rebel, Cocke was a flamboyant exception.

IBM nurtured this genial revolutionary because his innovations saved time and money. "I've always considered myself fantastically lazy," Cocke said. "No one should have to do [an arithmetic operation] when you can design a machine that does." Between 1968 and 1992 the company granted Cocke five corporate awards; in 1972 he was named an IBM Fellow; and in 1990 he won the company's ultimate tribute: the John E. Bertram Award for sustained excellence, awarded at a symposium in Cocke's honor. Many of these honors were for innovations arcane even to those familiar with the world of computer hardware and software, such as his creation of a logic simulation machine, used to test processor designs before fixing them in silicon. Nonetheless, everyone who uses a computer is in his debt.

The series of chips that Cocke developed in the early 1970s epitomized his unique contribution to computer design. The RISC (Reduced Instruction Set Computing) chip was designed to be "a more efficient machine," using a series of what Cocke modestly dismissed as a series of "numerical tricks" to execute the most common operations at top speed while relegating the less common operations to time-consuming subroutines. To understand the revolution created by the RISC chip, one must first recognize the original breakthrough of Cocke's career, the technique of compiler optimization.

The compiler is a software program that accepts instructions written in one of the higher-level computing languages, such as C++ or Pascal, and translates them into the language that the computer itself uses, called its "instruction set." A computer cannot read "multiply"; instead, the compiler translates that higher-level command into a machine command, expressed in a series of binary "instructions." Throughout the 1960s and 1970s computer designers demanded far more complex instruction sets, thinking that the greater demands on modern computers could be solved in that way only. These changes overloaded the pipeline with instructions flowing back and forth, slowing the compiler and effectively giving up the computer's speed advantage. The PL.8 compiler, developed as part of the IBM 801 Minicomputer Project, was the first to use Cocke's optimizing technology.

Creating a more efficient compiler, however, only

opened the pipeline of information flow; if the pump remained inefficient, there would be no net gain in speed or reduction of costs. That is where RISC architecture came in. Although a computer chip is small and its individual circuits infinitesimal, each operation consumes time and energy based on the distance the electronic impulse must travel from initiation to completion. By changing the design of the chip so the most common operations were clustered (the reduced instruction set), Cocke enabled the RISC computer to run twice as fast as a conventional machine.

Ironically, IBM did not embrace the possibilities Cocke opened for it. Throughout the 1960s Cocke worked on a project known as the Advanced Computing System, a scientific computer that would be a thousand times faster than existing machines. In 1969, however, IBM gave up the project. Similarly, after Cocke achieved his RISC breakthrough in the 1970s, companies such as Sun Microsystems, Hewlett-Packard, and Apple Computer were quick to exploit the new designs. IBM, however, did not introduce an RISC-based computer until 1986, and even then it was deliberately made slow so that it would not steal market share from IBM's other computers, the 360 and 370. Such lack of appreciation led over the years to the departure of many leading IBM computer designers, including Gene Amdahl, Donald Estridge, and R. Andrew Heller; but Cocke merely turned his attention to new problems, such as speech recognition or data storage.

For his accomplishments, Cocke was given the country's highest awards. In 1987 he received the Turing Award from the Association for Computing Machinery. In 1991 he received the National Medal of Technology, followed in 1994 by the National Medal of Science. He was named Inventor of the Year in 1992 and awarded memberships in the National Academy of Engineering and the National Academy of Sciences.

Cocke was a fine golfer and enjoyed working at IBM in part because it gave him access to nearby ski areas. In 1989 he finally gave up his lifelong bachelorhood to marry Anne Holloway; the couple had no children. His health began to falter after 1990, and a series of strokes darkened his last years and culminated in his death. Before that, though, Cocke wrote his own epitaph: "We did things that still haven't been done elsewhere in the computer industry today."

★

John Cocke and V. Markstein wrote "The Evolution of RISC Technology at IBM," *IBM Journal of Research and Development* 44, nos. 1 and 2 (Jan.–Mar. 2000): 48. For information about Cocke and his work, see "A Maverick Scientist Gets an IBM Tribute," *New York Times* (26 June 1990); Laurence Hooper, "The Wizards: A Look at the High-Tech Dream Team, as Chosen by a Survey of Their Colleagues," the *Wall Street Journal* (24 May

1993); and Jim Hoskins, *IBM RISC System/6000: A Business Perspective* (1991). Obituaries are in the *New York Times* (19 July 2002) and *IBM Research News* (17 July 2002).

HARTLEY S. SPATT

COHEN, Alexander H(enry) (*b.* 24 July 1920 in New York City; *d.* 22 April 2000 in New York City), producer of 101 theatrical productions in New York City and London, originator of the nationwide Antoinette Perry (Tony) Awards television broadcasts, and organizer of efforts aimed to promote the theater and revitalize the Broadway area.

Cohen was the elder of two sons born to Alexander H. Cohen, Sr., a banker, and Laura (Tarantous) Cohen, a homemaker. His father died when he was four years old, and his mother remarried, to a banker who lived in a spacious penthouse on Park Avenue. Despite the affluence of his surroundings, Cohen remembered his childhood as lonely and recalled that his relationship with his mother was remote. When his brother, Gerry, committed suicide in 1954, Cohen blamed his mother for it and never spoke to her again. Gerry's misfortune, he later said, was that he

Alexander H. Cohen, 1982. BETTMANN/CORBIS

had no family, whereas "I did have a family, and it was in the theater."

After graduating from Columbia Grammar School in Manhattan in 1938, Cohen attended New York University and Columbia University but earned no degree. He had become interested in the theater as a youth, thanks in large part to an uncle who made a point of taking him to shows once a week. As a young man he invested much of his inheritance on failed shows but enjoyed his first success as associate producer of *Angel Street* in 1941.

On 12 January 1942 Cohen married Jocelyn Newmark, with whom he had one daughter. He spent a year (1942–1943) in the army during World War II but was discharged owing to leg problems. For a time he worked as advertising and publicity director for the Bulova Watch Company, and throughout his career he had a habit of presenting wristwatches as gifts. The combination of his work for Bulova with his efforts in the theater proved so successful that he later took out an advertisement in *Variety* seeking other such employment with the promise "Have tux, will travel."

Cohen's career in the theater was characterized by a series of highs and lows. After *Angel Street,* almost two decades would pass before his next big success, *At the Drop of a Hat,* in 1959. Many successes, however, would follow in the 1960s for Cohen, often working with the Nine O'clock Theatre, which he founded. Notable productions included *An Evening with Mike Nichols and Elaine May* (1960); Lena Horne's *Nine O'clock Revue* (1961); *Beyond the Fringe* (1962), which introduced American audiences to the outrageous comedy of Peter Cook, Alan Bennett, Jonathan Miller, and Dudley Moore; *An Evening with Maurice Chevalier* (1963); *The School for Scandal* (1963), co-starring Sir John Gielgud and Sir Ralph Richardson; *Ages of Man* (1963), directed by Gielgud; *Hamlet* (1964), also directed by Gielgud and starring Richard Burton; Anton Chekhov's *Ivanov* (1965), starring Vivien Leigh; *At the Drop of Another Hat* (1966), which reprised the earlier success; Harold Pinter's Tony Award–winning play *The Homecoming* (1967); Jerry Herman's *Dear World* (1969), starring Angela Lansbury; and David Storey's *Home* (1970), co-starring Richardson and Gielgud.

Divorced from his first wife in February 1956, Cohen immediately (on 24 February) married Hildy Parks, an actress. The couple later had two sons and collaborated on numerous theatrical and television productions. Television shows produced by Cohen and Parks included the Tony Awards ceremonies, first presented on television in 1967 and broadcast under their direction for the next two decades. They also produced two dozen other television specials, including *Night of 100 Stars* (1982, 1985, and 1990), *Parade of Stars* (1983), and several presentations of the Emmy Awards. Cohen, or Cohen and Parks, produced numerous specials for all three networks, including the *NBC*

60th Anniversary Special for the National Broadcasting Company in 1986. Cohen also produced television specials for the actresses Marlene Dietrich and Liza Minnelli and the tenor Placido Domingo, and Parks served as writer on more than forty prime-time network specials.

Night of 100 Stars and *Parade of Stars,* according to Cohen, raised $3 million to build an Englewood, New Jersey, extended-care nursing facility for members of the Actors' Fund of America. *Happy Birthday Hollywood* (1987), a three-hour celebration that he and Parks produced for the American Broadcasting Company, raised a million dollars for the Capital Campaign Fund of the Motion Picture and Television Country Home and Hospital.

Long a promoter of the theater community, Cohen in the late 1950s oversaw the construction of the O'Keefe Center, a 3,100-seat theater commissioned by the O'Keefe Brewing Company of Toronto. He oversaw the booking and management for the O'Keefe Center for three years, beginning with the 1960 production of *Camelot,* starring Richard Burton and Julie Andrews. He later performed the same function in Philadelphia, Pennsylvania, where he resurrected the Erlanger and Locust Street Theaters and organized the Playgoers Club, which supported both theaters by providing a subscription base.

In the 1970s the city of Baltimore sought Cohen's help in the revitalization of the Inner Harbor and downtown areas. He supervised the redesign and construction of the abandoned Mechanic Theater, which returned to a prominent position in show business. In 1992 he undertook a three-year assignment opening and managing the Rich Forum for the Stanford Center for the Arts in Connecticut. He also conceived and administered the First American Congress of Theater (FACT), which brought together for the first time 300 representatives of American profit, nonprofit, and regional theatrical organizations for a week-long conference at Princeton University in 1974.

Cohen was an active and articulate spokesman for the legitimate theater's campaign to popularize and promote the Broadway theater and stem the deterioration of the Times Square area of New York City. His efforts led to the formation of the Mayor's Midtown Committee, on which he served for a decade in the 1970s and 1980s. In 1976 he conceived the plan of turning the abandoned and bankrupt Manhattan Plaza project on West Forty-second and Forty-third streets into a flourishing subsidized apartment colony for workers in the performing arts. He also coordinated the organization of the theater's participation in the successful "I Love New York" tourism promotion campaign.

Throughout his career, Cohen remained an innovator both in marketing and technology. In the mid-1950s he organized Theater Tours, a company that pioneered all-expense packaged tours to Broadway, which he merchandised through Braniff, Trans World Airlines, and Delta

Airlines. In 1959 he experimented with a traveling mechanized box office and became the first to install a telephone reservation system in a Broadway theater. Working with American Express in the early 1970s, he introduced the use of credit cards in all Broadway theaters. Cohen also introduced subtitles to the theater when he presented the Italian musical spectacle *Rugantino* in 1964. This system is now used at Lincoln Center and other opera houses throughout the world.

Rugantino proved to be one of many costly flops that ultimately cancelled out the financial benefits Cohen accrued from more successful productions. Among his most notorious failures was *Hellzapoppin'* (1977), starring Jerry Lewis, which closed in Boston before reaching Broadway and which reportedly cost Cohen $2 million. Cohen remained philosophical about his losses, however. "I can owe a million, and I have," he once said, "but when I put my head on the pillow at night, it's 'Goodbye Charlie.' I get up the next morning and start all over again."

Shortly before his death *Variety* magazine cited Cohen as one of the ten most important producers of the twentieth century. Cohen, who on numerous occasions received or was nominated for most of the major show business awards—particularly the Tony and the Emmy—was so much the quintessential theater producer that the producer and director Woody Allen cast him as such in *The Purple Rose of Cairo* (1985).

The producer himself became the focal point of the show in *Star Billing,* a one-man presentation Cohen wrote and produced. Presented off Broadway in 1998, the program featured his reminiscences of six decades in the theater. Wrote the *New York Times* theater critic Lawrence Van Gelder, "Mr. Cohen proves himself a splendid anecdotalist with a highly developed sense of comic timing." His 101st and final production, of Noel Coward's *Waiting in the Wings,* opened at the Walter Kerr Theater on 16 December 1999, the centenary of Coward's birth. Cohen died of emphysema at Lenox Hill Hospital and was cremated. His family scattered his ashes around the area he had loved most in life, Broadway.

Approximately five feet, ten inches in height and portly in his later years, Cohen had a fondness for the high life, which he seemed to manage to enjoy regardless of his current state of success (or lack thereof) in the theater. Long before the age of cell phones, he had his limousine equipped with its own telephone, an extravagance at the time. In addition to his base in Manhattan, he had homes at various times in Pound Ridge, New York; Fairfield, Connecticut; Saint Croix in the Virgin Islands; Mougins, France; and London. The critic Frank Rich called Cohen a "larger than life impresario who went with his own individual, often idiosyncratic taste . . . in placing his theatrical bets." To the producer Elizabeth McCann, Cohen was

"community minded . . . and charming and gregarious. It was impossible not to like him."

★

There is no biography of Cohen. Obituaries are in the *New York Times* and *Washington Post* (both 23 Apr. 2000). Long-playing recordings exist of numerous Cohen productions, and a 1997 interview with David Rothenberg and Betty L. Corwin was recorded on video and is available under the title *An Evening with Alexander H. Cohen.*

DAVID ROTHENBERG

COMO, Pierino Ronald ("Perry") (*b.* 18 May 1912 in Canonsburg, Pennsylvania; *d.* 12 May 2001 in Jupiter Inlet Beach Colony, Florida), immensely successful baritone pop singer and radio and television star whose career spanned six decades.

Born to Italian immigrants Pietro Como and Lucia (Travaglini) Como, Como was one of thirteen children. In the small town southwest of Pittsburgh where he was born and where his father worked in the Standard Tin Plate factory, Como began helping to support his large family at an early age. At age ten he was sweeping out a barber shop; at age twelve he was apprenticed to the barber; at age fourteen he had his own modest barber shop. Music was always

Perry Como. LGI STOCK/CORBIS

an important part of his life, however, and Como earned extra money in his teens singing at weddings, parties, and local meetings of the Sons of Italy and other fraternal organizations. Although financially strapped, his father insisted that all his children study music, and Como received instruction in baritone horn and organ, playing often with the Italian street bands that were common in the region. His father also insisted that his children be educated, and Como graduated from the local high school in 1929.

Como remained a barber and part-time musician in Canonsburg until the spring of 1933, when he successfully auditioned for the Freddie Carlone Orchestra. Como married his high school sweetheart, Roselle Beline, on 31 July 1933; they had three children. Como then toured the Midwest for several years with Carlone. By 1936 he was singing with the more prestigious Ted Weems Orchestra, with whom he made many radio appearances. Eventually the group had its own radio show, *Beat the Band,* from 1940 to 1941.

In late 1942, after the Weems Orchestra disbanded to join the war effort, Como was living in the borough of Queens in New York City, freelance singing in various clubs. Dissatisfied with the less-than-stable lifestyle and long evening hours away from his wife and their young son, Como planned to move back to Canonsburg and take up his barber's scissors once more. However, a booking agent saw his potential and arranged for singing jobs in more prominent clubs (including an extended engagement at the famed Copacabana), a regular radio spot on the Columbia Broadcasting System (CBS), and, most importantly, a recording contract with Radio Corporation of America (RCA) Victor in June 1943.

In the summer of 1943 Como's first single, "Goodbye Sue," was released, beginning a long and impressive recording career. His first Top Ten hit was the 1944 Jerome Kern song "Long Ago (and Far Away)," and in 1945 Como's recording of "Temptation" was his first to sell a million copies. (Over the course of his career he would have twelve million-selling singles.) Como's name became a household word because of such 1940s hits as "Till the End of Time" (based on Chopin's "Polonaise in A-Flat Major," this was the highest-selling record of 1945), "Dig You Later (A Hubba-Hubba-Hubba)," "I'm Always Chasing Rainbows," "Prisoner of Love," the 1898 song "When You Were Sweet Sixteen," "Because," " 'A'—You're Adorable," and "Some Enchanted Evening." His first album, called simply *Perry Como,* appeared in September 1946 and quickly reached the Top Ten. That same year, *Merry Christmas Music* was released and became a chart topper, not only in 1946, but also in 1947, 1948, and 1949. *Supper Club Favorites* (a spin-off from Como's television show) became a Top Ten album in March 1949. Como was heard on jukeboxes and radios throughout the country, and with fifteen records

on the charts in 1949, he was the top recording artist of that year. As one critic remarked about this period in Como's career, to a war-weary public, the novelty tunes, old ballads, and sentimental love songs that he delivered in his "low-keyed style became the sonic projection of the peaceful life, clean fun, controlled ebullience, and tranquil rather than passionate love."

During the 1940s Como was also busy with radio work and Hollywood films. In December 1944 he began both hosting and singing three nights a week on the radio program *The Chesterfield Supper Club,* which ran first on the Columbia Broadcasting System (CBS) and later on the National Broadcasting Company (NBC). His genial and relaxed manner, with his pleasant, soothing voice, made Como a natural for radio and later television. His film career, on the other hand, was perhaps his least successful undertaking. Signing a seven-year contract with Twentieth Century–Fox in August 1943, Como first appeared on the big screen in 1944 in *Something for the Boys.* He subsequently appeared in *Doll Face* (1945) and *If I'm Lucky* (1946). His radio and recording careers were much more important both to him and to his public, so Como was released from his contract in 1947 at his request.

Como made the leap from radio to television extremely successfully in December 1948, with the Christmas Eve premiere of *The Chesterfield Supper Club,* a weekly half-hour show on NBC. Two years later he moved to the Columbia Broadcasting System (CBS) for *The Perry Como Show,* which ran for five years and earned him an Emmy Award for best male singer in 1954. The show moved back to NBC in 1955 and ran until 1963, changing names in 1959 to *The Kraft Music Hall* to reflect its new sponsor. With music, mild comedy, and guest performers, the variety show was an American favorite and is considered by many to be the best of its kind in television history. Como earned two Emmy Awards for his work in 1955 (best male singer and best program host), and two more in 1956 and 1958 (best male personality in a continuing performance).

Off camera, Como continued to record huge hits during the 1950s, including the million-sellers "Don't Let the Stars Get in Your Eyes," "Wanted," "Papa Loves Mambo," "Hot Diggity," "Round and Round," and "Catch a Falling Star." This last recording won Como his only Grammy Award (best male vocal performance, 1958). Top-selling albums of these years included *I Believe* (a religious album) and *So Smooth* in 1954, *We Get Letters* (named after a popular regular segment of his television show) and *Merry Christmas Music* (a long-play version of his 1946 release) in 1957, and *Seasons Greetings* in 1959.

In June 1963 Como retired from weekly television work and thereafter was seen on the small screen only as a guest on other shows or hosting occasional broadcasts of *The Kraft Music Hall* and his own Christmas specials. *The Perry*

Como Christmas Album (1968), which eventually went gold, was another notable achievement of the decade. Golf, a particular passion of Como's, and spending time with his family were a big part of this hiatus from his career in the 1960s.

In June 1970 Como was back on stage for the first time in more than twenty years, performing live in Las Vegas. After this performance, he began making regular appearances in Las Vegas and elsewhere, and touring both nationally and internationally (he was especially popular in Australia and England). His 1970 recording of "It's Impossible" was his first hit in over a dozen years, and it appeared near the top on both the easy listening and pop charts. "And I Love You So" (1973) was his last significant single, and it soared to number one on the easy-listening charts of that year. His albums continued to be top sellers until 1983, with his last new album, *Perry Como Today,* released in 1987 on the RCA label. Como's receiving Kennedy Center Honors in 1987 was perhaps the highlight of this decade and was particularly fitting for a musician who was so much a part of the American sound for so long.

Into the 1990s Como performed occasionally and made guest appearances. After suffering from Alzheimer's disease for two years, he died peacefully in his sleep at home, six days short of his eighty-ninth birthday. He is buried near his wife in Riverside Memorial Park in Tequesta, Florida.

Slightly stocky, with black hair and black eyes, Como, who was famous for his gentle, engaging sense of humor, his serene temperament, and his cardigan sweaters, was dubbed the "man who invented casual" by the fellow crooner Bing Crosby. One critic remarked that "Nobody else was so intensely relaxed," and the singer Dean Martin, who often appeared on Como's television show, joked that he used to "go over to Perry's to borrow a cup of sleep." Como's popular television show, with its theme song "Dream Along with Me," was a reflection of its star: mellow, casual, and ingratiating. His smooth baritone voice (which was versatile and capable of dramatic as well as dulcet tones), the seemingly effortless grace of his singing style, and his good-friend-of-the-family personality charmed audiences for decades. With a career that included twenty-seven gold records and recording sales in the 100 millions, Como was an icon of American popular culture. He was, however, less impressed with himself, and in typical Como style, once told an interviewer, "I've done nothing that I can call exciting. I was a barber. Since then I've been a singer. That's it."

★

An excellent extended and illustrated interview with Como, covering both his professional and personal life, is in a series of issues of the *Saturday Evening Post* (12, 19, and 26 Nov. 1960).

An article on Como's music and recording career, with a discography and video list, is in Colin Larkin, ed., *The Encyclopedia of Popular Music* (1998). Obituaries are in the *Los Angeles Times* and *New York Times* (both 13 May 2001), and *Washington Post* (14 May 2001).

MICHAEL MECKNA

CONNOR, John Thomas ("Jack") (*b.* 3 November 1914 in Syracuse, New York; *d.* 6 October 2000 in Boston, Massachusetts), lawyer, chief executive officer of two Fortune 500 companies, and World War II officer who served as secretary of commerce under President Lyndon B. Johnson and resigned in opposition to the escalation of the war in Vietnam.

Connor, the oldest son of five children of Michael J. and Mary (Sullivan) Connor, attended Holy Rosary High School in Syracuse. In 1932 he entered Syracuse University, where he was captain of the golf team, managed the football team, was president of his class, was elected to Phi Beta Kappa, and graduated magna cum laude in 1936 with an A.B. in political science. Connor continued his education at Harvard Law School, graduating in 1939. A member of both the New York State and District of Columbia bar associations, Connor began his career in New York City with Cravath, Swaine, de Gersdoff, and Wood, a Wall Street law firm specializing in finance and business. In 1940 he married Mary O'Boyle, with whom he had three children.

In 1942 Connor moved to Washington, D.C., to join the Office of Scientific Research and Development as general counsel. As part of the defense effort under the direction of Vannevar Bush, Connor organized a consortium of university, private, and government research facilities focused on the development of penicillin and in 1948 was awarded the Presidential Certificate of Merit for this effort. Between 1944 and 1945 Connor served in the U.S. Marine Corps in the Pacific theater as an air combat intelligence officer connected to a dive-bombing squadron, rising in rank from first lieutenant to captain. Returning to Washington in 1945 from Japan, Connor joined the staff of Secretary of the Navy James V. Forrestal and helped write the legislation that led to the National Security Act of 1947, which created the Defense Department and the Central Intelligence Agency (CIA).

Recruited by Bush to the private sector in 1947, Connor joined Merck and Company, a major pharmaceutical firm in New Jersey, as general counsel and secretary. He held advancing corporate positions, including administrative vice president and general manager of the Merck, Sharp, and Dohme International division, and became president and chief executive officer (CEO) in 1955. In 1959 Connor

John T. Connor, 1965. BETTMANN/CORBIS

gained national recognition for his deft defense of the pharmaceutical industry against a hostile investigation led by Senator Estes Kefauver of Tennessee. At Merck, Connor expanded research and development leading to the introduction of life-enhancing drugs for treating polio, arthritis, and high blood pressure. In 1962 he established the Martin Luther King scholarship for outstanding African-American students at Harvard Law School.

In 1964 Connor was named secretary of commerce, the first member appointed to President Lyndon B. Johnson's new cabinet. Sworn in on 19 January 1965, Connor turned his energy to promoting federal policy that would check the inflation generated by the escalating war in Vietnam and to correcting the country's balance-of-payment problems. Marginalized by President Johnson, who Connor felt used his cabinet members as aides, and facing a merger, proposed by Johnson, of the Department of Labor and the Department of Commerce, Connor grew increasingly restive. Several divisions of the Department of Commerce were moved out to form a new Department of Transportation. As the war in Vietnam became more intense, its effect on both national and international economies became more negative. Connor, who believed the war was both morally and economically wrong, resigned from his post in January 1967. He continued to criticize the war policies of both Johnson and President Richard Nixon from the platforms of the Business Council, the Council on Foreign Relations, and the Committee of Business Executives Against the War; he also encouraged those administrations to reconsider wage and price controls.

After his resignation from Johnson's cabinet, Connor joined Allied Chemical Corporation, later Allied Signal, as president and CEO in January 1967. In 1969 he became Allied's chairman as well. Connor reorganized the administration of Allied and sold off unprofitable divisions. During his tenure, Connor moved the corporation toward greater profitability through heavier investment in energy and responded to increased pressure for environmentally careful corporate policies after Allied was fined $13.4 million for dumping chemical pesticide ingredients into the James River in Virginia. Continuing to protest government policies that seemed to discourage the participation of businesspeople in government, in 1977 Connor criticized the administration of President Jimmy Carter for not doing enough to encourage American development of clean coal and nuclear resources and for policies of high taxes and interest rates that encouraged inflation and discouraged growth. In 1975 President Gerald Ford named Connor to the Rockefeller Commission, which was charged with investigating domestic abuses by the CIA. Connor retired from Allied Chemical on 30 November 1979 to join Schroders Inc., the U.S. division of a British merchant banking firm, as non-executive chairman of the board. He served until his retirement from business in March 1986.

Connor received honorary degrees from more than fifteen colleges and universities. Active in golfing and as a board member of the Metropolitan Opera from 1974, Connor spent his retirement between homes in North Palm Beach, Florida, and Cape Cod, Massachusetts. Connor died of a form of blood cancer in Boston's Massachusetts General Hospital. He is buried at Christ the King Church near his home in Cotuit, Massachusetts, on Cape Cod.

★

Biographical sketches accompanying Connor's appointments to Johnson's cabinet and to the Rockefeller Commission appear in the *New York Times* (11 Jan. 1965 and 6 Jan. 1975, respectively). A lengthy interview with Connor, reviewing his interaction with three presidential administrations, is in the *New York Times* (1 Nov. 1977). Connor's career at Merck and Allied Chemical can be traced through *Business Week* and *Fortune* magazines. Obituaries are in the *Providence* (Rhode Island) *Journal-Bulletin* (9 Oct. 2000), the *Washington Post*, *New York Times*, and *Syracuse Post Standard* (all 10 Oct. 2000), and the *Barnstable* (Massachusetts) *Patriot* (19 Oct. 2000).

WENDY HALL MALONEY

CORSO, Gregory Nunzio   (*b.* 26 March 1930 in Manhattan, New York City; *d.* 17 January 2001 in Robbinsdale, Minnesota), poet closely associated with the Beat Generation.

Corso, the second of two sons of Fortunato Samuel (Sam) Corso and Michelina (Colonna) Corso, was born at 160 Bleecker Street in Greenwich Village. Before Corso's first birthday, his mother abandoned the family. He was told that his mother had returned to her native Italy, but six decades later he discovered that she had fled to Trenton, New Jersey, remarried, and raised a family there under the name of Margaret Davita.

Corso's father placed him in foster homes but refused to allow him to be adopted. During World War II the elder Corso regained custody of his son to avoid the draft, but he was drafted anyway in 1943, and the teenaged Corso ran away to live on the streets. His formal education ended before he entered high school. He had several run-ins with the law leading up to 1947, when he was sentenced to three years in Clinton State Prison in Dannemora, New York, for theft. In prison, Corso became interested in literature when sympathetic inmates gave him books with which he educated himself, taking delight in learning obscure, archaic words that he later used in his poetry.

Shortly after his release in 1950 and back in New York City, Corso met the poet Allen Ginsberg, who introduced him to Jack Kerouac, John Clellon Holmes, and William S. Burroughs, all members of the group later known as the Beat Generation. In 1952 Corso began to travel extensively and worked as a laborer, a cook, a salesman, and a cub reporter for the *Los Angeles Examiner*. During the summer of 1953, Corso and Kerouac had love affairs with the same woman. This conflict later became the central theme of Kerouac's novel *The Subterraneans,* in which the character Yuri Gligoric is based on Corso. Later in 1953, Corso's first child was born. Corso married Sally November on 7 May 1963; they had one child, separated in 1964, and eventually

Gregory Corso, 1981. CHRISTOPHER FELVER/CORBIS

divorced. He married again in 1968, to Belle Carpenter; they also had one child. His first son was born in 1976 to Jocelyn Stern and raised by another of his companions, Lisa Brinker. His last child was born in 1984 to the writer Kaye McDonough.

In 1954 Corso worked with a small theater company in Cambridge, Massachusetts, and wrote several plays, including *In This Hung-Up Age.* His first poems to appear in print were in the *Cambridge Review* and *Harvard Advocate.* His first book of poetry, *The Vestal Lady on Brattle, and Other Poems,* was privately published in 1955, but was not widely distributed until City Lights reprinted it in 1969.

In 1956 Corso visited Ginsberg in San Francisco and met the San Francisco Renaissance poets Michael McClure, Gary Snyder, and Philip Whalen. Lawrence Ferlinghetti, the publisher of City Lights Books, heard Corso read at the San Francisco Poetry Center and agreed to publish a book of his poems, *Gasoline* (1958). Corso also met Randall Jarrell, the poetry consultant to the Library of Congress, who invited Corso to visit him in Washington, D.C. Corso nurtured hopes of academic acceptance, but his outlandish behavior—disrupting poetry readings by interrupting and insulting the speakers; appearing disheveled and incoherent at his own readings due to drug and alcohol abuse—thwarted his ambition.

Early in 1957 Corso left for a two-year stay in Europe.

In Paris, he began to write longer poems on single themes, including "Bomb," "Marriage," and "Power," which were as much social criticism as poetry. When Ferlinghetti refused to publish "Power," Corso went to New Directions Books, which became his publisher for the rest of his life. In 1960 the company published *The Happy Birthday of Death*. Corso was very active during this period, and he compiled an anthology of new American writing, *Junge Amerikanische Lyrik* (1961).

Corso returned to New York City to help the photographer and filmmaker Robert Frank and the painter and filmmaker Alfred Leslie shoot the film *Pull My Daisy* in 1959. That same year he won the Longview Award for his poem "Marriage," which became his most anthologized work. Later in the year he returned to Europe, visiting Venice and Greece before settling into the Beat Hotel on Rue Git-le-Coeur in Paris. There, Corso helped Burroughs, Brion Gysin, and Sinclair Beiles develop the cutup method of composition. This process was accidentally discovered by Gysin when he sliced through a newspaper and glued the strips together in a random fashion to create new juxtapositions of words. Corso abandoned cutups after the group's first book, *Minutes to Go* (1960), was published. He felt that the technique, although yielding interesting results, was basically sterile. Corso's lyrical poetry was much more polished and refined than the cutups, with constant revision leaving little to chance. Corso also wrote his only novel in Paris, a surrealist narrative entitled *The American Express* (1961). He arranged for his *Selected Poems* (1962) to be published in England by Eyre and Spottiswoode, and his book *Long Live Man* was published by New Directions in the same year. Corso made several brief visits to the United States during the next decade. In 1964 he obtained a teaching position at the State University of New York at Buffalo, but he was dismissed in 1965 for refusing to sign a loyalty pledge. By 1966 Corso was back in Europe, spending most of his time in Greece and Paris. In 1969 he moved to San Francisco, which he found more hospitable than New York City.

During the 1960s Corso began a lifelong addiction to drugs, and his writing became much more sporadic. In 1970 New Directions published his *Elegiac Feelings American* and in 1981 *Herald of the Autochthonic Spirit*. Drugs took their toll on his literary output, and Corso's reluctance to give poetry readings further diminished his ability to earn a living. He often had to depend on friends for financial support. From the late 1970s through the mid-1980s, Corso lived in San Francisco, occasionally teaching at the Naropa Institute in Boulder, Colorado, where Ginsberg ran the poetics department. Returning to New York City during the 1990s, Corso moved to 64 Horatio Street, where he remained for the last decade of his life. His poetry was collected into *Mindfield/Gregory Corso* (1989), and *Library*

Journal made note of "Corso's lyric grace and ability to view life with enthusiasm and humor." After being diagnosed with prostate cancer, he went to Minnesota to live with his oldest daughter, Sheri Langerman, who nursed him through his final days. After his death, a funeral mass was held at Our Lady of Pompeii Church in Greenwich Village, and Corso's ashes were buried at the foot of the grave of the poet Percy Bysshe Shelley in the Protestant Cemetery in Rome.

Although Ginsberg considered Corso the greatest poet of his generation, other reviewers were less enthusiastic. Corso had a raw natural talent for verse but failed to produce a large body of work. His reputation as an *enfant terrible* was well earned, and his outrageous and sometimes obnoxious behavior charmed some but irritated others. Corso's ability to combine classical literature, archaic vocabulary, and popular culture within a beautiful lyric form is his most enduring legacy.

★

Corso's papers are scattered in more than a dozen libraries, including those at Stanford University in California, the University of Texas at Austin, and Columbia University in New York City. His selected letters are in Bill Morgan, ed., *An Accidental Autobiography: The Selected Letters of Gregory Corso* (2003), and they contain valuable information about Corso's life. There are no full-length biographies, but several critical books deal with some biographical issues. Longer biographical pieces appear in Thomas Parkinson, ed., *A Casebook on the Beat* (1961); Bruce Cook, *The Beat Generation* (1971); Donald J. Greiner, ed., *American Poets Since World War II* (1980); Frank N. Magill, ed., *Critical Survey of Poetry: English Language Series* (1982); Ann Charters, ed., *The Beats: Literary Bohemians in Postwar America* (1983); and Steven Watson, *The Birth of the Beat Generation: Visionaries, Rebels, and Hipsters, 1944–1960* (1995). Important interviews include those with Michael Andre in *Unmuzzled Ox* 2, nos. 1 and 2 (1973): 101–136, and *Unmuzzled Ox* 6, no. 2 (1981): 123–158; with Robert King in *Unspeakable Visions of the Individual* 5 (1977): 4–24; with Gavin Selerie in *The Riverside Interviews* 3 (1982): 21–25; and with Danny O'Bryan in the chapbook *Gregory Corso: Poems, Interview, Photographs* (1994). Obituaries are in the *New York Times* and *Los Angeles Times* (both 19 Jan. 2001), and *Village Voice* (30 Jan. 2001). Corso is featured in several films about the Beat Generation, including *Wholly Communion* (1965), *Fried Shoes, Cooked Diamonds* (1978), and *What Happened to Kerouac?* (1985).

BILL MORGAN

COVERDELL, Paul Douglas (*b.* 20 January 1939 in Des Moines, Iowa; *d.* 18 July 2000 in Atlanta, Georgia), director of the Peace Corps (1989–1991) and U.S. senator (1993–2000).

Born on the eve of World War II, Coverdell was a descendant of English and German families that had settled in the Midwest several generations earlier. His parents were Eldon Paul Coverdell, a traveling salesman, and Vonis (Wagner) Coverdell, a homemaker. Coverdell and his younger sister were raised as Methodists. Their father's occupation prevented the family from staying anywhere very long, and the children attended schools in six states. Although he was modest and soft-spoken, Coverdell excelled in his studies and attained recognition as a student leader. In 1957 he graduated from Lee's Summit High School in Lee's Summit, Missouri, and in 1961 he received a B.A. in journalism from the University of Missouri. Until 1964 he served as a lieutenant in the U.S. Army in East Asia.

Coverdell's interest in politics was first awakened by the party conventions that nominated Dwight Eisenhower and Adlai Stevenson for president in the 1950s. Although he was a lifelong Republican, he also was inspired by the emphasis of the administration of John F. Kennedy on youth and citizen outreach. While he was stationed in Okinawa, Japan, one Christmas, he decided to seek public office on returning home.

In 1964 Coverdell joined his father in a fledgling business in northern Atlanta to market insurance products to rural electric cooperatives. Later, this innovative concept was extended to banks and included affinity credit cards and other financial instruments. In his earlier years of struggling to make the family business profitable, however, Coverdell found local politics more interesting and rewarding. His first electoral contest came in 1968 when he unsuccessfully challenged the Democrat Jack Hardy for a Georgia state senate seat. By serving as campaign manager for the 1969 mayoral race of Rodney Cook, Coverdell not only gained valuable experience but also met Nancy Jane Nally, a flight attendant for Delta Air Lines, whom he married on 10 November 1972; the couple had no children.

Conducting a campaign based on personal rather than media contact, Coverdell beat the odds and won against Hardy in the 1970 senate race. His 1972 victory was even more impressive (he garnered 82 percent of the vote), and he held the seat for another seventeen years. Coverdell quickly came to the fore among Georgia Republicans, becoming minority whip in 1972, minority leader in 1974, and, eventually, party chair in 1985. Despite Coverdell's meager following in the legislature, his leadership was critical to the passage of insurance reforms, legislation to curb drunk driving and raise the legal age for drinking, and seatbelt legislation, as well as the blocking of tax increases and cutting of government waste. Secrets of his political success included his reliance on volunteers and such outreach strategies as town hall meetings, neighborhood visits, and a volunteer constituency office. Most important, as a moderate, Coverdell helped transform the Republican Party in Georgia from its traditional, right-wing image to a party of reform. To this end, and to wrest control from the cronies of the former segregationist governor Lester Maddox, he worked with a like-minded Democratic faction to enact procedural rules changes in the senate. Along with other progressive Republicans, such as Mack Mattingly, Rodney Cook, John Linder, and Newt Gingrich, Coverdell constructed a new power base, chiefly in the fast-growing Atlanta suburbs. By the mid-1980s Georgia was on the verge of becoming a two-party state.

Meanwhile, in further anticipation of political change, Coverdell cultivated a close friendship with the presidential aspirant George Herbert Walker Bush, then director of the Central Intelligence Agency. In 1980 and 1984 Coverdell served as chairman of state legislators for Ronald W. Reagan's presidential campaign (Bush was on the ticket as vice president), and in 1988 he headed the southern steering committee for the Bush presidential campaign.

Coverdell was awarded the directorship of the U.S. Peace Corps in 1989 and again displayed reformist zeal by reshaping this traditionally Democratic agency's role in world affairs. He dispatched volunteers to thirty new countries (including five former Communist states in Europe), secured increases in funding, and attracted more participants. The number of minority volunteers nearly doubled. Coverdell also linked the Peace Corps with a domestic agenda, instigating a program called World Wise Schools that connected Peace Corps volunteers with five thousand classrooms throughout the United States.

Coverdell's directorship of the Peace Corps provided enough national exposure and experience for him to make a bid in 1992 for the U.S. Senate seat held by a Democrat, Wyche Fowler, Jr. In addition to outcampaigning Fowler in a grassroots effort throughout Georgia, Coverdell successfully branded his opponent a "tax and spend" Washington insider in the style of the liberal Massachusetts senator Ted Kennedy, a strategy that subsequently would be employed by other Republican hopefuls in the South. Coverdell defeated Fowler by a narrow margin in a runoff election. As senator, he quickly gained respect from political veterans of both parties for organizing the defeat in 1994 of the health care plan sponsored by the administration of President William J. ("Bill") Clinton.

For his ardent advocacy of business interests, Coverdell received the Spirit of Enterprise Award from the U.S. Chamber of Commerce in 1997. He also favored a balanced budget amendment and term limits for legislators, and in 1997 he secured passage of his Volunteer Protection Act to insulate charitable and nonprofit organizations from lawsuits. *Georgia Trend* magazine recognized Coverdell as one of the state's top five elected officials for getting things done, much in the manner of the former Georgia senator Sam Nunn. For his crusade against drugs and domestic violence,

Paul Coverdell, 1989. BETTMANN/CORBIS

Gannett News Service in 1997 named Coverdell (along with Pennsylvania's senator Rick Santorum and Missouri's senator John Ashcroft) a leading spokesperson for "family values."

Increasingly viewed as an up-and-comer, Coverdell became chair of the Senate Agriculture Subcommittee on Marketing, Inspection, and Product Promotion and secretary to the Senate Republican Conference in 1997, and he handily won reelection in 1998. Coverdell died of complications from a cerebral hemorrhage at Piedmont Hospital in Atlanta, and his remains were cremated and buried at Arlington Cemetery in that city. At the time of his death, he was the Senate's fifth-highest-ranking Republican and liaison for the presidential contender George W. Bush.

Coverdell was an Atlanta businessman who, by hard work and tenacity, developed formidable political skills in the Georgia legislature and U.S. Congress. Despite his uncharismatic demeanor, he emerged from obscurity to enter the Republican mainstream as a fiscal conservative and social moderate. His hallmarks were availability and a genuine interest in people, including his minority constituents. Coverdell was widely regarded as rational, tough-minded, and approachable—a workhorse, not a show horse. He never shirked from his fair share of political responsibilities and willingly assumed some of his party's heaviest legislative burdens. His greatest legacy is the emergence of Georgia's two-party system. Coverdell's many years of party building led in 2002 not only to another Republican senator (Saxby Chambliss) from Georgia but also to a Republican Georgia governor (Sonny Perdue) and Republican control of the Georgia senate for the first time since Reconstruction.

★

Coverdell's U.S. Senate, Georgia senate, and Peace Corps papers are housed in the Ina Dillard Russell Library at Georgia College and State University in Milledgeville, Georgia. An informative biographical article is Peter H. Stone, "Rallying the Troops," *National Journal* 27 (2 Sept. 1995): 2,152–2,156. The most important memorial is a volume of addresses and tributes put out by the U.S. Government Printing Office (2000). An obituary is in the *New York Times* (19 July 2000). Three audiotapes of interviews with Coverdell, conducted on 4 and 10 Mar. 1989 by Clifford Kuhn for the Georgia Government Documentation Project, are in the William Russell Pullen Library at Georgia State University in Atlanta.

JOHN D. FAIR

CRAM, Donald James (*b.* 22 April 1919 in Chester, Vermont; *d.* 17 June 2001 in Palm Desert, California), chemistry educator who, with Jean-Marie Lehn of France and Charles J. Pedersen of the United States, shared the 1987 Nobel Prize for chemistry for the development and use of molecules with structure-specific interactions of high selectivity.

Cram grew up in Vermont, the fourth child of five, and the only son, of William Moffett Cram and Joanna (Shelley) Cram, both immigrants from Ontario, Canada, to rural Chester, Vermont. The family moved to Brattleboro, Vermont, two years after Cram was born. His father, of Scottish heritage, was described by Cram as a cavalry officer who later worked alternately as a successful lawyer and an unsuccessful farmer. His mother was of German descent. She was raised as a strict Mennonite but rebelled against the faith. She had a love of English literature, which she passed on to her son.

Cram's father died of pneumonia before he was four years old, leaving the family in dire financial straits. His mother was forced to rely on Aid to Dependent Children, a type of welfare program. Cram was encouraged to barter his services by doing odd jobs in exchange for anything he needed. He did any odd job available, from picking apples and digging potatoes to delivering newspapers. His early formal education was in small, one-room schoolhouses, but outside school he enjoyed a private world of classic books, from Charles Dickens to Shakespeare. He also bartered services for piano lessons.

Cram left home at age sixteen, by which time he was already six feet tall and weighed 195 pounds. Although he did not have a driver's license, he took a job driving two elderly ladies to Florida, where he stayed, working at odd jobs to support himself. He started secondary school in Florida but became homesick for New England and hitchhiked north to Massachusetts within a year. Cram spent his final year of high school at Winwood, a small private school on Long Island, New York, which significantly influenced his future. Cram worked as a factotum for his tuition and board. At Winwood he took a chemistry course, taught himself solid geometry, and won a $6,000 National College Honor Scholarship to Rollins College in Winter Park, Florida.

While at Rollins, Cram discovered the term "research," which to him meant that the only limitations would be his own resourcefulness and creativity. It was exactly what he wanted. Chemical research, he said, became his god, and conducting it was his act of prayer from 1938 to the end of his career. His first chemistry professor at Rollins thought Cram would be a good industrial researcher but not a good academic one. At that point, Cram became determined to have a career in academic chemical research. While at Rollins, Cram enjoyed many activities other than academics. In his junior year (1940) he had a leading role in the play *You Can't Take It with You,* written by Moss Hart and George S. Kaufman, in which the main character gives the advice, "Do what is in your heart, and you carry in yourself a revolution." Years later Cram's brilliance and creativity revolutionized chemistry.

On 22 December 1941 Cram married Jean Turner, a Rollins classmate who received her master's degree in social work from Columbia University. They divorced in 1969. Cram married his second wife, Jane Maxwell, a chemistry professor at Mount Holyoke College, on 25 November 1969. Cram described Maxwell as an "unsparing but inspiring critic and research strategist in ways beyond mention." Cram had no children, saying he chose not to, because he would be either a bad father or a bad scientist if he did.

Donald J. Cram. THE LIBRARY OF CONGRESS

After graduating from Rollins with a B.S. in chemistry in 1941, Cram took a teaching assistantship at the University of Nebraska in Lincoln, where he received an M.S. in chemistry in 1942. The United States had entered World War II by the time Cram earned his M.S. He went directly to work for the drug manufacturer Merck and Company, ultimately doing research on penicillin, working under the direction of Dr. Max Tishler, a Harvard-educated biochemist. When the war ended in 1945, Tishler arranged for Cram to attend Harvard University in Cambridge, Massachusetts, where he earned a Ph.D. in chemistry in 1947. That same year Cram started teaching at the University of California, Los Angeles (UCLA). He moved from assistant to associate professor in three years and then to full professor in six more. He remained at UCLA until he retired in 1990.

Cram did not view the achievement of winning the 1987 Nobel Prize for chemistry in his sixty-ninth year as the culmination of a career but rather as a prize that allowed him to continue research. It was in 1967 that he heard about crown ethers, which led to the field of host-guest chemistry. A chemist at the DuPont Company in Maryland, Charles J. Pederson, had developed methods to synthesize cyclic polyethers, called "crown ethers," and, starting with that discovery, the French chemist Jean-Marie Lehn and Cram subsequently each developed increasingly complex molecules with spaces inside that selectively bind ions within them. Cram called his work "host-guest chemistry" while Lehn called it "supramolecular chemistry." Their work has had enormous importance for the development of other branches of chemistry and biochemistry, particularly the explosive development in organic synthesis, which involves molecules that mimic the selectivity of enzymes. In all his work, Cram used visual representations of molecules to develop his deep understanding of three-dimensional space.

Cram has been described as always smiling, with a mischievous twinkle in his eye. When asked about winning a "Nobel Peace Prize in chemistry," he responded, "No, I won a piece of the chemistry prize." Cram was said to have filled a room with his enthusiasm and vigor, which spread contagiously among his students and colleagues. He was noted for having 150 trademark bow ties and for creativity in teaching as well as in research. Cram even taught introductory courses for nonscience majors, sometimes bringing his guitar and belting out a folk tune to relax the students. Cram did everything with the enthusiasm of a competitor. Outside the laboratory, he was an avid surfer and tennis player. He also enjoyed mountain climbing and swimming. On 15 September 2000, a few months after the death of his second wife, Cram married Caroline Cook. Cram died of cancer at his home in Palm Desert, California.

A prolific scientist and gifted teacher, he received many awards and honors, among them a Guggenheim Fellowship (1955), the California Scientist of the Year award (1974), and the National Medal of Science (1993). He received honorary degrees from Sweden's Uppsala University (1977) and the University of Southern California (1983). Cram was the author of more than 350 research papers and seven books, among them *Organic Chemistry* (1959; with George S. Hammond), *Elements of Organic Chemistry* (1967; with John H. Richards and George S. Hammond), and *Essence of Organic Chemistry* (1978; with Jane M. Cram). He revolutionized the teaching of the subject by reorganizing the presentation of the material. In 1998 Cram was ranked among the seventy-five most important chemists of the past seventy-five years by *Chemical and Engineering News,* a publication of the American Chemical Society.

★

For autobiographical information on Cram's life and work, see his *From Design to Discovery* (1990). For Cram's influence on chemistry, see Allison L. Byrum, "Donald Cram's Chemical Legacy," *Chemical and Engineering News* 79, no. 30 (23 July 2001):

38–40. Obituaries are in the *Los Angeles Times* and *New York Times* (both 20 June 2001).

M. C. NAGEL

CRANSTON, Alan MacGregor (*b.* 19 June 1914 in Palo Alto, California; *d.* 31 December 2000 in Los Altos, California), four-term U.S. Democratic senator from California (1969–1993) who was involved in a savings and loan industry scandal.

Cranston was one of two children of William MacGregor Cranston, a wealthy real estate agent, and Carol (Dixon) Cranston, a homemaker. Cranston graduated from Mountain View High School in Los Altos in 1932 and studied for one year at Pomona College in Claremont, California. In 1936 he earned a B.A. in English from Stanford University.

Cranston served as a foreign correspondent for the International News Service from 1936 to 1938 and worked in Washington, D.C., as a representative of the Common Council for American Unity from 1939 to 1941. He married Geneva McMath on 6 November 1940. They had two sons

Alan Cranston, 1990. AP/WIDE WORLD PHOTOS

before their 1977 divorce. Cranston headed the foreign language division of the Office of War Information from 1942 to 1944 and served in the U.S. Army in 1944 and 1945, achieving the rank of sergeant. He wrote *The Killing of the Peace* (1945), a highly acclaimed book recounting the failure of international diplomacy from 1916 to 1923.

Cranston helped pioneer the World Federalist movement after World War II and served as a director of the executive committee of Americans United for World Government. He returned to California in 1947 and made his fortune by expanding his father's successful Palo Alto real estate business. He later became president of Homes for a Better America and vice president of the Carlsberg Financial Corporation.

After chairing the northern California branch of the United World Federalists, Cranston served as national president of the United World Federalists from 1949 to 1952. He formed the California Democratic Council in 1952 to rebuild and invigorate the state Democratic Party and was its first president from 1953 to 1958. In 1954 Cranston joined the executive committee of the Democratic State Central Committee. In 1958 he became the first Democrat elected state controller in seventy-two years and won reelection easily in 1962.

Cranston lost narrowly to Pierre Salinger in the 1964 Democratic Party primary for the U.S. Senate and lost his bid for a third term as state controller in 1966. In 1968 Cranston easily won the Democratic Party primary for the U.S. Senate. The conservative Republican Max Rafferty upset the incumbent senator Thomas Kuchel in the Republican primary, and Cranston defeated Rafferty in the November election, garnering 51.8 percent of the vote. He won reelection, decisively defeating H. L. Richardson in 1974 and trouncing Paul Gann in 1980 with 4.7 million votes, the largest tally ever cast for a Senate candidate. Cranston was a grassroots politician in a media state and a liberal on Governor Ronald W. Reagan's home turf.

Cranston was assigned to the Labor and Public Welfare, the Banking and Currency, the Housing and Urban Affairs, and Veterans' Affairs committees of the Senate. The modest, energetic, hardworking, pragmatic, self-disciplined, health-conscious senator possessed vision, intellectual depth, skill, patience, and creative problem-solving skills. He served as the Democratic Party whip from 1977 to 1990, assisting Senate Minority Leader Robert Byrd, although Byrd differed ideologically with Cranston and was reluctant to delegate responsibilities. Cranston nurtured friendships with numerous senators and was one of the Senate's ablest vote counters. He finished first among the Senate's forty-six Democrats in a poll of Capitol Hill reporters to determine the ten best senators.

Cranston helped behind the scenes to secure adoption of the Panama Canal Treaty in 1977, supported arms reduction among superpowers, opposed the spread of nuclear weapons and arms sales to Arab nations, and backed the use of military force against Iraq in 1991. As Veterans' Affairs Committee chair, he expanded education, health, and housing benefits for veterans. Cranston cosponsored the Equal Rights Amendment and the Clean Air Act, and backed legislation benefiting organized labor, abused or adopted children, senior citizens, the handicapped, and the poor. He opposed President Reagan's and President George H. W. Bush's domestic economic programs and staunchly defended California's economic interests, delivering legislation for California's farmers, aerospace companies, banks and savings and loans, labor unions, entertainment industry, and new Silicon Valley industries.

Cranston's son Robin died in a 1980 automobile accident. His second wife, Norma Weintraub, whom he married in 1978, suffered from Parkinson's disease. Cranston and Weintraub divorced in 1989.

After years of carefully courting centrist voters while not alienating his liberal base, Cranston unsuccessfully sought his party's 1984 presidential nomination. He conducted a liberal campaign, pledging to reduce nuclear arms and to revitalize the struggling economy. The failed venture made Cranston vulnerable to attacks from Republicans, who claimed it exposed his true liberalism and alienated many Californians, who complained it distracted him from his Senate duties. He was reelected to a fourth Senate term in 1986, garnering only 49.3 percent of the vote against the moderate representative Ed Zschau.

In 1989 Cranston and four other senators were cited for intervening with federal thrift regulators to block an investigation of Charles Keating's bankrupt Lincoln Savings and Loan Company. Keating had contributed $1.3 million to their reelection bids and had been indicted on securities and fraud charges that cost taxpayers at least $1 billion. The Senate Ethics Committee held public hearings in November 1990 to determine whether any of the five senators had violated Senate rules against exerting improper influence in return for compensation. Cranston, having been diagnosed with prostate cancer and facing an uphill reelection battle, announced he would not seek reelection in 1992 and stepped down immediately as party whip. He underwent radiation therapy and was unable to testify at the February 1991 public hearings. The committee found that the five senators had violated no law or Senate rule but had exhibited poor judgment. The committee also accused Cranston of violating the Senate's code against improper behavior.

In an unusual plea bargain in November 1991, the Senate took no action on the Ethics Committee report and reprimanded Cranston for his "improper and repugnant" conduct. Cranston accepted the reprimand but seized upon a loophole in the Senate Conduct Code to justify his conduct as a service to constituents. This flouting of ethics cost Cranston his public confidence.

After leaving the Senate in 1993, Cranston chaired the

Gorbachev Foundation USA, a San Francisco–based think tank founded by the former Soviet president Mikhail Gorbachev to promote world peace and nuclear disarmament. An avid reader and physical fitness fanatic, Cranston was devoted to yoga, health diets, and running, and he held the world record for the 100-yard dash for men in his age group. He died of heart failure at his home in Los Altos Hills, California, and his remains were cremated.

Cranston left a mixed legacy. Although not in the mainstream of California politics, he was elected to four Senate terms and proved an effective Democratic Party whip. He exhibited a lifelong dedication to world peace and nuclear arms reduction. He underwent an unsuccessful presidential campaign in which his supposedly national stature netted him little support, and his Senate term ended under the cloud of a scandal.

★

Eleanor Fowle, *Cranston, the Senator from California* (1980), examines Cranston's life through the 1970s. For his pre-senatorial career, see *Current Biography* (1969). For his role in the 1984 presidential election, see Jack W. Germond and Jules Witcover, *Wake Us When It's Over: Presidential Politics of 1984* (1985), and *New York Times Biographical Service* 14 (Dec. 1983): 1,426–1,429. See Margaret Carlson, "Seven Sorry Senators," *Time* (8 Jan. 1990), and *New York Times Biographical Service* 21 (May 1990): 470–471, for information about his involvement in the Keating scandal. An obituary is in the *New York Times* (1 Jan. 2001).

DAVID L. PORTER

Carl T. Curtis, 1977. BETTMANN/CORBIS

CURTIS, Carl Thomas (*b.* 15 March 1905 near Minden, Nebraska; *d.* 24 January 2000 in Lincoln, Nebraska), fiscal conservative and staunch opponent of the New Deal and Great Society who served in the U.S. Congress from 1939 to 1979, longer than any other Nebraskan.

The youngest of eight children, Curtis was the son of Frank Curtis and Alberta Mae (Smith) Curtis. His father worked as a farmer and later as a custodian. Curtis attended public schools in Kearney County, Nebraska, graduating from Minden High School in 1923. From 1924 through 1930 he attended Nebraska Wesleyan University in Lincoln while also teaching public school and studying in a law office. He was admitted to the Nebraska bar in 1930.

Curtis had long had political ambitions. Even as a child he practiced speeches in front of the animals on his father's farm. He came from a Democratic family, and when he ran successfully for Kearney County attorney in 1930, his first political race, it was as a Democrat. He married Lois Wylie Atwater, a local schoolteacher, on 6 June 1931. They adopted two children. Curtis lost his bid for reelection as county attorney in 1934, the only electoral defeat of his career. An admirer of President Herbert Hoover, Curtis felt increasingly uncomfortable with President Franklin D.

Roosevelt's New Deal policies, which he considered wasteful and a threat to liberty. Poverty, hunger, and homelessness, he insisted, should be addressed by private charity and individual responsibility, not by expensive federal programs that increased the deficit. As citizens came to look to Washington, D.C., for help, government power would inevitably increase while individual freedom declined. Curtis derided Social Security, one of the New Deal's signal achievements, as "compulsory collective saving." "I wasn't a good Democrat," he said, explaining his switch to the Republican Party in 1936. Two years later he ran for Congress, beating the Democratic incumbent by a sizable margin. He was reelected seven times.

Curtis entered Congress as an isolationist who favored "strict and absolute" American neutrality in World War II. In his first speech before the House of Representatives, he deplored "America's drift toward war." He opposed Roosevelt's effort to amend the Neutrality Act to allow the export of arms and munitions to belligerent countries. Curtis's position found him, as it often would during his long congressional career, in the minority. In 1941 he voted against the Lend-Lease Act, a proposal to sell or lease military supplies to any nation whose defense the president deemed essential. Convinced that Roosevelt was leading the United States into war, Curtis remained an isolationist until the

Japanese attack on Pearl Harbor. At that point he realized that there was no avoiding conflict. Even so, he claimed that 8 and 11 December 1941, when he supported the congressional declarations of war against Japan and Germany, respectively, were "the worst two days I ever lived through."

A devastating flood of the Republican River in Nebraska in 1935 led to Curtis's most important legislation. While serving on the House Flood Control Committee, he sponsored a resolution that led to the creation of the Pick-Sloan Plan for the Missouri River basin, a blueprint for flood control, irrigation, recreation, and power generation. Although Curtis was an unrelenting critic of most government programs, he distinguished between "welfare programs," which in his view begat dependency, and "public works," which created jobs. Partly as a result of his efforts, the U.S. Army Corps of Engineers constructed numerous dams in the Missouri River basin.

Curtis thought that the expansion of federal power resulting from the New Deal and World War II was a threat to self-reliance, as Americans increasingly looked to Washington for help. He called himself a conservative, which he defined as someone who rejected "the need and the desirability of costly and paternalistic government." If, in forty years in Congress, little legislation bore Curtis's name, it was partly because of his conviction that government needed to be curtailed, not enlarged. Thus, he opposed the school-lunch program on the ground that parents, not the federal government, should provide food for their children. "It didn't hurt me to walk to school carrying a lunch pail," he insisted. He also opposed the food-stamp program and government-subsidized low-income housing.

In 1945 Curtis became a member of the House Ways and Means Committee, which had jurisdiction over tax and Social Security legislation, his focus for the next three decades. He frequently opposed increases in Social Security benefits and in 1951 proposed a constitutional amendment requiring a balanced federal budget. Although this measure was never adopted, he reintroduced versions of it many times.

Curtis decided to quit politics in 1954, but when one of Nebraska's senators died unexpectedly, he ran for the empty seat, winning the first of four terms in the Senate. As a member of the Senate Committee on Government Operations, he took a leading role in investigating labor racketeering. In 1959 he was appointed to the Senate Finance Committee, where he began considering alternatives to Social Security and other traditional pension plans. President Lyndon B. Johnson's Great Society programs of the mid-1960s, aimed in part at alleviating poverty, provided Curtis with numerous opportunities for dissent. On both fiscal and ideological grounds, he voted against Medicare, Medicaid, and federal aid to education. Despite his longstanding belief that reliance on government bred dependency,

however, he supported federal payments to farmers—an important part of his Nebraska constituency. Instead of Social Security, which he saw as a "compulsory collective saving" program, Curtis argued that individuals should have the freedom to invest for retirement as they wished. In 1971 he introduced a proposal for individual retirement accounts (IRAs). Two years later Congress passed a pension bill that included aspects of Curtis's IRA plan.

Curtis's wife died in September 1970. On 1 December 1972 he married Mildred Genier Baker, a registered nurse. Curtis was President Richard M. Nixon's staunchest defender during the Watergate crisis of 1973 and 1974, when a break-in at Democratic Party headquarters in the Watergate complex was traced to the White House. Curtis declared that Nixon was "totally innocent of any wrongdoing." Even after the release of White House tape recordings that implicated the president in a criminal cover-up, Curtis believed that the president had been falsely accused. When other prominent Republicans, including Senator Barry Goldwater of Arizona, turned against Nixon and impeachment loomed, Curtis remained steadfast. Nixon eventually resigned the presidency. In his political autobiography, *Forty Years Against the Tide* (1982), Curtis maintained that Nixon had been "lynched" by his political enemies and the "mass media."

After serving sixteen years in the House and twenty-four years in the Senate, Curtis retired from politics in 1979. He practiced law in Washington, D.C., for four years before retiring to Nebraska.

Curtis was a Republican conservative during four decades of Democratic control of Congress, a period that saw the implementation of Roosevelt's New Deal and Lyndon Johnson's Great Society. With the notable exception of the civil rights laws of the 1960s, which he supported, Curtis's main objective, expressed in the title of his memoir, was to resist what he saw as the dominant political liberalism of the era. Curtis entered Congress determined to oppose the growth of the federal government. While he did not succeed in this, his 1975 victory over Senator Jacob Javits, a moderate New Yorker, as chair of the Senate Republican Caucus, demonstrated the ascendancy of the conservative wing of the party, a dominance that would be confirmed five years later by the nomination of Ronald Reagan for president.

★

Curtis wrote two books: *To Remind* (1982), a daily devotional, and, with Regis Courtemanche, *Forty Years Against the Tide: Congress and the Welfare State* (1982). The second volume, which is part biography, part history, and part political argument, is indispensable for understanding Curtis's career from his perspective. Obituaries are in the *New York Times, Washington Post,* and *Omaha World-Herald* (all 26 Jan. 2000).

FRED NIELSEN

D

DALLIN, Alexander   (*b.* 21 May 1924 in Berlin, Germany; *d.* 22 July 2000 in Stanford, California), historian and political scientist who was one of America's foremost experts on Soviet Russia for half a century.

Dallin was the son of David Dallin, a leader of the moderate, so-called Menshevik, faction of the Social Democratic Party of pre-Soviet Russia. Although David Dallin continued to represent Menshevik interests following the revolution in late 1917, his position became increasingly untenable as Bolshevik (Leninist) control increased, and in 1921 he fled, with his wife, Eugenia (Bein) Dallin, to Berlin, where Alexander was born three years later.

With the approach of World War II, the Dallins fled again, first to France. But after the German victory over France in the summer of 1940, the Dallins felt forced to leave once again. Dallin and his mother crossed the Pyrenees in a southward journey, finally reaching Portugal in late 1940. There they were joined by David Dallin. The family arrived in New York City in late November 1940.

Dallin earned a B.S. from City College of New York in 1947. A year later he received an M.A. from Columbia University, and in 1953 he completed his Ph.D., also at Columbia. Thanks to his unusual background, Dallin was fluent in Russian, German, and French. From 1951 to 1954 he was the associate director of Columbia's research program on the USSR and from 1954 to 1956 director of research for the War Documentation Project in Washington,

D.C., where he worked with documents captured when the Germans surrendered in 1945.

In 1956 Dallin joined the Columbia faculty, becoming Adlai Stevenson Professor of International Relations in 1965, and heading Columbia's renowned Russian Institute from 1962 to 1967. Through most of the 1960s Dallin also served as a consultant to the federal government. In 1971 Dallin moved to Stanford University, where in 1983 he became chairman of the department of international relations. In 1985 he was named director of the Stanford Center for Russian and East European Studies, and in 1987 he became Raymond A. Spruance Professor of International History. Dallin was one of the organizers of the European University, established in Saint Petersburg, Russia, in 1994. He formally retired that same year.

A prolific author and editor, Dallin based his first major work, *German Rule in Russia, 1941–1945: A Study of Occupation Policies* (1957), on his studies of captured German army records and on numerous interviews with Soviet émigrés conducted as part of the Harvard Interview Project, funded by the U.S. Air Force. Reissued in 1981 in a revised edition, this massive work demonstrates his ability to handle a vast array of primary sources and to fashion them into a coherent narrative.

His other works were of three types. Original volumes of which he served as sole author, such as *The Soviet Union at the United Nations* (1962) and *The Soviet Union and Disarmament* (1965), tended to be more interpretive

Alexander Dallin, December 1968. AP/WIDE WORLD PHOTOS

Scientists, he concluded that Soviet foreign policy was determined more by internal forces than by the Soviet leaders' perceptions of America or the developing nations. In this assessment he differed from many American conservatives, who believed that America's rearmament during the 1980s was the primary force propelling the eventual dissolution of the Soviet system.

During the 1980s Dallin served as president of the International Council for Soviet and East European Studies, which became the World Congress for Central and East European Studies after the collapse of the Soviet Union. He was scheduled to make a presentation at a meeting of the group in Finland at the time of his death from a stroke suffered on the preceding day. He was survived by Lapidus and by his three children from his first marriage.

Following Dallin's death, his colleagues at Stanford and elsewhere created the Alexander Dallin Fund to support research on the subjects that engaged Dallin: the governmental policies of the USSR and its successor regimes, particularly the foreign policies of Russia and the fifteen other entities that made up the Soviet sphere of influence.

Widely known and esteemed by experts on Russian history and politics for his detached and scholarly approach to communism, Dallin was an unflagging participant in all kinds of collaborative efforts to investigate and explain Soviet Russia. He always maintained a scholarly balance laced with dry humor, a quality cited by all his associates, and his preference for the role of editor may reflect the self-effacing character that so many of his colleagues also cite in their remembrances of him.

★

Information on Dallin's work and life can be gleaned from both his *German Rule in Russia: A Study of Occupation Policies* (1957; rev. ed., 1981) and *Soviet Conduct in World Affairs: A Selection of Readings* (1960), which he edited. See also Daniel Abele, *Looking Back at Sovietology: An Interview with William Odom and Alexander Dallin* (1990), and *Reexamining the Soviet System: Essays in Honor of Alexander Dallin* (1996), edited by David Holloway and Norman M. Naimark. An obituary is in the *New York Times* (27 July 2000).

NANCY M. GORDON

than *German Rule* had been. Other works were collaborations, among them *Political Terror in Communist Systems* (1970), with George W. Breslauer. In the bulk of his later publications, however, he served as editor. Many of these were collaborative projects: *Soviet Politics Since Khrushchev* (1968), with Thomas B. Larson; *Women in Russia* (1977), with Dorothy Atkinson and Gail W. Lapidus (Lapidus became Dallin's second wife); and *The Gorbachev Era* (1986), with the future national security adviser Condoleezza Rice, then a colleague at Stanford. In *The Soviet System: From Crisis to Collapse* (1991), he and Lapidus presented an enormous collection of works by others, with an introductory essay by the two. A revised second edition appeared in 1995.

As a dominant figure in scholarly research on the Soviet Union, Dallin ensured that expert judgments on the central issue of American foreign policy would be informed by solid information. His linguistic skills enabled him to explore multiple sources, and he brought these to bear in writing about the many crises that characterized the U.S. relationship with the Soviet Union. In particular, Dallin highlighted the complex forces that dictated Soviet policy. In a 1983 article published in the *Bulletin of the Atomic*

DANA, Charles Anderson, Jr. (*b.* 7 January 1915 in New York City, *d.* 9 May 2001 in Manhattan, New York City), philanthropist of diverse interests, most noted for his work as director of the Dana Foundation.

Dana was the elder of two children born to Charles A. Dana, Sr., New York State legislator, industrialist, and philanthropist, and Agnes (Ladson) Dana, a homemaker. He came from a distinguished family that included not only

Richard Henry Dana, author of *Two Years Before the Mast,* but also the first Charles Anderson Dana, a journalist and member of President Abraham Lincoln's War Department. An attorney at the beginning of his career, Dana's father had represented a company that made universal joints, and made a wise investment in the firm that resulted in his accruing a fortune. He ran the company for years, and it was named for him in 1946. The elder Dana's humanitarian philosophy led him to contribute millions of dollars to a wide range of causes, and in 1950 he cofounded the Charles A. Dana Foundation, which became the center of his charitable activities.

Dana graduated from Saint Paul's School in Concord, New Hampshire, in 1933 and matriculated at Princeton University, from which he graduated with a degree in economics in 1937. He shared his father's interests and love of philanthropy and spent more than fifty years of his life channeling money to more than thirty charities. Dana signed the incorporation papers for the Dana Foundation with his father and was thus a founding member of a private, nonprofit, philanthropic organization that concentrated its giving in the fields of science, health, and education. Throughout his career as a director of the cash-rich foundation, Dana—who once remarked that his father was "a tough act to follow"—continued the tradition of philanthropy established by the elder Dana.

Dana married Marion "Bunny" Turrell in 1940; they had two children and divorced in 1951. In 1952 he married Eleanor Waters Langhore; they had one child and divorced in 1965. He married his third wife, Norma, in 1966; they had no children.

As a young man, Dana met Dr. Sidney Farber, a nationally recognized cancer expert, on a train trip, and urged his father to meet with him. That meeting resulted in the establishment of the Dana-Farber Cancer Institute, one of the leading cancer research and treatment centers in the country. Dana devoted his life to philanthropy. In addition to his work for the Dana Foundation and the Dana-Farber Cancer Institute, he served as a trustee of the Museum of the City of New York, the United Cerebral Palsy Research and Education Foundation, the New Canaan Nature Center, and the board of overseers of the Hoover Institution. He was a life trustee of the Mount Sinai–New York University Medical Center and Health System and served as honorary chairman of the Lyford Cay Foundation. A member of the advisory board of Hazelden, a New York drug treatment center, he also served on the board of the Alcoholism Council of New York as president for many years. Additionally, he sat on the board of Just One Break, a nonprofit agency representing disabled workers in the New York City area.

Dana was an active member of the James Madison Council of the Library of Congress, tasked with providing funding for an array of exhibitions, publications, and other outreach projects for the public. He was a member of the President's Committee on the Arts and Humanities during the administration of President Ronald W. Reagan and also was president of the Cadan Corporation, a private investment company. In 1986 the Dana Foundation instituted a program for "pioneering achievements" in health and education. The foundation contributed millions of dollars for the construction of educational facilities and funded research and experimental programs. In 1989 the foundation honored First Lady Nancy Reagan with a $50,000 award to the Nancy Reagan Drug Abuse Fund in recognition of her efforts to educate young Americans about the dangers of drug abuse.

In the early 1990s the Charles A. Dana Center, supported in part by major grants from the Dana Foundation and the National Science Foundation, was established at the University of Texas in Austin. The center operates more than forty interrelated projects focused on improving student achievement throughout Texas and provides educational resources for homeless children and youth in the state. During the latter part of the twentieth century and the beginning of the twenty-first, the Dana Foundation committed a large portion of its resources to research on the human brain and worked with leading scientists to focus global attention on the the progress being made against brain diseases.

At the time of its fiftieth anniversary in 2000, the Dana Foundation had appropriated $272 million for philanthropic purposes. At the anniversary celebration, the organization paid tribute to five of America's former first ladies, among other achievers, as winners of awards for their "pioneering achievements." Also in 2000, the Dana Foundation provided $7.4 million to establish a new center for neuro-oncology research at the Dana-Farber Institute. In more than four decades the Dana Foundation has awarded more than $33 million to the institute.

Among the numerous charitable organizations to which Dana donated, in addition to the Dana Foundation, were the Freedom Institute, the Museum of the City of New York, the Central Park Conservancy, and the Hospital for Special Surgery. For more than twenty years he supported the Dana Center for Orthopaedic Implants at the Hospital for Special Surgery, which enabled the hospital to make tremendous strides in musculoskeletal research. Dana further supported numerous programs at Columbia University College of Physicians and Surgeons, including the Dana post-doctoral program in brain and behavior, which brings new investigators into brain behavior research. In connection with his interest in the Central Park Conservancy in New York City, Dana helped restore the Upper Park and sponsored nature programs for Harlem residents. The

Charles A. Dana Discovery Center in Harlem serves more than seventy thousand children, teens, and adults each year.

When he was not working, Dana was an enthusiastic sportsman, riding horses until he was thrown and injured at the age of seventy-six and playing tennis and golf into his eighties. He had residences in New York City; New Canaan, Connecticut; and Nassau, Bahamas. At the age of eighty-six, Dana was struck by a vehicle on Madison Avenue and died at Bellevue Hospital. Following a memorial service at Saint James Episcopal Church in New York City, his cremated remains were buried in New Canaan.

Born into a wealthy family, Dana used his wealth to raise the quality of life for the less fortunate by being a loyal supporter of nonprofit organizations. After his death, the *Princeton Alumni Weekly* described Dana as an "entrepreneur and modest achiever, trout fisherman and ardent Princetonian." Edward Rover, president of the Dana Foundation, remembered him as "a wonderful director" who was always "clear on the importance of using our resources to the greatest advantage for the most people." The Dana Foundation chairman William Safire recalled, "He was always a force for better facilities for higher education." Said his son Charles A. Dana III of Newport, Rhode Island, "The essence of my father was his humanness. His warmth was always there."

★

While there are numerous books about Dana's well-known relatives, there are no biographies of Dana. A brief overview of the Dana Foundation awards for "pioneering achievements" is in the *New York Times* (9 Nov. 1989). An obituary is in the *New York Times* (12 May 2001), and a memorial tribute is in the *Princeton Alumni Weekly* (12 Sept. 2001).

HOPE E. YOUNG
MARIA RECIO

DANCER, Faye Katherine   (*b*. 24 April 1925 in Santa Monica, California; *d*. 22 May 2002 in Los Angeles, California), one of the best and most colorful players of the All-American Girls Professional Baseball League of the 1940s, who served as inspiration for a character in the film *A League of Their Own* (1992).

Dancer and her brother grew up in West Los Angeles with their parents, Lloyd Augustus Dancer, a Los Angeles Department of Water and Power inspector, and Olive Victoria (Pope) Dancer, a homemaker. She began playing softball in grade school, and at age eleven was playing in a merchant-sponsored softball league. As she later said, "I ate, slept, and dreamed about playing ball." She recalled practicing slides on the Santa Monica beach, and lying in bed at night visualizing her swing. From 1940 to 1942,

while still in high school, Dancer played for the Dr Peppers, a Class A amateur girls' softball team sponsored by the soft-drink manufacturer. The league played their games at Fiedler Field in Los Angeles. Dancer's brother remembered her playing in All-Star games against movie stars. She graduated from West Los Angeles University High School.

With male baseball players away fighting World War II, the chewing-gum magnate Phil Wrigley organized the All-American Girls Softball League (AAGSL) in 1943. The league's name was eventually changed to All-American Girls Professional Baseball League (AAGPBL). In 1944 a West Coast scout recruited Dancer. She was just eighteen, weighed 145 pounds, and stood five feet, six inches tall. Dancer and five other California girls reported to spring training in Peru, Illinois. Dancer then was assigned to play for the Minneapolis Millerettes, an expansion team, for their premier season. As a professional ballplayer, her salary was $75 a week, with an additional $2.50 a day for meals—impressive wages at the time, when baseball players' pay was modest at best.

Dancer's career lasted six seasons. She played for the Minnesota Millerettes in 1944, the Fort Wayne Daisies from 1945 through mid-1947, and the Peoria Redwings for part of 1947 as well as in 1948 and 1950. Over the course of her career she played outfield, infield, and pitcher. On the field Dancer was known for her skills as a player as well as for her clowning. A highly talented athlete, as her lifelong friend and fellow AAGPBL player Lavonne ("Pepper") Paire Davis remembered, "She was that rare breed of ballplayer that could lay down a perfect bunt, then steal second base. Then, the next time up, . . . knock it out of the ballpark." She earned the nickname "All the Way Faye."

Known as a power hitter and a base stealer, in 1945 Dancer shared the AAGPBL home-run record and in 1948 finished second behind Sophie Kurys in stolen bases, with 108. Sportswriters referred to her as a "fly-catching genius." Her picture appeared in *Life* magazine in 1945 with the caption "heavy hitter." A 1948 photo of Dancer sliding into third base is on display, along with her spikes and glove, as part of the Women in Baseball exhibit at the National Baseball Hall of Fame at Cooperstown, New York.

Dancer's antics made her popular with the fans but not with the AAGPBL chaperones. Loving the spotlight, she thrived on the attention of the crowd. To amuse them, she did splits, handstands, and cartwheels on the field. Once she caught fireflies and pinned them to her hat. Another time she called an unofficial time-out to get a drink of water. As Dancer recalled, "I'll probably be remembered as a crowd favorite, a little crazy . . . I always had fun."

Dancer also was known as a rebel. She and Davis were known to slip out for a few beers and then sneak back into the hotel after the 10:00 P.M. curfew. Team chaperones often were victims of her pranks. Some of her favorite gags included putting Limburger cheese on the light bulbs in their rooms, squeezing toothpaste into their Oreo cookies, and smearing peanut butter on their toilet seats. She was once fined for throwing a chaperone off a bus when the chaperone tried to take a beer from her. Dancer was also superstitious, or at least she led fans to believe she was. She claimed that having a fan rub a glass eye during a game brought the team luck. Consequently, she collected glass eyes wherever she went. She claimed that the most difficult glass eye she collected came from a carousel, and it took her eighteen rides to extract it. Stuffed animals and mounted fish also were fair game.

Among Dancer's most memorable experiences was playing baseball for a barnstorming team coached by the legendary athlete Jim Thorpe. Apparently, some of his ballplayers became disgruntled and walked out, leaving Thorpe in breach of contract. Dancer and some of the other AAGPBL players who were on their way to spring training came to his rescue.

Dancer's professional playing career ended in 1950, when she ruptured a spinal disc sliding into base. She was only twenty-five years old. After her AAGPBL career ended, she went to work full-time for Howard Hughes Aircraft as an electronics specialist, having previously worked for the company in the baseball off-season. Later she worked as a technician for Henry Electronics, retiring at age seventy-four. According to her brother, Dancer was an encyclopedia of baseball trivia. An avid fan of the Los Angeles Dodgers and Lakers, she often attended games with other AAGPBL players who lived in the Los Angeles area.

Dancer was reportedly thrilled with *A League of Their Own,* which depicted the exploits of AAGPBL players at the height of their wartime fame. The character of "All the Way" Mae Mordabito, played by Madonna, was based on Dancer. She also was delighted to have her photograph taken with Madonna and Geena Davis, who portrayed Pepper Davis in the film. In later years Dancer served as a member of the board of the AAGPBL Player's Association, which worked to bring public recognition of the league. She also was a member of the Golden Diamond Girls, a group of former players who traveled to card shows to sign autographs. Dancer, whose fiancé was killed in World War II, never married. She died at the age of seventy-seven after surgery for breast cancer at the University of California Los Angeles Medical Center. She is buried at Woodlawn Cemetery in Santa Monica.

★

Information on Dancer and the AAPGBL can be found in Sue Macy, *A Whole New Ball Game: The Story of the All-American Girls Professional Baseball League* (1993). See also Gai Berlage, *Women in Baseball: The Forgotten History* (1994); Susan E. Johnson, *When Women Played Hardball* (1994); and W. C. Madden, *The Women of the All-American Girls Professional Baseball League: A Biographical Dictionary* (1997). Obituaries are in the *Los Angeles Times* (1 June 2002) and *New York Times* (9 June 2002).

GAI INGHAM BERLAGE

DANIEL, (Elbert) Clifton, Jr. (*b.* 19 September 1912 in Zebulon, North Carolina; *d.* 21 February 2000 in New York City), foreign correspondent, Washington bureau chief, and managing editor for the *New York Times.*

Daniel, who grew up in the lumber-mill town of Zebulon in northeastern North Carolina, was the only child of Elbert Clifton Daniel, a pharmacist, and Elvah (Jones) Daniel, a homemaker. "I got the notion rather early in my life of going into journalism," he later recalled, "and I think I really picked up this notion from . . . reading about various careers in boys' magazines." Soon afterward, he began submitting reports about school athletic events to the local weekly, the *Zebulon Record.* "Some of these things were published, which was fatal," Daniel said, "because I never recovered from the delights of seeing my name in print." During his high school years, he worked summers for the *Record* and also in his father's drugstore.

Following his 1929 graduation from Wakelon School near Zebulon, Daniel attended the University of North Carolina at Chapel Hill, where he majored in English, studied journalism, reported for the *Daily Tar Heel,* served as editor of the *Carolina* literary magazine, joined Phi Delta Theta fraternity, and was elected vice president of the student body. He passed up an opportunity to run for the student body presidency "because I already had the notion—perhaps somewhat presumptuous—that I was a newspaperman, and that newspapermen should stay out of party politics."

Upon his graduation with a B.A. in 1933, Daniel became the associate editor of the *Daily Bulletin* in Dunn, North Carolina. From 1934 through 1937 he worked as a reporter and political columnist for the *Raleigh News and Observer.* At the beginning of his newspaper career, he used the by-line "E. C. Daniel, Jr.," because he had never cared for his first name. Daniel joined the Associated Press (AP) in 1937 and worked in its New York City bureau for two years, then transferred to the Washington, D.C., bureau, becoming its youngest member. He covered the U.S. War and Navy departments on the eve of World War II.

From late 1940 through 1955, Daniel lived abroad and gained renown for his international reporting. His first overseas assignment was as a member of the AP bureau in Bern, Switzerland. "That was at the very center of Europe,

Clifton Daniel (*right*), being congratulated by former president Harry Truman upon winning the Overseas Press Club Award, April 1956. BETTMANN/CORBIS

and a good listening post, but relatively inactive because Switzerland was a neutral country," he said years later. Daniel transferred to London in 1941 and made his reputation as foreign correspondent and news editor. "Clifton Daniel was not only a very fast and facile writer," Gay Talese wrote in *The Kingdom and the Power,* "but had often been put in charge of running the AP's London bureau during its most hectic hours and had always functioned calmly and efficiently."

In February 1944 Daniel began a thirty-three-year career with the *New York Times* when he was hired as a member of the newspaper's London bureau. He covered Supreme Headquarters of the Allied Expeditionary Forces, then followed the advance of the U.S. First Army through France into Belgium and Germany. "The big dirty trucks speed along the Rue La Fayette, their heavy tires singing on the cobblestones and their canvas tops snapping in the winter wind," he reported from Paris in March 1945. "The men [are] tired and cramped after eleven hours on the road. . . . But one of them peers out, sees the name of the street and says, 'La Fayette, we're here.'"

During the early postwar years, as the senior Middle East correspondent for the *Times,* Daniel covered the Soviet

withdrawal from northern Iran; the emergence of Arab nationalism, including the Egyptian revolution that toppled King Farouk; the battles between the Jewish underground and British forces in Palestine; and the creation of the State of Israel.

In 1952 Daniel returned to the London bureau and reported the death of King George VI and the coronation of Queen Elizabeth II. After a brief stint as chief of the *Times* bureau in West Germany, he went to Moscow in 1954 as the only full-time correspondent for a noncommunist western newspaper. Daniel reported on the power shift that followed Joseph Stalin's death, as Nikita S. Khrushchev began his rise to leadership. He described the "cruel snowladen wind blowing straight out of the pages of Russian history . . . and through the frozen streets of Moscow." In 1955 Daniel covered President Dwight D. Eisenhower's summit conference in Geneva with Khrushchev and British Prime Minister Anthony Eden. "That about terminated my foreign career," he recalled. "I came back to the United States with the idea of being prepared for and training for executive responsibilities."

Turner Catledge, the managing editor of the *Times,* groomed Daniel for senior management by naming him assistant to the foreign news editor in 1956, assistant to the managing editor in 1957, and assistant managing editor in 1959. "An important factor in my selection of Daniel was his proven ability as a reporter," Catledge later wrote. "One of the *Times'* biggest problems in those days was that almost all its editors came up from the copy desks and had little or no reporting experience." Daniel gained high marks for his coordination of the *Times* coverage of the 1963 assassination of President John F. Kennedy.

In September 1964, when Catledge was promoted to executive editor, Daniel moved up to managing editor, and served in this role for the next five years. As the senior news executive, Daniel made the *Times* more readable and lively through the innovative use of pictures and graphics, as well as expanded cultural coverage. He revolutionized the obituary section and added to the *Times* status as "the newspaper of record" by assigning writers to interview public figures for the preparation of advance obituaries. As managing editor, Daniel led his newspaper's coverage of the U.S. civil rights revolution, the escalation of the war in Vietnam, the Six-Day War between Israel and its Arab neighbors, the 1968 assassinations of the Reverend Dr. Martin Luther King, Jr., and Robert F. Kennedy, and the landing of the Apollo astronauts on the Moon. Daniel regarded the Moon landing as the most important event of the decade, and gave it the largest headline the *Times* had ever produced.

From late 1969 through 1972, Daniel served as associate editor, then moved to Washington, D.C., where he was chief of the *Times* bureau through 1976. In this role he strengthened the bureau's commitment to investigative reporting, improved political coverage, and played a major role in the newspaper's coverage of the Watergate scandal. Following his retirement from the *Times* in 1977, he wrote a memoir, *Lords, Ladies and Gentlemen* (1984), and edited the best-selling *Chronicle of the Twentieth Century* (1987).

Daniel, who had brown eyes and wavy gray hair, was of medium height. Distinguished-looking, he had a courtly manner, and spoke in a soft southern accent. Long known as the best-dressed man in American journalism, he wore Saville Row tailored suits.

On 21 April 1956 Daniel married the writer Margaret Truman, the daughter of President Harry S. Truman, at Trinity Episcopal Church in Independence, Missouri. Their marriage produced four sons. "I've often said that it was a good thing Clifton was a working newspaperman and understood the ways of the press," Mrs. Daniel wrote in her 1972 biography of her father. "Otherwise I think he might have developed a giant inferiority complex as an ex-president's son-in-law." Daniel, who liked and admired the former president, enjoyed their association. "Mr. Truman was not only a great president—but he was also a great father-in-law," Daniel wrote in his memoir. Daniel and his wife lived in New York City, where he died from complications related to a stroke and heart disease.

Daniel, who gained renown as a foreign correspondent, went on to make his mark as one of the more influential editors of his generation. His vision and leadership helped to bring the *New York Times* into the modern era, and enhanced its position as the dominant force in U.S. journalism.

★

The Clifton Daniel papers are housed at the Harry S. Truman Library in Independence, Missouri. Daniel published a memoir, *Lords, Ladies and Gentlemen* (1984). Margaret Truman, *Harry S. Truman* (1972), and Clifton Truman Daniel, *Growing Up With My Grandfather* (1995), are also illuminating. For more background on Daniel's career with the *Times,* see Gay Talese, *The Kingdom and the Power* (1969); Turner Catledge, *My Life and the "Times"* (1971); Harrison Salisbury, *Without Fear or Favor* (1980); James Reston, *Deadline: A Memoir* (1991); Richard F. Shepard, *The Paper's Papers: A Reporter's Journey through the Archives of the "New York Times"* (1996); and Max Frankel, *The Times of My Life and My Life with the "Times"* (1999). An obituary is in the *New York Times* (22 Feb. 2000). Daniel is also the subject of an oral history interview conducted in May 1972 by J. R. Fuchs for the Truman Library.

STEVE NEAL

DAVIS, Benjamin O(liver), Jr. (*b.* 18 December 1912 in Washington, D.C.; *d.* 4 July 2002 in Washington, D.C.), pioneering fighter pilot, commander of the Tuskegee Airmen during World War II, and the first African-American general in the U.S. Air Force.

Davis was the son of a career military officer, Benjamin O. Davis, one of only two African-American combat officers in the U.S. Army. At the time of Davis's birth, near his mother's family in Washington, D.C., his father was stationed with the Ninth U.S. Cavalry at Fort Russell, Wyoming. His mother, Elnora (Dickerson) Davis, was a seamstress prior to her marriage. Davis was the second of three children, and when his mother died in 1916, he and his siblings went to live with their grandparents until his father married Sadie Overton in 1919. Davis learned about discrimination in the military by observing his father's struggles in the army. For most of his career, the elder Davis was assigned to minor postings such as teaching military science at all-black colleges, instead of receiving the combat assignments he desired. Army policy dictated that he could not command white troops, or be placed in a situation in which he outranked white officers.

Davis attended Central High School in Cleveland, where he was the student council president. At age fourteen

Benjamin O. Davis, Jr.

and physically for the assignment, but he was rejected because there were no African-American flying units. The army would not allow Davis to train with white officers, and when he was advised to pursue a civilian career, he refused. "Still optimistic, and perhaps a little conceited," he wrote in his autobiography, "I thought that I had enough to offer that the Army might, under certain conditions, change its ridiculous policies and open its ranks to all who could contribute."

In September 1936 Davis was assigned to the Twenty-fourth Infantry, an all-black unit at Fort Benning, Georgia. There his isolation continued. He was refused admission to the officers' club because of his race, a slight that he considered "one of the most insulting actions taken against me during my military service." After completing advanced infantry training, Davis was assigned to teach the Reserve Officers Training Corps at Tuskegee Institute in Alabama, as his father had.

In 1940, as President Franklin D. Roosevelt sought a third term as president, pressure mounted to expand opportunities for African Americans in the armed forces. Roosevelt promoted Davis's father to brigadier general, making him the first African American to attain that rank. The U.S. War Department also announced that African Americans would be trained for all air corps specialties, including as pilots. After months of delay, plans were launched to create an aviation facility for African-American troops at Tuskegee. The younger Davis was sent to aviation school at the new base, where he became one of the first five African Americans to successfully complete the U.S. Army Air Corps flying program.

In May 1942 Davis was promoted to lieutenant colonel and given command of the Ninety-ninth Pursuit Squadron, the first all-black air unit. Standing a "trim six feet two inches, with a sometimes piercing gaze, a deep voice, and erect military bearing," according to a 2002 *New York Times* article, Davis was well suited to command. He supervised the men of the Ninety-ninth during their training and transit overseas to fight in World War II. The squadron saw its first combat over North Africa in June 1943, and soon afterward supported the Allied invasion of Sicily, Italy.

Davis went back to Tuskegee in August 1943 to assume command of the 332nd Fighter Group. At a Washington, D.C., press conference shortly after returning from the Mediterranean, Davis described the heavy burden the Tuskegee Airmen felt. Each man under his command had to forego the routine pleasures enjoyed by other servicemen because "his task is far greater, his responsibility is much heavier, and his reward is the advancement of his people." Davis defended his troops against reports that they had not performed well under fire, and persuaded military authorities to continue preparing his men for combat.

In January 1944 the 332nd arrived in Ramitelli, Italy,

he went for a ride in an open-cockpit airplane, and, as he later recalled, after that brief flight he was gripped by "a sudden surge of determination to become an aviator." After graduating from high school in 1929, he studied mathematics at Fisk University in Nashville, Tennessee, for the summer term and then attended Western Reserve University in Cleveland for one year. He spent the 1930–1931 academic year, as well as the autumn term of 1931, at the University of Chicago, and also attended Ohio State University in Columbus for the 1931 summer term. But what he wanted most was to become a pilot.

Deciding to follow his father into the army, Davis won an appointment to the U.S. Military Academy at West Point, New York, in 1932. West Point was a hostile environment for an African-American cadet. During his four years at the academy, Davis was completely shunned: no one spoke to him outside of the line of duty, and he lived alone because no other cadet would room with him. Despite this persecution, he graduated thirty-fifth in a class of 276 in 1936. He was only the fourth African American to graduate from West Point, and the first in the twentieth century. Two weeks after completing his studies, on 20 June 1936, he wed Agatha ("Aggie") Scott.

Early in his senior year, Davis applied for pilot training in the U.S. Army Air Corps. He was qualified academically

where they escorted U.S. bombers on more than 200 missions deep into German territory. Davis was proud of the outstanding combat record compiled by the Tuskegee Airmen—111 enemy planes shot down, 273 destroyed or damaged on the ground, and no U.S. bombers lost to enemy fighters. Davis flew sixty combat missions himself, receiving the Silver Star and Distinguished Flying Cross for bravery.

After World War II, Davis commanded Lockbourne Air Force Base outside Columbus, Ohio, from 1946 to 1949. Racial segregation was still the rule in the armed forces, but change was in the air. In 1948 President Harry S. Truman issued Executive Order 9981, preparing the way for desegregation of the military. Davis played a critical role in integrating the U.S. Air Force, which was formed from the U.S. Army Air Corps in 1947. He helped supervise the deactivation of all-black units, and the reassignment of their personnel. By December 1950, as other branches of the armed forces lagged far behind, the desegregation of the air force was nearly complete.

During the Korean War, Davis served as the chief of the Air Force Fighter Branch. In 1954 he became the first African-American general in the air force. In following years Davis held positions of increasing responsibility in the United States and abroad, completing his service as the assistant commander of the U.S. Strike Command. Wearing the three stars of a lieutenant general, he retired from the U.S. Air Force in January 1970, after thirty-seven years in the military.

Later that month Davis arrived in Cleveland to become the first African-American director of public safety for a major U.S. city. Mayor Carl Stokes (the first African-American mayor of a major city) asked Davis to stem a rising crime rate and ease tensions between the police and the city's African-American population. Davis lasted only six months in the job, however, resigning in July 1970 after differing with the mayor over his handling of black extremist groups. In his letter of resignation he wrote, "I am not receiving from you and your administration the support my programs require, and the enemies of law enforcement continue to receive support and comfort from you and your administration."

President Richard M. Nixon appointed Davis to the Commission on Campus Unrest in June 1970. As the director of civil aviation security for the U.S. Department of Transportation beginning in September 1970, Davis was responsible for developing anti-hijacking security measures, including the federal sky marshal program. He was the assistant secretary of transportation for safety and consumer affairs from 1971 until 1975. He remained active in retirement, sitting on numerous corporate and civic boards, including the Air Force Academy Board of Visitors, Commission on Military Compensation, and American Battle Monuments Commission.

In 1998 President Bill Clinton presented Davis with his fourth star, promoting him to full general. Clinton lauded his accomplishments, saying, "General Davis is here today as living proof that a person can overcome adversity and discrimination, achieve great things, turn skeptics into believers; and through example and perseverance, one person can truly bring extraordinary change." Four months after his wife of sixty-five years passed away, Davis died at age eighty-nine of Alzheimer's disease at Walter Reed Army Medical Center in Washington, D.C. He is buried at Arlington National Cemetery in Virginia.

Davis was a pioneer in many areas. He endured rejection and abuse to pursue a career in the segregated army, and persisted to attain his dream of becoming a fighter pilot. He led the most distinguished African-American fighting unit in World War II, and the record compiled by airmen under his command persuaded military leaders that, given proper training and leadership, African Americans could fight as well as any other servicemen. His leadership and personal integrity helped assure the smooth dismantling of military segregation. Due in large part to Davis's contributions, the U.S. armed forces were a model of successful racial integration at the end of the twentieth century.

★

Davis's papers are held at the Smithsonian Institution's National Air and Space Museum's Udvar-Hazy Center at Washington Dulles International Airport. His autobiography, *Benjamin O. Davis, Jr.: American* (1991), is the best single source for information about his life. Davis's post–World War II contributions are covered in Alan L. Gropman, *The Air Force Integrates, 1945–1964* (1998). Obituaries are in the *Washington Post* (6 July 2002) and *New York Times* (7 July 2002).

PAUL T. MURRAY

DAVIS, James Houston ("Jimmie") (*b.* 11 September 1899 [?] in Quitman, Louisiana; *d.* 5 November 2000 in Baton Rouge, Louisiana), two-time governor of Louisiana and singer and guitarist who recorded "You Are My Sunshine" and many other songs.

Davis was born to sharecropper parents Sam Jones Davis and Sara (Works) Davis, in such obscurity that his birth was not recorded. It may have taken place on 10 September or 11 September at any time between 1899 and 1903, although 1899 was finally declared the official year. A similar uncertainty applies to his place of birth; some sources say Quitman, Louisiana, some say he was born in Beech Springs. He was the eldest of eleven children, all of whom grew up together in a two-room shack.

Despite the family's poverty, Davis's father instilled in his children a love of learning. Davis graduated in a class of three from Beech Springs School, then attended Louisiana College, a small Baptist school in Pineville, Louisiana, where he earned a B.A. in history. He later received an M.A. in history from Louisiana State University. In 1927 he joined the faculty of Dodd College, a women's school in Shreveport, Louisiana, where he taught history.

One year later, Davis took a job as a court clerk in Shreveport, where he would remain for most of the 1930s. Throughout this time, he continued to pursue a career in country music. Although he could neither read nor write music, he picked out tunes on his guitar and recorded for RCA Victor Records. His first hit record was "Nobody's Darling but Mine" in 1934. In the mid-1930s Davis married Alverna Adams, a member of an old Shreveport family, who played classical piano and could write down his compositions for him. The couple had one son. In 1938 he ran a successful campaign for office as Shreveport's commissioner of public safety.

On 4 February 1940 Davis recorded the song that would make him famous, "You Are My Sunshine." He is widely believed to have written it, but Steven Tucker, a Tulane University historian, discovered that it was actually written by Paul Rice, who sold the rights to Davis for a sum variously reported as $250 and $17.50. The song soon became a hit for Davis's own recording and for versions recorded by Bing Crosby and Gene Autry. King George VI of England declared it his favorite song, and it was later recorded by more than 350 artists and translated into over thirty languages.

In 1942 Davis became Louisiana's public service commissioner, and in 1943 ran for governor. At first, he thought music was too undignified for a political campaign, and opponents tried to make hay of such Davis songs as "Honky Tonk Blues." He then realized that the electorate loved his music, and sang a few songs at each campaign stop. When one of his rivals, Earl Long, suggested that even if elected, Davis might run off to Hollywood if he got a good offer there, Davis cheerfully admitted that he probably would. He was elected. (Davis eventually appeared as himself in 1947 in *Louisiana,* a laughably clichéd portrayal of his political career, and had minor singing and acting roles in other films.)

As governor, Davis took action to support his state's timber industry, introducing a forestry act that mandated responsible harvesting practices. Another notable effort was to require the licensing of motor vehicle drivers, a first in Louisiana history. He also established a state retirement system. Although Davis did not raise taxes, at the end of his term there was a substantial surplus in the state treasury.

Forbidden by law from succeeding himself as governor, Davis returned to his farm and his musical career. In the 1950s, however, Davis saw a chance to return to politics, and he was again elected governor in 1959.

Jimmie H. Davis, 1960. BETTMANN/CORBIS

Davis celebrated his inauguration by riding his palomino horse, Sunshine, up the steps of the state capitol and into the legislature building, waving a white cowboy hat as he rode. His second term, however, was a step down from his first. Although he had recorded with black musicians in the 1930s and was not personally bigoted, he feared the changes integration was bringing and went along with the notorious Judge Leander Perez on a scheme to shut down the public schools of New Orleans rather than integrate them. That strategy failed, and Louisiana integrated with relatively little violence. During this term, the Sunshine Bridge over the Mississippi River and the Toledo Bend Reservoir were constructed, and more controversially, so was a new governor's mansion that overran its budget by $700,000.

After his term ended in 1964, Davis returned to performing, broadening his appeal with more Cajun and gospel music. In 1967 his wife died, and in the following year he married the fellow country singer Anna Gordon. In 1968 his successor as governor, John J. McKeithen, vetoed a bill that would have made "You Are My Sunshine" the state song, but in 1972 Davis was elected to both the Country Music Hall of Fame and the Gospel Music Association Hall of Fame. He made an effort to win a third gubernatorial term in 1971 but finished fourth in the race. In 1977 the state legislature decreed both "You Are My Sunshine" and Doralice Fontane's "Give Me Louisiana" as official state songs.

In his later years Davis's political sins were all but forgotten. His music was beloved, and there was a great celebration on 10 September 1999, which was declared to be his 100th birthday. One of his successors, Edwin W. Edwards, said, "He served two terms as governor of Louisiana and was never indicted. That's a genuine achievement." (Edwards himself was not so fortunate.) Davis died in his sleep at his home in Baton Rouge, Louisiana, and is buried at the Jimmie Davis Tabernacle Cemetery in Jonesboro, Louisiana.

Davis combined politics and music to perhaps a greater extent than any other American. As a governor, he was fairly benign in his first term, and although he let himself be dragged into the quagmire of segregation, he did relatively little harm in his second. "You Are My Sunshine" is one of the most beloved of American songs, and though he did not write it, he made it famous. And as a collector and performer of country, Cajun, and gospel music, Davis helped preserve Louisiana's folklore.

★

Davis's second wife, Anna, donated his papers and memorabilia, including several scrapbooks, photographs, and documents, as well as audio recordings, to the Louisiana State Archives in Baton Rouge. Memorial tributes are in *Billboard* (18 Nov. 2000) and *New Orleans* magazine (Jan. 2001). Obituaries are in the *New York Times* (6 Nov. 2000) and *Los Angeles Times* (7 Nov. 2000).

ARTHUR D. HLAVATY

DE CORDOVA, Frederick Timmins ("Fred") (*b.* 27 October 1910 in New York City; *d.* 15 September 2001 in Los Angeles, California), director and producer for stage, screen, and television who, as the executive producer of the late-night television series the *Tonight Show Starring Johnny Carson* from 1970 to 1988, was a consummate show-business insider and gatekeeper.

Well-known in show-business circles, but not to the general public, De Cordova seemed to enjoy romanticizing his childhood on the few occasions he spoke of it in public. In his autobiography, *Johnny Came Lately* (1988), he described his father, George, as a "successful con man" who loved the New York City nightlife and took his young son to Broadway opening nights and title prize fights. His mother, Margaret Timmins, was a lifelong friend of Catherine Dealy Shubert, whose husband's family at one time owned or controlled most of the legitimate theaters in North America, a connection that eventually led to De Cordova's career. Notwithstanding claims of a childhood spent among celebrities at Manhattan, New York City, nightspots, De Cordova was a good student, earning a B.A. from Northwestern University in Evanston, Illinois, in 1931 and admission to Harvard Law School.

While at Harvard, De Cordova met John Shubert, Jr.,

the son of one of his mother's friends, who convinced him to give up his legal studies and take a job with John Shubert Enterprises. Returning to New York City in 1933, De Cordova learned the entertainment business from the front office, serving as Shubert's assistant, and then spent several years in various production positions in regional theaters before returning to New York City. In 1943 he got the plum assignment of directing that year's edition of the *Ziegfeld Follies*. A tall, affable man, whom the actress Spring Byington once described as "built for evening clothes," De Cordova, sporting his trademark black horn-rimmed eyeglasses, became a familiar and well-liked figure in entertainment circles. The social connections he made during his long apprenticeship in the theater served him throughout his career.

De Cordova moved to Los Angeles in 1944 to begin his career's second phase—in the film industry. Signing on as a dialogue director with Warner Bros., he proved adept at handling actors and at editing dialogue to move along plot, a pair of complementary talents. Within a year he received his first directing assignment, *Too Young to Know*, a B-picture romance. De Cordova directed twenty-three Hollywood features (twenty-one of them between 1945 and 1953), none of which won much critical acclaim or public adulation. He did, however, impress the management at both Warner Bros. and, after 1949, Universal with his record of keeping pictures within budget, finishing them on time, and avoiding red ink at the bottom line, even under unlikely circumstances.

For example, in the *Desert Hawk* (1950), De Cordova managed to bring off a project that cast Rock Hudson as a villain and Jackie Gleason as Aladdin. He directed the comedies *Bedtime for Bonzo* (1951) and *Bonzo Goes to College* (1952), which starred Ronald Reagan as a college professor determined to demonstrate the ethical capacities of a chimpanzee; these movies gained attention years later because of Reagan's political success in becoming the U.S. president in the 1980s. Perhaps the most significant of De Cordova's films, in terms of cinema history, was *Here Come the Nelsons*, also known as *Meet the Nelsons* (1952), an early example of parlaying the popularity of a television series (*The Adventures of Ozzie and Harriet*) into a Hollywood theatrical release.

In 1953 De Cordova shifted his career emphasis again, this time to television production. His ability to meet deadlines and his familiarity and popularity among entertainers and industry operatives across the country made him well-suited for the new medium. He worked during the 1950s as the producer and/or director for a string of successful comedy shows starring blue-chip performers, including the *George Burns and Gracie Allen Show*, *Jack Benny Program*, and *George Gobel Show*. His ability to handle temperamental stars, such as Gobel, through the rigors of a thirty-

Fred De Cordova. AP/WIDE WORLD PHOTOS

nine-episode production season, made him a valuable asset in the industry. In 1957 he was brought onto the set of *Mrs. Adams and Eve* as the producer-director when the real-life marital troubles of its stars, Ida Lupino and Howard Duff, threatened to undermine the series. As expected, De Cordova charmed the stars and got the job done.

On 27 November 1963, at age fifty-three, De Cordova married Janet Thomas, an actress and model who had been his companion for years. De Cordova later joked that the secret to avoiding divorce in show business is to put off your wedding until no one else will have you. During the 1960s he continued to direct episodes of hit situation comedies, including *My Three Sons*, starring Fred MacMurray, and the *Smothers Brothers Show*. He briefly resumed feature film work as well, directing two United Artists comedies: *I'll Take Sweden* (1965), starring Bob Hope, and *Frankie and Johnny* (1966), starring Elvis Presley. De Cordova's career as a competent journeyman might have continued toward a successful, if unspectacular, end but for an assignment he was offered in 1970 that catapulted him into a position of power.

Johnny Carson, who had achieved unprecedented success with the *Tonight Show* on the National Broadcasting Company (NBC) since taking over as the program's host in 1962, had gone through four executive producers by the end of the 1969–1970 season. The network needed an executive producer for its late-night variety vehicle who was savvy and well connected enough to book top guest stars

and who could, at the same time, develop a rapport with Carson, a moody performer who had developed a reputation as a loner. Furthermore, the show's production schedule of daily ninety-minute episodes was arguably the most difficult in the business. All of these requirements played to De Cordova's strengths. He was offered the job and, at age fifty-nine, moved back to New York City to take on the challenge. Carson got along with De Cordova and was especially appreciative of his help .in convincing NBC to relocate the program permanently to Los Angeles in 1972, something the star had long wanted.

During De Cordova's seventeen years as the executive producer of the *Tonight Show Starring Johnny Carson,* the series developed into a leading promotional vehicle for performers as well as for films, television programs, and other media products, and De Cordova became an increasingly important figure in American entertainment. In a 1984 *People Weekly* interview, he described himself as the *Tonight Show*'s "chief traffic cop, talent scout, No. 1 fan, and critic all rolled into one."

De Cordova emerged as a show-business gatekeeper, choosing which guests to book and which to pass on. Moreover, he had charge of scheduling guest segments within each episode, a particularly significant role on a late-night show, which typically expects to lose hundreds of thousands of viewers after each commercial interruption as viewers tune out to go to sleep. During a taping, he could exercise discretionary power to prolong a lively interview, even if that meant bumping a guest who was due to appear later in the program. De Cordova came in for criticism from some quarters for favoring show-business cronies and not giving enough exposure to new talent. However, under his regime, the *Tonight Show* grew into one of NBC's most valuable properties, at one point accounting for 17 percent of the network's annual profits.

Back in the early 1950s, De Cordova had enjoyed making bit-part guest appearances as himself on the *Jack Benny Program*. In the 1980s he took up acting again as a hobby of sorts, appearing as himself in Martin Scorcese's film the *King of Comedy* (1983), as well as in several television episodes each of *Alf,* a sitcom about an alien living with an American family, and the *Larry Sanders Show,* a trenchant examination of the backstage workings of a late-night television series.

De Cordova retired as the executive producer of the *Tonight Show* in 1988 and spent his last years living with his wife in Beverly Hills, California, and playing golf. His death at age eighty-one is attributed to natural causes. De Cordova is buried at Holy Cross Cemetery in Culver City, California.

★

De Cordova's autobiography, *Johnny Came Lately* (1988), devotes almost as much space to a description of his duties as the executive producer of the *Tonight Show* as to the other parts of his life, and is arguably more instructive on that subject. An obituary is in the *New York Times* (18 Sept. 2001).

DAVID MARC

DERTOUZOS, Michael Leonidas (*b.* 5 November 1936 in Athens, Greece; *d.* 27 August 2001 in Boston, Massachusetts), educator, writer, and head of the Laboratory for Computer Science at the Massachusetts Institute of Technology, whose visionary work as a computer scientist facilitated the establishment of the World Wide Web Consortium.

Dertouzos was the son of Leonidas Michael Dertouzos, an admiral in the Greek navy, and Rozana G. (Maris) Dertouzos. Raised in the Greek Orthodox Church, he grew up in modest surroundings in the shadow of World War II. Dertouzos immigrated to the United States as a Fulbright scholar in 1954 and attended the University of Arkansas in Fayetteville, earning a B.S. in electrical engineering in 1957 and an M.S. in 1959. On 21 November 1961 he married Hadwig Gofferje, a chemist. They had two children, Alexandra and Leonidas. Dertouzos was naturalized as a U.S. citizen in 1965.

A contemporary of the computer-science pioneers Ray Kurzweil and Bill Joy, Dertouzos in the early 1960s attended the Massachusetts Institute of Technology (MIT)

as a doctoral student, working as an instructor and earning a Ph.D. in 1964, the year in which he founded a technology company, Computek. He also performed research as a Ford postdoctoral fellow through 1966. In the early 1960s Joseph Carl Robnett Licklider at the U.S. Department of Defense Advanced Research Projects Agency (ARPA) conducted the first studies of artificial intelligence to explore the potential of using computers as a tool for human communication. At MIT, whose staff Dertouzos had joined as an associate professor in 1964, the electrical engineering department merged gradually with the department of computer sciences, and Dertouzos quickly found his niche in the growing field of digital technology. In 1973 his faculty position changed from that of associate professor of electrical engineering to associate professor of engineering and computer science, and in 1974 he was named the fourth director of MIT's Laboratory for Computer Science (LCS). In that capacity he headed a project called Multiple Access Computer/ Machine-Aided Cognition (MAC), which marked the transformation of computers from their intended use as elaborate calculating machines to their role as the human communication systems of the twenty-first century.

By the early 1980s Dertouzos had formulated the vision of creating an open network environment for the purpose of providing connectivity between computers at multiple academic institutions. Users tapping into the configuration from any networked location might thereby obtain access to data in any of the other computers on the network. An unsensational first step toward this vision, taken by Dertouzos at the MIT lab, was already underway at that time as a project called Athena. Developed in conjunction with Stanford University in Palo Alto, California, Project Athena involved establishing communication between state-of-the-art time-shared computers located at multiple schools. Initially established for the purpose of sharing data between the institutions, the unbounded potential of this system became quickly apparent.

Parallel with Dertouzos's work at the LCS, in the early 1990s ARPA established a prototype computer network, called the Internet, for access by the general public. In 1993 Dertouzos invited the inventor Tim Berners-Lee to take up residence at MIT, where together they established the World Wide Web Consortium to develop standards and software for the use of the Internet by nontechnical users at the highest levels. Prior to the invention of the World Wide Web, Internet access remained limited to those persons willing and able to type cumbersome computer code sequences on a computer keyboard in order to communicate with other computers on the network. Although the invention of the Web is credited to Berners-Lee, Dertouzos, by establishing the Web Consortium, was largely responsible for bringing the power of the Internet into mainstream use.

In conjunction with his work at the LCS, Dertouzos

Michael L. Dertouzos, 2000. REUTERS NEWMEDIA INC./CORBIS

held multiple patents and founded more than fifty technology companies. Over the course of his career, he authored many works, including an award-winning paper, "Threshold Logic: A Synthesis Approach," in 1965.

In the late 1990s Dertouzos published two books for general audiences in which he elaborated his vision of the World Wide Web as an "information marketplace," a concept he had long-since introduced in academic circles. In 1997 the first of these books, *What Will Be: How the New World of Information Will Change Our Lives,* touted the notion of ubiquitous computing by which computers would be fully involved with the human environment so as to become completely transparent to the users. Because of this theory of fully incorporated computers, Microsoft Corporation, facing antitrust charges in 1998, called Dertouzos to testify as an expert witness regarding the importance of highly integrated, multipurpose software systems. However, fearful he might not support their case because of his concerns about technology vendors—he believed they would try to limit the consumer's ability to access products and services not compatible with their own—Microsoft dropped Dertouzos from the witness list in 1999.

With the resurrection of an MIT publication called *Technology Review* in 1998, Dertouzos wrote a column, "The People's Computer," for the bimonthly periodical. He used his column to critique the status quo of digital technology, and offered insights on his vision for the future of computers. Dertouzos addressed a variety of timely and diverse topics through these articles, the titles of which in-

cluded "Wire Our Schools? Not So Fast . . ."; "Privacy Is Not Doomed"; and "E-mail: Freedom or Jail?"

Firm in his belief that the full potential of digital technology remained almost entirely untapped, in 1999 Dertouzos undertook a futuristic project, called Oxygen, at the LCS. The goal of Oxygen, according to Dertouzos, would be to make using computers as easy as breathing. Around that same time he penned a second book about his vision, *The Unfinished Revolution: Human-Centered Computers and What They Can Do for Us* (2001). Soon after its release, Dertouzos died of heart failure. His remains were returned to Greece and buried at the First Athens Cemetery.

★

Interviews with Dertouzos are in Sami Lais, "Complete the Revolution," *Computerworld* (7 May 2001), and "Scope the Future," *Computerworld* (8 Oct. 2001). Memorial tributes include Otis Port, "Farewell to a Visionary of the Computer Age," *Business Week* (17 Sept. 2001). Obituaries are in the *New York Times* (30 Aug. 2001), *Interactive Week* (3 Sept. 2001), and *Technology Review* (Nov. 2001).

G. COOKSEY

DILLARD, William Thomas, Sr. (*b.* 2 September 1914 in Mineral Springs, Arkansas; *d.* 8 February 2002 in Little Rock, Arkansas), founder and chairman of Dillard's, Inc., a chain of department stores.

Dillard was born in Mineral Springs, a small town about 100 miles southwest of Little Rock. Working part time and summers in his father's hardware store for twelve years, he developed an interest in retailing. From this experience, Dillard knew that someday he wanted to own his own store. Dillard graduated with a B.B.A. in accounting from the College of Business Administration of the University of Arkansas in 1935, at the age of twenty, and earned an M.S. from Columbia University School of Business in 1937. After graduation he worked as a management trainee for Sears Roebuck and Company in Tulsa, Oklahoma, for nine months before returning to Arkansas to open his first store. In 1938 he borrowed $8,000 from his father and, despite the depression economy, opened a small store in Nashville, Arkansas, the hometown of his wife, Alexa. (He and his wife had five children.) From this modest 2,500-square-foot emporium in southwestern Arkansas grew one of the nation's largest retail chains. In 2002 Dillard's became the nation's third-largest upscale department store chain, behind Federated Department Stores Inc. and the May chain of department stores.

Dillard served in the navy during World War II. His store, aside from a short period during the war, continued operating and enlarging its Nashville location. Always looking for an opportunity to expand his business, in 1948 Dillard sold the Nashville operation and bought a controlling interest in a department store in Texarkana, Texas. His business strategy was to offer attractively priced national name-brand merchandise along with customer credit. By 1953 it was the leading store in Texarkana. He then opened another store in Magnolia, Arkansas, and purchased an existing store in Tyler, Texas, in 1956. In 1960 he expanded his business into Oklahoma, purchasing a store in Tulsa that was twice the size of the Tyler venture. As he did with his other acquisitions, Dillard was quick to make the Tulsa store profitable. By the time he was forty-five he was making more than $500,000 a year. "But," he stated, "I wasn't satisfied. I wanted to be a leading department store owner."

This goal led Dillard to increase his business pursuits in Arkansas. In 1963 he and some business associates purchased Pfeifer's of Arkansas, then one of the state's leading stores. Six months later he bought the Blass Department Store in downtown Little Rock. After these acquisitions Dillard moved to Little Rock and established his headquarters there. Key to his acquisition successes was the philosophy that store location was important. Foreseeing the trend toward suburban shopping malls, Dillard opened his first mall store in 1964 in Austin, Texas. His aggressive mall expansion tactic had significant implications in the chain's growth strategy. In 1969 the small family-owned venture of Dillard Department Stores, Inc., went public, and Dillard became the chair of the enterprise.

William T. Dillard, April 1993. AP/WIDE WORLD PHOTOS

By the early 1970s the chain had extended into Louisiana, Missouri, and New Mexico and expanded its operations in Texas, Arkansas, and Oklahoma. Dillard's personal work ethic and hands-on approach to management, his ability to turn marginal operations into profitable concerns, and his efficient system of distribution and inventory control allowed for further acquisitions. Through the 1980s he continued purchasing department stores and consolidating. By the late 1990s the company had more than three hundred department stores in twenty-eight states, employed more than forty-three thousand people, and enjoyed annual sales exceeding $6.6 billion.

Dillard was recognized and honored for his business acumen. In 1985 he was inducted into the Apparel Hall of Fame. In 1989 he received the National Retail Merchants Association Gold Medal for outstanding achievement. Among other citations, he was named Paul Harris Fellow by the Arkansas Rotary Club and received the lifetime achievement award from the Sam M. Walton College of Business Administration at the University of Arkansas. In addition to his business pursuits, Dillard, who had joined the Lambda Chi Alpha fraternity while he was a student at the University of Arkansas, remained active in the fraternity throughout his life.

A *Fortune* magazine article in 1989 described Dillard's

empire as "a quiet superstar . . . family run, highly computerized, extremely competitive, and great for investors." Dillard, who worked well into his eighties, turned over the day-to-day management of the company to his three sons before his death. The family still actively oversees the chain and holds seats on the company's board. Dillard died in his sleep at his home in Little Rock at age eighty-seven. Dillard's work ethic, keen attention to day-to-day organizational details, marketing philosophy based on his sound selling methods, alert selection of personnel, and hands-on approach to management laid the groundwork for his company's retailing success.

★

Information about Dillard is in Susan Caminit, "A Quiet Superstar Rises in Retailing," *Fortune* (23 Oct. 1989), and Bob Ortega, "Master Merchant: Nearing Eighty, Founder of Dillard Stores Seeks to Keep on Going," *Wall Street Journal* (11 May 1994). See also Leon Joseph Rosenberg, *Dillard's: The First Fifty Years* (1988). Obituaries are in the *New York Times* and *Los Angeles Times* (both 9 Feb. 2002).

REBECCA J. TIMMONS

DIXON, Julian C. (*b.* 8 August 1934 in Washington, D.C.; *d.* 8 December 2000 in Marina del Rey, California), U.S. congressman from Los Angeles who was a voice for minority issues in the U.S. House of Representatives.

Dixon was raised in a middle-class black neighborhood in Washington, D.C. His family moved to Los Angeles, where he graduated from Dorsey High School in 1953. He and his wife, Bettye Lee, had one child.

Dixon served in the U.S. Army from 1957 to 1960, rising to the rank of sergeant. He received a B.S. in 1962 from Los Angeles State College (now California State University) and an LL.B. from Southwestern University in Los Angeles in 1967. While in school, he worked for six years as a legislative aide to California state senator Mervyn M. Dymally. He practiced law from 1967 to 1973, and served in the California State Assembly from 1972 until 1978. At the 1984 Democratic National Convention, Dixon was appointed chairman of the convention's rules committee, and was successful at controlling the Reverend Jesse Jackson's efforts to challenge the delegate-selection procedure.

Dixon won election from west Los Angeles to the U.S. House of Representatives in 1989. His Thirty-second Congressional District encompassed dozens of distinct ethnic neighborhoods, from the wealthy northern sections to the poor areas of south central Los Angeles in the east. A strong advocate of civil rights, Dixon was willing to work across partisan lines to improve the lives of his constituents. He was chair of the House Ethics Committee in 1989, when

Julian C. Dixon. REUTERS NEWMEDIA INC./CORBIS

House Speaker Jim Wright was charged with sixty-nine counts of violating House rules in connection with the sales of a book he had written. Dixon was a stabilizing voice during the hearings, gaining bipartisan support in the process.

In 1999 Dixon was appointed to the Permanent Select Committee on Intelligence. As the ranking member of the Subcommittee on the District of Columbia of the House Committee on Appropriations, he fought for home rule and a representative voice. In the mid-1990s, Dixon, formerly a supporter of the Washington mayor Marion Barry, became one of his toughest critics, clamping down on the district government after Barry's reelection in 1994, and setting the scene for a federal takeover of the city's finances.

While serving on a defense spending panel, Dixon became known for his efforts to promote federal aid for communities hit by the closing of military bases. An advocate of the Los Angeles commuter rail system, Dixon was known as Los Angeles's "go-to" man in Washington, and Marc Littman of the Los Angeles County Metropolitan Transportation Authority later said that "Without Julian Dixon, there wouldn't have been a Metro Rail here."

Following the 1992 Los Angeles riots, Dixon led the support of emergency funds for damaged businesses. After the 1994 Northridge earthquake, Dixon authored a bill providing $8.6 billion in relief for earthquake victims that included, for the first time in federal law, language that specifically forbade discrimination on the basis of sexual orientation. He was a cosponsor of both the Employment Non-Discrimination Act, which bans job discrimination based on sexual orientation, and the Crimes Prevention Act. Dixon also supported aid to public schools, health care reform, and funding for police and fire departments.

As part of the Democratic Party's inner circle of national influence, Dixon chaired the Congressional Black Caucus in the 1980s, and worked hard to pass legislation to create a memorial for the Reverend Dr. Martin Luther King, Jr., in Washington, D.C. He served eleven terms in the House, winning reelection in November 2000 with an astonishing 84 percent of the vote. Dixon turned down an offer in 1997 to run for mayor of Los Angeles.

Dixon died from a heart attack suffered while undergoing minor surgery at Daniel Freeman Hospital in Los Angeles. At the time, he was the ranking Democrat on the House Intelligence Committee, and a key player on a panel that set defense spending. He is buried at Inglewood Cemetery in Los Angeles.

The first African-American congressman to chair an appropriations subcommittee, Dixon also authored resolutions that called for the awarding of the Presidential Medal of Freedom to Dr. Benjamin Mays, the former president of Atlanta's Morehouse College, who had delivered the eulogy at the funeral of Martin Luther King, Jr.; and the declaration of September 1983 as "Sickle Cell Anemia Awareness Month." He served as cosponsor for the Civil Rights Act and the Equal Rights Amendment. A bridge builder, Dixon maintained the dignity and professionalism of the House in the middle of intense partisan battles over ethics issues. In his local house district, he led the effort to connect the African-American and Jewish communities.

★

Profiles of Dixon include Tom Waldman, "Congressman Julian Dixon: Low-Profile by Choice," *California Journal* 20, no. 3 (Mar. 1989): 137–139. A profile of Dixon and several other black legislators is in *Ebony* (Dec. 1989). A statement by President William J. ("Bill") Clinton on Dixon's death is in the *Weekly Compilation of Presidential Documents* 36, no. 50 (18 Dec. 2000): 3,044. Obituaries are in the *New York Times* and *Los Angeles Times* (both 9 Dec. 2000).

REED MARKHAM

DONAHUE, Troy (*b.* 27 January 1936 in New York City; *d.* 2 September 2001 in Santa Monica, California), actor whose early 1960s films epitomized the wholesome side of the young American male.

Donahue was born Merle Johnson, Jr., to Merle Johnson, a vice president at General Motors, and Edith Johnson, a former stage actress. The family also had a daughter, Eve. Donahue was raised on Long Island, where visits by his mother's associates gave him his first taste of show business. He later told *People* magazine that he remembered watching guest Gertrude Lawrence reading reviews of *The King and I* at the family home.

After high school, Donahue attended Columbia University, where he studied journalism. He also began acting on the side, gaining experience working in summer stock productions. His acting dreams soon won out over his journalistic aspirations, and he quit college at age nineteen and moved to Los Angeles. His agent, Henry Wilson, rechristened him "Troy Donahue," as he had renamed such other clients as Arthur Gelien (Tab Hunter) and Roy Harold Scherer (Rock Hudson).

Donahue made his film debut as a newspaper reporter in the 1957 feature *Man Afraid*, though his performance was uncredited, as were subsequent roles in *Man of a Thousand Faces* and *The Monolith Monsters* (both 1957). The first time he received a screen credit came in the 1958 film *The Tarnished Angels*. Donahue's films of the period were solid grade-B features, many geared toward the growing adolescent market, with "racy" titles such as *Summer Love, Mon-*

Troy Donahue, 1958. THE KOBAL COLLECTION

ster on the Campus, and *Live Fast, Die Young* (all 1958). He also made guest appearances on numerous popular television shows, including *Wagon Train, Rawhide,* and *77 Sunset Strip.*

Donahue's break came when he signed with Warner Bros. in 1959 and was given a starring role in *A Summer Place,* released the same year. The film, a story of teen lovers (Donahue and Sandra Dee) who meet at a summer resort in Maine, put a modern twist on its age-old theme by actually allowing them to consummate their love prior to marriage. When Dee's character becomes pregnant, Donahue's naturally offers to "do the right thing," and the two wed. The film was a great success, making Donahue one of Warner Bros.' biggest stars, in addition to winning him a Golden Globe for most promising male newcomer.

Over the next six years, Donahue starred in seven other Warner Bros. films. Many followed the *Summer Place* formula of middle-class melodrama, with Donahue cast as a clean-cut "Mr. Nice Guy" always ready to come to the aid of the nice girl who may have strayed but who comes to her senses in the end. In *Susan Slade* (1961) he marries costar Connie Stevens to spare her the trauma of raising her out-of-wedlock son as a single parent. In *Rome Adventure* (1962) he chooses Suzanne Pleshette over "fast" girl Angie Dickinson, despite Pleshette's ill-chosen romance with an older man (Rossano Brazzi). Donahue and Pleshette were later married for eight months in 1964. *Palm Springs Weekend* (1963) tried to tap into the success of 1960's *Where the Boys Are,* following the frolics of college students on spring break. Donahue also starred in two Warner Bros. television series, *Surfside Six* and *Hawaiian Eye.*

By the mid-1960s such coy depictions of romance were becoming dated in the face of the burgeoning sexual revolution and the rise of the counterculture. Warner Bros., fearing that Donahue would no longer appeal to a youthful audience, did not renew his contract. He continued to work sporadically, appearing in such forgettable films as *Come Spy with Me* (1967) and *Sweet Savior* (1971), as well as the Columbia Broadcasting System soap opera *The Secret Storm* in 1970. During this turbulent period, Donahue married a second time, to actress Valerie Allen. The couple wed in 1966 and divorced in 1968.

In the year after his divorce, Donahue moved back to New York City. Depressed due to his lack of work, he indulged heavily in alcohol and drugs, having become a serious drinker during his Warner Bros. days. His drugs of choice also included marijuana, cocaine, painkillers, and amphetamines—"And I would use them in unison," he later told the *Toronto Star.* At the height of his addiction, he was homeless, and he spent a summer sleeping under a bush in Central Park. He tried marriage again with Alma Sharp, a city administrator in New York, but the couple divorced after three years.

The money he earned from one of his few appearances in a notable film during the 1970s, a small role in 1974's *The Godfather: Part II* (as an in-joke, his character was named Merle Johnson), enabled Donahue to move back to Los Angeles, where he found work in commercials and on television. He also married Vickie Taylor, a land development manager, in 1979. In 1981 the couple divorced. By then Donahue was ready to turn his life around. "I realized that I was going to die, and I was dying," he later told the *New York Times,* "or, worse than that, I might live the way I was living for the rest of my life." Donahue finally became clean and sober and fully returned to acting in the 1984 feature *Grandview U.S.A.*

Donahue's career never regained its former luster, but he worked steadily for the rest of his life, albeit mostly on such low-budget and/or straight-to-video exploitative fare as *Nudity Required* (1988), *Assault of the Party Nerds* (1989), and *Bimbo Movie Bash* (1997). One of his more memorable appearances was in John Waters's 1990 satire of teen musicals, *Cry-Baby.* He also worked as an acting teacher on Holland America Line cruise ships, and in 1991, on a cruise from Vancouver to Tahiti, met the Chinese-born opera singer Zheng Cao. The two became engaged in 1999.

On Thursday, 30 August 2001, after a gym workout, Donahue suffered a heart attack and was admitted to Saint John's Hospital and Medical Center in Santa Monica, California. He died there three days later, following heart surgery. Donahue had a daughter, Janine, and a son, Sean, the result of a brief affair with a woman he declined to name publicly.

★

There are no biographies of Donahue. Biographical information can be found in *People* (13 Aug. 1984). Obituaries are in the *New York Times* (3 Sept. 2001), *Variety* (10 Sept. 2001), and *People* (17 Sept. 2001).

GILLIAN G. GAAR

DONOVAN, Carolyn Gertrude Amelia ("Carrie") (*b.* 22 March 1928 in Lake Placid, New York; *d.* 12 November 2001 in New York City), flamboyant and astute fashion journalist and editor who, in semiretirement, became the "old lady of Old Navy."

Donovan and her sister never knew their father, who abandoned their mother, Margaret, when they were small children. Their maternal grandparents in Lake Placid, New York, raised them while their mother moved to Brooklyn, New York City, to work in a factory. As a child, Donovan was captivated by glamour. In the second grade, she made a paper-doll trousseau for Wallis Simpson, the American divorcée who married the Duke of Windsor. Donovan even

Carrie Donovan, ca. 1965. HULTON ARCHIVE/GETTY IMAGES

sent Jane Wyman sketches for a wardrobe and received a thank-you note from the actress. In 1942 Donovan and her sister moved to Brooklyn to join their mother, who now worked in a war production plant.

After graduating from high school in 1946, Donovan sold hats at the Saks Fifth Avenue department store in Manhattan and entered the Parsons School of Design. She never really learned to sew properly, so she bribed class-mates, including the future fashion designers Norman Norell and Jacques Fath, to stitch her designs. After gradu-ating in 1950, she designed junior dress lines for firms in the fashion district along Seventh Avenue. Briefly, she was an assistant to Fath in Paris. However, Donovan felt that creating fashion was not her true vocation; instead, she turned to fashion journalism.

From 1955 to 1963 Donovan was an editor for the woman's page of the *New York Times*, then associate fash-ion editor. She never mastered typing and wrote all her copy in longhand. "If something interested me," she said, "I figured it would interest the reader." Her prose helped make the Seventh Avenue fashion scene a subject of serious interest.

Donovan's status as a fashion authority was matched with an infectious, personal flair. "To know Carrie," *Times* editor Jack Rosenthal commented, "is to know a pronounced presence." Donovan turned routine editorial meetings into

performances of flamboyant pronouncements, insider gossip, and balanced decision-making. Her acerbic yet amusing wit was a trademark, as were her oversized, black-rimmed glasses, pearls, matching cuff bracelets, and black and leopard-print wardrobe. Even her Upper East Side apartment had leopard-patterned carpeting, red lacquered walls, and red furnishings. "Her sound," Rosenthal contin-ued, "is even more pronounced: crisp diction, animated in-to-NA-tion, a singular vocabulary drawing loosely from the French."

From 1963 to 1972 Donovan was an editor at *Vogue* and the protégée of the magazine's legendary editor in chief, Diana Vreeland. "My dear," Vreeland commented to Donovan, "you've got the common touch." In fact, Donovan did prefer plain food and even took the subway to work. She was always known as "Carrie," not "Ms. Donovan." She never married.

While at *Vogue,* Donovan was known for her eye for new talent, and was the first magazine journalist to high-light Paraphernalia, the most famous "mod" boutique in Manhattan during the 1960s. Her articles and pictorial fea-tures were the first to highlight designers such as Perry Ellis, and she introduced French designers such as Chris-tian Lacroix to American readers. She even convinced Ralph Lauren to begin designing clothes for women. Tire-less in her sense of journalistic duty, Donovan was usually the first to arrive at any fashion show.

When Vreeland was replaced at *Vogue,* Donovan be-came the senior fashion editor of *Harper's Bazaar.* From 1972 to 1976 she continued to launch emerging talents, including Donna Karan and Calvin Klein. She was the first to feature jewelry designs by Paloma Picasso. Donovan also convinced Tiffany and Co. to feature contemporary jewelry designs by Elsa Peretti. In 1977 Donovan worked briefly as the marketing vice president of Bloomingdale's department store but decided to return to journalism.

That year she became the style editor of the weekly *New York Times Magazine.* Her fashion shoots combined the latest news of Seventh Avenue with visits to the showrooms of emerging designers and the new opulence of the Reagan era. Jack Rosenthal, the *Magazine's* editor, recalled that once Donovan was about to present some picture layouts for approval, but found that there was not enough room on the table. "Undismayed," he remarked, "she spread the pages on the floor, then dropped to her knees to explain them, exclaiming, 'Let me excite you to madness!'"

As well as on fashion, Donovan also wrote articles on beauty, food, and home design. In 1981 she edited *Living Well: The New York Times Book of Design and Decoration.* Also that year Donovan became a fellow at the Rhode Is-land School of Design. In 1978 she had begun to edit "Fashions of the Times" insert supplements for the *New York Times Magazine.* Each issue was rich in advertisements, and these generated enormous revenue for the newspaper at a time when newspaper profits were plummeting. By 1990 there were nine such supplements, covering women's, men's, and children's fashions. Although Donovan thought about retiring in 1993, it was not to be. She continued to edit the supplements for another four years and also wrote an occasional guest column for the *New York Times Magazine.*

In 1997 a heart condition necessitated an operation. While she was still recovering, Dennis Leggett, the creative director of the Old Navy clothing retail chain, asked Donovan to write what he called "fashion memo" advertisements. Her forty-five-word columnettes appeared every Friday in the *New York Times,* accompanied by caricatures of her by the legendary show-business caricaturist Al Hirschfield. Donovan praised the company's "awe-fully" chic T-shirts, "fahb-ulous" slit-skirts, and "poopy-doop" fabrics, and her campy ads were a hit. "I devote my energies," Donovan said, "to convincing young people to dress oddly, it gives us old people a real hoot."

Donovan's new persona as the "old lady of Old Navy" was featured in television commercials. Upstaging spokesperson Morgan Fairchild and accompanied by an Airedale terrier, Magic, Donovan played herself to the hilt. In cartoon settings styled by the well-known photographic stylist Polly Hamilton, she could be seen riding an airplane or swirling a hula-hoop while breathlessly ad-libbing, "Pockets?! You can't have too many pockets!" In forty-two television ads, Donovan's retro flamboyance became a smashing success for Old Navy. People wondered, just who was that lady with the big glasses? She just happened to be, along with Diana Vreeland of *Vogue* and Carmel Snow of *Harper's Bazaar,* one of the most influential fashion journalist–editors of post–World War II America. After a long illness, Donovan died of heart failure at age seventy-three at New York Weill Cornell Center.

★

There is no full-length biography of Donovan. For more information about her life and career, see *Edwin Diamond, Behind the Times* (1993); Jack Rosenthal, "A Pro-Nounced Presence," *New York Times Magazine* (26 Feb. 1995); and Amy M. Spindler, "Cachet and Carrie," *New York Times Magazine* (17 Jan. 1999). Obituaries are in the *New York Times* (13 Nov. 2001) and (Manchester, UK) *Guardian* (3 Dec. 2001).

PATRICK S. SMITH

E

EARNHARDT, (Ralph) Dale (*b*. 29 April 1951 in Kannapolis, North Carolina; *d*. 18 February 2001 in Daytona Beach, Florida), professional race car driver who won seven Winston Cup championships and seventy-six National Association for Stock Car Automobile Racing (NASCAR) races between 1979 and 2001.

Earnhardt was the middle of five children of Ralph and Martha (Coleman) Earnhardt. He grew up in the textile mill town of Kannapolis, in the heart of NASCAR country. Earnhardt's father was a local legend as a stock car racer on small tracks in the Carolinas but never had the financial resources to compete at the highest levels. Dale began traveling with his father to races at around age ten. He worked in his father's garage at home in Kannapolis and on his father's pit crew at races. He attained a working knowledge of race cars that was equaled by few, if any, of his racing peers.

Earnhardt had little interest in team sports and was an indifferent student. He never wanted to be anything other than a stock car racer. He forced the issue when he dropped out of school at age sixteen. Earnhardt later regretted this decision, primarily because it disappointed his father, who died suddenly of a heart attack in 1973. By this time Earnhardt had begun racing on small tracks near his home. He drove in his first Winston Cup event in 1975, finishing twenty-second at the World 600 in nearby Charlotte, North Carolina. However, he was unable to convert this achievement into regular Winston Cup competition and dropped back to the minor league circuits. He won at this level but never made a significant profit. Earnhardt was chronically short of money during much of the 1970s and was forced to work a series of menial jobs to finance his racing career.

A short-lived marriage as a teenager to Latane Brown resulted in the birth of his son Kerry in 1969. Earnhardt married Brenda Gee in 1972. They had two children: Kelley, born in 1972, and Dale, Jr., born in 1974. They divorced in 1977. Earnhardt married Teresa Houston in 1982. Their daughter, Taylor Nicole, was born in 1988.

Earnhardt received his big break in 1979, when his talent was recognized by the owner Rod Osterlund, who made him the primary driver of his Chevrolet. He won the Southeastern 500 at Bristol, Tennessee, and finished seventh in the Winston Cup standings despite missing four races because of injuries suffered in a crash. Earnhardt was voted 1979 NASCAR Rookie of the Year.

He followed up with an outstanding 1980 season, winning five races, capturing the Winston Cup points race, and becoming the only driver to be NASCAR Rookie of the Year and Winston Cup winner in successive years. Earnhardt's rise to prominence was sidetracked when Osterlund sold his team in 1981 to J. D. Stacy. Earnhardt felt betrayed and quit the Stacy team after four races. He drove briefly with Richard Childress before signing in 1982 with Bud Moore. Earnhardt raced Fords for Moore without notable success.

Dale Earnhardt, 2001. AP/WIDE WORLD PHOTOS

Earnhardt rejoined the Childress team for the 1984 season, and the second time around proved to be the charm for this combination. The Childress team experimented in building vehicles using their own car parts rather than relying on factory parts. They consistently turned out cars equal to or superior to the competition. The high quality of Childress's Chevrolets, combined with Earnhardt's talents, enabled the team to dominate NASCAR for a decade.

Earnhardt won a pair of races in 1984 and four titles the following season. He then captured consecutive points titles in 1986 and 1987. Earnhardt won five races in 1986 and eleven the following season. At one point in the 1987 season, Earnhardt won four consecutive races. He finished third in the points race in 1988 and second the following year.

By this time Earnhardt had become both the most popular and the most controversial driver in NASCAR. Skilled, aggressive, and confrontational, he was an expert in "trading paint" with his rivals and coming out on top. Few NASCAR fans were neutral about Earnhardt, but even fans of other drivers acknowledged his skill and determination. His competitors always knew where he was on the track. It was said that the most fearsome sight a NASCAR driver could see was Earnhardt in his rearview mirror.

Earnhardt's first nickname was "Ironhead," a tribute to his legendary stubbornness. He was fined $3,000 for a controversial 1985 wreck with Darrell Waltrip in Richmond, Virginia. As he refined his innate abilities, the wins piled up, and "Ironhead" became better known as "The Intimidator" or "The Dominator."

Earnhardt's best-known move took place in the 1987 Winston, held in Charlotte. Late in the race he was bumped into the infield by Bill Elliott. Earnhardt somehow retained control of his car and passed Elliott before coming back onto the track. Earnhardt won the race, and the so-called Pass in the Grass became a NASCAR legend.

In 1988 GM Goodwrench replaced Wrangler as the sponsor of the Earnhardt-Childress team. Earnhardt's No. 3 car was painted black, and the "Man in Black" solidified his place atop NASCAR. Earnhardt captured Winston Cup titles in 1990, 1991, 1993, and 1994. The 1994 title was his seventh, which tied him with Richard Petty for the most in NASCAR history. A record-setting eighth title seemed inevitable, but it never happened. Earnhardt won five races in 1995 but was edged out for the points title by Jeff Gordon. He finished third in 1996.

Earnhardt's dominance occurred at a time when NASCAR was breaking out of its rural southern roots to become a national phenomenon. He parlayed his on-track dominance and his high name recognition into a wealth of endorsements. Despite his lack of formal education, Earnhardt became an adept public speaker.

By the middle 1990s he was making as much as $20 million annually. In 1997 he became the first driver to have his picture on a Wheaties cereal box. He started Dale Earnhardt Enterprises, which owned and managed two Winston Cup racing teams. He also owned a Chevrolet dealership, several farms, an air transport company, a minor league baseball team, and assorted real estate ventures. He still found time for hunting and fishing. His home in Mooresville, North Carolina, was only a few miles from where he grew up.

Earnhardt paid a physical price for his success. He was in numerous accidents, the most serious being a wreck in the 1996 DieHard 500 in Talladega, Alabama, that resulted in a broken sternum, a broken left collarbone, and a bruised pelvis. The following season he fainted at the beginning of the 1997 Southern 500. Tests were inconclusive, and he continued racing.

Earnhardt was plagued by a long inability to win the Daytona 500, the biggest race on the NASCAR circuit. Earnhardt had a number of excruciating near-misses, most notably in 1990 when he cut a tire on debris while leading on the last lap. He finally broke through with a win on 15 February 1998, his twentieth try at that title. The emotional victory was hailed by even his fiercest rivals. This was his only win of the season, however.

Earnhardt struggled to win in the latter 1990s. Other teams had caught up with Childress, and injuries and age were beginning to catch up with Earnhardt. His burgeoning business empire took time and energy.

Still, Earnhardt was competitive. He won the Winston 500 in Talladega in 2000 and finished that season second in the points race. He entered the 2001 season still hoping for that elusive eighth Winston Cup title. Earnhardt was close to the lead when the 2001 Daytona 500 entered its final lap. Realizing he couldn't win the race, Earnhardt attempted to block for Michael Waltrip and his son, Dale, Jr., both of whom were racing for Dale Earnhardt Enterprises. Sterling Marlin bumped Earnhardt, who lost control of his car and crashed directly into a wall. He was pronounced dead on arrival at Halifax Medical Center. The cause of death was massive head trauma.

Earnhardt's death devastated the NASCAR community. Impromptu memorials sprung up at almost every place that had a tangible connection with Earnhardt. Fans left flowers and wrote poetry. His funeral at Charlotte's Calvary Church was nationally telecast.

There also was controversy. Earnhardt's failure to wear a safety brace known as the Head and Neck Support (HANS) was criticized, although experts agreed that it would not have helped in this situation. Teresa Earnhardt fought a successful court battle to keep his autopsy photographs from becoming public. Debate raged over whether Earnhardt's seat belt had broken; it had not. Marlin received numerous death threats even though knowledgeable observers absolved him of blame for the fatal accident.

Earnhardt's career closed with seventy-six Winston Cup wins. He finished in the top ten in points nineteen times in twenty-one seasons and had career winnings of just over $41 million. His importance to NASCAR, however, lies in more than just statistics. His rags-to-riches success, take-no-prisoners style of racing, and down-to-earth personality made him one of NASCAR's most popular drivers and helped usher his sport into the modern age.

★

Numerous biographies, many written for a juvenile audience, are available. The best for adults probably is Leigh Montville, *The Fast Life and Tragic Death of Dale Earnhardt* (2001). Others include Frank Vehorn, *The Intimidator: The Dale Earnhardt Story* (1991), Frank Moriarity, *Dale Earnhardt* (2001), and John Regruth, *Dale Earnhardt: The Final Record* (2001). Mark Bechtel, "Crushing," *Sports Illustrated* (26 Feb. 2001), details his fatal race. Also useful are these *Sports Illustrated* articles: Sam Moses, "Dale Turns 'Em Pale" (7 Sept. 1987), and "Attitude for Sale" (6 Feb. 1995) and "Asleep at the Wheel" (15 Sept. 1997), both by Ed Hinton. An obituary is in the *New York Times* (19 Feb. 2001).

JIM L. SUMNER

EGAN, John Joseph ("Jack") (*b.* 9 October 1916 in New York City; *d.* 19 May 2001 in Chicago, Illinois), influential Catholic priest who, for almost four decades, balanced meticulous devotion to his church with innovative efforts to provoke social change.

Egan was the second of five children born to immigrant Irish parents, John Egan and Helen Curry Egan. His mother was a seamstress, and his father drove a bus for the Fifth Avenue Motor Coach Company. When Egan was six, the Chicago Motor Coach Company bought the New York City entity and transferred his father to Chicago, where he worked as chief clerk of the transportation department. Egan attended Our Lady of Lourdes Grammar School and DePaul Academy in Chicago. He went on from the academy to DePaul University, where he studied for a year before entering the diocesan seminary, Saint Mary of the Lake, in 1937.

At Saint Mary, he met the firebrand rector Monsignor Reynold J. Hillenbrand, who Egan recalled as "my first major intellectual influence." At a time when the notion of hierarchy still heavily pervaded the church, Hillenbrand, influenced by radical European religious movements, taught his seminarians to work for the empowerment of the laity. The community organizer Saul Alinsky taught another valuable lesson when he spoke to the seminarians: "On the day you are ordained, make up your mind whether you want to be a priest or a bishop. Everything else will follow." With his decision to work for the advancement of laypeople, Egan made the decision to be, as he said, "footwasher to the world."

In his first parish, Saint Justin Martyr, where he was assigned as an assistant in 1943, Egan mobilized laypersons to effect change in their world, one of returning war veterans and their new wives. Together, Egan and his parishioners developed marriage classes. Concurrently, he worked with Catholic Action cells of students, young workers, and teachers, who followed the formula for change of the French Cardinal Joseph Cardijn: to observe conditions around oneself, judge the morality of those actions against Gospel values, and act to change society.

Ten years into his parish work, in 1947, Egan was chosen by Samuel Cardinal Stritch, archbishop of Chicago, to direct Cana Conference, an innovative diocese-wide program for married couples. (The program also included pre-Cana classes for couples planning marriage.) By 1957, when he asked to be reassigned, Egan had developed a national reputation for his work in preparing couples for marriage. Most of the 410 parishes in the Chicago area sponsored Cana conferences, and more than thirty-nine thousand married couples had attended 803 such conferences between 1944 and 2000. In twelve years, mostly under

Egan's tutelage, Cana had spread to ninety-two dioceses in the United States and to Canada, France, Germany, Ireland, Australia, Japan, Malta, South America, and the Philippines. Almost thirty-six thousand engaged couples had attended a four-session pre-Cana conference between 1946 and 2000.

Egan was by then observing, judging, and acting within a wider world. Close to home, he saw what he regarded as a heinous injustice: the acquisition of land by the University of Chicago in the neighborhoods of Hyde Park and Kenwood surrounding its campus. This act displaced poor black families in the process. In criticizing the Hyde Park–Kenwood plan, Egan took on the university, the powerful *Chicago Tribune,* and his own church. Although he failed to stop the project, he resolved to have better success next time by building an interfaith coalition. In an unprecedented move, he called the director of the Chicago Board of Rabbis and the executive director of the Church Federation of Greater Chicago. Together they created the Interreligious Council on Urban Affairs to articulate the concerns of those who had little voice in the public arena. The three, along with African Americans from Chicago's South Side, soon made headlines by wading into Lake Michigan, under the protection of Chicago police, at tacitly segregated Rainbow Beach.

When Alinsky, a controversial community activist, invited him to engage full-time in community organization, Egan asked permission to create an archdiocesan Office of Urban Affairs (1958–1969). From that post, he became deeply engaged in the struggles over racial integration and urban renewal. The University of Chicago undertook a second plan to acquire land. This time African Americans asked to be included in the planning. Later, the Reverend Arthur Brazier, African-American pastor of the Pentecostal Apostolic Church of God, recalled that "with Protestant and Jewish support, Egan brought a sense of legitimacy to local community struggles and affirmed the right of people to organize and participate in the democratic process." As a result, African Americans, organized into the Woodlawn Organization, won concessions that specified that the demolition of the South Campus should be delayed until new units of low-cost housing were built, so that the people could be relocated out of the old housing of South Campus into the new. The writer Sanford Horwitt said that this was almost certainly the first time "that a black community in Chicago had, through sheer political power, won a major role in shaping an important urban-renewal program."

As pastor of Presentation Church (1966–1970), Egan worked with the Contract Buyers' League to help residents of the Lawndale neighborhood renegotiate $6 million in contracts for regular mortgages. At the University of Notre Dame (1970–1983) in South Bend, Indiana, Egan directed the Institute for Pastoral and Social Ministry to bring to-gether social activists from across the country. Back in Chicago, he directed the archdiocese's office of human relations and ecumenism until 1987. Upon retirement, he headed DePaul University's office of community affairs (1987–2001), where he was advocate for neighborhoods until his death. During his last decade, Egan was instrumental in bringing to Chicago an Alinsky-inspired group, United Power for Action and Justice, and was a major supporter for the National Interfaith Committee for Worker Justice. Egan died of heart disease at Holy Name Cathedral rectory in Chicago. He is buried at All Saints Cemetery, Des Plaines, Illinois.

Egan's life goal was to fight injustice wherever he found it and for as long as he found it. He marched for voting rights with the Reverend Martin Luther King, Jr., in Selma, Alabama; opposed urban renewal plans in the 1950s; challenged the Chicago Housing Authority in the 1960s; and fought excessive payday loan interest in the 1990s. As his colleague Ed Chambers said of him, "What Dorothy Day was for the poor, Egan was for the working class stiff."

★

Egan's papers are in the archives of the University of Notre Dame, South Bend, Indiana. The principal source of information on his life is Margery Frisbie, *An Alley in Chicago* (2002), based on a long series of interviews. Obituaries are in the *Chicago Tribune* and *New York Times* (both 22 May 2001).

Margery Frisbie

EIFLER, Carl Frederick (*b.* 27 June 1906 in Los Angeles, California; *d.* 8 April 2002 in Salinas, California), officer in the Office of Strategic Services who commanded an elite unit in the Far East, earning the sobriquet "the deadliest colonel."

Eifler, the fourth of five children born to Carl Frederick and Pauline (Engelbert) Eifler, dropped out of school at age thirteen. Bored and restless, he kicked around southern California doing odd jobs, including working in the same oil fields around Los Angeles in which his father worked. His mother was a homemaker. An army sergeant convinced Eifler that a military career would give him direction, so in 1922, when he was fifteen years old, he lied about his age and signed up. He spent almost two years in the Philippines working in the aerial photography unit before the army discovered his true age and discharged him.

Eifler returned to Los Angeles and again wandered through odd jobs until he enrolled in the Los Angeles Police Academy in 1926. For two years he worked as a police officer in Los Angeles and Newport Beach, California, before a chance encounter with a customs agent named Lee Echols. Even though Eifler was only twenty-two, thirteen years under the age limit, Echols recruited him. Eifler worked for the U.S. Customs Service on the Mexican border until 1934, including aiding in secret efforts against rum smugglers. While in Mexico, Eifler uncovered a Japanese spy ring, but his superiors dismissed his reports. Serving as a captain in the U.S. Army Reserves, Eifler brought his reports to his commanding officer, Colonel Joseph Stilwell, who was impressed with him and began to follow his career. In 1935 Eifler was promoted to the chief customs inspector position in Honolulu, Hawaii.

When the Japanese attacked Pearl Harbor, Hawaii, on 7 December 1941, Eifler, activated earlier that year as a captain in the Thirty-fifth Infantry, was the scheduled duty officer at Schofield Barracks, the nearby military base. His drive from his home to Schofield was indicative of his military career—he ran roadblocks, bullied guards, and dodged enemy fire, all to fulfill his duty. In March 1942 the Coordinator of Information (COI), the precursor to the Office of Strategic Services (OSS), wanted to form a new unit that would conduct guerrilla and espionage operations in Asia. General Stilwell, Eifler's former commander in California and now the commander of U.S. forces in the China/Burma/India theater, offered Eifler's name as the only acceptable commander for the new unit. The COI secured Eifler's transfer as the new commander of Task Force 5405-A, or Detachment 101.

Eifler, through his force of personality, sharp mind, and brute strength, created one of the most successful counterintelligence units in U.S. military history. He handpicked twenty-one men to form the core of the unit. They had no official training or practice to rely on and no reputation to precede them. Eifler, by then a major performing a general's job, had to create unit training and procedures from scratch at a whirlwind pace. Detachment 101 shipped out in the summer of 1942 and began operations shortly after arriving in India. In November, Eifler led the first U.S. foray into Burma, taking only one man with him to reconnoiter Japanese forces.

By January 1943, Detachment 101 was initiating numerous operations, usually with units of native Kachin. Eifler's command was responsible for tracking and harassing Japanese forces in Burma, gathering intelligence, and rescuing downed airmen. An accomplished pilot, he often flew behind Japanese lines to meet with inserted guerrilla teams, twice crashing, surviving, and hiking for days to friendly territory. He also led a rescue in Japanese-controlled waters using an experimental and untested boat, saving nine downed pilots. He even devised a plan to assassinate the Chinese general Chiang Kai-shek using Japanese prostitutes, but Stilwell rescinded his orders.

Detachment 101 achieved great success in World War II. Including 800 Americans and 10,000 native "Kachin Raiders," the unit cleared 10,000 square miles of Japanese-controlled territory and rescued more than 200 pilots. They were responsible for more than 16,000 Japanese casualties (killed and wounded), with the loss of only 22 Americans and 184 natives. Their success can be credited largely to Eifler and his refusal to accept the idea that something could not be done.

In December 1943 Eifler was recalled to Washington, D.C. The OSS had learned of the German nuclear program and asked Eifler to devise a plan to kidnap the German scientist Werner Heisenberg. Eifler planned to infiltrate Germany, escape to Switzerland, board a U.S. bomber, and rendezvous with a waiting submarine. The plan was canceled when the United States itself made spectacular progress in atomic energy with its Manhattan Project. The OSS then asked Eifler to prepare a plan to infiltrate the Japanese mainland in anticipation of a U.S. invasion. Under Project Napko, Eifler formed and trained ten units of Korean nationals as his infiltration teams and was ready to proceed when Japan surrendered.

During one of his operations in Burma, rough surf threw Eifler repeatedly against rocks, and he sustained a head injury that plagued him for the rest of his life. The injury caused bouts of amnesia and occasional violent rages. He fought through the symptoms during the war. After the end of World War II, he was hospitalized for more than a year. Physicians determined that he had permanent brain damage and required daily medication to control the amnesia and rages. Eifler returned to Honolulu to resume his customs position.

In 1952 Eifler enrolled at Jackson College in Hawaii. Despite his injury, he graduated with bachelor's and master's degrees in divinity in 1956. In 1963, after he received a Ph.D. in psychology from the Illinois Institute of Technology, he returned to California to work for the Monterey County Mental Health Services, retiring in 1973. Eifler's first wife, Lou, died in 1961; Eifler had adopted her son. On 30 June 1963 Eifler married Margaret Aaberg and adopted her son from a previous marriage. Eifler died of natural causes at age ninety-five and was cremated. His ashes are buried in Monterey.

Preston Goodfellow, his commander in the OSS, captured Eifler's essence when he gave him the nickname "the deadliest colonel." Eifler was a physically imposing man who instilled a mix of fear and respect in those he met. He was known for ordering his subordinates to punch him in the stomach, including a time he challenged seventy-seven men to knock him down with one punch, which they could not do. Eifler's military exploits earned him a Bronze Star, the Legion of Merit with two oak leaf clusters, and the Purple Heart. In 1988 he was inducted into the Military Intelligence Hall of Fame. Throughout his life he exhibited a "never say never" attitude that allowed him to overcome seemingly overwhelming opposition.

★

Thomas Moon, who served under Eifler in Burma, wrote his only full-length biography, *The Deadliest Colonel* (1975). Eifler's OSS exploits were the subject of numerous articles, including David Atlee Phillips, "The Toughest, Deadliest Hombre," *Military Intelligence: Its Heroes and Legends* (1987), and Troy J. Sacquety, "The Stuff of Intelligence Legend: Behind Japanese Lines in Burma," *Studies in Intelligence* (fall/winter 2001). An obituary is in the *Los Angeles Times* (20 Apr. 2002).

MICHAEL C. MILLER

ELIAS, Peter (*b.* 26 November 1923 in Brunswick, New Jersey; *d.* 7 December 2001 in Cambridge, Massachusetts), educator, information technology theorist, and pioneer of the computing sciences who, by means of his research, helped fuel the digital revolution of the final quarter of the twentieth century.

Elias was the son of Nathaniel Mandel Elias, an engineer at the Edison Laboratory, and Ann (Wahrhaftig) Elias. He attended Swarthmore College from 1940 to 1942 before enrolling at the Massachusetts Institute of Technology (MIT) in Cambridge. After graduating in 1944 with a B.S. in business engineering and management, he enlisted in the U.S. Navy. Elias, whose chosen specialty at that time was electrical engineering, spent the duration of World War II working with radar equipment at a base on a remote island in the South Pacific. He was rated as an electronic technician's mate first class at the time of his discharge.

After leaving the navy in 1946, Elias returned to Cambridge and enrolled in postgraduate studies at Harvard University, where he earned an M.A. in 1948. He completed an M.S. in engineering in 1949 and earned a Ph.D. in applied science in 1950, having served as an assistant professor of applied science during his postgraduate career. On 8 July 1950 he married Marjorie Forbes; they had three children. Also in 1950 Elias accepted a junior fellowship at Harvard, where he taught for three years, resigning in 1953 to join the faculty at MIT. He became an assistant professor in 1956.

In 1957 Elias participated in the founding of *Information and Control,* an academic journal committed to publishing original scientific papers on a variety of topics associated with the computational aspects of information theory, as well as the theoretical issues of computer science. Citing quality as the ultimate prerequisite for all articles, the journal was dedicated to logical programming, database technology, and verification of computer programs, with articles geared to electrical engineers, mathematicians, and other technical professionals. For the rest of his life, Elias served on the board of directors of the periodical, which distin-

guished itself as a pioneering publication on electronic systems. Later renamed *Information and Computation,* it boasted an estimated worldwide readership of ten million in the early twenty-first century and was included among the publications in an international clearinghouse of science documents archived by the prestigious Royal Library in the Netherlands.

Research into digital technology escalated rapidly at MIT during the 1960s and 1970s, and Elias undertook groundbreaking work in this area. In 1960, at the age of thirty-seven, Elias became both a full professor and head of the electrical engineering and computer science department at MIT. He was the youngest person ever to hold the latter position, a post he held until 1966. Elias served as a visiting professor at the University of California, Berkeley, in 1958, and at Harvard from 1967 to 1968. He was honored by MIT as the inaugural appointee to the Cecil H. Green professorship (1970–1972) and was named to the Edwin S. Webster chair at MIT, a position he held from 1974 to 1992. Elias also served as a visiting scientist at London's Imperial College of Science and Technology from 1975 to 1976.

When the electrical engineering department at MIT became the Laboratory for Computer Science in 1976, the school assumed a leadership position in the communication and technology revolution then under way. During those early years, much of the output from the MIT computer laboratory paved the way for subsequent practical applications of data-processing systems worldwide. It was a complex environment, in which only a select few proved capable of deciphering the intricate details of the machinery. In this world of prototypical technology, Elias was attuned to the vast spectrum of inscrutable details. An engineer and mathematician by profession, he was a communications expert in his own right, committed to the development of practical solutions through digital systems.

Elias assumed a pivotal role in the development of binary computer codes, with an ultimate focus on practical communication. He delved into information theory and, by means of his research, made inroads toward the development of data-verification methods to promote reliable electronic communications over unreliable channels. Likewise, he studied the feasibility of developing reliable computation systems despite the unreliability of the early components.

Elias served as the acting associate head of computer science at MIT from 1981 to 1983 and was a fellow of the American Association for the Advancement of Science. As a fellow with the Institute of Electronic and Electrical Engineers (IEEE), he chaired that group's information theory council and served on the editorial boards of the IEEE publications *Proceedings* and *Spectrum.* He held memberships in the National Academy of Science, the American Academy of Arts and Sciences, the Institute of Mathematical Statistics, and the National Academy of Engineering.

As a member of the Association for Computing Machinery (ACM), he was a contributor to the association's *Journal of the ACM,* and authored such articles as "Efficient Storage and Retrieval by Content and Address of Static Files" (April 1974) and "The Complexity of Some Simple Retrieval Problems" (July 1975), the latter written with Richard A. Flower.

Elias retired in 1991, becoming professor emeritus and maintaining his association with MIT as both an adviser to undergraduate students and a senior lecturer. Some time after the death of his wife in February 1993, Elias was stricken with a fatal brain infection, Creutzfeldt-Jakob disease. He died at his home at age seventy-eight.

Elias's research produced important data for future generations of computer scientists, and he contributed to systems for coding data compression and for economical storage and retrieval technology. Virtually all computer codes in modern mainstream technology are based on his efforts during the 1970s.

★

An MIT news release, a memorial tribute to Elias, appeared in *Tech Talk* (12 Dec. 2001). Obituaries are in the *Boston Globe* (12 Dec. 2001), *New York Times* (19 Dec. 2001), and *Washington Post* (21 Dec. 2001).

GLORIA COOKSEY

EPSTEIN, Julius J. ("Julie") (*b.* 22 August 1909 in Manhattan, New York City; *d.* 30 December 2000 in Los Angeles, California), witty and prolific screenwriter of Hollywood's golden age, best known for his work on the screenplay of *Casablanca.*

Epstein was born just minutes before his twin brother, Philip, at home on Manhattan's Lower East Side. His father, Henry Epstein, owned a livery stable, and his mother, Sarah (Gronenberg) Epstein, was a homemaker. Although the family was by no means wealthy, they summered in the Catskill Mountains, and both boys went to college. Epstein attended Pennsylvania State College (now Pennsylvania State University) for boxing and was the team captain and intercollegiate boxing champion (bantam featherweight) in 1929. He graduated with a B.A. in journalism in 1931. On 30 April 1936 Epstein married the actress Frances Sage (also known as Katherine Keating), with whom he had two children. The marriage ended in 1945, and in 1949 he married Ann Lazlo. Epstein and Lazlo had one child.

After graduating, Epstein boxed professionally three times in the featherweight division. Two wins and one draw later, he retired undefeated. He then got a job as an office boy and press agent for $15 per week for an orchestra

Julius J. Epstein, 1947. CORBIS

leader. In 1933 he was summoned to California by two college chums who had sold a story to Warner Bros. studio and then discovered they could not write. Epstein arrived on 14 October at 10:30 P.M. to ghostwrite the script; he was at work by midnight. The following day his two friends took him to a show at the Paramount Theatre and gave him a two-hour crash course in the technical aspects of screenwriting.

For the next nine months, Epstein wrote hundreds of ten- to twenty-page story ideas and finally sold one, *Living on Velvet* (1935), to Warner Bros. The studio offered him a contract for $100 per week. At the end of four weeks, Warner gave him a seven-year contract, which they subsequently renewed. He worked for Warner Bros. for seventeen years, during which time he had a stormy relationship with the studio head, Jack Warner.

His brother, Philip, arrived after Epstein, and the two cowrote numerous scripts. They became known as "the Boys" or "the Brothers" and were inveterate practical jokesters. The Boys generally arrived at the studio around noon and wrote for two hours. According to their contract, they were supposed to arrive at nine. Furious, Warner demanded that they come to work at the prescribed time, noting that even bank presidents arrive at nine. In response, the Epsteins wrote a partial scene and sent it off to Warner with a note advising him to have a bank president finish it.

Epstein was active in the Screenwriters Guild and the Committee for the First Amendment. In 1947 he traveled to Washington, D.C., to protest the legality of the House Un-American Activities Committee, which was investigating the alleged wide-ranging activity of Communist sympathizers in government and society. Warner named Epstein as a probable Communist. (He was, in reality, staunchly anti-Communist.) Once asked by the studio if he had ever belonged to a subversive organization, Epstein responded, "Yes, Warner Brothers."

Epstein wrote scripts for more than fifty films; in 1935 alone, five of his screenplays were produced. Epstein's many screen credits include *Stars over Broadway* (1935), *The Man Who Came to Dinner* (1941), *Mr. Skeffington* (1944), *Arsenic and Old Lace* (1944), *The Tender Trap* (1955), *Light in the Piazza* (1962), and *House Calls* (1978). In 1939 Epstein was nominated for an Academy Award for his script *Four Daughters* (1938) and then won the award in 1943 (with his brother and Howard Koch) for *Casablanca* (1942), an adaptation of the play *Everyone Comes to Rick's*. That Howard Koch shares the credit with the Epsteins for the script has garnered much controversy. What seems certain is that numerous writers had their hands on the project, and no one predicted that it would become a classic. Epstein referred to it as "slick shit" and claimed that it contained "not one moment of reality." Scenes were written just ahead of the shooting schedule, and no one could decide a suitable way to end the film. According to Epstein, he and his brother came up with the ending simultaneously in the car just east of Beverly Glen Boulevard. They turned to each other and said, "Round up the usual suspects," and then fleshed out the details in the remaining half-hour drive to the studio.

Although he was uncredited, Epstein played a major role in shaping the 1942 film *Yankee Doodle Dandy*. The actor James Cagney is reported to have refused to star in the picture until the Boys were brought in to add zip to the dialogue. Epstein thought the story was too sentimental but agreed to do the work for William Cagney, James's brother and associate producer of the film. The Boys put in one of the film's most famous lines, "My mother thanks you, my father thanks you, my sister thanks you, and I thank you," as a joke.

In 1952 Philip died of cancer. Epstein said that when they wrote, they were like one person—routinely finishing each other's lines—and he never collaborated with anyone after his brother's death. Epstein was nominated for an Academy Award again in 1972 for *Pete 'n' Tillie*, a combination of a Peter DeVries novella and one of his own plays (that flopped), entitled *But, Seriously*. He was nominated again in 1983 for *Reuben, Reuben* (based on another DeVries piece), which he considered his best work.

Epstein always wrote his screenplays in longhand and never read what he had written until the first draft was completed; he confessed that he modeled at least one char-

acter in every script after himself. Because Epstein wrote only two hours per day, his first drafts would take from two to three months. He dispensed with treatments (prose descriptions of the story) once the studios stopped demanding them but did use step outlines to construct the scripts. He once tried applying his abundant talent to directing but said he was so nervous that he could not speak to the actors. He preferred literate comedy to physical comedy, did not care for westerns, and detested science fiction. He likened the character E. T. in the Steven Spielberg film of the same name to the Israeli prime minister Menachem Begin, but without the sense of humor. He attributed his own sense of humor to being born Jewish. Epstein died at Cedars-Sinai Medical Center in Los Angeles and is buried in Hillside Memorial Park in Culver City, California.

Epstein was known as a witty and literate writer who could give flat dialogue zip and doctor any script. Modest, soft-spoken, and self-deprecating, eschewing credit and attention, he said, "If you're a storyteller, the structure is there. It comes as naturally as breathing." And if a writer has drawn a true character that the writer knows well, "the character writes your dialogue for you."

★

Patrick McGilligan, ed., *Backstory: Interviews with Screenwriters of Hollywood's Golden Age* (1986), provides entertaining and detailed information about Epstein's professional life. Aljean Harmetz, *Round Up the Usual Suspects, the Making of Casablanca: Bogart, Bergman, and World War II* (1992), contains anecdotes about Epstein's involvement in the writing and production of that movie. Pat McGilligan, ed., *Yankee Doodle Dandy* (1981), offers similar insights into that production. An obituary is in the *New York Times* (1 Jan. 2001). To experience Epstein's intelligence, humor, and wit, see *The Writer Speaks: Julius J. Epstein* (1995), from the Writer Speaks Video History Series, developed by the Writer's Guild Foundation.

KATHARINE FISHER BRITTON

EVANS, Dale (*b.* 31 October 1912 in Uvalde, Texas; *d.* 8 February 2001 in Apple Valley, California), actress, singer, composer, author, and Christian evangelist; wife and partner of Roy Rogers.

Christened Frances Octavia Smith, Evans was born to Walter Hillman Smith and Bettie Sue (Wood) Smith, farmers and hardware store owners. Her family moved to Osceola, Arkansas, where she finished high school, and later to Memphis, Tennessee. In January 1927 she lied about her age (she was fourteen) and married Thomas Frederick Fox. Their son was born a year later, and they divorced when Evans was sixteen.

Evans had difficult financial times during the Great De-

Dale Evans (*left*), with Roy Rogers. AP/WIDE WORLD PHOTOS

Oklahoma (1944; later retitled *The War of the Wildcats*). In the 1940s she made more than thirty-five films, including *Casanovas in Burlesque* and *Lights of Old Santa Fe* (both 1944). She began writing songs, both music and lyrics, and sang one of her own songs, "Will You Marry Me, Mr. Laramie?," at the Chez Paree nightclub in Chicago. A Paramount agent saw her there and invited her to audition for the lead opposite the crooner Bing Crosby in *Holiday Inn*. Although she did not get that part, she acted in two other films for Twentieth Century–Fox.

In 1944 Evans was cast opposite Roy Rogers in *The Cowboy and the Senorita* and *The Yellow Rose of Texas*. "The chemistry was just right between us, apparently," she recalled, "because after I made one picture with him, the exhibitors said, 'Don't break the team up.'" They followed this film with several other successful "horse operas," eight in 1946 alone. Evans and her second husband divorced in 1945. Meanwhile Rogers's wife, Arlene, died in October 1946, shortly after giving birth to their only son, thus leaving Rogers with three small children. In 1947 Rogers proposed to Evans on horseback while they were waiting for cues to enter as stars at a rodeo. They married on 31 December 1947 at the home of the governor of Oklahoma. Evans and Rogers both became born-again Christians in 1948.

On 26 August 1950 the couple's first child was born. She had Down's syndrome and congenital heart problems. Both parents cared for her at home, rather than institutionalize her, and she died shortly before her second birthday. Evans expressed her sorrow in her first book, *Angel Unaware* (1953), and donated all proceeds from it to the National Association for Retarded Children. In addition to Evans's son and Rogers's three children, the couple adopted four others over the next few years, among them, a girl from the Choctaw tribe of Native Americans and a Korean War orphan. Tragedies claimed two of the couple's adopted children: One was killed in a bus accident on a church outing, and another choked to death in 1965 while serving with the U.S. Army in Germany. Evans again worked through her grief by writing books, *Dearest Debbie: In Ai Lee* (1965) and *Salute to Sandy* (1967), with the proceeds again going to charity.

Rogers and Evans combined parenting with demanding and lucrative careers, appearing in such films as *Twilight in the Sierras* and *Trigger, Jr.* (both 1950), and *South of Caliente* and *Pals of the Golden West* (1951). Evans's favorite movie role was as Toni Ames in *Don't Fence Me In* (1945). Of that performance she told the *Saturday Evening Post* in 1951, "I . . . hate namby-pamby heroines. . . . Toni was a pleasant departure from the usual Western role, in which the girl just stands around while men do violent and admirable things." This focus on active female roles became a guiding principle of Evans and Rogers's television show.

pression, occasionally singing as "Frances Fox" but finally returning to her parents' home with her son. After studying at a business school in Memphis, she worked as a stenographer. Taking her boss's advice, she auditioned to sing on a local radio show sponsored by the company. She sang on the show a few times but soon moved on to WHAS in Louisville, Kentucky, where a station manager suggested she use "Evans" because it was easily understood. After singing on WFAA in Dallas, she became staff singer for Columbia Broadcasting System on WBBM in Chicago, where she moved in 1938 with her new husband, Robert Dale Butts. Butts, a pianist, was the source of her stage name "Dale." Evans then sang for a variety of radio shows, including that of the ventriloquist Edgar Bergen and his dummy, Charlie McCarthy.

After World War II began, Evans performed at more than 550 United Service Organizations shows, usually dressed in western regalia of her own design. At five feet, three inches tall and 127 pounds, with green eyes and brown or blonde hair, she was appealing on stage, wearing costumes with embroidery, sequins, and fringe. She almost always wore a short skirt or a split skirt to ride on horseback. Her big smile and attractive appearance enabled Evans to move easily from radio to movies. She played a minor part in *Swing Your Partner* (1943) and bit parts in several other films, singing to John Wayne in her first Western, *In Old*

While continuing to make films and occasionally entertain at rodeos and road shows, the couple expanded into radio and television with *The Roy Rogers Show* (1951–1956) and *The Roy Rogers and Dale Evans Show* (1962). The theme song was "Happy Trails to You," written by Evans and based, she said, on the trombone line in Ferde Grofé's *Grand Canyon Suite*. On one show the director wanted a song for a little girl to sing. Asking "How long do I have?" Evans retreated to her dressing room and twenty minutes later returned with "The Bible Tells Me So," still a familiar and beloved song.

The opening sequence of each television show portrayed Rogers and Trigger galloping along, followed by Evans on Buttermilk; Pat Brady in his jeep, Nellybelle; and Bullet, "the wonder dog." In most episodes, Brady was clumsy or provided comic relief, roles usually designated for the women in 1950s television—but not in Evans's show. Although her character owned a restaurant, she usually saddled Buttermilk and joined Rogers to solve crimes. In 2001 Evans told *Country Music,* "Before me, movie cowgirls were backdrop scenery for the cowboy, his horse and the action. You never saw a cowgirl with a guitar sitting on a horse singing." In the show, she was Rogers's companion but distinctly not his wife or girlfriend. The director and scriptwriters argued in one case that Roy should kiss her on the forehead as an apology, but Roy's image won out: cowboys—on his show, at least—kissed the horse, not the girl.

The wholesome scripted image of Evans and Rogers on the television show was consistent with their moral and Christian orientation. Evans was active in promoting Christianity, writing thirty-two books about her Christian faith, appearing in the 1950s with the evangelist Billy Graham, and later petitioning for a constitutional amendment to permit public school prayer. Evans received numerous awards and honors over the years, from the 1956 George Spelvin Award for humanitarian services from the Masquers' Club to citations from the National Association for Retarded Children, American Red Cross, American Legion, and other organizations. In 1966 the Texas Press Association named her Texan of the Year.

When her horse, Buttermilk, died, Evans had her stuffed and placed beside Trigger in the Roy Rogers–Dale Evans Museum in Victorville, California. (The museum moved to Branson, Missouri, in 2003.) Rogers passed away in 1998, and three years later Evans died of congestive heart failure at their home in Apple Valley, California. They are buried in Sunset Hills Memorial Park.

Evans was the first female movie and television star who dared to be strong and smart and whose personal life seemed to be consistent with that fictional role. She was a composer and singer of both western and Christian songs and, as an honest author, was open about shortcomings in her own life. In her *New York Times* obituary, James Barron

articulated her importance as an early role model: "Thousands and thousands of red-blooded American girls wore Dale Evans outfits and cast-iron six shooters in their matching holster sets as a kind of proto-feminist reach for equality with their brothers." Many of the little girls who watched Dale Evans in the 1950s became vocal feminists in the 1960s and 1970s, following Evans's image as a woman who—even while maintaining the difficult balancing act of mother and wife, composer, singer, actress, author, and Christian apologist—could ride into the sunset with her man.

★

Evans's papers are archived at the Roy Rogers–Dale Evans Museum, which in 2003 moved from Victorville, California, to Branson, Missouri. Autobiographical works include *Happy Trails: The Story of Roy Rogers and Dale Evans* (1979), with Rogers and Carlton Stowers, and *Happy Trails: Our Life Story* (1994), with Rogers and Jane and Michael Stern. A full-length biography is Elise Miller Davis, *The Answer Is God: The Inspiring Personal Story of Dale Evans and Roy Rogers* (1955). The couple also was profiled in Norman Vincent Peale, ed., *Faith Made Them Champions* (1955). See also Robert K. Oermann, "The Queen of the West," *Country Music* no. 211 (Oct./Nov. 2001). An obituary is in the *New York Times* (8 Feb. 2001).

DESSA CRAWFORD

EVANS, Rowland, Jr. ("Rowly") (*b.* 28 April 1921 in White Marsh, Pennsylvania; *d.* 23 March 2001 in Washington, D.C.), news commentator, television personality, newspaper columnist, and author.

Evans was the son of Rowland Evans, a well-to-do businessman, and Elizabeth Wharton (Downs) Evans, a homemaker. In 1939 he graduated from Kent School, an exclusive private academy in Connecticut, before enrolling at Yale University in New Haven, Connecticut. On 8 December 1941, the day after the Japanese attack on Pearl Harbor, Evans withdrew from the university and enlisted in the U.S. Marine Corps. Sent to the Pacific theater, he saw combat in the Solomon Islands and attained the rank of sergeant before contracting malaria in 1944, when he was discharged and sent home. His longtime friend and coworker Robert Novak said that Evans's wartime experiences helped him evolve from a privileged, aimless "society boy" into a mature man who became a hard-bitten realist.

Instead of returning to Yale, Evans became a copyboy for the *Philadelphia Bulletin,* leaving that job in 1945 to join the Associated Press wire service to cover national politics. In 1955 he left that position to become chief of the Washington bureau of the *New York Herald-Tribune.* Traveling often, Evans gained firsthand knowledge of Western Europe and the Soviet bloc and also traveled extensively in Asia. He became as knowledgeable of international affairs as he was of domestic politics.

On 18 June 1949 Evans married Katherine Winton; the couple had three children. In 1950 Evans entered George Washington University in the nation's capital, attending part-time and completing enough courses to receive an A.A. in 1952.

In 1962 Evans began his own six-days-a-week syndicated news column for the *New York Herald-Tribune*, still his home paper. Evans realized that he needed a partner to share the increased workload, and he contacted Novak, who was then working for the *Wall Street Journal*. Evans and Novak produced the first column of their "Inside Report" on 13 May 1963. Their first offering predicted that Barry Goldwater, a conservative senator from Arizona, would win the Republican nomination for president in 1964. Pundits considered the prediction unrealistic and extreme, but when it proved true, Evans and Novak gained stature as political analysts. "Inside Report," whose home paper became the *Chicago Sun-Times* in 1966, eventually appeared in more than 300 newspapers.

According to the former Democratic National Committee chairman Larry O'Brien, the "Inside Report" was the first thing that savvy Washington "insiders" read every morning. The column continued until 1993, when Evans went into semiretirement, and over time it became a launching pad for other work, as Evans and Novak produced newsletters on everything from domestic politics to foreign policy. While continuing with the column, Evans also served as a roving reporter and sometime editor for the *Readers Digest*.

In 1980 both Evans and Novak joined the fledgling cable news network CNN and became pioneers in transferring the influence of news columnists from the printed page to cable television. On their program *Evans and Novak*, the pair made an unlikely team, with Evans's persona of an elder patrician ready to educate, and Novak's of a scrappy little pit bull ready to fight.

Evans had great interview skills. His words and demeanor made television guests feel comfortable, after which he casually asked tough questions as easily as if he were talking about last week's weather. With Evans in semiretirement, in 1998 the program added the commentators Al Hunt of the *Wall Street Journal* and Mark Shields, a syndicated news columnist, and was renamed *Evans, Novak, Hunt, and Shields*. But even as his career activities declined, Evans continued with the show, appearing for the last time on 9 March 2001, just days before his death.

Like Novak, Evans began his career as a moderate liberal and knew several presidents well, including John F. Kennedy and Lyndon B. Johnson. But beginning in the 1970s both men became more conservative, and by 1980 both were supporters of President Ronald W. Reagan and believers in supply-side economics. Suspicious of communist countries, Evans believed that Reagan's military spending helped account for the collapse of the Soviet Union. Evans believed that his great calling was to devote his life to understanding U.S. politics, because he believed that the "heart and soul" of politicians "drive" the great movements in history. To elicit information, Evans developed a "signature" line: "So what do you know that is new?"

Evans wrote a number of books with Novak, including *The Reagan Revolution* (1981). Evans, with Novak as an occasional coauthor, also contributed articles to *Harper's*, the *New Republic, Atlantic Monthly, Saturday Evening Post*, and other magazines.

Near the end of his life, Evans developed esophageal cancer. He died at Georgetown University Hospital at age seventy-nine from complications caused by the cancer.

During a long career in which he evolved from a moderate to a conservative, Evans built and maintained a significant career as both a newspaper reporter and a television commentator. He became the model for objective reporting while adding his own interpretations of the political scene.

★

Sources on Evans and his views include his own books: *Lyndon B. Johnson: The Exercise of Power* (1966), with Novak; *Nixon in the White House: The Frustration of Power* (1971); and *The Reagan Revolution* (1981), with Novak. For a retrospective on Evans's career, see John Fund, "Remembering Rowly Evans," *Wall Street Journal* (26 Mar. 2001). For biographical sketches of Evans, see William H. Taft, *Encyclopedia of Twentieth-Century Journalists* (1986); Joseph P. McKerns, *Biographical Dictionary of American Journalism* (1989); and Robert B. Downs and Jane B. Downs, *Journalists of the United States* (1991). Obituaries are in the *New York Times* and *Washington Post* (both 24 Mar. 2001).

JAMES M. SMALLWOOD

F

FAHEY, John (*b.* 28 February 1939 in Takoma Park, Maryland; *d.* 22 February 2001 in Salem, Oregon), virtuoso acoustic guitar player known for his unorthodox fingerpicking style, which he named "American primitive."

Fahey was born in Takoma Park, a middle-class suburb of Washington, D.C. His parents worked for government agencies, and both were amateur piano players whose musical interests included country and bluegrass. They often took their son with them when they went to concerts. Fahey's formal musical training began when he learned to play the clarinet in school, but at the age of thirteen he bought a Sears, Roebuck Silver Charm guitar for $17. Instead of taking lessons, he bought a book of guitar chords and began to learn the basics. By his own admission, he was a slow learner.

Although rock-and-roll music and Elvis Presley were the rage in the 1950s, Fahey gravitated toward bluegrass and then traditional blues, much of it by the southern black artists of the 1920s and 1930s. Few record stores, however, stocked the hard-to-find blues recordings that Fahey and his fellow aficionados had come to love. Soon, Fahey and his friends were making excursions to the South in search of rare 78 rpm recordings of such blues artists as Blind Willie Johnson and Charley Patton.

Throughout the late 1950s Fahey was doggedly practicing the guitar and showing great improvement. His first recordings were made in the late 1950s by his friend Joe Bussard, who had a mail-order business selling copies of old blues recordings. To see whether any of his customers could tell if Fahey's recordings were "authentic," Fahey recorded under the name Blind Thomas. Often the customers could not tell the difference between Fahey and the authentic bluesmen. He recorded twenty-eight songs between 1958 and 1961, and these recordings were the only time that Fahey ever sang.

Fahey also had begun to compose. In 1959, while working as a gas station attendant in Maryland, he borrowed $300 to record an album. Only about a hundred copies of the album were pressed. One side the album said "John Fahey," while the other side featured Fahey under the pseudonym "Blind Joe Death." It took him three years to sell them all, peddling them out of the trunk of his car. Eventually, the album was rerecorded on Takoma Records, which Fahey established in Maryland in the early 1960s.

Fahey earned a B.A. in philosophy and religion from American University in Washington, D.C., and about 1963, soon after obtaining his degree, he moved to California to attend the University of California, Berkeley, to study philosophy. In 1964 he left Berkeley to attend the University of California, Los Angeles (UCLA), where he became the first UCLA student to earn an M.A. in folklore and mythology. His master's thesis focused on the music of the blues artist Charley Patton. After graduation Fahey went to Hawaii to become a teaching assistant in a university philosophy department but left after only three months.

Fahey decided to focus his attention on his tiny Takoma Records label. Fahey and others rediscovered and released recordings of Bukka White and Skip James, both renowned blues artists of the 1920s and 1930s. It was Fahey's recordings of himself playing solo acoustic guitar, however, that established the label as a thriving enterprise. His first two releases on the label were a rerecording of his amateur *Blind Joe Death* album (1959) and the album *Death Chants, Breakdowns and Military Waltzes* (1963).

Fahey's style was both eclectic and unclassifiable, as he borrowed from blues, classical, bluegrass, and eventually world music genres to develop his unique style and musical compositions. "I try and play anything I like, no matter what genre," Fahey commented. Although the recordings never sold in large enough numbers for him to hit the charts, Fahey soon developed a cult following for his dense fingerpicking style on the guitar. As one writer noted, "Fahey's Takoma years reveal a pastoral sense of beauty" with "infectious rhythmic undercurrents, exotic dissonances, and repetitive melodic interventions."

As well as recording on his own Takoma label, which he sold to Chrysalis Records in the mid-1970s, Fahey also recorded for numerous other labels. He made nearly forty albums and compact discs over a forty-year career, and among his most successful recordings were four Christmas albums. "I was in the back of a record store one July, and I saw all these cartons of Bing Crosby's *White Christmas* album," Fahey noted. "The clerk said it always sells out. So I got the idea to do Christmas albums that would sell every year." The first such album, *The New Possibility* (1968), included a version of "Silent Night" on the bottleneck guitar. "Nobody hears it the first time and doesn't get his socks knocked off," the pianist George Winston once noted. Winston was among several artists that Fahey "discovered." His other protégés included the guitarists Leo Kottke and Will Ackerman, who later founded Windham Hill Records.

Fahey continued to record throughout the 1970s and 1980s and had a hard-core following that included numerous musicians. He struggled with alcoholism for many years, was divorced three times, and fell on hard times financially. He was diagnosed with Epstein-Barr syndrome in 1986 and then with diabetes. He virtually disappeared from the music scene and lived in a Salvation Army shelter in Salem, Oregon, in the early 1990s. In 1994, however, Rhino Records released a retrospective of Fahey's recordings on two compact discs, called *Return of the Repressed: The John Fahey Anthology*. This recording, and a renewed interest by music journalists, led to a resurgence in his career. Fahey went on to perform and, with $50,000 he inherited after his father's death, established Revenant Records with Dean Blackwood, a lawyer and music promoter. He began to release new recordings for other labels and wrote the book *How Bluegrass Music Destroyed My Life:*

Stories (1960). Fahey died at age sixty-one after undergoing coronary bypass surgery and was buried in Restlawn Cemetery in Salem, Oregon. His final recording, *Red Cross*, was issued posthumously in 2003.

Although many musical artists like Kottke, who started out emulating Fahey's style, eventually went on to more success and fame than their mentor, Fahey stands alone for his idiosyncratic style and body of work. As one writer noted, "Every member of the fingerstyle guitar community acknowledges his 'American primitive' style as a direct or indirect influence." Although he was classified as a "folkie" early in his career, Fahey's style and music were essentially unclassifiable, as he incorporated a wide range of styles that included not only blues and jazz but Gregorian chant, Indian ragas, and classical guitar. Fahey's art will remain an inspiration for future generations of guitarists.

★

Fahey's memoir, thinly disguised as fiction, is *How Bluegrass Music Destroyed My Life: Stories* (1960). Profiles of Fahey and comments about his art and performances during his early years are "Syncopated Classics from the Underground," *Melody Maker* (Sept. 1969); Tim Ferris, "Why Fahey Wants to Kill Everybody," *Rolling Stone* (23 Dec. 1970); and Mark Humphrey, "An Existential Guitarist Packs His Bags," *LA Reader* (May 1981). Obituaries are in *Billboard* (10 Mar. 2001), *Acoustic Guitar* (June 2001), and *Guitar Player* (1 June 2001).

DAVID PETECHUK

FAIRBANKS, Douglas Elton, Jr. (*b.* 9 December 1909 in New York City; *d.* 7 May 2000 in New York City), film and television actor best remembered for his role as the villainous Rupert of Hentzau in *The Prisoner of Zenda* (1937).

Fairbanks was the only child of Douglas Elton Fairbanks, a theater actor, and Anna Beth (Sully) Fairbanks, an heiress and a homemaker. Living in New York City, the senior Fairbanks preferred acting on the stage. However, as his wife's fortune dwindled, financial concerns led him to move his family into a rented apartment near the Hollywood, California, foothills and to seek work in films. When not attending private military grammar schools, the young Fairbanks accompanied his father on movie sets and developed a love for films. Chubby and shy, Fairbanks admired the dashing, swashbuckling heroes his father portrayed.

Fairbanks first performed in silent feature films at age thirteen, starring in *Stephen Steps Out* (1923). Acting professionally at such a young age, Fairbanks had to quit school and be tutored on movie sets. Thomas S. Patton, a former postmaster of New York, instructed him, and though Fairbanks never graduated from high school, Patton instilled in him a lifelong love of learning.

Douglas Fairbanks, Jr., September 1947. AP/WIDE WORLD PHOTOS

Fairbanks acted in several more films, in which he often played the juvenile lead, including *Wild Horse Mesa* (1925), *Stella Dallas* (1926), *Padlocked* (1926), and *Broken Hearts of Hollywood* (1926). Soon, he received better quality parts. He was cast in *Women Love Diamonds* (1927) with one of his idols, Lionel Barrymore. Fairbanks's performance with Greta Garbo in *A Woman of Affairs* (1928) and his portrayal of a brash young reporter in *The Power of the Press* (1928) earned him the attention of important film executives. His first role in a talking picture came at age nineteen in *The Barker* (1928). The following year, he played the lead role opposite Joan Crawford in *Our Modern Maidens* (1929), and in June 1929 Crawford, whom he called "Billie," and Fairbanks were married. Her subsequent affair with the actor Clark Gable contributed to their divorce in 1934.

By that time Fairbanks had begun filming at Warner Bros.–First National, where his image as a callow youth quickly gave way to dramatic roles in such films as *Dawn Patrol, Outward Bound,* and *Little Caesar* (all 1930). Fairbanks had grown to a lean six feet tall, with dark hair, a thin mustache, and a captivating smile he inherited from his father. Never fully suited for tough-guy roles, he left Warner Bros. to form Criterion Films in England in 1934.

In 1936 Fairbanks's company produced its first film, *The Amateur Gentleman* (1936), followed by *The Accused* (1936),

and *Jump for Glory* (1937). Such efforts failed to advance the company and Fairbanks's acting career. Then in 1937 the producer David O. Selznick of Selznick International offered Fairbanks the role of Rupert of Hentzau in *The Prisoner of Zenda* (1937). Fairbanks balked at playing a supporting role after working so hard to become a leading man. He also disliked the idea of playing a swashbuckling swordsman for fear of negative comparisons with his father. However, at his father's urging, Fairbanks consented to the role. The film was a big success, and along with glowing reviews, Fairbanks received numerous new offers. He quickly made four romantic comedies: *The Joy of Living, The Rage of Paris,* and *Having a Wonderful Time* for Radio-Keith-Orpheum (RKO) Pictures, and *The Young in Heart* for Selznick International (all 1938).

In these films, Fairbanks had on-screen love affairs with such glamorous leading ladies as Irene Dunne, Paulette Goddard, Ginger Rogers, and Janet Gaynor. Offscreen, he had brief romances with the actresses Gertrude Lawrence and Marlene Dietrich. He fell deeply in love with Mary Lee (Epling) Hartford, the young ex-wife of The Great Atlantic and Pacific Tea Company (A&P) supermarket heir Huntington Hartford, and they married on 22 April 1939. They had three daughters, and their marriage lasted until Mary's death in 1988. On 30 May 1991 Fairbanks married his third wife, Vera Shelton.

Fairbanks returned to adventure films in *Gunga Din* (1939), in which he starred with Cary Grant and Victor McLaglen. Reminiscent of *The Three Musketeers, Gunga Din* was a professional and box-office triumph for Fairbanks, and his romantic character, Sergeant Thomas Ballantine, became one of his best-remembered roles. The growing threat of war in Europe and the death of his father in December 1939 overshadowed its success, however. Fairbanks made two more films before joining the U.S. Navy. He starred with Rita Hayworth in the black comedy *Angels over Broadway* (1940) and played twins in *The Corsican Brothers* (1941).

On 10 April 1941 Fairbanks was commissioned a lieutenant (junior grade) in the U.S. Naval Reserve. Fairbanks served with distinction, receiving several military honors for his participation in the invasions of Sicily, the Italian mainland, Elba, and the South of France. After the Battle of Salerno in 1943, Fairbanks received the Silver Star, a decoration that can be won only in combat. By war's end, Fairbanks had been promoted to commander. He also became involved in numerous charities and humanitarian organizations and was a founding member of the Cooperative for Assistance and Relief Everywhere (CARE) in 1945.

Having been away from his profession for four years, Fairbanks sought film opportunities in the postwar era. His big break came when he was offered the title role in the adventure epic *Sinbad the Sailor* (1947). Starring with Maureen O'Hara and Anthony Quinn, Fairbanks played the swashbuckling sailor, reminding moviegoers of his famous father. After *Sinbad,* his movie career waned, despite his producing and starring in other films. A lifelong Anglophile, Fairbanks moved to Britain in the early 1950s to host and produce the anthology television series *Douglas Fairbanks, Jr., Presents.* In 1957 he returned to the United States, where he made occasional television appearances on such programs as *Rowan and Martin's Laugh-In* (1968) and *The Love Boat* (1977). His last feature film role came in the contemporary thriller *Ghost Story* (1981), with costars Fred Astaire, Melvyn Douglas, and John Houseman. Fairbanks died of a heart attack and was buried in the same crypt as his father at Hollywood Forever Cemetery in Hollywood, California.

Although Fairbanks never achieved the larger-than-life screen persona of his father, his roles in films ranging from screwball comedies to gangster films and swashbuckling adventures established him as one of the most versatile actors of the prewar era. His illustrious war record and commitment to humanitarian service also represented notable achievements.

★

Fairbanks's manuscripts and personal papers are housed at the Boston University Library, Boston, Massachusetts. His first autobiography, *The Salad Days* (1988), covers his life up to World War II and is followed by *A Hell of a War* (1993), detailing his military experience. Fairbanks collaborated with Richard Schickel on *The Fairbanks Album* (1975), which displays family archival material. Schickel's biography of Douglas Fairbanks, Sr., *His Picture in the Papers: A Speculation on Celebrity in America Based on the Life of Douglas Fairbanks, Sr.* (1973), also provides helpful family information. An obituary is in the *New York Times* (8 May 2000).

ROBERT D. BALKEN

FANNIN, Paul Jones (*b.* 29 January 1907 in Ashland, Kentucky; *d.* 13 January 2002 in Phoenix, Arizona), businessman and statesman who reshaped Arizona's educational system, fostered better relations with Mexico, and fought for the rights of individual states to decide on open-shop or closed-shop workplaces.

At the time of Fannin's birth, his father was in poor health, and a doctor recommended that he move to Arizona probably because of the state's clean, dry air. In October 1907 the family, including two siblings, moved to Phoenix, where his father established a hardware store. He attended the University of Arizona for only two years (1925–1927) and then transferred to Stanford University in California, from which he graduated in 1930 with a B.A. in business administration. Fannin's experiences at Phoenix Union High School and the University of Arizona would influ-

Paul J. Fannin, 1964. AP/WIDE WORLD PHOTOS

ence his work as governor and U.S. senator, where he would work to make the system more fair to Spanish-speaking students and to Native Americans. He first put his education to work in the family hardware store, developing the interpersonal skills that would help him form successful working relationships.

In 1934 Fannin married Elma Addington, with whom he had three sons and one daughter. His son Bob later became chairman of the Arizona Republican Party. In the mid-1930s Fannin and his brother, Ernest, established the Fannin Gas and Supply Company. Propane gas was then becoming popular for heating, cooking, and other purposes, and the Fannins decided to become distributors not only of propane gas but also of the equipment required for using it. Paul Fannin was the company's president, a position he held until he sold his holdings in 1955. Starting a new business in the middle of the Great Depression was a terrific challenge, but the 1930s and 1940s turned out to be heady times for Fannin. He used his exceptional people skills to develop friendships and customer loyalty that resulted in the company's becoming a major supplier of gas and related supplies throughout the southwestern United States and much of northern Mexico, especially the state of Sonora.

By the 1950s Fannin had acquired a passion for developing good relations between Mexico and the United States, believing that his principles of building trust among people would lay the foundation for future success in trade and business enterprises. In 1959, addressing the first meeting of the Arizona-Sonora West Coast Trade Commission, which he founded, he summarized his view thus: "I believe every businessman and economist will agree that there can be no worthwhile economic relationship without the warmth and understanding of human relations based on mutual respect and friendship." When he retired at the young age of forty-eight, he chose to devote himself to creating such warm relations between Arizona and Sonora.

Frustrated by an Arizona government that he believed fomented resentment among its ethnic groups and hostility with Mexico and saying that he believed the state needed a good businessman in charge, Fannin decided to run as a Republican for governor in 1958. It was a surprise to almost every observer when he was elected by thirty thousand votes on 7 November 1958. He took office on 5 January 1959 and was elected to two more two-year terms in 1960 and 1962. His terms were productive ones, as he put his principles to work, and he had four major achievements that have continued to affect the lives of Arizonans. The first was his establishment in 1959 of the Arizona-Sonora West Coast Trade Commission, which became the modern Arizona-Mexico Commission. With the help of Sonora's governor Alvaro Obregon, he created a coalition of government and business that established connections between the states of Arizona and Sonora, and these resulted in hundreds of millions of dollars in increased trade between the two states over the next five decades.

The second major achievement was the equalizing of property taxes throughout Arizona, something that helped the impoverished areas of the state, especially in paying for schools. Fannin's third and perhaps greatest achievement was his reform of the state's educational system. He established a junior-college system, vital to the educational aspirations of working students such as he had been. He was determined to make the University of Arizona an institution to be esteemed, and he established the state's first medical school at the university. His fourth achievement was longer in coming. Fannin believed that much of the poverty in the state was due to the lack of water. Many businesses could not prosper without it, so he began his campaign to have water from the Colorado River Project piped to Arizona.

In 1964 Senator Barry Goldwater, a classmate and friend of Fannin's from high school, ran for president of the United States and declined to run for reelection as a U.S. senator from Arizona. Fannin ran to fill Goldwater's seat and was elected that November, taking office in the Senate as his third term as governor was about to expire. He was reelected to the Senate in 1970 but declined to run again

in 1976 because of the poor health of his wife. Fannin had three major achievements while in the Senate. The first came almost immediately. In 1965 several Senate Democrats tried to amend Provision 14(b) of the Taft-Hartley Act to force all states to have closed shops—places of employment where only members of a particular union could work—as opposed to open shops, or ones in which members of more than one union and nonunion members could work together. Fannin, who favored leaving the matter up to individual states, became the leader of the opposition to changing the law and formed a coalition of Republicans and Democrats to defeat the amendment.

His second major achievement was to foster educational reforms for Native Americans. Fannin and New York senator Robert F. Kennedy, a Democrat, worked together until Kennedy's assassination in 1968 to bring to reservations the full benefits of schooling without the negatives of forcing students to eschew their native cultures. This resulted in bills that defined the curriculum, established complete education from preschool to college, and provided the funds for the schools involved. The third major achievement was the completion of his efforts to bring more water to Arizona. Fannin authored the legislation that created the Central Arizona Project that brought Colorado River water to the state in 1968.

Upon his retirement from the Senate in 1977, Fannin served on the Central Arizona Water Conservation District Board and pursued his efforts to maintain a happy partnership between Arizona and Sonora. Only in the last few years of his life did his energy begin to flag. His wife passed away in 2001, and Fannin died of a stroke at his home the following year. His remains were interred with those of his wife at the Garden of Peace in the Serenity Mausoleum of Greenwood Memory Lawn in Phoenix.

Some journalists labeled Fannin an "ultra-conservative" because of his opposition to closed shops, but his achievements reveal someone who could not be neatly placed in an ideology. Instead, they show a man with a flexible mind, who was committed to including all Arizonans in the state's economic and educational opportunities and who strove to eliminate social barriers created by racism and poverty. He combined this flexibility of mind with the practicality of a thoughtful entrepreneur, resulting in reforms and initiatives that survived for decades and benefited millions of people.

★

There is little in print about Fannin. A sketch about his life is in Robert Sobel and John Raimo, *Biographical Directory of the Governors of the United States, 1789–1978* (1978). Another brief sketch is in John F. Goff, *Arizona Biographical Dictionary* (1983). Obituaries are in the *Washington Post* (16 Jan. 2002) and *New York Times* (17 Jan. 2002).

KIRK H. BEETZ

FARIÑA, Margarita Baez ("Mimi") (*b.* 30 April 1945 in Palo Alto, California; *d.* 18 July 2001 in Mill Valley, California), singer and social activist who founded the Bread and Roses Foundation, bringing entertainment to shut-ins.

The youngest of three daughters of Albert Baez, a physicist and science educator, and Joan (Bridge) Baez, a writer, Fariña was called Mimi from early childhood. Because of her father's profession and his association with the United Nations Educational, Scientific, and Cultural Organization (UNESCO), the family moved frequently. They lived briefly in Baghdad, Iraq, in 1951 and then returned to Palo Alto before moving in 1958 to Belmont, Massachusetts, where her father taught at the Massachusetts Institute of Technology.

Dyslexic and having difficulty in school, Fariña turned to music; she studied violin and harbored a desire to dance professionally. Before the cross-country move, her parents gave her a Goya classical guitar. Her sister Joan, four years older, also received a guitar, and the two girls learned to play, while their older sister, Pauline, gravitated toward nonmusical pursuits. Of the two younger sisters, Joan possessed a voice of unique clarity and, within a few years of moving to New England, was well established as a folksinger on the coffeehouse circuit. From the age of fourteen, Fariña occasionally performed with her older sister and, because of this lifestyle, developed into a precocious teenager. She socialized regularly with the college-age friends of her sister's and began smoking cigarettes.

When Fariña was sixteen, the family moved to the Paris suburb of Le Visinet, France. Still in high school, she completed her studies via correspondence courses through the University of Nebraska, earning a high school diploma in 1963. While in France in 1962 she met Richard Fariña, an adventurer and writer and the husband of the folksinger Carolyn Hester. The Fariña-Hester marriage disintegrated quickly after Richard met Mimi; within a year he had divorced Hester and married the eighteen-year-old Mimi in Paris in the spring of 1963. On their return to the United States later that year, a public ceremony was held in Carmel, California.

Together the couple embraced a folksinging career, making their professional debut at the Big Sur (California) Folk Festival in June 1964 and then signing with Vanguard Records and moving to Cambridge, Massachusetts. After appearing at the Newport (Rhode Island) Jazz Festival in 1965, they released a debut album, *Celebrations for a Grey Day,* in December. Fariña was widowed four months later on her twenty-first birthday in 1966, when her husband died in a motorcycle accident at Big Sur after a party to celebrate the publication of his first novel, *Been Down So Long It Looks Like Up to Me.*

Left with an unfulfilled recording contract, Fariña spent the years immediately following her husband's death preparing compilations of their work together, including live tracks from the various folk festivals at which they had performed. An album, *Memories,* was released on Vanguard in 1968; *Best of Mimi and Richard Fariña* appeared in 1971. Fariña performed with a San Francisco–based political satire troupe, the Committee, in 1967 and appeared at the Big Sur Folk Festival in 1968. She married the broadcaster Milan Melvin at the Big Sur Folk Festival, but they divorced two years later. She resurrected her folksinging career in the early 1970s by performing in clubs as a duo with Tom Jans; they released an album, *Take Heart,* on A&M Records in 1971. Her only major recording after this was *Solo,* released in 1986 on Rounder Records.

Despite Fariña's success as an entertainer, her musical career was but a youthful prelude to her life's work, which encompassed two and a half decades of social activism. This was a lifestyle inspired by earlier experiences, including an incident in 1967 in Santa Rosa, California, when Fariña, her mother, and her sister Joan were arrested while participating in an antiwar demonstration. On Thanksgiving Day 1972 Fariña joined her sister and the bluesman B. B. King in performing for inmates at Sing Sing Prison in Ossining, New York. In 1974 she participated in a similar concert program at a halfway house for teenagers. Fariña was inspired to establish a nonprofit foundation, Bread and Roses, committed to bringing musical entertainment to shut-ins.

With the support of colleagues in the entertainment industry, Fariña's foundation eventually organized more than five hundred musical events annually. In addition to appearances at penal institutions, she brought these programs to assorted institutional venues, including senior centers and psychiatric and children's hospitals, and expanded the venues later to include AIDS wards and homeless shelters. Working exclusively in California, Bread and Roses earned high visibility in the San Francisco Bay Area, where the actor Robin Williams threw his influence squarely behind the enterprise. The singer Boz Scaggs, the comedian Lily Tomlin, and the country artist Willie Nelson, among the many performers and others in the music industry affiliated with Bread and Roses, came forward to assist Fariña in this cause.

Established in 1974, by 1985 Bread and Roses had grown into a $200,000-per-year operation. By 1991 the organization supported four full-time staff members and four part-time assistants; the budget by that time had more than doubled, to $430,000. Fariña's arsenal of noteworthy supporters had grown to include more than 150 performers who remained on call for performances. The program served sixty institutions throughout northern California on

Mimi Fariña performing in Berkeley, California, September 1978. ROGER RESSMEYER/CORBIS

a regular basis, and Fariña maintained a waiting list of sixty others. Funded initially from donations, direct mail, and benefit fund-raisers, Bread and Roses grew dramatically when Fariña expanded her resources by soliciting corporate sponsorships, beginning in 1991 with Esprit Corporation.

In December 1999, as Fariña undertook the planning for a twenty-fifth anniversary celebration for Bread and Roses (held 20 March 2000) and made plans to retire from active involvement in the organization, she was diagnosed with lung cancer. She died the following year at her home in Mill Valley, where she lived with her partner, the writer Paul Liberatore. An estimated twelve hundred mourners attended a standing-room-only memorial service in her honor at San Francisco's Grace Cathedral.

Bread and Roses, which had an annual budget approaching $1 million by the time of Fariña's death, lived on as her legacy, reaching almost twenty-one thousand people at more than five hundred performances annually in the early 2000s, and with 125 institutions on the waiting list.

★

Highlights of Fariña's life are documented in David Hajdu, *Positively 4th Street: The Lives and Times of Joan Baez, Bob Dylan, Mimi Baez Fariña, and Richard Fariña* (2001). An interview with Fariña by Patrick Morrow appeared in *Popular Music and Society* 2, no. 1 (1972): 62–79. Among the numerous tributes are Chris Morris, "Folk Artist Mimi Fariña Remembered," *Billboard* (4 Aug. 2001). An obituary is in the *New York Times* (20 July 2001).

G. COOKSEY

FARRELL, Eileen Frances (*b.* 13 February 1920 in Willimantic, Connecticut; *d.* 23 March 2002 in Park Ridge, New Jersey), dramatic soprano, radio star, opera diva, concert soloist, and jazz and popular singer.

Farrell was the youngest of three children of Michael John Farrell, a singer and teacher, and Catherine Felicita (Kennedy) Farrell, a singer and organist, who traveled the vaudeville circuit as Farrell and Farrell or the Singing O'Farrells. Farrell's childhood was spent in Willimantic, Storrs, and Norwich, Connecticut. She made her stage debut in the second grade, playing a raindrop in the Saint Mary's school pageant. Throughout her childhood, Farrell took informal voice lessons from her mother. In 1935 she attended Norwich Free Academy, but at the end of the school year the family moved to her grandparents' house in Woonsocket, Rhode Island. At Woonsocket High, she sang with the band, and during her junior year she played Buttercup in the school's production of Gilbert and Sullivan's *H.M.S. Pinafore*. In her senior year Farrell sang "Sylvia" in a statewide competition and won first prize.

Following graduation in 1939, much to Farrell's surprise, her mother made arrangements for her to audition for Merle Alcock, a singing teacher in New York City. Alcock, a contralto who had sung more than thirty secondary roles at the Metropolitan Opera, accepted Farrell as a student, expecting her also to cook and sew for her. In her autobiography, *Can't Help Singing: The Life of Eileen Farrell* (1999), Farrell wrote, "She may not have taught me a whole lot I didn't know already, but at least she didn't do me any harm." Alcock recommended Farrell to a radio

Eileen Farrell, 1966. BETTMANN/CORBIS

executive at the Columbia Broadcasting System (CBS). Farrell's audition, singing "The Last Rose of Summer," secured her first professional singing job as a member of the CBS chorus. After three months it was apparent that Farrell was not a good fit in the chorus; her voice was too loud. Afraid of being fired, Farrell sang "Vissi d'arte" for another audition and was offered her own half-hour program with the CBS Symphony. In 1941 Farrell had a weekly show: *Eileen Farrell Sings,* which aired at 11:30 P.M. She did the same live show three hours later for the West Coast audience, singing one aria, one art song (usually in French or German), and one song in English. To learn all the music, and for language coaching, Farrell hired Charlie Baker, the musician and music director of the Rutgers Presbyterian Church.

In a 1958 article in *Life* magazine, Farrell said that when she sang in New York City, she knew only two arias. But, she continued, "Radio changed all that. For five years I sang everything from 'Oh Promise Me' to [Francis] Poulenc. Now, no matter what a conductor wants, I've usually sung it before." Although her show was a late-night one, Farrell gained popularity. She appeared as a guest on other radio shows, including André Kostelanetz's *Pause That Refreshes*

and *The Prudential Family Hour.* In 1944 a new teacher, Eleanor McLellan, "redirected" Farrell as a singer. McLellan instructed her in new breathing techniques, extended her upper register, and taught her to sing pianissimo and to project words in a meaningful way. The latter skill helped make her an effective pop singer later in her career.

On 5 April 1946 Farrell married Robert Vincent Reagan, a policeman and member of the New York Police Department forgery squad. They had a son and a daughter. When her radio show ended in 1947, Farrell went on the concert circuit, crisscrossing North America, singing with symphony orchestras. In 1949 she made her New York Philharmonic debut under the conductor Leopold Stokowski and toured South America with Thomas Schippers as piano accompanist. A recital at Carnegie Hall in 1950 received rave reviews, and the *New York Times* music critic Harold C. Schonberg wrote that Farrell's voice, renowned for its size, "could probably be heard in downtown Newark." During the 1950–1951 season she appeared sixty-one times with the New York Philharmonic. Her 1951 concert performance of Alban Berg's *Wozzeck* at Carnegie Hall has been described as a lasting contribution to opera. In 1953 Farrell joined the Bach Aria Group, "the smartest thing I ever did as a singer." Singing Bach was good for her voice, promoting lightness and agility.

Farrell continued guest appearances on radio, but she loved television, making her debut on the *Milton Berle Show* in 1950. She also appeared on the *Ed Sullivan Show* and the *Garry Moore Show;* a favorite skit on the Moore show was a song-and-dance number with Carol Burnett, playing two charwomen. In 1955 Farrell did the singing for Eleanor Parker in *Interrupted Melody,* the story of the Australian soprano Marjorie Lawrence. The soundtrack from the film sold well and later was reissued as *The Voice of Eileen Farrell* (1962).

In November 1955 Farrell sang the title role in Luigi Cherubini's *Medea* in a concert with the American Opera Society at New York's Town Hall. It was a great success and resulted in Farrell's venturing into staged opera productions. In 1956 she sang Santuzza in Pietro Mascagni's *Cavalleria Rusticana* in Tampa, Florida. Months later she played Leonora in Giuseppe Verdi's *Il Trovatore* for the San Francisco Opera. In 1957 she sang the title role in Amilcare Ponchielli's *La Gioconda* with the Lyric Opera of Chicago. Her long-awaited debut at the Metropolitan Opera in New York City was on 6 December 1960, singing Alceste in Christoph Gluck's opera of that name. Tickets were available only from scalpers, at $100 a pair, an enormous price at the time. The production was not distinctive, but Farrell's performance was. Her voice exhibited "matchless tone, clarity, and power," and twenty-two curtain calls resulted. Farrell had only five seasons at the Met, singing six roles in forty-five performances. She opened the 1962–

1963 season as Maddalena in Umberto Giordano's *Andrea Chénier.* Her final season was 1965–1966.

Opera was not Farrell's only interest. In 1959 she sang the Verdi *Requiem* in Spoleto, Italy. The jazz trumpeter Louis Armstrong also was scheduled to perform, but he contracted pneumonia, so Farrell sang "On the Sunny Side of the Street" with his band and was a hit. She recorded the album *I've Got a Right to Sing the Blues* (1960), which was a best-seller on pop charts for weeks. Another successful popular album, *Here I Go Again,* followed. Farrell became known as the "queen of crossover," succeeding in pop music, where most opera singers fail, by focusing on the meaning of the words and singing everything "very low."

In 1971 Farrell became distinguished professor of music at Indiana University School of Music in Bloomington, teaching opera and jazz. Farrell left Indiana in 1980 and moved to Castine, Maine, where she taught master classes at Peabody Institute and the University of Maine in Orono. Although Farrell gave up public performances after her husband died in 1986, she continued to record the music of Richard Rogers, Harold Arlen, and other "popular" composers. Her final album was *Love Is Letting Go* (1995). As the result of circulatory ailments, she entered a nursing home, where she died a week later at age eighty-two. Farrell was a versatile singer, equally effective in opera and pop music. Unlike many stars who sacrifice love and family for a career, Farrell had it all: "Much as I loved singing, the best part about it was coming home."

★

Farrell's autobiography, *Can't Help Singing: The Life of Eileen Farrell,* coauthored by Brian Kellow (1999), provides fascinating information about Farrell and the musicians with whom she worked. An interview with Farrell, focusing on her career, is in Deena Rosenberg and Bernard Rosenberg, *The Music Makers* (1979). On Farrell in opera see Winthrop Sargeant, *Divas: Impressions of Six Opera Superstars* (1973). For more information, see "Unpretentious Prima Donna," *Life* (24 Nov. 1958); Thomas Whiteside, "Eileen Farrell: Prima Donna with a Dustpan," *Coronet* (Dec. 1960), about her home life; Brian Kellow, "Blue Notes," *Opera News* (July 1992), concerning her crossover albums; and Richard Dyer, "Soprano Eileen Farrell Steps into the Spotlight Once Again," the *Boston Globe* (18 June 2000), a general overview of her career. Obituaries are in the *Los Angeles Times* and *New York Times* (both 25 Mar. 2002).

MARCIA B. DINNEEN

FEARS, Thomas Jesse ("Tom") (*b.* 3 December 1923 in Guadalajara, Mexico; *d.* 4 January 2000 in Palm Desert, California), Hall of Fame football player and coach whose prolific pass-catching for the Los Angeles Rams set the standard for subsequent generations of professional football receivers.

Fears was the second son born to an American government mining engineer, Charles Fears, Sr., and a Mexican homemaker, Carmen (Valdez) Fears. The family moved to South Central Los Angeles, a mostly Japanese-American neighborhood at the time, when Fears was six years old. He developed into an outstanding football player at Los Angeles Manual Arts High School, from which he graduated in 1942. As a teenager he also ushered at the Los Angeles Memorial Coliseum for fifty cents a game. After receiving many scholarship offers, Fears chose Santa Clara University in northern California. There, as a two-way end, he had two fine seasons, but then joined the U.S. Army Air Corps in 1944 during World War II. Fears was captain of the famed "service ball" Second Air Force Superbombers team in 1944 and 1945.

In 1945, after the war, Fears was drafted by the Rams, then located in Cleveland, of the National Football League (NFL). He elected to finish his college career rather than turn professional, and enrolled at the University of California at Los Angeles (UCLA), where he played football in 1946 and 1947. With the GI Bill to pay college costs, Fears enjoyed a good life, including small parts in movies. As an extra, he was visible for a few seconds in a Humphrey Bogart film, *Action in the North Atlantic* (1943). Fears was a solid player for the Bruins of UCLA but did not gain major All-America status. He graduated with a B.S. in business administration in the spring of 1948.

Tom Fears, 1951. BETTMANN/CORBIS

The Rams moved from Cleveland to Los Angeles for the 1946 season, and because they held the draft rights to him, Fears signed with the local NFL team in 1948 for a $500 bonus and a $6,000 annual salary. Fears said, almost seriously, "I took a pay cut going from college to the pros." For the Rams, he was a bargain. Fears led the NFL in receiving in each of his first three seasons in the league with fifty-one catches as a rookie, followed by seventy-two and eighty-four the next two seasons. His 1950 total (eighty-four receptions for 1,116 yards) set an NFL record that stood for fifteen years. He set another record, eighteen catches in a single game, that stood for over fifty years. Fears accomplished all of this while sharing the ball with another future Hall of Fame player, Elroy "Crazylegs" Hirsch.

A game that typified Fears's ability in the clutch was a Western Division playoff game against the Chicago Bears in 1950 for the right to play the Cleveland Browns for the NFL title. In defeating the Bears 24–14, Fears contributed touchdown catches of forty-three, sixty-eight, and twenty-seven yards. Unfortunately, the next week the Rams lost to the Browns, 30–28. The next season, Fears caught a seventy-three-yard touchdown pass from Norm ("Dutch") Van-Brocklin to help the Rams defeat the Browns 24–17 for the 1951 NFL championship. Fears said of the play, "It was the best thrown ball I've ever caught. Dutch laid it right there in full stride."

In an age when an athlete was considered old at thirty, Fears retired two games into the 1956 season at age thirty-three with an even 400 career pass receptions—at the time second only to the legendary player Don Hutson. He gained 5,397 yards and scored thirty-eight touchdowns. At six feet, two inches, and 215 pounds, Fears was big for an offensive end in his era and commanded the respect of both teammates and opponents. An outstanding blocker as well as a sure-handed receiver, he exemplified the competitiveness and work ethic that are still part of Rams folklore. The Rams linebacker Don Paul said, "He worked so hard and competed so hard, he wound up in the Pro Football Hall of Fame. Tom Fears was never one to get by on ability alone, although he had plenty of that." Fears was inducted into the Pro Football Hall of Fame in 1970.

Fears always stayed in peak physical condition. While coaching the Southern California Sun of the World Football League (WFL) during 1974 and 1975, Fears was challenged by Dave Roller, who considered himself the best tennis player on the team. Fears, then in his fifties, dispatched Roller in straight sets, 6–0, 6–0. An avid golfer, Fears once sank a long, crucial putt for par in an NFL alumni golf tournament. Referring to his clutch performance, Dick Daugherty, a former Rams teammate and member of the foursome that day, shook his head in re-

spectful awe and said, "Some guys just live for third down, and Tommy Fears is one of them."

Fears became an assistant for Vince Lombardi of the Green Bay Packers in 1959. Like Lombardi, his approach to coaching was of the no-nonsense variety. As part of the Packers dynasty—four NFL titles in a six-year span—Fears was a logical candidate to take over as head coach of the New Orleans Saints when they joined the NFL in 1967. Saddled with little talent, his record in New Orleans was an unimpressive 13–34–2 in three-and-a-half seasons. However, success eluded all subsequent Saints coaches for the franchise's first two decades. As a rookie head coach, Fears had the additional problem of having to deal with a mettlesome owner who was determined to have a feature-length movie, *Number One* (1969), starring Charlton Heston as an over-the-hill quarterback, filmed using Saints players and games as backdrops. Fears said, "You can't believe how much of a distraction it was. If that wasn't enough, it was a pretty poor film, too."

After football, Fears became a successful businessman, running several restaurants in southern California, renting condominiums, and overseeing avocado acreage in San Diego County. He developed symptoms of Alzheimer's disease in the early 1990s but functioned for several years before succumbing to complications of the disease in a Palm Desert convalescent facility. He was cremated and his ashes buried in Ascension Cemetery in Lake Forest, California. He was survived by his wife, LuElla Kathryn Wintheiser, whom he had married on 1 March 1952, and their six children.

In many ways Fears was a prototype for modern receivers. He combined the receiving ability of a "possession" receiver, the blocking ability of contemporary tight ends, and the work ethic that separates the great from the good.

★

There is no biography of Fears, but his career is discussed in Bob Oates, *The Los Angeles Rams* (1955); Jerry Izenberg, *Championship: The Complete NFL Title Story* (1966); George Sullivan, *Pro Football Immortals* (1969); and Mickey Herskowitz, *The Golden Age of Pro Football: A Remembrance of Pro Football in the 1950s* (1974). Obituaries are in the *Los Angeles Times* (6 Jan. 2000) and *New York Times* (8 Jan. 2000).

JIM CAMPBELL

FEEHAN, William M. (*b.* 29 September 1929 in Queens, New York City; *d.* 11 September 2001 in Manhattan, New York City), first deputy commissioner of the New York City Fire Department (FDNY), who served in more uniformed and appointive posts during his career than any other individual in the department's 138-year history and who died heroically while leading the emergency efforts at the World Trade Center after the terrorist attacks of 11 September 2001.

Feehan was the son of William Feehan, a New York fire-fighter from 1926 to 1958, and Katherine (Cashman) Feehan, a homemaker. Feehan grew up with his brother, James, in the Queens neighborhood of Jackson Heights and attended Saint Joan of Arc Elementary School and Cathedral High School. Although he was attracted to a number of possible careers, from early childhood he was fascinated by fires and firemen. For a while he thought of becoming a priest but was unwilling to give up the prospect of a family life.

Feehan was a lifetime resident of Queens, a borough long noted for its diversity of distinct neighborhoods, defined by ethnicity, race, and class. He met his wife, Elizabeth "Betty" Keegan, in the Rockaways, affectionately referred to as the "Irish Riviera," and married her in 1956. The Feehans lived in a modest home on Twenty-eighth Street in Flushing with their four children. Following a long tradition, one of his sons and his son-in-law became New York City fire-fighters.

After graduating from Saint John's University in 1954 with a degree in social studies, Feehan served in Korea. Returning in 1956, he joined the New York Fire Patrol and began a ten-year career as a substitute teacher in the New York City school system. On 10 October 1959 he was sworn in as a probationary firefighter, or "proby," in the FDNY.

Feehan's career in the fire department began in the tumultuous 1960s, a period of violent social unrest affecting neighborhoods in every borough, which was referred to by firefighters as "the War Years." Rising to captain, then battalion chief, borough commander, and eventually chief of department, Feehan responded to thousands of "runs" in every corner of the city. He was described as "a charismatic but quiet leader, a gentleman's fireman, who epitomized grace under pressure." A gentle giant at six feet, two inches tall, Feehan became the intelligent and compassionate voice of the fire department in speeches, lectures, and press conferences. The retired chief Henry McDonald, Feehan's executive officer for eight years, viewed him as a "true renaissance man, extremely honest, well read, a very, very smart guy. He could write like crazy. Everyone wanted him to write speeches for them."

In November 1993 Mayor David N. Dinkins appointed Feehan to the challenging post of fire commissioner. From its inception as a paid department in 1865, the FDNY had experienced bitter conflicts for managerial control between the uniformed force, politicians seeking the fulfillment of their own agendas, and bureaucrats attempting to impose private-sector values of order and efficiency on the department. Feehan was able to bridge the tensions between the administrative "bean counters" and those who put their lives on the line every day. Those who negotiated with Feehan when he was in charge of labor relations respected him as both "a tough son of a bitch" and "the guy who smoothed things over." McDonald noted that Feehan's success was in part due to his shy and modest nature. He said, "The key . . . was that no one ever thought he would climb their backs and take their jobs . . . [because] he had their trust." As fire commissioner, Feehan supported programs designed to encourage inner-city youth to join the ranks of "New York's Bravest," enacted cost-cutting managerial reforms, and restructured the department's fireboat division.

Feehan loved "the job" to the very end. When the Central Synagogue on Manhattan's East Side collapsed in August 1998, a reporter said, "Everyone was getting out of the way, and here was Bill, running into the smoke and fire—and he was 70 years old!" According to FDNY Lieutenant Daniel Maye, Feehan was regarded by all as the "grand old man of the fire department."

On the morning of 11 September 2001, hijackers flew passenger jets into the twin towers of the World Trade Center. Shortly after the attacks, Feehan raced from his headquarters in Brooklyn to the FDNY Command Center in the lobby of Tower One. Lynn Tierney, a former fire commissioner, noted that Feehan was seen "taking the elbow of a very frightened young lady in the lobby of lower number one, and calmly pulling her close and walking her through just like it was dinnertime."

At 10:29 A.M. Tower One collapsed, killing Feehan along with 342 of his "brothers" of every rank, from Peter Ganci, the chief of department, to seventeen young probationary firefighters fresh from the Fire Academy. Tower Two eventually collapsed as well. More than fifty New York Police Department and Port Authority police officers, and more than 2,400 civilians, were also buried with them in a nine-story-high "pile" of rubble. Ninety-six pieces of firefighting apparatus lay crushed amidst 1.8 million tons of debris.

Mourning the line-of-duty death of a firefighter, Feehan once wrote, "The truest form of love is to lay down your life for another but the purest form of love is to cherish each other every day." At the funeral mass held at Saint Mel's Roman Catholic Church in Bayside, Mayor Rudolph W. Giuliani described Feehan as "one of the most exceptional people that ever served the city." Feehan, he observed, "served in a war [in Korea] and he ultimately died in a war here on the streets of New York City." Feehan was buried in Saint Charles Cemetery in Farmingdale, Long Island. The French consul general in New York City presented his family with the Legion of Honor, and a street was named in his memory in Queens. Reflecting on Feehan's life and death, the historian Kenneth T. Jackson said, "We feel gratitude, we feel humbled, and we feel inspired by his example."

★

Full-length works about Feehan and the New York City Fire Department include Terry Golway, *So Others Might Live: A History of New York's Bravest; the FDNY from 1700 to the Present* (2002); David Halberstam, *Firehouse* (2002); Richard Picciotto and Daniel Paisner, *Last Man Down: A Firefighter's Story of Survival and Escape from the World Trade Center* (2002); Dennis Smith, *Report from Ground Zero: The Story of the Rescue Efforts at the World Trade Center* (2002); and Frank McCourt, Rudolph W. Giuliani, and Thomas Von Essen in their introduction to *Brotherhood* (2002). Brief references to the fire department are in Kenneth T. Jackson, ed., *Encyclopedia of New York City* (1995). For a lengthy article about Feehan's role in the World Trade Center incident, see "The Chief: William Feehan's Last Fire, After Four Decades on the Job," the *New Yorker* (8 Oct. 2001). An obituary is in the *New York Times* (13 Sept. 2001).

DONALD J. CANNON

FESHBACH, Herman (*b.* 2 February 1917 in New York City; *d.* 22 December 2000 in Cambridge, Massachusetts), theoretical nuclear physicist noted for his leadership in developing nuclear reaction theory and for his efforts to foster nuclear arms control and freedom for scientists throughout the world.

Feshbach received his B.S. from City College of New York in 1937. He went to the Massachusetts Institute of Technology (MIT) in Cambridge, Massachusetts, as a graduate student and earned his Ph.D. in physics in 1942. In his thesis he approximately derived the properties of tritium from nuclear forces, which was a difficult effort at the time. Tritium is a hydrogen isotope used in the release of nuclear energy through fusion, as in the hydrogen bomb. On 28 January 1940, Feshbach married Sylvia Harris; they had three children.

After serving as an instructor at MIT for four years, Feshbach was appointed an assistant professor and rose through the MIT ranks to institute professor in 1983. He remained at MIT for his entire career. Over the years Feshbach's work in physics focused on the theories underlying the structure and behavior of the nuclei of atoms. Working with the physicists Charles Porter and Victor Weisskopf, Feshbach revolutionized work in nuclear reactions with the development of the cloudy crystal ball model in 1954, also known as the optical model. This model provided a detailed description of the scattering of neutrons from nuclei. With the optical model, physicists can describe the scattering and also provide the wave functions needed to analyze a wide range of nuclear reactions.

In 1958 Feshbach developed a general nuclear reaction theory that became the backbone of complex nuclear reaction calculations developed over ensuing years. In particular, he discovered the analytical tool known as the "Feshbach resonance." Normally, when two atoms collide, they bounce off each other like billiard balls. With the Feshbach resonance, Feshbach described how two atoms adhere to form a temporary molecule, almost like reacting chemicals, when their kinetic energy is exactly equal to the energy required to bind them together.

In addition to his research, Feshbach and Philip M. Morse wrote the textbook *Methods of Theoretical Physics,* which was considered a seminal text long after its publication in 1953. "He was known in all of physics because of that book," said the MIT physics professor Arthur Kerman. Feshbach, with Amod deShalit, also wrote the textbook *Theoretical Nuclear Physics* (1974), which likewise is considered a classic work in the field. Feshbach's contributions to physics extended to the classroom, where he trained many well-known and respected physicists. In 1957 Feshbach and Morse cofounded the journal *Annals of Physics.* In the 1960s he also helped organize the American Physical Society's division of nuclear physics, which he chaired from 1970 to 1971. He was the founder and director of MIT's Center for Theoretical Physics from 1967 to 1973 and head of its physics department from 1973 to 1983.

Although much of Feshbach's work was important for the development of nuclear weapons, Feshbach turned down an offer from the physicist Edward Teller to work with him in the early 1950s on creating the hydrogen bomb at the Los Alamos Scientific Laboratory in New Mexico. "He was never in favor of nuclear weapons, except during World War II," said Feshbach's son, Mark Feshbach. Time did not change Feshbach's mind, and in 1969 he took part in a protest of military research at MIT. That same year he played a critical role in the founding of the Union of Concerned Scientists in an effort to represent some MIT faculty's beliefs about the Vietnam War and other issues. Feshbach served as the group's first chair, and the group continues as a national organization.

Named to the American Academy of Arts and Sciences in 1969, Feshbach served as president of the academy from 1982 to 1986, during which time he formed the Committee on International Security Studies. The committee focused on nuclear deterrence and policy issues and on advancing productive nongovernmental exchange with the Soviet Union and Eastern Europe. He was one of the signers of a 1981 letter to President Ronald W. Reagan from the Union of Concerned Scientists arguing for a halt to the arms race to deter nuclear war.

Feshbach's efforts to open communications between Western and Soviet scientists during the height of the cold war included championing the cause of refuseniks, Soviet citizens who were denied permission to emigrate, among them, notable Russian scientists supporting nuclear disarmament and human rights. Feshbach took a personal interest in fighting for the freedom of Andrei Sakharov, a 1975 Nobel Prize winner and internationally acclaimed physicist. After Sakharov spoke out against Russian intervention in Afghanistan, the Soviet government banished him to internal exile in Gorky in January 1980. Feshbach first met Sakharov in the mid-1970s and wrote an article published in *Physics Today* about visiting Sakharov in Moscow after he had returned from exile in 1987.

Feshbach also was a strong proponent of improving the position of women and minorities in physics and academia. Although he retired from MIT in 1987, he continued to do research and served on the MIT faculty Equal Opportunity Committee, making recommendations in 1991 for recruiting more women faculty members. Feshbach received many honors during his career. He was elected to the National Academy of Sciences in 1969 and received the National Medal of Science in 1986. He served as president of the American Physical Society from 1980 to 1981 and was the longtime editor of the journal *Annals of Physics*. In his book *Theoretical Nuclear Physics: Nuclear Reactions* (1992), Feshbach outlines the achievements of nuclear research over half a century, emphasizing the fundamental principles that led to new understandings of nuclear structure and interactions. Feshbach died at Youville Hospital in Cambridge of congestive heart failure.

Known during his career as one of the world's preeminent theoretical nuclear physicists, Feshbach made major contributions to advance the fields of nuclear reaction theory and nuclear structure. An educator who trained many prominent physicists, he also cowrote seminal textbooks in the field. As a nuclear scientist at the height of the cold war, Feshbach followed his conscience, speaking out against the proliferation of nuclear weapons and the Vietnam War, while championing the cause of freedom for the world's scientists.

★

Much of Feshbach's correspondence with Sakharov is in the Andrei Sakharov Archives and Human Rights Center at Brandeis University in Waltham, Massachusetts. Obituaries are in the *Boston Globe* (26 Dec. 2000), *MIT News* (27 Dec. 2000), *New York Times* (28 Dec. 2000), and *Physics Today* (Oct. 2001).

DAVID PETECHUK

FITCH, James Marston (*b.* 8 May 1909 in Washington, D.C.; *d.* 10 April 2000 in New York City), writer, preservationist, architect, and teacher who was widely admired as an activist driven to passionate and influential crusades centered on the built environment. He is generally regarded as the founder of the historic preservation movement.

Fitch was the elder of two children born to James Marston Fitch and Ellen (Payne) Fitch. He spent his childhood on a farm outside Chattanooga, Tennessee, where he was educated in the community public schools. His father provided steady support for the family through a variety of occupations. Fitch's mother, an accomplished gardener, supplemented the family income through her work in real estate and residential remodeling. Her influence on the young Fitch was significant. Upon the completion of his secondary education, Fitch attended the college of liberal arts at the University of Alabama (1925–1926) and, later, the school of architecture at Tulane University (1927–1928). The Great Depression interrupted Fitch's education, although he continued to read voraciously and broadly. He moved to Nashville, Tennessee, where he went to work for the interior design firm of A. Herbert Rogers, specializing in the restoration of the antebellum estates and gardens of the Belle Meade subdivision of Nashville.

Fitch spent the summer of 1932 in New Jersey, studying with the architect and housing advocate Henry Wright. There he met other leading figures (including Lewis Mumford, Clarence Stein, and Henry Klaber), worked with other promising students, and fell under the spell of the modernist movement. Returning to Nashville, he worked briefly for the Tennessee Valley Authority and then (1934–1935) as a low-cost housing analyst for the newly founded Federal Housing Administration in Washington, D.C.

Fitch's first published article, "These Houses We Live In: An Anonymous Lament," appeared in *Architecture* magazine in 1933. In the piece, he chafed against the superficiality of historical eclecticism in light of the more purposeful aims of modernism. His polemic and linguistic skill gained for him not only widespread attention in the architectural community but new professional opportunities as well.

On 7 February 1936 Fitch married Cleopatra Rickman, an archeological researcher. Also in 1936, he accepted the offer of a position as associate editor for *Architectural Record*. Disenchanted with the conservative milieu of the South, he was eager to move to New York City, where he became personally acquainted with the leading modernists of the day, including Walter Gropius, Frank Lloyd Wright, and others. Until 1942 he contributed prolifically to the *Record*, both as a writer and as a layout designer.

During World War II, Fitch served in the United States Army Air Force (1942–1945), but because of a bad ear he was exempt from combat. Instead, he worked as a meteorologist, stationed in the Midwest. Following the war, he returned to New York City as technical editor of *Architectural Forum* (1945–1949). The skills he gained as a meteorologist were put to good use in architecture, as he continued to press for greater functionality and technical excellence in construction as well as for the alignment of the built environment with the laws of nature.

Fitch joined the staff of *House Beautiful* (1949–1953) and established the Climate Control project, the principles of which he applied to the three houses he designed and built for himself and Cleo in Stony Point, New York. It was during this postwar period that his calling shifted from journalism to academia. He worked as an adjunct lecturer in the school of general studies at Columbia University and published his first major work, *American Building: The Historical Forces That Shape It* (1947).

In 1954 Fitch accepted a full-time appointment as assistant professor of architectural history at Columbia. He continued to focus his energies on modernism, documenting his convictions in acclaimed monographs on Gropius, Le Corbusier, Mies van der Rohe, and Wright in *Four Great Makers of Modern Architecture* (1963). At the same time, the combined flexibility of his work schedule and the incentives of new writing commissions prompted him to travel extensively to Africa, Europe, and the Middle East, where he studied traditional crafts, historical artifacts, and primitive architecture and witnessed for the first time the coordinated efforts of national governments toward the preservation of historic buildings and districts. The experience was transformative. He returned to the United States, where, by contrast, he was surrounded by the wholesale waste associated with the urban renewal movement of the period. He proposed restoration as a viable and economically resourceful alternative and articulated the new role of the preservationist as social activist. His collection of essays titled *Architecture and the Esthetics of Plenty* was published in 1961.

In 1964 Fitch and the architect Charles Peterson founded the graduate program in restoration and preservation at Columbia University. The cross-curricular program was a product of Fitch's uncompromising social conscience and comprehensive vision. He recruited a diverse and gifted student body that shared his inclusive approach to architecture as an agent to "act in favor of human beings." The discipline he forged awakened the architectural community to the practical logic of preservation and to preservation's didactic role in the perpetuation of "historical patrimony" and culture. Fitch headed the program until 1977, the year he retired from Columbia as professor emeritus.

In 1979, as the foremost preservationist in the United States, Fitch stepped into the position of director of historic preservation for the New York firm of Beyer Blinder Belle. He established the firm's philosophical approach to preservation projects and, as designer and critic, monitored many of its most celebrated projects, including the restorations of Grand Central Terminal, the South Street Seaport, and Ellis Island National Monument. He remained influential and active in preservation efforts and in historic district planning throughout the United States. His writing continued unabated, and in 1982 he produced his seminal work, *Historic Preservation: Curatorial Management of the Built World*. His final major work, coauthored with William Bobenhausen and published in 1999, was a new edition of *American Building: The Environmental Forces That Shape It*.

Fitch was consumed by his work. When he left the South as a young man, he maintained little contact over the years with his family. He and Cleo, who passed away in 1995, had no children. In June 1997 he married Martica Sawin, an art historian and critic. Fitch was a good-looking man (and a natty dresser), with a full head of brown hair that never grayed, a face that never seemed to age, and a manner of speaking that never quite lost the elegance and musicality of his southern roots. A series of small strokes precipitated his death just short of his ninety-first birthday. His ashes were interred in Chattanooga.

In the course of his career, Fitch received numerous honors, most notable among them the Louise du Pont Crowninshield Award (1985), the highest honor bestowed by the National Trust for Historic Preservation. As a pioneer in historic preservation, he was a founding member of the Association for Preservation Technology and the Victorian Society in America. The Fitch professorship in historic preservation at Columbia University was established in 2003, and the James Marston Fitch Charitable Foundation of New York City (set up in 1988) continues to fund new and worthy preservation projects.

Keenly intelligent, informed, and witty, Fitch invested his greatest energy in language, and as a writer and speaker he was supremely gifted. The range of his interests and the topics on which he wrote and spoke were boundless: primitive architecture, building construction, technology, anthropological theory, and history and social change. He had an extraordinary capacity to grasp and integrate core principles of all phenomena, which he converted compellingly and beautifully into a language that etched ideas indelibly on the minds of readers and listeners. He embodied the vision of a designer, the passion of an activist, the brilliance of a writer and speaker, and the intellect of an academic to transform, illuminate, and elevate the profession of historic preservation.

What had once been dismissed by the architectural establishment as an amateur activity of the lay community and an elitist diversion of the moneyed "blue-haired ladies" (Fitch's words) is now taken for granted as an important dimension of the architect's profession. In truth, the "blue-haired ladies" initially dominated the field, creating the template and setting the standard for historic preservation. Fitch unabashedly and repeatedly honored their contributions, citing their devotion to their task and the integrity of their work, best illustrated by Mount Vernon, Colonial Williamsburg, and Independence Hall. But for Fitch, who preferred democratic inclusiveness, humble components were as vital as landmarks. The graduate programs in historic preservation and restoration he helped create continue to imbue those principles among new generations of promising architects and preservationists, who in turn serve as "curatorial managers of the built world," as Fitch once noted. Fitch was an educator both in the classroom and out; his numerous writings circumscribe his vast and penetrating "synoptic vision" of a tangible and living culture, and his legacy is still very much in the making.

★

Information about Fitch is in the introduction, by Richard Blinder, to *American Building: The Environmental Forces That Shape It* (1999). An extensive analysis of his work and impact is presented in Beth Sullebarger, ed., *Historic Preservation: Forging a Discipline, the Proceedings of a Symposium in Honor of James Marston Fitch and Twenty Years of Historic Preservation at Columbia University, January 26, 1985* (1989). For a memorial tribute, see *Preservation* 52, no. 4 (July/Aug. 2000): 22. An obituary is in the *New York Times* (12 Apr. 2000).

ROBERT J. CHABORA

FOERSTNER, George Christian (*b.* 8 November 1908 in High Amana, Iowa; *d.* 16 January 2000 in Miami, Florida), innovative businessman who made Amana Refrigeration into a leading producer of home appliances.

Foerstner was one of two children of William Foerstner, a merchant, and Christine (Gernand) Foerstner. The family lived in one of seven villages of the Amana Colonies, a religious community in Iowa. Members of the community had separate homes but partook of joint meals and church services. Since church elders selected children for advanced education and Foerstner was not chosen, he ended his formal schooling when he was thirteen years old.

Foerstner went to work helping his father, who managed the High Amana General Store, by selling automobile accessories. In 1929 Foerstner became a salesman for the Amana Woolen Mills. He married Nora L. Jeck on 22 August 1932; the couple had a son and a daughter. In the same year, as the nation sank into the depths of the Great Depression, the Amana Society underwent the "Great Change" as its members voted to abandon communalism. They created two corporations: the Amana Church Society for religious matters and the Amana Society, Incorporated, a joint stock company for business enterprises. The latter operated for profit and was overseen by a board of directors, with society members holding stock.

The economic situation hurt Foerstner, his father, and many others, as the society had an oversupply of woolen goods and agricultural products, as well as unsold merchandise, in stores, and there were few buyers. Then in 1934 a restaurant owner in nearby Iowa City asked Foerstner if he could construct a walk-in beverage cooler for his beer. Working alone at first and then with one and, later, another employee, Foerstner labored in the corner of a small furniture shop. His product was well received, and soon he moved his new firm, the Electrical Equipment Company, to an old woolen mill. Foerstner began to produce not only coolers but also refrigerators and meat coolers for butchers and frozen food lockers for farmers.

In 1936 Foerstner sold his company to the Amana Society, which changed its name to Amana Refrigeration. Foerstner remained with the company as its principal manager, and Amana Refrigeration became the nation's largest producer of cool-storage units by 1942. With the onset of World War II, the company turned its efforts to making walk-in coolers and refrigeration units for the armed forces. When the war ended, Foerstner and Amana refocused on an earlier project, a home freezer chest. In 1947 Amana became the first appliance maker to offer upright home freezers, and in 1949 Amana marketed the first side-by-side refrigerator and freezer. Foerstner also displayed his advertising talent when he contracted Hollywood celebrities, such as Gary Cooper, Dorothy Lamour, Groucho Marx, and Cecil B. de Mille, to appear in promotional advertisements in the late 1940s. Later, the innovative Foerstner had home economists travel throughout the country educating housewives on how to "cook with cold."

In 1950 Foerstner and a group of investors bought the company back from the Amana Society. By that time Amana Refrigeration had become the world's largest producer of home freezers, and by 1954 the company was branching out and producing room air conditioners. Also in 1954 the company became the first to patent a self-defrosting refrigerator. By 1957 the Amana appliance line included central air conditioners and heat pumps. Foerstner and his associates sold Amana Refrigeration to the Raytheon Company in 1965. Raytheon had developed its "Radarange" tabletop microwave oven and needed an already well-established appliance manufacturer to produce and market it. Foerstner, who continued as chief manager at Amana, took on the task. In 1967 Amana produced the first 115-volt countertop microwave oven, which Foerstner had insisted should be shaped like a box and sell for less than $500.

In the same year, Foerstner created the Amana VIP Golf Tournament. To encourage the attendance of important appliance retailers, Foerstner made the event a professional-amateur affair, inviting professional golfers to play with corporate executives, celebrities, and noted politicians. The first tournament was held in West Virginia, but the next year Foerstner moved the Amana Open to Iowa City, where the one-day tournament continued until 1990. To promote the company further, Foerstner paid professional golfers $50 for every tournament in which they wore Amana hats, and he allowed participating golfers to be included in the health plan for Amana employees.

In 1976 Foerstner developed yet another promotional innovation, holding a convention in which Amana hosted and entertained distributors from all over the world for a full five days. The next year, however, he displayed a different side to his independent-mindedness and strong-willed competitiveness when he initiated a public contro-versy with the Association of Home Appliance Manufactur-ers (AHMA), accusing the organization of anticonsumerism and anti-energy conservation at a time when the nation faced an energy crisis. The dispute focused notoriety on Foerstner, who had voiced complaints concerning the AHMA for a decade, and provided positive publicity for Amana Refrigeration.

Foerstner stepped down as president of Amana Refrig-eration in 1978, and in 1982 retired as chairman of the board. Although he was a private man who lived modestly and shunned personal kudos, he nevertheless received rec-ognition for his achievements. In 1959 the West German government presented him with the German Order of Merit for his accomplishments in refrigeration. In 1985 he was inducted into the Iowa Business Hall of Fame. He counted many nationally known people, from former pres-idents of the United States and business colleagues to sports and entertainment personalities, as his friends and ac-quaintances. He served on many boards; contributed much to the creation of the Herbert Hoover Presidential Library in West Branch, Iowa; and provided significant donations to the University of Iowa in Iowa City.

His wife died in 1990, and Foerstner, having suffered heart problems for several years, died a decade later at age ninety-one near his home in Bal Harbour, Florida. He is buried in the Middle Amana Cemetery.

Foerstner left a legacy of business acumen, having founded and expanded Amana Refrigeration into a major, cutting-edge, high-quality appliance producer while prov-ing himself to be masterful and innovative in promotion, advertising, and salesmanship. At the same time, he led Amana Refrigeration to provide well-paying jobs for many in his home community, where he resided most of the year in a house across the street from the factory in Middle Amana.

★

There is no biography or autobiography for Foerstner. Some materials on his business life can be found at the Amana Heritage Society in Amana, Iowa. Information on the Amana Colonies is in Diane L. Barthel, *Amana: From Pietist Sect to American Com-munity* (1984). Magazine profiles of Foerstner include Michael A. Verespej, "Amana's George Foerstner Rocks Appliance Industry," *Industry Week* 194 (15 Aug. 1977): 45–47, and Joan Clark and Joan Liffring Zug, "A Success Story, Made in America," the *Iowan*

27 (summer 1979): 20–24. Obituaries are in the Des Moines, Iowa, *Register* (18 Jan. 2000) and the *New York Times* (24 Jan. 2000).

THOMAS BURNELL COLBERT

FRANCIS, Arlene (*b.* 20 October 1907 in Boston, Massa-chusetts; *d.* 31 May 2001 in San Francisco, California), actress and radio and television personality best known for the glam-our and wit she brought to the television quiz show *What's My Line?*

Francis was born Arline Francis Kazanjian, the only child of Aram Kazanjian and Leah Ethel (Davis) Kazanjian, a homemaker. Her Armenian-born father had studied art in Paris before emigrating to the United States and becoming a portrait photographer. Francis attended public school in Boston and spent considerable time with her English-born maternal grandfather, Albert Davis. A clothing store man-ager who had been a member of a Shakespearean acting company in his youth, Davis regaled her with stories of his experiences on tour in his native country, and encouraged her to recite poetry at family gatherings.

After the Kazanjians moved to New York City in 1914, Francis continued her formal education at Mount Saint Vincent Academy, a Roman Catholic convent school run

Arlene Francis, 1954. BETTMANN/CORBIS

by the Sisters of Charity in the Riverdale section of the Bronx, and subsequently at the Finch School for Girls, a finishing school in Manhattan. Attractive, spirited, and garrulous, she entertained her classmates at both schools, and impressed teachers with her acting ability. Her conservative father allowed her to take classes at the Theatre Guild Dramatic School, but also sent her to the Art Students League and set her up in a small gift shop on Madison Avenue in an attempt to divert her from a theatrical career. But her art classes failed to make Francis a painter, and the gift shop closed after only eight months.

While on a trip to California, Francis landed a small part in the horror film *Murders in the Rue Morgue* (1932), loosely based on the Edgar Allan Poe story. After learning that she had played a "woman of the streets" who is tortured and murdered by a mad scientist (played by Bela Lugosi), her father quickly put an end to her film aspirations. However, when she began seeking jobs in radio, a medium he viewed as more wholesome and family-oriented, Aram was supportive.

A gift for mimicry got Francis a job imitating birds and other animals on the program *King Arthur's Round Table*. She soon moved up to *The March of Time* and *The Cavalcade of America*, which presented re-creations of historical events and great works of literature for the listening audience. By the mid-1930s, she had become a regular on a number of daytime soap operas, playing the female lead on the popular *Betty and Bob* (1936), as well as supporting roles in *Big Sister, Central City*, and *Mr. District Attorney*.

By the mid-1930s the increasingly busy Francis, who had amended the spelling of her first name and dropped her family name, was serving as mistress of ceremonies for *The Hour of Charm,* a musical program that featured Phil Spitalny's All-Girl Orchestra, and cohosting the early game show *What's My Name?* The latter featured contestants chosen from a studio audience who tried to guess the identities of celebrities from a series of clues. The show gave Francis her first opportunity to ad-lib on the air and display the charm and spontaneity that made her famous in the coming decades. Radio "came easily," she later recalled, noting that it was a "crutch that paid well—and I never stopped working."

Even as she was rushing between radio studios, Francis was also trying to make a career in the theater, but in spite of her best efforts, she was most often just part of the scenery. Eventually she obtained somewhat meatier roles in works mounted by her fellow radio actor Orson Welles for the Federal Theatre Project at his Mercury Theatre. Francis later recalled that, while rehearsing for *Horse Eats Hat* (1936) and *Danton's Death* (1938), she received a thorough education in acting from Welles, Joseph Cotten, and especially Martin Gabel, a Philadelphian she had first met while working together on *Betty and Bob*. Francis had married Neil F. Agnew, the general sales manager for Paramount Pictures, on 28 November 1935. They divorced in 1945, and she married Gabel on 14 May 1946. They had one son.

Francis captured her first important Broadway role in *All That Glitters* (1938), but although she fashioned a credible Spanish accent as a South American call girl and received good critical notices for her performance, the play was unsuccessful. World War II led her to sacrifice some of her radio and theatrical appearances to sell war bonds and perform in benefit shows, but she found time to appear in *The Doughgirls* (1942), a Joseph Fields comedy directed by George S. Kaufman that became a Broadway smash. She also scored a wartime triumph on radio as the smooth host of *Blind Date* (1943–1946), a popular game show in which U.S. servicemen competed to date beautiful young actresses and models.

After the war, Francis continued to divide her time between radio and the stage. She was more successful with the former, starring in the serial *The Affairs of Anne Scotland* as a sexy private eye, and in the anthology series *There Was a Woman,* portraying female characters in a variety of predicaments. She also appeared regularly on *Leave It to the Girls,* a panel show that discussed male-female relationships and other subjects from a woman's point of view and invited prominent celebrities to provide a male response. In the theater, however, she suffered through a string of flops.

Francis turned to television in 1949 with a new version of *Blind Date,* which became even more popular than it had been on radio. Much in demand for additional hosting duties and appearances, she accepted the invitation of the producers Mark Goodson and Bill Todman to join the celebrity panel for *What's My Line?* On the live show, which debuted in 1950 and became an unexpected hit, the panelists tried to guess the unusual occupations of contestants, and the identities of well-known "mystery guests," by asking them yes-or-no questions.

To the television audience, the game and the small cash prizes awarded were secondary to the witty banter of Francis, the moderator John Daly, fellow regulars Dorothy Kilgallen and Bennett Cerf, and other members of the show-business elite who appeared on the panel. The viewing public also tuned in for the "fashion show," in which the panelists made their entrances in evening clothes and delivered effusive introductions of their colleagues. A diamond-encrusted, heart-shaped pendant worn by Francis for luck even inspired a mid-1950s fad.

What's My Line? lasted for an astonishing seventeen years (1950–1967) as a Sunday night staple for the Columbia Broadcasting System, and went on for eight more (1968–1975) in syndication. The only early panelist who remained at the show's end, Francis later wrote that her time on the show had been "some of the greatest fun I've ever had—in or out of a job. It turned out to be not so much a show for me . . . but a way of life."

Francis confessed to an interviewer in 1952 that she had largely given up her dream of becoming a successful stage actress. Instead, she had settled for the comfortable "cushion" of television, which she found more satisfying than radio. Aside from her work on *What's My Line?*, in the early 1950s she hosted *Talent Patrol* (later called *Soldier Parade*), which showcased aspiring performers from the armed forces, and *Who's There?*, which asked celebrities to try to identify other celebrities using physical clues.

In 1954 a more substantive opportunity came her way when National Broadcasting Company (NBC) president Sylvester ("Pat") Weaver chose Francis as "editor-in-chief" of *Home,* his new "women's magazine of the air." A daytime entry designed to attract sophisticated women uninterested in soap operas or game shows, *Home* used the latest technology and employed a team of experts for segments devoted to family affairs, health, fashion and beauty, cooking, gardening, and important issues of the day. As *Home*'s principal "communicator," Francis became one of the most famous women in the country, and her show attracted advertising for products never before seen on television. One year after Weaver's departure from NBC in 1956, however, his successors cancelled *Home.* Francis later wrote that the show's passing was a "great sadness. . . . To be that frantically busy for four years, and suddenly to find yourself all revved up and hear the race is called off—it's terribly unnerving."

The Arlene Francis Show, a modest potpourri of entertainment and chitchat, failed in 1958, and thereafter Francis found solace in her old haunts, theater and radio. She enjoyed success in *Once More, With Feeling* (1958), *Tchin-Tchin* (1962), and *Mrs. Dally Takes a Lover* (1965), all directed by her husband. On radio, she hosted a highly rated daily talk show on WOR in New York from 1960 to 1984, on which she chatted pleasantly with such disparate guests as Frank Sinatra, the Arizona senator Barry Goldwater, and the baseball player Curt Flood.

Late in her career Francis also gave two fine comic performances in motion pictures. In her best-known film role, she played the wisecracking wife of the philandering Coca-Cola executive James Cagney in Billy Wilder's frantic *One, Two, Three* (1961); and in *The Thrill of It All* (1965), a Doris Day–James Garner vehicle, she ably portrayed an ecstatic middle-aged expectant mother. Francis also wrote *That Certain Something: The Magic of Charm* (1960) and *No Time for Cooking: A New Kind of Cookbook* (1961).

Francis died following a long battle with Alzheimer's disease. Her remains were cremated and buried in Roosevelt Memorial Park in Trevose, Pennsylvania.

Francis had a busy acting career for three decades, with a few hits and a large share of theatrical misses. She flourished as an actress and host on radio, and was best known as a charming game-show panelist on television. The abrupt cancellation of *Home* probably prevented her from becoming a major television star, but her work on that show helped to pave the way to stardom for Barbara Walters and other women who followed.

★

Clipping files on Francis are at the Margaret Herrick Library of the Academy of Motion Picture Arts and Sciences in Beverly Hills, California, and in the Billy Rose Theatre Collection at the New York Public Library for the Performing Arts, Lincoln Center. *Arlene Francis: A Memoir,* written with Florence Rome (1978), is breezy, good-natured, and occasionally revealing about its engaging subject. Gil Fates, *What's My Line? The Inside History of TV's Most Famous Panel Show* (1978), is an entertaining chronicle of this television institution. Bernard M. Timberg and Robert J. Erler, *Television Talk: A History of the TV Talk Show* (2002), discusses the demise of *Home.* Obituaries are in the *New York Daily News* and *New York Times* (both 2 June 2001), and *Independent* (London) (4 June 2001).

RICHARD H. GENTILE

FRANKENHEIMER, John Michael (*b.* 19 February 1930 in New York City; *d.* 6 July 2002 in Los Angeles, California), television and movie director of legendary stature, best known as the director of classic 1960s films that were political thrillers about dark government conspiracies.

Frankenheimer was one of three children born to a German Jewish father, Walter Martin Frankenheimer, a stockbroker, and an Irish mother, Helen Mary (Sheedy) Frankenheimer, a homemaker. When he was about three years old, Frankenheimer's family moved from Manhattan to the small Long Island town of Malba, New York. He was brought up as a Catholic and educated at the La Salle Military Academy in Oakfield, Long Island, graduating in 1947.

At Williams College in Williamstown, Massachusetts, Frankenheimer's talent as a tennis player led him to contemplate a professional career in the sport. At six feet, three inches tall, the dark-haired, handsome young man with theater experience also had an interest in becoming an actor; he acted in dramatic productions while at Williams and worked in summer stock after his junior year. Instead, after graduating from Williams with a B.A. in English in 1951, Frankenheimer joined the U.S. Air Force. He served in the Motion Picture Squadron, where he learned fundamental filmmaking techniques. His interest shifted to working behind the camera.

In 1951, shortly after his enlistment, Frankenheimer

John Frankenheimer, ca. 1997. KURT KRIEGER/CORBIS

married his girlfriend, Joanne Evans, so that she could travel with him at government expense. The couple had an understanding that when Frankenheimer's stint in the military was over, they would divorce, since neither really wanted to be married. Following his discharge in 1953 as a first lieutenant, the union was dissolved.

That same year, Frankenheimer became an assistant director at the Columbia Broadcasting System (CBS) network in the still-new medium of television. He worked in a variety of programs and formats, from commercials to Edward R. Murrow's *Person to Person* series. As Frankenheimer's skills grew, his career advanced and he began working on prestigious dramatic anthology series, including *Studio One, Kraft Television Theater, DuPont Show of the Month,* and *Playhouse 90.*

Throughout the remainder of the 1950s, Frankenheimer directed a remarkable amount of live television drama and developed a signature style employing tight close-ups, which were known as the "Frankenheimer slash." Among his many notable productions were "The Comedian" (1957), with Mickey Rooney; "The Days of Wine and Roses" (1958), with Cliff Robertson and Piper Laurie; "The Browning Version" (1959), starring John Gielgud in his television debut; and "The Turn of the Screw" (1959), featuring Ingrid Bergman in her first television role.

On 22 September 1954 Frankenheimer married Carolyn Diane Miller. The couple had two daughters before they divorced in 1962. That same year he married the actress Evans Evans, and they remained together until his death.

By the early 1960s, as the era of live television drama faded, Frankenheimer was one of several young television directors who moved on to feature films. In 1962, with two motion pictures already under his belt (*The Young Stranger* in 1957 and *The Young Savages* in 1961), Frankenheimer directed *The Birdman of Alcatraz.* The film, starring Burt Lancaster as a murderer serving a life sentence, was a commercial and critical success. It was *The Manchurian Candidate,* though, also released in 1962, that launched Frankenheimer's reputation as a risk-taking Hollywood maverick. Angela Lansbury, who received an Academy Award nomination for best actress, and Frank Sinatra both turned in memorable performances. The movie, which Frankenheimer also coproduced, is the story of a decorated Korean War veteran who is brainwashed in a detention camp and programmed to kill a liberal politician. The movie had just recently completed its theatrical run when President John F. Kennedy was assassinated in 1963; the eerie similarities were apparent.

Frankenheimer, who was acquainted with the president, was deeply affected by his murder. A period of personal difficulties followed, including a problem with alcohol that Frankenheimer was later able to overcome. His next picture, *Seven Days in May,* was in production at the time of the assassination. This 1964 release was the story of a liberal army officer discovering a planned coup, organized by a right-wing general, against the U.S. president.

In 1966 Frankenheimer made his first color motion picture. *Grand Prix,* shot in France, was a big-budget, commercially successful release. The project indulged the director's great love of car racing and speed. Frankenheimer also spoke fluent French and was accomplished in cooking French cuisine.

When Senator Robert Kennedy ran for the Democratic presidential nomination in 1968, Frankenheimer volunteered to aid the cause by directing his campaign films. The two men became close friends in the time they spent together during the primary season. It was Frankenheimer who drove Senator Kennedy to the Ambassador Hotel in Los Angeles on the night the candidate was assassinated.

Following the trauma of Kennedy's death, Frankenheimer moved to France, where he worked on several introspective films that were met with audience indifference. He returned to the United States in 1973. Later in the 1970s, Frankenheimer achieved moderate commercial success with *French Connection II* (1975) and with *Black Sunday* (1976), the story of a terrorist attack during a Super Bowl football game, but his career floundered throughout the 1980s and early 1990s.

Frankenheimer's resurgence as an important director came with his return to television. Beginning in the mid-1990s, he directed and produced several made-for-television historical dramas that earned critical praise and large audiences. These projects included *The Burning Season* (1994), *Andersonville* (1996), *George Wallace* (1997), and *Path to War* (2002).

In 2001 Frankenheimer's Williams College graduating class celebrated its fiftieth reunion. His essay in the memory book expressed gratitude for the exciting career and life he had lived. Frankenheimer wrote that he felt he had much more to do. "I hope I continue to receive the gift of good health, which will enable me to continue to make films, for the idea of retirement holds no appeal for me." In less than one year, Frankenheimer's health had failed him. He died at age seventy-two after suffering a massive stroke due to complications following spinal surgery.

Frankenheimer was an active member of the Directors Guild of America and served as cochair of the Creative Rights Committee. He received myriad honors throughout his career, including four Emmy Awards and posthumous induction into the Television Hall of Fame in November 2002. Films that he directed garnered thirty-eight Academy Awards in various categories. Even though Frankenheimer was never nominated for an individual Oscar for motion picture direction, his legacy as a giant of the industry endures.

★

The most complete review of Frankenheimer's career is Charles Champlin, *John Frankenheimer: A Conversation with Charles Champlin* (1995). Another comprehensive resource is Gerald Pratley, *The Films of Frankenheimer: Forty Years in Film* (1998). Frankenheimer's work is discussed in numerous articles in film journals and periodicals, including B. Drew, "John Frankenheimer: His Fall and Rise," *American Film* (Mar. 1977), and John Thomas, "John Frankenheimer: The Smile on the Face of the Tiger," *Film Quarterly* 19, no. 2 (winter 1965–1966): 2. An article in the popular press is Bernard Weinraub, "Back to Hollywood's Bottom Rung, and Climbing," *New York Times* (24 Mar. 1994). An obituary is in the *New York Times* (7 July 2002).

MARY ANN WATSON

FRIEDMAN, Herbert (*b*. 21 June 1916 in Brooklyn, New York City; *d*. 9 September 2000 in Arlington, Virginia), astrophysicist known as the father of x-ray astronomy, who headed the U.S. Naval Research Laboratory (NRL) from 1963 to 1980.

Friedman was the second of three children of Samuel Friedman, an art dealer, and Rebecca (Seligson) Friedman,

Herbert Friedman. AP/WIDE WORLD PHOTOS

a homemaker. He attended public schools, enjoyed painting and drawing as a child, and enrolled as an art student at Brooklyn College in 1932. After changing to a science curriculum in his junior year, he graduated in 1936 with a B.A. in physics. From 1936 to 1940 he studied x-ray diffraction at the Johns Hopkins University, where he wrote a dissertation on solid-state physics and completed a doctoral program in 1940. That year he married Gertrude Miller, whom he met at Brooklyn College. They had two sons.

After teaching at Johns Hopkins for one year, Friedman joined the Naval Research Laboratory (NRL) in Washington, D.C., in 1941, just prior to the onset of U.S. involvement in World War II. Originally hired into the lab's metallurgy division, he studied gaseous discharges and developed x-ray and gamma-ray detection technology for use in Geiger counters. Assigned to head the NRL's electron-optics branch in 1943, he devised a way to use x rays to cut quartz crystals for radio filters. For this work he earned the navy's Distinguished Civilian Service Award in 1945.

For the next three decades Friedman pioneered rocket-based exploration of the upper atmosphere. Having conceived of this notion in order to facilitate the navy's post–World War II propulsion experiments of unarmed defense missiles, Friedman proposed loading the empty warheads with scientific detection equipment as ballast, in lieu of explosive devices. Using this method to collect data, he discovered x rays emanating from the Sun and studied aspects of stellar radiation that were previously inaccessible to researchers.

Beginning with the launch of a German-made V-2 rocket from the White Sands Missile Range in New Mexico in 1949, Friedman collected data in support of theories such as the ongoing generation of new stars. He studied the effects of stellar radiation on Earth and developed the first ultraviolet map of the heavens. In 1957 Friedman fashioned a radiation-detecting telescope from bundled tubes and designed a mechanically baffled Geiger counter in order to detect ultraviolet radiation from hot blue stars. In the late 1950s he studied x rays and ultraviolet radiation by means of Vanguard satellites that were specially equipped with these robotic telescopes. Also in 1957, as the head of the NRL's Project Sunflare, developed in conjunction with the International Geophysical Year (IGY) of 1958–1959, Friedman launched a Nike-Asp rocket combination to an altitude of 105 miles, a previously unattained distance, from which he utilized radiation detection technology to study the terrestrial effects of sunspots. For Project Sunflare, he likewise launched fourteen Nike-Deacon rocket combinations to altitudes of eighty miles from a base at San Nicolas Island near California.

Friedman presented his studies of the ultraviolet spectrum to the International Astronomical Union in Moscow in the summer of 1958. During a solar eclipse on 12 October 1958, he traveled to a vantage point in the Danger Islands near Samoa, using the USS *Point Defiance* as a floating base to launch a Nike-Asp missile to an unprecedented altitude of 150 miles. Using data he collected from the rocket when the eclipse blocked the chromosphere (inner atmosphere of the Sun), he isolated the Sun's corona as a source of atmospheric x-ray emission. The chromosphere, he then hypothesized, is the source of ultraviolet emissions.

On his return to Washington later in the fall of 1958, Friedman assumed superintendency of the NRL's atmosphere and astrophysics division, and with the establishment of the National Aeronautics and Space Administration (NASA) that year, he continued his quest to locate sources of ultraviolet radiation in the outer atmosphere. In December he placed a solar-radiation detector aboard NASA's *Explorer VII* satellite, and that same month, in addressing the American Association for the Advancement of Science, he presented a plan for rocket-based observatories to orbit Earth.

In April 1959 Friedman reported on rocket-based exploration at a symposium of the National Academy of Sciences, NASA, and the American Physical Society. In an IGY follow-up that summer, he inaugurated Project Sunflare II. Data from Sunflare II revealed sunspot temperatures as high as 190 million degrees Fahrenheit within the corona of the Sun, approximately ten times the anticipated

results. He further demonstrated the effect of sunspots in causing fadeout of earthbound radio transmission.

In 1960 Friedman took historic x-ray photographs of the Sun from cameras launched from White Sands aboard an Aerobee-Hi rocket in April, and on 22 June he launched a satellite to collect ongoing data of solar radiation. Data collected from a subsequent launch in August 1961 revealed 5,000 spectrum gradations in the Sun's ultraviolet radiation. He reported his findings to a symposium of the Committee on Space Research in May 1962 and presented his observations of Earth's helium belt to the National Academy of Sciences in 1963.

From 1963 to 1980 Friedman served as chief scientist at the E. O. Hulburt Center for Space Research, where he mapped x-ray sources in the outer atmosphere and established the existence of neutron stars. By 1965 he had charted thirty-seven sources, including thirty-five within the Milky Way. In 1966 he pinpointed the locations of the two sources outside the Milky Way.

A recipient of numerous major science awards, Friedman in 1960 was elected to the National Academy of Science and later was decorated with the Presidential Medal for Distinguished Federal Service by President Lyndon B. Johnson. He held approximately fifty patents during his lifetime and by 1967 had designed an x-ray observatory for the Moon. In 1965 and 1967 he contributed to early NASA projects to place solar laboratories in orbit, which were realized in the 1973 Skylab missions. He joined the University of Pennsylvania astronomy department in 1974 and served as adjunct professor at the University of Maryland from 1960 to 1980.

Unaffected and soft-spoken by nature, Friedman enjoyed classical music and throughout his lifetime was known to sketch with charcoal. Between 1975 and 1998 he wrote three books on astronomy for the nontechnical reader. He died of cancer at his home at age eighty-four.

★

"Herbert Friedman's Rocket Telescopes" is the story of Friedman's life and career, and is in Barbara Land, *The Telescope Makers: From Galileo to the Space Age* (1968). Obituaries are in the *Washington Post* (12 Sept. 2000) and *New York Times* (13 Sept. 2000).

G. COOKSEY

FUTCH, Eddie (*b*. 9 August 1911 in Hillsboro, Mississippi; *d*. 10 October 2001 in Las Vegas, Nevada), boxing manager and trainer who handled twenty-one world champions, including Joe Frazier, Ken Norton, Larry Holmes, Michael Spinks, Alexis Arguello, and Riddick Bowe.

Futch was the oldest of three children of Valley Futch, a Mississippi sharecropper who later worked in an automo-

Eddie Futch (top), shown with Riddick Bowe, ca. 1991. MICHAEL BRENNAN/CORBIS

bile plant, and Loy Laura Anderson, a domestic worker and entrepreneur. Futch was five years old when his parents moved to the Black Bottom section of Detroit. Futch's mother became the family's sole breadwinner when her husband left three years later.

As a young man, Futch excelled as a semiprofessional basketball player with the YMCA Flashes before turning to boxing, which he learned at the Brewster Recreational Center, the celebrated Detroit gym. Futch captured the Detroit Golden Gloves lightweight title in 1933, and his overall amateur record was 37–3. Because of Futch's speed and elusiveness, he became a favorite sparring partner for his Brewster teammate Joe Louis, then a promising amateur light heavyweight. "When I hit you," Louis told Futch, "I know I'm sharp."

After he was diagnosed with a heart murmur in 1936, Futch, then age twenty-five and the married father of three, became the head coach for the boxing program at the Brewster Recreational Center, in addition to working various jobs, including as a playground director and welder at the Ford Motor Company. In the early 1940s Futch taught boxing to a group of neighborhood kids who included Jimmy Edgar, later a middleweight contender, and Berry Gordy, the founder of Motown Records, who told *Sports Illustrated*, "Seems like all the principles that I used to build Motown came from him [Futch]."

During this time, Futch also seconded Holman Williams, a Detroit middleweight who Futch called "the greatest pure boxer I ever worked with." Futch was in Williams's corner in Cincinnati in 1942 against Charley Burley, another leg-

endary black middleweight of the era. "What a privilege it was to watch both men—the way they thought as well as fought," Futch recalled. Futch felt that Burley, whose greatest achievement was a 1944 victory over the future light heavyweight champion Archie Moore, was "the finest all-around fighter I ever saw."

In 1951 Futch moved to Los Angeles, where he worked with visiting East Coast fighters. His first champion was the welterweight Don Jordan, who won the title in a 1958 upset over Virgil Atkins. Futch's first marriage to Kathleen Jeter ended in 1951, and he then married Ethelyn ("Bobbie") Finney. He was the father of four children, all with Jeter.

Unable to make his living exclusively as a trainer, Futch joined the U.S. Postal Service in 1963. In 1966 he began working with Joe Frazier, the 1964 Olympic gold medalist who had won eight professional fights on the East Coast and was managed by Yank Durham. "Yank didn't know any of the fighters on the coast," Futch explained, "so he had to put his trust in me." Futch watched on television from Los Angeles as Frazier was knocked down twice before defeating contender Oscar Bonavena. "Yank, we've got to make this kid bob and weave," Futch told Durham after the fight. Futch took a leave of absence from the post office to prepare Frazier for his 1967 match with George Chuvalo. "I put a rope from one of the ring posts to the other," Futch said, "and I made him bob and weave under the rope."

Prior to the celebrated 1971 Muhammad Ali–Joe Frazier showdown at Madison Square Garden, Futch, now training Frazier full-time, helped to devise the strategy Frazier used to defeat Ali. Although Futch respected Ali's speed and courage, he detected a flaw in Ali's style. "Joe, here's a guy who doesn't know how to throw an uppercut," Futch told Frazier. "He stands up straight, drops his right hand and throws a punch. So the minute you see that right hand drop, you step in with a left hook." Years later Futch recalled, "That's the way Joe knocked Ali down in the fifteenth round." After Futch trained Ken Norton for his 1973 upset victory over Ali, Ali told reporters, "That Eddie Futch isn't as dumb as he looks."

Following Durham's death in 1974, Futch became Frazier's manager, while continuing as his trainer. Futch's most celebrated moment in the ring may have come when he halted the 1975 Ali-Frazier heavyweight championship "Thrilla in Manila" bout. After fourteen brutal rounds, Frazier's vision was severely diminished. Futch believed his fighter was leading on points but realized that Frazier could no longer see well enough to defend himself. Before the start of the fifteenth round, Futch told Frazier, "It's all over. No one will ever forget what you did here today." After the fight, Frazier said, "I wanted to go on, but I'd never go against Eddie."

Futch began training the heavyweight champion Larry Holmes in 1981 prior to Holmes's ninth title defense. "I told him we'd try to polish the things he does well," Futch recalled, "and what few faults he has we'll try to eliminate." That same year Futch was hired to work with the light heavyweight Michael Spinks. When Spinks challenged Holmes for the heavyweight title in 1985, Futch, passing up a significant payday, chose to work in neither corner.

Futch's final heavyweight champion was Riddick Bowe, the erratic 1988 Olympic silver medalist who Futch guided to a 1992 victory over Evander Holyfield for the heavyweight title. Futch's second wife died in 1989; he later married Eva Marlene Faldt on 21 March 1996. He retired from the ring in 1998, after sixty-two years in boxing. His many honors included induction in the International Boxing Hall of Fame in 1994. Futch died of natural causes at the age of ninety, and his ashes were spread in the Pacific Ocean.

A lifelong lover of poetry, Futch recited John Keats, Robert Burns, and Persian verse from memory. His demeanor was almost scholarly, although he could be stern and had little patience for fighters who failed to follow his instructions. A compact, graceful, and meticulous man with few enemies in the rough-and-tumble world of boxing, Futch said his proudest accomplishment was "I raised a great family." Futch was a mentor and father figure to many of the boxers and trainers who worked with him, but he also held himself apart from much of the fight crowd. "I am in boxing," Futch often said, "but not of boxing."

★

Dave Anderson, *In the Corner: Great Boxing Trainers Talk About Their Art* (1991), and Ronald K. Fried, *Corner Men: Great Boxing Trainers* (1991), both devote chapters to Futch. Valuable magazine profiles include Gary Smith, "Dear Mike," *Sports Illustrated* (27 Feb. 1989). An obituary is in the *New York Times* (12 Oct. 2001).

RONALD K. FRIED

G

GARDNER, John William (*b.* 8 October 1912 in Los Angeles, California; *d.* 16 February 2002 in Stanford, California), author, foundation executive, government official, and founder of Common Cause, the foremost nonpartisan citizen's lobby in the United States.

Gardner was the second of two sons born to William Frederick Gardner and Marie Flora (Glover) Gardner. Both parents were real estate brokers. Gardner's father left the family before Gardner was born and died within two years, and his mother bore the full responsibility for raising the children. A woman of great intellectual energy and business acumen, she not only sold real estate but designed and built homes. Shortly after John was born, she moved her two sons to a new home in the nascent rural community of Beverly Hills. While they were still young, Marie took them on a year-long world tour. For a short time in 1919, Gardner lived with his grandparents in Hawaii, where his love and talent for swimming was nurtured. In 1929, while at college, he set a number of Pacific Coast intercollegiate swimming records.

Gardner graduated from high school in 1929. Although intending to major in English at Stanford University in California, Gardner withdrew from college to write a novel, returning two years later to major in psychology. During this time he met Aida Marroquin, a Guatemalan woman who spoke little English. With neither of them proficient in the other's language, they married on 18 August 1934. Their marriage lasted until Gardner's death and produced two daughters. Gardner earned a B.A. in psychology from Stanford in 1935 and a M.A. in psychology the following year.

In 1938 Gardner received his Ph.D. in psychology from the University of California, Berkeley. Later that year the Gardner family, which now included a daughter, moved east, where Gardner had a brief, lackluster teaching career at the Connecticut College for Women and at Mount Holyoke College in Massachusetts. With the outbreak of World War II, Gardner moved his family to Washington, D.C., where he served as a military intelligence analyst with the Office of Strategic Services until 1943, when he enlisted in the U.S. Marine Corps. He was discharged in 1946 with the rank of captain. Gardner's military service triggered his interest in the complex strategic and moral requirements incumbent upon leaders, a field of inquiry he revisited in his writing throughout his professional career.

In 1946 Gardner moved to New York City to begin a long association with the Carnegie Corporation. An executive associate for nine years, he became Carnegie Corporation president and head of the Carnegie Foundation for the Advancement of Teaching in 1955. For the next ten years he helped chart the course of American education and influenced U.S. domestic and foreign policy. During these post-Sputnik, civil rights years, Carnegie naturally focused on high school preparedness in math and science, on cre-

John W. Gardner. GETTY IMAGES

ating equal educational opportunities, and on international education. Gardner was much sought after as a consultant, serving on several corporate and institutional boards. He also advised presidents Dwight D. Eisenhower and John F. Kennedy on several occasions.

In 1964 Gardner received the Presidential Medal of Freedom, the highest honor the nation can bestow on a civilian. In 1965 President Lyndon B. Johnson asked Gardner to come to Washington to serve as secretary of the U.S. Department of Health, Education, and Welfare (HEW), making him the only Republican cabinet member in Johnson's Democratic administration. As HEW secretary, Gardner became the chief expediter of Johnson's "Great Society" programs. For three whirlwind years, HEW was the driving force that produced hundreds of legislative initiatives designed to strengthen democracy, end discrimination, improve education, eliminate poverty, and provide health care for the elderly. These efforts also saw the establishment of Medicare, the Elementary and Secondary Education Acts, the Corporation for Public Broadcasting, and the White House Fellows Program. Gardner's unflagging optimism, which he credited to his youth in the

American West, was legendary. Having undertaken a seemingly impossible agenda for social reform, he said, "What we have before us are some breathtaking opportunities disguised as insoluble problems."

Because he could not unequivocally support Johnson in his bid for reelection, Gardner resigned as HEW secretary in 1968. He opposed the Vietnam War and anguished at the diversion of attention and resources away from the domestic imperatives of the Great Society initiatives. Although Gardner concluded that Johnson had lost his capacity to lead, he parted with Johnson on amicable terms.

From 1967 to 1968 Gardner led the National Urban Coalition, an umbrella organization for local and regional organizations dedicated to combat racism and poverty. With the establishment of Common Cause in 1970, and for the next seven years, Gardner spearheaded the first modern nonpartisan citizen's lobby in the nation. Common Cause operated through a uniquely designed governing board, on which sixty board members were elected by popular vote, and twenty were appointed. The appointees were women, minorities, and others who were not represented among the board members. It was vital that the Common Cause leadership accurately reflect the diverse nature of U.S. society. From the outset, Common Cause's action agenda was determined by its membership. After only two years, with an activist membership already approaching 200,000, it lobbied for the end of the Vietnam War and for equal opportunity, environmental protection, and reform of the government and the criminal justice system. In short, the Common Cause reform agenda was an amplification of the Great Society goals.

After seven years at the helm of Common Cause, Gardner continued to advise U.S. presidents and founded or directed a series of new advocacy groups. From 1976 to 1980 he chaired President Jimmy Carter's Commission on White House Fellowships, called The White House Fellows Program. In 1980, with Brian O'Connell, he founded the Independent Sector, a broad-based coalition of leaders of private-sector, civic-minded organizations. During this time he also chaired President Ronald W. Reagan's Task Force on Private Sector Initiatives.

In 1989 Gardner returned to Stanford as the Miriam and Peter Haas Centennial Professor of Public Service. In 1995 he began an active retirement career, serving in the Stanford University School of Education, while continuing to serve as the chairman of the National Civic League, an umbrella coalition of more than 200 activist organizations. In February 2002, after a two-year struggle with prostate cancer, Gardner died in his home on the Stanford campus. He is buried in the National Cemetery at the Presidio of San Francisco.

In each phase of his career, Gardner produced influential books. The Carnegie period is covered in *Excellence*

(1961) and *Self-Renewal* (1964). The HEW years are assessed in *No Easy Victories* (1968). Common Cause is treated in *Morale* (1978). *On Leadership* (1990), completed after Gardner returned to Stanford, is the most thorough exposition of his argument for the kind of dispersed leadership needed to revitalize U.S. democracy. In *Living, Leading and the American Dream* (2003), published posthumously and written with his daughter Francesca, Gardner came closest to giving detailed information about his personal and professional life. Here finally were some spare glimpses into the making of a public servant who for nearly six decades was a shaping influence in U.S. educational, social, and political life.

Gardner's approach to perfecting democracy in the United States was a pragmatic blend of action and reflection. Because of the unique perspective afforded him by his institutional leadership and government service, he understood more than many that fundamental change in U.S. institutions required strong activist organizations that could challenge the dominion of power wielded by special interests and lobbies.

★

There is no biography of Gardner. The John William Gardner Papers, 1961–1992, are housed at the Department of Special Collections and University Archives at the Stanford University Libraries. An obituary is in the *New York Times* (18 Feb. 2002).

JOSEPH G. FLYNN

GENNARO, Peter (*b.* 23 November 1919 in Metairie, Louisiana; *d.* 28 September 2000 in New York City), Tony Award–winning dancer and choreographer who gained fame as a specialty dancer on Broadway and later choreographed numerous shows for the stage and for television.

Gennaro was born in the New Orleans suburb of Metairie to Sicilian immigrants Gaetano Gennaro and Conchetta (Sabella) Gennaro, tavern operators. He was the youngest of three children. In his youth, Gennaro entertained and delighted audiences with his passion for dance and rhythmic talent, winning local dance contests by the age of four. Money earned from odd jobs allowed him to take tap and acrobatic lessons.

After enlisting in the U.S. Army during World War II, he began his army career as a company clerk posted in India. He said, "[The actor] Melvyn Douglas was there with an entertainment group, and when they asked me if I could dance, I said, 'Sure I can dance,' so I danced all over India for eight months." After the war ended, he worked for six months in a family-owned bar and restaurant. Determined to follow his passion for dance, Gennaro moved to New York City to pursue a professional career.

Peter Gennaro, 1979. AP/WIDE WORLD PHOTOS

Funded by the GI Bill, he studied ballet and modern dance as well as ethnic dance forms at the American Theatre Wing and the Katherine Dunham School in Manhattan. Although he wanted to concentrate in jazz dance, Gennaro knew that ballet was the fundamental training for any dancing career. In 1946, while studying at the Katherine Dunham School, he performed in many student recitals and performances. In 1947, while dancing with the corps de ballet of San Carlo Opera Company in Chicago, Gennaro met his future bride, Margaret Jean Kinsella, a fellow dancer. They married on 24 January 1948. They had two children—Michael Gennaro, later a theatre managing director, and Liza Gennaro-Evans, later a noted dancer and choreographer. Often described as a softhearted "family man," Gennaro avoided accepting jobs that required him to spend too much time away from his wife and children.

Gennaro was only five feet, six inches tall, but his upbeat personality and passion for dance contributed to the popularity of dance in both the Broadway musical and the television variety show during the 1950s and 1960s. In October 1949 Gennaro danced the title role in the New Orleans Opera House Association production of *Petrouchka*, costarring with his wife. During the late 1940s and early 1950s, Gennaro performed in the touring company of the revue *Make Mine Manhattan* (1949), and in musicals such as *Kiss Me Kate* (1950), *Guys and Dolls* (1950–1952), *Pretty Penny*, and *By the Beautiful Sea* (1950). In *Pajama Game* (1954), featuring the choreography of Bob Fosse, Gennaro's flashy style of dance was spotlighted in the famous "Steam Heat" number, danced with Carol Haney and Buzz Miller. He captivated audiences in the comic "Mu-cha-cha" duet with Judy Holliday in the musical *Bells Are Ringing* (1956), choreographed by Fosse and Jerome Robbins. Gennaro soon became one of Broadway's premier specialty dancers.

In 1957 Robbins asked Gennaro to cochoreograph the Broadway musical *West Side Story*. Drawing upon his experiences in dance and musical theater, Gennaro choreographed the Latin dance steps for the energetic song "America." His choreography for *Fiorello!* (1959) and *The Unsinkable Molly Brown* (1960, film version 1964) further extended his choreographing talent. Gennaro continued to choreograph Broadway musicals such as *Mr. President* (1962), *Bajour* (1964), *Jimmy* (1969), *Irene* (1973), *Annie* (1977; revival in 1997), *Carmelina* (1979), and the Broadway revival of the musical *Little Me* (1982). In 1977 he won the Tony Award for best choreographer for *Annie*.

To supplement his income during the early years of his performing career, Gennaro became one of the country's most popular dance instructors, teaching jazz dance to professional performers and to high school and college dance teachers. For his contributions to the teaching profession, he received the Dance Educators Award in 1957 and 1963, and the *Dance Magazine* award in 1964. Because of childhood ear infections, Gennaro was hearing impaired, and in 1974 he received the Eleanor Roosevelt Humanitarian Award from the New York League for the Hard of Hearing for overcoming his hearing loss in a field concerned with sound and movement.

In addition to performing, producing, and choreographing for Broadway, in the late 1950s and 1960s Gennaro began to dance and choreograph for television variety shows, including *Your Hit Parade*, *The Entertainers*, the *Judy Garland Show*, the *Andy Williams Show*, the *Bell Telephone Hour*, the *Bing Crosby Show*, the *Steve Allen Show*, the *Frankie Lane Show*, the *Arthur Murray Show*, the *Polly Bergen Show*, *Hollywood Palace*, and the *Red Skelton Show*. Gennaro also appeared in President Lyndon B. Johnson's campaigns to raise money for his election bids. During the 1960s, Gennaro and his troupe, the Peter Gennaro Dancers, appeared regularly on the *Perry Como Show* and the *Ed Sullivan Show*. He also produced audience-appealing commercials for Contac cold medicine, "The Colddiggers of 1969" (patterned after the film *Golddiggers of 1933*), and "I Love New York," in the 1970s. Gennaro produced and choreographed spectacular stage shows at New York City's Radio City Music Hall from 1971 to 1978. He also choreographed several *Miss America Pageants* (1973–1976, and 1984), a pas de deux for ballerina Natalia Makarova, and the London production of *Singin' in the Rain* (1985).

Gennaro thus became one of the most recognized and admired artists of his generation.

Gennaro received the 1997–1998 Distinguished Guest Artist award from the Loyola College of Music. The Tony Award–winning dancer and choreographer died at the age of eighty. In January 2002 Gennaro was inducted posthumously into the Theatre Hall of Fame.

Gennaro will be remembered for his choreographic contributions to *West Side Story* and *Annie*. But he perhaps will best be known for his dancing and choreography on Perry Como's *Kraft Music Hall* on television in the 1960s.

★

Photographs, reviews, films, and videotapes of Gennaro's dancing and choreography can be viewed at the Library of Congress in Washington, D.C., and the New York Public Library for the Performing Arts and the Museum of Television and Radio in New York City. "Introduction to Modern Jazz," a Labanotation score of a technique class Gennaro devised, is housed in the New York Public Library's Dance Collection. The Library of Congress has an audio recording of music and an illustrated manual for "A Dance Class with Peter Gennaro." Biographical information and insights into Gennaro's ideas about choreography are in Walter Terry, "The Choreographer's Job," *New York Herald Tribune* (8 Jan. 1961); Lydia Joel, "Conversation with Peter Gennaro," *Dance Magazine* (Aug. 1964); Harold Stern, "The Master of the Jazz Forms Turns to TV," *Dance Magazine* (June 1970); and Sidney Fields, "*Annie*'s Dance Master," *New York Daily News* (1 Dec. 1977). An affectionate look at Gennaro's life and career is in Sylviane Gold, "Peter Gennaro: Big Talent on a Small Screen," *Dance Magazine* (1 May 2001). Obituaries are in the *New York Times* (30 Sept. 2000), *Pittsburg Post-Gazette* (4 Oct. 2000), and *Independent* (London) (9 Oct. 2000).

REBECCA J. TIMMONS

GERSTENBERG, Richard Charles (*b.* 24 November 1909 in Little Falls, New York; *d.* 11 July 2002 in Paradise Valley, Arizona), chairman and chief executive officer of General Motors.

Gerstenberg was born to Richard Paul Gerstenberg and Mary (Booth) Gerstenberg. At the age of five, Gerstenberg moved with his family to the nearby town of Mohawk, New York, where he was raised and attended school. He graduated from the University of Michigan in 1931 with a B.A. In 1932 he became the timekeeper of General Motors' Frigidaire division in Dayton, Ohio, beginning a forty-two-year career with General Motors. Gerstenberg married Evelyn Hitchingham in December 1934; they had a son and a daughter.

Gerstenberg held many positions with General Motors. In 1934 he was transferred to the Fisher Body division in

Gerstenberg retired at the height of problems in the automobile industry, telling *Automotive News* in 1974, "I hate to leave all these problems to someone else."

After his retirement, Gerstenberg supported a variety of charitable causes, particularly in the field of education. He served on boards and committees for the United Negro College Fund, the University of Michigan, and the Alfred P. Sloan Foundation. In keeping with his ·work to help rebuild Detroit after the city's race riots in the late 1960s, Gerstenberg served as the chair of New Detroit and on the boards of several Detroit businesses. He also established a scholarship fund in honor of his father at Mohawk High School in New York. In between his work and charity commitments, Gerstenberg was an avid golfer and fly-fisherman.

Gerstenberg died at age ninety-two at his home in Paradise Valley, Arizona, following a long illness. When Gerstenberg entered college, his father told him, "I just hope that you won't have to work all your life like I had to work. I wish you could get a job with a big company and take things easy." While Gerstenberg did spend his career at a major corporation, he worked hard to solve the numerous problems encountered by General Motors and to keep the company profitable. In 2002 the General Motors chairman Jack Smith noted that Gerstenberg was "known for his high integrity and his deep concern for the well-being of the company and its employees."

★

Information about Gerstenberg's career at General Motors may be found in many of the company's press releases. Obituaries are in the *Automotive News* (22 July 2002) and *New York Times* (26 July 2002).

MARGALIT SUSSER

Richard Gerstenberg, 1973. AP/WIDE WORLD PHOTOS

Detroit and then to the central office in 1936. In 1949 Gerstenberg was appointed as the assistant comptroller, a position he held until April 1956, when he became the corporation's treasurer. In 1960 Gerstenberg became the vice president in charge of the financial staff. In 1967 he became the executive vice president of finance and a member of the board of directors, in which capacity he served as the chair of the finance committee. In January 1972 he became the chairman and chief executive officer (CEO) of General Motors, a post he held until his retirement in November 1974. Gerstenberg continued to serve as a director of the board until May 1980.

At a time when executives wore solid-color suits with white shirts and plain ties, Gerstenberg enjoyed going to work in striped shirts, bright ties, and, at times, plaid suits. Despite his unconventional apparel, Gerstenberg saw record profits for his company in 1972 and 1973, but all that changed after 16 October 1973, as an Arab oil embargo led to a U.S. oil crisis. With the rise in gasoline prices, consumers began looking for small, fuel-efficient vehicles, not the large automobiles offered by General Motors and the other major U.S. automakers. In 1974 Gerstenberg oversaw the extensive downsizing of General Motors' cars. As CEO he also testified in front of a U.S. Senate subcommittee on issues such as automobile safety, airbags, and fuel economy.

GIBSON, William Frank (*b.* 7 September 1933 in Greenville, South Carolina; *d.* 2 May 2002 in Greenville, South Carolina), civil rights advocate who fought for voting rights and economic reciprocity for African Americans, and who led the National Association for the Advancement of Colored People (NAACP) as chair of the board of directors from 1985 to 1995.

Gibson's father was a brick mason and his mother a school-teacher. He grew up with his sister in a comfortable middle-class home in the segregated South. His father was a successful and respected member of the community and a staunch supporter of the NAACP. Gibson's interest in the civil rights struggle became evident at age ten, after he accompanied his father to NAACP meetings.

After graduating from Mayo High School, the six-foot-tall youth was awarded a football scholarship by Allen Uni-

William F. Gibson, 1985. AP/WIDE WORLD PHOTOS

versity in Columbia, South Carolina. However, shortly after attending the university, Gibson injured his leg and was unable to play football. He transferred to North Carolina A&T State University in Greensboro, where he graduated with a B.S. in biology. In 1953 Gibson entered Meharry Medical College School of Dentistry in Nashville, Tennessee, earning a D.D.S. in dental surgery.

After completing his internship in 1959 at Harlem Hospital in New York City, Gibson returned to Greenville, where he established a private practice in general dentistry. At that same time, Gibson was active in local chapters of the NAACP, and in 1961 he was elected treasurer of the group. As treasurer, he organized the Black Council for Progress, which helped promote African Americans for political office. In 1979 Gibson negotiated for greater African-American representation in corporate America, playing a role in convincing major corporations to buy services from black-owned businesses and to hire blacks for managerial positions.

Although he had a successful career as a dentist, Gibson found time to serve the NAACP and the community. In South Carolina he served the organization and the state in numerous capacities, including a stint as president of the Greenville branch and of the South Carolina Conference of Branches. As a public servant Gibson served as chairman of the South Carolina Human Relations Committee, the

Voter Education Project, the Black Council for Progress, and the mayor's Human Relations Committee and Greenville Education Committee. He was also chairman of the South Carolina Committee to the United States Commission on Civil Rights. Gibson, who was vice chairman in 1983, headed South Carolina's NAACP chapter from 1977 to 1997, becoming chair of the board of directors in 1985. As chair, Gibson took the organization in a new direction by focusing on voter registration and economic parity for African Americans. He also served as a mentor to young professionals.

Gibson's leadership was not without controversy. In 1992 he repealed the term limit, which allowed him to serve a third term. Several members, including Benjamin Hooks, the executive director of the NAACP from 1977 to 1992, were opposed to Gibson's leadership and resigned. In 1994, during Gibson's third term, the NAACP experienced severe financial problems, and later that year it sunk into near bankruptcy. While still in the midst of financial crisis, the board learned that Gibson had approved hundreds of thousands of dollars to be paid to a former employee who complained that Benjamin Charvis, the executive director, sexually harassed her. The scandal led to questions regarding the organization's financial operations. After an intense scrutiny of Gibson's financial management, the board established that he had mishandled more than half a million dollars of the organization's funds since 1985. During this same time the NAACP had a deficit of about four and a half million dollars and had furloughed its staff. Leading donors such as the Ford Foundation threatened to withhold their contributions.

Responding to the financial misappropriations, critics called for Gibson's resignation. Carl T. Rowan, a syndicated columnist from the *Chicago Sun-Times,* accused Gibson of using his position as chairman for personal financial gain. After the financial mismanagement became public, many people within and outside the NAACP questioned the effectiveness of the organization's promotion of racial equality. Some board members felt that Gibson's leadership had hurt the NAACP's credibility. Others, like Leroy Warren Jr., chair of the NAACP Federal Task Force Committee, felt that the NAACP operated like a mafia, alienating supporting groups like organized labor, which was one of the organization's most important donors. In October 1994 the board of directors hired an independent audit group, Coopers and Lybrand, to audit the group's finances, but Gibson managed to block the audit.

In 1995 Gibson's ten-year tenure as NAACP board chairman came to an end when he was defeated with one vote and replaced by Myrlie Evers-Williams, the widow of the slain civil rights leader Medgar Evans. Despite the defeat, Gibson retained his seat on the board and continued to serve as president of South Carolina State Conference.

But the allegations and suspicion never subsided, and he spent his last years as an outcast.

Under Gibson, the NAACP accomplished many goals, and some people believe that despite his financial problems, he was a great political visionary. In 1993, for example, Denny's Restaurant, responding to complaints that it discriminated against African Americans, signed an agreement that gave employment and business opportunities to minorities. Gibson was particularly instrumental in negotiating dozens of agreements with corporations that opened up franchising, contracting, and employment opportunities for African Americans. It was also during Gibson's era that the NAACP released "Out of Focus, Out of Sync," a report that exposed the miserable treatment of minorities in the television industry. Gibson's greatest legacy was his dedication to racial justice and equal opportunity for all.

Gibson earned many honors and awards, including the Phillis Wheatley Association Award, the South Carolina Council on Human Relations Leadership Award, the South Carolina State Affairs Commission Recognition Service Award, the North Carolina Key to the City of Fayetteville Service Award, and the NAACP Leadership Award. Gibson was a member of Kappa Alpha Psi Fraternity and served in South Carolina's Democratic conventions for three years. In 1998 Gibson was honored with the Jefferson Award for his outstanding service to South Carolina.

Gibson died of cancer at age sixty-nine and was buried at Resthaven Memorial Gardens in Piedmont, South Carolina. His wife, Lottie, and four children survived him.

★

There are no full-length biographies of Gibson. For information about his life and career, see Phil W. Petrie, "William Gibson Remembered by National Leaders," *Crisis* 109 (July/Aug. 2002): 69, a tribute to Gibson. Jackie E. White, "Let's Scrap the N.A.A.C.P.," *Time* (13 Feb. 1995), and Paul Ruffin, "Binding the Ties at the N.A.A.C.P.," *Nation* (30 Oct. 1995), discuss the NAACP financial crisis. Also see Denise Crittedon, "Dr. Gibson Keeps NAACP on Course, with Change," *Crisis* 101 (Jan. 1994): 23. Obituaries are in the *New York Times* (3 May 2002) and *Jet* (27 May 2002).

NJOKI-WA-KINYATTI

GILBRETH, Frank Bunker, Jr. (*b.* 17 March 1911 in Plainfield, New Jersey; *d.* 18 February 2001 in Charleston, South Carolina), columnist and newspaper executive best known in South Carolina for his column "Doing the Charleston," and in the United States for the book *Cheaper by the Dozen* (1948), which he cowrote with his sister.

Gilbreth was the first son and fifth child born to Frank Bunker Gilbreth, an efficiency expert who originated "mo-

tion study" at the turn of the century, and Lillian (Moller) Gilbreth, a Brown University Ph.D. and accomplished engineering consultant who operated the family company, Gilbreth Incorporated, after her husband's death in 1924. When Gilbreth was nine, the family moved from Providence, Rhode Island, to suburban Montclair, New Jersey. Gilbreth and his five brothers and six sisters were often the subjects of their father's efficiency studies. The family became known for its family council, work charts, pranks, and travel escapades. They summered regularly in the Shoe, their house in Nantucket, Massachusetts, where the children learned astronomy, swimming, and sailing.

After graduating from Montclair High School in 1928, Gilbreth enrolled at Saint John's College in Annapolis, Maryland, to pursue a degree in engineering to please his mother. He was ill-suited for this course of study, however, and in 1929 he transferred to the University of Michigan to major in journalism. Here he found his passion in newspaper writing and edited and wrote for the college newspaper, the *Michigan Daily*.

After receiving his B.A. in 1933, Gilbreth spent a short time reporting for the *New York Herald Tribune,* before his future wife's brothers and fellow reporters invited him to work in Charleston, South Carolina, on the *News and Courier.* These brothers introduced him to Elizabeth Cauthen, whom Gilbreth married on 29 September 1934. The couple had one daughter. In 1936 Gilbreth and his wife's two brothers left the *News and Courier* and started their own newspaper, the *Star*, which lasted less than a year. In the wake of this failed venture, Gilbreth went to work for the Associated Press, first in Raleigh, North Carolina, then in New York City. Gilbreth also worked at the *Buenos Aires Herald* in Argentina.

With the onset of World War II, Gilbreth enlisted in the U.S. Navy in January 1942 and served in the South Pacific, participating in three invasions in the Admiralty Islands and the Philippines; he was decorated with two air medals and a bronze star. Gilbreth attained the rank of lieutenant commander before leaving the navy in 1945 at the end of the war. He then returned to his childhood hometown of Montclair and worked as a reporter for the Associated Press in nearby New York City.

In 1947 Gilbreth returned to the *News and Courier,* renamed the *Post and Courier* in 1991, as an editorial writer under the pseudonym Ashley Cooper, after Lord Anthony Ashley Cooper, who had been instrumental in founding Charleston. Gilbreth once described his pseudonym as a "fastidious, marcelled dandy . . . a fencing master, with his rapier-like thrusts against all that is evil, dull, boorish and humorless." He wrote the "Doing the Charleston" column until 1993, during which time he authored nearly 13,000 columns, advocating historic preservation, poking fun at tourists and blue bloods, challenging those people who supported flying the Confederate flag over the statehouse, and responding to readers' reactions to these and many other issues.

In 1948 Gilbreth and his sister Ernestine (Gilbreth) Carey coauthored the "life-with-father" memoir *Cheaper by the Dozen*, which recounts their story of growing up in a family of twelve children with parents who were efficiency experts. In 1950 Gilbreth and Carey wrote a sequel, *Belles on Their Toes*. Both books became Book-of-the-Month Club selections, excerpts were published in the *Ladies' Home Journal*, and they were made into movies. In subsequent years, Gilbreth wrote *Held's Angels* (1952), a novel lampooning the flappers and high-living youths of the Roaring Twenties, which was illustrated with 100 drawings by the cartoonist John Held, Jr. Gilbreth's other books include *I'm a Lucky Guy* (1951); *Innside Nantucket* (1954), a humorous story about his brother Bob buying and running Nantucket's Anchor Inn; *Of Whales and Women: One Man's View of Nantucket History* (1956); *How to Be a Father* (1958); *Loblolly* (1959); *He's My Boy* (1962), about his own young son; and *Time Out for Happiness* (1971), a biography of his parents.

After the death of his first wife in 1954, Gilbreth married Mary Pringle Manigault, the sister of the Charleston newspaper leader Peter Manigault, on 4 June 1955. Together they had a son and a daughter. Throughout his adult life, Gilbreth and his family continued his parents' tradition of summering on Nantucket, where they enjoyed clamming, blueberry picking, and sailing. During the middle 1960s Gilbreth became the assistant publisher of the *Post and Courier* and the vice president of the Evening Post Publishing Company. Using his brand of wit and facility with language, in 1970 he compiled the *Dictionary of Charlestonese*, a pamphlet that poked fun at the Charleston accent. More than 200,000 copies of the pamphlet sold, and the proceeds donated to the newspaper's Good Cheer Fund.

When Gilbreth retired at age eighty-two from writing his column, he continued to enjoy reading, golfing, and gardening, becoming something of an expert at growing camellias. Recognized for his lifelong literary contributions, he was inducted into the South Carolina Academy of Authors in 1998. Gilbreth died of a heart attack near his Charleston home and is buried in Magnolia Cemetery in Charleston.

During his more than forty years of writing "Doing the Charleston," one of the longest-running columns in American newspaper history, Gilbreth, a born Yankee, left his mark on his adopted town of Charleston. As one tribute noted, "He made us smile. He made us think. He made us angry—but never for long." As the best-selling author of eight books and the coauthor of two more, Gilbreth made many people laugh at his tall tales about growing up in his unique family.

★

Gilbreth humorously recounts his childhood in *Cheaper by the Dozen* and *Belles on Their Toes*. A collection of his "Doing the Charleston" columns was published in 1993 under the title *Ashley Cooper's Doing the Charleston,* Charles Rowe, ed. Obituaries are in the Charleston *Post and Courier* (19 Feb. 2001) and the *New York Times* (20 Feb. 2001).

JONATHAN A. GATES

GILLESPIE, Gregory Joseph (*b.* 29 November 1936 in Roselle Park, New Jersey; *d.* 26 April 2000 in Belchertown, Massachusetts), minutely realist painter who evoked the nightmarish through his irrational changes of scale and his alienated and sometimes grotesque figures.

Gillespie grew up in a strongly Catholic working-class family in what he called "an environment marked by extreme forms of behavior." His father, who had been a semiprofessional ballplayer, was an alcoholic; and his mother, a devout Catholic, was hospitalized for manic depression. Gillespie claimed that he renounced Catholicism "violently," but although he got over the "intellectual battle" with it at about the age of eighteen, he was not able to clear his mind entirely of it. In 1954, shortly after his graduation from Roselle Park High School, he enrolled in the Cooper Union for Advancement of Science and Art in New York City and studied there until 1960.

At first Gillespie's knowledge of art was limited to illustrations in comic books. He wanted to become a commercial artist but changed his mind upon seeing paintings in New York's Metropolitan Museum of Art and the Frick collection. He was especially taken with the fourteenth- and fifteenth-century Italian works and those of the nineteenth-century German expressionists. On 25 January 1959 he married the artist Frances Cohen. They had two children. In 1960 he moved to San Francisco to study at the Art Institute; his teachers included the figural artists Elmer Bischoff and Richard Diebenkorn. After receiving both a B.A. and an M.F.A. in 1962, Gillespie moved to Italy, residing in Florence in 1962–1963 and in Rome from 1964, where he lived and worked in the American Academy. He was drawn to the old masters, northern European as well as Italian. His favorite was the fifteenth-century Venetian painter Carlo Crivelli. Recalling his years in Italy, Gillespie said that he was "obsessive, morbid, and neurotic. . . . I was troubled by my childhood." In 1966 he was given his first one-person exhibition at the Forum Gallery in New York, and in 1977 he was given a retrospective at the Hirshhorn Museum and Sculpture Garden in Washington, D.C. In Italy he was supported by Tiffany, Chester Dale, and Fulbright-Hays fellowships.

Returning to America in 1970, Gillespie took up residence in a 100-year-old farmhouse in Belchertown in western Massachusetts. In 1983 his marriage came to an end. Around 1987 he stopped painting for six months to work with a spiritual teacher. His second wife, Peggy, was the founder and codirector of Love Makes a Family, an organization supporting and protecting the families of gay, lesbian, bisexual, and transgendered parents. They had one child.

Gillespie's work is marked by a heightened, often microscopic realism and is disturbingly mysterious. In it are fantasies reminiscent of the works of the Renaissance Flemish painter Hieronymus Bosch and subjects that are privately esoteric. Sometimes there are oblique references to Catholicism. Such is the case with the "shrine paintings," which Gillespie started toward the end of his stay in Italy. In these works a section of wall is opened up into a space resembling a reliquary containing arcane objects, as in *Exterior Wall with Landscape* (1967), where the niche holds a round mechanical object resembling an eye and a tiny nude figure standing beside it. Gillespie commented, "Maybe it's like our innards—gall bladder, liver, organs, organic life. It looks like it's getting buried in the wall." The shrine paintings and works similar to them appeared in the late 1980s and 1990s. In *Fertility Shrine* (1991) his bare-chested second wife sits in a niche-shaped portrait fastened onto a wall and is flanked by a shirt and a shovel, objects that seem to function as relics or devotional objects. In her right hand, which is missing a pinkie, she holds a wet artist's brush. Gillespie's paintings of women often include mutilation and torture, which might harken back to his Catholicism. Gillespie said that "maybe you never get over it completely."

Some of Gillespie's work portrays women whose arms are amputated above the elbow. Of *Woman in Brassiere* (1965) Gillespie said that "the brassiere is like a clamp," that there is "the notion of the flesh being constricted." In Gillespie's landscapes, people move about aimlessly, seldom communicating. In *Bathers in a Landscape* (1967) figures amble around a house. Two young women face each other in the foreground, and in the middle ground a heavy woman, her back to the spectator, walks purposefully into the background—all of the figures unconnected thematically or psychologically. Gillespie noted that the image of a woman walking away occurs often in his work, and "I always assumed it was an image of my mother."

Gillespie incessantly painted self-portraits. He showed himself in half-lengths, full-lengths, nude, clothed, seated, and standing. In *Self-Portrait in Circle* (1986–1988/97) he is depicted in a circular format within a rectangular frame in so markedly a realistic manner that the spectator looks to find his or her own image reflected in the mirror-like shape. *Myself Painting a Self-Portrait* (1980–1981) portrays Gillespie, nude from the waist up, painting a grimacing, hideous portrait that hardly resembles himself. In *Self-Portrait Triumphant* (2000), painted shortly before Gillespie committed suicide by hanging himself in his studio, the bare-chested, somewhat flabby artist, seated on a stool in the corner of a room, is shown with raised arms and clenched fists in a gesture of triumph. Referring to his self-portraits in an interview with the curator Abram Lerner, Gillespie observed, "The expediency of the situation is what starts it, but then . . . it becomes more fascinating precisely because the mind is looking at the outside, . . . observing its own exterior."

While he was not a household name in art circles, Gillespie's work is in major museum collections, and he always had his coterie of admirers, who rightfully regarded him as one of America's major realist painters in the second half of the twentieth century.

★

Abram Lerner, *Gregory Gillespie* (1977), contains a long, informative interview with the artist. Gillespie's work can be viewed in the following exhibition catalogs: Rose Art Museum, *William Beckman, Gregory Gillespie* (1984), and the Forum Gallery, *Gregory Gillespie, Recent Works* (1993). An obituary is in the *New York Times* (29 Apr. 2000).

ABRAHAM A. DAVIDSON

GILRUTH, Robert Rowe (*b.* 8 October 1913 in Nashwauk, Minnesota; *d.* 17 August 2000 in Charlottesville, Virginia), engineer and scientist who, during his forty-year career with the National Aeronautics and Space Administration (NASA), was instrumental in developing the Mercury, Gemini, and Apollo manned spaceflight programs.

Gilruth was the son of two high-school teachers: his father (later a school superintendent) taught science, and his mother taught mathematics. He showed an early aptitude for science and engineering, building model airplanes of his own design and constructing telescopes to view the planets as a teenager. He attended college in his native state, receiving a B.S. in aeronautical engineering in 1935 and a master's degree in 1936, both from the University of Minnesota.

Gilruth began his career shortly after graduation, specializing in research on rocket-powered aircraft. From 1937 to 1946 Gilruth worked with the National Advisory Committee for Aeronautics, a predecessor to NASA, at the Langley Aeronautical Laboratory in Virginia. In 1946 Gilruth moved on to Wallops Island, Virginia, where he worked as the chief of the pilotless aircraft research division and helped to develop a rocket launch range. One particularly important development made by Gilruth involved a new technique for gathering data on conditions in supersonic flight, an area about which little was known at the time. The wingflow test he developed remained top secret until his own presentation to the Royal Aeronautical Society of London in 1947.

From 1952 to 1959 Gilruth served as an assistant director of the Langley laboratory, where he and his team investigated high-temperature structures and dynamic loads. While still at Langley, Gilruth headed the Space Task Group and worked on developing a manned space program for the United States. His group of engineers and scientists developed and implemented most of the basic ideas that were used in NASA's Mercury program in the early 1960s. These principles included the shape of the spacecraft, the qualifications for astronauts, and the operational procedures from the time of launch through the end of the individual missions.

During this early phase of his career, Gilruth made important contributions that helped to solve the engineering difficulties of high-speed flight. The Space Task Group carried out innovative experiments on the design of new aircraft and built prototypes such as the X-15 and Dyna-Soar. The X-15 was a groundbreaking program in which rocket-powered airplanes flew above Earth's atmosphere and then glided back to Earth; the Dyna-Soar was a prototype, designed by Gilruth and his team to enter into orbit. The group's research and designs helped lay the groundwork for future projects such as the space shuttle.

The launching of *Sputnik 1,* the first artificial satellite to orbit Earth, by the Soviet Union on 4 October 1957 shocked the U.S. space program into action. When the Soviets put a dog into orbit one month later, the U.S. space scientists entered a race to put the first man into orbit, and the work that Gilruth and others were performing at various sites across the country took on a new importance. One direct consequence of the launch of *Sputnik 1* was the formation of NASA.

Gilruth joined NASA at its inception in 1958, leading a team for Project Mercury that succeeded in putting the first American into space. As the first director of NASA's Manned Spacecraft Center in Houston (later the Johnson Space Center) from 1961 to 1972, Gilruth directed twenty-five manned spaceflights as part of the Mercury, Gemini, and Apollo programs. Project Mercury was initiated to explore the effects of sending humans into space. The Mercury program's six flights from 1961 to 1963 included Alan Shepard's mission as the first American in space and John Glenn's successful attempt to become the first American to orbit Earth. During the Gemini program of 1965 to 1966, Gilruth and his NASA associates launched spacecraft with two astronauts aboard and perfected techniques used for linking spaceships in orbit. In June 1965, as part of the

Robert R. Gilruth, February 1962. AP/WIDE WORLD PHOTOS

Gemini 4 mission, Edward White became the first American to perform a space walk.

The Apollo program was initiated with President John F. Kennedy's announcement in 1961 that the United States would attempt to put a man on the Moon before the end of the decade. Gilruth and his team developed the idea to detach a lunar landing module from the main command ship as it orbited the Moon; this module would then land on the Moon and later return to dock with the main ship. After testing the lunar module concept and equipment on several Apollo missions in 1968 and 1969, Gilruth's group orchestrated the successful Moon landing of *Apollo 11* in June 1969. Gilruth also oversaw the famous rescue of *Apollo 13* in April 1970. His last mission was *Apollo 15,* in July 1971. The following year Gilruth moved to NASA headquarters in Washington, D.C., to became the director of key personnel development. After his retirement in 1973, Gilruth continued to serve as a consultant to NASA.

An avid seaman, Gilruth participated in many projects involving hydrofoils and is credited with building the first successful sailing hydrofoil. He also designed and built a fifty-two-foot, multihulled boat to sail around the world. Gilruth died at age eighty-six from complications due to Alzheimer's disease. He was survived by his second wife, Georgene Evans Gilruth.

During his lifetime Gilruth received some of the highest

honors granted by the aerospace industry, U.S. government, and academia, including the President's Award for Distinguished Federal Civilian Service and the National Aviation Club's Collier Trophy. He also received awards from the Institute of Aerospace Sciences, U.S. Chamber of Commerce, American Society of Mechanical Engineers, and National Rocket Club. He was a member of the National Academy of Engineering and the International Academy of Astronautics, a fellow in the American Astronautical Society, and a member of the prestigious National Academy of Sciences, as well as one of the first inductees into the National Space Hall of Fame.

In the 1950s and 1960s, in the infancy of the U.S. space program, placing a man on the Moon and bringing him home safely was a dream. Gilruth held together NASA's early efforts to make this dream a reality; his leadership style, meticulous attention to detail, and technical skills were critical to the success of the *Apollo 11* mission. The director of the Apollo lunar landing program, George Low, said in an interview, "[W]ithout Bob Gilruth there would not have been a Mercury, Gemini, or an Apollo program . . . he has been the leader of all that is manned spaceflight in this country."

★

A personal history of the Apollo program, including Gilruth's role, may be found in Glen E. Swanson, ed., *Before This Decade Is Out—: Personal Reflections on the Apollo Program* (1999). Obituaries are in the *Houston Chronicle* (17 Aug. 2000) and *New York Times* (18 Aug. 2000).

W. TODD TIMMONS

GINZBERG, Eli (*b*. 30 April 1911 in New York City; *d*. 12 December 2002 in New York City), economist who taught at Columbia University for more than sixty years and advised presidents from Franklin D. Roosevelt to Jimmy Carter.

One of two children of the Lithuanian émigré Louis Ginzberg, a celebrated Talmudic scholar at Jewish Theological Seminary, and Adele (Katzenstein) Ginzberg, who was active in social causes, Ginzberg was educated in the New York public schools. He graduated from DeWitt Clinton High School in 1927 and then went on to nearby Columbia University, where he received his B.A. in 1931, his M.A. in 1932, and Ph.D. in economics in 1934. On 14 July 1946 Ginzberg married Ruth Szold, a statistician; the couple had three children.

Ginzberg's parents hosted many renowned intellectual figures at their home, and the young Ginzberg became committed to linking ideas with action. Although his mentor, Wesley C. Mitchell, favored rigorous quantitative analysis, Ginzberg took every opportunity to explore the

Eli Ginzberg, 1967. AP/WIDE WORLD PHOTOS

social, cultural, and historical dimensions of economic behavior. He spent the 1928–1929 academic year at the University of Heidelberg in Germany, where the curriculum was still shaped by the recently deceased sociologist Max Weber's interest in the historical development of modern organizational and cultural forms. After returning to Columbia, Ginzberg continued to seek out alternatives to a narrowly economic conception of human behavior. Prominent among these was the "personality and culture" approach then being developed by reform-minded American social scientists, which Ginzberg imbibed in courses with the sociologist Robert M. MacIver and the anthropologists Franz Boas and Ruth Benedict.

Historical and philosophical concerns informed Ginzberg's earliest writings, a short rebuttal of the Marxist concept of primitive communism titled *Studies in the Economics of the Bible* (1932), and a dissertation, *The House of Adam Smith* (1934), which recaptured the socially progressive thrust of the Scottish economist's thought. Ginzberg also became increasingly convinced of psychology's role in economic life and spent much of his life working at the intersection of these two disciplines.

Ginzberg joined Columbia's Graduate School of Business in 1935 and rose steadily through the ranks, becoming the A. Barton Hepburn Professor of Economics in 1967. Although he was a dedicated and successful teacher, Ginzberg aspired to a broader social role. He styled himself as a scholar-activist in the mold of Columbia's E. R. A. Seligman, who helped develop the federal income tax during the 1930s. Ginzberg consistently argued that academic research should be informed by immediate policy needs, and hoped to serve as a nonpolitical adviser to those who could directly influence social change.

Ginzberg turned to practical matters in his own research, touring the nation in 1934 to examine economic conditions. The resulting book, *The Illusion of Economic Stability* (1939), advocated changes both in U.S. business culture and in federal policy. World War II offered new opportunities for public service. After leading a pioneering interdisciplinary study of unemployment, Ginzberg began his long association with the federal government in 1942, as a member of the Committee on Wartime Requirements for Scientific and Specialized Personnel. During the next few decades, he acted as a consultant for the U.S. Army and Air Force, the National Institute of Mental Health, and the Departments of State, Labor, and Defense.

In 1950 Ginzberg became the director of Columbia's new Conservation of Human Resources Project, in which government officials joined representatives of corporations, unions, and foundations to study employment from the standpoint of national manpower needs. Repudiating the idea that individuals choose careers on the basis of purely economic considerations, participants in the project generated a series of important empirical studies, including *The Uneducated* (1953) and *The Ineffective Soldier* (1959). Ginzberg synthesized the project's research in *The Human Economy* (1976), arguing that social change resulted from the interplay of government policies, educational initiatives, economic trends, and cultural forces.

Ginzberg also became involved in the federal government's attempts to develop a national manpower policy. Between 1962 and 1981 he chaired, successively, the National Manpower Advisory Committee, the National Commission for Manpower Policy, and the National Commission for Employment Policy. In 1974 Ginzberg expanded his reach into the private sector, becoming the first director of the Manpower Demonstration Research Corporation, which rigorously tested public policies.

Ginzberg strongly urged the integration of women and minorities into the workforce. He helped break down the resistance of military officials to desegregation in the 1950s, and later cowrote such volumes as *The Negro Potential* (1956), *Womanpower* (1957), *The Troublesome Presence: American Democracy and the Negro* (1964), and *Educated American Women: Life Styles and Self-Portraits* (1971). Deeply committed to Jewish causes, Ginzberg served as research director of the United Jewish Appeal in 1941, made numerous trips to Israel after 1953 under the auspices of the U.S. Technical Corporation Administration, and sat

on the board of governors for Jerusalem's Hebrew University twice during the 1950s. He published several books on the American Jewish experience, including *Agenda for American Jews* (1950); a memoir of his father's life, *Keeper of the Law: Louis Ginzberg* (1966); and the Hebrew-language *American Jews: The Building of Voluntary Community* (1980).

In addition to his work on manpower, Ginzberg became an expert on health care, consistently offering practical objections to sweeping reform proposals. He argued that liberal attempts to increase the overall supply of doctors would neither produce better care for the poor nor cut the overall social cost of health provision, but he also disapproved of conservative plans to expand the realm of choice and competition in the health industries.

Ginzberg remained director of the Conservation of Human Resources Project after becoming professor emeritus at Columbia in 1979, and took charge of the new Revson Fellows Program for the Future of the City of New York. He received numerous honors, including election to the American Association for the Advancement of Science and the American Academy of Arts and Sciences. Ginzberg also continued to teach at Columbia and Barnard College. He gave his last class on 3 December 2002, just days before dying in his sleep at his home. He is buried at Vineyard Haven on Martha's Vineyard.

With many others of his generation, Ginzberg helped develop a new public role for university professors that embodied the postwar marriage of academic expertise and governmental power. His emphasis on the psychological, philosophical, political, and historical dimensions of economic behavior brought him closer to figures in other disciplines but left him largely isolated from his own, with its increasing emphasis on narrow economic rationality and its sophisticated mathematical techniques. Ginzberg maintained that both the ideas and the social isolation of mainstream economic theorists made them irrelevant to the pressing problems of their day. By coupling his teaching with extensive consulting work and the production of more than 100 books, Ginzberg both defended and demonstrated an alternative model of economics as an applied behavioral science.

★

Ginzberg published three books that weave together autobiographical material with historical reflections. *My Brother's Keeper* (1989) deals with Ginzberg's life as a Jewish American, while *The Skeptical Economist* (1987) and *The Eye of Illusion* (1993) concentrate more heavily on his professional life. For personal testimony from friends and colleagues, see Iver Berg, ed., *Human Resources and Economic Welfare: Essays in Honor of Eli Ginzberg* (1972), and Irving Louis Horowitz, ed., *Eli Ginzberg: The Economist as a Public Intellectual* (2002). These books also contain extensive, although incomplete, bibliographies of Ginzberg's writings. An obituary is in the *New York Times* (16 Dec. 2002).

ANDREW JEWETT

GLICKMAN, Martin Irving ("Marty")

GLICKMAN, Martin Irving ("Marty") (*b.* 14 August 1917 in the Bronx, New York City; *d.* 3 January 2001 in Manhattan, New York City), collegiate athlete, member of the 1936 U.S. Olympic team, and career sports broadcaster who pioneered many of the techniques of play-by-play sports announcing for radio and television.

Glickman grew up in modest circumstances, the son of Harold Glickman, a cotton goods salesman, and Molly Glickman, a homemaker. His parents were Jewish immigrants from Iasi, Romania. Glickman attended James Madison High School in Brooklyn, where he excelled in short-distance running, winning several city and state title events. A B-plus student, he graduated in 1935 and might have had reason to hope for any number of offers of athletic scholarships but for long-standing prejudices against Jews in intercollegiate athletics.

In a 1998 interview for Syracuse's oral-history collection,

Marty Glickman. AP/WIDE WORLD PHOTOS

Glickman explained the unusual circumstance that led him to attend Syracuse University in New York, where he enrolled in 1935. "A Syracuse alumnus contacted me . . . to meet him and four others. . . . They wanted to back a Jewish athlete who would do well in school . . . and offered to pay my tuition and provide me a job," he said.

Glickman played tailback for the Orangemen's football team and ran the 100-yard dash on the track team. He capped off his freshman year by earning a spot on the 1936 U.S. Olympic team in the 400-meter relay event. That summer, in Nazi Berlin, his coaches were informed that the participation of Jewish athletes in the games would displease the German chancellor Adolph Hitler, who was in attendance. In a great historical injustice, acknowledged decades later by the U.S. Olympic Committee, Glickman and another Jewish runner, Samuel Stoller, were summarily benched. Glickman offered a detailed description of the incident in his autobiography, *Fastest Kid on the Block* (1996).

Glickman continued as a student athlete at Syracuse University and, while still in college, began his career as a professional sportscaster. "I had scored two touchdowns in a big game during my junior year," he said. "The following morning, I got a phone call from a local haberdasher who said, 'I want to cash in on your publicity. I want you to do a weekly radio sports round-up on WSYR under my sponsorship.'" Glickman was at first reluctant because of his tendency to stammer, but he agreed to take the job when he learned it would pay $15 per week. By the time Glickman graduated from Syracuse in 1939 with a B.A. in political science, he had almost two years of experience in commercial radio.

After graduation, Glickman moved back to New York City, where he would reside for the rest of his life. He played minor league football for the Jersey City Giants and worked, without pay, at radio station WHN. "We didn't call it an internship during the Depression," he said. "I just did it to be there, and to be known, when or if an opening developed." His break came in 1940, when he was hired by the station as a paid play-by-play announcer for a series of National Hockey League (NHL) games featuring the city's two teams, the Americans and the Rangers. When spring came, he was assigned to a program in which he offered verbal recreations of Major League Baseball highlights, using wire service accounts as scripts. In 1941 he married Marjorie Dorman; the couple had four children.

Although it was widely believed in the broadcasting industry that basketball, a game punctuated by many fakes and sudden reverses, was too quick and abrupt to be described coherently to a radio audience, Glickman believed it could be done by verbally "following the ball," without regard to the positioning movements of other players. In 1943 WHN agreed to carry an all-star basketball game that had been organized to benefit the Red Cross, and Glickman became the first radio announcer in history to give the play-by-play of a live basketball game. Later that year he joined the U.S. Marines, serving in the Pacific as an air traffic controller during World War II. He achieved the rank of first lieutenant.

Promoted to sports director at WHN in 1946, Glickman secured rights from the promoter Ned Irish to broadcast the college doubleheaders at Madison Square Garden that often matched the best teams in the country. When the National Basketball Association (NBA) was launched in 1946, he added the home games of the newly formed New York Knickerbockers to the schedule. Glickman called the action for all the games, college and professional, inventing the art of basketball announcing as he went along.

In the 1998 interview, Glickman explained his reliance on street terminology, which provided him with a ready-made vocabulary for describing the game to a general audience. "I spread the terminology of the city game: top of the key, elbow of the foul line, one-handed jump, two-handed set, and so on. . . . I could speak rapidly and I knew the game." In 1949 he added the first televised basketball game to his list of breakthroughs. The sportscaster Bob Costas credits Glickman with "laying out the geography" of the basketball court for future generations of announcers.

Glickman caught on early to the postwar professional football boom, leaving WHN in 1948 to become the voice of the National Football League (NFL) New York Giants on radio station WNEW, a job he relished for some twenty-three years. Despite his pioneering work and his popularity among metropolitan area fans, however, Glickman was never offered a network television contract for NFL or NBA announcing. He believed that the accent he developed in childhood, sometimes described as "New York Jewish," was the cause of this. He complained that the only role that network executives would consider him for was as "an abrasive, antagonistic color commentator, like a Howard Cosell," a role he rejected. "I'm strictly a play-by-play man," he said.

Although in many respects at the top of his craft, Glickman continued to take his share of bruises throughout his career. In 1971, after almost a quarter of a century at the microphone for the New York Giants, Glickman was unexpectedly let go by new management at WNEW. As always, he was ready for a comeback. In 1973 he began a six-year run as the radio voice of the New York Jets on WOR, ending when the Jets sold their radio rights to another station.

Throughout these situations, Glickman's voice remained familiar to New York sports fans. On local television, he called harness racing from Yonkers Raceway, indoor track meets from Madison Square Garden, and New York City high school football games on Saturday morn-

ings. When Time-Warner launched Home Box Office (HBO) in 1972, the first event ever shown on the pay-cable service was an NHL game featuring the New York Rangers hosting the Vancouver Canucks—with Glickman calling the action. "It was the first time I'd done a Rangers' game since before World War II," he said.

Despite the undeserved slights that marked his career on the field and in the booth, Glickman maintained a remarkable capacity to absorb psychological punishment and to continue to do what he did best. He died at Lenox Hill Hospital in Manhattan of complications from open-heart surgery performed in December 2000. His remains were cremated.

★

Glickman's autobiography, written with the sportswriter Stan Isaac, is *The Fastest Kid on the Block* (1996). Also see Peter Levine, "'My Father and I, We Didn't Get our Medals': Marty Glickman's American Jewish Odyssey," *American Jewish History* (Mar. 1989). Obituaries are in the *New York Times* and *Washington Post* (both 4 Jan. 2001). A two-hour interview with David Marc (recorded in 1998 on audiotape, with transcription) is held in the oral history archives of the Center for the Study of Popular Television at Syracuse University.

DAVID MARC

GONZALEZ, Henry Barbosa (*b.* 3 May 1916 in San Antonio, Texas; *d.* 28 November 2000 in San Antonio), the first Mexican American elected to the Texas Senate, who in 1961 became the first American from Texas of Mexican descent elected to the U.S. Congress.

Gonzalez was the son of Leonides Gonzalez Cigarroa and Genoveva (Barbosa) Gonzalez, descendants of the original Spanish settlers from Vizcaya, a small Basque province on the Bay of Biscay, who arrived in Mexico in 1534. They became silver miners as well as politicians, and eight generations of Gonzalez's forefathers were mayors of Mapimi in the state of Durango. Shortly after the Mexican Revolution in 1910, a band of insurgents under Pancho Villa arrested Gonzalez's father as a symbol of the deposed government. The elder Gonzalez was taken before a firing squad but was given a reprieve on the condition that he turn over almost all his possessions and leave the country. The father took his wife and two sons to San Antonio in 1911, planning to stay only until it was safe to return to their home in Mapimi. During this period, the couple had three more sons, including Henry, and a daughter.

The Gonzalez family lived in San Antonio's West Side, a predominantly Mexican-American working-class neighborhood. Gonzalez's father became managing editor of *La Prensa*, which for many years was the only Spanish-language daily newspaper published in the United States. The Gonzalez household was frequently full of visitors, including many of the politicians, landowners, military men, businessmen, and intellectuals who also had fled Mexico.

Gonzalez, who began working when he was only ten years old and still in grade school, endured the discrimination faced by Mexican Americans in Texas at the time. He was called a "greaser" and barred from areas reserved "for whites." Once, when he and a brother and a friend were ordered to leave a San Antonio swimming pool, Gonzalez refused. Years later, while serving on the San Antonio City Council, he sponsored an ordinance to end discrimination in the city's recreational facilities.

Gonzalez attended public schools in San Antonio, graduating from Thomas Jefferson High School in 1935. After two years at San Antonio Junior College, he enrolled at the University of Texas in Austin. He initially financed his education by a series of odd jobs, but because of the Great Depression he was forced to withdraw after one year at the university and return home to San Antonio. There he enrolled at Saint Mary's University School of Law as a member of the first full-time day law-school class, which consisted of just seven students. In 1940 he married Bertha Cuellar of Floresville, Texas, with whom he had eight children. Although Gonzales finished his coursework in 1942, he did not receive his LL.B. until he finished paying for his tuition and expenses in 1943. Even after completing law school, Gonzalez could not yet begin his career because World War II intervened, and he became a civilian cable and radio censor working in military intelligence.

After the war, in 1946, Gonzalez became chief juvenile officer of Bexar County, serving for several years before he began his political career when he was elected to the San Antonio City Council in 1953. Hard work and a reputation as a champion of the poor helped bring about his election in 1956 as the first Hispanic to serve in the Texas senate in a century. It was a close election that took three recounts to determine that Gonzalez had won—by only 309 votes. Although he was a freshman senator and a member of an ethnic minority in an era in which blatant racial discrimination was openly tolerated, Gonzales quickly established himself as a force to be reckoned with when he led a filibuster for a record twenty-two hours against a series of bills intended to resist desegregation. He also led the opposition to a state sales tax that would fall most heavily on the poor. Gonzalez developed a reputation as a serious legislator by introducing or cosponsoring forty-two bills, ranging from slum-clearance programs to the regulation of lobbying. He also was responsible for locating a branch of the University of Texas Medical School in San Antonio.

In a 1961 special election held to fill an unexpired term in the Eighty-seventh Congress, Gonzalez became the first American of Mexican descent elected to the U.S. Congress

Henry B. Gonzalez. AP/WIDE WORLD PHOTOS

from Texas. His Twentieth Congressional District subsequently returned him to office by overwhelming majorities in the next eighteen congressional elections. During his years in Congress, Gonzalez avoided the capital's social scene, preferring his small apartment filled with books. His family remained in San Antonio, so he commuted back and forth most weekends. A voice for the poor and downtrodden, Gonzalez was a champion of civil rights legislation in the House of Representatives. When he arrived in Washington to be sworn into office, he already had drafted a bill to end poll taxes, which discriminated against the poor and minorities. His proposal eventually became part of the Voting Rights Act of 1965.

Gonzalez sought the impeachment of President Ronald W. Reagan after the invasion of Grenada in 1983 and of President George H. W. Bush in connection with the Iran-Contra scandal in 1987. He also held hearings into the friendly relationship the Reagan and Bush administrations had had with Iraq before the first Gulf War. Gonzalez found evidence that those administrations provided agricultural credits and illegal loans that helped the Iraqi president Saddam Hussein build up his military before the invasion of Kuwait in 1990.

In 1989 Gonzalez became chairman of the House Banking Committee. He combined several characteristics that endeared him to his constituents. He was absolutely fearless in his fight against discrimination and on behalf of the disadvantaged. Gonzalez was willing to pressure his party to take a stronger stand on such issues and also zealously pursued the privileged who abused their trust regardless of party affiliation, such as those involved in the savings and loan scandal, most of whom were Democrats. Gonzalez drafted legislation to authorize a federal bailout of the savings and loan industry and impose new regulatory safeguards.

Throughout his long career, Gonzalez received numerous honors, but he particularly cherished the John F. Kennedy Profile in Courage Award, because he was an avid admirer of the late president. He received the award in 1994 for his investigations into the savings and loan industry and the Iraq scandal. Because of heart problems, Gonzalez did not file for reelection in 1998. He died of heart failure at age eighty-four and is buried at San Antonio's San Fernando Cathedral, the same church in which he was baptized. His third child, Charlie, succeeded him in the Twentieth Congressional District seat. In a memorial tribute for *Texas Monthly,* Jan Jarboe Russell summed up the congressman's view of life "as one long, tumultuous filibuster." Gonzales was, she wrote, "suited for the job: he had an ego that demanded life-or-death combat, the heart of a philosopher, and the bladder of an elephant."

★

The office of Representative Charlie Gonzalez has produced a sixty-six-page review of Gonzalez's life and career, with the most complete listing of his articles and the awards he received throughout his career. It is available from his office upon request. The best source on the first part of Gonzalez's career in Congress is Eugene Rodriguez, Jr., *Henry B. Gonzalez: A Political Profile* (1976). A less detailed but more recent work is Todd A. Sloane, *Gonzalez of Texas: A Congressman for the People* (1996), an unabashedly laudatory review. Russell's memorial tribute is in *Texas Monthly* (Jan. 2001). Obituaries are in the *New York Times* and the *Washington Post* (both 29 Nov. 2000).

CHARLES L. COCHRAN

GOODMAN, Louis Sanford (*b.* 27 August 1906 in Portland, Oregon; *d.* 19 November 2000 in Salt Lake City, Utah), pharmacologist who helped develop the first effective anticancer chemotherapy and who coauthored a seminal textbook on pharmacology and therapeutics.

Goodman grew up in Portland with his parents and two siblings. He attended Reed College in Portland, receiving a B.A. in 1928, and continued his education at the University of Oregon Medical School, graduating with an M.A. and an M.D. in 1932. Goodman married Helen Ricen in

1933, and the couple had two daughters That year Goodman interned at the Johns Hopkins Hospital in Baltimore, Maryland. In 1934 he was appointed National Research Council Fellow in Pharmacology at the Yale University School of Medicine in New Haven, Connecticut. Goodman joined Yale's faculty in 1935 as instructor in pharmacology and toxicology. He became assistant professor in 1937.

Soon after his arrival at Yale, Goodman met Alfred Gilman, another postdoctoral fellow. Their mutual interest in pharmacology led them to begin teaching the subject jointly. The pair quickly realized that the pharmacology textbooks of the time were outmoded and inadequate for the instruction of medical students, being either poorly written or not reflective of the latest findings in drug therapy. Goodman and Gilman decided to write a text to use with their students at Yale. Their goals were to correlate pharmacology with other medical sciences, to reinterpret the actions and uses of drugs in the context of then current medical advances, and to emphasize the application of pharmacodynamics to therapeutics. The time was ripe for this undertaking, as effective pharmaceuticals such as the sulfas and vitamins were just emerging.

The Macmillan Company agreed to publish the young doctors' book, expecting a manuscript of about 450,000 words, or 500 pages. Goodman and Gilman, however, submitted a handwritten manuscript of nearly a million words, or 1,200 pages! They staunchly refused to edit the text. Eventually, Macmillan conceded and, in 1941, printed three thousand copies to be sold at the then unheard of price of $12.50 per copy. *The Pharmacological Basis of Therapeutics: A Textbook of Pharmacology, Toxicology and Therapeutics for Physicians and Medical Students* was an immediate and huge success. It had an exceptional literary quality and emphasized the history of each drug's development, which made it highly readable. Its subtitle clearly indicated the audience for whom the book was written, and clinicians began to refer to it as the "blue bible," after the color of its cover. The first edition eventually sold more than eighty-six thousand copies, a record for a pharmacology textbook. Many experts later credited the book with establishing the discipline of pharmacology and strengthening its relevance to clinical medicine.

In 1942 Goodman, Gilman, and others began studying chemical warfare agents. Their team noted that the blood of soldiers exposed to nitrogen mustard had abnormally low levels of white cells. They were able to demonstrate in mice that the nitrogen mustard destroyed lymphatic tissue. Furthermore, nitrogen mustard treatments in mice caused regression of experimental lymphoma after just a few days. Clinical trials on humans followed, with equally dramatic results. Nitrogen mustard was determined to be effective against lymphosarcoma and Hodgkin's disease in patients who had not responded to radiation or for whom radiation was no longer effective. In 1946 Goodman's team published, in the *Journal of the American Medical Association,* the first paper on the use of a chemotherapeutic agent, nitrogen mustard, in the treatment of cancer. Nitrogen mustard became a model for the discovery of other classes of anticancer drugs, and chemotherapy joined radiation and surgery as standard treatments for cancer.

In 1943 Goodman became chairman of the Department of Pharmacology and Physiology at the University of Vermont College of Medicine. The following year he moved to Salt Lake City to become founding chairman of the Department of Pharmacology at the new University of Utah College of Medicine. Happy to move back west, Goodman was attracted by the opportunity to build a department from the ground up, with innovative teaching and research. In 1946 Goodman supervised a risky experiment that temporarily but totally paralyzed a colleague with the muscle relaxant curare. Doctors rarely used curare at that time, for fear of its paralyzing properties. Goodman's experiments helped broaden the use of curare and similar drugs as safe anesthetics that would allow surgeons to develop new operations.

From opposite sides of the country, in 1947, Goodman and Gilman began revising their textbook. Enormous advances in drug therapy had occurred in the 1940s, with the introduction of antibiotics and antihypertensive agents, among others. The authors were having difficulty keeping pace with the rapid changes in pharmacology and therapeutics. Each time the last of their chapters was rewritten, the earlier revised chapters once again were out of date. The second edition finally was published in 1955. It was clear to Goodman and Gilman that this was the last edition they could write on their own. The field of therapeutics had become too big. They called upon dozens of coauthors, mostly former associates who had become specialists in their fields, to participate in writing all future editions. With the fifth edition, in 1975, Goodman and Gilman added two associate editors, including Gilman's son, Alfred Goodman Gilman, whose middle name came from Louis Goodman.

Goodman's many accomplishments include significant research with alpha-adrenergic blocking agents. He developed methodologies for studying anticonvulsant drugs and became an authority on that drug class. He founded the journal *Pharmacological Reviews* and was its editor in chief for five years. He was president of the American Society for Pharmacology and Experimental Therapeutics from 1959 to 1960. Goodman was elected to the National Academy of Sciences in 1965. He served on committees of the National Institutes of Health and was a consultant for several drug firms. Goodman retired as chairman of Utah's pharmacology department in 1971 but remained on the faculty as distin-

guished professor. He kept his office there and continued to teach and work with students well into his eighties.

Goodman was described as having a keen wit and a gruff nature. He was outspoken and dedicated to his work. After sixty-two years of marriage, Helen Goodman died in 1996. Four years later, Goodman died of a heart attack in his Salt Lake City home at age ninety-four. At the time of his death, *The Pharmacological Basis of Therapeutics* was in its ninth edition and still considered the most authoritative textbook in its field. Although he was proud of his teaching and research programs at Utah, Goodman himself believed that the textbook was his most important contribution. Generations of doctors would agree.

★

Goodman's papers (1944–1977) are in the J. Willard Marriott Library at the University of Utah. A short biography and description of Goodman's research career is in Kenneth B. Castleton, *A Brief History of the University of Utah Hospital: With Biographies of Some Outstanding Professors* (1984). Goodman is interviewed in Allen B. Weisse, *Conversations in Medicine: The Story of Twentieth-Century American Medicine in the Words of Those Who Created It* (1984). Obituaries are in the *Salt Lake Tribune* (25 Nov. 2000) and the *New York Times* (28 Nov. 2000).

VICTORIA TAMBORRINO

GOTTI, John Joseph (*b.* 27 October 1940 in the Bronx, New York City; *d.* 10 June 2002 in Springfield, Missouri), underworld leader.

The fifth of thirteen children born to John and Fannie Gotti, first-generation Americans of Neapolitan origin, Gotti grew up in straitened circumstances. His father, a frequently unemployed construction worker, moved his family around before settling into a working-class section of Brooklyn in 1952. Young Gotti proved to be an indifferent student and, already a member of the Fulton-Rockaway street gang, dropped out of Franklin K. Lane High School at age sixteen. Five feet, ten inches tall, and powerfully built, Gotti was a naturally gifted brawler. By 1966 he had accumulated at least nine arrests for such activities as street fighting, intoxication, and automobile theft.

Gang activity soon brought Gotti to the attention of Aniello Dellacroce, a ranking operative in the organized crime "family" headed after 1957 by Carlo Gambino. In 1968 Federal Bureau of Investigation (FBI) agents arrested Gotti, along with his brother Gene and Angelo Ruggiero, Dellacroce's nephew, on charges of cargo theft and hijacking at Kennedy International Airport. In 1972, by the time Gotti had completed a three-year prison sentence on the hijacking charges, he had become a rising figure in the Gambino organization. He operated out of the Bergin

Hunt and Fish Club in Ozone Park, in the borough of Queens, New York City.

The charismatic Gotti's reputation for toughness served him well. In 1973, with Ruggiero, he allegedly murdered James McBratney, who the Gambino organization believed had kidnapped and killed Gambino's nephew. An appreciative Gambino hired the celebrated attorney Roy Cohn to defend Gotti and Ruggiero. Cohn negotiated the murder charges down to attempted manslaughter, and the two were sentenced to four years in prison.

During the period of his supposed incarceration at Green Haven Correctional Facility, Gotti was spotted dining in New York City restaurants and visiting his wife, Victoria (DiGiorgio) Gotti (married 6 March 1962), and their five children in their new home in Howard Beach, Queens. In 1980, after John Favara, a Howard Beach neighbor, accidentally killed Gotti's youngest son in an automobile/bicycle accident, Favara was beaten and disappeared. In 1984 an appliance repairman, Romual Piecyk, unaware of the mobster's identity, reported that Gotti had assaulted and robbed him. On learning of Gotti's reputation, Piecyk told court officials that he could not identify his assailant.

Paroled from Green Haven in 1977, Gotti claimed to have numerous legitimate jobs, including those of construction worker and plumbing-supply salesman. In fact, Gotti was an important associate of Dellacroce, especially after the death of Carlo Gambino in 1976. Gotti often met his underlings in the Bergin Club, where law enforcement officials had surreptitiously placed electronic surveillance and listening devices. In 1985 information from these sources prompted a federal racketeering indictment against Gotti and narcotics charges against his brother and Ruggiero. Gambino's successor, Paul Castellano, who supposedly wanted to nudge the organization toward legitimate activities and who held an aversion to narcotics trafficking, was said to have been deeply angered. Presumably, the strains between Gotti and the Gambino family "boss" factored into the gangland killing of Castellano outside a Manhattan steakhouse in December 1985. Salvatore Gravano, a close associate of Gotti, later testified that Gotti had arranged the murder and that the two men had witnessed the execution from across the street. Law enforcement and the press announced that Gotti had emerged as the new "father" of the Gambino organization.

Consequently, the national media paid considerable attention to Gotti's federal trial, which began in mid-1986. Prosecutors based their charges on the Racketeer Influenced and Corrupt Organizations (RICO) Act of 1970, which permitted surveillance and prosecution of individuals for membership in an ongoing criminal enterprise. Most observers anticipated a guilty verdict, but in 1987 the jury acquitted Gotti. Armed with still more-incriminating

John Gotti. AP/WIDE WORLD PHOTOS

tapes made at the Bergin Club, state prosecutors in 1990 indicted Gotti for the shooting of a labor union president involved in a conflict with the mobster. Once again, a jury found Gotti innocent. Later testimony pointed to brazen jury tampering by Gotti in both cases.

In the meantime Gotti enjoyed unprecedented notoriety. Given his repeated success in frustrating well-armed prosecutors, the press referred to Gotti as the "Teflon Don." Pleased, Gotti publicly taunted law-enforcement officials. Immaculately groomed, with his silver-streaked hair cut daily and styled into a swept-back coiffure, Gotti donned $2,000 doubled-breasted suits with $400 hand-painted silk ties. He preened when the media labeled him the "Dapper Don." According to underworld associates, Gotti compared himself to the Prohibition-era gangster Al Capone; confessed that his model had been Albert Anastasia, a notoriously violent New York underworld figure from the 1940s and 1950s; and claimed to have learned some of his guile from reading the Italian political philosopher Niccolò Machiavelli's *The Prince,* a treatise that suggested that rulers must exercise control through ruthless despotism and cunning.

Gotti's penchant for notoriety contributed to his downfall. He often encouraged underlings to report to him at the Ravenite Social Club on Mulberry Street in Little Italy in Manhattan, a situation that assisted investigators in videotaping and eavesdropping on his operations. Conversations recorded in this fashion provided the foundation for yet another series of arrests and indictments against Gotti and key subordinates. In the prosecutions, Gravano, who was said to be the "underboss" in the Gambino organization, testified against Gotti in exchange for a lighter sentence. In April 1992 a federal jury found Gotti guilty on thirteen counts, including charges of murder and racketeering, and he was sentenced to life imprisonment at the maximum-security facility in Marion, Illinois. Law enforcement experts reported that he appointed his son John A. Gotti as his successor in the Gambino organization, but the younger Gotti in 1999 pleaded guilty to racketeering charges and accepted a prison sentence. In 1998 physicians found that the senior Gotti was suffering from head and neck cancer. He died in a federal prison hospital in Springfield, Missouri, and was buried in Roman Catholic Saint John's Cemetery in New York City.

Gotti's death coincided with speculation that organized crime was undergoing major changes. Armed with the RICO statute, law enforcement officials had penetrated and disrupted the operations of the traditional underworld and imprisoned many of its leaders. Gotti's flamboyance strengthened the resolve of government officials to break the power of Italian Americans in organized crime. Unlike Gotti, however, most recognized leaders of organized crime encouraged their children to seek careers in legitimate professions.

★

Gotti's flair for publicity resulted in a substantial literature on the "Dapper Don." Among the best accounts are John H. Davis, *Mafia Dynasty: The Rise and Fall of the Gambino Crime Family* (1993), and Gene Mustain and Jerry Capeci, *Mob Star: The Story of John Gotti* (2002). On the conviction of Gotti, see Howard Blum, *Gangland: How the FBI Broke the Mob* (1993), and Peter Maas, *Underboss: Sammy the Bull Gravano's Story of Life in the Mafia* (1997). On the Gotti family, Jeffrey Goldberg, "The Don Is Done," *New York Times Biographical Service* (31 Jan. 1999), is especially insightful. An obituary is in the *New York Times* (11 June 2002).

WILLIAM HOWARD MOORE

GOULD, Stephen Jay (*b.* 10 September 1941 in Queens, New York City; *d.* 20 May 2002 in Manhattan, New York City), paleontologist and historian of science at Harvard University whose professional and popular articles, essays, and books revolutionized and popularized evolutionary theory.

Gould was the first son of second-generation Eastern European Jewish émigré parents Leonard Gould, a court stenographer, and Eleanore (Rosenberg) Gould, an artist. His only sibling, a younger brother named Peter, died in 1994. Gould was close to his maternal grandparents, Irene and Joseph Rosenberg, or "Grammy" and "Papa Joe" as he affectionately called them. Near the end of his own life, he wrote about their immigration to the United States in the last of 300 consecutive monthly pieces for *Natural History* magazine, noting with sad irony that their arrival date, 11 September 1901, was precisely one century before the greatest calamity of 2001, the terrorist attacks on the United States that killed approximately 3,000 people.

Gould was raised in the New York City borough of Queens and attended Public School 26 and Jamaica High School. When he was five years old, his father took him to the American Museum of Natural History in Manhattan, where he first set eyes on the *Tyrannosaurus* skeleton and vowed to dedicate his life's work to paleontology. Many young boys admire dinosaurs, but as Gould often noted, few retained that interest into adulthood. Gould did, earning a B.A. in geology from Antioch College in Ohio in 1963, finishing first in a class of 196 in the process. He went on to earn his Ph.D. in paleontology from Columbia University in New York City in 1967.

That same year, Harvard University in Cambridge, Massachusetts, appointed Gould assistant professor in invertebrate paleontology and assistant curator in its museum of comparative zoology. In 1971 he was promoted to associate professor, and in 1974 he earned tenure and a full professorship at the unusually young age of thirty-three. With the exception of a stint as visiting research professor of biology at New York University in 1996, Gould spent his entire career at Harvard, yet he remained a devoted New Yorker and Yankees fan who always considered himself a visitor in Massachusetts.

On 3 October 1965 Gould married a fellow Antioch student, Deborah Lee. They had two boys. After their divorce in 1995 he married the New York sculptor and art scholar Rhonda Roland Shearer.

Gould is best known for his prodigious output of writings, both professional and popular. In addition to the 300 essays for *Natural History,* he published over 500 scientific papers, more than 100 book reviews, and hundreds of editorial pieces, letters to the editor, and general commentaries. Of his twenty-five books, the first, *Ontogeny and Phylogeny* (1977), was a scholarly monograph, and the last, *The Structure of Evolutionary Theory* (2002), a technical synthesis of his life's work. The twenty-three books in between were works of popular science written in such a way as to be rewarding for scientists and nonscientists alike. At the heart of Gould's corpus are his eleven essay collections, drawn mostly from his monthly writings for *Natural His-*

Stephen Jay Gould. WALLY MCNAMEE/CORBIS

tory, beginning with *Ever Since Darwin* in 1977 and ending with *I Have Landed* a quarter-century later in 2002.

Gould's most important contribution to evolutionary theory began in 1972, when he and the fellow paleontologist Niles Eldredge first presented their hypothesis of punctuated equilibrium, arguing that Charles Darwin's linear model of change could not account for the apparent lack of transitional species in the fossil record. Historically, evolutionary theorists ignored this problem, usually dismissing it as an artifact of a spotty fossilization process. Eldredge and Gould suggested that the gaps in the fossil record are not missing evidence of gradualism but extant evidence of punctuation. Stability of species is so enduring, the two maintained, that species leave an abundance of fossils, comparatively speaking, in the strata while in their stable state. The change from one species to another, however, happens relatively quickly (on a geological time scale) in "a small sub-population of the ancestral form," and occurs "in an isolated area at the periphery of the range," thus leaving behind few fossils. Therefore, "breaks in the fossil record are real; they express the way in which evolution occurs, not the fragments of an imperfect record."

By going against the grain of accepted scientific theory, Gould's ideas earned him extensive criticism. In 1986 the Harvard biologist Bernard Davis devoted three essays in a collection to critiquing Gould's antihereditarian views, obliquely comparing him to the notorious Soviet pseudoscientist T. D. Lysenko. In one book, the philosopher

Daniel Dennett allocated fifty pages of a book to Gould, calling him "the boy who cried wolf," a "failed revolutionary," and—using capitalization to heighten the sarcasm—"Refuter of Orthodox Darwinism." The evolutionary biologist Richard Dawkins called Gould's hypothesis of punctuated equilibrium a "tempest in a teapot" and "bad poetic science." On the popular science front, the journalist Robert Wright maintained that "Gould is a fraud." According to Dawkins, "Among top-flight evolutionary biologists, Gould is considered a pest—not just a lightweight, but an actively muddled man who has warped the public's understanding of Darwinism." To most of these critics Gould responded enthusiastically and with literary brilliance, particularly in the pages of the *New York Review of Books.*

Another theoretical contribution of Gould's challenged the prevailing notion of "progress" in macroevolution. Contingency, chance, and accidents are as important in the history of life, Gould argued, as is the natural selection of adaptive features. He also railed against adaptationist arguments when they were applied to humans, most notoriously in the politically charged theory that differences in I.Q. test scores between blacks and whites had deep evolutionary significance. Gould argued in his most controversial book, *The Mismeasure of Man* (1981), that this is an example of "political" science at its worst.

This was just one of many liberal battles Gould fought throughout his life, starting in his youth when, he later said, he learned his Marxism at his "daddy's knee," and continuing at Antioch College. In his college years, he committed himself to the civil rights movement, and during a stint aboard a Woods Hole oceanographic ship, he brought two books with him—the Bible and Karl Marx's *Das Kapital.* Later, at Harvard, Gould and the liberal geneticist Richard Lewontin cofounded the organization Science for the People.

Gould's most lasting legacy, however, may rest in his popularization of evolutionary theory through his remarkable streak of 300 consecutive monthly essays in *Natural History* magazine from 1974 through 2001. In twenty-seven years Gould wrote approximately 1.5 million words, averaging about 5,000 words per essay. The range of subjects discussed in the essays was remarkably broad, touching on natural history, zoology, ecology, and environmental issues; geology and the social and behavioral sciences; and of course paleontology, paleobiology, and paleoanthropology. Foundational to the series were evolutionary theory and the history and philosophy of science.

Gould addressed significant historical elements in 220 of the essays, or about three-quarters of the total. For Gould, the pursuit of science was also the pursuit of the history and philosophy of science, and he was intensely interested in the interaction between individual scientists and their culture. This is why there were in these 220 historical essays no fewer than seventy-six major biographical portraits, a number of which include original contributions to the historical record, often utilizing primary documents in Latin, French, German, and Russian, all of which Gould translated himself.

In "This View of Life" (the title of the column) one sees most clearly the blending of popularization and professionalism that was distinctively Gouldian. In the prefaces to most of the essay collections, Gould—although he emphasizes the fact that he is first and foremost a serious scientist—balances this claim with a spirited defense of the importance of writing to a broader audience without reducing the intellectual quality of the content. "I intend my essays for professionals and lay readers alike," he explained. "I would not write these essays any differently if I intended them for my immediate colleagues alone."

Gould was a polymath of the highest order. His extrascientific writings covered such diverse subjects as baseball, choral singing, and music. Particularly notable is his 1978 "Narration and Précis of J. Dryden, 'King Arthur' for the Performance of Purcell's Incidental Music"; Gould had a respectable baritone voice and was a practiced choral singer.

Gould even conducted an extensive mathematical analysis of the reasons why modern baseball players are incapable of achieving a .400 batting average. For his study, Gould collected data from baseball archives and computed standard deviations between the worst hitters and the average, and the best hitters and the average, for over 100 years of the game's history. From these computations, he discovered a statistical trend of improvement in the average play over time such that the best contemporary players, while absolutely as good as—if not better than—players from earlier in the century, were relatively worse compared to the modern era's higher average level of play.

Similar creative conjoining of ideas can be seen in a 1980 article on "Phyletic Size Decrease in Hershey Bars," containing a light theme with a deep message—that long-term evolutionary trends may wash out short-term selective forces. It was a point that Gould hammered home time and again throughout his career in his struggle to balance the adaptationist program with other evolutionary factors. His most prominent presentation of his arguments was in the 1979 paper, "The Spandrels of San Marco and the Panglossian Paradigm: A Critique of the Adaptationist Programme," one of his most widely cited publications, in which he argued that many features of organisms are like spandrels—the empty, functionless space between two arches in a building's corner, often filled with decorative art.

Forty-four honorary degrees and sixty major fellowships, medals, and awards bear witness to the depth and scope of Gould's accomplishments in both the sciences and humanities. Among the many honors he accrued were a National

Book Award for *The Panda's Thumb* (1981), a National Book Critics Circle Award for *The Mismeasure of Man* (1981), and a Phi Beta Kappa Book Award for *Hen's Teeth and Horse's Toes* (1984). He even had a Jupiter-crossing asteroid named after him (Stephengould, discovered by Gene Shoemaker in 1992), and his impact in the popular arena is illustrated by his being featured in the television cartoon series *The Simpsons*.

"When my skein runs out," Gould once wrote, "I hope to face the end calmly and in my own way—and I find nothing reproachable in those who rage mightily against the dying of the light." He nearly died in 1982 from mesothelioma, an asbestos-induced cancer, but recovered after surgery and chemotherapy, as a result of which he later endorsed the medical use of marijuana. Twenty years later, Gould died of an unrelated cancer at his loft (once featured in a glowing review in *Architectural Digest*) in Manhattan's trendy SoHo district with his family at his side. Memorial services were held at both New York University and at Harvard. In his first collection of essays, *Ever Since Darwin*, Gould wrote that "Science is not a heartless pursuit of objective information. It is a creative human activity, its geniuses acting more as artists than as information processors." He was a literary genius who mastered the art of scientific creativity and composition.

★

There are no biographies of Gould, nor did he write an autobiography. Because of the personal nature of his essay style, aspects of his personal life appear here and there among the 300 essays, particularly the final one republished as the title piece in the last collection, *I Have Landed* (2002). Summaries of his career and scientific ideas by detractors include Daniel Dennett, *Darwin's Dangerous Idea* (1995), which is particularly critical of Gould, and Michael Ruse, *The Evolution Wars* (2000). A quantitative content analysis of Gould's work can be found in Michael Shermer, "This View of Science: Stephen Jay Gould as Historian of Science and Scientific Historian, Popular Scientist and Scientific Popularizer," *Social Studies of Science* 32, no. 4 (Aug. 2002): 489–524. Obituaries are in the *New York Times* and *Washington Post* (both 21 May 2002).

MICHAEL SHERMER

GRAHAM, Katharine Meyer (*b.* 16 June 1917 in New York City; *d.* 17 July 2001 in Boise, Idaho), publisher under whose stewardship the *Washington Post* became one of the leading newspapers in the United States.

Born Katharine Meyer, Graham was the fourth of five children of Eugene Meyer, an investment banker and the founder of Allied Chemical Company, and Agnes (Ernst) Meyer, an author and a patron of the arts and education.

Katharine Graham, 1997. AP/WIDE WORLD PHOTOS

She grew up amid great wealth: her family owned estates in Washington, D.C., where they lived during the year; in suburban Mount Kisco, New York; and near Jackson Hole, Wyoming, where they spent vacations. Her parents, characterized by formal manners, were detached with their children, and Graham later described her childhood as lonely. Her mother's stern reproaches, she recalled, inculcated a deep insecurity. Certain topics, including the fact that her father was Jewish, were never discussed. (The family belonged to an Episcopalian church but took little interest in religion.) Later in life, Graham would be surprised when she was the target of occasional anti-Semitic remarks or acts of discrimination.

As a child, Graham attended the Madeira School for Girls, first on Washington's Dupont Circle and then in Virginia, graduating in 1934. Although she later described her younger self as timid and possessed of the view that only men, not women, should have careers, her young adulthood displayed an independence uncommon for women of her time. She attended Vassar College for two years and then the University of Chicago for two more, graduating with a B.A. in 1938. She became politically active in college, breaking with her Republican parents to become a supporter of President Franklin D. Roosevelt's New Deal social programs.

In 1938 Graham moved to San Francisco and became a reporter for the *San Francisco News,* covering labor issues.

The next year her father, who six years earlier had purchased the ailing *Washington Post* at a bankruptcy auction, asked her to return home and work at his newspaper. She joined the *Post* and wrote what she called "light" editorials, on such subjects as horses and mixed drinks, and edited letters to the editor. Early in 1940, at a luncheon hosted by friends, she met Philip L. Graham, a twenty-five-year-old clerk to the U.S. Supreme Court justice Stanley Reed. The pair dated briefly before he proposed marriage to her. They married on 5 June 1940 and moved to a row house in Georgetown, the neighborhood favored by Washington's high society. Graham suffered a miscarriage in 1941, and the next year a baby boy died in childbirth, strangled by its umbilical cord. In 1943, however, a daughter was born, soon followed by three sons.

Her father came to like and admire her husband, and in light of the fact that Graham's only brother had chosen to become a doctor, Meyer decided that Philip Graham should be the one to take over the newspaper. In keeping with the expectations of the period, Graham herself did not think it unusual or take offense that her father would anoint his son-in-law instead of his own daughter as his successor. On 1 January 1946 Philip Graham became the *Post*'s associate publisher. Then, in June, President Harry S. Truman asked Meyer (who had served as a governor of the Federal Reserve Bank under President Herbert Hoover) to become the president of the newly created World Bank. Meyer ceased his active involvement with the paper, and Philip Graham assumed the role of publisher.

During his tenure, Graham's husband raised the *Washington Post*'s stature and quality. As the head of the Washington Post Company, he also purchased *Newsweek* magazine and two television stations. Building friendships with leading politicians, including President John F. Kennedy and Vice President Lyndon B. Johnson, he became a central player in Washington politics. He also suffered from severe depression. The first episode that Graham recalled came on 28 October 1957, when her husband awoke in the middle of the night sobbing inconsolably, saying that he could no longer go on. Over the next six years, despite psychiatric care, his behavior grew erratic. He began an extramarital affair with a *Newsweek* researcher and briefly left his wife. On 3 August 1963, while on weekend leave from a psychiatric institution to which he had been committed, he shot himself at the Grahams' country house in Marshall, Virginia. Graham heard the blast and discovered her husband's body in the bathroom.

On 20 September 1963 Graham, with some trepidation, became the president of the Washington Post Company. Over the next three decades, she would do far more to raise the newspaper's profile and expand the company's holdings than her husband ever had. One critical decision was the hiring in 1965 of Benjamin C. Bradlee, a former *Post* reporter then working at *Newsweek,* as a deputy managing editor. He was quickly promoted, first to managing editor and then to executive editor. Charismatic, tough, and enthralled with reporting, Bradlee assembled a roster of top-flight journalists—among them David Broder, Ward Just, and Stanley Karnow—several of whom he managed to lure from such top competitors as the *New York Times* and *Time* and *Life* magazines. Supportive of Bradlee's moves, Graham opened the corporate purse strings for him to make the hires.

Although she was tentative about assuming a public profile, Graham nonetheless emerged as one of the nation's leading executives. In 1966 the writer Truman Capote, a friend of hers, threw a gala ball in her honor that became the talk of high society. In the early 1970s, like many women, Graham began questioning her longstanding acceptance of various sexist cultural practices. Influenced by the activist Gloria Steinem, as well as by her own growing self-confidence and the discrimination she witnessed around her, Graham turned from an antifeminist to a feminist. After the *Post's* personnel director circulated a memo welcoming new employees in which he referred to the new male hires by their last names and the women by their first names, Graham sent him a memo of her own, upbraiding him for this practice.

The paper was changing, too. One significant shift was its turnabout on the Vietnam War. Initially the newspaper's editorials, in keeping with Graham's own views, supported U.S. military involvement in Indochina. As the war dragged on without progress, however, influential voices, such as those of the columnist Walter Lippmann and her new editorial page editor, Phil Geyelin, argued for an antiwar position, which Graham herself soon adopted. At the same time, she refused to violate the strict separation between reporting and opinion that she believed gave the paper its stature and credibility. "It isn't right for a publisher to tell an editor what to do or not to do," she once said. "But it is certainly the publisher's responsibility to see that the paper is complete, accurate, fair and as excellent as possible."

The paper's outspokenness brought on the wrath of President Richard M. Nixon, who was highly sensitive to criticism. In November 1969, as part of an administration campaign to discredit the news media, Vice President Spiro Agnew publicly denounced the press for its coverage of the war and other issues, heaping special opprobrium on the *Post.* Agnew's remarks, while deplored by most reporters, also triggered a round of soul-searching, as journalists—Graham included—sought to reconcile their duty to be skeptical with their commitment to be fair.

Relations between the paper and the Nixon administration worsened in 1971 with the publication of the so-called *Pentagon Papers,* a U.S. Department of Defense study of U.S. involvement in the Vietnam War. The *New York Times* was the first to obtain the study and began publishing articles about it on 13 June. After two days, the Nixon administration won a court order forbidding the *Times* to publish additional stories, but since the court had not barred other papers from doing so, a *Post* reporter acquired another copy of the study, and the paper prepared its own articles to run. The newspaper's lawyers advised Graham to wait until the *Times* case was settled, but she overruled their advice and chose to publish. The administration then sued the *Post* as well, but the Supreme Court soon ruled in favor of both newspapers in what was widely seen as a victory for the First Amendment and against prior restraint. Graham's decision to publish helped give her paper standing as a national newspaper second only to the *Times.*

The next coup for Graham and the *Post* came with the Watergate scandal. On 17 June 1972 five burglars were arrested breaking into the Democratic Party's national headquarters in the Watergate Hotel complex along the Potomac River in Washington, D.C. It would later emerge that the men belonged to a secret White House group, "the plumbers," that Nixon's aides had first set up to investigate Daniel Ellsberg, the former Pentagon aide who had given the *Pentagon Papers* to the *Post* and the *Times.*

At the outset, however, only a few journalists thought the Watergate break-in amounted to a consequential story. Among those few were two young reporters for the *Post,* Bob Woodward and Carl Bernstein, who investigated the story aggressively. Graham and Bradlee encouraged their reporters and defended them in the face of intense criticism from the administration as well as other journalists. Graham even replied personally to critics who wrote her blasting the *Post's* coverage. "If we are exaggerating minor peccadilloes," she wrote to one angry reader, "why has the majority of the White House staff had to be unloaded?"

At one point in 1972 John Mitchell, Nixon's campaign manager and the former attorney general, warned Bernstein on the phone that if the *Post* ran a story implicating Mitchell in a widespread effort of campaign sabotage, "Katie Graham's gonna get her tit caught in a big fat wringer." The line was made famous by Woodward and Bernstein's book about their Watergate reporting, *All the President's Men* (1974), and the film based on it. It became a favorite joke around the *Post* newsroom, and Graham even took to wearing a necklace with two pendants: a miniature gold wringer (a gift from a California dentist) and a miniature gold breast (a gift from the *Post's* longtime humor columnist, Art Buchwald).

Graham's editorial successes were matched by business triumphs. With help from Warren Buffett, a wealthy investor who also became one of her closest friends, Graham turned the *Post* into a robust, highly profitable corporation. She held a public offering of the company's stock in 1971, and it consistently fared well on the New York Stock

Exchange. The first woman to lead a Fortune 500 company, Graham raised her company's annual revenue from $84 million in 1963, when she became the president, to $1.4 billion in 1991, when she retired as the chief executive.

Some of the company's profits came at the expense of the blue-collar laborers who put out the *Washington Post.* The early 1970s were marked by a series of battles between labor and management at the newspaper, and, despite her liberal politics, Graham proved to be a tough, unforgiving bargainer. After a series of conflicts, the pressmen struck on 30 September 1975. The workers destroyed some of the machinery and even beat up one of their own foremen. In the 139 days that followed, they resorted to violence again, but Graham refused to budge. She joined white-collar employees of the paper in performing the strikers' jobs, at one point handling the telephones to take down classified ads. She decided to train replacement employees and eventually broke the pressmen's union. Many workers permanently lost their jobs.

With her clenched jaw and imperious bearing, Graham was seen as aloof in the newsroom, inspiring awe and sometimes fear. Many people referred to her always as "Mrs. Graham." But she also loved offering tips to reporters based on information she had learned from her powerful friends, and Bradlee jokingly referred to her, after the 1940s comic book character, as "Brenda Starr, Girl Reporter."

Graham also had a gregarious and playful side. With Meg Greenfield, the *Post*'s editorial page editor and another pioneering woman in the male-dominated world of journalism, she would sometimes sneak out of work to go to the movies. Maintaining a robust social life, she hosted dinners and parties at her Georgetown home. The friends and guests over the years amounted to a who's who of journalists, business leaders, and local, national, and international politicians, as well as notable intellectuals and artists.

In 1974 her son Donald joined the board of the Washington Post Company, and in 1976 began taking over some of his mother's duties. He succeeded her as publisher of the *Post* in 1979, as chief executive officer in 1991, and as chairman of the board in 1993. Graham, however, remained active on the board. In 1997, at the age of eighty, Graham published *Personal History,* a memoir. The book was widely praised as a lucid, engaging, and strikingly candid account of her development from what she called a "doormat wife" to perhaps the most powerful woman in journalism and business. It won the Pulitzer Prize for biography and became a best-seller.

On 14 July 2001 Graham was attending a conference of business executives in Sun Valley, Idaho, when she fell on a walkway and hit her head. She was hospitalized in Boise, where she died three days later from head injuries. Thousands of mourners, including some of the nation's most distinguished politicians and journalists, attended a memorial service for her at Washington's National Cathedral on 24 July. She was buried later that day beside her husband in a private ceremony at Oak Hill Cemetery, across the street from her Georgetown home.

★

The most informative book about Graham is her own autobiography, *Personal History* (1997). Also helpful is Ben Bradlee's memoir, *A Good Life: Newspapering and Other Adventures* (1995). Histories of the *Washington Post* include David Halberstam, *The Powers That Be* (1979); Howard Bray, *The Pillars of the Post: The Making of a News Empire in Washington* (1980); and Chalmers Roberts, *In the Shadow of Power: The Story of the Washington Post* (1989), an updated version of *The Washington Post: The First 100 Years* (1977). Obituaries are in the *Washington Post* and *New York Times* (both 18 July 2001).

DAVID GREENBERG

GRAY, Peter Wyshner ("Pete") (*b.* 6 March 1915 in Nanticoke, Pennsylvania; *d.* 30 June 2002 in Nanticoke, Pennsylvania), the only one-armed man to play major league baseball, whose on-field exploits and inspirational example for servicemen disabled in World War II captured national attention.

Gray was born Peter Wyshner, Jr., in Hanover, a Lithuanian and Polish enclave of Nanticoke, Pennsylvania, whose

Pete Gray, May 1945. AP/WIDE WORLD PHOTOS

economy revolved around the mining and production of anthracite coal for industrial and domestic use. He was the youngest of five children born to Lithuanian immigrants Peter Wyshner, Sr., a coal miner at the nearby Truesdale Colliery, and Antoinette (Keulewicz) Wyshner, an ambitious homemaker who once donned her husband's work clothes and went to work in the mines as well. Gray lost his right arm from above the elbow in a grocery truck accident at age six. Determined to realize a personal dream to play at Yankee Stadium, Gray, a natural right-hander prior to the mishap, learned to hit, catch, and throw left-handed. His fielding astounded fans as well as opposing players. After making a catch, he would place the glove under the stump of his right arm, roll the ball across his body with his left hand, and throw it into the infield.

After quitting school in his early teens, Gray, unable to work in the coal mines, began playing semiprofessional baseball in northeastern Pennsylvania's anthracite leagues. A visit to a tryout camp for the St. Louis Cardinals in the mid-1930s ended in rejection, as did an interview several years later with Connie Mack, the owner-manager of the Philadelphia Athletics. A cantankerous individual by nature, Gray, with relentless fire, willed himself to succeed to spite the naysayers. Believing that the rejections were motivated in part by ethnic discrimination, the one-armed outfielder changed his surname to Gray and left the coal region for Brooklyn in New York City, where he briefly played for the semiprofessional Bushwicks.

Gray made his minor-league debut in 1942 with Three Rivers in the Canadian-American League, batting .381 before breaking his collarbone while trying to steal home. His performance caught the attention of the Memphis Chicks, who signed him in 1943. The following year he was named the Most Valuable Player of the Southern Association, batting .333 with five home runs and sixty-eight stolen bases. Despite a gruff exterior, Gray had a soft spot for youngsters, especially those who were disabled. In Memphis, he developed a special friendship with Nelson Gary, Jr., a six-year-old amputee whose struggles reminded him of his own as a child. Dubbed the "One-Armed Wonder" by the sportswriters, Gray was purchased by the American League champion St. Louis Browns for $20,000 at the end of the 1944 season.

In 1945 the one-armed rookie played in seventy-seven games for the Browns, mostly as an outfielder or pinch-hitter. He collected fifty-one hits (eight for extra bases) and compiled a .218 batting average. A high point came on 20 May, when a crowd of 36,000 packed Yankee Stadium to see Gray go four for five with two runs batted in, as St. Louis swept a double-header from the Bronx Bombers. Pitchers tried to take advantage of Gray by blowing fastballs by him, but Gray's superb eye enabled him to excel as a fastball hitter. He only struck out eleven times during the

season. But infielders played in to counter Gray's skillful bunting, and he could be fooled on change-ups and breaking balls because he had to begin his swing early to compensate for his handicap. Defensively, Gray made 162 putouts, had three assists, and committed seven errors for a .959 fielding average. But he also gave runners an edge in the extra moment it took for him to transfer the ball from his glove to his hand for a throw from the outfield.

At a time when thousands of young men were sacrificing their lives on the battlefields of Europe and the Pacific, Gray became a heroic example on the home front. When the Philadelphia Sports Writers honored him as the "most courageous athlete," Gray, self-conscious about his 4-F status, told them: "Boys, I can't fight, and so there is no courage about me. Courage belongs on the battlefield, not on the baseball diamond." Still, Gray did his share for the war effort by visiting army hospitals and rehabilitation centers, speaking with amputees and reassuring them that they too could lead productive lives.

The conclusion of fighting in the Pacific on V-J Day, 2 September 1945, meant that many of baseball's stars would return from the battlefront, and thus peace brought with it the end of Gray's major league career. After 1945 he was a journeyman minor leaguer—with Toledo, Ohio; Elmira, New York; and Dallas, Texas—until 1949, when he retired. Left to wonder if he had made the majors on his playing abilities or been exploited by baseball, Gray shunned the limelight and struggled with alcoholism and a gambling addiction. With no baseball pension and a meager income, he returned to Nanticoke, where he spent the remainder of his life in near-poverty. At the age of eighty-seven, Gray died at Mercy Health Care Center in Nanticoke. He is buried at Saint Mary's cemetery in nearby Hanover Township. Having never married, he had no immediate survivors.

Many historians consider Gray a symbol of inferior wartime baseball. Some maintain that the St. Louis Browns purchased him as a gate attraction, while others view him as a curiosity item, a public-relations ploy to divert the attention of a war-weary nation. Nor did Gray enjoy the whole-hearted respect of his teammates, many of whom believed his presence in the line-up cost the Browns the opportunity to win another American League championship in 1945. But Gray's ability to rise above the humble circumstances of his birth, and his determination to overcome a physical disability, resonated far beyond the sports world and still stand as extraordinary testaments to the human spirit.

★

William C. Kashatus, *One-Armed Wonder: Pete Gray, Wartime Baseball, and the American Dream* (1995), is the definitive source

GRECO

on Gray's life and career. Other accounts deal strictly with Gray's significance to World War II–era baseball, among them Richard Goldstein, *Spartan Seasons: How Baseball Survived the Second World War* (1980); William B. Mead, *Baseball Goes to War* (1985); and Bill Gilbert, *They Also Served: Baseball and the Home Front, 1941–1945* (1992). The National Baseball Hall of Fame Library in Cooperstown, New York, has an extensive research file on Gray, including newspaper clippings from the entirety of his professional baseball career. *A Winner Never Quits* (1986), a television movie starring Keith Carradine as Gray, offers a moving account of his friendship with Nelson Gary, Jr., the six-year-old amputee.

WILLIAM C. KASHATUS

GRECO, Costanzo ("José") (*b.* 23 December 1918 in Montorio Nei Frentani, Italy; *d.* 31 December 2000 in Lancaster, Pennsylvania), dancer, choreographer, and teacher, who was responsible for introducing Spanish dance to the American consciousness.

Greco was one of two children born to Paolo Emilio Greco, a baker, and Carmela (Bucci) Greco. Both parents were from the same small town in Italy. When Greco was three, his father left for the United States, and in June 1928, by then a naturalized citizen, he settled the family in the New York City borough of Brooklyn, where Greco spent the remainder of his childhood. He attended various public elementary and junior high schools but did not go on to high school, instead studying briefly at the Leonardo da Vinci Art School in Manhattan.

In 1933 Greco began to study with the Spanish dance teacher Helen Veola, to whose studio he originally had chaperoned his sister. It was there that the ballet mistress from the New York Hippodrome Opera Company saw him, and he made his professional stage debut in *La Traviata* for the company in the mid-1930s. It was also at this studio that he met his first wife, Sarita, whom he married and divorced before he was twenty. Greco was by that time serious about dancing. He studied with Aurora Arriaza and briefly with Antonio Triana, who had been a partner to Encarnacion Lopez, the famous "Argentinita." Using the name "Ray Serrano," Greco also began to perform in numerous nightclubs, where Argentinita saw him dancing. In late 1942 she asked Greco to join her troupe, which included her sister, Pilar Lopez. He first performed with the company in January 1943, soon becoming one of Argentinita's two partners. He seemed to have been considered more valuable to the war effort as an entertainer and was never drafted for military service during World War II.

Greco learned much from Argentinita about the culture, dance, and music of Spain, and he choreographed his first dance for her company in about 1944. She also advised him to change his first name to José. Those who saw Greco in

José Greco. ALEX GOTFRYD/CORBIS

these early years were generally enthusiastic, with John Martin, the dance critic for the *New York Times,* exclaiming, "This young man can dance!" Greco stayed with the company until Argentinita died in 1945. Even before her death, Greco had planned to leave. He arranged a modest dance tour for the summer of 1945 with Lucille Peters, whom he had met in 1944 and who performed under the name "Nila Amparo." Meanwhile, Pilar Lopez returned to Spain to bury her sister and, once there, decided to start her own company. Greco and Amparo joined her, and in June 1946 the Ballet Español opened in Madrid. Greco danced throughout Spain with the company until 1948, occasionally returning to the United States. He married Amparo in New York on 16 August 1946; they had two children.

At this point Greco wanted to start his own company, which would be both authentic and versatile in combining the many styles of Spanish dancing from various regions of the world. To this end, he had assiduously continued to study all forms of Spanish dance and music while in Spain. In the meantime, however, Greco, Amparo, and several others were invited to perform in a film about the bull-fighter Manolete. Soon afterward, Greco formed the Ballets y Bailes de España de José Greco, which opened to poor reviews in Barcelona in January 1949. Nevertheless, the company gradually gained acceptance, with successful tours of South America and Europe, where Greco hired Lola de Ronda from the Ballet Español. De Ronda was a lead dancer for Greco's troupe for many years, and she and Greco eventually had three children together. They never married.

In 1951 Lee Schubert, the owner of a network of theaters, saw the movie about Manolete and persuaded Greco to bring his troupe to the United States, where they toured during the 1951–1952 season. Also in 1951 Greco was a recipient (with Carol Channing) of the New Broadway Personality of the Year Award. That season began a routine for the company that lasted for more than two decades, as they traveled throughout the United States in the winter months and toured Europe, Australia, and much of Asia in the summer. During these years Greco, in some cases with his company, danced in several movies, including *Sombrero* (1952), *Around the World in Eighty Days* (1956), *Holiday for Lovers* (1959), *Ship of Fools* (1965), and *The Proud and the Damned* (1968). Greco and his troupe also appeared on the television variety shows of Ed Sullivan, Perry Como, Johnny Carson, and others; performed on radio programs such as *Voice of Firestone;* and made several musical recordings on the Decca, Columbia, and RCA labels.

In his autobiography, Greco wrote about those years of ceaseless touring: "We performed. That's what it was all about. . . . Audiences came and applauded until their palms were raw . . . [and] that was our reward." In 1962 Greco received the Cross of the Knight of Civil Merit from the Spanish government for his contributions to Spanish culture and performing arts. That same year he hired Nana Lorca (Djenana Modrego-Vigaray) to dance with the troupe. After his divorce from Amparo in 1972, Greco and Lorca were married in June 1973. They had one child, Greco's sixth and last.

In 1972 Greco founded the José Greco Foundation for Hispanic Dance to promote the enjoyment and teaching of Spanish dance and culture. When he retired from dancing in 1974, he lectured extensively on the same subjects. In 1985, through the auspices of an old friend, Ana Borger-Reese, Greco went to Franklin and Marshall College in Lancaster, Pennsylvania, to lecture and teach. He was hired by the college theater and dance department in 1988 and received an honorary L.H.D. in 1994. After he saw three of his children dancing professionally in Spain, he formed the José Greco Dance Company (Second Generation), which in 1989 opened in New York City, featuring the three younger Grecos. The company continued until 1995, when Greco made his last appearance. Greco divorced

Lorca in about 1996 and married Borger-Reese, his fourth wife, in December 1998. He died two years later, at age eighty-two, of a heart infection brought on by an injury sustained on an Amtrak train. The family filed a lawsuit against Amtrak after his death.

Tall, dark, and good-looking, Greco was described by a friend as "gallant," "cosmopolitan," and "in love with life." He was much admired for his dancing, particularly for his dedication to Spanish dance and his ability to bring it to almost every city in the United States over such a long period. As Marita Benitez, a well-known flamenco dancer, said, "His contribution to Spanish dance will remain unparalleled forever in this country. He . . . put Spanish dance on the map."

★

Archival records about Greco and his company from the 1950s and 1960s, as well as numerous photographs and videotapes, are at the Dance Research Division of the New York Public Library. Other archive and journal materials are in the Shadek-Fackenthal Library at Franklin and Marshall College in Lancaster, Pennsylvania. Greco's autobiography, *The Gypsy in My Soul* (1977), is dated and poorly ghostwritten but remains a useful source for much of his career. More information about Greco's life and career can be found in Nancy Heller, "Jose Greco," *Flamenco International Magazine* (Jan.-Mar. 2001), and Rose Eichenbaum, "Remembering Jose Greco—Ambassador of the Spanish Dance," *Dance Magazine* 75 (1 Apr. 2001): 64. For details of the Amtrak accident, see Thomas Flannery, "Greco Death Called Homicide," *Intelligencer Journal* (29 May 2001). Obituaries are in the *New York Times* and *Los Angeles Times* (both 4 Jan. 2001).

SANDRA SHAFFER VANDOREN

GREEN, Adolph (*b.* 2 December 1914 in the Bronx, New York City; *d.* 23 October 2002 in Manhattan, New York City), ebullient lyricist, screenwriter, and playwright who, with Betty Comden, formed one of the most enduring professional partnerships on Broadway and in Hollywood.

Green was one of three children of Daniel and Helen (Weiss) Green, Hungarian immigrants. After graduating from DeWitt Clinton High School in the Bronx in 1934, he worked as a runner on Wall Street and dreamed of a life in the theater. Two new friends eventually helped him fulfill that dream. In the summer of 1937, at a camp in the Berkshire Mountains of Massachusetts, Green met a young music student named Leonard Bernstein. Discovering that they shared a knowledge of music and a sense of humor, they immediately forged a lifelong friendship. The following year Green met a stagestruck New York University student named Betty Comden, and Comden and Green soon began performing together in a group known as Six and Company.

In the fall of 1938 Comden and Green formed a new troupe of performers, known as the Revuers, which included a young woman named Judy Tuvim, soon to be known as Judy Holliday. Tuvim wangled the group an ongoing gig at a Greenwich Village coffeehouse known as the Village Vanguard, performing topical skits and songs. The Vanguard offered little in terms of pay, so Comden and Green began composing original (and therefore free) material for the group. The Revuers, who continued performing together until 1944, became popular among the arty set in New York. Bernstein was a frequent audience member, occasionally sitting in at the piano.

In 1943 the Revuers thought that they had made it big when they went to Los Angeles to appear in the film *Greenwich Village*. Unfortunately, most of their screen time was cut from the film, and only Holliday was offered a movie contract. The group split up, and Comden and Green ended up performing in New York again as a duo. Their career path changed in 1944. Bernstein, by then a celebrity composer and conductor, wanted to convert *Fancy Free,* a ballet he had composed with Jerome Robbins, into a musical comedy. He asked Comden and Green to write the book and lyrics for the show, which revolved around the romantic adventures of three sailors on twenty-four-hour shore leave in New York City. *On the Town,* which opened in December 1944 as a smash hit, included roles for Comden and Green that highlighted their comedic skills. Among its musical gems were "New York, New York" and "Some Other Time."

During rehearsals for the show, Green met Allyn Ann McLerie, an actress and singer. He had married Elizabeth Reitel (spelled "Reitell" in some sources) in 1940 or 1941 and divorced her shortly thereafter. In 1947 he married McLerie, to whom he would remain married until 1953. Neither marriage produced children. Comden and Green were lured to Hollywood by the prestigious Arthur Freed unit of Metro-Goldwyn-Mayer (MGM) to write the screenplay for the musical comedy *Good News* (1947). They then adapted their own *On the Town* for the screen in 1949. The two were saddened to learn that MGM deemed most of Bernstein's music too highbrow. Nevertheless, for the film, which pioneered in its use of location shooting, they agreed to write lyrics to several new songs by Roger Edens. Comden and Green went on to write many of MGM's most enduring musicals, including *The Barkleys of Broadway* (1949), *The Band Wagon* (1955), and *Singin' in the Rain* (1952).

Despite this productivity, Comden and Green did not neglect their Broadway roots. They never settled permanently in Hollywood and always considered New York City their home. Their second musical comedy, a 1920s-style pastiche known as *Billion Dollar Baby,* lasted only a few months in 1945 and 1946. Their third, a revue called *Two*

Adolph Green (*right*), with Betty Comden. THE KOBAL COLLECTION

on the Aisle, scored a moderate success in 1951, and they hit pay dirt by teaming again with Bernstein to write the lyrics for *Wonderful Town* (1953), a musical adaptation of the play *My Sister Eileen,* starring Rosalind Russell. They contributed lyrics to the musical version of *Peter Pan* (1954) and scored another hit with the book and lyrics for a play starring their friend Holliday, *The Bells Are Ringing* (1956). Late in 1958 they returned to the world of cabaret to appear in *A Party with Betty Comden and Adolph Green,* a revue that showcased material they had written over the years. The ever enthusiastic duo revived this format periodically throughout their joint careers.

On 31 January 1960 Green married the actress Phyllis Newman, with whom he had two children, a son in 1961 and a daughter in 1964. Green continued to work with Comden, writing books or lyrics or both for such musicals as *Do Re Mi* (1960), which featured Phil Silvers in a spoof of the record industry; *Applause* (1970), which starred Lauren Bacall in a reworking of the classic film *All About Eve;* and *On the Twentieth Century* (1978), which adapted another vintage film comedy, the screwball *Twentieth Century.* Comden and Green also wrote the film adaptations for *Auntie Mame* (1958) and *The Bells Are Ringing* (1960) as well as an original nonmusical screenplay, *What a Way to Go* (1964).

Not all of Comden and Green's work was successful. *A Doll's Life,* a musical about the further adventures of Henrik Ibsen's heroine in *A Doll's House,* lasted for only five performances in 1982. Nevertheless, they continued to produce work that generally appealed. Their last big original hit, *The Will Rogers Follies,* debuted on Broadway in May 1991, when Green was seventy-six years old. Green also acted from time to time, gaining particular kudos for his portrayal of an early television producer in the film *My Favorite Year* (1982). He and Comden were still getting together on a regular basis to think up new plots and lyrics when Green died of natural causes at age eighty-seven in his Manhattan home.

Green was a New York institution, a lively if hammy performer and the co-crafter of songs that would long endure in the popular imagination, among them "New York, New York," "Just in Time," and "Make Someone Happy." At their best, Comden and Green's spoken words and lyrics revealed an optimistic spirit and a mischievous sense of humor. The two were beloved among the literati of Broadway and Hollywood. They made headlines and commanded respect as a rare male-female pairing: partners who for many years shared work, friendship, and laughter but never a bed. In the foreword to a collection of their works, the film director Mike Nichols summed up their appeal: "I've always thought that when we all get to heaven that for state occasions they will probably play John Phillip Sousa, Irving Berlin, but at the party afterwards, God will say, 'Do you think we could get Betty and Adolph to do something?'"

★

The most comprehensive study of Green is Alice M. Robinson, *Betty Comden and Adolph Green: A Bio-Bibliography* (1993). Nichols's observations on the pair, as well as the scripts to three of their productions, may be found in *The New York Musicals of Comden and Green: On the Town, Wonderful Town, Bells Are Ringing* (1997). Green is discussed in the autobiography of his wife, Phyllis Newman, *Just in Time* (1988). Obituaries are in *Playbill* (24 Oct. 2002) and the *New York Times* (25 Oct. 2002).

TINKY "DAKOTA" WEISBLAT

GREENBERG, Joseph H(arold) (*b.* 28 May 1915 in Brooklyn, New York City; *d.* 7 May 2001 in Palo Alto, California), linguistic anthropologist noted for his groundbreaking classification of African and American languages and for significant research on language universals.

Greenberg was the second of two children born to Jewish immigrant parents. His father, Jacob Greenberg, whose original Polish surname of Zyto was dropped out of a desire for assimilation, earned his degree from the Columbia College of Pharmacy within three years of coming to the United States. After losing his drugstore during the depression, he became an insurance salesman. The piano playing of Greenberg's German-born mother, Florence (Pilzer) Greenberg, led him to learn to play. After performing at Carnegie Hall at age fourteen, he considered a career as a concert pianist and continued to play every evening throughout his life. He had absolute pitch in music, which eventually helped him interpret tonal languages.

Growing up, Greenberg and his older sister, Barbara, were exposed to German, Polish, Russian, Yiddish, English, and liturgical Hebrew. As a young child, he studied languages by examining grammar texts, dictionaries, and bilingual Greek plays from his local public library. In high school he took Latin and German. He also taught himself Greek after an unsuccessful attempt to transfer to another school that taught the language. In 1932 Greenberg entered Columbia College in New York City, where he excelled in Latin, Greek, Arabic, and other languages. Majoring in comparative philology, he initially considered a career in classical studies, but auditing a graduate-level course in American Native Languages taught by the pioneer anthropologist Franz Boas altered his career decision.

Following his graduation from Columbia in 1936, Greenberg chose to concentrate on linguistics from an anthropological perspective and began work at Northwestern University with a graduate fellowship from the Social Science Research Council. He spent a year at Yale University in New Haven, Connecticut (1937–1938), and conducted fieldwork among the Hausa people of northern Nigeria (1938–1939), a study that contributed to his dissertation, "The Religion of a Sudanese Culture as Influenced by Islam: A Study of Non-European Acculturation." Greenberg earned his Ph.D. from Northwestern in 1940 and returned to Yale as a postdoctoral student in the period 1940–1941.

On 23 November 1940 Greenberg married Selma Berkowitz, whom he had met while at Columbia. He entered the military in 1941 and served in the U.S. Army Signal Intelligence Corps. He deciphered German and Italian codes while stationed in North Africa until the Allied invasion of Italy (8 September 1943) and then served in Italy until his discharge in 1946.

After two years as an assistant professor at University of Minnesota (1946–1948), Greenberg returned to Columbia University and remained there through 1962. Exposure to linguists from the Prague school of structuralism, which focused on the structural basis of languages, was instrumental in solidifying Greenberg's perspective on the typology of languages. At Columbia he became involved with the linguistic circle of the New York journal *Word,* which he coedited from 1950 to 1954, and to which he contributed in the 1950s and 1960s.

In classifying languages and their relationships, Greenberg relied on his lifelong system of multilateral comparison. In this practice, which ultimately produced many bound notebooks, he patiently penciled the languages being compared down the left-hand margin with vocabulary words across the top of the page. He went beyond the nineteenth-century typology, which classified languages by their historical development from older source languages, recognizing that this typology was inexact, unclear, and ethnocentric. His "Studies in African Linguistic Classification," which appeared over several issues of the *Southwestern Journal of Anthropology* (1939–1940), classified the African languages into four distinct units: Niger-Congo, Nilo-Saharan, Afro-Asiatic, and Chadic. Although it was initially rejected by German and British scholars, this four-phylum system soon gained acceptance among nearly all students of African languages.

In 1962 Greenberg moved to Stanford University in Palo Alto, California, where he organized the African Studies Center in the 1960s and, in the 1970s, formed the Stanford/Berkeley Joint Center for African Studies. At the 1962 International Congress of Linguists, Greenberg and another prominent American linguist, Noam Chomsky, independently put forward opposing theories about the universals of grammar. Chomskyian and Greenbergian approaches to language universals eventually became known as the formalist and functionalist approaches, respectively. Greenberg's "Some Universals of Grammar with Particular Reference to the Order of Meaningful Elements" (1963) became one of the most cited papers in linguistics.

From 1968 to 1976, Greenberg served as codirector of the Stanford Project on Language Universals, which undertook cross-linguistic studies on grammar and phonology. The project also enabled research by postdoctoral fellows, nurtured the next generation of typologists, and produced two major published series: *Working Papers on Language Universals* (1969–1976), a twenty-volume set; and *Universals of Human Language* (1978). Greenberg served as chief editor of, and contributor to, the latter work, which was published in four volumes: *Method and Theory, Phonology, Word Structure,* and *Syntax.*

The publication of *Language in the Americas* (1987) sparked an ongoing debate in professional journals and created enough controversy that the scholarly disagreements engendered by Greenberg's work received coverage in the mainstream press. In classifying America's languages, Greenberg had spent more than thirty years analyzing lexicons and grammars in eighty languages, compiling information that he assembled in twenty-nine notebooks. A number of scholars vehemently rejected Greenberg's theory, which held that there were only three linguistic stocks in the Americas: Eskimo-Aleut, Na-dene, and Amerind. The controversy centered on the Amerind, or American

Indian, classification, which was a huge, widespread group, said to have derived from a single protolanguage. In defending his position against critics, Greenberg cited migration patterns, dentition, and genetic evidence.

Greenberg's last major work was the two-volume *Indo-European and Its Closest Relatives: The Euroasiatic Language Family* (2000–2001). Having investigated most of the world's languages, including those of Australia and Oceania in the 1950s, he lamented that he would not have the opportunity to classify the languages of Southeast Asia. Greenberg was the Ray Lyman Wilbur Professor Emeritus of the Social Science at Stanford, with emeritus professorial appointments in the departments of anthropological sciences, cultural and social anthropology, and linguistics. He was diagnosed with pancreatic cancer in late 2000, and six months later he succumbed at his home.

Although Greenberg's work often engendered controversy, he was a mild-mannered and self-effacing scholar. In addition, his peers recognized him with several awards. In 1970 he was named the first Distinguished Lecturer of the American Anthropological Association during its sixty-ninth meeting in San Diego. The American Academy of Arts and Sciences presented him with the Talcott Parsons Prize for Social Sciences in 1998, citing his visionary work in comparative linguistics and classification of languages, as well as his contributions to the typology of languages. A conference, "Global Perspectives on Human Language: Scientific Studies in Honor of Joseph H. Greenberg" (25–27 April 2002), welcomed scholars to Stanford from university departments of anthropology, linguistics, history, archaeology, and genetics throughout the world.

With a career spanning nearly seventy years, Greenberg was a diligent researcher, a broad reader, and a prolific writer, and had nearly 250 publications, including books, journal articles, reviews, and encyclopedia entries, to his credit. The Cecil H. Green Library at Stanford was his "office," where he generally worked six days a week, consulting resources and recording information in his notebooks.

★

Greenberg's papers from his tenure at Stanford University are housed at the Department of Special Collections and University Archives at Stanford. His journal articles and essays on typology and language universals, languages of Africa and the Near East, and a bibliography through 1989 are in Keith Denning and Suzanne Kemmer, eds., *On Language: Selected Writings of Joseph H. Greenberg* (1990). See also William Croft, Keith Denning, and Suzanne Kemmer, eds., *Studies in Typology and Diachrony: Papers Presented to Joseph H. Greenberg on his 75th Birthday* (1990). An obituary is in the *New York Times* (15 May 2001).

PAMELA HARPEL-BURKE

GREENE, Harold Herman   (*b.* 6 February 1923 in Frankfurt, Germany; *d.* 29 January 2000 in Washington, D.C.), U.S. federal judge best known for his civil rights decisions and for presiding over the 1981 trial that led to the breakup of the American Telephone and Telegraph Corporation.

Greene was born Heinz Grunhaus, the only child of Irving Grunhaus and Edith Spandau. The Jewish family left Germany in 1938, going through several European countries before arriving in the United States in 1943 and settling in Washington, D.C., where Greene's father opened a jewelry store. In 1944 Greene became a naturalized U.S. citizen, changed his name, and enlisted in the U.S. Army, serving largely in military intelligence, where he interrogated German prisoners. Greene was discharged from the army in 1946 with the rank of staff sergeant. He married Evelyn Schröer on 19 September 1948; they had a son and a daughter.

While supporting himself by working as a translator for the U.S. Department of Justice, Greene attended night school at George Washington University in Washington, D.C. He received a B.S. in 1949 and an LL.B. in 1952, finishing second in his law class. After clerking for Judge Bennett Champ Clark at the federal court of appeals in Washington, Greene served as an assistant U.S. attorney

Harold H. Greene, ca. 1979. WALLY MCNAMEE/CORBIS

from 1953 to 1957. He then moved to the Office of Legal Counsel at the Justice Department, and in 1958 he became the head of the appeals section of the department's newly established civil rights division.

The appointment of Robert F. Kennedy as the attorney general in 1961 reinvigorated the Justice Department. Kennedy captivated few more than Greene. Greene's arguments were central in persuading the solicitor general, Archibald Cox, to support reapportionment on behalf of the Kennedy administration in the Supreme Court, and Greene was one of the chief drafters of the Civil Rights Act of 1964 and the Voting Rights Act of 1965.

In 1965 President Lyndon B. Johnson appointed Greene as an associate judge of the D.C. Court of General Sessions. Greene immediately set up a federal payment system for court-appointed lawyers that gave indigent defendants a sense of hope. After becoming chief judge in 1966, he assisted the Justice Department in designing the reorganization of Washington's court system and lobbied Congress for its passage. "It was fun learning political maneuvering," Greene recalled.

The reorganization, which took effect in 1971, created a new trial court, the D.C. Superior Court. Greene aimed to insure defendants' rights. He resisted demands to arraign en masse the thousands arrested in the riots in 1967 and those following the assassination of the civil rights leader Dr. Martin Luther King, Jr., in 1968. Insisting on individual arraignments, he kept judges working literally around the clock, in shifts for five days straight in 1968. "I felt very strongly that the judiciary shouldn't cease to function as a judiciary merely because we were in the midst of a difficult civil disturbance," he said. "In criminal cases it is the individual that counts." He easily won reelection as chief judge in 1976, serving until 1978 when President Jimmy Carter named him to the federal district bench.

The first day on the court, Greene randomly drew from the docket of a deceased judge the government's antitrust suit against the American Telephone and Telegraph Corporation (AT&T). It became one of the most far-reaching cases in U.S. history. Filed in 1974 to end the regulated monopoly of the U.S. telephone network that AT&T had exercised for decades, the case had gone nowhere. Greene issued a pretrial order that put lawyers on both sides on strict schedules. What they intended to prove along with listings of evidence and witnesses totaled more than 4,000 pages alone. The trial began in March 1981. Greene was in complete control. He examined much of the "several millions pieces of paper" brought into court before admitting them into evidence and was "impatient with anyone wasting his time," recalled one witness. "He didn't have to raise his voice, but heaped scorn on his victim, and there was absolute silence in the courtroom."

In September 1981 Greene denied a move by AT&T to

dismiss the case. "The testimony and the documentary evidence produced by the Government," he wrote, "demonstrate that the Bell System had violated the antitrust laws in a number of ways over a lengthy period of time." This decision made it more difficult for the administration of Ronald W. Reagan to intervene in the case, despite its ardent antiregulatory fervor and predictions from several high-ranking generals that the country faced an imminent takeover if divestiture were ordered. It also pushed AT&T to work toward a settlement instead of risking a potentially devastating loss. After an eleven-month trial, the parties agreed to a proposed consent decree, breaking the world's largest corporation into pieces and creating the so-called Baby Bells to provide the same access as other carriers. Greene approved the decree, and its enforcement, including a review every three years of technological developments, occupied him for much of the rest of his career. This helped to reshape the whole telecommunications industry, ushering in a new world of competition that altered the daily lives of all users.

Greene won wide praise for his handling of the case. It "came out better than I expected," he thought, and he was runner-up for *Time*'s 1984 Man of the Year. He also received much criticism. Detractors considered him a "one-man regulatory agency," a "self-appointed telecommunications czar" who was "very cynical about big business." At the same time Greene was slightly disappointed that the settlement meant he would not write a major antitrust opinion, although he said he was never quite sure what he would have written.

"I hope they don't say that all I did was break up AT&T," Greene said about his career. "Some of the civil rights legal decisions were more interesting and important than the AT&T case." In 1984 he ruled that the government had to pay women in civil service jobs the same as men with the same duties and responsibilities. Greene tried to preserve the discretion of judges to tailor sentences in the face of rigid federal sentencing laws. In a series of cases in the late 1980s and early 1990s, he lowered sentences under what the guidelines set. In one case he declared them unconstitutional, only to be reversed on appeal. Greene's opinions emphasized the human face of justice and judging.

Short, slightly rotund, and with a wry sense of humor, Greene commanded his courtroom through his keen intelligence. He preferred hearing cases to reforming the judicial process. In both roles he had high expectations of the professionalism and ethics of government lawyers. His burning sense of social justice was always on display. He stopped hearing cases in 1998 and died at age seventy-six of a cerebral hemorrhage. He is buried in King David Cemetery in Falls Church, Virginia.

★

William Yurcik, "Judge Harold H. Greene: A Pivotal Judicial Figure in Telecommunications Policy and His Legacy," available on-line at <http://www.ieee.org/organizations/history_center/cht_papers/yurcik.PDF> (2001), provides a detailed review of Greene's life and career and includes a 1993 interview with Greene. For additional information about Greene's decisions and influence, see Victor S. Navasky, *Kennedy Justice* (1971), and Jeffrey B. Morris, *Calmly to Poise the Scales of Justice: A History of the Courts of the District of Columbia Circuit* (2001). Obituaries are in the *New York Times* and *Washington Post* (both 30 Jan. 2000). The Oral History Project of the Historical Society of the District of Columbia Circuit (1991–1997), available at the Library of Congress, includes transcripts of interviews with Greene.

ROGER K. NEWMAN

GREER, Jane (*b.* 9 September 1924 in Washington, D.C.; *d.* 24 August 2001 in Los Angeles, California), actress best remembered for her performance as Kathie Moffat in the classic film noir *Out of the Past* (1947), a role that made her an icon of the genre.

Born Bettejane Greer, Greer had a twin brother, Don. As a child Greer took part in several beauty contests, and as a teenager she dropped out of Western High School to pursue a career as a vocalist, thanks to her attractive contralto voice. She sang both on the radio and with important bands such as Enric Madriguera's orchestra in the Latin Club Del Rio in Washington, D.C. When Greer was fifteen an attack of palsy left her face partially paralyzed. Greer had to do numerous exercises to overcome the paralysis, and through these, she learned how important facial expressions could be in conveying human emotion: "I'd always wanted to be an actress, and suddenly I knew that learning to control my facial muscles was one of the best assets I could have as a performer."

Greer's mother, who wrote children's stories and traced her family back to the British metaphysical poet John Donne, worked in the U.S. War Department public information office and got her daughter a job modeling uniforms for women. In 1943, when the eccentric director and producer Howard Hughes saw a reproduction of a recruitment poster in *Life* magazine, showing the eighteen-year-old Greer modeling a new uniform, he told one of his aides to "find this girl as soon as possible and sign her up." In spite of Hughes's haste, Greer had to wait two more years to appear on screen because Hughes first kept her almost segregated from the outside world. "Hughes was obsessed with me," Greer would later recall. "But at first it seemed as if he were offering me a superb career opportunity." At

Jane Greer, 1957. THE KOBAL COLLECTION

the time Hughes was extremely powerful and could make and break an actress's career as he pleased.

Despite Hughes's obsession, in 1943 Greer met the crooner and comic actor Rudy Vallee and, after just a few weeks, on 2 December, they married. Predictably, Hughes was enraged, warning Greer that unless she divorced Vallee, she would never appear in a movie. The pressure Hughes put on the couple proved unendurable, and in July 1944 the couple divorced. Greer then moved in with Hughes. Since Hughes had been unable to find suitable roles for Greer, he leased her to RKO, which initially cast her under her real name in minor roles, the only jobs in her career where she exploited her skill as a singer. In *The Falcon's Alibi* (1946), for example, Greer played a lively band singer who is murdered by a mad disc jockey, played by Elisha Cook, Jr.

Greer joined Susan Hayward and Rita Johnson in her first important role as one of the three women betrayed by a murderous philanderer, played by Robert Young, in the film noir *They Won't Believe Me* (1947). Yet it was thanks to another film noir shot the same year that Greer became a star and an icon of the genre. In Jacques Tourneur's *Out of the Past* (1947), Greer played the femme fatale, Kathie Moffat, who seduces Whit Sterling (Kirk Douglas) before wounding him and absconding with $40,000, and then se-

duces Jeff Markham (Robert Mitchum), when Sterling sends him to look for her.

Greer was skillful in her portrayal of a deceptive character who, in the course of the movie, attains almost godlike status. Greer commented, "All through the picture they talk about you, so that by the time you come on screen, everyone thinks you're going to be nine feet tall." Film critics such as Marshall Deutelbaum argue that Tourneur's mise-en-scène favors the Greer character and underlines Kathie's importance through an elaborate series of allusions to the Renaissance painter Botticelli's *Birth of Venus,* casting the character in the Venus role. Although Kathie is constantly framed by male views of her, she repays the male characters with the same tools of financial theft and masculine brutality they have employed. The character of Kathie Moffat, and that of similar female figures in other films noir of the 1940s, later sparked the interest of feminist critics, who valued the characters' independence and unconventionality.

Greer's 1947 marriage to attorney and producer Edward Lasker once again enraged Hughes who, by then, had bought RKO and threatened to thwart her career; Greer and Lasker had three sons. Because her part in *Out of the Past* had made her a celebrity, at the end of the 1940s Greer became associated on screen with tough female characters. She played a gambling house owner responsible for the killing of two soldiers in *Station West* (1948). She teamed up again with Robert Mitchum in Don Siegel's *The Big Steal* (1949), playing the ex-girlfriend of a thief who robs the army payroll Mitchum is guarding. In *The Company She Keeps* (1950), her last film with RKO, Greer starred as a deceitful ex-con who seduces the boyfriend of her saintly parole officer.

During the 1950s Greer had fewer chances to use her sensual and deceitful persona to its full potential. After joining an all-star cast as the plotting Antoinette de Mauban in the undistinguished remake of the 1937 adventure classic *The Prisoner of Zenda* (1952), she retired to raise her family of three sons, Alex, Lawrence, and Steve, all of whom later took up careers in the movie and music industries. From then on, Greer made only sporadic appearances on screen: in John Boulting's lackluster *Run for the Sun* (1956), and as the second wife of Lon Chaney (James Cagney) in *Man of a Thousand Faces* (1957). She also appeared in television productions such as *Bonanza* and *Alfred Hitchcock Presents.*

In 1963 Greer divorced Lasker and went to live with the acting coach Frank London, with whom she remained until he died in January 2001. In 1964 she joined Susan Hayward and Bette Davis in Edward Dmytryck's heavy-handed melodrama *Where Love Has Gone*, in which she played a sympathetic probation officer. In the 1970s she guest-starred on the television series *Columbo* and *Quincy.*

During the 1980s and the early 1990s Greer continued

to take part in popular television series, such as *Murder She Wrote* and *Falcon Crest*, as well as in David Lynch's neo-noirish *Twin Peaks*. To the delight of noir buffs, she also appeared in Taylor Hackford's *Against All Odds* (1984), a remake of *Out of the Past*, in which she played the mother of Rachel Ward, who was cast in Greer's original role. Greer died of cancer at her home at age seventy-six and is buried in Westwood Memorial Park in Los Angeles.

Although Greer's association with film noir was brief, her performance in *Out of the Past* helped to define both a central character of the genre, the femme fatale, and a central motif, the inability of male leads to recognize that a woman who seems enslaved by their desires is in fact able to bring them to their demise.

★

For more information on Greer's life and career, see Ann E. Kaplan, ed., *Women in Film Noir* (1988). Marshall Deutelbaum, "The Birth of Venus and the Death of Romantic Love in *Out of the Past*," *Literature/Film Quarterly* 15, no. 3 (1987), provides a critique of *Out of the Past*. An obituary is in the *New York Times* (28 Aug. 2001).

LUCA PRONO

GROZA, Louis Roy ("Lou") (*b.* 25 January 1924 in Martins Ferry, Ohio; *d.* 29 November 2000 in Middleburgh Heights, Ohio), professional football player whose proficiency at placekicking made the field goal an integral part of the game.

Groza was one of three sons born to John and Mary (Koteles) Groza, the owners and managers of a family restaurant and bar in Martins Ferry. Both parents were Hungarian immigrants. Groza began his athletic career at Martins Ferry High School where he won ten letters in baseball, basketball, and football, and led the basketball and football teams to state championships.

Following his high-school graduation, Groza attended Ohio State University in Columbus on a football scholarship. Freshmen were ineligible to play varsity football, but Groza impressed the Buckeye coach Paul Brown with his placekicking skills in practice. In 1943, prior to his sophomore year, Groza was drafted into the U.S. Army. He served in the Pacific with the Ninety-sixth Division, fighting at the battles in Leyte Gulf, Philippines, and Okinawa, Japan. By the end of World War II Groza had become a master sergeant with a medical battalion. He was discharged in February 1946.

While still in Okinawa, Groza heard that Brown had left Ohio State to become the head coach of the Cleveland Browns, a professional football team in the new All-America Football Conference (AAFC). Since Groza's original college class had graduated, he was allowed to give up his

Lou Groza, 1961. AP/WIDE WORLD PHOTOS

amateur eligibility and move directly to professional football. After receiving a tryout, he signed a contract for $7,500 to play offensive tackle and kicker for the Browns. He continued to take classes at Ohio State in the off-season and graduated with a degree in business administration in 1949.

The Cleveland Browns dominated the AAFC. During the four years of the league's existence, the Browns won the championship four times and never lost more than two games per year. Groza spent the 1946 season as a starting kicker and back-up tackle. The following year he began to start at both positions. At six feet, three inches tall, and weighing 250 pounds, Groza was large for a lineman of his day, and exceptionally so for a placekicker. He had a unique, straight-on kicking style. Groza carried a tape measure in his helmet, and before each field goal and extra point he used it to line up the ball and measure his approach distance.

On 13 May 1950 Groza married Jackie Lou Robbins from Martins Ferry; they had three sons and one daughter. With the demise of the AAFC that same year, the Browns, San Francisco Forty-niners, and Baltimore Colts were absorbed into the older National Football League (NFL). Most experts predicted that the Browns would struggle against the more established teams. Instead Cleveland opened the season by defeating the defending NFL champions, the Philadelphia Eagles, 35–10, and continued on to a 10–2 record. Groza set a league record for field goals with thirteen, the first of five times he would lead the NFL in that category.

The Browns met the Los Angeles Rams in the 1950 championship game. In what is considered to be one of the

NFL's greatest contests, Groza's performance made the difference. His sixteen-yard field goal with twenty seconds left gave the Browns a 30–28 victory. Groza later said the clutch kick was "my biggest thrill in pro football." He had the shoe he used to make the kick bronzed as a keepsake.

Usually wearing uniform number "76" during his Browns career, Groza continued to play both offensive tackle and placekicker through the 1959 season. Such double duty was common at that time. Team rosters were limited to thirty-three players, and most could not imagine carrying a specialist who just kicked. Groza was named to the Pro Bowl every year except 1956, six times as a starting tackle. In 1954 he was named NFL Player of the Year. The Browns success also continued. They played in the championship game every year from 1951 through 1955, winning twice.

A back injury forced Groza to miss the 1960 season. He returned in 1961 and played seven more seasons just as a kicking specialist. Ironically, it was Groza's own success with field goals that began to convince teams to set aside a special roster spot for placekickers. In many ways he created his own job.

When Groza retired in 1967, his twenty-one-year career in professional football was the longest on record. He was the first NFL player to score 1,000 points, finishing with 1,349 career points on 244 field goals, 641 extra points, and one touchdown. Including his years in the AAFC, Groza had 1,608 career points. Groza's kicking talent earned him the nickname "the Toe." It was an honor he accepted graciously, using the name on his vanity license plates until he died. He always considered himself to be a football player who kicked, though, not just a kicker.

Following his retirement Groza spent several years with the Browns as an assistant coach, then opened a successful insurance agency in Berea, Ohio. He remained active in the team's alumni organization and often shared his kicking expertise with local high-school players. Groza wrote *How to Pass, Kick, Run, Block: The Game, the Techniques, of Pro Football* (1965), with Bart Starr and Yale Lary, and an autobiography, *The Toe: The Lou Groza Story* (1996), with Mark Hodermarsky. When the Browns owner Art Modell moved the Cleveland franchise to Baltimore following the 1995 season, Groza was one of several former Browns players instrumental in convincing the NFL to grant Cleveland a new team.

Groza was inducted into the Pro Football Hall of Fame in 1974. Although he never played a varsity game of college football, the Lou Groza Award is given annually to the best collegiate kicker. Groza suffered from Parkinson's disease during his later years. He died at age seventy-six of a heart attack in Middleburgh Heights and is buried in Berea.

During Groza's long career with the Cleveland Browns, he was part of the transition from part-time kickers who played another position to the modern kicking specialists.

He helped to make field goals and the kicking game a more central part of professional football. By remaining in the Cleveland area and being active in Browns alumni activities, Groza also became the public face of the franchise. At his funeral he was remembered as the quintessential Browns player, the one person above all others who best epitomized the team. The Browns franchise, not surprisingly, located the team headquarters at 76 Lou Groza Boulevard in Berea.

★

Memorabilia and newspaper clippings related to Groza are held by the Pro Football Hall of Fame in Canton, Ohio. Groza's autobiography, cowritten by Mark Hodermarsky, is *The Toe: The Lou Groza Story* (1996). Groza's early career is covered in Robert W. Peterson, *Pigskin: The Early Years of Pro Football* (1997), while a commemorative edition of *Sports Illustrated,* "Return of the Browns" (1 Sept. 1999), describes his role in returning the Browns franchise to Cleveland. Obituaries are in the *New York Times* and *Cleveland Plain Dealer* (both 1 Dec. 2000).

HAROLD W. AURAND, JR.

GUNTHER, Gerald (*b.* 26 May 1927 in Usingen, Germany; *d.* 30 July 2002 in Stanford, California), widely renowned constitutional law scholar.

Gunther grew up near Frankfurt, the son of Otto Gutenstein, a butcher, and Minna (Floersheim) Gutenstein, a homemaker. In grade school, Gunther was taught by a Nazi party official who referred to him as a "Jew pig" and who forced the boy to sit apart from his "Aryan" classmates to keep him from "polluting" them. Such firsthand experiences of Nazi persecution strongly influenced his subsequent principled and eloquent views on the First Amendment and other rights guaranteed by the U.S. Constitution. In 1938, after witnessing the destruction by arson of the town synagogue, the eleven-year-old Gunther and his family fled Germany for the United States, moving to Brooklyn, New York City.

Gunther came from a long line of butchers, but his intellectual acumen and curiosity led him to the world of academia. While teaching math and physics in the U.S. Navy, which he joined after graduating from Stuyvesant High School, he considered an engineering career. He later became interested in teaching history and immersed himself in the humanities at Brooklyn College. There he met his future wife, Barbara Kelsky, the daughter of Russian immigrants; they had two sons. After graduating from Brooklyn College in 1949, Gunther set his sights on a teaching career in political science and received an M.A. in public law and government from Columbia University. Believing that a law degree would help him become a better political science professor, Gunther applied to three law schools: Harvard, in Cambridge, Massachusetts; Columbia, in New York City; and Yale, in New Haven, Connecticut. In addition to money from the GI Bill and his wife's salary, Gunther needed an academic scholarship to finance his law school education. Only Harvard offered him one.

After graduating magna cum laude from Harvard in 1953 and serving as an editor of the *Harvard Law Review,* Gunther earned a judicial clerkship with Judge Learned Hand on the U.S. Court of Appeals for the Second Circuit. Hand, a renowned American jurist who never sat on the Supreme Court, became one of Gunther's heroes, and Gunther's experience as his clerk served as the inspiration for the award-winning biography, *Learned Hand: The Man and the Judge* (1994). The 818-page book was a two-decade labor of love based on 40,000 of Hand's letters and 4,000 of his legal opinions. It won the Erwin N. Griswold Triennial Prize from the Supreme Court Historical Society in 1995 and the Triennial Award of the Order of the Coif, a legal society, in 1999.

After his clerkship with Hand, Gunther obtained a Supreme Court clerkship with Chief Justice Earl Warren. From 1954 to 1955 Gunther worked on seminal decisions such as *Brown* v. *Board of Education,* the Supreme Court's revolutionary school desegregation decision. According to Warren, Gunther contributed significantly to the *Brown* decision.

Instead of returning immediately to academia after his clerkship with Warren, Gunther took a job with the legal firm Cleary, Gottlieb, Friendly and Hamilton, which later became the international legal powerhouse of Cleary, Gottlieb, Steen and Hamilton. Gunther allowed himself three years to decide whether private practice was the right path for him. After less than two years, Gunther returned to academia for good, joining the faculty of Columbia Law School, where he taught from 1956 to 1962. The Supreme Court Justice Ruth Bader Ginsburg was one of his students at Columbia. Gunther served as her mentor and testified on her behalf at the time of her appointment to the Supreme Court in 1993.

Gunther cut short his time at Columbia, moving to Stanford Law School in California in what is known among legal scholars as the "Great Raid of '62." Gunther and several other prominent scholars with secure futures at the top-rated Columbia became disenchanted with the administration at Columbia, and especially at the law school, so they decided to try their luck at the smaller, lesser-known Stanford. Their unexpected move shook the world of legal academia and lifted Stanford Law School out of relative obscurity.

At Stanford, Gunther became an extremely influential faculty member who, among other things, molded the law school's admission policies. Shortly after the Supreme Court approved the use of diversity criteria in affirmative-action programs in *Regents of the University of California* v. *Bakke,* Gunther pressed fellow faculty members to expand Stanford Law's admissions criteria beyond grade-point averages and LSAT scores to include such subjective factors as recommendations and life experiences. Gunther argued that doing so would advance the goal of diversity endorsed in *Bakke* and, just as importantly, enliven the classroom. Gunther's program was adopted and retained by the law school.

Perhaps Gunther's greatest professional accomplishment was the casebook *Constitutional Law.* Beginning in the late 1960s, it became the most widely used constitutional law text in U.S. law schools. The late Supreme Court Justice Lewis F. Powell, Jr., wrote in 1994 that the casebook was "the leading publication in the field, from which a generation of American lawyers have learned constitutional law." Gunther also wrote, cowrote, or edited over seventy other publications.

Outside the classroom, Gunther was an unwavering advocate of the First Amendment of the U.S. Constitution, regarding freedom of speech. In the 1970s he publicly defended the right of the American Nazi Party to march through suburban Skokie, Illinois—where a cluster of Holocaust survivors lived—even though he had directly felt the oppression of Adolf Hitler's Germany. The public dispute resulted in the Supreme Court's refusal to review the decision *Smith* v. *Collin,* which had allowed the Nazis to march. Gunther also criticized the efforts of Stanford and other universities to ban expressions of racial or religious hatred, saying, "The campus ought to be the last place to legislate tampering with the edges of First Amendment protections."

Throughout the 1970s and 1980s, Gunther was mentioned for possible nomination to the Supreme Court. In 1987, when the *National Law Journal* asked a group of lawyers who was most qualified to serve on the Supreme Court, Gunther's name emerged as the "best qualified" choice. However, like Judge Learned Hand, Gunther never reached the Court.

Gunther died at his home of lung cancer at age seventy-five. At the time of his death, he was William Nelson Cromwell Professor of Law, Emeritus, at Stanford University. Although he had emeritus status since 1995, he remained an active, popular, and highly influential professor.

★

For information about Gunther's life and career, see Luis Feldsten, "Gunther Has Left Indelible Mark on Stanford," *Stanford Law Journal* (May 1995). At a memorial service in October 2002, Supreme Court Justice David H. Souter made remarks about Gunther's life, which were reprinted in *Stanford Law Review* 55 (Dec. 2002). Obituaries are in the *New York Times* (1 Aug. 2002) and *San Jose Mercury News* (13 Aug. 2002).

REBECCA BILL CHAVEZ
PABLO L. CHAVEZ

H

HALL, Gus (*b.* 8 October 1910 in Iron, Minnesota; *d.* 13 October 2000 in Manhattan, New York City), the leading American Communist of the twentieth century and a four-time U.S. presidential candidate.

Hall was born Arvo Kusta Halberg, the fifth of ten children of the Finnish immigrants Matt and Susannah Halberg. Both of Hall's parents had been members of the Industrial Workers of the World, a radical labor organization, and his father was an iron miner who had been blacklisted during a 1904 strike in Minnesota. His father was also a skilled carpenter who built the log house where the family lived in "semi-starvation." In 1925 Hall left the eighth grade to help support his family, first working as a lumberjack and then as a steelworker and iron miner. In 1927, at the urging of his father, he joined the Communist Party and within a year became an organizer of the Young Communist League in the Upper Midwest. So successful was he that in 1931 he was selected to attend the Lenin Institute in Moscow, where he spent two years learning revolutionary theory and tactics. He then became the district organizer of the Young Communist League for Minnesota, Wisconsin, and northern Michigan.

Hall's many battles with the authorities began when he was arrested for inciting a riot during a Minneapolis Teamsters' strike in 1934. He spent six months in jail for that offense. Also in 1934 he became a member of the national committee of the American Communist Party. Hall then moved to Ohio where he became involved in the steelworkers organizing committee of the Congress of Industrial Organizations. In the 1930s he legally changed his name to Gus Hall when he wanted a job in the steel mills, because his birth name appeared on company blacklists. Hall also used aliases such as "John Hollberg" and "John Howell." In 1935 Hall failed in his election bids for both city councilman of Youngstown, Ohio, and governor of Ohio on the Communist ticket. Two years later he participated in a steel strike in Warren, Ohio, and was charged with using explosives and was fined $500 after pleading guilty to a lesser charge.

During World War II, Hall enlisted in the U.S. Navy as a seaman in 1942, and in 1944, while a machinist's mate on Guam, he was elected to the party's national committee. After being discharged in 1946 he was named to the national executive committee. He became the general secretary of the Communist Party of Ohio in 1947. Hall was soon back in court as he and eleven other leading Communists were indicted by a special grand jury in New York City on 20 July 1948 for willfully and knowingly conspiring to teach and advocate the violent overthrow of the U.S. government under the Alien Registration (Smith) Act. After defense motions for dismissal were denied by the Supreme Court on 11 January 1949, the acrimonious and contentious trial began six days later. During the trial Hall was jailed for contempt and remained incarcerated until the trial ended on

Gus Hall, June 1966. BETTMANN/CORBIS

14 October 1949, when all the defendants were found guilty and sentenced to five years in prison and fined $10,000 each.

In May 1950 Hall was named the national secretary of the party and was reelected to that post in December 1951. He urged the party to explore new ways and means to satisfy the public's yearnings for peace. He also urged an alliance of the "working class, allied with the Negro people, the poor farmers, the masses of women and youth." When his conviction was upheld by the Supreme Court, Hall fled to Mexico in an attempt to reach Moscow and sanctuary. But on 8 October 1951 he was apprehended by Mexican secret service agents and returned to the United States and federal prison at Leavenworth, Kansas, where he served an additional three years for jumping bail. He worked in the prison shoe factory and was released on 30 March 1957.

Hall achieved the highest post in the Communist Party at a party convention in New York City in December 1959 when he was named the general secretary. In an address to the convention and in an attempt to revitalize the party, Hall urged his fellow Communists along a "democratic road to socialism . . . within the developing and revitalized Constitutional process." However, Hall soon became entangled with the law when the Supreme Court held that membership in the Communist Party might be a violation of the Smith Act and that Communist action organizations must register their officers, members, financial reports, and publications with the Subversive Activities Control Board. Hall had to face a six-count indictment handed to him on

15 March 1962, but these charges were dropped after a long appeal process when on 15 November 1965 the Supreme Court ruled that registration violated the constitutional provision against self-incrimination.

By the mid-1960s the Communist Party was a shadow of its former self. From a high of 60,000 in 1939 its membership had declined to around 3,000 by 1960. Yet Hall continued the struggle and on 22 June 1966 at the party's first convention since 1959 he was reelected as the general secretary by acclamation. He ran for president of the United States four times in a row starting in 1972, gaining his best vote total in the 1976 election when he received 58,992 votes. The New Left radicals of the 1960s regarded him and his party as outmoded and stodgy and the Soviet Union as hidebound. Yet when Hall went on his annual trips to Moscow he was treated with dignity by Soviet leaders from Nikita Khrushchev to Mikhail Gorbachev. In the 1980s he denounced the liberalizing policies of Gorbachev. When Gorbachev was almost overthrown in 1991, Hall praised the plotters. This rigidity almost caused his own downfall as many American Communist Party members tried to get rid of him at the party's annual convention in Cleveland in 1991. Party membership had shrunk to about 1,000 members by the end of the century. Shortly before his death, Hall resigned as the party's general secretary.

Hall's personal life was conventional. On 13 September 1934 he married Elizabeth Turner, a colleague in the Young Communist League and of Hungarian-American background. They had a son and a daughter. At the time of his death, Hall was living in suburban Yonkers, New York. Not quite six feet tall, he weighed about 245 pounds and had grayish white hair and blue eyes. He died at age ninety from complications of diabetes at Lenox Hill Hospital in Manhattan, and his cremated remains were interred in Forest Home Cemetery near Chicago. His death came almost nine years after the demise of the Soviet Union that he admired so much.

During his career Hall authored several influential books about the Communist Party and its philosophy, including *Racism: The Nation's Most Dangerous Pollutant* (1971) and *Working Class USA: The Power and the Movement* (1987). He was the archetype of the unreconstructed Communist. Neither the Nazi-Soviet pact of 1939, nor the Hungarian uprising of 1956, nor the Warsaw Pact invasion of Czechoslovakia in 1968 disillusioned him as they did many other American Communists.

★

For information about Hall's life, see *Gus Hall Bibliography: The Communist Party, USA: Philosophy, History, Program, Activities* (1981), compiled and edited by Joseph Brandt, assisted by Sylvia Opper Brandt; and Mark Lapitsky and Nikolai Mostovets, *Gus Hall* (1985), translated from the Russian by Dmitri Belyavsky.

Biographical sketches appear in *Current Biography* (1973); *Political Profiles*, vol. 3, *The Kennedy Years*, and vol. 4, *The Johnson Years* (both 1976); and *American National Biography: Supplement 1* (2002). Obituaries are in the *New York Times, Washington Post,* and *Los Angeles Times* (all 17 Oct. 2000).

JOHN MORAN

HAMPTON, Lionel   (*b.* 20 April 1908 in Louisville, Kentucky; *d.* 31 August 2002 in New York City), musician and bandleader whose innovative playing on the vibraphone made him one of the major figures of the swing era.

Hampton was the son of Charles Edward Hampton, a railroad porter, and Gertrude (Morgan) Hampton, a waitress. He had a half-brother. As a youngster, Hampton absorbed the sounds of Louisville's black neighborhoods and grew familiar with rhythm instruments at his grandmother's church in Birmingham, Alabama. His favorite instrument was the drum: "Seemed to me that drumming was the best way to get close to God," he said in an interview before his death.

After his family moved to Chicago, Hampton joined the youth band established by the local black newspaper, the *Chicago Defender,* and there he acquired a strong grounding in reading music and in harmony. He was fourteen when he received his own set of drums from his grandparents. While he was a sophomore in high school, Hampton began to play with Les Hite's band at the Vendome Theater. Hite went to Hollywood, and soon after, so did Hampton.

In Hollywood, Hampton joined Hite in Reb Spike's band. Playing drums, he made his first recordings with Reb's Legion Club Forty-Fives in the fall of 1924. He had more opportunity to record with Paul Howard's Quality Serenaders, although he did not like the kind of music played by what he referred to as "the group that gigged at all the parties for the black middle class." In 1929, at the annual ball of the Antique Art Club, Hampton met Gladys Riddle Neal. A seamstress for such film stars as Joan Crawford, she was "a career woman" who had attended college. She was also three years older than Hampton and a divorcée. Neal soon became unofficial manager for the shy young man. Hampton liked to joke that after he met her, he never again saw a paycheck: she collected his pay and doled out money to him as she saw fit. She also assigned an acquaintance to act as unofficial watchdog over Hampton, who was inclined to disappear with his friends for days at a time.

While playing with Hite's band at Frank Sebastian's Cotton Club in suburban Culver City, Hampton met the jazz trumpeter Louis Armstrong, with whom he made several recordings in 1930. During an equipment breakdown, Armstrong noticed a vibraphone in the studio and asked whether Hampton could play it. Hampton had never before seen the instrument, which is similar to a marimba with electronically operated valves, but he noticed that it had the same keyboard as a xylophone, so he said, "Sure." He plugged it in and played an Armstrong solo note for note. When the studio equipment was repaired, he recorded Eubie Blake's "Memories of You" with Armstrong.

Hampton played drums with Armstrong's band for several months before Armstrong returned to New York. At Neal's urging, he then formed his own band, featuring the trumpeter Buck Clayton and the tenor saxophonist Herschel Evans. Hampton played several instruments, but he favored the vibraphone, on which Neal believed he would make his fame. She gave him his own set for his birthday. Hampton's unique sound and his dynamic stage presence attracted the attention of the famed bandleader Benny Goodman, who invited Hampton to record with him in 1936. Also in 1936, on 11 November, Hampton and Neal finally married, because her mother would not allow her to accompany Hampton to New York—where he was to join Goodman—unless they did so. At a time when most bands and audiences were segregated, the racially integrated roster of the Benny Goodman Orchestra, which included not only Hampton but also the pianist Teddy

Lionel Hampton. AP/WIDE WORLD PHOTOS

Wilson, was revolutionary. Goodman's was the only major integrated band of the era.

In 1940 Hampton formed a big band of his own, including such talented artists as Clifford Brown, Betty Carter, Arnett Cobb, Johnny Griffin, Charles Mingus, and Wes Montgomery. While performing in Seattle, he met the teenage Quincy Jones (who later was to gain fame as a composer and instrumentalist) but refused to take him on the road because of his youth. Recording often, his biggest hits included "Flying Home" and "Hey! Ba Ba Re Bop." While his musical talent was obvious, his success in maintaining a big band was due in no small measure to Neal, who was a sharp business manager. Not only did she help him earn and manage money, but she also helped him save it. She and Hampton lived in a middle-income housing complex in Harlem, and she never allowed her husband to carry around more than pocket change. Thanks to her efforts, the couple amassed a substantial estate.

Much of what the Hamptons had went to help others. Together they raised the funds to build public housing in Harlem. The first complex was called the Lionel Hampton Houses, and after Gladys's death in 1971, Hampton helped fund the Gladys Hampton Houses. A lifelong Republican, Hampton used his contacts with New York's governor Nelson Rockefeller to realize those projects. He was essentially nonpartisan, however, and was proud of having played at the inaugural celebrations of presidents from both parties and for every chief executive from Harry S. Truman to Ronald Reagan.

Hampton died of a heart attack at age ninety-four and is buried at Woodlawn Cemetery in the Bronx, New York. His life ended without his realizing the long-held dream of putting in place a chain of music schools across the country to teach young people "the natural rhythm and joy in music." He did, however, establish music scholarships at several colleges and universities. In 1989 he presided at the dedication of the Lionel Hampton Center for the Performing Arts at the University of Idaho.

Hampton was a consummate showman. While never losing sight of his audience, he seemed to commune with his instrument, looking down at his bouncing mallets, smiling and laughing as if they spoke to him. He lived to play music. In his last years, though tired and frail, he continued to perform frequently. He often appeared to be asleep backstage until the words "And now, ladies and gentlemen, Lionel Hampton" reached his ears. Suddenly, he would spring to life. Onstage at his beloved vibraphone his years slipped away, and he played as if he were twenty-two again.

★

The definitive source on Hampton is *Hamp: The Autobiography of Lionel Hampton* (1989), written with James Haskins. See also Robert Palmer, "Lionel Hampton Has No Time to Slow Down," *Chicago Tribune* (17 Sept. 1987), and Larry Birnbaum, "That's Entertainment: Tito Puente and Lionel Hampton," *Down Beat* 62, no. 11 (Nov. 1995): 16. An obituary is in the *New York Times* (1 Sept. 2002).

JAMES HASKINS

HANDLER, Ruth (*b.* 4 November 1916 in Denver, Colorado; *d.* 27 April 2002 in Los Angeles, California), cofounder of Mattel, Inc., and creator of the Barbie doll, the best-selling doll of all time.

Handler was the youngest of ten children of Jacob Mosko, a blacksmith, and Ida Mosko, a homemaker, Polish Jewish immigrants who arrived in the United States eight years before she was born. Shortly after her birth, her mother became gravely ill, and Handler lived with and was raised by an older sister and her husband, who owned a combination drugstore and soda fountain, where Handler worked after school. A tomboy, Handler never played with dolls but instead played baseball with her older brothers. During high school she worked in the law office of an older brother.

While she was still in high school, Handler met her future husband, Izzy "Elliot" Handler. In spite of misgivings from her family that she was too young to have a boyfriend, she continued to date him when she began attending the University of Denver. Attracted by the glamour of Hollywood, she took a summer trip to Los Angeles in 1937, where she landed a job as a stenographer at Para-

Ruth Handler. AFP/CORBIS

mount Pictures. A year later, her boyfriend moved to California, and they were married. They had three children.

Handler's husband was a plastics expert. On weekends in the family garage, he made Plexiglas furniture that Handler sold during the week. In 1942 they decided to form their own company, rented space, and hired 100 employees to manufacture plastic jewelry, clocks, and picture frames. With the advent of World War II and the rationing of plastic, they made their products with wood.

By 1945 the family business became Mattel, Incorporated. "Matt" was for Harold Mattson, a foreman, then partner, and "el" for Elliot. Mattson sold his partnership back to the Handlers in 1946. The company resumed using plastic after the war, and its best-known product was the Ukedoodle, a plastic toy ukulele, which by 1955 was advertised on television's *Mickey Mouse Club*.

Two years later, while vacationing in Switzerland, Handler bought an eleven-and-one-half inch doll, Blonde Lillie, an adult doll promoted as a sex novelty. Handler had wanted Mattel to sell a doll, but not the traditional baby type. "My daughter Barbara used to play with paper dolls as a young child," Handler told an interviewer. "She always chose the teenagers or grown-up working girls, and I often thought if we could three-dimensionalize that play pattern we'd have it made." In 1957 a Japanese company agreed to manufacture the adult-looking doll with an exaggerated, Brigitte Bardot figure (with the doll's proportions scaled to what would be, on a human, a 39-inch chest, 21-inch waist, and 33-inch hips), with blonde hair, blue eyes, a petite face, and arched feet. It was called "Barbie," after Handler's first child.

The genius of the concept of Barbie was not to formulate an adult doll for a child, but to develop it as an open-end concept. In the toy business, an "open-end concept" is a product that is multifunctional and has separately sold accessories. The first version of the doll was "Barbie the teenage model." Instead of a mere doll-as-baby, Mattel's Barbie was a girl's revelation, which could be constantly reinvented by a mere change of clothes. The doll, modeled by the designer Jack Ryan, and its clothes, designed by the stylist Charlotte Johnson, continuously changed.

Barbie made her debut at the 1959 American Toy Fair in New York City and became the hit of the convention. Because Mattel had a long-term contract with the *Mickey Mouse Club* show, Barbie was first featured on that program. Priced at three dollars, the doll sold 350,000 units its first year. It was packaged in a box with one outfit and a coupon for another outfit at a reduced price. (In 1967, when the Twist 'N Turn model appeared, the original doll could be traded in for a reduced price of the newer model.) Moreover, a child could also subscribe to an outfit-of-the-month club. Following the open-end concept, Barbie had not just an ever-changing wardrobe, but endless accessories, including a pink convertible, a camper, a house, furniture, and household equipment.

In 1960 Mattel went public, and in 1963 it was listed on the New York Stock Exchange. The company expanded its plants in Los Angeles and Japan. Handler knew all the California factory workers and lunched with them in the company's cafeteria; there was little employee turnover.

Although Barbie had everything a doll could want in the way of possessions, the doll still lacked a companion. In 1961 Mattel launched the Ken doll, named for Handler's second child. With a permanently painted swimsuit, the Ken doll had its own endless outfits, props, and vehicles. In 1963 Handler added another doll, Midge, as Barbie's best friend. Since Barbie and Midge were the same size, they could wear the same clothes. Mattel became the world's leading manufacturer of clothing, albeit on a miniature scale.

In 1964 Handler introduced Skipper, Barbie's younger and smaller sister, named after Handler's third child. This doll, of course, required a different set of clothes. Allan, Ken's friend, was also added in 1964. In 1967 Mattel modeled Twiggy Barbie after that year's real top model, and in 1968 Christie, Barbie's African-American friend, was launched. Handler continuously changed Barbie and her entourage according to market demand. By 2003 more than one billion dolls had been sold worldwide in 150 countries in over 100 editions.

As the first supermodel, it is appropriate that Barbie has worn clothes by, among others, the famous designers Ralph Lauren, Bill Blass, Bob Mackie, and Christian Dior. Handler commissioned the pop artist Andy Warhol to do Barbie's portrait in 1986. The doll has even been immortalized in a song, "Barbie Girl," by the Danish group Aqua ("Life is plastic/It's fantastic."). One woman fan has created a Barbie Hall of Fame, and the magazine *Barbie Bazaar* follows the history of the doll.

From the 1970s, feminists and some health-care advocates decried Barbie's image as a "bimbo" with an impossible-to-achieve, idealized body type. Defending the doll against such critical attacks, Handler always replied that her creation is a career woman. Indeed, Barbie's professional attire includes costume changes as a flight attendant, nurse, doctor, executive, rock singer, and princess. In 1998 Barbie's image had a major makeover, eliminating the waistline seam, making the breasts and hips smaller, and adding a more athletic appearance. Yet the open-end concept prevails. A talking Barbie asks, "Want to go shopping?" By 2003 Mattel was a Fortune 500 company with $2.5 billion dollars in sales. It absorbed toy manufacturers worldwide, and its portfolio had diversified to include keyboard musical instruments and the movie business (Radnitz/Mattel Productions).

In 1975 Handler was indicted by a grand jury on charges

of fraud and false reporting to the Securities and Exchange Commission, which accused her of falsifying accounting records to inflate the company's earings between 1969 and 1974. She pleaded no contest, paid a $57,000 fine, and performed 500 hours of community service. Handler claimed to have made poor business decisions as a result of breast cancer and a subsequent mastectomy. In any case, in 1975 she and her husband were forced out of the company they had cofounded. Immediately, she launched Ruthton Corporation, which manufactured prosthetic breasts for cancer survivors such as herself. She ran the company for fifteen years before selling it to Kimberly-Clark.

Handler died at age eighty-five from complications arising after colon surgery. "The mother of Barbie" created a timeless icon, owned by millions worldwide.

★

Handler's autobiography is *Dream Doll: The Ruth Handler Story* (1994). Also see M. G. Lord, *Forever Barbie: The Unauthorized Biography of a Real Doll* (1994); Craig Yoe, ed., *The Art of Barbie* (1994); and Sibyl De Wein and Joan Ashabraner, *The Collectors Encyclopedia of Barbie Dolls and Collectibles* (1994). Obituaries are in the *Los Angeles Times* (28 Apr. 2002) and *New York Times* (29 Apr. 2002).

PATRICK S. SMITH

HANNA, William Denby ("Bill") (*b.* 14 July 1910 in Melrose, New Mexico; *d.* 22 March 2001 in North Hollywood, California), prolific pioneer of animated television shows and cofounder of Hanna-Barbera Productions.

Hanna's father, William John Hanna, worked as a construction engineer, and his mother, Avice Joyce (Denby) Hanna, was a pious woman and an amateur writer of poems and essays. Hanna was the third of seven children and the only son. After living in Baker, Oregon, and Logan, Utah, the family moved to San Pedro, California, in 1917. By 1919 they had moved to the Watts neighborhood of Los Angeles, where Hanna joined the Boy Scouts, an organization important to him all his life.

Hanna began working manual jobs and by his sophomore year in high school had bought his own car. Hard work and a desire to learn and apply new skills characterized his entire life. He graduated from Compton High School in 1928, where he had studied piano, saxophone, and, later, piano composition. He enrolled in Compton Junior College in 1929, majoring in journalism, but the Great Depression forced him instead to find work. That year his father helped supervise the building of the Pantages Theater and moved his family to Hollywood, California. Hanna worked for his father, but his brief career in construction ended when he broke his arm.

Through a sister's boyfriend, Hanna heard of an animation studio started by the artists Hugh Harman and Rudolph Ising that produced cartoons, including *Looney Tunes* and *Merrie Melodies*. In 1930 Hanna landed his first job in animation, as a janitor for $18 per week. The Harman-Ising studio was small and production not as specialized as it later became, so it offered Hanna opportunities he was quick to seize. Within weeks he was supervising the small, all-female staff of inkers and painters. Soon he was contributing songs and jokes; he also learned to guide a cartoon's timing and synchronization to music.

In 1933 Hanna began to direct his own projects. His first, *To Spring*, featured flowers blooming. Much of the studio's work was produced for Metro-Goldwyn-Mayer (MGM). In 1937 MGM ended its contract with Harman-Ising and set up its own animation studio, headed by Fred Quimby, who immediately recruited Hanna and the New Yorker Joe Barbera. Eventually, Harman and Ising also joined the MGM crew. Meanwhile, a year after they met, Hanna married Violet Blanch Wogatzke on 7 August 1936 at Immaculate Conception Church in Hollywood. The couple had two children.

Hanna's first project for MGM, an animated version of the comic strip *The Katzenjammer Kids*, was his least successful. A later project, developed with Barbera, became the world-famous cat-and-mouse saga featuring Tom and Jerry. Hanna and Barbera differed in temperament, background, and skills but shared creativity, an ardor for work, and devotion to the art and business of animation. Barbera was the artist, dashing off experimental sketches of a character's expressions and attitudes. Beginning a partnership that lasted more than sixty years, the two developed the story and produced the short cartoon together. Because they were new at the studio, however, Ising garnered the production credit. *Puss Gets the Boot*, featuring Jasper the cat and Jinx the mouse, appeared in theaters in February 1940. The cartoon was nominated for an Academy Award ("Oscar"). Audiences delighted in the scheming cat and endearing mouse, who always fought yet sometimes revealed their underlying friendship. In 1941 *The Midnight Snack* used the names Tom and Jerry for the first time. Hanna and Barbera produced more than one hundred cartoons featuring their duo; between 1940 and 1957 these cartoons received seven Oscars and eight additional Oscar nominations.

Meanwhile, Hanna helped create flesh-and-blood as well as celluloid offspring. His first child, a son, was born in 1939, and a daughter in 1942. The Hannas built their own home in Sherman Oaks, California. During World War II Hanna worked on animated military training films. In 1945, approached by the actor and dancer Gene Kelly, Hanna and Barbera combined live action with animation for the first time when Kelly danced with Jerry the mouse

William Hanna (*left*), with Joe Barbera. CORBIS

in the film *Anchors Aweigh.* Beginning in 1955, Hanna and Barbera headed the MGM animation department. Television was increasingly stealing audiences from the theaters, however, and MGM closed the animation studio in 1957. "Television," Hanna wrote in his memoir, "could be our doom or our possible deliverance." As generations of Saturday morning TV-watching children know, it was the latter. The pair flipped a coin over whose name would go first and opened Hanna-Barbera Productions. Hanna developed a system called *limited animation* to cut costs to television-budget size. While many animation purists will never forgive him for this innovation, it allowed a variety of humorous new cartoons to fill the then-tiny screens in viewers' homes.

Limited animation also forced Hanna and Barbera to rely more on character development, scripting, and wise-cracks than on impressive visuals. Their first series, *Ruff and Reddy,* appeared on the National Broadcasting Company network on 14 December 1957; their first hit, *The Huckleberry Hound Show,* debuted on KPIX in New York on 2 October 1958. Besides the down-to-earth, southern-accented canine, the show featured Yogi Bear, Pixie and Dixie, and others who would soon get their own shows. It won an Emmy Award in 1960. That year, Hanna-Barbera's most renowned show, *The Flintstones,* premiering on the American Broadcasting Company (ABC) network on 30 September, brought animation to prime time. The Stone Age family, based in part on the comedian Jackie Gleason's situation comedy *The Honeymooners,* won a Golden Globe Award in 1965 and became an icon of American popular culture. Like Gleason's Ralph Kramden and his wife, Alice, Fred and Wilma Flintstone were a working-class couple, persevering through encounters with Fred's officious boss, their semi-helpful neighbors Barney and Betty Rubble, and Fred and Barney's half-baked schemes to achieve sucess. Going from the past to the future, in September 1962 Hanna-Barbera began *The Jetsons,* in which George Jetson drove a spaceship to work, and his wife, Jane, managed their robot maid. Their first action series, *The Adventures of Johnny Quest,* appeared on ABC in the fall of 1964.

Taft Broadcasting purchased Hanna-Barbera Productions in 1967, but Hanna and Barbera remained in charge. One of their longest-lasting characters, Scooby-Doo, debuted in 1969. The backing from Taft allowcd Hanna-Barbera to develop studios in other countries, beginning with Australia in 1971 and then Mexico, the Philippines, Argentina, Spain, Poland, and China. In 1977 their animated film of E. B. White's novel *Charlotte's Web* won an Annie Award. In the 1980s their cartoons of the Smurfs and animated stories from the Bible won numerous awards. Hanna and Barbera received stars on the Hollywood Walk of Fame in 1976; the Governor's Award, National Academy of Television Arts and Sciences in 1988; and election to the Television Academy Hall of Fame in 1993.

Hanna's health declined in the 1980s. In 1990 he underwent a heart bypass, although he still served as coproducer for Universal Pictures' 1990 film *The Jetsons: The Movie* and Amblin Entertainment's 1994 film *The Flintstones.* Hanna died at home at age ninety; he is buried in Ascension Cemetery in Lake Forest, California.

Over his long, creative lifetime, Hanna developed theater films, television features and specials, home videos, and more than 175 animated or live-action series for television. Naturally, that volume of work includes much that is forgettable, even regrettable. Still, all of his creations have appealed to generations of children, and key shows will never be forgotten by people of all ages. His work also provided technical innovations that shaped animation, especially for the small screen.

★

The best reference is Hanna's memoir, *A Cast of Friends,* written with Tom Ito (1996), which includes a comprehensive list of works through that year. The lavishly produced *The Art of Hanna-Barbera: Fifty Years of Creativity,* by Ted Sennet (1989), covers Hanna's life and his career. Obituaries are in the *New York Times* and *Los Angeles Times* (both 23 Mar. 2001).

BERNADETTE LYNN BOSKY

HANNUM, Alexander Murray ("Alex") (*b.* 19 July 1923 in Los Angeles, California; *d.* 18 January 2002 in Coronado, California), professional basketball player who became the first coach to win championships in both the National Basketball Association (NBA) and the American Basketball Association (ABA), and the first to lead two different teams to NBA titles.

Hannum was the son of Edward Hannum and Agnes Hannum. His father owned an Oriental rug cleaning business in Los Angeles, where Hannum grew up. Six feet,

Alex Hannum (*center, in tie*) and Philadelphia players celebrate 1967 championship. BETTMANN/CORBIS

seven inches tall, he played center on the Alexander Hamilton High School basketball team and was named All-Conference for the 1939–1940 and the 1940–1941 seasons. In his senior year he was also named to the All-City team.

Hannum attended the University of Southern California (USC) in Los Angeles, where he played basketball for two years before joining the U.S. Army Medical Department as a medical reconditioning instructor. He served in the army from April 1943 until March 1946, during which time he also played for the Los Angeles Shamrocks, an Amateur Athletic Union team. He then returned to USC and played basketball for two more years, leading the team in scoring during his senior season with an average of 11.4 points per game. Despite the presence of Hannum and Bill Sharman, another future inductee to the Basketball Hall of Fame, USC's two-year record was only 14–14.

After graduating from USC in 1948 with a B.S. degree in business, Hannum signed with the Oshkosh (Wisconsin) All Stars of the National Basketball League (NBL), for whom he averaged 5.7 points per game. When the NBL and the Basketball Association of America merged in 1949 to form the NBA, Oshkosh chose not to enter and sold Hannum to the Syracuse (New York) Nationals. Hannum ultimately played eight years of professional basketball with Oshkosh, Syracuse, Baltimore, Rochester (New York), Milwaukee (Wisconsin), and Fort Wayne (Indiana), averaging just under six points and 4.5 rebounds per game in his career. He was known as a rough player—he fouled out of eighty-two of the 580 games in which he played and usually had more fouls than rebounds—and his shooting was often derided. Hannum said that he would "clobber guys" and was correctly labeled a "hatchet man."

Hannum became the third coach of the 1956–1957 season for the St. Louis Hawks and ended the season as player-coach. He led the Hawks to the Western Division title, after which they took the Boston Celtics to seven games of the NBA finals before losing the seventh game in double overtime. The next season seemed a repeat of the preceding one, with a Western Division win that led to a face-off with the Celtics in the finals, but this time, outstanding play by Bob Pettit of the Hawks—combined with an injured ankle on the part of the Celtics star center, Bill Russell—proved the key to a Hawks triumph in six games.

Hannum later had contractual disagreements with the Hawks' owner, Ben Kerner, and quit to return to southern California and run a contracting business and coach the Wichita (Kansas) Vickers of the NIBL, an AAU team, from 1958 to 1960. In the fall of 1960 he came back to basketball as the coach of the Syracuse Nationals, compiling a three-year record of 135 wins and 122 losses, including the play-offs. When the Nationals moved to Philadelphia in 1963 and became the 76ers, Hannum returned to California as coach of the San Francisco Warriors, which he led to a Western Division title. In the playoffs the Warriors, behind the seven-foot, one-inch center Wilt Chamberlain, lost in five games to the Boston Celtics and Russell, but Hannum was named NBA Coach of the Year for the 1963–1964 season.

Under Hannum's guidance, Chamberlain altered his game to concentrate more on defense, with the result that the Warriors won the Western Division championship in 1964. The next year the team started badly, traded Chamberlain at mid-season, and finished last in the league. The Warriors improved during the next year but fired Hannum, who was then hired by the Philadelphia 76ers of the Eastern Division for the next season (1966–1967).

Reunited with Chamberlain and a superior cast of players, Hannum led the 76ers as they won forty-five of their first forty-nine games, finished the season 68–13, and cruised through the playoffs. In the process, they won eleven of fifteen games for the NBA title, breaking the Celtics streak of eight consecutive championships. Hannum's 76ers had the best record in basketball in 1967–1968 but were upset by the Celtics in the Eastern Division finals.

After the season ended, Hannum quit the 76ers to coach the Oakland Oaks of the American Basketball Association, which had begun in 1967. He got to return to California and was reunited with the All-Star Rick Barry, whom he had coached as a member of the Warriors during Barry's rookie season. The Oaks had the best record in the ABA and swept to the ABA title in 1968–1969, and Hannum was named ABA Coach of the Year. Financial problems, however, caused the Oakland franchise to fold after that year, and the last-place San Diego Rockets of the NBA hired Hannum to coach in the middle of the 1969–1970 season.

In the next season, Hannum led the Rockets to third place in the Western Division, just one game out of the playoffs. When the San Diego franchise moved to Houston before the 1971 season began, Hannum chose to return to the ABA as president, general manager, and coach of the Denver Nuggets. In that capacity, he compiled a record of 118 wins and 134 losses, losing in the first round of the playoffs in two of three years. Hannum remained with the Nuggets until the franchise was sold in 1974, and his contract was not renewed. He returned to Santa Monica, California, where he operated Alex Hannum General Construction.

Hannum was a popular coach with his players; he knew the game well and allowed them a great deal of latitude in their training regimen. He ended his coaching career with a record of 471 victories and 412 losses in the NBA, and 178 wins and 152 losses in the ABA. He was the only coach ever to win championships in both the NBA and the ABA, and was inducted into the Naismith Memorial Basketball Hall of Fame as a coach in October 1998. Hannum was married and divorced twice and had three daughters.

Chamberlain remembered Hannum as the greatest coach he had ever had. Hannum coached a dozen future Basketball Hall of Fame inductees, and five of his players—Larry Brown, Doug Moe, Larry Costello, Billy Cunningham, and Matt Goukas, Jr.—themselves became NBA coaches. Two nights after his death, the 76ers had a moment of silence to commemorate his passing.

★

Hannum's contributions and greatness as a coach are highlighted in Glen Macnow, *The Philadelphia 76ers Basketball Team,* and Ron Knapp, *Top 10 Professional Basketball Coaches* (both 1998). He figures prominently in Chamberlain's autobiography, *The View from Above* (1991), as well as in Wayne Lynch, *Season of the 76ers: The Story of Wilt Chamberlain and the 1967 NBA Champion Philadelphia 76ers* (2002). An obituary is in the *Philadelphia Inquirer* (20 Jan. 2002).

MURRY R. NELSON

HARSANYI, John Charles (*b.* 29 May 1920 in Budapest, Hungary; *d.* 9 August 2000 in Berkeley, California), economist, mathematician, philosopher, and Nobel laureate whose innovations in game theory influenced international relations, business, and politics.

Harsanyi was the only child of Charles Harsanyi and Alice Harsanyi, both pharmacists, who owned a drugstore in Budapest, Hungary. They could afford to send their son to the best schools, and did so. Harsanyi remembered with pride attending the Lutheran Gymnasium in Budapest, in those days one of the best schools in Europe. When he graduated in 1937, he had to make a difficult choice concerning the career he should pursue. Although he loved mathematics and philosophy, his parents had their hearts set on his becoming a pharmacist. Family always meant a great deal to Harsanyi, so he focused on pharmacology in college, rationalizing his choice by noting that the Nazis were likely to take over Hungary, and given the fact that the pharmacist's profession was considered a vital one, he might not be drafted into slave labor.

Although his parents had converted from Judaism to Roman Catholicism before he was born, and he himself was Roman Catholic, the Nazis regarded Harsanyi as Jewish. As long as Hungary remained independent, he was exempt from the draft because he was a pharmacist, but in May 1944, after Germany took over the government, Harsanyi was pressed into slave labor in Budapest, where he worked mostly in construction. In November the Germans decided to apply their "final solution" to Hungary, and Jews were taken by train to death camps. At the train

John C. Harsanyi, 1994. FORDEN PATRICK J/CORBIS SYGMA

ual laborer, mostly in factories. At night, he studied economics at the University of Sydney. He later recalled that he was drawn by the elegance of the mathematics of economics. While earning his M.A. in economics in 1953, he read and absorbed the writings of the Princeton mathematics professor John Nash on game theory.

By 1954, when he became a lecturer in economics for the University of Queensland, Harsanyi was at work on the theories that eventually would earn him the Nobel Prize in economics. Nash's work had, to Harsanyi's mind, a significant flaw: it required that all participants in a negotiation know everything that all the others knew. In 1956 Harsanyi received a Rockefeller Fellowship to attend Stanford University in California, where he earned a Ph.D. in economics in 1958. That year he moved his family to Canberra, Australia, to accept a professorship at Australian National University. During this period Harsanyi expanded game theory to include negotiations and conflicts in which none of the participants knew everything—in fact, when their understanding of events was flawed and differing information was available to different participants.

Kenneth Arrow, who had directed Harsanyi's dissertation at Stanford, helped him find a position as professor of economics at Wayne State University in Detroit in 1961. By then Harsanyi was becoming a legend in the field of economics and had also gained distinction as a teacher. He was noted not only for his brilliant mind, but also for his kindly personality and his ability to communicate with his students, a quality all the more impressive in light of the fact that he had not even known English when he first arrived in Australia a little more than a decade earlier.

In 1964 the U.S. government made Harsanyi an adviser to the U.S. Arms Control and Disarmament Agency. While working in Australia, he had developed mathematical models for welfare economics, and in the United States, both state governments and the federal government used the models to help policymakers choose where to spend money and how to focus their efforts for relieving poverty. In the late 1950s Harsanyi began building on Nash's ideas to develop simple algebraic formulae for the best conflict-resolution strategies. The U.S. government asked him to apply this work to international relations, and throughout the 1960s and 1970s his theory was put to use in negotiations for nuclear arms treaties.

Harsanyi left Wayne State in 1963, and in 1964 accepted a position at the Haas School of Business at the University of California, Berkeley. In 1966 he achieved tenure and a joint appointment in the school of business and the economics department. Thereafter he applied his theories to ethical questions, developing what he called "utilitarian ethics." His *Rational Behavior and Bargaining Equilibrium in Games and Social Situations* (1977) became standard reading for game theorists. In 1988 Harsanyi and his co-

station, Harsanyi removed his shirt with the yellow Star of David on it, which designated him as Jewish, and walked away. When a guard asked what he was doing, he boldly replied that he had been visiting a friend who was being deported, and the guard let him go. He then hid in the cellar of a Jesuit monastery for the remainder of World War II.

In 1946 Harsanyi enrolled at the University of Budapest, where he earned his Ph.D. in philosophy a year later. His outspoken anti-Communism did not sit well with Hungary's new Moscow-aligned regime, and although he secured a faculty position in September 1947 at the University Institute of Sociology, he was forced to leave in June 1948. While his period of teaching had been brief, he had time to meet his future wife, Anne Klauber, a student. The Communists tried to force her to abandon Harsanyi, but in April 1950 Klauber and Harsanyi made a harrowing escape through a marsh into Austria.

The couple migrated to Sydney, Australia, on 30 December 1950, and married three days later. They later had one son. Harsanyi's college degrees were not recognized in Australia, meaning that he could find work only as a man-author, Reinhard Selten, published *A General Theory of Equilibrium Selection in Games,* perhaps the most widely read book in its field.

Harsanyi retired from Berkeley in 1990. In 1994 he was awarded the Nobel Prize in economic sciences, sharing it with Nash and Selten. During the 1990s Harsanyi suffered from Alzheimer's disease, and died of a heart attack at his Berkeley home at the age of eighty. Harsanyi made major contributions toward the application of game theory to everyday events, to philosophy, to armed conflict, and to social problems.

★

Information on Harsanyi is in Marilu Hurt McCarty, *The Nobel Laureates: How the World's Greatest Economic Minds Shaped Modern Thought* (2001). Peter J. Hammond, *Harsanyi's Utilitarian Theorem: A Simpler Proof and Some Ethical Connotations* (1991), is a technical critique of his ideas. See also the memorial tribute by Kenneth Arrow, *John C. Harsanyi: May 29, 1920–August 9, 2000* (2001). Obituaries are in the *Washington Post* and *New York Times* (both 12 Aug. 2000).

KIRK H. BEETZ

HART, Leon (*b.* 21 November 1928 in Turtle Creek, Pennsylvania; *d.* 24 September 2002 in South Bend, Indiana), All-America football player at the University of Notre Dame, 1949 Heisman Trophy winner, and professional athlete who helped the Detroit Lions win three National Football League (NFL) titles in the 1950s.

Hart was the only child of Josephine (Lubert) Hart, a homemaker, and a plaster worker who divorced his mother when Hart was eight years old. He was raised by his mother and stepfather, Charles, a crane repairman for Westinghouse Corporation. The three established a firm bond during Hart's formative years; by contrast, as Hart later recalled, "I had no real relationship with my [biological] father. . . . He got a seat behind our bench when the Lions played in Pittsburgh. He wanted to see me, but I couldn't do it knowing the devastation it would mean to my mother."

Raised in the Pittsburgh suburb of Turtle Creek, Hart attended the local high school. At age fourteen, he learned the value of sustained effort. He recalled his mother's advice: "Son, you go to work in the steel mill, so you'll know what hard work is. Then when you go to college, you'll study harder." He spent two summers working in a steel mill. He maintained a B average, and mathematics was his top subject in high school. An excellent athlete, Hart won ten letters while playing football, basketball, baseball, and track. He led the Turtle Creek High School football team in four consecutive undefeated seasons. By his senior year

Leon Hart, 1951. BETTMANN/CORBIS

he had grown to almost six feet, five inches and weighed 225 pounds.

Hart was recruited by the universities of Pittsburgh, Tennessee, and Pennsylvania as well as by Columbia University and Virginia Military Institute. His high school academic record proved attractive to college coaches. Although, in his words, "Notre Dame did a lousy job of recruiting me," Hart fell in love with the campus and, more important, was fascinated with its famous coach, Frank Leahy. Hart later described Leahy as "the greatest man I ever met. I was afraid of him, so was everyone. But we worshipped the ground he walked on." Hart chose Notre Dame, and in his freshman year (1946) he served as backup right end to Jack Zilly. "He was a big freshman, he weighed about 260 pounds, we tried to fool him on a couple of plays and he wasn't very foolable [sic]," John Lujack, a quarterback who won the Heisman Trophy in 1947, fondly recollected. "We knew he was going to be a great player." In 1947 Hart stepped into the starting lineup. He combined with Jim Martin, another future Football Hall of Fame inductee, to form, in the words of the football writer and editor Lou Somogyi, "what can be deemed the greatest 'bookend' tandem in college football history."

Hart finished his Notre Dame career with forty-nine catches for 751 yards (an average of 15.1 yards per catch) and thirteen touchdowns. Those numbers would be modest by today's standards, but Hart was a versatile player. He also lined up at fullback to confuse defenses and was a dominant pass rusher and tackler. With his size, he could control both sides of the line of scrimmage. He was one of the greatest two-way players of his day and became the "centerpiece" of the greatest era in Notre Dame football history. In his four seasons at Notre Dame (1946–1949), the team posted a 36–0–2 record while winning national titles in 1946, 1947, and 1949 and finishing second to the University of Michigan in 1948.

In 1949 Hart established himself as one of the premier players in college football. His final game was particularly memorable. In a game against Southern Methodist University (SMU), the score was tied at 20 with nine minutes left to play. Hart moved from linebacker to fullback, powering for fifty-four yards and allowing Notre Dame to take the lead, 27–20. With time still left on the clock, Hart led the defense, stopping SMU on the Notre Dame one-foot line and thereby preserving the four-year winning streak of the Fighting Irish. Hart won the Heisman Trophy that year, becoming only the second and the last lineman (Larry Kelley of Yale was the first in 1936) to be thus honored.

Hart was one of the last two-way players in college football and the last non–skilled position player to win the Heisman until Michigan cornerback Charles Woodson did so in 1997. In the 1949 Heisman balloting, Hart easily outpolled two outstanding running backs: North Carolina's Charlie ("Choo Choo") Justice and Doak Walker of SMU. Hart also was selected by the Associated Press as its 1949 male athlete of the year, receiving more votes than Jackie Robinson, the first African-American professional baseball player, and Sam Snead, one of the greatest golfers of all time. Hart graduated from Notre Dame in 1950 with a degree in mechanical engineering. He was a recognized scholar-athlete. According to Somogyi, he joined his fellow Notre Dame graduate Angelo Bertelli as one of the only two players "in college football annals to: 1) win a national title in their senior year; 2) win the Heisman as seniors; 3) be the Number One pick of the NFL draft the ensuing spring."

Hart continued his football career on the professional level. Drafted by the Detroit Lions, he played for them from 1950 to 1957 and helped the Lions win titles in 1952, 1953, and 1957. In 1951, the year he earned All-Pro honors, Hart led the Lions in receptions, with thirty-five, and touchdowns, with twelve. In 1956 he also ran for 348 yards, a 4.6 average. An all-purpose player, Hart played end, defensive end, and fullback. In his eight seasons with the Lions, he had 174 catches for 2,499 yards and 26 touchdowns. He also accounted for four interceptions and eight kick returns and twice returned fumbles for touchdowns. Said the Lions

defensive back Jimmy David, "Leon was one hell of a guy—a great football player." Lou Creekmur, a Hall of Fame lineman for the Lions, noted: "Leon was probably a little more intelligent than the average football player. He had a degree in engineering, and he had an IQ that was a lot higher than the rest of us."

Hart married his hometown sweetheart, Lois Newyahr, on 17 February 1950. They had six children and lived in Birmingham, Michigan. After his retirement in 1957, Hart headed up a number of business enterprises. He founded and was president of Leon Hart Industries, which produced a variety of products, including tire-balancing equipment for the commercial trucking industry. In 1973 Hart was inducted into the College Football Hall of Fame.

In early September 2002, after attending a Notre Dame home game, Hart—suffering from prostate cancer and a heart condition—was admitted to Saint Joseph Medical Center in South Bend, Indiana. He died in the hospital a few weeks later, and a funeral service was held in Birmingham. He is buried in Cedar Grove Cemetery, Saint Joseph's County, Indiana. One son, Kevin, was a tight end on the Notre Dame 1977 national championship team, and one grandson, Brendan, was a walk-on tight end for the 2002 Notre Dame team.

Hart was one of the last two-way players on both the college and professional levels. He prided himself on "having often played a full sixty minutes," whereas one-way players are able to rest on the bench for part of the game. Until his death, he took a dim view of the free-substitution rule. "Today you ask a guy if he plays football and he says, 'No, I play left linebacker.' . . . The game used to belong to the players on the field. Now it's a puppet show, a chess game." Still, Hart loved the sport that made him famous. His modesty was impeccable: "I was just a guy who loved to play and put out the best effort he could all the time."

★

The richest repositories of information on Notre Dame football and its players are the Athletic Department Archives, Joyce Convocation Center, and the Sports Information Department. An abundantly illustrated work detailing Notre Dame's football success is Roland Lazenby, *College Football's Great Dynasties: Notre Dame* (1991). Also notable is Joe Garner, *Echoes of Notre Dame Football: Great and Memorable Moments of the Fighting Irish* (2001), which highlights Notre Dame's seven Heisman Trophy winners. Other important works include Francis Wallace, *Notre Dame: From Rockne to Parseghian* (1966); William Gildea and Christopher Jennison, *The Fighting Irish* (1976); and Jack Connor, *Leahy's Lads* (1994). An obituary is in the *New York Times* (25 Sept. 2002).

CHARLES F. HOWLETT

HAUGHTON, Aaliyah Dana. *See* Aaliyah.

HAY, Henry, Jr. ("Harry") (*b.* 7 April 1912 in Worthing, England; *d.* 24 October 2002 in San Francisco, California), gay rights pioneer who founded two pathbreaking organizations, the Mattachine Society and the Radical Faeries.

Born to American parents, Henry Hay, Sr., who managed mining operations in Africa and South America, and Margaret (Neal) Hay, a homemaker, Hay was the oldest of three children. After Hay's father lost part of his right leg in an accident in 1916, the family moved to southern California and settled in Los Angeles in 1919. Tall and precocious, the young Hay rebelled against his status-conscious mother and especially his authoritarian father, who, in the summer of 1925, sent the thirteen-year-old boy to work on a Nevada ranch. During this time, ranch hands who were members of the Industrial Workers of the World introduced Hay to progressive politics. Also during this time, Hay, who had a lifelong fascination with American Indian culture, received a blessing from a Northern Paiute Indian elder. Hay later learned that the elder was the prophet Wovoka, the onetime leader of the Ghost Dance religion.

Harry Hay. Mr. Daniel Nicoletta

Hay graduated from Los Angeles High School in 1929 and attended Stanford University from 1930 to 1932. While at Stanford, he discovered San Francisco's gay society, had a series of affairs with men, and defied conventions of the time by declaring his homosexuality to his classmates. Hay left Stanford without graduating and returned to a bohemian life in Los Angeles. For the next few years he held acting jobs in theaters and movies; wrote poetry and stories; worked as a ghostwriter; and, with two friends, made a surrealist film, *Even—As You and I* (1936). During this time, he became involved in leftist causes. Will Geer, one of Hay's many lovers in the early to mid-1930s (and who later played the grandfather in the 1970s television drama *The Waltons*), initiated Hay into Los Angeles labor circles and the Communist Party. Together they participated in labor demonstrations and political theater. Hay described his experiences at the San Francisco general strike of 1934—where the police shot dead two protesters—as a life-changing event.

Like most gay men of his time, Hay married. A disaffected Roman Catholic, he married Anita Platky, a Jewish woman and fellow Communist Party member, in 1938. To their circle of progressive friends, the Hays seemed a model couple. They were active in Communist Party functions, both in New York (1939–1942) and after returning to Los Angeles. They adopted two girls. Hay taught Marxism and folk music history at leftist organizations and in 1948 landed a job as a production engineer at Leahy Manufacturing, where he worked until 1964.

Hay continued to have gay dalliances. In 1948, following the publication of Alfred Kinsey's *Sexual Behavior in the Human Male* (which suggested that homosexuality was more prevalent than was previously thought), Hay began formulating an idea for a gay organization. At a time when gays were forbidden to assemble in public and were frequently harassed by police, Hay asserted that homosexuals constituted a cultural minority and, like racial and ethnic minorities, deserved equal civil rights with the majority.

Hay found few sympathetic ears until 1950, when he met and began a two-year relationship with Rudi Gernreich, an Austrian refugee and fashion designer who would become famous in the 1960s and 1970s. With Gernreich and five others, Hay founded a secret organization based in Los Angeles that became known as the Mattachine Society (named after the all-male troupes of masked clowns in medieval France who mocked social conventions). The first significant and long-lasting gay rights organization in the country, the society held discussion groups and encouraged political action. In 1952 it won a historic legal victory when Dale Jennings, one of the Mattachine founders, was acquitted in a police-entrapment case. The society spun off satellite chapters and ONE Incorporated, which

HAYES

published *ONE Magazine: The Homosexual Viewpoint,* the first widely distributed gay publication in the United States.

With his role in the fledging homophile movement (as this first wave of gay organizing activities is often called), Hay made a break from his former life. In 1951 he and Platky divorced, and he resigned from the Communist Party (although he remained a dedicated Marxist throughout his life and continued to fight for various oppressed groups). The anticommunist hysteria of the 1950s caught up with him in 1953. A faction of the Mattachine Society that favored adapting to the mainstream forced out the founders, citing their communist roots. In 1955 Hay made a short but dramatic appearance before the House Un-American Activities Committee.

From 1952 to 1962 Hay was in a relationship with Jorn Kamgren, a Danish milliner who did not share his intellectual or political interests. Hay devoted this period to the study of gay anthropology and wrote voluminous notes on the roles of gay people in non-western cultures.

In 1963 he met John Burnside, with whom he would spend the rest of his life. For the next ten years Hay helped run a factory that manufactured a type of kaleidoscope that Burnside, an engineer, had invented. Although he remained politically active, Hay increasingly turned his attention to defining gay spirituality. He grew his hair long and wore colorful clothes and bold accessories. In 1965 Hay founded the Circle of Loving Companions, a small but enduring collective made up mostly of friends. The next year Hay helped organize the first gay protest parade in Los Angeles.

In 1969 a more militant and visible chapter in the gay rights movement opened with the Stonewall riots in New York City, named after a Greenwich Village gay bar, the Stonewall Inn, at which a routine police raid in June touched off riots when the bar's patrons resisted arrest. Later that year, Hay was elected the first chair of the Gay Liberation Front of Los Angeles. In 1970 Hay and Burnside moved to San Juan Pueblo in northern New Mexico, where they stayed until 1979. During this time Hay continued his study of Indian culture, successfully led a campaign to stop a dam project on the Rio Grande, and developed a theory of gay consciousness that led to the first Radical Faerie conference in 1979.

In settings ranging from small gatherings to large rural retreats, the Radical Faeries encouraged gay men to free themselves from the constraints of straight society and its "gay clones," and to redefine their relationships with one another, nature, and the spiritual world. Although internal strife marred Hay's leadership in the growing movement, he stayed involved in the group, his utopian vision of gay brotherhood. After moving back to Los Angeles with Burnside in 1979, Hay continued to lecture, organize, and protest in the 1980s and 1990s. In 1999 the couple moved to

San Francisco, where Hay died of lung cancer at age ninety. His body was cremated.

Hay was at times cantankerous, autocratic, and idealistic. Some of his core ideas, like his thesis that homosexuals are intrinsically different from heterosexuals and his insistence that the gay community not exclude its fringe groups, were and remain controversial. Nonetheless, his ideas and actions drew a road map for gays and lesbians to realize their individual potential and exercise their collective power. In the process Hay helped reshape the social and political landscape of twentieth-century America.

★

Hay's personal papers are housed in the San Francisco Public Library's James C. Hormel Gay and Lesbian Center. His major speeches, papers, and interviews are collected in *Radically Gay: Gay Liberation in the Words of Its Founder* (1996), ed. by Will Roscoe. Stuart Timmons, *The Trouble with Harry Hay: Founder of the Modern Gay Movement* (1990), is a detailed account of Hay's life. Obituaries are in the *New York Times* and *Los Angeles Times* (both 25 Oct. 2002). There is also a documentary film, *Hope Along the Wind: The Life of Harry Hay* (2001), directed by Eric Slade.

JEFFREY H. CHEN

HAYES, Robert Lee ("Bob") (*b.* 20 December 1942 in Jacksonville, Florida; *d.* 18 September 2002 in Jacksonville, Florida), Olympic 100-meter-dash champion and professional football player whose speed and ability forced revolutionary changes in the way National Football League (NFL) coaches defended against the passing game.

Hayes was born to Mary (Green) Hayes and George Sanders. His father never legally adopted him, and Hayes and his mother and three siblings lived with Joseph Hayes, a disabled World War II veteran who earned a living running a shoeshine stand and an illegal numbers operation in the Bottom, or Hell's Hole, section of Jacksonville's east side ghetto. Hayes's speed was evident at an early age. Although he often was truant, he attracted the notice of the track coach at Matthew W. Gilbert High School in Jacksonville when he far outdistanced the squad's sprinters while wearing street shoes. Encouraged to join the team, Hayes entered seven events in a track meet—the long jump, the high jump, the 4 × 100-yard relay, and the 100-, 200-, 440-, and 880-yard runs. Hayes won six individual events and anchored the winning relay team.

During this time Hayes and his friends also cashed in by betting on his abilities in hastily arranged street-match races against all comers. He never lost. Still, football was his main athletic interest. It was said later in his career that what made Hayes so successful on the gridiron was that he "was a football player first, who had sprinter's speed."

Bob Hayes, 1964. BETTMANN/CORBIS

Other track performers—Frank Budd, Ray Norton, Henry Carr, John Carlos, Jimmie Hines, Harvey Nairn, and Tommie Smith—were primarily track stars trying to make the conversion to football, none with much success.

A four-sport performer in high school, Hayes attracted the attention of college recruiters in all four sports—football, basketball, baseball, and track and field. While he had some scholarship offers from major schools—the University of Southern California, Ohio State, Nebraska, Oklahoma, and Penn State—he elected to attend Florida Agricultural and Mechanical University (FAMU). At the time, FAMU was the most storied of the historically black football-playing schools. The legendary Jake Gaither was coach of the Rattlers, and Hayes was one of a handful of lightning-fast running backs at FAMU. While he was there, he came under the astute tutelage not only of Gaither but also of the track coach Robert ("Pete") Griffin, under whose watchful eye he became an Olympic hopeful. He progressed for several seasons under Griffin and tied the world record in the 100 yards (the race later would be lengthened to 100 meters) with a 9.2-second clocking in early 1962. Because a standard-caliber starting pistol was not used, Hayes's time was not officially

recognized, so in 1963 he ran in St. Louis with practically no wind blowing to set a new, and recognized, world record of 9.1 seconds.

Meanwhile, Hayes also was making a name for himself as a football player. Before his senior season the blisteringly fast running back was drafted in the seventh round by the Dallas Cowboys of the NFL as a "red shirt," or future selection. He also was taken in the fourteenth round by the Denver Broncos of the rival American Football League (AFL). Hayes still had the 1964 Olympics and his final year of football ahead of him. At the 1964 Olympic Games in Tokyo, Hayes cruised to victory in the 100 meters with a world record–setting 10.0 seconds and anchored the U.S. 4 × 100-meter relay. The football writer Paul Zimmerman wrote that the American team was in fifth place when Hayes got the baton, a few yards behind the pack, "but Hayes pulled even with thirty meters to go, shifted into overdrive, and finished ahead of everyone with an explosive burst that made the greatest sprinters in the world look sluggish."

As the "World's Fastest Human," a title bestowed on the reigning 100-yard and 100-meter champion, Hayes was a target for the opposition in his final season of college football. He turned in spectacular games, combining running, receiving, and kick returning. Although he was still willing to run track in the spring, both Gaither and Griffin advised him to "take the money and run," literally. Hayes did, signing with the Cowboys for a three-year deal at $100,000 and a Buick Riviera as a bonus. On 9 July 1965 Hayes and a fellow FAMU student, Altamease Martin, were married in Dallas. They divorced in 1972. Hayes later married Janice McDuff, with whom he had a son.

Hayes burst onto the NFL scene as a rookie in the 1965 season, when he gained 1,003 yards on 46 catches. His 21.8 yards per catch and his twelve touchdown receptions were both the highest in the NFL that season, and his speed immediately earned him the nickname "Bullet." The next year his yardage increased to 1,232, while his total catches rose to sixty-four and his touchdown catches to thirteen. Hayes had a decided effect on the game. Collectively, defensive coordinators were staying up late at night to devise ways to contain him; certainly, there was no sure way of stopping him. Because no one could stay with him in man-to-man coverage, teams came up with "zone" schemes to cope with his blazing speed. These strategies proved only moderately successful.

The speedy Hayes also was a dangerous punt returner. In 1967 he led the league in punt-return yardage (276 yards) and in 1968 in punt-return average (20.8 yards). Hayes continued to have seasons of thirty-five to fifty catches each, and his average yards per catch was always quite high, a league-leading 24.0 in 1971. Most other years it hovered around 20.0. Eventually, his numbers tailed off, and in 1975 he was traded to the San Francisco 49ers. He played only four games in that season—after which he retired from football—and caught just six passes, but his per-catch average was still 19.8 yards. He finished his career with 371 receptions for 7,414 yards and seventy-one touchdowns; his average of 20.0 yards per catch for his entire career is outstanding.

Unfortunately, Hayes's post-playing career was difficult. He had problems with alcohol, and in 1979 he was convicted on a questionable drug-trafficking charge, serving ten months in prison. He underwent rehabilitation and later spent much time involved in youth drug-prevention programs. In his final years he battled liver and kidney ailments as well as prostate cancer. Hayes died of complications from those diseases in a Jacksonville hospital and is buried in Edgewood Cemetery in Jacksonville.

Hayes's track and field credentials are undeniable, and his football credentials were such that, at the time of his death, many considered him deserving of induction into the Pro Football Hall of Fame. He was selected for the Cowboys' Ring of Honor and remains the only athlete with an Olympic gold medal and a Super Bowl ring. Perhaps the honor of which Hayes was most proud was one he earned in 1994, at age fifty-one—his B.A. in elementary education from FAMU. At the time, he told a reporter from *Jet,* "I take great pride in this accomplishment. I challenge all athletes to get their diploma."

★

Hayes, with Robert Pack, wrote an autobiography, *Run, Bullet, Run* (1990). His career is discussed further in Carlton Stowers, *Journey to Triumph* (1982), and Peter Golenbeck, *Cowboys Have Always Been My Heroes* (1997). Obituaries are in *USA Today* and the *New York Times* (both 20 Sept. 2002) and the *Times* of London (21 Sept. 2002).

JIM CAMPBELL

HEARN, Francis Dayle ("Chick") (*b.* 27 November 1916 in Buda, Illinois; *d.* 5 August 2002 in Northridge, California), sports broadcaster on radio and television, known principally as the longtime play-by-play announcer of basketball's Los Angeles Lakers.

Hearn, one of two sons of a railroad track worker, grew up mostly in Aurora, Illinois, where his family moved in 1925; it was then a small town at the outer edge of metropolitan Chicago. A star athlete at East Aurora High School, he had realistic hopes of winning a basketball scholarship to attend college. At the beginning of his senior year, however, his father was seriously injured in a car accident and could no longer work, circumstances that forced Hearn to quit the basketball team and find an after-school job. He graduated in 1936. Soon after, Hearn was involved in an automobile

Chick Hearn, 2002. REUTERS NEWMEDIA INC./CORBIS

collision as well, which resulted in broken ribs and required a full body cast. His recovery was complicated by an emergency appendectomy and pneumonia, which almost cost him his life.

Upon regaining his health, he found work as a salesman in the Aurora area and played basketball and refereed in the Amateur Athletic Union (AAU). Known as Fran Hearn until his twenty-second birthday, he gained his nickname as the result of a practical joke that was pulled on him by his AAU teammates. He was given a gift-wrapped shoebox that appeared to contain a new pair of sneakers. "It was an old maggoty chicken," Hearn recalled in an interview with *Sports Illustrated.* "I got it all over my hands and under my nails. It was awful." After that, he was called "Chicken" by members of the team, which eventually stuck to him as "Chick."

Hearn married his high-school sweetheart, Marjory Jeffers, on 13 August 1938. The couple had a son and a daughter, both of whom met with tragic deaths as adults. During World War II, Hearn joined the U.S. Army and served in the Pacific. While stationed in the Philippines, he volunteered to work at an Armed Forces Radio station, where he learned basic radio engineering skills and was given opportunities to announce on the air. Discharged in

1946, he returned to Aurora and took a job selling pharmaceuticals for a regional distributor. Hoping to find his way back into radio, he took an opportunity at WMRO, a 250-watt station, to broadcast high-school basketball games. This led to a full-time job as an on-air announcer and disc jockey, allowing him to quit his sales job and embark on a career in broadcasting.

Hearn combined a player's knowledge of basketball and football with a knack for colorful description into a distinctive professional style while covering high-school sports in north central Illinois for WMRO and later WBNU. A break came in 1950 when he was offered a job by WEEK in Peoria as a play-by-play basketball announcer for Bradley University. College sports were experiencing a tremendous boom during this period, and Bradley was playing a national schedule, including major tournaments around the country, giving Hearn his first opportunities to meet major broadcasting executives. In 1955 he received an offer from the Columbia Broadcasting System (CBS) to become the play-by-play announcer for University of Southern California (USC) football on CBS's West Coast regional radio network. He relocated to southern California and held that job for eight years.

Hearn already was well known in Los Angeles when the Minneapolis Lakers of the National Basketball Association (NBA) moved there after the 1959–1960 season. In a town whose sports scene was dominated by the perennially powerful college teams of the University of Southern California and the University of California, Los Angeles, professional basketball did not get much attention. The Lakers had no local radio or television contracts during their season in southern California. "The Lakers had Jerry West and Elgin Baylor on that team—but nobody cared," said the sportscaster Lynn Shackleford. When the team made the 1960–1961 NBA play-offs, the owner Robert Short called on Hearn to travel to St. Louis to call the action on a hastily arranged broadcast of their series with the Hawks.

Attendance improved significantly when the teams returned to Los Angeles to continue their series, and although the Lakers lost, Short was convinced that radio coverage was crucial to the team's success. Convinced of Hearn's ability to paint vivid pictures of the Lakers' stars in action, he hired him to do play-by-play on KFWB for the full schedule of games the following season. It was a turning point for what would soon become one of the most successful franchises in U.S. professional sports. Hearn would be the Lakers' only regular play-by-play announcer on local radio and television for the next forty-two years. This included a thirty-six-year period (1965–2001) during which he called every game the Lakers played, without exception. From 1972 to 1979, while the team was owned by Jack Kent Cooke, Hearn also served as an assistant general manager for the Lakers, helping to negotiate player contracts.

Hearn and Marty Glickman, who did local radio play-by-play for New York Knicks games, generally are credited with creating the rhetoric of basketball broadcasting. What probably endeared Hearn most to many Lakers fans was his invention and repetitive use of phrases to describe archetypal Laker moments. For example, he coined the term "slam dunk" specifically for Wilt Chamberlain, feeling that the existing terms, "dunk" and "stuff," did not adequately convey the overpowering way in which Chamberlain put the ball through the basket. He also is credited with inventing the terms "air ball," for a shot that misses both the backboard and the rim, and "charity stripe," for the free-throw line. On a team known through the years for its many stylish ball handlers, Hearn would exclaim, "The mustard's off the hot dog," when an overly fancy move backfired. The NBA star Bill Walton, who grew up listening to Hearn, said, "When Chick said, 'You can put this one in the refrigerator,' I knew that no matter how many minutes were on the clock, the game was over and I could go to sleep."

Although he was identified in the minds of most sports fans with Lakers broadcasts, Hearn was at the microphone for a variety of other sporting events, most notably the first Muhammad Ali–Joe Frazier heavyweight boxing championship fight in 1971 and the 1992 Olympic basketball tournament from Barcelona, Spain. From 1977 to 1991 he called selected University of Nevada, Las Vegas, basketball games on evenings when they did not conflict with Lakers games. Many Angelinos knew him as the host of *Bowling for Dollars,* a local television game show during the 1970s. Hearn also appeared in thirteen Hollywood feature films, usually playing himself or a broadcaster, including *The Gambler* (1974) and *White Men Can't Jump* (1992).

Hearn received many honors for his broadcasting work, including being inducted into the American Sportscasters Association Hall of Fame (1995) and the Naismith Memorial Basketball Hall of Fame (posthumously in 2003). His long streak of 3,338 consecutive games at the microphone for the Lakers was broken on 20 December 2001, when he was hospitalized for emergency heart valve surgery. During Hearn's recovery at his home in Encino, California, he slipped and fell, causing new injuries that resulted in his death at a hospital in nearby Northridge. His funeral in Brentwood was attended by dozens of Lakers players and officials from over the years, many of whom counted him as a personal friend. The former Lakers player Earvin ("Magic") Johnson eulogized Hearn, saying, "Some people grow bigger than their sport, bigger than their job."

★

Bruce Newman, "From High Above the Western Sideline," *Sports Illustrated* (9 Apr. 1984), is one of the few pieces written about Hearn that explores his personality in any depth. An obituary is in the *Los Angeles Times* (6 Aug. 2002); it is extensive and includes comments about Hearn from many athletes, sportscasters, and friends.

DAVID MARC

HEARST, Randolph Apperson (*b.* 2 December 1915 in New York City; *d.* 18 December 2000 in New York City), communication company executive credited with helping save the Hearst Corporation, the newspaper publishing empire founded by his father, William Randolph Hearst. He came to wider public notice in the 1970s when his daughter Patty was kidnapped by a group of political radicals.

Hearst enjoyed the advantages of great wealth in childhood, as he did throughout his life. He and a twin brother were the youngest of five sons of Millicent (Wilson) Hearst and William Randolph Hearst, the famous newspaper publisher whose life was the thinly veiled subject of Orson Welles's film *Citizen Kane* (1941). A capable student, he graduated from the private Lawrenceville School in New Jersey and entered Harvard University in 1933 but did not complete a degree. Instead, he moved to San Francisco, the flagship city of the Hearst newspaper chain, to begin learning the

Randolph A. Hearst (*right*), with his wife, Veronica, August 1999. AP/WIDE WORLD PHOTOS

family business as a reporter for the *Call-Bulletin*. Hearst married Catherine Campbell in 1938; the couple had five daughters.

In 1939 Hearst was appointed by his father as an assistant to the publisher of the *Atlanta Georgian*. Some have interpreted this first executive position as a model for his career. He served as a watchdog for the Hearst Corporation, helping oversee the sale of the newspaper, which took place the following year. Hearst joined the U.S. Army Air Forces during World War II, serving as a pilot and flight instructor in the Air Transport Command from 1942 to 1945 and achieving the rank of captain.

After the war he returned to the San Francisco Bay Area and filled a series of upper-echelon positions at the *Oakland Post-Enquirer* and the *Call-Bulletin,* which culminated in his being named the publisher of the latter in 1950. By the time of his father's death the following year, it had become clear to Hearst that his interests and talents lay in corporate management, which complemented the inclinations of his brother William Randolph Hearst, Jr., a journalist strongly committed to the editorial side of the business. Neither of them, however, would dominate the company. Under the terms of their father's will, a thirteen-member board of trustees was set up to control the Hearst Corporation, with only five of the seats going to family members.

While his older brother's journalistic orientation often led him to quarrels with the trustees over business matters, Hearst provided welcome family support for a corporate business plan that was resigned to the shrinking role of the newspaper in American life during the age of electronic media. During the 1950s and 1960s, this entailed the gradual sale or closing of the majority of the Hearst daily newspapers. Print operations were restructured to favor the company's demographically targeted magazines, including *Cosmopolitan*, *Good Housekeeping*, and *Redbook* for women and *Esquire, Motor Week,* and *Popular Mechanics* for men.

During this period the corporation executed a major push into electronic media, buying a collection of television and radio stations in broadcast markets from New England to Hawaii. Considerable investments also were made in noncommunications businesses, such as urban real estate and timberlands to produce paper for Hearst publications. As a result, the Hearst Corporation went from a net money-loser at the time of Hearst's father's death to one of the largest and most profitable privately held companies in the world, with estimated assets of $4.5 billion at the end of the twentieth century. Meanwhile, Hearst moved through a succession of management jobs within the corporation and its many properties. In 1965 he became the chairman of the Hearst Corporation's executive committee and was made a director of the board, positions he held until 1973, when he was made the chairman of the board.

In February 1974 Hearst's youngest child, Patricia, was kidnapped from her Berkeley, California, apartment the day before she was to be married to Steven Weed. The abductors, an obscure cell of self-styled political radicals who called themselves the Symbionese Liberation Army (SLA) and whose leader was known as Commander Cinqué, demanded that Hearst distribute food, free of charge, to California's poor as "ransom" for his daughter, while she was kept under lock and key in a dark closet.

Before the abduction, if Hearst's name appeared in the corporation's newspapers any place beyond the editorial masthead, it was likely to be on the social page. In 1974, however, the sedate corporate executive and socialite suddenly was thrust into the harsh glare of the media limelight. He appeared daily on television news programs, pleading for his daughter's release, responding to the SLA's demands by purchasing $2 million of food packages, and arranging for their distribution in poor neighborhoods in the San Francisco and Los Angeles areas. Commander Cinqué dismissed Hearst's action as a "mockery."

The affair took a bizarre turn some two months after the abduction when Patty Hearst appeared on a video surveillance tape, carrying a rifle and apparently aiding the group in the robbery of a branch of the Hibernia Bank in San Francisco. In a message delivered to the *San Francisco Examiner,* of which Hearst was then the president, she denounced her parents as "fascist pigs" and announced that she had taken on the nom de guerre "Tania." For almost a year, as police pursued the SLA, Patty Hearst was shuttled around the Bay Area to a succession of safe houses. When captured, she was tried and convicted of bank robbery along with other members of the group, despite the belief of her parents and many others that she had been terrorized or "brainwashed" into participating. Hearst visited her in prison daily. He was able to persuade President Jimmy Carter to have her sentence commuted after twenty-one months.

The prolonged strain of these events proved to be too much of a burden for Hearst's forty-four-year marriage; he and Campbell were divorced in 1982. Three months later, Hearst wed Maria Scruggs. This union ended in a 1986 divorce. Hearst's third marriage, to Veronica de Uribe, took place in 1987. Several colleagues claimed that Hearst was changed by the events surrounding his daughter's kidnapping. Raul Ramirez, a reporter whom Hearst had hired just after the kidnapping, told the *New York Times,* "I remember he pointed to his window and said, 'There is a city out there that I didn't know existed.'" In the years that followed, Hearst took a particular interest in public education. As a director of the William Randolph Hearst Foundation, he authorized millions of dollars in grants for early childhood education, curriculum research, and the purchase of computers for school districts that could not afford them.

Hearst retired in 1996, after serving as chairman of the Hearst Corporation for twenty-three years. He was the sole surviving son of the founder. The company's media holdings at the time included just twelve daily newspapers, as well as sixteen magazines and twenty-seven television stations, and his personal wealth was estimated by *Forbes* to be $1.8 billion. He died of a stroke just weeks after his eighty-fifth birthday and is buried in the Hearst family plot at Cypress Lawn Memorial Park in Colma, California. Hearst's lack of sentiment at the passing of the American newspaper from its position of crucial importance in society is interpreted by some as a bloodless acceptance of the rule of cash and by others as a realistic attitude that saved one of America's great fortunes from ruin. The contrast between the father, one of history's swashbuckling individualists, and the son, a consummate organization man, is a stark and perhaps cautionary tale.

★

There is no autobiography or biography of Hearst. See the autobiography by William Randolph Hearst, Jr., with Jack Casserly, *The Hearsts: Father and Son* (1991), for his brother's impressions. There are several books about the Patty Hearst kidnapping; Shana Alexander, *Anyone's Daughter* (1979), is perhaps the most thoughtful. Obituaries are in the *New York Times* and *San Francisco Chronicle* (both 19 Dec. 2000).

DAVID MARC

HELMS, Richard McGarrah (*b.* 30 March 1913 in Saint Davids, Pennsylvania; *d.* 22 October 2002 in Washington, D.C.), consummate intelligence officer who was the director of the U.S. Central Intelligence Agency from 1966 to 1973.

Helms was the second of four children of Herman and Marion (McGarrah) Helms, a homemaker. After his father, an executive for the Aluminum Company of America (Alcoa), returned from serving in World War I, the family moved from suburban Saint Davids to New York City and then to the affluent suburb of South Orange, New Jersey. After Helms finished his junior year at Carteret Academy, his parents took the family to Europe, convinced that immersion in foreign languages and culture was indispensable to their children's education. Helms was enrolled in Le Rosey preparatory school in Switzerland, where all courses were conducted in French. The following year his parents moved to Freiburg im Breisgau, Germany, where Helms learned German by attending the local gymnasium (a secondary school). Helms returned to the United States in 1931 to attend Williams College in Williamstown, Massachusetts. He served as the class president, editor of the college newspaper and yearbook, and president of the senior honor society.

Richard Helms, 1973. AP/WIDE WORLD PHOTOS

Helms found journalism exciting and upon graduation in 1935, magna cum laude with a B.A. in English and history, landed his first job as a reporter in London. Unable to obtain a work permit, however, he moved to Berlin, where, at age twenty-three, he interviewed the German leader Adolf Hitler as a correspondent with United Press International (UPI). In pursuit of his ambition to own an American newspaper, Helms left UPI in 1937 to work for the *Indianapolis Times* on the advertising staff. On 8 September 1939 he married Julia Bretzman Shields, a divorcée with two children. The couple had a son of their own. After divorcing Shields in 1968, Helms married Cynthia McKelvie later that year.

When the United States entered World War II, Helms resigned from the *Indianapolis Times* and in January 1942 volunteered for the U.S. Navy. In 1943 he was assigned to the Office of Strategic Services (OSS), the forerunner of the Central Intelligence Agency (CIA). Helms left the navy as a lieutenant commander in January 1946, aware that his ambition to own a newspaper had evaporated and that he was "hooked on intelligence." He stayed on during the transition from the OSS to the CIA in 1947, and by the early 1950s he was promoted to deputy head of covert operations.

In 1965 Helms became the deputy director of the CIA. The following year President Lyndon B. Johnson appointed him as CIA director, making Helms the first career spy to hold that post. Helms received favorable attention in the press and from Congress for his professionalism. In

his one public speech to newspaper editors, he said, "The nation must, to a degree, take it on faith that we, too, are honorable men, devoted to her service." His reputation rose as a result of his refusal to allow President Richard M. Nixon's administration to use the CIA to thwart the Federal Bureau of Investigation's (FBI) examination of the 1972 Watergate break-in, when burglars with White House connections were caught inside Democratic Party headquarters at the Watergate office complex. (The scandal led to Nixon's resignation.)

As Helms wrote in his memoirs, *A Look over My Shoulder* (2003), Nixon's chief of staff, H. R. Haldeman, wanted the CIA to put forward the notion that the FBI's Watergate investigation would uncover sensitive information regarding the CIA's Bay of Pigs operation that had failed to overthrow the Cuban leader Fidel Castro in 1961. Helms resisted, stating, "The Bay of Pigs hasn't got a damned thing to do with this, and what's more, there nothing about the Bay of Pigs that's not already in the public domain." Helms further refused to use unvouchered CIA funds to provide bail money for the jailed Watergate burglars. Helms's conclusion was that Nixon's order to Haldeman for the meeting was a presidential attempt to obstruct justice. Nixon, furious that Helms would not go along, forced his resignation from the CIA and appointed him as the U.S. ambassador to Iran in 1973.

Helms was hardly settled in Tehran, Iran, when congressional investigators looking into the Nixon administration and intelligence misdeeds required him to make more than a dozen trips back to Washington, D.C., to provide testimony. Helms noted in his memoirs that when Salvador Allende Gossens was elected as the president of Chile in 1970, Nixon ordered Helms to do whatever was necessary to see that Allende, a Marxist, never took office. Helms later testified under oath before the Senate Foreign Relations Committee that the CIA had never tried to overthrow Allende or to funnel money to his political foes. In 1973 Allende was killed in a right-wing military coup. Although Helms testified that the CIA had no dealings with the Chilean military, Senate investigators later discovered that the CIA had funneled more than $8 million to Allende's opponents through the International Telephone and Telegraph Corporation.

In 1976 Helms resigned his post in Tehran and returned to Washington to a plea of no contest to two misdemeanor counts of perjury that he had lied to a congressional committee, resulting in a fine of $2,000 and a two-year suspended sentence. Helms claimed he was put in an impossible position. He had sworn an oath to keep the CIA's secrets. He also swore before the Senate committees to tell the truth. He believed that his vow to keep secrets to protect the security of the nation was more important. He professed to wear his conviction as a "badge of honor."

In his memoirs, Helms emphasized the frustration of providing intelligence to Johnson and Nixon when it challenged their policy decisions, especially with regard to U.S. involvement in the Vietnam War. He also defended the CIA against the charge that it was a "rogue elephant," insisting that policy makers sometimes used the CIA to achieve covertly what they could not do overtly. In 1967 President Johnson had instructed Helms to find proof that foreign agents and funds were at the root of the racial and political unrest rampant in America. During Johnson's and Nixon's administrations, all such reporting of foreign influence was funneled directly through Helms. The operation, code-named CHAOS, became a symbol of all that critics objected to in government policy. The CIA, violating its charter at the behest of the president, ultimately failed to find any foreign connection; the discovery of their effort, made by a congressional committee, shocked many Americans.

Efforts were made to restore Helms's reputation in the 1980s when President Ronald W. Reagan asked him to serve on the Commission on Strategic Forces and awarded him the National Security Medal in a 1983 White House ceremony. Helms considered the award an "exoneration." Helms died in his sleep of multiple myeloma at age eighty-nine at his home in Washington, D.C., and was buried with full honors in Arlington National Cemetery in Virginia.

Helms was keenly aware that, ideally, the proper use of intelligence in policy making is to enlighten the process and help policy makers avoid mistakes by shunning prejudice and partisan judgments. As Helms said, it helps "keep the game honest." Unfortunately, policy makers too often look to the intelligence community to find support for their policies and suppress findings that do not. Helms testified before Congress, however, that despite all the criticisms of the structure and functioning of the intelligence community, if one were to create it from scratch, what would emerge would bear a striking resemblance to what we now have.

★

Helms's posthumously published autobiography, with William Hood, *A Look over My Shoulder: A Life in the Central Intelligence Agency* (2003), provides sharp observations about how power and information is used and misused in Washington, D.C. See also Thomas Powers, *The Man Who Kept the Secrets: Richard Helms and the CIA* (1979), for an earlier profile of Helms's career. Christopher Andrew includes extensive vignettes of Helms's relationships with presidents in his work *For the President's Eyes Only: Secret Intelligence and the American Presidency from Washington to Bush* (1995). Obituaries are in the *New York Times* and *Los Angeles Times* (both 24 Oct. 2002).

CHARLES L. COCHRAN

HENDERSON, Joseph A. ("Joe") (*b.* 24 June 1937 in Lima, Ohio; *d.* 30 June 2001 in San Francisco, California), African-American tenor saxophonist whose popularity with jazz audiences in the 1990s eclipsed his triumphs of the 1960s.

Henderson was born into a family of fifteen children. His music-loving parents introduced him to classical music and jazz at an early age, but not until he entered high school did he become interested in playing music, at which time he selected the tenor saxophone as his instrument. Henderson developed rapidly on the instrument, and he composed music for the school concert band as well as for local jazz and rhythm and blues groups.

At the behest of his older brother James, Henderson decided to go to college to study music. After one year at Kentucky State College, he transferred to Wayne State University in Detroit. He studied flute and string bass at the university and learned theory and advanced sax techniques from Larry Teal of the Teal School of Music. While in Detroit, Henderson worked with up-and-coming musicians such as Donald Byrd and Yusef Lateef. By 1959 he had his own group and was being contracted to write scores for local orchestras.

In 1960 Henderson joined the U.S. Army and continued his musical development in the service. While he was stationed at Fort Benning, Georgia, his four-piece ensemble won the post's talent contest and later competed in the All

Joe Henderson (foreground), with Carnell Jones, ca. October 1964. MOSAIC IMAGES/CORBIS

Army entertainment contest. After serving at Fort Belvoir, Virginia, Henderson toured with a musical group that entertained troops around the world. The group spent a year traversing the globe, and, while they were in Paris, Henderson had the opportunity to sit in with Kenny Clarke and Kenny Drew.

Discharged from the army in 1962, Henderson moved to New York City and quickly became involved with the city's jazz community. At a party he befriended the trumpeter Kenny Dorham, who engineered a meeting between Henderson and Dexter Gordon. The twenty-five-year-old saxophonist's sets with Gordon's group at Birdland immediately established him as a new force on the instrument.

Dorham also introduced Henderson to the staff at Blue Note Records, where the trumpeter was under contract. Henderson attracted national attention with his stunning debut solo on the title track of Dorham's *Una Mas* (1963), an album that also featured two other talented youngsters, Herbie Hancock and Tony Williams. Henderson also appeared on Dorham's final album as a bandleader, 1964's *Trompeta Tocatta*.

Henderson's work on Dorham's albums marked the beginning of a long and prolific career with Blue Note. He spent much of the 1960s recording for the label, both as a bandleader and a sideman, eventually appearing on thirty-four Blue Note releases. Henderson's rich tone, ability to effortlessly absorb the ideas of bandleaders, and remarkable capacity to perform at high levels on everything from bop dates to avant-garde sets made him one of the label's most in-demand players. Henderson appeared on classic albums such as Lee Morgan's *The Sidewinder* (1963), Andrew Hill's *Point of Departure* (1964), Horace Silver's *Song for My Father* (1964), and McCoy Tyner's *The Real McCoy* (1967).

Henderson's own Blue Note albums from the mid-1960s display a style that mixes hard bop with occasional experimental outside-inside flourishes. He typically worked in a quintet setting, with Dorham, Tyner, and the drummer Elvin Jones among his favorite sidemen. His two 1964 albums, *In 'n' Out* and *Inner Urge,* were particularly strong and well received.

After recording *Mode for Joe* in 1966, Henderson joined Horace Silver's Quintet. He stayed with Silver until 1968 and was an integral part of the pianist's second great band. He was part of a potent front line that included the trumpeter Woody Shaw. Henderson, who also composed many of the group's songs, was particularly effective on *Cape Verdean Blues* (1967).

Henderson spent the next several years moving through a variety of groups in search of musical challenges. In 1967 and 1968 he and the trumpet player Freddie Hubbard jointly led the Jazz Communicators. He played in Herbie Hancock's band in 1969, and in the following year appeared on two of Hubbard's best works, *Red Clay* and *Straight Life*. Henderson's adventurous spirit led him beyond the orbit of jazz, and he spent part of 1971 performing with the rock band Blood, Sweat, and Tears.

Although he frequently appeared as a sideman during this period, Henderson also recorded a diverse series of albums under his own name. He signed with Milestone in 1967 and recorded for that label until 1976. He earliest dates for the label featured a sound reminiscent of his work for Blue Note, but by the early 1970s he had pushed the boundaries of his music with electronics, overdubbing, unusual instrumentation, and early examples of world music. He maintained no consistent band and brought in well-known players—including Shaw, the drummer Jack DeJohnette, and the multi-instrumentalist Alice Coltrane—for "one-off" performances.

Henderson moved to San Francisco in 1972 and resided there for the rest of his life. While in California he became involved in music education, but he continued to tour and record for a variety of labels. He toiled in relative obscurity, even though he released some excellent albums, particularly *The State of the Tenor (Live at the Village Vanguard),* released in 1985. In the late 1980s Henderson made a calculated effort to regain some measure of his former stature by leading an otherwise all-female band.

Henderson's career, however, did not reignite until he signed with Verve in 1991. His album of Billy Strayhorn tunes, *Lush Life* (1991), sold 450,000 copies worldwide. In 1992 the readers of *Down Beat* magazine named Henderson both the top tenor saxophonist and the jazz musician of the year, and selected *Lush Life* as the album of the year.

Also in that year, Henderson won his first Grammy Award, for best instrumental jazz solo. He repeated these triumphs in 1993: not only did *Down Beat* readers again award him the same three honors as in 1992, including the selection of his 1993 release *So Near, So Far (Musings for Miles)* as the album of year, but Henderson won another Grammy, this time as best jazz instrumentalist.

His "third period" continued with a successful 1995 album, *Double Rainbow: The Music of Antonio Carlos Jobim,* which, like its predecessor, celebrates a legendary jazz musician. Henderson's playing career ended in 1998 after he suffered a stroke. He died of heart failure exacerbated by emphysema, and is buried in San Francisco. Six months after his death, Henderson was inducted into the *Down Beat* Hall of Fame.

Henderson spent almost forty years as one of the top tenor saxophonists in jazz. His innovative style blended hard bop and the avant garde with classical and world music references. During the 1990s, at an age when many musicians retire, he was one of the most critically respected and commercially successful performers in jazz. *Down Beat* noted his passing by remarking that Henderson's "luminous tone, telling improvisations and handful of evergreen originals placed him firmly in the modern jazz pantheon."

★

There is no biography of Henderson. Information related to him can be found in David Rosenthal, *Hard Bop: Jazz and Black Music* (1992), and Richard Cook, *Blue Note Records: The Biography* (2001). See also Paul de Barros, "Joe Henderson: Hall of Fame," *Down Beat* 68, no. 12 (Dec. 2001): 40–43. An obituary is in the *New York Times* (3 July 2001). Henderson can be seen performing in the film *Antonio Carlos Jobim: An All-Star Tribute* (1994).

SCOTT M. BEEKMAN

HERBLOCK. *See* Block, Herbert Lawrence.

HEWLETT, William Redington ("Bill") (*b.* 20 May 1913 in Ann Arbor, Michigan; *d.* 12 January 2001 in Palo Alto, California), pioneer in modern electronics and cofounder of the Hewlett-Packard Company who became one of the fifty richest men in the world, as well as one of its leading philanthropists.

Hewlett was the son of Dr. Albion Walter Hewlett, a professor of medicine at the University of Michigan, and Louise (Redington) Hewlett, a homemaker. In 1916 the family moved to California, where Hewlett's father taught at Stanford University Medical School. After his father's death in 1925, Hewlett's mother took the family on a year-long European trip. They returned to San Francisco just in time for Hewlett to attend Lowell High School, where he graduated in 1930 with mediocre grades. Hewlett suffered from dyslexia, a condition he struggled to overcome

throughout his life. It was only through his father's previous affiliation that he was able to enter Stanford University.

Introduced to engineering, Hewlett found a realm of knowledge unmarred by linguistic misprision; he flourished, obtaining his B.A. from Stanford in 1934, followed by an M.S. from the Massachusetts Institute of Technology in 1936, and a M.E. in electrical engineering from Stanford in 1939. His Stanford master's thesis, an investigation into the new field of negative feedback, would pave the way for Hewlett-Packard's first commercial product, a resistance-tuned audio oscillator that used feedback from an incandescent bulb to control the output.

Hewlett met David Packard early in his Stanford career, and they became close friends; they shared a love of the outdoors that continued throughout their lives. Packard, an ex-football player, was a better skier, but Hewlett, a competitive wrestler, was a better climber. On 23 August 1937 the two held what Packard later remembered as their first "official" business meeting, drawing up papers for a proposed "Engineering Service Company." A year later, when Hewlett moved into an apartment at 367 Addison Avenue in Palo Alto, he and Packard rented the garage out back and, with $538 in assets, began one of the great partnerships in U.S. business history. Hewlett won a coin toss that put his name first.

The Hewlett-Packard (HP) audio oscillator, which Hewlett first demonstrated at a regional Institute of Radio Engineers conference in November 1938, could be used in the calibration of motion picture sound equipment. The company's first large sale was to Walt Disney Studios, which bought at least eight for use during the filming of *Fantasia* (1940). Total sales by the fledgling company in 1939 were only $5,369. However, the next year they introduced seven new products, including a vacuum-tube voltmeter, a wave analyzer, and a frequency counter. As Hewlett remembered in later years, "We did anything to bring in a nickel." With the help of a contract to provide the International Telephone and Telegraph Company (ITT) with fixed-frequency oscillators, sales soared to $34,000.

Hewlett, a member of the U.S. Army Reserve, was called to active duty in 1941; he served with the Signal Corps until the end of 1945. After a year spent adjusting to the peacetime economy, Hewlett-Packard incorporated in 1947, with Hewlett as vice president. At that point sales had grown to $679,000. By the time he was named executive vice president in 1957, sales had reached $30 million. He became president in 1964 (sales were $165 million), and chief executive in 1969 (sales had reached $1 million a day). By the time Hewlett retired from all but emeritus positions in 1987, Hewlett-Packard's annual sales had reached the $10 billion mark.

Despite its vast size, however, HP remained true to its roots in what Packard and Hewlett called "The HP Way."

William R. Hewlett (*right*), with H. Ross Perot, April 1988. BETTMANN/CORBIS

Hewlett's offices were laid out in an open plan, with workspaces separated only by low partitions. Hewlett once used bolt cutters to cut a padlock on a supply room, leaving a note reading, "Please don't chain this again—Bill." In 1967 a twelve-year-old called to ask if the company could spare some used electronic parts. Hewlett himself took the call, sent the young man the parts, and promised him a summer job; the caller was Steve Jobs, future cofounder of Apple Computer. Engineers knew that their projects were sure to develop "the Hewlett effect"—a hidden flaw that would come to light only after the boss had poked and prodded, challenging his employees not just to do their jobs but to do their best.

Hewlett's most famous challenge occurred in the early 1970s, after an extremely productive five-year stretch. Hewlett-Packard had entered the computer market in 1966 with the HP 2116A, and followed that with a successful $5,000 desktop calculator, the HP 9100, in 1968. Hewlett praised his engineers, then asked, "Can you make a calculator that will fit in my shirt pocket, and can you make it affordable?" The result was the HP 35, the first pocket scientific calculator, introduced in 1972 at only $395.

Hewlett never forgot the opportunity that Stanford had given him, or the inspiration of his professor and mentor, Frederick E. Terman, who was the first to suggest that he and Packard might make a good business team. Hewlett served as a trustee of the university from 1963 to 1974. In 1994 Hewlett and Packard each gave $12.5 million to establish a fellowship in Terman's honor, and later that year they jointly gave $77.4 million to complete Stanford's state-of-the-art science and engineering complex. All told, the two men donated some $300 million to Stanford. Hewlett established the William and Flora Hewlett Foundation in 1966 and later endowed the Public Policy Institute of California with an initial grant of $70 million.

Hewlett married his childhood sweetheart, Flora Lamson, on 10 August 1939; they had five children. She died in 1977, and a year later Hewlett married Rosemary Bradford, assuming fatherhood of five stepchildren. As he aged, Hewlett reluctantly gave up his commitment to the active outdoor life, exchanging mountain climbing for photography and skiing for the study of Sierra wildflowers. He received many honors in later life, including the National Medal of Science in 1985, the Founders' Award of the National Academy of Engineering in 1993, and an honorary lifetime membership in the Instrument Society of America.

Hewlett died in his sleep at home from the lingering effects of a stroke.

★

David Packard, *The HP Way: How Bill Hewlett and I Built Our Company* (1995), recounts the history and development of Hewlett-Packard. An obituary is in the *New York Times* (13 Jan. 2001).

HARTLEY S. SPATT

HIBBLER, Albert George ("Al") (*b.* 16 August 1915 in Tyro, Mississippi; *d.* 24 April 2001 in Chicago, Illinois), blind singer best known for the 1955 song "Unchained Melody" and for his earlier vocal work with Duke Ellington (1943–1951).

Born blind, Hibbler was the third of five children of farmers Hubert Hibbler, Sr., and Lucy (Propst) Hibbler. He added the middle name George as a child because he liked the way it sounded. Hibbler's parents sold their farm in the early 1920s and moved from Mississippi to Dell, Arkansas, to become sharecroppers. Hibbler picked cotton and did not attend school until 1929, when he enrolled at the Arkansas School for the Blind in Little Rock, where he sang soprano in the school choir until his voice deepened into a baritone. Hibbler's early vocal influences were Pha Terrell (of Andy Kirk's band Twelve Clouds of Joy), Arthur "The Street Singer" Tracy, and the popular radio crooners Bing Crosby and Russ Columbo.

In approximately 1933, when Hibbler was still a student at the Arkansas School for the Blind, a local promoter began to arrange auditions for Hibbler with bands visiting Little Rock, including Fletcher Henderson and Fats Waller. With financial support from a Little Rock department-store owner, Hibbler left school before graduating and studied voice for two terms at the New England Conservatory in Boston from 1935 to 1936. After returning to Little Rock, he began singing the blues in roadhouses, and his first professional job was with Monroe Fingers and His Yellow Jackets. Hibbler's local notoriety led to him hosting his own weekly radio show on KGHI-AM from 1936 to 1938. He then moved to Memphis, Tennessee, where he sang with Dub Jenkins and His Playmates before going to San

Al Hibbler. Mr. Jack Vartoogian

Antonio, Texas, where he performed with Boots and His Buddies and then formed his own outfit. Near the end of 1941, Hibbler met the pianist Jay McShann and sat in with his band, impressing both McShann and his young sax player, Charlie Parker. Hibbler joined McShann's band in 1942 for one year; their first recording together was "Get Me on Your Mind" for Decca (1943).

After leaving McShann in early 1943, Hibbler briefly went solo in New York City, where he crossed paths with Duke Ellington for the third time (he had auditioned for Ellington earlier in both Little Rock and Memphis). Hibbler sat in with Ellington's band at the Hurricane Club, and this time was hired. During his eight years in the band, which was the longest tenure of any of Ellington's male vocalists, Hibbler was featured on such notable songs as "Do Nothin' Till You Hear From Me" (written especially for him), "Don't Get Around Much Anymore," and "I'm Just a Lucky So and So." While with Ellington, Hibbler made several solo recordings with Mercer Ellington (including the 1948 hit "Trees"), as well as recordings with various Ellington sidemen, such as Billy Kyle, Harry Carney, and Billy Strayhorn, and other jazz greats, such as Billy Taylor.

Hibbler's idiosyncratic "scoop and swoop" vocal style was praised by some and panned by others. His voice reached from deep baritone to high tenor, and although he used very precise diction, he often included vibrato, grunts, growls, and a vague cockney accent. Ellington described Hibbler's voice as "tonal pantomime" and clearly appreciated him, paying Hibbler $250 per week and referring to him in a 1973 memoir as "our major asset." Singer Mel Tormé praised Hibbler's vocals on "I Like the Sunrise" (1947; from Ellington's "Liberian Suite") as "one of the gentlest, most moving vocals ever put on wax." Some critics, however, thought Hibbler's singing was exhibitionist—the jazz historian Leonard Feather described Hibbler's vocals as "grotesque tonal distortions," and in 1990 the writer Will Friedwald likened Hibbler to how Billy Eckstine "might sound if he were drunk." Nevertheless, Hibbler was named a "New Star" jazz male vocalist by *Esquire* (1947) and was twice voted best male band vocalist by *Down Beat* (1948 and 1949).

Hoping to earn more money as a solo act, Hibbler left Ellington's band in September 1951 and recorded several albums, including *Al Hibbler Sings Love Songs* (Verve, 1952) and *Al Hibbler Sings Duke Ellington* (Norgran, 1954), as well as collaborating with Count Basie on *Basie/Jazz* (Clef, 1953). He was not an immediate solo success, however, and had to return to singing in small clubs for little money. In 1955 Hibbler's new manager signed him with Decca, which recorded him with choirs and strings. "Unchained Melody" (which reached number three on the pop chart) and its follow-up single, "He" (which reached number four), were both million-sellers, enabling Hibbler to purchase a house in suburban Teaneck, New Jersey, where he lived for nearly forty years.

Hibbler made numerous television appearances, including the *Ed Sullivan Show* and Alan Freed's *Big Beat,* and was one of the first artists signed by Frank Sinatra's Reprise record label, releasing the album *Monday Every Day* (1961), recorded with the Gerald Wilson Orchestra. Hibbler preferred to sing songs with intelligent lyrics that could be understood by listeners—he thought rock and roll to be "a passing fancy"—while the musical tastes of young people began moving toward rhythm and blues and then rock and roll. The single "After the Lights Go Down Low" (1956), which reached number ten on the pop chart, was his last major hit.

At the time Hibbler's commercial success was beginning to wane, he began to take an active role in the fight for civil rights. Responding to an invitation from Martin Luther King, Jr., Hibbler led a picket line in Birmingham, Alabama, in 1963, carrying a placard with the inscription, "Equal Opportunity and Human Dignity," and was briefly arrested along with fellow protestors. Police officials immediately released him because of his blindness, however, which Hibbler complained was "segregation at its highest level." Two days later, he held an outdoor concert as a movement fund-raiser. In an earlier bizarre incident in New Jersey, Hibbler was arrested in 1960 for being drunk and disorderly after accepting a ride home from a Harlem bar with a man who (unbeknownst to him) turned out to be a burglar. A disoriented Hibbler had been abandoned and was found alone by police at the third gas station the burglar had broken into on the ride home.

Although chronic drinking and smoking had coarsened Hibbler's voice, he continued to record and give concerts sporadically, including albums with the blind multi-instrumentalist Rahsaan Roland Kirk (*A Meeting of the Times,* Atlantic, 1972) and the pianist Hank Jones (1984), and he performed at the Newport Jazz Festival in 1973 and 1976. Hibbler sang "Nobody Knows the Trouble I've Seen" and "When the Saints Go Marching In" at Louis Armstrong's 1971 funeral. One of his last appearances was at New York City's Lincoln Center (1999) as part of the centennial celebration of Ellington's birth. Hibbler received a Pioneer Award from the Rhythm and Blues Foundation (1991) and a Lifetime Achievement Award from the Arkansas Jazz Heritage Foundation (1995).

Hibbler married Jeanette McAden on 23 January 1949; they separated in approximately 1966 but never divorced. The couple had no children, and she died in 1982. Hibbler lived with Cetire Streater from the 1970s until her death in a fire that destroyed his house in 1994, after which he went to live with his sister in Chicago. He died at Holy Cross Hospital in Chicago and was buried in Lincoln Cemetery in Worth, Illinois.

Hibbler never used a white cane and only wore dark glasses when performing on stage. A gregarious man, Hibbler wanted no special treatment, for he did not consider his lack of sight a handicap. As he frequently pointed out, "Anything can be a handicap if you let it." Hibbler's singing transcended many different types of music (blues, jazz, and popular standards), but he worked with some of the greatest jazz musicians of the twentieth century. His success and acceptance by the public helped to pave the way for the blind entertainers who followed him.

★

Hibbler discussed his life and career in two autobiographical articles, "What Love Can Do," *Tan* (Aug. 1956), and "A Blind Man Can Get Rich," *Sepia* (Dec. 1958). Early profiles include "Al Hibbler: Blind Bard Bounces Back," *Hue* (Feb. 1956); "New Pop Crop on Top," *Time* (3 Sept. 1956); and "Al Hibbler Says: A Blind Man Can 'See' Beautiful Women," *Ebony* (Aug. 1957). Valuable information also appears in Barry Kernfeld, ed., *The New Grove Dictionary of Jazz* (2002). An overview of Hibbler's career, written by Joseph F. Laredo, is in the booklet accompanying the 1998 Varese compact disc *Unchained Melody: The Best of Al Hibbler.* Felix Grant conducted a far-reaching audio interview with Hibbler (23 Apr. 1968) for *The Album Sound* radio program on WMAL-AM, which is in the Felix E. Grant Jazz Archives at the University of the District of Columbia in Washington, D.C. Hibbler's involvement in the Birmingham civil rights protests is briefly discussed in Diane McWhorter, *Carry Me Home: Birmingham, Alabama, the Climactic Battle of the Civil Rights Revolution* (2001), which also contains a photograph of Hibbler leading a picket line. Brief footage of Hibbler's Birmingham arrest can be seen in the Public Broadcasting System documentary *Eyes on the Prize,* episode four, "No Easy Walk" (1986). Obituaries are in the *Chicago Sun-Times* (26 Apr. 2001), *New York Times* (27 Apr. 2001), and *Los Angeles Times* (28 Apr. 2001).

JOHN A. DROBNICKI

HILL, George Roy (*b.* 20 December 1921 in Minneapolis, Minnesota; *d.* 27 December 2002 in New York City), film director best known for the box-office hits *Butch Cassidy and the Sundance Kid* (1969) and the *Sting* (1973), both of which won Oscars.

Hill, one of three sons of George Roy Hill, Sr., the secretary of a Minneapolis auto club, and Helen Frances Owens (Murphy) Hill, a homemaker, was born into the newspaper business on his mother's side of the family. Hill had several passions creatively channeled into his future work as a film director. Aeronautics represented adventure to Hill, who earned his pilot's license by age seventeen and was attracted to the barnstorming feats of stunt pilots. He majored in music at Yale University in New Haven, Connecticut,

George Roy Hill (*left*) with Robert Redford on the set of *The Great Waldo Pepper*, 1975. THE KOBAL COLLECTION

where he became the president of the dramatic society and was a member of the glee club.

After graduating from Yale with a B.A. in 1942, Hill entered the U.S. Navy and then flew combat air support for the U.S. Marines during World War II. Upon his discharge, Hill spent a few months in Texas working as a cub reporter at a family newspaper. He then made a life-changing trip to Ireland, his ancestral home, where he discovered the country's rich literary culture. His experiences in Ireland included performing in Lyric Theater productions staged at the legendary Abbey Theater. He also earned a B.Litt. from Trinity College, Dublin, in 1949. Hill returned to the United States, where he performed with Cyril Cussack's repertory and Margaret Webster's Shakespearean Company. On 7 April 1951 he married Louisa Horton. They had two sons and two daughters before their marriage ended in divorce. During the Korean War, Hill served a two-year stint as a pilot for the marines and attained the rank of major.?

In 1953 Hill wrote the teleplays *Keep Our Honor Bright* and *My Brother's Keeper,* concerning the night landing of an airplane. From 1954 to 1959 he established a successful career as a television writer, assistant producer, and director. In 1956 Hill directed the docudrama *A Night to Remember,* a large-scale production about the sinking of the *Titanic* that aired on Kraft Television Theater and won the Sylvania and Christopher awards as well as two Emmys for

directing and writing. Hill directed *Judgment at Nuremberg* (1957) and *A Child of Our Time* (1958) for Playhouse 90. He became known as a director who consistently received strong performances, including in the Broadway stage productions of *Look Homeward, Angel* (1957), *The Gang's All Here* (1960), *Greenwillow* (1960), *Period of Adjustment* (1960), and *Moon on a Rainbow Shawl* (1965).

Hill began his career as a feature film director with screen adaptations of two plays, Tennessee Williams's *Period of Adjustment* (1962) and Lillian Hellman's *Toys in the Attic* (1963). *The World of Henry Orient* (1964), starring Peter Sellers as a boy from Brooklyn, New York City, who lives the fantasies of being a concert pianist, further transformed Hill into a cinematic artist. The duality of the boy's world is expressed by a playful use of camera and editing technique. The film became the official U.S. entry in the 1964 Cannes Film Festival. This attention led to Hill's work on *Hawaii* (1966), a $10 million epic based on the James Michener novel. Hill attempted to fashion the film into a metaphor for the U.S. military involvement in Vietnam by emphasizing the theme of a clash of cultures, but he quit the project before shooting because of a dispute with the producers, the Mirisch brothers. He was not replaced, because the largely Polynesian cast refused to work with anyone else, but he was never able to gain artistic control over the film. Hill tried to transform *Thoroughly Modern Millie* (1967) from a traditional Hollywood musical into a sophisticated farce, but he was unable to get his vision totally on the screen in the face of the producer Ross Hunter's powerful will.

Butch Cassidy and the Sundance Kid (1969) was Hill's breakthrough. The revisionist western starred Paul Newman and Robert Redford and defined the buddy film genre. The memorable bicycle sequence, shot and edited to the song "Raindrops Keep Falling on My Head," was a crowd-pleaser, as was the chemistry between the lead actors. Hill balanced light-hearted comedy with western myth and an anti-Hollywood conclusion that did not offer a happy ending. Hill next directed a screen adaptation of Kurt Vonnegut's time-tripping World War II novel, *Slaughterhouse-Five* (1969). He was able to translate the book's complex narrative skillfully, capturing the author's unstuck-in-time continuum, which propelled the character Billy Pilgrim through the past and present of his life, the American experience, and beyond. *Slaughterhouse-Five* (1972) was poorly received upon release, but Hill's next film, *The Sting* (1973), a period con-man film, again paired Redford and Newman and was a blockbuster that garnered seven Oscars, including one for best picture and another for Hill as the movie's director.

With the *Great Waldo Pepper* (1975), Hill directed a film about his obsession with aviation, after years of reluctance to engage in such a personal project. Redford starred in this tribute to the barnstorming pilots of post–World War I. Again Hill examined the theme of the falsity of myth and heroes, as he had in *Butch Cassidy and the Sundance Kid.* *Slapshot* (1977) was a profane and raucous look at bush league hockey, in which Hill exploited the sport subject to examine male relationships, violence, and the grassroots American lifestyle. He continued to explore a wide range of stories. *A Little Romance* (1979) featured a teenaged Diane Lane and Thelonious Bernard in a story of young love in Europe. The roguish charm of Sir Laurence Olivier as Julius, the force who brought the two together, and the music of Antonio Vivaldi allowed Hill to focus on the innocence of young lovers rather than on overt sexuality.

The loyal readership of John Irving's novel the *World According to Garp* (1978) worked against acceptance of the 1982 film, but Hill again succeeded in finding a cinematic equivalent for a literary narrative. *The Little Drummer Girl* (1984) was based on the political thriller by John le Carré. Hill was attracted to this story of an individual, played by Diane Keaton, caught up in a labyrinth of agents, terrorists, and antiterrorists in the Middle East, humanizing the polemics of the subject. *Funny Farm* (1988) starred Chevy Chase as a sports journalist who moves to a farm in Vermont to write the great American novel and satirized the peculiarities of country life. This was to be Hill's final film. He became ill with Parkinson's disease, which kept him confined to his New York City apartment and away from his work as a film director; the illness took his life at age eighty-one.

Hill will be best remembered for his blockbusters, but he was a sophisticated film director with literary, theatrical, and musical sensibilities. He was a Hollywood filmmaker independent in spirit who, as a professional, managed to incorporate his many passions into entertaining motion pictures that educated audiences to the sublime cultural and social issues he discovered during his adventurous and civilized life.

★

Edward Shores, *George Roy Hill* (1983), is a critical study of Hill's films through *A Little Romance* (1979). Andrew Horton, *The Films of George Roy Hill* (1984), covers Hill's life and career through the shooting of *The Little Drummer Girl* (1984). An obituary is in the *New York Times* (28 Dec. 2002).

VINCENT LOBRUTTO

HILLEGASS, Clifton Keith (*b.* 18 April 1918 in Rising City, Nebraska; *d.* 5 May 2001 in Lincoln, Nebraska), businessman who created *Cliffs Notes,* a series of literary study guides used widely by high school and college students.

Hillegass was the son of Pearl Clinton Hillegass, a rural mail carrier, and his wife, Rosena (Dechert) Hillegass. He grew up in Rising City, a small town of 450. Even as a boy, Hillegass was an avid reader and a hard worker. Forced into inactivity for two months after an operation when he was seven years old, he passed the time by reading everything he could, a habit that continued after his recuperation. He read virtually every book in the local libraries— "some with regret," he later said—before his graduation from Rising City's high school in 1934. An industrious youngster, Hillegass earned money delivering papers, selling magazines, and milking cows. When the local bank closed, fourteen-year-old Hillegass lost $714, a sizable sum in the Great Depression. He earned the money back within two years.

In 1934, at age sixteen, Hillegass entered Midland College, a Lutheran school in Fremont, Nebraska. Despite working full-time at a Woolworth store and at other jobs, he graduated in three years. The store manager tried to persuade him to remain with the company, saying that he might soon have a store of his own. Hillegass declined the offer, instead accepting a graduate assistantship to study physics and geology at the University of Nebraska. He completed the course work for an M.S. but left school before writing a thesis. He began working as a sales clerk for Long's Bookstore (later Nebraska Book Company) in Lincoln. Hillegass married Catherine Galbraith on Christmas Day 1939. They had three children.

Hillegass served as a meteorologist in the U.S. Army Air Forces during World War II, rising to the rank of captain. After the war, he rejoined Nebraska Book Company, where he was manager of the wholesale division from 1946 to 1964. He crisscrossed the country, buying and selling college textbooks. His travels brought him into personal contact with hundreds of bookstore managers, 90 percent of whom he knew on a first-name basis. One of his most important friendships, at least from a business standpoint, was with Jack Cole, a Toronto bookstore owner who had developed *Cole's Notes,* a series of study guides published in Canada. Cole suggested that there might be a market for similar books in the United States, and he offered Hillegass his outlines for sixteen of Shakespeare's plays. Hillegass used a $4,000 loan and Cole's books to create *Cliff's Notes* (the apostrophe was later dropped) in August 1958.

Working from the basement of his Lincoln home, he wrote, and his wife typed, a thousand letters to college bookstore managers asking them to stock the *Notes.* The managers' acquaintance with Hillegass induced many of them to put aside their skepticism and give his guides a try. Eighteen thousand *Notes* sold in 1958. Sales reached 129,000 in 1961 and doubled during each of the next four years. Because of this success, Hillegass quit his job at Nebraska Book in 1964. Hillegass's years of bookstore sales experience served him well. He understood that both managers and customers wanted prompt, accurate shipments. He accepted orders by phone and sent them out on the day he received them, and he promised to buy back any unsold copies. With their distinctive yellow and black covers, *Cliffs Notes* soon became a familiar sight in bookstores and dorm rooms.

Hillegass hired college professors and high school teachers to revise the *Cole's Notes* he had published and to prepare guides for other classic works. In addition to plot outlines, the *Notes* came to include authors' biographies, lists of characters, critical commentaries, review questions, and suggested essay topics. After his divorce from his first wife, Hillegass married Mary D. Patterson on 17 April 1968. He adopted her daughter.

In a note to readers of his guides, Hillegass urged that they be used "responsibly," as starting points for further study and thought. "A thorough appreciation of literature allows no short cuts," he insisted. His *Notes* were to be aids for the understanding of literature, not a substitute for reading the works themselves. Critics were not so sure. Many teachers forbade their students from using *Cliffs Notes,* and a few colleges banned their use as well. A survey in the 1990s revealed that one-third of "high achieving" American high school students had used *Cliffs Notes* or similar guides instead of reading the assigned text.

By the time Hillegass entered semiretirement in 1984, annual sales of *Cliffs Notes* had reached five million copies. Seventy percent of the guides were bought by high school students. Although there were more than two hundred *Cliffs Notes* in print, the thirty-five most popular study guides accounted for almost half of the company's sales. Annual sales of the top titles, including *The Scarlet Letter, Huckleberry Finn, Hamlet, Macbeth,* and *A Tale of Two Cities,* exceeded 100,000 copies each. By the late 1990s *Cliffs Notes* had more than three hundred titles in print, with total sales of 100 million copies.

In 1999 Hillegass sold his company to IDG Books Worldwide, publishers of the popular *For Dummies* series of how-to books, for $14 million. In the same year, he and his wife donated $500,000 to create an endowed chair in English and to support literary research at the University of Nebraska. A life-long Nebraskan, Hillegass died at his home at age eighty-three from complications of a stroke suffered the month before.

★

For Hillegass's own account of his life and business, consult Clifton K. Hillegass, *Cliffs Notes, Inc.: Quality of Product . . . Service . . . Policy* (1985), originally presented as an address to a meeting of the Newcomen Society of the United States. See also

Norman Atkins, "Fast Food for Thought," *Rolling Stone* (26 Mar. 1987), and Meeks Fleming, "Shakespeare, Dickens, and Hillegass," *Forbes* (30 Oct. 1989). An obituary is in the *New York Times* (7 May 2001).

FRED NIELSEN

HINTON, Milton John ("Milt") (*b.* 23 June 1910 in Vicksburg, Mississippi; *d.* 19 December 2000 in New York City), jazz bassist and photographer.

Hinton was only three months old when his young, unmarried parents, Milton Dixon Hinton, born in Liberia, and Hilda Gertrude Robinson, separated. His mother and her extended family of thirteen brothers and sisters, all childless, raised him. In 1919 he and the family moved to the South Side of Chicago, where his mother became a department store clerk and piano teacher. She bought him a violin in 1923, which he embraced, admiring the virtuosity of a neighborhood friend, Quinn Wilson (later the powerhouse bassist of the Earl Hines Orchestra). The next

Milt Hinton, June 1990. AP/WIDE WORLD PHOTOS

year he entered Wendell Phillips High School, where he learned harmony and musical theory from Major N. Clark Smith and played the violin in the school orchestra. He eventually became first violin (succeeded by Ray Nance, later a trumpeter and violinist for the Duke Ellington Orchestra). He graduated from high school in 1929.

Before the end of his sophomore year Hinton had decided to join the school's Reserve Officer Training Corps marching band, requiring him to learn a brass instrument. He settled on the bass horn or tuba (as had his friend Wilson), and also played the sarrusophone (a bass instrument of the oboe family). His formal training deepened his interest in musical theory and arranging rather than soloing, a view shared by several schoolmates, notably Scoops Carry (later the lead alto saxophonist for the Hines band). Hinton also played tuba in the band assembled by Major Smith for the *Chicago Defender,* the city's leading African-American newspaper. Its drummers included Lionel Hampton and Nat (later "King") Cole, future jazz greats as vibraphonist and pianist and singer, respectively.

Chicago was the center of jazz music during the 1920s, and Hinton was drawn to the rhythmic bass violin—the string bass—in 1927, inspired partly by Ellington's bassist Wellman Braud and Steve Brown of the Jean Goldkette Orchestra. He mastered the instrument between formal instruction and early professional contacts in the Chicago area. He studied it at Crane Junior College (1929–1930), then briefly at Northwestern University (1933), and finally with Paul Steinke (1933–1936) and Dmitri Shmuklosky (1936–1945). On the violin, which he continued to study until 1936, he played melody, an ability he transferred to the bass by using his bow on the bass strings. In the late 1920s the Chicago bassist Bill Johnson taught him to "slap" the strings against the neck of the instrument. Unlike others, who used their arms to slap, Hinton employed his wrists to achieve multiple "slaps"—up to four per beat instead of the usual one. From Steve Brown's cross-rhythms he developed fast "slap-style solos," even alternating his hands.

Hinton, along with the contemporary bassist Walter Page, initiated a revolution in jazz bass playing. He played with small bands around Chicago, mostly playing the tuba; on this fading jazz instrument he made his first recordings with the Tiny Parham band in late 1930, after which he dropped the tuba completely. His next major work was with his idol on jazz violin, Eddie South, who taught him much, improving his bowing technique. With South, Hinton made his first recordings on the bass (and a rare vocal) in 1933. He joined the quartet of the drummer Zutty Singleton at Chicago's Three Deuces club in 1935, which included a nightly number with the pianist Art Tatum. He credited South and Singleton as "the two musicians who influenced me most." Hinton was briefly married to Oby

Allen during the late 1930s; they had no children and divorced.

In the spring of 1936, the touring bandleader Cab Calloway, passing through Chicago, hired Hinton after only one hearing at the Three Deuces. His driving bass immediately transformed the sound of the orchestra, whose members dubbed him "Fump"—according to Calloway, "the fump-fump of his heavy bass gave the band a depth it hadn't had before." His nickname later became "the Judge." A small man, Hinton could barely be seen "bent over his bass, virtually hugging it, sweating, squeezing that last ounce of acoustic energy out of his instrument." He invariably wore a smile, playing with immense enthusiasm. He made his first of dozens of records with Calloway's band in May 1936.

The Cab Calloway Orchestra opened at New York's Downtown Cotton Club that year and began adding leading jazz soloists, including the tenor saxophonist Ben Webster, whom Hinton idolized. Because playing for the club's floorshows was not difficult, after hours the newer men like Hinton challenged each other with different musical ideas. No one was more innovative than the trumpet player Dizzy Gillespie, who joined in mid-1939, in time to play a solo on the band's first recording, "Pluckin' the Bass," which showcases Hinton. Another Hinton showpiece is "Ebony Silhouette" (1941), which features the bow instead of the slap. Calloway also included Hinton in the Cab Jivers, a quartet within the band.

During the intermissions between Cotton Club shows, Hinton maneuvered his bass up the stairs to the roof with Gillespie, where he endeavored to absorb Gillespie's experimental and unorthodox chord changes (a step toward the "bebop" phenomenon). It was Hinton who grabbed the knife away from Gillespie after Gillespie had jabbed Calloway in the buttocks during a famous confrontation involving a thrown spitball. Gillespie was fired, but he and Hinton performed together on several of the many recording sessions of pickup combos led by Lionel Hampton, and by the pianist Teddy Wilson, backing the songstress Billie Holiday. In about 1939 Hinton married Mona Clayton, a member of his mother's church choir; they had one daughter. They lived briefly in Harlem, across the street from Minton's Playhouse, the jazz club where Gillespie invited Hinton to sit in as bop was evolving there. Owing to his availability, if nothing else, Hinton became the virtual house bass player.

Although the Cab Calloway Orchestra disbanded in 1948, Calloway formed a sextet, the Cabaliers, that included Hinton until it, too, broke up in 1951. Hinton played gigs with different groups around New York, including the Count Basie Orchestra in 1953, followed by a tour of Japan with the jazz trumpeter Louis Armstrong. His old acquaintance the comedian Jackie Gleason then hired him to play on a recording session of mood music. Hinton's excellent ability to read all kinds of music, showcased in this session, led in 1954 to his joining the band on the Robert Q. Lewis daily television show—thereby breaking the racial color line of that medium.

For the next three decades Hinton freelanced on records, tours, festivals, and club dates with jazz-oriented musicians, popular singers, and rhythm-and-blues groups. He played in Eddie Condon's band at the first Newport Jazz Festival in 1954 and was a part of the all-stars who played for Duke Ellington's seventieth birthday at the White House in 1969. In the early 1970s the talk-show host Dick Cavett gave Hinton television prominence as part of Bobby Rosengarden's band. Hinton began a long association with the clarinetist Benny Goodman on the first of several record albums together in 1955, as well as television appearances, culminating in a White House concert for President Ronald W. Reagan in 1981. He recorded his first of many albums under his own name in 1955; his last, *Laughing at Life*, was released in 1995.

In the mid-1930s Hinton had taken up photography, and in 1935 he started making visual recordings of his fellow musicians as they lived and worked. In time, the trombonist and fellow photographer Keg Johnson of the Calloway band taught him to process his film even while he was on the road. Hinton preferred black-and-white images but used color in the 8-mm movie camera he purchased later. The result is an archive of more than 60,000 negatives, the best of which have been exhibited in galleries and featured in two books Hinton cowrote, *Bass Line* (1988) and *OverTime* (1991). Beginning in the 1980s Hinton taught jazz workshops at Skidmore College in Saratoga Springs, New York, and at Baruch College and Hunter College in New York City. His playing declined only in the late 1990s. Hinton died at a Queens, New York, hospital after an extended illness.

★

Hinton's autobiography, with David G. Berger, is *Bass Line: The Stories and Photos of Milt Hinton* (1988), and has a select discography. A shorter essay introduces *OverTime: The Jazz Photographs of Milt Hinton* (1991), by Hinton, Berger, and Holly Maxson. Largely autobiographical segments are quoted in Nat Shapiro and Nat Hentoff, eds., *Hear Me Talkin' to Ya: The Story of Jazz Told by the Men Who Made It* (1955); Cab Calloway and Bryant Rollins, *Of Minnie the Moocher and Me* (1976); Stanley Dance, *The World of Earl Hines* (1985); and Dizzy Gillespie with Al Fraser, *To Be or Not to Bop: Memoirs* (1985). Gunther Shuller, *The Swing Era: The Development of Jazz, 1930–1945* (1989), provides an analysis of Hinton's style. Obituaries are in the *New York Times* (21 Dec. 2000) and *Mississippi Rag* (Feb. 2001).

CLARK G. REYNOLDS

HOOKER, John Lee (*b.* 22 August 1917 near Clarksdale, Mississippi; *d.* 21 June 2001 in Los Altos, California), blues singer, guitarist, and songwriter who recorded over 100 albums in a career that spanned six decades.

One of eleven children born to William Hooker, a sharecropper and part-time Baptist preacher, and Minnie (Ramsey) Hooker, a homemaker, Hooker was raised in the Mississippi Delta, the birthplace of the most primal blues music. A shy youth who stuttered, he began singing in his father's church but became enamored of the blues when his sister Alice dated Tony Hollins, an itinerant bluesman. Hollins gave Hooker his first guitar, to the disapproval of his father, who considered blues the devil's music. Hooker's parents separated, and in 1931 his mother married Will Moore, a local bluesman who played with the legendary Charlie Patton. Moore gave Hooker a new guitar and schooled him in his own distinctive brand of rhythmic one-chord blues that would become Hooker's own. "Whatever I'm doing is his style," Hooker later acknowledged.

Uninterested in school (he remained a lifelong illiterate) or working in the fields, Hooker ran away to Memphis, Tennessee, at age fourteen to become a musician. Staying with an aunt, he worked as an usher in the New Daisy Theater on Beale Street before moving in 1935 to Cincin-

John Lee Hooker, ca. 1992. NEAL PRESTON/CORBIS

nati, where he worked as a janitor at a cesspool-draining company, and played at house parties and juke joints. In 1943 Hooker settled in Detroit, where he found janitorial work at several automotive plants, including those of Ford and Dodge, while performing in his spare time. He soon married Alma Hopes, and although they had a daughter, the marriage failed after a few months. Following a second short-lived marriage, to Sarah Jones, he married Maude Mathis in 1946. They had eight children before separating in 1969. In the late 1970s Hooker was also briefly married to Millie Strom.

By the late 1940s Johnny Lee, as Hooker called himself at that time, was playing regularly at Detroit nightspots such as Henry's Swing Club and the Apex Bar. He was "discovered" by Elmer Barbee, a local record dealer, who brought him to the attention of Bernie Besman, head of Sensation Records. Besman agreed to record Hooker, and on 3 November 1948 "Boogie Chillen" was released. A boogie-driven tour of rough-and-tumble Hastings Street, black Detroit's main drag, "Boogie Chillen" was an overnight sensation, climbing to number one on *Billboard*'s rhythm and blues chart. "The thing caught fire," Hooker proudly recalled. "It was ringin' all across the country." The song exemplified Hooker's signature style: largely improvised, unrhymed lyrics; a rough-hewn voice at once full of menace and allure; and rhythmic, one-chord riffing on electric guitar driven by incessant foot-stomping and punctuated by blistering staccato runs. It was, according to the blues writer Pete Welding, "tough, ferocious, magnificent music and immediately established Hooker's mastery of the blues."

Despite a string of hits including "Hobo Blues" and "Crawlin' King Snake" (1949) and "I'm in the Mood for Love" (1952), Hooker had difficulty collecting royalties, and he began recording for various labels under an array of aliases to avoid contractual problems. He appeared as Texas Slim on the King label, John Lee Booker on Chance, Birmingham Sam and His Magic Guitar on Savoy, The Boogie Man on Acorn, and Little Pork Chops on Danceland. Whatever the name, however, the Hooker sound was unmistakable. Hooker left Sensation in 1952, and after short stints with Modern, Chess, and Specialty Records, signed in 1955 with Chicago-based Vee Jay, where he remained until 1964.

At Vee Jay, Hooker toned down the fierce intensity of his earlier work, aiming for the lighter, more polished style of rhythmic blues then popular. He began recording with a small backup band—second guitar, bass, and drums— with varying degrees of success. Although his Vee Jay sides usually sold well, and he produced classics such as "Dimples" (1956) and "Boom Boom" (1962), Hooker's career might have flagged had it not been for the folk music and blues revivals of the early 1960s. While on leave from Vee Jay, he cut an album of traditional blues, alone with an acoustic guitar, for Riverside. *The Country Blues of John Lee Hooker* (1959) garnered rave reviews, and Hooker, after an auspicious debut at the 1960 Newport Folk Festival, became a fixture on the folk circuit, playing coffee houses, colleges, and festivals. In 1962 he toured Europe for the first time as part of the American Folk Blues Festival. Hooker proved wildly popular in Europe, especially in England, where he was idolized by fledgling rockers such as the Rolling Stones, the Animals, and the Yardbirds.

Hooker moved to Oakland, California, in 1970, following his breakup with his wife Maude. He continued recording for various labels into the 1970s, although the work came to seem run-of-the-mill and desultory, and Hooker himself seemed adrift, recycling much of his earlier material but without the searing brilliance of the original. Notable exceptions include *Live at Café Au Go-Go* (1967), on which he is backed by Muddy Waters and his band, and *Hooker 'n' Heat* (1971), his rocking collaboration with Canned Heat. Hooker eventually abandoned recording to work the blues circuit, a string of small clubs that still showcased blues performers, with his Coast to Coast Blues Band.

In 1980 Hooker made his movie debut in *The Blues Brothers* (1980) as the funky musician "Street Slim." He also sang on the soundtrack of *The Color Purple* in 1986. Returning to the studio, he hit gold in 1989 with *The Healer,* a collaborative effort that included such artists as Carlos Santana, George Thorogood, and Bonnie Raitt. A commercial and critical success, the album rose into the U.S. Top 100 pop chart and won Hooker his first Grammy Award for his duet with Raitt on "I'm in the Mood" in 1990. The following year, he was inducted into the Rock and Roll Hall of Fame.

Invariably resplendent in a pin-striped suit, raffish Homburg hat, and wraparound sunglasses, Hooker was now a respected elder statesman of the blues. Subsequent albums, including *Mr. Lucky* (1991), and the Grammy winners *Chill Out* (1995) and *Don't Look Back* (1997)—all collaborative efforts—also sold well. In 1997 he opened John Lee Hooker's Boom Boom Room, a blues venue in San Francisco, where he could often be seen performing. In 2000 he received the Grammy Award for lifetime achievement, solidifying his reputation as godfather of the blues. Hooker died peacefully in his sleep of natural causes. On 28 June 2001 he was honored with a memorial service at the Inter-Stake Center Auditorium at Oakland's Mormon Temple. He is buried in the Chapel of the Chimes Cemetery in Oakland.

Hooker is widely regarded as the last of the great Delta bluesmen. He brought the undiluted blues of his native Mississippi to the harsh electric glare of the big city in postwar America and produced some of the most magnificent, brutally emotional blues of the period. Although he showed an ability to adapt to changing musical tastes throughout his career, Hooker never abandoned the dark, Delta-laced beat that was the bedrock of his style. His slow blues and house-rocking boogies helped popularize rhythm and blues and proved an inspiration to a generation of blues musicians and rock and rollers such as the Rolling Stones, Led Zeppelin, Robert Cray, Van Morrison, and countless others. "When I die," Hooker was fond of saying, "They'll bury the blues with me. But the blues will never die."

★

The definitive biography of Hooker is Charles Shaar Murray, *Boogie Man: The Adventures of John Lee Hooker in the American Twentieth Century* (2000). An extremely well-written and exhaustive account of Hooker's life, personal and professional, *Boogie Man* includes a selective discography of the best of Hooker's music available on compact disc. For additional biographical material, see "Living Blues Interview: John Lee Hooker," *Living Blues* (autumn 1979), and "John Lee Hooker, Continuing Saga of the Boogie King," *Down Beat* (Feb. 1990). A memorial tribute is in *Rolling Stone* (2 Aug. 2001). An obituary is in the *New York Times* (22 June 2001).

MICHAEL MCLEAN

HORSTMANN, Dorothy Millicent (*b.* 2 July 1911 in Spokane, Washington; *d.* 11 January 2001 in New Haven, Connecticut), research scientist, epidemiologist, virologist, and pediatrician credited with being the first scientist to show that the poliovirus enters the nervous system through the bloodstream.

Horstmann, the daughter of Henry Horstmann and Anna (Humold) Horstmann, earned her B.A. at the University of California, Berkeley, in 1936 and her M.D. at the University of California, San Francisco, Medical School in 1940. She completed her internship at the San Francisco City and County Hospital and her residency at Vanderbilt University in Nashville, Tennessee. Her long tenure with Yale University began in 1942 as a Commonwealth fellow and researcher in John Rodman Paul's preventive medicine group, after which she became an internal medicine specialist. In 1943 she became part of Paul's poliomyelitis study group and helped fight a polio epidemic in New Haven, Connecticut. She was appointed instructor in 1944, assistant professor in 1945, and associate professor in 1948. In 1961 she became the first woman to hold a full professorship at the Yale School of Medicine. Then, in 1969, she became the first Yale woman to receive an endowed chair in epidemiology and pediatrics when she was named John Rodman Paul Professor.

Horstmann is most widely recognized for her contribution to the development of the polio vaccine. In the 1950s polio struck fear into the heart of the American nation. The dreaded disease seemed to rise in epidemic proportions primarily in summer and predominantly in children. People affected by polio became paralyzed and were unable to breathe. Scores died; survivors usually were left seriously crippled. It was classed as a "luxury" disease, one that ravaged communities that had virtually been purged of illnesses typically attributed to poverty.

The first scientific breakthrough toward eradicating the disease came in the early 1900s, when Karl Landsteiner transmitted the disease from the spinal cord of a nine-year-old boy, who had died after a brief illness, into two Old World primates, thereby determining that the disease was caused by a virus. Researchers firmly believed that the virus somehow penetrated the nervous system without first entering the bloodstream, a conclusion drawn from the fact that polio victims showed no sign of the virus in their blood.

In 1952 Horstmann made a monumental discovery. She had begun investigating viremia, the blood-borne transmission of viruses, after research by William McDowell Hammon of the University of Pittsburgh had demonstrated that injections of gamma globulin—a serum extracted from plasma and rich in antibodies—temporarily prevented the disease. Horstmann believed that Hammon's findings indicated that the disease was indeed carried through the bloodstream. In her laboratory at Yale and despite popular scientific dogma, Horstmann pursued her theory. She administered small amounts of the virus to primates and determined through blood tests that the virus was present in the animals' blood before any symptoms developed. Symptoms did develop, however—in particular, paralysis—suggesting that the virus was carried to the brain by the bloodstream. Horstmann and her team discovered that antibodies totally removed the virus from the bloodstream by the time paralysis occurred.

Horstmann's research, and similar studies by David Bodian at the Johns Hopkins University, showed that the disease was spread orally, causing an intestinal infection that was followed by viremia. Although Horstmann's findings were disregarded initially by many researchers, she had uncovered the true etiology of the disease. If the virus could be killed in the blood before it attacked the nervous system, thousands of lives would be spared worldwide.

Hammon showed that it took relatively few antibodies to kill the virus, and in 1953 Jonas Salk—also at the University of Pittsburgh—developed a vaccine made of small amounts of killed polio viruses. These dead viruses stimulated polio antibodies, but would it be effective enough to prevent the disease in humans? In the summer of 1954, 440,000 children in forty-four states across the nation were vaccinated, and another 210,000 were given placebo shots. Blood tests were performed in dozens of laboratories; study results proved Salk's vaccine to be 80–90 percent effective.

Soon thereafter, Albert Sabin of Children's Hospital in

Cincinnati developed an oral vaccine from weakened live polioviruses. A large field test of this vaccine was conducted in Russia during the late 1950s in what has been called a "remarkable example of cold war diplomacy" between the Soviet Union and the United States. Horstmann was intricately involved in this scientific and diplomatic mission, which included Poland and Czechoslovakia. By 1960 millions of Russian, Polish, and Czechoslovakian children had received the vaccine, and Horstmann was responsible for evaluating and validating its safety. Only after that validation was Sabin's vaccine approved for licensing in the United States. By the year 2000 the vaccine had virtually eradicated polio worldwide. The crippler had been conquered, in large part owing to a determined woman who ignored popular opinion and followed her scientific intuition.

After her appointment as professor, Horstmann focused her research on diagnostic virology and rubella, establishing the effectiveness of a rubella vaccine. Her contributions to science and public health earned her four honorary doctorate degrees, the James D. Bruce Award of the American College of Physicians in 1975, the Thorvold Masden Award from Denmark in 1977, and the Maxwell Finland Award of the Infectious Diseases Society of America in 1978. She served as that society's president from 1974 to 1975, was elected to the National Academy of Sciences, and was a member of the American College of Physicians, the Royal Society of Medicine, and the American Society of Clinical Investigations.

Besides papers published in other journals, her manuscripts "The Poliomyelitis Story: A Scientific Hegira" and "The Sabin Live Poliovirus Vaccine Trials in the USSR, 1959" were published in the *Yale Journal of Biology and Medicine* in 1985 and 1991, respectively. In 1982 Yale named her senior research scientist and emeritus professor, titles she held until her death of Alzheimer's disease at the age of eighty-nine. Never married, she was described by colleagues as a "very elegant woman in addition to being a perfectly disciplined scientist," and a "remarkable woman . . . very inspiring, very dedicated to her work . . . a trailblazing person."

★

Horstmann's papers from 1946 to 1995 are housed in the Yale University Library, Manuscripts and Archives, New Haven, Connecticut. They include correspondence, research data, notes, writings, memorabilia, and photographs documenting her career. An early perspective on polio and those researching it, including Horstmann, appeared in *Newsweek* (1955). The article, entitled "The Polio Vaccine," is reprinted in Lewis L. Gould, Edward L. Ayers, Jean R. Soderlund, and David M. Oshinsky, *American Passages* (1999). Obituaries are in the *New York Times* (21 Jan. 2001) and *Washington Post* (22 Jan. 2001).

MARIE L. THOMPSON

HORWICH, Frances Rappaport ("Miss Frances") (*b.* 16 July 1908 in Ottawa, Ohio; *d.* 22 July 2001 in Scottsdale, Arizona), innovative educator, broadcasting pioneer, television personality, and author who wrote and hosted *Ding Dong School,* the first educational television program for preschool children.

The youngest of six children, Horwich was the daughter of Samuel Rappaport and Rosa (Gratz) Rappaport. After receiving her elementary and high school education in Ottawa, Ohio, she attended the University of Chicago, where she earned a bachelor's degree in early childhood education in 1929. Horwich then went to New York City to complete an M.A. at Columbia University's Teachers' College in 1933. She returned to Chicago to work as a nursery school supervisor with the Works Progress Administration (WPA) from 1933 to 1935. Horwich earned a Ph.D. in child development, parent education, and teacher education from Northwestern University in 1942, with a dissertation entitled "Parent Education in the Teachers' College, and Practices in the Nursery School, Kindergarten, and Primary Grade." Meanwhile, she married Harvey L. Horwich, an attorney, on 11 June 1931.

Horwich began her teaching career in 1929 as a first-grade teacher in suburban Evanston, Illinois. She was also

Frances R. Horwich, 1955. BETTMANN/CORBIS

a kindergarten director in Winnetka, Illinois, where she resided until 1938. That year she became dean of education at Pestalozzi Froebel Teachers College in Chicago, and she then served as supervisor of student teachers at Chicago Teachers College from 1940 to 1943. Moving to New York in 1943, she served as director of Hessian Hills School in Croton-on-Hudson until 1945. She spent the period 1945–1946 at the University of North Carolina, Chapel Hill, as a visiting professor of education, and then moved to Roosevelt College in Chicago, where she served as associate professor from 1946 to 1947 and professor of education and department chair from 1947 to 1952.

With nearly twenty-five years of experience, Horwich was recommended by Judith Waller, central division educational director at the National Broadcasting Company (NBC), to become television's first schoolteacher with a program for preschool children. The show, *Ding Dong School,* first aired on 3 October 1952 on WNBQ, the Chicago-area NBC affiliate. Producer Reinald Werrenrath, Jr.'s three-year-old daughter coined the program's title, inspired by the opening shot of Horwich ringing an old-fashioned school bell. *Ding Dong School* featured an active, rather than passive, learning style with developmentally appropriate activities, including a variety of art projects, simple crafts, songs, and short films. A unique feature included Horwich posing direct questions to the children, reinforcing her belief that speaking clearly and directly to children stimulated their language skills. Horwich's emphasis was on demonstration as she introduced children to exercises involving clay, scissors, paste, and finger paint, while also including movement segments to keep the children active. The last five minutes of the program were devoted to the parents, mainly mothers, requesting special materials for the next day's activities and summarizing the content of the current program.

Within seven weeks, the network syndicated the program, showing it in more than thirty-six cities, with a viewing audience of more than three million. *Ding Dong School* won the George Foster Peabody Award in 1953, *Look* magazine's TV Award for best children's program during 1953–1954, and four Emmy nominations between 1954 and 1959. For her part, Horwich was named 1953's Woman of the Year in Educational Programming by the Associated Press. She also received an honorary doctorate from Bowling Green State University in 1954, the *Parents' Magazine* Medal Award in 1955, and the Silver Trophy Award from the National Audience Board in 1956.

Ding Dong School's popularity also generated the production of supplies that were, per Horwich's request, educational and affordable. Her control over the show was so great that when she was informed by the network that a manufacturer of BB guns was interested in being a sponsor,

she refused to approve the advertisement. In addition, she rejected a request to advertise flavored children's aspirin because the product had been linked to the deaths of young children who mistook the tablets for candy.

In 1959, when informed by NBC that the program was to be cancelled, Horwich, who owned rights to *Ding Dong School,* moved it first to New York and then Los Angeles, taping 130 episodes. The program continued in syndication until 1967.

Horwich produced other televised children's programs in the 1960s, including *Time for Children with Miss Frances* and *Time for Parents with Miss Frances* during 1966 and 1967. Hosting the television special *Seeing the World from Three Feet High* in the 1970s gave Horwich the airtime needed to be vested in the pension plan of the American Federation of Television and Radio Artists (AFTRA).

A strong advocate of innovative programs for young children, Horwich explained the difference between her shows and others in a 1966 interview. "Too many programs on television rob children of their own ideas, without giving them a chance to create and think for themselves." She felt there were three fundamental principles for working with young children: "We must have faith in children; we can't work with children alone, but must work with parents at the same time; and what happens to children up to the age of six is terribly important."

During her career she authored many books for children, including *Miss Frances' Ding Dong School Book* (1953), *Stories and Poems to Enjoy* (1962), and a series of twenty-six other *Ding Dong School* books. Horwich also wrote and narrated *Ding Dong School* records produced by RCA-Victor (1953–1956) and Golden Records (1960). She authored many books for adults, including *Portfolio on More and Better Schools for Children Under Six* (1949), *Have Fun with Your Children* (1954), and *The Magic of Bringing Up Your Child* (1959).

Professionally active throughout her career, Horwich served as secretary-treasurer for the National Association for Nursery Education in 1943 and as president of the National Association for the Education of Young Children from 1947 to 1951. She served as director of children's activities for Curtis Publishing Company from 1962 to 1963 and as an educational consultant for Field Enterprises Educational Corporation beginning in 1965.

After retiring in 1964, Horwich remained an educational and political consultant as well as a summer lecturer at Northwestern University, the University of North Carolina, and the University of California. In 1973 she and her husband moved to Scottsdale, Arizona, where he died in 1974. The couple was childless. Horwich died of congestive heart failure at age ninety-three at Scottsdale Healthcare Center in Scottsdale. Shortly before her death, Horwich was honored with the Silver Circle Award from the National Academy of Television Arts and Sciences.

Standing five-feet, five-inches tall with dark brown hair and brown eyes, Horwich was frequently described as matronly yet possessing "a mysterious alchemy of personality." Her demeanor was one of gentleness and kindness. She had many interests, including cooking, baking, ceramics, and knitting. Later in life, Horwich suffered from severe arthritis.

Horwich's work with preschool children centered on appealing to their interests and "opening new doors and windows of enlightenment," while enabling children to draw on their innate sense of resourcefulness. Leaving her legacy for children's programming, *Ding Dong School* gave way to successors such as *Sesame Street, Romper Room,* and *Mr. Rogers' Neighborhood,* fostering a unique niche in the history of children's television.

★

Articles about Horwich and *Ding Dong School* include "Teacher on TV," *Time* (27 Oct. 1952); "A 'Ding Dong' Rings TV Bell: Teacher Gets Close to the Kids," *Life* (16 Mar. 1953); and Robert Lewis Shayon, "Miss Frances from Chicago," *Saturday Review* (18 Apr. 1953). Obituaries are in the *Chicago Tribune* (25 July 2001), *New York Times* (26 July 2001), and *Washington Post* (27 July 2001).

CONNIE THORSEN

HOVHANESS, Alan (*b.* 8 March 1911 in Somerville, Massachusetts; *d.* 21 June 2000 in Seattle, Washington), prolific composer whose music embraced Eastern musical and spiritual dimensions, especially those of Indian, Armenian, and Japanese origins.

Born Alan Vaness Chakmakjian in a Boston suburb, Hovhaness was the only child of Haroutiun Chakmakjian, an Armenian who taught chemistry at Tufts University, and Madeline Scott, a homemaker of Scottish descent. While Hovhaness's mother helped him to acclimate to American life, his father privately nurtured the boy's curiosity about Armenian language and culture. After his mother's death, Alan dropped his given surname and adopted Hovhaness, an Armenian variation on Johannes.

Hovhaness learned to read music and began composing in elementary school. There is disagreement as to how much his parents encouraged his musical pursuits. He told one interviewer that they sent him to a piano teacher who promoted his composition but informed another that they were terrified that he would actually pursue a musical career. Hovhaness attended public schools in Arlington, Massachusetts, graduating from high school there in 1929. After two years at Tufts University, he transferred to the New

Alan Hovhaness, 1955. GORDON PARKS/TIME LIFE PICTURES/GETTY IMAGES

England Conservatory of Music, where he studied with Frederick Converse starting in 1932. Through the years, Hovhaness earned no college-level academic degrees aside from honorary doctorates.

The multitalented musician supported himself in the 1930s by playing piano for choruses, a chamber orchestra, and various instrumentalists. During the summer of 1942 he was a student at the Berkshire Music Center at Tanglewood in Lenox, Massachusetts. He had planned to study with Bohuslav Martinů, but the Czech composer was indisposed, and sessions were led by the American composer Aaron Copland, who did not welcome Hovhaness's compositions warmly. Returning home to Boston, Hovhaness met Herman DiGiovanno, a Greek mystic painter who encouraged him to study Armenian music.

Hovhaness acknowledged many artistic influences. As a child, he took an avid interest in George Frideric Handel, spending allowance money on the baroque composer's complete works. He also admired the twentieth-century Finnish composer Jean Sibelius, especially his Symphony no. 4. Gradually, Hovhaness became fascinated with Eastern musical idioms. In 1936 he met the North Indian musician Vishnudas Shirali and the traveling Armenian folksinger Yenovk Der Hagopian, whose music he transcribed into Western notation. Hovhaness also explored ancient and modern compositions from the Armenian Orthodox church. He scrutinized works by the priest Komitas Vartabed and was an organist at an Armenian church in the 1940s.

Prone to relentless creative activity, such as jotting down themes in restaurants or wherever he happened to be, Hovhaness eventually amassed at least five hundred compositions—an extraordinary achievement, begging comparison with such workhorses as Johann Sebastian Bach or Darius Milhaud. Hovhaness's opus list would be even longer had he not destroyed many early pieces in the 1940s as he reshaped his compositional style.

At a time when other art-music composers were writing complex works that were not always accessible to general audiences, Hovhaness focused on communicating and making music "beautiful." He claimed not to think about "programs" or themes but took inspiration from and named pieces after nature, especially mountains. In his music, listeners can sense a confluence of Eastern and Western influences. From the cultures of India, Armenia, Japan, and Korea, he drew on spirituality, modes, rhythms, and harmony not based on three-note chords, integrating them into a Western structure rich in counterpoint. Hovhaness described his music as "giant melodies in simple and complex modes around movable and stationary tonal centers." Rather than write music identifiable with a particular century or country, he hoped to share the best of what he heard within himself.

A concert of Hovhaness's compositions was organized in Boston in 1944 to benefit an Armenian charity. That event led to what has been dubbed his "Armenian period," marked by output that includes *Lousadzak*, or *The Coming of Light*, and Armenian Rhapsody no. 1. With an Armenian student group in 1945, he organized another concert of his music in New York. There he attracted attention from the avant-garde composers John Cage and Lou Harrison, the latter also being a critic for the *New York Herald Tribune*.

Hovhaness lived briefly in New York and then moved back to Boston, where he taught at the Boston Conservatory of Music from 1948 to 1951. At that time his music began to come into its own, and apart from teaching summer school at the Eastman School of Music in Rochester, New York, in the mid- to late 1950s he managed to survive mainly by composing. He was commissioned to write a ballet, *Ardent Song*, for the choreographer Martha Graham, who took it on tour. He received three Guggenheim Fellowships in the 1950s. A 1959 Fulbright Fellowship funded a tour of the Orient; after which he returned on a 1962 Rockefeller grant to study ancient Japanese and Korean court music and to give the premiere performance of his Symphony no. 16 for strings and Korean instruments.

Hovhaness's best-known orchestral work may be his Symphony no. 2, subtitled *Mysterious Mountain*, which the Houston Symphony premiered in 1955. Other symphonic pieces include *Meditation on Orpheus* (1957); *And God Created Great Whales* (1970), which incorporated the recorded voices of humpback whales; and the *Mount St. Helens* Symphony no. 50 (1982). The 1957 *Magnificat* ranks among his better-known choral pieces.

Many major orchestras continued to play Hovhaness's music throughout the rest of his life. During the 1967–1968 season he was composer in residence with the Seattle Symphony Orchestra, and he chose to move to that city in the early 1970s. In 1976 his violin concerto, *Ode to Freedom,* was introduced by the National Symphony Orchestra in Washington, D.C., on the occasion of the U.S. bicentennial. Hovhaness's Symphony no. 65 premiered at Carnegie Hall in New York City in 1991, for an eightieth birthday tribute. Hovhaness died at age eighty-nine at Swedish Medical Center in Seattle, after suffering from a longtime stomach ailment.

A tall man with large hands, a long face, and a scruffy beard in later years, Hovhaness was described variously as agreeable, aloof, and artistically demanding. Some sources say that he married six times. He was survived by his last wife, the soprano Hinako Fujihara, and a daughter. At different times he took responsibility for recording and marketing his music. Recording companies were administered by two of his wives—Elizabeth Whittington, who founded Poseidon Records in the 1960s, and Fujihara, director of Fujihara Music. Eventually, more mainstream labels took up Hovhaness's cause and began releasing recordings by him.

★

Hovhaness has not been profiled in a comprehensive, full-length book form, but several volumes on contemporary music contain chapters on him. Among them are "Alan Hovhaness" in Richard Kostelanetz, *On Innovative Music(ian)s* (1989), and "Mysterious Mountain," in William Duckworth, *20/20: 20 New Sounds of the 20th Century* (1999). Peter Westbrook's informative late-life interview, "Alan Hovhaness, Angelic Cycles," is in *Down Beat* (Mar. 1982). Notable career developments from 1949 appear in the fifth edition of Nicolas Slonimsky, *Music Since 1900* (1994). Obituaries are in the *New York Times* and *Los Angeles Times* (both 23 June 2000).

WHITNEY SMITH

HOWE, Harold, II ("Doc") (*b.* 17 August 1918 in Hartford, Connecticut; *d.* 29 November 2002 in Hanover, New Hampshire), U.S. commissioner of education during the Lyndon Baines Johnson administration and eminent educator who presided over sweeping changes in American schools and championed the disadvantaged.

Howe was born in Hartford, Connecticut, but spent his formative years in Hampton, Virginia. His father, Arthur Howe, was a Presbyterian minister and the president of the Hampton Institute (now Hampton University), a historically black college. His mother, Margaret (Armstrong) Howe, was the daughter of Samuel Chapman Armstrong, who had founded the Hampton Institute in 1868 as a trade school for freed slaves. Margaret Howe was a leading citizen of Hampton and managed a summer colony in New Hampshire. While in Hampton, Howe developed an easy relationship with young blacks along with a lifelong concern for equal education opportunities.

Howe earned a B.A. from Yale University in 1940 and took a position at the Barrow School in Lebanon, New York. He married Priscilla ("Sibby") Lamb on 4 September of that year; they had three children. Howe joined the navy in 1942, serving as a minesweeper captain in both the Atlantic and the Pacific theaters during World War II. After the war Howe attended Columbia University, completing an M.A. in history in 1947. That same year he joined the faculty of Phillips Academy in Andover, Massachusetts. In 1950 he moved into the public school system in Andover as principal of the junior and senior high schools. He moved on to be principal at Walnut Hills High School in Cincinnati from 1953 to 1957 and Newton High School in Newton, Massachusetts, from 1957 to 1960. While working at these two schools, Howe did postgraduate work in education at the University of Cincinnati and at Harvard University.

His career took a noticeable turn in 1960, when he became the superintendent of schools in suburban Scarsdale, New York, one of America's most affluent communities. There he met and befriended John Gardner, who later was appointed secretary of the Department of Health, Education, and Welfare. In 1964 Howe took over as director of the Learning Institute in North Carolina for Governor Terry Sanford, who had founded it. In 1966, on the recommendation of Gardner, President Lyndon B. Johnson appointed Howe as the U.S. commissioner of education. In this position he was charged with distributing federal funding to public schools under the Elementary and Secondary Education Act of 1965. This act provided financial support to nearly twenty-seven thousand school districts. "I had the job of setting up a system for doing something nobody had ever done before," recalled Howe in 2000. He also directed the federal effort to reduce school segregation. Under the 1964 Civil Rights Act, federal funding was provided to school districts that did not discriminate on the basis of race. Howe resigned as commissioner in 1968 when President Johnson declined to run for reelection.

Howe next worked for the Ford Foundation, first as an adviser in India and then as vice president for education. At Ford, Howe quickly earmarked $100 million to support the nation's historically black colleges. His projects fol-

Harold Howe II, January 1985. BETTMANN/CORBIS

lowed his belief that Ford should focus on teachers and teaching and ways to develop and sustain educational leaders. He also supported projects in school finance reform.

Howe left the Ford Foundation in 1981 to become a senior lecturer at Harvard University's Graduate School of Education. There he played an influential role in developing and establishing programs to certify teachers, principals, and superintendents. In 1982 he was a major influence in establishing the Principals' Center at Harvard, which is dedicated to the professional and personal development of school leaders. In 2000 a professorship in Howe's name was established at Harvard University.

Always a staunch advocate for improving educational opportunities for children from poor families, Howe in 1986 organized and chaired the Commission on Work, Family, and Citizenship, which studied the experiences of non-college-bound youths. The commission, with support from the W. T. Grant Foundation, published the report "The Forgotten Half: Pathways to Success for America's Youth," which outlined the needs and problems of this group and recommended a number of solutions. Howe published two major educational works, *Picking Up the Options* (1968) and *Thinking About Our Kids: An Agenda for American*

Education (1993), in which he called on the country to reassess its educational goals by recognizing the educational roles and responsibilities of families and communities. He also wrote extensively for professional journals.

Howe was a trustee at Yale University, Vassar College, the Taft School, the College Entrance Examination Board, the John Hay Whitney Foundation, and the Kennedy Center in Washington, D.C., and chairman of the National Council on Education Research, the Institute for Educational Leadership, and the Educational Testing Services.

Howe received honorary degrees from Princeton University, the University of Notre Dame, and other schools. He retired in 1994 and died at age eighty-four at Kendal at Hanover, a retirement community in Hanover, New Hampshire. His death followed a long illness resulting from a blood disorder. Memorial services were held in Cambridge, Massachusetts, and Washington, D.C. He is buried at Pine Grove Cemetery in Holderness, New Hampshire.

"Doc was Doc, not a carbon copy of anyone else, not even like anyone else. He was just himself. He knew who he was, what he valued, what he enjoyed, what he stood for," according to a friend. Howe was steadfast in his determination to help disadvantaged children and never wavered when his views were unpopular. Few people have had a greater impact on the beliefs and practices of American educators. He always advised policy makers to stop attempting to motivate students by failing them and to stop trying to improve teachers by telling them they are no good.

★

For an understanding of Howe and his ideas and ideals, consult his own books and articles, including *Picking Up the Options* (1968) and *Thinking About Our Kids: An Agenda for American Education* (1993). Articles about Howe include Nancy Hoffman and Robert Schwartz, "Remembrance of Things Past: Interviews with F. Keppel and H. Howe," *Change* 22 (Mar.–Apr. 1990): 52–57; Cynthia Thompson, "Equal Opportunity—Past and Present: An Interview with Harold Howe II," *Journal of Developmental Education* 1 (Jan. 1988): 16–19; and Erik Robelen, "Howe Pioneered New Federal Role in U.S. Education," *Education Week* (11 Dec. 2002). Obituaries are in the *New York Times* and *Boston Globe* (both 3 Dec. 2002).

JOAN GOODBODY

HUNTER, Kim (*b.* 12 November 1922 in Detroit, Michigan; *d.* 11 September 2002 in New York City), actress of stage and screen who established her reputation with her iconic performances as the sensuous Stella Kowalski in the Broadway (1947) and film (1951) versions of *A Streetcar Named Desire*.

Born Janet Cole in 1922, Hunter was the daughter of Donald and Grace (Lind) Cole. Her father died when she

Kim Hunter, 1952. AP/WIDE WORLD PHOTOS

was four years old. After her mother remarried, the family, including Hunter's brother, moved to Miami Beach when she was ten. According to Hunter, she was "lonely growing up" and would fill the time portraying pretend characters in front of the mirror.

By the time she entered high school, Hunter was studying acting and, at the age of seventeen, she made her stage debut playing the title role in *Penny Wise* at the Miami Women's Club. Hunter soon was working with stock theater companies around the country and was performing in *Arsenic and Old Lace* at the Pasadena Playhouse in California when a talent scout spotted her. After signing a contract with the producer David O. Selznick, she appeared in her first film, *The Seventh Victim* (1943), in which her character battled devil worshipers. She also appeared in the Ginger Rogers film *Tender Comrade* (1943), about women living communally during World War II. Her other early film roles included *When Strangers Marry* (1944) and *Stairway to Heaven* (1946).

On 11 February 1944 Hunter married William Baldwin, with whom she had a daughter. She and Baldwin divorced in 1946. During the mid-1940s she also studied acting under Konstantin Stanislavsky, who established and taught the "method" introspective approach to acting, at the Actors Studio in New York. Hunter remained at the Actors

Studio for five years but left shortly after Lee Strasberg became artistic director in 1951.

Hunter had already established herself as a talented stage actor when she appeared opposite Marlon Brando in Tennessee Williams's play *A Streetcar Named Desire* on Broadway in 1947. As Stella, Hunter portrayed the tormented wife of Brando's character, Stanley Kowalski, a bully and rapist. Both Hunter and Brando left the cast after two years but reprised their roles in the 1951 film version, directed by Elia Kazan. Although Hunter commented years later that the film version was highly censored in terms of depicting the play's strong sexual context, including homosexuality, she added, "It was the best film experience I ever had." Hunter won the 1951 Academy Award as best supporting actress for her strong portrayal of sexual and emotional hunger. Also in 1951, on 20 December, Hunter married Robert Emmett, a writer, with whom she had a son.

Hunter next appeared opposite Humphrey Bogart in *Deadline U.S.A.* (1952) but soon was blacklisted by Hollywood and television. Although she was never a member of a communist organization, she was named as a communist sympathizer in a pamphlet called *Red Channels*. The evidence against her was circumstantial at best and based largely on the prevailing fears of the day. For example, some critics considered *Tender Comrade* to be pro-Soviet. Hunter also had been a strong supporter of civil rights and peace movements, both of which were believed to be (and often were) infiltrated by Communists. She signed many petitions, and in 1949 helped sponsor a world peace symposium. Hunter later pointed out that the conference had 400 other sponsors, including the physicist Albert Einstein and Eleanor Roosevelt, the widow of President Franklin D. Roosevelt.

Although Hunter had won an Academy Award, she did not work in movies again until 1956, when she starred with Bette Davis in *Storm Center,* a film about book burning. Fortunately, Hunter's stage career remained intact. She appeared in several plays while blacklisted, including *The Children's Hour,* by Lillian Hellman, in 1954. As the blacklist fervor faded, Hunter began to work again. She was praised for her strong performance in films *The Young Stranger* (1957), as the mother of a troubled teenager, and for her role as the director of a mental institution in *Lilith* (1964). Hunter also appeared in various television films and series, including *The Closing Door* (1960), *Give Us Barabbas* (1961), and *Lamp at Midnight* (1966).

In 1966 Hunter appeared in the science fiction movie *Planet of the Apes* as Dr. Zira, a chimpanzee psychiatrist who has sympathy for the humans captured and kept in slavery by the ruling apes. To prepare for her role, she spent many hours at the Bronx Zoo studying chimpanzee and ape behavior. Despite disliking the cumbersome makeup she was required to wear, Hunter also starred in the film's two sequels. Over the next three decades, Hunter appeared in numerous made-for-television movies and as a guest actor on several series, including *Columbo, Ellery Queen,* and *Mad About You.* She also took a role on the soap opera *The Edge of Night,* playing Nola Madison during the 1979–1980 season. Her film roles, however, were few and far between and included parts in *The Kindred* (1986) and *Midnight in the Garden of Good and Evil* (1997).

Hunter always maintained that she preferred stage acting over movie and television roles, and her later career included numerous stage credits, among them *The Penny Wars* (1969) and *To Grandmother's House We Go* (1981) on Broadway. She also performed throughout the United States in numerous regional productions, including a one-woman show about the poet Emily Dickinson, *The Belle of Amherst.* In 1996 she played Lady Markby in the Broadway production of *An Ideal Husband.* Her husband died in 2000, and in the following year Hunter made her last stage appearance in the off-Broadway revival of *The Madwoman of Chaillot.* She died of a heart attack at her home in Greenwich Village, New York City, above the Cherry Lane Theatre.

Hunter, who once said "acting is my life," had an eclectic career spanning five decades, during which time she amassed numerous stage, screen, and television credits. Although she was accused of being a Communist and blacklisted for a time in the 1950s, she always maintained a forgiving attitude to colleagues who had cooperated with congressional investigators by naming people as communist sympathizers. Hunter will be remembered by fans for her versatile performances, which showed through even when she was smothered beneath an incredible amount of makeup.

★

Hunter wrote a combination cookbook and autobiography called *Loose in the Kitchen* (1975). She reminisced about her early work in *American Theater* (Sept. 1966) and discussed her acting training and technique in *Back Stage* (7 Sept. 2001). Obituaries are in the *New York Times* (12 Sept. 2002) and *Variety* (16 Sept. 2002).

DAVID PETECHUK

J

JACK, Beau (*b.* 1 April 1921 in Waynesboro, Georgia; *d.* 9 February 2000 in Miami, Florida), professional boxer who twice held the New York State Boxing Commission lightweight championship in the 1940s, fought twenty-one main events at Madison Square Garden, and became a member of the Boxing Hall of Fame.

Born Sidney Walker to poor parents who separated when he was eight months old, Jack, together with his brother and sister, was raised on a farm outside Augusta, Georgia, by an octogenarian grandmother, Evie Mixom. Jack never attended school. Starting at age eight, he walked three and a half miles into Augusta and worked as a shoeshine boy. Jack once returned home crying after his shoeshine box was stolen by another youth. He was admonished by his grandmother to fight for what was his. She gave him the nickname "Beau Jack" after he successfully fought to retain his location on an Augusta street corner. The name remained with him throughout his professional boxing career.

Jack often received money from white men after fighting with other bootblacks, defending his turf. At age fifteen he entered battle royals, a crude form of sporting entertainment in which a group of five to ten young African-American boys was blindfolded and placed in a boxing ring to fight each other, with the survivor winning prize money offered by patrons. In one such contest, Jack knocked out his brother to win the prize money. After winning several battle royals, Jack won one held for the patrons of the Mas-

ters golf tournament, bringing home $1,000 to his grandmother. He was noticed by several Augusta National Golf Club members and offered a job shining shoes at the club by the club steward, Bowman Milligan. At age fifteen Jack married his first wife, Josephine, with whom he had nine children. In the mid-1960s he married a second time. He eventually fathered fifteen children, ten boys and five girls.

When he was eighteen, Jack received financial assistance from Bobby Jones, Clifford Roberts, Jimmy Demaret, Grantland Rice, and other members of Augusta National to travel north and begin training for a professional boxing career. The Augusta steward, Milligan, accompanied him to Springfield, Massachusetts, where Milligan became the club steward and Jack a caddie at the Longmeadow Country Club. Jack also trained evenings at a Holyoke, Massachusetts, boxing club. He began his professional career on 20 May 1940 and was successful on the small fight-club circuit with his pressing, swarming, crowd-pleasing tactics. This success led to bouts in New York City, where Jack defeated several leading lightweights. On 18 December 1942, Jack knocked out Tippy Larkin to win the New York State Boxing Commission's version of the lightweight championship, the title having been vacated by Sammy Angott.

Jack was a tireless campaigner. He fought three leading contenders in a three-month span in 1943, and fought three Madison Square Garden main events within a month in March 1944. Jack engaged in a four-bout series with Bob

Beau Jack (*left*) fighting Morris Reif, January 1946. BETTMANN/CORBIS

Montgomery in 1943 and 1944, twice losing and once regaining the lightweight title. In their final bout on 4 August 1944, fought several months after each man had entered the U.S. Army, Jack won a ten-round decision in a nontitle bout at Madison Square Garden that raised $35.9 million in war bond sales, the largest gate in boxing history.

During World War II, Jack was stationed at Fort Benning, Georgia. After being discharged from the service, he resumed his boxing career in December 1945, but suffered a serious knee injury while training to fight Willie Joyce in Chicago in November 1946. After a knee operation, he returned to fight Tony Janiro at Madison Square Garden on 21 February 1947. In the fourth round, Jack fell to the canvas after missing a punch, his left knee broken in five places. He was unable to continue and lost the bout by a technical knockout. After a second operation, Jack returned to the ring, but with restricted mobility, suspect stamina, and recurring weight problems. His final attempt to regain the lightweight championship ended in a sixth-round technical knockout at the hands of the world champion, Ike Williams, on 12 July 1948. In four bouts against Williams, Jack was never victorious.

Jack's knee problems and the relentless nature of his boxing style limited his longevity, and after two defeats to Gil Turner in 1951 he left the ring. His boxing career finally came to an end in 1955 after a four-bout comeback. Jack had a career eighty-three wins, twenty-four losses, and five draws. Always a fan favorite in Madison Square Gar-

den, he fought there twenty-seven times, including twenty-one main events, a record that had not been equaled at the end of the twentieth century.

The Augusta sporting fraternity that initially bankrolled Jack's boxing career supposedly banked his ring earnings, and enabled him to leave boxing owning a drive-in barbecue stand, a thirty-two-acre farm, a $10,000 annuity, and a trust fund. Yet within five years Jack had returned to shining shoes, working initially at the Fontainebleau Hotel and later at the Doral Hotel in Miami Beach, Florida. Although he neither smoked nor drank, Jack reportedly squandered much of his ring earnings during the prime of his career, spending freely on clothes, women, and friends.

In the 1980s Jack trained fighters at the Fifth Street Gym in Miami Beach, and for a time, was also manager. In 1972 he was elected to the *Ring Magazine* Hall of Fame, and in 1991 to the International Boxing Hall of Fame. In his final years Jack became friendly with another former world champion, Gerardo Gonzalez, better known as "Kid Gavilan," the Cuban-born welterweight champion of the early 1950s, and a former opponent. Jack died of complications from Parkinson's disease at age seventy-eight. His body was cremated and his ashes spread at the grave of a daughter who predeceased him.

Jack was a true boxing primitive—a man with no formal education who was barely literate and who lived totally for his profession. According to his longtime manager, Chick Wergeles, Jack would have fought for nothing. To boxing critics, the arc of Jack's career represented all that was wrong with the sport: a young, unlettered fighter of promise achieves success but, because of his naive, good-hearted, trusting nature, is exploited by shadowy figures and malign forces, and spends the final phase of his life as he started it, shining shoes. Yet Jack never publicly voiced any bitterness or regrets, nor did he express anger toward anyone regarding his fate. He wanted only to be remembered as a fighter who always gave the full measure and never left his fans displeased with his performance in the ring.

★

W. C. Heinz wrote about Jack years after his greatest boxing successes in "The Primitive," in *Once They Heard the Cheers* (1979). Additional biographical material can be found in John D. Windhausen's entry on Jack in David L. Porter, ed., *Biographical Dictionary of American Sports: Indoor Sports* (1989), and in James B. Roberts and Alexander G. Skutt, *The Boxing Register* (2002). Contrasting views regarding Jack's financial status at the end of his boxing career can be found in Beau Jack, as told to Charles Samuels, "Maybe Somebody Did Rob Me, But I Don't Know Who," *Sports Illustrated* (29 Nov. 1954), and Randy Russell, "The Truth About Beau Jack," *Sport* (Sept. 1955). See also the appreciation by W. C. Heinz, "The Late, Great Beau Jack," *Ring Magazine* (July 2000). An obituary is in the *New York Times* (12 Feb. 2000).

EDWARD J. TASSINARI

George Jackson. MOTOWN RECORDS

JACKSON, George Anthony (*b.* 6 January 1958 in Manhattan, New York City; *d.* 10 February 2000 in Manhattan, New York City), cofounder of Jackson-McHenry Entertainment, Elephant Walk Entertainment, and Urban Box Office Network, and president and chief executive officer of Motown Records.

Jackson was the son of Melvin Jackson, a postal worker, and Henrietta (Hogan) Jackson Stancil, a production supervisor at the *Amsterdam News.* Jackson, who had a sister and a brother, was born and raised in the Harlem section of Manhattan. He attended Fordham Preparatory High School, graduating in 1976. After high school, he enrolled at Harvard University and earned a B.S. in sociology and economics in 1980.

Jackson began his career at Proctor and Gamble, where he worked in marketing and sales for two years. In 1982 Jackson, who was known as "Poppa George," moved to Los Angeles to work for Paramount Television's situation comedy *The New Odd Couple,* which aired from 1982 to 1983. After only one year he became executive assistant to the president of worldwide production at Universal Pictures. Jackson's steady progress continued when he spent 1984 to 1986 as executive vice president of production at

Indigo, the actor and comedian Richard Pryor's production company at Columbia Pictures. He then headed Grio Entertainment Group, a Warner Bros.–based partnership with the producer Quincy Jones and Clarence Avant. Jackson was instrumental in the early career development of several African-American filmmakers, including Robert Townsend, Reginald Hudlin, and Roy Campanella, Jr. He also worked with LL Cool J, Russell Simmons, Ice-T, Wesley Snipes, and Mario Van Peebles.

With Doug McHenry, Jackson cofounded the production and management company Jackson-McHenry Entertainment, and served as its chairman. Jackson-McHenry produced and directed youth- and music-oriented films that were notable for their box office returns. Formed in 1985, the company's first hit was *Krush Groove* (1985), a rap-oriented film. They followed that with the gangster epic *New Jack City* (1991), starring Wesley Snipes, and the popular hip-hop–based films House Party II (1991) and House Party III (1994), all coproduced by Jackson. *New Jack City,* a controversial movie portraying the drug culture in Harlem, which some felt advocated youth violence, was the most successful film produced by Jackson-McHenry Entertainment.

In 1996 Jackson and McHenry founded Elephant Walk Entertainment, a film and television company. Elephant

Walk Entertainment is credited with the syndicated television program *Motown Live* (originated in 1959), the critically acclaimed love story *Jason's Lyric* (1994), Martin Lawrence's hit *A Thin Line Between Love and Hate* (1996), and the successful United Paramount Network television comedy *Malcolm and Eddie* (1996). From 1980 through 1990 Jackson coproduced more than twelve films, including *Krush Groove* (1985), the first major movie to focus on hip-hop and rap culture. He is credited as the creator of the New Jack Swing era, also known as the hip-hop era, which was introduced by *Krush Groove*, and for bringing hip-hop and rap music to Hollywood. Films such as *Krush Groove* and *New Jack City* brought break-dancing and hip-hop culture from the South Bronx to Main Street.

Jackson lived in Los Angeles until 1997, when he moved back to New York City. In November of that year he became president and chief executive of Motown Records, based in New York. He oversaw Motown's music operations and helped to revive the careers of legendary artists such as Diana Ross and Stevie Wonder. Faced with the huge challenge of reestablishing the label's profitability, Jackson expanded Motown and forged into hotter music styles like hip-hop and rap. He promoted the careers of the teen group 98 Degrees and the classic Motown group the Temptations. Although carrying the legendary record label through its fortieth anniversary and producing memorable urban blockbusters, Jackson left Motown in 1998 when Seagram Company bought Polygram. He married Yuko Sumida in March 1998; they had one daughter.

In 1999, after leaving Motown, Jackson cofounded Urban Box Office Network (UBO) with Frank Cooper and Adam Kidron. UBO, an Internet company aimed at urban minorities, was the first major Internet business to move its headquarters to Harlem. One year after the company was formed, it had 175 employees and had planned thirty websites. The first group of Internet sites was expected to be launched in February 2003, but Jackson died of a stroke at Saint Luke's Roosevelt Hospital in New York prior to the launch. He is buried in Hackensack Cemetery, New Jersey.

Jackson was active in the Producer's Guild, the American Film Institute Third Council, and the Independent Film Project West. In addition, he oversaw fundraisers for the Black Filmmaker Foundation and Big Brothers Association of America. Among his numerous awards and honors were the National Association for the Advancement of Colored People (NAACP) Image Award, Black American Cinema Society Award, and Communications Excellence to Black Audiences (CEBA) Award. Jackson was a founding member of De La Salle Academy, a private school for talented children, and served on its board. A memorial scholarship fund was created at De La Salle to honor Jackson.

By the time of his death at age forty-two, Jackson had realized numerous accomplishments. His interest in film and entrepreneurial aspirations took him a long way from production assistant at Paramount Television to president and chief executive of Motown Records. Jackson was instrumental in producing the movies of some of Hollywood's leading African-American actors. He is best remembered as the chairman and president of the successful Elephant Walk Entertainment, a leader in the resurgence of youth music–oriented filmmaking during the 1990s. The Reverend Jesse Jackson referred to Jackson as a tremendous talent and an inspiration to many young people. Because of his commitment to film and music, Jackson left a great legacy of excellence and creativity for future generations.

★

There is no full biography of Jackson, but a biographical sketch can be found in *Contemporary Black Biography* 19 (1998). Jackson's career is discussed in "Successful Film Producer George Jackson to Head Motown," *Jacksonville Free Press* (11 Nov. 1997); Don Thomas, "George Jackson Named President and CEO of Motown Records," *New York Beacon* (12 Nov. 1997); Roy S. Johnson, "Motown: What's Going On," *Fortune* (24 Nov. 1997); and Terry Pristin, "Downloads from Uptown: a Web Portal in Harlem," *New York Times* (27 Feb. 2000). Obituaries are in the *Los Angeles Times* (12 Feb. 2000), *Washington Post* (13 Feb. 2000), *New York Times* (15 Feb. 2000), and *New York Amsterdam News* (17 Feb. 2000).

NJOKI-WA-KINYATTI

JAM MASTER JAY (JASON WILLIAM MIZELL) (*b.* 21 January 1965 in Brooklyn, New York City; *d.* 30 October 2002 in Queens, New York City), member of the landmark rap group Run-D.M.C., which popularized and defined the musical style.

Jam Master Jay was born Jason William Mizell to Jesse Mizell, a social worker, and Connie Thompson Mizell, who would later become a first-grade teacher. Connie's two children from a previous marriage rounded out the close, loving family of five. In 1975 the Mizells moved from Brooklyn to the middle-class Hollis section of Queens. Jam Master Jay stumbled in his mid-teens, whiling away his time on the corner as a petty criminal and street tough until his guilt over disappointing his parents effected a change in his course of action. He attended Andrew Jackson High School, eventually earning a GED, and enrolled at Queens College as a computer science major.

Throughout his teens, Jam Master Jay was mesmerized by early rap DJs (disc jockeys), artists who performed various aural tricks with turntables—for instance, manually "scratching" the vinyl across the needle to produce rhythmic bursts of sound. This, in turn, provided the accom-

Jam Master Jay (*center*) with the other members of the rap group Run-DMC, 1988. Lynn Goldsmith/ CORBIS

paniment for rappers, whose art centers on the spoken word. Among the DJs that the young Jam Master Jay admired were Grandmaster Flash, whose 1982 single "The Message" is considered the first important rap record, and Davy DMX. He obsessively practiced with headphones on in his bedroom in the middle of the night, blending records together into a musical collage. Soon the streetwise teen was being smuggled into clubs to display his prodigious talents. His friends Joseph ("Run") Simmons and Darryl ("D.M.C.") McDaniels often rapped in accompaniment.

The trio's big break came courtesy of Run's older brother, the future media mogul Russell Simmons, who arranged for his brother's group to record for Profile Records in 1983. Their early singles were modest hits, including "It's Like That," "Sucker MCs," and "Jam Master Jay," an homage by the rappers to their DJ. The group toured relentlessly to promote its aggressive, hard-driving sound. Their 1984 self-titled debut album was the first long-playing rap record in history and the first to attain gold status. One year later *King of Rock* was the first rap album to go platinum.

Run-D.M.C.'s biggest hit broke open the mainstream market for rap. "Walk This Way" from 1986's *Raising Hell,* a remake of Aerosmith's 1976 hit with the band members Steven Tyler and Joe Perry, reached the number-four position on the pop charts. The song's landmark video was the first by rap artists to receive significant play on the cable network Music Television and introduced a world of suburban teens to rap.

Run-D.M.C. played increasingly larger venues to support the album, but its breakout popularity was tarnished by violence that erupted among fans at concerts. Most notably, rival Los Angeles gangs rioted at a show at Long Beach Arena, bringing an abrupt end to the event. As a result, the media tended to associate the trio with street thuggery despite their music's clear anti-violence message. The fact that rap was mostly an African-American art form already engendered negative reactions by many white observers, and the putative connection of its biggest act with street violence only furthered racist bias against it.

By the time the group released its fourth album, *Tougher Than Leather,* in 1988, the rap world had moved on to edgier, more political acts, such as Public Enemy and N.W.A. *Back from Hell* in 1990 was Run-D.M.C.'s first album not to achieve platinum status. Soon thereafter, Run fell victim to a false rape accusation that would cost him hundreds of thousands of dollars before it was dismissed. Meanwhile, D.M.C. struggled with alcoholism.

Jam Master Jay, however, worked tirelessly during this period. Throughout the trio's career, he continued to perform as a solo DJ, often spinning at local clubs after Run-D.M.C. concerts and flying to other cities to play during off days. Run-D.M.C.'s *Down with the King* album in 1993 afforded a brief popular comeback and tour, but Jam Master Jay worked through the remainder of the 1990s mostly as a DJ and producer for other artists in his Hollis recording studio. His productions include Onyx's hit *Bacdafucup* in 1993, and in the twenty-first century some of 50 Cent's early singles, including the 2003 hit "Wanksta."

Jam Master Jay's first child, a son, was born in 1985 to his girlfriend, Lee Bullock. On 24 June 1991 he married Terri Corley, with whom he had two more sons. In the fall of 2002, just as his new Hot Ta Def record label was taking off and a nostalgic renewal of interest in Run-D.M.C. promised another comeback, Jam Master Jay was shot in the head by an unknown assailant who burst into the DJ's studio, opened fire, and fled without being identified. He is buried in Ferncliff Cemetery in suburban Hartsdale, New York.

More than six months later, police were still unable to identify Jam Master Jay's killer. The unsolved murders of the "gangsta" rappers Tupac Shakur in 1996 and Chris ("Notorious B.I.G.") Wallace in 1997 were believed to be the result of rap business feuds, but Jam Master Jay's life was largely free of such discord. Despite his experimentation with street life as a teenager, Jam Master Jay was a well-loved, peaceful family man, a popular figure in Hollis, and a pillar of the community.

Jam Master Jay is remembered as a generous, caring man who often gave free studio time to young artists and made time for Hollis's youth. His musical legacy literally lives on in the Scratch Academy, a New York City school for young DJs that he began shortly before his death. As rap's first super-group, Run-D.M.C. profoundly shaped the genre, in large part through Jam Master Jay's contributions. His choice of spinning hard, fast rock music instead of the slower soul and rhythm and blues of his predecessors formed the template for the hardcore rap of Public Enemy and N.W.A. and the rap rock of later acts such as Korn, Limp Bizkit, Linkin Park, and Kid Rock. Through Run-D.M.C., rap spawned a second popular music revolution that rivaled that of rock and roll and became the dominant influence in American youth culture by the mid-1990s.

★

Bill Adler, *Tougher Than Leather: The Rise of Run-D.M.C.* (1987), provides detailed coverage of the group and its members up to 1987. David Thigpen, *Jam Master Jay: The Heart of Hip-Hop,* hastily written in January 2003, covers Jam Master Jay's entire life. Jim Tremayne's oft-quoted June 2000 interview in *DJ Times*, "King of Rap," offers a wealth of insight from Jam Master Jay himself. Obituaries are in *Entertainment Weekly* (15 Nov. 2002) and *People* (18 Nov. 2002).

FRED MEYER

JENNINGS, Waylon Arnold (*b.* 15 June 1937 in Littlefield, Texas; *d.* 13 February 2002 in Chandler, Arizona), country-and-western recording artist, songwriter, and leader of the anti-Nashville "outlaw" rebellion among country musicians in the 1970s.

Jennings was the son of William Alvin Jennings, who worked a succession of jobs, from cotton farming to truck driving, but who also played the guitar. Waylon grew up sharing a two-room, dirt-floored house with eleven relatives, and picked cotton while still a child. He got his start in the music business as a teenage disc jockey and performer who loved both the country music of Hank Williams and the blues of B. B. King. In 1955 he met his fellow

Waylon Jennings. MR. KEN SETTLE

West Texan Buddy Holly and joined his backup band, the Crickets. Jennings was not on the flight that claimed Holly's life, along with the lives of the rising stars Richie Valens and J. P. ("The Big Bopper") Richardson, on 3 February 1959: at the last minute, he gave up his seat on the single-engine plane to Richardson.

Jennings performed around the Southwest, gaining the attention of talent scouts with the A&M label, who signed him in 1963. After he moved to the capital of country music—Nashville, Tennessee—he switched to the Radio Corporation of America (RCA) in 1965. In Nashville he became the friend and roommate of another artist destined for greatness, Johnny Cash. Over the decade that followed, Jennings chafed against the heavy-handed, formulaic overproduction in studios bent on creating a homogenized, nonthreatening "Nashville sound" that some people described as "countrypolitan." This would prove to be just one instance of the country "crossover" phenomenon, which resulted in music that was less and less recognizable as "country." Whereas Nashville's power establishment at the time favored songs that sounded like those of the pop crooners, Jennings, with his increasingly scruffy appearance and rough-edged baritone, wanted to create and perform music that brought country back to its simple roots. That desire necessitated a move away from the Tennessee capital.

Jennings fought the pop-crossover tendencies of country music with his own form of musical fusion, reaching into his rock and roll past for instrumental and vocal methods but relying mostly on traditional country themes for his lyrics. His songs, including "Only Daddy That'll Walk the Line," "Ain't Living Long Like This," "I've Always Been Crazy," "Good-Hearted Woman," and "Mamas, Don't Let Your Babies Grow Up to Be Cowboys," revolve around the images of the rambling man and the long-suffering woman who tries to put up with him. They extol the pleasures and perils of drinking and general rowdiness and continually return to the notion that tranquility can be found in the simplicity of country living.

Usually accompanied by a small group somewhat reminiscent of the Crickets, Jennings formulated a musical style based on simplicity itself. The Jennings aesthetic reflected more than just a rejection of Nashville's overly decorative recordings; rather, it gave expression to a powerful, eclectic form of music that sounded unlike that of anyone else. His trademark sound, which he called "chicken-pickin'," featured a driving, unadorned rhythm, very often employing a heavy combination of drums, bass, and rhythm guitar on a song's every beat. This was best illustrated on his 1975 hit and Nashville protest song "Are You Sure Hank Done It This Way?"

Jennings represented a strange mix of traditionalism and innovation, and generated irony and paradox with the same fervor with which he created hit songs. Traditionalism mixed with a love of innovation on his 1974 hit "Bob Wills Is Still the King." Wills and his path-breaking Texas Playboys were a formative influence on Jennings from the time of his childhood in the 1930s until Wills's retirement in 1969 and during the band's reconstitution after Wills's death in 1975. Jennings appeared on *Wanted: The Outlaws,* a watershed album with Willie Nelson, Tompall Glaser, and his wife, Jessi Colter. Released in 1976, the album amounted to a musical declaration of independence from Nashville, but the fact was lost on many observers that this "anti-Nashville" statement was produced from material previously recorded in that city. In a further irony, the fact that it was the first country record ever to achieve platinum status (one million copies sold) certainly was not lost on the Nashville establishment. The Country Music Association, which had named Jennings male vocalist of the year for 1975, showered him with further awards.

Jennings and Nelson collaborated on "Luckenbach, Texas," a 1977 hit that became one of the anthems of the Texas "progressive country" music community. The song celebrated the goodwill and simplicity possible in small-town relationships, yet most of the people who created—and listened to—such music lived in urban areas. This, just one of the continuing paradoxes of country music that Jennings helped perpetuate, never seemed to concern him or his fans.

Further, Jennings's rejection of industrial approaches to music never suggested a devotion to noncommercialism. His efforts produced sixteen number-one country singles, and his records, personal appearances, and songwriting royalties netted him a handsome income over a career that lasted the better part of a half-century. He appeared on television shows and in films; wrote and performed the theme song and did the opening narration on the television program *The Dukes of Hazard* in the late 1970s to early 1980s; and cocreated a one-person autobiographical stage show, *A Man Called Hoss.* In the mid-1980s Jennings, Nelson, Cash, and Kris Kristofferson toured internationally and recorded as a country supergroup, the Highwaymen. In their material and staging, they hinted at the swagger, independence, and potential lawlessness of the highwaymen of legend, further perpetuating the "outlaw" image.

Jennings's personal life mirrored the triumphs and tragedies of the characters he portrayed in his songs. Marrying for the first time at eighteen, he had three wives and five children before marrying Colter in 1969. He battled substance addiction for years, but in 1989 he completed work on his general equivalency diploma, undoing the part of the hell-raiser image that had prompted him to drop out of high school. Despite his long identification with rebellion against the country music establishment, he was inducted into the Country Music Hall of Fame in 2001. Jennings died in his sleep from complications related to diabetes at age sixty-four.

★

Jennings's autobiography, written with Lenny Kaye, is *Waylon: An Autobiography* (1998). For insight into Jennings's personality and music, see R. Serge Denisoff, *Waylon: A Biography* (1983). See also Bob Allen, *Waylon and Willie: The Full Story in Words and Pictures of Waylon Jennings and Willie Nelson* (1979), and John L. Smith, *The Waylon Jennings Discography* (1995). The best source for putting Jennings's career in context is Bill C. Malone, *Country Music, U.S.A.* (2002). An obituary is in the *New York Times* (14 Feb. 2002).

DAVID STRICKLIN

JONES, Horace Allyn ("Jimmy")   (*b.* 24 November 1906 in Parnell, Missouri; *d.* 2 September 2001 in Maryville, Missouri), Thoroughbred horse trainer who, with his father, Ben, trained two Triple Crown winners, five Horses of the Year, eight Kentucky Derby winners, and eighteen national champions.

Jones's father, Benjamin Allyn Jones, and mother, Etta (McLaughlin) Jones, a schoolteacher, raised cattle and racehorses in Parnell. Ben began racing his stock on local circuits and eventually moved to larger venues in New Orleans, Maryland, Kentucky, Mexico, Cuba, and Canada. In 1914 Jones watched his first official races, including the match race between Iron Mask and Pan Zareta in Juárez, Mexico. Starting at age nine, he galloped horses before school and trained and occasionally rode horses on local race circuits in the summer.

Jones graduated from Parnell High School in 1924 and attended Northwest Missouri State Teachers College, where he studied veterinary science and animal husbandry for two years. In 1926 he left school and, after a brief stint working in Battle Creek, Michigan, at a threshing machine factory, joined his ill father in New Orleans. There, Jones obtained his horse trainer's license and saddled his first winner, Nose Dive. He and his father would work together until Ben's death in 1961. Jones met Margaret Mary ("Peggy") Keenan while delivering horses to the Aurora, Illinois, racetrack. They were married in Ohio on 4 June 1929; the couple had no children.

Ben's racing stable, Jones Stock Farm, relied primarily on Seth, an American top-twenty sire from 1925 through 1929, and his progeny to rank no lower than ninth in races won between 1922 and 1931. In 1925 the stable's leading money winner, two-year-old Captain Seth, died of pneumonia, for which there was no effective treatment then. Seth died in 1927 and proved to be irreplaceable for the stable. Ben was soon looking for better horses to train and found them with Herbert Woolf, a Kansas City businessman and the owner of Woolford Farms, who hired the Joneses in 1931. After serving a term as the mayor of Parnell

Jimmy Jones (*left*), holding the bridle of Citation following a race, June 1950. BETTMANN/CORBIS

in 1932, Jones began working with his father again. In 1938 they won their first Kentucky Derby for Woolf with Lawrin, who defeated the pre-race favorite, Calumet's Bull Lea.

In September 1939 Warren Wright, the owner of Calumet Farm in Lexington, Kentucky, hired Ben as a trainer and Jones as an assistant trainer. Wright had hired nine trainers prior to the Joneses, and they were eager to make a good initial impression. Calumet horses had won nine races that year prior to their arrival. The Joneses had a second-place finish and then seven winners in their first eight races with Calumet. Jones later noted that Whirlaway's win in the 1941 Kentucky Derby gave them their first sense of job security. That year Whirlaway earned the Triple Crown, winning the Preakness and Belmont Stakes in addition to the Kentucky Derby.

Often Jones and his father would be racing separate strings of Calumet horses in different parts of the country. Jones eventually became a licensed pilot and flew his own plane to keep up with his hectic schedule. He returned to Calumet Farm after serving in the U.S. Coast Guard from 1943 to 1944 during World War II. In 1947 he was promoted to the trainer position as his father's health deteriorated. Ben became the farm general manager and fully relinquished all of his training duties in 1953.

In the twenty-five years that Jones and his father trained at Calumet, the stable was the North American champion owner twelve times, with 1,619 wins and $17.8 million in earnings, and the champion breeder fourteen times. The trainers experienced particular success at the Kentucky Derby, saddling seven winners, three second-place finishers, one third-place horse, and only two unplaced horses. They trained their horses to peak for the Kentucky Derby. "If we saw that they were getting too much [work], we would back off. I would rather be in front of the schedule than behind. If you get behind, you don't just catch up."

The outstanding Calumet horses trained by the Joneses included the Horses of the Year Whirlaway (1941, 1942), Twilight Tear (1944), Armed (1947), Citation (1948), and Coaltown (1949), and the champions Bewitch, Barbizon, Tim Tam, and Two Lea. Their top money winners included Citation ($1,085,760), Armed ($817,475), and Bewitch ($462,605). According to Jones, the secret to their success was recognizing that "training each horse is an individual act. You do it by knowing your horse. . . . Keep your horses as fresh as possible and eager to race."

Jones trained the Triple Crown winner Citation, although his father saddled the horse for its victories in the Derby Trial and the Kentucky Derby. In 1948 Citation won a world record nineteen stakes and features races and earned purses totaling $709,470, the largest amount earned by any stable that year. Citation also became the first Thoroughbred to win purses worth $1 million. After saddling the 1956 second-place finisher, Fabius, Jones won

consecutive Kentucky Derby races with Iron Liege and Tim Tam; the latter nearly won the Triple Crown, finishing second in the Belmont Stakes after breaking a sesamoid bone in the stretch run.

In October 1964 Jones retired as Calumet's head trainer to become the director of racing at Monmouth Park in Oceanport, New Jersey. In 1977 he saddled the winner Bolero's Orphan as a favor for the trainer Jimmy Iselin. Two months later, Jones underwent heart surgery and retired to his Parnell ranch with his wife, who died in 1983. In retirement he attended many racing events, visiting Gulfstream Park in Miami for the winter racing season and attending the Kentucky Derby each May before heading back to Parnell. Jones died at age ninety-four at Saint Francis Hospital in Maryville of kidney failure. He is buried at Rose Hill Cemetery in Parnell.

As a Calumet trainer, Jones saddled 1,034 winners, including fifty-four stakes winners, with earnings of $12,792,676 (through 31 July 1964). In 1947 he set a trainer's single-year earnings record with $1,334,805—the first time a trainer had exceeded $1 million. He led the nation in earnings for five years (1947–1949, 1957, 1961). He was named the Thoroughbred Racing Association's Man of the Year in 1952 and elected to the National Museum of Racing's Hall of Fame in 1959, joining his father, who had been elected the year before.

★

Joe Hirsch and Gene Plowden, *In the Winner's Circle: The Jones Boys of Calumet Farm* (1974), is a rich biographical source. Hirsch wrote several later articles on Jones for the *Daily Racing Forum*. Gerald Holland, "Say Hello to Jimmy Jones," *Sports Illustrated* (17 Mar. 1958), describes a day in the life of Jones at Hialeah Race Track. Susan Rhodemyre, "When Calumet Was King," *Thoroughbred Record* 215 (21 Apr. 1982): 2,137–2,140, is an interview with the seventy-five-year-old Jones, focusing on his time at Calumet Farm. Jim Bolus, "Two Fellows from Missouri," *Thoroughbred Record* 224 (May 1990): 84–89, describes the family's early history in Missouri, their accomplishments, and their work with Citation. An obituary is in the *New York Times* (2 Sept. 2001).

STEVEN P. SAVAGE

JONES, Robert Trent, Sr. (*b.* 20 June 1906 in Ince, England; *d.* 14 June 2000 in Fort Lauderdale, Florida), the "father of modern golf architecture" and the premier golf course architect of the second half of the twentieth century.

Jones was born to Welsh parents who had immigrated to East Rochester, New York, when Jones was six years old. His father was an engineer who worked for the New York Central Railroad. Jones became an accomplished golfer who, at age sixteen, set a course record at the Western New

Robert Trent Jones, Sr. AP/WIDE WORLD PHOTOS

York Open at Genesee Valley Park in Rochester and in 1927 scored as low amateur in the Canadian Open. A premature case of ulcers convinced him, however, that his health would not stand the strain of professional competition. Golf architecture was a happy alternative that had first attracted his attention when he had the opportunity to meet and watch the golf architect Donald Ross oversee the construction of Oak Hill in Rochester.

When Jones matriculated at Cornell University in Ithaca, New York, he knew that he wanted to be a golf architect, and he persuaded the dean to allow him to shape a relevant program of study. He took courses in horticulture, agronomy, and land drainage at the College of Agriculture. He studied engineering and surveying in the College of Engineering. He took courses in chemistry, public speaking, and journalism in the College of Liberal Arts. And he studied landscape architecture in the College of Architecture. After his graduation in 1930 Jones returned to Rochester, where he took courses in sketching, a skill he used to good advantage in his presentations to prospective clients. In 1930, after building greens at Sodus Bay Golf Club in New York, Jones joined the Canadian designer Stanley Thompson in business. During the next eight years

of the depression, they built nine courses and renovated eight others. Jones married Iona Tefft Davis; the couple had two sons, both of whom became golf architects.

In 1938 Jones went solo and had seven commissions in as many years. With the end of World War II, golf course construction began anew, and Jones had two commissions in 1946, five in 1947, and six in 1948, including Peachtree Golf Club in Atlanta, in collaboration with the golfing legend Bobby Jones. In 1949 he had eleven commissions, and in 1950, among his other commissions, he teamed up with Jones again, remaking numbers eleven and sixteen at Augusta—the famed Georgia club and site of the Masters Tournament—into dramatic water holes by damming Rae's Creek.

With a clear vision of how a golf course should properly play and a robust approach to constructing the layout for such a course, Jones shaped golf architecture into a profession with the same deliberateness he applied to sculpting his courses. In a career that spanned almost seven decades, he flew an estimated eight million miles and left a legacy of more than four hundred new courses in forty-three states and thirty-four countries and redesigned 160 others.

The sun never sets on a Jones course, he was proud to proclaim. Jones believed firmly that "every hole should be a hard par but an easy bogey," a philosophy that often stirred the ire of Professional Golfers' Association (PGA) members, who preferred tough birdies and easy pars. "If your husband had to play this course for a living he'd be in the poor house," the golfer Ben Hogan grumbled to Jones's wife after winning the U.S. Open at Oakland Hills (Michigan) in 1951, a course that Jones had toughened up the previous year in preparation for the championship. After his Oakland Hills reconstruction, Jones's reputation for imaginative and challenging designs (and redesigns) made him the "Open Doctor," the architect of choice to oversee alterations to courses in preparation for major championships. "When we build a course," he explained, "we [are] in combat with the golfer. We're on the defense and he's on the attack."

By the end of Jones's life, seventy-nine championships had been played on courses he either had built or had reconstructed, including twelve PGA championships, twenty U.S. Opens, and, abroad, six courses that hosted the World Cup of Golf. To challenge the professionals while at the same time being fair to less skilled golfers, after World War II Jones began to build longer courses with exceptionally long tee boxes ("runway tees") that provided multiple distance options. From tee to green, he firmly believed that "the line of play should be obvious from the tee," and he moved a lot of earth to set up his courses to offer a clear set of "risk-reward" options that made him the leader of the "heroic school" of golf architects. Jones also was the first architect to promote the construction of extensive water hazards, which he preferred over bunkers for the certainty with which they imposed a penalty. "On my courses the tournament winner will be the man who has played the most good shots the best," he asserted. "We don't want somebody to win who's spraying his shots over in the next fairway, then knocking a wedge over a tree or two to the green and ramming in a putt for a birdie, scoring a sixty-five when he would have scored a seventy-five if the proper penalties had been exacted." "Ramming in a putt" on one of Jones's greens, however, was not easy.

While his greens were large, their contours were complex. Several courses that most clearly reflect his philosophy are Peachtree in Atlanta; Spyglass Hill in Pebble Beach, California; Firestone South in Akron, Ohio; Valderrama in Sotogrande, Spain; and, most assertive of all, Ballybunion, in Ballybunion, Ireland, an undulating links layout that critics harshly criticize as far too punishing.

By 1950, Robert Trent Jones, Inc., was an established premier architectural firm that eventually set up offices in Montclair, New Jersey; Fort Lauderdale, Florida; Palo Alto, California; and Leeds, England. Among his more unusual assignments, Jones built a putting green at the White House for President Dwight D. Eisenhower and courses for the Rockefeller family, Aga Khan IV, and King Hassan II of Morocco. In 1974 he built the first golf course in the Soviet Union, about twenty miles northwest of Moscow. One of his last projects was the Robert Trent Jones Golf Trail in Alabama, a series of eighteen public courses. In 1987 Jones was the first architect inducted into the World Golf Hall of Fame.

Jones was a founding member and a former president of the American Society of Golf Course Architects and the first recipient of its Donald Ross Award for outstanding contributions to the profession. A man with an irrepressible sense of humor, when he awoke in the hospital in July 1999 to be told by his sons that he had had a stroke, he replied, "Do I have to count it?" He died just short of his ninety-fourth birthday, from the aftereffects of a stroke.

★

Herbert Warren Wind wrote a profile of Jones for the *New Yorker* (4 Aug. 1951). See also Leonard Schecter, "The Jones Idea of a Golf Course," the *New York Times Magazine* (7 July 1968). John Garrity, "The Jones Boys," *Sports Illustrated,* discusses the careers and difficult relationships between father and sons. An obituary is in the *New York Times* (16 June 2000).

MARTIN J. SHERWIN

JORDAN, June (*b.* 9 July 1936 in Manhattan, New York City; *d.* 14 June 2002 in Berkeley, California), poet, novelist, and author of children's books.

Jordan was the only child of Granville Ivanhoe Jordan, a postal clerk and immigrant from Panama, and Mildred Maude (Fisher) Jordan, a nurse and immigrant from Jamaica. Born in the Harlem section of Manhattan, Jordan relocated with the family to Bedford-Stuyvesant in Brooklyn when she was five.

Although Jordan's father was physically abusive, Jordan assisted him with chores and carpentry, and he taught her how to box. When Jordan was a child, her father introduced her to literature with sets of secondhand books by such authors as William Shakespeare, Zane Gray, Sinclair Lewis, Edgar Allan Poe, and the poet Paul Laurence Dunbar, whose use of black dialect made a lasting impression on her. Jordan's mother was dutiful and self-sacrificing but in denial about her husband's physical abuse of Jordan. She committed suicide in 1966.

Jordan began writing poetry at age seven. She attended Midwood High School, where she was the only African American in a student body of 3,000, and then Northfield School for Girls in Massachusetts, where her interest in writing was encouraged. Jordan attended Barnard College in New York City from 1953 to 1955, the University of Chicago from 1955 to 1956, and returned to Barnard in 1956. She apparently never earned a degree. She married

June Jordan. AP/WIDE WORLD PHOTOS

Michael Meyer on 5 April 1955. Their only child, a son, was born in 1958; the marriage ended in divorce in 1966. Jordan would later write about her and Meyer's experience as an interracial couple.

During the early to mid-1960s, Jordan worked as a research associate and writer for the Technical Housing Department of Mobilization for Youth in New York City. In 1967 she began teaching English at the City College of New York. She also taught at Connecticut College and Sarah Lawrence College, where she remained until 1974 before joining Yale University. She joined the African-American Studies Department at the University of California, Berkeley, in 1986.

Jordan's first book of poetry, *Who Look at Me?*, was published in 1969. Her first and only novel, *His Own Where* (1971), was nominated for a National Book Award. The book is representative of her interest in urban planning and commitment to Black English, years before the Ebonics debate of the 1990s. *His Own Where* can also be interpreted as an autobiographical reference to Jordan's relationship with her parents. *Civil Wars* (1981) covers self-determination in Angola and the concept of power—its abuse by those who have it and the rebellion against that abuse by those who do not. *Civil Wars* also describes Jordan's turbulent relationship with her husband and the problem of public intolerance of interracial marriages. Critics have described *Civil Wars* as illuminating, combative, and educational.

Some of Jordan's poetry, particularly that in *Passion: New Poems, 1977–1980* (1980), has been denounced by critics as radical. The collection includes forceful pieces on police brutality, racism, genocide, the Cuban leader Fidel Castro, and a man's descriptive confessional comparing the theft of a Porsche to rape. Jordan also criticizes the poetry establishment for excluding, through critical and economic censorship, important work by minority poets. Written mostly in free verse, the poems share the themes of her essays of the same period.

Jordan's collections of essays include *On Call: New Political Essays* (1985), in which she discussed a variety of international and domestic political subjects concerning Nicaragua and Israeli foreign policy with regard to South Africa; *Technical Difficulties: African-American Notes on the State of the Union* (1994); *June Jordan's Poetry for the People: A Revolutionary Blueprint* (1995); and *Affirmative Acts: Political Essays* (1998). In addition to *Passion,* her books of poetry include *Things That I Do in the Dark: Selected Poetry* (1977); *Living Room: New Poems* (1985); *Naming Our Destiny: New and Selected Poems* (1989); *Haruko/Love Poems* (1994); and *Kissing God Goodbye: Poems, 1991–1997* (1997).

Jordan also composed lyrics for twenty-two songs as well as the libretto for *I Was Looking at the Ceiling and Then I Saw the Sky: Earthquake/Romance* (1995), an opera by the composer John Adams and the director Peter Sellars. In the opera, Jordan gave voice to seven characters in present-day Los Angeles, who are struggling to fill their lives with love as they deal with racial tensions and a catastrophic earthquake.

Jordan also contributed significantly to children's literature. Among her children's works are *Dry Victories* (1972), *Fannie Lou Hamer* (1972), and *New Life: New Room* (1975). In her children's literature, she did not patronize young readers but emphasized social realities and survival in a racist society.

Jordan received numerous honors and awards, including the Rockefeller Fellowship for Creative Writing (1969–1970), a Yaddo Fellowship (1979), a National Endowment for the Arts Fellowship (1982), and the Achievement Award for International Reporting from the National Association of Black Journalists (1984). She also received the Chancellor's Distinguished Lectureship from the University of California, Berkeley (1986), and the International Association of Poets, Playwrights, Editors, Essayists and Novelists (PEN) Center USA West Freedom to Write Award (1991). She also won the Ground Breakers–Dream Makers Award from the Women's Foundation in San Francisco (1994) and the *Reader's Digest* Lila Wallace Writers Award.

Jordan published twenty-eight books, mostly poetry and political essays, as well as novels, plays, children's books, and countless articles. This body of work ranks her among the most published of African-American writers. She was passionate but did not allow her artistry as a writer to be overshadowed by her political positions. Jordan described her politics as the "politics of survival and change," while terming her religion "humanitarian." According to Jordan, the role of the poet in society is to earn the trust of the people and assure them that their words will not be twisted. The role of the black poet or poet of color is to rally the spirit of one's people in the face of being hated and despised. Politically adept poetry can be useful to revolution.

Jordan died of breast cancer at her home at age sixty-five. *Some of Us Did Not Die: New and Selected Essays of June Jordan* (2002), released after Jordan's death, discusses Jordan's thoughts on her cancer and the reaction of the United States to the terrorist attacks of 11 September 2001.

The writer Alice Walker said, "June Jordan makes us think of Akhmatova, of Neruda. She is the bravest of us, the most outraged. She feels for all. She is the universal poet." For the writer Toni Morrison, the sum of Jordan's career was "Forty years of tireless activism coupled with and fuelled by flawless art."

★

Jordan's *Civil Wars* (1981), a collection of essays, letters, and speeches published in periodicals between 1964 and 1980, is an important source of biographical information, as it serves as a record of her development as a writer and addresses each of the author's main concerns: feminism, racism, violence, homosexuality, children, and education, as well as her personal experience as a single mother. Her personal memoir is *Soldier: A Poet's Childhood* (2002). For further biographical information, see Joy Harjo, "An Interview with June Jordan," *High Plains Literary Review* 3, no. 2 (fall 1998): 60–76. Obituaries are in the *New York Times* (18 June 2002) and (Manchester, U.K.) *Guardian* (20 June 2002). Refer also to the audio recording of Jordan's radio interview with David Barsamian, "June Jordan: Childhood Memories, Poetry and Palestine," Alternative Radio (11 Oct. 2000).

LEE MCQUEEN

JOVANOVICH, William Ilija ("Bill") (*b.* 6 February 1920 in Sunnyside, Colorado; *d.* 4 December 2001 in San Diego, California), author, publisher, and chairman of the publishing house Harcourt Brace Jovanovich.

Born Vladimir Jovanovich in Sunnyside, a company town near Louisville, Colorado, Jovanovich was the only son and one of three children of Ilija M. Jovanovich, a Serbian immigrant coal miner, and Hedviga (Garbatz) Jovanovich, a Polish immigrant whom his father had met when she was running a rooming house in Pueblo, Colorado. She continued to run rooming houses throughout the marriage. Jovanovich grew up in the mining camps speaking Serbian and Polish but mastered English quickly and did well in school. He graduated from Manual High School in Denver and won a scholarship to the University of Colorado, graduating with an A.B. in English in 1941. He received a two-year graduate fellowship to Harvard in 1941 but left a year later to join the U.S. Navy.

During World War II Jovanovich underwent naval officer training in San Diego. He served from 1942 to 1946, primarily as a supply officer. For a short time he was stationed in Mobile, Alabama, where he met Martha Evelyn Davis. They were married on 21 August 1943 and had three children. After his service in the navy, during which he attained the rank of lieutenant, he enrolled at Columbia University in New York City, but he soon ran out of funds. He joined Harcourt, Brace, and Company in 1947, working for $50 per week as a high school textbook salesman. During his early years with the firm, he edited many successful texts, including the popular Adventures in Literature series. In 1953 he became vice president and director, and just two years later he was named president and director. Remarkably, he became president within eight years of starting with the company.

"My preparation [for work] began . . . when I first passed through the doorway of an elementary school," said Jovanovich. "I had a distinct impression that I had just been

William Jovanovich. AP/WIDE WORLD PHOTOS

hired." His son once said that Jovanovich "was still selling books ten years after he became president." During his tenure as a salesman, he talked to the teachers, not just to the superintendents or the board members. He strove to know his schools and what they needed, and he encouraged those in authority to purchase the books that their teachers wanted.

By 1964 it had become evident to Jovanovich that his first priority had to be his administrative responsibilities, so he gave up his one remaining sales territory, Washington, D.C. As president, Jovanovich worked for diversity in the materials produced for schools and created books designed for the African-American market. To this end, in 1968 Jovanovich created the Division of Urban Education at Harcourt, thus pioneering the concept of devoting a publishing group to underprivileged, inner-city kids. He based it in San Francisco, a move that surprised many of his East Coast publishing contemporaries.

Jovanovich was an author as well as an editor. His better-known works include the essay collection *Now, Barabbas* (1964) and the novel *Madmen Must* (1978). He also is credited with bringing about the publication of the aviator Charles Lindbergh's memoirs. In 1970 he became the chair and chief executive officer (CEO). That same year the board changed the name of the company to Harcourt Brace Jovanovich. In 1976 Jovanovich became president, CEO, and director of the company. His last position with Harcourt was as chairman of the board and the executive committee.

Jovanovich was noted for his business acumen, and his tenure at Harcourt was marked by financial success and rapid expansion. After 1970 the company branched out into nonpublishing enterprises, such as Sea World theme parks, broadcasting, office supplies, and insurance. The company also expanded its legal, medical, and scientific book divisions and became one of the largest and most profitable publishing houses in the world. The company prospered until 1990, when Jovanovich spent billions to stave off a hostile takeover attempt, creating serious financial problems in the process. He retired that year, and the company was sold in 1991. Jovanovich was a member of the editorial board of Phi Beta Kappa; the chairman of Longmans Canada Limited (1961); a visiting professor at the University of California, Berkeley (1967); a lecturer at Pace University and Adelphi University; and a regent of the State of New York (1974–1977).

Jovanovich spent his retirement years reading, studying, and writing for his own pleasure. He kept in contact with many authors and developed a close relationship with his grandchildren. He died at his home in San Diego of complications from kidney failure and is buried next to his father in Riverside Cemetery in Denver, where immigrants were buried during the time he was growing up. Jovanovich was a man who stuck to his goals and his personal belief that "everyone deserves a good education." His groundbreaking work was the foundation for many of the diversity programs and textbooks that we see today. Jovanovich believed that publishing was an art form—that art and commerce should work together and that the publisher was responsible for all aspects of the process.

★

There is no biography of Jovanovich. For insight into his life, read his books *Now, Barabbas* (1964) and *Serbdom* (1998). An obituary is in the *New York Times* (6 Dec. 2001).

JOAN GOODBODY

JUDGE, Mychal Fallon (*b.* 11 May 1933 in Brooklyn, New York City; *d.* 11 September 2001 in Manhattan, New York City), Roman Catholic priest, who, as chaplain for the Fire Department of New York City, was killed in the line of duty in the terrorist attack on the World Trade Center on 11 September 2001.

Born Robert Emmett Judge, Judge changed his first and middle names after he joined the Franciscans. His parents, Michael Judge and Mary (Fallon) Judge, were immigrants from County Leitrim, Ireland, who settled in Brooklyn in the 1920s. His father ran a grocery store in Brooklyn; his mother was a homemaker. Judge had a twin sister who was born two days after him, and an older sister. Judge's birth name was a tribute to one of Ireland's most famous heroes, Robert Emmett, who led an ill-fated rebellion against British rule in 1803.

When Judge was three, his father became ill and spent the next three years in a hospital. According to Judge's biographer, the children could visit their father only from a distance, waving to him from an interior window in the hospital. Judge's father died when Judge was only six. Even during his last years, Judge would tell friends how much he missed having a father and a male role model in the house. His mother, left with three young children to rear, rented spare rooms to boarders to make ends meet. As an adolescent, Judge worked odd jobs in Brooklyn and across the East River in Manhattan, where he shined shoes to help his mother pay bills.

Judge's mother, like many Irish immigrants, was a devout Catholic who passed her faith along to her children.

Mychal Judge, July 2001. JIM LORD/GETTY IMAGES

Judge was a seventh-grade student in Saint Paul's Roman Catholic School when he first considered a vocation in the priesthood. He enrolled in a Catholic high school in Brooklyn, Saint Francis Preparatory School, but in 1948 he transferred to a junior seminary in upstate New York. After graduating and spending a year in a monastery, Judge became a Franciscan friar in 1954. Franciscans, in keeping with the spirit of their patron, Saint Francis of Assisi, are known for their outreach to the poor, their brown cloaks and sandals, and their spartan lives. According to Franciscan tradition, Judge was required to change his name when he turned his life over to the church. He chose to call himself Fallon Michael, a tribute to his parents. Later, in the mid-1960s, he reversed the order of his new names but changed the spelling of his first name to Mychal in order to distinguish himself from his contemporaries.

By then Judge was a Franciscan friar, a member of a religious community, but not yet a priest. He enrolled in classes at Saint Francis College in New Hampshire and earned a bachelor's degree from Saint Bonaventure University in Olean, New York, in 1957. Later that year, he began studies in theology at Holy Name College in Washington, D.C. After more than a decade of training and study, he was ordained a priest on 25 February 1961.

Judge moved around a great deal early in his career, serving three parishes in New Jersey—Saint Joseph's in East Rutherford from 1962 to 1966, and again from 1970 to 1976; Sacred Heart of Rochelle Park from 1967 to 1969; and Saint Joseph's of West Milford from 1979 to 1985. Between these postings he also worked at Siena College in Loudonville, New York. In 1986 he was assigned to the friary at Saint Francis of Assisi Church on West Thirty-first Street in Manhattan, just steps away from the bustle of Madison Square Garden and Pennsylvania Station.

In New York City, Judge ministered to AIDS victims and to gay Catholics who wished to retain a connection to the institutional church. Judge himself apparently told friends and colleagues before his death that he was gay. He also was an alcoholic, and he ministered to others who shared his affliction. The son of immigrants, he reached out to newcomers who often visited the friary for a meal or for legal advice. His work on behalf of the sick, the suffering, and the poor did not go unnoticed. To his delight, he was invited to White House prayer breakfasts during the administrations of Presidents William J. ("Bill") Clinton and George H. W. Bush. New York mayor Rudolph Giuliani asked Judge to preside over a prayer service after the crash of TWA Flight 800 in 1996.

The ministry that Judge would grow to love and would lead to his death began in 1992, when he was appointed as a temporary chaplain in the Fire Department of New York (FDNY). Two years later, that temporary assignment became permanent, and Judge became a familiar presence in the city's firehouses and at fires, with his white helmet and rubber turnout coat with his name on the back. On 10 September 2001 Judge presided over a mass at a rebuilt firehouse in the South Bronx. During his homily, he reminded the gathered firefighters that when an alarm sounded, they never knew what God might have in store for them.

The following morning, two hijacked planes struck the twin towers of the World Trade Center. Judge responded immediately to the emergency and was in the lobby of the North Tower when the South Tower collapsed (the North Tower later collapsed as well). The lobby instantly filled with debris. Firefighters found Judge within minutes, but he was already dead. Rescue workers placed his body in a chair and reverently took him to nearby Saint Peter's Church. In death, Judge became a symbol of the heroism and sacrifice of the 343 firefighters who died at the World Trade Center that day. He also became a hero for gay rights advocates. In June 2002 the U.S. Congress passed, and President George W. Bush signed, the Mychal Judge Act, which provides federal death benefits to the same-sex partners of firefighters and police officers who die in the line of duty.

Judge was buried on 15 September in Holy Sepulchre Cemetery in Totowa, New Jersey, after a funeral Mass at Saint Francis of Assisi Church on West Thirty-first Street in Manhattan. A few weeks later, Judge's helmet was presented to Pope John Paul II. A group of lay Catholics began a movement to declare Judge—the gay, alcoholic son of Irish immigrants—a saint of the Roman Catholic Church.

★

The only biography of Judge is Michael Ford, *Father Mychal Judge: An Authentic American Hero* (2002). Books that discuss Judge's role as fire department chaplain include Dennis Smith, *Report from Ground Zero: The Story of the Rescue Efforts at the World Trade Center* (2002), and Terry Golway, *So Others Might Live: A History of New York's Bravest—The FDNY from 1700 to the Present* (2002). Magazine and newspaper articles about Judge include Jennifer Senior, "The Firemen's Friar," *New York* (12 Nov. 2001); Jesse Green, "Requiem for a Heavyweight," *Talk* (Dec. 2001); John Bookser Feister and John Zawadzinski, "No Greater Love," *Saint Anthony's Messenger* (Dec. 2001); and Charisse Jones, "The Making of Father Mychal," *USA Today* (19 Feb. 2003). Obituaries are in the (New York) *Daily News* (14 Sept. 2001) and the *Boston Herald*, *Sunday Times* (London), and *Toronto Star* (all 16 Sept. 2001).

TERRY GOLWAY

K

KAEL, Pauline (*b.* 19 June 1919 in Petaluma, California; *d.* 3 September 2001 in Great Barrington, Massachusetts), movie critic for *The New Yorker* who heralded a flowering of American film in the 1970s and influenced a generation of critics.

Kael was the youngest of five children born to Isaac Paul Kael and Judith (Friedman) Kael, Polish immigrants who owned a farm in California's Sonoma County. When Kael was eight years old, the family sold the farm and moved to San Francisco. She attended the University of California, Berkeley, majoring in philosophy but, before graduating, set out for New York City with a friend, the poet Robert Horan.

After three years Kael returned to San Francisco, where she became a part of the artistic avant-garde. She wrote plays, worked on experimental films, and supported herself by taking jobs as an advertising writer, bookstore clerk, cook, and seamstress. She married and divorced three times and had one daughter. Kael, a lifelong movie fan, began to publish essays on film in the 1950s for such publications as *Sight and Sound* and *Partisan Review.* She broadcast weekly reviews on KPFA, a listener-supported radio station in Berkeley, and between 1955 and 1960 she managed, scheduled the offerings of, and wrote the program notes for a revival movie house in the city. The program notes attracted a wide readership.

In 1965 Kael published a collection of her essays in a book called *I Lost It at the Movies,* thus establishing a tradition—continued in such works as *Kiss Kiss Bang Bang* (1968), *Going Steady* (1970), and *When the Lights Go Down* (1980)—that a Kael title would contain a sexual double entendre. That same year she moved to New York City with her daughter and began to freelance for such magazines as *Life, Holiday,* and *Mademoiselle.* She was briefly the movie critic for *McCall's* but was fired for being too negative (characterizing *The Sound of Music,* for example, as "sugar-coated lies for the masses"). She published two essays about film in the *New Yorker* in 1967—the second, a rave review of the film *Bonnie and Clyde,* which had been condemned or ignored by most critics. The following year, the magazine's renowned editor, William Shawn, hired her as movie critic.

Initially, Kael shared the job with Penelope Gilliatt, and she reviewed only films released between September and March. But even at six months a year, Kael made an immediate impact. Her conversational writing style, marked by hyperbole, slang, and a frankly impressionistic approach, contrasted with the traditionally buttoned-down prose of the *New Yorker.* Kael's work had an improvisational quality, which was not surprising, given her lifelong love of jazz. She set great trust in her own visceral reaction to a movie (a word she preferred to the more pretentious "film"), scrawling her pieces in pencil on a yellow legal pad after a single viewing. Her sensibility was ideally suited to the groundbreaking films of the late 1960s and 1970s by such

Pauline Kael, 1968. MARTHA HOLMES/TIME LIFE PICTURES/GETTY IMAGES

directors as Sam Peckinpah, Robert Altman, Peter Bog-danovich, Hal Ashby, William Friedkin, Francis Ford Coppola, Steven Spielberg, George Lucas, Martin Scorsese, and Brian DePalma. These films not only were artistically interesting but also reflected and, to some extent, generated the enormous changes going on in American society. Kael was their perfect chronicler. She would not just describe or critique a film but *confront* it—as if she were bringing to bear everything she knew about movie history and all her intelligence and critical and literary talent.

By the middle of the 1970s Kael was the most talked about film critic in the country. Her rave reviews of such works as *The Godfather, Last Tango in Paris,* and *Nashville* attracted almost as much attention as the films themselves. She became a mentor to a group of younger critics, including James Wolcott, Greil Marcus, and Elvis Mitchell. She also was condemned frequently for what her critics considered sloppy writing and sloppy thinking and, to some, an anti-intellectual tendency that exalted "trash" at the expense of self-consciously artistic films. Most notably, in 1980 her *New Yorker* colleague Renata Adler wrote an essay in the *New York Review of Books* denouncing Kael's work as "piece by piece, line by line, without interruption, worth-

less." Whether readers loved Kael or hated her, she could not be ignored. As one of her colleagues once remarked, "A whole generation of film critics has had to respond to her either by imitating her or resisting her."

Kael published more than a dozen books, most of them collections of her *New Yorker* reviews and essays. *Deeper into Movies* (1973) won the National Book Award. *The Citizen Kane Book: Raising Kane* (1971) was an expansion of her *New Yorker* essay about Orson Welles's classic film, in which she argued that the screenwriter Herman J. Mankiewicz's contribution to the finished product had been undervalued by film historians and critics. In 1979 Kael took what proved to be a five-month leave of absence from the *New Yorker*, working as an "executive consultant" for Paramount Pictures. When she returned to the magazine, it was as the sole movie critic. By that time, she and her daughter had moved to western Massachusetts, from which she made weekly moviegoing trips to New York City. She stayed in the *New Yorker* post until 1991, when illness forced her to step down. She died at the age of eighty-two of Parkinson's disease.

In her twenty-three years of writing for the *New Yorker,* Kael became the most influential movie critic in the country. Indeed, she probably was the most influential movie critic in American history. She did not have much of an impact on a given film's box-office performance (the *New Yorker*'s circulation when she left was only about 600,000), but she did set the terms and the tone of discussion.

★

Kael's *For Keeps* (1994) is a collection of thirty years of reviews that includes an autobiographical introduction. A book-length interview by Francis Davis is *Afterglow: A Last Conversation with Pauline Kael* (2002). Nineteen interviews, originally published between 1966 and 1994, are collected in *Conversations with Pauline Kael* (1996), edited by Will Brantley. Ben Yagoda, *About Town: "The New Yorker" and the World It Made* (2000), gives an account of Kael's hiring at the *New Yorker* and her working relationship with William Shawn. An appreciation by David Denby is in the *New Yorker* (17 Sept. 2001). Obituaries are in the *New York Times* (4 Sept. 2001) and *Variety* (10 Sept. 2001).

BEN YAGODA

KAMEN, Martin D(avid) (*b.* 27 August 1913 in Toronto, Canada, *d.* 31 August 2002 in Santa Barbara, California), pioneer in the use of radioactive tracers for biochemical research and codiscoverer of carbon-14.

Kamen was the only son and one of two children of Aaron Kamenetsky, a portrait photographer, and Goldie (Achber) Kamenetsky, his assistant. His mother had traveled from Chicago to her family's home in Toronto for his birth and neglected to have his identity recorded upon her return, beginning what would be a lifelong series of misadventures with U.S. government officials. He undertook all his schooling in Chicago, where he graduated from Hyde Park High School in 1930. He went on to the University of Chicago, where he earned a B.S. in physical chemistry, graduating cum laude in 1933. Kamen continued his education at the University of Chicago, from which he earned a Ph.D. in chemistry in 1936. By that time, he already had achieved his first publication, coauthorship of a short journal article on "Scattering of Protons in Collisions with Neutrons," in 1935.

During these formative years, Kamen was known far more widely as a concert violist than as a scientist. He received violin lessons from the age of eight and gave his first public concert a year later, "playing with absolutely sure intonation and good musicianship," according to *Music News*. He was concertmaster of the orchestra in high school, where he switched to the viola, and his initial scholarship at the University of Chicago was from the department of music, for whose orchestra he was first violist. During these years he also played with the Gary (Indiana) Symphony Orchestra, the traveling orchestra of the Girvin Conservatory, where he had been a student, and numerous chamber groups. Through his continuing devotion to the viola, he would over the years become a close friend of many world-renowned musicians.

Upon completing his doctoral work, Kamen traveled to Berkeley, California, to work with the series of cyclotrons then being constructed by E. O. Lawrence at the Radiation Laboratory of the University of California. He did not start receiving a salary until six months after his arrival, by which time his services as a radiochemist had proved essential. He formed a research partnership with Samuel Ruben, a chemist, and together they set out to solve the secrets of photosynthesis. In their research, they studied carbon-14, a radioactive isotope with a remarkably long half-life of 5,700 years. Researchers before that time had been forced to use isotopes whose half-lives were measured in minutes, making complex experiments impossible.

In mid-1939, in response to the growing international need for long-lived radioisotopes, Lawrence assigned Kamen's carbon-14 project top priority. Over the next six months, the pair experimented with the irradiation of numerous media, finally achieving the hoped-for result on 27 February 1940. The news was announced during the presentation of the Nobel Prize in physics to Lawrence. That same year, using oxygen-18 as a tracer, the pair was able to demonstrate that the oxygen used in photosynthesis came from water, not from carbon dioxide.

With America's entry into World War II, Kamen became part of the Manhattan Project, focusing on obtaining uranium-235 through the synthesis of uranium tetrachlo-

Martin D. Kamen. THE LIBRARY OF CONGRESS

ride. The work brought his life under the scrutiny of military intelligence—with disastrous results. Kamen was a liberal Jew, a musician who associated with other Jews, liberals, internationalists, and artists, among them Yehudi Menuhin and Isaac Stern. Once, after he had arranged for some radioactive phosphorus to be sent to Seattle to treat a Russian consular official who had leukemia, he had gone out to dinner with the Soviet vice-consul in San Francisco. The combination of leftist connections and direct contact with Soviet officials flagged Kamen as a potential spy.

Furthermore, his active brain often achieved insights that led military intelligence to feel he knew too much. For example, on a 1943 trip to Oak Ridge, Tennessee, he observed that a sample of radioactive sodium from the nuclear laboratory there glowed far more brightly than irradiation in a cyclotron would produce; he inferred that Oak Ridge must have a functioning nuclear reactor. He was immediately suspected of having been leaked the information. In July 1944 Kamen was declared a security risk and removed from his position with the Radiation Laboratory. Three years later his passport was confiscated, and for a year he was forced to work as an inspector at the Kaiser Shipyards.

Kamen was stunned by these actions, even attempting suicide in 1951; he would spend the next ten years attempting to restore his damaged reputation. During the hearings of the House Un-American Activities Committee (which was set up to find and expose Communists in various areas of government), he was deliberately smeared, leading to a libel suit by Kamen against the *Chicago Tribune* and the *Washington Times-Herald,* which he won in 1955. That same year, after an unprecedented court battle, his passport finally was returned to him. Despite these severe blows, Kamen retained his dedication to science. In 1945 he accepted a position at the Edward Mallinckrodt Institute of Washington University in St. Louis, overseeing their cyclotron and developing the new sciences of biogeochemistry and molecular biology. He shifted his own research toward bacterial photosynthesis and then toward the study of bacterial cytochromes, an area he would pursue for the rest of his career.

In 1957 Kamen helped develop a graduate department of biochemistry at Brandeis University and four years later became the founding chairman of the chemistry department at the new University of California, San Diego. Even after he reached emeritus status in 1977, he continued his research work. His accomplishments were finally recognized on 12 December 1995, when President Bill Clinton presented Kamen with the Enrico Fermi Award, the Department of Energy's highest honor.

Kamen was married three times. He married Esther Hudson the night of the 1938 California-Stanford football game, but the marriage collapsed under the pressure of his war work, and they were divorced in 1943. After his move to St. Louis, Kamen met Beka Doherty, a journalist, and they were married on 16 March 1949. They had one son. Beka died in November 1963, and four years later, on 29 April 1967, he married Virginia Swanson. She died in 1987.

Kamen was an essential figure in the development of radiochemistry in the mid-twentieth century, a prime contributor to the developing science of biochemistry, and a brilliant nurturer of academic programs. That he accomplished all this while battling the forces of bureaucratic suspicion and cold war paranoia makes his scientific work all the more remarkable. His story exemplifies the conflict between scientific inquiry and military secrecy in the years during and immediately after World War II. It also demonstrates the work that can be accomplished, despite official harassment, by a dedicated scientist. In the decades after Kamen and Ruben's success, carbon-14 became the dominant radioactive tracer for scientific investigation into fields as diverse as photosynthesis and archeology.

★

Kamen's memoir is *Radiant Science, Dark Politics: A Memoir of the Nuclear Age* (1985). See also Nathan Oram Kaplan and Arthur Robinson, *From Cyclotrons to Cytochromes: Essays in Molecular Biology and Chemistry* (1982). An obituary is in the *New York Times* (5 Sept. 2002). An oral history transcript of interviews conducted by Horace Albert Barker and Sally Smith Hughes, *Scientist and Professor of Microbial Chemistry at Berkeley* (2001), is at Stanford University in Palo Alto, California.

HARTLEY S. SPATT

KARSKI, Jan (*b.* 24 April 1914 in Lódz, Poland; *d.* 13 July 2000 in Washington, D.C.), courier for the Polish underground in World War II who provided the West with one of the first accounts of the Holocaust.

Born Jan Romuald Kozielewski, Karski was the youngest of eight children born to Stefan Ignacy Kozielewski and Walentyna (Burawska) Kozielewska, a homemaker. Although Karski's manners often seemed aristocratic, his father owned a tannery and leather goods factory, and his family was solidly middle class. His father died when Karski was five years old, and thereafter he was raised largely by his mother and his oldest brother, Marian, who was eighteen years his senior.

In 1935, after graduating from Jan Kazimierz University in Lwów, where he studied law and diplomacy, Karski took an internship in Germany with the Polish ministry of foreign affairs and enrolled in an artillery training school, where he was chosen as the top cadet. He went on to diplomatic positions in Geneva, London, and Warsaw. By February 1939 he was an administrative assistant to the director of personnel for the Polish foreign ministry. Not yet twenty-five years old, Karski was advancing rapidly toward a position as an ambassador, but world events would dramatically change the course of his career.

When Nazi soldiers crossed the Polish frontier in September 1939, Karski reported to his mounted artillery division in Oßwiêcim (Auschwitz), but as the Polish military disintegrated, he fled eastward, eventually finding himself a prisoner of war in Soviet Ukraine. As a native of a part of Poland annexed by the Third Reich, he was among the refugees exchanged by Germany and the Soviet Union. He thus avoided execution by the Soviet dictator Josef Stalin's troops, and, by escaping a camp for displaced persons in German-occupied Kielce, he once again avoided death at the hands of the Nazis.

Karski made his way on foot to Warsaw and joined the nascent Polish underground, for which he became a courier using a number of identities and surnames, including Karski, the name by which he became known to the world. In late 1939 he traveled to various Polish cities to establish contact among the grassroots resistance movements, and in early 1940 he slipped through the border to deliver communications from the resistance to the government-in-exile.

After a journey that took him to Slovakia, Hungary, Yugoslavia, Italy, and France, Karski returned to Warsaw in May 1940 to learn that his brother Marian, the Warsaw police chief and a member of the underground, had been arrested and the Polish police conspiracy broken. (Marian was sent to Auschwitz but eventually was released, apparently owing to a clerical error.) Karski immediately became a trusted mediator among the various Polish political groups, which set out to build an underground state. On his second clandestine trip abroad, Karski was captured by the Germans in Slovakia. Badly beaten, he attempted suicide and was transferred to a hospital in Poland, where the underground rescued him. The Germans executed thirty-two Poles in reprisal.

In 1942 the Polish resistance gave Karski the tasks of keeping the government-in-exile informed of Communist infiltration and delivering substantive information to the West about the Nazis' systematic murder of the Jewish population. In preparation for his mission, Karski met with Jewish leaders, visited the Warsaw ghetto twice, and, disguised as a Ukrainian guard, infiltrated a sorting station near a concentration camp. Using the papers of a French worker, Karski traveled by train through Berlin, Brussels, and Paris, from whence he passed through Spain and Gibraltar to London.

The microfilm Karski carried delivered convincing evidence of the Holocaust, but it took the Allies a month to acknowledge the extermination of the Jews, and acknowledgement did not bring action. Pope Pius XII, for instance, said that he had done all he could for the Jews, and the U.S. Supreme Court Justice Felix Frankfurter, himself a Jew, did not believe Karski when the two met in June 1943. President Franklin D. Roosevelt was impressed, however, and, as a result of his meeting with Karski, he established the War Refugee Board to help Jewish escapees from Europe.

Karski had become a de facto ambassador, although not the kind he had devoted his youth to becoming. Nor could he be allowed to return to Poland. The Germans had become aware of his activities, and while he was in Britain he had learned of Allied plans to accede to Stalin's demands for annexation of the eastern half of Poland. This news could have sparked a national insurrection if the Polish people learned that they had been sold out by their putative defenders. Karski therefore returned in February 1944 to the United States, where he became a celebrity. Although his plans to produce a cinematic epic about the Polish underground foundered, he did publish *Story of a Secret State* (1944) and was extremely popular on the lecture circuit and in American magazines.

In 1945 Karski began to teach classes on underground movements for the Federal Bureau of Investigation, but his fame faded as the war ended, and he had difficulty obtaining work. At first the new Hoover Institution at Stanford University hired him to gather documents from Poland and the Baltic states, and he was successful in this endeavor,

Jan Karski, April 2000. AFP/CORBIS

but the United States withdrew its recognition of the Polish government in London, leaving Karski without a state. Full-time employment at the U.S. State Department was blocked by his origin from what was now a Communist country. Employment offered by the United Nations required that he give his formal thanks to the Communist government in Poland, which Karski refused to do. An academic career seemed impossible, since credits from his formerly prestigious university in Lwów were no longer recognized.

A marriage to the daughter of a Latin American diplomat ended quickly, and although Karski assisted his brother Marion and his sister-in-law's move to the United States, his brother never adapted and committed suicide in 1964. Memories of his wartime experiences were so traumatic that Karski vowed never to speak about them. A new, meaningful life did emerge in the United States, however, and ultimately Karski became a powerful witness to the atrocities of the wartime years. The School of Foreign Service at Georgetown University offered him a full scholarship in 1949, and upon earning his Ph.D. in 1952 he began a thirty-two-year career at the university, lecturing on comparative government and communism. Although his strong anti-Communist views brought him the nickname "McCarthyski" (after the U.S. Senator Joseph McCarthy, who initiated a witch-hunt for Communist sympathizers in government circles during the 1950s), Karski was regarded as among the best of the faculty at Georgetown.

Karski became a U.S. citizen in 1954. The State Department and the United States Information Service sent him on lecture tours of Asia and Africa during the 1960s, and even though he declined the Central Intelligence Agency's (CIA) offer of a job in psychological warfare, he did write a report for the CIA about the connection between Radio Free Europe and the suppressed Hungarian Revolution of 1956. In 1965 Karski married the dancer Pola Nirenska, whom he had known since 1950. He traveled to Poland for the first time since the war as a Fulbright scholar in 1974, to conduct research for his second book, *Great Powers and Poland (1919–1945): From Versailles to Yalta* (1985). Three years after his return from Poland, Karski was approached by Claude Lanzmann to break his silence on the Holocaust. The interviews with Lanzmann, conducted in 1978, were extremely painful, as Karski ended more than thirty years of bitter silence.

By the time Lanzmann's documentary, *Shoah,* was released in 1985, Karski had begun a new career as a speaker. He captivated his first audience at the October 1981 International Liberators Conference and ended his extensive speaking career in Auschwitz twelve years later. Karski's stories of the Warsaw ghetto and the death camps and his narrative of efforts by the Polish underground to aid Jews communicated both the inhumanity of the Holocaust and the humanity of those who tried to stop it. Tragedy once again befell Karski in 1992, when his wife, at the age of eighty-one, leaped to her death from the balcony of their Bethesda, Maryland, apartment. Karski died of heart and kidney failure at Georgetown University Hospital in Washington, D.C., at the age of eighty-six, two months after traveling to his hometown to receive an honorary citizenship.

As well as the honorary citizenship of Lódz, Karski was twice awarded the Order Virtuti Militari, the highest military honor bestowed by the Polish government, and the Order Białego Orla ("Order of the White Eagle"), the highest civilian honor in Poland. He was also recognized as a "Righteous Among Nations" by the State of Israel and was made an honorary Israeli citizen in 1994.

Diplomat, resistance activist, and educator, Karski influenced the United States as a powerful voice for victims of Nazism and as an expert on the political struggles he had personally experienced. He made the country aware of Polish resistance against German occupation in World War II, the inhumanity of the Holocaust, and the human rela-

tionship between the two tragedies. Karski served as a living example of the "righteous among nations."

★

Works about Karski include E. Thomas Wood and Stanislaw Jankowski, *Karski: How One Man Tried to Stop the Holocaust* (1994). He also is discussed in Harry J. Cargas, *Voices from the Holocaust* (1992), and Susan Glick, *Heroes of the Holocaust* (2002). Obituaries are in the *New York Times* and *Washington Post* (both 15 July 2000). Karski is featured prominently in the documentary *Shoah* (1985).

JANUSZ DUZINKIEWICZ

KEMPER, James Scott, Jr. (*b.* 8 April 1914 in Chicago, Illinois; *d.* 2 July 2002 in Pauma Valley, California), former head of the Kemper Insurance Companies, an organization he expanded from a company started by his father in 1912.

Kemper was one of three children, and the only son, born to James Scott Kemper, Sr., and Mildred Estelle (Hooper) Kemper. Kemper's mother died in 1927, and his father remarried in 1931 to Gertrude Ziesing Stout, whose son became Kemper's stepbrother.

Kemper received a B.A. from Yale University and then a law degree from Harvard University. He was admitted to the bar in 1940. During World War II, Kemper served in a naval aviation unit in the Pacific as an intelligence officer. After the war, Kemper was a special attorney in the antitrust division of the U.S. Department of Justice and practiced law in New York City, Chicago, and Los Angeles before coming to the Kemper organization. There, Kemper would follow in the tradition of his father and his paternal ancestors in his career path, beliefs, philanthropic causes, and activities.

Kemper joined his father's business in 1960. In 1967 he was instrumental, according to a Kemper Insurance Companies press release, "in the formation of the publicly held Kemper Corporation, a holding company designed to provide flexibility in diversification." Kemper became chairman and chief executive officer of the Kemper organization in 1969, a position he held until his retirement in 1979. During his reign as chairman, Kemper expanded the insurance company founded by his father into a major financial services organization. He kept his father's offerings of property-casualty policies and included low-cost term life insurance, making Kemper Insurance a leading provider of such coverage. That same year, Kemper started the policy of reinsurance and formed the Kemper Reinsurance Company. He continued to expand the Kemper organization by forming Kemper Financial Services in 1970. He also expanded the company by buying regional property-casualty insurance companies in the Midwest and on the West Coast.

Like his father, Kemper brought new ideas, views, and innovations to the organization. He put into effect the concept of an alcoholism rehabilitation program for his employees, making Kemper the first corporation to offer this benefit to employees. Today, the program has expanded to deal with "a variety of 'living' problems" and is used as a program model for other companies. In 1975 Kemper was also one of the first to implement a corporate code of ethics. He publicly encouraged the U.S. Chamber of Commerce and the National Association of Manufacturers "to adopt ethical codes and to develop enforcement procedures" for corporations. An avid golfer, Kemper also built the Kemper Lakes Golf Course, located next to the Kemper organization headquarters in Long Grove, Illinois. He used golf as a promotional tool for his company, which has sponsored the Kemper Insurance Open golf tournament since 1968.

Though retiring as chief executive officer in 1979, Kemper continued to serve as chairman of the board for the Kemper Insurance Companies and Kemper Corporation until 1986. The latter holding was sold to Zurich Insurance Group in 1996. He remained active by becoming a consultant for Kemper on public policy and external affairs. He also continued as chairman of the board of Kemper Sports Management, Inc., which manages the Kemper Lakes Golf Course. In addition, he belonged to the advisory board of the Professional Golfers Association (PGA). As an honorary member of the PGA of Illinois, Kemper chaired the 1989 PGA championship held at Kemper's golf course.

Kemper overcame an alcohol addiction and became involved in many committees involved with the issue of alcohol abuse. President Jimmy Carter appointed Kemper to the Commission on Alcoholism and Other Related Problems. President Ronald Reagan assigned him to the Presidential Commission on Drunk Driving, which he chaired under its new name, the Commission Against Drunk Driving. He was a member of the Department of Health, Education, and Welfare's interagency committee on federal activities for alcohol and alcoholism. In addition, Kemper was the director for both the Council on Alcoholism and the Betty Ford Center. For his work against alcohol abuse, Kemper received the Gold Key from the National Council on Alcoholism, and in 1990 he received the Order of Lincoln, Illinois' highest honor.

His other charitable works included being honorary chairperson of the James S. Kemper Foundation. Kemper also served on the boards of Boys and Girls Clubs of America, the Lyric Opera of Chicago, the Illinois Institute of Technology, the Museum of Science and Industry, and the Eisenhower Medical Center. He garnered many awards for his various activities, among which were the Silver Plaque from the National Conference on Christians and Jews.

Like his father, Kemper was a staunch Republican. He served as a delegate to several GOP national conventions.

He believed that the business community needed to be active in politics and government concerns. He acted on this belief by often going to Washington, D.C., to discuss public policy in the insurance industry.

Kemper resided in Golf, Illinois, and had a vacation home in Pauma Valley, California, where he suffered a heart attack and died at age eighty-eight. Kemper was survived by his wife, Joan, and their five children.

★

Information about Kemper is available in "Kemper Head Retires," *New York Times* (27 Mar. 1986), and the *Washington Post* (9 July 2002). Obituaries are in the *Chicago Sun-Times* (5 July 2002) and *American Banker* (10 July 2002).

MARGALIT SUSSER

KENNEDY, Florynce Rae ("Flo") (*b.* 11 February 1916 in Kansas City, Missouri; *d.* 21 December 2000 in Manhattan, New York City), African-American lawyer and women's, civil, and gay rights advocate.

Kennedy was the second of five daughters born to Wiley Kennedy, a Pullman porter who later owned a taxi business, and Zella Kennedy, who worked outside the home, as a domestic, only during the depression. Kennedy credited her parents with instilling in their children a sense of pride and self-confidence. "We were taught early on not to take any shit from anyone," she wrote in her 1976 autobiography, *Color Me Flo: My Hard Life and Good Times.*

By the time she entered Lincoln High School in Kansas City, Kennedy had decided that she would become a lawyer. After graduating at the top of her class in 1934, she held several jobs and owned a hat shop with one of her sisters. Kennedy was readily recognizable for her cowboy hat and pink sunglasses. Her first political protest was to organize a boycott of a local Coca-Cola bottling plant that refused to hire black truck drivers.

After her mother died of cancer in 1942, Kennedy moved to the Harlem section of New York City with her sister Grayce. While holding several jobs, she studied prelaw at Columbia University, where she first examined the similarities between the oppression of women and the oppression of blacks. After earning a B.A. in 1948 with an "A" average and being rejected by Columbia's law school, she claimed racial discrimination and vowed to fight the decision. She was subsequently admitted—one of eight women and the only black person in her class—and received a J.D. in 1951. Despite her negative attitude toward marriage, in 1957 she married the writer Charles Dudley Dye, who was ten years her junior. The marriage was brief, and they had no children; Dye died a few years later.

After law school, Kennedy clerked with the law firm of

Hartman, Sheridan, and Tekulsky. She opened a law practice in 1954. She often helped abused women and represented the legendary black performers Billie Holiday and Charlie Parker in efforts to recoup money withheld by record companies. "Handling the Holiday and Parker estates taught me more than I was really ready for about government and business delinquency and the hostility and helplessness of the courts," Kennedy wrote in her book. She realized that the law, which seemed to favor big business, did not provide justice for the people about whom she cared.

Recognizing the influence that the media had on public opinion, Kennedy left law to pursue political activism. She established the Media Workshop in 1966 to combat racism in advertising and journalism, and she hosted *The Flo Kennedy Show,* a cable access television program. Bold actions, such as providing legal representation for the civil rights leader H. Rap Brown in 1966 and for twenty-one members of the Black Panthers, a militant African-American group, facing a bombing conspiracy and other charges in 1969, heightened her visibility.

In one memorable action, Kennedy led women in a mass urination to protest the lack of women's restrooms at Harvard University. During a 1967 anti–Vietnam War rally in Montreal, Canada, the Black Panther Bobby Seale was denied the right to speak because he wanted to address racial issues. "I went berserk," Kennedy wrote in her book. "I took the platform and started yelling and hollering." Soon thereafter, she was invited to speak in Washington, D.C. Thus began a twenty-year-long career during which she and the feminist icon Gloria Steinem formed a lecturing team referred to by Steinem as "the Thelma and Louise of the '70s," in reference to the feminist buddy film from 1991. Steinem recalled Kennedy's reaction when, almost inevitably, some man would ask if they were lesbians: Kennedy would ask, "Are you my alternative?"

Among Kennedy's causes were decriminalization of prostitution and legalization of abortion. In the 1971 book *Abortion Rap,* coauthored with Diane Schulder, Kennedy wrote, "If men could get pregnant, abortion would be a sacrament." The book was one of the first to relate painful stories of unwanted pregnancies and botched back-alley abortions. It also presented class action suits filed by Kennedy and other women lawyers calling New York's abortion laws unconstitutional. A year later, the state legislature legalized the procedure.

In 1971 Kennedy founded the Feminist Party, which nominated the black congresswoman Shirley Chisholm for president. Kennedy moved to San Francisco in 1972, opening another Pandora's box when—on behalf of the party—she filed a complaint with the Internal Revenue Service accusing the Roman Catholic Church of abusing its tax-exempt status by using funds to influence political de-

Flo Kennedy. AP/WIDE WORLD PHOTOS

cisions, particularly abortion. These actions, Kennedy claimed, violated the First Amendment, which mandates the separation of church and state. She later campaigned for David Dinkins when he won the New York city mayoral election in 1989, as well as for the clergyman and politician Jesse Jackson.

By the late 1980s Kennedy had suffered two heart attacks and three strokes. Although she was confined to a wheelchair, she continued campaigning, signing a statement against the Persian Gulf War in 1990–1991 and protesting that the war on drugs was, instead, a war on the people. In 1974 *People* magazine called Kennedy "the biggest, loudest, and, indisputably, the rudest mouth on the battleground where feminist activists and radical politics join in mostly common causes." Kennedy died at her Manhattan apartment at age eighty-four. Following Kennedy's death, Marie Wilson of the Ms. Foundation called her "one of the most wonderfully outrageous pioneers of feminism in America."

Of herself, Kennedy wrote in *Color Me Flo,* "I never stopped to wonder why I'm not like other people. The mystery to me is why more people aren't like me."

★

Insight into Kennedy's life can be found in her autobiography, *Color Me Flo: My Hard Life and Good Times* (1976). See also Debbie Lang, "Remembering Flo Kennedy: 'Sweetie, If You're Not Living on the Edge, Then You're Taking Up Space . . . ,'" *Revolutionary Worker* 1095 (18 Mar. 2001). An obituary is in the *New York Times* (23 Dec. 2000).

MARIE L. THOMPSON

KESEY, Kenneth Elton ("Ken") (*b.* 17 September 1935 in La Junta, Colorado; *d.* 10 November 2001 in Eugene, Oregon), writer who is best known for his novel *One Flew over the Cuckoo's Nest* (1962) and for his zealous promotion of psychedelic drugs.

Kesey was the first of two sons born to Fred A. Kesey and Geneva (Smith) Kesey. He was raised a Baptist in Springfield, Oregon, where his father operated a cooperative for dairy farmers and his mother kept house. As a child he took part in the life of the farm and sought adventure in the tales of Zane Grey and the pages of comic books. The comic books, full of superheroes and arch-villains embodying a desperate struggle between good and evil, clearly influenced the themes he would later explore in his fiction. Early on, Kesey developed a love for the outdoors, spending much of his adolescence hunting, fishing, and swimming. He wrestled and played football at Springfield High School, where he was voted "most likely to succeed" upon graduation in 1953.

While at Springfield High, Kesey met his future wife, Faye Haxby. They married on 20 May 1956 and remained together for forty-five years, raising four children, including a daughter Kesey fathered out of wedlock with Carolyn Adams. Adams, better known as "Mountain Girl," later married the Grateful Dead bandleader Jerry Garcia. In the fall of 1953 Kesey entered the University of Oregon in Eugene, where he majored in speech and drama. He performed in college plays and continued wrestling, winning the Fred Lowe Award, a prize given to the best wrestler in the Northwest. After receiving his B.A. in 1957, Kesey went to Hollywood to pursue an acting career. Between film jobs, he began writing "End of Autumn," a novel about college athletics. Pleased with his progress on the novel, which remained unpublished as of 2003, he went to Stanford University to study creative writing on a Woodrow Wilson Fellowship.

Kesey's teachers at Stanford included Wallace Stegner, Richard Scowcroft, Frank O'Connor, and Malcolm Cowley, who later took *One Flew over the Cuckoo's Nest* to Viking. His fellow students in the writing seminar were an extraordinarily gifted group. Among them were the future novelists Larry McMurtry and Robert Stone, who frequently socialized with Kesey at his home in Perry Lane, then

Ken Kesey, 1990. JEFF BARNARD. AP/WIDE WORLD PHOTOS, INC.

Stanford's bohemian quarter. Vic Lovell, a neighbor and a graduate student in psychology, changed Kesey's life forever when he told him about a government-sponsored research project at the Veteran's Administration hospital in Menlo Park. There, Kesey was paid $20 a session to ingest various hallucinogenic drugs, including mescaline, psilosybin, IT-290, LSD, and peyote. After taking a night job as an aide on the psychiatric ward in 1961, he noticed that the mind-altering drugs gave him a new perspective on the mental patients, "a sense that maybe they were not so crazy or as bad as the sterile environment they were living in." The job allowed him time to work on "Zoo," an unpublished novel that was awarded Stanford's Saxton Prize ($2,000) and provided him with the inspiration for *One Flew over the Cuckoo's Nest*.

Viking released *One Flew over the Cuckoo's Nest* in February 1962 to generally favorable reviews. The *New York Times* declared it "a work of genuine literary merit," while *Time* hailed it as "a roar of protest against middlebrow society's Rules and the invisible Rulers who enforce them." Randle P. McMurphy's heroic battle against the controlling forces of Nurse Ratched and the "Combine" appealed to a generation of rebellious baby boomers about to launch a cultural revolution, and the book enjoyed brisk sales. Its popularity led to a stage production starring Kirk Douglas, which opened on Broadway in November 1963, and to a film version featuring Jack Nicholson, which was released in 1975. The movie, directed by Milos Forman, garnered five Academy Awards. Ironically, after a disagreement over script changes, Kesey sued the producers and swore never to see the film.

In the fall of 1962 Kesey returned to Oregon, where he worked on *Sometimes a Great Notion* (1964), an elaborate saga set in the Pacific Northwest that recounts a logging family's struggles against nature, union organizers, and each other. Although the book never achieved the popularity of *Cuckoo's Nest*, it won high praise from literary critics, including Leslie Fielder, who commended Kesey for attempting to "redeem the big book, the Great American Novel—replete with virgin landscapes and swelling with virile assertion." Kesey agreed with the critics: "It's my best work," he said, "and I'll never write anything that good again." A film version with Paul Newman, Henry Fonda, and Lee Remick was released in 1971.

In the summer of 1963 Kesey used some of the earnings from *Cuckoo's Nest* to buy a place in La Honda, California. He also spent $1,500 on a 1939 International Harvester school bus, which he painted in Day-Glo colors and outfitted with film and recording equipment. In the summer of 1964, with a supply of LSD and other drugs on board, Kesey and his friends—a group that called themselves the "Merry Pranksters"—headed to New York City to see the World's Fair and celebrate the publication of *Sometimes a Great Notion*. The bus driver was Neal Cassady, the model for Dean Moriarty in Jack Kerouac's book *On the Road* (1957). After their arrival in New York City, Cassady brought Kerouac and Kesey together at a Park Avenue party. Kerouac left early, however, put off by the noise, the wild antics of the Pranksters, and what he considered their disrespect for the American flag. The Pranksters later drove to Millbank, New York, to visit the psychologist Timothy Leary, where they again received a cool reception.

After returning to California, Kesey and the Pranksters joined with the Grateful Dead in promoting "acid tests," huge public parties with rock music, light shows, and Kool-Aid spiked with LSD. Kesey's growing notoriety, his advocacy of drugs, and his involvement with the San Francisco chapter of the motorcycle group Hell's Angels soon attracted the attention of law enforcement. After a second arrest on drug charges in January 1966, Kesey faked his own suicide and fled to Mexico. He returned to the United States in September, crossing the border near Brownsville, Texas, disguised as a drunken cowboy on horseback. Apprehended after publicly taunting the FBI, he took a plea bargain at trial and served five months in jail.

Upon his release in November 1967, Kesey moved to a farm in Pleasant Hills, Oregon, which became his lifelong home. In March 1969 he traveled to London, working briefly on a short-lived project at the Beatles' Apple Records. While he wrote little over the next twenty years, he continued to publish sporadically. He coedited *The Last Supplement to the Whole Earth Catalog* (1971) with *Realist* editor Paul Krassner and in 1974 launched *Spit in the Ocean* (SITO), a small magazine that included the serialized version of his unfinished novel "Seven Prayers by Grandma Whittier." *Kesey's Garage Sale,* an eclectic selection of letters, interviews, stories, and drawings, which includes "Over the Border," a screenplay based on Kesey's flight to Mexico, appeared in 1973. *Demon Box,* a collection of articles originally written for popular magazines, including *Esquire, Rolling Stone,* and *Playboy,* was published in 1986. Kesey dedicated *Demon Box* to his son Jed, who had died in an automobile crash in 1984. He later characterized this period in his life as "the comedown years—my gonzo time."

In 1989 Kesey accepted an invitation to teach creative writing at the University of Oregon. The result was *Caverns* (1990), an experimental mystery novel authored by Kesey and thirteen graduate students under the pseudonym O.U. Levon (an anagram for University of Oregon novel). Teaching may have helped to jump-start Kesey's creative juices. Several books followed in rapid succession, including *The Further Inquiry* (1990), a screenplay focusing on Neal Cassady and the legendary 1964 bus trip; two children's books, *Little Tricker the Squirrel Meets Big Double the Bear* (1990) and *The Sea Lion: A Story of the Sea Cliff People* (1991); and *Sailor Song* (1992), Kesey's first major novel in eighteen years. He followed it with *Last Go Round* (1994), a rodeo novel he coauthored with Prankster Ken Babbs.

The book was to be Kesey's "last go round" as well. Diagnosed with liver cancer in October 2001, he sought treatment at the Sacred Heart Medical Center in Eugene, where he died of complications following surgery at age sixty-six. At the funeral service, held in Eugene's McDonald Theater on 14 November 2001, Kesey's body lay on stage in a psychedelically painted coffin. In a grave they dug with their own hands, his friends buried him on his Pleasant Hill farm.

Kesey's literary reputation rests primarily on *One Flew over the Cuckoo's Nest* and *Sometimes a Great Notion*. In life, as in art, he sought to celebrate freedom and individuality and to strike a blow against mechanization, conformity, and control. Choosing to be "a lightening rod" rather than "a seismograph," he advocated the use of drugs, not to dull the senses but to open them wide in an unrelenting quest for unmediated experience. The trip (in both senses of the word) that Kesey and the Merry Pranksters took across

America in the summer of 1964 embodied that quest. Brilliantly chronicled by Tom Wolfe in *The Electric Kool-Aid Acid Test* (1968), the trip turned Kesey into an instant folk hero for the generation that came of age in the 1960s.

★

Kesey's archives are on deposit at the University of Oregon's Knight Library. There is no full-length biography, but Barry Leed, *Ken Kesey* (1981), and Stephen L. Tanner, *Ken Kesey* (1983), provide serviceable introductions to the man and his work. Books covering Kesey's years with the Merry Pranksters include Tom Wolfe, *The Electric Kool-Aid Acid Test* (1968), and Paul Perry, *On the Bus: The Complete Guide to the Legendary Trip of Ken Kesey and the Merry Pranksters and the Birth of the Counterculture* (1990). Interviews include Gordon Lish, "What the Hell You Looking in Here For, Daisy Mae? An Interview with Ken Kesey," *Genesis West* (fall 1963): 17–29; Paul Krassner, "An Impolite Interview with Ken Kesey," the *Realist* (May–June 1971): 46–53 (reprinted in *Kesey's Garage Sale,* 1973); and Robert Fagen, "Art of Fiction" *Paris Review* (spring 1994): 59–94 (reprinted in *Beat Writers at Work: The Paris Review*, 1998). See also John Riley, "Bio: Novelist Ken Kesey Has Flown the 'Cuckoo's Nest' and Given Up Tripping for Farming," *People* (22 Mar. 1976). Posthumous tributes include Larry McMurtry, "On the Road," *New York Review of Books* (5 Dec. 2002), and Carl Lehmann-Haupt, "Ken Kesey," *My Generation* (Mar.–Apr. 2002): 83–87. Obituaries are in the *New York Times* and *Los Angeles Times* (both 11 Nov. 2001). Kesey appears in several videos, including *Still Kesey* (1986).

WILLIAM M. GARGAN

Hank Ketcham, February 1984. AP/WIDE WORLD PHOTOS

KETCHAM, Henry King ("Hank") (*b.* 14 March 1920 in Seattle, Washington; *d.* 1 June 2001 in Pebble Beach, California), syndicated cartoonist who created *Dennis the Menace.*

Ketcham was the son of Weaver Vinson Ketcham and Virginia Emma (King) Ketcham. When he was about six years old, he saw one of his father's artist friends scribbling characters from the funny papers—Barney Google, Moon Mullins, and Andy Gump. "I couldn't wait to borrow his 'magic pencil' and try my own hand at drawing," Ketcham later recalled. He would trace comics that appeared in the Seattle newspapers, and by the second grade he was impressing classmates with his skill. At Queen Anne High School in Seattle, he became cartoonist for the student newspaper.

Ketcham matriculated at the University of Washington but dropped out in 1938 after his freshman year to seek an illustrating job in Hollywood. He found work for $16 a week as an illustrator for Walter Lantz, who had created Woody Woodpecker. Ketcham worked as an "in betweener," an illustrator who draws motion between plot points, like the dozens of panels that might make up a cat-and-mouse chase. In 1939 he moved to the Walt Disney Studios for $25 a week, where he worked on Donald Duck movie cartoons and on the movies *Fantasia* and *Pinocchio* (both 1940).

After the Japanese attack on Pearl Harbor, Ketcham enlisted in the navy and spent World War II as a photographer's mate, third class, in Washington, D.C., where he did publicity work for war bonds. He courted an admiral's daughter, Alice Louise Mahar of Malden, Massachusetts, and they wed on 13 June 1942. The next year he created *Half-Hitch,* a comic about a diminutive sailor that ran in the *Saturday Evening Post.* The Ketchams' first child, a son named Dennis, was born in 1946 while the family was living in suburban Westport, Connecticut, where Ketcham was a struggling freelance cartoonist. Ketcham's success continued to grow, and he sold cartoons to top magazines, including *Collier's, Ladies' Home Journal,* and the *New Yorker.*

The family later moved to California, settling into a Carmel Woods cottage near Monterey. It was there, on an October afternoon in 1950, as Ketcham labored over a cartoon for the *Saturday Evening Post,* that his son spent his naptime quietly dismantling his bedroom down to the curtain rods. Ketcham's wife stormed into her husband's studio with the news, adding, "Your son is a menace!" It was an inspiration. Ketcham roughed out drawings for a panel called *Dennis the Menace* and sent them to his New York agent. The Post-Hall syndicate bought it, and the first panel of *Dennis the Menace* appeared on 12 March 1951 in sixteen U.S. newspapers. By year's end it was in a hundred papers, plus newspapers in Frankfurt, Germany; Helsinki, Finland; and Istanbul, Turkey.

The storyline for the comic was simple: a dirt-smudged whirling dervish with a loving heart unintentionally terrorizes a suburban neighborhood through his endless quest for excitement, which usually lay on the same path as trouble. Dennis often could be found clutching a teddy bear and sitting in a rocker facing the corner as punishment for bad behavior. With his cowlick and freckles, he explored an idyllic world of picket fences and permanent neighbors. His ever flummoxed dog was named Ruff, and his playmates were the adoring Joey, the prissy know-it-all Margaret, and the adventurous Gina. His parents were Alice and Henry Mitchell, and the childless elderly neighbors were the Wilsons. Mr. Wilson was the neighborhood grump who disliked children, but Dennis never seemed to realize it and inflicted himself upon Wilson unsparingly. In one panel, Dennis stands on a chair in his pajamas in the darkened house, speaking into the telephone. "Are you awake, Mr. Wilson?" he asks innocently.

With the success of *Dennis the Menace,* the Ketchams soon had enough money to move to a seventy-acre ranch in Carmel Valley, California. In contrast to the idealized postwar suburban family in the cartoon, however, the Ketcham family was coming unglued. His wife grew increasingly dependent on alcohol and barbiturates, and in early 1959 they divorced. Before the year ended, she was dead at age forty of an overdose. It was also the year that Ketcham was sent by Vice President Richard Nixon to the Soviet Union on a "humor exchange" of cartoonists, Ketcham's first trip outside the United States and one that would prove to be formative. He decided to take up residence in Geneva, Switzerland, and married Jo Anne Stevens on 1 July 1959, a union that later ended in divorce.

His son, Dennis, then twelve years old, did poorly in private school in Geneva. Ketcham sent him to a boarding school in Connecticut and remained in Switzerland with his new wife. Dennis later served a tour of duty in Vietnam as a marine but returned with post-traumatic stress disorder and drifted from job to job. He had little contact with his father. "Dennis has been out of my life for a number of years," Ketcham said in a 2001 interview with the *Orlando Sentinel.* "It's regrettable—there's no communication."

Ketcham's third marriage gave him a new lease on fatherhood, one that he embraced. He married Rolande Praeprost on 9 June 1970, and they had two children, a daughter and a son. "In my family now, I'm much more active with the kids and their schooling than I was before. I listen better.

And I think I'm more patient," Ketcham told the *Pittsburgh Post-Gazette.* The Ketchams returned to the United States in 1977, in part because the cartoonist felt that he was out of touch with American culture. They settled in Pebble Beach, California.

Under King Features, the cartoon strip reached a peak of one thousand newspapers in forty-eight countries and nineteen languages by the year 2000, making it one of the most successful comics of all time. The character became a spokesman for the United Nations Children's Fund and the International Red Cross. The cartoon spawned a television series that ran from 1959 to 1963, starring Jay North as Dennis, as well as animated programs and two films, including a 1993 version starring Walter Matthau as the hapless Mr. Wilson. Ketcham's books of recycled Dennis cartoons, including *I Wanna Go Home* (1965), *Well, God, I Goofed Again* (1975), and *Someone's in the Kitchen with Dennis* (1978), sold more than fifty million copies. Ketcham eventually hired artists to draw the cartoon after his health began to fail, although he still penned a few when inspiration struck, which are recognizable by his notch in the upper-right border of the panel.

Golf was Ketcham's passion. He was a member of the Royal and Ancient Golf Club of Saint Andrews, Scotland; the Geneva Golf Club in Switzerland; and the Cypress Point Golf Club in Pebble Beach. He was a recipient of the 1952 Reuben Award, the highest honor bestowed by the National Cartoonist Society. He died of heart disease and cancer at the age of eighty-one and was cremated.

Ketcham found the secret of eternal youth at the end of a pen. His Dennis the Menace, a mischievous, slingshot-toting scamp, has endured more than five decades on newspaper comic pages, though the boy is forever young at five. An accomplished artist, Ketcham distinguished himself among cartooning peers with his command of depth and perspective, intricate backgrounds, and variation of line in his single-panel drawings.

★

Ketcham's autobiography is *The Merchant of Dennis the Menace* (1990). Information about Ketcham is in M. S. Mason, "Illustrator Moves from Laugh Lines to Fine Lines," *Christian Science Monitor* (28 May 1999), and "Menace Maker," *People* (18 June 2001). Other sources include the International Museum of Cartoon Art in Boca Raton, Florida. Obituaries are in the *New York Times, Los Angeles Times,* and *Washington Post* (all 2 June 2001).

Mark Washburn

KIAM, Victor Kermit, II (*b.* 7 December 1926 in New Orleans, Louisiana; *d.* 27 May 2001 in Stamford, Connecticut), owner and spokesperson of Remington Products, the electric shaver company.

Kiam was born to Victor Kiam and Nanon (Newman) Kiam, millionaire parents who divorced shortly after his birth. Growing up in predominantly Roman Catholic New Orleans, he fended off the stigma of divorce by pretending that his father and mother were away when friends came to visit; in reality, he was raised by his grandparents. He made his first profits as a child, buying cans of Coca-Cola at three cents and selling them on the streets of New Orleans for nine. At age eight he set up a soft-drink stand. When he was a teenager, his grandparents sent him to Phillips Academy in Andover, Massachusetts, where George H. W. Bush, who became president of the United States, was a classmate.

Kiam served in the U.S. Navy during World War II and in the U.S. Naval Reserve from 1947 to 1956. He earned a B.A. from Yale University in 1948 and a certificate of languages from the Sorbonne in Paris in 1949. He received an M.B.A. from Harvard University in 1951. At the Sorbonne, he made money by using his own car to serve as a personal tour guide to tourists. He married Ellen Lipscher on 26 November 1956; they had three children.

Kiam's first job was at Lever Brothers, which he joined in 1951. He left Lever Brothers in 1955 as the marketing director of its Pepsodent toothpaste line, then spent thirteen years at Playtex before buying his first company, Benrus Watch Company. Benrus, struggling financially before Kiam bought it, became a miniconglomerate of luxury products after Kiam ended discount-store marketing and price reductions that he felt made the watches less desirable to affluent consumers. He left Benrus after eight years and, with his wife, founded the Friendship Collection, which imported jewelry and antiques from China.

Kiam bought Remington Products from Sperry Rand in 1979. In a television commercial for Remington's electric shavers, Kiam told consumers that he liked the shavers so much he "bought the company." The "liked it so much I bought the company" line entered popular culture as the simple explanation of why he bought the struggling shaver company, but that was not quite true. Kiam was preparing to buy another company when he read that Sperry Rand's chairman wanted to get out of the razor business and instead focus on the company's burgeoning computer business. Kiam had never actually used an electric shaver, and Remington, based in Bridgeport, Connecticut, sold one of every five electric shavers in the United States. His wife bought him a Remington shaver, and he was so impressed with the product that he paid more for the company than he later thought he should have. Spending $25 million in a highly leveraged buyout, which included $500,000 from his own art fortune, he acquired a company that had lost $30 million in the previous five years.

Telling customers that a Remington shaver would shave "as close as a blade or your money back," Kiam took the company to a $4 million profit in its first year, cutting staff, offering generous incentives, and beginning his personal advertising campaign, a direct pitch from him to consumers. Remington's market share quickly doubled, and when Kiam sold the business in 1996, he was paid nine times his original investment. He retained the chairmanship of the board of directors until his death, and his family retained 52 percent ownership of the company stock.

Kiam's other later ventures did not work out as well. Two years after buying the New England Patriots football team in 1988, a sexual harassment scandal involving several players and a female sportswriter led to a boycott of Remington products and several embarrassing verbal gaffes on Kiam's part. At one point he called Lisa Olson, the accusing sportswriter, a "classic bitch." On another occasion, he said that Olson, who had accused a Patriots player of exposing himself to her, had one thing in common with the Iraqis, with whom the United States was at war—they had both seen "Patriot missiles up close." His $85 million purchase of the team led to estimated losses of $20 million, forcing the football zealot to sell his 51 percent interest in the team in 1991, along with his personal stake in Remington, to recoup losses.

The loss of the Patriots visibly drained Kiam, but his energy quickly rebounded. After attempting to retire in

Victor Kiam, March 2000. AP/WIDE WORLD PHOTOS

1994, Kiam predictably grew itchy for more sales and more deals. He renewed his ties to China by becoming the chairman of ITI China Holdings, a company that distributed Western-made goods in China and a joint venture with the Chinese Army.

Throughout his career, Kiam maintained a consistent global focus, even promoting his Remington advertisements abroad while joking that he could do "29 seconds in 15 languages." Kiam also bought the Ronson cigarette lighter company but found mixed financial results. In 1999, when the London *Daily Mirror* suggested it was time for Kiam to retire, he sued the newspaper, winning £105,000 plus costs.

Throughout his life, Kiam maintained a grueling work schedule, starting at 8 A.M. and working until 9 P.M., six days a week. On Sunday he filled orders. Near the end of his life, he was the chair of the National Sales Hall of Fame. Despite his gregarious personality, Kiam hated parties. He preferred to restrict his conversation to money or tennis, at which he excelled. Kiam and his son once won the American Eastern Area tournament for fathers and sons, and in 1988 he launched a father-son, mother-daughter tournament in the Soviet Union.

Kiam, a chain smoker, suffered several heart attacks before he died of a heart condition at age seventy-four at his home.

★

Kiam has not been written about extensively, but he wrote several books about winning sales approaches and achieving wealth. *Going for It! How to Succeed as an Entrepreneur* (1986) was his first, and best-selling, but other similarly upbeat-sounding titles followed, including *Keep Going For It: Living the Life of an Entrepreneur* (1988) and *Live to Win: Achieving Success in Life and Business* (1989). An obituary is in the *New York Times* (29 May 2001).

ALAN BJERGA

KINGMAN, Dong (*b.* 31 March 1911 in Oakland, California; *d.* 12 May 2000 in Manhattan, New York City), watercolorist and teacher whose work is represented in the permanent collections of more than fifty museums and institutions in the United States.

Kingman, the second of eight children, was born Dong Moy Shu, of Chinese descent; his parents came to the United States from Hong Kong in 1900. His father, Dong Chun-Fee, owned a small laundry in Oakland and later a dry goods business; his mother, Lew Shee, was an artist. At age five Kingman moved to Hong Kong with his family, where his father sought to give his children a traditional Chinese education. According to Chinese custom, Kingman was given his new name when he entered school. Hearing that he aspired to be an artist, his teacher gave him the name King (scenery) Man (composition). In later years, he combined the two words into Kingman, and following Chinese custom, he used the family name first and the given name second, thus Dong Kingman.

Kingman studied art and calligraphy with Szeto Wai, the Paris-trained painting master, at the Lingnan School in Hong Kong. Wai taught him both Chinese classical and French impressionist styles of painting.

In 1929, at age eighteen, Kingman returned home to Oakland at the beginning of the depression. He attended the Fox Morgan Art School while working as a newsboy, dishwasher, and houseboy. Kingman decided to concentrate on watercolors, and he painted every spare moment. A 1936 solo exhibition at the San Francisco Art Association brought him critical success and instant recognition. From 1936 to 1941 he was a project artist for the Works Progress Administration, created by the government in part to help support the arts and artists. In 1942 Kingman won the first of two Guggenheim Fellowships, which allowed him to travel and to paint American scenes. His first one-man show in New York City, at Midtown Galleries in 1942, was well received by the media.

During World War II Kingman served in the U.S. Army as a cartographer for the Office of Strategic Services (OSS) in Washington, D.C. After his honorable discharge in December 1945, he settled in Brooklyn in New York City, and he became a guest lecturer and then an art instructor at Columbia University (1946–1958). Hunter College also appointed him an instructor in watercolors and Chinese Art (1948–1953). He also taught at the Famous Artists School in Westport, Connecticut (1955–1978), and received an honorary doctorate from the Academy of Art College in San Francisco in 1987.

In 1954 Kingman became a cultural ambassador for the United States in an international lecture tour for the U.S. State Department. In 1955 he moved across the East River from Brooklyn to Manhattan, where he maintained the same residence and studio until 2000. Kingman's first wife, Janice Wong, whom he married on 28 September 1929, passed away in 1954, and in 1956 he married Helena Kuo. Kuo died in 1999. He had two children with Wong.

During the 1950s and 1960s Kingman became involved in the film industry, serving as a technical adviser. He painted mood-setting scenes for such films as *Flower Drum Song* (1961) and *55 Days at Peking* (1963), and contributed artwork to several motion pictures. He also produced, directed, and animated the short film *Hong Kong Dong*. More than 300 of his film-related works are permanently housed at the Fairbanks Center for Motion Picture Study in Beverly Hills, California.

In 1981 the Ministry of Culture of the People's Republic

Dong Kingman, March 1984. AP/WIDE WORLD PHOTOS

of China hosted an exhibition of Kingman's paintings in Beijing, which was attended by over 100,000 people. It was the first one-man show by an American artist held in China after the resumption of diplomatic relations between the United States and China. In the 1990s Kingman's paintings were the subject of two major exhibitions in Taiwan: one at the Taipei Modern Art Museum in 1995 and the other at the Taichung Provincial Museum in 1999. Kingman's work appears in *San Francisco: City on Golden Hills* (1967), *Dong Kingman's Watercolors* (1980), *Paint the Yellow Tiger* (1991), and *Portraits of Cities* (1997).

Kingman died at age eighty-nine of pancreatic cancer at his home in Manhattan. His ashes were placed at the Church of Saint Mary the Virgin in New York City. Since his death, Kingman has been honored with several major exhibits. The American Academy of Motion Picture Arts and Sciences presented a special exhibition, "Dong Kingman: An American Master in Hollywood" (2000). This was followed by a national touring retrospective, "Dong Kingman: An American Master" (2000–2002), and "Dong Kingman: Watercolor Master" (2002–2003) in China. The Chinese Historical Society of America launched its new facilities with the "Dong Kingman in San Francisco" ex-

hibit (2001–2002). Also, Columbia University's School of Visual Arts and the American Watercolor Society established awards named after him.

Kingman's artwork has been collected by major institutions such as the Boston Museum of Fine Arts, the Art Institute of Chicago, and the M. H. de Young Memorial Museum of Art in San Francisco. New York City's Whitney Museum of American Art, the Metropolitan Museum of Art, and the Museum of Modern Art have also collected his work.

Kingman was one of the world's finest watercolorists, whose fresh, bold, vibrant paintings of urban scenes were appreciated by viewers worldwide. His work, which can energize the heart and calm the mind, shows not only the artist's mastery of the medium, but also tells a story of his quest to unite the best of the Western and Eastern cultures. His skill and techniques and his enthusiasm and sense of humor inspired and influenced thousands of students, art professionals, and friends.

★

Kingman's books and exhibits are important sources for information about his life and work. Alan Gruskin, *The Water Colors of Dong Kingman, and How the Artist Works* (1958), contains useful material about Kingman's life. Monte James, *Dong Kingman: An American Master* (2000), contains information about Kingman and his watercolors. See also Monte James, "Dong Kingman: Master Watercolor Artist," *Arts of Asia* 33, no.1 (Jan.–Feb. 2003): 130–133. Obituaries are in the *New York Times*, *San Francisco Chronicle*, and *Chicago Tribune* (all 16 May 2000). See also *Dong Kingman* (1954), a fifteen-minute documentary by James Wong Howe.

JUDY X. XIAO

KLEINDIENST, Richard Gordon (*b.* 5 August 1923 near Winslow, Arizona; *d.* 3 February 2000 in Prescott, Arizona), U.S. Attorney General noted for the scandals in which he was involved and suspected by historians of being the mysterious "Deep Throat" of the Watergate scandal.

Kleindienst was born on a farm owned by his parents, Alfred R. Kleindienst, a postmaster and brakeman for a railroad, and Gladys (Love) Kleindienst, a homemaker. Kleindienst was an only child. His mother died when he was a small boy, and his father hired a Navaho woman to keep house. From her, the boy learned to speak Navaho fluently. His association with this woman, as well as with ethnic minorities at school, may have influenced the remarkably tolerant racial policies he supported in his later career.

Kleindienst was a hard worker in and out of class, working on two paper routes in grammar school and at a gas

Richard G. Kleindienst, January 1969. BETTMANN/CORBIS

station in high school. From 1941 to 1943 Kleindienst attended the University of Arizona, where he joined the U.S. Army Reserve Officer Training Corps. In 1943 he was called to active duty during World War II, serving as a navigator in Italy for the U.S. Army Air Forces. Discharged in 1946, he enrolled at Harvard University in Cambridge, Massachusetts, where he earned a B.A., graduating magna cum laude in 1947. He then entered Harvard Law School.

On 3 September 1948 Kleindienst married Margaret Dunbar, with whom he had four children. The Kleindiensts made a point of enrolling their children in ethnically mixed public schools. In 1950 Kleindienst received his LL.D. and then moved the family to Phoenix, where he joined the law firm of Jennings, Strauss, Salmon, and Trask. While in Arizona, he met Senator Barry Goldwater, who urged him to become involved in politics.

In 1952 Kleindienst was elected a delegate to the Republican Party's national convention, where he supported Dwight D. Eisenhower's nomination as presidential candidate. Later that year, Kleindienst was elected to the Arizona House of Representatives and served one term. In 1955 he became chairman of the Arizona Young Republican League and remained active in state Republican politics thereafter. He became a senior partner in the law firm of Shimmel, Hill, Kleindienst, and Bishop in 1958.

From 1956 to 1963 Kleindienst served on the Arizona Republican Central Committee and, with the exception of 1962, on the Republican National Committee. In 1964 Kleindienst left his committee positions to concentrate on Goldwater's campaign for the presidency and his own run for Arizona governor. He was the director of "field operations" for Goldwater's campaign and during the primaries was accused of employing "dirty tricks" to discredit Goldwater's Republican opponents. The accusations, however, were unproven.

The Democratic Party proved much more adept at dirty tricks than the Republican during the presidential campaign, inventing what is now known as the "hit piece," a deceptive television commercial intended to discredit an opponent. The spot showed a sweet-looking little girl, whose daisy picking is interrupted—permanently—by a nuclear explosion, the implication being that Goldwater would incinerate little girls with nuclear bombs. The impact of the "daisy commercial" was devastating. Although 1964 proved to be a bad election year for Republicans nationally, in Arizona they did well, except for the race for the governorship, which Kleindienst lost to Sam Goddard. In 1966 he ran John R. Williams's victorious campaign for governor of Arizona.

In 1968 Kleindienst became the national director of Richard Nixon's campaign for the presidency. Nixon claimed a narrow victory over the Democrat Hubert H. Humphrey that year, with some of the credit going to Kleindienst's savvy campaign decisions. At the urging of Goldwater, President Richard M. Nixon appointed Kleindienst deputy U.S. Attorney General.

Kleindienst, who took office 31 January 1969, quickly became a focus for controversy. Although notably articulate and a fine administrator, he was defensive and abrasive and supported repressive tactics against those who publicly protested U.S. involvement in the Vietnam War. Kleindienst's achievements became even more visible when he became U.S. Attorney General on 12 June 1972. He had already made a hard-driving, successful push to hire members of ethnic minorities into the Justice Department and to enlist lawyers from ethnic minorities, now he pressed the department to enforce civil rights laws.

In spite of these positive efforts, Kleindienst became involved in a scandal involving the industrial giant International Telephone and Telegraph (ITT). In early 1972, during confirmation hearings with the Senate Judiciary Committee, Kleindienst testified that he had not brought an end to a Justice Department antitrust prosecution of ITT because it had contributed to Nixon's 1968 presidential campaign. Documents later revealed that Nixon had telephoned Kleindienst and demanded that the ITT prosecution be dropped, soon after which the Justice Department settled out of court with ITT. Many casual observers attributed Kleindienst's resignation as attorney general on 30 April 1973 to the ITT scandal, but a more likely cause was his tenuous position because of Watergate. When Kleindienst was informed in 1973 of the break-in at the Democratic Party headquarters in the Watergate Hotel, he immediately launched an investigation that, at his express direction, was to leave out no suspect. He refused to call off the Federal Bureau of Investigation probe, instead encouraging it, and pressed for Justice Department prosecutions. This placed him at odds with Nixon and the president's inner circle, putting Kleindienst in an almost impossible position. The result was his resignation.

In March 1974 the special prosecutor Leon Jaworski charged Kleindienst with not fully answering the Senate's queries about ITT, a misdemeanor to which Kleindienst pleaded guilty (he later expressed regret for this decision) on 16 May 1974. He received a $100 fine and a thirty-day suspended sentence. Kleinsienst then returned to Arizona. In 1981 he became involved in an insurance scandal, and was suspended from practicing law for one year by the Arizona Bar Association. He also briefly lost his right to argue cases before the U.S. Supreme Court, but was later acquitted on all charges and restored to full rights as a practicing attorney.

Kleindienst continued to practice law, amid ever increasing speculation that he was "Deep Throat," a secretive government figure who clandestinely revealed the facts of the Watergate cover-up to the press. The speculation was fueled by evidence that he had resisted the cover-up of the break-in and had pressed for a full investigation, no matter where it would lead. In 1995 Kleindienst was diagnosed as having lung cancer, of which he died five years later.

Although Kleindienst was caught up in scandals during his career, and his treatment of First Amendment rights during the Vietnam War made him a controversial figure,

he was almost universally regarded as a good man, even by political opponents. He was gregarious and made friends easily, and was admired by most of those who worked with him. His principal character flaw may have been allowing his feelings of loyalty to override his common sense, although in the acid test of the Watergate scandal he took the high moral ground and stubbornly held to it throughout his dismissal from office and public humiliation. His most enduring legacy may be the bettering of civil rights for ethnic minorities, and his finest hour may have been when he refused to involve the Justice Department in a cover-up of government misdeeds. A strong supporter of law and order, Kleindienst insisted that the law should apply to everyone, no matter how powerful.

★

Kleindienst's autobiography, *Justice: The Memoirs of Attorney General Richard Kleindienst* (1985), is mostly an account of the people he knew and admired. Obituaries are in the *Chicago Tribune, New York Times,* and *Washington Post* (all 4 Feb. 2000).

KIRK H. BEETZ

KNOWLES, John (*b.* 16 September 1926 in Fairmont, West Virginia; *d.* 29 November 2001 near Fort Lauderdale, Florida), fiction and travel writer whose coming-of-age novel *A Separate Peace* (1959) became required reading for generations of high school students.

The third child of James Myron Knowles, a vice president of Consolidation Coal Company, and Mary Beatrice (Shea) Knowles, a homemaker, Knowles grew up in privileged wealth in the rural Appalachian Mountains of West Virginia. After attending a primary school in Fairmont, Knowles was expected to follow his older brother to a preparatory school in Pennsylvania; instead, on a whim, at the age of fifteen, he applied and was accepted to the prestigious Phillips Exeter Academy in New Hampshire. His few years there were, in his words, "more crucial in my life than in the lives of most members of my class, and conceivably, than in the lives of almost anyone else who ever attended the school."

The decisive time there was the summer of 1943, when Knowles completed remedial class work after earning poor grades during his first year at the school. He and his classmate friends formed a group known as the Super Suicide Society of the Summer Session. Members were initiated by jumping off a high tree branch into an adjacent river. The memories of that summer became the vivid set pieces of his novel *A Separate Peace* (1959) and its sequel, *Peace Breaks Out* (1981).

After graduating from Exeter in 1945, Knowles served for several months in the U.S. Army Air Force's Aviation

Cadet Program and later enrolled as an English major at Yale University in New Haven, Connecticut, earning a B.A. in 1949. From 1950 to 1952 he worked as a reporter and drama critic for the *Hartford Courant* in Connecticut. Another reporter there at that time was the journalist and cultural critic David Halberstam. After a three-year grand tour of Europe, in 1955 Knowles became an associate editor at *Holiday* magazine.

When he was not writing travel pieces, Knowles wrote short stories and a novel-length manuscript that was laden with symbols. While in Europe, Knowles befriended the playwright Thornton Wilder, who read the manuscript. Wilder told Knowles that it lacked vivid character portraits based on the author's real memories of past events. Knowles scrapped the manuscript and then wrote what would become *A Separate Peace.*

After the novel was published in 1959, Knowles received both the William Faulkner Foundation Award and the Rosenthal Award from the National Institute of Arts and Letters. The coming-of-age book, set in a prep school, was hailed as a worthy successor to *The Catcher in the Rye* (1951), by J. D. Salinger, and *Lord of the Flies* (1954), by William Golding. The novel has remained a perennial best-seller, with more than ten million copies sold during Knowles's lifetime. Paramount Pictures made it into a film in 1972. With the book's success and with financial security, Knowles quit *Holiday* magazine and traveled widely.

Knowles's autobiographical novel describes an idyllic summer term at a New England prep school, where a "separate peace" reigned while the United States was swept into World War II. The narrator recounts retrospectively his teenage allegiance to two fellow students. One is a buttoned-down, conservative student leader, a character based on the novelist Gore Vidal, one of Knowles's classmates at Exeter. The second student is an athletic eccentric who is crippled when he is pushed from a tree. With simple, but nuanced words, the novel explores the competitive good and evil natures underlying the novel's personalities. Critics and millions of readers still debate the ambiguity of the narrator's guilt concerning his classmate's fall and eventual death. Knowles never revealed the truth of the narrator's responsibility in the incident.

During the 1960s Knowles was a writer in residence at the University of North Carolina at Chapel Hill and at Princeton University in New Jersey. *Morning in Antibes* (1962) concerns the moral dilemmas of Americans living on the French Riviera. Most critics felt that it was a major disappointment, as was *Indian Summer* (1966), about two childhood best friends meeting again in middle age. Knowles's *Paragon* (1971) was set at his alma mater, Yale University, where two roommates, one arrogant and wealthy and the other modest and poor, compete melodramatically. *Spreading Fires* (1974) was a psychological thriller set in the south

John Knowles, 1972. AP/WIDE WORLD PHOTOS

of France. In both *Paragon* and *Spreading Fires,* the characters and their emotional natures create events pitting active against passive people in disjointed scenes that draw parallels between a character's past and some present event. Most critics thought that *Paragon* was more successful because it offered a satirical look at college life. Critics viewed *Fires* as a jumble of hackneyed situations and stagy dialogue. Both books were thought to be too derivative of *A Separate Peace.*

In 1978 Knowles published a sprawling saga set in his native coal-mining West Virginia. *A Vein of Riches* portrays the waning fortunes of two generations of a coal baron's family contrasted with the misfortunes of a coal miner's family. Most critics thought that the family melodrama and events of the mines were trite and that any narrative imagination had been mined out.

From the 1980s, Knowles lived in Fort Lauderdale, where he taught creative writing at Florida Atlantic University. *Peace Breaks Out* (1981) was a sequel to his first novel, and it treats malevolence leading to murder at a boarding school. *A Stolen Past* (1983), set at Yale University, is a reminiscence of college friendships. His last novel, *The Private Life of Axie Reed* (1986), concerns an aging actress suddenly confronting her own mortality, just as Knowles had done in a near-fatal auto accident in 1983.

Knowles's travel pieces are collected in *Double Vision: American Thoughts Abroad* (1964); his short stories are collected in *Phineas: Six Short Stories* (1968).

After the extraordinary success of *A Separate Peace*, Knowles's subsequent novels were unfavorably compared to his first book, which he often called "my albatross." A skilled stylist, Knowles explored the emotional and psychological connections of contrasting characters. He died after a short illness at age seventy-five. He never married.

★

Knowles donated his early longhand manuscripts to the library of the Phillips Exeter Academy. Other manuscripts are at the Beinecke Rare Book and Manuscript Library at Yale. His autobiography is *Backcasts: Memories and Recollections of Seventy Years as a Sportsman: Fishing, Hunting and Other Stories* (1993). For information on Knowles's life and the historical background of *A Separate Peace,* see Hallman Bell Bryant, *A Separate Peace: The War Within* (1990). Obituaries are in the *Los Angeles Times* and *New York Times* (both 1 Dec. 2001).

PATRICK S. SMITH

KOCH, Kenneth Jay (*b.* 27 February 1925 in Cincinnati, Ohio; *d.* 6 July 2002 in Manhattan, New York City), avant-garde poet, playwright, and novelist who received the Bollingen Prize in poetry and was a principal figure in the New York School of poetry.

The son of Stuart J. Koch, a furniture store owner, and Lillian Amy (Loth) Koch, an amateur literary reviewer (whose surname is pronounced "coke"), was raised in a middle-class family in Cincinnati. He was an affable and brilliant student. His poor eyesight kept him from becoming a military meteorologist in World War II but not from being drafted into the army in 1943, where he served as a rifleman in the Philippines until hepatitis forced his evacuation in 1945. After the war Koch enrolled at Harvard University in Cambridge, Massachusetts, where he earned an A.B. in 1948. Koch went on to earn an M.A. in English and comparative literature in 1953 and a Ph.D. in 1959, both from Columbia University in New York City.

While at Harvard, Koch became a lifelong friend and rival of the poet John Ashbery. After graduation, Koch moved to New York City and joined the thriving art, literature, and music scene of the 1950s. An early poem, "In Love with You," captures the high spirits of the time: "As if the world were a taxi, you enter it, then / Reply (to no one), 'Let's go five or six blocks.'" Koch, Ashbery, Frank O'Hara, and James Schuyler became known as the New York School of poets. Koch's poetry embodied all of the movement's elements; his mix of surreal imagery, slapstick humor, wide-ranging cultural allusiveness, and graceful

Kenneth Koch. MR. CHRIS FELVER

lyricism revolted against the prevailing literary formalism of the day. Koch's writing was especially engaged with avant-garde work in other media: his first book, *Poems* (1953), was published by the Tibor de Nagy Gallery, with accompanying prints by the artist Nell Blaine.

In 1950–1951 Koch held a Fulbright Fellowship in France, where his imperfect command of French inspired him to write poetry with the same energetic and buzzing confusion of language he had experienced firsthand. After returning to the United States, he began a long teaching career, first as a lecturer in English at Rutgers University (1953–1958) and Brooklyn College (1957–1959) and then as a professor of English and comparative literature at Columbia University (1959–2002). He married Mary Janice Elwood on 12 June 1954; they had one daughter.

In 1959 Koch published his mock epic *Ko; or, A Season on Earth.* Modeled partly after the Romantic British poet George Gordon Byron's *Don Juan* and delighting in absurd rhymes ("oranger" with "porringer," for instance), it followed the mishaps of such characters as Ko, a Japanese student who becomes a pitcher for the Dodgers baseball team. It was followed by *Thank You, and Other Poems* (1962), *The Pleasures of Peace, and Other Poems* (1969), *When the Sun Tries to Go On* (1969), and *Sleeping with Women* (1969), books that reveled in love and ordinary urban life and derided solemn poetry. In "Variations on a Theme by William Carlos Williams," Koch parodies and celebrates a famous modern poem: "Last evening we went dancing and I broke your leg. / Forgive me. I was clumsy, and / I wanted you here in the wards, where I am the doctor!"

During the 1960s and 1970s Koch wrote, cowrote, and produced numerous off- and off-off-Broadway plays. Experimental in technique, the plays often poked fun at avant-garde sensibilities in order to show the comic potential of experimentation. Around this time Koch also led poetry workshops for children in a New York City public school, an experience that inspired several pioneering books on teaching poetry to children, including *Wishes, Lies and Dreams: Teaching Children to Write Poetry* (1970). This devotion also drew Koch to teach poetry to elderly nursing home residents in the mid-1970s, an experience he recounted in *I Never Told Anybody: Teaching Poetry Writing in a Nursing Home* (1977).

With *The Art of Love* (1975), Koch's poetry began showing a reflective turn. While never falling into the confessional mode, his poems nevertheless look back on his early life in New York City, his friendships and artistic discoveries, as well as his more personal experiences, including his military service and his love for his wife, who died in 1981. His poetic production slowed somewhat in the 1980s, but after marrying Karen Culler on 29 December 1994, Koch wrote several important books of poetry, including *One Train: Poems* (1994), *Straits: Poems* (1998), *New Addresses: Poems* (2000), and *A Possible World: Poems* (2002).

Significant recognition of Koch's career came late. *One Thousand Avant-Garde Plays* (1988) was nominated for the National Book Critics Circle Award in 1988. In 1995 Koch received the Bollingen Prize from Yale University, and in 1996 he was elected a member of the American Academy of Arts and Letters. In 2000 his book *New Addresses* was a finalist for the National Book Award in poetry. A series of apostrophes, or direct addresses, to themes that occupied Koch's career, it includes a hauntingly clear statement about the link between Koch's life and art in "To Breath": "I want to understand certain things and tell them to others. . . . / Stay with me until I can do this. // Afterwards, you can go where you want." Koch died of leukemia in Manhattan.

In an era dominated by the personal expressive lyric, Koch's blend of linguistic verve, wide-ranging allusiveness, and irreverence made him perhaps the most significant comic poet after World War II. Fighting against the solemnity of lyric solitude, Koch favored all forms of collaboration. His theater productions brought him together with set designers, his collaborative writings energized the play of ideas, and his efforts to teach poetry to children and the elderly demonstrated the importance of taking pleasure in

the process of poetry rather than its product. While Ashbery and O'Hara have garnered much of the praise for the New York School, Koch's work remains mysteriously undervalued for such a major poet. A crucial figure in the American avant-garde, his lyricism and wild humor never seem to age, and his ceaseless delight in the act of creation mocks all that is somber and sober in modern literature.

★

Kenneth Koch, *The Art of Poetry: Poems, Parodies, Interviews, Essays, and Other Work* (1996), is an excellent introduction to the poet's work and thought. David Lehman offers an engaging biography and memoir of Koch in *The Last Avant-Garde: The Making of the New York School of Poets* (1998). Dean Young, "In Defiance of Gravity: A Final Interview with Kenneth Koch," *Poets and Writers* (Sept./Oct. 2002), is a recorded conversation that provides good biographical detail. An obituary is in the *New York Times* (7 July 2002).

TEMPLE CONE

KRAMER, Stanley Earl (*b.* 23 September 1913 in Manhattan, New York City; *d.* 19 February 2001 in Woodland Hills, California), independent motion picture producer and director who consistently challenged the Hollywood system, highlighting such social problems as racism, greed, and McCarthyism.

Kramer was born and raised in New York City's Hell's Kitchen, a notoriously tough neighborhood on Manhattan's west side in the 1920s and 1930s. An only child, he was raised by his mother, Mildred, and his maternal grandparents; his father abandoned the family, and Kramer never had any contact with him. The family lived in a one-bedroom apartment while Kramer's mother worked as a secretary in the New York offices of Paramount Studios. Kramer grew up poor, but his mother instilled in him the need for education. A bright student, he attended local public schools and graduated from DeWitt Clinton High School in 1928 at age fifteen; he also was active in the gang life of Hell's Kitchen. On the streets he learned about racism firsthand: the gangs in the area divided along racial lines. This experience also taught him about crossing racial barriers.

Kramer's street education was combined with a swift transition from school to the work world. Kramer remarked on his one major regret about his early life: "I was shoved through Manhattan's schools, and through New York University from the age of fifteen to nineteen, so fast that I forgot my youth." He graduated from New York University (NYU) in 1933 with a B.S. in business administration. During his years at NYU, he wrote for the school's literary magazine, the *Medley*. This experience gave him a taste for

Stanley Kramer. THE KOBAL COLLECTION

writing, and, with the depression in full swing, he moved to California in the hope of becoming a screenwriter.

Kramer's efforts to create screenplays were not successful initially. He spent several years working on sets before landing a job in the research department at Metro-Goldwyn-Mayer (MGM). He worked his way into the editing department and by 1938 was a senior editor. He then left MGM to write screenplays for Columbia and Republic Pictures while also contributing to several radio programs. In 1942 he went back to MGM to help produce films with David L. Loew.

In 1943, during World War II, Kramer joined the U.S. Army Signal Corps, made training films, and learned the craft of making movies quickly and cheaply. After the war he went back to California, and by 1947 he had started his own independent production company, called Screen Plays, Inc. He quickly secured the rights to two stories by Ring Lardner, "The Big Town" and "Champion." They became the basis for his first motion pictures.

In 1948 "The Big Town" became *So This Is New York,* a light comedy about the luckless adventures of a family in the great city. Filmed in just forty-eight days, it was the beginning of Kramer's quickly produced films, but it was a commercial failure. His next production, *Champion,* was his first commercial and critical success. Appearing in 1949,

Champion starred Kirk Douglas in his first major role, as Midge Kelly, a savage boxer who works his way from the street to the championship of the world. The film depicts a dark world of brutality and greed; Midge becomes the champion only at the price of his humanity. Classified as film noir, *Champion* was Kramer's first critique of American commercialism. The film was critically lauded and received an Academy Award for best editing.

Kramer quickly followed *Champion* with the first major motion picture to use racial epithets onscreen and the first to discuss racism in the military. *Home of the Brave* starred James Edwards as an African-American soldier who is shell-shocked and partially paralyzed after a fierce battle in the Pacific. The soldier's paralysis in the hospital is psychological, caused by a lifetime of systematic racism, which is epitomized by the way he is treated by his combat buddies. The film continued Kramer's investigation of the American value system. It also was critically praised and commercially successful.

The early 1950s were busy for Kramer: he married Ann Pearce, with whom he had two children. And he quickly produced a succession of films through his independent company and through an arrangement with Columbia. In these years he made *The Men* (1950), the first film starring Marlon Brando; *Cyrano de Bergerac* (1950); the first film production of Arthur Miller's play *Death of a Salesman* (1951); *My Six Convicts* (1952); *The Sniper* (1952), an influential film noir directed by Edward Dmytryk, who had been out of work before Kramer hired him; and the classic western *High Noon* (1952), an allegory of McCarthyism. McCarthyism was named after Senator Joseph McCarthy, who during the 1950s conducted a wide-ranging investigation of alleged communists in the U.S. State Department and the broader American society. *High Noon* depicted the political reaction and the social paranoia of the 1950s under the guise of the Western genre. Kramer employed many "blacklisted" writers and directors—branded as politically questionable by McCarthy and those who feared the influence of communism in Hollywood—during this period.

Kramer followed *High Noon* with *The Happy Time* (1952); *The Four Poster* (1952); *Eight Iron Men* (1952); *The Member of the Wedding* (1952), based on the play by Carson McCullers; *The Juggler* (1953); *The 5,000 Fingers of Dr. T* (1953), from a story and screenplay by Dr. Seuss; *The Wild One* (1954), starring Marlon Brando in the first biker movie; and *The Caine Mutiny* (1954), starring Humphrey Bogart in one of his most critically praised roles.

By the mid-1950s Kramer's reputation as a maker of "message films" was established. His version of *Death of a Salesman* was, as he put it, the first major film to be "picketed by Communist-hunting right wingers." As well as producing films, he began directing films with *Not as a Stranger* (1955), starring Robert Mitchum and Frank Sinatra. This first film was a financial success, but it was quickly followed by the biggest failure in his career, *The Pride and the Passion* (1957), a big-budget disaster that failed with critics and bombed at the box office.

In 1958 Kramer countered the failure of *The Pride and the Passion* with *The Defiant Ones,* one of the most powerful films of his long career. This film became his personal favorite, and it has remained one of his best known. *The Defiant Ones* is the story of two convicts, played by Tony Curtis and Sidney Poitier. The men, who are handcuffed together on a chain gang, escape. Prison iron binds them, but racial hatred separates them. Throughout their escape, they come to realize their common humanity and toss aside the prejudices separating them. The film is one of the most powerful statements about race relations ever produced in Hollywood. Poitier, who received an Academy Award nomination for his role, believed the movie was an important social statement. He remarked that Kramer's producing such films as *The Home of the Brave* and *The Defiant Ones* showed that he "was a man who made hard choices, choices based on his own conscience. He made one hell of a commitment to things when commitment was difficult for everyone."

Kramer ended his 1950s films with *On the Beach* (1959), a movie about the end of the world. Gregory Peck and Ava Gardner starred in this film about nuclear holocaust, a relevant topic at the height of the cold war. Kramer moved into the 1960s with *Inherit the Wind* (1960), starring Spencer Tracy, an actor who would figure prominently in later Kramer productions. Tracy starred in Kramer's *Judgment at Nuremberg* (1961), one of the first films to depict the Nazi war crime trials. That same year, Kramer received a special Oscar: the Irving G. Thalberg Award for "consistently high quality in filmmaking."

After directing *Judgment at Nuremberg,* Kramer produced three films in quick succession: *Pressure Point* (1962), starring Poitier as a psychologist experiencing the pathology of racism via a young Nazi played by Bobby Darin; *A Child Is Waiting* (1963), starring Burt Lancaster; and a western called *Invitation to a Gunfighter* (1964). In 1963 Kramer directed a comedy, *It's a Mad, Mad, Mad, Mad World*—the first since he had produced *So This Is New York* in 1948. He loaded it with comedians, including Milton Berle, Sid Caeser, Buddy Hackett, Dick Shawn, Phil Silvers, Terry-Thomas, and even the Three Stooges. A sprawling chase film, it inspired many later chase comedies.

Kramer followed *It's a Mad, Mad, Mad, Mad World* by directing an adaptation of a Katherine Anne Porter novel, *Ship of Fools* (1965). In 1966 he married Karen Sharpe; they had two daughters. *Guess Who's Coming to Dinner* (1967) was the most important film of Kramer's late career. Starring Tracy, Katharine Hepburn, and Poitier, *Guess Who's Coming to Dinner* was a light comedy with a serious theme: interracial marriage. This was a forbidden topic in Hollywood (only the renegade filmmaker Samuel Fuller had tackled it in his 1959 crime drama *Crimson Kimono*). The film did well at the box office but was blasted by critics, who saw it as simplistic and moralizing. Poitier again believed in Kramer, calling *Guess Who's Coming to Dinner* a "totally revolutionary movie."

Kramer ended his directing career with a series of uneven films that may have harmed his reputation: *The Secret of Santa Vittoria* (1969), starring Anthony Quinn; *RPM* (1970), a film about student unrest on American campuses that the critic Donald Spoto called "the nadir of Kramer's directorial career"; *Bless the Beasts and Children* (1971); *Oklahoma Crude* (1973); *The Domino Principle* (1976); and *The Runner Stumbles* (1979). In 1991 Kramer received the Producers Guild's David O. Selznick Award and the Lifetime Achievement Award from the American Foundation for the Performing Arts.

Critical appraisals of Kramer's career have always been divided. For the critic David Thompson, Kramer's "films are middlebrow and overemphatic; at worst, they are among the most tedious and dispiriting productions the American cinema has to offer." As Donald Spoto has noted, however, "He was the first to make mainstream Hollywood films about pressing and often unpopular issues." Kramer also was one of the founding figures of independent moviemaking. As a producer and director, he put social problems on the screen that had never been seen in a Hollywood film; he hired blacklisted writers and directors and, in *High Noon,* produced one of cinema's strongest attacks on political hypocrisy; and he brought to almost every film he made a sense of social conviction. He once said, "What grabs me in cinematic terms is the idea of telling a story against a background of social or political conflict." Kramer gave "social or political conflict" a place in popular Hollywood filmmaking. He died at the Motion Picture and Television Fund Hospital following a brief bout with pneumonia.

★

Kramer told the story of his filmmaking life in *A Mad, Mad, Mad, Mad World: A Life in Hollywood* (1997). A comprehensive survey of Kramer's films can be found in Donald Spoto, *Stanley Kramer: Filmmaker* (1978). An obituary is in the *New York Times* (21 Feb. 2001).

JOHN ROCCO

KRIENDLER, H. Peter ("Pete") (*b.* 8 July 1905 in Brooklyn, New York City; *d.* 21 December 2001 in Manhattan, New York City), restaurateur of the family-owned "21" Club, a legendary restaurant in New York City.

Kriendler was the fourth of eight children of Austrian-Jewish immigrants Kieve (Carl) Kriendler, a metalworker, and Sadie Kriendler, a midwife. He grew up in a fifth-floor walk-up tenement apartment in New York City's Lower East Side. His father, a welder at the Brooklyn Navy Yard, died of influenza in 1917, leaving the family dependent on his mother's income as a midwife and on money from his uncle Sam, a saloonkeeper. In his memoir, Kriendler depicts his uncle as being the inspiration for his family's business, because his uncle served only quality liquor and food, charged top dollar, and created a congenial and hospitable atmosphere.

After leaving Public School 120, Kriendler attended DeWitt Clinton High School. In 1920 the Eighteenth Amendment, known as the Volstead Act, outlawed the making and selling of liquor. Illegal drinking establishments, called speakeasies, flourished until 1934, when the Twenty-First Amendment repealed the Volstead Act. In 1922 Kriendler's brothers, Jack and Mack, as well as their partner, Charles A. Berns, opened a speakeasy called the Red Head in Manhattan's Greenwich Village. Along with his two other brothers, Kriendler worked there sweeping the floor, serving food, and tending bar. Kriendler wrote in his memoir that at age sixteen, "all I could do was sip a soft drink and hang around trying to act like a big cheese while hoping to catch a dance with one of the 'flappers.'"

While attending night classes at City College of New York, Kriendler became a broker on the New York Curb Market (now the American Stock Exchange). In 1929 he earned a law degree from Saint Lawrence University in Canton, New York. In 1933 he married Jeannette Epstein, who died in 1991. They had no children. Instead of pursuing a career in law, Kriendler worked at his family's speakeasy. Its name and locale changed several times. On New Year's Eve 1930, it opened at 21 West Fifty-second Street. By then called the "21" Club, it was housed in a brownstone building refashioned by the architect Francis Buchanan, who devised the club's ingenious raid-proof hidden closets and vaults, as well as drop-away shelving and chutes. A wine cellar, hidden in an adjacent brownstone, contained more than 25,000 wine bottles. The first floor bar served quality liquors smuggled from Europe. Mixed drinks invented at "21" include the Southside, Bloody Mary, Ramos Gin Fizz, and B and B (Benedictine and brandy). Later, it became the first East Coast restaurant to showcase California wines.

Kriendler was known as "Mr. Pete" to employees and as "Pete" to patrons. In 1938 he became a partner; in 1946, when his brother Jack died, he became the executive manager and host of the club. During the 1930s and the 1940s the adjoining brownstones were annexed to provide more rooms for the club. The facade had an elaborate iron gate and twenty-one trademark cast-iron jockeys. Kriendler was a congenial host to countless authors, politicians, business tycoons, and celebrities, including the writers Ernest Hemingway, Robert Benchley, and John O'Hara; the actors Clark Gable and Joan Crawford; and presidents Franklin D. Roosevelt and Richard M. Nixon. With an aura of cordial hospitality, the "21" Club was the place to meet and dine, to see and to be seen.

During World War II the columnist Ed Sullivan hosted a weekly radio program from "21." The club was also featured in movies, including *All about Eve* (1950), *The Sweet Smell of Success* (1957), and *Wall Street* (1987). In the club, trademark red-and-white checkerboard cloths covered small tables that were set against paneled walls. The first floor bar was decorated with *New Yorker* magazine cartoons by Peter Arno. Elsewhere, Kriendler adorned the "21" Club with his own extensive collection of artworks by Frederic Remington. American western art was a passion for Kriendler, who donated other Remington works to the Whitney Gallery of Western Art at the Buffalo Bill Historical Center in Cody, Wyoming. During many summers Kriendler visited Wyoming to hunt and fish.

The "21" Club served only the freshest game and fish prepared by a succession of renowned executive chefs (Henri Geib, Yves-Louis Ploneis, Anthony Pedretti, and Michael Lomonaco). Kriendler constantly searched worldwide for just the right delicacy, such as freshly killed grouse, placed on the lunch menu the day after the shooting season opened in Scotland. Meals were astronomically expensive, with the least costly item—the "21" hamburger—priced at more than $40 at the time of Kriendler's death. Although the liquor and meals were always of high quality, it was Kriendler's legendary hospitality that brought patrons back as regular customers.

Kriendler took genuine care of his loyal staff and famous patrons. A master of studious elitism, Kriendler instinctively knew just where to seat one of his achiever patrons. Indeed, a good table was considered a badge of honor and esteem of café society. Kriendler installed a telephone hookup at every table, and a switchboard operator handled the calls and messages of customers. Kriendler perfected the art of diplomacy, chatting with patrons, introducing people, and solving problems. If the actor Cary Grant felt like having a peanut butter and jelly sandwich, that is what he got. Once an unruly customer lingered long past closing time. Kriendler turned up the lights, but the patron refused to take the hint. Kriendler presented the check, and the customer paid with a $1,000 bill. Kriendler counted out the change in small bills and coins. The following evening, the same customer returned and apologized about the incident. With a smile, Kriendler replied, "Last night? What incident?"

After viewing a documentary about Albert Schweitzer and his medical clinic in the Congo, Kriendler made several visits and asked how he could help. Schweitzer replied that the clinic patients needed shoes. Kriendler called the chairman of U.S. Rubber, a "21" patron, and arranged to have hundreds of shoes shipped to the clinic.

Kriendler helped transform a family speakeasy into a restaurant that became a legend. When he retired in 1985, the "21" Club was sold for $21 million to General Felt Industries, a holding company headed by Marshall S. Cogan and Stephen Swid, who then invested another $10 million to renovate the restaurant. Kriendler and his wife spent their retirement in New York, Wyoming, Alaska, and Scotland. He died of natural causes at his home at age ninety-six. He is buried in Mount Carmel Cemetery in Glendale, New York.

★

Kriendler's autobiography is *"21": Every Day Was New Year's Eve: Memoirs of a Saloon Keeper* (1999), with H. Paul Jeffers. See also Michael Lomonaco, *The "21" Cookbook: Recipes and Lore from New York's Fabled Restaurant* (1995), with Dona Forsman. An obituary is in the *New York Times* (22 Dec. 2001).

PATRICK S. SMITH

L

LAKE, Harriette. *See* Sothern, Ann.

LAMARR, Hedy (*b*. 9 November 1913 in Vienna, Austria; *d*. 19 January 2000 near Orlando, Florida), internationally acclaimed beauty and movie star of the 1930s and 1940s as well as an inventor.

Born Hedwig Eva Maria Kiesler, Lamarr was the only child of Emil Kiesler, a bank director, and Gertrud (Lichtwitz) Kiesler, a concert pianist; Lamarr was Jewish. (Some sources state that she was born in 1914 or even 1915, and it seems that she never revealed her true age.) She attended Vienna's most exclusive schools but was an indifferent scholar with a propensity to run away from home and a generally rebellious nature. At fifteen she skipped school one day and went to the nearby Sascha Film Studios, Vienna's version of Hollywood. (Lamarr dropped out of school and never attained a high school degree.)

Lamarr's remarkably good looks led to an audition and subsequent small parts in several films. A raven-haired beauty with large, lustrous eyes and alabaster skin, Lamarr was declared by Max Reinhardt, the famous German director, to be the most beautiful girl in the world. In 1932, at age sixteen, Lamarr starred in *Ecstasy*. An almost silent film, it featured a nude swim; a naked romp through the forest outside Prague, Czechoslovakia; and Lamarr in the throes of an orgasm the likes of which had never been seen before in the cinema. It became an international sensation and was banned by the pope and scores of cities and towns in the United States. Frederick ("Fritz") Alexander Mandl, the proprietor of one of central Europe's leading munitions manufacturing plants, saw *Ecstasy* and petitioned Lamarr's parents for her hand in marriage. He then tried to buy up all the copies of *Ecstasy* and destroy them. He did not succeed with this latter quest.

Lamarr married Mandl on 10 August 1933 and became hostess at lavish dinner parties with the high and mighty of Europe, including the German dictator Adolf Hitler and the Italian leader Benito Mussolini. She soon became bored by her marriage to the much older Mandl and took off for London, obtaining a Parisian divorce in 1937. In London she met the visiting head of the Hollywood studio Metro-Goldwyn-Mayer (MGM), Louis B. Mayer, who had seen *Ecstasy* and offered Lamarr a film contract, changing her name to "Hedy Lamarr" after Barbara Lamarr, a silent-screen actress he admired.

Lamarr made several pictures at MGM, but her career did not take off until 1938, when she met the French actor Charles Boyer at a party and he offered her the starring role opposite him in *Algiers,* a remake of the gritty French film *Pepe le Moko. Algiers* and Lamarr were a smash hit. Harvard University students voted Lamarr "the girl they would most like to be marooned on a desert island with," and women all over the United States copied her parted-in-the-middle hairdo and began wearing turbans and pearls.

Hedy Lamarr. AP/WIDE WORLD PHOTOS

In 1940 Lamarr met the French musician George Antheil at a Hollywood dinner party, and she began to talk with him about her desire to aid the burgeoning U.S. defense effort. (She was naturalized as a U.S. citizen in 1953.) Remembering conversations she had overheard between Mandl and Nazi arms manufacturers at parties, Lamarr came up with a way to prevent an enemy from jamming a radio signal that was being used to steer torpedoes. The next day she and Antheil implemented her idea, now known as frequency hopping, using Antheil's expertise with player pianos. Lamarr and Antheil were awarded a patent for the technology in 1942. The U.S. Navy used it during the 1962 Cuban Missile Crisis, but the patent had expired in 1958, and Antheil and Lamarr never made any money from their invention. The technological descendents of the patent are used today to speed satellite signals across the globe, and frequency hopping remains at the heart of the U.S. Department of Defense's Milstar communication satellite system. There were some doubts that Lamarr had the technical expertise to contribute much to the project, but Antheil always credited her. Lamarr and Antheil were awarded the prestigious Pioneer Award from the Electronic Frontier Foundation in 1997. All Lamarr was to say about the award was "It's about time."

Married six times, Lamarr's second marriage, on 5 March 1939, was to the Hollywood writer and producer Gene Markey; they adopted a son. She married Markey on their first date, a trip to a Mexican beach. She divorced him in 1940 and on 27 May 1943 married John Loder, a British-born actor with whom she had two children. She divorced Loder in 1947 and on 12 June 1951 married Ted Stauffer, a former bandleader; they divorced in 1952. She married husband number five, the Texas oilman W. Howard Lee, on 22 December 1953; they divorced in 1960. Husband number six, whom she wed on 4 March 1963, was the lawyer Lewis W. Boies, Jr., but that marriage, too, did not last long, and they divorced in 1965. Of her many marriages, Lamarr famously announced, "I married all my lovers; that is what you did back then."

A sampling of Lamarr's movies and famous leading men includes *Lady of the Tropics* (1939) with Robert Taylor, *Comrade X* and *Boom Town* (both 1940) with Clark Gable, *Crossroads* (1942) and *The Heavenly Body* (1943) with William Powell, *Tortilla Flat* (1942) with Spencer Tracy, and *Copper Canyon* (1950) with Ray Milland. In *White Cargo* (1942) with Walter Pidgeon, Lamarr's pronouncement "I am Tondelayo" provided fodder for comedians for months to come. Also, only when it was discovered in the picture that the native girl Tondelayo was the product of an Arab father and an Egyptian mother—and therefore not black—was she permitted to marry the white coffee planter. Lamarr did, however, use poor judgment in turning down starring roles in *Casablanca* and *Gaslight,* films that made her contemporary Ingrid Bergman a star.

In contrast to other sex goddesses of the time, Lamarr consistently played strong, independent women who knew their value in the marketplace of erotic exchange and were not afraid to bargain. In 1949, her extraordinary beauty intact, she made *Samson and Delilah*. Directed by Cecil B. DeMille, who chose Lamarr for the part, the film was a big hit. In 1951 Lamarr made another highly successful movie, *My Favorite Spy,* opposite Bob Hope.

The return to the home in the 1950s of American women who had entered the workforce during World War II brought about a diminished interest in Lamarr's portrayals of aggressive and erotic women. The last half of her life was an endless round of bad husbands and courtroom scenes. In 1966 Lamarr published her autobiography, *Ecstasy and Me: My Life as a Woman,* an uninhibited account of her many sexual encounters with both sexes. She later sued her ghostwriters and publisher for defamation of character but lost the suit. She also was arrested twice in her later years for shoplifting inexpensive articles from Los Angeles and Florida stores, but she served no prison time. Her final years were spent in a two-room apartment on the outskirts of Orlando, Florida, living on Social Security and a small pension from the Screen Actors Guild. Lamarr was found dead of natural causes in her apartment, and her ashes interred in Vienna.

A highly intelligent woman, Lamarr's beautiful face and impulsive nature were her downfall. As she said near the end of her autobiography, "My face has been my misfortune. . . . It has attracted all the wrong people into my boudoir and brought me heartache and tragedy for five decades. My face is a mask I cannot remove. I must always live with it. I curse it."

★

Lamarr's autobiography is *Ecstasy and Me: My Life as a Woman* (1966). A children's biography with an emphasis on her role as inventor is Ann Gaines, *Hedy Lamarr* (2002). Her films are discussed at length in Christopher Young, *The Films of Hedy Lamarr* (1978), and Jan Christopher Horak, "High Class Whore," *CineAction* (spring 2001). Lamarr's career as an inventor also is detailed in Fleming Meels, "I Guess They Just Take and Forget About a Person," *Forbes* (14 May 1990), and Ludwig Siegele, "What's the Frequency, Hedy?" *Die Zeit* (11 Apr. 1997), reprinted in *World Press Review* (July 1997). Obituaries are in the *New York Times* (20 Jan. 2000) and *Variety* (24 Jan. 2000).

DOROTHY L. MORAN

LANDERS, Ann (Esther Pauline Lederer) (*b.* 4 July 1918 in Sioux City, Iowa; *d.* 22 June 2002 in Chicago, Illinois), advice columnist who influenced and reflected American mores in the second half of the twentieth century.

Ann Landers, 1955. MARK ELIAS. AP/WIDE WORLD PHOTOS

Ann Landers (the pen name of Eppie Lederer), was born Esther Pauline Friedman. She and her identical twin sister, Pauline Esther, were the youngest of four surviving children of Abraham Friedman, a grocer, and his wife, Rebecca (Rushall) Friedman, a homemaker, who were immigrants from Russia.

The twins, nicknamed Eppie and Popo, attended public schools in Sioux City and graduated from Central High School in 1936. From 1936 to 1939, they attended Morningside College, a Methodist-affiliated school where the Friedman twins stood out because they were Jewish. During their junior year, Popo became engaged to Morton Phillips, heir to a multimillion-dollar liquor fortune. Not long after, Eppie made a very different choice: Jules Lederer, a salesman at the T. S. Martin Department Store in Sioux City. The twins were married in a double wedding on 2 July 1939. Neither returned to college after marriage.

Eppie's only child, Margo, was born in 1940. The Lederers moved frequently: from Sioux City to St. Louis and back; to Little Rock, Arkansas; and then to New Orleans, Milwaukee, Los Angeles, Chicago, and Eau Claire, Wisconsin.

In Eau Claire, Eppie became involved in Democratic Party politics and was elected party chairwoman for the county in 1954. Not long after that, the Lederers moved to Chicago, where Jules became president of Autopoint, a manufacturer of ballpoint pens, and Eppie found herself frozen out of local politics by the entrenched Chicago Democratic machine.

Looking for something to do, Eppie became interested in an advice column in the *Chicago Sun-Times*. Newspaper advice columns, derisively called "lovelorn columns," had been around for a long time and tended to be ridden with sentiment. This one, by a columnist who went by the name of "Ann Landers," was different. The prose was straightforward, and the advice was direct. Eppie called a friend at the *Sun-Times* to see if Ann Landers, who promised to answer every letter, needed help with her mail. She learned that Ruth Crowley, who had created the column, had died suddenly, and a competition was being held to replace her. The *Sun-Times* reluctantly allowed Eppie, who had no journalistic experience, to join it. She won the contest, and her first column ran on 16 October 1955.

In Eppie Lederer, it turned out, the *Sun-Times* had found someone who could take the tired genre of the lovelorn column and give it a fresh spin. The new Ann Landers continued Crowley's innovation of practical, straight-talking advice, but added to the formula sass, wit, and an unusual ability to cut to the chase.

Inundated with mail—the Ann Landers column was syndicated in some thirty newspapers by Field Enterprises, the *Sun-Times* syndicate—the new columnist called on her twin for help. Eppie showed Popo what she had learned about putting together a column, and after Popo returned to her home in California, Eppie sent her a portion of the mail. When the *Sun-Times* learned, however, that confidential Ann Landers mail was being sent across the country to a person who was not even employed by the paper, Eppie was told that her sister's participation in the column would have to end.

Newspaper management did, however, acknowledge that the column was more work than one person could handle, and provided Landers with three assistants. Over the years, the number of assistants grew. They answered the vast majority of the mail, sorting out about 500 letters a day for the attention of Landers herself. From those 500, she chose the letters that went into the column. Much of the advice that did not make the paper involved referring readers to places where they could get help, and Landers's staff kept detailed records on every social-service organization in every town where her column was syndicated.

Meanwhile Popo, finding herself frozen out of her sister's column, launched her own advice column, called "Dear Abby," under the pen name of Abigail Van Buren. It made its debut in the *San Francisco Chronicle*, just eighty-five days after the publication of Eppie's first column.

Both columns exploded in popularity. They were re-markably similar, but Dear Abby was perhaps a bit funnier—Popo had a facility for risqué one-liners—while Ann Landers resonated a bit more as a real person. It is impossible to give the exact number of newspapers in which each column appeared, because syndicate numbers are notoriously unreliable, but both eventually appeared in well over 200 papers worldwide. The intense rivalry between the two columns, however, caused serious problems between the sisters, who did not speak to each other for several years, although from 1964 on their relationship was generally amicable.

The new Ann Landers was not shy about speaking her mind. When "Concerned Parents" wrote that their thirteen-year-old son had made some unsettling discoveries when he examined the wallet of their daughter's boyfriend, she replied: "You have a right to be deeply concerned—about that little punk you're raising. Teach the kid to mind his own business."

When "Still Paying" wrote that he had not married the girl he had impregnated because "We were worlds apart—intellectually, socially, and financially," Landers replied: "Since you and the girl were 'worlds apart intellectually, socially, and financially,' it's too bad you didn't stay worlds apart physically. Of course you didn't get off easy. Why should you?"

To women complaining of miserable marriages, she would pose what became known as "the Ann Landers question": "Are you better off with him or without him?" Correspondents who seemed to willfully ignore the obvious were told: "Wake up and smell the coffee." One piece of advice, "Mind your own business," was repeated so often that she shortened it to MYOB.

Landers stood for traditional morality, but she also urged tolerance and forgiveness. In 1965 she told a reader who was angry that her pregnant-but-unmarried cousin had continued to go to work until two weeks before her baby's delivery: "Your cousin was trying to hold her head up, and you knocked it down. Please be kind to her from now on." And to a girl who considered her life ruined because she had had an out-of-wedlock baby at age sixteen, Landers wrote: "One mistake does not brand you as worthless."

Her column also served as a forum on her previous advice. If subsequent letters convinced her that she had been wrong, she would amend her advice and cheerfully sentence herself to "forty lashes with a wet noodle." Over the years, there were spirited debates in her column about wives who undressed in the closet, women who did housework in the nude, whether it was gauche for people to perform musical numbers at their own weddings, and even the proper way to hang toilet paper.

Landers's advice shifted over the years. In the early days of her column, she opposed divorce; by the 1970s, however, she had come to consider it an acceptable option. She never wavered in her opposition to premarital sex for teenagers, but she amended her position for unmarried adults. "When I first got into this work," she said in 1981, "I thought a woman should remain a virgin until she married or died, whichever came first. Well, I changed my mind about that." She believed strongly, however, in making birth control available to teenagers, and supported legalized abortion, perhaps because her mail was testament to the misery that could result from unwanted pregnancies.

In the early 1970s her own marriage began to fall apart, due to business reversals her husband had suffered, the punishing hours both worked, and his eventual involvement with another woman. In a column in 1975 she announced her own divorce: "How did it happen that something so good for so long didn't last forever?" she wrote. "The lady with all the answers does not know the answer to this one." She asked her readers not to write to ask for details. They did write, however. She received 30,000 letters, which were so supportive and compassionate that she kept them for the rest of her life.

Landers stood just under five feet, two inches tall, had a trim figure, and wore her dark hair in a signature lacquered style, with a flip on the side. Her voice was penetrating, with a strong midwestern twang, but its distinctiveness proved to be an asset, and she was a highly effective public speaker.

Through the years, acrimonious debates periodically cropped up in her column on the merits of having children. In 1976 she invited all parents to respond to a one-question poll: "Parenthood—if you had a choice would you do it again?" An overwhelming 70 percent of respondents said no. Landers, as surprised as anyone, wrote: "I believe the logical explanation for this phenomenon is (a) the hurt, angry and disenchanted tend to write more readily than the contented, and (b) people tell me things they wouldn't dare tell anyone else."

Landers's career included some missteps, although her stumbles did her little damage with her readers. She was criticized for compromising her journalistic integrity in 1974 after she took a trip to China that was sponsored by the American Medical Association and wrote articles on the trip for the *Sun-Times* without disclosing that an outside organization had paid for the trip. In 1982, when a newspaper culled old columns to put together a feature on her, it was discovered that she had occasionally recycled letters and answers, slightly rewritten and not labeled as repeats. After the ensuing controversy, she ended that practice.

Landers was the author of eight books: *Since You Ask Me* (1961); *Ann Landers Talks to Teenagers About Sex* (1963); *Truth Is Stranger* (1968); *Ann Landers Speaks Out* (1975); *The Ann Landers Encyclopedia, A–Z* (1978); *Wake Up and Smell the Coffee: Advice, Wisdom and Uncommon Good*

Sense (1996); and *Best of Ann Landers: Her Favorite Letters of All Time* (1996). In 1987, after a change in ownership at the *Sun-Times*, she moved her column to the *Chicago Tribune*, where it remained for the balance of her career.

She continued to write her column up until her death of multiple myeloma, a cancer of the bone marrow. Her last column ran on 27 July 2002, a month after she died. She was cremated, and her ashes were scattered over Lake Michigan near Chicago.

For nearly half a century, from 1955 through 2002, Landers's column not only amused the world with its chronicling of the absurdities of human nature, but helped define decent behavior. She brought sass and humor to the advice column, but she did not sacrifice the sense that she took every problem seriously and cared deeply for her readers. Few advice columnists have been able to walk that line.

★

The most complete biographical information on Landers is in Jan Pottker and Bob Speziale, *Dear Ann, Dear Abby: The Unauthorized Biography of Ann Landers and Abigail Van Buren* (1987). See also Margo Howard, *Eppie: The Story of Ann Landers* (1982), written by her daughter. Virginia Aronson, *Ann Landers and Abigail Van Buren* (2000), was written for the juvenile market but contains solid information. David I. Grossvogel, *Dear Ann Landers: Our Intimate and Changing Dialogue with America's Best-Loved Confidante* (1987), examines the changes in American society reflected over the years in Landers's column. An obituary is in the *New York Times* (23 June 2002).

LYNN HOOGENBOOM

LANDRY, Thomas Wade ("Tom") (*b.* 11 September 1924 in Mission, Texas; *d.* 12 February 2000 in Dallas, Texas), innovative professional football coach who molded the Dallas Cowboys into "America's Team" while revolutionizing the game's offensive and defensive systems.

Born to Ray Landry, an auto mechanic and volunteer fire chief, and Ruth (Coffman) Landry, a homemaker, Landry was the second of two children; an older brother, Robert, was killed in World War II. Landry was an outstanding student-athlete at Mission High School, winning All-District honors in football and serving as class president. He also was a member of the National Honor Society. In his senior year the Mission High team—against which no opponent managed to score a single point, let alone win a game—became district champions.

Landry, a solid if not spectacular player, matriculated at the University of Texas at Austin in the fall of 1942. Before he could earn a varsity letter, he enlisted in the U.S. Army Air Corps and piloted a B-17 bomber on thirty missions over Europe, eventually attaining the rank of first lieuten-

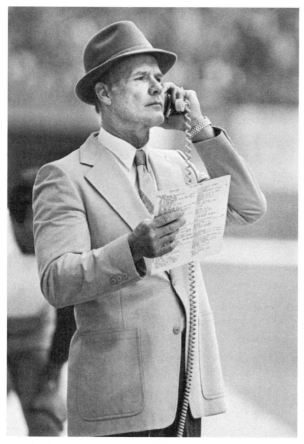

Tom Landry, 1980. BETTMANN/CORBIS

ant. A decorated veteran, Landry returned to Texas after the war to again play football for the Longhorns. During his junior season (1947), when he was a starting defensive halfback, he met Alicia Wiggs, a first-year student and model whose picture had appeared in *Seventeen* magazine. Landry starred in the 1 January 1948 Sugar Bowl, a 27–7 victory over Alabama. A cocaptain as a senior, he capped a fine season with an outstanding performance in the Orange Bowl, a 41–28 victory over Georgia. Landry took on the fullback duties in addition to playing defensively in the game and rushed for 117 yards on twenty-eight carries. Before graduating with a B.S. in business administration (he would later earn an M.S. in industrial engineering from the University of Houston), Landry married Wiggs on 28 January 1949. They had three children. Landry's wife was very much a part of her husband's career, accompanying the coach and team on all their away games. Their son, Tom, was a defensive back at Duke until knee surgery ended his career.

Landry signed with the New York Yankees of the All-America Football Conference (AAFC) to play professional football. He started as a rookie defensive back for the Yankees, a team that finished third in the league's last year

of existence. Landry then was chosen by the New York Giants when four AAFC teams were folded into the established National Football League (NFL) in 1950. He became a "spoke" in coach Steve Owen's "Umbrella Defense." So vast was Landry's knowledge and grasp of Owen's defense that he became a player-coach in 1954, the same year he was voted to the All-Pro team. He also was voted to the Pro Bowl All-Star game team.

After the 1955 season Landry retired as a player but remained as the defensive coordinator under his Giants mentor, Jim Lee Howell. Another figure destined for greatness, the future Green Bay Packers coach Vince Lombardi, served as offensive coordinator. It was during this time (1956–1959) that Landry developed the 4–3 defense, still a staple in the NFL. This defense was innovative in that there were only four defensive linemen, as opposed to prior defenses that featured five-, six-, or even seven-man lines. The three linebackers in the 4-3 defense assumed additional duties as pass defenders, which had never been done before. Landry was such a keen student of the game— breaking down film and charting tendencies—that he knew how opposing teams and players would react in certain situations. Once, after he told the Hall of Fame linebacker Sam Huff that a particular opponent would have a certain reaction to a specific play, Huff questioned, "What if he does something else?" Self-assured, without a trace of arrogance, Landry said, "Sam, he won't." When the situation came up on the field, it unfolded exactly as Landry had said it would.

Landry had great leeway as an assistant coach. Howell said, "I got Landry to coach the defense. I got Lombardi to coach the offense. All I do is pump up the football." Lombardi left New York in 1959 to take over the moribund Green Bay Packers. A year later Landry left to head up the expansion Dallas Cowboys. With a roster populated by other teams' castoffs, Landry had a tough start. In his first season the future five-time Super Bowl coach managed only a tie against his old team, with no victories and eleven losses. The Cowboys gradually improved and by 1966 recorded a 10-3-1. It was the first of twenty consecutive winning seasons, an NFL record. While football-mad Texas fans clamored for Landry's scalp in the early years, general manager Tex Schramm resisted the criticism, and in the middle of the losing years, he signed Landry to an unheard-of ten-year contract. Later, football observers would note that the role of front-office continuity in the Cowboys' success could not be overestimated. The thirty-year tenures of Landry, Schramm, and—to a lesser extent—player personnel director Gil Brandt produced outstanding results.

Expectations were high when the Cowboys started winning, but they could not seem to "win the big one." The title of a 1969 Steve Perkins book about the Cowboys, *Next Year's Champions*, was a reference akin to the long-standing lament of Brooklyn Dodgers baseball fans: "Wait till next year." Another book of the period was Sam Blair's *The Dallas Cowboys: Pro or Con?* (1970). Likewise, the title of Perkins's 1972 book *Winning the Big One*, a chronicle of Dallas's first NFL championship and first Super Bowl victory, in Super Bowl VI, signified the changes in the team's fortunes. Prior to that time, Lombardi's Packers had kept Landry's Cowboys from success much of the time. The teams met in several championships, all of them won by the Packers, including the famed Ice Bowl game of 1967 on the frozen turf of Lambeau Field, Green Bay's home stadium.

The sustained success of the Cowboys was unrivaled. Landry's dignified demeanor, enhanced by his immaculate attire—including his trademark fedora—were a vital part of the Cowboys' (and the NFL's) image. His stoic appearance was interpreted by some as a sign of aloofness, but this was not the case. Rather, he was fully immersed in the ebb and flow of the game—"thinking two or three plays ahead," as he put it. Nevertheless, his seriousness prompted jokes. Once someone asked the fullback Walt Garrison if he ever saw Landry smile. Garrison replied, "No, but then I've only been with the team for eleven years."

As the rest of the league caught on to Landry's methods, winning became harder. His final three seasons (1986–1988) produced a 17–30 mark. When the new owner Jerry Jones took over in 1989, he unceremoniously sacked the only coach the Cowboys had ever had. Understandably, Landry was somewhat miffed and resisted Jones's efforts to have him recognized in the Cowboys' Texas Stadium "Ring of Honor" until 1993. A devout Christian, Landry made countless no-fee speeches on behalf of the Fellowship of Christian Athletes. His faith was strongly tested when he contracted acute myelogenous leukemia in 1999. He died a year later at Baylor University Medical Center at the age of seventy-five and is buried in Sparkman-Hillcrest Cemetery in Dallas.

Landry was one of the game's great innovators and coaches. His record of 270–178–6 speaks for itself, as do his two Super Bowl victories, thirteen division championships, and two Coach of the Year awards. He was inducted into the Pro Football Hall of Fame in 1989. Perhaps the greatest tribute came from the man who ended his coaching career: of Landry, Jones said, "He is the single most important person in the history of this franchise."

★

Landry, with Gregg Lewis, wrote *An Autobiography: Tom Landry* (1990). See also Dave Klein, *Tom and the 'Boys* (1990); Skip Bayless, *God's Coach* (1990); and Bob St. John, *Landry: The Legend and the Legacy* (2000). Obituaries are in the *New York Times* and *USA Today* (both 14 Feb. 2000).

JIM CAMPBELL

LANE, Richard ("Dick"; "Night Train") (*b.* 16 April 1927 in Austin, Texas; *d.* 29 January 2002 in Austin, Texas), Pro Football Hall of Fame cornerback, acknowledged as one of the greatest defensive backs in National Football League history, and holder of the record for most interceptions in one season.

Lane was the product of starkly grim beginnings. His mother, Johanie Mae King, a prostitute, and his father, Will Lance, a pimp also known as "Texas Slim," abandoned him at the age of three months. Ella Lane, a widow with two children, heard Lane's cries coming from a trash can, found him, and raised him in poor but loving circumstances. He attended Keating Junior High School and L. C. Anderson High School in Austin where, despite his small size at the time (135 pounds), he played football and basketball while working odd jobs after practice. In 1944 he played offensive and defensive end on the Texas high school championship football team, developing a reputation as a deadly open-field tackler, fast and agile with a gambling, aggressive style of play.

After graduating from high school, Lane entered Scottsbluff Junior College (now Western Nebraska Community College) in 1947. He received Junior College All-America

Dick Lane, 1964. BETTMANN/CORBIS

293

recognition as an offensive end. Problems with his birth mother, with whom he was living at the time but who he discovered had returned to a life of prostitution, led him to drop out of junior college after one semester in 1947. He entered the U.S. Army in 1948 and served for several years, mostly at Fort Ord, California, working as a special services assistant. At Fort Ord, Lane began to gain weight and played offensive end on the base football team, participating in three military bowl games. In 1951 Lane caught eighteen touchdown passes and was scouted by the San Francisco 49ers. After leaving the army, Lane received a football scholarship to attend Loyola University of Los Angeles, but after the 1951 season, the school dropped football.

Lane married his first wife, Geraldine Dandridge, in 1948 while he was in the military. They had one child and divorced in 1959. After his discharge, he found work in a Los Angeles aircraft assembly plant, stacking aluminum sheets coated with lubricant into metal bins and playing basketball for the company team at night. Growing disenchanted with his job, and with his wife pregnant, Lane noticed the office of the Los Angeles Rams one day while riding the bus to work. Armed with a scrapbook of his football exploits, he walked into the Rams' offices seeking a chance to make the team. The coaching staff was impressed enough to offer him a $4,500 contract.

Lane tried out as an offensive end but had a difficult time mastering the team's complex offensive schemes and intricate terminology. His chances as a pass receiver also were limited by the presence of the All-Pro starters Elroy Hirsch and Tom Fears, both eventual Hall of Fame selections. Worried and depressed, Lane often visited Fears's room at training camp, and it frequently happened that a popular recording of the song "Night Train" was playing on Fears's record player. Fears's roommate, Ben Sheets, gave Lane his nickname, and it stuck.

The Rams coaches switched Lane to defensive end during an intersquad scrimmage and were impressed by his aggressive play. With the Rams defensive backfield depleted by injuries, Lane was moved to cornerback. It would be the start of a fourteen-year career in which his instinctive combative play would revolutionize the position. In 1952 Lane set the all-time season interception record with fourteen interceptions. He achieved this in a twelve-game season, and more than half a century later—even with a sixteen-game schedule—that mark remained intact. He also returned five interceptions for touchdowns over the course of his career, with two of these in 1952.

Lane played for the Rams (1952–1953), the Chicago Cardinals (1954–1959), and the Detroit Lions (1960–1965). His best seasons came under coaches who gave free rein to his talents. He was less effective under coaches and systems that sought to discipline his freelancing methods. His chafing under more restrictive defensive schemes led to a mal-

content reputation. Lane led the National Football League (NFL) in pass interceptions in 1952 and 1954 but received his greatest recognition playing for the Lions. He was an All-Pro selection in 1956 and from 1960 to 1963, and he played in six Pro Bowls. Tough and courageous, he was suffering from stomach pains the night before the 1961 Pro Bowl, but he scored its first touchdown on a forty-two-yard interception return. Two days later he underwent an appendectomy.

Lance missed much of the 1964 and 1965 seasons with injuries and retired before the beginning of the 1966 season. His sixty-eight interceptions placed him third on the all-time list of NFL defenders. In addition to his defensive exploits, he was used as a pass receiver at times, and in 1955 he was involved in a ninety-eight-yard touchdown reception. In 1970 sportswriters nationwide named Lane the top NFL cornerback of all time. He was a unanimous choice for the Pro Football Hall of Fame in 1974.

After he divorced his first wife, Lane married the blues singer Dinah Washington on 2 July 1963 in Las Vegas, Nevada, with the famed basketball player Wilt Chamberlain as his best man. The marriage was Washington's seventh and last. While attempting to lose weight in preparation for a forthcoming concert appearance that year, Washington died from an accidental overdose of sleeping pills on 14 December. Lane later married Mary Opal Cower, a schoolteacher, from whom he was divorced in 1964 and with whom he had one child. From 1966 to 1972 Lane was a special staff assistant for the Lions. Seeking opportunities to coach, he held assistant coaching positions at Southern University in Baton Rouge, Louisiana, in 1972 and Central State University in Ohio in 1973. For a time, he was the road manager for the comedian Redd Foxx. In 1975 Lane returned to Detroit as the executive director of the Detroit Police Athletic League, a position he held until his retirement in 1983. Lane suffered from diabetes and chronic knee problems. In 2001 he entered an assisted living facility in Del Valle, Texas. He died from a heart attack and is buried at Evergreen Cemetery in Austin.

At six feet, two inches and 210 pounds, Lane was the first defensive back with the size and speed to match fast and agile wide receivers. His signature "necktie" tackles, in which he grabbed the opponent around the head, neck, or shoulders and wrestled him to the ground, instilled fear in all who played against him. Lane also became adept at grabbing running backs and receivers by the facemask and wrenching them to the turf, a tactic that was banned after a vicious 1961 tackle of Jon Arnett at the Los Angeles Coliseum that left Arnett unconscious for several minutes. Lane transcended his troubled origins to become the premier athlete at his position. He remains the standard by which all defensive backs are judged.

★

Information about Lane is in Mike Burns, *Night Train Lane* (2000). A perceptive description of Lane at the height of his career with the Detroit Lions can be found in George Plimpton, *Paper Lion* (1965). See also Joe Falls, *The Specialist in Pro Football* (1966); Mickey Hershkowitz, *The Golden Age of Pro Football* (1974); and George Allen with Ben Olan, *Pro Football's 100 Greatest Players* (1982). An obituary is in the *New York Times* (1 Feb. 2002).

EDWARD J. TASSINARI

LARDNER, Ringgold Wilmer, Jr. ("Ring") (*b.* 19 April 1915 in Chicago, Illinois; *d.* 31 October 2000 in Manhattan, New York City), Hollywood screenwriter and author best known for the film *Woman of the Year* (1942) and the novel *The Ecstasy of Owen Muir* (1954), who achieved notoriety as a member of the "Hollywood Ten."

Lardner was the third of four sons born to Ring Lardner, a well-known humorist and sports writer, and Ellis (Abbott) Lardner, a homemaker. The family moved from Chicago to suburban Greenwich, Connecticut, and then to Great Neck, Long Island (also a suburb of New York City) early in Lardner's childhood. Both parents possessed a sense of humor, which they transmitted to their sons along with an appreciation of reading and writing. All four siblings became successful writers in their own right. However, after the deaths of Jim in 1938 and David in 1944 (both died as war correspondents in Europe), then of John in 1960, Lardner was left to carry on the legacy alone.

Despite opposition from Ring, Sr., Ellis had succeeded in naming their third son after his father. Because of his father's fears that he would receive abuse over his given name, Lardner was called "Bill" for most of his childhood. The topic of his son's name, and other stories about the brothers, became the subject of the senior Lardner's columns. At the age of four, Lardner received his first byline for "The Young Immigrunts," despite the fact that his father actually wrote the piece.

Lardner had a difficult adolescence because he expanded horizontally almost as fast as he grew vertically. He was in his mid-twenties before he lost forty pounds and evolved into the tall, lean, distinguished-looking man that Hollywood would know. His intense eyes, later framed by glasses, enhanced the aura of intellect surrounding him. Following graduation from Phillips Academy in Andover, Massachusetts, Lardner attended Princeton University from 1932 to 1934. While at Princeton, he joined the Socialist Club. Shortly after his father's death on 24 September 1933, Lardner left Princeton on a tour of Europe to observe socialism in action. His experiences in the Soviet Union confirmed his devotion to communism. Lardner labored

Ring Lardner, Jr., 1985. AP/WIDE WORLD PHOTOS

as a reporter with the New York *Daily Mirror* when he returned in 1935. After meeting the film producer David O. Selznick, Lardner moved to California to work at Selznick International.

Lardner's big break came when he and Budd Schulberg were asked by Selznick to rewrite *A Star Is Born*. Lardner credited Schulberg with recruiting him into the Communist Party in 1937, although he had already embraced Marxist-Leninist theory. Lardner married Selznick's secretary, Silvia Schulman, on 19 February 1937. They had two children, Peter and Ann. Warner Bros. employed Lardner as a scriptwriter during this period until Jack Warner fired him for raising money to fund ambulances during the Spanish Civil War, and for picketing the studio visit of Vittorio Mussolini, son of the Italian dictator. In 1942 Lardner worked with Michael Kanin on *Woman of the Year,* produced by Metro-Goldwyn-Mayer (MGM). After the film won an Academy Award for best original screenplay, MGM overlooked Lardner's political leanings long enough for him to work on *The Cross of Lorraine* (1944). During the remainder of World War II, questions concerning Lardner's political background and his leftist leanings prevented him from working on most projects, and he was relegated to assisting the U.S. Army Signal Corps with training films. Lardner and Schulman divorced in

1945. The following year, after the release of *Cloak and Dagger,* Lardner married Frances Goldwyn Lardner, his brother David's widow, on 28 September 1946.

Immediately after Lardner obtained a contract from Twentieth Century–Fox and purchased a house in Santa Monica, California, the House Un-American Activities Committee (HUAC) subpoenaed him in the spring of 1947. Of those brought before the committee to testify on communist activity in the United States, fourteen "friendly witnesses," including Schulberg and Warner, named Lardner as a communist. Of the nineteen Hollywood figures called to testify as "unfriendly" witnesses, ten chose to challenge the HUAC by claiming protection under the First Amendment. Known as the "Hollywood Ten," they exercised an option that kept them from admitting wrongdoing or naming others, while challenging the constitutionality of the committee.

The HUAC finally called Lardner to the stand on 30 October 1947, the final day of the hearings. Upon being prompted by Congressman J. Parnell Thomas, the committee head, to answer the question "Are you or have you ever been a member of the Communist Party?" Lardner gave the now-famous response, "I could answer the way you want, Mr. Chairman, but I'd hate myself in the morning." Less than a month later, the major movie studios, including Fox, instituted the "blacklist" and fired Lardner and other listed employees. Lardner and Frances's son James, their only child together (she had two from her marriage to David), was born amid this crisis. The House of Representatives found the ten in contempt of court and sentenced Lardner to one year in prison, which was shortened by two months and fifteen days for good behavior. His incarceration at the Federal Correctional Institution in Danbury, Connecticut, during 1950 allowed Lardner to begin the novel *The Ecstasy of Owen Muir* (1954).

Following Lardner's release, the family moved briefly to Mexico, then to New York to live with his mother. Frances, ostracized because of her marriage to Lardner, managed to locate some acting jobs in New York. The Lardners found aid in the movie business from sympathizers who hired Lardner under conditions of anonymity; he also worked under various pseudonyms until he could use his own name again in the early 1960s. By then he had returned to Hollywood to script *The Cincinnati Kid* (1964) and *M*A*S*H* (1970), which won him an additional Academy Award (for best writing of a screenplay based on material from another medium), along with other honors.

After writing the memoir *The Lardners: My Family Remembered* (1976), Lardner published the novel *All for Love* (1985). Plagued by deafness, arthritis, and a heart condition, he retired with Frances to New York, where he died of cancer in their Manhattan apartment. His remains were cremated. At the time of his death, Lardner was awaiting the publication of his memoir *I'd Hate Myself in the Morning* (2000), an enlightening and satirical look at his life.

Lardner carried his role as the last Lardner and a member of the "Hollywood Ten" with aplomb and courage. Although his identity as a communist served to diminish his early career, he never gave up on his writing and instead assembled an impressive list of credits. Lardner demonstrated impressive knowledge and political dedication, as well as humor in his scriptwriting, qualities that enabled him to stand out from others. Perhaps his greatest significance came from his role as an outcast during a time of conformity. He never regretted his actions, and his extensive work and unwavering convictions became an example to those willing to stand up publicly for their beliefs.

★

Lardner wrote about his family background and life in *The Lardners: My Family Remembered* (1976) and *I'd Hate Myself in the Morning: A Memoir* (2000). Many books are available on the Hollywood Ten, among them Robert Vaughn, *Only Victims: A Study of Show Business Blacklisting* (1972); Larry Ceplair and Steven England, *The Inquisition in Hollywood: Politics in the Film Community* 1930–1960 (1980); and Patrick McGilligan and Paul Buhle, *Tender Comrades: A Backstory of the Hollywood Blacklist* (1997). An obituary is in the *New York Times* (2 Nov. 2000).

SARAH JANE ROSENDAHL

LAWRENCE, Jacob Armstead (*b.* 7 September 1917 in Atlantic City, New Jersey; *d.* 9 June 2000 in Seattle, Washington), painter and printmaker whose works focused on the biographies of several famous African Americans, as well as the daily lives of blacks and other Americans.

Lawrence, the eldest of three children born to Jacob Lawrence, a railroad cook, and Rose Lee (Armstead) Lawrence, moved with his parents to the coal mining town of Easton, Pennsylvania, when he was two years old. In 1924 his parents separated, and his mother settled with her children in Philadelphia, Pennsylvania. Shortly afterward, she moved to New York and left the children in foster homes, but in 1930 she brought her family to the Harlem section of New York City. Lawrence attended grammar school at Public School (P.S.) 68; junior high school at the Frederick Douglass School, P.S. 139; and the High School of Commerce, from which he graduated in 1934.

An early mentor was Charles Alston, under whom he studied in the Works Progress Administration–sponsored Harlem Art Workshop in 1932 and from 1934 to 1937. As a teen, Lawrence frequented the Metropolitan Museum of Art on Fifth Avenue, where he came to admire the techniques of Italian Renaissance artists as well as the work of the contemporary Mexican muralists and of such American

Jacob Lawrence, 1993. AP/WIDE WORLD PHOTOS

modernists as Arthur G. Dove and Charles Sheeler. In 1937 he obtained a two-year scholarship to the American Artists School in New York City, where he studied with Anton Refregier. Along with Ben Shahn, William Gropper, Jack Levine, and a few others, Lawrence became one of the principal social realist artists of the 1930s and 1940s, who saw America, despite its opportunities, as a place of injustice and exploitation of the powerless.

Inspired by W. E. B. Du Bois's play *Haiti*, Lawrence produced *Toussaint L'Ouverture* (1936–1938), a series of forty-one paintings dealing with the black hero's struggle for political power and Haiti's fight for independence. In his *Frederick Douglass* series (1938–1939), he illustrated in thirty-two paintings the life of the famous black orator, from his painful childhood in slavery and his escape through his disguise as a sailor, his association with the abolitionist William Lloyd Garrison, his meetings with the abolitionist John Brown, his fight for the better treatment of black soldiers during the Civil War, and his appointment in 1877 by President Rutherford B. Hayes to the post of U.S. Marshal of the District of Columbia. In the thirty-one paintings of the *Harriet Tubman* series (1939–1940), Lawrence depicted the brutalizing of Tubman by an overseer when she was a young girl, her dramatic escape from slavery, her establishment of the Underground Railroad to lead slaves to freedom, and her nursing of Union soldiers during the Civil War.

The best known of Lawrence's works is *Migration of the Negro* (1940–1941), a series of sixty paintings that depict the large-scale migration of blacks from the South to the North early in the twentieth century. In this work the forms

are flatter and more abstract than in his previous series, and there is a sense of their dynamic interaction. One image, captioned "One of the largest race riots occurred in East St. Louis," presents individuals whose arms and hands appear to have become one with the knives and clubs they are using as weapons against each other. In contrast to these early series, some of Lawrence's work from the 1940s was less confrontational and less concerned with black people as victims.

On 24 July 1941 Lawrence married the painter Gwendolyn Clarine Knight. They had no children. Shortly after marrying, he made his first trip to the South, visiting New Orleans, where he began a series on John Brown. The next year he produced his *Harlem* series, in which he showed a wide variety of commonplace activities—a woman carrying grocery bags, a man passing out from too much whiskey. In 1943, during World War II, Lawrence entered the U.S. Coast Guard and served on a weather patrol ship with Boston as its home port. Working as a ship's artist, he created a series of paintings depicting life in the coast guard, the subject of his first one-person exhibition in New York's Museum of Modern Art in 1944. He attained the rank of petty officer, third class, before his discharge in 1945.

In 1946 Lawrence began his extensive teaching career by teaching during the summer session at Black Mountain College in North Carolina. In October 1949 he admitted himself to Hillside Hospital in the New York City borough of Queens, seeking treatment for what his doctor diagnosed as nervous difficulties. Lawrence spent nine months in the psychiatric ward. In the 1950s Lawrence reworked earlier themes. He produced egg tempera paintings in 1967 dealing with the Harriet Tubman story and twenty-two screen prints in 1977 recounting once again the story of John Brown. A favorite subject from the 1940s through the 1970s was vigorous and powerful black workmen shown drilling, sawing, carrying boards, and so on.

From 1954 to 1970 Lawrence taught at the Skowhegan School of Painting and Sculpture in Maine; the Pratt Institute in New York City; Brandeis University in Waltham, Massachusetts; the New School for Social Research in New York City; and other institutions. In 1971 he was appointed full professor at the University of Washington School of Art in Seattle, where he taught until his retirement in 1987. Beyond the studio and classroom, Lawrence was active in art organizations: in 1954 he was elected national secretary in the Artists Equity Association, and in 1957 he became president of the Artists Equity Association of New York. His first retrospective exhibition, which began at the Brooklyn Museum in 1960, toured nationally. In 1962 he visited Nigeria and returned to live and paint there from April to November 1964.

He kept active after retirement, producing his fifteenth series, *Eight Sermons of the Creation from the Book of Genesis,* in 1990, the year after he received the National Medal of Arts from President George H. W. Bush. Lawrence's other awards included the coveted Spingarn Medal from the National Association for the Advancement of Colored People as well as honorary degrees from eighteen colleges and universities. Lawrence died of cancer at his home in Seattle.

★

Ellen Harkins Wheat, *Jacob Lawrence, American Painter* (1986), is an authoritative work enhanced with photographs from the 1920s and 1930s. See also Wheat's *Jacob Lawrence, The Frederick Douglass and Harriet Tubman Series of 1938–1940* (1991); Patricia Hills, *Jacob Lawrence, Thirty Years of Prints (1963–1993), A Catalogue Raisonné* (1994), which is marred by small reproductions; *Jacob Lawrence: The Migration Series* (1993), ed. Elizabeth Hutton Turner, which includes large, full-page reproductions; and *Over the Line: The Art and Life of Jacob Lawrence* (2000), ed. Peter T. Nesbett and Michelle DuBois. An obituary is in the *New York Times* (10 June 2000).

ABRAHAM A. DAVIDSON

LE CLERCQ, Tanaquil ("Tanny") (*b.* 2 October 1929 in Paris, France; *d.* 31 December 2000 [some sources say 1 January 2001] in New York City), celebrated twentieth-century ballerina and muse for choreographer George Balanchine, whose instinctive musicality and brilliant technique made her one of the New York City Ballet's first great ballerinas.

Le Clercq, the only child of the poet and writer Jacques Le Clercq and Edith (Whittemore) Le Clercq, a homemaker,

Tanaquil Le Clercq in *Bourree Fantasque*, 1950. HULTON-DEUTSCH COLLECTION/CORBIS

was named Tanaquil by her father after an Etruscan queen. Le Clercq's father, the godson of the French Premier Clemenceau, was born in Austria. He graduated from the University of California, Berkeley, and became a naturalized U.S. citizen. Her mother was from St. Louis, Missouri. Le Clercq was born in Paris while her father was on a Guggenheim Fellowship, and the family remained there till she was three years old. They then moved to New York City, where her father taught Romance languages at Queens College. Le Clercq's mother exposed her to ballet at an early age and sought out good teachers. Le Clercq also attended the progressive King-Coit theater school in New York City, but did not finish high school.

At the age of four, Le Clercq began studying with the renowned ballet master Mikhail Mordkin, who had trained at the Bolshoi in Moscow and was later a star of Serge Diaghilev's Ballet Russes in Paris. Mordkin had immigrated to the United States in 1924 and founded the Mordkin Ballet, which became the forerunner to the American Ballet Theatre. In 1940, at age eleven, Le Clercq won a competitive scholarship to the School of American Ballet (SAB), established in 1934 by George Balanchine and Lincoln Kirsten. She became among the first generation of ballerinas to be personally trained by Balanchine, who had come to the United States in 1933 at the urging of Kirsten. Trained at the Imperial Ballet School in Russia and later the Petrograd Conservatory of Music, Balanchine had left Stalinist Russia to join Diaghilev's Ballet Russes in Paris. Among his conditions for coming to the United States was a ballet school to promote his repertoire of abstract choreography. Le Clercq would become one of Balanchine's leading stylists, as her tall, lithe appearance epitomized the Balanchine ballerina.

Balanchine cast Le Clercq in SAB student performances. One in particular, *Resurgence,* was prophetic. In the ballet, which Balanchine choreographed for a March of Dimes benefit in 1944, Le Clercq portrayed a dancer paralyzed by a black-clad monster, Polio, danced by Balanchine. Although Le Clercq's character was confined to a wheelchair, she miraculously recovered when showered with silver coins. Years later, Balanchine recalled the ballet as an omen.

Le Clercq's first professional performance was in 1945 at Ted Shawn's Jacob Pillow Festival in Lee, Massachusetts. In 1946, at age seventeen, Le Clercq became an original member of the Ballet Society, the precursor of the New York City Ballet, which was established in 1948. Never in the corps, Le Clercq immediately began to dance an assortment of ballets, beginning with the role of the dynamic Choleric in *Four Temperaments* (1946). Over the next ten years, she danced some thirty-eight soloist roles, mainly in Balanchine ballets and principle roles in such Balanchine creations as *Divertimento* (1947) and *Orpheus* (1948). Le Clercq's performances ranged from the fragile Dewdrop in Balanchine's *Nutcracker* (1954) to the theatrical dancehall girl in his *Western Symphony* (1954). Critics described her performance in Balanchine's *La Valse* (1951) as compelling, like one dancing on the edge of a volcano. In the ballet, Le Clercq danced to the music of Maurice Ravel as a doomed heroine who dramatically plunges her hand into a long black glove to convey her impending fate.

Le Clercq also appeared in New York City Ballet performances of ballets by other celebrated choreographers, including Jerome Robbins, Sir Frederick Ashton, Antony Tudor, and Merce Cunningham. Robbins later commented, "Tanny could do anything."

Critics responded enthusiastically to Le Clercq's dancing from the first. An ideal muse for Balanchine, she married him on 31 December 1952, becoming his fourth wife. Balanchine's previous wives had also been ballerinas, but Le Clercq in particular seemed his creation. Her elegant style, lyrical yet energetic performances, and perfect long-legged body predicted a bright future. Le Clercq trusted Balanchine and entered their marriage confident in their collaboration. However, on 28 October 1956, during a European tour, tragedy struck. After dancing a matinee and evening performance in Copenhagen, she was taken to the hospital, where physicians diagnosed polio and put her in an iron lung. Paralyzed from the waist down, Le Clercq spent the next forty-three years in a wheelchair. Devastated, Balanchine remained by her side during the first year. After returning to the United States, he took her to Warm Springs, Georgia, hoping the therapeutic waters would improve her condition. Nothing worked. Le Clercq once confided to a friend that "it took her ten years to decide not to commit suicide."

Le Clercq eventually came to terms with her condition. She coached ballerina Patricia McBride to dance *La Valse* in 1962. She and Balanchine shared a large, sun-filled apartment near the SAB and a house in Connecticut. Balanchine trained their large yellow-and-white cat Mourka to perform jetés and various other ballet steps. Le Clercq compiled photographs of the cat taken by Martha Swope and wrote a clever narrative that was published in 1964 as *Mourka: The Autobiography of a Cat*. Le Clercq later published *The Ballet Cookbook* (1967). She accepted an invitation to teach at the Dance Theatre of Harlem in 1970. Whatever these successes, her marriage to Balanchine ended in divorce in 1969 (they had no children), by which point Balanchine had begun his obsession with ballerina Suzanne Farrell.

Although at first despondent over her condition, Le Clercq rarely indulged in self-pity and refused the pity of others. Sophisticated and elegant, she could also be earthy and unpretentious, and she enjoyed gardening and crossword puzzles. She lived alone after her divorce and rarely talked about her failed marriage or her condition. When Balanchine died in 1983, he left to Le Clercq and two others 70 percent of the rights to his ballets. Meanwhile, she remained dedicated to the City Ballet and in love with Balanchine, describing herself as a one-man woman. She promoted two City Ballet programs, one to bring homeless children to performances as guests complete with treats and photo opportunities, and another to bring talented teachers from remote areas to attend performances. In 1998 the New York City Ballet opened its fiftieth anniversary with a tribute to Le Clercq as a charter member of the company.

Le Clercq died from pneumonia in New York Hospital on her wedding anniversary at age seventy-one. Hers was a dramatic life that began with "kinetic genius" and ended with undiminished spirit. Le Clercq's dancing epitomized Balanchine's choreographic legacy of speed, technique, and athleticism. Her versatility and theatricality bound her in an artistic and emotional relationship with Balanchine, whose contribution to modern ballet is unequaled.

★

Bernard Taper, *Balanchine: A Biography* (1984), offers photographs of Le Clercq and a brief personal history. Information about Le Clercq's ballet background and personal life can be found in Richard Buckle and John Taras, *George Balanchine: Ballet Master* (1988). Holly Brubach et al., "Remembering Tanaquil Le Clercq" in *Ballet Review* (summer 2001): 35–66, offers reminiscences, letters, and Frank O'Hara's poem "Ode to Tanaquil Le Clercq." Obituaries are in the *New York Times* (1 Jan. 2001) and *Los Angeles Times* (5 Jan. 2001).

ELOISE F. MALONE

LEE, Peggy (*b.* 26 May 1920 in Jamestown, North Dakota; *d.* 21 January 2002 in Los Angeles, California), renowned jazz artist known for her soft, seductive vocal technique, who was the only female singer to record number-one hits in the 1940s, 1950s, and 1960s.

Christened Norma Deloris Egstrom, Lee was the seventh of eight children born to Marvin Egstrom, an employee for the Midland Continental Railroad. Her biological mother died suddenly during childbirth in 1924. Eleven years of a chronically abusive stepmother and an alcoholic father may have persuaded the young Lee to seek acceptance in her music. She sang her first professional concert at age fourteen, earning fifty cents at an event held by the local Parent Teachers Association. "It beat shucking grain," she later observed.

Lee graduated from high school in 1938, borrowed a railroad pass from her father, and headed for Hollywood. She tried to build a career as an actress while waiting tables and even worked as a carnival barker. She sang briefly at the Jade Room, a supper club on Hollywood Boulevard, but made no impression on the movie studios. A severe throat illness forced her to return to North Dakota to recuperate in 1940. Settling briefly in Fargo, Lee sang regularly on the local radio station WDAY, where the station manager Ken Kennedy gave her the name Peggy Lee. After a year of modest tours and radio shows in the Midwest, Lee caught another ride back to California.

During a short engagement in Palm Springs, Lee despaired of trying to sing every night above the typical clatter of a supper-club audience, so one night she simply sang quietly and then even more quietly. The audience listened, and Lee began the lifelong perfection of her seductively soft, emotionally packed, uniquely precise style. The entertainment manager for the Ambassador West Hotel heard her and invited her to sing back in Chicago. Benny Goodman was then in the Windy City, looking for a replacement for his lead vocalist, Helen Forrest, who had quit his band for the Harry James Orchestra. Goodman hired Lee the same evening he first heard her. Lee spent 1942 and 1943 touring and recording with Goodman's nationally acclaimed jazz ensemble. In a span of just fifteen months, she recorded her first hit, the million-selling "Why Don't

Peggy Lee (*right*), with Dean Martin, October 1967. BETTMANN/CORBIS

You Do Right?," and eight other songs that topped the nation's popular charts.

In 1943 Lee married Dave Barbour, a guitarist for the Goodman band. They resigned the tour and moved to California, where their daughter was born. Lee signed a recording contract in 1945 with Johnny Mercer's new label, Capitol Records; switched to Decca Records in 1951; and then returned to Capitol in 1958. During that time she recorded nearly thirty nationally acclaimed records, including "Mañana" and "It's A Good Day," both coauthored with Barbour. Although Lee and Barbour divorced in 1951, their fruitful artistic collaborations continued. At the same time, Lee began her film career, appearing in a 1953 remake of *The Jazz Singer*. In 1955 she costarred in *Pete Kelly's Blues,* poignantly cast as a fading 1920s jazz singer who had turned to drink. Her acting and singing earned her an Academy Award nomination as best supporting actress.

In addition to acting, Lee also composed and sang for the movies, including the curious 1954 cult film *Johnny Guitar* and Walt Disney's 1955 feature-length cartoon *The Lady and the Tramp*. In 1959, with the jazz great Duke Ellington, she cowrote the song "I'm Gonna Go Fishing" for the movie *Anatomy of a Murder*; her music can also be heard in *Pieces of Dreams* (1969) and *After Hours* (1985).

Lee was married three more times between 1955 and 1965: to Brad Dexter on 4 January 1955 (they were divorced later that year); to Dewey Martin on 25 April 1956; and later, after her divorce from Martin, to Jack del Rio in March 1964. The marriage to del Rio lasted just a few months, and she planned to remarry Barbour, but after his sudden death in 1965, she never married again.

In 1958 Lee received the first of twelve Grammy Award nominations, for her hit recording of "Fever." Eleven years later, she won the Grammy for best female vocal performance for her rendition of "Is That All There Is?" by Jerry Lieber and Mike Stoller. Less successful was the autobiographical musical *Peg,* for which Lee cowrote twenty-two songs. It opened in New York City in 1983 and closed after just a few performances. "The audiences loved it," she reflected afterward. "The critics didn't."

Beginning in the late 1970s, recurrent health problems gradually reduced her public appearances. Pneumonia, diabetes, poliomyelitis, and heart disease all hindered her. In 1976, while performing in Las Vegas, Lee slipped on a steel floor plate and fractured her pelvis. Although she was seriously injured, she called for a chair onstage and finished the show seated. Lee retired from recording in 1988 but sang several final orchestral concerts in London, seated this time in a wheelchair. After a debilitating stroke in 1994, she spent the next eight years quietly with her daughter, grandchildren, and great-grandchildren in Los Angeles, where she died at home from a heart attack. She is buried in the Westwood Village Memorial Park Cemetery near Los Angeles.

Lee remains perhaps the single most influential singer across all pop styles in the middle of the twentieth century. Her subtlety and immediacy continue to inspire generations of performers, writers, and listeners. She was the only female vocalist to have number-one hit recordings in the 1940s, 1950s, and 1960s, and by 1970 she had published more than one hundred musical compositions. Along the way, in addition to Ellington, she collaborated with Victor Young, Johnny Mandel, Neal Hefti, Harold Arlen, Marian McPartland, Quincy Jones, Frank Sinatra, and Dave Grusin, among others.

Along with Ella Fitzgerald and Billie Holiday, Lee challenged the stereotype of swing-band singers. She performed and improvised, she composed and arranged, she acted and authored. She also perfected an instantly identifiable musical style that blended pop and jazz, rather than differentiating them. Her touring and television concert appearances demonstrated her lifelong commitment to thorough planning and artistic versatility. She was renowned for designing and implementing nearly every aspect of a performance—costuming, coiffure, melodic nuance, musical arranging, lighting, blocking, and shooting.

Whitney Balliett, jazz reviewer for the *New Yorker*

magazine, wrote of Lee: "Many singers confuse shouting with emotion. Peggy Lee sends her feelings down the quiet center of her notes. . . . She does not carry a tune; she elegantly follows it." The jazz critic Leonard Feather remarked, "If you don't feel a thrill when Peggy Lee sings, you're dead, Jack."

★

The most notable book on Lee is her own *Miss Peggy Lee: An Autobiography* (1989). See also Gene Lees, *Singers and the Song* (1987); Fred Hall, *Dialogues in Swing: Intimate Conversations with the Stars of the Big Band Era* (1989); and Paul Roland and Roy Carr, *Jazz Singers: The Great Song Stylists in Their Own Words* (2000). An obituary is in the *New York Times* (23 Jan. 2002).

JAMES MCELWAINE

LEMMON, John Uhler, III ("Jack") (*b.* 8 February 1925 in Boston, Massachusetts; *d.* 27 June 2001 in Los Angeles, California), multifaceted American actor whose boyish Everyman persona accommodated both broadly comedic and quietly dramatic roles.

Born in the Back Bay area of Boston, Lemmon came from Scotch-Irish ancestry. He was the only child of John Uhler Lemmon, Jr., general sales manager and vice president of the Doughnut Corporation of America, and Mildred LaRue (Noel) Lemmon, a homemaker. His acting debut came when he was four and appeared in an amateur production of *Thar's Gold in Them Thar Hills.* His father, whom Lemmon described as "a frustrated entertainer," had volunteered him, and the boy became hooked on performing. Besieged by health problems as a child—he had been born premature and with acute jaundice—he had three mastoid and seven adenoid operations by age thirteen. Of his condition during his early years, Lemmon said, "I just wanted to get a little attention, I guess. Actors are impossible, you know."

Lemmon was raised in the suburb of Newton, attended such select New England institutions as Rivers Country Day School, and graduated in 1943 from the elite Philips Andover Academy. He was eighteen years old and America was at war when he entered Harvard University. As a member of the Reserve Officers Training Corps (ROTC), Lemmon was forced to major in "war service sciences" (physics, chemistry, and other hard sciences). In 1946 he interrupted his studies to serve three months aboard the aircraft carrier USS *Lake Champlain,* as a communications officer. Back at Harvard, Lemmon distinguished himself in college theatrics and, during his senior year, was elected president of the Hasty Pudding Club, for which he wrote an original depression-era musical revue titled *The Proof of the Pudding.* He jokingly billed himself as "Timothy Orange."

As a struggling actor in New York in the early 1950s,

Jack Lemmon in a scene from *The Apartment*, 1960. THE KOBAL COL-
LECTION

Lemmon studied with the legendary Uta Hagen and supported himself by playing piano for the silent movies shown
at a beer hall on Second Avenue called Old Nick. "I hardly
made anything," he said of those times, "but watching
[Charlie] Chaplin and [Buster] Keaton night after night
was like a Harvard education in comedy technique." It was
during this time that Lemmon met his first wife, Cynthia
Stone, a Finch College graduate working as a radio actress.
They married in her hometown of Peoria, Illinois, on 7
May 1950. They had one son.

Lemmon made his stage debut in an off-Broadway production of Leo Tolstoy's *Power of Darkness* and performed
often on live television in New York during the medium's
golden age. Discovered by Harry Cohn of Columbia Pictures while performing in a revival of *Room Service,* he
signed with Columbia and became a contract player there.
He made his movie debut in 1954 opposite Judy Holliday
in a comedy called *It Should Happen to You,* under the
direction of George Cukor. Cohn promoted Lemmon with
the prophetic tagline "A Guy You're Gonna Like."

A year and two films later, Columbia "loaned" Lemmon
to Warner Bros. for its 1955 film version of *Mister Roberts,*
for which he earned an Academy Award for best supporting
actor with his portrayal of the hapless layabout ensign

Frank Thurlowe Pulver. Columbia featured Lemmon in
seventeen films, all starring roles, although he turned in his
most high profile performances for other studios during this
time period. He was loaned out to United Artists for *Some
Like It Hot* (1959), *The Apartment* (1960), and *Irma la
Douce* (1963)—three films directed by Billy Wilder, who
would become Lemmon's mentor—and to Warner Bros.
for *Days of Wine and Roses* (1962).

Lemmon and Stone divorced in December 1956, and at
Columbia in 1958 he met his second wife, the actress
Felicia Farr, with whom he would have a daughter. (He
also had a stepdaughter, Felicia Farr's child by a previous
marriage.) They married on 17 August 1962 in Paris, where
Lemmon's best men were Wilder and the director Richard
Quine. "They are both my dearest friends," Lemmon said.
"I couldn't choose between them."

Although much was made of Lemmon's enduring relationships with Wilder and Walter Matthau—his costar
in *The Fortune Cookie* (1966), *The Odd Couple* (1968), and
eight other films—he had equally important collaborations
with Quine and his frequent costar Ernie Kovacs. Quine
first directed Lemmon in a 1955 musical remake of *My
Sister Eileen* and subsequently in such other Columbia titles
as *Operation Mad Ball* (1957); *Bell, Book, and Candle*
(1958); *It Happened to Jane* (1959); and *The Notorious
Landlady* (1962), as well as United Artists' *How to Murder
Your Wife* (1965). Wilder may have been the director who
put Lemmon on the map, but Quine was an important
recurring thread throughout his life and career. When
Kovacs joined the mix, appearing alongside Lemmon in
Operation Mad Ball; Bell, Book, and Candle; and *It Happened to Jane,* it was a teaming that would serve as a prototype for the Lemmon-Matthau acting relationship.

Lemmon's parents also were a significant influence during the 1950s and 1960s. He revealed that the inspiration
for his comic performance as "Daphne," the cross-dressing
musician in *Some Like It Hot,* was his mother, Millie. His
father, who was dying of cancer at the time, joined Lemmon for a small, nonspeaking part in *The Notorious Landlady* during filming in Carmel, California, in 1961. By 1964,
thanks to the back-to-back release of three consecutive box-
office hits—*Irma la Douce, Under the Yum Yum Tree*
(1963), and *Good Neighbor Sam* (1964)—Lemmon was the
number-one male box office star in the nation. As both an
actor and a personality, he defined an era, refining the
1960s idea of comedy for "the buttoned-down mind." The
Lemmon "character," as *Saturday Review* put it in its 1961
review of *The Wackiest Ship in the Army* (1960), was "the
outranked, outnumbered, outmanipulated little fellow with
sound instincts and bad judgment. . . . And if . . . he
emerges triumphant, it's because of a basic decency rather
than superior cunning or sudden inspiration." The men he
played—George Denham in *It Happened to Jane,* C. C.

("Bud") Baxter in *The Apartment*, William Gridley in *The Notorious Landlady*, Joe Clay in *Days of Wine and Roses*, Sam Bissell in *Good Neighbor Sam*, Harry Hinkle in *The Fortune Cookie*, Howard Brubaker in *The April Fools* (1969), and George Kellerman in *The Out-of-Towners* (1970)—were recognizable specifically because of their flaws.

His popularity with audiences freed Lemmon to take on roles in more serious, socially relevant films, *The China Syndrome* (1979) and *Missing* (1982) among them. He won his second Academy Award, this time for best actor, in 1973 for one such portrayal, as Harry Stoner, a conflicted businessman who has lost his way and longs to regain his idealism, in *Save the Tiger*.

Lemmon participated in the making of eighty-two movies in his lifetime, including titles for television and films he narrated; although he was known primarily as a screen actor, he was not limited to just that. Also a businessman, he organized his own film production company, Jalem, with Richard Carter in 1966. Its first picture was *Cool Hand Luke*, starring Paul Newman and released by Warner Bros. in 1967, followed by *Luv*, starring Lemmon himself and released by Columbia, also in 1967. He also tried his hand behind the camera, directing his friend Matthau in *Kotch* (1971). This was Lemmon's only movie as a director, although he came close to directing Susan Sarandon and Jill Clayburgh in a film version of John Ford Noonan's play *Coupla White Chicks Sitting Around Talking*, from a script by Wendy Wasserstein. The film was never made.

Lemmon liked to keep his acting muscles flexed, as he once put it, and he would often abandon Hollywood's back lots for the stage. He knew that taking roles in plays would help compensate for the dry spells that often came with film work, and—perhaps more important—would help him keep the world of Hollywood in perspective. For example, he opted to appear on stage in 1960 in Robert L. Joseph's *Face of a Hero* just as he was breaking through on-screen. The play, which he first performed on television in 1958, came just after *Some Like It Hot* and *The Apartment* and right before *Days of Wine and Roses*. In the 1970s Lemmon took three more breaks to refresh himself in the theater, starring in *Idiot's Delight* and opposite Matthau and Maureen Stapleton in *Juno and the Paycock*, both staged by the Center Theater Group in Los Angeles, and in *Tribute*, on Broadway in 1978.

During most of the 1960s and 1970s, however, movies remained Lemmon's principal medium, and he was duly rewarded for his efforts. Aside from his two Academy Awards, Lemmon won innumerable other acting honors, including assorted Golden Globe Awards and lifetime achievement awards from the American Film Institute and the Film Society of Lincoln Center. He also received Oscar nominations for six other roles—in *Some Like It Hot, The Apartment, Days of Wine and Roses, The China Syndrome*, the film version of *Tribute* (1980), and *Missing*.

His last Oscar nomination came in 1982, and because the roles that followed were in forgettable films—*Mass Appeal* (1984), *Maccheroni* (1985), and *Dad* (1989)—Lemmon elected to return to the stage. He appeared first with Estelle Parsons in an ill-fated play titled *A Sense of Humor* (written by Ernest Thompson, of *On Golden Pond* fame), staged in Los Angeles in 1983, and then on Broadway, playing the plum role of the patriarch James Tyrone in a much anticipated 1986 revival of Eugene O'Neill's towering tragedy *Long Day's Journey into Night*. In 1989 Lemmon traveled to London to make his British debut opposite Michael Gambon in *Veteran's Day* by Donald Freed, his last stage role.

As a senior actor in the early 1990s, Lemmon experienced a second wind and secured choice parts with noted directors in such films as Oliver Stone's much touted *JFK* (1991), James Foley's adaptation of the David Mamet play *Glengarry Glen Ross* (1992), and Robert Altman's *Short Cuts* (1993). Thereafter, his roles were divided between serious parts in television and cable productions—Mamet's *Life in the Theater* (1993) and remakes of *12 Angry Men* (1997) and *Inherit the Wind* (1999)—and more frivolous ones for the big screen, usually opposite his partner of choice, Matthau. These films included *Grumpy Old Men* (1994) and its sequel, *Grumpier Old Men* (1995), as well as *Out to Sea* (1997) and *The Odd Couple II* (1998).

One of his more provocative roles of this September period was in a little-seen 1996 film, *Getting Away with Murder*, in which Lemmon played Max Mueller, an elderly suburban man suspected by a neighbor (Dan Aykroyd) of being the former commander of a German death camp during World War II. Lily Tomlin and Bonnie Hunt also starred in the film, adding to its pedigree, but given the sensitive (and highly dubious) nature of the material, *Getting Away with Murder* received only a limited theatrical release, becoming something of a lost movie.

Lemmon's last major acting role was in the 1999 television version of *Tuesdays with Morrie*, based on the best-selling book by Mitch Albom and presented by Oprah Winfrey. For his title performance as Morrie Schwartz, a man dying of amyotrophic lateral sclerosis (Lou Gehrig's disease), Lemmon won his last award, an Emmy. His final role in a theatrical feature—a cameo for the director Robert Redford in *The Legend of Beggar Vance*, which Lemmon also narrated—came in 2000. Following a long, unpublicized battle with cancer, Lemmon died at age seventy-six. He is buried at Westwood Memorial Park in Los Angeles.

When he was not acting, Lemmon was a self-taught pianist who liked to tool around on the keys but was serious enough to make a few recordings. He also had a fine singing voice. Offscreen, he was known as a humanitarian and philanthropist, qualities that complemented the Everyman image that remained with him throughout his fifty-year career. He was an active supporter of animal rights, including endorsement of the Protect Paws and Wildlife (ProPAW) initiative to ban cruel traps and poisons. Lemmon, who prided himself on being a particularly bad golfer, also participated regularly in the National Football League Almuni Charity Golf Classic Tour, which benefits various charities and foundations. Politically, Lemmon was an outspoken liberal who often campaigned for the Democratic Party and spoke out for the environment. In 1969 he narrated *The Slow Guillotine,* a controversial, Emmy-winning television documentary made for Los Angeles's KNBC-TV that was an exposé of how, through ignorance, the environment was permitted to go into disarray.

★

Lemmon was that rare American celebrity who did not write an autobiography. Biographies include Don Widener, *Lemmon* (1973); Joe Baltake, *The Films of Jack Lemmon* (1977); Will Holtzman, *Jack Lemmon* (1977); and Joe Baltake, *Jack Lemmon: His Films and Career* (1986). Obituaries are in the *New York Times* and *Los Angeles Times* (both 29 June 2001), and *Variety* (9–15 July 2001).

JOE BALTAKE

LEMON, Robert Granville ("Bob") (*b.* 22 September 1920 in San Bernardino, California; *d.* 11 January 2000 in Long Beach, California), baseball player who made the switch from an infielder/outfielder to become a Hall of Fame pitcher and later a manager who led his team in one of the game's greatest comeback seasons of all time.

Of Scotch-Irish descent, Lemon grew up in Long Beach, California. He was the younger of two children of Earl Lemon, a former minor league shortstop and catcher who eventually became an ice vendor at a time when refrigerators were not common, and Ruth Edith (West) Lemon, a homemaker. As a child, Lemon enjoyed golf, tennis, and football, but not baseball. His father loved the game, however, and afternoons spent practicing with him helped win over the young Lemon.

While attending Woodrow Wilson High School in Long Beach, Lemon began to attract attention for his skill as a baseball player. Although his coaches used him primarily as a shortstop, thanks to his phenomenally strong right arm, he also played the outfield and pitched occasionally. While he was still in high school, seventeen-year-old Lemon signed a contract with the Cleveland Indians for $1,000. The six-foot-tall Lemon began his professional baseball career in 1938 with the class C Springfield (Ohio) Indians of the Middle Atlantic League, where his short seven-game

stay included stints in the infield and outfield. For the next several seasons he played for several minor-league teams, including the Class C Oswego (New York) Netherlands of the Canadian-American League; the Class A New Orleans Pelicans of the Southern Association; and the Class A Wilkes-Barre (Pennsylvania) Barons of the Eastern League. This minor-league success led to a big-league call-up and his major league debut with the Cleveland Indians on 9 September 1941. Another all-around productive season in the minors in 1942, this time with the International League's Baltimore Orioles, led to another end-of-season appearance with the Indians.

In 1943 Lemon entered the U.S. Navy and joined a service team in Aiea, Hawaii. When a number of pitchers got hurt, the team's manager, who knew that Lemon had a good curveball, started him and soon realized that he had a star on his hands. Lemon married Jane McGee on 14 January 1944; they had three sons. After more than three years of navy duty, Lemon reported to spring training with the Indians in 1946, but his third-base skills had deteriorated enough while he was in the service that he was switched to center field. His switch to the outfield was not a success, but while Lemon was languishing on the bench, Cleveland's manager, Lou Boudreau, began hearing positive reports from big leaguers who had faced Lemon in the service. These included such formidable players as Bill Dickey, Birdie Tebbetts, and Ted Williams, and therefore Boudreau decided to take a chance on Lemon.

Soon a somewhat reluctant Lemon, who still pined to be an everyday player, was on the mound, using an assortment of pitches and striking out big-league hitters. He did well in that first season as a hurler, but the best was yet to come. By 1948 Lemon was a staff ace thanks to a superb sinker and curveball. He finished the season with a 20–14 mark, leading the league in complete games, shutouts, and innings pitched. He also tossed a no-hitter against the Detroit Tigers on 30 June 1948, was named to his first of seven straight All-Star games, and won the second and sixth games in Cleveland's six-game World Series triumph over the Boston Braves.

Beginning in 1948 Lemon started a stretch with the Indians in which he won at least twenty games per season in seven of nine years. He also was a key factor in Cleveland's 1954 pennant drive, posting a 23–7 record, while part of the famed rotation of Early Wynn, Bob Feller, and Mike Garcia, as Cleveland won a record 111 regular-season games before being swept by the New York Giants in the World Series. Injuries to his leg and arm forced Lemon to retire after the 1958 season. In fifteen big-league seasons, he compiled a 207–128 record, 188 complete games, 1,277 strikeouts in 2,850 innings, and a 3.23 earned run average. He also hit thirty-seven home runs and was inducted into

Bob Lemon, March 1955. BETTMANN/CORBIS

the National Baseball Hall of Fame in Cooperstown, New York, in 1976.

Lemon's post-playing career soon found him involved with the national pastime again, as a scout (1959) and coach (1960) with the Indians, a coach with the Philadelphia Phillies (1961), a minor-league manager in Hawaii (1964) and Seattle (1965–1966), a coach for the California Angels (1967–1968), a minor-league manager with Vancouver (1969), a scout with the Kansas City Royals (1973), a minor-league manager in Sacramento (1974) and Richmond (1975), and a major-league coach with the New York Yankees (1976). The always unflappable Lemon got his first chance as a major-league manager with the Royals when he replaced Charlie Metro on 9 June 1970, lasting through the 1972 season. In 1971 he led Kansas City to an 85–76 record and a second-place finish in the American League West. His next chance to skipper a big-league club came in 1977 with the Chicago White Sox. The team's 90–73 record and third-place finish in the American League West helped Lemon win the American League Manager of the Year award. Despite these successes, in the early part of the next season, he garnered a 34–40 mark, which led to his dismissal by the White Sox on 29 June 1978.

A new and surprising chapter in Lemon's life began in the summer of 1978. The defending World Series champion Yankees were suffering through a tumultuous season, and after the resignation of their manager, Billy Martin,

Lemon took over on 25 July. The team was in fourth place with a 52–43 record, ten and a half games behind the Boston Red Sox. Lemon's calm and relaxed personality proved to be just what the team needed to catch the Red Sox and eventually win the American League East after a one-game playoff punctuated by Bucky Dent's famed home run at Fenway Park. New York went on to defeat the Royals in the American League Championship Series and then defeat the Los Angeles Dodgers in the World Series.

In the same month as the 1978 World Series, tragedy struck when the youngest of Lemon's three sons, only twenty-six years old, died on 31 October as the result of injuries he had suffered in an automobile accident four days earlier. The good times did not last for Lemon in New York. After getting off to a 34–31 start in 1979, he was replaced by Martin on 18 June and took a scouting and personnel job with the team. Lemon was back in the dugout when once again he became Yankees manager, this time replacing Gene Michael on 6 September 1981. He helped the team get to the World Series, where they lost to the Dodgers. Only fourteen games into the 1982 season, he once more was reassigned to scouting. He finished his major-league managing career with a 430–403 record.

In failing health during the late 1990s, Lemon suffered a stroke in December 1998 and two in 1999. He died of complications of liver disease at the age of seventy-nine at Palmcrest North Convalescent Hospital in Long Beach and was cremated but not interred.

Baseball has rarely seen one of its combatants change positions, especially the tough transition from an infielder/outfielder to pitcher, midstream in his playing career and become successful, but Lemon did exactly that. He not only made the switch with little prior pitching experience but also made it at the major-league level. Proving more than adequate, he became a workhorse member of one of the game's greatest pitching rotations of all time, leading his team to a World Series triumph. When his playing career was over, he took on the challenge of managing and, after working his way up through the minor leagues, was at the helm when he helped another team to one of the greatest regular-season comebacks ever seen.

★

The only biography of Lemon is Ed McAuley, *Bob Lemon: The Work Horse* (1951); published only midway through his playing career, it leaves more than forty years of his baseball life uncovered. Lemon's clippings files, which include numerous newspaper and magazine stories from throughout his long career, are stored at the National Baseball Hall of Fame Library in Cooperstown, New York. An obituary is in the *New York Times* (13 Jan. 2000).

BILL FRANCIS

LEMONS, A. E. ("Abe") (*b.* 21 November 1922 near Ryan, Oklahoma; *d.* 2 September 2002 in Oklahoma City, Oklahoma), successful collegiate basketball coach whose sharp wit and unorthodox style made him a fan and media favorite and a revered mentor to his players.

Lemons was born on a farm and raised in poverty in southern Oklahoma, the seventh of eight children of Abraham Eldridge Lemons and Johnnie (Thompson) Lemons, who sewed quilts and took in washing. He was named A. E., the initials not standing for any name, not even for Abraham Eldridge (his father's name). Later, when he applied for admission to the Merchant Marines and was told that he needed a first name, Lemons added a "b" to his initials and became "Abe."

Lemons's father gave up farming before Lemons was a year old and moved the family to Walters, Oklahoma, where he took a job as a butcher. Lemons attended Walters High School, where he was a member of the basketball team, earning starter status in his senior year. He graduated in 1941. He spent 1941 and 1942 at Southwestern State Teachers College in Weatherford, Oklahoma, where he cleaned President James Boren's office and some other rooms in exchange for tuition, books, room, and board. Following his freshman year, Lemons joined the merchant

Abe Lemons, 1963. AP/WIDE WORLD PHOTOS

marine after being rejected by the U.S. Navy and the U.S. Army Air Corps for medical reasons. Upon his discharge in 1946, he enrolled in Hardin College in Wichita Falls, Texas, following Boren, who had left Southwestern. Boren arranged for Lemons to have a full scholarship at Hardin. On 24 August 1946 Lemons married Betty Jo Bills, whom he had met during his freshman year at Southwestern while on a trip to Temple, Oklahoma. The couple had two daughters.

After the birth of their first child in July 1947, Lemons investigated the possibility of obtaining a larger scholarship at another institution to help pay the family's mounting bills. Texas Wesleyan offered a full scholarship, but it was matched by Doyle Parrack, an old friend of Lemons's from southwestern Oklahoma, who had just become head coach of the Oklahoma City University (OCU) Chiefs. A six-foot, three-inch forward, Lemons served as team captain in his senior year, and when he became the first member of his family to graduate from college in May 1950 (with a B.A. in history and physical education), Parrack invited him to stay on as freshman basketball coach. In 1955, when Parrack accepted the head coaching position at the University of Oklahoma, Lemons was elevated to head coach of the Chiefs.

In his first eighteen-year stint at OCU, Lemons had a record of 311–181, with only two losing seasons, 1959–1960 (12–13) and 1970–1971 (9–16). During that period, OCU earned invitations to seven National Collegiate Athletic Association (NCAA) tournaments and four National Invitational Tournaments (NIT). In spite of his team's success, attendance was disappointing, especially in his last season, in which the team had a 21–6 record and earned a bid to the NCAA tournament.

In 1973 Lemons received and accepted an offer at about twice his OCU salary to become head basketball coach at Pan American University in Edinburg, Texas. He inherited a team (the Broncs) still on a severe NCAA probation and coming off a dismal record of 4–22. He turned the program around in dramatic fashion. During Lemons's three-year tenure, he recorded season records of 13–9, 22–2, and 20–5. Although prevented by the lingering probation from receiving a post-season bid in 1975, Pan American finished the season ranked third nationally.

In the spring of 1976 Darrell Royal, director of athletics at the University of Texas at Austin (UT), invited Lemons to become head men's basketball coach. After a rebuilding year and a 13–13 record in 1977, Lemons's 1977–1978 Longhorn squad finished the regular season at 22–5 and then scored four victories to win the NIT title.

A colorful rivalry developed between Lemons and then-Arkansas coach Eddie Sutton, probably because of statements made by Lemons that alienated the Arkansas fans. The day before an away game against the Razorbacks,

Lemons announced, "The guy who plays the worst has to stay in Fayetteville for a week." During an Arkansas-Texas game in Austin, won by Sutton's team, the coaches engaged in a heated discussion that almost led to fisticuffs, and Lemons once appeared at a "roast" of Eddie Sutton dressed in overalls and a wig similar to Sutton's hairstyle. Even the Arkansas legislature became involved when, in March 1979, a tongue-in-cheek resolution honoring Lemons was introduced, failing by a vote of 93–0.

Although his teams were successful on the court, Lemons's off-court persona, long-drawn stories, quick wit, and caustic humor did not find the same favor with the new athletics administration at UT after the retirement of Darrell Royal in January 1980. Royal (also from Oklahoma) had been one of Lemons's staunchest supporters, but his successor as director of athletics, DeLoss Dodds, and others at the University of Texas did not appreciate Lemons's behavior and image. On 10 March 1982 Dodds summoned Lemons to his office and fired him, claiming that the basketball program needed new leadership and new direction. Stunned, Lemons sat out the 1982–1983 season, calling it his "red-shirt" year. During his six years at UT, Lemons had compiled a record of 110–63. His team made the NCAA Tournament in 1979 and the NIT in 1980. Lemons was named Southwest Conference Coach of the Year twice.

In April 1983 Lemons was invited to return to Oklahoma City University, where he coached for seven more years, with a creditable record of 123–83. He retired at the end of the 1990 season, with a career record of 599–343, twenty-eighth best for all NCAA Division I coaches at that time. Lemons received many honors during his career. In January 1976 the Texas Sports Writers Association honored him as Senior College Coach of the Year, and in April of that same year he began a term as president of the National Association of Basketball Coaches. In 1978 Lemons and the Duke University coach Bill Foster shared the title of National Basketball Coach of the Year. In September 1990 Lemons was inducted into the Oklahoma Sports Hall of Fame. In 1994 he was inducted into the University of Texas Longhorn Hall of Honor, and in the summer of 1997 he was named to the Oklahoma Coaches Association Hall of Fame. On 5 May 1990 he was awarded an honorary L.H.D. from Oklahoma City University.

Lemons died at his home after a four-year battle with Parkinson's disease and was buried in Oklahoma City. A basketball coach at the collegiate level for thirty-four years, with a career won-loss record of 599–343, Lemons coached at three different institutions, inheriting at each a poor basketball program that he took to national prominence. His off-court wit and his laid-back attitude toward his players obscured for some his true skill as a coach. In the foreword to *Abe Lemons: Court Magician* (1999), the former Indiana basketball coach Bob Knight put into perspective the

coaching success that Lemons attained with his unorthodox style: "Abe has, throughout his entire career, been far and away the most entertaining person I have ever seen in athletics. . . . Abe has one of the . . . best basketball minds I have encountered during my time in coaching."

★

Information about Lemons's way with words can be found in Robert Heard, *You Scored One More Point Than a Dead Man: The Irresistible, Sardonic Humor of Abe Lemons* (1978). For more information, see Bob Burke and Kenny A. Franks, *Abe Lemons: Court Magician* (1999). Obituaries are in the *Houston Chronicle* and *Austin American-Statesman* (both 3 Sept. 2002). A video, compiled by Nike Sports Productions, is *Abe and Eddie: A Basketball Story* (1981).

JIM CASTAÑEDA

LEVI, Edward H(irsch) (*b.* 26 June 1911 in Chicago, Illinois; *d.* 7 March 2000 in Chicago, Illinois), provost and president of the University of Chicago who, as U.S. attorney general in the administration of Gerald R. Ford, helped restore confidence in government after the scandals of the previous administration.

Levi was the son of Gerson B. Levi, a rabbi, and Elsa (Hirsch) Levi, a homemaker. He was raised in the Hyde Park neighborhood on Chicago's South Side, where he attended the University of Chicago Laboratory School from kindergarten through his graduation from high school. He entered the University of Chicago, where he received his Ph.B. in 1932 and his J.D. with honors in 1935. Levi went on to Yale University on a Sterling Fellowship and received his J.S.D. in 1938.

Levi began his career by gaining admission to the bar in Illinois in 1936. He enjoyed teaching and returned to the University of Chicago as an assistant professor of law from 1936 to 1940. A brilliant scholar and teacher, Levi is remembered by students for his witty putdowns of those who displayed sloppy thinking. Appointed special assistant to U.S. Assistant Attorney General Thurman Arnold, a vigorous antitrust prosecutor, in 1940, he became a first assistant in the War Division in 1943. In 1944 he was appointed chairman of the Interdepartmental Committee on Monopolies and Cartels. He also served as first assistant in the Antitrust Division and contributed to efforts to stop the growth of business monopolies. Levi was admitted to the U.S. Supreme Court bar in 1945. He married Kate Sulzberger on 4 June 1946; the couple had three sons.

Levi returned to academia in 1945 and was a professor of law at the University of Chicago until 1975. An adviser to the so-called Chicago school of physicists, Levi assisted in drafting the U.S. Atomic Energy Act in 1946, which led to the establishment of the Atomic Energy Commission. In 1949 he published *Introduction to Legal Reasoning,* still considered a significant legal textbook. As a leading authority on antitrust activity, he served as counsel to the House Judiciary Committee's antitrust subcommittee in 1950.

Also in 1950, Levi became dean of the law school at the University of Chicago, and in 1958 he founded the prestigious *Journal of Law and Economics.* Promoted to university provost in 1962, he served for six years before becoming the eighth president of the University of Chicago in 1968. Levi was the first scholar of the Jewish faith to be chosen to head a major American university. *Newsweek* magazine described him as a "cunning administrator," admired for his deftness in handling student protests during the epidemic of student unrest in the late 1960s. When students occupied his office during one such protest in 1969, Levi simply moved to another building. After sixteen days of waiting, the demonstrators drifted away. Levi served as president until 1975, increasing the already high reputation of the university. He also assisted in the redevelopment of the impoverished neighborhood surrounding the university.

Levi gained experience in the mid-1960s with the White House panel on education and as a consultant for the Office of Education under the Department of Health, Education, and Welfare. A few years later Levi was offered the position of U.S. attorney general. Following the resignation of President Richard M. Nixon, Gerald R. Ford became president in August 1974, promising to overhaul the Justice Department. Ford's appointment of Levi as his first cabinet member on 14 January 1975 was widely praised by legal and government analysts.

Levi was confirmed by the Senate on 5 February 1975. One of his first objectives was to establish guidelines for the Federal Bureau of Investigation (FBI) and the Central Intelligence Agency, whose involvement in clandestine activities had posed serious problems under the Nixon administration. Levi established a commission to evaluate the FBI, and the committee issued guidelines for domestic security and the handling of civil disorders. Among his many other activities as attorney general, Levi worked to enforce antitrust legislation. Through his efforts, the Justice Department was given increased review responsibilities over the activities of the Civil Aeronautics Board. He also contributed to legislation on school busing. According to Levi's bill, busing should be implemented only in cases where it could clearly be shown that segregation had resulted from government actions. His bill also included court review of busing effectiveness.

Levi left his position with the Department of Justice following the inauguration of President Jimmy Carter in January 1977. He returned to the University of Chicago as a Glen A. Lloyd Distinguished Service Professor and de-

Edward H. Levi, January 1975. BETTMANN/CORBIS

voted himself to several educational and community causes. In 1986 he served as a member of the Martin Luther King, Jr., Federal Holiday Commission, and he was vice president of the American Philosophical Society from 1991 to 1994. The Stanford professor Herbert L. Packer listed Levi as one of the two most brilliant antitrust law scholars of his generation. His honors included the Legion of Honor (France), the Learned Hand Medal of the Federal Bar Council, the Fordham-Stein Award, the Brandeis Medal, and honorary degrees from several colleges. He died at his home at age eighty-eight and is buried in Chicago.

As an educator, Levi believed that lawyers should have an interdisciplinary background to give them knowledge of more than just the law. As Gerhard Casper, a former colleague who went on to become president of Stanford, recalled, Levi maintained that "universities are the custodians not only of the many cultures of man but of the rational process itself." As the nation's leading attorney, he is credited with helping restore Americans' respect for government.

★

A number of documents relating to Levi are housed at the University of Chicago. In addition to papers from his presidency, these include a bibliography of his works from 1936 to 1992 and a series of tributes given at a 6 Apr. 2000 memorial service. Further information on Levi can be found in Robert Sobel, ed., *Biographical Directory of the United States Executive Branch, 1974–1977* (1977), and Eleanora W. Schoenebaum, ed., *Profiles of an Era: The Nixon/Ford Years* (1979). See also John Paul Stevens, "Professor Edward H. Levi," *University of Chicago Law Review* 52, no. 2 (spring 1985): 290. Obituaries are in the *New York Times* and *Chicago Sun-Times* (both 8 Mar. 2000).

REED MARKHAM

LEWIS, Flora (*b.* 29 July 1922 in Los Angeles, California; *d.* 2 June 2002 in Paris, France), award-winning journalist and columnist, noted as an astute foreign correspondent reporting on crucial twentieth-century events in a male-dominated profession.

Lewis was the only daughter of Jewish parents, Pauline (Kallin) Lewis, a pianist, and Benjamin Lewis, an attorney. She had a younger brother. Lewis showed her precocity early, graduating from high school in Los Angeles at age fifteen. After first spending time in Switzerland, she graduated from the University of California, Los Angeles, summa cum laude and Phi Beta Kappa with a B.A. in political science (1941) and received an M.S. from the Columbia University School of Journalism the following year. After having been a college stringer (local correspondent) and cub reporter for the *Los Angeles Times*, she joined the Associated Press (AP) in 1942.

Based in New York and then Washington, D.C., she was posted to London in 1945, arriving on VJ Day (Victory over Japan Day, 15 August 1945). That same month she married Sidney Gruson, a correspondent and future executive for the *New York Times*. Prevailing rules at the *Times* meant that Lewis could not write for the same paper, so after leaving the AP in 1946, she established herself as a contract and freelance reporter as the couple traveled across the countries of western and eastern Europe, the Middle East, and Mexico. Their two daughters and a son were born in three different countries. Lewis interviewed important Polish and Vietnamese leaders and reported on the Shah of Iran's 1951 wedding.

After a stint as an editor at McGraw-Hill in New York City in 1955, Lewis became the *Washington Post*'s first female foreign correspondent, going on to head the *Post* offices in Bonn and London. Known as a determined investigative reporter and skilled writer with a moderate attitude, she was appointed bureau chief when the *Post* first opened its New York office in 1965. Her first two books contained her observations of the Hungarian and Polish revolts against communism that had taken place while she lived in Europe. *Case History of Hope: The Story of Poland's Peaceful Revolutions* (1958), an analysis of the forces that affected Poland's mood after the death of the Soviet dictator Joseph Stalin, was praised for Lewis's reportorial interpretation and absorbing writing. *Red Pawn* (1965), which traced the disappearance from the Eastern Bloc of the American Quaker Noel Field (a prisoner and, possibly, a communist agent) and his family, is an account full of many characters, clues, and changing politics. A later book, *One of Our H-Bombs Is Missing* (1967), received mixed reviews; it recounts the aftermath of the 1966 airplane crash that released four hydrogen bombs over Spain. Lewis received awards from the Overseas Press Club for magazine and foreign reporting in 1956 and 1962 as well as the Columbia Journalism School's Fiftieth Anniversary Award in 1963.

After leaving the *Washington Post* in 1966, Lewis became a foreign affairs columnist. She wrote the syndicated column "Today Abroad" for the *New York Post, Newsday,* and international newspapers. She traveled to Vietnam five times in five years to report and write on general strategy rather than specific battles, and she covered the 1967 Six-Day War in Israel. Only after she and Gruson were divorced in 1972 did Lewis become the *New York Times* bureau chief in Paris. In 1976 she also was named diplomatic correspondent. From 1980 to 1990 she was only the third foreign affairs columnist, replacing the Pulitzer Prize winner and *Times* family member C. L. Sulzberger; from 1990 to 1994 she was the *Times* senior columnist. She continued to write for such American, British, and French periodicals as *Time,* the London *Observer,* and *France-Soir.* Calling herself a "hard-nosed . . . bleeding-heart moderate," Lewis strongly criticized President Ronald M. Reagan's foreign policies. Her last book, *Europe: A Tapestry of Nations* (1987), updated and republished as *Europe: Road to Unity* (1993), consists of separate chapters on the national character of twenty-five European countries.

Lewis earned a third award from the Overseas Press Club for foreign reporting in 1978, was made a Chevalier de la Légion d'Honneur by the French government in 1981, won the Fourth Estate Award for "a lifetime of contribution to American journalism" from the National Press Club in 1985, and received the Elmer Holmes Bobst Award in Arts and Letters from New York University in 1987. She garnered honorary doctorates from several universities, including Princeton and Dartmouth, and won numerous other awards in journalism, foreign affairs, and international studies. A woman of varied intellectual interests, Lewis believed that learning languages was "an education not only in words, but an education in how to think, how minds work." A brilliant, fluent, tough competitor, she was also a slim, chic woman. Having lived most of her life abroad, Lewis died of cancer at her home in Paris, near the Louvre. Her ashes were distributed from a boat off the Florida coast.

In a field where women were not readily honored or even accepted on the literal and figurative front lines, Lewis achieved success while combining journalism, marriage, and motherhood. Realizing that "truth is the hardest substance to pin down," Lewis investigated and assessed major political trends and events of the second half of the twentieth century. With "dream writing," incisive analysis, and a nonideological position, she followed her "unerring instinct for news" through Europe, Israel, and around the world.

★

A section of Julia Edwards, *Women of the World: The Great Foreign Correspondents* (1988), includes personal observations by its author, a Columbia classmate of Lewis's. An extensive biographical sketch is in *Current Biography Yearbook* (1989). A posthumous tribute by Terence Smith is in the *Columbia Journalism Review* (July/Aug. 2002). Obituaries are in the *New York Times* (2 June 2002) and *Washington Post* (3 June 2002).

RACHEL SHOR

LEWIS, John Aaron (*b.* 3 May 1920 in La Grange, Illinois; *d.* 29 March 2001 in Manhattan, New York City), celebrated pianist and composer who changed jazz by synthesizing European classical and baroque keyboard styles with African-American bebop and blues to yield the style known as "third stream," most frequently identified with his group, the Modern Jazz Quartet.

Lewis was born into a musical family. His father was an optometrist who played violin and piano, and his mother was an operatic singer who had studied in Chicago with Madame Schumann-Heink. Within a year of his birth, the family moved to Albuquerque, New Mexico, to reside near his maternal grandparents. Lewis's parents divorced soon after their arrival in New Mexico, and his mother died unexpectedly the next year. He grew up with his grandmother and great-grandmother in a comfortable middle-class environment, far from America's teeming urban musical centers.

Lewis began to study piano in 1927, encountering music mostly through radio and phonograph. He also received private lessons, something he resisted at first. He performed professionally at the age of ten (for his Boy Scout merit badge in music), playing a three-hour nightclub concert with wages of $1, along with all he could eat. By age fifteen he was performing blues-oriented jazz piano regularly in local clubs and taverns throughout New Mexico.

In 1938 Lewis enrolled at the University of New Mexico, majoring in anthropology and directing the university jazz band. Six months before graduation he was drafted into the U.S. Army. Lewis survived the invasion of Normandy in 1944 and was assigned to Army Special Services because of his musical ability. During this time he met Kenny Clarke, a jazz drummer and avid proponent of the newly emergent bebop style.

Lewis returned to Albuquerque in 1945 to finish college. In the meantime, bebop—which Lewis ambiguously termed "unbelievable" when he first heard it—had replaced the swing style of music on the radio. Determined to pursue a future in music, he relocated to New York City and, by 1946, was performing the "unbelievable" at legendary Fifty-second Street jazz clubs with Oran ("Hot Lips") Page, a trumpeter from the famed keyboardist and orchestra leader Count Basie's band.

When Clarke returned to New York from the army, he introduced Lewis to the composer and arranger Dizzy Gillespie, who hired him as arranger and pianist to replace Thelonious Monk, who was launching his solo career as a pianist and composer. As a member of Gillespie's renowned band, Lewis met the vibraphonist Milt Jackson and the bassist Ray Brown. Lewis, Clarke, Jackson, and Brown soon began performing short interludes between the big-band sets featuring Gillespie. The future Modern Jazz Quartet had been formed.

In 1947 Lewis performed as pianist on the trumpeter Miles Davis's first recordings, and in 1949 he played for Davis's historic *Birth of the Cool* project, collaborating with the saxophonists Gerry Mulligan and Lee Konitz and the pianist and arranger Gil Evans. Lewis continued to perform and record with the Gillespie rhythm section, now billed as the Milt Jackson Quartet.

The bassist Percy Heath replaced Ray Brown in 1952, and the group changed its name (but not its initials) to the Modern Jazz Quartet (MJQ). Lewis's writing shifted conceptually from bebop's freely conceived, high-energy arrangements to tightly woven contrapuntal restraint. His polyphonic composition and arranging style emphasized subtle timbral combinations of piano and vibraphone, with large amounts of orchestrated interaction among all four artists. His compositional forms expanded the predominantly binary song structures of conventional Broadway "standards" long popular with bebop artists. Lewis's songs would often feature three or more sections, carefully balanced and modulated. Brief solos were contrasted against complexly intertwined quartet interludes.

Clarke resigned from the quartet in 1955 and was replaced by Connie Kay. For the next forty years, except for

John Lewis, February 2000. Mr. Jack Vartoogian

a seven-year sabbatical from 1974 to 1981, the Modern Jazz Quartet continued its extraordinary musical synthesis of baroque, jazz, and blues. The group performed mostly at festivals and concerts, invariably in formal concert dress and always bowing to the audience. Whitney Balliett, the jazz critic for the *New Yorker,* noted that such a formal approach often "misled the unknowing into regarding [the MJQ] as a cocktail group, and the knowing into scoffing at it as staid and stuffy." Yet no less a figure than Davis compared the MJQ to "a boxer stepping into the ring dressed in a tuxedo."

In 1955 Lewis and the composer Gunther Schuller founded the Society of Jazz and Classical Music, an agency for commissioning new work from jazz composers for chamber ensembles. In 1956 Lewis composed for the seminal third-stream album *Two Degrees East, Three Degrees West,* first released as *Grand Encounter,* and in 1957 he wrote the score for Roger Vadim's film *Sait-on jamais? (No Sun in Venice).* The following year Lewis began a long affiliation with the Monterey Jazz Festival and composed an orchestral suite, *European Windows,* for the Stuttgart Symphony. In 1959 he wrote a jazz ensemble score for the Harry Belafonte film noir *Odds Against Tomorrow.*

In 1960 Lewis won *Metronome* magazine's award for best jazz arranger and received a Grammy nomination for best jazz composition for *Sketches from Third Stream Music.* In 1961 he premiered a choreographic score, *Original Sin,* with the San Francisco Ballet. In 1962 he cofounded Orchestra U.S.A., a twenty-eight-piece experimental orchestra of both jazz and traditional players. From 1968 until 1972 Lewis served as director of the Lenox (Massachusetts) School of Jazz, where he championed the music of the jazz great Ornette Coleman. Between 1974 and 1981 he taught

at Harvard University and City College of New York and in 1984 began recording J. S. Bach's *Well-Tempered Clavier,* using carefully arranged jazz rhythm sections as new basso continuo accompaniments to the keyboard. In 1985 he cofounded the American Jazz Orchestra and in 1987 recorded a keyboard duet, *Chess Game,* based on Bach's *Goldberg Variations,* featuring his wife, Mirjana, as harpsichordist.

Lewis continued recording notable albums into the mid-1990s. During this time he received honorary degrees from the Manhattan School of Music, the Berklee School of Music, the New England Conservatory, and the University of Northern New Mexico. In 1989 he was named Officier des Arts et Lettres by the French government. In 2001 he received the Jazz Master Award from the National Endowment for the Arts and the Award for Artistic Excellence from the Jazz at Lincoln Center Foundation. Lewis died of prostate cancer in Manhattan at age eighty. He was survived by his wife and two children.

Leonard Feather wrote in the *Encyclopedia of Jazz:* "Lewis is regarded as one of the most brilliant minds ever applied to jazz. Completely self-sufficient and self-confident . . . an unusual, quiet firmness, coupled with modesty and a complete indifference to critical reaction." Lewis's creative output stands as a unique monument: blues-based polyphonic individuality wedded to formal mastery and melodic invention.

★

Information on the Modern Jazz Quartet can be found in Leonard Feather and Ira Gittler, *The New Edition of the Encyclopedia of Jazz* (1960), and Gary Giddins, *Visions of Jazz: The First Century* (1998). Obituaries of Lewis are in the *New York Times* and *Chicago Tribune* (both 31 Mar. 2001).

James McElwaine

LINCOLN, C(harles) Eric (*b.* 23 June 1924 in Athens, Alabama; *d.* 14 May 2000 in Durham, North Carolina), author, educator, and scholar who wrote several important works on African-American religion and social experience.

Born in the small rural town of Athens, Lincoln was an out-of-wedlock child whose parents gave him to his maternal grandparents, Less Charles Lincoln and Mattie (Sowell) Lincoln, to raise. His grandmother became the anchor and stabilizing force of his life. She was a lay leader at the Village View United Methodist Church, which shaped Lincoln's religious life. Growing up in extreme poverty, he did not own a pair of shoes until he was six years old; he often said that his greatest fear was becoming poor again. Despite such hardship, Lincoln was extremely bright and possessed a gift for writing. Because there was no public schooling for black students in his county at the time, he spent twelve years at Trinity High School, a private institution founded by the American Missionary Association, and graduated as the valedictorian of his class.

Seeing education as a path out of poverty, he eventually earned many degrees: an A.B. from Lemoyne-Owen College in Memphis, Tennessee, in 1947; an M.A. in the sociology of religion from Fisk University in Nashville, Tennessee, in 1954; a B.D. from the University of Chicago in 1956; and an M.Ed. and Ph.D. in social ethics, both from Boston University in 1960. At Boston he befriended his classmate Martin Luther King, Jr., and the two went on double dates with their future wives, Lucy Cook and Coretta Scott. He also studied at the University of Chicago Law School and Brown University in Providence, Rhode Island. In order to support himself, he worked as a Pullman porter on the railroad, a sales manager for Pepsi-Cola, a nightclub manager, a road manager of the Birmingham Black Barons baseball team of the Negro Leagues, and a stringer and journalist for black newspapers and magazines.

Lincoln's first teaching job was at Clark College in Atlanta in 1954, where he also served in the dean's office. He subsequently taught at Portland State College, Union Theological Seminary, Brown University, Vassar College, the University of Ghana, Fisk University, and Duke University, where he was a professor of religion and culture from 1976 to 1993. He received honorary doctorate degrees from Boston University, where he served on the board of trustees; Clark-Atlanta University; and Emory University. Lincoln married Lucy Cook on 1 July 1961; they had two children. Lincoln also had two children from a previous marriage in 1947 to Minnie Coleman Reeves.

A prolific author and scholar, Lincoln published twenty-three books and hundreds of articles. Several of his books are classics in the study of black religion, a field that he played a pivotal role in developing. As the only scholar given official permission to do a study of the Nation of Islam, his *Black Muslims in America* (1961) became the standard text on the subject. He also coauthored *The Black Church in the African American Experience* (1974), which won the Distinguished Book Award from the Society for the Scientific Study of Religion in 1991. His novel *The Avenue: Clayton City* (1987) won the Lillian Smith Book Award for best southern fiction in 1988. His *Race, Religion, and the Continuing American Dilemma* (1984) and *Coming Through the Fire: Surviving Race and Place in America* (1996) contain Lincoln's insights as a moral philosopher. Lincoln, who suffered from high blood pressure and diabetes, died of a heart attack at his home at age seventy-five. His last published work, the "Song of Reconciliation," which summarized his optimism about racial relations in America, was sung at his memorial service in the chapel of Duke University. He was also the founder of an interracial congregation, the Reconciliation United Methodist Church, in Durham.

A Renaissance man, Lincoln was also a poet, gourmet cook, and fisherman. His hymns appeared in the *United Methodist Hymnal,* the *African Methodist Episcopal Church Hymnal, Songs of Zion,* and *Lift Every Voice and Sing.* He also wrote "Kerry's Song," which was sung at the wedding of Kerry Kennedy, the daughter of the slain U.S. senator Robert F. Kennedy, and Andrew Cuomo, the son of the former New York governor Mario Cuomo. Lincoln's many distinguished friends included the civil rights leader Martin Luther King, Jr., the Kennedy family, the black activist Malcolm X, and the author Alex Haley. As an ordained Methodist minister, Lincoln was honored by Pope John Paul II at the Vatican in 1990 for his "scholarly service to the church." His ashes were interred at a special memorial site in Athens, renamed the Lincoln-Bridgeforth Park in his honor, where his childhood home once stood.

★

C. Eric Lincoln, *Coming Through the Fire: Surviving Race and Place in America* (1996), contains autobiographical information. An interview with Lincoln is Yvonne Odillo, "The Universal Black Experience," *Journal of Negro History* 75, nos. 3–4 (summer–fall 1990): 112–119. Obituaries are in the *Los Angeles Times* (16 May 2000) and *New York Times* (17 May 2000).

LAWRENCE H. MAMIYA

LINDBERGH, Anne (Spencer) Morrow (*b.* 22 June 1906 in Englewood, New Jersey; *d.* 7 February 2001 in Passumpsic, Vermont), pioneer aviator and author whose complex marriage to Charles A. Lindbergh brought her fame and tragedy and whose books found a wide audience.

Morrow was the second of four children born to Dwight Whitney Morrow, a partner in J. P. Morgan and Company,

Anne Morrow Lindbergh. AP/WIDE WORLD PHOTOS

and Elizabeth Reeve (Cutter) Morrow, a writer and poet. Her liberal Republican father was a power on Wall Street, ambassador to Mexico (1927–1930), and U.S. senator from New Jersey (1930–1931). Her mother was an author of children's books and an advocate for women's education who served as acting president of Smith College (1939–1940). Grounded in the morality of the Presbyterian Church and cosseted by nannies and servants at Next Day Hill, the Morrows' fifty-four acre estate in suburban Englewood, Lindbergh, along with her two sisters and her brother, grew up in the insulated, well-protected world of the genteel upper class. She attended the Dwight School in Englewood and graduated from Miss Chapin's School in New York City in 1924. At Smith College in Northampton, Massachusetts, where she earned a B.A. in English with honors in 1928, she discovered a talent for writing and won two literary prizes for her poetry and prose.

The shy young woman who emerged from college was little different from the unworldly young girl who had entered four years earlier. Her diaries from those years, *Bring Me a Unicorn: Diaries and Letters of Anne Morrow Lindbergh, 1922–1928* (1972), reveal a gifted writer who, despite her travels abroad with her parents, had little awareness of the political and literary currents of her time or of the larger world beyond her own. Years later she wrote that she was

still, at twenty-one, the "sheltered Emelye" of Geoffrey Chaucer's "Knight's Tale," living in a walled garden.

Her life changed dramatically during the Christmas holiday of her senior year at Smith, when she traveled to Mexico City, where her father had invited the aviator Charles Lindbergh for a visit. His solo flight from Long Island to Paris in May 1927 was the stuff of legend, and the international press in a few short months had made Lindbergh into a mythic hero, calling him "Lucky Lindy" and the "Lone Eagle." When Anne met him, he was the most famous man in the world, and she instantly fell in love. They were married in her parents' home on 27 May 1929 in a simple ceremony before a small gathering of family and friends.

For the next several years the Lindberghs were easily the most famous couple in the United States and made a handsome "all-American pair." Charles was tall and slender, with a movie star's good looks, while blue-eyed Anne stood five feet tall and glowed with good health. They were photographed everywhere and hounded daily by strangers and the press. To escape, they often resorted to backdoor exits and decoy cars as if they were—in her words—"criminals or illicit lovers." As newlyweds they spent the early months of their marriage aloft, crisscrossing the continent and the Caribbean to survey routes for commercial aviation while Charles taught her the skills and confidence she needed to serve as his copilot, navigator, and radio operator. In 1930 she received the first glider pilot's license granted to a woman, and her private pilot's license came the following year. More important to her was her husband's praise of her competence in flight.

Flying was for both of them a spiritual experience, one that in time the two captured in prose, and it temporarily freed them from the unsolicited celebrity they had known from the day they met. *Hour of Gold, Hour of Lead: The Diaries and Letters of Anne Morrow Lindbergh, 1929–1932* (1973) reveals her ambivalence in embracing the grand adventure of their flying partnership against her yearning for "a home, family life, privacy, a baby." When, on 20 April 1930, they set a transcontinental speed record, flying from Los Angeles to New York in forty hours and forty-five minutes, she was seven months pregnant.

Charles Augustus Lindbergh III was born on Anne's birthday, 22 June 1930. A year later, leaving the baby with her parents, she and her husband set off in a single-engine Lockheed "Sirius" for Japan and China by way of Alaska and the Bering Sea to map air routes to Asia. They endured freezing cold, thick fog, and moments of great danger and exhilaration—all of it lyrically described in her first bestselling book, *North to the Orient* (1935). They cut short their tour on news of her father's death from a cerebral hemorrhage at age fifty-eight on 4 October 1931. By early 1932 they were in their new home in Hopewell, New Jersey, their privacy assured—they thought—by four hundred acres of land and a driveway nearly a mile long.

To many Americans mired in the Great Depression, the Lindberghs' life seemed the perfect idyll, filled with glamour, wealth, and excitement. At 10:00 P.M. on 1 March 1932, that illusion was shattered when the Lindberghs' nurse went upstairs to check on the baby before bed and found his crib empty. Charles III had been kidnapped, and Anne would never see him again. Calling the kidnapping the "Crime of the Century," an army of photographers, reporters, and curiosity-seekers descended on Hopewell and turned the subsequent ten weeks of frantic investigations and negotiations into a national circus. Over twelve thousand people claimed that they had dreamt the exact location of the missing child. Al Capone and other criminals offered their help. Newspapers had extras ready at every hour, prepared to announce the baby's safe return, but on 12 May 1932 Charles, insisting that Anne remain at home, identified a body found in a ditch not far from their home as that of their son.

Locked Rooms and Open Doors: Diaries and Letters of Anne Morrow Lindbergh, 1932–1935 (1974) details the family's attempts to recover from the tragedy. The first easing of pain came with the birth on 16 August 1932 of Jon, their second child. At the urging of her husband, Anne set to work in autumn on *North to the Orient,* and in the summer of 1933 the couple flew the single-engine "Sirius" on a five-and-a-half month, thirty thousand-mile survey of North and South Atlantic air routes. That hazardous flight became the subject of her next book, *Listen! The Wind* (1938). In 1934 she received the Hubbard Gold Medal from the National Geographic Society for her accomplishments in exploratory flying. "All these factors," she wrote, "were restoring."

Whatever peace the Lindberghs found that year was lost with the trial, conviction, and execution of the alleged kidnapper, Bruno Hauptmann, in the period 1935–1936. Once again they were hounded by the paparazzi. They took refuge in England in January 1936, living in self-imposed exile in Kent, where Lindbergh returned to her writing and gave birth to another son, experiences she recorded in *The Flower and the Nettle: Diaries of Anne Morrow Lindbergh, 1936–1939* (1976). In the spring of 1938 she and Charles retreated to Illiec, a tiny island they purchased on the Brittany coast.

The next two years brought new pain. Assessing the strength of German air power for the U.S. government (1936–1939), Charles regularly cast the Third Reich in a positive light and suggested that Britain and America were ill prepared to meet its military power. He urged both countries to make peace with the German dictator Adolf Hitler to avoid war. When he accepted a medal, in 1938, from Hermann Göring—who, in addition to being one of the

highest-ranking Nazi leaders, was also chief of the German air force, or Luftwaffe—the American and British press criticized him as a Nazi sympathizer. On their return to Lloyd Neck, New York, in 1939, Charles became an active isolationist who worked to keep America out of the war, and this further brought his patriotism into question.

Anne contributed to the debate over their loyalty with a widely read and widely condemned essay, *Wave of the Future* (1940). In it she urged America to concentrate on domestic reform, not war. She offered a naïve and weakly developed isolationist argument that Italy, Germany, and the Soviet Union, whatever their flaws, were new worlds struggling to be born; they were the wave of the future, and the United States could do little to prevent their birth. The controversy worsened when Charles was accused of anti-Semitism after an ill-conceived September 1941 speech in Des Moines, Iowa, in which he suggested that Jews risked retaliation because of their agitation for war against Germany.

Alienated by the isolationism issue, old friends spoke publicly against them, and strangers again threatened the Lindbergh children with retribution for their parents' politics. Through it all, Anne stood by husband. In her introduction to *War Within and Without: Diaries and Letters of Anne Morrow Lindbergh, 1939–1944* (1980), she wrote that she had attempted to dissuade Charles from making the Des Moines speech. At the time, she said nothing publicly, but wrote in her diary that she had faced three challenges in her life: "The first was sorrow (the kidnapping case), the second was fear (the flights), and the third is bitterness (this whole war struggle). And the third is the hardest."

After the United States entered the war in December 1941, Anne devoted herself to her growing family, which by 1945 numbered three sons and two daughters. Alone much of the time—her husband, no longer an isolationist, was serving as a civilian adviser to the U.S. Army Air Forces in the Pacific—she returned to her writing, sending her poetry to the *Atlantic* and completing her fifth book, *The Steep Ascent* (1944), a well-received novel based on a dangerous flight the Lindberghs had made in 1937. At war's end the family moved to a secluded house on three wooded acres in Scott's Cove on Long Island Sound in suburban Darien, Connecticut.

A decade later Anne produced *Gift from the Sea* (1955), a poetic meditation on her decades-long search for an inner life. Using a variety of seashells picked from the sands of Florida's Sanibel and Captiva Islands to represent the stages of marriage and a woman's life, she wrote about the uneasy balance between men and women, the absence of silence and leisure in the modern world, the competing demands of family and career, and the need for periods of solitude and creativity to revitalize the spirit. The book was a publishing sensation, appearing on the *New York Times* best-seller list for eighty weeks, forty-seven of them in first place. It became Lindbergh's best-known work and earned her a generation of devoted readers. By the time of her death, *Gift from the Sea* had sold seven million copies and continued to sell into the next century at a rate of thirty-five thousand copies a year.

The Unicorn and Other Poems, 1935–1955 (1956) was published to mixed reviews but healthy sales. In 1962 Lindbergh published her second novel, *Dearly Beloved: A Theme and Variations,* in which she explored the meaning of love, marriage, and divorce as seen in the lives of nine wedding guests. It was a critical failure—dismissed by many reviewers as weak "women's fiction"—but a success with readers, who purchased more than a hundred thousand copies. She returned to nonfiction with *Earth Shine* (1969), a lyrical two-essay meditation on her visit to Cape Kennedy for the first Moon-orbiting flight of Apollo 8, whose pictures of Earth, she wrote, gave the world "a new sense of Earth's richness and beauty." The book reflected both Lindberghs' strong commitment to conservation and their shared belief, in her words, that "human values spring from earth values."

After the death of her husband from cancer in 1974, Anne Lindbergh completed editing her dairies and letters for publication. Released singly over the next six years, the five volumes found both a welcoming audience and critical acclaim. In 1986 she wrote the introduction to *Wartime Writings 1939–1940,* a collection of essays by her old friend the pilot and writer Antoine de Saint-Exupéry, who had disappeared in 1944 while on a mission over Germany. She was named to the National Aviation Hall of Fame (1979), among other honors, and received a special Aerospace Explorer Award from Women in Aerospace for her lifetime contributions to flight (1993). During those years she lived in seclusion in Darien, retreating each summer to her chalet overlooking Lake Leman near Vevey, Switzerland, until she became too frail to make the journey. In 1999 Lindbergh moved from Connecticut to a small house on her daughter Reeve's farm in Passumpsic, Vermont. A decade of debilitating strokes, the first in 1991, led to her death at age ninety-four. Her body was cremated and her ashes scattered at an undisclosed location.

Lindbergh wrote in a lyrical voice that spoke to a worldwide audience of women through the middle third of the twentieth century and beyond. One of the nation's most admired women, both for her exploits as a pilot and her finely wrought prose as a writer, she was a precursor of the feminists of the 1960s and 1970s. Her diaries remain an important historical record of three decades in the life of an exceptionally gifted woman.

★

The papers of both Anne Morrow Lindbergh and Charles Augustus Lindbergh are in Manuscripts and Archives, Yale University Library, New Haven, Connecticut. The family correspon-dence is closed until 2051, and the remaining papers are restricted. Anne Morrow Lindbergh's diaries are indispensable, as are Reeve Lindbergh's *Under a Wing: A Memoir* (1998) and *No More Words: A Journal of My Mother, Anne Morrow Lindbergh* (2001). The family disavowed Susan Hertog's *Anne Morrow Lindbergh: Her Life* (1999) and forced Hertog to retract all family quotations and delete all passages from Lindbergh's journals. Also denied the use of the Lindbergh papers were Dorothy Herrmann, who wrote *Anne Morrow Lindbergh: A Gift for Life* (1992), and Joyce Milton, author of *Loss of Eden: A Biography of Charles and Anne Morrow Lindbergh* (1993). The only biographer to have unrestricted access to the family papers and the cooperation of the family was A. Scott Berg, for *Lindbergh* (1998). See Alden Whitman's interview with Anne Lindbergh in the *New York Times* (12 Oct. 1969). An obituary is in the *New York Times* (8 Feb. 2001). A television interview with Morley Safer for *60 Minutes* (20 Apr. 1980) is at the Museum of Television and Radio, New York City.

ALLAN L. DAMON

LINDSAY, John Vliet (*b.* 24 November 1921 in New York City; *d.* 19 December 2000 in Hilton Head, South Carolina), controversial 103rd mayor of New York City, who aspired to be the voice of urban America in a time of financial crisis and racial turmoil.

Lindsay was one of five children born to George Lindsay and Florence (Vliet) Lindsay, and was raised with his twin brother in relative prosperity on West End Avenue in the borough of Manhattan. Boasting both English and Dutch ancestry, Lindsay often claimed he was an "ASP" (Anglo-Saxon Protestant), a variant of "WASP," since all Anglo-Saxons were white. His father, an investment banker, later moved the family to Park Avenue and won a Social Register listing, but Lindsay was never as rich or socially prominent as many people believed.

Educated at the Buckley School on the Upper East Side of Manhattan and Saint Paul's School in Concord, New Hampshire, Lindsay entered Yale University (New Haven, Connecticut) as the nation faced World War II, and graduated a year early (1943) with a B.A., owing to wartime acceleration. He entered the navy as a gunnery officer, received five battle stars for combat in Europe and Asia, and was mustered out (March 1946) as executive officer of the destroyer *Swanson*. He graduated from Yale Law School in 1948 with an LL.B. On 18 June 1949 he married Mary Anne Harrison; the couple settled into an apartment in the Stuyvesant Town section of New York City, and Lindsay began to practice law at the firm of Webster, Sheffield, Fleischmann, Hitchcock, and Chrystie. Lindsay and his wife had four children.

Lindsay believed in Republican Party principles, especially individualism and human rights, and entered politics during Dwight D. Eisenhower's 1952 presidential campaign. He became leader of the New York Young Republicans and in 1955 joined U.S. Attorney General Herbert Brownell's Justice Department. His duties included work on the 1957 Civil Rights Act and aiding persons displaced by the Hungarian Revolution. Encouraged by Brownell, in 1958 Lindsay declared his candidacy in the so-called silk-stocking district (the Seventeenth Congressional District of New York), in which the Republican incumbent was retiring. After winning the primary, he defeated his Democratic opponent by extensively walking around the district and preaching the liberal values dear to residents of Manhattan's East Side. Before entering Congress, he was among the "bright hopes" of East Coast Republicanism.

As a member of the House of Representatives from 1959 to 1965, Lindsay proved indifferent to party discipline, a maverick concerned with urban affairs and civil rights. He defended the record of the liberal Supreme Court led by Chief Justice Earl Warren; supported creation of the Department of Urban Affairs; and endorsed the goals of the Great Society, the domestic agenda of President Lyndon B. Johnson intended to secure social justice. The self-styled "Congressman from the Constitution" often delivered moral sermons resented by his colleagues. From 1963 to 1964 Lindsay voted with his party only a third of the time, and then he refused to support the presidential candidacy of the conservative Barry Goldwater. Hailed as an independent Republican in New York, where he held a "safe seat," he was isolated and alienated from national party concerns. His candidacy for mayor of New York City in 1965 offered a better opportunity to confront America's urban crisis.

New York was the richest city in the world, but Lindsay saw a metropolis that was ill governed by "machine" Democrats who preferred party regularity to effective programs. Unopposed for the Republican nomination, he offered the vision of a "Proud City" where every minority person could rise. Although Democrats held a three-to-one registration edge, Lindsay faced a lackluster Democratic opponent, Abraham Beame, and benefited from the candidacy of the conservative political journalist William F. Buckley, who drew thousands of potential Democratic voters. He ran as a Fusion candidate, with strong support from Nelson Rockefeller, the governor of New York. Lindsay preached a liberal agenda that attracted middle-class Jews and tirelessly worked the minority precincts of the city. "He is fresh and everyone else is tired," said campaign ads, and a last-minute endorsement by the politician (and later mayor of New York City) Edward Koch attracted liberal Democrats. Lindsay won with 43.3 percent of the vote, and *Time* and *Newsweek* covers designated him the new spokesman for the urban American even before his inauguration.

No leader ever had his dreams shattered so immediately.

John V. Lindsay. THE LIBRARY OF CONGRESS

On New Year's Day 1966, his first day in office, the Transit Workers Union struck New York's transportation system. A bitter quip said Lindsay miraculously ended subway crime in a single day, but the twelve-day strike was a disaster that overwhelmed his promise. The new mayor denounced "power brokers" and jailed a contemptuous union leader, but he finally accepted a too generous settlement. Powerful municipal unions perceived Lindsay as soft, and his tenure saw ever larger contracts awarded to municipal workers. He was weakened further when the Civilian Review Board, created to deal with complaints against policemen, was defeated by the voters. Winning approval of a city income tax to deal with the precarious fiscal state of New York City was hardly a vote-getting program. Nor was the mayor wise to favor election of a Democrat over Rockefeller in the gubernatorial election of November 1966. Lindsay's other major program, merging city services into ten "superagencies," was administratively sensible but poorly implemented.

From 1967 to 1968, as other American cities experienced race riots, New York City remained relatively peaceful. Lindsay bravely appeared in ghetto "hot spots" and worked to provide adequate community services. He was the driving force behind the incisive report of the Kerner Commission (1968), which pointed out the racial division in American society. In 1968 many people believed that he would be appointed to complete the senatorial term of Robert F. Kennedy, who had been assassinated in June 1968, but Rockefeller did not ask Lindsay to step into that seat.

Instead, Lindsay experienced the horrific months of New York's "Great School Wars" in 1968, battles that shattered racial and religious cooperation and accelerated the decline of public education. The decentralized system created out of that conflict lasted until 2003. Many whites came to believe that Lindsay programs favored minorities, and this perception—along with rising crime rates, doubled welfare rolls, and "quiet riots" that led to decay and abandonment within minority neighborhoods—fostered an exodus from New York. Manufacturing jobs declined, corporations relocated, and "white flight" began to undermine the city. When Lindsay's reorganized sanitation services failed to clear snow from outer boroughs after a February 1969 snowstorm, pundits pronounced his tenure a failure. Lindsay himself noted that his atoning visits to the affected boroughs produced "fascinating speculation about my ancestry."

In 1969 Lindsay was defeated in the Republican primary for mayor. He was effectively a man without a party, virtually at war with Rockefeller and totally against the Vietnam War policy of President Richard M. Nixon. Nonetheless, he could legitimately list as accomplishments four balanced budgets, rent-stabilization legislation, the "911" emergency system, and air-conditioned subway cars. He also had revived the city's appeal as a Hollywood movie location. He created an Independent/Liberal/Fusion candidacy and gained some union support because of the generous wage settlements. Fortunately for him, the Democrats selected a weak candidate who competed with the Republicans for conservative votes. Lindsay appealed to liberals and minorities and was reelected with only 41.1 percent of the vote; some attributed his win to the euphoria stemming from the 1969 World Series victory of the Mets baseball team.

In his second term Lindsay was unable to reverse the downward spiral of the city he loved. The rushed imposition of open-admission requirements at City University (1970) led to a decline of standards. Welfare costs and crime rates continued to rise, and the city endured a six-day police strike. Violence erupted in the "hard-hat" riot against war protesters and in the municipal prisons. Still, Lindsay remained immensely admired outside New York, and his campaign book, *The City* (1970), was widely read. In February 1971 the Gallup poll named him the most popular American politician. On 11 August 1971 he formalized what had long been apparent by joining the Democratic Party, just before his program of "scatter site" housing in

the Forest Hills section of Queens caused a resurgence of tension between blacks and Jews. When the new Democrat contended for the presidential nomination in 1972, his mystique was shattered in a series of humiliating primary defeats. He returned to persistent attacks on the city's borrowing practices and the credibility of its fiscal solvency. During 1972 the Lindsay-appointed Knapp Commission, examining the police department, reported that a "sizeable majority" of city police officers were accepting bribes.

New Yorkers were relieved when Lindsay announced that he would seek a third term, and in November 1973 voters reestablished the normal Democratic majority. Two years later New York City went bankrupt. Lindsay collected more money than ever before from taxes and state and federal government subsidies, yet he quadrupled city debt by doubling welfare rolls and granting munificent union contracts. Although segments of his administrative reorganization endure, the full plan proved ineffective. When part of the West Side Highway collapsed in December 1973, it symbolized the decaying municipal infrastructure. Racial tensions worsened despite his efforts. In retirement Lindsay claimed that he would have prevented New York's bankruptcy, but his administration became a convenient target for blame. Mayor Koch admitted his delight in "tormenting" Lindsay. Although Lindsay brought many talented people into city government, his cool personality did not inspire them. Instead, many of them left prematurely, along with thousands of ordinary city government workers. During his tenure, "Fun City" became "Run City."

Lindsay rejoined his original law firm in 1974, and he also was a commentator for the American Broadcasting Company. He wrote a novel, appeared in a movie, and made a half-hearted effort at the Democratic senatorial nomination in 1980. His most effective work was done as chairman of the Lincoln Center Theater from 1984 to 1991, but declining health plagued his later years. Parkinson's disease, heart trouble, and two strokes drained his strength, and Mayor Rudolph Giuliani appointed him to city commissions so that he could qualify for a city pension. Accompanied by his wife, who was always his most ardent advocate, Lindsay spent his last days by the ocean and died of complications from pneumonia and Parkinson's disease.

★

The most important collection of Lindsay's papers is at Yale University, New Haven, Connecticut, and in New York City's Municipal Archives. Biographies include Nat Hentoff, *A Political Life: The Education of John V. Lindsay* (1969), and Vincent J. Cannato, *The Ungovernable City: John Lindsay and His Struggle to Save New York* (2001). His approach to urban problems is the subject of "The Fate of the American City," *Saturday Review* (8 Jan. 1966), and of his books *Journey into Politics: Some Informal Observations* (1967) and *The City* (1970). Lindsay's ambiguous legacy and the lack of consensus regarding his accomplishments made him the subject of many volumes, including Barry Gottenhrer, *New York City in Crisis* (1965) and *The Mayor's Man* (1975), and Woody Klein, *Lindsay's Promise: The Dream That Failed* (1969). (Gottenhrer and Klein were among the many dedicated people he drew into government.) Critical analysis of Lindsay's terms as mayor is in Jack Newfield and Paul Du Brul, *The Abuse of Power: The Permanent Government and the Fall of New York* (1977); Charles Morris, *The Cost of Good Intentions: New York City and the Liberal Experiment, 1960–1975* (1980); and Mark Schefler, *Political Crises/Fiscal Crisis: The Collapse and Revival of New York City* (1987). Obituaries are in the *New York Times, Chicago Tribune,* and *Washington Post* (all 21 Dec. 2000).

GEORGE J. LANKEVICH

LOEB, Nackey Scripps (*b.* 24 February 1924 in Los Angeles, California; *d.* 8 January 2000 in Goffstown, New Hampshire), publisher of the *New Hampshire Sunday News* and the *Union Leader.*

As the granddaughter of the publishing baron Edward Willis ("E. W.") Scripps, it is no surprise that Loeb ended up as a newspaper publisher. Loeb was the fourth of six children born to Robert Paine Scripps, a newspaper owner, and Margaret Lou (Culbertson) Scripps. Loeb's father became one of the most prominent men in the newspaper world, joining forces with Roy Howard to create the Scripps-Howard newspaper chain, which owned more than thirty daily newspapers.

When Loeb was born, her parents named her Elizabeth, but later they changed her name to Nackey in honor of her grandmother. Loeb was raised in California and enjoyed a secluded, upper-class upbringing at the Scripps family ranch in Miramar. She attended San Diego's Wayland Parker School and La Jolla's Bishop's School for Girls before matriculating at Scripps College in Claremont, California, an institution her grandfather and great-aunt had founded in 1926.

Loeb married George Gallowhur, with whom she had a daughter. Before they divorced, she met William Loeb, Jr. Their relationship got off to a rocky start, because they began seeing each other while they were both still married. One night in 1949 police interrupted the couple's dinner to serve William Loeb papers for a $200,000 alienation-of-affection lawsuit brought by Loeb's husband. After things settled down, the couple married on 15 July 1952 in Reno, Nevada; they had one daughter, and the family subsequently divided its time between a ranch in Reno and a 100-acre, thirty-room mansion in Prides Crossing, Massachusetts.

Although Loeb had grown up saying that she was sick of hearing about newspapers and wanted nothing to do with the family business, she found herself in the newspaper world when she married William Loeb. He was the owner and publisher of the *Union Leader* and the *New Hampshire Sunday News.* As a newspaperman, Loeb dashed off ultraconservative editorials and used his newspaper to advance his causes. He also attempted to influence presidential primaries by penning front-page editorial attacks on candidates he did not support. William Loeb also was known for poking fun at former presidents Gerald R. Ford and Lyndon B. Johnson, calling one "Jerry the Jerk" and the other "Snake Oil Johnson." He also referred to former president John F. Kennedy as the "Number One Liar in the USA."

As a couple, the Loebs enjoyed the outdoors. Loeb rode horses, loved to ski, relished duck and goose hunting, and went salmon fishing and skeet shooting. An accomplished marksman, she was a member of the Massachusetts Rifle Association. The couple also played tennis and once was featured on the television show *60 Minutes* lobbing balls at each other. Loeb's involvement in sports, however, came to an end following a December 1977 car accident in Reno that left her partially paralyzed. After months of rehabilitation, she learned to use a wheelchair to get around and never complained about her fate. She sponsored the annual Union Leader Millyard Classic Road Race, which every year attracted elite runners. Loeb especially supported the wheelchair competitors, offering cash prizes to the winners and inspiring many wheelchair users not to give up on life.

During her marriage to William Loeb, Loeb's involvement with the newspapers was largely ceremonial. When her husband died of prostate and bone cancer in 1981, however, Loeb became president and publisher of the Union Leader Corporation and proved to be an avid businesswoman. She purchased a state-of-the-art color press, and she kept her husband's tradition of publishing front-page editorials and using the paper as a vehicle to influence politics. An endorsement from Loeb could make or break a candidate, since her newspaper was the largest in the state and the only one with statewide circulation. The political consultant Mary Anne Marsh told the *Boston Herald* that for decades Loeb and her husband defined New Hampshire politics. Because the New Hampshire primary was the first major polling test for a candidate, presidential hopefuls wanted the Loebs' consent. "For many elections, they were kingmakers," Marsh said.

So important was an endorsement from the paper that former president George H. W. Bush, then vice president under President Ronald W. Reagan, spoke at a memorial banquet in honor of William Loeb in the 1980s, even though Loeb had maligned him in print. Loeb, however, backed Pete DuPont that year. In 1996 the conservative presidential candidate Pat Buchanan called Loeb his "political godmother," because he believed her endorsement helped him win the New Hampshire presidential primary over Senator Bob Dole. When the former president William J. ("Bill") Clinton visited New Hampshire following his impeachment, Loeb created a storm with her controversial headline "Mr. President, You're a Disgrace." This ran in conjunction with an editorial, "Don't Come Back, Kid."

Loeb kept her husband's name alive by signing her correspondence "Mrs. William Loeb." She followed her Baptist roots in 1993 by yanking the cartoon *For Better or for Worse* from the paper's pages when the cartoon began featuring a homosexual character. In 1999 Loeb founded the Nackey S. Loeb School of Communications in Manchester, New Hampshire, to offer courses in journalism. She retired from the *Union Leader* in May 1999. Loeb was in poor health in the last few months of 1999, partly owing to complications related to her partial paralysis; she died at her home, and her remains were cremated. Following her death, the School of Communications created an award named in her honor that will recognize individuals who show an outstanding commitment to the First Amendment to the U.S. Constitution, respecting freedom of speech.

Loeb will be remembered as a proponent of freedom of the press. As the school's executive director, Holly Babin, told the *Union Leader,* "She encouraged an exchange of opinions. In her honor, we would like to recognize others who protect and put to good use this basic American freedom."

★

For information on Loeb and her career, see Dave Wedge, "Nackey Loeb, Union Leader Legend, Dies," *Boston Herald* (9 Jan. 2000); "Mrs. Loeb Remembered for Power, Courage," *New Hampshire Sunday News* (9 Jan. 2000); Shawne K. Wickham, "State Bids Its Farewell to Mrs. Loeb," *Union Leader* (15 Jan. 2000); and "Loeb Award to Honor First Amendment," *Union Leader* (4 Feb. 2003). An obituary is in the *New York Times* (12 Jan. 2000).

LISA FRICK

LOGUE, Edward Joseph (*b.* 7 February 1921 in Philadelphia, Pennsylvania; *d.* 27 January 2000 in West Tisbury, Massachusetts), urban planner who oversaw major redevelopment projects in Boston, New York City, and New Haven, Connecticut, among other locations.

Logue was one of four sons born to Edward J. Logue, a real estate assessor for the city of Philadelphia, and Resina (Fay) Logue. He attended Yale University in New Haven, Connecticut, where he received his B.A. in 1942. From 1943 to 1945 he served as a second lieutenant in the U.S. Army Air Forces. As a bombardier with the Fifteenth Air Force in Italy during World War II, he was the recipient of the Air Medal with clusters, eight Battle Stars, and a Presidential Unit Ci-

Edward J. Logue, 1974. AP/WIDE WORLD PHOTOS

tation. After World War II he studied law at Yale and earned his LL.B. in 1947. On 7 June of that year he married Margaret DeVane, the daughter of William Clyde DeVane, dean of Yale College. They had two children.

Married and with a law degree, Logue returned to Philadelphia to work in the office of M. H. Goldstein, a firm specializing in labor law. In 1949 he left Goldstein to serve as staff assistant to Governor Chester Bowles of Connecticut. With Bowles's defeat in the 1950 election, Logue moved to the position of chief of staff to the Connecticut state senate majority. In 1952 he again joined Bowles, who was by then U.S. ambassador to India, as his principal staff assistant. This position gave him an opportunity to travel extensively in India and Southeast Asia. He returned to the United States in 1953 to work on the campaign of his friend, Richard C. Lee, for mayor of New Haven. Lee won and, in 1954, brought Logue into his administration. The next year Lee called upon Logue to serve as development administrator for the New Haven Redevelopment Agency, a position he held until 1960.

Proportionately the largest program of its kind in the nation, the work in New Haven attracted national attention. Boston's mayor, John F. Collins, asked Logue to serve as development administrator for the Boston Redevelopment Authority, and Logue accepted the position, which he held from 1960 to 1967. Under his leadership, major redevelopment projects were undertaken throughout Boston. Most of them had to do with neighborhood revitalization, but projects that attracted the most national attention were in public areas, such as Government Center, Faneuil Hall–Quincy Market, Waterfront, Central Business District, and Prudential Center. Logue's critics claimed that neighborhood revitalization often came at the expense of the destruction of communities and the relocation of their residents, but in actuality most land clearance had taken place prior to his tenure at the redevelopment authority.

It has been pointed out that Logue's transformation of Boston was as significant as that brought about by the great architect Charles Bulfinch at the beginning of the nineteenth century. In Boston, as in New Haven, Logue was adept at securing federal funds for these undertakings. Logue worked with the strong support of Collins, so when Collins chose not to run for reelection in 1967, Logue resigned his position with the Boston Redevelopment Authority. He decided to run for the office of mayor but was unsuccessful. During the next year Logue served as visiting Maxwell Professor of Government at Boston University.

Meanwhile, New York governor Nelson A. Rockefeller decided to address his state's problems of decaying business districts and proliferating substandard housing by establishing an authority that could borrow funds without the necessity of obtaining voter approval. He approached Logue to head that agency, which was to be known as the Urban Development Corporation (UDC). Logue agreed and served as president and chief executive officer until 1975. The agency was endowed with significant powers, most notably the authority to issue its own bonds and the power to override local zoning and building codes. Under Logue's leadership the UDC built thirty-three thousand units of housing in 115 developments in twenty-seven communities around the state. The UDC also developed three new towns: Roosevelt Island in New York City; Radisson, near Syracuse; and Audubon, near Buffalo. Additionally, the corporation undertook a wide variety of nonresidential projects. Logue's insistence on including low-income residents in the UDC-built housing often brought him into conflict with neighboring home owners.

By 1975, however, federal funding, essential to the UDC's activities, had been severely diminished, and the corporation defaulted on $100 million in bond anticipation notes. Faced with these financial problems and lacking support from the newly elected governor Hugh Carey, Logue tendered his resignation. He taught at New York University Law School in the fall of 1975 and at the University of Pennsylvania's department of city and regional planning from 1975 to 1977. He also served as a consultant to Rockefeller's Commission on Critical Choices for America, which hoped to develop new national policies in a variety of areas. In 1976 he formed his own private consulting firm, Logue Development Company.

His next major urban development undertaking began in September 1978, when New York mayor Edward I. Koch appointed Logue director of the South Bronx Development Office (SBDO; called the South Bronx Development Organization after January 1981). His efforts in the South Bronx resulted in the construction of ninety single-family homes in an area known as Charlotte Gardens. Frustrated by bureaucratic delays and a lack of sufficient federal funding, Logue resigned from his position with the SBDO in 1985. He moved back to Boston, where he formed a new consulting company, Logue Boston, which undertook several local projects. When he died, he was in partial retirement at his home in West Tisbury, Cape Cod, Massachusetts.

Logue often has been compared to Robert Moses, the powerful mid-twentieth-century planner who carried out many major projects in New York. Both men thought in terms of large-scale developments that they were determined to complete in a timely and efficient manner, and both were stubborn, impatient, and demanding. Unlike Moses, however, Logue was concerned with social planning as well as physical planning. Over time, he came increasingly to emphasize economic diversity among the residential populations of his developments, especially on Roosevelt Island, his personal favorite. Logue's work, though often controversial, clearly resulted in substantial changes in the appearance of New Haven, Boston, New York City, and many communities throughout New York State.

★

Logue's papers are in the Yale University Library Manuscripts and Archives, New Haven, Connecticut. There is no biography of Logue, but several books deal with his major projects: Allan R. Talbot, *The Mayor's Game: Richard Lee of New Haven and the Politics of Change* (1967); Eleanor L. Brilliant, *The Urban Development Corporation: Private Interests and Public Authority* (1975); and Thomas H. O'Connor, *Building a New Boston: Politics and Urban Renewal, 1950–1970* (1993). A substantial obituary is in the *Boston Globe* (28 Jan. 2000). In addition to an obituary (29 Jan. 2000), the *New York Times* ran several articles in connection with a 23 Apr. 2000 memorial service. Extensive interviews with Logue concerning his work with the New York State Urban Development Corporation are held by the Oral History Program, University at Albany, State University of New York.

IVAN D. STEEN

LOMAX, Alan (*b.* 15 January 1915 in Austin, Texas; *d.* 19 July 2002 in Sarasota, Florida), renowned ethnomusicologist, scholar, and social activist.

Lomax was the third of four children born to John Avery Lomax, a celebrated ethnomusicologist and folklorist, and Bess (Brown) Lomax. In 1917 his father's career in an administrative position at the University of Texas became entangled in a political struggle. John Lomax was summarily fired, and the Lomaxes moved to Chicago, where John sought to establish a career in investment banking. Within a short time, the governor of Texas was impeached, John's academic termination was rescinded, and the family returned to Austin.

In 1928 the Library of Congress established the Archive of American Folk Song. John Lomax was appointed curator of the collection in 1932, and Alan took a leave from college to assist in his father's next song-hunting foray. He completed his studies in 1936, when he graduated with a B.A. summa cum laude from the University of Texas at Austin.

John and Alan Lomax coauthored *American Ballads and Folk Songs* in 1934. The 1935 Lomax expedition in search of American folk songs included the author Zora Neale Hurston and the folklorist Mary Elizabeth Barnicle. While recording at Louisiana State Penitentiary at Angola, John and Alan recommended leniency for a talented inmate named Huddie Ledbetter. Leadbelly, as he was known in prison, was pardoned, and the Lomaxes recorded *Negro Folk Songs as Sung by Leadbelly* (1936). They documented the robust blues traditions of the Delta, Memphis, and Piedmont styles. By 1940 they had recorded Eddie James, Jr. ("Son House"); Booker T. Washington ("Bukka") White; McKinley Mor-

ganfield ("Muddy Waters"); and scores of other American country, bluegrass, folk, and mountain music artists, including Aunt Molly Jackson, Pete Seeger, the Golden Gate Quartet, Burl Ives, and Woody Guthrie.

In 1936 Alan married Elizabeth Lyttleton Harold, and while they honeymooned in Haiti, they documented that island's vibrant *vodun* musical tradition. Alan Lomax succeeded his father as curator of the Archive of American Folk Song, and in 1939 he began broadcasting his own segment, called "Wellsprings of Music," for the *School of the Air* radio series for the Columbia Broadcasting System (CBS). He also hosted the CBS prime-time folk music series *Back Where I Come From,* frequently featuring the performer Woody Guthrie. Lomax secured sizable grants from the Guggenheim and Carnegie Foundations that financed the construction of a recording studio at the Library of Congress, enabling easier on-site recordings. To stabilize funding, Lomax sometimes asked songwriters to share copyright royalties with the archive. This controversial practice of "holding" intellectual property frequently embittered the artists.

In 1938 Lomax recorded eight hours of interviews and performances with the New Orleans jazz innovator Ferdinand LaMenthe ("Jelly Roll Morton"). These recordings served as the foundation for his 1950 picaresque study *Mister Jelly Roll,* which later inspired two Broadway musicals. Lomax repeated this same synthesis of recorded music, interview, and book format with the Alabama singer Vera Hall for *The Rainbow Sign* (1959; field recordings done in

Alan Lomax. CORBIS

1945). In 1946 he recorded performances, interviews, and philosophical discussions with the blues artists John Len Chatman ("Memphis Slim"), "Big Bill" Broonzy, and Aleck Ford Miller ("Sonny Boy Williamson II"), collectively published as *Blues in the Mississippi Night.*

From 1932, the year of the first Lomax song-hunting expedition (which covered sixteen thousand miles in four months throughout the Deep South), until 1942, Alan Lomax; his stepmother, Ruby Terrill Lomax; and his father, John, published more than three thousand discs of indigenous music from forty-seven of the forty-eight states, as well as Haiti, Canada, and the Bahamas. The name Lomax had become permanently identified with Pan-American musical scholarship.

After a stint in Army Special Services as a radio commentator, Lomax returned to Mississippi in 1947, armed with an early portable tape recorder. This time he documented the extraordinary African panpipes and fife-and-drum ensembles, as well as inmates' songs, at the Parchman, Lambert, and Angola penitentiaries. He recorded series of compilation discs for Decca and Brunswick Records while hosting a folk music show called *On Top of Old Smokey* for Mutual Radio.

Lomax advocated what he called "cultural equity: the right of every culture to have equal time on the air and equal time in the classroom." He believed that sound recording could greatly empower folk musicians and their audiences by giving "a voice to the voiceless . . . [putting] neglected cultures and silenced people into the communications chain." Audio recording "added the voice of the common man to the written history of America." Such idealistic beliefs, accompanied by his opportunistic and manipulative style, helped persuade Lomax to relocate his research to Europe from 1950 to 1958. He thus avoided the possibility of being blacklisted by Senator Joseph McCarthy's House Un-American Activities Committee, which was engaged in ferreting out suspected communist influences in society and government. Lomax recorded in Spain and Portugal in 1953 and Italy in 1954 (eleven volumes of folk music for Westminster). In England he recorded a similar series, *Folksongs of Great Britain* (ten volumes for Caedmon Records).

Upon his return to the United States in 1959, Lomax recorded the *Southern Heritage Series* (seven volumes for Atlantic) and *Southern Journey* (twelve volumes for Prestige), incorporating new stereophonic recording techniques. In 1961 he married Antoinette Marchand. In 1962 he recorded throughout the Caribbean, including the Hindu *chaupai* communities in Trinidad and African *garífuna* colonies in Guatemala. Lomax's recordings were influential in establishing the skiffle band style in England, a style that gave rise to the rock music of the Beatles and the Rolling Stones. Ironically, Lomax could not tolerate the increasing influence on folk artists of rock and other electric music styles. He suspended his support of the folksinger Bob Dylan after hearing the 1965 "electric" concert with Dylan and the Paul Butterfield Blues Band at the Newport Folk Festival.

In 1967 he published *Hard-Hitting Songs for Hard-Hit People,* a labor and folk song collection that he had begun collecting in 1940 with Guthrie and Seeger. In 1978 Lomax commenced ten years of videotaping in the West and the Deep South for the Public Broadcasting Service series *American Patchwork,* which was broadcast in the early 1990s. Lomax served as a research associate at Columbia University and Hunter College in New York City, establishing the Association for Cultural Equity in New York in 1989. In 1991 Lomax began assembling *The Global Jukebox,* an interactive database for folk music, dance, and theater. Lomax published *The Land Where Blues Began* in 1993, expanded from a video documentary he had produced in the 1980s. Lomax won the National Book Critics Circle award for general nonfiction for this book.

In 1995 Lomax suffered two debilitating strokes and moved from New York to Florida. Despite his condition, he continued supervising Rounder Records' retrospective compilation the *Alan Lomax Series.* In 2000 two of his 1959 Parchman Farm recordings (including James Carter's "Po' Laz'rus") were featured prominently in the Grammy Award–winning score for the film *O Brother, Where Art Thou?* In 2002 seven more Lomax recordings were featured in Martin Scorsese's film *Gangs of New York.* At age eighty-seven, after a third stroke, Lomax died from lingering circulatory problems in a nursing home.

Lomax was the world's principal recorder of folk music. For nearly seventy years he traveled throughout the world, capturing the music of oral traditions with sound recording technology, just as the inventor Thomas A. Edison had envisioned it would be. Lomax was America's preeminent song catcher.

★

For more information about Lomax, see John and Alan Lomax, *American Ballads and Folk Songs* (1934), *Negro Folk Songs as Sung by Leadbelly* (1936), *Folk Song USA* (1983), and *Our Singing Country* (2000). Articles about Lomax are "The Good and the Beautiful in Folksong," *Journal of American Folklore* (July–Sept. 1967); "Choreometrics and Ethnographic Filmmaking: Toward an Ethnographic Film Archive," *Filmmakers Newsletter* 4, no. 4 (Feb. 1971); "The Evolutionary Taxonomy of Culture," *Science* 177 (21 July 1972): 228–239; and "Cinema, Science, and Cultural Renewal," *Current Anthropology* 14 (1973): 474–480. Obituaries are in the *Los Angeles Times* and *New York Times* (both 20 July 2002).

JIM MCELWAINE

LORD, Walter (*b.* 8 October 1917 in Baltimore, Maryland; *d.* 19 May 2002 in Manhattan, New York City), historian best remembered for his 1955 book *A Night to Remember,* about the sinking of the *Titanic,* and whose many books introduced millions of citizens to American history.

Lord was the only son of John Walterhouse Lord, a lawyer, and Henrietta Mactier (Hoffman) Lord; he had one sister. He attended the Gilman School in Baltimore, where he ran track and participated in debating and graduated in 1935. Lord entered Princeton University that same year, and after he graduated with a B.A. in history in 1939, he enrolled at Yale University Law School. When the United States entered World War II in 1941, Lord joined the Office of Strategic Services, serving as a code clerk in Washington, D.C., and between 1944 and 1945 as an intelligence analyst in London. Lord returned to Yale in 1945 and received an LL.B. the following year. However, Lord did not intend to practice law. Instead, he went to work for the Research Institute of America, a business-information service where, he wrote, "it seemed I might better combine my legal education with an interest in writing," adding, "I was not disappointed."

For the next seven years (1946–1953), Lord was foreign editor at the institute, working in New York City, and later editor in chief for business reports, working in Washington, D.C. In both capacities he wrote and edited newsletters on legal subjects of interest to businessmen. He also joined the tax expert J. K. Lasser in writing several books, chiefly for businessmen. In 1953 Lord, in his words, "crossed the Great Divide" to write a series of case histories for the advertising agency J. Walter Thompson, and subsequently wrote copy for the agency in almost every conceivable form, from newsletters and tax manuals to television commercials.

While at the Research Institute, Lord had spent his evenings and weekends editing the *The Fremantle Diary: Being the Journal of Lieutenant Colonel Arthur James Lyon Fremantle, Coldstream Guards, on His Three Months in the Southern States,* a British officer's account of his travels through the Confederate states in 1862. Published in 1954, the *Fremantle Diary* was followed one year later by his famed book on the *Titanic* disaster, *A Night to Remember.* Told in an enthralling fast-paced, "you are there" style, *A Night to Remember* vividly describes the collision of the "unsinkable" super ship with an iceberg, and the aftermath of the ship's destruction, including the loss of 1,500 lives. The book was based on years of research in documentary evidence and on interviews with some sixty survivors. Lord observed—and he was the first to do so—that a higher percentage of first-class male passengers were rescued than were women and children from third class. Indeed, as a reviewer pointed out, the "sinking of the *Titanic* . . . played a part in the social revolution of the twentieth century; never again would the Western world take it for granted that class discrimination was normal in the sphere of safety precautions and rescue work."

Walter Lord, March 1957. AP/WIDE WORLD PHOTOS

Impressed by the success of *A Night to Remember*, a Book-of-the-Month Club selection and a best-seller, *Life* magazine offered Lord a contract to write a book about the Japanese attack on Pearl Harbor that led the United States into World War II. Accepting, he exploited the same research techniques he used when writing *A Night to Remember*. The result, *A Day of Infamy* (a phrase drawn from President Franklin D. Roosevelt's war message to Congress), was published in 1957. It lacked the years of intensive investigation Lord had devoted to the sinking of the *Titanic* and failed to achieve the popularity of *A Night to Remember*. However, Lord was the first historian to interview Japanese participants in the attack.

In his next publication, *The Good Years* (1960), also a Book-of-the-Month Club selection, Lord centered his account on the first fifteen years of the twentieth century. Once again, by relying on thorough research and eyewitness accounts, Lord was able to capture in fascinating detail such events as the Boxer Rebellion in China (1900), the assassination of President William McKinley (1901), and the San Francisco earthquake (1906). *The Good Years* also succeeded in imparting the sense of breezy confidence Americans of these years had in the operation of the moral law in God's universe, and in the inevitability of progress. Although lively and readable, the book provided little evidence of the dark side of this era, of the "currents of protest that underlay the cheerful facade of progressivism," as one reviewer observed.

Lord returned to the subject of World War II with his next book. *Incredible Victory* (1967) recounted a stunning triumph by the U.S. Navy over a Japanese armada at the Battle of Midway. Skillfully shifting the vantage point from fleet to fleet and from ground to air, Lord showed how a badly outmanned and outgunned U.S. fleet under the command of Admiral Chester W. Nimitz was able to sink four of the largest aircraft carriers in the fleet of the Japanese admiral Isokoru Yamamoto. One crucial factor in the U.S. victory, which Lord reported publicly for the first time, was the work of the U.S. Navy's Combat Intelligence unit in cracking the Japanese code. In researching his account, Lord traveled over 30,000 miles and interviewed some 400 participants, both American and Japanese. He also did a prodigious amount of research in government reports, as well as studying maps and perusing diaries and personal letters. *Incredible Victory* was not only a remarkable account of the Battle of Midway, but also, in the words of one scholar, a "wonderfully human" book.

Lord wrote two other volumes about World War II, *Lonely Vigil: Coastwatchers of the Solomons* (1977) and *The Miracle of Dunkirk* (1982). The former recounts the adventures of an intrepid band of Allied coastwatchers who spotted Japanese ships and planes during the Solomon Island campaign. Lord's history was measurably improved by the "rich haul of stories involving [narrow] escapes and rescues," as well as heroic and "exotic adventures." *The Miracle of Dunkirk*, based largely on interviews with some 500 British and German survivors of the evacuation of the British Expeditionary Forces in June 1940, was judged by a reviewer as "contemporary history at its best."

Lord's other books include *A Time to Stand* (1961), *Peary to the Pole* (1963), *The Past That Would Not Die* (1965), *The Dawn's Early Light* (1972), and a companion volume to *A Night to Remember, The Night Lives On* (1986).

Lord was one of a handful of post–World War II writers who pioneered the extensive use of oral interviews in the preparation of histories. And his books, especially the "definitive" *Night to Remember* and his four volumes about World War II, demonstrate the value of personal memory. Scrupulously researched and immensely readable, Lord's books tell the reader "all he wants to know about what happened (and sometimes more), very little about why." One can certainly reply that Lord, writing in a tradition that reached back to Herodotus and earlier to the preliterature era where a tribal bard would relate tales that contained his people's history, was basically a storyteller; that he wrote one classic and several first-class histories; and that his books continue to delight and inform readers.

In addition to his writing career, Lord served as president of the Society of American Historians and as trustee of the New York Historical Society and the South Street Seaport Museum. A bachelor, Lord died in his elegant apartment on West Sixty-eighth Street in Manhattan after a long struggle with Parkinson's disease. He was cremated and his ashes were interred at Green Mountain Cemetery in Baltimore.

★

Steven Biel, *Down with the Old Canoe: A Cultural History of the Titanic Disaster* (1996), covers Lord's role in reviving interest in the sinking of the *Titanic*. A *Washington Post* article by Ken Ringle (10 Sept. 1987) on Lord contains material from an interview. "Tribute to Walter Lord: He Had an Eye for Humanity," *Naval History* (Oct. 1992), emphasizes Lord's influence on other authors and historians. Obituaries are in the *New York Times* and *Washington Post* (both 21 May 2002).

RICHARD HARMOND

LOVELACE, Linda Susan (*b.* 10 January 1949 in the Bronx, New York City; *d.* 22 April 2002 in Denver, Colorado), adult film actress whose role in the notorious 1972 film *Deep Throat* changed the adult film industry by bringing the genre into the American mainstream, and who later spoke out against the industry.

Linda Lovelace, ca. 1974. HENRY DILTZ/CORBIS

Lovelace was born Linda Boreman and spent her youth in suburban Yonkers, New York. She attended a private Catholic high school until she was sixteen, when her parents moved to Fort Lauderdale, Florida, to retire. At age twenty she gave birth to her first child. After giving the child up for adoption, she returned to New York City to begin computer training. She suffered severe injuries in a car crash shortly after her arrival in New York, which led to her return to her parents' home in Fort Lauderdale in 1969. During this recuperative period, Lovelace met Chuck Traynor, the man who would involve her in prostitution, pornography, and drug addiction and who also would become her first husband in 1971. Traynor countered Lovelace's claims of abuse by stating that Lovelace was a willing participant in the violence he inflicted upon her. Although Traynor's claims were corroborated by several of Lovelace's costars in her early films, her account of Traynor's violence remains the more viable of the two arguments.

For the next three years, according to Lovelace, Traynor beat, raped, and forced her into prostitution and adult films. This period is marked by the production of the film that brought Lovelace her fame, *Deep Throat,* released in 1972.

Although it was not the first hard-core film in which Lovelace acted, *Deep Throat* revolutionized the adult film industry in a variety of ways. The film opened in both adult and mainstream theaters, and Lovelace embarked on a public relations tour intended to market her as a star, no different from a studio actress hitting the talk-show circuit to promote the latest box-office hit. Historians cite evidence of the film's impact on so-called Middle America, stemming from the *Washington Post* journalist Bob Woodward's use of the name "Deep Throat" for his source of information during his investigation of the Watergate scandal that led to the resignation of President Richard M. Nixon. (The scandal involved a break-in at Democratic Party headquarters in the Watergate complex that was traced to the White House through information provided by a person who was never named.) *Deep Throat* did not succeed in mainstreaming the adult film industry, as its director, Gerard Damiano, had hoped. Nevertheless, the film remains the most lucrative X-rated moneymaker of all time, yielding nearly $100 million in revenue from theater and video distribution from an initial production cost of only $25,000.

Although *Deep Throat* appealed to an audience that traditionally had not patronized adult theaters, its success was short-lived, and Lovelace's role in the film did not catapult her to Hollywood success. In 1973 she appeared in a pictorial spread in *Playboy* magazine and as a cover model for *Esquire* magazine, and she tried her hand at journalism by writing a series of sexual-advice columns. That same year she and Traynor were divorced. She published her first autobiography, *Inside Linda Lovelace,* in 1973. In 1974 Lovelace starred in *Deep Throat II,* an R-rated film with a minimal amount of nudity and sexual content. The tamer rating of the sequel stemmed from the successful prosecution on obscenity charges of several key figures involved in *Deep Throat's* production. The trial, held in the heart of the Bible Belt, in Memphis, Tennessee, marked a turning point in the adult film industry and in Lovelace's career.

Lovelace faced legal difficulties after her appearance in *Deep Throat II.* She was arrested in Las Vegas, Nevada, early in 1974, charged with possession of narcotics. Lovelace soon began work on her second autobiography, *The Intimate Diary of Linda Lovelace,* and the filming of the movie that would end her motion picture career, *Linda Lovelace for President* (1976). Audiences did not respond to a clothed Lovelace, and she fell out of public sight for several years after the film's release.

Lovelace published *Ordeal,* her third autobiographical volume, in 1980, written with the help of Mike McGrady. In it Lovelace alleged that she had suffered abuse at the hands of Traynor, and she also condemned the pornography industry as inherently violent toward and exploitative of women. In 1986 she testified before the U.S. attorney general's Commission on Pornography (known as the Meese Commission), where she described the violence that characterized the pornography business. President Ronald W. Reagan called the Meese Commission to explore the possible options available to the federal government in limiting the general public's access to pornographic material, basing his concerns about pornography on his belief that the material was inherently violent in nature.

Lovelace's testimony, which was extremely well publicized, drew considerable media and public attention to the commission's hearings, yet it did not help the commission overall. Although Lovelace pointed to her own experiences in the world of adult film as indicative of the violence that permeated it, the Meese Commission failed to provide factual data to back up its assertion that pornographic material should be further restricted.

Lovelace's fourth and final autobiographical work, *Out of Bondage* (1986), chronicles her life with her second husband, Larry Marchiano, whom she had married in 1976, and the difficulties she encountered—particularly for a born-again Christian—in trying to escape the notoriety that her earlier work had given her. These writings were yet another aspect of her crusade against pornography, which included public-speaking engagements as well as testifying before investigative bodies examining pornography and its effect on women and American society. Lovelace's activism also included opposition to the use of silicone implants for breast augmentation, a concern she linked to her own feminist beliefs that such physical alterations served as further evidence of American society's penchant for objectifying women.

Lovelace and Marchiano had two children together before divorcing in 1996. Throughout this activist phase of her life, she worked at a variety of clerical positions to support herself and her family, which expanded to include Lovelace's first granddaughter, born in 1998. Lovelace continued this work until her death from injuries sustained in a car accident near Denver on 3 April 2002. Lovelace was fifty-three at the time of her death nineteen days later. She is buried in Parker Cemetery in Parker, Colorado.

As the star of one of the most popular, notorious, and financially successful adult films in history, Lovelace symbolized the explosion of the adult film industry in America. Nonetheless, her life story also corroborates the claims of opponents of that same industry, who believe that pornography exploits and objectifies women.

★

Lovelace wrote several books about her life: *Inside Linda Lovelace* (1973); (with Mike McGrady) *Ordeal* (1980); and (with McGrady) *Out of Bondage* (1986). For more information on Lovelace, see Ronald J. Berger, Patricia Searles, and Charles E. Cottle, *Feminism and Pornography* (1991); Frederick S. Lane, III, *Obscene*

Profits: The Entrepreneurs of Pornography in the Cyber Age (2000); and Nadine Stossen, *Defending Pornography: Free Speech, Sex, and the Fight for Women's Rights* (2000). Obituaries are in the *Chicago Tribune* and *Los Angeles Times* (both 23 Apr. 2002) and the *New York Times* (24 Apr. 2002).

KIMBERLY LITTLE

LUDLUM, Robert (*b.* 25 May 1927 in New York City; *d.* 12 March 2001 in Naples, Florida), Broadway and television actor, theatrical producer, and one of the most popular and commercially successful authors of international suspense and espionage thrillers of the twentieth century.

Ludlum grew up in Short Hills, New Jersey. His father, the businessman George Hartford, died when Ludlum was seven, and his mother, Margaret (Wadsworth) Ludlum, sent him to private schools in Connecticut, including the Rectory School in Pomfret, the Kent School in Kent, and the Cheshire Academy in Cheshire. He acted in school productions and appeared in his first professional production in 1941 at age fourteen, when he landed the role of Sterling Brown in the Broadway show *Junior Miss*. While

Robert Ludlum. GETTY IMAGES

on tour in Detroit in the summer of 1943, he ran away to Toronto to join the Royal Canadian Air Force. Caught falsifying his name and age, Ludlum had to wait two years before enlisting in the U.S. Marine Corps, serving in the South Pacific from 1945 to 1947.

At the end of his service, Ludlum entered Wesleyan University in Middletown, Connecticut, supporting himself by acting in summer stock theaters and on Broadway. While at Wesleyan, he met Mary Ryducha, a fellow actor whom he married 31 March 1951, shortly before completing his B.A. and receiving the New England Professor of Drama award.

The Ludlums acted in minor roles throughout the 1950s. Their three children, Michael, Jonathan, and Glynis, were born in this decade. Ludlum appeared in over 200 television plays on shows such as the *Kraft Television Theater* and *Studio One*. His deep voice made him perfect for television commercial voice-overs (a toilet-cleaner commercial paid a son's college expenses). Back on Broadway, Ludlum produced successful plays such as *The Front Page*. He received various grants and awards from the American National Theatre and Academy (1959), including the Scroll of Achievement (1960), and awards from the Actor's Equity Association and the William C. Whitney Foundation (1960).

Wanting creative control and encouraged by his wife, Ludlum turned to theater production, first at the North Jersey Playhouse in Fort Lee (1957–1960), then at his own theater, the Playhouse-on-the-Mall in Paramus, New Jersey (1960–1970), the first shopping-mall theater. A careful balancing act kept the theater going—theatrical chestnuts to finance the occasional exciting, underattended, experimental play. The as yet–undiscovered actor Alan Alda played the lead in Ludlum's *Owl and the Pussycat* at the Playhouse. Ludlum also produced plays in New York City.

In the late 1960s, at age forty-four, and frustrated with theater management, Ludlum discovered a new calling, writing blockbuster political thrillers. With Henry Morrison as his literary agent, he rose at 4:30 A.M. and wrote longhand 2,000 words a day (he never typed) for fifteen months. His first book, *The Scarlatti Inheritance* (1971), arose from Ludlum's speculation about two 1926 *Illustrated London News* photographs of smiling Nazis in new uniforms and a German buying bread with a wheelbarrow full of money; he postulated that Hitler's Third Reich had been secretly financed by cutthroat western businesses. The intentionally confusing *Osterman Weekend* (1972), with its topical, and at the time shocking, suggestion of the domestic activities of the Central Intelligence Agency (CIA), was followed by *The Matlock Paper* (1973), which explored the socio-political ramifications of drugs on campuses and exploitative professors with questionable loyalties. *Trevayne* (1973), written under the pseudonym Jonathan Ryder, responded to the Watergate scandal, hitting hard at the political amorality of international financiers. These quick successes confirmed Ludlum's genius for anticipating the fears and conspiracies that troubled readers. The income the novels produced enabled Ludlum to give up the theater, yet his acting and producing experience helped him to delineate setting, develop character, and pace plot, evoking gut-wrenching anticipation.

Global domination is a recurring Ludlum theme. For example, his plots included Nazi and neo-Nazi villains double-dealing in Argentina (*The Rhinemann Exchange*, 1974); debunking Christianity (*The Gemini Contenders*, 1976); and reviving fascist goals in modern ultraconservatives (*The Holcroft Covenant*, 1978, and *The Apocalypse Watch*, 1995). There are spies in the White House (*The Parsifal Mosaic*, 1982); rogue generals (*The Aquitaine Progression*, 1984); an arranged presidential election (*The Icarus Agenda*, 1988); a Basque terrorist attempting to assassinate the U.S. president (*The Scorpio Illusion*, 1993); computer surveillance gone amuck (*The Prometheus Deception*, 2000); and government agencies out of control. *The Chancellor Manuscript* (1977) debunks the secret blackmail methods of the former Federal Bureau of Investigation director J. Edgar Hoover, while the Bourne trilogy (*The Bourne Identity*, 1980; *The Bourne Supremacy*, 1986; and *The Bourne Ultimatum*, 1990) studies a trained agent suffering personality disintegration, post-traumatic stress syndrome, and confusion produced by chemical debriefings as he confronts the notorious assassin the Jackal, Red Chinese targeting Hong Kong, and the CIA. Jason Bourne is one of Ludlum's most compelling creations, brought to life by Richard Chamberlain in a 1998 television miniseries based on *The Bourne Identity* and by Matt Damon in a 2002 film adaptation of the same book. Ludlum explores the changes wrought by aging, personal loyalty amid illusion and betrayal, the power of love, and the kindness of strangers. Yet the world he depicts is violent, treacherous, and deceptive.

Ludlum had a triple by-pass in the mid-nineties; his wife died in 1996 after forty-six years of marriage. Two years later Ludlum remarried.

After twenty years with Bantam Publishing, Ludlum signed a three-book contract with St. Martins Press in November 1998 to produce four books for $4 million per book and to provide a set of six-page book descriptions to be written by others, developing his key ideas into what would be called "Covert-ONE" novels. Ludlum finished two of the contracted books before he died, *The Prometheus Deception* (2000) and *The SIGMA Protocol* (2001). *The Janson Directive* came out in 2002.

Ludlum died of a heart attack at age seventy-three. Each of his twenty-three novels was a *New York Times* best-seller, and his books were translated into thirty-two languages in over forty countries. Six have been filmed, and over 210 million copies have been printed. Despite biting criticism of Ludlum's plotting and characterization as sensational, wooden, and melodramatic, most critics agree that his books are compelling, catapulting readers forward at breathtaking speed in global settings and reflecting the fears of our time. A good Ludlum novel captures an individual's "outrage" at the violation of human dignity, human rights, and simple justice by monolithic companies, power-hungry politicians, and agencies beyond government control. In his books, helpless individuals are caught in behind-the-scenes conspiracies that challenge their wits, and Ludlum's values reflect the nightmare possibilities of modern paranoia. Yet Ludlum finds hope in the integrity and courage of competent individuals as they battle tyrannical foes. Hunters become the hunted, and the seemingly unconquerable are indeed defeated—at least for a while. Ludlum captured the globalization of American culture and the psyche of the "Age of Conspiracy." His stories of the individual triumphing over the impersonal corporate mind echo in the subconscious.

★

The Robert Ludlum Companion (1993), ed. by Martin H. Greenberg, is mainly an omnibus of works, but it contains some biographical material; and Gina Macdonald, *Robert Ludlum: A Critical Companion* (1997), contains a chapter on Ludlum's literary influences, a biography, and an analysis of his key works. Roy S. Goodman, "Robert Ludlum," in *Mystery and Suspense Writers: The Literature of Crime, Detection and Espionage* (1998), ed. by Robin W. Winks, emphasizes Ludlum's literary significance. An obituary is in the *New York Times* (13 May 2001).

GINA MACDONALD

LUISETTI, Angelo Enrico ("Hank") (*b.* 16 June 1916 in San Francisco, California; *d.* 17 December 2002 in San Mateo, California), basketball player who catapulted the college game into the national limelight and popularized the one-handed jump shot that became the foundation of the modern-day game.

Luisetti was the only child of Italian immigrants Steffan Luisetti, a laborer and chef who became a restaurant owner, and Amalia (Grossi) Luisetti, a homemaker. He began playing basketball at age eight at a playground near his home and often competed against taller youngsters. Luisetti normally shot from a distance and developed a one-handed push shot rather than using the two-handed set shot of that era. He graduated in 1934 from Galileo High School, where he refined his unusual shooting style.

Luisetti earned a basketball scholarship to Stanford University in Palo Alto, California, and enrolled there in the fall of 1934. He starred on the undefeated freshman team,

scoring 305 points and averaging 16.9 points in eighteen games. Luisetti earned extra money by waiting on tables and working security at football games. Under the coach John Bunn, the six-foot, two-inch, 184-pound forward led the Indians varsity team to three consecutive Pacific Coast Conference championships between 1935 and 1938. He earned consensus First Team All-America honors all three seasons. In the 1935–1936 season, Luisetti scored 416 points and averaged 14.3 points per game (ppg) to pace Stanford to a 22–7 record. He tallied thirty-two points against the University of Washington, making twenty-four points in the final eleven minutes, after his coach urged him to shoot the ball rather than pass it.

During his junior and senior seasons, Luisetti led the nation in scoring and earned Helms Athletic Foundation Player of the Year honors. In the 1936–1937 season, he scored 410 points and averaged 17.1 ppg for a 25–2 Stanford record. The Indians finished 21–3 in 1937–1938, as Luisetti scored 465 points and averaged 17.2 ppg. Essentially, he became the game's first modern player. The fierce competitor combined excellent hand-eye coordination, tremendous spring in his legs, excellent speed, and quick reactions. Besides using the jump shot, he was the first player to dribble and pass behind his back and switch positions on the court to meet changing conditions.

The birth of Luisetti as a national star, and the emergence of the West Coast game as a rival to eastern-style play, came on 30 December 1936, when Stanford played Long Island University (LIU) before seventeen thousand fans at Madison Square Garden in New York City. LIU, coached by the legendary Clair Bee, had won forty-three consecutive games over a two-year span. Combining strong drives to the basket and patented one-handed jump shots, Luisetti scored fifteen points to help the Indians upset the heavily favored Blackbirds 45–31. Many New Yorkers had never seen the one-handed jump shot before. He also dazzled the media and partisan crowd with his tough defense and stellar passing to open teammates. The crowd gave him a standing ovation when he walked off the floor.

Elected team captain as a senior, Luisetti became the first collegian to score fifty points in a game. On 1 January 1938 he made twenty-three field goals and four free throws to help Stanford trounce Duquesne University 92–27 at Public Auditorium in Cleveland, Ohio. His teammates refused to take shots and continually passed the ball to him so that he could break the record. A team player, Luisetti disliked hogging the ball, but this time he was forced to take open shots. He returned to Madison Square Garden to help Stanford defeat the powerful City College of New York team 45–42 and LIU by fourteen points.

Luisetti completed his Stanford career as the leading varsity scorer in college basketball history, with 1,291 points in eighty games and an average of 16.1 ppg. Despite these

Hank Luisetti, 1940. AP/WIDE WORLD PHOTOS

achievements, he arrived on the scene too early to compete on a national stage that might have provided him with greater individual glory. The postseason National Invitation Tournament and National Collegiate Athletic Association (NCAA) events were launched during the first two seasons after his graduation. By then coaches at western schools had embraced Luisetti's one-handed jump shot and the Stanford style of play, and soon the West gained the upper hand in college basketball: between 1939 and 1944 the universities of Oregon, Oklahoma, Wyoming, and Utah won NCAA tournaments.

For Luisetti, however, with no existing national-scale professional arena in which to star and earn a comfortable living, the only real opportunity to excel in basketball beyond the college level was in Olympic competition. To maintain his amateur status, therefore, he turned down opportunities to play in the fledgling National Basketball League. His hopes to participate in the 1940 Olympic Games, planned for London, were dashed, however, when the Games were canceled because of World War II. (Called off for the same reason in 1944, the Olympics did not resume until 1948.)

Meanwhile, Luisetti had graduated from Stanford in

1938 with a B.S. in social science and went to work for Standard Oil of California. During this time, he played Amateur Athletic Union (AAU) basketball but was suspended for the 1938–1939 season because he had appeared in a movie: capitalizing on his fame, Hollywood had paid him $10,000 to appear in *Campus Confessions* with Betty Grable in 1938. He returned to AAU competition in the 1939–1940 season and was named outstanding player for the 1940 AAU national tournament. He played for the San Francisco Olympic Club in the 1940–1941 season and the Phillips 66ers in the 1941–1942 season, but he was sidelined with an injured knee during the latter season.

Luisetti married Jane Rossiter on 18 April 1941. They had a son and a daughter before her death. In 1943, during World War II, he enlisted in the U.S. Navy and was assigned to preflight school in Saint Mary's, California. He was at the height of his scoring powers, averaging thirty points per game and often outplaying the future National Basketball Association (NBA) star Jim Pollard. In 1944 Luisetti was scheduled for deployment overseas when he contracted spinal meningitis. He was hospitalized in a coma for one week and lost forty pounds. Although he had a miraculous full recovery, doctors advised him against playing competitive amateur or professional basketball again.

He worked for John Hancock Life Insurance Company from 1946 to 1948 and for Stewart Chevrolet in San Francisco from 1948 to 1959, coaching the latter's AAU basketball team from 1949 to 1951. Luisetti's squad, led by the future NBA star George Yardley, won the AAU crown in 1951. Luisetti left coaching after that season and conducted basketball clinics for several years in the San Francisco area. He served as president of the western region for E. F. McDonald Travel Company for many years and retired in the mid-1980s.

A 1950 Associated Press poll named Luisetti the second-greatest basketball player of the twentieth century's first half, behind the legendary center George Mikan. He was elected to the Naismith Memorial Basketball Hall of Fame as a charter member in 1959 and was selected for the Helms Athletic Foundation All-America team and the Stanford Hall of Fame. In 1988 Stanford dedicated a bronze statue of Luisetti, by his former teammate Phil Zonne, in his history-making shooting pose.

★

Luisetti's papers and clippings are at the Naismith Memorial Basketball Hall of Fame in Springfield, Massachusetts. There is no full-length biography. Sandy Padwe, *Basketball's Hall of Fame* (1970), has a chapter on him. Don E. Liebendorfer, *The Color of Life Is Red* (1972), and Gary Cavalli, *Stanford Sports* (1982), briefly examine his Stanford career. Obituaries are in the *San Francisco Chronicle* (21 Dec. 2002) and *New York Times* (23 Dec. 2002).

DAVID L. PORTER

M

MAAS, Peter Guttrich (*b.* 27 June 1929 in New York City; *d.* 23 August 2001 in Manhattan, New York City), investigative journalist and best-selling author whose most successful works include *The Valachi Papers* (1969) and *Serpico* (1973).

Maas was the son of Carl Maas and Madeleine (Fellheimer) Maas, a Roman Catholic couple of primarily Dutch and Irish ancestry. He first demonstrated his journalistic skills while writing for the student newspaper at Duke University in Durham, North Carolina, when he not only managed to sneak into the guarded hospital room of the United Auto Workers (UAW) leader Walter Reuther (who was recovering from an attempted assassination), but convinced Reuther to grant an exclusive interview. In addition to making the student paper, the interview netted Maas $100 when it was sold to the Associated Press.

In 1949, after receiving a B.A. in political science from Duke, Maas conducted postgraduate work at the Sorbonne and did assignments for the Paris bureau of the *New York Herald Tribune*. Drafted during the Korean conflict, he served from 1952 to 1954 in the U.S. Navy before returning to New York, where he became a contributor to *New York* magazine and an associate editor for *Collier's* magazine. By the early 1960s, he had a reputation for character-based in-depth reporting. On 4 April 1962 Maas married the screenwriter and producer Audrey Gallen; they had one son.

While interviewing the U.S. Attorney General Robert F. Kennedy in 1963 for an article on the attorney Roy Cohn, who often defended members of the Mafia crime syndicate, Maas received official confirmation that the mobster Joe Valachi, whose name he had first heard from his *New York* editor, had agreed to testify against the Mafia. Maas authored a series of well-received articles based on his interviews with Valachi for the *Saturday Evening Post*, but his primary research and writing at the time concerned the obscure story of the first submarine rescue in 1939. The latter formed the basis of his first book, *The Rescuer* (1968), which was ignored by both critics and the public.

Convinced his Valachi interviews merited further development, Maas, against the advice of his agent, decided to base his second book on the informant's inside stories of the $40 billion-per year Mafia syndicate. The finished product, titled *The Valachi Papers*, was rejected by two dozen publishers before being accepted by Putnam and published in 1968. It sold more than 2.5 million copies, was translated into fourteen languages, paved the way for the blockbuster success of Mario Puzo's novel *The Godfather*, and was converted by Hollywood into a commercially successful film that Maas called "one of the worst movies I've ever seen."

Maas next became obsessed with the story of Frank Serpico, a police officer who was nearly killed for exposing corruption in the New York Police Department. *Serpico* (1973) was every bit as successful as *The Valachi Papers* and spawned a better motion picture as well as a television series. Two years later, a series of articles for *New York* magazine on the bizarre subculture of the sixty gypsy clans across the United States developed into Maas's fourth book, a biography of Steven Tene, the grandson and heir of Tene Bimbo, the bulibasha ("king") of a particularly violent Romany tribe in New York City. *King of the Gypsies* (1975) became Maas's third consecutive best-seller, although his happiness was marred by the death of his wife in a car accident just before the book was released. The book also generated numerous lawsuits from the outraged Romany community.

At age fifty Maas completed his first novel, *Made in America* (1979), a "labor of love" (he turned down a $1 million advance to write a book on the Shah of Iran to work full time on the novel) that became his fourth best-seller as well as his most critically successful venture. The novel was not as commercially popular as his nonfiction, however.

Despite wealth and success, Maas never lost his anger at the corruption and injustice around him, and he continued to write investigative pieces on subjects ranging from the rights of American Indians to the exploitation of children by U.S. factories. He wrote articles prolifically for the next two decades, and his books continued to enjoy wide sales, though none approached the numbers of his Valachi and Serpico biographies. His next four nonfiction works were *Marie: A True Story* (1983), about Marie Ragghianti, who received death threats after exposing political corruption in Tennessee; *Manhunt* (1986), the true tale of a Central Intelligence Agency (CIA) turncoat; *In a Child's Name: The Legacy of a Mother's Murder* (1989), based on a true custody case (and adapted into a television movie); and *Killer Spy: The Inside Story of the FBI's Pursuit and Capture of Aldrich Ames, America's Deadliest Spy* (1995).

Maas also wrote two espionage novels: *Father and Son* (1989), about an American youth who becomes a gun runner for the Irish Republican Army (IRA), and *China White* (1994), about a Hong Kong heroin syndicate. Although popular, neither achieved the critical or commercial success of his previous efforts.

Maas returned to the top of the best-seller charts with 1997's *Underboss*, which generated controversy when the Mafia boss Sammy Gravano testified at his trial that he had received a portion of the royalties. (Maas denied the allegations; he admitted that he had split his advance and movie rights proceeds with Frank Serpico—although, strangely, he stopped speaking to Steven Tene when the latter asked to borrow $700 during the writing of *Gypsies*.) Maas's final book, *Terrible Hours* (1999), is a reworking of his failed first book, *The Rescuer;* the second incarnation was a best-seller and became a movie.

Maas married Laura Parkins on 14 September 1976. They separated three years later, and Maas married his third wife, Suzanne, with whom he had a son. Maas died of complications from ulcer surgery at Mount Sinai Medical Center in Manhattan at age seventy-two.

Peter Maas. MR. JERRY BAUER

At his best, Maas was a genre unto himself, combining the edge of an angry social commentator with the skills of a seasoned journalist and the aesthetic of a first-rate prose writer. He is often compared to Truman Capote, Norman Mailer, and Tom Wolfe for his use of concentrated nonfiction to convey a much broader message, as well as to writers as diverse as the anthropologist Margaret Mead and the novelist Richard Adams for using a microcosm to gain perspective on a macrocosm. More than 150 works of nonfiction have been published on the Mafia since Maas's groundbreaking *Valachi Papers*, while *Serpico* continues to influence both cutting-edge journalism and pop culture more than a generation after its publication. Maas was the literary equivalent of a musical "cross-over" artist.

★

There is no shortage of criticism of Maas's ten nonfiction books and three novels, while a complete bibliography of his articles and editorials would require several pages. *Contemporary Literary Criticism*, vol. 29 (1984), includes select criticism of his most popular works through *Marie: A True Story*. Obituaries are in the *Los Angeles Times* and *New York Times* (both 24 Aug. 2001).

JON DARBY

MacARTHUR, Jean Marie Faircloth (*b.* 28 December 1898 in Nashville, Tennessee; *d.* 22 January 2000 in Manhattan, New York City), wife of General Douglas MacArthur, the leader of U.S. military forces in the Philippines, Japan, and South Korea during World War II and the Korean War.

Born at the turn of the twentieth century, the woman who would accompany General Douglas MacArthur on a wartime Pacific Ocean odyssey gained respect for the military early in life. Her father, Edward Cameron Faircloth, was a banker and business owner who divorced MacArthur's mother, Sarah (Beard) Faircloth, a homemaker, when MacArthur was eight. After the divorce, MacArthur's mother took her daughter and two sons to her hometown of Murfreesboro, Tennessee, where the family lived with MacArthur's grandfather Richard Beard, a former captain in the Confederate Army. In 1907 "Sally" Faircloth married Frederick Smith; they had four children together.

After spending one year at Ward-Belmont College in Nashville, MacArthur returned to Murfreesboro to graduate from Soule College in 1917. Her birth father died and left her a substantial fortune, which she used to travel widely, visiting friends in Manila, the Philippines, in 1928 and touring Europe in 1930. In 1933 and 1935 she again visited the Far East, and on that second trip she met Douglas MacArthur, who was traveling to Manila to become U.S. military adviser to the Philippine Commonwealth. Then thirty-six years old, MacArthur was en route to Shanghai to visit friends when she was assigned to sit next to the general at a dinner on the USS *President Hoover.* Mesmerized by the confident fifty-five-year-old who sent her flowers the next day, MacArthur rented a hotel suite in Manila to be near him, beginning a courtship that culminated with their wedding in New York City on 30 April 1937.

The newlyweds had no honeymoon. With tensions rising between the United States and Japan, they immediately returned to Manila. Their only child, Arthur, was born in 1938, and General MacArthur readied the Philippines for possible war with Japan. War came on 7 December 1941, with the Japanese attack on Pearl Harbor; an attack on the Philippines followed within hours. The Japanese invasion army drove the badly outgunned U.S. forces to the island fortress of Corregidor, where the MacArthurs lived in the Manila Tunnel from Christmas Eve 1941 until March 1942. Living under daily bombardment, MacArthur did needlework while her son played and her husband coordinated defensive operations. During the siege MacArthur learned that President Manuel Quezon of the Philippines had offered her and their son passage to Australia. In her most famous remark, the general's wife refused, saying, "We have drunk from the same cup; we three shall stay together." In March 1942, however, they did leave when President

Jean Faircloth MacArthur, November 1947. AP/WIDE WORLD PHOTOS

Franklin D. Roosevelt ordered General MacArthur off the island, not wanting one of his leading generals held captive.

The family escaped by patrol boat, navigating through a Japanese naval blockade to Mindanao Island in the Philippines. They then flew to Australia, where MacArthur lived in Brisbane until her husband returned to the Philippines in 1944. She joined him in Manila shortly afterward and in 1945 moved with him to Tokyo, where General MacArthur took the post of Supreme Commander for the Allied Powers to administer the occupation of Japan. There, MacArthur served not only as a social bridge to Japanese leadership but also as a recognized link between the general and those who appealed to him for help. When North Korean forces unexpectedly surged across the Thirty-eighth Parallel, attacking South Korea in 1950, she stayed behind as her husband rushed to command beleaguered U.S. forces struggling to hold the country near the southeast city of Pusan. General MacArthur's amphibious landing at Inchon dramatically turned the tide of the war, but the general also ran afoul of President Harry Truman, who relieved the outspoken, sometimes arrogant general of his command in 1951. The MacArthurs moved to New York

City and took residence on the thirty-second floor of the Waldorf Towers, where General MacArthur lived until his death in 1964.

General MacArthur was not buried in New York City or in Washington, D.C., a city against which he held a grudge until his death. Instead, he was buried in Norfolk, Virginia, the hometown of his mother, who was widely considered the most influential woman in Douglas MacArthur's life. Jean MacArthur took over planning for the museum at the MacArthur Memorial in Norfolk when he died six weeks before its dedication. She also took an active role in creating the General Douglas MacArthur Foundation, a philanthropic trust for which she served as honorary chairwoman. She received frequent visits from her son, who had disappeared from public view after receiving a music degree from Columbia University in 1961. Rumored at different times to be a ballet dancer or a musician, Arthur MacArthur has led a private life cloaked in mystery and, it is thought, under an assumed name.

MacArthur made speeches and public appearances well into her nineties, continuing to live at the Waldorf and making frequent visits to Norfolk to monitor foundation activities. In 1984 she received the Distinguished Public Service Award from the U.S. Department of Defense, and in 1988 President Ronald W. Reagan gave her the Presidential Medal of Freedom, the nation's highest civilian award. She also was seen frequently at New York Mets games, cheering for the baseball team that had become her favorite after the Brooklyn Dodgers left for Los Angeles. She suffered various ailments in her later years and outlived most of her friends and contemporaries. She died at Lennox Hill Hospital in New York at the age of 101 and was buried at her husband's side in the MacArthur tomb at the MacArthur Memorial in Norfolk.

As the wife of one of America's pivotal figures, Jean MacArthur shared the public spotlight with her husband, General Douglas MacArthur, during a dark time in the nation's history, the loss of the Philippines to the Japanese. Her significance to contemporaries was as an example of poise and loyalty under difficult circumstances. Her lasting significance may be that of someone who stands as an example of a gender role that has declined. Jean Faircloth's role in life was to be "Mrs. Douglas MacArthur," subsuming her own career and interests beneath her husband's while Douglas was alive and serving as the caretaker of his memory after his death. It was a role in which she excelled.

★

MacArthur's papers are housed with those of her husband in the Jean MacArthur Research Center in the General Douglas MacArthur Memorial in downtown Norfolk. Further writings on MacArthur can be found in biographies of the general, including William Manchester, *American Caesar: Douglas MacArthur,*

1880–1964 (1978), who referred to MacArthur as a "poem of womanhood" for her devotion to the general, a phrase that recurred in many later descriptions; and D. Clayton James, *The Years of MacArthur,* 3 vols. (1970–1985), which covers the years the MacArthurs were married. Other biographies of General MacArthur containing information about his wife are Michael Schaller, *Douglas MacArthur: The Far Eastern General* (1998); Geoffrey Perret, *Old Soldiers Never Die: The Life of Douglas MacArthur* (1996); and Richard Connaughton, *MacArthur and Defeat in the Philippines* (2001). Obituaries are in the *New York Times* and *Washington Post* (both 24 Jan. 2000).

ALAN BJERGA

McGUIRE, Dorothy Hackett (*b.* 14 June 1918 in Omaha, Nebraska; *d.* 14 September 2001 in Santa Monica, California), actress best remembered for her roles as soft-spoken, steadfast, and intelligent women in films of the 1940s and 1950s.

McGuire was the daughter of Thomas Johnson McGuire, a lawyer, and Isabelle Flaherty McGuire. Revealing an early talent for the stage, McGuire began acting with the Omaha Little Theater while still in her teens, making her stage debut opposite Henry Fonda in a production of James M. Barrie's *A Kiss for Cinderella.* After her father's death when she was fourteen, she was sent first to a convent school in Indianapolis and then to Pine Manor Junior College in Wellesley, Massachusetts.

Graduating from Pine Manor at nineteen, McGuire moved to New York City to find work as an actress. Her first break came when she was selected as Martha Scott's understudy in Thornton Wilder's classic play *Our Town.* When Scott went to Hollywood to reprise her role in the film version, McGuire took over the role on stage. In the late 1930s she played in the road company of *My Dear Children,* a vehicle for the aging John Barrymore. She also appeared with Benny Goodman and Louis Armstrong in *Swingin' the Dream,* a failed musical version of Shakespeare's *A Midsummer Night's Dream.*

McGuire's biggest break came in 1941, when she was selected over many other young actresses to portray the leading role in *Claudia,* Rose Franken's stage adaptation of her two novellas and twenty-two short stories about the title character. As the naive young wife who finds a degree of maturity, McGuire gave an appealing performance that won praise from the critics. After touring with the play in June 1942, she went to Hollywood the following year to recreate her role in the film version opposite Robert Young as her husband, David. The movie was a huge success and prompted a sequel, *Claudia and David,* in 1946. In 1943 McGuire married the famed photographer John Swope; they had two children, Mark and Mary Swope. Both chil-

Dorothy McGuire. THE KOBAL COLLECTION

dren would appear in films, with Mary known professionally as Topo Swope.

One of McGuire's most memorable roles came in 1945 when she played Katie Nolan, a resilient tenement wife and mother, in *A Tree Grows in Brooklyn*, adapted from Betty Smith's best-selling novel. The film, which marked the directorial debut of Elia Kazan, led to Academy Awards for James Dunn as McGuire's alcoholic husband and to Peggy Ann Garner as her sensitive daughter, Francie. McGuire's subsequent roles in the 1940s established her as a leading actress, especially adept at playing sensitive women. In *The Enchanted Cottage* (1945), she portrayed a shy, homely spinster who finds happiness in a mysterious cottage with her war-scarred husband, played by Robert Young. In *The Spiral Staircase* (1946), where McGuire played a mute servant girl stalked by a serial killer, she never spoke a word until the film's final scene. She won an Academy Award nomination for best actress for her performance as Kathy, the fiancée of a writer played by Gregory Peck, in the film version of Laura Z. Hobson's novel *Gentleman's Agreement* (1947). As a society woman who is ambiguous about her future husband's investigation into anti-Semitism in the United States, she brought substance to a one-dimensional role. The film won that year's Academy Award for best picture.

McGuire was kept busy throughout the 1950s, although few of her films were exceptional. She nevertheless brought warmth and conviction to *I Want You* (1951), *Old Yeller* (1957), and *A Summer Place* (1959). She won a New York Film Critics Circle nomination for best actress for playing a lovelorn secretary to an acerbic author played by Clifton Webb in the Rome-set *Three Coins in the Fountain* (1954), and played another secretary, caught up in an explosive murder trial, in *Trial* (1955). Perhaps her finest film of the period was William Wyler's *Friendly Persuasion* (1956), in which she was the compassionate wife of the Quaker patriarch played by Gary Cooper, confronted with the travails of the Civil War.

As McGuire devoted more time to her personal life, her film roles became fewer, but she appeared in such movies as *The Dark at the Top of the Stairs* (1960), *Swiss Family Robinson* (1960), and *The Greatest Story Ever Told* (1963), in which she played the Virgin Mary. She provided one of the voices for the 1973 film version of Richard Bach's best-selling novel *Jonathan Livingston Seagull*. McGuire also began to appear more regularly on television. In the 1970s she played prominent roles in the television films *She Waits* (1972), *The Runaways* (1975), the miniseries *Rich Man, Poor Man* (1976), and *The Incredible Journey of Doctor Meg Laurel* (1979). She excelled as Marmee March, the stalwart mother in Louisa May Alcott's *Little Women*, in a 1978 television adaptation of the novel. She repeated her role the following year in a miniseries version of the book.

Over the years, McGuire continued to return to the stage. In the mid-1940s she joined with Joseph Cotten, Jennifer Jones, and other actors to form the La Jolla Players, a repertory company in California. In 1950 she toured with the company in Tennessee Williams's *Summer and Smoke*, and the following year, returned briefly to Broadway, co-starring with Richard Burton in Jean Anouilh's *Legend of Lovers*. In 1958 she starred in an adaptation of Sherwood Anderson's *Winesburg, Ohio*, and in 1976 she appeared in Tennessee Williams's *The Night of the Iguana*. Her last stage performance was in a 1982 Los Angeles production of Lillian Hellman's *Another Part of the Forest*.

In later years, McGuire confined herself to sporadic television appearances. She was especially notable as an embattled widowed farmer in *Ghost Dancing* (1983), and as a frail mother in *I Never Sang for My Father* (1988). In 1986 she appeared in a three-part episode of the television drama *St. Elsewhere*. Her final television appearance was in the 1990 play *The Last Best Year*. McGuire died of heart failure at age eighty-three. Her remains were cremated and her ashes scattered at sea.

At the peak of her film career in the 1940s and 1950s, McGuire exuded a quiet elegance and an effortless charm that made her a popular favorite with audiences. In the movie world of fantasy and dreams, she was always real and always believable.

★

A clipping file on Dorothy McGuire can be found in the Performing Arts Library at Lincoln Center in New York City. Obituaries are in the *New York Times* (15 Sept. 2001) and *Variety* (17 Sept. 2001).

TED SENNETT

McINTIRE, Carl Curtis (*b.* 17 May 1906 in Ypsilanti, Michigan; *d.* 19 March 2002 in Voorhees, New Jersey), Protestant fundamentalist leader best known for his right-wing politics and attacks on the ecumenical movement.

McIntire was one of four children of Carl Curtis McIntire, a Presbyterian minister, and Hettie Hotchkin, a missionary who worked with Native Americans. He lived with both parents in Ypsilanti and Salt Lake City, Utah, where his father held pulpits, and later (upon the divorce of his parents) with his mother in Durant, Oklahoma, where he lived on Indian reservations.

For three years McIntire attended Southeastern State Teacher's College in Durant, where his mother was dean of women. He spent his senior year at Park College in Parkville, Missouri, from which he graduated in 1927. During the academic year 1928–1929, he attended Princeton Theological Seminary in New Jersey, after which he transferred to the newly formed Westminster Theological Seminary in Philadelphia, which he found more orthodox than Princeton, and from which he graduated in 1931.

First ordained in the Presbyterian Church of the United States of America (PCUSA), the leading northern Presbyterian body, he pastored two New Jersey congregations: Chelsea Presbyterian Church in Atlantic City (1931–1933) and the Collingswood Presbyterian Church in Collingswood (1933–1938). In the meantime, McIntire had become a follower of J. Gresham Machen, a leading conservative scholar at Princeton and later at Westminster. In 1934 McIntire joined the Independent Board for Presbyterian Foreign Missions, a group spearheaded by Machen in protest against the more liberal theology of PCUSA's Foreign Missions Board. In 1935 the West Jersey Presbytery suspended McIntire from the PCUSA ministry, a decision upheld by the PCUSA general assembly in 1936. After a trial before the presbytery, McIntire, along with other members of the independent board, was held guilty of defying denominational discipline and formally deposed from the PCUSA ministry.

McIntire's Collingswood parish voted to leave the PCUSA. Both pastor and congregation affiliated with a small new body, the Presbyterian Church in America—soon renamed the Orthodox Presbyterian Church (OPC)—

which was led by Machen. When Machen died in January 1937, McIntire, together with several other pastors, broke from the OPC. Finding the OPC inadequate in such matters as total abstinence from alcoholic beverages, dispensational theology (which centers on the imminence of Christ's second coming), and a more interdenominational mission board, in September 1938 they formed another denomination, the Bible Presbyterian Church. McIntire made the 11 April 1938 issue of *Time* magazine when, after losing a court battle over ownership of the Collingswood church edifice, he led 1,223 parishioners to a hastily erected tent, where the communion grape juice was served in paper cups.

In 1936 McIntire began editing a weekly eight-page tabloid, the *Christian Beacon,* and in 1937 he founded Faith Theological Seminary, first based in Elkins Park, Pennsylvania, and later in the Germantown section of Philadelphia. In 1941 he established the American Council of Christian Churches (ACCC), a federation of small fundamentalist bodies, and in 1948 set up its global counterpart, the International Council of Christian Churches (ICCC). Through the Christian Beacon Press, he began publishing a series of books, each of which attacked the National Council of Churches, the World Council of Churches, and various mainline Protestant bodies, all of which McIntire viewed as being permeated by communism and "modernism." Sample titles include *The Rise of the Tyrant* (1945), *"Author of Liberty"* (1946), *Modern Tower of Babel* (1949), *Servants of Apostasy* (1955), and *The Death of a Church* (1967).

McIntire was at the height of his fame in the 1960s. By then he had added two colleges to his orbit: Shelton (named the National Bible Institute until 1950; campus located at various times in Ringwood, New Jersey, and Cape May and Cape Canaveral, Florida) and Highland (Pasadena, California). His holdings also included two conference centers (Cape May and Cape Canaveral, Florida) and a daily radio broadcast, *The Twentieth-Century Reformation Hour,* heard on more than 600 stations. At one point he was receiving 4,000 letters a day. He strongly criticized his fellow evangelicals, describing Billy Graham as "a cover for the apostates," and the Southern Baptists as "soggy" compromisers.

McIntire was nothing if not flamboyant. In 1948 he endorsed a preventive nuclear strike against the Soviet Union. In 1970 he led 14,000 demonstrators to Washington, D.C., to urge victory in Vietnam. A year later, he took a table-tennis team to Taiwan in response to President Richard M. Nixon's "ping pong diplomacy" with the People's Republic of China. In 1975 he was expelled from Kenya, having accused its leaders of being communist. During his career he described the Roman Catholic Church as "fascist"; pro-

Carl McIntire, September 1970. BETTMANN/CORBIS

claimed that the comet Kohoutek (visible to the unaided eye from the end of November 1973 until late January 1974) marked the Second Coming; expressed suspicions that creatures in UFOs resembled beings described in the Book of Revelation; and opposed the civil rights movement, the teaching of evolution, and fluoridated water.

However, McIntire's empire already contained the seeds of decline. In 1956 and 1977 the Bible Presbyterian Church experienced schism, as did Faith Seminary in 1956 and 1971. In 1971, under pressure, McIntire relinquished control of the ACCC, at which point he formed the American Christian Action Council, which in 1987 became the National Council of Bible Believing Churches in America. In 1984 McIntire himself withdrew from his own wing of the Bible Presbyterians, establishing a separate synod of several congregations. When the Federal Communications Commission (FCC) terminated his broadcasts in 1973 because the station he broadcast on violated the Fairness Doctrine requiring both sides of an issue to be heard, he sought to broadcast twelve miles off the New Jersey shore from a converted World War II–vintage minesweeper that he called "Radio Free America." Despite his announcement, "This is Radio Free America. The silence of the sea is broken at 1160 on the AM dial," an FCC injunction closed him down within ten hours. In 1985 the U.S. Supreme Court supported the action of New Jersey, taken twenty years before, to withdraw recognition of Shelton College. Highland College was also closed, and his "Christian Admiral" Hotel in Cape May was razed to the ground. In 1986 the *Christian Beacon* ceased publication.

McIntire remained a separatist to the last. At age ninety-two, when Collingswood parish declared his pulpit vacant, he started holding Sunday services in his own home.

McIntire was over six feet tall and of stocky build and possessed, in the words of one observer, "the polished grace of a successful businessman." In 1931 he married Fairy D. Davis, with whom he had three children. She died in 1992, and in 1995 he married Alice Goff, his secretary. He died of natural causes and is buried at Harleigh Seminary in Camden, New Jersey.

The church historian Martin E. Marty described McIntire, with his penchant for schism, as "the most consistent fundamentalist of the twentieth century." Certainly he took the causes of doctrinal purity and rightist patriotism to their ultimate conclusions.

★

Princeton Theological Seminary is the official repository of the Carl Curtis McIntire Papers, holding more than 300 feet of records and manuscripts. Other collections containing extensive McIntire correspondence include the papers of Allan A. MacRae, R. Laird Harris, Max Belz, and James Oliver Buswell, Jr., all held in the Presbyterian Church of America Historical Center, St. Louis, Missouri, which also holds a small McIntire collection. For scholarly articles concerning McIntire, see John Fea, "Carl McIntire: From Fundamentalist Presbyterian to Presbyterian Fundamentalist," *American Presbyterians* 72 (1994): 253–268, and Thomas J. Ferris, "Christian Beacon, 1936–," in Ronald Lora and William Henry Longton, eds., *The Conservative Press in Twentieth-Century America* (1999): 141–151. A memorial tribute is "Fundamentalist with Flair," *Christianity Today* 46 (21 May 2002): 52–57. Obituaries are in the *New York Times* and *Philadelphia Inquirer* (both 22 Mar. 2002).

JUSTUS D. DOENECKE

McINTOSH, Millicent Carey (*b.* 30 November 1898 in Baltimore, Maryland; *d.* 3 January 2001 in Tyringham, Massachusetts), educational administrator and early feminist.

The daughter of two leading Quakers, Anthony Morris Carey, a machinery supply merchant, and Margaret Cheston (Thomas) Carey, a homemaker, Carey was also the niece of M. Carey Thomas, the first president of Bryn Mawr College. Bryn Mawr had been established outside Philadelphia in the 1880s by the Quaker community of Pennsylvania and Maryland to provide a liberal education for women comparable to that offered by the Ivy League colleges for men.

Carey attended the Bryn Mawr School in Baltimore and then Bryn Mawr College, where her aunt was still president (she would retire in 1922). She graduated magna cum laude with a B.A. in English and Greek from Bryn Mawr in 1920. After a year in Baltimore working as a social worker, Millicent accepted an offer arranged for her by her aunt to study abroad. She chose Newnham College, one of the women's colleges at Cambridge University in England. In 1923 she entered the graduate school of the Johns Hopkins University in Baltimore, receiving her Ph.D. in English in 1926.

Carey was appointed as an instructor in English at Bryn Mawr in 1926. She became dean of freshmen there in 1928. In 1930 she moved to New York City to become the headmistress of the Brearley School, a highly regarded private institution for girls. During her seventeen-year tenure, Carey transformed Brearley into an outstanding college preparatory school, with a solid grounding in the humanities yet also offering courses in "modern living" and sex education.

In 1932 Carey married Dr. Rustin McIntosh, a professor of pediatric medicine at Columbia University and director of services at Babies Hospital. The McIntoshes had five children, all of whom went on to distinguished professional careers.

In 1947 McIntosh was appointed dean of Barnard College, the women's division of Columbia University, becoming the first married woman to head one of the seven preeminent women's colleges. At Barnard she made the faculty an integral part of the college administration and gave them primary responsibility for the instructional program. She raised substantial sums for the college endowment, including two large contributions from the philanthropist John D. Rockefeller, Jr. These funds enabled the college to pay its faculty competitive salaries and to enlarge the physical fa-

Millicent Carey McIntosh, December 1953. AP/WIDE WORLD PHOTOS

cilities in which Barnard was housed. McIntosh made a particular point of creating a new facility for Barnard's day students, who outnumbered the residential students two to one.

McIntosh had made a particular point of encouraging Barnard graduates to teach in public schools, particularly at the senior high level. She instituted a program at Barnard to provide all the education courses that students would need to qualify for certification in New York State, together with the necessary practice teaching in cooperation with the Dalton School in New York City.

During McIntosh's tenure as dean, Barnard grew closer to Columbia College, the men's undergraduate division of Columbia University. Numerous courses were offered by one or the other college but not by both, thus providing a richer choice for the undergraduates in each. She also promoted interdepartmental majors, notably in foreign area studies and international relations, areas in which Columbia enjoyed a national reputation.

In 1952 McIntosh became the president of Barnard. The post was no different from that of dean, but the title recognized her outstanding contributions to the college and, through it, the university. McIntosh retired in 1962 and went to live with her husband on their farm in Tyringham, in the Berkshires of western Massachusetts. However, she continued her involvement with Barnard as an adviser to its board of trustees, helping them resist the pressure to merge Barnard into the general university system. Barnard remained a separate college within Columbia. McIntosh died at her home in Tyringham at age 102.

McIntosh did much to create the greater role for women in society that characterized American culture in the latter half of the twentieth century. She showed, thanks to her intense energy, that it was possible to be professionally active and to raise children to be contributing members of society. Her ability to lead the faculty and students at Barnard through the many changes characterizing college education in the post–World War II era led many other women to pursue similar combinations of career and family. At the same time, she cultivated an informality that endeared her to students who knew her as "Mrs. Mac." The esteem in which McIntosh was held was graphically illustrated in the celebrations of her one hundredth birthday, in which she, together with the current leaders of the school and of the college, took an active part. A student center at Barnard is named in her honor.

McIntosh rejected the narrow concept of feminism that set women against men and that enjoined those who wanted to have a professional career to remain single. Rather, she and her husband were exemplars of the two-earner family that came to be a characteristic of American society at the end of the twentieth century.

★

McIntosh reveals much about herself in the foreword she wrote to Marjorie Housepian Dobkin, ed., *The Making of a Feminist: Early Journals and Letters of M. Carey Thomas* (1979), a book widely used in courses on women's studies. McIntosh's accomplishments at Barnard are described extensively, if somewhat fulsomely, in Marian Churchill White, *A History of Barnard College* (1954). She appeared on the cover of *Newsweek* (15 Oct. 1951) and in an accompanying article ("Dean McIntosh Proves Point: Women's Colleges Are of Age") about the growth of college education for women, especially in the "Seven Sisters" institutions, the women's equivalent of the Ivy League. An obituary is in the *New York Times* (5 Jan. 2001).

NANCY M. GORDON

MCKAY, John Harvey (*b.* 5 July 1923 in Everettsville, West Virginia; *d.* 6 October 2001 in Tampa, Florida), college and professional football coach, noted as much for his sometimes biting one-liners as he was for his gridiron successes.

McKay was one of five children born to John McKay, a mine superintendent, and Gertrude (Lavery) McKay, a

John McKay. UNIVERSITY OF SOUTHERN CALIFORNIA

homemaker, in the bituminous coalfields of West Virginia. His parents were both of Scotch-Irish ancestry and had moved to West Virginia from Pennsylvania before McKay was born. The town in which he was born no longer exists: once the mines played out, the people left. The McKays moved several times before settling in Shinnston, West Virginia, after his father's death.

At Shinnston High School, from which he would graduate in 1940, McKay earned All-State honors in football and basketball. Although he was small (five feet, nine inches tall and 172 pounds), he earned an athletic scholarship to Wake Forest University, but when his mother became ill, he returned home before classes began. He then went to work at Bethlehem Mine in Shinnston as part of an electrical substation construction crew. Shortly after the Japanese attack on Pearl Harbor, McKay joined the Army Air Forces. Shipped to San Antonio, Texas, he was classified "GDO" (ground duty only) because of depth-perception problems. He later went to gunnery school and eventually was sent to the Pacific; however, as he later recalled, "I was a tail-gunner, but never saw action—the war was winding down by then." At Maxwell Field in Alabama, he played basketball and football until his discharge in January 1946.

While McKay was in the service, a physical education commander, Duane Purvis, an All-America fullback at

Purdue University, persuaded him to matriculate there. McKay played halfback as a freshman in 1946 and was second on the team in pass receptions, with ten catches for 196 yards. When Purdue changed coaches the next year, McKay transferred to the University of Oregon and played under the coach Jimmy Aiken. After losing a year of eligibility because of transferring, McKay played the 1948 and 1949 seasons for the Ducks. He graduated with a B.S. in physical education in 1950.

Despite injuries, McKay was drafted by the New York Yankees of the All-America Football Conference (AAFC) for the 1950 season. Twenty-seven years old at the time, McKay turned down the pros' offer of $6,000 and instead took a job as an assistant coach at Oregon for a salary of $2,800. On 24 June 1950 McKay married Nancy ("Corky") Hunter, with whom he had four children. One son, John, or "J. K.," played wide receiver for his father at the University of Southern California (USC) and later with the Tampa Bay Buccaneers, while another, Rich, became the Buccaneers' general manager, a position he held at the time of his father's death.

McKay worked as an assistant at Oregon until 1959, when he took a similar job at USC. When the head coach, Don Clark, resigned, McKay succeeded him in 1960. What occurred over the next sixteen years, with McKay at the head of the Trojans, was the stuff of legend. His teams, with their pulverizing running game, compiled a record of 127–40–8. The Trojans were crowned national champions in 1962, 1967, 1972, and 1974. They won Rose Bowls in 1963, 1968, 1970, 1973, and 1975 and won national Coach of the Year awards twice. He coached forty All-America honorees and two Heisman Trophy winners, Mike Garrett and O. J. Simpson.

Perhaps the greatest triumph of McKay's years at USC was his 10–5–1 record against the Trojans' intracity rivals, the University of California, Los Angeles (UCLA), Bruins, a team that had beaten USC regularly before McKay's arrival. When USC faced the Bruins in McKay's first season, the Trojans had a dismal 3–5 record, and UCLA was ranked eleventh in the nation. Nonetheless, USC, keyed by the sophomore quarterback Bill Nelson and the end Marlin McKeever, upset the Bruins 17–6 in the homecoming game. McKay, who had a one-year contract at the time, said of that contest, "It only saved my job."

Although UCLA was a "must win" game, McKay, a Roman Catholic, took great delight in getting the better of Notre Dame and allowed the Irish only six victories in sixteen games. While he enjoyed the confidence and adulation of the vast Trojan following, he did not believe that he could support his family adequately on his salary as a USC coach and began listening to offers from the National Football League (NFL). Rumors began to spread and, in what he later acknowledged was "a big mistake," he quelled

speculation by admitting that he had taken a job as head coach for the Tampa Bay (Florida) Buccaneers. Distracted by this news, his team, which had started the season 7–0, lost the last four games of the 1975–1976 season.

Life was not easy with the Bucs, an expansion team. McKay tasted defeat twenty-six times before the team won its first game, and between 1976 and 1984 the team's record was an abysmal 45–91–1. During the initial losing streak, he remarked, "The mail is running three-to-one that I'm not a stupid S.O.B., but there are a lot of ones." Still, there were successes in the Tampa years. In 1979 the Bucs accrued a 10–6 record and defeated the Philadelphia Eagles to compete in the National Football Conference title game against the Los Angeles Rams. They lost to the Rams, however, and thus missed the opportunity to play in Super Bowl XIV.

Perhaps McKay's most famous and best one-liner was from his early days in Tampa. A reporter asked, after an inept performance, what he thought of his team's execution. McKay quipped, "I'm in favor of it." He died of heart failure as a result of diabetes in a Tampa hospital, and his remains were cremated.

★

McKay's *Football Coaching* (1966) is a coaching techniques book. There is no biography that includes his NFL coaching career, but *McKay: A Coach's Story* (1974), written with Jim Perry, deals with most of his USC career. A memorial tribute is in the *Los Angeles Times* (13 Nov. 2001), and an obituary is in the *New York Times* (11 June 2001).

JIM CAMPBELL

McLEAN, Malcom Purcell (*b.* 14 November 1913 in Maxton, North Carolina; *d.* 25 May 2001 in New York City), entrepreneur who changed the shipping industry, and consequently world trade, with the revolutionary concept of containerizing freight for shipment by sea.

McLean was the fourth child and second son of Malcom Purcell McLean, a farmer who also worked a mail route, and Almena McLeod Currie, a homemaker. McLean grew up poor on a farm in Maxton, along with three sisters and three brothers. At age eight he sold eggs for his mother, keeping a commission for himself. After graduating from Maxton High School in 1931, he worked as a grocery store clerk and then borrowed money for a gas station in the nearby town of Red Springs and to buy a used truck to haul dirt for the Works Progress Administration (later renamed the Works Projects Administration, or WPA). With the money he earned, McLean bought another truck to drive goods to as far away as New York. Eventually he added

In 1940 McLean Trucking had a fleet of thirty trucks and was earning $230,000 annually. McLean's older sister, Clara, and younger brother, Jim, worked with him. By 1950 the company employed 2,000 people and had thirty-seven terminals on the East Coast. Based in Winston-Salem, North Carolina, and by then grossing $12 million annually, it was the largest motor-freight company in the southern United States.

McLean wanted to implement his ideas for putting truck-size boxes onto vessels called trailer ships. The boxes would be specially built steel trailers, later called containers, stronger than a truck trailer, that could be loaded without wheels and stacked. When McLean tried to purchase the Pan-Atlantic Steamship Company of Mobile, Alabama, the railroad industry lobbied the Interstate Commerce Commission (ICC) to enforce a ban on same ownership of different modes of transportation. Consequently, in 1955 McLean sold his 75 percent share in McLean Trucking for $6 million and purchased Pan-Atlantic. The company had coastwise shipping rights, but two tankers had to be converted from break-bulk vessels to container ships. McLean was opposed by labor unions, railroads, ports, and truckers, all of whom would lose income through the implementation of containerized shipping.

On 26 April 1956, when the *Ideal X*, a converted World War II tanker, loaded with fifty-eight trailers, sailed from Port Newark, New Jersey, to Houston, containerization was born. The ship also carried oil below deck. Four more trailer ships operated on this run until 1957. Between 1956 and 1958 more vessels were converted and sailed coastwise. In 1958, under the name McLean Industries, Inc., the company moved its headquarters to Port Elizabeth, New Jersey.

In 1960 Pan-Atlantic's Sea-Land service was renamed Sea-Land Service, Incorporated, and it was at about that time that the nomenclature changed to containers and container ships. To qualify to ship between domestic ports, vessels could not be built abroad. McLean circumvented the issue by ordering ships' midsections built in Germany to be grafted onto American-built surplus tankers in U.S. shipyards. McLean then set his sights on Europe, but U.S. Lines sent the first container ship to Europe on 18 March 1966, while Sea-Land's SS *Fairland* sailed for Rotterdam on 28 April 1967. Despite doubts and anticontainerization sentiment, McLean converted a terminal in Rotterdam for handling containerized shipments. Meanwhile, by 1966 McLean had traveled to Vietnam in his own jet and obtained lucrative contracts to carry cargo and supplies for the U.S. military in Southeast Asia. While other U.S. shipping companies received government subsidies, McLean refused them.

In 1969 McLean sold his shares in Sea-Land for $500 million in R. J. Reynolds stock and a seat on its board. He worked in real estate, invested in electron microscopes and

Malcom P. McLean. TIME LIFE PICTURES/GETTY IMAGES

five trucks to his fleet, hired drivers, and named the business McLean Trucking Company. In 1934 a bad winter ruined the business. In debt, McLean went back to driving by himself and managing the service station.

In 1937 McLean drove a truck loaded with bales of cotton from Fayetteville, North Carolina, to Hoboken, New Jersey. Waiting all day to unload the truck, McLean envisioned loading the whole truck onto a ship rather than moving individual crates of goods by sling from trucks onto ships, a system known as break-bulk cargo. Eliminating this step would speed the transportation of goods, create a more economical method of shipping, and reduce pilferage. McLean's idea involved using specially designed cranes to load the sealed containers onto ships. The only modern precedent was a company called Seatrain, which had been loading rail boxcars, with wheels still attached, onto ships since 1929.

On 23 November 1938 McLean married Margaret Britton Sikes. They had two daughters and one son. After more than fifty years of marriage, McLean's wife died in 1992. On 11 December 1995 McLean married Irena Serafin.

lasers, and invented a device to move hospital patients from a stretcher to a bed. In 1973 he started a hog farm in North Carolina that earned a reputation as the cleanest in the United States. In 1978 he bought his arch-rival, U.S. Lines. McLean wanted to create an around-the-world service that would load and unload in ports along the way, but the plan failed, and U.S. Lines declared bankruptcy in 1986. In 1991 he started Trailer Bridge, a freight service to Puerto Rico, using specially designed large multimodal containers. On 11 December 1995 McLean married Irena Serafin.

Among the awards McLean received were the Elmer A. Sperry Award (1991), for "a distinguished engineering contribution which, through application proved in actual service, has advanced the art of transportation whether by land, sea, or air." In 1994 *American Heritage* magazine selected McLean as one of the ten most important "agents of change" for having sparked "a fundamental change in the world economy." That same year, the College of Charleston (South Carolina) gave McLean the W. Don Welch Medallion for "meritorious contributions to intermodal transportation." In 1997 the U.S. Secretary of Transportation Rodney Slater presented McLean with a plaque reading "To the father of containerization, whose vision sparked a global revolution." In 1999 the Navy League of the United States gave McLean the Nimitz Award, which "honors a leader of industry who has made a major contribution to the Untied States' maritime strength." In 2000 McLean was named "Man of the Century" by the International Maritime Hall of Fame. That same year he received an honorary degree from the U.S. Merchant Marine Academy in New York.

McLean died at his home at age eighty-seven of heart failure brought on by complications from pneumonia. A memorial service was held at the Fifth Avenue Presbyterian Church in Manhattan. McLean's ashes were dispersed at sea in June 2002 from the U.S. Merchant Marine Academy at King's Point, Long Island. There is a headstone in the family plot in Maxton.

McLean was a private man who rarely gave interviews. He believed in the importance of his rural roots, remembering that loans from local people gave him the opportunity to start and build his business during the depression. He was a keen cost analyst who built a safe and profitable trucking business. His innovative contribution to the transportation industry has been compared to the impact of the change from sail to steam shipping. Containerization and intermodalism (transportation involving different modes, such as trucks and ships) became mainstays of the shipping industry. An independent straight talker, who hated business jargon and preferred face-to-face communication to talking by telephone, McLean succeeded because he was an outsider to the ocean-shipping industry and could ignore doubtful experts.

★

The nascent Malcom McLean Foundation of Virginia holds McLean's papers. McLean, who rarely gave interviews, wrote an autobiographical article about the beginnings of his businesses in North Carolina for *American* magazine (May 1950). The spring 1994 issue of *Audacity* features an article with an interview by Oliver E. Allen. A substantial article is in *American Shipper* (May 1996). Obituaries are in the *Washington Post* (27 May 2001); *New York Times* and *Journal of Commerce* (both 29 May 2001); and *Economist* (2–8 June 2001).

JANE BRODSKY FITZPATRICK

McVEIGH, Timothy James   (*b.* 23 April 1968 in Lockport, New York; *d.* 11 June 2001 in Terre Haute, Indiana), decorated veteran of Operation Desert Storm who was convicted of masterminding the 19 April 1995 bombing of the Alfred P. Murrah Federal Building in Oklahoma City, Oklahoma.

McVeigh was the middle of three children and the only son of William ("Bill") McVeigh, a laborer in an automobile manufacturing plant, and Mildred ("Mickey") McVeigh (now Frazer), a travel agent. McVeigh was influenced most by his paternal grandfather, Eddie McVeigh, who taught him how to hunt and who first introduced the young

Timothy McVeigh. AP/WIDE WORLD PHOTOS

McVeigh to guns. McVeigh's first firearm was a .22 caliber hunting rifle he received at age thirteen from his grandfather, and his interest in, and collection of, firearms grew quickly. McVeigh is reported to have often taken guns from his growing collection to his high school to impress his friends.

Although he was reported by his former neighbors to be a congenial young boy and by his teachers to be a good student, McVeigh had a troubled early family life. Conflicts between his parents ultimately led to divorce in 1986. While his sisters decided to live with their mother, McVeigh, who blamed his mother for the breakup, stayed with his father. That same year McVeigh graduated from Starpoint Central High School with a perfect attendance award for the entire four years. He was awarded a $500 New York State Regents Scholarship and briefly attended Niagara County Community College but quickly dropped out in 1986. He went to work briefly for Burger King but soon switched to a career more consistent with his interests when he obtained a job with Park Security driving an armored car, a position facilitated by his having obtained a permit to carry a concealed weapon. Seemingly adrift, McVeigh began researching the "right of the people to keep and bear arms" as set forth in the Second Amendment to the U.S. Constitution. He became obsessed with *The Turner Diaries*, a fictional account of a truck bombing of Federal Bureau of Investigation (FBI) headquarters by a white supremacist upset over federal gun laws, written by William Pierce, not coincidentally a former American Nazi Party official and an avowed white supremacist. Inspired and seeking access to bigger guns and targets, McVeigh enlisted in the U.S. Army in May 1988. He went through basic training at Fort Benning, Georgia, hoping ultimately to become a Special Forces "Green Beret." While at Fort Benning, he met Terry Lynn Nichols and Michael Fortier, two men who would eventually assist or otherwise facilitate McVeigh's bombing of the federal building.

After basic training, the three, who had become friends, were transferred to Fort Riley, Kansas, where McVeigh and Nichols were assigned to the First Infantry Division, Second Battalion, Sixteenth Infantry. There McVeigh excelled at marksmanship, scoring an unprecedented perfect score of 1,000 points during a live-fire test. McVeigh was such an excellent marksman that he was invited to try out for the Special Forces. Before he could try out, however, McVeigh, who had been promoted to sergeant in 1990, was sent in 1991 to the Persian Gulf, where he saw action in Operation Desert Storm as a gunner on a Bradley Fighting Vehicle. On the second day of the campaign, McVeigh hit an Iraqi machine gunner in the chest from nearly 2,000 yards away, killing him instantly. He served with distinction and was awarded the Combat Infantry Badge and the Bronze Star. Ironically, he found killing to be distasteful once he came to understand that most of the Iraqi soldiers were forced to serve the dictator Saddam Hussein.

Upon his return to the United States, McVeigh finally tried out for the Special Forces, but because he had not allotted himself sufficient time to train for it, he failed to make the cut. Disappointed and dejected, he decided to leave the army and was honorably discharged in December 1991, less than one year after his return from the Persian Gulf. Increasingly disillusioned with his life and the federal government, and becoming more obsessed with *The Turner Diaries*, conspiracy theories, and survivalist training, in early 1993 McVeigh left the Buffalo area in his car, carrying with him all his possessions that he had not sold. He sought out his former army buddies, Nichols and Fortier, who also had left the army. During this time McVeigh began to frequent gun shows.

While he was on his way to visit Fortier in Kingman, Arizona, federal agents attempted to raid the Branch Davidian compound in Waco, Texas, on 28 February 1993. The result was a prolonged standoff. McVeigh, upset by the government's actions, decided to travel to Waco to lend moral support to the Davidians. While there, McVeigh ominously told a student reporter that "the government is continually growing bigger and more powerful, and the people need to prepare to defend themselves against government control."

After a brief stay in Waco, McVeigh visited Fortier and then traveled to Decker, Michigan, to visit Nichols. He and Nichols watched on 19 April 1993 as government agents finally raided the Davidian complex; flames quickly erupted, engulfing the compound and causing the deaths of about eighty members, including children. The events at the Davidian compound, along with the standoff at Ruby Ridge, Idaho, the year before, when federal officials shot and killed the wife of the survivalist Randy Weaver and their fourteen-year-old son, incensed McVeigh and inflamed his antigovernment rhetoric. In 1994 he informed Nichols and Fortier that he was moving into his "action phase."

At 9:02 A.M. on 19 April 1995, exactly two years after the raid on the Branch Davidian compound, McVeigh detonated a rented Ryder truck packed with more than 4,000 pounds of an explosive he and Nichols had mixed from a combination of fuel oil and fertilizer. The explosion ripped apart the Alfred P. Murrah Federal Building in Oklahoma City, killing 168 people, including nineteen children in a day-care facility on the second floor.

McVeigh was arrested within hours of the bombing. After two years of court hearings, his case went to trial in Denver in 1997. On 2 June 1997 he was convicted of, among other charges, eight counts of first-degree murder. He was sentenced to death on 15 August 1997. After four years on death row, during which his lawyers sought unsuccessfully to appeal his case, McVeigh was executed by lethal injection at the Federal Penitentiary at Terre Haute, Indiana, on 11 June 2001, the first inmate executed by the federal government in thirty-eight years. In lieu of the traditional "last words," McVeigh offered a written statement, the poem "Invictus" by William Ernest Henley, which ends with these lines: "It matters not how strait the gate, / How charged with punishments the scroll, / I am the master of my fate: / I am the captain of my soul."

McVeigh's coconspirator Nichols was convicted and sentenced to life imprisonment by the federal government for his role in the bombing. On 13 May 2003 an Oklahoma state judge ruled that Nichols also could be tried in state court for the offense; prosecutors indicated that they would seek the death penalty. Fortier was the prosecution's star witness, testifying about hearing McVeigh talk of his hatred for the government and his plans to blow up the federal building in Oklahoma City because he believed the orders for the government siege at the Branch Davidian compound were issued there. Fortier was sentenced on 27 May 1998 to twelve years in prison and fined $200,000 for failing to warn authorities of the plot to bomb the federal building.

★

For more information about McVeigh and the bombing of the federal building, see Brandon M. Stickney, *All-American Monster: The Unauthorized Biography of Timothy McVeigh* (1996); Peter Israel and Stephen R. Jones, *Others Unknown: The Oklahoma City Bombing Conspiracy* (1998); Richard A. Serrano, *One of Ours: Timothy McVeigh and the Oklahoma Bombing* (1998); John Douglas and Mark Olshaker, *The Anatomy of Motive: The FBI's Legendary Mindhunter Explores the Key to Understanding and Catching Violent Criminals* (1999); and Lou Michel and Dan Herbeck, *American Terrorist* (2001).

MARK H. ALLENBAUGH

MANSFIELD, Michael Joseph ("Mike") (*b.* 16 March 1903 in New York City; *d.* 5 October 2001 in Washington, D.C.), Senate majority leader who shifted from support to skepticism regarding American intervention in South Vietnam and from private to public opposition to the war.

Mansfield was the oldest of three children born to the Irish-Catholic immigrants Patrick Mansfield, a hotel porter, and Josephine (O'Brien) Mansfield. After his mother died in 1906, Mansfield went to live with relatives in Great Falls, Montana. He attended public and parochial schools, but he dropped out at age fourteen to enlist in the U.S. Navy during World War I and made seven convoy crossings of the Atlantic Ocean before he was discharged for being underage. He then served in the U.S. Army from 1919 to 1920 and in the U.S. Marine Corps from 1920 to 1922. The

Mike Mansfield, January 1967. THE LIBRARY OF CONGRESS

marines sent him to the Philippines, Japan, and China, experiences that influenced his lifelong interest in Asia.

After the war Mansfield returned to Montana, where he worked as a copper miner and attended the Montana School of Mines to become a mining engineer. A local high-school teacher, Maureen Hayes, persuaded him to complete his high-school education through correspondence courses and enroll at the University of Montana in Missoula. They married on 13 September 1932, while he was a student, and had one daughter. Mansfield earned a B.A. in 1933 and an M.A. in 1934, and remained at the university as a professor of Far Eastern and Latin American history and political science while studying for his doctorate.

At his wife's urging, Mansfield ran for the Democratic nomination for the U.S. House of Representatives in 1940 and suffered his only electoral loss. The Republican Jeannette Rankin won the seat, but as a pacifist she voted against declaring war on Japan after their attack on Pearl Harbor and did not seek reelection in 1942. This time Mansfield won the Democratic nomination and the election, ending his academic career.

As a member of the House Foreign Affairs Committee, Mansfield earned recognition as an authority on Asian affairs. In late 1944 President Franklin D. Roosevelt sent him on a five-week inspection tour of China. Mansfield's report realistically outlined conditions in China but called the

Chinese communists "more reformers than revolutionaries," a characterization that his political opponents later would hold against him. He also served as a delegate to the United Nations Assembly in Paris.

When Mansfield, as a liberal Democrat, challenged the conservative Republican incumbent senator Zales Ecton in 1952, Senator Joseph R. McCarthy went to Montana to campaign against "China Mike," who nevertheless won a narrow 50.7 percent victory. Mansfield received a seat on the prestigious Senate Foreign Relations Committee and began to follow events in Southeast Asia. In 1953 he met the South Vietnamese nationalist Ngo Dinh Diem, then in exile in the United States. Mansfield admired Diem as an anticolonialist as well as an anticommunist and believed that Diem's brand of nationalism could withstand communist insurgency. Later in 1953 Mansfield went on his first fact-finding mission to Indochina, establishing personal acquaintances with most of the leaders in the region. Following the French defeat at Dien Bien Phu in May 1954, he called on the United States to recognize Vietnam, Laos, and Cambodia as independent governments.

Mansfield served as a U.S. delegate to the Manila conference in 1954 that established the Southeast Asian Treaty Organization (SEATO). He called on the State Department to support Diem's government in South Vietnam against the communist North Vietnamese government under Ho Chi Minh. On another visit to Southeast Asia in 1955, Mansfield called Diem the "right man in the right place" and warned that the alternative probably would be a military regime. At home, Mansfield diligently attended to constituent services and Montana-related issues. He won reelection in 1958 with 76 percent of the vote, a third term in 1964 with 64 percent, and a fourth in 1970 with 60.5 percent. In 1957 Senate Democrats elected Mansfield assistant majority leader, or whip, second to the dynamic majority leader, Lyndon B. Johnson.

In 1960 Mansfield's close friend John F. Kennedy won the Democratic presidential nomination and selected Johnson as his running mate. The ticket's narrow victory thrust Johnson into the vice presidency. At the urging of both Kennedy and Johnson, Mansfield reluctantly accepted the majority leadership. He then stunned the Senate Democratic Conference by proposing that the vice president preside at their meetings. Senators voiced such strong opposition that Johnson rarely attended conference meetings thereafter. Mansfield also retained Johnson's top aide, Bobby Baker, as secretary to the majority, but in 1963 Baker was forced to resign for improper financial activities.

As majority leader, Mansfield adopted a starkly different style from that of Johnson, who had concentrated power in his own hands. Believing that the Senate operated best by accommodation, respect, and mutual restraint, Mansfield widely distributed power and perquisites. He insisted that all senators were equal and must share the legislative burden. By spreading legislative responsibilities among junior senators, he also sought to reduce the influence of their more conservative senior colleagues, who chaired powerful committees. He quietly abolished most patronage positions to establish a professional staff; assigned office space by seniority; and refrained from handing out committee assignments as favors in exchange for support.

When Kennedy's legislative program stalled, some senators blamed Mansfield for not being a more aggressive leader, but after Kennedy's assassination elevated Johnson to the presidency, the legislative logjam broke, and Mansfield's decentralized style of leadership facilitated a deluge of bills. Mansfield teamed with the Republican leader Everett Dirksen to break a protracted southern filibuster and pass the landmark Civil Rights Act of 1964, and over the next two years Congress enacted most of Johnson's War on Poverty and Great Society programs.

Meanwhile, Mansfield was increasingly troubled over the deteriorating situation in Southeast Asia. He had urged Kennedy to seek a negotiated settlement in Laos and to concentrate U.S. attention on South Vietnam, but he preferred economic aid to military assistance. On his return to Vietnam in 1962, Mansfield heard pessimistic reports from newspaper correspondents stationed in Saigon. Transmitting these findings to Kennedy, he warned against U.S. military intervention on the grounds that only the Vietnamese could solve their problems. Kennedy told his aides that he was initially angry with Mansfield for disagreeing so completely with the administration's policy and later with himself for agreeing with Mansfield. In November 1963 the assassinations of both Diem and Kennedy profoundly shocked Mansfield, who delivered a moving eulogy at Kennedy's state funeral.

As soon as Johnson became president, Mansfield began warning him that military victory in Vietnam was illusory. Mansfield endorsed French proposals for the neutralization of Vietnam, which Johnson dismissed as "milquetoast." Citing an attack by North Vietnamese torpedo boats on American destroyers in the Tonkin Gulf in 1964, Johnson requested a congressional resolution in support of military retaliation. When Johnson met with a bipartisan delegation of congressional leaders, Mansfield was the sole dissenter. At that private gathering, he recommended taking the matter to the United Nations. Publicly, he voted for the Tonkin Gulf Resolution.

After Johnson's reelection in 1964, Mansfield continued to send him a stream of memoranda that questioned and dissented from administration policies. He warned that applying more U.S. military pressure on the Vietcong would make a peaceful settlement less likely and cause military actions in South Vietnam to spread into neighboring Laos and Cambodia. In February 1965, following a Vietcong raid on an American base at Pleiku, Mansfield attended a meeting of the National Security Council. Everyone but Mansfield endorsed a retaliatory bombing of North Vietnam.

Mansfield led another fact-finding mission to Vietnam in December 1965, a trip that reinforced his belief that the United States should convene an international conference to seek a diplomatic solution. He disappointed Senate doves, however, by not breaking with Johnson publicly, and he would not advocate a military withdrawal until a diplomatic solution assured South Vietnamese independence. Mansfield similarly distanced himself from antiwar demonstrations: he shared their view of the war but opposed tactics that disregarded the law. Although he doubted that U.S. interests in Southeast Asia justified the cost in American lives and resources, he rejected the label of "isolationist" and instead described the U.S. position in Vietnam as "isolated internationalism."

Following the Tet Offensive in 1968, when the Vietcong launched their biggest strike, infiltrating the city of Saigon and even occupying the U.S. embassy, Johnson called Mansfield to the White House to gain his support for sending more troops to Vietnam. Mansfield declared that he would oppose the measure in the Senate, and Johnson thanked him for his honesty and candor. Four nights later, Johnson announced his decisions to limit the bombing of North Vietnam and not seek another term as president.

The Republican Richard Nixon, who won the presidency in 1968, differed with Mansfield on most issues, except for the need to restore diplomatic relations with China. As majority leader, Mansfield attended monthly breakfast meetings with the president that often dealt with China and other foreign policy issues. Following Nixon's visit to China in 1972, Mansfield and the Senate Republican leader Hugh Scott led the first congressional delegation to Beijing. Mansfield also pledged his support for American disengagement from the Vietnam War. If the United States withdrew its troops, he promised to declare it the "best possible end of a bad war." Nixon understood that by rejecting this concession from an opposition party leader, he would turn Kennedy's and Johnson's war into his own. He declined, however, not wanting to lose the war.

That decision on Nixon's part brought Mansfield into open opposition against further combat. He sponsored an amendment prohibiting the use of U.S. troops in Laos and Thailand, endorsed repeal of the Tonkin Gulf Resolution, and supported passage of the Cooper-Church amendment, which set a date for removal of all U.S. troops from Cambodia. A Mansfield bill calling for the phased withdrawal of U.S. troops cleared the Senate 57–42. Although it was rejected in the House, a modified version was enacted, marking the first time that a twentieth-century Congress had urged an end to a war still in progress.

The arrest of five burglars armed with wiretapping equipment at the Democratic Party headquarters in the Watergate complex in 1972 prompted Mansfield to call for a Senate investigation into Nixon's involvement. Mansfield's judicious appointments to the committee and avoidance of partisan rhetoric helped focus national attention on the evidence the Watergate investigators uncovered and led the way to the president's resignation in advance of impeachment. When Nixon's successor, Gerald Ford, proposed additional U.S. aid to South Vietnam, Mansfield opposed him and for the first time voted against a defense appropriation bill. Without continued American support, the South Vietnamese government soon collapsed.

To reestablish congressional authority, Mansfield cosponsored the War Powers Act of 1973, enacted over a presidential veto. Under his leadership in the 1970s the Senate also adopted a series of reforms to strengthen the institution. "Sunshine" legislation opened almost all committee meetings to public view. The Senate staff was vastly expanded to provide legislators with expertise independent of the executive branch. The number of votes needed to invoke cloture on filibusters was reduced from two-thirds to three-fifths.

After a record sixteen years as majority leader, Mansfield announced his retirement in 1976. He cited his inability to stop the Vietnam War as his greatest regret and the Twenty-sixth Amendment, which lowered the voting age to eighteen, as his proudest achievement. In 1977 he went to Hanoi on a mission for President Jimmy Carter to seek an accounting for Americans missing in action. From 1977 to 1989 Mansfield served as ambassador to Japan under Carter and President Ronald Reagan. President George H. W. Bush presented him with the Presidential Medal of Freedom in 1989, and President Bill Clinton called on his advice in normalizing relations with Vietnam. Mansfield spent his last years as an East Asia specialist for the investment firm Goldman Sachs. He died at age ninety-eight of congestive heart failure and is buried in Arlington National Cemetery in Arlington, Virginia.

Mansfield always credited his wife for his success. When parks, centers, and other sites were dedicated in his honor, he requested that they be named for her, too, and Montana erected statues of both Mike and Maureen Mansfield in the state capitol. Unusually modest, reflective, and taciturn for a party leader, Mansfield generated admiration and respect on both sides of the aisle for his fairness and integrity. He redefined the Senate majority leadership and set the model for his successors.

★

Mansfield's papers are at the University of Montana in Missoula. Biographies include Louis Baldwin, *Honorable Politician: Mike Mansfield of Montana* (1979); Gregory Allen Olson, *Mansfield and Vietnam: A Study in Rhetorical Adaptation* (1995); Francis R.

Valeo, *Mike Mansfield, Majority Leader: A Different Kind of Senate, 1961–1976* (1999); and Don Oberdorfer, *Senator Mansfield: The Extraordinary Life of a Great Statesman and Diplomat* (2003). Other relevant volumes include Robert Mann, *A Grand Delusion: America's Descent into Vietnam* (2000); Robert A. Caro, *Master of the Senate: The Years of Lyndon Johnson* (2002); and Randall Woods, ed., *Vietnam and the American Political Tradition* (2003). Congress issued *Tributes to Mike Mansfield of Montana: Commemorating the Longest Tenure as Majority Leader of the United States Senate* (1970) and *Tributes to the Honorable Mike Mansfield of Montana in the United States Senate upon the Occasion of His Retirement from the Senate* (1976). Obituaries are in the *New York Times* and *Washington Post* (both 6 Oct. 2001). Oral histories and other recorded interviews are in the John F. Kennedy and Lyndon B. Johnson presidential libraries and at the libraries of Princeton University and Mississippi State universities and the universities of Georgia and Maryland.

DONALD A. RITCHIE

MAPLE, John Edward ("Jack") (*b.* 23 September 1952 in Queens, New York City; *d.* 4 August 2001 in Manhattan, New York City), New York City deputy police commissioner who devised Compstat, a system for tracking and storing crime information that transformed police crime-fighting tactics nationwide.

Jack Maple, November 1999. AP/WIDE WORLD PHOTOS

Maple was the eldest son of George Maple, a postal employee, and Gladys Maple, a nurse's aide. He grew up with his three brothers and three sisters in Richmond Hill in the borough of Queens, attending Catholic grade schools. Maple was accepted at Brooklyn Technical High School, a prestigious public high school for math and science, but he was frequently truant. He eventually earned a G.E.D from Fort Greene Night School. When he was a teenager, Maple's father took him to Grand Central Terminal to view coffins of soldiers returned from Vietnam, and urged Maple to make something of himself so as to avoid a similar fate. At his father's insistence, Maple took all the civil service exams when he was sixteen.

Maple joined the New York City Transit Police in 1970, first as a trainee in Brooklyn and later as a "cave cop" patrolling the subway platforms in the Times Square area of Manhattan's Forty-second Street. Although transit police were not supposed to make arrests on the street while off-duty, the maverick Maple compiled 400 arrests by late 1980, and at age twenty-seven became the department's youngest detective.

Deciding he needed a more dignified image, Maple dieted on espresso and minnow-size bites of fish and lost fifty-five pounds in five weeks. Standing five feet, seven inches tall, he then adopted a wardrobe of designer suits, bow ties, two-tone spectator shoes, and homburgs. A 1983 *New York* magazine profile detailed how Maple, thinking he was entitled to the good life, obtained a $20,000 loan on the two-bedroom Queens home he shared with his wife and young daughter, borrowed $8,000 more, and spent the sum (which exceeded his annual salary) buying an Alfa Romeo Spider sports car, attending Broadway shows, eating chocolate cheesecake, drinking Dom Perignon champagne at the Plaza Hotel's Oak Bar, and spending nights at the Waldorf Astoria. His first marriage ended, as did his second.

In 1985 Maple commanded a new handpicked plainclothes unit that worked as decoys, mostly from 10 P.M. until 5 A.M., to go after the "wolf packs"—gangs of teenagers who roamed the subways, robbing and often attacking their victims. "Treat every case as if your mother was the victim," Maple told those he supervised. Believing police had to fight crime rather than respond to it, Maple papered his walls with fifty-five feet of hand-drawn maps he called "charts of the future," color coded to detail each subway stop and occurrences of each robbery and crime so that police could go after criminals where crimes occurred.

Bostonian William "Bill" Bratton took command of the New York Transit Police in April 1990. Impressed with a ten-page proposal from Maple on how to reduce crime in the subways, Bratton named Maple, then a lieutenant, a special assistant to the commissioner and gave him command of one hundred transit police to put his ideas into action. During Bratton's two years as commissioner, subway gang robberies fell 99 percent from 1,200 to 12, felony crime dropped 22 percent, robberies decreased 40 percent, fare evasion was halved, and ridership increased. Maple followed his mentor back to Boston in 1992 when Bratton was named superintendent in chief, and later, police commissioner, of the Boston Police.

In 1994, following his election as mayor of New York City in November 1993, Rudolph Giuliani appointed Bratton commissioner of the New York City Police Department (NYPD). Bratton believed the war on crime could be won and vowed to carry out the new mayor's promise to reduce disorder and fear in the Big Apple. Bratton named Maple to the new position of deputy commissioner for crime control strategies. Maple equated this promotion to that of an ensign in the coast guard waking up as a three-star admiral in the navy.

At Elaine's, an expensive Upper East Side hangout he frequented with friends to sip champagne on ice or drink double espressos, Maple scribbled on a napkin the four principles that redefined the objectives, methods, and outcomes of the NYPD: 1) accurate, timely intelligence; 2) rapid deployment; 3) effective tactics; and 4) relentless follow-up and assessment. Once a reluctant reader, Maple built a library of military histories and studied the strategies deployed by great military leaders including Sun-tzu, Hannibal, Horatio Nelson, Erwin Rommel, and George Patton.

With Chief of Department Louis Anemone, Maple, and others in attendance, Bratton presided at weekly 7 A.M. meetings of top police officials, detectives, and precinct commanders and held them accountable for the crimes occurring in their precincts and for strategies to combat them. Compstat, a database based on Maple's "charts of the future," generated daily crime numbers by precinct that helped the police to compare statistics, identify trends early, and respond rapidly. Compstat is credited as a major factor in the reduction of the New York City murder rate (which plummeted 50 percent) and of the overall crime rate (which dropped 39 percent) in the first two years of Giuliani's administration, when Bratton was police commissioner.

Under pressure from Giuliani, Bratton resigned in early 1996, and Maple's resignation soon followed. That year, New York City's murders dropped below 1,000, falling to 629 in 1997. Compstat was honored by Vice President Al Gore's National Performance Review for government reform and won a 1996 Innovations in American Government Award from the Ford Foundation.

Later in 1996, John Linder, a former Bratton consultant, asked Maple to join the firm that became known as the Linder/Maple Group. As self-styled specialists in "crime-reduction services," they counseled police departments in New Orleans; Newark, New Jersey; Baltimore; and international cities on how to apprehend more criminals and improve the operations of their police departments. The crime rate in New Orleans dropped 22 percent in the first nine months of their contract. Maple published his crime-fighting strategies and advocated better-trained, better-paid, and more diverse police forces in *The Crime Fighter: Putting the Bad Guys Out of Business,* written with the journalist Chris Mitchell (1999). Maple also cowrote and coproduced episodes of the television drama *The District,* whose crime-fighting character Jack Mannion was based on Maple.

In March 2001 Maple married NYPD Sergeant Brigid O'Connor, his long-term girlfriend. He died of colon cancer at home at age forty-eight and was survived by O'Connor and his three children. Maple was honored with a full police inspector's funeral in Saint Patrick's Cathedral in midtown Manhattan. His body was cremated.

In his eulogy, Giuliani praised Maple's genius for crime fighting, an ability that earned the former deputy police commissioner the reputation as "the man who cleaned up New York."

★

William J. Bratton, with Peter Knobler, *Turnaround: How America's Top Cop Reversed the Crime Epidemic* (1998), details Maple's career, crime fighting, and the development of Compstat. Maple's consulting work with the New Orleans police is profiled in David Remnick, "The Crime Buster," the *New Yorker* (24 Feb. 1997), and long-time friend Michael Daly wrote of the young Maple in "The Cop Who Loved the Oak Bar," *New York* (Apr. 1983). An obituary is in the *New York Times* (6 Aug. 2001).

RITA ORMSBY

MARCUS, Stanley (*b.* 20 April 1905 in Dallas, Texas; *d.* 22 January 2002 in Dallas, Texas), the "Merchant Prince" who, through his fashion and merchandising innovations, developed Neiman Marcus into an international symbol of quality and elegance.

Marcus was the eldest of four sons of Herbert Marcus and Minnie (Lichtenstein) Marcus. He grew up in a close-knit extended family of German and Russian Jewish second-generation immigrants. Herbert Marcus, with his sister Carrie and her husband, Al Neiman, a flamboyant salesman and marketer, all had some retail experience in Dallas stores. This young trio envisioned a specialty store that featured the new concept of ready-to-wear garments instead of custom-made apparel. Dallas in 1907 was an unremarkable small city with flat topography, scorching summers, and freezing winters. The young entrepreneurs advertised the opening of the "Neiman Marcus" store that year in the local papers, promising the best-quality merchandise with the customer's satisfaction guaranteed.

As Marcus grew up, Neiman Marcus weathered economic hard times and a fire that destroyed the original store. His father pushed for a new, larger store in the center of the retail district at the corner of Main and Ervay Streets, where the flagship opened on 15 September 1914. Marcus began working in the new store on Saturdays and school holidays as a messenger, cashier, and junior floorwalker. His father taught him the store philosophy that there was never a good sale for Neiman Marcus unless it was a good buy for the customer.

Marcus attended public schools in Dallas and then entered Amherst College in Massachusetts, where he spent an unhappy year. Frozen out of fraternity life because of anti-Semitism, he transferred to Harvard University in Cambridge, Massachusetts, where a more tolerant atmosphere prevailed. He joined a Jewish fraternity and served as president in his senior year. At Harvard, Marcus was an average student, but a course on the history of the printed book sparked a lifelong interest in books. While a student, he started a successful mail-order book company. After graduation his father convinced him that his future was with Nciman Marcus, rather than as a bookseller. To prepare for a career in retailing, he spent a year at the Harvard Graduate School of Business Administration, where he earned an M.B.A. in 1926.

Before enrolling in graduate school, Marcus traveled with his father to Europe on a buying trip in 1925. During the trip Marcus observed his father on a constant quest for the best dressmakers, tailors, craftsmen, and manufacturers. This philosophy guided Marcus during more than fifty years at the helm of Neiman Marcus.

Among the many innovative merchandising ideas Marcus put into practice was personalized gift wrapping; Neiman Marcus was the first store in the United States to offer the service. He staged weekly fashion shows; Neiman Marcus was the first store outside New York City to advertise in national magazines. In 1926 the first Neiman Marcus Christmas booklet was a sixteen-page mailing to the stores' best customers. Since that time, the catalog has evolved into a beautifully designed wishbook that reaches nearly two million customers. All of Marcus's ideas for Neiman Marcus, highlighted in the media, enhanced the store and the growing reputation and economy of Dallas. His goal was to serve an increasing number of wealthy consumers as well as a rising middle class.

Marcus also realized the importance of Dallas's location, midway between the East and West Texas oil fields, and recognized the benefits of the booming cotton market—

Stanley Marcus. BETTMANN/CORBIS

two factors that helped lead to the rise of the Neiman Marcus stores.

In 1932 Marcus married Mary Cantrell, known as Billie; they had three children. One son, Richard, later became Neiman Marcus president. In 1938 he awarded the first Neiman Marcus Award for Distinguished Service in the Field of Fashion.

In 1959 Marcus and his brother Edward, who was in charge of the mail-order part of the store, collaborated on the offering of a Black Angus steer, dressed or "on the hoof," as an unusual gift in the catalog. The response from customers as well as the media was remarkable. The following year Marcus surmised that deliberately unusual gifts in the catalog would generate even more publicity. He and his staff created the "His and Hers" matching gifts. His and Hers Beechcraft airplanes were the first offering. This was followed over the years by pairs of Chinese junks, hot-air balloons, mummy cases, camels, and limited editions of luxury Cadillac automobiles. Although not many of these items actually sell, they regularly bring the company worldwide publicity.

Marcus made yearly buying trips to Europe and Asia, seeking the finest merchandise. In Stockholm he noticed a store promoting French fashion, merchandise, and cooking. He returned to Dallas and created the Neiman Marcus fortnight, which is held each October. Every year, these two-week events feature merchandise, arts, crafts, fashions, cultural exhibits, and performers from a featured country.

After his father's death in 1950, Marcus was appointed chief executive and began to develop new stores. A lack of capital led to a merger with Broadway-Hale stores, followed by another merger with Carter, Hawley, Hale, Inc., where Marcus was a top executive. Richard Marcus became Neiman Marcus president in 1972. Marcus continued in executive positions for several years and headed his own consulting business. He also wrote books and a weekly editorial column for the *Dallas News*.

Marcus contributed much to Dallas and its cultural life. A heartfelt liberal in a conservative city, he took out a full-page ad in the Dallas newspapers after the Kennedy assassination headed, "What's Right with Dallas," which defended the city but asked for more tolerance. He opened the store's Zodiac Restaurant to African Americans in the 1960s, to begin integration in the city.

Marcus dedicated his 1979 book, *Quest for the Best*, to his wife Billie, who had died in 1978. He married Linda Cumber Robinson Marcus, an anthropologist, who shared his appreciation of art. Marcus had amassed a collection that included modern and contemporary art; with Linda he expanded the collection by acquiring American Indian art, New Mexican devotional art, and African and Latin American arts and crafts. Marcus's collection of 5,000 miniature books was donated to Southern Methodist University in Dallas.

Marcus was an articulate and candid writer as well as a noted lecturer. His first book, *Minding the Store: A Memoir* (1974), tracks the growth of the store as well as his life and career. *Quest for the Best* (1979) explores his pursuit of the best products and services worldwide. *His and Hers: The Fantasy World of the Neiman Marcus Catalogue* (1982) tells the history of the Christmas catalog. *Stanley Marcus from A to Z: Viewpoints Volumes I and II* (2000) offers essays by Marcus on subjects as diverse as gardening, education, his dislike of cocktail parties, and the problems of aging.

Marcus died at age ninety-six. His funeral was attended by 2,000 friends and associates. It was held in the Meyerson Symphony Center—a location large enough for Dallas to bid farewell to a favorite son.

★

Marcus's memoir is *Minding the Store: A Memoir* (1974). For more information, see his books *Quest for the Best* (1979) and *His and Hers, the Fantasy World of the Neiman Marcus Catalogue* (1982). Also see Michael Hazel, ed., *Stanley Marcus from A to Z: Viewpoints Volume I and II* (2000). An obituary is in the *New York Times* (23 Jan. 2002).

ROSEMARIE S. CARDOSO

MARRIOTT, Alice Sheets (*b.* 19 October 1907 in Salt Lake City, Utah; *d.* 17 April 2000 in Washington, D.C.), cofounder of the hotel group Marriott International, Incorporated.

Marriott was born to Edwin Spencer Sheets, a lawyer and a bishop in the local ward of the Mormon church, and Alice (Taylor) Sheets. When Marriott was twelve, her father died in the influenza epidemic of 1918–1919. Four years later, at age sixteen, Marriott entered the University of Utah in Salt Lake City. While she was a junior, Marriott began dating a graduating senior, J. Willard Marriott. In June 1927, at age nineteen, Marriott graduated with honors with a B.A. in Spanish (which would prove beneficial in later years) and as a member of Phi Kappa Phi Honor Society. On 9 June, just after graduation, she married J. Willard Marriott in the Salt Lake Temple. The couple had two sons. The eldest, J. W. Marriott, Jr., became chair and chief executive officer of Marriott International, Inc.; the other, Richard E. Marriott, became the chair of Host Marriott Corp. Following the ceremony, the newlyweds loaded the groom's Model T Ford with their belongings and set off for Washington, D.C., where, on 27 May, J. Willard had opened a nine-stool A&W root beer stand.

Marriott was involved immediately in the business, serving as bookkeeper and making the daily deposits. Although it was profitable during the summer months, the business needed more than root beer sales to stay afloat in the fall and winter months. The Marriotts discussed the idea of serving Mexican and southwestern food. Marriott, who was fluent in Spanish, spoke with the chef at the Mexican embassy, who provided her with recipes for chili con carne and hot tamales and told her where she could order the ingredients. Marriott practiced cooking the recipes in their apartment, while her husband renovated the stand for food service.

Determined to have everything ready so they would not lose their patronage, the stand opened for business in the fall of 1927 as the "The Hot Shoppe." The Hot Shoppe was the first in a chain of popular family restaurants, with Marriott as the chef. Hot Shoppes offered the first curbside service and originated the Mighty Mo "double hamburger" sandwich. Although the Hot Shoppes eventually grew to one hundred restaurants in eleven states, they lost business to competition from fast-food restaurants, such as McDonalds. Meanwhile, the chain formed the foundation for a string of ventures in the hotel and resort industry and in airline catering.

In 1937 the Marriotts were the first to offer airline catering by providing passengers with box lunches. In 1957 they opened the Marriott Twin Bridges Motor Hotel, just

Alice Sheets Marriott, July 1968. AP/WIDE WORLD PHOTOS

vice chair of President Richard M. Nixon's 1969 Inaugural Committee and honorary chair of the 1973 Inaugural Committee. Marriott also was actively involved with various charitable and artistic organizations, serving as a trustee for the John F. Kennedy Center for the Performing Arts. She was on the board of directors of the National Ballet Society and a member of the Women's Committee of the National Symphony Orchestra.

Marriott was a member of several philanthropic organizations, including the Goodwill Industries Guild, International Neighbors Club, and the honorary board of the National Committee for Prevention of Child Abuse. She served on the board of the Metropolitan Washington chapter of the Arthritis Foundation, winning its first Lifetime Achievement Award. Honoring her personal philosophy of volunteerism, the Alice S. Marriott Award for Community Service is awarded annually to a Marriott business unit that exemplifies the volunteer spirit.

Marriott's endowments fund educational institutions, charitable endeavors, and foundations conducting medical research. The University of Utah was the recipient of the Marriotts' support and generosity for many years. For the Marriott Library's twentieth anniversary in 1988, Marriott made a sizable donation and chaired the university's capital campaign. In 1989 she dedicated the Alice Sheets Marriott Center for Dance at the University of Utah as well as the J. Willard and Alice S. Marriott School of Management at Brigham Young University in Provo, Utah. Under her guidance, the family also established the Marriott Foundation for People with Disabilities in 1989.

Marriott was inducted into the Hospitality Industry Hall of Honor posthumously in 2001, joining such industry leaders as Conrad N. Hilton and her husband, J. Willard Marriott. She held two honorary degrees, one from the University of Utah (1974) and one from Mount Vernon College (1980). In 1990 she was awarded the Chi Omega Woman of Achievement. Marriott died at age ninety-two at Georgetown University Hospital of complications after a stroke. Her determination and work ethic helped the nine-stool root beer stand she and her husband opened in 1927 grow into a global hospitality empire.

outside Washington, D.C., in Arlington, Virginia. The night before the grand opening Marriott assisted in hanging pictures in each of the guest rooms. By January 2003 Marriott International had more than 2,600 operating units in the United States and in sixty-six other countries and territories, with annual sales of more than $2 billion.

Although the births of her sons took Marriott away from the day-to-day operations of the company, J. Willard, Sr., often sought his wife's counsel. Her soft-spoken but no-nonsense style, good judgment, and knack for analyzing business concepts proved invaluable as the company grew and diversified. During a time when most wives stayed in the background, Marriott was a full partner in the development of the Marriott Corporation. She became company vice president and the matriarch of the Marriott holdings. Throughout her life she was an active member of the Church of Jesus Christ of Latter-Day Saints.

In addition to her corporate and family responsibilities, Marriott devoted time and money to many civic and charitable organizations and causes. She had several high-ranking roles in the Republican Party and was treasurer of three national conventions (1964, 1968, and 1972). She was also

★

The J. Willard and Alice Sheets Marriott Papers (1924–1989) at the Marriott Library at the University of Utah contain materials documenting Marriott's personal, professional, political, religious, and charitable activities. See also J. Willard Marriott, Jr., and Kathi Ann Brown, *The Spirit to Serve: Marriott's Way* (2001). An obituary is in the *Washington Post* (19 Apr. 2000).

REBECCA J. TIMMONS

MARTIN, Donald Edward ("Don") (*b.* 18 May 1931 in Clifton, New Jersey; *d.* 6 January 2000 in Miami, Florida), wry illustrator best known for his hilarious cartoon drawings, which for three decades contributed to the mayhem of *Mad* magazine.

Martin was the son of Wilbur Lawrence Martin, a salesman, and Helen Henrietta (Husselrath) Martin. He and his brother grew up in New Jersey, where Martin attended the Newark Institute of Fine and Industrial Arts from 1948 to 1951. He transferred to the Pennsylvania Academy of Fine Arts in Philadelphia, taking his degree in 1952. Despite his original aspiration to become a painter, Martin was increasingly attracted to the zany world of cartoons. He moved to New York City in 1953, where he worked as a freelance artist and greeting-card designer and held a job as a paste-up artist. Martin married Rosemary Troetschel on 14 December 1956; they had one son.

In the early 1950s, when Martin was becoming established in New York, a new and unorthodox comic-book startup, called *Mad*, remained relatively obscure. By 1955, however, the publication had evolved into a glossy-covered magazine with black-and-white pages. Around that time Martin submitted a few samples of his cartoons, with goofy and moronic-looking characters, to *Mad*. The magazine's owner, William M. Gaines, appreciated the artistic style as well as the parodies that permeated Martin's cartoons, and in 1956 the first Don Martin comic to be published in *Mad* appeared in issue number 29. The strip, called "Alfred E. Newman Answers Your Questions," was a clever takeoff on advice columns. The title of the feature made reference to the *Mad* mascot, Alfred E. Newman, who came to be portrayed in later issues as an odd-looking man with an idiotic expression on his face. Thus, Martin and his goofy cartoon characters seemed to fit perfectly with the format of *Mad*, and before long he was contributing comic strips, called "Don Martin Department," to the magazine on a regular basis.

Dubbed "Mad's Maddest cartoonist" and billed by editors of the magazine as one of *Mad*'s "usual gang of idiots," Martin created a world filled with human menageries of inept bunglers. Quick-witted with quips and visually expressive, Martin drew oddball cartoon characters that were virtually devoid of shoulders, a feature that was emphasized by their exaggerated waistlines. He drew nerdy-looking people with bulbous noses, pelican jaws, and feet that were steamroller flat, with enormously wrinkled arches and toes. A typical character in one of Martin's cartoon strips might stand calmly, with an ax lodged in the top of his head and an expression of gaping bewilderment on his face. As Martin conceived these funny-looking people, he endowed each character with a name equivalent to his or her appearance. Martin's flagship schlep was a quizzical-looking gent

named Fonebone. Other Martin characters were saddled with such names as Karbunkle, Dr. Dork, and the good-natured Festerand. In Martin's cartoons the simplest word or phrase might be taken literally to a disastrous consequence, as in "Cat got your tongue?"—the cue for a cat to walk by gripping a human tongue in its mouth.

It was Martin's ongoing implication, through the respective titles of his comic strips, that the central characters were modeled after him. In truth, these cartoon clowns represented Martin's alter ego at best, because he was known to his friends as shy; his characters, in contrast, were knuckleheaded buffoons who lived in a madcap world of outrageous puns.

In 1962 Martin published a compilation of all new cartoons in paperback form. Cowritten with E. Solomon Rosenblum, the volume was called *Don Martin Steps Out*. Martin and Rosenblum followed with *Don Martin Bounces Back* in 1963 and *Don Martin Drops Thirteen Stories* in 1965. In 1977 he published *Don Martin Forges Ahead* in his ongoing series of paperbacks, which by 1986 totaled thirteen publications.

By means of his off-the-wall parodies, Martin helped bring *Mad* magazine to a peak circulation of more than two million copies in 1972, and he contributed to the modern American culture with hilarious inventions, such as National Gorilla Suit Day. Martin and Troetschel divorced in January 1976, and Martin married Norma Haimes, an artist and librarian, on 23 August 1979. They had no children. In 1987 a disagreement between Martin and *Mad* management over copyright ownership of his cartoon strips resulted in a permanent rift between Martin and *Mad*. He continued as a freelance cartoonist, publishing his wacky comic strips in a rival magazine, called *Cracked*, which was similar in content and style to *Mad*. Despite the circumstance of Martin's departure, the editor of *Mad* never applied the "maddest cartoonist" appellation to another artist, according to the *Mad* chronicler Maria Reidelbach.

Suffering from failing eyesight in his later years, Martin underwent corneal transplant surgery; wearing special contact lenses and using a magnifier, he continued to draw his maniac characters. He also worked as a television animator and in 1994 launched a cartoon magazine on his own, called *Don Martin*. A member of the Graphics Artists Guild and the National Cartoonists Society, Martin was an executive committee member of the Cartoonist Guild. In 1980 he was honored with the Ignatz Award at the Orlando Comicon, an international comic-book convention. Over the years his various paperbacks sold more than seven million copies. He died of cancer at age sixty-eight at Baptist Hospital in Miami.

In an obituary in the *Independent* (London), Denis Gifford compared the slapstick humor of Martin with the comedic style of the silent movie stars Charlie Chaplin and

Buster Keaton. Martin wrote into his cartoons a witty rep-artee of sound effects, such as the classic "Shtoink!" This descriptive noise, once used by Martin to represent the sound of a nurse drawing blood, became well known as the personalized license plate on his car. In 2001 Edward Norris, John E. Hett, and a team of editors compiled a sixty-page dictionary of Don Martin sound effects—from the AAAAGH! EEEEEOOOOWACK of a dentist removing a tooth to the ZZZZOOWNT sound of a drill penetrating a fence.

★

Maria Reidelbach discusses Martin's contributions to *Mad* in *Completely Mad* (1991), a chronicle of the history of the magazine. John Hett, "Don Martin Dictionary," was published in *The Journal of MADness* 12 (Nov. 2001). Obituaries are in the *New York Times* (8 Jan. 2000) and *Independent* (London) (11 Jan. 2000).

G. COOKSEY

MASTERS, William Howell (*b.* 27 December 1915 in Cleveland, Ohio; *d.* 16 February 2001 in Tucson, Arizona), sex researcher and therapist who, with his colleague Virginia Johnson, wrote the best-selling book *Human Sexual Response* (1966), which provided both popular and scientific support for the sexual revolution of the late 1960s and early 1970s.

William H. Masters. AP/WIDE WORLD PHOTOS

Masters was the son of affluent parents, Francis Wynne Masters and Estabrooks (Taylor) Masters. He attended seventh and eighth grade in Kansas City, Missouri, then spent four years at the Lawrenceville School in Lawrenceville, New Jersey, graduating in 1934. As a premedicine student at Hamilton College in Clinton, New York, he was a member of the football, basketball, and debating teams and a member of the literary society Alpha Delta Phi. After receiving his B.S. in 1938 with majors in science and literature, Masters became a medical student at the University of Rochester School of Medicine and Dentistry in New York, earning his M.D. in 1943. In the 1970s both his undergraduate and medical alma maters awarded him honorary Sc.D. degrees.

Master's mentor at Rochester was the anatomist and endocrinologist George Washington Corner, the discoverer of the hormonal basis of menstruation in 1928, the codiscoverer of progesterone in 1929, and the chair of the National Research Council's Committee for Research in Problems of Sex from 1947 to 1956. Corner encouraged Masters to pursue the scientific study of reproduction, first in animals, then in humans. Corner was also an early supporter of Alfred Kinsey's sex research, and could be regarded as the godfather of the serious academic scrutiny of human sexual behavior.

On 13 June 1942 Masters married Elisabeth Ellis; they had a son and a daughter. That same year he was commissioned as an ensign in the U.S. Naval Reserve and was promoted to lieutenant in 1943. Discharged, he moved to St. Louis, where he held a series of internships and residencies in obstetrics, gynecology, pathology, and internal medicine at the St. Louis Maternity Hospital and at Barnes Hospital. In 1947 Masters joined the clinical faculty of obstetrics and gynecology at the Washington University School of Medicine in St. Louis and established a private gynecological practice in the city. He began conducting sex research under laboratory conditions at Washington University in 1954. He hired Virginia Johnson as his assistant in 1957 because he wanted the mature perspective of a mother.

With funding from the National Institutes of Health (NIH), Masters and Johnson recorded photographic, electrocardiographic, electroencephalographic, biochemical, metabolic, and other scientific data on hundreds of paid volunteers as they copulated and masturbated in the laboratory. In 1964 in St. Louis they founded the Reproductive Biology Research Foundation, which they renamed the Masters and Johnson Institute in 1973.

Masters and Johnson described and analyzed the sex act

in four chronological phases: excitement, plateau, orgasm, and resolution. After writing only a few professional journal articles, they published their results as a book, *Human Sexual Response*. Released on 18 April 1966, it sold more than 300,000 hardcover copies in the next four years. The work fostered a new frankness about sex, a willingness to discuss it openly in mixed company, and a relaxing of social inhibitions that eventually led to the publication of popular sex manuals such as Alex Comfort's *The Joy of Sex* (1972).

Human Sexual Response superseded both of the so-called Kinsey Reports: *Sexual Behavior in the Human Male* (1948) and *Sexual Behavior in the Human Female* (1953). Its main advance over these earlier studies was that Kinsey only interviewed his subjects, while Masters and Johnson actually observed human sexual action and measured its phenomena. Their perspective was quantitative, physiological, and psychological, whereas Kinsey's was qualitative and sociological.

As well as their laboratory research, Masters and Johnson were also concerned with clinical therapy and psychological healing. In 1959 they began to develop a method of sexual counseling that emphasized the teamwork of a male therapist, a female therapist, and the sexually dysfunctional couple, and integrated medical diagnosis, laboratory tests, and roundtable discussion. Masters and Johnson preferred a two-week program of cotherapy with a five-year follow-up. They described this technique in their second book, *Human Sexual Inadequacy* (1970).

Masters and Johnson also wrote *The Pleasure Bond* (1975); *Homosexuality in Perspective* (1979); and, with Robert C. Kolodny, *Textbook of Sexual Medicine* (1979), *Human Sexuality* (1982), *Masters and Johnson on Sex and Human Loving* (1986), *Crisis: Heterosexual Behavior in the Age of AIDS* (1988), *Biological Foundations of Human Sexuality* (1993), and *Heterosexuality* (1994).

A major paradox of Masters's life was that he shunned the limelight but was not afraid to rock the boat. This paradox can be explained by viewing him foremost as a medical professional, dedicated to the Hippocratic ideal of healing his patients, whatever the consequences. He regarded the ability to talk frankly and guiltlessly about sex as an essential component of healthy human relationships, and believed that true morality, especially sexual morality, must be built upon accurate science.

Masters was deeply concerned with preventing the abuse of patients, clients, spouses, and children by those whom they most trusted. He fought quackery in the sex-therapy profession, judged his medical colleagues sternly, and urged that patients seduced by their physicians should neither submit quietly nor bring merely civil charges of malpractice, but should bring criminal charges of rape. Late in his career he developed methods to treat the victims and perpetrators of child abuse. In the 1980s Masters's published

results and therapeutic methods came under increasingly harsh criticism, especially his findings about AIDS, and his views generally fell out of favor.

Masters and his first wife divorced in 1970; he married Johnson on 7 January 1971; they divorced in 1993. That same year he married Geraldine Baker Oliver, the sister of his Hamilton roommate. In 1994 he closed the Masters and Johnson Institute and retired to Tucson, Arizona. He died at the Tucson Medical Center Hospice from complications of Parkinson's disease.

In spite of the apparently liberal or even radical overtones and implications of his research, Masters was a conservative Republican and devout Episcopalian. He remained constantly under fire from other conservatives, especially for his spirited defense of rights for homosexuals in the 1970s and 1980s. He was a private, quiet individual who did not seek to make social waves, but to conduct what he and his colleagues believed to be serious physiological, psychological, and gynecological research with beneficial clinical and therapeutic impact.

★

There is no single repository for Masters's papers and correspondence. Some are held by the Library of Congress in Washington, D.C., and the University of Michigan in Ann Arbor. The alumni archives of Hamilton College contain a significant amount of biographical information, as do the feature stories on *Human Sexual Response* in *Life* (24 June 1966) and *Newsweek* (10 June 1966). See also Paul A. Robinson, *The Modernization of Sex: Havelock Ellis, Alfred Kinsey, William Masters, and Virginia Johnson* (1976), and Vern L. Bullough, *Science in the Bedroom* (1994). An obituary is in the *New York Times* (19 Feb. 2001).

ERIC V.D. LUFT

MATHEWS, Edwin Lee ("Eddie") (*b*. 13 October 1931 in Texarkana, Texas; *d*. 18 February 2001 in La Jolla, California), Hall of Fame third baseman who, along with teammate Hank Aaron, formed one of the most prolific power-hitting duos in baseball history.

Mathews was the only child of Edwin Mathews and Eloise Mathews. Texarkana, a blue-collar city of factories and textile mills located on the Texas-Arkansas border, was on the eastern edge of what came to be known as the Dust Bowl. When drought conditions ruined the local economy in 1935, the Mathews family joined millions of other Americans during the Great Depression in migrating west, eventually settling in Santa Barbara, California. Edwin Mathews found work as a wire chief for Western Union, where his responsibilities included telegraphing the play-by-play accounts of minor league baseball games. Occasionally, he would bring his young son into the press box, and it was there that "Eddie" Mathews was first introduced to the national pastime.

An indifferent student but a standout athlete, in his senior year of high school Mathews was named to the All–Southern California team in both football and baseball. That spring Mathews received offers of football scholarships from the University of California, Los Angeles, and the University of Southern California. But his first love was baseball, and on the night of his graduation in 1949, he accepted a $6,000 offer to play in the Boston Braves farm system. In signing with the Braves, Mathews rejected a $30,000 offer from the Pittsburgh Pirates, because the bonus rules of the time stipulated that players who signed for over $6,000 could not spend more than one year in the minor leagues.

Mathews made his professional debut at third base for the High Point–Thomasville Hi-Toms of the North Carolina State league. He quickly established himself as one of the game's best prospects, hitting .363 with seventeen home runs in just 240 at bats. In 1950 he moved up to the Atlanta Crackers of the Southern Association, where he continued his powerful hitting, blasting thirty-two home runs and helping Atlanta to the league pennant. His progress through the minor leagues was briefly curtailed in 1951, when he was drafted into the U.S. Navy during the Korean War. After spending a few months playing baseball for the Navy Training Center team in San Diego, Mathews received a discharge from the service when his father became ill with tuberculosis. Mathews would later say his greatest regret was that his father, who remained an invalid until his death in 1954, never got to see him play in the major leagues.

After splitting the remainder of the 1951 season between Atlanta and the minor league Milwaukee Brewers of the American Association, Mathews was invited to the Boston Braves' spring training camp in 1952. A few days before the start of the season, the Braves traded away their regular third baseman, and the twenty-year-old Mathews was thrust into the starting lineup in his first season as a major leaguer.

Like his boyhood idols Stan Musial of the St. Louis Cardinals and Ted Williams of the Boston Red Sox, baseball's two best left-handed hitters during the 1940s, Mathews initially employed a closed stance at the plate. Also similar to those great hitters, Mathews had a short stride and quick, powerful wrists that were so impressive that one sportswriter quipped, "More ballplayers talk about Mathews' wrists than about Marilyn Monroe's legs." In his rookie season, which would also be the Braves last year in Boston, Mathews belted twenty-five home runs. But his closed stance made him vulnerable to inside pitches, and he led the league in strikeouts.

When the Braves franchise moved to Milwaukee in

Eddie Mathews, May 1956. BETTMANN/CORBIS

1953, Mathews opened up his stance, and the adjustment paid immediate dividends. Not only did his strikeout totals go down, but he also connected for a league-leading forty-seven home runs, while driving in 135 runs and batting .302. He was still only twenty-two years old, but already pundits were comparing him to some of the greatest sluggers in the history of the game, with one writer going so far as to suggest that Mathews might be "the second Babe Ruth."

Mathews was not that good, but during his thirteen-year stay in Milwaukee, he averaged better than thirty-four home runs and ninety-eight runs batted in (RBI) a season. He twice led the league in home runs and paced the circuit in walks four times. His offense helped turn Milwaukee into a perennial contender in the National League. From 1953 to 1965 the Braves finished with a winning record every year, claiming back-to-back pennants in 1957 and 1958 and winning the World Championship in 1957. Soft-spoken and aloof with the media, Mathews was often overlooked on a team that included a future 300-game winner in Warren Spahn and the future all-time home-run king in Hank Aaron. Yet during their thirteen years as teammates, Mathews hit just twenty-one fewer home runs than Aaron; together the pair collected 863 round-trippers, the most ever hit by two teammates. At least one publication took notice; in 1954 *Sports Illustrated* put Mathews and his powerful swing on the cover of the magazine's inaugural issue.

After the Braves moved from Milwaukee to Atlanta prior to the 1966 season (Mathews was the only Brave to play in Boston, Milwaukee, and Atlanta), Mathews's offensive production began to slip, and for the first time in his career he failed to hit twenty home runs. "If I'd been a horse, they would have shot me a long time ago," Mathews joked to one reporter. Prior to the 1967 season, the Braves traded Mathews to the Houston Astros of the National League, where he continued to struggle, batting just .238 before being shipped in midseason to the Detroit Tigers of the American League. Warming the bench for the Tigers for parts of two seasons, Mathews retired after Detroit won the 1968 World Series.

Mathews's personal life and postretirement activities were chaotic. Divorced three times, his ex-wives included Virjcan Lauby, whom he married in 1954 and with whom he had three children, and Elizabeth Busch Burke, the daughter of the St. Louis Cardinals owner August Busch, Jr. His fourth marriage, to Judy Mathews, lasted until his death.

After his retirement as a player, Mathews was a coach for the Atlanta Braves in 1971. Promoted to manager in 1972, he was fired in 1974 after compiling a 149–161 record. Later he worked for the Milwaukee Brewers as a scout, but tales of his excessive drinking hurt his reputation and likely prevented him from getting more opportunities. When the Atlanta Braves hired him as a minor league hitting instructor in 1987, the club included a sobriety clause in his contract. Mathews kept drinking anyway, and the organization fired him in 1989. It was his last job in baseball.

For his part, Mathews refused to apologize for his drinking; the first sentence of his autobiography reads, "I was born during Prohibition, and I've spent most of my life trying to get caught up." Misfortune struck Mathews again in 1996 when his pelvis was crushed in a fall while disembarking from a cruise ship. In failing health after that, Mathews died of complications from pneumonia at age sixty-nine. He is buried in Santa Barbara Cemetery.

Mathews was elected to the National Baseball Hall of Fame in 1978, on his fifth time on the ballot. Upon his retirement, no third baseman in history could match Mathews in career home runs (512), runs (1,509), RBI (1,453), and slugging percentage (.509). Mathews was one of greatest power hitters in the history of the game, and one of the two or three best third basemen who ever lived.

★

The National Baseball Hall of Fame Library in Cooperstown, New York, maintains a clipping file on Mathews. His autobiography, written with Bob Broeg, is *Eddie Mathews and the National Pastime* (1994). A highly readable account, it offers Mathews's

perspective on his career accomplishments and later struggles. The definitive source for all baseball statistics is John Thorn et al., eds., *Total Baseball*, 7th ed. (2001). Obituaries are in the *New York Times* and *Chicago Tribune* (19 Feb. 2001).

DAVID JONES

MATTHAU, Walter (*b.* 1 October 1920 in New York City; *d.* 1 July 2000 in Santa Monica, California), beloved performer who originated the role of Oscar Madison in *The Odd Couple* on Broadway (1965) and earned a best supporting actor Academy Award for *The Fortune Cookie* (1966).

Throughout his life, Matthau concocted fabrications about his past. Among the many untruths he told journalists: his original surname was "Matuschanaskayasky"; his father was a Russian Orthodox priest; his mother was a Romanian Gypsy; his middle name was "Foghorn," which he claimed to have noted on his Social Security card application; and his hobby was collecting hospital bedpans. Actually, he was born Walter Matthow on New York's Lower East Side. His father, Melas, also known as Milton, had been a peddler in Kiev, then part of the Russian Empire. Upon arriving in the United States in the early part of the twentieth century,

Walter Matthau, 1986. AP/WIDE WORLD PHOTOS

he worked as an electrician, a process server, and a photographer. Matthau's mother, Rose (Berolsky) Matthow, was born on a farm in Lithuania.

In 1923, when Matthau was three and his older brother, Henry, was five, Milton abandoned his family. To support her children, Rose Matthow toiled in the Lower East Side sweatshops, sewing women's underwear. The Matthows resided in a series of tenements, often moving because Rose was unable to pay the rent. "When my mother bought socks," Matthau recalled, "she didn't buy seconds. She bought fourths." As a youngster, he earned pennies by shining shoes, selling newspapers, and peddling ice cream and soda pop. While he loved sports—he was particularly adept at playing handball—he also was an avid reader who began reciting Shakespeare at age seven and developed a love of classical music and opera. Mozart became his preferred composer. He also fantasized about becoming an actor. In the mid-1930s, while working as a concessionaire in the Lower East Side Yiddish theaters, he had walk-on roles in several productions.

In his youth, Matthau began indulging in what would become a lifelong habit: gambling. At first, he wagered pocket change on handball games. Through the decades, he constantly bet on baseball games, horse races, and boxing matches. In the 1990s he wagered $10,000 on whether the Los Angeles Lakers center Shaquille O'Neal would make a free throw. At a black-tie event, he bet the talk-show host Larry King $20 that Matthau's limousine would arrive first. It would be impossible to estimate how much money Matthau lost in his lifetime, but a conservative figure would be $5 million.

Matthau graduated from Seward Park High School in January 1939 and took odd jobs in and around the Lower East Side. He joined the Civilian Conservation Corps and worked as a forester in Montana. In April 1942, four months after the Japanese attack on Pearl Harbor that brought the United States into World War II, he enlisted in the United States Army Air Corps. Eventually, he was shipped overseas, where he was assigned to the 453rd Bomb Group of the Eighth Air Force and worked as a link-trainer instructor at Royal Air Force station 144 in Old Buckenham, England.

After the war the GI Bill enabled Matthau to pursue his dream of becoming an actor. He returned to New York and enrolled in the Dramatic Workshop of the New School for Social Research, where he studied with the director-producer-playwright Erwin Piscator. His acting school roles ranged from Sir Toby Belch in *Twelfth Night* to "1st Soldier" in Jean-Paul Sartre's *Flies*. While at the New School, he altered his surname from "Matthow" to "Matthau." He began appearing in summer-stock productions and made his Broadway debut in 1948, playing a candle bearer in *Anne of the 1000 Days*. That same year, he

married Geraldine Grace Johnson, a fellow acting student. The union produced two children. Their son, David, became an actor in the 1970s.

The 1950s found Matthau frequently appearing on Broadway. While most of the plays in which he appeared were flops, he generally earned positive reviews, and he began to establish a reputation as a reliable character actor. This stage work proved invaluable as he continued learning his craft and evolving as an actor. During one of his more successful runs, in *Will Success Spoil Rock Hunter?* (1955), he met and fell in love with Carol Marcus Saroyan, an ex-debutante and sometime actress who was twice divorced from the writer William Saroyan. Matthau eventually divorced his first wife, and he and Carol were married on 21 August 1959. A son, Charles, was born four years later.

During the 1950s Matthau also had starring and supporting roles in scores of television shows. In 1950 he played various characters during a thirteen-week run on *Mr. I. Magination,* a children's program. One of his favorite parts was Iago in a 1953 *Philco Television Playhouse* production of *Othello.* It was his lone professional Shakespearean role. Matthau almost made his screen debut starring opposite Marilyn Monroe in *The Seven-Year Itch* (1955). He screen-tested for the part but lost it to Tom Ewell. He did, however, make his initial screen appearance in *The Kentuckian* (1955), playing a whip-wielding heavy. Most of his early movie roles were dramatic ones, as either villains or sympathetic observers of the hero.

At this point in his career, Matthau preferred stage acting, taking film and television roles only to supplement his income. To pay off gambling debts, he accepted starring roles in *Gangster Story* (1960), an ultra-low-budget melodrama that he also directed, and *Tallahassee 7000* (1960–1961), a syndicated television series. Meanwhile, his standing in the world of theater rose steadily, and he earned a Tony Award nomination for best supporting actor for his performance as a Russian-accented conductor's manager in *Once More, With Feeling* (1958). He won the award for *A Shot in the Dark* (1962), in which he played a debonair aristocrat.

Then in his mid-forties, Matthau might have remained a well-respected New York stage actor and Hollywood supporting player. In 1965, however, he won the role that earned him stardom: Oscar Madison, New York sportswriter and slob extraordinaire, in Neil Simon's hit comedy *The Odd Couple*. For his performance, Matthau earned another Tony Award, this one for best actor. "That was the plutonium I needed," he once remarked. "It all started happening after that."

The Odd Couple was Matthau's final New York stage credit. His next role also made him a movie star: *The Fortune Cookie,* a Billy Wilder comedy in which he played "Whiplash Willie" Gingrich, a shyster lawyer. *The Fortune*

Cookie was his first credit opposite Jack Lemmon, with whom he would often be partnered onscreen during the next thirty-two years. With ten days left in the shoot, however, Matthau suffered an almost fatal heart attack. Wilder refused to replace him with another actor, and after a five-month recuperation, he returned to the set to complete filming.

Formerly a diehard New Yorker, Matthau permanently abandoned the East Coast for California in 1968, eventually settling in Pacific Palisades. His first starring screen role was in *A Guide for a Married Man* (1967), in which he played a husband who tentatively considers committing adultery. He reprised the Oscar Madison role onscreen in *The Odd Couple* (1968), with Lemmon replacing Art Carney, Matthau's Broadway costar, as Felix Ungar. In the screen version of the hit Broadway musical *Hello, Dolly!* (1969), Matthau played Horace Vandergelder to Barbra Streisand's Dolly Levi. The on-set friction between the two actors made headlines.

The 1970s was a busy decade for Matthau. He had some of his best screen roles, including *Kotch* (1971), directed by Lemmon, in which he played a widower in his seventies; *The Sunshine Boys* (1975), which featured him as a cantankerous vaudevillian; and *The Bad News Bears* (1976), in which he played a broken-down Little League coach. His performances in the first two earned him Academy Award nominations for best actor. Matthau also gave solid dramatic performances in *Charley Varrick* (1973), playing a stunt pilot turned bank robber, and *The Taking of Pelham One Two Three* (1974), in which he was cast as a New York City transit detective. Amid all these professional accolades, he again was plagued by ill health and underwent coronary bypass surgery in 1976.

Matthau's career began to slump during the 1980s. None of his films from this period ranks with his earlier successes, and by decade's end his stardom had faded. He even returned to dramatic television, which he had abandoned after his *Odd Couple* success, appearing in several made-for-television movies. The 1990s saw a resurgence of his screen career, as he won over a new generation playing Mr. Wilson in the children's comedy *Dennis the Menace* (1993). More important, he and Lemmon scored a hit playing aging antagonists in *Grumpy Old Men* (1993), *Grumpier Old Men* (1995), and *Out to Sea* (1997). One final pairing, in *The Odd Couple II* (1998), was less successful. Perhaps Matthau's favorite 1990s credit was *The Grass Harp* (1995), based on a Truman Capote novella and directed by his son Charles, with whom he shared a close, intensely loving relationship.

As he aged, Matthau's health continued to fail. Starting in the late 1980s, he suffered from a multitude of afflictions, including heart blockage, anemia, colon cancer, pneumonia, sepsis, and acute respiratory distress syndrome. His final screen credit was *Hanging Up* (2000), in which he played a self-absorbed screenwriter. He died of a heart attack at the age of seventy-nine and is buried in Pierce Brothers Westwood Memorial Park in Los Angeles.

Because of his roles in comedies, Matthau often is thought of as a comedian. Actually, he was a comic actor, and it frequently is forgotten that he was equally adept in dramatic roles. Rarely did he ever give a stale performance, even when his material was less than first-rate. Matthau was a character actor who became a star and who was adored by audiences for his lovable grouchiness, his definitive portrayals of grumpy old and middle-aged men, and his onscreen chemistry with Lemmon.

★

An important early Matthau interview appears in Lillian and Helen Ross, *The Player: A Profile of an Art* (1962). His wife, Carol Matthau, cites him extensively in her memoir, *Among the Porcupines* (1992), and his life story is told in Rob Edelman and Audrey Kupferberg, *Matthau: A Life* (2002). Obituaries are in the *New York Times* and *Washington Post* (both 2 July 2000).

ROB EDELMAN

MAXWELL, William Keepers, Jr. (*b.* 16 August 1908 in Lincoln, Illinois; *d.* 31 July 2000 in Manhattan, New York City), novelist and longtime fiction editor at the *New Yorker*, where he helped shape the careers of the writers Sylvia Townsend Warner, John O'Hara, Eudora Welty, John Cheever, Frank O'Connor, John Updike, Harold Brodkey, and many others.

Maxwell, the son of William Keepers Maxwell, an insurance executive, and Eva Blossom (Blinn) Maxwell, a homemaker, spent the first fourteen years of his life in Lincoln, a typical midwestern small town that provided, he later remarked, "three quarters of the material I would need for the rest of my writing life." When Maxwell was ten, his mother died in the influenza epidemic of 1918–1919. It was a wrenching experience he would return to again and again in his writing, most directly in the novel *They Came Like Swallows*. With his mother's death, he wrote in a biographical essay, "the beautiful . . . world of my childhood was swept away. . . . And so . . . I began to cherish in my mind the people and scenes of the past."

Maxwell received a B.A. from the University of Illinois in Urbana in 1930 and an M.A. in English literature from Harvard University in Cambridge, Massachusetts, in 1931. He returned to the University of Illinois to pursue a doctorate and teach English composition. Two years later, he left school with the intention of becoming a writer. He so enjoyed working on a biographical project that he abandoned his intention of becoming a poet and embarked on *Bright Center of Heaven,* a novel published in 1934.

William Maxwell. MAX AGUILERA-HELLWEG/TIME LIFE PICTURES/
GETTY IMAGES

In 1936 Maxwell moved to New York City, where, armed with a letter of reference from his publisher, he applied for a job at the *New Yorker*, an eleven-year-old weekly that was just becoming an outlet for serious fiction and poetry. Hired as a junior editor, his first principal duty was to meet every week with the magazine's regular cartoonists and explain why their submissions had been rejected. Soon he was also working with short-story writers and receiving some valuable advice from the editor who had hired him, Katharine Angell White (who became a close and lifelong friend). He noted, "I learned [from White] that it is not the work of an editor to teach writers how to write." Over a forty-year career as an editor at the magazine, Maxwell put this lesson into practice. He always felt that his job was not to put his own stamp on a short story or in any way to instruct writers, but rather, through Socratic questions and minimal editorial changes, help them achieve their best work. As he explained in an interview with the *Paris Review,* "I came to feel that real editing meant changing as little as possible."

Maxwell was devoted to his writers. In conversation, his strong feelings were sometimes masked by his characteristic courtly reserve. But they flourished in correspondence, where Maxwell's warmth and enthusiasm shone through.

A typical effusion was in a 1941 letter to the short-story writer Nancy Hale: "Whenever I read anything of yours, in manuscript here, or at my dentist's, I am convinced against a mountain of evidence that there is such a thing as the human heart." Not surprisingly, Maxwell developed intimate and lasting friendships with many of his writers (including all those named previously). His twenty-year correspondence with Frank O'Connor was published under the title *The Happiness of Getting It Down Right* (1996), and his forty-year correspondence with Sylvia Townsend Warner under the title *The Element of Lavishness* (2001). However, Maxwell could be caustic when necessary. Before J. D. Salinger had succeeded in publishing a story in the *New Yorker,* Maxwell wrote to Salinger's agent, "We think Mr. Salinger is a very talented young man and wish to God you could get him to write simply and naturally."

Maxwell met his wife, Emily Gilman Noyes, when she applied for a job as poetry editor of the *New Yorker.* They married on 17 May 1945 and had two daughters.

Maxwell completed his second novel, *They Came Like Swallows* (1937), by the time he started his job at the *New Yorker.* During his first few years at the magazine, he had little time for his own fiction writing. Eventually, he moved to a three-day-a-week work schedule and devoted two days a week to writing. He wrote in the morning in the study of his Manhattan apartment, wearing his pajamas and a bathrobe. Much admired in the literary world for his quiet precision of language and emotion, although not well known outside of it, he wrote the novels *The Folded Leaf* (1945), *Time Will Darken It* (1948), and *The Chateau* (1961), and a family memoir, *Ancestors* (1971). Maxwell retired from the *New Yorker* in 1976. Subsequently he concentrated on shorter fiction—including the novella *So Long, See You Tomorrow* (1980), which won the William Dean Howells Award from the American Academy of Arts and Letters for the most distinguished work of American fiction published in the last five years; and the short stories in *Over by the River and Other Stories* (1977) and *Billie Dyer and Other Stories* (1992). Displaying a new force and gravity in these works, while retaining his customary gentle irony and attention to the past, he gained more readers and critical attention than ever before. In the years after he retired as editor, he also published a collection of essays and reviews, *The Outermost Dream* (1989), and a children's book, *Mrs. Donald's Dog Bun and His Home Away from Home* (1995). Maxwell's collected stories, *All the Days and Nights,* was published in 1994.

Perhaps Maxwell's most widely read piece of writing was an essay, "Nearing Ninety," which was published in the *New York Times Magazine* on 9 March 1997, when he was eighty-eight, and was accompanied by a full-page photographic portrait. "I have regrets," he wrote, "but there are not very many of them and, fortunately, I forget what they are." On the other hand, Maxwell reported that his memories of his boyhood were nearly unclouded by age. He recalled a time when his father hitched up the horse and took him and his mother for a sleigh ride. "I was bundled up to the nose, between my father and mother, where nothing, not even the cold, could get at me. The very perfection of happiness." Maxwell died at his home in Manhattan at age ninety-one, eight days after the death of his wife.

Along with his colleagues Katharine White, Gustave Lobrano, and Roger Angell, Maxwell was responsible for establishing the *New Yorker* as the preeminent periodical for short fiction in the English-speaking world. More than any of them—indeed, perhaps more than any other editor in history—Maxwell took his writers' literary struggles to heart. In the process, he helped to shape some of the most memorable short fiction of the twentieth century.

★

Maxwell's papers are held at the University of Illinois at Urbana-Champaign. The *New Yorker* records at the New York Public Library contain many letters to and from Maxwell. Maxwell figures prominently in two memoirs by *New Yorker* writers: Alec Wilkinson, *My Mentor: A Young Man's Friendship with William Maxwell* (2002), and Larry Woiwode, *What I Think I Did: A Season of Survival in Two Acts* (2000). Maxwell's interview for the *Paris Review* is in George Plimpton, *Writers at Work: The Paris Review Interviews, Seventh Series* (1986). An obituary is in the *New York Times* (1 Aug. 2000).

BEN YAGODA

MERRICK, David (*b.* 27 November 1911 in St. Louis, Missouri; *d.* 25 April 2000 in London, England), one of the most successful independent producers in the history of Broadway theater, known for the high quality of his shows and the masterful publicity stunts that extended their runs.

Merrick was born David Lee Margulois, the youngest of six children of Russian-Jewish immigrant parents Samuel Margulois, the owner of several grocery stores, and his wife, Celia Margulois. Raised by his married sister, Sayde, after his parents divorced, he saw every touring show he could; when he moved to New York City to pursue a career in the theater, he changed his name to Merrick, with conscious reference to David Garrick, the eighteenth-century English actor.

After graduating from Central High School in St. Louis in 1930, Merrick attended Washington University for two and a half years. He completed his undergraduate studies at St. Louis University, continuing on for a law degree in 1937. While in law school, he played the role of Tubal in a student production of Shakespeare's *Merchant of Venice*. He also acted in the Young Men's Hebrew Association pro-

David Merrick, 1970. AP/WIDE WORLD PHOTOS

duction of Clifford Odets's *Awake and Sing* in 1936, but putting on the show appealed to him more than acting in it. After graduation, he set up a desk in another attorney's office, but spent considerable time in New York attending plays and pursuing an involvement in the theatre.

In 1938 Merrick married Leonore Beck, a St. Louis resident he had known as a student, and her modest inheritance supported his dream of becoming a Broadway producer. Merrick was married six times altogether. His first five marriages ended in divorce. His second marriage was to Jeanne Gilbert (1963); they had one daughter. The third marriage was to Etan Aronson (1969), with whom he had another daughter. The fourth marriage was to Karen Prunczik (1982). The fifth was his remarriage to Etan (1983). The last marriage was to Natalie Lloyd in November 1999.

In 1939 the Merricks took up residence in New York City. In 1940, after studying the market, Merrick invested $5,000 in Herman Shumlin's production of *The Male Animal*. The investment paid back $20,000 and, more importantly, led to his apprenticeship as Shumlin's general manager from 1945 to 1949. Shumlin noted Merrick's passion for the theater, his artistic sense, and his keen understanding that theater was a business. Ulcers kept Merrick from serving in World War II.

As a fledgling producer in 1949, Merrick (with Irving L. Jacobs) presented *Clutterbuck*, a romantic comedy. Despite lukewarm reviews, he kept the show running for 218 performances with a clever publicity stunt. Each night during cocktail hour, bellboys paged "Mr. Clutterbuck" in the lounges of Manhattan hotels. Tourists bought tickets, and the investors recouped their money. Merrick's next venture was the musical *Fanny* (1954), an adaptation of Marcel Pagnol's film trilogy, which opened to negative reviews. To promote the show, during the wedding of Grace Kelly and Prince Rainier in Monaco, a sky-written message appeared: "WHEN IN NEW YORK SEE FANNY." And back in New York, a life-size nude statue of Nejla Ates, the show's belly dancer, mysteriously appeared in Central Park opposite the bust of Shakespeare, attracting widespread front-page coverage. Ticket sales soared, and *Fanny* ran for 888 performances.

Merrick's promotional stratagems were legendary. In 1955 Tyrone Guthrie's production of *The Matchmaker* received enthusiastic reviews, but taking no chances, a man in a chimpanzee outfit drove around New York in a Rolls Royce with a sign that read: "I'm Driving My Master to see *The Matchmaker*." When ticket sales slowed for John Osborne's *Look Back in Anger* (1957), a young woman jumped from the audience to the stage, in a carefully rehearsed outburst, to belt the young protagonist (Kenneth Haigh) in the midst of his portrayal of an unfaithful husband; the run was extended for fifteen months. In 1961 Merrick solicited seven men who shared the name of the seven New York theater critics, printing their rave reviews for *Subways Are for Sleeping*. When grosses dipped for *Hello, Dolly!* (1964) after a series of cast replacements, Merrick brought the show back to sellout performances with an all-black cast featuring Pearl Bailey and Cab Calloway. When the show finally closed, it had outdistanced *My Fair Lady* with a run of 2,844 performances and had earned ten Tony awards.

In 1957 Merrick began to produce several attractions in one season. In little more than one month, he presented Osborne's *Look Back in Anger*, which won the New York Drama Critics Award; Peter Ustinov's *Romanoff and Juliet*; and the musical *Jamaica*, with Lena Horne and Ricardo Montalban. During that same 1957–1958 season, Merrick also produced a limited engagement of Osborne's *Entertainer*, with Laurence Olivier. Extremely profitable, all these productions were presented on Forty-fifth Street between Broadway and Eighth Avenue, which thereafter became known as "Merrick Parkway," a pun on the Merritt Parkway, a regional highway connecting New York City and Connecticut.

The 1958–1959 season brought six new attractions: *The World of Suzie Wong*, with France Nuyen as Suzie; Osborne's controversial *Epitaph for George Dillon;* John-Carlo

Menotti's opera *Maria Golovin*; and three musicals—*La Plume de Ma Tante* (which won the Drama Critics Award), *Destry Rides Again*, with Delores Gray and Andy Griffith, and *Gypsy*, with Ethel Merman. A seventh production, also a musical, opened in October 1959: *Take Me Along*, with Walter Pidgeon and Jackie Gleason.

During the 1960–1961 season, three productions opened in less than one week: *Irma la Douce*, a London and Paris musical success that starred Elizabeth Seal; *A Taste of Honey*, which won the Drama Critics Circle Award; and *Becket*, with Olivier and Anthony Quinn, which won four Tonys. Two musicals followed: *Do Re Mi* in December 1960 and *Carnival!* (Drama Critics Circle Award) in April 1961. At one point in 1960, eleven Merrick shows were running simultaneously. From *Fanny* in 1954 through *Carnival!* in 1961, he had produced a record twenty shows, establishing himself as the most active presenter of plays on Broadway, the creator of musical entertainments, and the importer of plays. In 1961 the American Theatre Wing bestowed on Merrick a special Tony Award "in recognition of a fabulous production record in the past seven years."

Although Merrick had determined early in his career that only comedies and musicals were profitable, not all his shows were high-gloss entertainment. In 1959 he established the David Merrick Arts Foundation, which enabled him to produce serious plays that were commercial risks. The first venture to receive full backing was Bertolt Brecht's *The Resistible Rise of Arturo Ui* (1962). Next came Osborne's *Inadmissible Evidence* (1965) and Peter Weiss's *Marat/Sade* (1966). By 1966 three of the year's top dramatic offerings, *Marat/Sade*, *Inadmissible Evidence* from England, and Brian Friel's *Philadelphia, Here I Come!* from Ireland were presented under the auspices of the foundation. The foundation also contributed to the experimental theater at Brandeis University in Waltham, Massachusetts, which Merrick helped to organize, and to the theater department at Catholic University of America in Washington, D.C.

In 1983 Merrick suffered a severe stroke that affected his speech and left him unable to carry on as a producer. His last production was an unsuccessful all-black revival of the Gershwin musical comedy *Oh, Kay!* (1990). It marked the eighty-eighth production in the master showman's unparalleled career. Merrick had homes in New York, London, and Paris. He died in his sleep at age eighty-eight in a London rest home. He is buried at the Pinelawn Memorial Park and Cemetery in Farmingdale, New York.

Merrick's other musical successes included *Oliver!* (1963; 774 performances), *Promises, Promises* (1968; 1,281 performances), and *42nd Street* (1980; 3,486 performances). "Without a doubt, he was truly the greatest producer of the old-fashioned musical," noted Jerry Herman, who wrote the score for *Hello, Dolly!* Also an important source for serious theater, Merrick's imported hits included Tom

Stoppard's *Rosencrantz and Guildenstern Are Dead* (1967) and *Travesties* (1975); *A Midsummer Night's Dream* (1971); and Leslie Bricusse and Anthony Newley's musical *Stop the World—I Want to Get Off* (1962). Merrick's brief excursion into film produced *Child's Play* (1972), with James Mason, Robert Preston, and Beau Bridges; *The Great Gatsby* (1974), with Robert Redford and Mia Farrow; *Semi Tough* (1977), with Burt Reynolds; and *Rough Cut* (1980), also with Reynolds.

Merrick believed that a successful producer was a man who chose a good property and then fought to keep it alive after opening night. His weapon was the publicity stunt. Accused by some of the shameless hucksterism of circus promoter P. T. Barnum, Merrick learned his trade in his own way, carefully researching and questioning past procedures. He found ways to cut costs and stood up against unfair union practices, while his sheer number of productions gave him the power to bargain in his business dealings. He was known as the grand master of litigation and manipulation (his law degree served him well) and for making enemies of colleagues, associates, and critics. And yet he was a valuable force and the most vital producer and showman to come along in years. For a quarter-century that ended with the musical *42nd Street* in 1980, Merrick was the dominant showman in the Broadway theater, producing or coproducing more than eighty plays (including many foreign hits), and his record of productivity and profitability remains unmatched. His estate in 1983 was assessed at between $50 and $70 million.

★

The Billy Rose Theatre Collection at the New York Public Library for the Performing Arts, Lincoln Center, New York City, contains uncataloged newspaper clippings and magazine articles about Merrick and his productions. For biographical information about Merrick, see Howard Kissell, *David Merrick: The Abominable Showman* (1993). For a compilation of journalistic literature and data on productions, including credits, runs, synopses, and review citations, see Barbara Lee Horn, *David Merrick: A Bio-Bibliography* (1992). Obituaries are in the *New York Times* and *Manchester Guardian* (both 27 Apr. 2000), and *Variety* (1 May 2000).

Barbara Lee Horn

MILLER, Merton Howard (*b.* 16 May 1923 in Boston, Massachusetts; *d.* 3 June 2000 in Chicago, Illinois), economist widely regarded as the father of modern financial analysis who shared the 1990 Nobel Prize in economics and whose work epitomized the "Chicago school" of economics and its unflinching belief in the efficiency of competitive markets.

Miller was the only child of Joel L. Miller, an attorney, and Sylvia F. (Starr) Miller. After completing the Boston Latin

School, Miller followed in his father's footsteps, entering Harvard University in Cambridge, Massachusetts, in 1940, and graduating with a B.A. magna cum laude in economics in 1943 (class of 1944). During the war years he married Eleanor Cohen; the couple had three daughters. Eleanor Miller died in 1969; the next year Merton married Katherine Dusak, who survived him.

His first job after college was as an economist in the U.S. Treasury's Division of Tax Research, a position he held until 1947. After the Treasury, Miller spent two years with the Division of Research and Statistics of the Board of Governors of the Federal Reserve System. In 1949 he entered graduate school at the Johns Hopkins University in Baltimore to study economics, "primarily because [the economics theoretician] Fritz Machlup was then a leading member of its small, but very distinguished faculty."

After earning his doctorate from Johns Hopkins in 1952, Miller taught for one year at the London School of Economics before moving to Pittsburgh to become assistant professor of economics in the Graduate School of Industrial Administration (GSIA) at Carnegie Institute of Technology (now Carnegie-Mellon University). At the time, the GSIA was the first and most influential of the new wave of research-oriented business schools. Among Miller's colleagues were Herbert Simon, who won the Nobel Prize in economics in 1978, and Franco Modigliani, who won the economics prize in 1985.

Miller and the somewhat older Modigliani formed a research team that worked on a variety of theoretical projects in corporate finance from 1958 through the mid-1960s. The product of their partnership was a set of mathematically rigorous propositions, dubbed "M&M theorems," that proved that the market value of a firm is independent of its capital structure. Specifically, the M&M theorems showed that a corporation's value is determined by its investment decisions, not its financing decisions. This conclusion ran counter to conventional wisdom, which maintained that the value of a firm depends on the ratio of equity (stocks) to debt (bonds). The M&M theorems transformed the field of finance, which, before Miller, was largely narrative, consisting primarily of the study of such legal arrangements as the contents of legislation and descriptions of financial institutions such as banks.

Miller stayed at Carnegie until 1961, when he left to become a professor of finance and economics in the Graduate School of Business at the University of Chicago, where he remained until his retirement in 1993. He was a visiting professor at the University of Louvain in Belgium during the academic year 1966–1967. Miller was named the Edward Eagle Brown Professor of Banking and Finance at Chicago in 1966.

Between 1981 and 1987 Miller was the Leon Carroll Marshall Distinguished Service Professor, and he finished his active career at Chicago as the Robert R. McCormick

Merton H. Miller, July 1994. RALF-FINN HESTOFT/CORBIS SABA

Distinguished Service Professor, retaining that title when he gained emeritus status in 1993. The crowning achievement of Miller's academic career came in October 1990, when he was named a winner of the Nobel Prize in economics. He shared the award with Harry Markowitz, who was recognized for developing the theory of portfolio choice, and William Sharpe, who was honored as the author of the capital asset pricing model and creator of the beta concept.

Miller received his Nobel Prize for the theorems he had developed with Modigliani. Although the M&M theorem is immensely complicated, Miller would often tell the following story when asked to summarize it in a quick, concise, and understandable way: A pizza deliveryman comes to the baseball manager Yogi Berra after a game and asks Yogi if he would like his pizza cut into quarters or eighths. After pausing for a second, Yogi declares, "cut it in eight pieces. I'm feeling hungry tonight." "You can understand the M&M theorem," Miller would say, "if you know why this is a joke."

As his fellow laureate Sharpe observed, Miller had "a wonderful and wicked sense of humor." His wit achieved legendary status following an incident that took place during one of Miller's tours of Europe. A friend arranged for Miller to give a presentation at the Hochschule der Bundeswehr, the German army's staff school in Hamburg. Prepared to give a technical talk to finance professors, Miller was surprised to discover that his audience consisted almost exclusively of students. "I looked . . . at the rows of young uniformed faces sitting politely . . . and the only thing I could think to say was: 'Gentlemen: Tomorrow we invade Poland!'" Gales of laugher filled the hall.

Despite his easygoing manner, Miller could be tough and outspoken when the situation called for it. This is precisely the position he found himself in after the stock market plunge of 19–20 October 1987. Shortly after the infamous "market meltdown," several Wall Street leaders placed the blame for the collapse on the Chicago markets. Specific accusations were leveled at the Chicago Board of Trade and the Chicago Mercantile Exchange, where many new financial products had been created. Financial instruments such as forward transactions, futures, and currency interest rate swaps are called "derivatives," because their value derives from that of other assets, such as stock or commodity prices. Wall Street leaders claimed that the volatility of derivatives and related products caused the 1987 crash.

With Miller as their point man, the Chicago exchanges, citing his studies and those of other prominent economists, were able to deflect the Wall Street charges. As Miller saw it, the dispute between the securities and futures markets was less about the crash and more about the realization on Wall Street that the Chicago exchanges, with their innovative products, had taken business from East Coast dealers. As he said in a 1992 interview, "If these markets don't remain fast and cheap . . . they risk losing their discount chain status, becoming instead a fancy department store, and that would make them uncompetitive." Miller died of lymphoma at age seventy-seven. A memorial service was held at the Rockefeller Chapel of the University of Chicago on 14 October 2000.

Profiles of Nobel laureates often portray them as individuals consumed with their work and devoid of a life outside their discipline. This was certainly not true of Miller.

A loving husband, devoted father, doting grandfather, and a season-ticket-holding fan of the Chicago Bears, Miller was a renowned economist who had an indefatigable sense of humor and a genuine lust for life.

★

Miller's Nobel-winning contributions, as well as those of the other winners, are described in David Warsh, "Nobel-est in Economics: Three Americans Share Prize for Corporate Finance Theories," *Boston Globe* (17 Oct. 1990). Additional information about Miller's contributions is in Peter J. Tanous, "An Interview with Merton Miller," *Investment Gurus* (1997). Obituaries are in the *Chicago Tribune* (6 June 2000) and *Policy* (winter 2000).

JAMES CICARELLI

MINK, Patsy Matsu Takemoto (*b.* 6 December 1927 in Paia, Maui, Hawaii; *d.* 28 September 2002 in Honolulu, Hawaii), first Japanese-American U.S. congresswoman and senator, as well as lawyer and activist, best known as a trailblazer for women, minorities, children, the environment, education, and the poor.

Mink was one of two children and the only daughter of Suematsu Takemoto, a civil engineer, and Mitama (Tateyama) Takemoto, both of Japanese descent, whose own parents had emigrated from Japan to work in Maui's sugar plantations. Mink's persistence and tenacity were evident at an early age, especially when she decided to attend school a year early. In addition, she was advised by her family to do well academically and to work hard for her beliefs. Both as a child and as an adult, Mink faced racial and sexual discrimination. All the while, however, her intelligence and abilities enabled her to make the best of the situations in which she found herself. She became the first female student body president at Maui High School where she also graduated as valedictorian in 1944.

After commencing her studies at the University of Hawaii, Mink transferred to Wilson College in Chambersburg, Pennsylvania, in 1946 and then to the University of Nebraska at Lincoln in 1947. She was instrumental in ending discriminatory practices there, before becoming ill and returning to the University of Hawaii, where she received a B.A. in zoology and chemistry in 1948. Mink was denied her dream of becoming a medical doctor after having applied to twenty medical schools and being refused by all of them because she was a woman.

In the interim, Mink began working at the Honolulu Academy of Arts, where the female director suggested that she apply to law school. She was officially accepted as a foreign student at the University of Chicago Law School because, at that time, school officials had not realized that Hawaii was a part of the United States. At Chicago, Mink

Patsy T. Mink. UPI/BETTMANN

met her husband, John Francis Mink, a hydrologist and geologist: they married on 27 January 1951. She graduated that same year and was admitted to the Hawaii bar in 1953.

Mink was refused a position at all the law firms to which she applied, so she began working at the University of Chicago Law School Library. She remained there until her eighth month of pregnancy. Six months after her only daughter, Gwendolyn, was born, Mink and her family returned to Hawaii, where she opened her own practice and became the first Japanese-American woman lawyer in Hawaii. She taught law at the University of Hawaii from 1952 to 1956. In 1955 she served as an attorney for the Hawaii House of Representatives. She also founded the Oahu Young Democrats and later, the Hawaii Young Democrats. After unsuccessfully running for a seat in the Territory of Hawaii House of Representatives in 1954, Mink won a seat in 1956—the first Asian-American woman to do so. She also served as Vice President of the National Young Democrats of America from 1957 to 1959.

In 1958 Mink was elected to the Territory of Hawaii Senate. When Hawaii became the fiftieth state in 1959, the territorial legislature was dissolved and Mink ran for U.S. Congress, losing to Daniel Inouye. From 1959 to 1962 she continued to teach law at the University of Hawaii until she won a state senate seat. In 1960 Mink attended the

Democratic National Convention, for which she had been selected to present a civil rights speech. During this time she became a member of the National Association for the Advancement of Colored People (NAACP).

After winning a seat in U.S. Congress in 1964, Mink served continuously for the next twelve years. She introduced the first comprehensive Early Childhood Education Act (ECEA) and was a vocal opponent of the Vietnam War. In 1972 she co-authored Title IX , as part of the Higher Education Act Amendments, which prohibited gender discrimination by federally funded institutions, guaranteeing the equality of women in education and athletic programs by 1977. In 1972 Mink ran for the U.S. presidency. Her bid ended unsuccessfully, but she was able to highlight social issues she considered important. In 1976 she was the primary author of the Surface Mining and Reclamation (Stripmining) Act and the Mineral Leasing Act. Also in 1976, she ran for a U.S. Senate seat but was not victorious. Instead, President Jimmy Carter appointed her assistant secretary of state for oceans and international environmental and scientific affairs, in which capacity she served effectively until 1978.

That same year Mink returned to Hawaii and re-entered the world of local politics. For the next three years she was president of Americans for Democratic Action and taught law at the University of Hawaii. From 1983 to 1987 Mink was on the Honolulu City Council, serving as chair from 1983 to 1985.

Senator Spark Matsunaga died in 1990 and Daniel K. Akaka was chosen to fill his seat, which left his own House seat vacant. Convinced by her husband to run once again, Mink returned to Congress and remained there almost until her death.

For her relentless efforts, Mink received honorary degrees from Chaminade College (1975); Syracuse University (1976); and Whitman College (1981). She was also accorded numerous accolades, including the Leadership for Freedom Award from Roosevelt College, Chicago (1968), the Freedom Award, Honolulu Chapter of the NAACP (1971), the Distinguished Humanitarian Award YWCA, St. Louis (1972), the Creative Leadership in Women's Rights Award, NEA (1977), the Hispanic Health Leadership Award (1995), the Justice in Action Award from the Asian American Legal Defense and Educational Fund (1996), and the Hawaii Women Lawyers Lifetime Achievement Award (1997). She was named one of the ten best politicians in Congress in 1992 by *McCall's* magazine. After her death, Title IX was renamed the Patsy T. Mink Equal Opportunity in Education Act in her honor.

Mink died at age seventy-four at the Straub Clinic and Hospital in Honolulu of viral pneumonia after contracting chicken pox. She is buried at the National Memorial Cemetery of the Pacific at Punchbowl in Honolulu.

Mink will be remembered as a petite woman with the heart of a warrior; one who never gave up on any cause worth fighting for, especially where education, childcare, the environment, and equal opportunity for women and minorities were concerned. She said it best herself when describing her own life: "My career in politics has been a crucible of challenges and crises where in the end, the principles to which I was committed, prevailed."

★

There is no biography of Mink. For information about her life and career, see Patsy Sumie Saiki, *Japanese Women in Hawaii: The First 100 Years* (1985); and Mari J. Matsuda, ed., *Called From Within: Early Women Lawyers of Hawaii* (1992). See also "First Congresswoman from Overseas," *Life* 58 (22 June 1965): 49–50 + ; Rudolf Engelbarts, *Women in the United States Congress, 1917–1972: Their Accomplishments with Bibliographies* (1974); and Brian Nutting and H. Amy Stern, eds., *CQ Politics in America 2002, The 107th Congress* (2001). Tributes to Mink include Daniel K. Akaka, "Honoring Patsy T. Mink," *Congressional Record* (30 Sept. 2002). Obituaries are in the *Washington Post* and *New York Times* (both 29 Sept. 2002).

ADRIANA C. TOMASINO

MIZELL, Jason William. *See* Jam Master Jay.

MOAKLEY, John Joseph ("Joe") (*b.* 27 April 1927 in Boston, Massachusetts; *d.* 28 May 2001 in Bethesda, Maryland), fifteen-term U.S. congressman from South Boston who led the investigation proving that Salvadoran military forces, backed by the U.S. government, were responsible for the murder of Jesuits in El Salvador in 1989.

Moakley was the oldest of three sons of Joseph Ambrose Moakley, a truck driver, and Mary Rita (Scappini) Moakley, a homemaker. He grew up in the Old Harbor Village housing project in South Boston ("Southie"), a strongly blue-collar Irish-Catholic district. He studied sheet metal at South Boston High School. At age fifteen, with his father's blessing, he obtained a false birth certificate so that he could join the U.S. Navy, serving in the Pacific from 1943 to 1946, during World War II. After the war Moakley went to Newman Preparatory School and then attended the University of Miami (Florida) from 1950 to 1951, when he left, saying that he was "sick of it."

In 1950 Moakley ran for Massachusetts state representative and lost. In 1953 he was elected to the Massachusetts House of Representatives, where he served until 1963, acting as majority whip in 1957. In 1956 he received a J.D. from Suffolk University Law School in Boston, and he was admitted to the Massachusetts bar in 1957, the same year he married Evelyn Duffy; the couple had no children. He served in the Massachusetts Senate from 1964 to 1970.

J. Joseph Moakley (*left*) with his wife, Evelyn, November 1972. AP/WIDE WORLD PHOTOS

Moakley ran for the seat from the Ninth Congressional District in 1970 but lost to a popular antibusing candidate, Louise Day Hicks. In 1971 Moakley won a seat on the Boston City Council. Then, in a daring political move, he ran for a seat in the U.S. Congress in 1972 as an Independent-Democrat to avoid facing Hicks in a primary. He thus broadened his base, and although he lost some of the Southie wards he had won previously, Moakley was able to run on a more liberal platform than Hicks. He had overwhelming support from African-American voters in the Roxbury and Mattapan areas, and he split the Irish vote, winning the general election by 5,000 votes.

When Moakley took office in January 1973 he switched back to the Democratic Party. Moakley won most of his subsequent elections with 70 percent or more of the vote, with the exception of 1982, when his margin was 67 percent. In the next four elections, no Republican opposed him. Moakley headed the Democratic Patronage Committee, having control of 800 jobs, including elevator operators, doorkeepers, and the capitol police. Thomas P. ("Tip") O'Neill, Speaker of the House and a fellow Massachusetts Democrat, was Moakley's mentor in Washington.

A local connection drew Moakley into international affairs. Before that, he quipped, "foreign affairs to me was going to East Boston and getting an Italian sandwich." In 1983 he met a group of Salvadorans from his district who had been denied refugee status. He began to investigate and invited two Jesuit priests from the University of Central America to testify before the House Rules Committee, on which he had a seat. Both men were later among six priests

and two women murdered in El Salvador in 1989. That year, Speaker of the House Tom Foley appointed Moakley to head the investigation into the murder of the priests, in which high-ranking Salvadoran military and government officials were implicated. Moakley's investigation forced him to seriously challenge the U.S. policy in El Salvador, which was designed to fund the anti-Communist Salvadoran government despite the human rights abuses of its army. In 1990 Moakley won "temporary protective status" for Salvadorans. The investigation also resulted in a cut of funding to the School of the Americas at Fort Benning, Georgia, a U.S. Army training school that nineteen of the twenty-six assassins had attended.

In 1989 Moakley became chair of the House Rules Committee, a position he held until the Republicans won the majority in 1994. The powerful Rules Committee decides which bills reach the floor for debate and how those debates are conducted. Moakley enabled the Democratic liberal leadership to carry out the party agenda, but he never made personal enemies of Republican opponents. As a ranking Democrat under Republican rule, he was still able to get funds for local projects, such as the Boston Harbor cleanup and Boston's "Big Dig," the Central Artery/Tunnel Project involving the construction of an underground expressway. He also cochaired the Organ and Tissue Donation Task force. In 1992 Moakley was exposed for writing more than ninety bad checks drawn on the House bank. He recovered from the potential scandal with typical humor, saying that he should "have majored in accounting rather than sheet metal when I was at Southie High."

Moakley had many health problems. Over the years, he lost a kidney, suffered from colon cancer, and had a hip replacement. In 1995 he was given just two months to live after he was diagnosed with hepatitis B, which he probably contracted during a trip to China in the 1980s. He had a liver transplant in July, around the same time that his wife was discovered to have a brain tumor. She asked him to retire to stay with her in Boston, but thirty minutes before a scheduled press conference to announce his retirement she recanted her wish, asking only that he spend more time with her, which he did. She died in March 1996 after thirty-nine years of marriage.

Moakley was a friend to the U.S. Merchant Marine, helping pass the 1996 Maritime Security Act, which created the $1-billion, ten-year Maritime Security Program. In 1998 he traveled to Cuba with colleagues from the Massachusetts House to meet the Cuban leader Fidel Castro. The group ultimately recommended lifting the U.S. embargo on food and medicine. Lobbied by firefighters in his district, Moakley worked to require tobacco companies to produce self-extinguishing cigarettes.

Moakley was a liberal in the classic Democratic tradition. Known by local unions as "Jobs" Moakley, he was still working on appropriations and helping constituents from his hospital bed in the last week of his life. Socially, however, he opposed busing and voted to ban the so-called partial-birth abortion procedure, although by 1995 he said he no longer unequivocally supported anti-abortion groups. He also supported a bill to ban "desecration" of the American flag. In 1995 he suggested as his own epitaph "This is a kid who was born in South Boston, lived in South Boston, loved South Boston, and even though he served in Washington, he never left South Boston." He was well known for his wit and had friends in both the Republican and Democratic parties.

In 2000 Moakley was awarded the prestigious Distinguished American Award by the Kennedy Library Foundation. In March 2001 the federal courthouse in Boston was renamed for him. A chair in political science was established in his name at Boston College, and he was honored for his role in leading Congress to fund research into diseases of the aging eye by the establishment of a fund for a Moakley Scholar at Harvard Medical School's Schepens Eye Research Institute. Moakley received honorary doctorates from Suffolk University, the New England School of Law, Northeastern University, and the University of Central America in El Salvador.

In February 2001 Moakley announced that he had high-grade myelodysplastic syndrome, an incurable type of leukemia. He died in Bethesda Naval Hospital at the age of seventy-four. The funeral mass, held on 1 June 2001 at Saint Brigid's Church in South Boston, was attended by President George W. Bush and former presidents George H. W. Bush and William J. ("Bill") Clinton, among others. Moakley is buried in Blue Hill Cemetery in Braintree, Massachusetts, south of Boston.

★

Moakley's papers are held at the Suffolk University Moakley Law Library in Boston. There are two profiles of Moakley in the *Boston Globe*: one by John Robinson (2 Aug. 1990), and another by Daniel Golden (29 Sept. 1991). Obituaries are in the *Boston Globe, New York Times, USA Today,* and *Washington Post* (all 29 May 2001).

JANE BRODSKY FITZPATRICK

N

NASH, Gerald David (*b.* 16 July 1928 in Berlin, Germany; *d.* 11 November 2000 in Albuquerque, New Mexico), leading historian and interpreter of modern American and western American history.

Nash was the only child of Alfred B. Nash, a lumber supply merchant, and Alice (Kantorowicz) Nash. The family was comfortably middle class. The family name was originally Nashon, a traditional Jewish name, but was converted to Nachschoen over time so that it sounded more German. The rise of Nazism under Adolf Hitler made life increasingly unstable for Jews, and the family immigrated to Palestine in October 1937 and then to New York City in March 1938. In the United States, Nash's father contracted the family name to Nash in order to facilitate assimilation into the new society.

Living on savings, the family settled among a community of German-Jewish émigrés in Washington Heights in Manhattan, where they learned English at night school and through the assignment of a student tutor at public school. The family later leased a town house on West 103rd Street in Manhattan. The large dwelling, originally built by the composer George Gershwin, was divided into apartments and proved to be an attractive address for other German refugees, many of whom were the foundation of the business and intellectual life of the city.

By 1940 the war in Europe was affecting the United States, and Nash felt again the venom of anti-Semitism and Nazi sympathizers. Nash continued through middle school, working as a school sales representative for the *New York Times,* among other small jobs. He was rewarded for his studies and work ethic by being admitted to one of the most selective institutions in the city, Stuyvesant High School. Nash became a naturalized U.S. citizen in 1944.

After graduating from Stuyvesant in 1945, Nash went on to New York University, where he majored in history and minored in public policy and administration. A member of the undergraduate honors organization Phi Beta Kappa, Nash earned a B.A. in 1950. Still short of money, he did some teaching and sought out scholarships to graduate schools. Ohio State University offered him a fellowship, but he found the town of Columbus and the university openly hostile to Jews. After a quarter, Nash enrolled at Columbia University in New York City.

Columbia was a welcome change for Nash, and he came to know such well-known professors as Richard Hofstadter, Richard B. Morris, Henry Steele Commager, Allan Nevins, Dumas Malone, and Garrett Mattingly. In 1952 he earned an M.A. in history, and with an offer of financial aid from the University of California, Berkeley, Nash headed west.

His mentor at Berkeley was John D. Hicks, who was part of the University of Wisconsin "frontier" theory laboratory begun by the historian Frederick Jackson Turner, who in turn was succeeded by Frederic L. Paxson. Hicks had been one of Paxson's students and brought to California a fresh interest in western politics and social development. He turned Nash to a study of California public administration, which provided an opportunity to examine stores of primary public documents. Like Columbia, Berkeley was a burgeoning academic establishment with such distinguished faculty as Carl Bridenbaugh, Armin Rappaport, Henry May, Dwight Waldo, and Frank Freidel. Nash received his Ph.D. in history from Berkeley in 1957. His doctoral thesis was published as *State Government and Economic Development: A History of Administrative Policies in California, 1849–1933* in 1964. After teaching briefly at Stanford, Nash took a position at Northern Illinois University in DeKalb, which allowed him to live in Chicago. In 1961 he moved to the University of New Mexico in Albuquerque. Nash married Marie Norris on 19 August 1967. They had one child.

In a department of eight faculty members, Nash's workload was not light. By 1970 the department had tripled in size, and Nash served as chairman from 1974 to 1980. He also took over the editorship of *The Historian,* the journal of the history honor society Phi Alpha Theta, a position he held from 1974 to 1984. The society created an annual prize in his name for undergraduate history research.

By now an established historian, Nash was naturally sought to join the formation in the 1980s of a center for the study of western history. The University of New Mexico provided funding and brought Richard Etulain to the campus as its star western scholar. Nash and Etulain became close colleagues, and with Ferenc Szasz and others on the faculty, formed a cohesive cadre of western researchers. The resourceful Nash sought to develop further his California studies to include the entire Far West region. The rise of a "new" western history in the 1980s saw an intense interest in western ethnicity, nativism, class conflict, environmentalism, and gender issues, all of which had lain dormant since Turner's seminal 1893 thesis, which declared that frontier America was closed by virtue of census statistics. The new history, however, left Nash unmoved, for he could not accept the notion of social dramatics taking precedence over harsh economic and physical realities. He was quick to point to the influence of the federal government in transforming the West, especially after World War II. The rise of urban and suburban enclaves, as well as the rise of industry, agribusiness, and transportation innovations, were all part of Nash's insight to the meaning of the West in the twentieth century.

Nash's view was that the federal government, rather than self-reliance and rugged individualism, was crucial to the making of the modern West. He hazarded the argument that since World War II the American West had led as a cultural pacesetter. However, this argument was contested by practitioners of the "new" western history. In turn, the excesses of these historians were rejected by Nash, who saw them as being enamored with arguing about Turner's failure to look into the social dynamics of the

West. The aspects of gender, ethnicity, race, and class were not rejected by Nash; rather, they were viewed as diversions from what he regarded as a focus more central to understanding the new West.

Nash displayed his pedantic but professional style of writing in *The American West in the Twentieth Century: A Short History of an Urban Oasis* (1973); *The American West Transformed: The Impact of the Second World War* (1985); *State Government and Economic Development* (1979); *Creating the West: Historical Interpretations, 1890–1990* (1991); *The Federal Landscape: An Economic History of the Twentieth Century West* (1999); and *A Brief History of the American West Since 1945* (2001). He also edited several works and served as president of the Western History Association in 1990 and 1991.

Nash retired from the University of New Mexico in 1995 after thirty-four years. He died of pancreatic cancer and his remains were cremated.

★

Richard W. Etulain and Ferenc Morton Szasz, eds., *The American West in 2000: Essays in Honor of Gerald D. Nash* (2003), is especially useful in that Nash provides an autobiographical section. Obituaries are in the *Albuquerque Journal* (13 Nov. 2000), *Washington Post* (18 Nov. 2000), and *Western Historical Quarterly* (spring 2001).

JACK J. CARDOSO

NASON, John William (*b.* 9 February 1905 in Saint Paul, Minnesota; *d.* 17 November 2001 in Kennett Square, Pennsylvania), college president who led an interfaith group to get Japanese Americans out of World War II detention camps and into colleges and universities.

Nason was the son of Albert John Nason, a businessman, and Mary Ethel (Eaton) Nason, a homemaker. He attended Saint Paul public schools until 1918, when his family moved to Chicago. There he attended the Chicago Latin School and, among other jobs, worked as a bank messenger and sold birdhouses for twenty-five cents. Nason also attended the Phillips Exeter Academy in New Hampshire and Carleton College in Minnesota, where he earned a B.A. with honors in philosophy in 1926. After graduating from Carleton, Nason attended Yale Divinity School in New Haven, Connecticut, where he was elected Fellow of the National Council on Religion in Higher Education. He also studied at Harvard University in Cambridge, Massachusetts, where he received an M.A. in philosophy in 1928. As a Rhodes scholar, Nason studied at Oxford University in England for three years.

In 1935 Nason married Bertha Dean White, a Quaker; they had two sons. After his marriage, he also became a Quaker. Discussing the Quaker perspective with the *New*

John W. Nason (*left*), shown with British ambassador Oliver Franks (*center*) and his wife and Earnest Patterson (*right*), May 1949. AP/WIDE WORLD PHOTOS

York Times, Nason observed that the Quakers "have always emphasized the spiritual quality of . . . daily life. Little interested in creeds and ritual, they have kept a deep concern for the religious character of daily living." In 1957 he married Elizabeth Mercer.

In 1931 Nason began teaching philosophy at Swarthmore College in Pennsylvania, which had been founded by Quakers during the U.S. Civil War. He was appointed president in 1940 at age thirty-five. Speaking of the institution's heritage, Nason said, "Character cannot be handed over in lecture courses, nor can a religious spirit be forcibly instilled. They come, if at all, . . . by what Quakers themselves call the inward working of the spirit."

Nason quickly became a distinguished educational leader and an advocate for reason and idealism, guiding Swarthmore during the difficult years of World War II and the rapid expansion of higher education in the late 1940s and early 1950s. As Swarthmore's leader, he was a constant source of inspiration and wisdom and an advocate for academic rigor, inclusion, and humanity. Discussing World War II in his first annual report in 1941, Nason addressed the pacifism followed by many Quakers. He wrote, "the College should neither institute military training nor yet set obstacles in the way of students or faculty who may wish to enlist." He also served on a committee that managed the program for conscientious objectors to the war.

Nason was best known for his activities on behalf of Japanese-American students during World War II. He served for three years as chairman of the national Japanese American Student Relocation Council, which liberated more than 4,000 interned students from War Relocation Authority camps and found places for them in over 600 colleges and universities, including Swarthmore. As well as obtaining scholarships, free tuition, and funds for the students, Nason set up welcome committees on the campuses.

Nason resigned as Swarthmore president in 1953 to become president of the Foreign Policy Association, a national organization that resisted McCarthyism, the anticommunist movement led by the Wisconsin senator Joseph McCarthy. Nason wanted to see the United States develop and support an intelligent foreign policy, not only for its own interests, but for the interests of the world as a whole. Under Nason's leadership, World Affairs Councils were established in large cities and the "Great Decisions" discussions programs, which continue to involve several hundred thousand participants each year, were initiated. Nason later returned to Carleton College, his alma mater, serving as its fifth president from 1962 to 1970.

Nason was chair of the Philadelphia Committee for Federal Union. He was also president of the United Nations Council of Philadelphia and the World Affairs Council of Philadelphia, as well as a member of the board of directors of the National Council of Christians and Jews in Philadelphia and the board of the Philadelphia Branch of the United States Committee for the Care of European Children. Nason served on the editorial board of the *Amer-*

ican Scholar, the committee of the Friends Civilian Public Service, and the Commission to Study the Organization of Peace. In recognition of his leadership and his contributions to education, Nason received honorary doctorates from many institutions, including Swarthmore; Carleton College; the Johns Hopkins University in Baltimore; the College of Wooster in Wooster, Ohio; Saint Olaf College in Northfield, Minnesota; Hamilton College in Clinton, New York; Muhlenberg College in Allentown, Pennsylvania; and Hahnemann Medical College and the University of Pennsylvania, both in Philadelphia.

Nason's publications include *The Nature and Content of a Liberal Education* (1941), *Leibniz and the Logical Argument for Individual Substances* (1942), and *Foundation Trusteeship: Service in the Public Interest* (1989). Nason's writings on higher education administration include a study of the effectiveness of search and screening committees in hiring higher education professionals.

After retiring to the Adirondack Mountains in 1970, Nason became actively involved with environmental and conservation issues. He became a trustee of the Adirondack Nature Conservancy in 1977 and subsequently helped to found and direct the New York State Conservancy. He died of natural causes at age ninety-six at Crosslands, a Quaker community in Kennett Square, Pennsylvania.

Nason was a vibrant and deliberative leader who shaped Carleton and Swarthmore colleges in significant and enduring ways. His work led to changes in student services and academic administration. He will be remembered most for his role in assisting Japanese-American students to get out of internment camps and back into college.

★

There is no biography of Nason. His papers are held in the Swarthmore College library. Obituaries are in the *Boston Globe* (29 Nov. 2001) and *Los Angeles Times* (7 Dec. 2001).

REED MARKHAM

NEEL, James Van Gundia (*b.* 22 March 1915 in Hamilton, Ohio; *d.* 1 February 2000 in Ann Arbor, Michigan), pioneer in the field of human genetics who discovered the genetic basis for sickle cell anemia and headed long-term studies of atomic bomb survivors in Hiroshima and Nagasaki, Japan.

Neel, the eldest of three children, was born to Hiram Alexander Neel, metallurgist and executive at a steel mill, and Elizabeth (Van Gundia) Neel, a homemaker. When Neel was ten years old his father died of pneumonia, and the family moved to Wooster, Ohio, a halfway point between his mother's hometown and McKeesport, Pennsylvania, where a large part of his father's family lived. Neel won a scholarship to the College of Wooster, Ohio, which he

started attending at age sixteen, graduating in 1935 with a B.A. While an undergraduate, he developed an interest in genetics, a field that was dominated at that time by studies of the fruit fly *Drosophila melanogaster*. Neel did his graduate work at the University of Rochester in New York, where he studied under one of the world's leading authorities on *Drosophila* genetics, Curt Stern.

After receiving a Ph.D. in 1939, Neel taught zoology at Dartmouth College, New Hampshire, before enrolling in the University of Rochester's Medical School at age twenty-seven. He supplemented his medical studies with a National Research Council Fellowship in Zoology at Columbia University, 1941–1942, and as Cramer Fellow at Dartmouth College, 1942–1943. While in medical school, Neel married Priscilla Baxter on 6 May 1943; they had three children. He was awarded an M.D. in 1944; that same year he published his research on the inheritance of thalassemia, a hemoglobin disorder. He completed his internship and residency in internal medicine at Strong Memorial Hospital and Rochester Municipal Hospital.

Neel served in the U.S. Army Medical Corp as a lieutenant from 1943 to 1944 and 1946 to 1947. He and his family had moved to Ann Arbor, Michigan, where in 1946 he accepted a position at the University of Michigan as assistant geneticist at the Laboratory of Vertebrate Biology. He remained with the University of Michigan until his retirement in 1985.

In November 1946 President Harry Truman directed the National Academy of Sciences (NAS) and the National Research Council's division of medical science to begin a study of the genetic and medical effects of the Hiroshima and Nagasaki bombings on the survivors. The result of this directive was the establishment of the NAS Atomic Bomb Casualty Commission (ABCC), of which Neel was the first acting director of field studies. He also designed the initial studies assessing the continuing effects of the nuclear bombs on survivors, specifically, initiating a survey to assess genetic damage from radiation exposure. The project's results, published in 1956, showed that there was no increased rate of inherited genetic mutations in children of survivors but raised grave concerns about the carcinogenic (cancer-causing) effects of ionizing radiation. The ABCC, and its successor, the Radiation Effects Research Foundation (RERF), are estimated by the NAS to be the "longest running binational research program in modern history." Neel was involved with the project for more than forty years. Neel's studies in Japan also looked at the children born to consanguineous couples, that is, those who were first cousins or shared an even closer blood relationship. Surprisingly, the conclusions were that the children born from these unions were less likely to have genetically related illnesses than had been believed.

In 1948 Neel became director of the Heredity Clinic at

James V. Neel. ASSOCIATED PRESS

the University of Michigan, a part of the Institute of Human Biology. One of the two projects he decided to research was the inheritance of hemoglobin diseases, chief among them sickle cell anemia. In sickle cell anemia the hemoglobin, which carries oxygen in the red blood cells, is defective. Once oxygen is released from the defective hemoglobin molecule, it becomes elongated, causing the red blood cell to assume a sickle shape and leading to clogged blood vessels, organ damage, and severe pain. In 1949 Neel was able to demonstrate that the disease is a recessive trait inherited through simple Mendelian inheritance. This means that a person needs two defective copies of a single gene in order to manifest the disease. Those who carry only one defective copy of this gene (and have one normal copy) do not make enough defective hemoglobin to cause a health problem (this is known as sickle cell trait). Neel's discovery, and his subsequent work with the Liberian Institute of Tropical Medicine, also paved the way for research that showed that carriers of the sickle cell trait in Africa had more resistance to malaria, explaining the high frequency of the sickle cell gene in African Americans.

In 1956 Neel established the Department of Human Genetics at the University of Michigan in place of the Heredity Clinic, the first such academic department in the United States. He remained the department chair for twenty-five years. Beginning in the 1960s Neel turned his attention to evolutionary genetics, working with the Xavante and Yanomami Amazon tribes. These tribes represented the closest groups one could find to original hunting-gathering societies, and Neel's work among them strengthened, among other things, his idea of the "thrifty gene." According to this hypothesis, diseases such as diabetes and obesity are caused by genetic controls that were once beneficial in societies whose day-to-day nutrition was uncertain; some ongoing studies support this theory.

Neel died of prostate cancer at his home. Less than one year after his death, a controversial book called into question Neel's ethics as a scientist, among other concerns, his work with the Amazon tribes. *Darkness in El Dorado: How Scientists and Journalists Devastated the Amazon,* by Patrick Tierney, was published in November 2000. The book alleged, among other things, that Neel intentionally spread measles among the Yanomami tribe in Venezuela, who had never been exposed to the virus and therefore suffered severe loss of life. Neel was conducting research on the Yanomami in 1968 when the measles epidemic broke. The book created a firestorm in scientific circles, with various bodies, such as University of Michigan, the American Society of Human Genetics, and the NAS, launching official investigations into the allegations. All the investigations found Tierney's allegations to be baseless. The measles epidemic had reached the Yanomami territory before Neel arrived, and Neel and his team vaccinated the population appropriately and quickly. The vaccine Neel used, the Edmonston B vaccine, was not, as Tierney claimed, unsafe, nor was it capable of causing an epidemic. Although every investigating body found that the book contained inaccuracies and misrepresentations, the controversy and media coverage cast a pall over Neel's long and distinguished career. In July 2002 the American Anthropological Association concluded its own eighteen-month-long investigation, supporting the findings from other committees regarding the accuracy of Tierney's book but faulting Neel for his failure to obtain informed consent for the blood samples he took from the Yanomami.

Neel is considered by many to be one of the founding fathers of modern human genetics, paving the way for our current understanding of issues ranging from the inheritance of diseases to evolutionary genetics. For a man who modernized the science, he was somewhat of a technophobe—he never took to computers and continued to write his manuscripts in longhand. He was an astonishingly prolific researcher, producing more than six hundred published works. His students and colleagues found him inspiring, with an infectious love for the beauty of science. Among his many distinguished awards are the Albert Lasker Award (1960) and the National Medal of Science (1974).

★

Neel's papers relating to his association with the ABCC are held at the John P. McGovern Historical Collections and Research Center at the Houston Academy of Medicine–Texas Medical Center Library, in Houston, Texas. Other papers, including those relating to his work with the Amazonian tribes, are held in the manuscripts department at the American Philosophical Society Library in Philadelphia. Neel's autobiography is *Physician to the Gene Pool: Genetic Lessons and Other Stories* (1994). Further information about his career is in William J. Schull, "James Van Gundia Neel," *Biographical Memoirs of the National Academy of Sciences* 81 (2002): 3–21; and Kenneth M. Weiss and William J. Schull, "Perspectives Fulfilled: The Work and Thought of J. V. Neel (1915–2000)," *Perspectives in Biology and Medicine* 4, no. 1 (winter 2002): 46–64. An obituary is in the *Los Angeles Times* (3 Feb. 2000).

ADI R. FERRARA

NEUBERGER, Maurine Brown (*b.* 9 January 1907 in Cloverdale, Oregon; *d.* 22 February 2000 in Portland, Oregon), the third woman elected to the U.S. Senate.

A descendant of Oregon pioneers, Neuberger was the daughter of Walter T. Brown, a country doctor, and Ethel (Kelty) Brown, who taught education at Oregon Normal School. Neuberger grew up in Polk County and worked summers picking fruit in Willamette Valley orchards. She graduated from Bethel High School in 1923 and then studied at Oregon College of Education in Monmouth, where she received a teacher's certificate in 1925. She taught physical education and modern dance before resuming her education at the University of Oregon in Eugene. She graduated with a degree in English in 1929. In 1936 and 1937 she took graduate courses in education at the University of California, Los Angeles. From 1932 through 1944 she taught English and physical education in Oregon public schools, including Lincoln High School in Portland. During World War II she helped operate her family's 120-acre dairy farm.

On 20 December 1945 Neuberger married the writer and former state legislator Richard L. Neuberger, whom she had known for nearly a decade. They settled in Portland Heights. Neuberger often collaborated with her husband in his writing and took photographs to illustrate his articles for national magazines and newspapers. As a couple, the Neubergers also sparked a revival of the Democratic Party in a state that had long been a Republican stronghold. Before their marriage, Neuberger had been active in the League of Women Voters and had served on a Democratic precinct committee. In 1948 Richard Neuberger was elected state senator. Neuberger herself ran successfully for the Oregon House of Representatives in 1950, and thus in 1951

Maurine Brown Neuberger, October 1965. BETTMANN/CORBIS

the Neubergers became the first husband and wife in U.S. history to serve simultaneously as legislators.

During three terms in the Oregon House (1951–1955), Neuberger made her mark as an advocate for consumers, twice taking on the dairy industry. Her first battle was an attempt to repeal a law that prevented stores from selling milk below the home delivery price. After the dairy lobby blocked her legislation, she launched a petition drive to place a repeal measure on the statewide ballot, and the voters overturned the milk-control act. Neuberger won an even more celebrated victory over the dairy lobby in arguing for the repeal of a 1915 law that banned the sale of yellow margarine. In making her case, Neuberger brought a mixing bowl and a pound of margarine to a meeting of the House Agriculture Committee and showed her colleagues what a messy and time-consuming job it was to mix food coloring into a block of white margarine. Her legislation passed, and the ban was lifted. Neuberger also successfully sponsored the first tax credit for child care. As chairman of the House Education Committee, she sponsored legislation to establish Portland State College. In 1953, when the Oregon Senate overwhelmingly approved a loyalty oath for teachers, Neuberger and other House liberals prevented it from becoming law by blocking it in committee.

In 1954 Richard Neuberger became the first Democrat in forty years to be elected to the U.S. Senate from Oregon. Following the 1955 state legislative session, Neuberger resigned from the House and joined her husband as his unpaid assistant and political partner. On the eve of the filing deadline for the 1960 Oregon Democratic primary, her husband died unexpectedly of a cerebral hemorrhage, and Neuberger was urged by state and national party leaders to run for his seat. Vowing to continue her husband's legacy, she waged a strong campaign and defeated the former governor Elmo Smith with 55 percent of the vote in the general election, becoming only the third woman elected to the U.S. Senate. Hattie Carraway of Arkansas and Margaret Chase Smith of Maine preceded her.

During her six years in the Senate, Neuberger proved more interested in getting results than in grabbing headlines. "She has . . . a traditional view of the Senate, ironically far more like that . . . of Senator Russell of Georgia than like that of those senators with whom she normally votes," William S. White observed in *Harper's.* A Democratic loyalist, Neuberger generally supported the policies of Presidents John F. Kennedy and Lyndon B. Johnson. She voted for the 1964 Tonkin Gulf Resolution, which authorized the expansion of the U.S. military presence in Vietnam, but later became a critic of the war. Neuberger's initial support of the resolution and later opposition to the war were influenced by her friendship with Senator J. William Fulbright, the chairman of the Foreign Relations Committee.

Neuberger achieved some notable victories, including her 1961 legislation eliminating billboards from federal highways, which passed over the opposition of the powerful outdoor advertising lobby. After the release of the report of the Surgeon General's Advisory Committee on Smoking and Health in 1964, Neuberger successfully sponsored the 1966 Federal Cigarette Labeling and Advertising Act. Because of her efforts, all cigarette packages were labeled with the warning, "Caution: Cigarette Smoking May Be Hazardous to Your Health." Neuberger, a former pack-a-day smoker, wrote *Smoke Screen: Tobacco and the Public Welfare* (1963).

Selected by President Kennedy as a member of the Commission on the Status of Women, Neuberger was a strong proponent of a federal law to guarantee equal pay to women for performing the same work as men. In 1963 she was among the sponsors of the Equal Pay Act, which was endorsed by Kennedy and approved by Congress. This law required firms engaged in interstate commerce to pay the same wages to men and women for doing the same work.

Neuberger was ahead of her time when she proposed legislation in 1961 that would have provided public funding to presidential and congressional candidates and set limits on the amounts of money that could be spent in campaigns. She chose not to run for a second term in 1966, explaining that she was did not want to seek special interest money in what would have been an expensive campaign. In 1964 Neuberger married Philip Solomon, a Boston psychiatrist; they divorced in 1967. Also in 1967, she moved to Cambridge, Massachusetts, where she taught at Radcliffe College. She moved back to Portland two years later, where she lectured at Reed College and remained politically active into her nineties. Neuberger died of a bone marrow disorder at a Portland nursing home at age ninety-three. She is buried in Beth Israel Cemetery in Portland.

As a trailblazer in national politics, Neuberger served as a mentor and role model to a new generation of political women and did much to rebuild the Democratic Party in Oregon. The former first lady Eleanor Roosevelt observed that Neuberger was "a genuine leader in liberalism and in enlightened good works."

★

Neuberger's papers are at the Oregon Historical Society as well at the University of Oregon in Eugene. For more information about here career, see Richard L. Neuberger, *Adventures in Politics: We Go to the Legislature* (1954), and Steve Neal, ed., *They Never Go Back to Pocatello: The Selected Essays of Richard Neuberger* (1988). See also Robert Cahn, "Madam Senator from Oregon," *Saturday Evening Post* (7 Jan. 1961); William S. White, "The Lady from Oregon," *Harper's Magazine* (Oct. 1961); and Steve Neal, "Maurine Remembers," a three-part series in the *Oregon Journal* (2–4 Aug. 1971). Obituaries are in the *Oregonian* (23 Feb. 2000) and *New York Times* (24 Feb. 2000).

STEVE NEAL

NICHOLAS, Harold Lloyd (*b.* 17 March 1921 in Winston-Salem, North Carolina; *d.* 3 July 2000 in New York City), one of the two Nicholas Brothers, a dancing duo.

Nicholas was the youngest of three children born to Ulysses Nicholas, a jazz drummer, and Viola (Harden) Nicholas, a stride pianist. His older brother, Fayard Antonio, chose his name, which was based on that of the white silent-comedy star Harold Lloyd. Both parents played in the pit bands of black vaudeville theaters throughout the eastern United States. Within one year of the family's 1924 move to Baltimore, young Harold added his voice to Fayard's and sister Dorothy's singing and dancing as the "Nicholas Kids" at the Lincoln Theater. In 1926 the family moved to Philadelphia, where Ulysses formed a ten-piece pit band for the Standard Theater. The children watched the dance acts and visiting jazz musicians when not attending private school. Dorothy dropped out of their act, but Fayard shared his tap and acrobatic dance steps with Harold. The two

Harold Nicholas (*right*) and his brother Fayard in a scene from the movie *Sun Valley Serenade*, 1941. BETT-
MANN/CORBIS

boys first performed together on stage at the Standard, probably in early 1929.

A "class act," with their impeccable attire, rhythmic exuberance, and penchant for tasteful good fun (an attribute taken from their parents), the Nicholas Brothers achieved immediate success. Harold had an appealing soprano voice and garnered most of the attention because of his youthful spirit. They joked, bantered, and sang, but everything was built around their unique and mature dancing style. This included not merely acrobatic and tap but swing dancing, based on the swing music style already being performed by popular black dance bands and soon to be embraced by white America.

Within a year the Nicholas Brothers were appearing at theaters in Washington and Baltimore, drawing such large crowds and critical acclaim that late in 1931 their parents decided to give up their own careers in order to manage their sons. The family relocated to the affluent Sugar Hill section of New York City's Harlem district, where the children received private tutoring as their careers soared. In March 1932 the brothers opened at Harlem's Lafayette Theater with Eubie Blake's orchestra, which also backed them in the first of several film shorts, *Pie, Pie Blackbird*. Like the jazz musicians who improvised on their instruments and in song, the Nicholas boys improvised with their feet, hands, and their entire torsos—most dramatically with airborne leaps and landing "splits." In October they

advanced to the Cotton Club, which became their home base for the rest of the decade, even after it moved downtown in 1937. They were backed on different occasions by the bands of Cab Calloway, Jimmie Lunceford, and particularly Duke Ellington, whose varied fare most appealed to them. In 1938 Harlem's Apollo Theater became an alternate second home, thus adding Count Basie's ensemble to the roster of bands that gave them musical support.

Trips to Hollywood began in 1934, when Harold appeared with Paul Robeson in the motion picture *Emperor Jones,* and both brothers in *Kid Millions,* for which Harold sang with a black-faced Eddie Cantor. Both boys danced, and Harold sang, in the film *Big Broadcast of 1936,* which featured the dancer Bill "Bojangles" Robinson. In such major movies, though the Nicholas Brothers were denied speaking roles because of their race, they were never stereotyped like most black actors as fools or servants. They were instead portrayed as the "precocious innocent," in the words of the Nicholas Brothers' biographer Constance Valis Hill, and again Harold stood out for his nearly ageless "youthful charm."

The brothers appeared on the Broadway stage with Josephine Baker in the *Ziegfeld Follies of 1936* and the comedy *Babes in Arms* (1937), choreographed by George Balanchine. Showtime was 8:00 P.M., and afterward they were rushed to the Cotton Club for midnight and 2:00 A.M. performances. During this time they traveled to London to appear as part of Lew Leslie's *Blackbirds of 1936,* an all-black revue. The brothers made four records of their singing and tap-dancing, two in London in 1936 and two in New York, accompanied by the cornetist Bobby Hackett's band, in 1937. Their appearance with Carmen Miranda in the motion picture *Down Argentine Way* (1940) led them to add Afro-Brazilian rhythms to their repertoire.

Constantly in demand, Fayard and Harold also fit in theater appearances with the big bands of Basie, Louis Armstrong, and Artie Shaw, choreographed by Nick Castle. A five-year film contract with Twentieth Century–Fox resulted in two excellent collaborations with the Glenn Miller Orchestra—*Sun Valley Serenade* (1941) and *Orchestra Wives* (1942)—and the all-black extravaganza *Stormy Weather* (1943). In the first of these, Harold sang with Dorothy Dandridge, whom he married in September 1942. They had a daughter before divorcing in 1949.

Standing five feet, two inches, Harold was too short to be drafted into the wartime army, unlike the taller Fayard. A year after Fayard entered the military in 1943, Harold appeared in two motion pictures, *Carolina Blues* and *The Reckless Age.* Upon Fayard's return, both of them toured the South with Dizzy Gillespie's bebop band (1945), appeared on Broadway in *St. Louis Woman* (1946) with Pearl Bailey, and danced with Gene Kelly in the movie *The Pirate* (1948). The brothers made a three-year tour of Europe, initiated by a 1948 Royal Command Performance alongside Ellington and Basie before King George VI at the London Palladium and ending with their role in the Italian film *Botta et Riposta* (1951).

Returning to the United States on the eve of the rock and roll era, the Nicholas brothers found that their postwar style of dance had gone out of fashion. They enjoyed little exposure, aside from brief television appearances, and in 1956 they returned to Europe. Though Fayard went home after a year, Harold continued working as a solo act, finding venues for his singing as well as his dancing. Between 1956 and 1964 he recorded two albums in France, starred in a stage show in Amsterdam, performed with Josephine Baker in Paris, and costarred in the French film *L'Empire de las nuit* (1963). In France he married Elayne Patronne, by whom he had one son before their divorce in 1971.

After Harold's return to America in 1964, he and Fayard reunited for occasional television appearances and tours, although the younger and healthier Harold worked mostly as a solo act. He appeared in the Sidney Poitier comedy film *Uptown Saturday Night* (1974) and on stage at home and in Europe, including his own Italian television show (1983). He was conversant in several languages. In 1979 he met Rigmor Alfredsson Newman, who soon became his manager; they were officially married on 30 December 1999 after having lived together for nearly two decades. From her he gained two stepchildren. Harold died of heart failure following surgery at age seventy-nine.

Numerous awards and accolades heaped upon the Nicholas Brothers culminated with *From Harlem to Hollywood,* a special 1998 Carnegie Hall tribute at which Harold himself sang. His voice, in the words of Jennifer Dunning in the *New York Times,* was "as sweet and subtle as ever." In a 1992 television special, *Nicholas Brothers: We Sing and We Dance,* the dancer Mikhail Baryshnikov observed that both had "choreographic minds," and that their work transformed the future of dance.

★

Nicholas's widow, Rigmor Newman Nicholas, maintains a Harold Nicholas archive. The definitive work is Constance Valis Hill, *Brotherhood in Rhythm: The Jazz Tap Dancing of the Nicholas Brothers* (2000). The brothers are treated within a broader context in Marshall and Jean Stearns, *Jazz Dance: The Story of American Vernacular Dance* (1968). An obituary is in the *New York Times* (4 July 2000). The Nicholas Brothers' two American recordings are on the compilation *Cotton Club Stars.*

CLARK G. REYNOLDS

NOMELLINI, Leo Joseph   (*b.* 19 June 1924 in Lucca, Italy; *d.* 17 October 2000 in Palo Alto, California), Hall of Fame offensive and defensive lineman for the San Francisco 49ers who retired in 1963 as the all-time record holder for consecutive games played in the National Football League (NFL).

Nomellini was born in Italy to Paul and Julia Nomellini, and at the age of four immigrated to the Chicago suburb of Gilman, Illinois, with his mother and two sisters. His father remained in Italy with an incurable disease, and after his death, Nomellini's mother remarried. The couple operated a candy store, and young Leo played sports in the sand lots of Chicago's tough West Side. After the stout teenager entered Crane Technical High School in 1938, his family encouraged him to work in a foundry after school instead of competing in athletics. Only after graduation, as an eighteen-year-old U.S. Marine at Cherry Point, North Carolina, did Nomellini play organized sports. Recruited for the base football team, the Leathernecks, Nomellini played at left tackle. That experience, and an earlier fascination with the film *Knute Rockne—All American* (1940), stimulated Nomellini's passion for football.

After completing his enlistment, which included combat in the South Pacific at Saipan and Okinawa, Nomellini accepted a football scholarship in 1946 to play for Bernie Bierman's University of Minnesota Golden Gophers. The untested twenty-two-year-old freshman became an instant force at offensive guard. The next year Nomellini moved to offensive tackle, a position at which he started from 1947 to 1949. It was at Minnesota that Nomellini earned his most enduring nickname, "Leo the Lion." College teammate

Bud Grant, later head coach of the Minnesota Vikings, said Nomellini "would just roar" when pulling around the corner on a running play. Nomellini play was unpolished, but he compensated for his inexperience by using the colossal strength and quickness of his six-foot, three-inch, 265-pound body to "run you over like a truck." Nomellini earned consensus All-America honors in 1948 and 1949.

Nomellini also wrestled for Minnesota but lost the Big Ten heavyweight wrestling championship match his senior year. Further demonstrating his unusual combination of size, speed, and power, he competed in track and field as a shot-putter and as anchor for the 440-yard relay team.

In January 1950 Nomellini played in the College Football All-Star Game in Chicago, and then became the San Francisco 49ers first-ever NFL draft choice. Later that spring, he received his B.A. in education from the University of Minnesota.

The twenty-six-year-old started at offensive tackle and made an immediate impact on a mediocre San Francisco team. Nomellini held that position for his first three seasons and was named All-Pro in 1951 and 1952. In 1953 coach Buck Shaw moved Nomellini to his favorite position, defensive tackle, where he again was named All-Pro in 1953, 1954, 1957, and 1959. At the peak of his career in 1955, severe injuries to the 49ers offensive line forced Nomellini to play both ways for nearly all sixty minutes of each of the team's twelve games. Still, despite Nomellini's best efforts and those of four future Pro Football Hall of Fame inductees on offense, the 49ers put together playoff-caliber seasons only in 1952 and 1956.

Nomellini remained relatively injury-free despite a decision in 1952 to wrestle professionally. Wrestling, like football, was a rough sport that suited Nomellini well. Unlike the later World Wrestling Federation, professional wrestling during the 1950s was unpredictable, and Nomellini risked injury—not to mention his football career—when he joined the fledgling National Wrestling Alliance (NWA). In March 1952 Nomellini teamed up with Hombre Montana to defeat Ben and Mike Sharpe for the NWA tag-team title. Nomellini won and lost the title repeatedly during the 1950s, often conceding because of interference with the football season. Wrestling almost exclusively on the West Coast, Nomellini demonstrated his extraordinary physical skills in winning his most famous match in 1954, when he handed the professional wrestling legend Lou Thesz his only NWA career defeat. A rematch, which ended in a loss to Thesz, drew gate receipts of $72,000, a Bay Area record.

Nomellini continued to punish quarterbacks and wrestling opponents into the early 1960s. In 1960 fragmentation within the NWA caused the formation of the American Wrestling Association (AWA), which Nomellini immediately joined. In July 1960 Nomellini teamed up with Verne Gagne to defeat the AWA's original tag-team champions,

Murder Inc. (Tiny Mills and Stan Kowalski). One month later Nomellini again forfeited a title because of football. Nomellini regained the AWA tag team title one last time in May 1961, when he and Wilbur Snyder defeated Hard Boiled Haggerty and Gene Kiniski.

On 9 December 1962, in a game between the 49rs and Green Bay, NFL Commissioner Pete Rozelle presented the thirty-eight-year-old Nomellini, sporting his usual crew cut and wide smile, with a plaque for breaking Emlen Tunnell's record of 158 consecutive games played. Nomellini retired from football after the 1963 season with ten Pro Bowl appearances and a total of 174 consecutive games played. In 1969 Nomellini was elected to the Pro Football Hall of Fame and to the NFL's fiftieth anniversary and all-time teams.

His durability and passion to compete continued throughout his career, yet Nomellini's personal warmth was unmistakable to those who knew him. "Leo was one of the kindest, gentlest, biggest tough men you'd ever want to meet," said 49er teammate Y. A. Tittle. Despite Nomellini's strength and size, most considered him a "gentle giant."

In 1949 Nomellini married Ruth Benson, with whom he had three children. After filing for divorce in 1963, Ruth attested to her husband's hard-nosed, football-first attitude, claiming that he loved the game more than he did her or their children. After they divorced, Nomellini never remarried, but he remained close to his ex-wife and children for the remainder of his life.

Nomellini remained in San Francisco after retirement, working for more than thirty years as the head of public relations for Northwestern Title Company. He was enshrined in the College Football Hall of Fame in 1977 and the National Italian American Sports Hall of Fame in 1979. He also briefly worked as a professional wrestling promoter in the Bay Area during the early 1980s. Late in life, Nomellini underwent hip surgery and experienced heart ailments. In late September 2000 Nomellini suffered a stroke and was admitted to Stanford University hospital, where he remained until he died of complications.

Looking back at Nomellini's life, longtime teammate and friend Bob St. Clair remarked, "He loved people, he loved having fun. . . . He just enjoyed life so much." Perhaps the greatest testament to Nomellini's character was the fact that, despite health problems in his later years, he vigorously participated in charity functions around the Bay Area and remained loyal to numerous alumni associations. Although his consecutive games record has been surpassed many times over, Nomellini's name regularly appears on the rosters of nearly every college and professional all-time team.

★

Biographical information on Nomellini can be found in the Pro Football Hall of Fame archives in Canton, Ohio. Additional sources detailing Nomellini's life include Bob Carroll, *Football*

Legends of All Time (1997), and Don Smith and Pete Fielre, *Total Football II* (1999). Obituaries are in the *San Francisco Chronicle* (18 Oct. 2000) and *New York Times* (27 Oct. 2000).

RUSTY ATON

NOZICK, Robert (*b*. 16 November 1938 in Brooklyn, New York City; *d*. 23 January 2002 in Cambridge, Massachusetts), Harvard philosopher whose first book, *Anarchy, State, and Utopia* (1974), made libertarianism respectable in academic philosophy.

Nozick was the son of Max Nozick, a Jewish immigrant from Russia who owned a small business, and Sophie (Cohen) Nozick, a homemaker. He attended public schools in Brooklyn and joined the youth branch of Norman Thomas's Socialist Party. In high school he encountered Plato's *Republic*, which inspired him to study philosophy, although he later admitted that he read little of the book and understood less.

At Columbia University in New York City, Nozick founded a chapter of the Student League for Industrial Democracy (later known as Students for a Democratic Society). He received his B.A. in 1959. Also in 1959, on 15 August, he married Barbara Fierer, a teacher. They had two children. Nozick continued his philosophical studies at Princeton University in New Jersey, where he received an M.A. in 1961 and a Ph.D. in 1963. He became an instructor in philosophy at Princeton in 1962, served as a Fulbright scholar at Oxford University in England in 1963 and 1964, and in the latter year became an assistant professor at Princeton. In 1965 he took a position as an assistant professor at Harvard University in Cambridge, Massachusetts, and then moved to Rockefeller University in New York City in 1967 as an associate professor. He returned to Harvard as a full professor in 1969 and remained there for the rest of his career. In 1971 and 1972 he was a fellow at the Center for Advanced Study in the Behavioral Sciences at Stanford University, in Palo Alto, California.

His studies at Princeton led Nozick to question his earlier assumption that labor was the sole source of value and that the market was merely a means for capitalists to extract that value from others. He wrestled with these political questions for years, and in 1974 he published a groundbreaking philosophical response to his former politics. In *Anarchy, State, and Utopia*, Nozick set out to establish that the greatest amount of justifiable government intervention in the lives of individuals is what has been called a "nightwatchman state," the only powers of which are to prevent theft, assault, and breach of contract. Such a government could have evolved from a theoretical state of nature, he maintained, without violating anyone's natural rights. The main focus of the book was a thorough and respectful rejoinder to his Harvard colleague John Rawls, whose *Theory of Justice* (1971) called upon the state to redistribute income for the general good.

Perhaps the best-known part of Nozick's book was a demonstration that if a government set out to enforce a particular distribution of rewards, a single popular athlete (his example was the basketball player Wilt Chamberlain) could ask individuals to pay more to watch him play, thus changing the intended pattern of rewards. Therefore, a government that wanted to enforce distributive justice would have to forbid or at least regulate all "capitalist acts between consenting adults," lest they overturn the carefully designed balance. Nozick further suggested that the true utopia would be a framework in which individuals could explore their own vision of utopia, as long as they did not interfere with others.

Anarchy, State, and Utopia was a polymath work that brought together ethics, economics, game theory, psychology, and even a discussion of the application of his theories to the children's writer Dr. Seuss's *Thidwick, the Big-Hearted Moose*. Thinkers on many sides, particularly the political left, questioned Nozick's approach. Anarchists insisted that his arguments justifying even a minimal state were illegitimate, while liberals and socialists maintained that he gave insufficient weight to noneconomic values and freedoms. The book won the National Book Award in 1975 and established Nozick's reputation. Divorced from his first wife in 1981, Nozick married Gjertrud Schnackenberg, a poet, on 5 October 1987.

Rather than continue the political debates his first book had started, Nozick moved on to other areas of inquiry. *Philosophical Explanations* (1981) dealt with issues ranging from the philosopher Martin Heidegger's famous question "Why is there anything at all, rather than nothing?" to science-fiction scenarios in which one might be a brain in a vat being tricked into believing that his "world" really exists. The book won the Ralph Waldo Emerson Award from Phi Beta Kappa. In 1989 he published *The Examined Life: Philosophical Meditations*, a popularly written treatment of topics outside the usual range of academic philosophy, including love, creativity, and the Holocaust. In this work he pulled back from some of the libertarian statements in his first book, suggesting that there were communal goals that could not be attained without more government than the minimal sort he had advocated.

From 1981 to 1984, as chairman of the Harvard philosophy department, Nozick became known for the range of courses he offered, teaching with members of the psychology, government, and economics departments as well as the divinity and law schools. In 1997 he delivered six John Locke Lectures at Oxford University under the title "Invariance and Objectivity." In 1998 he was named University Professor, Harvard's most distinguished professorial title; at the time he was one of only eighteen such professors. In the 1990s Nozick published *The Nature of Rationality* (1993) and *Socratic Puzzles* (1997). His final book, *Invariances: The Structure of the Objective World* (2001), was something of a philosophical summa, an attempt to construct a unified philosophical theory that took into account such scientific areas as evolution, cognitive theory, and quantum physics. Nozick died at age sixty-three of complications from stomach cancer.

Throughout his career, Nozick produced theories that are discussed in academic circles, but he remains known primarily for his first book, *Anarchy, State, and Utopia.* While he did not win the day for libertarian theory (and indeed came to express doubts about aspects of it), he brought it to the academic mainstream, producing arguments that had to be taken seriously and answered. As Jonathan Wolff said in his monograph about Nozick, "It is no longer acceptable to criticize capitalism by platitude." The theories expressed in *Invariances* may become more influential if a biology-based view of humanity prevails.

★

Jeffrey Paul, ed., *Reading Nozick* (1981), is a collection of essays on *Anarchy, State, and Utopia.* See also Jonathan Wolff, *Robert Nozick: Property, Justice, and the Minimal State* (1991); A. R. Lacey, *Robert Nozick* (2001); and David Schmidtz, *Robert Nozick* (2002). An obituary is in the *New York Times* (24 Jan. 2002).

ARTHUR D. HLAVATY

OAKES, John Bertram (*b.* 23 April 1913 in Elkins Park, Pennsylvania; *d.* 5 April 2001 in Manhattan, New York City), journalist and editor who directed the *New York Times* editorial page from 1967 to 1976 and who created the "op-ed" page.

Oakes was the younger of two sons of George Washington Ochs and Bertie (Gans) Ochs, a homemaker. His father was editor of the *Philadelphia Public Ledger* and the brother of Adolph Ochs, publisher of the *New York Times*. His mother died of an infection one week after his birth, and an unmarried aunt, Bertha Ochs, moved into the household and helped raise him. In 1917, in the intense anti-German atmosphere of World War I, his father legally changed his sons' surnames from Ochs to Oakes.

Known to his friends as "Johnny," Oakes attended the Collegiate School in New York City (to which the family had moved in 1915) and the Laurenceville School, a boarding school in New Jersey. His father also required that he and his brother attend Sunday school at Emanu-El, the Reformed Jewish Temple in Manhattan, where he studied Jewish theology and history. Oakes graduated from the Laurenceville School in 1930, and in 1934 earned a B.A. in English literature from Princeton University in New Jersey. In addition to graduating magna cum laude, he was chosen "most brilliant" by his classmates. He continued his studies at the University of Dijon in France, earning a diploma in French in 1933, and at Oxford University on a Rhodes

scholarship, earning a B.A. and M.A. in 1936. Oakes married Margery C. Hartmen on 24 October 1945. They had four children.

His career in journalism began in 1936 as a reporter covering the New Jersey legislature for the *State Gazette and Trenton Times*. In 1937 he moved to the *Washington Post*, working the police beat and eventually covering Congress and the Supreme Court. In 1941, when the United States entered World War II, Oakes joined the U.S. Army as a private, believing that Americans of his background and education should begin service in the lower ranks. By 1946 he had risen to the rank of major. Such rapid promotions were not uncommon for the intelligence services, in which he served. He took an oath of secrecy concerning his counterintelligence missions. Over the course of his term of service, he earned the Bronze Star, the Order of the British Empire, and the Croix de Guerre. As a young lieutenant training recruits in Arkansas, Oakes had observed that a surprising number of young Americans could neither read nor write, "an absolutely shocking experience." His wartime service also included two years as a counterintelligence officer in France and Germany, where he worked with the Office of Strategic Services, the forerunner of the Central Intelligence Agency.

After the war Oakes joined the *New York Times* Sunday department, serving as editor of the "Week in Review" from 1946 to 1949, when he moved to the editorial board. During the 1950s, in addition to writing editorials, he distinguished

John B. Oakes, July 1986. AP/WIDE WORLD PHOTOS

himself as a pioneer in environmental journalism. He created and wrote a monthly environmental column and was an active member of the Interior Department's Advisory Board on National Parks, Historic Sites, Buildings, and Monuments from 1955 to 1962. In 1961, after almost a year in Europe and Africa, he wrote, *The Edge of Freedom,* a study of U.S. foreign relations with emerging African and Eastern European nations.

On 25 April 1961 Oakes was appointed editor of the editorial page under the new president and publisher of the *Times,* Orvil Dryfoos, who expected Oakes to overhaul the page. A committed progressive, Oakes reinvigorated the editorials, writing many of them himself. Several of these, "John Fitzgerald Kennedy" (23 November 1963), "Ad Astra" (on the lunar landing, 21 July 1969), and "Environmental Security" (8 November 1971) became classics in the field. He recruited a talented and diverse editorial staff that included the seasoned labor reporter A. H. Raskin; a conservationist, Ada Lousie Huxtable; and the first African American on the editorial board, Roger Wilkins. Under Oakes, the *Times* editorial page shifted to the left as he demonstrated an unflagging commitment to such liberal causes as environmental protection, literacy, civil rights, and support for the United Nations.

Long before most newspapers became concerned about the U.S. involvement in Vietnam, the *Times* expressed its opposition to escalation of the conflict. Familiar with France's Indochina experience, Oakes felt that the United States was repeating the French catastrophe. From 1946 to

1954, France had fought a colonial war against a range of Indochinese nationalists, among whom the communists were the most effective. By 1954, with the siege of Dien Bien Phu, at which some fifteen thousand of France's best troops found themselves hopelessly trapped, the French public had grown weary of the war, and France withdrew. Soon President Dwight D. Eisenhower sent U.S. military advisers, and as Oakes predicted, the process began to repeat itself.

Oakes's most significant contribution to the *Times* was an institutional one: the creation of the "op-ed" page. Before becoming editor of the editorial page, Oakes had received an article on the Middle East that was too long for the "Letters to the Editor" section and too short for the newspaper's Sunday magazine. He subsequently proposed a page that would provide a format for such articles by outside contributors. A decade-long debate over space and editorial control ensued, ending in the fall of 1970 when the page was inaugurated. Oakes adopted the designation "op-ed" for the page, a term that had been used briefly by the *New York World* in the 1920s, though the modern op-ed page is Oakes's creation. In Oakes's modern format, one page of the newspaper featured editorials, and the page opposite included a variety of essays and columns by *Times* staff writers and outside contributors. The format has since been adopted by newspapers across the nation.

By the mid-1970s considerable tension had developed between Oakes and the *Times* management. For his part, Oakes insisted that his editorial and opinion pages remain independent from the news department, and he expressed concern about advocacy reporting in the *Times* news stories, particularly those on the Vietnam War. At the same time, the *Times* publisher Arthur Ochs Sulzberger (Oakes's cousin) and other executives became increasingly disturbed by the stridency of some of Oakes's editorials and the antibusiness tone of others. Things came to a head in March 1976, when Sulzberger announced that he was removing Oakes as editor of the editorial page. Oakes stepped down at the end of that year and became senior vice president of the *Times*. He retired in 1978 but continued writing for the op-ed page until 1993. Oakes died of complications from a stroke in Mount Sinai Hospital, New York City.

Oakes was the recipient of many journalistic awards and other honors, including the Princeton Distinguished Service Award (1964) and Woodrow Wilson Award (1970) from Princeton University and awards from the Sierra Club and the National Audubon Society. He was honored with two George Polk Awards, in 1965 and in 2000. His 1965 Polk Award for editorial comment commended him for making the *Times* editorial page "the most vital and influential journalistic voice in America."

Born into one of the most powerful families in American journalism, Oakes was an outstanding reporter and a respected editor. A lifelong progressive, he brought commitment, courage, and a keen intellect to bear on all his work. During his tenure on the editorial page, the *New York Times* reached an unequalled position of influence in American politics and culture.

★

For further information on Oakes's life and career, see Gay Talese, *The Kingdom and the Power* (1969), and Susan E. Tifft and Alex S. Jones, *The Trust: The Private and Powerful Family Behind the New York Times* (1999). Obituaries are in the *New York Times* and *Washington Post* (both 6 Apr. 2001).

KEVIN O'KEEFE

O'CONNOR, Carroll (*b.* 2 August 1924 in New York City; *d.* 21 June 2001 in Culver City, California), actor on stage, screen, and television best known for his Emmy Award-winning television role as the loudmouthed, bigoted Archie Bunker in the situation comedy *All in the Family* (1971–1979).

O'Connor grew up in an Irish-Catholic family in middle-class neighborhoods of the Bronx and Queens in New York City. He was one of three children of Edward Joseph O'Connor, an attorney, and Elise Patricia O'Connor, a teacher. Despite an emphasis on education at home that helped both of his brothers become physicians, he was an indifferent student, rarely making grades above C. In his autobiography, O'Connor wrote that although he enjoyed

reading and writing and was eager to learn, he was "impossible to teach" because of an aloof attitude, probably a form of rebellion.

After graduating from high school in 1941, he made a series of false starts at college, which included intermittent enrollments over the next decade at Wake Forest University, the U.S. Merchant Marine Academy, and the University of Montana. Rejected by the Naval Air Corps because of his poor academic record, he spent much of World War II as a merchant seaman, serving in the North Atlantic and Mediterranean war zones.

O'Connor reached his late twenties without completing college or fixing on a vocation. In 1950 he traveled to Ireland, where he discovered a fascination with his family's heritage, which had the effect of focusing his energies. He enrolled at the University College in Dublin, studying history, literature, and theater, and became active in the drama society, receiving his B.A. in 1952. Moreover, O'Connor discovered himself as an actor while studying in Ireland. Taking the stage name of George Roberts, he worked under the direction of Michael MacLiammoir and Hilton Edwards, the founders of the Gate Theatre in Dublin, appearing in several plays at the Gate as well as in other productions in Ireland and Britain.

Despite these successes, his return to New York in 1954 was anything but triumphal. Unable to find work beyond a few bit roles, O'Connor returned to the University of Montana, where he had taken several undergraduate courses some years earlier, and earned an M.A. in speech communication in 1956. He used this as a credential to teach English in the New York City public school system. Although he continued to audition for stage roles, he believed at the time that it was more than likely that teaching would be his life's work.

A turning point in O'Connor's belated struggle to become an actor occurred in 1958 when he won a role in the off-Broadway production of *Ulysses in Nighttown*, an adaptation of a scene from the James Joyce novel *Ulysses*. Receiving positive reviews and the enthusiastic recommendation of the play's director, Burgess Meredith, O'Connor found himself taken seriously at auditions for the first time. His next role was in *The Big Knife* (1959), a revival of a Clifford Odets play about corruption in the Hollywood film industry. Cast as a ruthless blackmailer by the director Peter Bogdanovich, O'Connor was lauded by New York critics, including Judith Crist of the *Herald Tribune*, who found his performance "sharply cruel and unctuously powerful." Roles followed in several television anthology drama series, including a production of the *Armstrong Circle Theatre* in which he played a prosecutor in the trial of Nicola Sacco and Bartolomeo Vanzetti, political radicals who were arrested, convicted, and executed in the 1920s for payroll robbery and murder.

Carroll O'Connor, 1998. AP/WIDE WORLD PHOTOS

New York–based anthology drama was rapidly disappearing from prime-time television at the beginning of the 1960s in favor of filmed series produced in Los Angeles. Having played the role of starving actor long enough, O'Connor did not hesitate to respond when Hollywood beckoned. He appeared in guest roles, usually as a villain, in dozens of prime-time drama series, including some of the most popular of the 1960s: *The Untouchables, Naked City, Dr. Kildare, Ben Casey, Bonanza, The Fugitive, The Man from U.N.C.L.E., I Spy, Gunsmoke, The Wild, Wild West*, and *Mission: Impossible*. He was equally active in the movies throughout the decade, appearing in supporting or character roles in a score of mostly undistinguished features. The most remembered of these films was probably the Elizabeth Taylor–Richard Burton extravaganza *Cleopatra* (1963), in which he played the scheming Casca.

By the early 1970s O'Connor was financially secure for the first time in his life and had developed a reputation for professional competence. Nonetheless, he had not yet starred in his own television series or in a theatrical feature film, so his name was virtually unknown to the public. This journeyman status was about to change dramatically on the strength of a single role.

Norman Lear, a veteran American television comedy writer who had spent much of the 1960s in London, approached O'Connor with a starring part in a situation com-edy he had adapted from a British Broadcasting Company hit about a Cockney family in London's East End, *'Til Death Us Do Part*. Transplanting the setup to an American working-class family in the New York City borough of Queens, Lear titled the proposed series *All in the Family*. On the surface, it seemed conventional sitcom fare. O'Connor's character, Archie Bunker, had a job, a house, neighbors, and a family consisting of a wacky wife and a live-in daughter married to a man he did not especially like.

If the form was familiar, the content was not. Archie was to be portrayed as a political Neanderthal, carrying overtones and undertones of racism, sexism, and other traits previously taboo in American television right into the nation's living rooms. Making the role even more difficult to play was the understanding that as the principal of a comedy, Archie could not be completely unsympathetic. He would have to demonstrate that beneath his blustering about "coloreds" and "homos" and "commies" there beat the good, if somewhat confused and ignorant, heart of a decent husband and father.

Lear produced two pilot episodes of *All in the Family* for the American Broadcasting Company network in 1970, with O'Connor in the starring role. After many front-office debates about how the public would react to the show's radical disregard for conventional boundaries, the network dropped the project. The Columbia Broadcasting System

(CBS) bought an option in the summer of 1970 but declined to put the show on its fall schedule. Faced with the failure of several other programs at midseason, however, CBS programmers finally gave the series a prime-time slot in January 1971.

The controversial subject matter, which brought the viewer such subjects as menopause, euthanasia, and criticism of a sitting president, did provoke protests, as predicted. On the political left were those who thought Archie's utterance of ethnic and racial slurs constituted a form of validation for such speech as well as the thinking behind it. The political right charged that conservative values were being caricatured and ridiculed in the malapropisms of an uneducated, uncultured buffoon. Surprisingly, a steadily building audience accepted the show as a refreshingly honest airing of the nation's dirty laundry.

Much of the credit for the *All in the Family*'s survival and its ultimate success was given by Lear, as well as many critics, to the bravado comic performances of O'Connor and the other members of the ensemble cast. *All in the Family* became the highest-rated show on all of television for 1971–1972, its first full season, and held that position for an unprecedented five consecutive years. Its weekly audience was projected by the A. C. Neilsen Company to be as large as fifty million viewers at the height of its popularity.

As often happens in hit television series, many viewers confused character and actor, believing that O'Connor held the views Archie espoused. This was far from the truth. O'Connor held mostly liberal political views and was active in the 1968 presidential campaign of Eugene McCarthy. "Both of my father's law partners, who were two of his best friends, were Jews, and it would have been unthinkable to utter a word such as 'hebe,' [one of Archie's favorite epithets] even in a joke in our home," he said. Few viewers knew that O'Connor had performed Shakespeare at the Edinburgh Festival or held an M.A. in speech communication. The actor claimed to have based Archie's accent on that of an acquaintance of his father's from the Canarsie section of Brooklyn.

"The funniest thing about Archie was that he would never change his mind," O'Connor told the *Los Angeles Times,* referring to the lessons about race, sex, politics, and other topics he was repeatedly taught in the hundreds of episodes of *All in the Family.* "Archie never laughed at anything himself. The world was a painful place to him. Painful to him; funny to you."

At the end of the 1978–1979 season, with other members of the cast departing for new projects, O'Connor chose to stick with the character by repackaging the series as *Archie Bunker's Place,* in which Archie, now widowed, opens a neighborhood bar. O'Connor hoped to keep the series vital by continuing to explore television taboo, but he found himself continually involved in battles with CBS executives who felt that controversial material had exhausted its popularity in television comedy. After four seasons the show was cancelled, with O'Connor, who had been receiving more than $100,000 per sitcom episode for more than a decade, now anxious to leave television behind.

Hoping to realize a lingering dream, he returned to New York in 1983 to make his Broadway debut in *Brothers,* a play concerning an Irish family, which he also produced. Despite strong box-office pre-sales based on the star's celebrity, the play had only a short run. The following year he was back on Broadway in another family drama, *Home Front.* This was an even more embarrassing failure, closing in less than two weeks.

O'Connor returned to television, which proved the only medium in which he would find commercial success. In 1987 he was back in a starring prime-time role in the crime drama series *In the Heat of the Night.* In the feature film on which it is based, an old-school racist southern sheriff is forced to work with an urbane African-American agent of the Federal Bureau of Investigation. O'Connor did not want to create a southern version of Archie Bunker, so he reshaped Bill Gillespie into a character who gradually transcends racist attitudes, finds positive value in all his colleagues, and consequently grows as a person. In the show's sixth season, Gillespie marries an African-American woman. "A kind of insight and enlightenment happened to Gillespie," O'Connor said. Having won four Emmy Awards as best actor in a comedy series for *All in the Family,* O'Connor won his fifth in 1989 as best actor in a dramatic series. The following season he received the National Association for the Advancement of Colored People (NAACP) Image Award.

O'Connor married Nancy Fields in 1951, a year after they met at the University of Montana. Their only child, Hugh O'Connor, whom they adopted as an infant in 1962, developed an addiction to cocaine and committed suicide in 1995. O'Connor then became active in the antidrug movement, making television spots and personal appearances to promote antidrug messages. He died of a heart attack, complicated by diabetes, at age seventy-six. O'Connor is buried at Westwood Memorial Park in Santa Monica, California.

★

O'Connor published his autobiography, *I Think I'm Outta Here: A Memoir of All My Families,* in 1998. An article of interest is a remembrance of O'Connor by William F. Buckley, "The Laughter of Archie Bunker," *National Review* (23 July 2001). Obituaries appear in most major newspapers, including the *New York Times* (22 June 2001).

DAVID MARC

O'CONNOR, John Joseph (*b.* 15 January 1920 in Philadelphia, Pennsylvania; *d.* 3 May 2000 in Manhattan, New York City), theological conservative and ardent advocate for the poor and working class, who as archbishop and cardinal of New York led the most visible and important Catholic diocese in the United States from 1984 to 2000.

O'Connor was fourth of five children born to Thomas Joseph O'Connor, a skilled painter specializing in gold leafing, and Dorothy Magdalene (Gomple) O'Connor. Raised in a Philadelphia row house, as a youth he loved baseball, ran a bicycle repair shop in his basement, and hoped to become a police officer. O'Connor's father, "who overwhelmingly shaped my life," O'Connor later recalled, led a family devoted to what liberals call "pay, pray, obey" Catholicism.

After he transferred from public high school to West Catholic High School for Boys, O'Connor found his vocation. Despite a seminary experience that he "cordially disliked," he never wavered in his priestly commitment. He enrolled in Saint Charles Borromeo Seminary in Philadel-

John Joseph O'Connor, September 1984. ROBERT MAASS/CORBIS

phia in 1936 and was ordained on 15 December 1945. In the next seven years, still in Philadelphia, he was an assistant pastor and a guidance counselor at Saint James High School, served in a psychiatric ward, hosted two radio programs, and received an M.A. in theology from Saint Charles Borromeo Seminary (1949). O'Connor's work with mentally retarded children fostered a diocesan center, and treatment for retarded children remained a lifelong concern for O'Connor.

The turning point of O'Connor's life came in 1952, when he followed his bishop's suggestion and enlisted as a U.S. Navy chaplain in a program created by Francis Cardinal Spellman. During his twenty-seven-year military career, O'Connor saw combat in both Korea and Vietnam, often celebrating mass on the hood of a Jeep. After the Korean armistice, he obtained a second M.A., this one in clinical psychology, at Catholic University of America in Washington, D.C. (1954); wrote *Principles and Problems of Naval Leadership* (1958); and instituted a program for retarded children in the Monterey, California, Diocese (1962). O'Connor's Vietnam service with the Third Marine Division won him the Legion of Merit. He wrote a book defending American intervention, *A Chaplain Looks at Vietnam* (1968), which he later regretted.

In 1970 O'Connor earned a Ph.D. in political science from Georgetown University in Washington, D.C. His professors included the distinguished thinker and diplomat Jeane Kirkpatrick, who considered him one of her "two or three smartest" scholars. O'Connor learned to play golf while serving as the first Catholic senior chaplain at the U.S. Naval Academy in Annapolis, Maryland, and then moved to Washington, D.C., as navy chief of chaplains. Appointed auxiliary bishop of the Military Ordinariate and assigned to New York, O'Connor retired from the navy on 1 June 1979 with the rank of rear admiral.

O'Connor was always a Catholic traditionalist, but his learning and intellectual curiosity, his devotion to workers' rights, and his combative nature made him more than the "simple parish priest" he aspired to be. An enthusiastic supporter of the reforms of Vatican II, he enjoyed celebrating mass in English and facing the congregation, and he decried the medieval thinking that blamed all Jews for the death of Christ. His devotion to "life, at every stage of its existence" led him to condemn the death penalty, euthanasia, assisted suicide, and abortion. His book *The Defense of Life* (1981) condemned abortion as a "national Holocaust." His pastoral letter in January 1986 proclaimed the anniversary of *Roe* v. *Wade,* the court case that essentially legalized abortion, to be a day of "national infamy." He challenged a Harvard University audience to explain why a bishop would be applauded for indicting racism but damned for indicting abortion.

Appointed bishop of Scranton, Pennsylvania, in May

1983, O'Connor announced that ending abortion was his primary goal. He also fought for higher teacher salaries, more women in important leadership positions, and regular meetings with every priest. When he left after only nine months, the city named a plaza in his honor. With regard to matters of national defense, O'Connor tended to be hawkish. In 1983, when American bishops collectively considered the arms race and nuclear war, O'Connor regularly consulted with the conservative, pro-defense administration of President Ronald M. Reagan. Although he served on the drafting committee, he could not alter the pacific tone of the bishops' report, *The Challenge of Peace: God's Promise and Our Response* (May 1983). O'Connor voted for the final document and came to consider nuclear policy as "rationalizing insanity."

Pope John Paul II named O'Connor as the sixth archbishop of New York on 19 March 1984, in so doing allegedly choosing someone whom he described as "a man like me"—one who could "say no." O'Connor arrived at the famed diocese with 1.8 million Catholics amid controversy. In recent interviews he had likened abortion to the Holocaust and asserted that he could not vote for any Catholic politician who supported such a policy. Assailed by the *New York Times* for breaching the barrier between church and state, he was the implicit target of a major September 1984 speech by Governor Mario Cuomo, a Catholic. He fought with Mayor Edward Koch, rejecting the city's mandated preference for hiring gays in city-funded, church-sponsored programs. By the time O'Connor became a cardinal on 21 March 1985, he was a front-page celebrity.

New Yorkers gradually discovered that O'Connor was no mere dogmatist. Widely read, politically sophisticated, and supportive of unions, he led a bishop's group to Nicaragua and condemned aid to the anticommunist Contras; denounced Reagan's reduction of public housing funds; and criticized spending on the MX missile. O'Connor also quietly visited hospital patients, counseled wounded police officers, and cared for AIDS patients. He appointed the first Hispanic and first black laywomen vice chancellors and the first woman communications director. He initiated sanctification proceedings for Terence Cardinal Cooke, his predecessor, and Dorothy Day of the Catholic Worker Movement.

When Koch suffered clinical depression in 1986, the cardinal personally intervened. Two very different men, who frequently battled each other in their official capacities, they became good friends and ultimately collaborated on a bestselling book, *His Eminence and Hizzoner: A Candid Exchange* (1989). O'Connor firmly supported papal authority, even in cases in which it infringed on American academic freedom and clerical independence, yet by circumventing curial instructions during his 1986 trip to Israel, he advanced the Vatican recognition process. Scorned by femi-

nists and targeted by gay activists, he endured the disruption of Sunday mass at Saint Patrick's Cathedral in November 1989 by activists from the AIDS organization ACT UP.

O'Connor was a conservative who flouted tradition by allowing altar girls (not just boys), attending the wedding of an AIDS sufferer in his cathedral, and permitting liturgical dancing by blacks within Saint Patrick's Cathedral. He was the first cardinal to join the Salute to Israel parade. As an administrator, the "Boss," as subordinates often called him, found it intolerable to close schools or cut church services. Cuomo said O'Connor "resisted the insistence of fiscal reality" with vehemence.

During a tenure marked by headline controversies, O'Connor always celebrated daily mass and preached the worth of every individual. Diagnosed with a brain tumor in August 1998, he was disfigured by treatment but continued working until his death at age eighty in his residence near Saint Patrick's Cathedral on Fifth Avenue. His national stature was such that George W. Bush, then governor of Texas, sent him a written apology for visiting Bob Jones University, an anti-Catholic college, during the 2000 primary campaign. O'Connor is buried at Saint Patrick's in a tomb bearing his motto, "There can be no love without justice."

★

O'Connor's papers are deposited at Saint Joseph's Seminary in Yonkers, New York. Insights into his thoughts are found in his books *Principles and Problems of Naval Leadership* (1958), *A Chaplain Looks at Vietnam* (1968), *In Defense of Life* (1981), and *A Moment of Grace* (1995). His most systematic and enlightening writing appears in dialogues with sometime opponent Edward Koch, *His Eminence and Hizzoner: A Candid Exchange* (1989), and in a more spiritual context in conversations with Elie Wiesel, *A Journey of Faith* (1990). The primary biography by Nat Hentoff, *John Cardinal O'Connor: At the Storm Center of a Changing American Church* (1987), does not cover his later years. Personal reminiscences are collected in Terry Golway, *Full of Grace: An Oral Biography of John Cardinal O'Connor* (2001). An obituary is in the *New York Times* (4 May 2001).

GEORGE J. LANKEVICH

O'FARRILL, Arturo ("Chico") (*b.* 28 October 1921 in Havana, Cuba; *d.* 27 June 2001 in Manhattan, New York City), composer, arranger, and orchestra leader who was one of the founding fathers of Latin jazz.

O'Farrill's parents, of Irish, Cuban, and German extraction, were solidly middle class; his father was a lawyer. After completing elementary education in Cuba, O'Farrill moved to the United States in 1937 to attend the Riverside Military

Chico O'Farrill, December 2000. MR. JACK VARTOOGIAN

Academy in Gainesville, Georgia. At school "Artie" became enthralled with the swing band music of such American artists as Benny Goodman, Artie Shaw, Glen Miller, and Tommy Dorsey. (Goodman later gave him a new nickname, "Chico.") It inspired him to pick up the trumpet, which he played in the school dance orchestra, concert band, and chapel orchestra. He graduated in 1940, planning to study law at the University of Havana.

The lure of North American jazz music, however, proved too strong. O'Farrill persuaded his father to allow him to study harmony and orchestration with the noted Cuban composer Félix Guerrero. By 1943 he was playing trumpet with the René Touzet and Armando Romeu dance orchestras in Havana. In 1944 he went to Mexico, where he played with Luis Alcaraz. In 1946 he toured Europe with Armando Oréfiche's Havana Cuban Boys. While in Europe, O'Farrill began to hear the records of Charlie Parker, Dizzie Gillespie, and other pioneers of post–World War II jazz music and bebop, with their new harmonic changes and asymmetrical phrasings. Soon thereafter he gave up the trumpet to concentrate on composing and arranging.

O'Farrill moved to New York City in 1948 and began soaking up various musical influences: the Gillespie–Chano Pozo fusion of Cuban rhythms and North American jazz (Cubop), the Frank ("Machito") Grillo–Mario Bauzá collaborations in Afro-Cuban big-band music, as well as classical works by Béla Bartók and Igor Stravinsky. He later studied orchestration with Bernard Wagenaar of the Julliard School. Meanwhile, O'Farrill was beginning to

make his name in Manhattan music circles. His breakthrough came when his idol Goodman bought his arrangement of "Undercover Blues." This led to an arranging job with the bandleader Stan Kenton and brought him to the attention of the jazz producer Norman Granz.

In 1950 O'Farrill created his most enduring work, "Afro-Cuban Jazz Suite." It consisted of eight movements: introduction-canción, mambo, transition, introduction to 6/8, 6/8, transition and jazz, rhumba abierta, and coda. Produced by Granz, it was recorded by the Machito band and featured solos by Parker on alto sax, Flip Phillips on tenor sax, and Buddy Rich on drums. Released as a 10-inch LP ("long-playing" record), it is one of the finest extended Latin jazz compositions ever committed to vinyl, and it established O'Farrill as a major force on the jazz scene. In 1954 he arranged the Gillespie-Pozo Cubop classic "Manteca" as a four-part movement, called "Manteca Suite." The six albums he issued through Verve, a division of Polygram, between 1950 and 1954 (including the "Second Afro-Cuban Jazz Suite") have been collected on compact disc as *Cuban Blues: The Chico O'Farrill Sessions* (1996).

O'Farrill and his band performed regularly at the New York jazz mecca Birdland, but with the era of big bands waning he returned to Cuba in 1955. For the next two years he played posh places such as the Havana Yacht Club and recorded with major Cuban stars, among them, the bassist Israel ("Cachao") López. Between 1957 and 1965 he lived in Mexico City, where he provided music for television. He also composed another of his major works, *Aztec Suite,* for the trumpeter Art Farmer.

In 1965 O'Farrill returned to the United States, living in Los Angeles before settling permanently in New York City. He was the arranger and musical director for a television show, *Festival of the Lively Arts,* during the mid-1960s. O'Farrill also kept busy with television jingles and occasionally arranging for artists as disparate as the Argentinean tenor saxophonist Gato Barbieri (*Viva Emiliano Zapata,* 1974) and British rock star David Bowie (*Black Tie White Noise,* 1993). In 1984 he provided the musical score for the Cuban director Jorge Ulla's film, *Guaguasí.* In 1991 he arranged the Machito-Bauzá composition "Tanga" in five movements. John Storm Roberts, in his book *Latin Jazz,* refers to "Tanga" as "rich ensemble sonorities with a rhythmic range from classic mambo and creamy bolero to Afro-Cuban religion, and secular rumba abierta—a journey back that inverted the normal progression of such works."

The decades of the seventies and eighties were lean both artistically and financially, however, and it was not until the mid-1990s that O'Farrill and his music became widely heard once again. His musical comeback began in 1995 with *Pure Emotion,* which was nominated for a Grammy Award in the best Latin jazz category. The album was one of a trio he made for Milestone Records, including *Heart of a Legend* (1999) and *Carambola* (2000), the former nominated for a Latin Grammy for best jazz recording. His composition for the trumpeter Wynton Marsalis, "Trumpet Fantasy," was performed at Lincoln Center in 1996. He also made weekly appearances with his band at Birdland until 1998. O'Farrill was inducted into the International Latin Music Hall of Fame in April 1999. In 2001 he appeared in Ulla's Latin-Jazz documentary, *Calle 54,* which

includes a performance of "Afro-Cuban Suite." Before his death in 2001, he had been working on the score for a Broadway version of Oscar Hijuelos's novel *The Mambo Kings Play Songs of Love.*

Commenting on his newfound fame, O'Farrill quipped, "Success is fickle and arrives when you least expect it." Unfortunately, it came too late for him to reap all its rewards. He died at New York Weill Cornell Hospital in Manhattan from complications of pneumonia. He was survived by his wife, Lupe (Valero) O'Farrill, a singer he married during his time in Mexico; his son, Arturo, Jr., a jazz pianist and director of the Afro-Cuban Orchestra at Lincoln Center; and his daughter, Georgina, a television writer and producer.

In his final years O'Farrill was one of the last living links between Latin jazz pioneers, such as Machito and Gillespie, and a new generation of players that included the Cuban trumpeter Arturo Sandoval and the saxophonist Paquito D'Rivera. Oscar Hijuelos, in his liner notes to the *Cuban Blues* compact disc, writes: "O'Farrill's compositions are like pocket symphonies, loaded with the widest possible range of tonalities, surprise rhythms, and haunted melodies."

★

There are no biographies of O'Farrill. For information about his career, see the biographical sketch in Scott Yanow, *Afro-Cuban Jazz* (2000) and the liner notes for *Cuban Blues* (1996), written by Oscar Hijuelos. More information is in the Arturo O'Farrill interviews in *Hispanic Magazine* (June 2000), and *Latin Jazz Club* (Mar. 2003). Obituaries are in the *New York Times* and *Washington Post* (both 29 June 2001).

RUBIL MORALES-VAZQUEZ

P-Q

PAIS, Abraham (*b.* 19 May 1918 in Amsterdam, the Netherlands; *d.* 28 July 2000 in Copenhagen, Denmark), physicist who helped build the theoretical foundations of elementary particle physics and historian of science, whose acclaimed *Subtle Is the Lord: The Science and the Life of Albert Einstein* is considered a masterpiece of scientific biography.

Pais (pronounced Pice) was one of two children and the only son of Jesaja and Kaatje (van Kleeff) Pais, both schoolteachers and both Jewish. He had a happy childhood and excelled in school. He attended the University of Amsterdam, where he heard two guest lectures on radioactive decay by George Uhlenbeck, a physics professor at the University of Utrecht and codiscoverer of the spin of the electron. For Pais, the intensity of an encounter with the frontiers of science convinced him that physics was his calling. In 1938 he graduated with two degrees—one B.S. in physics and another in mathematics.

Pais started graduate work at the University of Amsterdam and then transferred to the University of Utrecht to study under Uhlenbeck. Uhlenbeck left in 1938 to spend the fall semester at Columbia University in New York and in 1939 took a permanent position at the University of Michigan. Meanwhile, Pais earned an M.S. in physics on 22 April 1940, just three days before the German invasion of the Netherlands; in another five days the Dutch army capitulated. Supported by an assistantship, Pais began his doctoral studies under Uhlenbeck's successor, Leon Rosen-feld, attempting to describe meson theory using projective relativity. Shortly after the Nazi occupation, the authorities began imposing restrictions on Jews, and one of the new regulations forbade Jews from earning doctoral degrees after 14 July 1941. Pais worked feverishly on his dissertation and was awarded a Ph.D. in physics just five days before the deadline.

On 19 May 1942, after the Nazi regime began transporting Jews out of the Netherlands, Pais went into hiding with the aid of a non-Jewish friend, Tina Bucher or Tineke Buchter. For two years he hid in five different locations, moving each time there appeared to be danger of discovery. During this period he read novels, studied physics, and exercised. In March 1945 the Gestapo found and arrested Pais and his friend Leon Nordheim, an old friend of Pais's and a radical Zionist. Nordheim was executed, but Pais—thanks to the intervention of Bucher, who met with a Nazi official in Amsterdam on his behalf—was released at the end of April. Many of Pais's friends and relatives, including his sister, did not survive the Holocaust. His parents, who also had been in hiding, did survive. On 8 May 1945 Germany surrendered to the Allied Forces, and in June, Pais returned to the University of Utrecht to resume his position. Shortly thereafter he began publishing scientific papers—approximately 150 in all.

The Nobel Prize winner Niels Bohr, a physicist, invited Pais to come to Copenhagen to work at what was later named the Niels Bohr Institute, the mecca for quantum physicists. While in Copenhagen, Pais and Christian Moller published a paper in which they coined the word "lepton" for light particles (in the electron-neutrino family). The term is now standard in physics. Pais spent a great deal of time with Bohr and his family, discussing Bohr's idea of complementarity (which poses the question of whether an electron is a wave or a particle) and elementary particle physics.

Pais spent the academic year 1946–1947 at the Institute for Advanced Study at Princeton, New Jersey, where he met and befriended the celebrated physicist Albert Einstein. In 1947 J. Robert Oppenheimer, the newly appointed director of the Institute for Advanced Study, asked Pais to stay at the institute for a five-year term as an institute professor. Even better, during the 1948–1949 academic year Uhlenbeck was at the institute, and he and Pais collaborated on several papers. In one they provided a means of handling the troublesome infinities of quantum electrodynamics. This paper is still considered to be of major significance. In January 1951 Pais's status at the institute was changed from a five-year term to a permanent appointment as a professor of physics. He became a naturalized citizen in 1954 and remained at the institute until 1963.

With the advent of the new particle accelerators and detectors, physicists began discovering many short-lived subatomic particles. Pais devoted himself to the study of this subject and became known as the father of particle physics. In one of his papers he coined the term "baryon" for protons, neutrons, and other "heavier" subatomic particles. This term also became standard in physics. In another paper he introduced the radical and crucial idea known as the principle of associated production (1952), which explained why some newly discovered particles were produced in great quantities in accelerators by "strong" interaction but whose decay was relatively slow, indicating "weak" interaction. Basically, associated production theorizes that accelerators produce certain "strange" particles only in pairs and that the individual particles decay in a "slow" manner that depends on the preservation of a new quantum number. This number was later redefined by Murray Gell-Mann and called "strangeness."

On 15 December 1956 Pais married Lila Atwill, a fashion model; the couple had one son. They were divorced in 1962, the same year Pais was elected to the National Academy of Sciences. In 1963 Pais left the institute for a professorship at Rockefeller University in New York City. He and two colleagues produced a spectacular result in 1964, using the mathematics of symmetric groups: a computation of the magnetic moments of the neutron and proton to within 3 percent of the experimental value.

In 1976 Pais married Sara Ector, a French teacher who later became a television executive. They were divorced in 1985, and on 15 March of that year he married Ida Benedicte Nicolaisen (née Edelberg), an anthropologist in Copenhagen. They divided their time between Copenhagen and New York.

In the late 1970s Pais shifted his research from theoretical physics to physics history. With exacting scholarship he produced his masterpiece, *Subtle Is the Lord: The Science and the Life of Albert Einstein* (1982), for which he won an American Book Award. His *Inward Bound: Of Matter and Forces in the Physical World* (1986) is a more technical history of particle physics. In 1988 Pais became an emeritus professor of Rockefeller University. Pais spent his retirement writing. He published *Niels Bohr's Times: In Physics, Philosophy, and Polity* (1991), *Einstein Lived Here* (1994), *Paul Dirac: The Man and His Work* (1998), and *The Genius of Science: A Portrait Gallery* (2000). His autobiography, *A Tale of Two Continents: A Physicist's Life in a Turbulent World*, was published in 1997. Pais attended many conferences throughout the world and did extensive touring and mountain climbing. He was a member of the National Academy of Sciences and the American Academy of Arts and Sciences and a Fellow of the American Philosophical Society. Pais died of a heart attack in Copenhagen and is buried there.

Pais will be remembered both as a physicist and a historian of physics. His pioneering work in the theory of elementary particle physics was ingenious and groundbreaking. With his award-winning *Subtle Is the Lord,* he set the standard for scholarship and eloquence in scientific biography.

★

Pais's papers are at the Rockefeller University Archives. In addition to his autobiography, *A Tale of Two Continents* (1997), and his book *Inward Bound* (1986), material on his life and work appears in Helge Kragh, *Quantum Generations: A History of Physics in the Twentieth Century* (1999); Ellen Land-Weber, *To Save a Life: Stories of Holocaust Rescue* (2000); and Fulvio Bardossi and Judith N. Schwartz, *God's Pickpockets: The Rockefeller University Research Profiles* (winter 1982–1983). Obituaries are in the *New York Times* (31 July 2000), the *Guardian* (4 Aug. 2000), and *Physics Today* (May 2001).

HOWARD ALLEN

PALMER, R(obert) R(oswell) (*b.* 11 January 1909 in Chicago, Illinois; *d.* 11 June 2002 in Newtown, Pennsylvania), historian and educator whose numerous publications won him recognition as a major historian.

Palmer was the elder of two sons born to Roswell Roy Palmer, an accountant, and Blanche Genevieve (Steere) Palmer. After his mother died in 1919, the father raised the children largely by himself. Educated in Chicago's public schools, Palmer excelled in his studies, winning a citywide contest with a play written in Latin. His success earned him a four-year scholarship to the University of Chicago, where he received a Ph.B. in history in 1931. As a senior, Palmer studied with the eminent historian Louis Gottschalk, who persuaded him to pursue graduate work at Cornell University. He accepted this advice, and under the direction of Gottschalk's own teacher, Carl Becker, obtained his Ph.D. in history in 1934 for a dissertation titled "The French Idea of American Independence on the Eve of the French Revolution."

His thesis work led Palmer to continue his study of eighteenth-century France. In 1935 and 1936 he did research in Paris on the intellectual conflict between Enlightenment rationalists and Christian apologists during the late 1700s. Published in 1939 as *Catholics and Unbelievers in Eighteenth-Century France,* the work earned him a reputation as a scholar of the first rank. Three years earlier, Palmer had accepted an instructorship at Princeton University. The school's extensive library provided him with the material for another substantial work, *Twelve Who Ruled: The Committee of Public Safety During the Terror* (1941). A collective biography of the members of the Committee of Public Safety, which ruled France during the Reign of Terror (1793–1794), this well-written study demonstrated Palmer's mastery of the source material and his ability to write well for a general audience.

World War II interrupted Palmer's academic career. Because of his weak eyesight, he was assigned to service as a civilian on the staff of the historical division of the U.S. Army from 1943 to 1945. In collaboration, he produced two considerable volumes, *The Organization of Ground Troops* (1947) and *The Procurement and Training of Ground Combat Troops* (1948).

By the time these studies appeared, Palmer had resumed his teaching at Princeton, where he was promoted to full professor (1946), then Dodge Professor of History (1952). With the authorization of the French scholar Georges Lefebvre, he translated *Quatre-vingt-neuf,* written in 1939 to mark the 150th anniversary of France's great revolution. Ably rendered as *The Coming of the French Revolution* (1947), the volume unexpectedly became a classic. It remained continuously in print in paperback for more than half a century.

An even greater success was *A History of the Modern World,* first published in 1950, which traced the course of western civilization from its origins to the mid-twentieth century. The volume rapidly gained a wide readership because of its balanced judgments concerning political, diplomatic, and military affairs, as well as its careful organization and literate style. Widely adopted in college history classes, it appeared in revised and updated versions that kept the content current. A ninth edition, written by Palmer

in collaboration with Joel G. Colton and Lloyd S. Kramer, appeared shortly before Palmer's death. It also gained an international audience thanks to translations into seven foreign languages.

After completing his general history, Palmer undertook a large-scale project based on extensive research. Stimulated by the work of the French scholar Jacques Godechot, he explored the concept of an Atlantic community shaken by four decades of political upheaval at the end of the 1700s. The two historians jointly delivered a paper at the Tenth International Congress of Historical Sciences, held in Rome in 1955, that dealt with the "Problem of the Atlantic" from the eighteenth to the twentieth century. Palmer developed the theme in two substantial volumes collectively titled *The Age of the Democratic Revolution: A Political History of Europe and America, 1760–1800.* The first volume, *The Challenge* (1959), detailed the conflict among privileged and wealthy members of the upper classes, reforming monarchies, and popular forces, which resulted in the outbreak of revolution, most notably in Britain's thirteen North American colonies. The second volume, *The Struggle* (1964), traced the course of upheaval across Europe, beginning in France. The work earned Palmer the prestigious Bancroft Prize in history in 1960. He would later condense his study in *The World of the French Revolution* (1971).

Palmer left Princeton in 1963 to become dean of arts and sciences at Washington University in St. Louis. After three years, however, he returned to Princeton, where he remained until 1969. He then taught at Yale University, where he completed *The School of the French Revolution: A Documentary History of the College of Louis-le-Grand and Its Director, Jean-François Champagne, 1762–1814* (1975), a study of a major secondary school in Paris. He retired as professor emeritus in 1977. After serving as adjunct professor at the University of Michigan for three years (1977–1980), Palmer returned to Princeton, where he was affiliated with the Institute for Advanced Study.

Despite advancing age, Palmer remained highly productive in the 1980s and 1990s. He completed translations of two important French historical works, Louis Bergeron's *France Under Napoleon* (1981) and Jean-Paul Bertaud's *The Army of the French Revolution* (1988). In addition, he wrote four other studies of eighteenth-century France. *The Improvement of Humanity: Education and the French Revolution* (1985) presented a detailed synthesis of projects for, and achievements in, educational reform during the revolutionary era. His *Two Tocquevilles: Father and Son* (1987) compared the writings on the French Revolution produced by Count Henri de Tocqueville and his famous offspring Alexis. In 1993 Palmer published *From Jacobin to Liberal: Marc-Antoine Jullien, 1775–1848,* a documentary biography of a durable politician and writer who shifted his loyalties as one regime succeeded another. Palmer's final work, in which he selected and translated writings by the liberal French economic theorist Jean-Baptiste Say, was published as *J.-B. Say: An Economist in Troubled Times* (1997).

On 19 December 1942 Palmer married Esther Caroline Howard. The couple had three children. Palmer died at the age of ninety-three, and his body was cremated.

A plainspoken midwesterner, Palmer disliked abstract theory and obscure language, preferring clear, straightforward prose. A Democrat in his politics, he abhorred the extremism of right and left, infusing his writings with a deep respect for liberal values. The extent and quality of his work earned him the esteem of his professional colleagues, who elected him president of the Society for French Historical Studies in 1960 and the American Historical Association in 1970. Palmer's international reputation earned him honorary degrees from the universities of Toulouse (1965) and Uppsala (1977). In 1990 Palmer received the Antonio Feltrinelli Prize from the Italian National Academy of the Incei for his distinguished contributions to history.

★

Palmer's papers are in his family's possession. He paid tribute to the professor who introduced him to French history in "The Great Inversion: America and Europe in the Eighteenth-Century Revolution," published in Richard Herr and Harold T. Parker, eds., *Ideas in History: Essays Presented to Louis Gottschalk by His Former Students* (1956). Palmer discussed his writing of *A History of the Modern World* in an interview in the *New York Times Book Review* (30 July 1950). An essay by Palmer in L. P. Curtis, ed., *The Historian's Workshop* (1970), discusses the origins of *The Age of the Democratic Revolution*. Obituaries are in the *New York Times* (18 June 2002) and the American Historical Association newsletter *Perspectives* (Sept. 2002).

JAMES FRIGUGLIETTI

PARTON, James (*b.* 10 December 1912 in Newburyport, Massachusetts; *d.* 20 April 2001 in Hanover, New Hampshire), journalist, editor, cofounder, president, and publisher of *American Heritage* magazine (1954–1970).

Parton was the older of two children born to Hugo Parton, a publisher, and Agnes (Leach) Parton, an artist. His grandfather and namesake was a well-known nineteenth-century biographer of the American statesmen Aaron Burr, Andrew Jackson, Benjamin Franklin, and Thomas Jefferson and the French writer Voltaire; it was from his grandfather that Parton acquired his love for writing and history. From an early age he showed an interest in publishing.

Parton attended Loomis Institute of Windsor, Connecticut (later known as Loomis-Chaffee), from 1926 to 1930; there he was the managing editor of the yearbook,

Loomiscellany. He attended Harvard University from 1930 to 1934 and graduated with an A.B., distinguishing himself with an honors thesis in English. Parton then went into journalism as assistant to Edward L. Barneys, a public relations specialist in New York City. Over the next two decades Parton worked for Time, Inc., and the New York *Herald Tribune* as assistant general manager, cinema critic, and aviation editor and as editorial director of the Pacific Coast News Bureau for *Time, Life,* and *Fortune.*

From 1942 until 1945, during World War II, Parton interrupted his career to serve in the United States Army Air Forces (USAAF). He served as aide de camp to Lieutenant General Ira C. Eaker, commander of the Eighth Air Force in England and the Mediterranean Allied Air Forces; as historian of the Eighth Air Force; and as chairman of the U.S. Army commission that produced a book about the Eighth Air Force entitled *Target—Germany*. Parton rose to the rank of lieutenant colonel and earned the Legion of Merit, the Bronze Star, and the European Theatre ribbon with four battle stars. He was invited to the first reception after the war at England's Buckingham Palace, where he collected signatures from important dignitaries, including the British prime minister Sir Winston Churchill.

After his discharge from the USAAF in 1945, Parton returned to journalism at Time-Life International, becoming promotional and editorial director. He spent a short time (1948–1949) as editor and publisher of the Los Angeles *Independent* and served for a few months as a consultant to the U.S. State Department. In 1950 Parton married Jane Audra Bourne; they had three children, including a son who died in 1991. His wife died of cancer in 1962. Parton later married Ruth Dawkins; they did not have children. In 1953 Parton and two of his colleagues from Time-Life International founded Thorndike, Jensen, and Parton, Inc., a consulting and publishing firm, to serve a variety of corporate clients. Parton served as vice president and treasurer until 1957.

In 1947 the American Association for State and Local History founded a popular magazine called *American Heritage*. Two years later the Society of American Historians (SAH), led by Allan Nevins, a history professor at Columbia University, proposed the creation of a popular history magazine in hardcover. Parton spotted a copy of the *American Heritage* magazine at the Loomis School in 1953, which piqued his interest, because his firm was looking for a new magazine to publish. He envisioned growth possibilities of a magazine meant to acquaint Americans with their own history. Further, he could use the existing subscription base with new promotional strategies to his advantage. In 1954 Parton and his associates established the American Heritage Publishing Company, Inc., and acquired the modest quarterly publication. The SAH remained as a sponsor.

The magazine company started with a "puny capital of $60,000," as Parton later recalled, and became a success with Parton as corporate president and publisher, Thorndike as editorial director and vice president, and Jensen as editor. Shortly after the establishment of the company, Bruce Catton, a Pulitzer Prize–winning historian, became the chief editor, and Alexander Hehmeyer, a New York lawyer, joined the staff. Parton took vigorous promotional steps to ensure the success of the magazine. A full-page ad in the *New York Times Book Review* of 17 October 1954 emphasized, among other fascinating and exciting aspects of the *American Heritage,* that it also would be entertaining. Parton threw his profit-making abilities and his influence behind a direct-mail campaign with the assistance of others, including Frank Johnson, a copywriter. The subscriber base rose to 40,000 by the time the first issue was published in December 1954 and to 100,000 by the printing of the third issue. As early as 1962 subscriptions rose to more than 350,000.

Contributors to the publication included journalists, historians, and researchers. The magazine was designed to enrich the readers' appreciation of the panorama of the American experience and sought to capture the whole history of the country and its people. The magazine was published bimonthly in hardcover, with lavish color illustrations. Each issue covered a wide range of topics, carried no advertising, and was sold almost entirely by direct mail with a yearly subscription rate of $12–15.

For fifteen years Parton's foresight, style of writing history, and imaginative leadership as president and publisher brought success and phenomenal popularity to *American Heritage.* Under his leadership the company also produced books on American history, including the Pulitzer Prize–winning *American Heritage Picture History of the Civil War.* With a changing economy and the rising cost of paper and production over the years, however, the hardcover magazine began to face a financial challenge. Since the company published annual books on major periods in American history, Parton decided in 1969 to sell his company to McGraw-Hill.

Subsequently the magazine underwent several changes and had several owners. In 1978 the magazine switched to soft cover, and in 1982 it began selling ads. Roy Rosenzweig, writing in *Radical History Review* (1985), observed that "as the most influential and successful post–World War II historical publication, *American Heritage* . . . comprises an important chapter in the largely untold story of popular history . . . in the United States."

After 1970 Parton never strayed far from his vocation. He served as president of the Encyclopaedia Britannica Educational Corporation from 1970 to 1973 and then as chair of its executive committee. He also served as assistant Librarian of Congress for public education, in charge of publications, exhibits, and media from 1976 to 1977. After leaving the

Library of Congress he edited the multivolume *Impact: The Army Air Forces Confidential Picture History of World War II,* published in 1980. Parton moved to Hanover, New Hampshire, in 1983 and authored a biography, *Air Force Spoken Here: General Ira Eaker and the Command of the Air* (1986). At age eighty-eight Parton suffered a fatal heart attack. He is buried in the family plot in Newburyport.

Parton was an active alumnus of Harvard and a trustee and an ardent supporter of the Air Force Historical Foundation. The genius of Parton's vision is the *American Heritage* magazine and its mandate to inform U.S. citizens about their own history. Throughout Parton's life, his spirit of organization and dedication to his work, family, and friends was reflected in his leadership and publications.

★

Parton's papers (1914–1986) are in the Harvard University Houghton Library in Cambridge, Massachusetts; they include personal and professional writings, correspondence, photographs, military service, and publishing materials. Other holdings and related materials are located at the United States Air Force Academy Library in Colorado Springs, Colorado, and at Columbia University in New York City. There is no definitive biography of Parton. An appraisal can be found in Roy Rosenzweig, "Marketing the Past: *American Heritage* and Popular History in the United States," *Radical History Review* 32 (1985). A short biographical sketch is in Parton, *The Legacy of Neglect,* Lewis Case Lecture Series (1968). Obituaries are in the *New York Times* (25 Apr. 2001) and *Air Power History* 48 (2001).

HOPE E. YOUNG

PASTORE, John Orlando   (*b.* 17 March 1907 in Providence, Rhode Island; *d.* 15 July 2000 in North Kingston, Rhode Island), Rhode Island governor and U.S. senator, the first Italian American elected to this position.

Pastore was the second of five children born to Michele Pastore, a tailor, and Erminia (Asprinio) Pastore, a seamstress. Both parents were Italian immigrants. In 1916 his father died suddenly of a heart attack, forcing his mother and older brother to support the family. Pastore looked after his younger brother and sisters after school each day. Three years later his mother married her husband's younger brother, Salvatore Pastore, also a tailor. Salvatore wanted his nephews to leave school after the eighth grade, but Pastore's mother encouraged him to continue his education. While attending Providence public schools, he delivered coats and suits for his stepfather and worked as a drugstore delivery boy, as an office boy for a law firm, and as a footpress operator in a jewelry shop. In 1925 he graduated with honors from Classical High School, but could not afford to attend college. He worked as a claims adjuster for Nar-

John O. Pastore, March 1966. BETTMANN/CORBIS

ragansett Electric Company, and in 1927 began to attend Northeastern University's evening law school in the Providence YMCA. He earned his LL.B. in 1931 and was admitted to the Rhode Island bar on 18 May 1932.

Depression-era Providence produced almost no paying clients for young lawyers, so in 1933 Pastore turned to politics. Supported by the local Democratic Party, he was elected to the Rhode Island House of Representatives in 1934. He served on the judiciary and education committees (1935–1936) and after his reelection chaired the corporations committee in 1937. As more Italian Americans supported the Democratic Party, their leaders demanded that they fill more political offices, and Pastore was offered the office of fifth assistant state attorney general. He accepted because the job provided a regular salary, and resigned from the legislature to take the new position. In 1938, however, the Republicans captured all state general offices and replaced all prosecutors.

Pastore practiced law privately from 1939 to 1940, and after the Democrats returned to power in 1940, he was appointed assistant attorney general, a position in which he served until 1945. On 12 July 1941 Pastore married Elena Elizabeth Caito, with whom he had three children.

Ethnic politics also contributed to Pastore's selection for his next political office. The outgoing lieutenant governor was Italian American, and the state Democratic convention nominated Pastore for the position. Initially reluctant because he would have to take a 50 percent pay cut, he was elected in 1944 and became lieutenant governor in January 1945. In October, after J. Howard McGrath resigned to become U.S. solicitor general, Pastore became governor.

To pay for highway improvements and other public works projects that had been put off during World War II, Democrats in the legislature demanded a tax on corporations, and Republicans a state sales tax. Pastore supported a compromise, enacted in May 1947, which included a 4 percent corporate tax and a 1 percent sales tax, the state's first. Other legislation included the state's first primary election law, $5 million to fight water pollution, a $20 million veterans' bonus, and a fair employment practices act. Pastore ate lunch every day at the state house cafeteria and maintained good relations with the press, sometimes inviting reporters into his office more than once a day. He was reelected by a 22,000-vote plurality in 1946, and by 73,000 votes in 1948, setting a Rhode Island record.

Another job change by McGrath contributed to Pastore's next, and most significant, career move. Elected to the U.S. Senate in 1946, McGrath resigned in August 1949 to become U.S. attorney general. Pastore appointed the state budget director Edward L. Leahy to fill the vacant senate seat, with the understanding that Leahy would not seek reelection, and in July 1950 Pastore announced his own candidacy for the Senate. After he was elected in November, he resigned the governorship on 18 December, and was sworn in as a senator the next day, thus gaining two weeks' seniority over other freshmen.

From 1953 Pastore served on the Joint Committee on Atomic Energy, which he cochaired with House colleagues from 1963 to 1976. He supported the development of nuclear power plants but tried to limit nuclear weapons. A strong supporter of the Limited Nuclear Test Ban Treaty, he went to Moscow for the treaty's signing and was a floor manager for its Senate ratification in September 1963. He helped lead the Senate in its March 1970 ratification of the Nuclear Non-Proliferation Treaty.

Pastore, who chaired the Communications Subcommittee of the Commerce Committee from 1955 to 1976, supported the development of new communication technologies and public television broadcasting. In 1960 he managed the Senate resolution that suspended the equal time provisions of the Federal Communications Act, thus allowing the televising of the John F. Kennedy–Richard M. Nixon presidential debates. He supported the Communications Satellite Act of 1962; pushed for the passage of the Public Broadcasting Act of 1967, which created the Corporation for Public Broadcasting; and supported public television for the rest of his career. In the late 1960s and early 1970s he opposed excessive sex and violence on television and held hearings, but he opposed federal controls, telling the networks to police themselves.

A longtime political ally of President Lyndon B. Johnson, Pastore supported the Great Society and its attendant "war on poverty." He served as floor manager for debate and voting on Title VI of the Civil Rights Act of 1964, which enforced the act by withholding federal funds from state and local entities that practiced racial discrimination. The most memorable moment of his political career occurred on 24 August 1964, when Pastore, at the request of Johnson, delivered the keynote address at the Democratic National Convention in Atlantic City, New Jersey. Emotionally recalling what he, a child of immigrants, had achieved, the senator praised the accomplishments of the Kennedy and Johnson administrations and in a rousing peroration called for the president's reelection. The reaction to Pastore's speech was so positive that he was briefly considered for the vice presidency. A member of the leadership and the Senate Democratic Policy Committee, he was an unsuccessful candidate for majority whip in 1965.

Pastore initially supported U.S. participation in the Vietnam War, but soon developed ambivalence toward it, partly as a result of increased combat deaths, and partly because of cuts in domestic spending to pay for the war. After Johnson withdrew his reelection bid in 1968, Pastore began to push for peace. By 1972 he was supporting proposals to limit military spending and cut off funds for the war.

In October 1975 Pastore announced that he would not seek reelection to the Senate in 1976. He said he did not want to overstay his welcome, was looking forward to spending more time with his family, and wanted to leave when he could walk out by himself. He had not enjoyed seeing his senior colleagues propped up by aides and vowed not to let the same happen to him. Also, the Senate was changing; members elected in 1972 and 1974 had less respect for seniority, and campaigns were increasingly expensive. To give

his successor the advantage of seniority he had enjoyed years before, Pastore resigned on 28 December 1976.

Having no desire to remain in Washington as a lobbyist, as did many retired legislators, Pastore returned to Rhode Island. He became chairman of Columbus National Bank of Rhode Island in 1977 and maintained an office in its Providence headquarters, but he was not involved in its day-to-day operations. He called for the nonproliferation of nuclear weapons and for an end to underground testing. Slowed in his last three years with Parkinson's disease, he contracted pneumonia and died of kidney failure at age ninety-three. He is buried in Saint Ann's Cemetery, Cranston, Rhode Island.

A first generation Italian American, the meticulously groomed and impeccably dressed Pastore was intelligent, ambitious, and hardworking. Standing five feet, four inches tall, with a commanding voice, he evoked emotion and argument with his oratory, and spoke flawlessly, without resorting to slang. He was always open to modifying his positions, as he did on state taxes, nuclear power, and the war in Vietnam. He had a good sense of self and knew when to retire. Never tainted by any scandal, Pastore was a state and national Democratic leader who looked after his constituents and supported his party's programs from the 1930s through the 1970s.

★

Pastore's papers, which chiefly cover his service in the U.S. Senate, are in the Archives and Special Collections of Phillips Memorial Library at Providence College in Rhode Island. The files on constituent service, however, were destroyed to preserve privacy. A biography, Ruth S. Morgenthau, *Pride Without Prejudice: The Life of John O. Pastore* (1989), is in part based on interviews the author conducted with Pastore and his associates between 1985 and 1988. Duane Lockard, *New England State Politics* (1959), and Samuel Lubell, *The Future of American Politics* (1965), help put Pastore's early career in political context. Patrick J. Conley, "Tradition and Turmoil: Government and Politics in Rhode Island, 1636–1986," *Rhode Island Rhetoric and Reflection: Public Addresses and Essays* (2002), provides an overview of the political environment in which Pastore operated. Samuel Lubell, "Rhode Island's Little Firecracker," *Saturday Evening Post* (12 Nov. 1949), covers Pastore's early career. Obituaries are in the *Providence Journal, New York Times,* and *Washington Post* (all 16 July 2000).

WILLIAM A. HASENFUS

PEARL, Daniel ("Danny") (*b.* 10 October 1963 in Princeton, New Jersey; *d.* January or February 2002 in Karachi, Pakistan), *Wall Street Journal* reporter kidnapped and killed by Muslim militants while on assignment in the Middle East.

Pearl was the only son of three children born to Judea Pearl and Ruth (Rejwan) Pearl, college sweethearts who had met at the Technion (Israel Institute of Technology) in Haifa, Israel. Pearl's mother, a computer consultant, was born in Baghdad, Iraq, and his father, a computer scientist and leader in the field of artificial intelligence, was born in Tel Aviv, Israel. The couple came to the United States in 1960 to do graduate work at Princeton University. In 1966, when Pearl was three years old, the family moved to southern California, where Pearl's father later joined the faculty at the University of California, Los Angeles (UCLA).

As parents, the Pearls strove to cultivate the creative and the intellectual sides of their children. Pearl's violin lessons, which he began in 1970, helped him develop a love of music. During his journalism career, Pearl was known for treating fellow reporters to impromptu concerts on the violin and mandolin. The family also regularly traveled abroad to Europe and Israel. At age thirteen Pearl journeyed to Jerusalem, where he studied for one year at a high school in Rehovot. Because of his exposure to this area of the world, Pearl developed a lifelong interest in the Middle East.

Pearl graduated from Birmingham High School in suburban Van Nuys, California, as a National Merit Scholar in 1981. His talent for verbal communications became clear when he placed fifteenth in the United States on the English portion of the Preliminary Scholastic Aptitude Test

Daniel Pearl. CORBIS

(PSAT). Pearl attended Stanford University, where he wrote for the school newspaper and cofounded a nonpartisan political quarterly called the *Stanford Commentary*. He graduated with a B.A. in communications in 1985.

Following graduation, Pearl spent the summer completing an internship at the *Indianapolis Star*. From there, he moved to Massachusetts and worked at several papers over the next few years. His first stop was the *North Adams Transcript*. By 1987 he had joined the *Union News*, and in 1988 he became a business reporter for the *Berkshire Eagle* in Pittsfield. While at the *Eagle*, Pearl won a 1988 American Planning Association Award for a five-part series on land use.

Pearl joined the *Wall Street Journal* in 1990 and spent the next decade helping readers become better acquainted with the crooks, leaders, downtrodden, and everyday people of the world. Reporting from the *Journal*'s Atlanta office, Pearl quickly made a name for himself, staying with stories other reporters would throw away, and his offbeat, thought-inspiring feature stories began to appear on the *Journal*'s front page. During this time Pearl also kept busy with music and played lead violin in a band.

Handsome, bespectacled, and intelligent, Pearl moved up the ranks at the *Wall Street Journal*. In February 1993 Pearl moved to the paper's Washington, D.C., office to cover transportation and telecommunications, and by January 1996 he was stationed in London, working as a foreign correspondent. In February 1998 Pearl joined the paper's Paris bureau and met the Dutch-Cuban journalist Mariane Van Neyenhoff, a French citizen. They married in August 1999. In 2000 Pearl was stationed in Bombay, India, as the *Journal*'s South Asia bureau chief.

Pearl was able to reveal the human side of complicated international issues. He strove to give a voice to the voiceless and yearned to promote understanding between dissident groups of people. Following the terrorist attacks on the twin towers of the World Trade Center in New York City on 11 September 2001, Pearl became interested in explaining the viewpoints of the Muslim world to the American people. To this end, Pearl traveled to Karachi, Pakistan, in January 2002, because the area was home to many Muslim militant groups. While there, Pearl was investigating a possible link between the militant groups and Richard C. Reid, a British man who allegedly had attempted to detonate a "shoe bomb" aboard an American Airlines flight the previous December. Pearl had heard that Reid might be associated with Al Qaeda, the militant group responsible for the "9/11" attacks.

On 23 January, Pearl arranged to meet with a key figure in Pakistan's Islamic movement, a man who Pearl thought would tell him more about Reid. Instead, Pearl was kidnapped. Days later, his kidnappers sent messages to media outlets depicting Pearl in chains with a gun to his head. The group, calling itself the National Movement for the

Restoration of Pakistani Sovereignty, demanded that the United States release Taliban and Al Qaeda prisoners being held at Guantanamo Bay, Cuba. In the end, Pearl died at the hands of his abductors, who filmed the gruesome murder on videotape and sent it to the U.S. Consulate in Karachi on 21 February 2002. In the video Pearl decries his religion as well as his country for its foreign policies.

Pearl's murder became a symbol of the devastation caused by terrorist hostility. At least four men have been convicted in connection with his murder. Pearl's remains were returned to the United States, and his body was buried in an undisclosed location in Los Angeles. On 30 May 2002 Pearl's wife gave birth to a son, their only child. That year his family set up the Daniel Pearl Foundation to promote cross-cultural understanding.

★

At Home in the World: Collected Writings from the Wall Street Journal (2002), ed. by Helene Cooper, with a foreword by Mariane Pearl, includes a brief but informative biography of Pearl. For descriptive profiles, see Suzanne Herel, "Peninsula Recalls Pearl as Young Reporter," *San Francisco Chronicle* (22 Feb. 2002); "Reporter Daniel Pearl Is Dead, Killed by His Captors in Pakistan," *Wall Street Journal* (24 Feb. 2002); Tom Tugend, "Family of Slain Journalist Daniel Pearl Never Lost Hope," *Jerusalem Post* (26 Feb. 2002); and Patrick Rogers and Karen Brailsford, "Daniel's Song," *People* (14 Oct. 2002). Obituaries are in the *Wall Street Journal* (22 Feb. 2002) and (London) *Daily Telegraph* (23 Feb. 2002).

LISA FRICK

PETTY, Lee Arnold (*b.* 3 March 1914 in Randleman, North Carolina; *d.* 5 April 2000 in Greensboro, North Carolina), professional race car driver who in 1959 won the inaugural Daytona 500 and, at retirement, had fifty-four first-place finishes in National Association for Stock Car Auto Racing (NASCAR) events.

Petty was the son of Judson E. Petty and Jessie M. Petty, who were Carolina farmers. Judson Petty was remembered by his grandson, the race car driver Richard Petty, as "a quiet, God-fearing Quaker gentleman." Lee Petty's real education was embedded in an interweave of work, family, and community in a cultural landscape dominated by automobiles. The writer Mark D. Howell has described the Petty home as a place "where automobiles and speed were commonplace, a part of everyday life."

Following his school years, Petty worked in sales and for a short time ran the family trucking business. In the late 1940s (during the pre-NASCAR era) he took part in midnight races, more akin to high-speed chases, where souped-up cars took on challenges for purses, or wagered monies, that could amount to several thousand dollars.

Later, Petty and his brother Julie found themselves involved in more formal versions of this type of automobile competition. A Petty history describes these early track races: "Eventually these nocturnal events evolved into more organized free-for-alls in someone's cow pasture, complete with paying spectators, large fields of cars, and the typical shady promoters."

Petty was fascinated by this format of auto racing and was convinced that he could compete as both a car builder and a driver. He built a 1937 Plymouth with a Chrysler engine that had all cylinders arranged in a row—known as an inline engine—and won the first race he entered. Just at the time Petty was setting out on a career as a stock-car racer, Bill France was incorporating NASCAR, whose first officially sanctioned race took place in Charlotte, North Carolina, on 19 June 1948. Exactly one year later NASCAR held its first Grand National Championship on the same track.

This race set the tone for NASCAR's embrace of fanciful rhetoric and the crafting of myths and legendary folktales out of surreal happenings. In this case, for example, the original winner was disqualified because he used a vehicle with illegally modified rear springs, and Petty had "a spectacular wreck." Tim Bongard and Bill Coulter in *The Cars of the King* underscore the fact that thrills and spills and danger were an inherent aspect of stock-car racing. Roll bars, car design, and driver helmets were primitive and afforded minimal protection. "[Petty's] Buick swerved and barrel-rolled four times, spewing parts and pieces in all directions. When the pile of crumpled metal finally came to rest, Lee Petty emerged with only a minor cut."

Petty was a smooth but not flamboyant driver who stood out because of his conservative persona. He preferred "consistency to flash." This is borne out by race photographs showing him with a 1954 Chrysler, a 1956 Dodge, and a 1960 Plymouth. While the vehicles are eye-catching, with brightly colored numerals and the beginnings of advertisement decals, Petty blends into the pictures. He is dressed in slacks and a short-sleeved shirt, and his body language is low-key. The contrast with his racing son, Richard Petty, is extraordinary. The son came to be known as "the King," and his dark glasses and rakish cowboy hats adorned with hawk feathers transformed him into a poster figure for NASCAR. For Lee Petty, the focus was strictly on racing. He wanted no part of a theatrical landscape.

Petty dominated NASCAR in the 1950s. He won Grand National point victories in 1954, 1958, and 1959 and took second place in 1949 and 1953. Of equal importance were "most popular driver" category successes in back-to-back years (1953–1955). Petty's approachable manner created a culture in which it was expected, even assumed, that drivers would make themselves available and accountable to race fans. Petty presented himself as a common man with the

Lee Petty, ca. 1960. AP/WIDE WORLD PHOTOS

common touch. In dress, manner, and gesture he was of, not apart from, the fans who cheered him on. In this respect, NASCAR carved out a spectator-friendly sport in which driver and fan seemed to be cut from the same cloth. This stands in contrast to Formula One Grand Prix drivers, who, in the 1950s, were remote celebrities whose lifestyle was that of the rich and the famous.

In terms of racing, Petty's forte was on short tracks. His first NASCAR triumph was at just such a setting, the half-mile Heidelberg Speedway in Pittsburgh. Driving a Plymouth on 2 October 1949, he won by an astounding margin of five laps. Petty's consistency made him a stellar racer. For example, in 1954, alongside twelve first-places victories, he had thirty-four top-five finishes. In 1959 he had eleven wins and twenty-seven top-five slots. Arguably, 1959 was Petty's premium season. He won consistently against rivals and racing teams that were more professional, more technically competent, and more competitive than those of ten years earlier. His career-defining moment was winning the inaugural Daytona 500 in 1959. Three cars crossed the finish line as if "in one," and it took photo-finish experts at NASCAR three days to declare Petty the victor.

In 1960, while Petty won only three races, his prize monies were just a little less than his earnings for 1959. Quite simply, his presence throughout the 1950s paved the way for race sponsors and NASCAR backers to increase prize money and make stock-car racing increasingly attrac-

tive. At the 1961 Daytona 500, Petty's no. 42 Plymouth took evasive action to avoid a driver called Banjo Matthews. Petty flew through a track fence at over 150 miles per hour and landed in a parking lot. He spent four months in a hospital recovering from a punctured lung and a crushed left leg. His career was almost over. His last race was at Watkins Glen, New York, on 19 July 1964.

Petty married Elizabeth Toomes in 1936. Their two sons, Richard and Maurice, both became NASCAR icons for their driving and mechanical skills, respectively. The Pettys eventually raced against each other and were intensely competitive. Indeed, in 1959 Lee Petty was awarded a first place after protesting that his son Richard had received the checkered flag one lap early. A 1972 Hollywood movie entitled *Smash-Up Alley: The Petty Story* featured Richard Petty playing himself and the actor Darren McGavin as Lee Petty. Petty died of complications from an abdominal aneurysm at Moses H. Cone Memorial Hospital in Guilford County, his home for many years.

A member of the North Carolina Sports Hall of Fame and the International Motorsports Hall of Fame, Petty drove Buicks, Plymouths, Chryslers, Dodges, and Oldsmobiles. As he did so, racing evolved into a modern, high-speed, technically sophisticated sport. In 1953 rollover bars were recommended for competitors; in 1954 Chrysler developed a 300-horsepower engine; in 1956 Martinsville Speedway was paved; and in 1958 Goodyear and Firestone both claimed to have produced the best, safest, and fastest tires.

★

Mark D. Howell explores the intergenerational Petty clan in *From Moonshine to Madison Avenue: A Cultural History of the NASCAR Winston Series* (1997). Jim L. Sumner's profile of Lee Arnold Petty appears in David L. Porter, ed., *Biographical Dictionary of American Sports* (1995). Richard Pillsbury's classic study of NASCAR is in *The Theater of Sport* (1995). A wealth of information, especially on technology and mechanics, is presented in Tim Bongard and Bill Coulter, *The Cars of the King* (2002). The 1959 Daytona 500 finish is examined in Ron Smith's *Chronicle of Twentieth-Century Sport* (1992). An obituary is in the *New York Times* (7 Apr. 2000).

SCOTT A. G. M. CRAWFORD

PHILLIPS, John Edmund Andrew (*b.* 30 August 1935 on Parris Island, South Carolina; *d.* 18 March 2001 in Los Angeles, California), songwriter, musician, and founder of the pop-rock group the Mamas and the Papas.

Phillips was the youngest of three children of Claude Andrew Phillips, a career officer in the U.S. Marine Corps, and Edna Gertrude (Gaines) Phillips, a Cherokee Indian. His father's heart disease forced him to take a medical discharge in 1939, after which he began to drink heavily. Phillips's mother was a homemaker until she opened a dress shop, and later worked in a department store to help support the family.

Growing up in suburban Alexandria, Virginia, Phillips was educated in Catholic schools up to the ninth grade and served as an altar boy for a time. He spent second through sixth grade at Linton Hall Academy, a military school run by nuns. In early adolescence he thought briefly of entering a seminary to study for the priesthood, an idea quickly quashed by his father. Phillips went to George Washington High School where, having grown more than six feet tall, he played varsity basketball. He also began playing the guitar. He was expelled from George Washington High School in the spring of 1953 and spent his senior year at the Bullis School in Silver Spring, Maryland.

Upon graduation from high school in 1954, Phillips entered the U.S. Naval Academy at Annapolis, Maryland, but was unhappy there. He found a way out by claiming to have blind spots in his eyes from a childhood accident. After Annapolis he enrolled in a number of colleges but did not stay at any of them for long.

By 1956 he was out of college and working in a series of jobs in Alexandria, including selling sewing machines, encyclopedias, burial plots, and Corvette automobiles. In May 1957 he married Susan Adams. They had two chil-

John Phillips, ca. 1967. HENRY DILTZ/CORBIS

dren, Jeffrey and Laura (later known as the actress MacKenzie Phillips). Phillips formed a group called the Abstracts, which included his friend Phil Blondheim. Later, the group changed its name to the Smoothies, had a single called "Softly," and appeared on the television show *American Bandstand*.

In the late 1950s groups such as the Kingston Trio brought folk music new popularity. In 1961 Phillips formed a folk trio called the Journeymen with Blondheim (who had changed his name to Scott McKenzie) and Dick Weissman. They had moderate success, recording three albums for Capitol Records and playing the folk-music circuit of clubs and college campuses. During a Journeymen show at the Hungry i in San Francisco, Phillips met and became entranced with a seventeen-year-old beauty, (Holly) Michelle Gilliam. Phillips and his wife soon divorced, and on New Year's Eve 1962 he married Gilliam. Their marriage produced one daughter, Chynna, who in the 1980s sang with the group Wilson Phillips. After the Journeymen split up in 1964, Phillips formed the New Journeymen with Michelle Phillips and Marshall Brickman. Brickman was eventually replaced by Denny Doherty, who had been with the Halifax Three and with the Mugwumps.

In 1965 Phillips took his group to the Virgin Islands to rehearse new songs. There, the singer Cass Elliot, who had also been with the Big Three and the Mugwumps, joined the group. Phillips and the group returned to California, and in October 1965 they had a successful audition with the producer Lou Adler, who signed them on as the Mamas and the Papas to his record label, Dunhill Records, in 1965. The Mamas and the Papas made all of their records with Dunhill, and Adler became their manager as well as their producer. By March 1966 the group had a number-one hit with their first single, "California Dreamin'." Within months a second single, "Monday, Monday," also hit number one, and the group's popularity expanded with their first album, *If You Can Believe Your Eyes and Ears.* "Monday, Monday" went on to win the 1966 Grammy Award for best contemporary group performance. A series of hits followed. However, even as the group had its first astounding success, the seeds of disruption—marital discord, individual ambition, and drug use—were already in evidence.

In 1967 Phillips helped to organize the first Monterey International Pop Festival, and the Mamas and the Papas performed on the last night of the show. This festival is credited with introducing the performers Jimi Hendrix, Janis Joplin, and the Who to U.S. audiences. The same year, another song written by Phillips, "San Francisco (Be Sure to Wear Flowers in Your Hair)," became a big hit for the former Journeyman Scott McKenzie, who debuted the song at Monterey.

In 1968 Phillips and Michelle separated, and the Mamas and the Papas disbanded. The Phillips' divorce became final in 1970, and the same year Phillips put out a country-flavored solo album called *John Phillips: The Wolfking of L.A.* Although the album was not a commercial success, one song, "Mississippi," became a minor hit. The Mamas and the Papas reunited for a short time in 1971 to fulfill contractual obligations with Dunhill. The album, *People Like Us,* was the band's last with the original members; Cass Elliot, known as Mama Cass, died in 1974.

Phillips married for a third time in 1972 to Genevieve Waite, a model and actress from South Africa. They had two children, a son, Tamerlane, and a daughter, Bijou, later a model and actress. In 1975 a Broadway musical, *Man on the Moon*—with book, words, and music by Phillips and with Waite and Denny Doherty among the cast—opened to negative reviews and closed after five performances. In 1976 Phillips wrote music for the film *The Man Who Fell to Earth.*

After the breakup of the Mamas and the Papas, Phillips increasingly misused drugs, including heroin, and in July 1980 he was arrested on federal drug trafficking charges. The next year Phillips received an eight-year sentence, which was suspended except for thirty days in Allenwood Federal Prison Camp, a minimum-security facility, and five years of probation. He agreed to do 250 hours of public service and tour the country speaking out about the dangers of drugs.

In 1981 Phillips reunited the Mamas and the Papas with Denny Doherty, Spanky McFarlane filling in for Cass Elliot, and Mackenzie Phillips taking Michelle's parts. The group toured through much of the 1980s. Phillips's marriage to Waite ended in 1985. The next year his autobiography, *Papa John,* was published, as was former-wife Michelle's version of their story, *California Dreamin': The True Story of the Mamas and the Papas.* In 1988 the Beach Boys had a number-one hit with "Kokomo," a song Phillips co-wrote.

By 1992 Phillips's hard living had caught up to him, necessitating a liver transplant. In 1995 he married his fourth wife, Farnaz Arasteh. In 1998 the Mamas and the Papas were inducted into the Rock and Roll Hall of Fame. In later years Phillips completed work on a set of recordings he had made from 1973 to 1979 with Mick Jagger and Keith Richard of the Rolling Stones. These recordings were released as the album *Pay, Pack and Follow* in 2001. He recorded a new album, *Phillips 66,* also released in 2001. Phillips died of heart failure at age sixty-five at the University of California Medical Center and is buried in Palm Springs Mortuary in Palm Springs, California.

Phillips wrote a number of the most memorable songs of the second half of the twentieth century. Performers as varied as the Grateful Dead, the Lennon Sisters, and Wes Montgomery have made covers of his songs, an indication of their wide appeal. The charismatic Phillips was a perfectionist, coaxing singers he worked with to produce the intricate harmonies he envisioned. Along with Brian Wilson of the Beach Boys, Phillips wrote songs that defined the California myth of the 1960s.

★

Phillips's memoir, *Papa John: An Autobiography* (1986), written with Jim Jerome, is the main source for information about his life. The shorter *California Dreamin': The True Story of the Mamas and the Papas* (1986), by Michelle Phillips, and *Go Where You Want to Go: The Oral History of the Mamas and the Papas* (2002), by Matthew Greenwald, add to the story. Obituaries are in the *Los Angeles Times, New York Times,* and *Washington Post* (all 19 Mar. 2001).

William L. Keogan

PHILLIPS, William   (*b.* 14 November 1907 in Manhattan, New York City; *d.* 12 September 2002 in Manhattan, New York City), writer, critic, and cofounder and editor of *Partisan Review* (1934–2002).

Phillips was born in East Harlem in Manhattan. His parents, as he put it, "combined an abysmal provinciality." Both came from Russia; his father, Edward Phillips, emigrated from Odessa in his teens, changing his name from Litvinsky (a common practice among immigrant Jews) on the advice of friends. He lived in Oregon for a time, then moved to New York City, where he became a lawyer, a profession for which he was sorely unsuited. As failure overwhelmed him, he gradually withdrew from the world and indulged in "the standard varieties," as Phillips recalled, "of therapy and palliation," including yoga and mesmerism. In better days, he served as chairman of a local school board and once served as an officer of a Jewish fraternal organization. Late in life, he became a Christian Scientist.

Phillips's mother, Marie (Berman) Phillips, came from Kiev in her twenties. When Phillips was a year old, she separated from his father and took the boy to live in Kiev with her mother and family, returning to New York in 1912. A hypochondriac, she daily felt besieged by numerous nervous pains and paralyses and so pursued strange diets and consulted quack doctors to help alleviate her condition. Unlike her husband, she kept a few friends, and even managed, despite her troubles, to write a novel in her spare time. She died at age ninety-six.

As a boy, Phillips moved to the top of his class at P.S. 40, and later, attending the predominantly Jewish Morris High School in the Bronx, played football and water polo, ran track, and swam. Following high school, he attended the City College of New York (now City College of the City University of New York), "the poor boy's stepping stone to the world," where he earned a B.S. in 1928, and then New York University (NYU), where he received his M.A. in 1930. In 1930 and 1931 he did graduate work at Columbia University in New York City, and taught expository writing at NYU from 1929 to 1932. During this time, he met Edna Greenblatt; they married in 1933. Like many couples during the depression, they decided not to have children, and Edna worked as a schoolteacher to help them stay afloat during the depression. She died in 1985.

Outside of that economic crisis, several signal events combined to form Phillips's mature worldview and to determine his life's course. The first event encouraged him to become a writer and literary critic. In his final year at City College, he was introduced by a fellow student to the work of T.S. Eliot, and found himself, as he recalled, "swimming in the exotic waters of modernism and pondering the new, complex questions of criticism." Further, while a graduate student at New York University, he took a course in philosophy from Sidney Hook and began to embrace Marxism.

Teaching as a part-time instructor at New York University also helped radicalize Phillips and exposed him to Greenwich Village, where he would get his first taste of literary and intellectual life outside the classroom. His earliest work for the radical press, under the pen name William Phelps, included two book reviews for the *Communist* and a critical essay for the *Dynamo*. (He also published numerous articles and editorials in *Partisan Review*, as well as a 1968 book of essays, reviews, and stories entitled *A Sense of the Present*, using his real name.)

In 1934 Phillips joined the John Reed Club, an organization of writers and painters under the aegis of the Communist Party, eventually becoming secretary of the club's writer's group. He soon discovered, to his dismay, that what passed for literature among club members was crude and propagandistic. He dreamt of a magazine, as he once recalled, "to express my views and to mobilize a group of writers looking for a similar direction." It was then that he met Philip Rahv, a Russian immigrant also engaged in radical left-wing culture and who, like Phillips, held modern, avant-garde literature in high esteem. Soon after, the two founded *Partisan Review*, the first issue of which appeared in February 1934. This "first" *Partisan Review*, however, was short-lived, and the John Reed Club closed in 1935. Unable to raise money, uneasy with the prospects of proletarian literature, and disturbed by the Moscow trials and Stalinism in general, Phillips and Rahv suspended the bimonthly in October 1936, hoping to find financial backing to publish a journal independent of the Communist Party. "We were cocky kids," Phillips later recalled, "driven by a grandiose idea of launching a new literary movement, combining the best of the new radicalism with the innovative energy of modernism."

In December 1937 the "new" *Partisan Review* appeared, and it would become, arguably, the most influential literary and cultural journal of twentieth-century America. Its circulation never exceeded 15,000, but it was known and consulted by countless academics, writers, and intellectuals across the world. "P.R.," as it was commonly called, committed itself to modernist movements in art and culture, while at the same time pursuing an antitotalitarian, anti-Stalinist political agenda. The journal took issue with, among other things, naturalism, pragmatism, and mass culture, demanding that intellectuals rise in "permanent mutiny" against "the petty regime of utility and conformity" infecting American thought. Many of the pressing issues of the time were discussed in its pages: Trotskyism versus Stalinism, World War II, the hostile reaction to Communism, the war in Vietnam, neoconservatism, and the New Left. In addition, the magazine attracted and printed most of the talented figures of the century, both European and American, and many for the first time.

In its heyday, the 1940s and 1950s, *P.R.* was famous for being the house organ of the New York Intellectuals, a group of writers and critics, primarily Jewish, whose work appeared regularly in its pages. The more famous among them, other than Phillips and Rahv, included the novelists Saul Bellow and Mary McCarthy; the art historian Meyer Schapiro; the poet Delmore Schwartz; and the critics Clement Greenberg, Irving Howe, Dwight MacDonald, Harold Rosenberg, and Lionel Trilling.

In 1969 Rahv retired from *P.R.* as co-editor, leaving Phillips alone at the top of the masthead. Rahv died in 1972. In 1963 *Partisan Review* moved to Rutgers University, where Phillips also taught; in 1978 the journal moved to Boston University. In the late 1990s Phillips handed the editorial duties to his wife, Edith Kurzweil, whom he had married in 1995. Phillips died at the age of ninety-four. With its April 2003 issue, *Partisan Review* ended publication.

As the voice of opposition to "debilitating liberalism," and all manifestations of philistinism it could identify, *Partisan Review* invited attacks from the beginning. In its later years, it was accused of not supporting radical feminism, black and gay liberation, and other radical causes. Yet, for its rejection of any politics that might sacrifice intellectual freedom, as well as for its devotion to high literary standards and intellectual ideals throughout its career, its cultural importance cannot be overestimated. Although overshadowed by many of those he published, Phillips, "the soul of *Partisan Review*," helped orchestrate the intellectual conversation of twentieth-century American culture for nearly seventy years.

★

Phillips's memoir is *A Partisan View: Five Decades of the Literary Life* (1983). Studies of *Partisan Review* and the New York Intellectuals include James Burkhart Gilbert, *Writers and Partisans: A History of Literary Radicalism in America* (1968); Alexander Bloom, *Prodigal Sons: The New York Intellectuals and Their World* (1986); and Terry A. Cooney, *The Rise of the New York Intellectuals: Partisan Review and Its Circle* (1986). An obituary is in the *New York Times* (14 Sept. 2002).

ROB HOUSE

PIERCE, Samuel Riley, Jr. (*b.* 8 September 1922 in Glen Cove, New York; *d.* 31 October 2000 in Silver Spring, Maryland), lawyer, bank founder, and secretary of Housing and Urban Development in the administration of President Ronald Reagan.

Pierce was the eldest of three sons born to Samuel and Hettie Elenor (Armstrong) Pierce. The senior Pierce, who influenced his son's later political affiliation with the Republican Party, used initiative and ingenuity to parlay his Nassau Country Club position as groundskeeper into a valet service for members, then a dry cleaning business, and finally a real estate enterprise, providing concrete examples

of a drive for excellence and self-sufficiency. In his high school years in suburban Glen Cove, Pierce was highly successful as both a scholar and an athlete; he was not only his class salutatorian but also a regional champion in the 100-yard dash, a football player, and captain of his basketball team. In 1948 Pierce married Barbara Penn Wright, a New York physician; they had one daughter.

A Cornell University (Ithaca, New York) scholarship began his education, but it was interrupted by World War II. Distinguishing himself in North Africa and Italy during World War II from 1943 to 1946 as the first African American to staff the army's Criminal Investigation Unit for the Mediterranean Theaters, Pierce began a long line of firsts in a four-decade career. After the war Pierce earned an A.B. in 1947 from Cornell University and, in 1949, a J.D. from Cornell Law School. Membership in the New York Bar Association came in 1950, and in 1952 he earned an LL.M. from New York University.

Following the family political path by joining the Republican Party in 1949, Pierce increased his involvement in the 1950s, earning a reputation as a "loyal Republican, who made no waves." A Ford Foundation Fellowship at Yale University in New Haven, Connecticut, in the late 1950s enhanced his legal studies and prepared him for duties as an assistant U.S. attorney in New York City. There, he participated in the formation of the indictment of the congressional representative Adam Clayton Powell, Jr., for income tax evasion. Respected widely in legal and political circles, Pierce made his public sector debut in 1955 as an assistant to Secretary of Labor Arthur Larson in the Dwight D. Eisenhower administration. This experience prepared him for his next public posts, as associate counsel and then counsel for the House Judiciary Antitrust Subcommittee (1956–1957).

Civil rights literature does not widely acknowledge Pierce, but his many achievements paved the way for African Americans who followed. Differing from Democratic colleagues in the civil rights struggle, Pierce focused on helping the poor while remaining loyal to the Republican Party. J. Edgar Hoover, director of the Federal Bureau of Investigation, identified Pierce "as a preferable 'moderate' alternative to more 'radical black' leaders such as Roy Wilkins and the Rev. Dr. Martin Luther King, Jr." Pierce was an asset in most political and public activities during the era. Governor Nelson A. Rockefeller appointed him as a municipal judge for the New York Court of General Sessions, a position he held from 1959 to 1960. In 1961 Pierce joined the firm of Battle, Fowler, Stokes, and Kheel, where he became a partner. In his partnership role, his educational background and public sector experience permitted a focus on labor, tax and antitrust law, and civil and criminal litigation.

In 1964 Pierce became the first African American on a

Samuel R. Pierce, 1981. CORBIS

legal team to argue and win a case before the Supreme Court; he defended King, other black ministers, and the *New York Times* in a landmark dispute, *New York Times v. Sullivan*, that established limitations on the use of defamation lawsuits. Pierce remained a valued and quiet contributor to the civil rights movement by serving on two mayoral panels seeking increased construction industry jobs for African Americans (1963–1964) and recommending judicial appointments (1966) and by chairing a committee to improve the operations of the Harlem antipoverty agency Haryou-Act (1964–1966). With the 1964 formation of the Freedom National Bank, the first black-owned commercial bank in New York State, Pierce added valuable banking and finance expertise to his repertoire. This caught the eye of Republican Party officials, who moved him into yet another public post in the 1970s.

Pierce's work in the 1970s combined his academic, public sector, and legal experience. He worked hard as a trustee of Cornell University. Impressing President Richard M. Nixon with his banking and finance expertise, he became general counsel at the U.S. Treasury Department, serving from 1970 to 1973 and receiving its highest honor, the Alexander Hamilton Award. Then Pierce returned to New York and served on a multitude of major corporate boards, including U.S. Industries and Prudential Insurance Com-

pany. New York University honored him in 1972 with an honorary doctorate of laws.

Marking another career first in 1981, Pierce was named by President Reagan as the secretary of Housing and Urban Development (HUD). The only African American in the cabinet, he served two complete terms and was considered its most effective member. Pierce initially strove to improve the department's management and efficiency, reduce the debt, improve financial forecasting, and slash its budget from $26 billion in 1981 to $8 billion in 1989. He is credited with helping the poor by replacing Section 8 new construction with a voucher system for existing housing, upgrading housing for low-income individuals, increasing housing for the elderly and handicapped, and establishing homeless programs.

In his final years at HUD, the inspector general conducted an agency audit that triggered congressional investigations into abuses, favoritism, and mismanagement of federal housing subsidies. Pierce's integrity and competency were questioned, and the department was engulfed in scandal. He was never convicted, but other staff members were. Syracuse University (1983) and Pratt Institute (1987) later honored Pierce with honorary degrees. Other honors included the prestigious Salute to Greatness Award given by the King Center for excellence in leadership and commitment to social responsibility (1989), the Reagan Revolution Medal of Honor, and the Presidential Citizens Medal.

Pierce died of complications from a stroke at age seventy-eight at Holy Cross Hospital in Silver Spring, Maryland.

★

Biographical data is in Jack Salzman, David L. Smith, and Cornell West, eds., *Encyclopedia of African American Culture and History,* vol. 4 (1966); Charles L. Sanders, ed., *The Ebony Success Library: 1000 Successful Blacks,* vol. 1, (1973); and Jessie Carney Smith, *Black Firsts: 2000 Years of Extraordinary Achievement* (1994). Obituaries are in the *Chicago Tribune* (3 Nov. 2000) and *Washington Post* (4 Nov. 2000).

Ann E. Pharr

PIORE, Emanuel Ruben ("Mannie") (*b.* 19 July 1908 in Vilnius, Lithuania; *d.* 9 May 2000 in New York City), physicist, computer scientist, pioneer in government and science relations, and first director of the International Business Machines (IBM) research division.

Piore was born to Ruben Piore and Olga (Gegusin) Piore. He was educated by a personal tutor and attended local schools in his hometown of Vilnius, Lithuania, until German occupation during World War I persuaded his mother

Emanuel R. Piore, 1967. GETTY IMAGES

to move with her son to the United States in 1917. The Piores survived a harrowing trip that included a six-month internment by the Germans at Rotterdam. After arrival in the United States, Piore studied at New York public schools and at the private Ethical Culture School. He became a naturalized citizen in 1924. Later, at the University of Wisconsin, Piore obtained an A.B. in 1930 and a Ph.D. in 1935, both in physics.

Piore married a fellow University of Wisconsin student, Nora Kahn, on 26 August 1931. They had three children. After college Piore began his professional career at the Radio Corporation of America (RCA) electronic research laboratory. From 1938 to 1942 he directed the television lab at Columbia Broadcasting System (CBS). During World War II, Piore served on the staff of the deputy chief of naval operations for air and led the Special Weapons group in the Bureau of Ships. He continued his association with the navy after the end of the war, serving as chief scientist of the newly formed Office of Naval Research from 1946 to 1955. Piore became the first civilian head of the Office of Naval Research, an important innovator in the nascent relationship between American government and American science. Future organizations, such as the National Science Foundation (which Piore also played a part in forming), emulated the Office of Naval Research in its support of research done by universities across the nation. As chief

scientist and, later, director of the Office of Naval Research, Piore had a large role in the development of this new model for cooperation between government and academia. He was largely responsible for persuading the navy and the government to provide financial support for peacetime science in America.

In the decade after the war, Piore played a vital role in the development of this new model for cooperation. As chairman of the High Energy Physics Committee, Piore supported federal funding for the new particle accelerators critical to the understanding of the basic particles of matter. Before the war, American science and American government maintained a certain distance. Scientists often were reticent about accepting money from government sources, owing primarily to their concern that accepting support would jeopardize their independence. Government, for its part, also was hesitant in supporting science. But the immensity of the wartime projects, such as the Manhattan Project to build the first atomic bomb, helped change many minds about government support of science. Piore helped mold a new model of cooperation between government and science with his work at the Office of Naval Research, with his efforts on the High Energy Physics Committee, and with his service on the Science Advisory Committee during both the Dwight D. Eisenhower and John F. Kennedy administrations.

After 1955 Piore returned to private industry. After a brief stint as vice president for research of the Avco Manufacturing Corporation, he began a longtime association with International Business Machines (IBM) as its first director of research. From 1956 to 1961 Piore led IBM in new directions, with emphasis on basic research and on emerging technologies. His first job was to separate the new research division from the manufacturing and development labs, eventually locating the research division in suburban Yorktown Heights, New York. Piore also encouraged other IBM laboratories to focus on basic research, to hire large numbers of young Ph.D. scientists, and to give them the freedom to pursue basic research. Indeed, young scientists were encouraged to perform their research in settings similar to those of the graduate schools they had just left. In keeping with these priorities, the IBM research division under Piore encouraged the publication of research results and the acquisition of patents for technological innovations.

Under Piore's leadership, IBM researchers made many important advances in the field of digital computers, among them projects involving the use of microwaves as the basis for computers, a cryogenics-based computer using superconducting wire, and the use of computers to make translations from the written word. Indeed, Piore and his team of scientists and engineers laid the groundwork for IBM's becoming a world leader in industrial research. Piore became a vice president of IBM in 1960 and served on the board of directors from 1962 to 1973.

During his lifetime, Piore was a Life Fellow of the Institute of Electrical and Electronics Engineers (IEEE). He also received the Distinguished Civilian Service Award, the highest honor given to a citizen by the U.S. Navy. In 1976 the IEEE established the Emanuel R. Piore Award for outstanding work in the field of computer science information processing. Piore died after a long illness in New York City, only a few months after the death of his wife of seventy years.

Piore's involvement with the new model of government support for science helped set the tone for research in the twentieth century. Later, his leadership at IBM helped make that corporation into a world leader in industrial scientific research.

★

The American Philosophical Society holds the Emanuel Ruben Piore Papers, a collection that includes professional correspondence, lectures given by Piore, and material from his tenure at IBM. Piore's scientific autobiography is titled *Science and Academic Life in Transition: Emanuel Piore* (1990). An obituary is in the *New York Times* (12 May 2000).

W. Todd Timmons

POTOK, Chaim Tzvi (*b.* 17 February 1929 in the Bronx, New York City; *d.* 23 July 2002 in Merion, Pennsylvania), best-selling novelist who enjoyed worldwide acclaim for his novel *The Chosen* (1967), and for other works that explored the confrontation between traditional Jewish and modern culture.

Potok was born Herman Harold Potok to Benjamin Max Potok, a jeweler and watchmaker, and Mollie (Friedman) Potok, a homemaker; both were Hasidic Jews who had emigrated from Poland. Max Potok's business failed during the depression, and his four children grew up poor. Potok, the eldest, attended Jewish parochial schools, and in high school began calling himself by his Hebrew name, Chaim, which means "life." Throughout his life, Potok wrote both lovingly and critically of the strict Orthodox Judaism in which he was raised.

As a boy, Potok expressed an interest in painting, a hobby his father tolerated until he reached his bar mitzvah, or coming of age, at thirteen. Potok switched to writing, which bothered his parents less. But like Danny Saunders, the Hasidic boy in his best-known novel, *The Chosen*, Potok hid his love for secular literature from his parents. When he was sixteen, Potok read Evelyn Waugh's *Brideshead Revisited* and was entranced by its portrayal of an upper-class English Catholic family at odds with the larger British culture. With that book, and James Joyce's *Portrait of the Artist As a Young*

Man, Potok came to appreciate an author's power to grapple with ideas and communicate with strangers.

Against his father's wishes, Potok pursued a secular education while he continued his Jewish one. He earned a B.A. in English literature summa cum laude in 1950 from Yeshiva University in Manhattan, New York City. Four years later, he received a M.H.L from the Jewish Theological Seminary in New York City, and was ordained as a Conservative rabbi. The seminary, part of Judaism's Conservative movement, taught a course of study too liberal for Potok's father. But Max Potok did not disown his son, as is the case with some of Potok's characters who challenge their ultra-Orthodox parents.

In interviews, Potok explained that he sought the rabbinical degree not because he wanted to lead a Jewish congregation, but because he wanted to make himself a better writer. "I knew . . . I wanted to write fiction and . . . that my subject was going to be, in one way or another, Jews and Judaism and its interplay with the twentieth century," Potok said in a 1981 interview. "I decided at that point to go to the seminary to get a broader and deeper understanding of the nature of things Jewish."

Shortly after he was ordained as a rabbi in 1954, Potok entered the U.S. Army and served in Korea from 1955 to 1957 as chaplain and first lieutenant attached to a frontline medical battalion that worked with an engineer combat

Chaim Potok. Mr. Jerry Bauer

battalion. Upon his return, he moved to California, accepting a teaching position at the University of Judaism in Los Angeles, as well as the directorship of Camp Ramah in Ojai, working at both institutions until 1959. He had met his wife, Adena Sara Mosevitzsky, a psychiatric social worker, at another Jewish camp in the Poconos in 1952. They married on 8 June 1958, and had three children.

Potok spent the rest of his life working within Jewish institutions. Unlike other contemporary Jewish American writers, such as Philip Roth and Saul Bellow, whose characters live on the periphery of the religion, Potok's are imbued with it. "It is woven into the fiber of my being," Potok said of his Orthodox background. "There is a great deal of passion and beauty in that sort of faith." He was a scholar in residence at Har Zion Temple in Philadelphia from 1959 to 1963. He helped promote and chart the course of much of American-Jewish scholarship in the ensuing decade, as managing editor of *Conservative Judaism* from 1964 to 1965, and as editor in chief of the Jewish Publication Society of America from 1965 to 1974.

Potok received a Ph.D. in 1965 from the University of Pennsylvania. He studied Western philosophy, he said, to better understand the "umbrella" culture in which he and his Jewish characters lived.

With the publication of his first novel, *The Chosen,* in 1967, Potok won a devoted audience that also placed many of his ensuing works on best-seller lists. In the novel, the story of friends raised in two different Jewish traditions in the 1940s, Potok introduced millions of readers worldwide to the insulated Hasidic communities of Brooklyn. The success of the book, written in short, straightforward sentences, surprised him. He thought it would appeal only to a few hundred Jewish readers. *The Chosen* became a popular feature film in 1981, starring Rod Steiger and Robby Benson. Potok had a cameo role as a teacher of Talmud, the collection of Jewish law. A musical version of *The Chosen* played briefly off-Broadway in 1988.

The Promise, a sequel to *The Chosen,* was published in 1969. *My Name Is Asher Lev,* the story of a young Jewish artist, followed in 1972. Potok drew on his Korean experience in *The Book of Lights* (1981), the story of a rabbi who delves into the Kabala, the Jewish book of mysticism. He won the National Jewish Book Award with the sequel to *My Name Is Asher Lev, The Gift of Asher Lev,* in 1990. His last published work was *Old Men At Midnight* (2002).

Potok also wrote nonfiction, including *Wanderings: Chaim Potok's History of the Jews* (1978), and *The Gates of November* (1996), the chronicle of a Soviet Jewish family. He also helped the violinist Isaac Stern write his memoirs and is credited as a contributor to *My First Seventy-nine Years: Isaac Stern* (1999).

Potok branched into playwriting in the 1990s, when three of his plays, including *Out of the Depths,* were produced in Philadelphia. His first children's book, *The Tree of Here,* which deals with a child's fear of moving to a new house, appeared in 1993.

Potok was a much sought-after speaker at universities and on radio programs for his scholarly, yet down-to-earth, manner. His academic talks sometimes surprised audiences used to the plain language of his novels. As Potok explained, "[P]rose . . . has to be transparent. You've got to be able to look right through it. If it's somehow thick and unwieldy, it's bad writing and you're hiding something."

Potok died of brain cancer at his home, and was buried at Shalom Memorial Park in Philadelphia.

Potok's most widely read works feature religious young men whose fascination with aspects of modernity causes strife within their homes. The novels are autobiographical in that both Potok's parents came from long lines of Hasidic rabbis, and his father expected him to become an Orthodox rabbi himself. Potok owed the popularity of his fiction to the seeming exoticism of Hasidism, with its embrace of emotional religious expression and rejection of secular influences. But he considered its deeper attraction its universal theme: the difficulties of negotiating between a traditional community and the modern, secular world.

★

Daniel Walden, ed., *Conversations with Chaim Potok* (2001), is an illuminating collection of interviews conducted between 1976 and 1999, in which Potok discusses his upbringing, his writing style, and the themes of his works. Obituaries are in the *Los Angeles Times, New York Times,* and *Philadelphia Inquirer* (all 23 July 2002).

LAUREN MARKOE

PRICE, Cecil Ray (*b.* 15 April 1938 in Flora, Mississippi; *d.* 6 May 2001 in Jackson, Mississippi), deputy sheriff who participated in the notorious murders of three civil rights workers in 1964.

Neighbors described Price, who had one sibling and was raised in rural Neshoba County, Mississippi, as a nice young man who was helpful to those in need. A deputy in the county sheriff's department, he had a wife, Conner, and a son, Cecil, Jr. He was also a member of the Ku Klux Klan. Price was heavyset with powerful shoulders and a doughy face; his grin was big and self-assured.

Price's life was unremarkable until June 1964. That year, James Chaney, an African American from Meridian, Mississippi, established a center in his hometown to assist African Americans in registering to vote. The Klan kept a list of individuals targeted for violence due to their efforts on behalf of blacks in the state, and Chaney's name was on that list. A spy for the quasi-governmental Mississippi State

Cecil R. Price, October 1967. BETTMANN/CORBIS

Sovereignty Commission had procured the application forms of those who had volunteered to participate in "Freedom Summer," a voter registration drive to be conducted by young people—mostly college students—in the South. The forms, which were passed on to the Klan, included photographs of the applicants, meaning that not only Chaney but also his white coworkers, Robert Goodman and Michael Schwerner, could be recognized by Klansmen. The State Sovereignty Commission also obtained the license-plate numbers for automobiles driven by civil rights workers in Mississippi.

On 21 June 1964 Chaney, Goodman, and Schwerner visited Longdale in Neshoba County to investigate the burning of an African-American church that had served as a voter registration center. After talking with the locals, they climbed into their blue station wagon to return to Meridian. Deputy Price spotted their car on a rural road, noted that the automobile had a license plate number on the State Sovereignty Commission's list, and pulled it over. After charging the young men with going sixty-five miles per hour in a thirty-five mile per hour zone, he arrested all three and took them to the sheriff's office in the town of Philadelphia. They were held there for about two hours, during which time they were fed dinner. They paid their fine, then returned to their vehicle at 10:25 P.M.

Unbeknownst to the three young men, Price had sent word to the local Klan, whose leader, the Reverend Edgar Ray Killen, arranged to have him deliver them into the hands of Klan members on a remote road. As the three men drove toward the boundary with Lauderdale County, Price followed them in his sheriff's car. Eventually he pulled them over and forced them into his vehicle, then delivered the young men to Rock Cut Road, where waiting Klansmen tortured them and eventually shot them. (Chaney was most likely beaten to death.)

The Federal Bureau of Investigation (FBI) did not begin investigating the disappearance of Chaney, Goodman, and Schwerner until after their burned car was discovered in a thicket. On 4 August 1964 U.S. Attorney General Robert F. Kennedy ordered the FBI to give the investigation priority. President Lyndon B. Johnson took a personal interest in the case, putting additional pressure on the FBI. During the investigation, Price appeared to be a model of professionalism and cooperation.

An important turning point occurred when a local alcoholic reported that, soon after the killings, he had seen and heard Killen saying an insane-sounding prayer over an earthen dam. This proved the clue the authorities needed, and FBI special agents—assisted by local law enforcement personnel, including Price—began digging into the dam. Soon they uncovered the corpses of the missing young men.

The governments of both Mississippi and Neshoba County refused to prosecute for the murders, but the Justice Department applied an 1870 law that allowed the federal government to prosecute for civil rights violations, with maximum penalties including a $10,000 fine and ten years in prison. In 1965 Price and eighteen other men were indicted for violating the civil rights of Chaney, Goodman, and Schwerner. A judge tried to throw out the charges, but the Justice Department appealed to the U.S. Supreme Court, which ruled that all the indicted men had to face the charges against them.

The trial began in a segregated courtroom, with blacks on one side and whites on the other, on 7 October 1967. Co-conspirator James Jordan had confessed to the crime and testified for the prosecution, detailing Price's role in setting the victims up to be murdered. On 20 October the jury returned convictions for five defendants, including Price. (The jurors also returned acquittals for seven of the defendants, while seven others were acquitted by default, due to hung juries in each instance.)

Price was sentenced to ten years in prison but released after only four and a half years, and he returned to Philadelphia to become a watchmaker. He also worked as a market manager, and during the last years of his life was a truck driver. Meanwhile, he established a reputation for compassion and helpfulness and was reportedly tormented by memories of the June 1964 slayings. He claimed that he had been "brainwashed" by the Klan in the 1950s and 1960s and stated publicly that he had repented of his actions.

In the mid-1990s the papers of Mississippi's State Sovereignty Commission (which was abolished in 1977) were opened to the public. Mississippi Attorney General Mike Moore and Neshoba County District Attorney Ken Turner found in them enough evidence to prosecute the nine murderers still living, even though some physical evidence such as bullets had disappeared over the years. Price cooperated with the prosecutors, confessing to his role in the murders and identifying his fellow conspirators. He was to be the prize witness at the murder trial when he died suddenly.

Price sustained a skull fracture when he fell about fourteen feet from a man-lift, or cherry picker, while at work. He was first taken to Neshoba General Hospital and later died at University Medical Center in Jackson. Services were held on 8 May 2001 at McLain-Hays Funeral Home in Philadelphia, and Price's remains were buried in Eastlawn Cemetery.

Price's crimes had the unintended consequence of opening up the means for federal prosecution of civil rights violations by forcing prosecutors to dig up the 1870 law. Thanks to its success in the Price case, that statute has been invoked many times since in civil rights proceedings.

★

Seth Cagin and Philip Dray, *We Are Not Afraid: The Story of Goodman, Schwerner, and Chaney and the Civil Rights Campaign for Mississippi* (1988), covers the activities of Price's victims and the context of their achievements. David Oshinsky, "Should the Mississippi Files Have Been Reopened?," *New York Times* (30 Aug. 1998), provides an account of the issues involved in the prosecution of the murderers over thirty years after the fact. Obituaries of Price are in the *Neshoba Democrat* (2 May 2001) and the *New York Times* (9 May 2001).

KIRK H. BEETZ

PUCINSKI, Roman Gordon (*b.* 13 May 1919 in Buffalo, New York; *d.* 25 September 2002 in Park Ridge, Illinois), chief investigator into the Katyn massacre (1952), U.S. congressman (1959–1973), and Chicago alderman (1973–1991).

Born in Buffalo to Polish immigrants, as a child Pucinski moved to the Wicker Park neighborhood of Chicago, a heavily Polish part of town. Pucinski's father abandoned his mother, Lydia Pucinski, and his siblings when he was a child, and to help his family through the Great Depression, Pucinski sold Magic Washer soap to grocery stores and chocolate to office workers after school. Later, his mother ran the family-owned radio station "Godzina Sloneczna" (WEDC-AM 1240), which broadcast Polish-language programs. He graduated from Wells High School in Chicago in 1938.

Pucinski's first calling was journalism. He attended Northwestern University in Evanston, Illinois, after graduating from high school, but started reporting at the *Chicago Times*, soon to become the *Sun-Times*, in 1939 while still a student. His years at the newspaper grounded him in politics and also kept him from graduating from John Marshall Law School in Chicago—he never took the bar exam because he was too busy with the 1948 presidential election.

World War II interrupted Pucinski's education and his career. He joined the U.S. Army Air Forces and flew forty-

Roman C. Pucinski, August 1961. AP/WIDE WORLD PHOTOS

nine bomber missions over Japan, serving as the lead bombardier on the first B-29 raid on Tokyo in 1944 under General Jimmy Doolittle. He attained the rank of captain and was awarded the Distinguished Flying Cross.

In 1952 Pucinski took a leave from the *Sun-Times* for his first Washington assignment, as chief congressional investigator for a special congressional committee set up to inquire into the massacre of 14,000 Polish soldiers at Katyn Forest at the beginning of the war. Believed by some to be a Nazi atrocity, Pucinski gathered evidence in five European countries to help persuade the congressional panel that the Soviets were responsible. The recognition he received for his work resulted in his appointment as Illinois division president of the Polish American Congress, and those connections led him into politics for his first congressional run in 1956. Urged to run and backed by then–Chicago mayor Richard J. Daley, he lost his first bid to the incumbent, Republican Timothy Sheehan, but won an election to represent Chicago's northwest side in 1958, the first of seven terms in Congress. He was known as a hardworking congressman and outspoken in the press. His greatest achievement, he said, was to get more funding for public education, an area of his expertise. Legislation he sponsored gave Chicago schools $38 million in 1971.

In 1972, forced by redistricting into a race with a fellow Democrat, the incumbent Frank Annunzio, Pucinski gave up his congressional seat to run an underdog campaign for the U.S. Senate, which he lost to the incumbent, Republican Charles Percy, who outspent him ten-to-one. He ran in part because he promised Mayor Daley he would—in return for near-certain defeat, he asked for a seat on Chicago's city council, which at that time was considered better than a congressional seat in local eyes.

Pucinski started the first of six terms as an alderman in 1973, serving the heavily Polish Forty-first Ward. In 1977, after Daley's death, Pucinski ran for Chicago mayor but lost in a six-way primary to Michael Bilandic, who had succeeded Daley. A lifelong Democrat, he found himself more out of step with his party in his later years, as he represented his conservative constituents as one of the last of the old machine politicians. He declined a second mayoral bid in 1983, but rather than support the fellow Democrat and eventual winner, Harold Washington, he backed the Republican, Bernard Epton.

Pucinski continued to oppose Washington throughout Washington's tenure as mayor, working with a majority of aldermen to greatly reduce the effectiveness of Chicago's first African-American mayor. He also kept up his ties with Poland, raising $1.5 million for the Solidarity trade-union movement and speaking with the leader of Solidarity, Lech Walesa, on the telephone on New Year's Eve 1982 to test the easing of Polish government restrictions on telephone communications. But in 1991 Pucinski's own electoral string ran out. The Republican Brian Doherty, a fresh face in a changing ward, beat Pucinski in Doherty's first run for elective office, running an expensive campaign arguing that northwest Chicago residents spent too much in taxes for the services they received.

The Polish community itself lost political clout in Pucinski's later years, as assimilation, the rise of the Latino community, and changing class demographics made Polish identity and political affiliation less advantageous. Pucinski limited himself in his later years to ceremonial appearances and support for his daughter, Aurelia, who shared her father's taste for politics and served as Cook County Circuit Court Clerk. When Aurelia was running for the office, Pucinski became a short-time Washington supporter to secure support for his daughter.

Pucinski married twice. His first wife, Aurelia, died in 1983; they had two children. His second marriage was to the Wisconsin poet Elizabeth Simpson, who died in 1990. Pucinski died of pneumonia in a nursing home at age eighty-three. He had Parkinson's disease. He is buried at Saint Joseph Cemetery and Mausoleums in River Grove, Illinois.

Pucinski's twin experiences as a journalist and airman both heavily influenced his career in Congress. In a city of towering political figures, no Chicago politician was more quotable than Pucinski—he was known for calling journalists in the morning, asking them what the big story was, then calling back half an hour later with a quote for a story. And as a freshman congressman, he pressured the government to require cockpit voice recorders in all airplanes that carry at least six passengers. In 1999, forty years later, the Federal Aviation Administration gave him its Silver Medal of Distinguished Service for that action during a ceremony in the Polish Museum of America.

Throughout his fourteen years in Congress and his eighteen years as an alderman, Pucinski, or "Pooch," as he was affectionately known, epitomized Chicago's unique ethnic flavoring. A leader of the city's close-knit and politically influential Polish community, Pucinski fit the mold of the city's Democratic machine of the Daley era, looking out for his constituents, his city, and his party through a career that saw defeats that were as grand as his victories.

★

There is no biography of Pucinski, but references to him appear in books on the Daley era, including Mike Royko, *Boss: Richard J. Daley of Chicago* (1988); Bill Granger and Lori Granger, *Lords of the Last Machine: The Story of Politics in Chicago* (1992); and Adam Cohen and Elizabeth Taylor, *American Pharaoh: Mayor Richard J. Daley, His Battle for Chicago and the Nation* (2000). Obituaries are in the *Chicago Tribune* (26 Sept. 2002), and the *Washington Post* and *New York Times* (both 27 Sept. 2002).

ALAN BJERGA

PUENTE, Ernest Anthony, Jr. ("Tito") (*b.* 20 April 1923 in the Bronx, New York City; *d.* 1 June 2000 in Manhattan, New York City), legendary Latin and jazz bandleader and percussionist, widely acknowledged as the king of Latin music.

Puente was born at New York City's Harlem Hospital to Ernest Anthony Puente, a factory foreman, and Ercilla (Ortiz) Puente, a homemaker, both migrants from Puerto Rico. His brother died in a fall from a fire escape at the age of four, and his sister died in her teens, leaving Puente an only child. Raised in the neighborhood known as Spanish Harlem, or El Barrio, Puente attended Public Schools 43 and 184, Cooper and Galvanni Junior High Schools, and Central Commercial High School. His also studied at the New York School of Music on 125th Street and Lenox Avenue, received private drum lessons, and listened religiously to the music of the jazz greats Benny Goodman, Artie Shaw, Duke Ellington, and others on the radio. He had an opportunity to hear many of these musicians perform live at such New York theaters as the Paramount and the Strand. A particular hero was the drummer Gene Krupa: Puente won a drum contest with a note-for-note rendition of Krupa's solo on "Sing, Sing, Sing."

In 1939 the sixteen-year-old Puente dropped out of school and began working with the orchestra of the Cuban bandleader Jose Curbelo, a mentor both in music and in business. Three years later, he took a job with another Cuban bandleader, Machito (Frank Grillo), who would become his principal musical model. Drafted into the U.S. Navy in 1942, Puente served on the USS *Santee.* In addition to loading ammunition, he played alto saxophone and drums in the ship's band and learned arranging techniques from a pilot who had arranged for the big band of Charlie Spivak. After seeing action in nine battles in both the Atlantic and the Pacific, Puente was discharged in 1945 with a presidential commendation.

A federal law required that all returning servicemen be offered their prewar jobs, but Puente's replacement as percussionist for the Machito Orchestra had a family to support, and both Machito and Puente agreed that it would be best if he kept the position. Puente worked for several bands before joining Pupi Campo's orchestra in September 1947. There he met the trumpeter Jimmy Frisaura, who became a close friend and played in Puente's own band for forty years.

During this time, Puente studied at the Julliard School of Music under the GI Bill and learned to use the vibraphone. In March 1949 he launched his own band, originally known as the Piccadilly Boys and renamed the Tito Puente Orchestra in the early 1950s. The group, which included several former members of Campo's orchestra, played its first date in Atlantic Beach, New Jersey, on 4 July 1949.

Tito Puente. AP/WIDE WORLD PHOTOS

They later became regulars at the Palladium Ballroom in Manhattan, a showcase for Latin bands such as those of Puente, Machito, and Puente's longtime friend (and sometime rival) Tito Rodríguez. In 1949 Puente had his first major hit with "Abaniquito." That same year Puente signed an exclusive contract with Radio Corporation of America (RCA), which issued the single "Ran Kan Kan," destined to become a Puente classic, and eventually rereleased many of his earlier recordings, formerly available only on the old 78-rpm disks.

The 1950s were a fruitful period for the Puente orchestra. Early in the decade the conga player Mongo Santamaría and the bongoist Willie Bobo, both of whom would later have highly successful solo careers, joined the band. Puente had numerous important releases, none more significant than *Puente in Percussion* (1955), one of the first albums ever to use only bass and percussion.

Puente's first highly successful album with RCA was *Cuban Carnival* (1956), which he followed later that year with *Puente Goes Jazz.* In 1957 he released *Night Beat,* which included the trumpeter Doc Severinson, and *Top Percussion,* which explored the Afro-Cuban drumming and chants of the Santeria religion. The music and teachings of Santeria remained an interest for Puente throughout his life. Also in 1957 Puente was the only non-Cuban recognized in a Cuban government ceremony honoring the country's great musicians of the past half-century.

In late 1957 Puente and his orchestra recorded his most commercially (and, in the view of some, artistically) successful album of the era, *Dance Mania,* which sold over half a million copies. One of its major hits was "Cuyuco," which became a favorite among dance aficionados, and

"Hong Kong Mambo," featuring Puente on marimba playing a riff that imitated the melodies of the Far East. By the end of the decade Puente had left RCA and returned to his Tico Records, on which he had also recorded in the early 1950s. In 1961 he recorded one of his personal favorites, *Puente in Hollywood* (retitled *Puente Now*), and in 1962 made the first of many concert tours in Japan, where he helped to popularize Latin music. He recorded numerous significant long-playing records in the 1960s with two important female vocalists, Cecilia Cruz and La Lupe, and La Lupe became a featured vocalist throughout most of the late 1960s.

In 1967 Puente presented a concert of his own compositions at New York's Metropolitan Opera and in the late 1960s hosted his own television program, *El Mundo de Tito Puente* (The World of Tito Puente) on a Spanish-language network. He served as grand marshal for the 1968 Puerto Rican Day parade in New York City and received the keys to the city in 1969 from Mayor John Lindsay. Over the decades that followed, Puente survived and incorporated many new rhythm trends, including cha-cha, pachanga, boogaloo, salsa, Latin soul, and disco. Of these styles, the one with which he became most identified was salsa, but he had reservations about it. Noting in an interview that "salsa" means "sauce" in Spanish, he said, "My problem is that we don't play sauce, we play music." Nevertheless, he recognized that its popularity with mainstream audiences helped increase the exposure of Latin music in general.

By that point rock music was dominant, and the early 1970s witnessed Carlos Santana's reinterpretation of hits by Puente and Bobo for a younger generation. A cover of Bobo's "Evil Ways" appeared on Santana's first album, and *Abraxas* (1970) included a version of Puente's 1960s standard "Oye Como Va." Santana also covered Puente's "Pa' los Rumberos," originally recorded in 1956, on *Santana III* (1972). In 1977 Puente and Santana played together at New York's Roseland Ballroom.

Puente received his first Grammy Award in 1978, for *Homenage a Beny More* and was honored after the awards ceremony with a testimonial "roast" by members of the Latin music community. Funds given by sponsors of the roast provided the basis for a scholarship fund, in Puente's name, to support the musical education of talented young people. Over the years that followed, the project held annual fundraisers and awarded more than a hundred scholarships. In the early 1980s Puente signed with Concord Records, which released the first album by the newly renamed Tito Puente Latin Jazz Ensemble (later called Tito Puente and His Latin Ensemble). That album, *On Broadway,* received a Grammy in 1983. Another Grammy followed in 1985, for *Mambo diablo,* and in 1990 for the track "Lambada Timbales."

The readers of *Down Beat* voted Puente percussionist of the year in 1989, and he received the magazine's "musician of the month" award several times in the late 1980s and early 1990s. In 1987 the National Academy of Recording Arts and Sciences honored him with the Eubie Award, and on 4 August 1990 Puente received a star on the Hollywood Walk of Fame. Puente appeared in the films *Armed and Dangerous* (1986) and *Radio Days* (1987), and provided music for several films, most notably *The Mambo Kings* (1992). The latter was based on the Oscar Hijuelos novel *The Mambo Kings Play Songs of Love,* in which Puente himself is depicted as the king of the New York mambo scene in the 1950s. While Puente was working on music for the movie, a consortium of famous Latin artists gathered to join him on his 100th album, *The Mambo King,* released in 1991.

In the early 1990s Puente organized his third major group, after the orchestra and the Latin Jazz Ensemble, the Golden Latin Jazz All Stars. The latter released a live album as well as the highly successful studio album *In Session* (1994). He continued to tour throughout the 1990s, performing at twenty to thirty jazz festivals a year in Europe, Russia, the Far East, Australia, Latin America, and North America. The 1997 three-CD boxed set *50 Years of Swing* featured tracks representing Puente's half-century of recording and performance, and the liner notes included tributes from a variety of artists.

In 1993 Puente was honored with an all-star jazz tribute at Carnegie Hall; in 1994 with the prestigious Founder's Award from the Association of Songwriters, Composers, Authors, and Publishers; and in 1995 with a Lifetime Achievement Award from *Billboard* magazine. In July 1996 he performed before the largest television audience in history at the Centennial Olympic Games in Atlanta, and upon receiving the Smithsonian National Museum Medal of Honor and Lifetime Achievement Award in October, Puente donated to the museum the timbale he had played at the Olympics.

On 29 September 1997 Puente, who had performed for four presidents—Jimmy Carter, Ronald W. Reagan, George H. W. Bush, and William J. ("Bill") Clinton—received the National Medal of Arts from Clinton at a White House ceremony. Clinton commented that the mere mention of Puente's name "makes everyone want to get up and dance." Puente also earned Grammys in 1999, for *Mambo Birdland* and, as coproducer with Eddie Palmieri, for *Masterpiece/Obra Maestra* in 2000. Puente died at New York University Medical Center, of complications following heart surgery. He is buried at Saint Anthony's Church in Nanuet, New York.

His personal life was as eventful as his career. During wartime shore leave, he married his longtime girlfriend Mirta Sanchez, with whom he had a son in 1947. They later divorced. In 1953 he and Ida Carlini, a dancer with whom he engaged in a long-term relationship, had a son, Richard Anthony Puente, who went on to become a musician. For the last three decades of his life, Puente was involved with Margaret Acencio. Their daughter, Audrey Puente, became a weather forecaster on New York City's Channel 4, and their son, Tito Puente, Jr., also became a musician. During the mid-1990s, Puente and Acencio were married, with their son and daughter serving as best man and maid of honor.

At the time of his death Puente, known as "El Rey" (the king), had 118 albums, over 450 compositions, more than 2,000 arrangements, and some 10,000 live performances to his credit. His durability as a musician was a result of several factors, including his enormous talent and musical knowledge, his innovative creativity, his resilient and consistent affinity for the promotion of his enterprise, his competitive verve, and, most of all, his powerful charisma. In the eyes of many musicians and critics, he will go down in history as the greatest Latin music artist of the twentieth century.

★

The principal source on Puente is Steven Loza, *Tito Puente and the Making of Latin Music* (1999). See also Ruth Glasser, *My Music Is My Flag: Puerto Rican Musicians and Their New York Communities, 1917–1940* (1995). Articles on Puente include Bobby Sanabria and Ben Socolov, "Tito Puente: Long Live the King," *Hip: Highlights in Percussion* 5 (spring/summer 1994): 1–7, 22–23; "Tito Puente: The Early Years," *Latin Beat* 4, no. 1 (1994): 14–20; and Max Salazar, "Tito Puente: The Living Legend," *Latin Times* 3, no. 3 (1977): 15–18. An obituary is in the *New York Times* (2 June 2000).

STEVEN LOZA

PUSEY, Nathan Marsh (*b.* 4 April 1907 in Council Bluffs, Iowa; *d.* 14 November 2001 in Manhattan, New York City), twenty-fourth president of Harvard University, who led the university through dramatic changes from 1953 to 1971.

Pusey was the third child and second son born to John Marsh Pusey, a county court clerk, and Rosa (Drake) Pusey. His father died within a year of his birth, and his mother, who had taught school before her marriage, returned to teaching to support her family. A gifted student, Pusey graduated in 1924 from Abraham Lincoln High School in Council Bluffs, where he was a member of the debate and basketball teams and editor of the school paper. He entered Harvard on scholarship, earning a B.A. in English and graduating both magna cum laude and Phi Beta Kappa in 1928. He spent a year in Europe and, when he was unable to find work in publishing on his return home, taught for two years at the Riverdale Country School in New York

City. There he discovered, as he later recalled, that he was "seriously interested in education."

Pusey returned to Harvard for a master's degree in 1931. To qualify for admission to a program in classical literature, he taught himself Greek over the summer. Intrigued by the ancient world, he shifted his course of study to Athenian civilization, earning an M.A. in ancient history in 1932 and a part-time assistantship in the history department. Two years later he won a fellowship to the American School of Classical Study in Athens.

Pusey became an instructor at Lawrence College in Wisconsin in 1935. He received his Ph.D. from Harvard in 1937; his unpublished dissertation, written in Greek on a Greek typewriter, was a study of Athenian law.

On 10 June 1936 Pusey married Anne Woodward of Council Bluffs, whom he had tutored in algebra when she was thirteen years old and he an undergraduate. They had two sons and a daughter.

Pusey taught classical history and literature at Scripps College in California (1938–1940) and classics at Wesleyan University in Connecticut (1940–1944). While at Wesleyan, he also taught physics in the U.S. Navy V-5 program, which provided enlisted personnel a basic technical education in specialized shipboard skills. In the fall of 1944 he returned to Lawrence as its eleventh president, quickly making his mark with a series of curriculum reforms that emphasized the liberal arts. His doubled the college's endowment and earned a national reputation for his vigorous support of academic freedom.

On 1 June 1953 the Harvard Corporation appointed Pusey the twenty-fourth president of the university, making him the first non–New Englander to hold that prestigious position. His call to Cambridge came at an auspicious moment in the nation's life, a period he later called "the most creative . . . in the history of higher education in the United States." Beginning with the GI Bill (legislation passed during World War II to ease the return of millions of servicemen to civilian life) and continuing into the Eisenhower years, when Congress and the Supreme Court expanded the educational role of the federal government, student populations in U.S. schools and colleges swelled to near unmanageable levels, and a shortage of teachers and facilities developed nationwide. College presidents, particularly in the Ivy League and the small liberal arts colleges in the northeast, took on the role of public advocates, making the case for educational reforms and increased financial support at all levels of schooling.

As president of Harvard, Pusey moved to the forefront of such advocacy. Nearly six feet tall, physically fit, with patrician features and a commanding intelligence, he was, at forty-six years of age, well equipped for the role. He had an unbending faith in the liberal arts as "a source of inward strength" and in the power of education to transform the self. He firmly believed that education was "at root an informed search for truth—passionately pursued," but he balanced this with a deep religious faith, saying on one occasion, "We need to know, but also to believe, and what we want especially to do is to believe knowingly." An Episcopalian, he was the last Harvard president to read the Scriptures every Sunday during services in Memorial Church.

As he took up his duties in the fall of 1953, Pusey consolidated the reforms of his predecessor, James Bryant Conant. Conant had introduced the concept of meritocracy into admissions practice, improved both science teaching and laboratory facilities, and given special attention to the graduate schools of business, law, and medicine. Within weeks Pusey took on Senator Joseph McCarthy, who had asserted that the Harvard faculty was riddled with Communist sympathizers and demanded the immediate firing of four professors. Pusey had publicly opposed McCarthy's reelection in 1952, thereby earning the senator's continuing enmity. In a series of speeches and press releases, he dismissed the senator's latest charges as groundless. Harvard, he said, had no communists teaching in its classrooms because the university was a place where young minds were taught to search freely for the truth, and communists sought only indoctrination.

No tenured faculty member at Harvard was fired; McCarthy went elsewhere for targets; and the American Civil Liberties Union, among others, honored Pusey for his courageous stand. But this was the public face of the university. Years later, several former graduate teaching assistants and untenured instructors came forward to assert that Harvard had, in private, capitulated to government pressures, demanding that jobseekers cooperate with the Federal Bureau of Investigation and reveal to them and to McGeorge Bundy, the dean of faculty, names of radical associates in their past. Failure to do so meant denial of employment and, for those already teaching, nonrenewal of their contracts. Pusey's role in these activities is unclear, because Harvard's archival policies restrict outside access to certain administrative papers for up to eighty years after an event.

Otherwise, Pusey's achievements at Harvard were both progressive and sweeping. He strengthened the undergraduate humanities program and reshaped Harvard College, which had been too long neglected in favor of graduate programs. He also revitalized the divinity school and the graduate school of education. He upgraded campus facilities, nearly doubling the university's floor space and adding specialized libraries and centers for the arts. In all, thirty buildings were constructed, and another seventy were modernized or refurbished.

In 1957 Pusey announced "The Program for Harvard College," the most ambitious fundraising effort by any uni-

Nathan M. Pusey, December 1963. BETTMANN/CORBIS

versity up to that time. In contrast to the low-key approaches of the past, "The Program" aggressively targeted wealthy alumni worldwide for money. Its professional staff enlisted hundreds of graduates on a scale never before attempted to solicit their classmates for annual gifts at specified levels. Within five years it generated $100 million from 28,000 alumni, setting a standard for other schools and making fund-raising thereafter a key measure of a college president's success. Under Pusey's leadership, Harvard's budget and endowment each quadrupled in value. Faculty salaries and benefits reached new levels, and the number of faculty and staff more than doubled to 8,500. Pusey increased the hiring of female faculty and initiated a "need-blind" admission policy so that even the poorest applicant could be admitted on the strength of intellect or talent alone. He also initiated discussions in the late 1960s that led to an eventual merger of Radcliffe and Harvard.

Pusey's widely praised stewardship was openly challenged by student radicals in 1969. In that tumultuous year, opposition to the war in Vietnam on college campuses moved from speechmaking and pamphleteering to acts of violence that saw faculty offices trashed, administration buildings occupied, and laboratories set on fire. Harvard's violence began in late April 1969, when Students for a Democratic Society took control of University Hall, the administrative heart of the campus, seeking to change the university's system of governance. They manhandled deans and secretaries, driving them from the building, and conducted a sit-in with the intention of shutting Harvard down until their "non-negotiable demands" were met. These demands included elimination of reserve officers training corps, establishment of a department of black studies, and changes in Harvard's policy on the conversion of nearby residential areas to university use.

Pusey saw these leftist students as being no different from McCarthy and his right-wing supporters: both violated the terms of civil discourse, substituted force or raw power for reasoned argument, and threatened academic freedom in unacceptable ways. He refused to negotiate with the demonstrators and instead called in state and local police in riot gear to remove them from the building. Forty-five students were injured and 197 arrested to face charges of trespass and assault. Asked to ratify Pusey's action, the faculty, many of them troubled that off-campus police had violated the sanctuary of the campus with tear gas and clubs, refused. A general strike paralyzed the campus for several days but, in the end, charges were dropped, and no students were dismissed.

The campus remained divided well into the next academic year. Members of the faculty and some well-placed alumni complained that Pusey had panicked and, without faculty consent, had violated Harvard's traditional autonomy by calling in outsiders to settle an internal dispute. Other faculty critics spoke out against his leadership in other areas. Finding himself increasingly isolated and certain that his continued presence might harm the institution he loved, Pusey tendered his resignation, effective in 1971.

Retiring to New York, Pusey served as head of the Andrew Mellon Foundation (1971–1975) and was active in a variety of philanthropic causes until his death. His *American Higher Education, 1945–1970: A Personal Report* (1978) analyzed the momentous changes in colleges and universities that had so altered the course of higher education. He died of heart disease at New York Weill Cornell Center in Manhattan.

Pusey earned national praise for his defense of academic freedom in the McCarthy era but widespread criticism years later for bringing riot police on campus to arrest student radicals. In the memorial services that followed his death, his many triumphs on behalf of Harvard took center stage, and his sad final years in Cambridge, when many of the faculty and students had turned against him, were largely ignored. His severest critics knew that Pusey's seventeen-year tenure had reenergized and extended the worldwide reach of an institution he dearly loved. As James Reston wrote in the *New York Times,* Pusey was not "a popular president with the students or the faculty—but his record

in defending the integrity of a free university cannot be seriously challenged."

★

Pusey's papers are in the Harvard University Archives at the Pusey Library, Harvard University. Under the university's policy of closing certain archival holdings for a period of fifty to eighty years, some papers relating to Harvard's official response to McCarthyism became available in 2003; others remain closed. Papers relating to the 1969 riots, only some of which are open to scholars, are held in the university archives under the title, "The Harvard University Student Strike, 1969." For selected speeches and occasional papers, see Pusey's *The Age of the Scholar* (1964). Pusey's "A Presidential Autobiography," written for the twenty-fifth anniversary of his class, is in the *Harvard Alumni Bulletin* (6 June 1953). See also Roger Rosenblatt, *Coming Apart: A Memoir of the Harvard Wars of 1969* (1997); John T. Bethell, *Harvard Observed* (1998); and Morton Keller and Phyllis Keller, *Making Harvard Modern: The Rise of America's University* (2001). Obituaries are in the *New York Times* and *Harvard University Gazette* (both 15 Nov. 2001). The university archives hold a two-cassette sound recording, "An Interview with Nathan M. Pusey," conducted by a reporter from the *Harvard Crimson* (27 Mar. 1989).

ALLAN L. DAMON

QUINN, Anthony Rudolph Oaxaca (*b.* 21 April 1915 in Chihuahua, Mexico; *d.* 3 June 2001 in Boston, Massachusetts), two-time Oscar-winning actor who appeared on stage, screen, and television for over half a century, including in a signature role in the film *Zorba the Greek* (1964).

Quinn, the son of Francisco Quinn and Manuela (Oaxaca) Quinn, was born into poor circumstances. His father was of Irish and Mexican extraction; his mother was Mexican with some Indian inheritance. At the time of his birth, his father was serving in Pancho Villa's insurgent army during the Mexican revolution.

While searching for his father, Quinn and his mother were smuggled north to Juarez, Mexico, then into El Paso, Texas, where they lived in a tiny hut along a refuse-filled canal. His mother supported them by doing laundry and house cleaning until she eventually found her husband when Quinn was about two years old. It took another few years for the family to be accepted by Quinn's paternal grandmother; by that time, Quinn's sister was born.

The family moved to Nevada, where Quinn's father and a cousin were employed laying railroad track through the desert. When the crew lost a member, Quinn's mother took over the vacant position. Shortly after that, Quinn's father suffered an injury at work. Unable to continue with the railroad, he tried crop picking before settling into a Los

Angeles barrio. By then Quinn's grandmother had become a permanent member of the household.

Quinn's father worked at odd jobs until he started caring for animals at a zoo, then working as a camera operator when the animals were used in movie scenes. In the meantime, Quinn grew up on the street, attending school when he had to, fighting, and picking up whatever odd jobs were available. His relationship with his father was somewhat tumultuous, varying from harsh discipline to being doted upon. When Quinn was ten his father died in an accident.

In his father's absence, Quinn began supporting the family, working at various odd jobs. Although born into a Roman Catholic household, at one time he played saxophone, preached, and acted as a Spanish interpreter for the Protestant evangelist Aimee Semple McPherson. Like many children growing up in poverty, he resented those whom he felt looked down upon him because of his background. For the rest of his life, he felt a need to show that he had risen above his roots. When his mother remarried, Quinn found it impossible to accept his stepfather and went to live with his sister and grandmother.

During Quinn's occasional attendance at Polytechnic High School, he showed his talent for drawing and won a contest for a design for a supermarket. This led to a meeting with the architect Frank Lloyd Wright, who, noticing a speech impediment, recommended that Quinn have surgery and speech lessons to correct it. Trading janitorial services for acting lessons, which he hoped would improve his speech, Quinn worked at the studio of Katherine Hamil, a former actress. There he was given a part in a school production of Noel Coward's *Hay Fever,* his first acting job. Later, Mae West recommended him for a role modeled on John Barrymore's character in *Clean Beds* (1936). When Barrymore saw Quinn's performance, he added the young man to his circle of friends. In 1936 Quinn got his first part in a film, a nonspeaking role in *Parole* that lasted less than a minute.

In 1937 Quinn was given a small part as an Indian in the Cecil B. De Mille epic *The Plainsman* (1936). This led to a confrontation on the set, during which the brash young Quinn won an argument with the director about how a scene should be played. Becoming a contract player with Paramount, he played gangster roles in the studio's remarkably popular B films, as well as a number of minor ethnic roles. After a few years, however, Quinn quit Paramount because of these limited roles, and because he felt that his relation to De Mille had become a drawback.

Meanwhile, Quinn met the director's adopted daughter, Katherine, whom he married on 21 October 1937. Although marital tensions quickly developed because of Quinn's indiscretions, they had five children. Both parents had difficulty overcoming the death of their first child, Christopher, who drowned in a swimming-pool accident.

After several more films as a freelancer, Quinn signed a

Anthony Quinn. SYGMA PHOTO NEWS

three-year contract with Twentieth Century–Fox. His second film with that company was as a Mexican cowboy in the classic *The Ox Bow Incident* (1942). This was followed by a number of less-than-memorable roles in films during the World War II period. In one of these films, *Ladies in Washington* (1944), Quinn had his first on-screen kissing scene. Attempting to revitalize his career, Quinn then moved to New York to try the legitimate stage and television. He lost the role of Stanley Kowalski in *A Streetcar Named Desire* to Marlon Brando, but played that role for more than a year in the touring company before getting the lead on Broadway. Quinn was naturalized as a U.S. citizen in 1947.

In 1952, paired as the younger brother to Brando in *Viva Zapata!,* Quinn earned his first Oscar for best supporting actor. Frustrated by continually being cast in ethnic roles, he went to Italy to play a strongman in Federico Fellini's *La Strada* (1953). For the next several years Quinn was constantly on the go making films. In *Lust for Life* (1956), the story of Vincent Van Gogh, Quinn played the artist Paul Gauguin. His performance earned him his second Oscar as best supporting actor.

Over the next decade and a half, few actors were as

prolific as Quinn, both in the number of films and the variety of his roles. He played a Greek officer in *The Guns of Navarone* (1961), and appeared as the aging boxer, Mountain Rivera, in *Requiem for a Heavyweight* and as the Arabian chieftain, Auda abu Tayi, in *Lawrence of Arabia* (both 1962). Two years later, Quinn starred in *Zorba the Greek* (1964) as the title character, an exuberant Greek who teaches a staid young Englishman to unwind; this became the role with which Quinn was always identified. Despite the film's low budget, *Zorba the Greek* had an impressive cast, and many felt that Quinn was denied an Oscar because he admitted that he had fathered a child with Iolanda Addolari, an Italian costume designer. Quinn terminated his marriage to his first wife in 1965 and married Addolari the following January.

In 1968 Quinn gave a remarkable performance as a Russian prelate elevated to the papacy in *The Shoes of the Fisherman*. Even in what are considered minor films, Quinn showed himself to be a consummate actor. He played opposite Ingrid Bergman in the chilling film noir *The Visit* (1964), and was a bumbling Italian mayor in *The Secret of Santa Vittoria* (1969). In *The Twenty-Fifth Hour* (1967), Quinn played to perfection the role of a peasant who is dragged through the turmoil of World War II Europe. The persistent struggle to cope with life is also evident in his role as the aging Cuban fisherman, Santiago, in the television adaptation of Ernest Hemingway's *The Old Man and the Sea* (1990).

In a career that spanned sixty-six years, Quinn acted in over 175 films; he directed one and produced several. He also made appearances on and off-Broadway and in plays with touring companies. He was also active in television, from talk shows and dramatic performances to one short series. His last film appearance was in *Avenging Angelo,* released after his death in 2002. Late in his career, Quinn took up painting and exhibited his work in a number of well-reviewed shows in various parts of the world. He also developed a reputation as a serious collector of fine art.

Quinn wrote two autobiographies. In *The Original Sin: A Self-Portrait* (1972), he focuses primarily on his early life, which he relates as a series of vignettes with his counselor. He brought his life up to 1995 in *One Man Tango* (1995), using the device of a bicycle ride near his home south of Rome to trigger his memories. After fathering a child by his secretary, Kathy Benvin, Quinn divorced his second wife in 1997 and married Benvin. In all, Quinn had thirteen children by three wives and two unnamed women. He died of respiratory failure at Brigham and Women's Hospital in Boston and was buried at his estate in Bristol, Rhode Island.

Constantly driven by self-doubt and feelings of inferiority, Quinn drove himself to become one of the major screen actors of the twentieth century. Despite his myriad talents, and against his own efforts to avoid being typecast, he will be most remembered for a wide variety of ethnic roles.

★

The Anthony Quinn Library, a branch of the Los Angeles Count Public Library at 3965 Cesar Chavez Avenue in Los Angeles, has over 3,000 items, including photographs, scrapbooks, scripts, screenplays, and other memorabilia, relating to Quinn. Both of Quinn's autobiographies, *The Original Sin: A Self-Portrait* (1972), and *One Man Tango* (1995), written with Daniel Paisner, are readable; although the latter repeats most of the material in the first. Alvin H. Marill, *The Films of Anthony Quinn* (1975), is an excellent source for plots and screen credits for Quinn's films through the mid-point of his career. Melissa Amdur, *Anthony Quinn* (1993), is much too brief. Obituaries are in the *New York Times* and *Washington Post* (both 4 June 2001).

ART BARBEAU

R

RAMONE, Joey (*b*. 19 May 1951 in Forest Hills, New York; *d*. 15 April 2001 in New York City), lead singer and songwriter for the Ramones, regarded by many critics as the first important punk-rock band.

Ramone was born Jeffrey Hyman, the son of Noel Hyman, who owned a trucking company in Manhattan, and Charlotte (Lesher) Hyman, an artist and owner of an art gallery on Queens Boulevard. He had one younger brother. Ramone's parents divorced when he was just entering adolescence, and when his mother remarried, he felt alienated and withdrew into music. As he later put it, "I was spending a lot of time by myself. Rock 'n' roll was my salvation." He was attracted to musicians such as Del Shannon, Buddy Holly, Phil Spector, Gene Vincent, the Rolling Stones, the Beach Boys, and the Beatles. These influences provided the underpinning for the Ramones' later assault on the stagnant pop music aesthetic of the 1970s.

Ramone attended local public schools and Forest Hills High School, and although academics did not interest him, his passion for art and music grew. He felt like an outsider in middle-class Queens, and his appearance further set him apart: he was tall and gawky, grew his hair long, and perennially wore sunglasses. His first instrument was a drum kit, which he set up in the basement of his mother's art gallery. By the time he was seventeen, he was out of his mother's house and looking for work. He also experimented with LSD and ended up spending two brief stays at psychiatric hospitals because of it. These experiences only heightened his sense of alienation.

In the early 1970s Ramone moved to Greenwich Village in Manhattan and worked in an art gallery, but times were hard and he ended up back in Queens, living with his mother and working for her. He joined a band called the Snipers, a glam rock group influenced by David Bowie and T-Rex, and while this provided an outlet, he needed something more—or, as he put it, "I wanted more realism."

He got more realism in 1974 when he met the other future members of the Ramones. All Queens natives, the four had many things in common, including a sarcastic sense of humor, a love of raw rock like that of the Stooges, and an upbringing filled with comic books, horror movies (they sang about *The Texas Chain Saw Massacre* on their first album), and borderline juvenile delinquency. As the rock critic David Fricke put it, "They could not have existed in any other country, or in any other city, or been born in any other borough than Queens."

In homage to 1950s bands made up of brothers, the band members styled themselves as "the Ramones," complete with fraternal identities and names. Hyman, who became Joey Ramone, started on the drums but quickly took over on lead vocals, bringing to bear a distinctive vocal quality that would remain a signature aspect of the group for the next three decades. John Cummings became Johnny Ramone, whose guitar playing was fast and furious and formed a kind of punk template. Douglas Colvin took up the bass as Dee Dee Ramone, and Tommy Erdelyi became the drummer Tommy Ramone. They assumed a Ramones uniform, which they wore for the entire life of the band: ripped jeans, T-shirts, sneakers, and leather motorcycle jackets. They never appeared on stage dressed in any other clothes.

On 16 August 1974 the Ramones played their first gig at CBGB, the Lower East Side club that would become the home of New York punk. Along with such groups as Television, Blondie, the Dictators, Richard Hell and the Voidoids, and the Dead Boys, the Ramones helped give birth to a native New York punk that would eventually alter the course of rock history. As the rock critic John Rockwell put it, the Ramones stood out from the rest of the New York bands because they were "the purest conceptual band of the bunch, and possibly the wittiest." The concept behind the Ramones was simple: according to Ramone, "We wanted to kind of save rock 'n' roll, keep it exciting and fun and the whole bit." The Ramones on stage were rock dynamos. All their songs were under two and a half minutes in length, they played fast, and they gave their all during every performance. It was not uncommon to hear them play fifteen songs in thirty minutes. The songs were about deviant behavior ("Now I Wanna Sniff Some Glue"), outsiders ("Pinhead"), and the emerging punk aesthetic ("Judy Is a Punk," "Blitzkrieg Bop").

The Ramones quickly established a loyal following at CBGB, and 1976 saw the appearance of their first album, titled simply *Ramones.* Constantly touring, the band played a now legendary show in London on 4 July 1976, a performance famous for its influence on British punk: as a result of exposure to the Ramones, the members of the Sex Pistols, the Clash, and the Buzzcocks all took up instruments.

The band toured frequently, and it was not uncommon for the Ramones to play over 150 shows a year. In 1977 they released two more albums, *Leave Home* and *Rocket to Russia.* Along with their debut, these recordings have been called classic punk statements, and they helped shape the emerging punk subculture. Songs such as "Teenage Lobotomy," "Sheena Is a Punk Rocker," and "Rockaway Beach" quickly became punk standards. In 1978 Tommy Ramone left the band and was replaced by Marky Ramone (Marc Bell) on drums. The band's forth album, *Road to Ruin,* which included the quintessential Ramones anthem, "I Wanna Be Sedated," was also released that year. In 1979 the group starred in the Roger Corman–produced film *Rock 'n' Roll High School.*

Although the Ramones never had a hit record, their reputation and fan base grew during the 1980s, partly due to their constant touring. In 1980 Joey Ramone got to work with one of his music heroes when Phil Spector produced the Ramones' fifth studio album, *End of the Century.* Joey took the first political stance in his decade-long career in

Joey Ramone, 1996. STEVE JENNINGS/CORBIS

1985, when he wrote "Bonzo Goes to Bitburg," criticizing President Ronald W. Reagan's visit to the graves of SS troops on a tour of a German military cemetery. Also in 1985, he joined nearly fifty international artists on the antiapartheid single "Sun City."

Major shifts occurred in 1989, as another of the Ramones' founding members, Dee Dee, left the band to be replaced by CJ Ramone (Chris Ward), a former fan who had grown up listening to the group. Also in 1989, the band composed the title song for the Stephen King film *Pet Sematary,* reportedly at the request of King, a Ramones fan, and Joey appeared as himself in the cult film *Roadkill.* The band also appeared on the television series *The Simpsons* in 1993.

The Ramones reached the apex of their popularity as a performing band in the early 1990s, when they released three albums that solidified their reputation and influence: *Mondo Bizarro* (1992), *Acid Eaters* (1993), and *Adios Amigos* (1995).

The latter album was a fitting good-bye, coming as it did in the year when Joey was diagnosed with lymphoma. He was given three to six months to live, but though the Ramones officially ceased performing in 1996, he remained active for an additional half-decade. Always a prominent figure in New York music circles, he continued to sponsor bands and music events. In the winter of 2000 he broke his hip after a fall while leaving one of the music events he had sponsored. He died on Easter Sunday in 2001 at the age of forty-nine. He had never married or had children.

Ramone left behind an unfinished solo album, *Don't Worry About Me,* which was released in 2002, the same year the Ramones—the band from Queens that used to ride the 7 train to gigs with their instruments in shopping bags—were inducted into the Rock and Roll Hall of Fame. Also in 2002, the corner of Second Street and the Bowery in Lower Manhattan was renamed Joey Ramone Place. The spot is half a block from CBGB, where the Ramones started their careers as New York's most notorious and beloved punks. It was a fitting tribute to an artist who helped create the sound of New York punk and changed the course of rock and roll history.

★

There are several full-length studies of the Ramones and their influence on rock culture, including Jim Bessman, *Ramones: An American Band* (1993), and Dick Porter, *Ramones: The Complete Twisted Story* (2003). The most comprehensive work on the band, and on Ramone's contribution to it, is Everett True, *Hey Ho Let's Go: The Story of the Ramones* (2002). Dee Dee Ramone wrote about his life in the *Ramones in Lobotomy: Surviving the Ramones* (2002). Obituaries are in the *Village Voice* (16 Apr. 2001) and *New York Times* (17 Apr. 2001).

JOHN ROCCO

RAWLS, John Bordley (*b.* 15 February 1921 in Baltimore, Maryland; *d.* 24 November 2002 in Lexington, Massachusetts), political philosopher whose book *A Theory of Justice* (1971) is considered one of the major twentieth-century works in the field.

Rawls, the son of William Lee Rawls, a constitutional lawyer, and Anna Abel (Stump) Rawls, a social activist, was born into a wealthy family. Of his four brothers, two died from sicknesses they acquired from him. Rawls later developed a stutter, which he blamed on his guilty feelings over their deaths.

As a young man, Rawls was inspired by the progressive, feminist politics of his mother, who ran the local League of Women Voters chapter. In 1939 he graduated from Kent School in Connecticut. He then entered Princeton University in New Jersey, where he became interested in political philosophy under the tutelage of Norman Malcolm. Rawls received his B.A. from Princeton in 1943 and his Ph.D. in 1950.

On 28 June 1949 Rawls married the painter Margaret Warfield Fox; they had four children. From 1950 to 1952 Rawls was an instructor at Princeton. He then spent a year as a Fulbright fellow at Oxford University in England. From 1953 to 1959 he served as an assistant professor, then associate professor at Cornell University in Ithaca, New York; as a professor at the Massachusetts Institute of Technology (MIT) in Cambridge from 1960 to 1962; as a visiting professor at Harvard University in Cambridge from 1959 to 1960; and as a professor there from 1962 to 1995.

Rawls began discussing the concept of "Justice as Fairness" in an October 1957 article by that title published in the *Journal of Philosophy*. This notion gradually evolved into his most celebrated book, *A Theory of Justice* (1971), which argues that justice must be the basis for a modern society. "Justice is the first virtue of social institutions, as truth is of systems of thought," he wrote. To define "justice," Rawls proposed a "thought experiment" wherein a hypothetical group of people who know nothing about themselves are asked to design the basic political structure for a new society they will inhabit, without knowing their future social status (for example, whether they will be rich or poor). Inspired by rational choice theory and game theory, Rawls concluded they would design a society that offered the best conceivable outcome in the event that fate consigned them to the least fortunate social stratum. To oversimplify, in a worst-case scenario they would be comfortably poor rather than miserably poor.

A Theory of Justice presents two vital principles. The more important, in Rawls's view, is personal liberty. The second principle requires a distribution of services and wealth that maximizes the comfort of the least advantaged as much as possible—that is, as much as is compatible with the liberty of others and the economic health of the overall society. Rawls, in translating these ideas into guidelines for action, said the government must establish a minimum standard of living (say, by means of "family allowances and special payments for sickness and unemployment") as well as support public schools or subsidize private ones. However, he did not take this to an extreme. Although his work raised questions about the legitimacy of the notion of "property," and although many perceive a democratic-socialist outlook in his writings, Rawls did not insist that everyone receive the same amount of goods, nor did he reject a market-capitalist economy per se. He opposed the Soviet-style "command" economy because it infringed on personal liberty.

A Theory of Justice won effusive praise. In a front-page article for the *New York Times Book Review*, the philosopher Marshall Cohen called the book a "peerless contribution to political theory," which disproved the widespread claim that "systematic moral and political philosophy are dead." The *Times* in 1972 later chose *Theory of Justice* as one of the five most significant books of the preceding year.

John Rawls. COURTESY OF MARGARET FOX RAWLS

Even the book's best-known critic, the libertarian philosopher Robert Nozick, commented, "It is a fountain of lovely ideas." In 1985 Alan Ryan, a political philosopher, noted that the book "is written with tremendous clarity and care, but there's nothing about it to provoke instant excitement," further observing that it nevertheless "has been more widely cited by sociologists, economists, judges and politicians than any work of philosophy in the past hundred years." Rawls's notions seem to convince readers of the basic goodness of human beings and the potential improvement of society.

A Theory of Justice has not lacked for critics, on either the right or the left. Conservatives feel Rawls went too far; leftists feel he did not go far enough. In the conservative *National Review*, John Kekes wrote that Rawls failed to address the possibility that some persons are more deserving than others of social help. Comparing two equally poor people—one a vicious mugger, the other a devoted parent—Kekes said that according to his reading of Rawls, both, being impoverished, are equally entitled to society's beneficence. On the other hand, many leftists complained Rawls was too stodgy: He had the right values, but he didn't push them far enough. They especially disliked his ranking of personal liberty over socioeconomic equality. The leftist-feminist critic Maureen Ramsey pointed out that poor, un-

employed, or uneducated people may not be in a position to "give pride of place to political and legal rights," as rich liberals are.

By the early 1990s "liberal" had become a dirty word to many Americans. Many liberal social programs of the 1960s had bogged down or been shut down, and Rawls faced vigorous attacks from the right. In 1993 he published *Political Liberalism*, which asked, "How is it possible for there to exist over time a just and stable society of free and equal citizens, who remain profoundly divided by reasonable religious, philosophical, and moral doctrines?" Reviewing the book for the *New York Times*, John Gray cited its "utter political emptiness," which offered an "abstract schema" that glossed over "the political conflicts that have raged in recent years [which] have turned on issues of cultural identity—ethnic, nationalist, and religious."

Rawls loved sailing and mountain climbing. A "modest, tweedy man," he "turned down hundreds of honorary degrees," according to the *New York Times*. Unlike many celebrity intellectuals, Rawls kept a low profile and rarely gave interviews. However, true to his values, he signed petitions backing affirmative action, which he saw as an example of the government's responsibility to aid the historically downtrodden. In 1997 he joined in a published statement supporting the legalization of physician-assisted suicide. Rawls also defended the citizen's right to engage in peaceful civil disobedience against the government. Writing in the leftist journal *Dissent,* he criticized the 1945 atomic bombing of Hiroshima.

Rawls formally retired from Harvard in 1991 but continued to teach for four more years. He suffered several strokes beginning in 1995. In a White House ceremony in September 1999, Rawls received the National Humanities Medal from President William J. ("Bill") Clinton. He died of heart failure at his home at the age of eighty-two, and was buried in Cambridge, Massachusetts.

Although the moral philosopher Martha Nussbaum hailed Rawls as "the most distinguished philosopher of the twentieth century," his legacy is contested. By the time of his death, American liberalism had fallen on hard times. The White House and Congress were dominated by hardcore conservatives. The terrorist attacks of 11 September 2001 undermined confidence in Rawls's dream of a peacefully pluralistic world. Still, his many remaining admirers share his vision of a "realistic utopia," one in which (as he put it) the "great evils" of "unjust war, oppression, religious persecution, slavery and the rest" will "eventually disappear" thanks to the elimination of political injustice. Recalling the Holocaust and other historical horrors, Rawls warned against allowing these evils to override hope for the future of society. "Otherwise, the wrongful, evil, and demonic conduct of others destroys us too and seals their victory."

★

A famous and engaging conservative critique of Rawls is Robert Nozick, *Anarchy, State, and Utopia* (1974). An excellent chapter on Rawls's work is in Quentin Skinner, ed., *The Return of Grand Theory in the Human Sciences* (1985). A rich introduction to Rawls is Samuel Freeman, ed., *The Cambridge Companion to Rawls* (2003). An important early review of *Theory of Justice* is Stuart Hampshire, "A New Philosophy of the Just Society," *New York Review of Books* (24 Feb. 1972). See also Brian C. Anderson, "The Antipolitical Philosophy of John Rawls," *Public Interest* (spring 2003). Helpful left-wing assessments of Rawls include Rodney G. Peffer, "Rawlsian Theory, Contemporary Marxism, and the Difference Principle," in Mark Evans, ed., *The Edinburgh Companion to Contemporary Liberalism* (2001). An attempt to reinterpret Rawls's work in terms of the debate over international human rights is Patrick Hayden, *John Rawls: Towards a Just World Order* (2002). A rare published interview with Rawls is in *Commonweal* (25 Sept. 1998). An obituary is in the *New York Times* (26 Nov. 2002).

KEAY DAVIDSON

REBER, Grote (*b.* 22 December 1911 in Wheaton, Illinois; *d.* 20 December 2002 in Bothwell, Tasmania, Australia), electrical engineer who pioneered radio astronomy.

Born in suburban Chicago, the only child of Schuyler Reber and Harriet (Grote) Reber, a grade school teacher, Reber took an early interest in radio and was an enthusiastic radio ham by age fifteen. He attended the Armour Institute of Technology (now the Illinois Institute of Technology), graduating in 1933 with a B.S. in electrical engineering,

and went to work for a series of Chicago radio manufacturers. Reber could be described as the electronic Galileo, using radio receivers to examine and chart the invisible universe, where matter makes its presence known through bursts of radiation and cosmic waves. He not only developed the science of radio astronomy but also built the first backyard parabolic reflector, a forerunner of what would become an ubiquitous appliance the world over—the home satellite dish.

In 1933 Reber learned of a revelation by Karl Guthe Jansky of Bell Telephone Laboratories that would change his life. Jansky had been assigned to find the source of a low hiss that interfered with transatlantic radiophone reception, and traced part of the interference to what appeared to be a powerful radio source at the center of the Milky Way galaxy. Jansky did not have the opportunity to continue his work on stellar radio waves, but Reber recognized that Jansky's discovery was revolutionary and devoted his spare time to studying the phenomenon.

In the summer of 1937 Reber built the world's first radio telescope in the backyard of the suburban Wheaton, Illinois, home he shared with his mother. A junior high school teacher, she once taught Edwin Hubble, who grew up to become one of the most celebrated astronomers of the twentieth century. Reber's crude backyard contraption cost $1,300—half his yearly salary. The dish was thirty-one feet in diameter and was made of two-by-fours and sheet metal. It rotated on an axis driven by an old Model T engine. Because he had dismantled his mother's clothesline to make space for the dish, he had to let her hang laundry on it on Mondays. Long before Reber's contraption began locating mysterious signals from the heavens, it became a

Grote Reber, May 1986. AP/WIDE WORLD PHOTOS

tourist attraction, with motorists stopping on the street to view the curiosity. "I considered placing a juke box out front with a sign, 'Drop quarter in slot and find out what this is all about,'" Reber recalled in a 1987 interview.

It took two years of painstaking engineering to coax the symphonies of the heavens from the radio dish. Reber published his first paper on the subject, "Cosmic Static," in 1940 in the *Astrophysical Journal*, describing a universe awash in enigmatic radio sources. He confirmed Jansky's observation that the center of the Milky Way galaxy emitted radio waves, and found other sources in the constellations Cassiopeia and Cygnus. Meanwhile, he undertook a radio survey of the sky and, in 1943, based on his observations, produced the first radio map of the celestial sphere, in effect, an atlas of major radio wave sources. It showed that some radio sources matched the positions of stars and others did not. One of the mysterious hot spots identified by Reber appears to be a distant pair of colliding galaxies. Reber realized that the brightness of a star has nothing to do with the strength or location of the radio waves it emits. He concluded that some radio waves come from the gas clouds of neutral hydrogen between the stars, where ionized hydrogen atoms are present.

In 1944 Reber detected emissions from the Andromeda galaxy and from the Sun. In 1947 he moved to Virginia, donating his original telescope to his new employer, the National Bureau of Standards, where he worked for four years. In 1951 Reber began to support himself through scientific grants and moved to Hawaii to escape radio interference from human-made sources. There he developed a larger radio telescope to find new sources of radio waves. In 1954 he moved farther from the radio emissions associated with civilization to remote Tasmania in Australia, where interference was minimal. He joined the Commonwealth Scientific and Industrial Research Organization, and built yet a bigger version of his satellite dish to listen to distant galaxies. It consisted of eight-story poles in a circle linked by fifty-seven miles of wire. With it, Reber was able to map the universe above the Southern Hemisphere. From 1957 to 1961 Reber worked at the National Radio Astronomy Observatory in Green Bank, West Virginia, and then returned to Tasmania to continue his studies.

The science writer and populist Isaac Asimov wrote, "If Jansky gave birth to radio astronomy, Reber nursed it single-handed through its infancy." Reber's pioneering work has led scientists to some of the most dramatic discoveries in all of astronomy, including pulsars, which are collapsed stars that whirl at fantastic speeds, spewing torrents of radiation with each rotation. Jupiter was found to be the solar system's second-largest source of radio energy after the Sun, and remnants of the big bang have been detected, echoes of the birth pangs of the universe. Reber disagreed with Hubble's "big bang" theory, writing in a 1977 paper at the University of Tasmania: "Time is merely a sequence of events. There is no beginning nor ending. . . . I am attempting to instill thinking about the endless, boundless, stable universe."

Reber spent the rest of his days in Bothwell in remote Tasmania, where conditions were ideal for reception. He erected a solar-powered house and traveled about in contraptions of his own design: a battery-powered bicycle and three-wheeled cars that would travel no faster than thirty miles per hour in order to achieve maximum fuel economy. Known to neighbors and scientific colleagues as fiercely independent and cantankerous, he was socially awkward and never married. Many of the 400 residents of Bothwell regarded him as a hermit, a brilliant recluse who had little need for the society of others. He died from natural causes at age ninety; his remains were cremated and his ashes placed in his adopted hometown in Tasmania.

In 1962 Reber received the Bruce Medal of the Astronomical Society of the Pacific and was the American Astronomical Society Russell Lecturer. In 1975 he received the National Radio Astronomy Observatory's Jansky Lectureship and in 1983 the Royal Astronomical Society's Jackson-Gwilt Medal. His research was published in *Nature,* the *Astrophysical Journal,* the *Proceedings of the Institute of Radio Engineers,* and the *Journal of Geophysical Research.* Reber's original backyard dish antenna is on display at the National Radio Astronomy Observatory in West Virginia.

★

Reber's scientific papers and records, as well as his personal and scientific correspondence, are held by the National Radio Astronomy Observatory Library in Charlottesville, Virginia. For information on Reber's life, see Isaac Asimov, *Asimov's Biographical Encyclopedia of Science and Technology: The Lives and Achievements of 1510 Great Scientists from Ancient Times to the Present Chronologically Arranged* (1982). Obituaries are in the *New York Times* (25 Dec. 2002), the (Melbourne, Australia) *Age* (28 Dec. 2002), and *Sunday Tasmanian* (5 Jan. 2003).

MARK WASHBURN

REEL, A(dolf) Frank (*b.* 30 June 1907 in Milwaukee, Wisconsin; *d.* 3 April 2000 in Norfolk, Virginia), labor lawyer, media company executive, and author of two controversial books—one concerning the trial and execution of a Japanese general accused of war crimes during World War II and the other about network television.

Reel was one of two children, both boys, born to Herman Reel (a merchant) and Blanche (Ullman) Reel. He received his B.S. in 1928 and his LL.B. in 1931 from Harvard University, immediately entering private-practice law in Boston. He was partner in the Roewer and Reel law firm from 1934 until 1947 but put his civilian career on hold during World War II, when he became an army captain in the claims division in the Pacific theater. At the end of the war, as a captain in the Judge Advocate General Corps, he was appointed defense counsel for the Japanese general Tomoyuki Yamashita, conqueror of the Philippines and Malaya who was accused of war crimes.

Reel resumed civilian life in 1946, returning to Boston to practice labor law. One union he represented was the American Federation of Radio Artists. He left private practice in 1947 to work with the federation full-time, eventually becoming its executive secretary. On 29 March 1947 Reel married Virginia Wentworth, a nurse, and the couple settled in suburban Tarrytown, New York, where they reared four children. In 1954 Reel became executive vice president of Ziv Television Programs in New York City, leaving that company in 1968 to assume the presidency of Metromedia Producers Corporation, also in New York City. He returned to private practice in 1977 as an attorney with Hess, Segall, Guterman, Pelz, and Steiner in New York City, a position he held until his retirement.

Reel was always politically active. At Harvard, he formed the "Brown Derby" brigade to support Democratic New York governor Al Smith in his 1928 presidential bid. In Tarrytown, where he lived until close to his death, Reel succeeded in freeing the village from its Republican stronghold in 1958, when he and two others became the first Democrats elected to village government. He served as member of the village's board of trustees until 1962 and as its corporate counsel from 1977 to 1983. In 1962 he made an unsuccessful bid for Congress against the Republican Robert Barry. Undaunted, he contributed to any activity that would advance the Democratic cause—from writing letters to newspaper editors in support of local candidates to organizing one of the largest rallies Tarrytown ever experienced in support of Robert F. Kennedy's presidential bid. In fact, Reel would have become one of Kennedy's New York delegates at the Democratic National Convention had Kennedy not been assassinated in 1968.

Following his defense of the accused Japanese war criminal Yamashita, Reel wrote his controversial book *The Case of General Yamashita* (1949). In it, he called the trial "unjust, hypocritical, and vindictive," accusing General Douglas MacArthur of scripting the entire trial and the verdict, which found Yamashita guilty and resulted in his execution by hanging on 23 February 1946.

Yamashita undoubtedly was one of the twentieth-century's outstanding military commanders and led Japanese troops in their conquest of Malaya and the Philippines in 1941–1942. Later, during the battle of Manila in January and February 1945, Japanese troops raped and murdered more than 100,000 Filipinos and two hundred American prisoners of war. Yamashita, who was not present during the battle, surrendered to General MacArthur in September 1945 and was tried one month later in Manila before a U.S. military commission of five generals untrained in law.

Yamashita was not accused of authorizing, committing, condoning, or aiding in the atrocities but of failing to control troops under his command. Reel noted in his book that the atrocities were committed primarily by Japanese naval troops whose admiral ignored Yamashita's orders. He also pointed out that Japan's communication system was severely disrupted during the battle and, not being present, Yamashita had no way of controlling the troops.

In an article published in the *Journal News,* Herb Geller, vice president of the North Salem Historical Society, recalls a Democratic meeting he and his wife hosted in their apartment in 1962. At the meeting were Reel and—ironically—three other people who had been intricately involved in Yamashita's trial. One, the guest of honor at the meeting, was Congressman Samuel Stratton, who was seeking the Democratic nomination for governor of New York and who had been interpreter at the trial. Reel and Stratton had not seen each other since the trial. According to Geller, all four of his guests who had been involved with the trial agreed that Yamashita was innocent and that the guilty admiral went free.

Following his conviction, Yamashita was permitted an appeal to the U.S. Supreme Court, which denied his appeal 6–2. Two justices dissented—Justice Francis Murphy, U.S. governor-general of the Philippines in the 1930s, and Justice Wiley Rutledge, who, Geller noted, "vigorously dissented, claiming that Yamashita had not been given a fair trial and the charges did not warrant his conviction and execution." Reel commented in his book, "We do not hang people for crimes that others commit." Professional historians have tended to agree with Reel's judgment about the case.

In 1979 Reel wrote a second controversial book, this time about television, titled *The Networks: How They Stole the Show.* Following Reel's death of natural causes at age ninety-two at an assisted living home, Pat Pilla, a former Tarrytown mayor, commented of his colleague of prior years: "He was very intelligent, but also very practical. He was down to earth whenever you talked to him about any problems."

★

Herb Geller's article in the *Journal News* (29 Aug. 2002) recounts the meeting attended by Reel and Stratton in the Geller home in 1962. Obituaries in the *Los Angeles Times* (11 Apr. 2000) and the *Journal News* (12 Apr. 2000) provide overviews of Reel's life and activities.

MARIE L. THOMPSON

REUSS, Henry Schoellkopf (*b.* 22 February 1912 in Milwaukee, Wisconsin; *d.* 12 January 2002 in San Rafael, California), liberal Democratic U.S. congressman from Wisconsin (1955–1983) who helped to create the Peace Corps.

Reuss was born into a prominent German family and grew up in inner-city Milwaukee. His father, Gustav Reuss, a banker, maintained a lifelong commitment to progressive Republican Party politics, and his mother, Paula (Schoellkopf) Reuss, was a disciple of the social reformer Jane Addams. Reuss attended a Lutheran parochial school and the Milwaukee Country Day High School, from which he graduated in 1950. He earned a B.A. in history and government from Cornell University in 1933 and an LL.B. from Harvard University in 1936, where he was a member of the Harvard Law Review.

Reuss became a member of the Democratic Party and a dedicated public servant who gave most of his professional career to advancing a wide range of progressive causes. While in college and law school, he developed a life-long interest in history and government policy, especially foreign affairs. His intense interest in and dedication to honest government and progressive policy initiatives provided the foundations of his career.

Following law school graduation, he returned to Milwaukee and began work for Quarles, Spence and Quarles; he also served as assistant corporation counsel for Milwaukee County from 1939 to 1940. In late 1940 he moved to Washington, D.C., to serve as an assistant counsel for the Office of Price Administration (OPA), where he served under the economist John Kenneth Galbraith from 1941 to 1942. While in Washington, he met Margaret Magrath, an

economist for the OPA. They married on 24 October 1942 and had four children.

Reuss enlisted in the U.S. Army in 1943 as a private and was later commissioned as second lieutenant. During World War II he was first assigned to Supreme Headquarters of the Allied Expeditionary Force in London and then followed the advancing Allied armies to procure supplies. He later transferred to a combat division, earning the Bronze Star for action at the Rhine Crossing. After the end of hostilities, he worked in the office of price control for the military government occupation in Germany.

Reuss left the army in 1945 and became active in local Milwaukee politics and community development. He was a founding member of the American Veterans Committee and helped to launch the Milwaukee Urban Development Corporation. During this period he worked with other Democratic activists such as Gaylord Nelson, who became a Wisconsin state senator in 1949, and James E. Doyle, who became a federal judge in 1965, to rebuild the party. He ran unsuccessfully for mayor of Milwaukee in 1948 (and again in 1960). After his first unsuccessful bid as mayor, Reuss returned to Washington to join the legal staff of the European Cooperation Administration of the Marshall Plan. Eventually, he served as its deputy general counsel and was stationed in Paris until 1950.

Moving from Paris to Milwaukee and returning to private legal practice, Reuss intensified his participation in political affairs. In addition to serving as a special prosecutor for the commission charged with investigating corruption in Milwaukee city government in 1950, he continued to be a party activist. He ran unsuccessfully for attorney general of Wisconsin and as a candidate for nomination to the U.S. Senate in 1952. Throughout this period Reuss was an outspoken critic of Senator Joseph R. McCarthy, who in the 1950s led a government effort to root out communist influences in American society, and a leader in the "Joe Must Go" movement. In 1954 Reuss was finally successful in his bid for election to the U.S. House of Representatives and began a congressional career that lasted from 1955 to 1983. In the House, his primary concern was foreign policy. Early on, he was critical of the cold war foreign policy of President Dwight D. Eisenhower and Secretary of State John Forster Dulles, because of its focus on militarism and pacts with dubious allies. He especially disliked the "One-China" policy of the Eisenhower administration, which advocated treating Taiwan as the only legitimate Chinese government. Reuss argued for recognizing both Taiwan and the communist-led People's Republic of China, which controlled mainland China. He pushed for U.S. disengagement from Europe and was one of the most vociferous opponents of Eisenhower's approach to the new Cuban leader Fidel Castro, an approach designed to destabilize and if possible overthrow Castro's regime.

Henry S. Reuss, December 1964. AP/WIDE WORLD PHOTOS

In the late 1950s Reuss argued for a more humane foreign policy and began to advocate a youth volunteer service that would serve in developing foreign countries and help start such basic services as health care and education. His ideas were adopted by the presidential candidate John F. Kennedy and became a reality as the Peace Corps shortly after Kennedy became president. During the administrations of Kennedy and Lyndon B. Johnson, Reuss was a strong supporter of liberal domestic reform. He particularly advocated civil rights, the Medicare program, and the War on Poverty. He was deeply committed to an activist government working to improve the lives of all Americans. However, consistent with his philosophy, he was an early and consistent opponent of U.S. involvement in Vietnam. Gradually, he became a leader of a group of dissident congressional Democrats and was one of the first to endorse the 1968 "peace candidacy" of Eugene McCarthy, for whom he campaigned actively.

Reuss's congressional career was also marked by leadership on other issues. He was an early exponent of a more aggressive environmental policy through his chairmanship of the Subcommittee on Conservation and Natural Resources. He joined with several other young Democrats in 1970 to lead an assault on the seniority system. As result of this successful revolt, he became chair of the Committee on Banking, Finance, and Urban Affairs (1975–1981). In 1972–1973, while a ranking member of this committee, he led an investigation of the money-laundering activities of the Committee to Re-Elect President Richard M. Nixon, which opened the door for a fuller Watergate scandal investigation. The committee also did an extensive study of the operations of the Federal Reserve Board, resulting in a series of 1977 laws that reformed domestic and international monetary and banking policies. Reuss also chaired the Joint Economic Committee (1981–1983) and served on the boards of several environmental organizations. He also published several small works on the environment, foreign affairs, and economic issues.

After choosing not to run for re-election in 1982, Reuss returned to private law practice in Washington but stayed active in public affairs. He moved from Washington to Belvedere, California, in 1995. During the 1980s and 1990s he emphasized urban redevelopment, energy programs, and housing for the poor. This work continued until his death of congestive heart failure in a hospital at age eighty-seven. His remains were cremated, with some ashes buried at his family plot at Forest Home Cemetery in Milwaukee and the rest scattered at the family home in North Lake, Wisconsin.

During his long career in public service, Reuss championed the rights of ordinary Americans and became an influential voice on foreign affairs, banking reform, and the environment.

★

The Henry S. Reuss Papers (1959–1982) are largely housed at the Milwaukee Area Research Center at the University of Wisconsin, Milwaukee, and include films and audiotapes. He has not been the attention of much scholarly work. A slim autobiography, *When Government Was Good: Memories of a Life in Politics* (1999), is the best source of information about his life and work. Obituaries are in the *Milwaukee Journal Sentinel, New York Times,* and *Washington Post* (all 15 Jan. 2002), and the *Chicago Tribune* (16 Jan. 2002).

R. DAVID MYERS

RHODES, James Allen ("Jim") (*b.* 13 September 1909 in Coalton, Ohio; *d.* 4 March 2001 in Columbus, Ohio), longest-serving governor of Ohio, known for his involvement in the Ohio National Guard shooting of Vietnam War protesters at Kent State University in May 1970.

Born in a small Appalachian village in the southeastern Ohio county of Jackson, Rhodes grew up in a middle-class Methodist family of Welsh ancestry. The third of five children of James Rhodes, a coal miner, and Susan (Howe) Rhodes, a restaurateur, only Rhodes and two sisters survived to adulthood. Both parents had deep ties to the Republican Party, with Rhodes's father serving as a precinct committeeman. The young Rhodes attended local schools in Jasonville, Indiana, and enjoyed an ordinary boyhood until the age of nine, when his father died.

The emergency created by the 1918 death of the family breadwinner forced Rhodes to enter the working world. The family moved to Springfield, Ohio, where Rhodes carried newspapers, cut grass, delivered groceries, and took every other possible odd job to help make ends meet. The experience turned Rhodes into a lifelong entrepreneur and undoubtedly contributed to his later gubernatorial passion for job creation. Rhodes graduated high school in Springfield.

Tall and athletic, Rhodes won a basketball scholarship to Ohio State University (OSU) in Columbus in 1932. More skilled on the court than in the classroom, he wound up on academic probation after one quarter and dropped out. Rhodes stayed in the campus area to run a restaurant called Jim's Place, sell desk blotters, run an employment agency, and serve as a journal clerk of the Ohio House of Representatives. He also claimed to have acquired a roundabout legal education by monitoring law classes at OSU.

Rhodes harbored a boyhood ambition to become Ohio governor, and he began a steady climb to the top. After a door-to-door campaign in 1934, he won election as a Republican ward committeeman in the state capital of Columbus. In 1937 he beat four opponents to join the Colum-

James A. Rhodes, February 1975. BETTMANN/CORBIS

bus Board of Education. Elected city auditor in 1939, he was reelected in 1941.

Rhodes also found time in 1941 to marry his childhood sweetheart, Helen Rawlins. The couple had three children. A devoted family man, Rhodes rarely spent a night apart from his wife, who died in 1987.

Rhodes's political career took a considerable jump in 1943, when he won the Columbus election and became the youngest mayor of any large U.S. city. Columbus had the largest land area of any city in the state and, because Rhodes allowed suburbs to obtain waterlines only if they agreed to be annexed into the city, a strong fiscal base as well. Rhodes served three terms as mayor before making a failed bid for governor in 1950.

To reach the governor's chair, Rhodes needed to establish statewide name recognition. He accomplished this by becoming state auditor in 1952. In this position he bore responsibility for monitoring every aspect of state and local government. Rhodes won reelection as auditor in 1956 and 1960. He tried again for governor in 1954, but lost to the Democratic incumbent, Frank Lausche. Rhodes had better luck in the 1962 gubernatorial contest against the incumbent, Michael V. DiSalle. Finally capturing the statehouse, Rhodes became Ohio's sixty-first governor. He spent sixteen years as governor, from 1963 to 1971 and from 1975 to 1983.

Rhodes cast a long shadow across Ohio. As governor, he upgraded Ohio's highway system, built an airport for each county, developed a network of community and technical colleges, and improved the state park system. He tirelessly sought industry for the state and persuaded such interna-

tional firms as Honda to open plants within Ohio. Although laudable, these achievements were not enough to make Rhodes into a nationally known figure.

In 1970 President Richard M. Nixon's escalation of the Vietnam War into neighboring Cambodia set off protests nationwide. At Kent State University, students held a mock funeral for the U.S. Constitution and burned a Reserve Officer Training Corps building. The mayor of Kent declared a state of emergency and requested assistance from the governor. Rhodes, running for the U.S. Senate, held a press conference, during which he called the demonstrators "the worst type of people we harbor in America." He sent the Ohio National Guard to restore order. Once on campus, the guardsmen panicked and fired into a crowd on 4 May 1970. Four students died and nine were injured. Kent State immediately closed for the remainder of the school year, while demonstrations in response to the shooting forced other universities to suspend classes.

Rhodes never apologized for Kent State. He saw the event as an accident and regarded the day as the saddest day of his career. Rhodes lost the Senate election. In 1979 the state of Ohio settled a civil suit, with the defendant Rhodes signing a statement that the incident was a tragedy that should never have occurred. Monetary damages were paid to the families of the victims.

By 1974 Rhodes's business investments had made him a millionaire. A notably vigorous man who avidly golfed and helped found the National Caddie Association, he left politics after 1983 but could never remain quiet. In 1987 he patented a residential air-purification system and unsuccessfully tried to market it. Rhodes succumbed to heart disease at Ohio State University Medical Center and, following a Lutheran funeral, was buried at Greenlawn Cemetery in Columbus.

Although one of the most significant Ohio governors of the twentieth century, Rhodes would probably have remained an obscure Midwestern leader to the majority of Americans had the killings at Kent State not catapulted him into national prominence. The notoriety gained that day overshadows the enormous contributions that he made to Ohio in education, recreation, transportation, and industrial development.

★

There is no central collection of Rhodes's papers. Some materials relating to his gubernatorial administrations, including a 1994 television interview, are housed at the Ohio Historical Society. Papers about the Kent State shooting, including court documents, are part of the May 4 Collection at Kent State University. The best biography of Rhodes is in Alexander P. Lamis, ed., *Ohio Politics* (1994). Edward J. Mowery and James Allen Rhodes, "Taxpayer's Governor" (1963), is campaign literature. R. Dean Jauchius and Thomas H. Dudgeon, "Jim Rhodes's Big Win!: The Making of an Upset" (1978), is a report of the 1974 gubernatorial contest written by two strategists for the Rhodes campaign. Stanley J. Aronoff and Vernal G. Riffe, Jr., "James A. Rhodes at Eighty" (1989), is a tribute produced by two longtime friends. Obituaries are in the *Columbus Dispatch* (5 Mar. 2001) and *New York Times* (6 Mar. 2001).

CARYN E. NEUMANN

RICHARDS, Faith Buchner ("Bucky") (*b.* 25 May 1921 in Chicago, Illinois; *d.* 20 September 2002 in Albuquerque, New Mexico), one of the first members of the Women Airforce Service Pilots (WASP).

Richards's was the only child of Elkanah Buchner, a dentist, and Pearl (Woodford) Buchner, a college English teacher. Her interest in flying was piqued at the age of eight, when her father and grandfather took her to an air show and she rode in a barnstormer. Later, when Richards was about twelve years old, she observed a female pilot in an air-show race; this experience convinced her that flying was to be her lifelong passion. She graduated from Kelvyn Park High School in Chicago in 1939.

Richards became involved in the Civilian Pilot Training program in 1941 while still a student at Morningside College in Sioux City, Iowa. A year later she earned her private pilot license and flew with the Civil Air Patrol in Sioux City—a member of the last class permitted to join by the government. Richards heard of the record-setting pilot Jacqueline Cochran's program for women pilots from a U.S. Marine recruiter after the United States entered World War II. She applied and was accepted into WASP class 43-W-4. In 1943 Richards received her college diploma on the tarmac at the airfield. Her first assignment was ferrying aircraft from Wilmington, Delaware; other job duties included test-hopping aircraft (flying planes after they have been damaged to check that they are airworthy) and shuttling personnel. Although women were allowed to fly combat airplanes from their factories to army air bases and elsewhere in the United States, they were forbidden to do so overseas and in combat zones.

In December 1943 Richards was stationed with the Second Ferrying Command in Greenwood, Mississippi, after being trained in Sweetwater, Texas. She remained there for the next twenty-two months and became an engineering test pilot. She was one of only two women at the base and earned the nickname "Bucky." Richards briefly returned to Sweetwater to receive her instrument certification before being stationed in Romulus, Michigan, and being transferred back to the Greenwood base. She remained at Greenwood until the deactivation of the WASP on 20 December 1944. As a member of the WASP, Richards flew sixteen different aircraft, including training planes such as the BT-13 and the AT-6, as well as B-24 and B-26 bombers. She married John Richards on 11 May 1951. They had no children and divorced in 1971.

On 13 June 1964 Richards earned her helicopter rating in a Brantley B-2 in Oklahoma City, Oklahoma. This was an extremely difficult task because the flying techniques differed from those she had learned as an airplane pilot. As the seventy-fourth woman to receive a helicopter rating, she became number seventy-four of the Whirly-Girls, an organization of female helicopter pilots. She also became a LINK (flight simulator) instructor as well as a map plotter in meteorology and a crew scheduler with United Airlines in Chicago. After moving to the Dallas–Fort Worth area of Texas in 1950, she joined Braniff Airlines and later, American Airlines, before her retirement in 1986.

Legislation to continue to allow the WASP in the military had failed on numerous occasions in the 1940s and thereafter. However, Richards helped pass a law in 1977 that granted members of the WASP military veteran status with full benefits. Around this time, Richards adopted a daughter, Nancy.

In 1995 Richards earned a glider rating in Boulder, Colorado, at the age of seventy-four—her love of flying intact after all those years. Four years later she was inducted into the Aviation International Forest of Friendship in Atchison, Kansas, under the auspices of The Ninety-Nines, an international organization of female pilots. In 2001 Richards represented the women of World War II in her own float in a Fourth of July parade in Ewing Township, New Jersey. On 6 December 2001 the New Jersey Advisory Committee for Women Veterans presented her with the "Minute Woman" Award.

Richards was a past president of the WASP and served on the board as education chairwoman. She was also a former board member of the Women Military Aviators and a member of the Governor's Advisory Board for Women Veterans for the State of New Jersey, as well as a member of the local chapter of The Ninety-Nines. Richards has also been featured in many exhibits throughout the United States and Europe. Her uniform and wings are on display at the Smithsonian Air and Space Museum in Washington, D.C., and she is included in the Women's Memorial at Arlington National Cemetery in Virginia. During 1998 and 2000 two museum exhibits in Frankfurt, Germany, featured Richards, with the second exhibit dedicated as a tribute to her. In addition, in 2002 a blimp that belonged to a film-production company in Germany was named "Bucky."

This remarkable woman spent her later years as a volunteer at the local Veteran's Hospital, where she counseled other female veterans. She could always be found giving seminars about aviation and flying. She even owned a travel agency and took to the skies in a balloon. She also dedicated herself to children and to answering questions by email on "WASP on the WEB"—a website begun as a tribute to the women of the WASP during World War II.

Richards died at a nursing home at the age of eighty-one. Although most of her ashes are in the columbarium at St. Michael's and All Angels Episcopal Church in Albuquerque, some, at her own request, were scattered from an aircraft. Richards will always be remembered as a pioneer whose search led her to the heavens.

★

The Woman's Collection of the Blagg-Huey Library at Texas Woman's University in Denton, Texas, contains a folder with biographical material on Richards, as well as an oral history and interview by Dora Strother. For further information about Richards, see Richard Benke, "World War II 'WASP' Female Bomber Pilot Dies at 81," *The Associated Press State & Local Wire* (24 Sept. 2002). Obituaries are in the *Newark Star Ledger* (25 Sept. 2002) and *Albuquerque Journal* (29 Sept. 2002).

ADRIANA C. TOMASINO

RIDDER, Bernard Herman, Jr. ("Bernie") (*b.* 8 December 1916 in New York City; *d.* 10 October 2002 in San Mateo, California), newspaper executive who built Ridder Publications into a major media organization and initiated a merger with Knight Newspapers to form Knight Ridder, the nation's second largest newspaper group.

Ridder was one of four children born to the newspaper magnate Bernard Herman Ridder, Sr., and his second wife,

Nell Hickey, a homemaker. The family lived on Park Avenue near Eighty-fifth Street in Manhattan, and Ridder attended private school at Saint Bernard's, where he studied Latin but rebelled at studying German, which some other members of the family embraced. Ridder's grandfather, Herman Ridder, had established the family newspaper business as publisher of *Die Staats-Zeitung,* a German-language newspaper in New York City. Ridder showed his athletic prowess early, becoming captain of the baseball team and a member of the school's soccer team. He was sent to Canterbury boarding school in New Milford, Connecticut, when he was thirteen. From then on he spent much of his time away from home at boarding and prep schools until he entered Princeton University, where he majored in history.

Upon completing his B.A. at Princeton in 1938, Ridder began his newspaper career at the *New York Journal of Commerce,* where he was paid $15 a week for working in the dispatch room handling plates and mats for the advertising department. During this time he also improved his squash game, and he won both the New York State Squash Rackets championship and the Metropolitan Squash Rackets championship. Tall and lanky—at six feet, four and a half inches tall and 165 pounds—Ridder entered the national squash championship and made it to the semifinals, where he was beaten by a man who had been his squash tutor.

Ridder's father urged him to go to the *Aberdeen American News* in South Dakota to "work out his business career." That was Ridder's intention when he arrived in Saint Paul, Minnesota, on 9 February 1939. But Jane Delano, Ridder's girlfriend, encouraged him to postpone his career in Aberdeen so that he could marry her in Chicago. Ridder had met and fallen in love with Delano, a relative of President Franklin D. Roosevelt, eight months earlier at a golf tournament. They married on 24 February 1939 in Chicago and had five children together; Ridder's two sons also became newspaper executives.

Ridder worked in the advertising department of the *Aberdeen American News,* where he also learned about newspaper circulation. He left Aberdeen for Duluth, Minnesota, in August, where he was assigned to the advertising department. Within two years he was named advertising director. An avid golfer, Ridder was playing in a golf tournament in Duluth when his wife delivered their first child. He lost the tournament on the thirty-fourth hole and officials drove him directly to the Duluth hospital. Soon after the Japanese attack on Pearl Harbor in 1941, Ridder joined the U.S. Navy. He was a gunnery officer aboard the aircraft carrier USS *Bunker Hill* in the Pacific and rose to the rank of lieutenant, earning nine battle stars. After the war he returned to Duluth as advertising director of the *Duluth Herald* and the *Duluth News Tribune.* In 1952 he was

Bernard H. Ridder, Jr., March 1939. AP/WIDE WORLD PHOTOS

named publisher of the two papers, which eventually merged in 1982. In 1958 he moved to Saint Paul to become publisher of the *St. Paul Dispatch* and the *St. Paul Pioneer Press,* which merged in 1985. Ridder held the publisher positions in both Minnesota cities until 1973.

Ridder was instrumental in the expansion of Ridder Publications when the company moved westward in 1952, purchasing newspapers in California, Kansas, and Colorado. Under his leadership the company grew from ten newspaper and radio and television facilities to twenty-two when, as president and chief executive officer of Ridder Publications, Inc., he took the company public in 1969. He was a leading negotiator for Ridder Publications when it merged with Knight Newspapers in 1974. His managerial and negotiating skills were well demonstrated in both cases. Some members of the Ridder family were hesitant to take the firm public, and there was major opposition by a brother and a cousin to the merger with Knight. Ridder served on the Knight Ridder board until 1994 and was chairman from 1979 to 1982.

A director of the Associated Press from 1954 to 1964, he also was president of the Inland Daily Press Association in 1954. Ridder was active in civic affairs in Duluth and Saint Paul, where he formed a group to finance a new downtown

Hilton Hotel. Ridder's interest in sports took the company into a five-way partnership that brought the Minnesota Vikings professional football team into the state for an investment of $600,000. He was chairman of the team's board from 1961 to 1967. As part of his golfing career, he served on the United States Golf Association executive committee from 1958 to 1964 and on the Tournament Policy Committee of the Professional Golf Association. Ridder died of complications from a stroke at his home in San Mateo, California, and was cremated.

Ridder's success as a publisher came because he selected good people and then let them do their jobs. He took a hands-off approach toward news coverage and editorial policies, but he was always well informed about his newspapers' operations and their bottom line performance.

★

Information about Ridder is available in William Swanson, "The Paper Lions," *Corporate Report* 5, no. 6 (June 1974): 17. Obituaries are in the *Saint Paul Pioneer Press* (11 Oct. 2002) and the *New York Times* and *Washington Post* (both 12 Oct. 2002).

JOHN R. FINNEGAN, SR.

RIESMAN, David, Jr. (*b.* 22 September 1909 in Philadelphia, Pennsylvania; *d.* 10 May 2002 in Binghamton, New York), sociologist whose landmark studies of American culture and higher education strongly influenced subsequent work in those fields.

Riesman was the eldest of three children born to David Riesman and Eleanor (Fleisher) Riesman. His father was a hardworking German-Jewish immigrant who had risen to become one of the most eminent physicians in Philadelphia, a professor of clinical medicine at the University of Pennsylvania, and a medical historian. His mother, a homemaker, was a graduate of Bryn Mawr College and had a strong and informed interest in modernist literature and art. The Riesmans were members of Philadelphia's upper middle class, residing in the fashionable Rittenhouse Square neighborhood.

Riesman received his early education at the William Penn Charter School and, after a preparatory year at the Evans School in Arizona, attended Harvard College in Cambridge, Massachusetts, from which he graduated in 1931 with a B.S. in biochemical sciences. Rather than follow in his formidable father's path, Riesman enrolled at Harvard Law School, from which he graduated in 1934. Although he excelled in his legal studies and attracted the patronage of the future Supreme Court justice Felix Frankfurter, Riesman was always restless in the law, drawn instead to the larger world of ideas.

431

More than a decade would pass, however, before Riesman felt free to devote himself to those intellectual pursuits. After a year as a research fellow at Harvard Law School, a subsequent year as a clerk to the Supreme Court justice Louis D. Brandeis, and then a year in private legal practice in Boston, Riesman took a position in New York as a professor of law at the University of Buffalo Law School, which he held from 1937 until 1941. With the U.S. entry into World War II, Riesman made another series of changes, first going to work for the district attorney's office in New York, then joining the executive staff of the Sperry Gyroscope Company.

None of these varied experiences was wasted on the ever-observant Riesman, who acquired a vast knowledge of American white-collar culture and who became widely known for his articles in law reviews and in political science journals. But it was not until the prominent sociologist Edward Shils invited Riesman to join the social science faculty of the University of Chicago that he finally found a venue adequate to the exercise of his prodigious energies. Riesman started out in 1946 as a lowly visiting assistant professor, but by the time he left in 1958 he was moving back to Harvard as the Henry Ford II Professor of Social Sciences and as one of the most famous sociologists in the world.

What happened between those two dates was the 1950 publication of Riesman's masterwork, *The Lonely Crowd: A Study of the Changing American Character,* which became one of the most widely read and most influential social science works in the twentieth century. Coauthored with Nathan Glazer and Reuel Denney, *The Lonely Crowd* was not only an examination of the changing structures and folkways of U.S. society at the mid-twentieth century, but also a searching exploration of the changes taking place within the souls of individual Americans. The book's very title seemed to sound a resonant chord in the public mind, capturing in a single haunting phrase many of the most troubling features of the organized, corporatized, bureaucratized, suburbanized, and homogenized society that the United States was becoming.

The dominant social character of Americans, Riesman argued, had changed dramatically since the nineteenth century, in response to declining fertility rates and the emergence of an economy based on service and consumption. The change, as Riesman expressed it, was from inner-directed personality types—self-reliant and purposeful souls who navigated through life relying upon the firm principles implanted in them by parents—to other-directed types, who were brought up to rely upon the cues of others, particularly peer groups, coworkers, and mass media, in addition to parents, to find their way in the world.

Inner direction had been appropriate for the era of imperial and industrial-capitalist expansion, an era that turned productive energies to the task of conquering the

David Riesman. THE LIBRARY OF CONGRESS

"hardness" of the material world. But with the transformation from an economy oriented toward production and extraction to one oriented toward service and consumption, and dominated by large bureaucratic business corporations and governments, inner direction was outmoded. A new kind of social character was required for an emerging new social order.

Riesman found the consequences of this change in myriad aspects of American life, from the content of children's stories and the culture of suburban schools to the golf-course behavior of businessmen and the pathologies of American political discourse. In so doing he produced one of the classic broad-gauge examinations of the American character.

By the time Riesman returned to Harvard in 1958, he had decided to narrow his scholarly interests to the study of higher education, paying particular attention to educational strategies and reform, student development and welfare, and the relationship between the university and the larger society. Such concerns were at the center of his *Constraint and Variety in American Education* (1956), and of such later works as *The Academic Revolution* (1968) and *Academic Values and Mass Education* (1970).

Riesman also was much revered at Harvard for his popular and long-running undergraduate course, Social Sciences 136, "Character and Social Structure in America," which reflected his multidisciplinary view of sociology, combining it with excursions into history, psychology, anthropology, economics, political science, and popular culture. He retired from teaching in 1980 but remained actively involved in university affairs, including service on undergraduate prize committees, until his health began to fail in the late 1990s.

No account of Riesman's life would be complete without mention of his many political involvements, ranging from the resettlement of German refugee lawyers during the war years to his opposition to nuclear weapons and to the Vietnam War. Nor can one omit mention of his long and affectionate marriage to Evelyn (Thompson) Riesman, known to their friends as Evie, whom he married on 15 July 1936. Their union produced four children and lasted until her death in 1998. A Bryn Mawr graduate and a talented writer and musician, Evelyn was a devoted partner in her husband's many activities and coauthored their *Conversations in Japan* (1967).

★

Several of Riesman's essays offer autobiographical insights, most notably "A Personal Memoir: My Political Journey," in Lewis Coser, ed., *The Idea of Social Structure: Papers in Honor of Robert K. Merton* (1975), and "Two Generations," *Daedalus* 93 (spring 1964). A haunting and insightful appreciation of Riesman's career by his former colleague Orlando Patterson is in the *New York Times* (19 May 2002). Obituaries are in the *New York Times* (11 May 2002) and *Boston Globe* (12 May 2002).

WILFRED M. MCCLAY

RIPLEY, S(idney) Dillon, II   (*b.* 20 September 1913 in New York City; *d.* 12 March 2001 in Washington, D.C.), ornithologist, biologist, ecologist, writer, and secretary of the Smithsonian Institution from 1964 to 1984.

Ripley was born to Louis Arthur Ripley, a stockbroker, and Constance Baillie (Rose) Ripley, a homemaker. His great-grandfather, Sidney Dillon, was a founder of the Union Pacific Railroad. The Ripleys were wealthy and were able to provide their son with trips overseas, a private education, and the means to indulge his growing fascination with wildlife and nature. At age ten Ripley demonstrated his interest in waterfowl by building a duck pond on a family estate. During this time his family took Ripley to Paris, where he visited the Louvre and the Tuileries Gardens. When Ripley was thirteen his family took him and his sister to India, a trip that included a walking tour of western

Tibet. Ripley's lifelong interest and dedication to the Indian subcontinent resulted from this trip.

Ripley was educated at the prestigious Saint Paul's School in Concord, Massachusetts, where he maintained his interest in observing, collecting, and breeding birds. He graduated from Saint Paul's in 1932 and entered Yale University, where he studied history and received a B.A. in 1936. He then joined an eighteen-month Academy of Natural Sciences expedition to New Guinea, where he was introduced to tropical ornithology. After the expedition was completed, Ripley began working in the Department of Ornithology at the American Museum of Natural History in New York City in 1939. Shortly afterwards, Ripley accepted a fellowship at Harvard University, where he received his Ph.D. in ornithology in 1943. Ripley next joined the Office of Strategic Services (OSS), where he coordinated intelligence activities in Burma, India, and Thailand. While working for the OSS, he met Mary Moncrieffe Livingston, a photographer, orchidologist, and amateur entomologist. They married on 18 August 1949 and had three daughters. Throughout their marriage, she assisted him with his work and traveled with him on ornithological expeditions. She died in 1996.

After the war ended, Ripley taught biology at Yale and quickly established himself as an expert in ornithology and ecology. In 1946 Ripley became the first curator of ornithology at Yale's Peabody Museum of Natural History. During his tenure at the Peabody, the ornithology program earned an international reputation for its comprehensive collection. Ripley's scholarly work led to his becoming a Fulbright Fellow in 1950 and a Guggenheim Fellow in 1954. He was appointed director of the Peabody Museum in 1959. In 1964 Ripley was invited to become the eighth secretary (chief executive officer) of the Smithsonian Institution.

The attractions Ripley introduced to the Smithsonian, along with his managerial policies, assisted in creating a museum that was engaging, enjoyable, and hospitable to the public. Drawing upon his childhood experiences at the Louvre and the Tuileries Gardens in Paris, Ripley set up a carousel on the Washington, D.C., Mall. In addition, he encouraged youngsters to play on a life-size fiberglass triceratops, nicknamed Uncle Beazley, which was located in front of the Natural History Museum. These attractions created a playful and whimsical environment at the Smithsonian. Ripley also instituted programs such as the American Folklife Festival, which showcased regional and international dancing, singing, and arts and crafts, and the Smithsonian Associates, in which specialized classes, lectures, and tours were offered to the public. In 1970 he founded the *Smithsonian Magazine,* which quickly reached millions of subscribers. Ripley's philosophy that the American people should feel that the Smithsonian belonged to them was enhanced by his refusal to shut down the buildings when the Poor People's Campaign (1968) and anti–Vietnam War protests of the 1960s and early 1970s were held in Washington, D.C.

During his twenty years as the Smithsonian secretary, Ripley oversaw an impressive expansion of the Smithsonian institution that included the foundation of the National Portrait Gallery (1962), the Hirshhorn Museum and Sculpture Garden (1966), the Anacostia Museum (1967), and the National Air and Space Museum (1976). In 1976 the institution acquired the National Museum of African Art (1979). In addition, Ripley renovated many of the museums, including the Renwick Gallery and the Smithsonian American Art Museum. In 1973 the Smithsonian assisted Harvard in the creation of the Center for Astrophysics in Cambridge, Massachusetts. The Smithsonian also established ecological research centers in Florida, Maryland, and Panama. He retired in 1984 but continued to promote environmental protection and wildlife conservation through organizations such as the Charles Darwin Foundation, of which he was a founding member.

Ripley enjoyed an influential reputation not only for his contributions to the Smithsonian but also for his research in ecology and ornithology. He was a prolific writer of articles and books. His first book, *Trail of the Money Bird: 30,000 Miles of Adventure with a Naturalist* (1942), was published shortly before he graduated from Harvard. He wrote numerous books on ornithology with a specific focus on Asia. These include *Search for the Spiny Babbler: An Adventure in Nepal* (1952) and *The Land and Wildlife of Tropical Asia* (1964). Ripley worked with Salim Ali of the Bombay Natural History Society to produce influential scholarship on the ornithology of the Indian region. Their definitive work was the ten-volume *A Synopsis of the Birds of India and Pakistan, Together with Those of Nepal, Sikkim, Bhutan and Ceylon* (1961).

While Ripley was secretary, the number of yearly visitors to the Smithsonian grew to more than thirty million. Although critics of Ripley believed that he demonstrated a populist approach to museum management, Ripley maintained that the public would benefit from museums as living and interactive repositories of education in the arts, the sciences, and history. In recognition of his work, Ripley was the recipient of numerous awards and honorary degrees. He was elected into the National Academy of Sciences in 1968, and in 1985 he received the nation's highest civilian honor, the Presidential Medal of Freedom.

★

There is no biography of Ripley. Obituaries are in the *New York Times* (13 Mar. 2001) and *Washington Post* (13 Mar. 2001).

JULIA CHENOT GOODFOX

RITTS, Herbert, Jr. ("Herb") (*b.* 13 August 1952 in Los Angeles, California; *d.* 26 December 2002 in Los Angeles, California), prominent photographer known for portraits of celebrities, supermodels, athletes, and political and spiritual leaders.

Ritts was born to Herbert Ritts and Shirley Ritts, who owned a successful furniture business. Ritts Furniture provided the family a home in the tony Brentwood section of Los Angeles and vacation houses in Malibu and on Catalina Island. Although Ritts would eventually go on to study economics in college, he showed an interest in photography as a child, snapping pictures of his friends and family, including three siblings, with a single-lens reflex Miranda camera.

After finishing high school and studying economics at Bard College in New York City, Ritts announced his homosexuality to his family, who were supportive. When he returned to California after graduating with a B.S. in 1975, he took a position as a sales representative for the family's furniture business.

His father's company serviced the film industry, which afforded Ritts access to countless movie sets. But tables and chairs did not fuel his passions, so he enrolled in photography classes and learned the craft by snapping pictures of his friends, many of whom were actors. His first published

Herb Ritts, December 1999. BEMBARON JEREMY/CORBIS SYGMA

photo, of nine-year-old Ricky Schroder and Jon Voigt on the set of the 1979 film *The Champ,* appeared in *Newsweek.*

Ritts's real break, however, came one afternoon in 1979 as he drove around in the desert with the then-unknown actor Richard Gere and Gere's girlfriend. While waiting for a flat tire to be changed, Ritts snapped a picture of a brooding, sweat-beaded Gere, who was clad in a white sleeveless top and well-worn jeans. The picture—of Gere leaning against a jacked-up Buick with arms stretched up, hands behind his head, and a cigarette dangling from his lips—would eventually be published in major magazines and would earn Ritts respect as a celebrity portraitist. Before long Ritts was shooting covers for *Vanity Fair, Vogue, Interview, Harper's Bazaar,* and *Elle.*

His subjects were no less impressive in terms of their star power. Among his most notable images was a 1987 shot of the pop star Madonna in Japan, lying in bed wearing Mickey Mouse ears and a cheeky grin. Other celebrated works include a 1991 portrait of the actress Elizabeth Taylor that drew a parallel between the star's glimmering eyes and a chunky, sparkling diamond; a 1986 shot of the actor Jack Nicholson with his notorious grin accentuated by a magnifying glass; and a *Vanity Fair* cover shot of the supermodel Cindy Crawford giving the singer k. d. lang, who was dressed in a man's suit, a mock shave.

Ritts did not limit himself to magazine work. His images were prominent on album covers and in numerous advertising campaigns, including those for the fashion designers Gianni Versace and Calvin Klein. His work on a GAP clothing ad campaign earned him the 1991 Infinity Award for Applied Photography from the International Center of Photography in New York City.

The photographer also dabbled in video directing for top pop acts. His video credits include Madonna's "Cherish," Britney Spears's "Don't Let Me Be the Last to Know," and 'NSYNC's "Gone." Two sultry videos, Janet Jackson's "Love Will Never Do (Without You)" and Chris Isaak's "Wicked Game," earned him MTV awards in 1991. Both videos were awash in Ritts's signature style—shot mostly in black and white, overflowing with fit human specimens, and heavy on sand and sexiness.

Ritts also published numerous coffee-table books of his photographs, including *Men/Women* (1989), in which he explores the simple beauty of the male and female forms; *Duo: Herb Ritts Photographs Bob Paris and Rod Jackson* (1991), which chronicles the life of a gay couple; and *Notorious* (1992), a collection of celebrity shots, many of which had never been published before. For his book *Africa* (1994), Ritts took a slight detour from his usual work of celebrity snaps and pop videos. Although the tome highlights a subject far removed from the world of celebrities and pop culture—the Masai people—the stylized, geometric, sparse images nevertheless bear Ritts's signature.

In the fall of 1996 Ritts was honored with his first ever retrospective at a major museum, the Museum of Fine Arts in Boston. The show, titled *Herb Ritts: Work,* featured more than 200 images, from his interpretations of the musicians Dizzy Gillespie and Courtney Love to his shots of African landscapes and fashion spreads.

In December 2002 Ritts completed one of his final photo shoots, capturing the actor Ben Affleck for an upcoming *Vanity Fair* cover. Two weeks later Ritts died at the University of California, Los Angeles, Medical Center from acquired immunodeficiency syndrome (AIDS)–related pneumonia. He was fifty years old. Ritts was survived by his partner of seven years, Erik Hyman.

Ritts's work teetered between commercial and high art and was embraced by both everyday people and art scholars. His photographs celebrated the human body and celebrity, often with a smidge of humor. When away from the camera, he was dedicated to AIDS and antidrug charities. Before dying, he established the Herb Ritts, Jr., Foundation, which provides grants to young photographers and arts organizations.

★

Writings about Ritts's work and an audio interview with the artist are at the Museum of Fine Arts, Boston, which held a retrospective, *Herb Ritts: Work,* from 22 Oct. 1996 through 23 Feb. 1997. Obituaries are in the *Los Angeles Times* and *New York Times* (both 27 Dec. 2002).

JEN DARR

RIVERO, Horacio, Jr. ("Rivets") (*b.* 16 May 1910 in Ponce, Puerto Rico; *d.* 24 September 2000 in Coronado, California), first Hispanic four-star admiral in the U.S. Navy, who served as vice chief of naval operations as well as commander of allied forces in southern Europe. Rivero also was the first American of Spanish descent to serve as U.S. ambassador to Spain.

The son of Horacio Rivero, Sr., a merchant, and Margarita (DeLucca) Rivero, Rivero graduated from Central High School in San Juan, Puerto Rico, and entered the U.S. Naval Academy in Annapolis, Maryland, in June 1927. He was about five feet, four inches tall and weighed 112 pounds. On one occasion, an instructor had difficulty reading Rivero's name on his oversized jumpsuit. The officer asked gruffly, "What's your name, Mister? Rivets?" Thus he acquired the nickname "Rivets." He graduated from Annapolis in 1931 with distinction, ranking third in his class of 441.

From 1933 to 1938 Rivero served aboard five ships as either a communications officer or an assistant gunnery officer. In 1938 he studied electrical engineering at the Naval Postgraduate School at Annapolis, Maryland, and

Horacio Rivero. U.S. Department of Defense

earned an M.S. in electrical engineering from the Massachusetts Institute of Technology in 1940. From June 1940 to January 1942 he served brief tours with the Naval Gun Factory and the Bureau of Ordnance in Washington, D.C., and at the Naval Proving Ground in Dahlgren, Virginia. Rivero married Hazel Hooper in 1941; they had one daughter.

In January 1942, shortly after the United States entered World War II, Rivero assisted in fitting out the USS *San Juan,* a light cruiser on which he served as assistant gunnery officer after its commissioning. He also served as gunnery officer on the *San Juan* during 1943 and 1944, participating in U.S. Marine Corps invasions at Guadalcanal and the Marshall Islands; he received the Bronze Star Medal with Combat "V" for directing naval gunfire in support of the landings. In late 1944 he returned to the United States to assist in fitting out the cruiser USS *Pittsburgh,* which saw combat at Iwo Jima and Okinawa. On 5 June 1945 a severe typhoon ripped the bow from the ship, but quick action by Rivero helped keep the vessel afloat without any loss of life. He was awarded the Legion of Merit for his role in saving the ship.

Rivero returned to Washington in August 1945 to work on the navy's incipient nuclear weapons program and participated in atomic weapons tests in the South Pacific in

1948. Also in 1948 he received his first sea command as skipper of the destroyer USS *William C. Lawe.* During the Korean War, he served as commanding officer of the USS *Noble,* an amphibious transport. He completed the course at the National War College in 1953 and for the next two years served on the staff of the commander in chief, Pacific Fleet. In October 1955 he received a promotion to rear admiral and was named deputy chief of the Armed Forces Weapons Project. In 1957 he became commander of a destroyer flotilla and took charge of long-range objectives in the Office of the Chief of Naval Operations.

In December 1960 Rivero became the deputy chief of staff for plans and operations to the commander in chief, Atlantic, with additional duty on the joint staff, commander in chief, Atlantic, and the staff of the commander in chief, western Atlantic area. He was promoted to vice admiral in 1962 and on 15 October of that year assumed command of the amphibious force, Atlantic Fleet. A week later President John F. Kennedy declared a blockade of Cuba after the discovery of Soviet missiles on the island nation, and Rivero participated in the enforcement of this blockade.

In 1963 Rivero returned to the Office of the Chief of Naval Operations, and on 31 July 1964 he became the first Puerto Rican and first Hispanic to reach the rank of four-star admiral. (Naval historians point to Admiral David G. Farragut, whose father was from Spain, as the first Hispanic admiral in the U.S. Navy. When Farragut was promoted to admiral in 1866, however, the rank of four-star admiral did not exist.)

Rivero served from 1964 through 1968 as the vice chief of naval operations, the second-highest post in the U.S. Navy. The final position he held in his forty-five-year naval career was as commander in chief of the allied forces in southern Europe for the North Atlantic Treaty Organization. While he was in this position, he paid a courtesy call on General Francisco Franco, knowing that the Spanish dictator was often dismissive. Surprisingly, Franco talked with Rivero, who was fluent in Spanish, for forty-five minutes.

After his retirement from the navy in 1972, Rivero received an appointment from President Richard M. Nixon to serve as U.S. ambassador to Spain. He held this position until 1974. Rivero spent the remainder of his life in Coronado, a popular naval retirement community in San Diego. During this time he served for two years as president of the World Affairs Council and was Honorary Chairman of the American Veterans' Committee for Puerto Rico Self-Determination, an organization committed to a permanent political status for the commonwealth. He continued to be active in naval affairs, serving as an adviser to the chief of naval operations, the U.S. Naval Academy, and the U.S. Naval War College.

"Admiral Rivero was by far the most brilliant individual

I've ever had the privilege of working for in the navy," recalled Captain Bill Russell, a former personal aide. According to retired Admiral Thomas Moorer, who headed the navy when Rivero held the number-two position, "He has one of those minds that anticipates problems and works out the answers in advance." Rivero died from natural causes at his home in Coronado and is buried at Fort Rosecrans National Cemetery in San Diego.

Rivero played a major role in the U.S. Navy's development of nuclear weapons and became the vice chief of naval operations, the navy's second highest position. His career put him at key places during pivotal junctures of twentieth-century history—as a naval officer in the Pacific theater of World War II, as an admiral during the Cuban Missile Crisis, and as an ambassador to Spain at a time when that country was undergoing a transition from dictatorship to democracy. By any measure, Rivero's achievements were remarkable.

★

A small collection of Rivero's papers is housed at the Naval Historical Center in Washington, D.C. Karl Schuon, *U.S. Navy Biographical Dictionary* (1964), has a brief biography. Obituaries are in the *San Diego Union-Tribune* (26 Sept. 2000), *Los Angeles Times* (27 Sept. 2000), and *New York Times* (28 Sept. 2000).

PAUL A. FRISCH

RIVERS, Larry (*b.* 17 August 1923 in the Bronx, New York City; *d.* 14 August 2002 in Southampton, New York), artist, writer, and jazz musician whose iconoclastic work presaged Pop Art.

Rivers, born Yitzroch Loiza Grossberg, was the eldest of the three children of Shiah Grossberg, a plumber and truck company owner, and Sonya (Hochberg) Grossberg, a homemaker. The Grossbergs were an immigrant Jewish couple from Ukraine who fostered their son's early interest in music, and by the age of seventeen he was playing baritone saxophone in touring jazz bands. At about that time he acquired his professional name when an emcee dubbed his combo "Larry Rivers and His Mudcats."

In 1942 Rivers enlisted in the U.S. Army Air Corps but in 1943 received a medical discharge for a mysterious nervous condition that caused tremors in his left arm. These tremors, however, did not deter him from pursuing his musical career. His disability payments enabled him to study, in 1944 and 1945, at the famed Juilliard School of Music in Manhattan, where he met Miles Davis and, through him, other notable jazz musicians.

In 1945 Rivers married Augusta Burger. But the relationship was stormy and, after the birth of a child, the couple separated in 1946. While playing in a band at a summer resort in Maine, Rivers met a young artist, Jane Freilicher, who introduced him to painting and to her artist friends in New York City. With their encouragement, in 1947 he enrolled for a brief time in Hans Hofmann's School. Still relying on his music to earn a living, Rivers inhabited two worlds: the daylight milieu of art studios, museums, and an erratic family life; and the nighttime demimonde of jazz clubs, where drugs and nervous energy fueled his creativity. In 1948 Rivers enrolled at New York University, graduating in 1951 with a B.A.

Although Rivers continued to work as a professional sax player throughout his life and was also a serious, although largely unpublished, poet, he began to make a name for himself as a visual artist. His first one-man exhibition at the Jane Street Gallery in Greenwich Village in 1949 was favorably reviewed by the influential critic Clement Greenberg (although he later retracted his praise). By the early 1950s Rivers was represented by the Tibor de Nagy Gallery in Manhattan, and his circle of friends included poets as well as painters and musicians. But even in bohemia, Rivers stood out for his scandalous behavior, including the use of hard drugs and a penchant for sexual adventures with both women and men. His intimate friendship with the poet Frank O'Hara provided creative stimulus for them both, and led to the 1957 lithographic series *Stones,* one of Rivers's many collaborative projects with poets.

Much of Rivers's early notoriety stemmed from his iconoclasm, which was not only social and sexual but also artistic. At a time when abstract expressionism was the dominant force in American art, he depicted recognizable figures, albeit with the panache of an action painter. Moreover, his works were often narrative, reflecting his interest in historical and literary themes. His 1953 canvas *Washington Crossing the Delaware,* an ambitious effort to reinvigorate a hopelessly corny image, initially provoked scorn from fellow artists, who admired his technique but sneered at his subject.

Soon, however, others started to mine iconic Americana as a rich lode of source material, and with the advent of Pop Art in the late 1950s Rivers began to look prophetic. His work had been acquired by such New York museums as the Museum of Modern Art, the Metropolitan Museum of Art, and the Whitney Museum of American Art, and he was the subject of a profile in *Life* magazine that emphasized his versatility. In addition, Rivers appeared on a television quiz show, experimented with sculpture and printmaking, designed theater sets, and continued to play the sax.

Rivers's painting career blossomed in the 1960s, a time when his paintings and sculptures were often based on printed source material, including advertisements, textbook illustrations, bank notes, and product packaging. He was also fond of quoting the Old Masters, and wittily combined both gambits in a series of paintings derived from a cigarbox version of Rembrandt's *Syndics of the Drapers Guild* (1662). His first retrospective exhibition, which made a nationwide tour (1965–1966), revealed the scope of his ambition, but it also invited charges of superficiality from those who considered his subjects shallow, clichéd, or dictated by his mercurial personality rather than aesthetic dedication. Notwithstanding critical ambivalence, Rivers's work—now represented by the Marlborough Gallery in New York—continued to sell well. His monumental mixed-media *History of the Russian Revolution: From Marx to Mayakovsky* (1965), which was made for the retrospective, was acquired by Joseph H. Hirshhorn, who donated it to the museum that bears his name.

In 1961 Rivers married Clarice Price, an art teacher. After the birth of two daughters, the couple separated in 1967. Also in the 1960s, Rivers traveled to Europe, the Soviet Union, and Africa; exhibited widely; made films; and executed commissions for murals, set designs, and publications.

During the 1970s and 1980s, seemingly oblivious to developments in minimal and conceptual art, Rivers devoted himself to historical subjects, social and political issues, and material drawn from his own artistic and personal history. Abandoning freehand drawing, he relied on projected photographs and tracings to create complex montages. Works during this period include *Some American History* (1969–1970), a multipart critique of race relations commissioned by the Menil Foundation; *Golden Oldies* (1978), which reprised many of his earlier motifs; and *History of Matzah: The Story of the Jews* (1982–1984), commissioned by the East Coast collector and dealer Jeffrey Loria. In 1981 he began a relationship with a young painter, Daria Deshuk; their son was born in 1985.

In the final decade of his life, Rivers concentrated on portraits of figures in recent cultural history, from movie stars to prominent artists. By this time he had given up his longtime studio residence on East 13th Street in Manhattan and was living year-round in Southampton, Long Island, where he had summered since the early 1950s. He died there of liver cancer and is buried in the Jewish cemetery in Sag Harbor, Long Island.

Three months before Rivers's death, the Corcoran Gallery of Art in Washington, D.C., mounted a comprehensive exhibition, *Larry Rivers: Art and the Artist,* which illustrated the power of his imagination and virtuosity as well as his capacity to shock, amuse, titillate, beguile, and infuriate. Outrageous and often provocative, even when his antics distracted attention from his artistic achievements, Rivers fervently wished for a place among the respected masters whose work he admired and often paraphrased. Equally intrigued by high art and popular culture, he was a pioneer in mediating their differences.

★

Rivers wrote two memoirs: *Drawings and Digressions,* with Carol Brightman (1979), which deals largely with his artistic development; and *What Did I Do?: The Unauthorized Autobiography,* with Arnold Weinstein (1992), a madcap collection of revealing anecdotes. Monographs include Sam Hunter, *Larry Rivers* (1969); Helen A. Harrison, *Larry Rivers* (1984); Sam Hunter, *Larry Rivers* (1989); and Barbara Rose et al., *Larry Rivers: Art and the Artist* (2002). For a profile, see "Wonder Boy and His Many Sides," *Life* (20 Oct. 1958). An obituary is in the *New York Times* (16 Aug. 2002).

HELEN A. HARRISON

Larry Rivers.

ROBARDS, Jason Nelson, Jr. (*b.* 26 July 1922 in Chicago, Illinois; *d.* 26 December 2000 in Bridgeport, Connecticut), stage and screen actor whose performances are widely credited with the mid-twentieth–century revival of interest in the playwright Eugene O'Neill.

Robards was born in Chicago, where his father, Jason Nelson Robards, Sr., also an actor, performed in a road show. But Robards, Sr.'s career was at this time mainly focused on film, so he was able to raise his two sons in

Jason Robards, January 1994. AP/WIDE WORLD PHOTOS

the urging of his father, who had studied there in 1910. Robards remained only eight months, but during that time met the fellow actors Charles Durning and Colleen Dewhurst, who would later play opposite him on stage and screen, most notably in the 1973 production of *A Moon for the Misbegotten.*

Professionally, Robards did not meet with immediate success. He married his first wife, Eleanor Pitman, and had his first child, Jason Robards III, in 1948 (the couple eventually had two more children), but he did not receive any noteworthy roles until he was cast in *American Gothic,* directed by José Quintero at Circle in the Square in New York City in 1953. The role was important mainly because it established a long relationship between Quintero and Robards.

In 1956 Quintero staged O'Neill's *The Iceman Cometh* and made the historic decision to cast Robards in the role of Hickey despite the discrepancy between the actor's appearance and the playwright's description of the character. By 1956 O'Neill's reputation had fallen from its earlier heights; *Iceman* had been a failure on Broadway ten years earlier. But Quintero's production helped O'Neill regain his place in American drama, and Robards's portrayal of Hickey, for which he won an Obie Award, was at the heart of the production's success. The link between Robards's and O'Neill's stature was further strengthened the same year, when Robards portrayed Jamie in the world premiere of *A Long Day's Journey into Night*, again with Quintero as director. For that performance, Robards won the New York Drama Critics Award and a Tony nomination in 1957.

In 1958 Robards and his wife divorced. Robards married three more times, beginning in 1959 with Rachel Taylor (divorced in 1961); then the famous actress Lauren Bacall, in 1961, with whom he would have one child before divorcing in 1969; and finally Lois O'Connor, in 1970, with whom he had two more children.

Robards's first film was *The Journey* (1959), in which he played a Hungarian freedom fighter. Although he insisted he did movies just to "grab the money and go back to Broadway as fast as I can," Robards would nevertheless garner back-to-back Oscars for Best Supporting Actor in 1977 for his portrayal of Ben Bradlee in the Watergate saga *All the President's Men,* and in 1978 for his portrayal of Dashiell Hammett in *Julia.*

As time went by, Robards seemed to embody the American patriarch, benign or malevolent, with his gravelly voice and eyes that looked as though they held several lifetimes worth of unutterable experiences. Although most of his parts on stage and in film took advantage of his genteel exterior, at least two of his more memorable roles belonged to acclaimed Westerns. In 1969 he played opposite Henry Fonda and Charles Bronson in *Once Upon a Time in the West,* directed by Sergio Leone, and a year later he por-

Hollywood, California. After Robards, Sr., divorced his wife, Hope Maxine (Glanville) Robards, a homemaker, in 1927, he raised his sons as Christian Scientists. Robards would long remember the negative aspects of his father's career; Robards, Sr., began acting in silent movies, finding success as early as 1921, but his cachet in Hollywood plummeted by the mid-1930s, and a sense of insecurity pervaded the house.

Immediately after graduating from Hollywood High School in 1939, Robards joined the U.S. Navy, in which he served for seven years. Over the course of his service, Robards survived the Japanese attack at Pearl Harbor and took part in thirteen large naval engagements; at the end of the war he received the Navy Cross, the service's second-highest decoration.

Shortly before engaging in the Philippines campaign, at the age of twenty-two, Robards was first exposed to the work of Eugene O'Neill when he found a copy of *Strange Interlude* in his ship's library. The play impressed Robards, and he began to think about becoming an actor. After leaving the navy in 1946, Robards enrolled at the American Academy of Dramatic Arts (AADA) in New York City at

trayed a ragged prospector in *The Ballad of Cable Hogue,* directed by Sam Peckinpah. His antipathy to film may have been overstated, given that he shot his last movie, *Magnolia* (1999), while suffering from cancer.

Robards died of lung cancer at Bridgeport Hospital in Connecticut. He was survived by his widow and six children, two of whom (Jason Robards III and Sam Robards, the son of Robards's union with Bacall) became actors. As of his death, Robards held the record for accruing the most Tony nominations, although he won the award only once, in 1959, for *The Disenchanted*. In 1997 he won the National Medal of Arts, and in 1999 was recognized for his "lifetime of contribution to arts and culture" with the Kennedy Center Honors Award.

Robards stands out among twentieth-century actors by virtue of his style of performance and by the way he used his career not only to interpret roles but to advocate a certain set of values and aesthetics. He always championed the stage over the screen, and his insistent return to plays by O'Neill signified a love for the playwright stemming from a sense of kinship with the characters O'Neill created and with the playwright himself. Robards was also one of the last holdouts against what he referred to as "Lee Strasberg and the lousy Method." Robards dismissed the self-analysis encouraged by the Method, instead retaining the fluid sense of ease typical of actors earlier in the century. As such, he provided a countermodel for actors performing psychological realism.

★

An extensive interview with Robards is in Yvonne Shafer, comp., *Performing O'Neill: Conversations with Actors and Directors* (2000). The most thorough source of information is Stephen A. Black et al., eds., *Jason Robards Remembered: Essays and Recollections* (2002), which includes interviews as well as essays, reviews, and obituaries, as well as a tribute by the actor Kevin Spacey, originally published in the *New York Times* (14 Jan 2001). The *New York Times* commemorated his death in its Arts section (27 Dec. 2000), and on its editorial page (28 Dec. 2000).

DANIEL MUFSON

ROGERS, William Pierce   (*b.* 23 June 1913 in Norfolk, New York; *d.* 2 January 2001 in Bethesda, Maryland), U.S. attorney general during the administration of President Dwight D. Eisenhower (1957–1961), and U.S. secretary of state during the administration of President Richard M. Nixon (1969–1973).

Born in a small town near the Canadian border, Rogers was the only child of Harrison Alexander Rogers, a paper mill executive, and Myra (Boswick) Rogers, a homemaker. When Rogers was thirteen his mother died, and he moved

in with his grandparents in nearby Canton, New York. His father's business fell off during the depression, so Rogers had to earn his own pocket money. In 1930 he graduated from Canton High School as valedictorian and received a scholarship to Colgate University, in Hamilton, New York.

Rogers graduated from Colgate in 1934 with a B.A. and entered Cornell Law School, where he edited the *Cornell Law Review*. On 27 June 1936 he married Adele Langston, a member of his law class; they had four children. In 1937 he graduated fifth in his class at Cornell, earning an LL.B., then worked briefly for a Wall Street firm before becoming an assistant district attorney for Thomas E. Dewey, Manhattan's chief criminal prosecutor. Rogers tried over 1,000 cases before joining the U.S. Naval Reserve in 1942. He served on the aircraft carrier USS *Intrepid* in the Pacific, attaining the rank of lieutenant commander.

Rogers left military service in 1946 and spent about a year with the district attorney's office before moving in 1947 to Washington, D.C., to work on the staff of a U.S. Senate committee investigating the defense program, becoming its chief counsel in July 1947. Rogers took a bipartisan approach and stayed on even after the committee changed leadership. He also became friendly with the California congressman Richard M. Nixon. They admired each other for making significant achievements in the legal profession despite their inconspicuous origins in small-town America. Rogers advised Nixon to pursue the case against Alger Hiss, a State Department official accused of spying for the Soviet Union, although Nixon's pursuit of Hiss remains questionable to this day.

Rogers left Washington for New York City, where he played a pivotal role in Dwight D. Eisenhower's campaign for the 1952 Republican presidential nomination. Rogers led the credentials committee fight to seat Eisenhower's delegates in four key Southern states, ousting those loyal to Robert Taft. This was perhaps the last of the great political convention fights over delegate credentials and had enormous implications for the Republican Party. Eisenhower's supporters were seated, and Rogers spent part of the presidential campaign touring the West with the vice presidential nominee, Richard Nixon. Rogers was with Nixon when the allegation that Nixon had received improper campaign contributions arose. The furor escalated to such a level that Nixon made the then-unprecedented move of giving a nationwide television speech to defend himself (which Rogers had helped him prepare), arguing that the only gift he had personally received was his daughters' "little dog Checkers." Eisenhower thought Nixon's performance was weak, but it was well received by the public and Nixon survived the ethical challenge.

In 1953 Eisenhower appointed Rogers deputy U.S. attorney general, acting as a liaison with other agencies. In 1956 he accompanied Nixon to Austria following the Hun-

William P. Rogers, January 1961. AP/WIDE WORLD PHOTOS

garian uprising. In January 1958, after Herbert Brownell resigned as attorney general, Rogers replaced him. Rogers had developed expertise in civil rights legislation, and he sought to enforce school integration orders, a particularly sensitive area because of the 1954 Supreme Court decision requiring public schools to integrate. He urged Eisenhower to resist political pressure in appointing judges, and opened antitrust suits against the electronics giants Westinghouse and General Electric. Rogers's diplomatic career began when he represented the United States at the independence ceremony for the Republic of Togo.

When John F. Kennedy, a democrat, became president in 1961, Rogers returned to private practice. He was general counsel for the Washington Post Company and argued several libel suits, including the successful defense of the Associated Press against charges by General Edwin Walker, a conservative army general who retired in 1961 at Kennedy's suggestion for passing out right-wing literature to his troops, that the Press had defamed him. Rogers also filed a brief in support of the *New York Times* in the U.S. Supreme Court, in *Times* v. *Sullivan* (1964), in which the Court ruled that public figures could recover damages only for "reckless" or malicious misstatements. Although a Republican, Rogers was named to brief posts at the United Nations, serving for a while as a U.S. delegate to the General Assembly, and was appointed to President Lyndon B. Johnson's Commission on Law Enforcement and Administration.

In 1969, with the United States torn over the Vietnam conflict, President Nixon appointed Rogers secretary of state because he was "a superb negotiator," although he was inexperienced in foreign affairs. Nixon appointed Henry A. Kissinger, who had been an adviser to Nixon's Republican rival Nelson Rockefeller, as his special assistant for foreign affairs. As Nixon tells it in his memoirs, he and Kissinger agreed that Kissinger would handle the intense conflicts, leaving Rogers to handle the day-to-day workings of the State Department, with its large and often uncontroversial missions. On 22 January 1969 Rogers became the fifty-fifth secretary of state. Kissinger assumed the lead of the National Security Council, which had not played a major role in the Johnson administration. Kissinger became the president's man on foreign policy issues, negotiating with the Russians on arms limitation and with the Vietnamese and Chinese on the Indochina situation.

Although the political columnist Stewart Alsop called Rogers "The Ghost at Foggy Bottom" (the Washington neighborhood where the State Department building rests), Rogers did have important responsibilities. He took the main role in Nixon-era Middle Eastern policy but was criticized by fellow cabinet officer Elliot Richardson as viewing foreign policy as a lawyer would—on a case-by-case basis with no overall view. Rogers also dealt with crises in Korea and with the Southeast Asia Treaty Organization, the international organ the United States sought to use to back U.S. policy in Vietnam and the rest of nearby Asia.

Nixon continued to turn to Rogers for advice at critical moments. When agents broke into the Democratic National Committee headquarters at Washington's Watergate Hotel, Nixon sought Rogers's advice about how to handle H. R. Haldeman and John Ehrlichman, who had played prominent roles in the break-in. Rogers counseled Nixon to demand their resignations but refused to sit in on the meeting. Rogers was then asked to review Nixon's resignation speech.

The Chinese communists also contributed to Rogers's discomfort. When Nixon visited China in 1972 as part of the opening up of Sino-American relations, the Chinese pointedly refused to give Rogers a significant role in the negotiations. In fact, Rogers had not been in on the initial overtures. At the start of his second presidential term in 1973 Nixon asked Rogers to resign. Predictably, he was replaced by Kissinger. Despite Rogers's long service, Nixon, in his memoirs, is dismissive of his old friend.

Rogers returned again to private practice, this time with his own law firm. In 1988 he led the committee investigating the explosion of the space shuttle *Challenger,* which killed seven astronauts. In 1996, on Nixon's death, Rogers praised his abilities but noted that he was not much of a friend.

Rogers was senior partner of the firm Clifford Chance Rogers and Wells in Washington, D.C., when he died at his Maryland home of heart failure. He is buried at Arlington National Cemetery in Virginia.

★

Some of Rogers's papers are at the Eisenhower Library in Abilene, Kansas. Earl Mazo, *Richard Nixon: A Political and Personal Portrait* (1959), treats the early years of the Nixon-Rogers friendship. Richard M. Nixon, *The Memoirs of Richard Nixon* (1978), and Henry Kissinger, *Years of Upheaval* (1982), describe the Nixon administration years. Stanley I. Kutler, ed., *Abuse of Power: The New Nixon Tapes* (1997), contains transcripts of Nixon-Rogers conversations. Stewart Alsop's column about Rogers is "The Ghost at Foggy Bottom," *Newsweek* (29 Mar. 1972). An obituary is in the *New York Times* (4 Jan. 2001).

JOHN DAVID HEALY

ROSENBERG, William ("Bill") (*b.* 12 October 1916 in Boston, Massachusetts; *d.* 20 September 2002 in Mashpee, Massachusetts), fast-food industry entrepreneur who founded Dunkin' Donuts, Incorporated and was a major influence on franchising in the United States.

Rosenberg was the third of four children born to Nathan Rosenberg and Phoebe (Swart) Rosenberg. Rosenberg's father owned a grocery store in the Dorchester section of Boston; his mother was a homemaker. As a young child Rosenberg often joined his father on pre-dawn trips to the wholesale market in Boston's historic Faneuil Hall to buy

William Rosenberg, March 2000. ASSOCIATED PRESS

fresh fish, meat, and produce. Often his father would buy him a jelly doughnut, a treat that Rosenberg remembered for the rest of his life.

Rosenberg's early years were rough-and-tumble. Street fights, some provoked by anti-Semitism, others the result of petty thievery and gang rivalries, were part of the crime, corruption, poverty, and prejudice that stained the social fabric of Boston in the 1920s. One of Rosenberg's boyhood rivals eventually became one of the most wanted criminals in America. During Rosenberg's grade school years, he worked at many jobs and endured long hours, starting before school and continuing after school into the late evening. Rosenberg quipped that these work days lasted from "can't see to can't see." Nathan Rosenberg's business failed during the Great Depression, so Rosenberg, who was in the eighth grade, quit school to help support the family. He delivered newspapers and worked as a Western Union delivery boy. He also competed with people who had the legitimate concessions at public events. One summer day at the racetrack, he sold ice chips in paper cups at ten cents a cup and made $71.00, a substantial amount for a day's work during the depression.

In the early 1930s Rosenberg landed a lucrative Jack and Jill ice cream–truck route in the wealthy town of Milton, Massachusetts. On the front of the truck he painted "Here Comes Bill," on the rear, "There Goes Bill." Rosenberg developed a popular following in the town, and the company viewed him as a go-getter. Rosenberg admired the company's chief accountant, Harry Winokur, who later introduced him to his sister-in-law, Bertha "Bookie" Greenburg. A few years later, at the age of twenty-one, Rosenberg was chosen as the company's national sales manager, in charge of developing and selling truck routes. Bookie and Rosenberg eloped to Brewster, New York, and married on 27 April 1937. They had three children.

With the advent of World War II, Rosenberg worked as part of the defense industry at the Hingham shipyards. Soon he became the first Jewish person in his union to be elected delegate. In this position he worked as a contract coordinator, where his experience with Jack and Jill helped him to bring his "win-win" approach to labor-management relations. After World War II Rosenberg founded and expanded Industrial Luncheon Services to serve factories without cafeterias. Using a military-style field-kitchen operation, the business deployed a fleet of former telephone company trucks retrofitted with stainless interiors to deliver and serve hot lunches to factory workers. In 1950, using savings he had accumulated during World War II, Rosenberg opened the first Open Kettle, a drive-in coffee and donut shop in Quincy, Massachusetts.

Partnering with Rosenberg in the early days of this venture was his now brother-in-law Harry Winokur (who later started Mr. Donut). Rosenberg had a vision of opening many donut shops. His architect came up with a new name to help speed the project—Dunkin' Donuts. Rosenberg, stealing a feature from the restaurant chain Howard Johnson's, which offered twenty-eight ice cream flavors, imagined the distinctive appeal of providing fifty-two different kinds of donuts, one for each week of the year. As the number of Dunkin' Donuts stores increased, Rosenberg became interested in franchising. In 1960 he founded and eventually chaired the International Franchise Association, which grew to include more than 30,000 members. In 1963, when Rosenberg's son Robert graduated with an M.B.A. from Harvard Business School, Rosenberg offered him the company presidency. Rosenberg stayed on as chief executive officer.

With the opening of the 300th Dunkin' Donuts store in 1966, Rosenberg had his sights set on taking the company public. In 1968, with Paine Webber as the lead brokerage house (the same company that had handled McDonald's a few years earlier), the negotiations began. Rosenberg disagreed with Paine Webber's president, Nelson Darling, about the opening price of the stock, claiming that the analysts had undervalued the company's worth and insisting that the opening price be $20.00 a share, "not a penny more or less." Paine Webber finally agreed. The day Dunkin' Donuts, Incorporated opened on Wall Street at $20.00 a share, it closed at $26.00, making Rosenberg and many of his early backers millionaires. His optimism was vindicated,

and the company soon became what some investment analysts call a "ten-bagger," one of the best ten investments in thirty-year period, returning a tenfold profit on its initial purchase price.

As Dunkin' Donuts prospered, Rosenberg's lifelong passion for horses and for riding led him to become involved in breeding standardbreds, the horses used in harness racing. He acquired Wilrose Farm in New Hampshire and produced a number of champions. Once again, Rosenberg's commitment to improving quality through organization came to the fore. He was successful in 1974 in establishing the New Hampshire Sire Stakes, an association that improved marketing and quality standards for harness-racing owners and trainers, and in later years he established the International Horse Racing Association.

In April 1978, after a long separation, Rosenberg and his wife divorced. On 24 June he married Ann Marie Miller, who had been his personal assistant and companion since the founding days of his horse-breeding business. In the 1970s Rosenberg fought a series of battles with cancer. He underwent successful surgery on both lungs in 1971 and extensive radiation for lymphatic cancer in the late 1970s. During these times he remained a mainstay of the horse industry and played an active role in the international expansion of Dunkin' Donuts.

Rosenberg's business ventures and illnesses led to sustained philanthropic activities. He donated Wilrose Farm to the University of New Hampshire, which named an International Center for Franchising in his honor. With Harvard Medical School and the Dana-Farber Cancer Institute, he forged donor links between Dunkin' Donuts franchise owners. In 1986 he created the William Rosenberg Chair in Medicine at Harvard Medical School, and in 1999 assisted in funding the William and Ann Rosenberg Clinical Vector Production Laboratory at the Harvard School of Human Genetics. After a long battle with several cancers, Rosenberg died at his home. He is buried in Sharon Memorial Park in Sharon, Massachusetts.

Rosenberg did indeed rise from "rags to riches." He did nothing halfway. He organized individuals and groups who initially saw no benefit in working collaboratively. He created a major franchise when franchising was in its infancy. Moreover, with Dunkin' Donuts, Rosenberg instilled in his customers a brand loyalty that approximates old-time fan allegiance to a sports team. Especially in New England, as the area's coffee and donut class wars escalated, Dunkin' Donuts customers continue to "man the barricades" against the high-priced incursions of Starbucks and Krispy Kreme (which Rosenberg once attempted to acquire).

★

There is no biography of Rosenberg. Biographical material can be found in *Time to Make the Donuts* (2001), an autobiography written with Jessica Brilliant Keener. An obituary is in the *New York Times* (23 Sept. 2002).

JOSEPH G. FLYNN

ROSTOW, Eugene Victor Debs (*b.* 25 August 1913 in Brooklyn, New York City; *d.* 21 November 2002 in Alexandria, Virginia), lawyer, economist, and undersecretary of state for political affairs (1966–1969).

Rostow, one of three sons of Victor A. Rostow and Lillian (Helman) Rostow, Russian-Jewish immigrants, was raised in New Haven, Connecticut. His younger brother was Walt Rostow, the economist and a foreign adviser to President Lyndon B. Johnson. Their parents were politically active socialists who named Rostow after the socialist politician and presidential candidate Eugene V. Debs.

In 1933 Rostow graduated from Yale University in New Haven, Connecticut, as a Phi Beta Kappa—he was nineteen years old—then studied graduate economics at King's College at Cambridge University in England from 1933 to 1934. Also in 1933 he married Edna Greenberg; they had three children. Returning to the United States, Rostow re-

Eugene V. Rostow, 1965. BETTMANN/CORBIS

ceived his LL.B. in 1937 from Yale University Law School. He worked briefly for a private law firm before joining the Yale law faculty in 1938, becoming a full professor six years later and dean in 1955, a position he held for ten years.

During World War II, Rostow served as a legal adviser in the U.S. State Department, working for Assistant Secretary of State Dean Acheson. Rostow criticized the Supreme Court's ruling that supported the internment of Japanese-Americans; he later wrote an article for the *Yale Law Review* that was influential in persuading the federal government to restore the property and the citizenship of the Japanese-Americans who had been confined in detention camps.

Rostow also called for the reorganization and increased governmental regulation of oil companies in his 1948 book, *A National Policy for the Oil Industry*. As the dean of Yale Law School, he helped make the school into one of the most liberal law programs in the country. He remained an important link between the academic community and the federal government, demonstrating particularly strong support for President Lyndon B. Johnson's foreign policy.

In 1966 Johnson appointed Rostow undersecretary of state for political affairs. Three months later he was named an alternative governor of the International Monetary Fund and the World Bank. During his tenure in the federal government, Rostow consistently defended the U.S. involvement in the war in Vietnam and criticized its opponents, comparing the isolationism of U.S. intellectuals in the 1960s to that of the United States in 1938 in relation to the German dictator Adolf Hitler. Rostow likewise supported the 1965 invasion of the Dominican Republic.

As undersecretary of state for political affairs, Rostow's job was to provide "as much intellectual input" as possible. According to Rostow, Johnson "wanted me to produce ideas, work on European problems, NATO [North Atlantic Treaty Organization] problems, and the economic problems of the [State] Department." Thus, in January 1967, Rostow visited India and other countries to discuss U.S. food assistance. In February 1968 he participated in a United Nations conference that recommended a system of preferential tariffs meant to encourage industrial growth in developing countries.

In May 1968 Rostow represented the United States in negotiations about the financing of U.S. troops in West Germany, with the result that in 1969 the West German government agreed to reimburse the United States for a large part of these costs. Rostow saw this as especially important, noting, "We have to keep the troops there in order to be able to have some options other than the nuclear option." He felt that the United States had two "fundamental national interests" in Europe: to keep the Soviet Union from obtaining access to European capital and to enlist the support of Europe in various projects of U.S. interest around the world.

In 1969 Rostow left government service and returned to Yale as Sterling Professor of Law and Public Affairs. In the 1970s he wrote extensively on nuclear proliferation and was a member of the Committee on the Present Danger. His defense of postwar U.S. diplomacy was published in 1972 as *Peace in the Balance: The Future of U.S. Foreign Policy.* He also wrote *Toward Managed Peace: The National Security Interests of the United States, 1759 to the Present* (1993).

Rostow served in the administration of President Ronald W. Reagan as the head of the Arms Control and Disarmament Agency beginning in 1981. Senior administration officials thought that he was inadequately hawkish, however, and he was caused to resign in 1983. In the 1990s Rostow served as a fellow at the U.S. Institute for Peace in Washington, D.C. He died at age eighty-nine from congestive heart failure at an assisted-living facility in Arlington, Virginia.

★

For information about Rostow's career, see Myres S. McDougal, ed., *Power and Policy in Quest of the Law: Essays in Honor of Eugene Victor Rostow* (1985). An oral history interview with Rostow (2 Dec. 1968) is at the Lyndon Baines Johnson Presidential Library at the University of Texas, at Austin. Obituaries are in the (Manchester) *Guardian* (28 Nov. 2002) and *Seattle Times* (1 Dec. 2002).

KIM RICHARDSON

ROTE, (William) Kyle, Sr. (*b.* 27 October 1928 [some sources say 1927] in Bellevue, Texas; *d.* 15 August 2002 in Baltimore, Maryland), All-America college football player and record-setting receiver for the New York Giants who became one of the first professional athletes to work as a sportscaster.

Rote grew up in San Antonio, Texas, the younger of two sons of Jack Tobin Rote, a construction worker, and Emma Bell (Owens) Rote, a homemaker. Like many youngsters growing up during the Great Depression, Rote went without many material things. He recalled, "I had the kind of love that makes you not notice the absence of other things. The only thing I ever wanted that I had to do without was a bike."

Rote, who played mostly with his older brother and his friends, showed no early athletic ability. By the time he was a senior at Thomas Jefferson High School in San Antonio, however, he was All-State in football and basketball and a star in baseball. Because there were no college scholarship offers, and Rote could not afford college any other way, he and some of his basketball teammates decided to do a postgraduate, or fifth year, of high school. Rote further blossomed in these extra months, becoming one of the South-

Kyle Rote, August 1951. BETTMANN/CORBIS

west's most sought-after schoolboy athletes. With "forty or fifty" offers from which to choose, Rote decided to matriculate at Vanderbilt University in Nashville, Tennessee. Nonetheless, Rote missed his girlfriend, Betty Jamison, who would become his first wife, and left Vanderbilt after "four or five weeks" of a summer session.

He then contacted Southern Methodist University (SMU) in Dallas and enrolled there in the fall of 1947. He shared backfield space with one of college football's all-time greats, Doak Walker, a three-time consensus All-American. On 3 December 1949 Rote had a game that was voted by the Texas Sportswriters Association as "the finest performance by a Texas athlete in the first half of the [twentieth] century." It was the last game of the season, and the SMU Mustangs were playing a Notre Dame team that was in the midst of a thirty-seven-game unbeaten streak and was a twenty-seven-point favorite. Still worse, Walker was injured and not suited up. Rote rose to the occasion by rushing for 115 yards, passing for 146 yards, and punting for a forty-eight-yard average. He scored all three of SMU's touchdowns and was driving for a fourth and possible tying score when time ran out. The Fighting Irish escaped with a 27–20 victory. Since no other major college games were played on that late date, Rote received tremendous media exposure for his spectacular performance. He and Walker were named to most All-America teams.

When Walker moved up to the National Football League (NFL), Rote was looked upon for a stellar senior season. He was again a consensus All-America and runner-up for the Heisman Trophy. Meanwhile, he was a good enough catcher to play minor league baseball for Corpus Christi (Texas) of the Gulf Coast League following graduation. He also ran the sprints for the Mustangs' track and field squad. Rote left SMU in 1951 with outstanding and versatile statistics. In his three-year career he ran for 2,038 yards at a 5.0-yard average. He passed for 648 yards in just two seasons as a passer and caught sixty-one passes for 733 yards. He returned twenty-one kickoffs for 562 yards and scored thirty-two touchdowns and two extra points. Long after he was gone from the Dallas campus, the highest praise a Mustang prospect could receive from an SMU coach was, "He's *almost* as good as Kyle." Fred Benners, an SMU quarterback, said of Rote, "He had the greatest God-given physical equipment of anybody I ever played with. . . . He could run, pass, punt, and catch. I never saw anybody better." While Rote was starring at SMU, his cousin, Tobin Rote, was a stellar quarterback at Rice University and later had a long professional career.

Rote was the first player taken in the 1951 NFL draft, by the New York Giants. He signed a three-year deal with the Giants, calling for $20,000 as a rookie and $15,000 for each of the next two years. He injured both knees in his rookie season and was never the runner he was in college, but he developed into a reliable receiver and a respected team leader as the Giants became one of the NFL's elite teams in the 1950s and early 1960s. Rote also was a man of principle. When team owners were vehemently opposed to the NFL players forming a union, Rote risked his career as an organizer of the NFL Players Association. He became the union's first president in 1956, when the team owners finally recognized the labor organization. With the Giants contending and the popularity of pro football exploding at about this time, Rote began his sportscasting career—first in radio and then in television—while still an active player.

His gimpy knees robbed him of his speed, but his knowledge of the game and precise pass patterns allowed him to retire in 1961 as the Giants' all-time leading receiver. In his eleven-year career he had 300 receptions for 4,797 yards and forty-eight touchdowns. He served as a Giants assistant coach in 1962 and 1963 before becoming a full-time football analyst for National Broadcasting Company television. Rote had four children with his first wife, including Kyle, Jr., who was a seven-year star in the North American Soccer League. Rote was divorced in 1964 and married the television personality Sharon Ray Ritchie on 2 August 1965. After they divorced in 1971, Rote and his third wife, Nina, were married. Rote was elected to the Texas Sports Hall of Fame in 1962 and the College Football Hall of Fame in 1964. He eventually moved to the

Baltimore area and died there in Sinai Hospital after experiencing cardiopulmonary complications following emergency hernia surgery. He is buried in National Memorial Park Cemetery in Falls Church, Virginia. The charismatic Rote was held in such high esteem by his teammates that fourteen Giants named their sons after him. He authored two books, *Pro Football for the Fan* (1964) and *The Language of Pro Football* (1966).

★

There is no biography of Rote. His career is discussed in Barry Gottehrer, *The Giants of New York: The History of Professional Football's Most Fabulous Dynasty* (1963); Gerald Eskenazi, *There Were Giants in Those Days* (1976); and Dave Klein, *The Game of Their Lives* (1976). Obituaries are in the *Houston Chronicle*, *New York Times*, *San Antonio Express-News*, and *Seattle Times* (all 16 Aug. 2002).

JIM CAMPBELL

ROWAN, Carl T(homas) (*b.* 11 August 1925 in Ravenscroft, Tennessee; *d.* 23 September 2000 in Washington, D.C.), journalist, syndicated columnist, radio commentator, author, and campaigner for racial justice.

Rowan was born in a dying coal mining town, the eldest of the five children of Thomas David Rowan, a lumber stacker, and Johnnie (Bradford) Rowan, a homemaker. When Rowan was still an infant, the family moved to McMinnville, Tennessee, hoping for greater economic opportunities. As Rowan grew, he supplemented the family's meager income by doing menial jobs. He excelled in school, graduating from Bernard High School in 1942 as class president and valedictorian. He moved to Nashville, Tennessee, and worked odd jobs to earn money for college.

Rowan attended Tennessee A&I University in Nashville (now Tennessee State University) from 1942 to 1943 and in 1943 passed a competitive naval examination to enter the V-12 program for officer training. On 1 November 1943, as part of this program, Rowan reported for duty at Washburn Municipal University in Topeka, Kansas, and learned that he would become the only black in a unit of 335 sailors. He eventually moved to the Naval Reserve Midshipman School at Fort Schuyler in the Bronx, New York City, where in 1944 he became one of the first African Americans to become a commissioned officer in the U.S. Navy. He served in several assistant officer positions and then as communications officer, before receiving an honorable discharge on 18 June 1946.

Rowan earned a B.A. in mathematics from Oberlin College in Ohio in 1947. When he learned of the brutal beating of a African-American U.S. Army sergeant by lawmen in South Carolina and that the sheriff involved in the beating,

Carl T. Rowan, December 1996. AP/WIDE WORLD PHOTOS

Linwood L. Shull, was found not guilty, Rowan concluded that white Americans did not know how bad it was for blacks and that they would "never know until we get some Negroes on the white newspapers and magazines." He stated that "the Woodard case, as much as any event, steeled my resolve to be a writer, to bust open the lily-white journalistic establishment in America." Reporting was then one of the most discriminatory professions in the United States, a profession that in 1947 barred the African-American correspondent for the only black newspaper in the country from the press galleries of Congress. Rowan received an M.A. in journalism in August 1948 from the University of Minnesota in Minneapolis-St. Paul, and became a copy editor for the *Minneapolis Tribune.* On 2 August 1950 Rowan married Vivien Louise Murphy, a public health nurse. They had three children.

In 1950 Rowan, one of only five African-American journalists in the United States, became the first general assignment black reporter for the *Tribune.* Resolving to present "truths that only he could tell," he traveled more than 6,000 miles through the South, writing a series of articles entitled "How Far from Slavery?" This series resulted in the publication of his first book, *South of Freedom* (1952). Rowan then traveled to India and Southeast Asia for the

U.S. Department of State to lecture on the role of a free press in a free society. His Asia travels were recorded in his second book, *The Pitiful and the Proud* (1956). His third book, *Go South to Sorrow* (1957), details his follow-up trip to the South. By the end of the decade Rowan published regularly in the *Saturday Evening Post, Redbook, Reader's Digest,* and *Ebony.* In 1961 he resigned from the *Tribune* to pursue a career in the government.

From 1961 to 1963 Rowan was the deputy assistant secretary of state for public affairs in the administration of President John F. Kennedy, the first African American to hold such a high position in government. He served as U.S. ambassador to Finland from 1963 to 1964. After Kennedy's assassination, President Lyndon B. Johnson appointed Rowan director of the U.S. Information Agency. In 1965 Rowan resigned from government and began writing three columns each week for the *Chicago Daily News* and recording three three-minute television commentaries each week for Westinghouse Broadcasting. Rowan got his own daily radio program, the *Rowan Report,* and became a regular panelist on *Meet the Press* and *Inside Washington.*

In 1987 Rowan founded Project Excellence, a college scholarship program for high-achieving African-American high school students in the Washington area. He was charged with violating the district's gun laws when he shot and wounded an intruder, but the trial ended with a hung jury. In 1987 he hosted and coproduced the television special "Searching for Justice: Three American Stories" in celebration of the anniversary of the U.S. Constitution. The amputation of his right leg as a consequence of diabetes, in 1997, did not slow down this defender of affirmative action. He wrote his last column a few days before his death, at age seventy-five, in the Washington Hospital Center. He died from natural causes, although he had suffered from a variety of diseases, including diabetes and heart and kidney ailments. His body was cremated.

The author of eight books, Rowan was the recipient of many honors, including the Sidney Hilman Award for the best newspaper reporting in 1951. He was the only journalist to win the medallion of Sigma Delta Chi, the professional journalism society, three years in a row (1953, 1954, and 1955) for both foreign and domestic correspondence. He won the Alfred I. Dupont–Columbia University Silver Baton, one of the most coveted awards in American television, for the documentary *Thurgood Marshall: The Man,* in 1987. In 1990 Rowan was inducted into both the National Association of Black Journalists (NABJ) and the Delta Chi Hall of Fame. He was the recipient of the NABJ Lifetime Achievement Award. He also served as president of the Gridiron Club and director of the Gannett Company.

Plainspoken and direct, Rowan was a good-humored individual who always stressed the importance of education and who was an unwavering champion of the poor and minorities. A passionate reporter on race, he spent his life challenging the status quo as a newspaperman and commentator.

★

Rowan's papers are housed in the Oberlin College Archives at the Mudd Center in Oberlin. His autobiography, *Breaking Barriers: A Memoir* (1991), is the leading source for information about his life and career. Another excellent source is Dan Nimmo and Chevelle Newsome, *Political Commentators in the United States in the 20th Century: A Bio-Critical Sourcebook* (1997). Obituaries are in the *New York Times* and *Washington Post* (both 24 Sept. 2000).

JOYCE K. THORNTON

RUDIN, Lewis ("Lew")   (*b.* 4 April 1927 in the Bronx, New York City; *d.* 20 September 2001 in New York City), real estate tycoon and cheerleader for New York City businesses, cultural institutions, and neighborhoods.

Rudin, the youngest of the two sons of Samuel Rudin, a property developer, and May (Cohen) Rudin, a homemaker, was born in the Throgs Neck section of the Bronx and brought up on Manhattan's Upper West Side. He was part of a family real estate business founded by his paternal grandfather, Louis Rudinsky, an immigrant from Eastern Europe who came to the United States in 1883 and settled on Chrystie Street in New York's Lower East Side. Rudinsky, a tailor by trade, bought his first apartment building in 1902. When he had the opportunity to buy property on East Fifty-fourth Street, he did so without bothering to take a look. He later told his son that any property that was good enough for John D. Rockefeller (whose mansion was on West Fifty-fourth) was good enough for him.

In 1924 Rudin's father, Samuel, purchased a lumberyard in the Westchester Square section of the Bronx to construct one of the first six-story elevator apartment buildings in the Bronx. The family business centered on building and managing apartment buildings. When May Rudin grew unhappy living in the Bronx, Samuel built apartment houses on Manhattan's Upper West Side, where the family lived for many years. Rudin attended DeWitt Clinton High School, graduating in 1944, and then enrolled in New York University School of Commerce. Rudin's undergraduate education was interrupted by service in the U.S. Army in Europe during World War II. Having risen to the rank of sergeant, he returned to New York University after the war and graduated in 1949.

Rudin joined his brother, father, and uncle in the family real estate business, building and managing multiple-family dwellings during the housing shortage that followed World War II. In 1955 their organization purchased land to build its first office building, at 415 Madison Avenue. The family business, now called Rudin Management, gave Rudin's brother, Jack, responsibility for development and construction, and Rudin responsibility for financing and leasing. The Rudins established a pattern of limiting their investments to New York City, of not selling their buildings, and of maintaining their reputation as quality landlords. Over time, Rudin buildings came to be regarded as significant for their distinctive ambience.

As investment builders and owners with all their assets connected to New York City, the Rudin family business was threatened by the negative perception of Gotham in the 1970s. A garbage workers' strike, a crippling snow storm, and riots during a blackout shook consumer confidence, exacerbated by major corporations terminating their leases on city office space in their flight to suburban corporate headquarters. As Rudin later said, "Well, we couldn't very well pick up our buildings and move them across the George Washington Bridge."

With the city vulnerable to financial disaster, Rudin, with several other prominent local business people, raised $2.5 million to establish and chair the Association for a Better New York (ABNY) in October 1971. Through ABNY, Rudin, now the executive vice president of Rudin Management, focused individual, group, and media attention on what was exciting and profitable about living and working in the metropolis. Relying on his charm and goodwill, Rudin began to use ABNY's monthly breakfast meetings as a forum for business, political, and cultural leaders to meet, talk, and promote New York. He gave away thousands of golden apple lapel pins, and leaders in every field made it their business to be seen and heard at ABNY's breakfast meetings. Rudin created the "I Love NY" campaign and became active in the New York Conservancy, preserving neighborhoods and landmark structures. The effort awarded him "Living Landmark" status.

In 1975, as the city faced bankruptcy, Rudin persuaded major corporations and utilities to pre-pay $600 million in local real estate taxes so that New York would not default on the city payroll. Rudin continued to intercede on behalf of the city by offering his financial support as well as his personal commitment to improving life in New York. In 1976, with his brother, and in honor of their father, Rudin financed the New York City Marathon, an annual race through all five boroughs that draws thousands of runners and millions of spectators. An avid sports enthusiast, Rudin convinced the executives of the U.S. Tennis Association that it was in their best interest to keep the U.S. Open in Queens. In 1977 Rudin brought his son, William, and his daughter, Beth (both children from his marriage to Gladyce Largever), into the family business. After his marriage to Largever dissolved, Rudin married Basia Szmanska on 4

Lewis Rudin (*center*) with Mario Cuomo (*left*) and Arthur Mitchell (*right*), September 1983. AP/WIDE WORLD PHOTOS

January 1973. At the time of his death, he was married to Rachel Rudin.

Tension created by city and state residential rent laws and by rising fuel and maintenance costs led Rudin to turn from investing in apartment houses to commercial space. In 1983 Rudin Management was forced to sell cooperative shares in their apartment buildings, although the family continues to hold the deed to the property the buildings stand on. Rudin bitterly criticized state and city laws that protected rent rates in unoccupied apartments, laws that discouraged landlords from continuing to invest in such properties.

In the early 1990s, when an economic recession and high crime rates again threatened New York businesses and residents, Rudin again led the rally to bring the city back to prosperity and safety. He organized a campaign to provide police officers with protective vests, and he lent support to social action programs like Meals on Wheels. For his continuing efforts on behalf of New York City, Mayor David Dinkins awarded Rudin the Bronze Medallion, New York City's highest civilian honor, in 1994.

In 1996 Rudin created a state-of-the-art technology facility at 55 Broad Street in lower Manhattan, attracting new media tenants and making New York a competitor to Silicon Valley. Until shortly before his death, Rudin continued to actively promote New York as the site for the 2012 Olympic Games. Rudin died at home from bladder cancer, and was buried in Central Synagogue ten days after the terrorist attack on the World Trade Center.

★

There is no biography of Rudin. Obituaries are in the *New York Times* and (New York) *Daily News* (both 21 Sept. 2001). A memorial essay by James Taub is in the *New York Times* (30 Dec. 2001), and one by Clem Richardson is in the *Daily News* (24 Sept. 2001).

WENDY HALL MALONEY

RUTHERFORD, Maude Russell (*b.* 1897? in Texas; *d.* 8 March 2001 in Atlantic City, New Jersey), African-American singer and dancer credited for introducing the Charleston.

Information about Rutherford's early years is vague. She confided to friends that she had been born in 1897, although the date inscribed on her headstone is 1902. Rutherford was the daughter of a white father, William Mc-Cann, and an African-American mother, Margaret Lee.

Because Texas law prohibited interracial marriages, Rutherford's parents never wed or lived together.

While a teenager, Rutherford worked as a ticket taker at a local theater, where she met Sam Russell, a noted African-American comic actor. When Russell asked her to travel with him, she refused unless he married her. He agreed, although the union proved to be violent and short-lived. Weary of repeated beatings from her husband, Rutherford left him, taking $100.00 with her to New York City, where she tried to break into show business. Tall and possessed of a good singing voice, she went from audition to audition, usually performing the popular song "I'm Forever Blowing Bubbles." One producer's attempts to mold her into a blues singer failed, and Rutherford later admitted that she was told to "stick to the bubbles." But because of her talent, looks, and stage presence, Rutherford eventually won roles, often being cast as a "good-time" girl or a comic character. Rutherford was fast on her feet and soon began making a name for herself as a dancer, in addition to her growing reputation as an actor and a singer.

Rutherford's ascent in the theater came during the 1920s, when the Harlem Renaissance was at its peak and the Broadway stage played host to a number of productions featuring African-American performers. Her good looks earned her billing as the "Slim Princess," and she soon appeared with such stars as Josephine Baker, Fats Waller, and Pearl Bailey. Rutherford was a perennial favorite at the famed Cotton Club in Harlem.

Rutherford established her place in American theater in the 1922 Broadway production of *Liza,* an all-black revue in which she introduced the signature dance of the decade, the Charleston. Mistakenly, many dance historians credit the 1923 Broadway production *Runnin' Wild* with introducing the Charleston, but Rutherford did so a year earlier.

Rutherford was most proud of her talent as a dancer. Describing her dancing to an interviewer, Rutherford stated, "I used to kick thirty-two times across the stage, and my legs would hit my nose. I was a dancing fool." Throughout the 1920s she danced in a series of popular musicals, among them *Dixie to Broadway* (1924), *Chocolate Scandals* (1927), and *Keep Shufflin'* (1928). She also performed in the 1936 London stage production of *Blackbirds,* with Josephine Baker.

Rutherford's private life was colorful. She married five times, the last time in 1953 to Septimus Rutherford, a chief steward for the Moore-McCormack shipping line. A flamboyant performer, Rutherford was known for the sharp contrasts that defined her life—her elegance on stage, and her brusque demeanor and colorful language off stage. She left show business during the 1950s and later went to work as a switchboard operator at a hotel in Atlantic City, where she died. At the time of her death, she was believed to have been 104 years old.

Rutherford's stage performances illustrate the growing influence of African-American music and dance in American theater during the 1920s and for years thereafter. *Liza* was just one of many shows with an African-American cast that acquainted white audiences with songs and dance steps that became popular. These performances, and the shows at the Cotton Club, helped to revolutionize American musical and dance theater; many of the groundbreaking steps and routines of the 1920s became a permanent part of the modern stage.

★

Information on Rutherford is woefully scarce. The one source of biographical information is *Who's Who Among African Americans* (2002). An obituary is in the *New York Times* (29 Mar. 2001).

MEG GREENE MALVASI

S

SADDLER, Joseph ("Sandy") (*b.* 23 June 1926 in Boston, Massachusetts; *d.* 18 September 2001 in the Bronx, New York City), longtime world featherweight boxing champion whose diminutive physique concealed an extraordinary knockdown and knockout capability.

Saddler's parents were West Indians and part of a remarkable Caribbean migration that saw significant numbers of islanders relocate to London as well as to East Coast American cities such as Boston, New York City, and Philadelphia. Though born in Boston, Saddler was raised in Harlem in New York City, a special place within the American landscape, as it was a community that both embraced and encouraged African-American involvement in all sorts of creative enterprise ranging from dance, theater, and music to athletic activity.

In contemporary boxing, across all weight divisions there is an obsession with "bringing on" young fighters so that they can, earlier rather than later, force their way onto the rankings lists. Saddler is the classic exemplar of a previous era in which an apprenticeship was viewed as being the best fistic education for teenage boxers. By the time he was seventeen, Saddler had taken part in about fifty amateur bouts. Such an extensive baptism of fire meant that, at least in the early part of his career, Saddler fought with remarkable levels of pugilistic savoir faire.

At five feet, eight and a half inches, weighing from 116 to 119 pounds, Saddler fought regularly during the spring and summer of 1944—three times per month in May, June, and July. In all, Saddler fought on twenty-two occasions that year, and his modus operandi was stunning hitting power with a deadly finishing punch. While he lost his second fight (the only knockout of his career) and his ninth contest, he floored, and had counted out, ten fellow boxers. As 1944 waned, Saddler's punching ferocity waxed. In his last six fights of the year, every win was by knockout, and he only fought fourteen rounds in all six fights combined.

In 1945 Saddler moved up a weight division to the featherweight level. With twenty-four fights, he won seventeen by knockout. In 1946 Saddler fought on fewer occasions (fifteen), but he took on more highly regarded boxers. By the end of 1946, *Ring,* the premier boxing magazine and a publication that could literally make or break contender aspirations, placed Saddler as the seventh-best featherweight boxer in the world.

To look at Saddler's itinerary in 1947 is to retrace the intriguing geography of post–World War II boxing and to recognize the fact that a onetime regional boxer (Saddler's road trips in 1944 took him only as far afield as Hartford, Connecticut, and Jersey City, New Jersey) had now embarked on an international career. He fought in Mexico City; New Orleans; Caracas, Venezuela (three times); and Havana, Cuba (twice).

On 29 October 1948 Saddler fought Willie Pep in New York City for the world featherweight crown. *The Boxing Register* noted: "Saddler dominated the fight. He cut Pep

Sandy Saddler, September 1951. BETTMANN/CORBIS

in the first round, knocked him down twice in the third, and finally knocked him out in the fourth." A year later, on 11 February 1949, in a tumultuous rematch with Saddler that went fifteen rounds, Pep survived quite a beating—he needed eleven stitches—and regained his title.

In many respects, Saddler's career cannot be accurately assessed unless seen as an adjunct to Pep's. They fought twice more—8 September 1950 and 26 September 1951—and while Saddler won both times, the contests were tumultuous. Boxing historians speak of the Pep-Saddler 11 February 1949 fight as one of the great ring encounters of all time. Madison Square Garden in New York City hosted a capacity crowd of 19,097, setting a record for a featherweight fight with $87,563 in gate receipts. The third Pep-Saddler battle (8 September 1950) drew a crowd of 38,781 at Yankee Stadium, with $262,150 being taken in at the turnstiles. This was a new featherweight box office record.

The final Pep-Saddler encounter (26 September 1951) was the most controversial of the four. In *Boxing Greats: An Illustrated History of the Legends of the Ring* (1998), Steve Bunce and Bob Mee describe it as a "wild fight," with both boxers perfecting "boxing infringements" and "inventing a repertoire of new ones." Gouging and illegal striking were part of both fighters' skill armory. Such was the level of the irregularities that the New York State Athletic Commission suspended Saddler's license for sixty days. Pep's lifetime ban was eventually commuted to twenty months.

Saddler was featherweight champion of the world from 1950 to 1957, including three years during which he completed his military service, serving in the U.S. Army. In both 1955 and 1956 he defended his world title. His career was permanently halted in 1957, when he received serious eye injuries in a taxi crash.

In 1973 Saddler and Pep returned to the Madison Square Garden for an exhibition bout. Saddler was forty-seven, and Pep was fifty. Fortuitously, the fight lasted only one round. Bunce and Mee comment on the Pep-Saddler rivalry: "The two men were friends but it upset Saddler that whenever they were introduced before fights his name always came second." Saddler pointed out that he was the one who retired as the undefeated featherweight champion of the world.

Saddler was a muscular, linear boxer with lithe legs and long arms. His seventy-inch reach undoubtedly helped him towards 103 career knockouts. His career record was 144 wins, sixteen losses, and two draws. After his boxing career ended, he trained several professional boxers and, for a period during the early 1970s, worked with George Foreman. He was elected to the International Boxing Hall of Fame in 1990. In his later years he suffered from Alzheimer's disease. Saddler died in his sleep at Schervier Nursing Home in the Bronx at age seventy-five. He was survived by his wife, Helen, and three children.

For nearly a decade, Saddler decimated the ranks of featherweight boxing and, pound for pound, could be considered in an elite group with the likes of Sugar Ray Robinson and Henry Armstrong. Pete Ehrmann, in a February 2002 tribute in *Ring* magazine, said of Saddler that he stood "head and shoulders above most other fighters in an era filled with so many great ones."

★

James B. Roberts and Alexander G. Skutt, *The Boxing Register: International Hall of Fame Official Record Book* (1997), is an excellent resource and contains a full listing of Saddler's boxing career statistics. Nat Fleischer and Sam Andre, *An Illustrated History of Boxing* (1997), examines the Pep-Saddler brouhahas and contains revealing photographs of these encounters. Steve Bunce and Bob Mee, *Boxing Greats: An Illustrated History of the Legends of the Ring* (1998), includes a chapter entitled "Unkind History Neglects Saddler." For insights on Cuba as a boxing center—Saddler fought there twice in 1947 and once in 1951—see John Sugden, *Boxing and Society: An International Analysis* (1996). Pete Ehrmann's tribute to Saddler in *Ring* (Feb. 2002) is a comprehensive minibiography. An obituary is in the *New York Times* (22 Sept. 2001).

SCOTT A. G. M. CRAWFORD

SAGAN, Ginetta Teresa Moroni ("Topolino") (*b.* 1 June 1923 in Milan, Italy; *d.* 25 August 2000 in Atherton, California), antifascist political prisoner, human rights activist, founder of the first western U.S. chapter of Amnesty International, and founder of the Western Region of Amnesty International.

Sagan was the only child of Rosa Levy and Dario Cicogona, both physicians. Cultured people, they traveled extensively, taking their daughter all over Europe and even visiting Africa. They went to museums, theaters, and the opera and engaged in lively discussions on history and culture. When the fascist dictator Benito Mussolini came to power in Italy in 1922, her parents became active in the Italian resistance movement. This was dangerous work, and in 1943 they were caught. Her Catholic father was shot to death in a public execution, and her Jewish mother was sent to the concentration camp in Auschwitz, Poland, where she died in fewer than six months. In September 1943 Sagan herself joined the resistance. She assisted in helping people safely across the Italian border into Switzerland, provided food and clothing to people in hiding, and transported newspapers and messages to the Allies. If she was caught, she risked imprisonment or even death. Her small size (she was barely five feet tall) was a big advantage, allowing her to dart in and out of places without being noticed. Her comrades in the movement nicknamed her "Topolino" ("Little Mouse").

In February 1945 Mussolini's fascist police caught Sagan and imprisoned her in a dark villa, where, for more than forty-five days, she was interrogated, beaten, raped, and tortured. One day a loaf of bread was thrown into her cell. As she had been denied food, this event was quite remarkable. Inside the bread was a matchbox, which held a piece of paper with the single word "*coraggio*" (courage). This kind gesture gave her hope.

On 23 April 1945 two Nazi soldiers told Mussolini's guards that she was needed for further questioning, and they took her away. Sagan thought that she was about to be executed, but the Germans in fact were deserters, and they took her to a Catholic hospital in Switzerland. Sagan spent several months recuperating from the injuries that she had suffered at the hands of the fascists. In 1948 she went to Paris, where she lived with her godfather, the American banker Joshua Campbell. She studied child development at the Sorbonne. In 1951 she entered the University of Chicago, where she met Leonard Arthur Sagan, a doctor, scientist, and human and environmental rights activist. They were married in 1952 and had three sons.

During the 1960s, while living in Washington, D.C., Sagan contributed to the establishment of Amnesty International in the United States (AIUSA). The group, which

Ginetta Sagan, May 1979. AP/WIDE WORLD PHOTOS

was founded in London in 1961, publicizes the plight of people who are oppressed by their governments, regardless of political point of view. When the Sagan family moved to suburban Atherton, California, in 1968, Sagan founded the first Amnesty International chapter in the western United States. Until then, all eighteen chapters had been in the East. During the early and mid-1970s, Sagan was instrumental in establishing seventy-five Amnesty International chapters in the western United States.

Sagan served on the national board of AIUSA from 1973 to 1976 and from 1983 to 1987. She founded the Aurora Foundation in 1981 to provide support to the families of political prisoners. Its report on the abuse of human rights in Vietnam from 1975 to 1988 is an important document that led to the release of more than six hundred prisoners who had been in "reeducation" camps, in which the communists who ruled the country sentenced their former political rivals to hard labor and forced them to undergo political indoctrination.

Over the years, Sagan supported the Solidarity movement in Poland, opposed the military government in Greece in 1971, helped reveal the activities of the Central

Intelligence Agency in the 1973 coup in Chile, and worked to secure the release of prisoners in the Czech Republic, including the playwright Vaclav Havel, who later became the country's president. In 1990 she spoke out against the Iraqi leader Saddam Hussein, and she campaigned on behalf of apartheid victims in South Africa. For her activism, she was harassed on a number of occasions and received many death threats. In 1987, while in Poland, her car lost its steering and turned over; she was seriously hurt. This incident is believed to have been a deliberate attempt to silence her.

In 1994 Amnesty International established the Ginetta Sagan Fund and Award for those who campaign against the maltreatment of women and children. Women in such countries as Bhutan, Peru, Rwanda, Pakistan, and Afghanistan have received awards of $10,000 from the fund. Sagan's work resulted in honors over the years, including the Italo-American Woman of the Year (1980), the Jefferson Award (1987), the Albert Schweitzer Award of Distinction (1990), the Grande Ufficiale del Merito della Repubblica Italiana (1996), and the Presidential Medal of Freedom (1996).

Sagan was afflicted with cancer in the latter half of the 1990s. After undergoing surgery and chemotherapy, she decided not to take further treatment but to devote her remaining time to working for Amnesty International. She succumbed to pancreatic cancer at the age of seventy-seven and was cremated. A tireless activist on behalf of those unjustly imprisoned and tortured, Sagan was essential to the establishment of Amnesty International on the West Coast. She once said, "silence in the face of injustice is complicity with the oppressor."

★

Mary Peace Finley, *The Matchbox* (1995), a children's biography, provides insight into Sagan's childhood. Many articles chronicle Sagan's activism, including Samuel Totten, ed., "Planting the Seeds of Freedom: An Interview with Ginetta Sagan," *Social Education* 49 (Sept. 1985): 465–469; Bill Billiter, "Rights Honoree Calls for Hussein Protest Recognition: Chapman College's Albert Schweitzer Award Recipient, a Former Nazi Prisoner, Asks the World to Denounce the Iraqi President's Human-Rights Abuses," *Los Angeles Times* (7 Sept. 1990); and Sam Whiting, "Ginetta Sagan—A Meddler in the Business of Human Rights—For Ginetta Sagan, Fighting the Abuses of the World's Governments Is Almost Second Nature: The Amnesty International Leader Has Been at It Since a Teenager in Mussolini's Italy," *San Francisco Chronicle* (4 Aug. 1996). Obituaries are in the *New York Times* (30 Aug. 2000) and the *Guardian* (14 Sept. 2000).

JENNIFER THOMPSON-FEUERHERD

SALMON, Wesley C(harles) (*b*. 9 August 1925 in Detroit, Michigan; *d*. 22 April 2001 in Madison County, Ohio), philosopher of science noted for his theories of scientific explanation and probability.

Salmon was the only child of Wallis Samuel Salmon, an engineer, and Ruth (Springer) Salmon, a homemaker. He studied at Wayne State University in Detroit in 1943 and 1944, and earned an M.A. at the University of Chicago in 1947. On 26 November 1949 he married Nancy Huston Pilson; they had one child.

In 1950 Salmon earned his Ph.D. at the University of California, Los Angeles (UCLA), studying under the philosopher Hans Reichenbach, whose ideas would have a profound influence on Salmon's future work and thought. Over the first quarter century of his career, Salmon worked as an instructor at UCLA (1950–1951), as an instructor and later assistant professor at Washington State College (1951–1954), as an assistant professor at Northwestern University (1954–1955), as an assistant professor and later associate professor at Brown University (1955–1963), and as Hanson Professor of the History and Philosophy of Science at Indiana University at Bloomington (1963–1973).

In the decades after World War II, the prevailing schools of thought in the philosophy of science were those of the logical positivists, such as Rudolf Carnap, and their close cousins, the logical empiricists, including Reichenbach. Both groups treated scientific knowledge as the only type of knowledge concerning facts and maintained that the choices scientists make in accepting certain theories over others could be explained in purely rational, even mathematical, terms.

Thomas Kuhn's *Structure of Scientific Revolutions* (1962) challenged these notions. According to Kuhn, scientists throughout history have supported theories not so much because of their demonstrated practical superiority, but often because of personal preferences or outright prejudices. When Salmon first read Kuhn's book, he once recalled, he was so flustered by the opening pages that he shut the book and did not return to it for some time. Later, however, he revisited the work and recognized the importance of the questions it raised.

Amidst this intellectual tempest, Salmon rose to an international position of influence for his effort to bridge the chasm between the Kuhnians, on the one hand, and the traditional view of science as a largely rational enterprise, on the other. His most important area of focus lay in the realm of scientific explanation, which at the time was dominated by the revered logical empiricist Carl G. Hempel.

According to Hempel, a truly scientific explanation is a correct deductive or inductive argument in which at least one premise is a general scientific "law" and which has as its conclusion the event to be explained. Hempel said explanations and predictions are "symmetric." To offer a crude example, wet streets can be explained by a recent rainfall; conversely, if one sees falling rain, then one can predict the streets will soon be wet. Philosophers began to doubt Hempel's "explanations-as-arguments model" when they realized it could be misused to justify absurd "explanations"—for instance, that a man failed to become pregnant because he took birth-control pills. Also, contrary to Hempel's dictum, some valid-sounding explanations are asymmetric. To cite a notorious example (offered by Sylvain Bromberger), the height of a flagpole explains the length of its shadow, but the length of the shadow does not explain the height of the flagpole.

In 1963, while teaching at Indiana, Salmon learned about the emerging criticisms of Hempel's models during conversation with the philosopher J. J. C. Smart and began to develop alternatives to Hempel's models. Salmon became a leading figure in the "causality" school of explanation, according to which a proper explanation must incorporate a "causal" account of the phenomenon to be explained. Thus, for example, the flagpole's height can be explained by the actions of the person who made it, not by the length of its shadow. Logical empiricists, following in a tradition established by the great eighteenth-century empiricist David Hume, had long resisted talk of "explanations"—even ones as seemingly self-evident as this. They feared that a penchant for explanation would allow the intrusion of metaphysical thinking or the attempt to assign explanations beyond what the facts warranted. Salmon attacked this problem by providing a careful analysis of physical causation.

Watching Kuhn and Hempel sharing the podium as "the most distinguished living advocates for their respective viewpoints" at a 1983 meeting of the American Philosophical Association's eastern division, Salmon was struck by the idea that a probability theorem developed by the eighteenth-century mathematician Thomas Bayes could be used to build a bridge between the two differing worldviews. Salmon's proposal reflected the spirit of his mentor, Reichenbach, who was a major advocate of a probabilistic approach to scientific logic. Salmon outlined his Bayesian approach to Kuhn in an essay, "Rationality and Objectivity in Science or Tom Kuhn Meets Tom Bayes." According to Salmon, rough numerical probabilities could be assigned to Kuhn's vague criteria for subjective theory choice, and thus it could be possible to show that a core of rationality existed in the processes by which scientists chose certain theories over others.

Divorced from his first wife in 1970, Salmon married Merrilee Hollenkamp Ashby, herself a scholar of philosophy and the social sciences, on 26 July 1971. The couple did not have children. Salmon spent the latter part of his career as a professor at the University of Arizona (1973–

1981) and at the University of Pittsburgh (1981–1999). A professor emeritus from 1999, he taught his last class at Kyoto University in 2000. He died from injuries sustained in a car accident at age seventy-five.

Salmon's books included *Logic* (1963); *Foundations of Scientific Inference* (1967); *Statistical Explanation and Statistical Relevance* (1971); *Space, Time, and Motion: A Philosophical Introduction* (1975); *Scientific Explanation and the Causal Structure of the World* (1984); *Four Decades of Scientific Explanation* (1990); and *Causality and Explanation* (1998). Another book, *Reality and Rationality,* was almost complete when he died. He was president of the Philosophy of Science Association (1971–1972), the Pacific division of the American Philosophical Association (1976–1977), and the International Union of History and Philosophy of Science (1998–1999).

★

In addition to Salmon's books, information on his work and ideas can be found in Robert McLaughlin, ed., *What? Where? When? Why?: Essays on Induction, Space and Time, Explanation: Inspired by the Work of Wesley C. Salmon and Celebrating His First Visit to Australia, September–December 1978* (1982); James H. Fetzer, ed., *Probability and Causality: Essays in Honor of Wesley C. Salmon* (1987); Maria Carla Galavotti and Alessandro Pagnini, eds., *Experience, Reality, and Scientific Explanation: Essays in Honor of Merrilee and Wesley Salmon* (1999); and Giora Hon and Sam S. Rakover, eds., *Explanation: Theoretical Approaches and Applications* (2001). An obituary is in the *New York Times* (4 May 2001).

KEAY DAVIDSON

SAWHILL, John Crittenden (*b.* 12 June 1936 in Cleveland, Ohio; *d.* 18 May 2000 in Richmond, Virginia), energy official under the administrations of presidents Richard M. Nixon, Gerald R. Ford, and Jimmy Carter; twelfth president of New York University; and president and chief executive officer of the Nature Conservancy.

Sawhill was the eldest of four children born to James Mumford Sawhill and Mary (Gipe) Sawhill. His family moved to Baltimore, where he attended private elementary and secondary schools. He earned his B.A. in 1958 from the Woodrow Wilson School of Public and International Affairs at Princeton University, graduating cum laude. Also in 1958, on 13 September, Sawhill married Isabel ("Belle") Van Devanter, the granddaughter of Willis Van Devanter, an associate justice on the U.S. Supreme Court from 1910 to 1937. The Sawhills had one son.

Upon graduating from Princeton, Sawhill moved to New York City, where he worked for Merrill, Lynch, Piece, Fenner, and Smith. Then, in 1960, Sawhill enrolled in the graduate school of business administration at New York University (NYU), where he also taught introductory economics and statistics and worked as the assistant to the dean. In this position Sawhill was responsible for the process governing admission and for coordinating the development of a new master of business administration (M.B.A.) program. Sawhill received his Ph.D. in economics, finance, and statistics in 1963 and soon afterward went to work as director of credit and research planning for the Commercial Credit Company in Baltimore. In 1965 he joined the management-consulting firm of McKinsey and Company in Washington, D.C. In 1968 Sawhill rejoined the Commercial Credit Company as vice president in charge of planning and a year later became senior vice president. From 1971 to 1973 he was a member of the five-man executive office, which had overall responsibility for managing the company.

Sawhill began his career in government in 1973, when he was named associate director for natural resources, energy, and science in the Office of Budget and Management. At the end of the year, he became deputy administrator, under William Simon, of the newly created Federal Energy Office, helping expand the staff from two hundred to more than three thousand employees in just sixty days. Sawhill came to national prominence in April 1974, when he was appointed federal energy administrator and presided over the development of Project Independence, a government-wide plan aimed at moving the United States toward energy self-sufficiency. In this post Sawhill exhorted Americans to lower thermostats and turn down air conditioners. He also advocated a policy of higher fuel prices and faster licensing of atomic power plants. However, after an appearance on the national news program *Face the Nation,* in which he endorsed a steep gasoline tax and criticized the administration for not developing a fully conceived energy plan, he had to resign his post under pressure from President Ford.

In 1975 Sawhill returned to NYU to become the university's twelfth president, the only alumnus to hold that position. Sawhill took over the university amid a severe budget crisis, sagging enrollment figures, and low staff and faculty morale. During his tenure, which ended in 1979, he led a huge fund-raising drive, collecting over $150 million in gifts. The educational efforts of Sawhill, who was named one of the 100 most respected emerging leaders in higher education in 1978, led Edward B. Fiske, the education editor of the Sunday *New York Times,* to observe that he had "engineered perhaps the most dramatic rescue operation in the history of American education. . . . NYU now has a balanced budget, a substantial endowment, growing enrollment, and high faculty morale."

Sawhill returned to government in 1979, when he went to work as deputy energy secretary under President Carter. He then became chairman and chief executive of the United States Synthetic Fuels Corporation, a government-

John C. Sawhill, September 1974. BETTMANN/CORBIS

sponsored energy company. After President Ronald Reagan took office in 1981, Sawhill returned to the private sector as director of McKinsey and Company, focusing on national and international energy issues, including conservation and exploration of new energy sources.

In 1990 Sawhill embarked on a new challenge as president and chief executive officer of the Nature Conservancy. An admirer of the ecologist and nature writer Aldo Leopold's land ethic, which stressed an active human role in the natural world, Sawhill distinguished himself as a conservationist. He maintained that business had a central role in righting the environmental wrongs it had helped create. In a published speech made to the Business Council on 11 May 1990, titled "How to Think About the Environment: The Impact of New Behavior," Sawhill reasoned that business must rethink its defensive environmental stance, suggesting that business opportunities awaited those who embraced an environmental approach. He also held that economic development was essential for curing environmental ills. "I believe," Sawhill wrote, "that we will never be successful in cleaning up the environment unless we have sustained real growth in per capita income."

Under Sawhill's leadership, the Nature Conservancy

bought or brokered sales that protected approximately seven million acres in the United States, raised more than $315 million under the conservancy's Last Great Places campaign (the largest campaign in the history of the conservation movement), doubled its membership to 1.1 million people, and oversaw a threefold increase in the conservancy workforce to more than three thousand. Sawhill often told audiences that "the fundamental way that we protect the environment, frankly, is to buy it," and while the core mission of the conservancy was to protect land and water habitats by purchasing them, under Sawhill's leadership it took broader approaches to environmental conservation. For example, when the Nature Conservancy purchased a string of fourteen barrier islands off the coast of Virginia near lower Chesapeake Bay, the project also steered resources toward economic development on the mainland that promoted environmentally friendly businesses, organic farming, and sustainable fisheries, while controlling coastal development. Like the conservancy's approach that protected ecosystems, Sawhill's conservation ethic expressed an acute understanding of the interconnectedness between economic development and land conservation.

Sawhill's nonprofit leadership served to underscore his legacy as a managerial innovator. In the latter capacity, he shared his wisdom with students as a senior lecturer at the Harvard Business School from 1997 until his death. After launching the conservancy's $1 billion fund-raising campaign, the largest effort in the history of private conservation, Sawhill died of complications from diabetes at the Medical College of Virginia in Richmond.

During his life Sawhill was an avid runner and, as NYU president, was a fixture of the Washington Square Park jogging community. He was equally active intellectually, maintaining a vigorous curiosity that enabled him to bridge the widening gap between business interests and environmental concerns. As an advocate for developing new energy sources, a tireless campaigner for environmental and energy conservation, and a free-market champion, Sawhill was one of the leading and most provocative environmental intellectuals of the late twentieth century.

★

Additional information on Sawhill is in the New York University Archives' John Sawhill Collection. A memorial tribute is "Remembering John Sawhill 1936–2000," *Nature Conservancy* (Sept./Oct. 2000): 6–7. An obituary is in the *New York Times* (20 May 2000).

DAVID KINKELA

SCHAAP, Richard Jay ("Dick") (*b.* 27 September 1934 in Brooklyn, New York City; *d.* 21 December 2001 in Manhattan, New York City), sports reporter, author, editor, and television and radio broadcaster.

Schaap was born into a Jewish household in the Flatbush neighborhood in Brooklyn. His father, Maurice William Schaap, was a graduate of Cornell University and a salesman; his mother, Leah (Lerner) Schaap, a homemaker, earned her master's degree in her forties and became a French teacher. The oldest of three children, Schaap was six when his parents moved the family to Freeport, Long Island.

By age twelve, the precocious Schaap wanted to be a sportswriter. As a high school junior, he worked toward that goal by writing a weekly sports column for the *Freeport Leader* and serving as a sports reporter at the *Nassau Daily Review-Star* under the direction of the twenty-year-old deputy sports editor Jimmy Breslin, who would go on to an equally impressive career in journalism.

After graduating from high school in 1951, Schaap followed his father's footsteps at Cornell University, where he cultivated his interest in sports by playing as a goalie on the varsity lacrosse team. He also joined the Reserve Officers Training Corps. Most significantly, he continued his pursuit of journalism by becoming the editor of the student newspaper, the *Cornell Daily Sun*. In 1955 Schaap graduated with a B.S. in industrial and labor relations.

Dick Schaap, January 2001. AP/WIDE WORLD PHOTOS

The following fall, Schaap entered the Columbia Graduate School of Journalism as a Grantland Rice Fellow. He distinguished himself when *Sports Illustrated* published his article on the tawdry aspects of recruiting elite high school basketball players in New York City. Outside the classroom, Schaap displayed an impressive work ethic by cobbling together three part-time jobs at the *Long Island Press*, the *New York Times*, and Columbia University, where he served as assistant sports information director. Schaap graduated from Columbia in 1956 with an M.S. in journalism.

From 1956 to 1963 Schaap worked at *Newsweek*, where ability and ambition drove him quickly up the ranks. During these years, the young writer honed his craft at the feet of master sports journalists such as Roger Kahn. In this bygone era when athletes and sportswriters still frequently socialized together, Schaap's engaging personality enabled him to forge close relationships with prominent athletes such as the boxer Cassius Clay (later known as Muhammad Ali). In 1960 he moved from assistant sports editor to sports editor. Soon thereafter he advanced to general editor before becoming the youngest senior editor in the magazine's history. By the time Schaap left *Newsweek* in 1963, he had demonstrated that he was as comfortable covering stories about the comedian Lenny Bruce or the civil rights movement as he was handling sports. He also had established credibility as a free-lance writer and published the first three books in a prolific writing career that ultimately would include thirty-four volumes.

In 1964 Schaap joined the *New York Herald Tribune*, serving briefly as city editor before becoming a full-time columnist. Schaap relished his time with the *Tribune*, where he introduced the term "Fun City" to describe New York City and worked with practitioners of the pathbreaking New Journalism such as Tom Wolfe and Breslin. However, with the *Herald Tribune* folding and its successor, the *World Journal Tribune*, at the brink of extinction, Schaap left in 1967 to write a book on Robert F. Kennedy.

Over his career, Schaap developed a reputation for being "king of the ghostwriters." In 1968 he published *Instant Replay*, an exposé on professional football based on the diary of the Green Bay Packer Jerry Kramer. Written in the "as told to" genre, it was at the time the best-selling sports book ever published. In 1969 he formed his own publishing company, Maddick Manuscripts, which published several sports books before going defunct. Undeterred by this setback, Schaap eventually wrote twelve different "autobiographies" about famous athletes, including ones about the gay Olympian Tom Waddell and the two-sport star Bo Jackson.

In the late 1960s the raspy-voiced Schaap began a lengthy career as a versatile television and radio broadcaster. He had an affable personality, a self-deprecating wit, and a breadth of knowledge that allowed him to feel comfortable with topics ranging from sports to entertainment to politics. After ghostwriting Joe Namath's autobiography in 1969, he joined the star quarterback as a cohost on the *Joe Namath Show,* where the two interviewed guests from sports and show business. In 1971 Schaap joined the National Broadcasting Company (NBC), where he delivered local sports reports for WNBC television in New York City. In time, his responsibilities grew and included national programming with his own baseball show, football show, and contributions on the *Nightly News* and *Today* show. The indefatigable Schaap, uncomfortable with having only one job, also served as editor for *SPORT* from 1972 to 1976.

In 1980 Schaap joined the American Broadcasting Company (ABC), where he worked under the innovative executive Roone Arledge. In addition to sports coverage, Schaap contributed stories to the network's *World News Tonight* and news magazine *20/20*. In 1989 he became the host of ESPN's *Sports Reporters* and helped turn the fledgling show into a sports institution. In the 1990s his duties continued to expand: hosting ESPN Classic's *Schaap One on One,* working as a theater critic on ABC's *World News Tonight,* and cohosting with his son Jeremy a weekly ESPN radio show called *The Sporting Life with Dick Schaap.* Over the course of his broadcasting career, Schaap won six Emmys, including one for reporting on the comedian Sid Caesar's struggles with drugs and alcohol and another on Waddell's battle with acquired immunodeficiency syndrome (AIDS).

Late in his career, appearances on television and in a few films made Schaap a celebrity. Surprised by his own stardom, Schaap put it in perspective by joking that people would come up to him and say, "I know you. Who are you?" Schaap recognized that his appeal was not his own status but his connection to larger stars. His autobiography, *Flashing Before My Eyes* (2001), reflects this sentiment. Indeed, Schaap's great strength was that he tried to keep the people he covered more important than himself.

On 20 June 1956 Schaap married Barbara M. Barron. Schaap and Barron divorced in 1967. Schaap married Madeleine Gottlieb on 29 August 1967. They divorced in 1980. Schaap married his third wife, Patricia Ann McLeod, on 17 May 1981. He had six children—two with each of his wives. He died from complications following hip replacement surgery at the age of sixty-seven. His body was cremated and his remains scattered at a few locations of significance to him.

★

Schaap's autobiography, *Flashing Before My Eyes: Fifty Years of Headlines, Datelines and Punchlines, by Dick Schaap as Told to Dick Schaap* (2001), is by far the best source on Schaap's life. An obituary is in the *New York Times* (22 Dec. 2001).

ALAN BLOOM

SCHINDLER, Alexander Moshe (*b.* 4 October 1925 in Munich, Germany; *d.* 15 November 2000 in Westport, Connecticut), Reform rabbi and longtime president of the Union of American Hebrew Congregations, the umbrella organization of North America's Reform Jews.

Schindler was one of two children born to Eliezer Schindler and Sali (Hoyda) Schindler. His father, who had roots among the German *Hassidim,* was a Yiddish author of religious and romantic poetry and worked as a journalist and editor for *Agudath Israel,* a devoutly orthodox Jewish organization. The family fled Germany in 1932, just before the Nazis took power, and after sojourns in Italy and France, arrived in the United States in 1938. Hoping to become an engineer, Schindler enrolled at City College of New York (CCNY), but his studies were interrupted by World War II. He joined the U.S. Army and served as a ski trooper in an Alpine patrol, earning three combat ribbons for bravery as well as a Purple Heart and a Bronze Star. At the end of the war, he searched for surviving relatives in Germany, ending up at the concentration camp at Dachau, where some of them had perished.

By the time he returned home, Schindler's career goals had shifted. He graduated from CCNY in 1950 with a bachelor's degree in social science. His 1949 honors thesis in history, *From Discrimination to Extermination,* a study of the German government's anti-Jewish policies from 1933 to 1945, was published in 1950. He received a bachelor's degree in Hebrew literature from the Jewish Institute of Religion at Hebrew Union College in 1951, a master's degree in Hebrew literature from the Jewish Institute in 1952, and rabbinic ordination in 1953.

Schindler served at Temple Emanuel in Worcester, Massachusetts, as assistant rabbi (1953–1956) and associate rabbi (1956–1959). During this time, he also served as director of the B'nai B'rith Hillel Foundation at Clark University and at Worcester Polytechnic Institute, both located in Worcester.

In 1956 Schindler met Rhea Rosenblum and proposed marriage to her that night. Three months later, on 29 September 1956, they were married. They had five children.

In 1959 Schindler moved on to direct the New England Federation of Reform Temples of the Union of American Hebrew Congregations (UAHC), simultaneously serving as literary editor of the *CCAR Journal,* the publication of the Central Conference of American Rabbis (CCAR). In 1963 he became director of education for the UAHC in New York, where he also led the Joint Commission on Jewish Education of the UAHC and the CCAR. He became founding editor of *Dimensions,* a Reform Jewish quarterly of religious thought, in 1966. From 1963 to 1967 he edited a pioneering series of Reform Jewish textbooks.

Elevated to the vice presidency of the UAHC in 1967,

Schindler assumed the presidency in 1973, becoming the leader of a denomination of some eight hundred congregations with 1.25 million members, more than one-third of the affiliated Jews in North America. At age forty-seven Schindler was one of the youngest men ever to head a major American religious organization. Drawing on his family's poetic heritage, he composed his consecration sermon in blank verse.

As president of the UAHC, Schindler sought to enrich Reform Judaism with some of the tradition, emotion, and ritual abandoned by earlier generations of Reform Jews. At the same time, he challenged some long-held beliefs. For example, in 1978 he created a furor by spearheading the acceptance of patrilineal descent in the definition of what makes a person Jewish. For centuries, Jews considered a child Jewish only if his or her mother was a Jew, but Schindler advocated accepting as Jews the children of Jewish fathers and non-Jewish mothers, as long as they had been raised as Jews. The CCAR officially recognized patrilineal descent in 1983, a move criticized by more traditional Jews.

Schindler further defied tradition by advocating outreach (not proselytization) to the unchurched, the intermarried, and those who had ceased to be practicing Jews. These initiatives were a response to disturbing statistics. Fully half of American Jews were marrying outside the faith, and Schindler was seeking to stem the tide. Going one step further, he reached out to gay and lesbian Jews, urging that they be welcomed by Reform Judaism as both congregants and clergy. He also encouraged the idea of women becoming Reform rabbis, the first one having been ordained the year before he became president of the UAHC.

Beyond reaching out to those on the fringes of the Reform movement, Schindler admonished those within his flock that they should set a better example of religious commitment. "Reform Judaism by its very nature has accorded a good deal of authority to the individual," he said. "The tragedy is that too many Reform Jews at every level have seized on this right to opt to do nothing." He urged greater observance of the Sabbath both at home and in the sanctuary.

In 1976 Schindler became the first Reform Jew to be elected president of the Conference of Presidents of Major American Jewish Organizations (CPMAJO), a coalition of leading religious and secular groups. Although widely assumed to be a dove on Middle Eastern politics because of his position as the head of the liberal Reform movement, Schindler, who believed that unity on Israel's behalf was critical, embraced the leadership of the hawkish Israeli prime minister Menachem Begin. He and Begin eventually became close friends.

Schindler, who remained president of the UAHC until 1996, was involved with numerous other Jewish organiza-

Alexander M. Schindler, 1982. DAVID RUBINGER/CORBIS

tions during the remainder of his life. He served on the executive boards of CPMAJO (1967–1996) and the Hebrew Union College–Jewish Institute of Religion (1967–2000). He was a member of the executive committees of the World Zionist Organization (1973–2000) and the Join Distribution Committee (1987–2000) and a vice president of the Memorial Foundation for Jewish Culture (1967–2000). In addition, he maintained a busy schedule of speaking engagements at conferences and congregations throughout the United States.

Schindler was a heavyset silver-haired man of great personal warmth, and his European accent and frequent use of Yiddish phrases in conversation projected a very traditional persona. Rabbi Eric Yoffie, who succeeded Schindler as president of the UAHC in 1996, noted that "this most reformed of reformers . . . a promoter of dramatic change, was also someone who was seen as possessing . . . [a] Jewish soul. . . . That's what made him so acceptable in the general community. It gave him a measure of credibility."

Rabbi Arthur Hertzberg, a leader of Conservative Judaism who disagreed profoundly with Schindler on many issues, said of him, "He knew the secret of how to disagree, very fundamentally, without being disagreeable. Alex Schindler had many critics—but he had no enemies." Once asked to give his own thoughts on life, Schindler wrote, "To live life fully, clinging to its many gifts with all my might and then, paradoxically, to let go when life compels us to surrender what it gave."

He died of a heart attack at his home in Westport, Connecticut, and is buried there.

★

Correspondence with Schindler can be found in the papers of Irvin Fane in the National Union Catalog Manuscript Collection, Library of Congress, Washington, D.C. A short memorial tribute is in the *Christian Century* (6 Dec. 2000). Obituaries are in the *New York Times* and *Washington Post* (16 Nov. 2000).

NATALIE B. JALENAK

SCHULZ, Charles Monroe (*b.* 26 November 1922 in Minneapolis, Minnesota; *d.* 12 February 2000 in Santa Rosa, California), the most successful cartoonist of his time and the creator of the comic strip *Peanuts,* which, at its height, was the most widely syndicated cartoon strip in history

Schulz was the only son of Carl Schulz and Dena (Halverson) Schulz, a devoted and hardworking couple, neither of whom had progressed beyond the third grade. His father was a barber in Saint Paul, Minnesota, and his mother was a homemaker. An uncle nicknamed the boy "Sparky," after Spark Plug, a horse in the "Barney Google" comic.

Young Schulz proved to be a superior student. At Saint Paul's Richard Gordon Elementary School, he was selected as the outstanding boy student in the second grade and was skipped ahead by half-grades in the third and fifth grades, an achievement that would backfire on the timid youngster. When he entered junior high, he was the youngest and smallest boy in his class, covering his loneliness and insecurity by becoming stubborn and sensitive to life's injus-

Charles M. Schulz, 1981. AP/WIDE WORLD PHOTOS

tices. By the time he entered Saint Paul Central High School, Schultz was a skinny, 136-pound teen who regarded himself as plain and unattractive. He had difficulty making friends and felt invisible. "I never regarded myself as being much and I never regarded myself as being good-looking and I never had a date in high school, because I thought, 'Who'd want to date me?'" he recalled years later.

His lifelong catalog of rejections began to be compiled at Central. He would cite to the end of his days that the editors of the school yearbook, the *Cehisean,* rejected his drawings, even though a sketch of his dog was published in 1937 in the syndicated strip "Ripley's Believe It or Not."

Schultz graduated from Central in 1940 and took up art courses at Federal Schools, later named Art Instruction Schools. He was drafted into the U.S. Army as a private in 1943, about the time his mother was diagnosed with colon cancer. He was twenty when she died in February 1943 at age forty-eight. He was still in despair three days later when he boarded a train for Camp Campbell, Kentucky, and during World War II, where he served as a machine-gun squad leader in France, Germany, and Austria. "The Army taught me all I needed to know about loneliness," he wrote in later years. The secure nest his parents' home represented to him was forever gone, a loss he would grieve for the rest of his life.

After the war, Schultz returned to Saint Paul and began teaching at Art Instruction Schools. In 1947 he sold his first comics—a weekly series of single-panel cartoons about kids called "Li'l Folks"—to the *Saint Paul Pioneer Press.* In 1948 one of his cartoons was published in the *Saturday Evening Post.*

After an editor at the *Pioneer Press* told Schulz that he could not have a raise and that "Li'l Folks" would not be moved from the back page of the women's section to the comics pages, he quit drawing for the paper and tried to interest syndicates in a four-panel strip about children. After numerous rejections, United Feature Syndicate bought the idea but decreed that it needed a new name. The syndicate decided to call it "Peanuts," contemporary slang for children, a title that Schulz forever loathed as undignified. United Features paid Schulz $90 for the first month of strips, and on 2 October 1950 *Peanuts* debuted in seven newspapers. The first strip showed a boy named Shermy saying, "There goes good old Charlie Brown," as a round-headed kid passed. "How I hate him," Shermy said in the final panel.

Shy, unassuming, and incurably melancholy, Schulz sketched a world of childhood cruelty leavened with slapstick gags, a suburban realm where kids philosophized with an adult consciousness and a beagle took flights of fancy atop his doghouse. *Peanuts* became the world's most successful comic strip, one that yielded two famous figures: Charlie Brown and his dog, Snoopy. Nonetheless, professional success never erased the intricate pain at Schulz's core, which bled through into the cartoons he crafted with crow-quill pens dabbed into an inkwell. Schulz once said that he based the initial theme of *Peanuts* on the cruelty that exists among children: "I recall all too vividly the struggle that takes place out on the playground. This is a struggle that adults grow away from and seem to forget about."

Schulz never forgot. To the end of his days, he could recite the many slights and disappointments that had beset him: the redheaded woman who spurned his proposal for marriage, the uncaring editor who let one of his early cartoons die rather than give a token raise. He was burdened with feelings of inferiority, anxiety, and depression. Through Charlie Brown, he espoused a brooding Scandinavian stoicism in which the pursuit of triumph led to doom. Craig Schulz, the cartoonist's son, said in a 2000 interview that Schulz used his depression as a tool. He noted that his father tried not to let his depression control his life, "but if it wasn't for the depression, he wouldn't have drawn the cartoons for fifty years and gotten some of the ideas he did."

Schulz married Joyce Halverson on 18 April 1951. They moved to Colorado Springs, Colorado, but Schulz did not like it there, and after a year they returned to Saint Paul. The couple had five children.

The first Sunday *Peanuts* strip was published on 6 January 1952, and later that year the characters Lucy and Linus were introduced. Pig Pen, the archetypal messy kid, arrived in 1954, and Linus took up his security blanket—a term that would be added to American slang and eventually to dictionaries—on 1 June 1954.

By this time, the *Peanuts* characters were developing stronger personalities. Lucy, modeled after Schulz's bossy daughter Meredith, became a fussbudget and crabby know-it-all. Lucy soon fell for Schroeder, a piano prodigy, and spent her days leaning on his piano, dreamily listening to him play Beethoven while he ignored her. Schulz's favorite composer was Brahms, but he decided to go with Beethoven for Schroeder's music because, he acknowledged, "Brahms just isn't funny."

By 1955 the strip was gathering momentum and growing in popularity. It hit a benchmark of 100 newspapers, and Schulz was honored with the Reuben Award, the highest honor of the National Cartoonists Society. The following year would see the invention of two running gags in the strip, both reflecting the hapless ordeals that ever shrouded Charlie Brown. On 12 April 1956 Charlie Brown ran afoul of a kite-eating tree, and on 16 December, Lucy pulled the football away just as Charlie Brown was about to kick it. For the next four decades, Lucy would offer to hold the football every autumn and then pull it away, testing, and ultimately betraying, Charlie Brown's faith.

In 1958 the Schulz family moved to Sebastopol, California, and the *Peanuts* gang went into merchandizing, a move that made the cartoonist a millionaire. Soon the characters were on plastic dolls and greeting cards, and selling Ford Falcons. In the years to come, *Peanuts* characters were licensed on more than 20,000 products. The strip also had begun to present understated satire on contemporary life. As psychology enjoyed a renaissance in the 1950s, Lucy began dispensing tough-love advice from her lemonade-stand-style kiosk with the sign "Psychiatric Help 5 Cents."

In 1959 Charlie Brown acquired a sister, Sally, and Linus acquired a legendary idol, the Great Pumpkin, a specter said to rise from the pumpkin patch each Halloween night to distribute toys to children. This commentary on the commercialization of Christmas began with Charlie Brown's ridiculing the idea of the autumn spirit. "All right, so you believe in Santa Claus and I'll believe in the 'Great Pumpkin,'" Linus said. "The way I see it, it doesn't matter what you believe just so you're sincere." Linus waited in the pumpkin patch each fall, in vain, falling asleep before the phantom could appear.

In 1961 Schulz invented an unseen, unnamed character known only as the Little Red-Haired Girl, the object of Charlie Brown's unrequited adoration. She was based on Donna Mae Johnson, a woman who turned down his proposal of marriage. Throughout the life of the strip, Charlie Brown struggled to summon the courage to talk to the girl but could only admire from afar. One day he mused what

would happen if he walked over and asked her to eat lunch with him. "She'd probably laugh in my face," he decided. "It's hard on a face when it gets laughed in."

One of the most popular of all *Peanuts* books was published in 1962, *Happiness Is a Warm Puppy*. It was a collection of single-panel cartoons that illustrated simple delights. One panel had Snoopy sitting on the doghouse with two birds. "Happiness is getting together with your friends," the caption said. The book shot onto the *New York Times* best-seller list in 1962 and was number one for forty-five weeks.

In 1964 Schulz became the first cartoonist to win the Reuben Award for a second time. By then, his characters had so permeated the national conscience that they became instructional models for the book *The Gospel According to Peanuts* (1965), by Robert L. Short, a Methodist minister. It was one of many philosophical interpretations of the strip, and although Schulz publicly disagreed with some of Short's points, the two men became friends.

A Charlie Brown Christmas first aired on the Columbia Broadcasting System (CBS) on 9 December 1965, with a jazz soundtrack and Linus reading a Bible passage from the book of Luke, explaining the Christmas story. The show played to huge ratings and won two Emmy Awards in 1966, one for outstanding children's program and the other a special "classifications of individual achievements" award for Schultz. Other Peanuts specials followed—*Charlie Brown's All-Stars* and *It's the Great Pumpkin, Charlie Brown*, both in 1966. In 1967 *Peanuts* went off-Broadway with the play *You're a Good Man, Charlie Brown*. A narcoleptic underachiever named Peppermint Patty joined the strip that year and introduced racial diversity to *Peanuts* when she brought a Hispanic kid from her neighborhood named Jose Peterson to play second base on Charlie Brown's team. His tenure lasted only a week, but in 1968 Franklin, the first black character, arrived. Integrating a comic strip was such a radical idea at the time that his appearance merited an article in *Newsweek* magazine.

In 1969 a feature movie was made called *A Boy Named Charlie Brown*, but the real measure of the strip's popularity came not in Hollywood but in outer space; Apollo X astronauts named their command capsule "Charlie Brown" and their lunar module "Snoopy."

Schulz had reached the pinnacle of his profession. He was the highest paid, most widely read cartoonist in history. He was earning more than $30 million a year, and his characters had cut a swath across culture and commerce. But his home life was suffering. He and Joyce Schulz had long grown apart. She was outgoing, eager for adventure and travel; he panicked aboard jetliners and suffered anxiety attacks in hotels. They divorced in 1972, and the following year, Schulz married Jean Forsyth Clyde.

Peanuts was picked up by its two-thousandth newspaper

in 1984, and in 1990 the Louvre museum in Paris hosted an exhibition of Schulz's art. The cast had grown to include Marcie, a formally polite sidekick who addressed Peppermint Patty as "Sir"; Snoopy's bohemian brother Spike, named for Schulz's boyhood dog; and Woodstock, Snoopy's flighty bird pal. Schulz gave often to charity, including a $1 million donation toward construction of a D-day memorial in Virginia.

At its height, Schulz's strip was the most widely syndicated in history, appearing in newspapers with a combined readership of 355 million people. His characters appeared on television, on Broadway, on blimps, and in books, and they even went to the Moon. They became part of the American psyche and were exported in dozens of languages. But Schulz's health began to decline. In November 1999 he was diagnosed with colon cancer, which spread to his stomach. Strokes left his vision and speech impaired. On 14 December 1999 he announced that he was retiring. Schulz had never employed assistants to draw the cartoon, and when he quit, he said that *Peanuts* would end. The last fresh daily strip ran on 3 January 2000.

He died in his sleep at home at age seventy-seven as newspapers containing the final Sunday *Peanuts* strip were on the press. The strip had a letter from Schulz thanking his fans for their support through the years and was surrounded by indelible *Peanuts* images—Snoopy on his doghouse, and Lucy pulling the football away from Charlie Brown. Schulz is buried in Pleasant Hills Cemetery in Sebastopol, California.

Posthumous honors include the Milton Caniff Lifetime Achievement Award from the National Cartoonists Society, a Congressional Gold Medal, and a U.S. Postal Service stamp featuring Snoopy as the Flying Ace. *Peanuts* did not die but lived on, like classic television shows, in reruns. Newspapers kept running old strips distributed by the syndicate, and readers ranked it among their favorites in periodic surveys, a reflection of the timeless, personal themes the strip embodied.

People asked Schulz why he could not have Charlie Brown kick the football. Schulz responded, "Well, I could. It would make him happy. And happiness is neat. I wish we could all be happy. But unfortunately, happiness is not very funny."

★

Rheta Grimsley Johnson, *Good Grief: The Story of Charles M. Schulz* (1989), is regarded as the best biography of the cartoonist. Other biographical sources include M. Thomas Inge, ed., *Charles M. Schulz: Conversations* (2000), and Michael A. Schuman, *People to Know: Charles M. Schulz: Cartoonist and Creator of Peanuts* (2002). Obituaries are in the *San Francisco Chronicle* and *Los Angeles Times* (both 14 Feb. 2000).

Mark Washburn

SCOTT, Roland Boyd (*b.* 18 April 1909 in Houston, Texas; *d.* 10 December 2002 in Washington, D.C.), African-American pediatrician, allergist, researcher, educator, and devoted champion in the fight against sickle cell anemia, for which he gained international acclaim and became known as the "father" of research into the disease.

Scott was the son of Ernest John Scott and Cordie (Clark) Scott, a nurse. He graduated from high school in Kansas City, Missouri, and earned his B.S. in 1931 and his M.D. in 1934, both from Howard University in Washington, D.C. On 24 June 1935 he married Sarah Rosetta Weaver; their union lasted until her death in 1969. The couple had three children. After a year as an intern at the Kansas City General Hospital, Scott fulfilled his pediatric residency at Provident Hospital in Chicago and was a fellow in pediatrics at the University of Chicago Children's Memorial Hospital and the Chicago Municipal Hospital for Contagious Diseases from 1936 to 1939. During that time he became board certified in allergy and immunology and in pediatrics.

In 1939 Scott returned to Howard as assistant professor of pediatrics, focusing his research primarily on childhood allergic disorders. He became chief of the Division of Pediatrics in 1945 and served as chair of the Department of Pediatrics from 1949 to 1973. He was professor of pediatrics from 1952 to 1977 and became distinguished professor of pediatrics and child health in 1977, a position he held until he retired in 1990. In 1950–1951 he took a twelve-month sabbatical to study at the Institute of Allergy at Roosevelt Hospital in New York City. Owing to his growing reputation in sickle cell research in the 1950s, he became one of the first black physicians granted privileges at such institutions as Children's and Providence Hospitals in Washington, D.C., during an era when there was an unwritten ban by many hospitals against black doctors.

While continuing his teaching and research duties at Howard, Scott studied pediatric dermatology at the Skin and Cancer Hospital from 1956 to 1959. He also maintained a private practice. "He was an academic by day and a physician who had office hours every night, and he even made house calls," commented Dr. Duane R. Bonds, who headed the Sickle Cell Disease Scientific Research Group at the National Heart, Lung, and Blood Institute (NHLBI).

Scott's interest in sickle cell anemia began when he became aware of how many children were being admitted to Howard University Hospital with symptoms now known to be caused by the disease. Although he had not trained as a hematologist, he plunged headlong into researching the painful genetic blood disorder, characterized by unusual red blood cells shaped like sickles. The disease occurs primarily in black people of African descent but also is found in people of South American, Arab, and Mediterranean descent. Although James B. Herrick of Chicago first described the disease in western literature in 1910, there was a lack of interest, research, and funding devoted to it, because it affected primarily African Americans. In 1970 in the United States, 1,155 new cases of the disease were recorded, while research funding totaled just $50,000. In comparison, new cases of muscular dystrophy totaled 813, and research funding exceeded $7,900,000.

During the 1960s and 1970s, in particular, considerable political and medical controversy surrounded the disproportionate attention the disease received. "Sickle cell was not a popular subject because of about 350 years of white brainwashing," Scott told a *Washington Post* reporter in 1972. "Black people were taught to look down on practically everything that was part of their heritage." Although his achievements in researching the disease and lobbying for research funding were major, Scott believed that one of his most important contributions was in helping blacks understand that they were not the only ones affected by the disease. After Scott's death, Dr. George Dover, professor and chair of the Department of Pediatrics at Johns Hopkins Hospital in Baltimore, said that Scott "treated individuals, not the disease. In particular he constantly reminded me to pay attention to the social and emotional implications of sickle cell on each patient and their family."

One of Scott's biggest challenges was convincing the U.S. government of the need for research funds. Dr. Wendell F. Rosse of Duke University Medical Center in Durham, North Carolina, commented on Scott's "relentless advocacy for sickle cell disease and for the rightful place of those of African descent in American life." Scott's lobbying culminated in Congress's passing the Sickle Cell Anemia Control Act of 1971. His efforts were largely responsible for legislation authorizing the establishment of several comprehensive centers for the disease as part of the NHLBI of the National Institutes of Health. The act provided funding for those centers. With his grant, Scott established Howard's Center for Sickle Cell Disease in 1972, of which he remained director until he retired. When federal funding began to diminish near the end of the 1970s, Scott commented, "Interest in sickle cell, like other major diseases, is like the latest hairstyles, fashions and dances—it goes in cycles."

Scott died at Washington Adventist Hospital from congestive heart failure at age ninety-three. Over the course of his career, he wrote more than three hundred articles on sickle cell disease, allergy, and childhood growth and development. He established the first growth and development norms for African-American children and conducted genetic research into thalassemia, a disorder of hemoglobin metabolism seen in several types of anemia among people of African and Mediterranean descent. A member of many associations and societies, he received the Noteworthy Service and Illustrious Career in Sickle Cell Education and Research Award (1982), the Distinguished Service to Health Award, the National Association of Medical Minority Educators Award (1982), and the American Academy of Pediatrics Jacobi Award (1985).

★

No biography of Scott has yet been written. For overviews of his life and work, see obituaries in the *Washington Post* (12 Dec. 2002), the *New York Times* (14 Dec. 2002), and the *Lancet* (15 Mar. 2003).

MARIE L. THOMPSON

SEGAL, George (*b.* 26 November 1924 in the Bronx, New York City; *d.* 9 June 2000 in South Brunswick, New Jersey), sculptor known for his white, plaster-cast sculptures of people situated in everyday environments made out of real objects.

Segal was the younger of two sons born to Jacob Segal, a Russian-Polish immigrant who owned a kosher butcher shop in the Bronx, and Sophie (Gerstenfeld) Segal, a homemaker. After attending Public School 70 near his home on 174th Street, Segal entered one of New York City's most prestigious schools, Stuyvesant Technical High School. In 1940 his family moved to South Brunswick, New Jersey, to operate a chicken farm, and Segal stayed with an aunt in Brooklyn to finish high school. In the fall of 1941 he entered Cooper Union School of Art, commuting from New Jersey, but he left school to help out on the farm after his brother was drafted into the army. He also began part-time study at nearby Rutgers University. Segal married Helen Steinberg, the daughter of a neighboring farmer, on 7 April 1946, and they returned to New York City. From 1947 to 1948 he attended Pratt Institute of Design, transferring to New York University, where he graduated in 1949 with a B.S. in art education.

This period was an exciting one for Segal, who was both inspired and frustrated by abstract expressionism, the dominating aesthetic at that time. He regularly visited the hangouts of the artists closely identified with that movement and reveled in his studies with such artists as Tony Smith (known for his minimalist sculptures of the 1960s) and William Baziotes (a New York School painter), among others. Nevertheless, after graduation Segal bought a chicken farm on Davidson's Mill Road across the street from his parents' place, believing that he would not be able to support his family through art. He spent the first six months building chicken sheds and then a family; his two children, a son and a daughter, were born in 1950 and 1953, respectively. In 1953 Segal met Allan Kaprow, one of the founders of Hansa Gallery, an artists' cooperative in New

George Segal, 1979. GETTY IMAGES

York City. Kaprow introduced him to a "completely different world," to other artists who were reacting against the legacy of abstract expressionism with bold ideas and radical forms. Segal began to paint seriously again, transforming the chicken sheds into studios.

Despite the attention he was receiving—solo exhibitions at the Hansa Gallery in 1956, 1957, and 1958, and inclusion in the art historian Meyer Schapiro's 1957 exhibition "The New York School: The Second Generation"—Segal was dissatisfied with his work. He desired a return to a synthesis of the figure, without abandoning tenets of modernism. Kaprow's 1958 staging at Segal's farm of the first "Happening," a nonverbal performance art piece that made use of the surrounding environment, provided a catalyst. Later that year Segal constructed partial figures out of plaster, burlap, and wire, which he placed adjacent to his paintings in his 1959 Hansa Gallery and 1960 Green Gallery solo exhibitions. He even included some props in the latter show, to create minimal environments.

Segal's breakthrough came in 1961 when one of his students in a local adult painting class introduced him to plaster medical bandages. That July, Segal used himself as his first subject by wrapping himself in the bandages, which he then removed in sections, with the help of his wife, and reassembled. He placed the seated figure in a chair in front of a table onto which he attached a window frame, calling the environmental tableau *Man Sitting at a Table*. He included this and other sculptures in Sidney Janis's groundbreaking 1962 exhibition, "The New Realists," which highlighted artists that were identified as "pop," heralding a movement that dominated the 1960s. These artists shared an interest in representing commercial, popular culture in a nonemotive fashion, but Segal focused on the consumers and their role in contemporary society. The artist's technique of making sculptures out of plaster casts of actual people allowed him to capture directly the essentials of his subject. "Casting left me free to compose and to present content," he stated. "I could report on my model and not on me." In 1963 Segal earned an M.F.A. from Rutgers University in New Jersey with a thesis about his new work.

Segal's sculptures, which seemed so clearly to elucidate the ambiguity and isolation of modern life, quickly gained the attention of dealers, critics, and collectors. He received his first international solo exhibitions in 1963 at the Galerie Illeana Sonnabend in Paris and the Galerie Schmela in Düsseldorf, Germany, followed by one in New York City at the Green Gallery in 1964. Included in the latter show was *Gas Station* (1963–1964), in which Segal placed the station attendant holding a can of motor oil at one end of the twenty-four-foot panoramic environment and another figure sitting next to a Coca Cola machine at the other. Janis, who became his dealer in 1965, included Segal's *Cinema* (1963)—a man standing in front of a brightly lit movie-theater sign in the act of placing the first letter of the upcoming movies—in his group show "4 Environments by 4 New Realists." This signature work of Segal's was also placed at the entrance to the 1969 exhibition "Pop Art" held at the Hayward Gallery in London, which was one of the first historical shows exploring the movement.

In the 1970s Segal began making inside casts of his body molds so that he could achieve a higher degree of realism in his figures. He also developed an interest in chromatic effects, painting his figures and props in contrasting colors, as, for example, in his 1977 relief torso portrait of Meyer Schapiro. In this work the subject's suited torso is the same blue as the rough stone background, with the forward jut of the flesh-toned head and hands suggesting his intellectual achievements. In the next decade Segal began a series of still-life sculptures that were free copies of paintings by the French artist Paul Cézanne, works that explored notions of reproduction and reality.

In 1976 Segal made the first of many public sculpture commissions, which he continued to receive over the course of his life, despite the controversy he sometimes faced. For example, his 1979 allegorical *Kent State: Abraham and Isaac,*

465

intended as a commissioned gift to the university in recognition of the students killed during anti–Vietnam War demonstrations, was rejected by Kent State officials as being too critical of the government; the bronze version found a home at Princeton University. But his 1982 *Holocaust,* which is situated outside the Palace of the Legion of Honor in San Francisco and whose plaster version is in the Jewish Museum in New York City, has received wide approbation, as have his three depression-era tableaux for the Franklin Delano Roosevelt Memorial in Washington, D.C., which was dedicated in 1997.

Segal's long, productive career was filled with many honors and awards, including several honorary doctorates, the first in 1970 from Rutgers University. Other awards were the Israel Achievement Award and the Jewish Museum's Mayer Sultzberger Award (both 1986), the International Lifetime Achievement Award for Sculpture given by President William J. ("Bill") Clinton (1992), the Tokyo *Praemium Imperiale* Award for Lifetime Achievement in the Arts (1997), the National Medal of Arts (1999), and the Federal Design Achievement Award (2000). He continued to create art until his death, at home, from bone cancer. Segal is buried in Washington Cemetery in the Deans section of South Brunswick.

Segal's ghostly "people" continue to inhabit public squares and other urban spaces. They are always startling but pleasurable to come across, because they strike a chord with the viewer, a sharing of common experiences. "Everybody was looking for a new way to represent reality," remembered Segal. "The only space I could be convinced about was the physical distance between my body and the canvas—the space in which I walked."

★

There are several good monographs of Segal's work, including Jan van der Marck, *George Segal* (1975); Phyllis Tuchman, *George Segal* (1983); and Sam Hunter and Don Hawthorne, *George Segal* (1984). Also useful are two exhibition catalogues: Martin Friedman and Graham W. J. Beal, *George Segal: Sculptures* (1978), with commentary by Segal; and Marco Livingstone, *George Segal Retrospective: Sculptures, Paintings, Drawings* (1997). An obituary is in the *New York Times* (10 June 2000). The transcript of an interview (26 Nov. 1973) with Segal, conducted by Paul Cummings, is in the Archives of American Art at the Smithsonian Institution in Washington, D.C.

LEIGH BULLARD WEISBLAT

SHANNON, Claude Elwood (*b.* 30 April 1916 in Petoskey, Michigan; *d.* 24 February 2001 in Medford, Massachusetts), electrical engineer and mathematician whose theory of information laid the foundation for modern digital telecommunications.

Claude E. Shannon, May 1952. HULTON ARCHIVES/GETTY IMAGES

Shannon was born to Claude Elwood Shannon, a probate judge, and Mabel (Wolf) Shannon, a high school principal. His fascination with both mathematics and gadgetry emerged at an early age. Growing up in Gaylord, Michigan, Shannon played with radio kits and erector sets supplied by his father. He also enjoyed solving mathematical problems given to him by his sister, who also became a mathematician. "I was always interested, even as a boy, in cryptography and things of that sort," Shannon said. One of his favorite stories was "The Gold Bug," an Edgar Alan Poe mystery with a rare happy ending: by decoding a mysterious map, the hero finds a buried treasure. Shannon graduated from Gaylord High School in 1932.

After graduating with a B.S. from the University of Michigan in Ann Arbor in 1936, Shannon entered the Massachusetts Institute of Technology (MIT) in Cambridge, Massachusetts, for graduate studies in electrical engineering and mathematics. His brilliance first manifested itself in his MIT master's thesis, titled "A Symbolic Analysis of Relay and Switching Circuits," in which he showed how an algebra invented by the nineteenth-century British mathematician George Boole—which deals with such concepts as "if X or Y happens but not Z, then Q results"—could represent the workings of switches and relays in electronic circuits.

The implications of the paper by the twenty-two-year-old student were profound. As a result, circuit designs could be tested mathematically before they were built, rather than through tedious trial and error. Engineers could routinely design computer hardware and software, telephone networks, and other complex systems with the aid of Boolean algebra. Shannon's paper has been called "possibly the most important master's thesis in the century." Shannon, typically, downplayed it. "It just happened that no one else was familiar with both those fields at the same time," he said.

Shannon earned his Ph.D. from MIT in 1940. After a one-year stint at the Institute for Advanced Study in Princeton, New Jersey, he went to Bell Laboratories in 1941 and remained there for fifteen years. During World War II he helped to develop encryption systems, including one used by Winston Churchill and Franklin D. Roosevelt for transoceanic conferences. This encryption work inspired Shannon's theory of communication. He realized that, just as digital codes could protect information from prying eyes, they could shield it from the ravages of static and other forms of interference. The codes could also be used to package information more efficiently so that it could be carried over a given channel. Recalling this period, Shannon said, "My first thinking . . . was how you best improve information transmission over a noisy channel." However, as he continued to work on the problem, he noted, "you begin to generalize in your head about all these broader applications."

In 1948 Shannon published "A Mathematical Theory of Communication," a two-part article that appeared in the *Bell System Technical Journal*. With this highly technical paper, Shannon created what is now known as information theory and helped bring about the information age. The heart of this seminal paper is Shannon's precise, quantitative definition of information. The amount of information in a given message, he proposed, is determined by the probability that out of all the messages that could be sent, that particular message would be selected. He defined the overall potential for information in a system as its "entropy," which in thermodynamics denotes the randomness—or "shuffledness," as one physicist put it—of a system. (The great mathematician John von Neumann reportedly persuaded Shannon to use the word "entropy," arguing that because no one really understands the concept of entropy, Shannon would have an edge in debates over his theory.)

Shannon defined the basic unit of information—which John Tukey of Bell Laboratories later dubbed a "binary unit," or "bit" for short—as a message representing one of two states. One could encode a great deal of information in relatively few bits, just as in the old game Twenty Questions, when one could quickly zero in on a correct answer through deft questioning. Building on this mathematical foundation, Shannon demonstrated that any given communications channel has a maximum capacity for reliably transmitting information. Although one can calculate this maximum and approach it through clever coding, one can never quite reach it. The maximum has come to be called the "Shannon limit."

Shannon and others then took up the challenge of suggesting ways to approach the Shannon limit. The first step was to eliminate redundancy from the message. Just as a laconic Romeo can get his text message across with a mere "i lv u," so does a good code compress information to its most efficient form. A so-called error-correction code then adds just enough redundancy to ensure that the stripped-down message is not obscured by noise. For example, an error-correction code processing a stream of numbers might add a polynomial equation on whose graph the numbers all fall. The decoder on the receiving end knows that any numbers diverging from the graph have been altered in transmission.

Shannon's ideas were almost too prescient to have an immediate impact. One problem was that primitive vacuum-tube circuits of the time could not handle the complex codes needed to approach the Shannon limit. In 1956, however, members of the Institute for Electrical and Electronics Engineers (IEEE) recognized the significance of Shannon's work by forming the IEEE Information Theory Society. With the advent of high-speed integrated circuits in the 1970s, engineers began to fully exploit information theory. Shannon's insights helped to shape almost all systems that store, process, or transmit data in digital form, from compact disks and cells phones to supercomputers and satellites.

Information theory has influenced many other fields, including linguistics, economics, biology, and even the humanities. Its intellectual impact has been compared to that of two other profound and much-misunderstood scientific insights: Heisenberg's uncertainty principle and Einstein's theory of relativity. In the early 1970s, the Information Theory Society published an editorial, sardonically titled "Information Theory, Photosynthesis, and Religion," deploring the overextension of Shannon's ideas.

Shannon himself was skeptical of some uses of his theory, such as interpreting works of literature or music. He often emphasized that information theory could not address questions related to meaning, and was not intended to do so. But applying the theory to scientific fields such as biology made sense to him. "The nervous system is a complex communications system, and it processes information in complicated ways," he said. When asked whether he thought machines could "think," he replied, "You bet. I'm a machine, and you're a machine, and we both think, don't we?" He added, "it is certainly plausible to me that in a few decades machines will be beyond humans" in intelligence.

Indeed, Shannon's fascination with intelligent machines anticipated and helped to spawn the field of artificial intelligence. He was one of the first scientists to propose that a computer could compete with humans in chess. In 1950 he explained in *Scientific American* how that task might be accomplished. He also built a "mind-reading" machine that could play the game of penny-matching, in which one person tries to guess whether the other has chosen heads or tails; the machine recorded and analyzed its opponent's past choices, looking for patterns that would foretell the next choice. The machine won more than 50 percent of its games, even against the smartest engineers at Bell Laboratories.

Colleagues who knew Shannon in his prime said that he had a genius for avoiding that "strangest place." "There are doable problems that are trivial, and profound problems that are not doable," Elwyn Berlekamp, an engineer who cowrote several papers with Shannon, said. "Claude had a fantastic intuition and ability to formulate profound problems that were doable."

In 1956 Shannon left Bell Laboratories to become a professor of communications at MIT. He published little on information theory thereafter. Although he continued to explore information theory through the 1960s, and did not fully retire from Bell Laboratories until 1972, he simply did not feel most of his research was worthy of publication. "Most great mathematicians have done their finest work when they were young," he pointed out. In 1957 Shannon was named Donner Professor of Science at MIT, where he taught until 1978. He received numerous awards and honors, including the National Medal of Science in 1966 and the coveted Kyoto Prize in 1985.

In the 1960s Shannon stopped attending meetings dedicated to the field he had created. One reason may have been that he was quite shy and feared public speaking. In 1973, after agreeing to give a lecture at a major conference on information theory, he almost backed out at the last second. "I never saw a guy with so much stage fright," recalled his friend Berlekamp. "In this crowd, he was viewed as a god-like figure, and I guess he was worried he wouldn't live up to his reputation." Shannon eventually gave an inspiring speech about feedback and self-referential systems.

By the late 1980s Shannon had dropped almost entirely out of sight. He spent most of his remaining years tinkering with his beloved gadgets at his home in Winchester, Massachusetts. On 27 March 1949 Shannon married Mary Elizabeth Moore, an engineer whom he had met at Bell Laboratories. They had three children. In the early 1990s Shannon's wife revealed to friends that her husband was suffering from Alzheimer's disease. Shannon died of complications from the disease at the Courtyard Nursing Care Center in Medford, Massachusetts.

One of Shannon's last public appearances was in 1985, when he unexpectedly dropped in on the International Information Theory Symposium in Brighton, England. The meeting was proceeding smoothly, if uneventfully, when news raced through the halls and lecture rooms that the snowy-haired man with the shy grin wandering in and out of sessions was none other than Shannon. Some participants at the conference had not even known he was still alive.

At the banquet, the meeting organizers somehow persuaded Shannon to address the audience. He spoke for a few minutes and then—fearing he was boring everyone—pulled three balls from his pocket and juggled them. The crowd cheered and lined up for autographs. Trying to explain how he and others felt, Robert McEliece, the chairman of the symposium, said: "It was as if Newton had showed up at a physics conference."

Shannon was renowned among colleagues for his self-deprecating humor and playfulness. He was an avid juggler, unicycler, and gadget-builder. Among his favorite inventions was a juggling W.C. Fields robot, a mechanical mouse that could navigate a maze, and a computer that calculated in Roman numerals and was called Thrifty Roman Numeral Backward Computer, or THROBAC. "I've always pursued my interests without much regard for financial value or value to the world," he told a journalist in 1989. "I've spent lots of time on totally useless things." He even dabbled in poetry, producing a whimsical homage to the Rubik's Cube, a three-dimensional puzzle popular during the 1970s.

Although many scientists are better known than Shannon, arguably none have had a greater impact on modern life. After his death, the journal *Nature* eulogized Shannon as "the man who started the digital revolution." Solomon Golomb, one of countless engineers whose work has built on Shannon's, said that Shannon's influence on computers, telecommunications, and other information-processing technologies cannot be overstated. "It's like saying how much influence the inventor of the alphabet has had on literature," Golomb remarked.

★

Shannon's papers are in N.J.A. Sloane and Aaron D. Wyner, eds., *Claude Elwood Shannon: Collected Papers* (1993). Shannon and Warren Weaver helped to popularize information theory in *The Mathematical Theory of Communication* (1949). For a longer assessment of Shannon's legacy, see Mitchell Waldrop, "Reluctant Father of the Digital Age," *Technology Review* (July–Aug. 2001). Obituaries are in the *New York Times* (27 Feb. 2001) and *Nature* (12 April 2001).

JOHN HORGAN

SHAPIRO, Karl Jay (*b.* 10 November 1913 in Baltimore, Maryland; *d.* 14 May 2000 in New York City), Pulitzer Prize–winning poet and poetry editor.

Shapiro, who legally changed the spelling of his first name from Carl to Karl, was born "under the roof where Poe expired," as he put it in later years. His father, Joseph Shapiro, was a salesman who gave his family a life of feast or famine; no sooner would they get comfortable in Baltimore than they would move to Chicago, then to Norfolk, then back to Baltimore. Shapiro was closer to his mother, Sarah (Omansky) Shapiro, a homemaker, particularly in the critical period just after he finished high school, when his father abandoned the family to live with his mistress. In 1936, partly in reaction to this family crisis, the budding poet rode cross-country with his girlfriend and sailed on a tramp steamer to Tahiti.

Shapiro boasted that he attended three high schools and two universities, and yet had no degrees. He had graduated from high school in 1932 and entered the University of Virginia, where his older brother was a student. He left the University of Virginia after one year (1932–1933), then enjoyed a four-year hiatus that included his Tahiti excursion and the private publication of his first book of poetry, *Poems* (1935), which helped win him a scholarship to Johns Hopkins University. There, beginning in 1937, he "studied English literature, Greek, Latin, French and History," but left with a "spotty" education. He also studied librarianship at the Enoch Pratt Free Library School in Baltimore; his studies there were also cut short, this time by the draft. He entered the U.S. Army Medical Corps in 1941 and, since he had attended college, was made a company clerk. Although he served for the full term of World War II, he never saw action.

Nevertheless, it was Shapiro's military service that made him a great poet. Accepted among his comrades, who did not see him as the victim of a nasty domestic scandal or a Jew filling a quota, he was finally able to feel like an initiate. The sense of himself as "being both in and out of society at the same time" was something Shapiro thought essential to the act of poetry. He declared, "[T]he poet is in exile whether he is or he is not. . . . Isolated within my own world, like a worm in an apple, I became a poet."

As a Medical Corps clerk stranded on a South Pacific island, far behind the front lines with days of inaction before him, Shapiro turned to writing: "Every day I went to the office and wrote . . . thirty lines." The result, as transmitted in the V-Letters that were the only means of communication with his girlfriend and agent, Evalyn Katz, was four books of poetry: *Person, Place, and Thing* (1942), *The Place of Love* (1942), *V-Letter and Other Poems* (1944), and *Essay on Rime* (1945). *V-Letter,* published while he was serving in New Guinea, won the Pulitzer Prize for poetry in 1945, and Shapiro was praised as the "true spokesman for our generation." His poetry combined the ironic distance of prewar modernism with a new, vernacular directness that would become the authentic voice of midcentury poetry. In the sonnet "Full Moon: New Guinea," for example, the formal correctness of the poem's formal structure stands in acute tension with its violent content, a dialectic repeated throughout these volumes.

Karl Shapiro, 1944. AP/WIDE WORLD PHOTOS

Shapiro returned from World War II in 1945 a famous poet, and was named a Fellow in American Letters (1945–1946) and then Consultant in Poetry to the Library of Congress (1946–1947). In 1947 Johns Hopkins, where he had failed to graduate eight years before, invited Shapiro to become a professor of writing. As he wrote in his autobiography, "He was catapulted into a tenured professorship after having dropped out as a sophomore." Then in 1950 he assumed the most prestigious administrative post in American poetry, the editorship of *Poetry* magazine. He held this position for six years, then in 1956 took on the editorship of *Prairie Schooner,* which he helped elevate to similar prestige before returning to full-time teaching and writing in 1966, first at the University of Illinois at Chicago Circle (1966–1968), and then at the University of California, Davis (1968–1985).

These years of Shapiro's career as an editor were marked by controversy. In late 1948 Shapiro was one of only two voters for the Bollingen Prize to vote against Ezra Pound for the award, on the grounds of his anti-Semitic broadcasts during World War II and offensive passages in his *Cantos.* As Shapiro later recalled, "I was suddenly forced into a conscious decision to stand up and be counted as a Jew." His resignation from *Prairie Schooner* generated similar public furor. He had accepted a short story that dealt in part with homosexuality in the academic community; the University of Nebraska, which published the journal, ordered him to eliminate the references or omit the story. He resigned instead, and read the story in its original form over the local radio.

More fatefully, between these events Shapiro had written a polemic against the impersonal modernist voice in poetry, entitled *In Defense of Ignorance* (1960), in which he compared T.S. Eliot and Pound to Jekyll and Hyde, two faces of the same "disease." He dismissed their works as "frozen poems with an ice-pick at the core." Such attacks on academic intellectuals led to Shapiro's dismissal from the academic pantheon; his poems were dropped from the *Oxford Book of American Verse*. An article on Sylvia Plath in the *Saturday Evening Post* included Shapiro among a group of American authors who had committed suicide, and a *New York Times* crossword puzzle listed him as a "late American poet." His attacks on cultural academe did, perhaps, amount to intellectual suicide.

Shapiro's own poetic voice was changing during these years. He had made his reputation by writing in the sonnet form and in a terza rima that he had borrowed from Dante via William Carlos Williams; their formal constraints lent intensity to his messy vision of reality. However, in *The Bourgeois Poet* (1964), he turned to Walt Whitman and his beloved W.H. Auden for models. Some critics praised *The Bourgeois Poet* as Shapiro's finest collection, pointing to its "poetic integrity," while others lamented what they saw as apostasy. Shapiro defended his work, insisting that "the two traditional attributes of poetry—rhyme and versification—were not only nonessential, but artificial impediments to the poetic process."

Shapiro led an active personal life. He married Evalyn Katz on 25 March 1945, immediately after his return from the Pacific; they had one son and two daughters. He would later mourn the death of his youngest daughter, who committed suicide in 1993. But Shapiro was unable to remain faithful to one woman, a trait he recorded at length in the second volume of his autobiography, *Reports of My Death* (1990). The breakdown of his relationship with the University of Nebraska paralleled the breakdown of his marriage to Evalyn; the couple separated and eventually divorced in January 1967.

On 31 July 1967 Shapiro married Teri Kovach, whom he had met shortly after his separation from Evalyn. Kovach died of cancer in July 1982, and Shapiro lived in deep mourning until Sophie Wilkins, "former wife of his oldest friend," called him one day and he discovered a late-blooming passion. Shapiro and Wilkins married on 25 April 1985 and moved to New York City, where they lived together in relative obscurity until Shapiro's death, in a hospice, at age eighty-six.

Ultimately, Shapiro's quest for a key to the poetic pro-

cess was a failure: "The modern poets . . . all had one goal . . . to discover a form, or the form. . . . Auden found his form . . . . But Eliot and Pound never succeeded. . . ." In addition to the Pulitzer, Shapiro won four prizes from *Poetry,* the Shelley Memorial Prize, and the Bollingen Prize in 1969. In spite of such accolades, however, Shapiro "could never decide whether he was really happy." His career was not about awards, it was about "prosody," and there could be no final resolution to that—only an occasional triumph.

★

Shapiro's autobiographies are *The Younger Son* (1988), *Poet: An Autobiography in Three Parts* (1988), and *Reports of My Death* (1990). Information about Shapiro is in Lee Bartlett, *Karl Shapiro: A Descriptive Bibliography* (1979), and Joseph Reino, *Karl Shapiro* (1981). An interview with Shapiro, conducted by Robert Phillips, is in "The Art of Poetry XXXVI," *Paris Review* (spring 1986). An obituary is in the *New York Times* (17 May 2000).

HARTLEY S. SPATT

SHULL, Clifford Glenwood (*b.* 23 September 1915 in Pittsburgh, Pennsylvania; *d.* 31 March 2001 in Medford, Massachusetts), physicist who won the 1994 Nobel Prize in physics for contributions to the development of neutron scattering in condensed matter research.

Shull was the youngest of three children born to David H. Shull, a hardware business owner, and Daisy (Bistline) Shull. Shull claimed that his middle name referred to the Glenwood section of Pittsburgh, where he was born and enjoyed a happy childhood. He attended school in Glenwood through junior high, then commuted by public streetcar to Schenley High School, in a different neighborhood, where his first interest in aeronautic engineering was replaced with an interest in physics because of a physics course taught by a dynamic teacher, Paul Dysart.

Since family finances were limited, Shull enrolled at the Carnegie Institute of Technology (now Carnegie Mellon University) located in the same Schenley Park area of Pittsburgh as his high school, enabling him to live at home. It was 1933, the heart of the depression, and Shull had a half-tuition scholarship based on his good high school record. At Carnegie, Shull's interest in physics grew under the influence of the exciting lectures in his freshman year given by Harry Hower, chairman of the physics department.

In January 1934 Shull's father died unexpectedly. His brother had just finished college and was going to teach art, but changed his plans to operate the family business. Shull worked at a number of summer jobs to help pay his expenses during his college years. During his junior and senior years he was encouraged by his counselor at Carnegie to attend graduate school. He completed his B.S. at

Clifford G. Shull, October 1994. KRAFT BROOKS/CORBIS SYGMA

Carnegie in 1937 and entered the physics department of New York University (NYU) in the fall, where he had a teaching assistantship to provide for his expenses. As graduate assistants participated in ongoing research, Shull became associated with a nuclear physics group that was in the process of building a 200 kilo-electron volt (keV) Cockroft-Walton generator for accelerating deuterons. (The latter are the nuclei of deuterium atoms, or atoms of a heavy hydrogen isotope that has one neutron in addition to its one proton.)

During Shull's third year of graduate school, the physics department started construction of a 400 keV generator to be used for accelerating electrons. Working with Frank Meyers, the head of the nuclear physics group, Shull undertook an electron-double-scattering (EDS) experiment that became his thesis work. He received his Ph.D. from NYU in June 1941. Although he did not work on the project, Shull was aware of others in the physics department who were working on neutron scattering and their initial experimental efforts.

While still a graduate student at NYU, Shull met Martha-Nuel Summer of Newberry, South Carolina, who was in a master's program in history at Columbia University. They married on 19 June 1941 and moved to Beacon, New York, in July, where Shull had obtained a job as a research physicist with the Texas Company (now Texaco). His work at the Texas Company was with x-ray diffraction and small-angle scattering techniques to study powder samples, work that gave him valuable background for his later work with neutrons. The study related to catalysts used in making high-octane aviation fuel.

With the start of the Manhattan Project, the secret U.S.

research program that led to the development of the first atomic bomb at the end of World War II, Shull wanted to join the team at the University of Chicago, but the Texas Company told the War Manpower Board that his research related to aviation fuel was critical to the war effort. Shull stayed with the company until 1946, when he joined the Clinton Laboratory (now Oak Ridge National Laboratory) in Oak Ridge, Tennessee. By this time, the Shulls had the first of their three sons.

Shull's work at the Oak Ridge Laboratory between 1946 and 1955 led to his receiving the Nobel Prize in physics years later for his pioneering work in neutron scattering, a technique that answered the question of where atoms "are" within liquid and solid matter. In simple terms, when a beam of neutrons is directed at a given material, the neutrons are scattered by atoms in the sample to form a diffraction pattern that can be interpreted to identify the positions of the atoms. The magnetic properties of matter were also revealed in the studies. Following World War II, research in the scientific community changed from using neutrons emitted by radioactive sources for atomic bombs to using them as a new resource for tools to study matter at the atomic level. Shull shared the 1994 Nobel Prize with Bertram Brockhouse, a Canadian.

In 1955 Shull spent time at the Brookhaven National Laboratory before going to the Massachusetts Institute of Technology (MIT) as a professor of physics, where he remained until his retirement in 1986. Shull was described by colleagues as a modest, kind, and generous man who was a consummate experimentalist and teacher. He received numerous awards and honors, including the Buckley Prize from the American Physical Society in 1956. He was also elected to the American Academy of Arts and Sciences in 1956 and to the National Academy of Science in 1975.

Shull died of liver failure at Lawrence Memorial Hospital; his wife died following an extended illness four days later. Although the couple lived in Lexington, Massachusetts, they were buried in her family's hometown of Newberry, South Carolina, in Rosemont Cemetery.

Shull's career in physics started early in his life. He was the right person at the right time to take advantage of the developing field of condensed matter after World War II, using the resources of nuclear reactors for peacetime research. He always acknowledged those who influenced his life and those who worked with him.

★

Biographical information on Shull is in *The Tech* 115 (7 Feb. 1995). Information on Shull's work can be found in "The Nuclear Reactor as a Research Instrument," *Scientific American* 189 (Aug. 1953): 23. Obituaries are in the *Boston Globe, New York Times,* and *Washington Post* (all 4 Apr. 2001).

M. C. NAGEL

SIMON, Herbert A(lexander) (*b.* 15 June 1916 in Milwaukee, Wisconsin; *d.* 9 February 2001 in Pittsburgh, Pennsylvania), diversely brilliant social and computer scientist who pioneered the study of organizational decision-making, business administration, and artificial intelligence, and who won the Nobel Prize in economics in 1984.

Simon was born to Arthur Simon, a German-born electrical engineer and patent attorney, and Edna (Merkel) Simon, a pianist. A gifted student, Simon skipped three semesters at the Milwaukee public school he attended. He graduated early, enrolling at the University of Chicago, where he earned his B.A. in political science in 1936. While at Chicago, Simon met Dorothea Isobel Pye, a graduate student, whom he married on 25 December 1937; they had three children.

Simon had become interested in public administration while conducting a study of the Milwaukee Recreation Department as an undergraduate. He subsequently worked for the International City Manager's Association (ICMA) in Chicago under Clarence Ridley, one of his former instructors, with whom he developed mathematical methods for evaluating the efficacy of administrative techniques. During this time, Simon began using computers, then in their infancy, to tabulate statistical data and tables. In 1939 he went to the University of California at Berkeley to preside over a three-year grant-funded study of local government. This work permitted Simon to complete a Ph.D. from the University of Chicago in 1943. His dissertation was published in 1947 as *Administrative Behavior,* a seminal

Herbert A. Simon, October 1978. BETTMANN/CORBIS

work on organizational decision-making. This book and another, *Organizations* (1958), became staples in courses on business education, public administration, and organizational sociology.

In 1942 Simon went to the Illinois Institute of Technology to teach political science. He became chair of the political science department in 1946, and in 1949 went to the Carnegie Institute of Technology (now Carnegie Mellon University) in Pittsburgh to join the faculty of its new Graduate School of Industrial Administration. Although trained as a political scientist, in the late 1940s Simon began work in economics, especially econometrics (the application of statistical methods to the study of economic data and problems), for which he was awarded the 1978 Nobel Prize in economics.

In the mid-1950s Simon began research on the psychology of problem solving, for which he would later receive the American Psychological Association's highest award for lifetime achievement. Also in the mid-1950s, he wrote his first computer programs, starting down a path that would lead him and his colleague Allen Newell to receive the Association for Computing Machinery's Turing Award, that discipline's highest honor. In both psychology and computer science, Simon is best known as a forceful advocate of the idea that the human mind is an information-processing machine, functionally similar to a digital computer.

Simon's career path straightened out after the mid-1960s, as he eased into an endowed chair at Carnegie Mellon University (CMU) in computer science and psychology. Simon was a polymath, though he did not like the term, who made fundamental contributions to a wide range of fields. In addition to his primary fields of study, he found time to deepen his explorations into the philosophy of science, the theory of design, and sociobiology. His list of publications runs to over 800 items, and if they had to be categorized by discipline, the fields involved would include political science, public administration and management, operations research, systems theory, organization theory, decision theory, economics (including the theory of the firm, game theory, economic history, and econometrics), sociology, sociobiology, social psychology, cognitive psychology, pure mathematics, philosophy, linguistics, and computer science. The word "diverse" does not even begin to describe his intellectual interests or achievements.

Simon was a positivist's positivist: in every field he entered he sought to bring the complex and chaotic world of human thought and action within the ambit of rational, empirical science. To Simon, the place to begin this quest was with the "atomic phenomena of human behavior in a social environment." The most atomic of such phenomena, he believed, was the essential act of choice, an act that he understood to be strongly shaped by the social environment. Eventually, his research into decision-making led him to see strong parallels between the way in which information was processed in computers, in large bureaucracies, and in the human mind.

Simon's work with Newell at the Rand Corporation involved efforts to write computer programs that simulated human decision-making, becoming one of the first significant forays into the creation of "thinking machines," or artificial intelligence. In 1955 Simon and his colleagues announced the creation of a computer program that could solve mathematical theorems in Bertrand Russell and Alfred North Whitehead's *Principia Mathematica*.

By the late 1950s, Simon had come to define mind and machine, organism and organization, and individual and institution as highly specialized, yet tightly integrated, hierarchical systems, each locked in a continual struggle to adapt to its environment as best it could, given its limited powers. To Simon, the mind and the computer were model bureaucracies, and a bureaucracy was a model mind.

The conceptual pillars of Simon's propositions were the ideas of "system" and of "bounded" rationality. To Simon, the economy, the family, the individual organism, the cell, and the atom were all complex, hierarchically structured systems. That they were systems meant that their component elements were strongly interdependent. That they were

hierarchical meant that they had a treelike structure and so were decomposable into subsystems, sub-subsystems, and so on. That they were complex meant that the behavior of the system at one level of the hierarchy was difficult to predict from knowledge of the properties of the elements at lower levels.

The second pillar was Simon's trademark principle of bounded rationality. To Simon, human reason was bounded. These bounds were not set by the passions or the unconscious, but by the inherent limits of the human organism as an information processor. Simply put, "the capacity of the human mind for formulating and solving complex problems is very small compared with the size of the problems whose solution is required for objectively rational behavior in the real world." As a result, Simon asserted, the human actor must "construct a simplified model of the real situation in order to deal with it." Humans behave rationally with regard to these simplified models, but such behavior does not even approximate objective rationality. Thus, rational choice exists and is meaningful, but it is severely bounded. These ideas and the modeling techniques Simon developed to test their implications became widely influential in the behavioral sciences in the 1960s and 1970s, and their legacy continues to this day.

Simon was also influential in the world of science policy. He was a key adviser to the Ford Foundation regarding its program in the behavioral sciences, an effective lobbyist for the behavioral sciences in the National Academy of Sciences, and an important member of the Academy's Committee on Science and Public Policy. He was an influential member of the Social Sciences Research Council, serving on its central policy and planning committee and on its board of directors, including a three-year stint as chairman. In addition, he was the first behavioral scientist to serve on the President's Science Advisory Committee. He used these positions to encourage both the behavioral revolution in social science and the inclusion of behavioral scientists among the nation's science-policy elite.

Simon died at Presbyterian University Hospital in Pittsburgh of complications from surgery to remove a cancerous abdominal tumor.

Simon was an effective institution-builder and a strong advocate for his vision of behavioral science in the realm of science policy. As a founding faculty member at CMU's Graduate School of Industrial Administration, he pioneered the introduction of concepts and methods from the behavioral sciences into management education. The ideas and techniques advocated by Simon and his colleagues soon found their way into almost every business school, helping to create the modern degree of Master of Business Administration (M.B.A.). Simon was also a leader in the transformation of CMU's psychology department from a second-tier program into one of the most influential departments in the nation, and he was one of the founders of its renowned department (now school) of computer science.

★

Simon's autobiography is *Models of My Life* (1991). Information about Simon is in David Klahr and Kenneth Kotovsky, *Complex Information Processing: The Impact of Herbert A. Simon* (1989); Stephen Waring, *Taylorism Transformed: Scientific Management Theory Since 1945* (1991); and Peter E. Earl, ed., *The Legacy of Herbert Simon in Economic Analysis* (2001). For more information, see Esther-Mirjam Sent, "Herbert A. Simon as a Cyborg Scientist," *Perspectives on Science* 8, no. 4 (2000): 380–406; and Mie Augier, "Models of Herbert A. Simon," *Perspectives on Science* 8, no. 4 (2000): 407–443. Obituaries are in the *New York Times* (10 Feb. 2001) and *Washington Post* (11 Feb. 2001).

HUNTER CROWTHER-HEYCK

SIMON, William E(dward) (*b.* 27 November 1927 in Paterson, New Jersey; *d.* 3 June 2000 in Santa Barbara, California), secretary of the U.S. Treasury from 1974 to 1977.

Simon, the grandson of a French immigrant textile-dyeing manufacturer, was the son of Charles Simon, Jr., an insurance broker, and Eleanor (Kearns) Simon, a homemaker.

William E. Simon, 1974. GETTY IMAGES

Simon attended the Newark Academy in Livingston, New Jersey, graduating in 1946. During the next two years he served as an infantryman in the U.S. Army, swimming with the army team in the Pacific Olympics while stationed in Japan. Upon discharge from the service, he attended Lafayette College in Easton, Pennsylvania, where he earned a B.A. in government and law in 1952. On 9 September 1950 he married Carol Ann Girard, a member of an old Philadelphia banking family; they had seven children.

In 1952 Simon joined Union Securities, becoming an assistant vice president and manager of the Municipal Trading Department in 1955. From 1957 to 1964 he was vice president of Weeden and Company. He then joined the investment firm Salomon Brothers in 1964, where six years later he became senior partner in charge of the government bonds and municipal bonds department, as well as one of the seven partners on the firm's executive committee. He was also active in various business organizations and served as national chairman of the U.S. Olympic Committee.

Nationally known for his knowledge of securities markets and his conservative economic views, Simon was appointed by President Richard M. Nixon as deputy secretary of the Treasury on 6 December 1972; he was sworn in on 2 February 1973, in the midst of the energy crisis. He directed the administration's program of restructuring U.S. financial institutions. In early 1973 Simon was appointed chairman of an interdepartmental Oil Policy Committee, established to confront the increasing shortage of oil and gasoline. Later that year he asked the Federal Trade Commission to withdraw its antitrust suit against eight major oil companies, denying that they were in collusion and arguing that the suit would worsen the energy crisis; he became a hero to conservatives, also decrying increased U.S. dependence on foreign oil.

After the October 1973 Yom Kippur War and the subsequent boycott of oil shipments to the United States by the Organization of Petroleum Exporting Countries (OPEC) in December 1973, President Nixon appointed Simon to replace John Love as chairman of the newly created Federal Energy Office as well as to be head of the Emergency Energy Action Group, a new cabinet-level committee. As "energy czar," Simon rapidly implemented government controls over gasoline use, announcing that the administration wanted a 30 percent reduction in private gasoline use in the first three months of 1974; later he called for a ten gallon per week limit on private drivers. The embargo was lifted in June 1974. After George Shultz resigned as secretary of the Treasury, Simon was appointed to succeed him, taking the oath of office on 8 May 1974, and continuing in office after Nixon's resignation under President Gerald R. Ford until Ford's term expired on 20 January 1977.

In July 1974 Simon toured the Middle East, negotiating treaties and agreements with Egypt, Saudi Arabia, and Kuwait, and persuading the governments of the latter two countries to invest their petrodollars in U.S. government securities rather than in direct corporate investment, which would have involved control over the policies of U.S. corporations. Simon moved to demonetize gold and to abolish restrictions on individual ownership of this metal. In August 1974 Simon met with the chairmen of the Federal Reserve Board and of Citibank to arrange for bonds whose interest rates could be adjusted for inflation. Later that month President Ford appointed Simon to the Council on Price and Wage stability, in connection with Ford's unsuccessful "WIN" (Whip Inflation Now) program.

In late September 1974 Simon was appointed to the new Economic Policy Board and was widely considered to be Ford's chief economic adviser. That month Simon met with a number of foreign treasury ministers, proposing a plan to establish a $25 million lending facility to help nations pay their oil deficits. He also used grain sales as a weapon to persuade the Soviet Union to relax pressures on dissidents. During the 1974–1975 recession, Simon used funding to help nations finance oil deficits as a device to influence their foreign policies. On the question of demonetizing gold, a compromise agreement with France was reached. Agreements providing for debt relief for less-developed nations followed in 1975.

Both internationally and nationally Simon favored moderate growth, a position which critics felt deepened the recession. In early 1975 Simon expressed opposition to the "double taxation" resulting from federal taxation of both corporate profits and dividend income. He also emphasized the need for price stability, warned of social security deficits in future years, and attacked the food stamp program as encouraging cheating and laziness. Simon strongly opposed federal aid during the New York City fiscal crisis of 1975 ("Ford to City: Drop Dead" was a famous headline at the time), rejecting pleas for federal guarantees of city bonds. After the creation of the Municipal Assistance Corporation and the Emergency Financial Control Board, Simon reluctantly conceded the need for federal aid to prevent the city from going bankrupt and thus creating a worldwide financial crisis.

Talk of Simon as the Republican vice-presidential nominee in 1976, or as a candidate for governor of New Jersey, came to nothing, and in 1977 he became president and trustee of the nonprofit John M. Olin Foundation, as well as a consultant to such firms as Booz Allen and Hamilton, an international management consultant firm. Later, Simon cofounded Wesray Corporation, pioneering leveraged buyouts and acquiring over thirty companies, including Avis, Wilson Sporting Goods, and Gibson Greeting Cards.

Meanwhile, Simon wrote two best-selling books defending his conservative economic ideas and policies, *A Time for Truth* (1978), and *A Time for Action* (1980). Critics were bemused at Simon's statements, expressed in these books and elsewhere, that he and his fellow conservatives were frustrated to the point of helplessness by the liberal left's control over the media, the bureaucracy, and American culture. Other critics, noticing that Simon, after leaving office, moved to California while leaving his family in New Jersey, implied that he was at fault in what they characterized as the breakdown of his marriage.

On the other hand, in his later years Simon, a devout Roman Catholic, practiced as a Eucharistic minister, personally attending to AIDS victims and other seriously ill people in hospitals in New York and California; the majority of these patients never knew who he was. He also gave over $80 million to charities and educational institutions, including the University of Rochester and Thomas Aquinas College in Santa Barbara, California. Later in life, with the help of his two sons, Simon decided to give his entire fortune, amounting to $350 million, to educational and health-related charities, especially those oriented toward people with low incomes. After his wife's death in June 1995, Simon married Tonia Adams Donnelly on 2 June 1996.

In 1987 Simon founded and became president of WSGP International, which concentrated on investments in real estate and financial service organizations in the western United States and Pacific Rim. The next year he founded Simon and Sons, a global merchant bank with offices in New Jersey, Los Angeles, and Hong Kong. From 1981 to 1985 Simon was president of the U.S. Olympic Committee, and created the U.S. Olympic Foundation with an endowment of $125 million. A number of academic chairs, and the business administration school at the University of Rochester, were named after Simon, and he was awarded numerous honorary degrees. He was a director of many corporations, universities, and hospitals. He died at Cottage Hospital in Santa Barbara of complications from pulmonary fibrosis, a lung disease. He also had a serious heart condition. His funeral took place at Saint Patrick's Cathedral in New York City, and he is buried in a Catholic cemetery in New Vernon, New Jersey.

Simon was a controversial secretary of the Treasury. Vilified by liberals for putting the interests of big business ahead of the national interest, he was praised by conservatives for favoring sound financial policies and trying to rein in aggressive government power. His opposition to irresponsible inflationary policies and his emphasis on energy independence, policies receiving support in later years from both Republican and Democratic administrations, as well as his philanthropic activities, involving personal service and financial support, will be remembered.

The William E. Simon Papers, covering the years 1972 to 1977, as well as some later papers, are housed at Lafayette College in Easton, Pennsylvania. Loren Galanter discusses Simon in Eleanora W. Schoenebaum, ed., *Political Profiles: The Nixon-Ford Years* (1980). Obituaries are in the *Los Angeles Times, New York Times,* and *Washington Post* (all 4 June 2000), *Thomas Aquinas College Quarterly Newsletter* (summer 2000), and *University of Rochester Review* (fall 2000).

STEPHEN A. STERTZ

SITTER, Carl Leonard (*b.* 2 December 1922 in Syracuse, Missouri; *d.* 4 April 2000 in Richmond, Virginia), U.S. Marine Corps officer who won the Medal of Honor for heroism during the Korean War.

Carl L. Sitter, 1951. AP/WIDE WORLD PHOTOS

Sitter was the son of William A. Sitter, a steelworker who also worked in construction, and Luvilla H. Sitter. His family moved to Pueblo, Colorado, when he was six. He graduated from Pueblo Central High School in 1940 and on 22 June 1940 enlisted in the U.S. Marine Corps. Following duty in Iceland, he was serving as a corporal on Wallis Island in the Pacific area when he was commissioned a second lieutenant in the Marine Reserves on 12 December 1942. He later received a regular Marine commission.

During World War II, Sitter saw action in the Pacific while serving with the Twenty-second Marine Infantry Regiment as an infantry platoon leader. On 20 February 1944 he was slightly wounded at Eniwetok in the Marshall Islands, winning the first of his four Purple Hearts. In July 1944 he was seriously wounded in the shoulder at Guam in the Mariana Islands while leading his platoon in an assault against the Japanese defending Orote Peninsula, earning the Silver Star medal for exposing himself to enemy fire and refusing to be evacuated until his platoon had accomplished its mission.

Following World War II, Sitter served in various assignments at San Diego, California; Quantico, Virginia; the Brooklyn Naval Shipyard; the Panama Canal Zone; Key West, Florida; Camp Lejeune, North Carolina; and Camp Pendleton, California. After the Korean War broke out, Sitter, then a captain, participated in the Inchon landing in September 1950 while attached to the staff of the First Marine Regiment.

In November and December 1950, Sitter took part in the Chosin Reservoir campaign as commander of Company G, Third Battalion, First Marines, which was part of the First Marine Division. The marines and other troops from the U.S. X Corps were charged with severing the main supply route of the Chinese communists from Manchuria into North Korea. By late November the X Corps was strung out along the narrow road from Hungnam on the

east coast of North Korea to the Chosin Reservoir, more than sixty miles to the north. When the Chinese counterattacked on 27 November, most of the Third Battalion had already been ordered to advance to Hagaru-ri, a crucial crossroads at the southern end of the reservoir and the site of an airstrip the Marines intended to use to ferry in supplies and to evacuate wounded men.

During the night of 27 and 28 November, the Chinese cut the road between Hagaru-ri and Koto-ri to the south, and the next night they launched two major assaults against Hagaru-ri. On 28 November, Sitter's company, which had been left behind because of a shortage of transportation, was attached to Task Force Drysdale, a makeshift force of 900 officers and men that was ordered to advance north from Koto-ri to reinforce the defenders of Hagaru-ri. Leaving Koto-ri on 29 November, the task force immediately came under heavy automatic weapon and mortar fire, and although Sitter's men were able to drive the Chinese from Hill 1236 in fierce fighting, the task force was forced to stop farther up the road to wait for tanks to arrive from Koto-ri. Resuming the advance later in the day, the task force edged forward, with Sitter's men following the tanks and dismounting their trucks to charge Chinese positions whenever opposition was encountered. Finally, at 9:00 P.M. on the evening of 29 November, twelve hours after leaving Koto-ri, the tanks, Sitter's company, and other units that were able to free themselves from the melee along the road reached Hagaru-ri. Sitter lost one-third of his men in the fight.

On the morning of 30 November, after scant sleep for his men, Sitter was ordered to attack East Hill. Overlooking Hagaru-ri, it was a major threat to the U.S. position at the Chosin Reservoir. Using machine guns and mortars placed on the crest of the hill, the Chinese had frustrated all previous attempts by the marines to capture its heights. Sitter's men attacked the southwest slope with the aid of two engineer platoons in two assault elements, but they were stopped halfway to the summit by intense Chinese fire and the icy ground. At nightfall Sitter pulled his men back, dug in, and waited for reinforcements before resuming the attack the next morning. During the night of 30 November and 1 December, the Chinese counterattacked in a furious effort to drive the marines completely from the hill. Despite exacting a heavy toll on the onrushing Chinese and supported by artillery and mortar fire, Sitter's company was nearly overrun. However, reinforced by a company of Royal Marines, it threw back the Chinese in close fighting, sometimes hand to hand, in which Sitter was wounded in the face, arms, and chest by grenade and mortar fragments. Refusing to be evacuated and visiting every gun position and foxhole, Sitter inspired his men to hold on even after the Chinese reached his command post. By noon on 1 December, the Marines had recovered the ground the Chinese had captured, although the battle for East Hill continued until the X Corps began to pull back to Hungnam on 6 December. During the battle on 30 November and 1 December, Sitter was in almost constant combat for thirty-six hours and had sixty killed and wounded in his command. For his inspiring leadership, battle tactics, and personal valor at East Hill, Sitter was awarded the Medal of Honor by President Harry Truman at a White House ceremony on 29 October 1951.

Sitter returned to the United States in February 1951 and during the next two decades held a variety of staff and command posts in the United States, England, and Okinawa while rising to the rank of colonel. While serving in England, he received a B.A. in 1960 from the extension program of the University of Maryland. Following his retirement from the marines on 30 June 1970, Sitter worked with the Virginia Department of Social Services until 1985, retiring as chief of the research and reporting branch. At the time of his death, he was attending the Union Theological Seminary and Presbyterian School of Christian Education in Richmond in preparation for entering the ministry.

A stoic, unflappable combat leader, Sitter was married to Ellen Louise Herren. They had three children. He later married Velma Ruth Tichenor. Sitter died of pneumonia and is buried at Arlington National Cemetery in Arlington, Virginia.

★

A biographical sketch summarizing Sitter's career is available from the U.S. Marine Corps History and Museums Division. Sitter's service during the Chosin Reservoir campaign is described in Lynn Montross and Nicholas Canzona, *The Chosin Campaign*, vol. 3 in *The U.S. Marine Operations in Korea, 1950–1953* (1957); Roy E. Appleman, *Escaping the Trap: The US Army X Corps in Northeast Korea, 1950* (1990); and Martin Russ, *Breakout: The Chosin Reservoir Campaign, Korea 1950* (1999). An obituary is in the *New York Times* (8 Apr. 2000).

JOHN KENNEDY OHL

SLAUGHTER, Enos Bradsher ("Country") (*b.* 27 April 1916 in Roxboro, North Carolina; *d.* 12 August 2002 in Durham, North Carolina), baseball player whose constant hustling and offensive skills over a nineteen-year career, primarily with the St. Louis Cardinals, earned him election to the National Baseball Hall of Fame.

Slaughter was the fourth of six children born to Zadok Slaughter and Lonnie (Gentry) Slaughter, who were farmers. He worked on the family farm as a youngster and learned how to play baseball from his father, who had played semiprofessionally as a barehanded and barefooted

Enos Slaughter, 1954. BETTMANN/CORBIS

catcher. He played baseball and basketball at Allensville High School and joined his brothers on the Collins and Aikman textile mill team in a local industrial baseball league. He transferred to Bethel Hill High School to play football and graduated in 1934.

Declining an athletic scholarship to play baseball and football at Guilford College, Slaughter chose to work in the mill and play second base for the company team. In the fall of 1934 the sports editor of the *Durham Morning Herald* secured an invitation for him to attend a tryout camp run by the St. Louis Cardinals. He showed enough promise to be offered a contract for the following spring. Over the winter he married Hulo Powell, his high school sweetheart, the first of his five wives. Four of his marriages were short-lived; the fifth, to Helen Spiker, lasted twenty-three years until their divorce in 1980. Slaughter fathered five daughters and had one adopted son.

At spring training in Asheville, North Carolina, Billy Southworth, a coach and former player, noticed that Slaughter ran flat-footed and suggested that he run on the balls of his feet. This increased Slaughter's speed dramatically and probably saved his nascent career. The Cardinals assigned him to Martinsville, Virginia, in the Class D Bi-State League and turned him into an outfielder. In 1936, having been promoted to Columbus, Georgia, in the Class B South Atlantic League and not playing very well, Slaughter drew a warning from his manager for walking in from the outfield to the dugout. A player who did not run, said Eddie Dyer, could easily be replaced. It was during this period that Slaughter earned his nickname, "Country."

Slaughter took this admonition to heart and never sulked again. Moreover, he decided to run everywhere on the ball field, a promise to himself that he kept. After a final year of seasoning in the minors, he joined the Cardinals in 1938. He batted .276 and then hit better than .300 four years consecutively. He enlisted in the Army Air Forces late in 1942, but color blindness kept him from becoming a pilot. Assigned to Lackland Air Force Base in San Antonio, Texas, as a physical training instructor, he played for two years in a service league and then, late in 1944, joined an all-star Air Force team touring the Pacific and playing games to entertain the troops.

Returning to St. Louis after the war, Slaughter hit .300 in 1946, helped the Cardinals win the National League pennant, and sparked them during the World Series against the Boston Red Sox. Despite breaking his elbow in Game 5, he stayed in the lineup and got a key hit in Game 6, which St. Louis won. Then, with the scored tied in the deciding game, he opened the eighth inning with a single. After two Cardinals made outs, Slaughter tried to steal second base as Harry Walker stroked a hit, scored as a double, into center field. Slaughter never stopped running,

the Boston defense hesitated, and the "Mad Dash," as it was immortalized, gave the Cardinals the game's winning run.

Slaughter's career was tainted by an incident with racial overtones. Journalists and historians have disagreed over how many players disapproved of the African-American player Jackie Robinson's promotion to the Brooklyn Dodgers in 1947, but the Cardinals were implicated in an alleged plot to strike rather than play against him. In Slaughter's autobiography, he denied that any such plan existed, but in a close game with Brooklyn that season, Slaughter hit an infield ground ball, ran hard toward first base, Robinson's position, and spiked him on the foot. Slaughter claimed Robinson's foot was improperly placed in the middle of the base and there was no deliberate intent to injure, but the episode and its implications dogged him the rest of his life.

Slaughter remained with the Cardinals through the 1953 season. He hit .300 three more times, including .336 in 1949, but St. Louis did not win any more pennants. In April 1954 the Cardinals shocked Slaughter by trading him to the New York Yankees. He spent a season and a half in New York and parts of two seasons with the Kansas City Athletics before rejoining the Yankees in August 1956. At the advanced age of forty, he helped New York win the pennant, and in that year's World Series against the Dodgers, he won Game 3 with a three-run home run. Slaughter played for the Yankees for three more seasons, mostly as a pinch hitter, and finished his major league career with the Milwaukee Braves in 1959. He returned to the minors for two years as a player-manager and then retired. From 1971 through 1977 he coached baseball at Duke University.

In his nineteen-year career, Slaughter batted an even .300. He collected 2,383 hits, scored 1,247 runs, and walked 1,019 times. A fine defensive outfielder, he played in ten All-Star games and five World Series, and the *Sporting News* named him to its Major League All-Star team in 1942 and 1946. Slaughter was elected to the Baseball Hall of Fame in 1985. He raised tobacco on a farm in Roxboro and frequently returned to St. Louis to recount the highlights of his career. He succumbed to complications arising from colon and stomach surgery at Duke University Medical Center and is buried in Allensville United Church Cemetery in Allensville, North Carolina, near Roxboro.

★

Slaughter's autobiography is *Country Hardball* (1991), written with Kevin Reid. Another account of his life is in *Baseball: The Biographical Encyclopedia* (2000), ed. by David Pietrusza, Matthew Silverman, and Michael Gershman. Obituaries are in the *New York Times* and *St. Louis Post-Dispatch* (both 13 Aug. 2002).

STEVEN P. GIETSCHIER

SMITH, Howard K(ingsbury) (*b.* 12 May 1914 in Ferriday, Louisiana; *d.* 15 February 2002 in Bethesda, Maryland), award-winning journalist, pioneer of broadcast news on radio, and a widely respected television news commentator during the third quarter of the twentieth century.

Smith was the second of two sons born to Howard K. Smith, a railroad conductor, and Minnie (Cates) Smith, a homemaker. It was a troubled and loveless household, marked by poverty and unfulfilled expectations after Smith's father was fired from his railroad job and the family moved to New Orleans. Long an indifferent student, Smith caught fire in his junior year at Alcee Fortier High School, graduating as valedictorian and winning a scholarship to Tulane University. At Tulane, he again excelled academically. Elected student body president, he captained the track team, setting a college record for the 110-meter high hurdles that stood until the 1980s.

Graduating from Tulane in 1936 with a B.A. in journalism, Smith, by then fluent in German, spent the summer on a fellowship at Heidelberg, where he became a close observer and critic of Adolf Hitler's Nazi Germany. Returning to the United States as a rewrite man for the *New Orleans Item-Tribune,* he won a three-year Rhodes Scholarship to Oxford's Merton College in England in the spring of 1937. In his second year he assumed leadership of the Oxford University Labour Club, from whose ranks key figures in the postwar British Labour government would emerge. Between academic terms, he regularly visited Germany, sharpening his understanding of the Nazi regime.

In 1939, as World War II began, Smith abandoned his studies to work for United Press, first in London and then in Berlin, where in the spring of 1941 he joined Columbia Broadcasting System (CBS) Radio. Like other foreign journalists, Smith was shadowed by the Gestapo, Hitler's political police, who confiscated and burned his notebooks and papers before allowing him to leave Germany for Switzerland on 6 December 1941, just hours before the Japanese attacked Pearl Harbor. Settling in the Swiss city of Berne, he wrote *Last Train from Berlin* (1942), recounting his experiences with the Nazis. As a foreign national from a warring state in neutral Switzerland, he was not permitted to use Swiss broadcasting facilities but was allowed to cable reports on occupied Europe to CBS and to contribute articles to *Time* and *Life* magazines for nearly three years. He married Benedicte ("Bennie") Traberg, a Danish journalist, on 4 March 1942. They had a son and a daughter.

Following the liberation of Paris in August 1944, CBS assigned Smith as a war correspondent to the U.S. Ninth Army. Among the events he covered were the Battle of the Bulge in December 1944 and the surrender of the German army to the Russians in Berlin on 8 May 1945. Beginning in November 1945, he reported on the Nuremberg war

Howard K. Smith. AP/WIDE WORLD PHOTOS

crimes trials and witnessed the execution of ten convicted Nazi war criminals on 1 October 1946. In 1946 he replaced Edward R. Murrow as CBS's London-based chief European correspondent, a position he held for eleven years.

Smith was particularly sympathetic to the new Labour government in Britain, and in *The State of Europe* (1949) he proposed the creation of socialist welfare states on the Continent. He was sharply critical of U.S. foreign policy in Greece and elsewhere in the early stages of the cold war. As a result, he was named a Communist sympathizer in the right-wing publication *Red Channels* (1950), and was later denounced by Senator Joseph McCarthy, who led a wide-ranging investigation into the influence of Communism in various arenas of American society. CBS dismissed the allegations as false.

In 1957 Smith returned to the United States as CBS's chief Washington correspondent. He covered stories for the televised evening network news, beginning with the integration of the Little Rock, Arkansas, public schools in 1957, and hosted such programs as *Eyewitness to History* (1960–1962) and *Face the Nation* (1960–1963). Although he reported the news evenhandedly, he frequently provided clearly identified, opinionated analyses of the day's events. In his view, such opinions were essential to free journalism. There were certain times, Smith argued, that required a reporter to take sides, and he maintained that no one could be nonjudgmental about Hitler or silent in the face of racial segregation. He was aware of the cost of that freedom, especially when program sponsors threatened to withdraw their support. His documentary attacking apartheid in South Africa led to CBS being briefly banned in Pretoria, and his sympathetic presentation of the Arab position on Palestine on the television show *See It Now* generated controversy in Israel and the United States.

In 1961 Smith covered the civil rights movement in Birmingham, Alabama, where the police chief Bull Connor had given the anti-civil rights group the Ku Klux Klan a free hand in severely beating six student "freedom riders" who had come to the city to challenge the "Jim Crow" segregation laws. In a series of radio broadcasts, transcripts of which were published each day in the *New York Times,* Smith denounced Connor's brutal tactics. Outraged at Smith's comparison of Birmingham to Nazi Germany, the city sued CBS for $1 million, and a number of southern stations left the network. Smith was subsequently barred from ending a hard-hitting CBS report, *Who Speaks for Birmingham?,* with a statement by the eighteenth-century British statesman Edmund Burke, "The only thing required for the triumph of evil is for good men to do nothing." After a fiery exchange with William S. Paley, the head of CBS, who feared a further loss of viewers and sponsors, Smith resigned, ending his twenty-two-year association with the network on 29 October 1961.

When the American Broadcasting Company (ABC) obtained a sponsor for *Howard K. Smith—News and Commentary,* Smith found a new home on 14 February 1962. An instant hit with audiences and critics alike, the program was cancelled at year's end after Smith presented "The Political Obituary of Richard Nixon." The documentary, which aired following Nixon's defeat in the California gubernatorial race, included a controversial interview with Alger Hiss, a former U.S. State Department official whose perjury trials in 1949–1950 made Nixon a national figure. As a member of the congressional House Committee on Un-American Activities (HUAC) in 1948, Nixon believed the testimony of witnesses who accused Hiss of spying for the Soviet Union during and after World War II, but despite a series of well-publicized hearings, he was unable to secure an admission of guilt or clear-cut evidence of espionage. Instead, a federal court found Hiss guilty of lying during the HUAC interrogations and in 1950 sentenced him to five years in prison. For the remainder of the century, Hiss carried the taint of the unresolved spy charges, and his appearance on the Nixon documentary brought immediate protests from various patriotic groups across the country, leading the sponsors of Smith's program to withdraw their support. Although he remained on the ABC payroll, Smith had virtually no assignments over the next seven years but, with a change in network management,

became co-anchor of *ABC Evening News* (1969–1975), during which time he was a hawk on Vietnam, where his son had almost been fatally wounded in 1965.

Smith was one of the first journalists to call for President Nixon's resignation during the Watergate scandal, a controversy stemming from a break-in at the headquarters of the Democratic National Committee in Washington, D.C. The burglary eventually was traced to the Committee to Re-elect the President and led to Nixon's resignation in the face of impeachment. In 1975 Smith's role on *ABC Evening News* was limited to a brief commentary. Unhappy with further reductions in airtime three years later, Smith resigned from ABC on 20 April 1979. In retirement, he lectured at colleges and wrote his memoirs, *Events Leading Up to My Death: The Life of a Twentieth-Century Reporter* (1996). He died of pneumonia aggravated by congestive heart failure and is buried at Aspen Hill, Maryland.

One of the legendary Murrow Boys—the elite team of journalists Murrow assembled for CBS on the eve of World War II—Smith helped pioneer news reporting on radio and television. For nearly three decades he was one of the nation's most admired and talented broadcasters. He was honored with, among others, six Overseas Press Club awards (1951–1954, 1961, and 1963); the George Polk Memorial Award (1960), a Peabody Award (1960), and an Emmy (1960) for his high standards of news coverage and analysis and for his graceful language. As a journalist, Smith adhered to standards that were abandoned in later years, when the major networks replaced hard news with light entertainment features, making his kind of reporting and commentary obsolete.

★

The Howard K. Smith Papers are in the Archives Division of the State Historical Society of Wisconsin in Madison. His memoir, *Events Leading Up to My Death: The Life of a Twentieth-Century Reporter* (1996), is indispensable. His work during and after World War II is described in Stanley Cloud and Lynne Olson, *The Murrow Boys* (1996). An obituary is in the *New York Times* (19 Feb. 2002). "Reminiscences of Howard K. Smith (1968)" are in the Oral History Project, Butler Library, Columbia University in New York.

ALLAN L. DAMON

SNEAD, Samuel Jackson ("Sam") (*b.* 27 May 1912 in Ashwood, Virginia; *d.* 23 May 2002 in Hot Springs, Virginia), golfer who won more Professional Golf Association (PGA) Tour victories than any other player, with a swing universally admired as the most natural and graceful in the history of the game.

Snead was one of six children born to Harry Snead and Laura Snead. His father kept chickens and cows on a small farm to supplement his salary from a local hotel, where he maintained boilers; his mother was a homemaker. Growing up in the foothills of Bath County, Virginia, in a village of 400 inhabitants three miles from Hot Springs, Snead spent his early years hunting and fishing, recreations that he cherished throughout his life. "Fishing is a lot like golf," he told a reporter in 1967. "You got to know where the fish run and that takes a lot of time: just like golf takes [a lot of] practice." Standing five feet, eleven inches tall, with long arms and incredibly limber tendons, Snead was a natural athlete who excelled at a wide range of sports, including football, baseball, basketball, golf, and track. But a high school football injury, and impatience with teammates who were not as talented, led him to concentrate on golf, which he particularly liked because of the solitary, self-dependent nature of the game.

Snead began his career as a golfer during the depression at The Homestead, a course near his home in Hot Springs. He started as a caddie when he was seven, worked his way up to course handyman, and in 1934 became a professional by virtue of accepting an unpaid position as a apprentice professional at the nearby Cascades Course. He earned what he could from lessons, but with more opportunity to practice than to teach, his game improved faster than his economic circumstances. When the golf manager of the Greenbrier Hotel in White Sulphur Springs saw him swing, he offered Snead an assistant's job at $45.00 a month plus room and board. From 1936 to 1939 and from 1947 to 1974, Snead was Greenbriar's head professional.

Snead joined the PGA Tour in 1937 at age twenty-five. In his rookie year he finished second in the U.S. Open and won five tournaments, including the Oakland Open. (His last PGA victory, the Greater Greensboro Open, was in 1965, at age fifty-two years and ten months, making him the oldest winner of an official PGA Tour event.) In his youth he was the youngest professional player to shoot his age or better, and completed rounds of sixty-seven and sixty-six at age sixty-seven in the 1979 Quad Cities Open. Cofounder of the Senior PGA Tour, he won the PGA Seniors' championship six times, in 1964, 1965, 1967, 1970, 1972, and 1973.

In 1942 Snead entered the U.S. Navy and served until a back injury led to his medical discharge in September 1944. In August 1940 he had married Audrey Karns; they had two sons. The second, Terrence, developed a serious learning disability from a childhood fever. His condition weighed heavily on Snead. "As much as I like money," he once told his friend Johnny Bulla, "I'd give it all up if Terry could be all right."

Snead's achievements as a competitive golfer are unlikely to be matched. He won a total of 135 victories, eighty-

Sam Snead, June 1949. CORBIS

one of them on the PGA Tour, eleven more than Jack Nicklaus (winner of the "Golfer of the Century" award). He won three PGA championships (1942, 1949, and 1951), three Masters tournaments (1949, 1952, and 1954), and the British Open in 1946. He made eight Ryder Cup teams from 1937 to 1969, and captained three. He also won the Vardon Trophy for low stroke average in 1938, 1949, 1950, and 1955, and was the leading money winner in 1938, 1939, and 1950, the year in which he won eleven tournaments. In the forty-two years from 1937 to 1979, Snead won money every year he played on the U.S. tour.

The admiration of the golfing world for Snead's graceful swing highlights the aesthetic nature of the game. He was golf's version of the dancer Rudolph Nureyev, personifying the mastery of the demands of rhythm, balance, and coordination that are required to play the game at the highest level. He was the first really long driver to win tournaments; he was an accurate iron player, a precise chipper, and a good long putter who occasionally twitched when close to the hole, a condition he dubbed the "yips." He "made holes-in-one with every club in his bag but the putter," according to the golf writer Bill Fields. He "had all the shots: wedges that would dance, one-irons that would soar, drivers off the deck struck so solidly—and curving on demand—that even a superb shotmaker like Lee Trevino would watch with eyes agape." He was a natural. "Watching Sam Snead practice hitting golf balls is like watching a fish practice swimming," quipped John Schlee, the runner-up in the 1973 U.S. Open.

But for all Snead's skills and achievements, his failure to win a U.S. Open title, the ultimate challenge on the PGA Tour, barred him from the front rank of the pantheon of the greatest golfers of the twentieth century. Finishing second three times, he was dubbed the "Great Runner-up." This is a flip analysis at best; his U.S. Open losses have been overblown. In 1939, at the seventy-second hole, Snead believed he needed a birdie to win. Throwing caution to the wind, he landed in a bunker, took two to get out, and shot an eight, which put him in fifth place, only to discover afterward that a cautious par five would have won. In 1947 he lost the play-off to Lew Worsham by missing a putt; in 1949 he failed by one stroke to catch Cary Middlecoff; and in 1953 he was the runner-up to a dominant Ben Hogan. But a year later, at the Augusta National Golf Club, he beat Hogan 70–71 in a playoff that won Snead his third Masters, a feat that should have put his runner-up reputation to rest. The U.S. Open jinx was painful, but Snead was philosophical about it: "I thought if I lost it wasn't my turn. But I never gave up trying."

Snead wrote several books that contain golf instruction and personal anecdotes, including *Golf Begins at Forty* (1978), with Dick Aultman, and *The Game I Love: Wisdom, Insight, and Instruction from Golf's Greatest Player* (1997), with Fran Pirozzolo. He died at his home in Hot Springs after suffering a series of small strokes, and is buried in the Snead Family Cemetery in Hot Springs.

★

Information about Snead's life and career is in Mike Towle, *I Remember Sam Snead: Memories and Anecdotes of Golf's Slammin' Sammy* (2003). Obituaries are in the *New York Times* and *Washington Post* (both 24 May 2002).

MARTIN J. SHERWIN

SOTHERN, Ann (*b.* 22 January 1909 in Valley City, North Dakota; *d.* 15 March 2001 in Ketchum, Idaho), vivacious actress, comedienne, and singer who moved from glamour roles in the 1930s to play colorful, spirited women on stage, film, and television.

Sothern, born Harriet Arlene Lake (as a young girl, she began spelling her first name "Harriette"), was the oldest of three girls of Walter J. Lake, a traveling salesman, and Annette (Yde) Lake, a Danish-born opera singer. By 1912 the family had moved to Waterloo, Iowa, and in 1917 Sothern began third grade in Minneapolis. As a child she staged backyard musicals, sometimes accompanied her mother on tour, and later studied at the MacPhail School of Music.

Ann Sothern. THE KOBAL COLLECTION

She graduated from Central High School in 1926 with several prizes in composition.

After her parents divorced in 1927, Sothern lived with her father in 1928 and 1929 while attending the University of Washington in Seattle. Her mother became a vocal coach at Warner Bros. Studios in Los Angeles, and when Sothern visited her in the summer of 1929, she did a screen test. This led to small roles for producer Paul Bern at Metro-Goldwyn-Mayer (MGM), and when Florenz Ziegfeld heard Sothern sing at a party, he offered her work in a Broadway musical. Six months later, Sothern moved east to accept Ziegfeld's offer.

Cast as third female lead in *Smiles,* Sothern opened in Boston on 28 October 1930, and her musical numbers proved so popular that the leading lady demanded she be replaced. Then Sothern landed the lead in Richard Rodgers and Moss Hart's satire of Hollywood, *America's Sweetheart,* and in late 1931 starred in *Everybody's Welcome.* In 1932 she toured for seven months in *Of Thee I Sing* by Hart and George S. Kaufman, and was invited to take over the Broadway lead.

In 1933 Sothern returned to Hollywood and appeared briefly in two films before Harry Cohn at Columbia Pictures signed her to star in *Let's Fall in Love* (1934), a Harold Arlen musical about a sideshow girl masquerading as a Swedish actress. Cohn stipulated that she change her name, and Harriette Lake became Ann Sothern. The film's success led to a contract at Columbia, but the studio confined her to B pictures—or, as she later described them, "Z pictures." Sothern moved to RKO Pictures in 1936 but, finding herself cast in equally disappointing films, left after one year. By then she had appeared in twenty-six films, and had become known as "Queen of the Bs."

During *Of Thee I Sing,* Sothern met the bandleader Roger Pryor. They met again in Hollywood in 1935 and married on 27 September 1936. They had no children. After leaving RKO, Sothern traveled with Pryor, performing with his orchestra.

In 1938 producer Walter Wanger offered Sothern a part in *Trade Winds,* a brassy role in which Sothern made wisecracks written by Dorothy Parker. Her performance was so acclaimed that MGM revived a project originally planned for the recently deceased Jean Harlow: the role of Maisie Ravier, a good-natured, hard-boiled showgirl adventuress. *Maisie* (1939) grew into a highly successful series of ten pictures. Sothern used their success to bargain for better parts, notably leads in the musical *Lady Be Good* (1941), in which she introduced the Oscar-winning song "The Last Time I Saw Paris," and the army-nurse drama *Cry "Havoc"* (1944).

Sothern and Pryor separated in September 1941. The same year, Sothern filmed *Ringside Maisie*—another installment in the successful series—with actor Robert Sterling, whom she married on 23 May 1943, six days after her divorce from Pryor became final. The couple had one child, Tisha Sterling, who later became an actress and sometimes worked in films with her mother. Sothern and Sterling divorced on 8 March 1949.

In 1947, after MGM did not renew her contract, Sothern freelanced through nine more pictures, including what many consider to be her best role, that of Kirk Douglas's wife in Joseph Mankiewicz's *A Letter to Three Wives* (1949).

In January 1950 Sothern collapsed while skiing and was diagnosed with severe infectious hepatitis. Depressed and unable to work for nearly two years, she made radio broadcasts of Maisie stories recorded from her bedroom. Sothern was befriended by the actor Richard Egan, who influenced her to convert to Roman Catholicism in 1952. Still weak from illness, she played opposite Robert Cummings in the Broadway comedy *Faithfully Yours,* which opened on 18 October 1951 for sixty-eight performances. In the following year she made television appearances on *Schlitz Playhouse of Stars* and *Hollywood Opening Night*. These roles brought offers to star in her own series, and after a supporting role in Fritz Lang's stylish murder tale, *The Blue Gardenia* (1953), Sothern left films for television.

The series Sothern chose was *Private Secretary,* the first program in television history to feature a career woman in the business world. It ran for 104 episodes, from February 1953 to March 1957, and brought Sothern three Emmy nominations and a bronze shorthand book from the National Secretaries Association. Astutely, she insisted on part ownership and began her own production company, sometimes directing episodes.

In 1954 Sothern starred in Max Liebman's early color television production of Hart's *Lady in the Dark.* In 1958, in addition to recording her album *Sothern Exposure* and starting a music publishing business, Sothern began a second series that quickly came to resemble *Private Secretary.* In *The Ann Sothern Show* she played the assistant manager of a New York hotel, supported by actors from the earlier series. Sothern composed the theme song and coproduced the show, which won a Golden Globe in 1959 and brought her a fourth Emmy nomination.

After the final episode aired in September 1961, Sothern returned to New York, where she studied acting with Stella Adler to prepare for more demanding dramatic roles. She played a battered prostitute in *Lady in a Cage* and an overbearing party chairwoman in Gore Vidal's *The Best Man* (both 1964), for which she was again nominated for a Golden Globe. In 1965 she played the manager of a penny arcade in the film *Sylvia* and had a short television run as a soul reincarnated in the form of an automobile in *My Mother the Car.* She also made seven guest appearances with her friend Lucille Ball on *The Lucy Show,* playing the sort of comic role she had perfected in *Maisie*—the penniless Countess Framboise, formerly Rosie Harrigan.

After 1965 Sothern played character roles in minor theatrical and television films (notably *Chubasco* in 1968 with her friend Egan), and starred in plays and musicals at regional theatres. In Jacksonville, Florida, in 1973, she suffered a broken back from a falling piece of scenery. In intermittent pain for the rest of her life, she learned to walk with a cane. Nevertheless, the next year she went to Hong Kong to play the hostess of a mahjong parlor in *Golden Needles,* and in 1975 performed with her daughter in Jonathan Demme's *Crazy Mama,* destined to become a cult favorite.

In spite of her disability, Sothern played featured roles in three more films and two television dramas. One of these was a 1985 remake of *A Letter to Three Wives.* Her cameo role caught the attention of the director Lindsay Anderson, who gave her a major part in *The Whales of August* (1987) as the nosy neighbor of Bette Davis and Lillian Gish. For her performance Sothern received an Academy Award nomination for best supporting actress. It was her last picture.

At her home in Ketchum, Idaho, close to her daughter and granddaughter, Sothern supported civic affairs and pursued painting. In 1993 she narrated a documentary on American folk art, and in 1999 the Museum of Modern Art in New York City celebrated her with a retrospective. She died of heart failure at ninety-two and is buried in Ketchum Cemetery.

"Hollywood," Sothern once said, "doesn't respond to a strong woman, not at all." She described herself as "a Hollywood princess, never a Hollywood queen." By her own effort, in the 1930s she broke free from the glamour ingénue stereotype; in the 1940s popularized a feisty female character; and, against the cultural climate of the 1950s, made a heroine of an unmarried career woman. As independent offscreen as on, she gained a reputation for generosity to her costars. Lucille Ball, whose career often paralleled Sothern's, described her as "the best comedienne in this business, bar none." Of her remarkably varied career, Sothern said in 1987, "I've done everything but play rodeos."

★

The Margaret Herrick Library of the Academy of Motion Picture Arts and Sciences maintains a collection of Sothern's clippings, photographs, and studio biographies. Margie Schultz, *Ann Sothern: A Bio-Bibliography* (1990), features a good biographical essay and an exhaustive bibliography of articles about Sothern, with full lists of her films, theatrical performances, radio and television programs, and records. David Shipman gives an excellent overview of Sothern's films in *The Great Movie Stars: The Golden Years* (1979). See also Michael Buckley, *Films in Review* (1988). Obituaries are in the *New York Times* and *Los Angeles Times* (both 17 Mar. 2001). Mike Kaplan filmed a documentary retrospective, *The Sharpest Girl in Town: Ann Sothern,* which premiered at the Museum of Modern Art in 1999.

ALAN BUSTER

Floyd D. Spence, August 1962. AP/WIDE WORLD PHOTOS

SPENCE, Floyd D(avidson) (*b.* 9 April 1928 in Columbia, South Carolina; *d.* 10 August 2001 in Jackson, Mississippi), Republican congressman from South Carolina who served as chair of the House Armed Services Committee.

Spence was born to James Wilson Spence and Addie Jane (Lucas) Spence. He graduated from Lexington High School in 1947, and then attended the University of South Carolina at Columbia, where he was a star football player and student body president. He earned a B.A. in English in 1952. He was commissioned as an ensign in the U.S. Naval Reserve that same year, serving during the Korean Conflict. (He retired from the reserves as a captain in 1988.) On 22 December 1952 Spence married Lula Hancock Drake; they had four children. After earning an LL.B. from the University of South Carolina School of Law in 1956, he was elected to the state house of representatives as a Democrat. He switched parties and became a Republican in 1962, two years before Senator Strom Thurmond, also from South Carolina, changed parties.

Spence narrowly lost a U.S. House race that year to a Democrat who later switched parties. Spence was then elected to the state senate as a Republican in 1966. When the incumbent ran for governor in 1970, Spence ran again for the House seat and won. A pollster who sampled Spence's congressional district when he first ran for Congress found that 21,000 people claimed him as a "personal friend." He seemed to know everybody. With his cheerful smile and spunky outlook, Spence was able to connect instantly and deeply with people of all ages and backgrounds. "Getting along with people is the best way to get along in life, and I work hard at getting along with people," he said. Spence was reelected as representative from South Carolina's Second District fifteen times, serving continuously in this seat from 1971 until his death in 2001.

During his thirty years in Congress, Spence kept a low profile. He introduced few bills, rarely spoke on the House floor, issued few press releases, and did not have a press secretary. Even though he served as chair of the House Armed Services Committee (1995–2000), one of the most influential and powerful committees, he was never invited to appear on the Sunday television talk shows. That was not Spence's forte, and he was not comfortable doing it. Known for his good cheer, he was not a visible fighter in congressional battles. He had an eye for women, and often in their presence would sniff the air and say, "You smell nice tonight"; or, he would warn them, "Watch out for these hairy-leg men in Washington." With men, he would roll the cloth of their coats between his fingers and say, "That's a nice jacket." Ask him how he was doing, and he would respond, "Oh, about half way." This amicable demeanor won him friends and elections all his life, and he became invincible at the ballot box.

Spence advocated a strong national defense and had a solidly conservative voting record. He supported displaying the Ten Commandments in federal buildings and a ban on partial-birth abortions, but opposed background checks before the purchase of a gun. In 1971 Spence was the first House member to introduce legislation calling for a constitutional amendment requiring a balanced federal budget. Although he served on the Committee on Standards of Official Conduct (Ethics Committee) for thirteen years as the ranking Republican, his greatest energy was devoted to military issues. He gained fame for his lead role in the fight to develop a missile-defense system, for which he long advocated.

During the 1980s, Spence supported the defense buildup under President Ronald W. Reagan, and during the 1990s called for "responsible downsizing of defense expenditures rather than drastic cuts." But that downsizing went much farther than Spence considered wise. As chair of the Armed Services Committee, Spence peppered the administration of President William J. ("Bill") Clinton with criticism, even as he managed complex and lengthy defense-authorization bills. He argued that defense cuts were too deep, twice as deep as Clinton promised in 1992, and he worried about the erosion of the U.S. nuclear weapons stockpile.

Spence argued that the cuts jeopardized U.S. military superiority, whose dominance was displayed during the 1990–1991 Gulf War. He said in 1998, "Our national strategy is to be able to simultaneously fight and win two major regional contingencies. But we've cut back so much since Desert Storm that I don't think we could do even one." Spence was particularly concerned when retention rates in the armed forces declined and standards for enlistment were lowered. "The decline in military quality of life is approaching a state of crisis," he said, and indicated that he would support a military draft if retention rates and readiness did not improve. Spence also criticized the Clinton administration for selling high-tech devices to China, and Clinton's policy toward North Korea as "appeasement and bribery." Spence secured money to support U.S. troops in Iraq and Bosnia despite faulting the conduct of North Atlantic Treaty Organization (NATO) operations in the latter country.

"We don't have a defense against weapons of mass de-struction, and the president has blocked all of our efforts to increase national security," Spence warned in 1998. Although efforts to declare missile defense as a national priority were frustrated by a Democratic filibuster that year, Spence moved missile defense significantly forward by creating the Commission on Missile Defense, headed by the former defense secretary Donald Rumsfeld. In July 1998 the panel unanimously concluded that rogue states could develop missiles with the capacity to deliver nuclear weapons without U.S. intelligence agencies knowing. This changed the conversation, and in 1999 the House passed legislation that would commit the U.S. to building a missile-defense system as soon as technologically possible. Later, again defense secretary under President George W. Bush, Rumsfeld was in a position to move missile-defense forward, a development for which Spence deserved much credit.

Spence's support for the military was legendary, stretching far beyond legislation to the everyday world of politics. During the 2000 presidential election recount in Florida, he voiced concern when Democrats stopped counting absentee military ballots without postmarks. Spence's tenure as chair of the Armed Services Committee ended in 2001, when the Republican's three-term limit on committee chairmen forced him to step down. He then became chair of the Armed Services Military Procurement Subcommittee.

From 1990 to 1996 Spence did not have a Democratic opponent. In 1998, however, he was opposed by Jane Frederick, a Beaufort County architect and self-styled feminist who attacked Spence's "archaic, insensitive and unacceptable view toward women" and his stands on abortion, family leave, and the minimum wage. Spence campaigned vigorously around the district, but his campaign organization was rusty, and Democrats made their best South Carolina showing in years. Spence won 58 percent to 41 percent, a solid, but not overwhelming, margin. He ran ahead of the state ticket, but despite years of helping local black officials, he lost in three black majority counties. Frederick ran again in 2000, and the result was virtually the same, with Spence winning six of eleven counties and taking Richland and Lexington counties by 38,000 votes, as well as Frederick's Beaufort County base by 6,000.

Spence's first wife died in 1978, and on 3 July 1988 he married Deborah Ellen Williams. That year, at age sixty, Spence underwent a rare double lung transplant. Then in May 2000, after two months of kidney failure, he received a transplant from his oldest son. Spence died at Saint Dominic-Jackson Memorial Hospital from complications following the removal of a blood clot on his brain while being treated for Ramsay Hunt Syndrome, a viral infection that causes paralysis of the facial muscles. He is buried in Saint Peter's Lutheran Church Cemetery in Lexington, South Carolina. At the time of his death, he was second in seniority among House Republicans, trailing only Phil Crane of Illinois and tying Bill Young of Florida.

★

The Floyd D. Spence Papers are held in the Modern Political Collections at the South Carolina Library Annex on 720 College Street in Columbia. For information about Spence's life and career, see "Time to Rebuild," *The American Legion* 149, no. 4 (Oct. 2000); and "The Gentleman from the Land of the Palmetto," *The Officer* 78, no. 8 (Sept. 2001). Obituaries are in the *New York Times* and *Washington Post* (both 17 Aug. 2001).

LEE BANDY

STANLEY, Kim   (*b.* 11 February 1925 in Tularosa, New Mexico; *d.* 20 August 2001 in Santa Fe, New Mexico), actress who won distinction on the Broadway stage, on television, and in film.

Stanley was born Patricia Beth Reid to Dr. J. T. Reid, a professor, and Ann (Miller) Reid, an interior designer. She grew up in Albuquerque, New Mexico, and attended the University of New Mexico from 1942 to 1944, majoring in drama. She left the university in the middle of her junior year to study acting at the Pasadena Playhouse, where she changed her name to distinguish herself from another Patricia Reid in her class.

In 1947, with $21.00 in her pocket, Stanley took a Greyhound Bus to New York City to launch her acting career. For two years she supported herself as a waitress and fashion model. In 1950 she joined the Actors Studio to train under Elia Kazan and Lee Strasberg. After appearing on Broadway in *Montserrat* (1949), *The House of Bernarda Alba* (1951), and *The Chase* (1952), Stanley received the 1954 Drama Critics Award for her work as the tomboy Millie in William Inge's *Picnic* (1953). The *New York Herald Tribune* critic Walter Kerr wrote that Stanley was "one of the most promising performers on Broadway." Stanley won further praise in Inge's *Bus Stop* (1955) as Cherie, the Ozark chanteuse. In 1958 Stanley thrilled audiences in New York City and London as Sara Melody in Eugene O'Neill's *A Touch of the Poet* and as Maggie in Tennessee Williams's *Cat on a Hot Tin Roof*. However, she did not reprise these roles on film, thus giving Marilyn Monroe, Elizabeth Taylor, and Susan Strasberg their opportunity to play coveted roles.

Stanley's film debut was as Emily Ann in *The Goddess* (1958), Paddy Chayefsky's naturalistic character study of a Marilyn Monroe–type sexpot. According to John M. Clum in his biography of Chayefsky, Chayefsky's script assumed the emptiness of Hollywood success but, more interestingly, investigated people's dependency upon that illusion. Despite Stanley's riveting performance, *The Goddess* "never had the success it deserved."

Kim Stanley, 1957. JOHN SPRINGER/CORBIS

Although Stanley married four times, Strasberg was perhaps the most influential man in her life, as she worked with him for fifteen years at the Actors Studio. Commenting on her acting technique, Stanley said of Strasberg, "He made it possible for the whole world to open up for me." Yet, the Actors Studio's 1964 production of Anton Chekhov's *Three Sisters,* in which Stanley played Masha under Strasberg's direction, was, according to Arthur Penn, "a major disappointment in her life. She expected the work of the Studio to carry over into the production." The cast included Geraldine Page and Shirley Knight. Although the play was a hodgepodge of brilliant moments, a *Newsweek* critic wrote that Stanley "seizes this role and takes it to its limit." In the restaged 1965 London production, Stanley felt betrayed that Strasberg had not "been there" to stand behind her, and also guilty, for she and Page had originally convinced Strasberg to direct. The London performance was a fiasco. Paul Bogart's rarely seen 1964 film adaptation is the only record of any Actors Studio production.

Stanley was the adult voice of Scout Finch in *To Kill a Mockingbird* (1962) and was nominated for an Academy Award as the crazed medium in *Séance on a Wet Afternoon* (1964). Although the award went to Julie Andrews, Stanley won the National Board of Review Best Actress Award in 1964 and a British Academy Award and the New York Film Critics Award in 1965.

Early in her career Stanley appeared on television programs such as *Goodyear TV Playhouse* and *Magnavox Theater*. According to biographer Jon Krampner, in the 1960s and early 1970s Stanley worked intermittently in television. "Many were quality shows," Krampner said, "but much of her work during this period was on cookie-cutter series dramas." However, Stanley's role in "A Cardinal Act of Mercy" (1963), a two-part episode of *Ben Casey,* earned her an Emmy Award.

In 1972 Stanley left New York City and returned to New Mexico, where she taught acting at the College of Santa Fe. Back in New York City in 1978, she taught acting at the Lee Strasberg Institute. One student described Stanley as both "personal and far away . . . unapproachable—yet she wrapped us in her magic gauze." Stanley dreamed of directing her own repertory company, an ambition that never materialized.

Back in Hollywood in 1982, Stanley did her final film and television work, beginning with *Frances* (1982), which earned her an Academy Award nomination for best supporting actress for her role as Lillian Farmer, the mother of Frances Farmer, who was played by Jessica Lange. Lange and Stanley discovered a close kinship during their work together. Stanley subsequently appeared as the barnstorming pilot Pancho Barnes, who inspired the early NASA astronauts, in Philip Kaufman's *The Right Stuff* (1983). Her final performance came as Big Mama in a 1985 Public Broadcasting System telecast of *Cat on a Hot Tin Roof,* with Lange as Maggie, a role Stanley had received rave reviews for in London years earlier. Stanley won a second Emmy award for her performance.

In the mid-1990s Stanley returned to Santa Fe, where she died of uterine cancer at age seventy-six. Her remains were cremated. Stanley had three children: a daughter by her second husband, Curt Conway, whom she married on 28 January 1950; a son by Brooks Clift, the brother of the actor Montgomery Clift; and a daughter by her third husband, Alfred Ryder, whom she married on 1 August 1958. Stanley's first marriage to Bruce Hall (1946) and fourth marriage to Joseph Siegel (1964) were childless.

Arthur Penn called Stanley the "American Duse," after Elenora Duse, the great Italian actress. Though regarded by theater professionals as the most outstanding stage actress of her generation, many wondered why Stanley's career was frustratingly uneven. The writer and director Arthur Laurents blamed it on Stanley's ongoing battle with alcohol. Yet perhaps the keen sensitivity and personal intensity that served Stanley as an actress led her to see through the Hollywood illusion, as in *The Goddess,* making a consistent career impossible.

★

Information about Stanley can be found in John M. Clum, *Paddy Chayefsky* (1976); David Garfield, *A Player's Place: The Story of the Actors Studio* (1980); and Foster Hirsch, *A Method to Their Madness: The History of the Actors Studio* (1984). Additional information is in Gabriel Miller's interview with Nicholas Martin, "Nicholas Martin's On Directing: Arthur Laurents," *American Drama* 12, nos. 1–2 (winter–summer 2003): 140–160. Obituaries are in the *New York Times* (21 Aug. 2001) and *Washington Post* (22 Aug. 2001).

ROBERT VELLANI

STARGELL, Wilver Dornel ("Willie") (*b.* 6 March 1940 in Earlsboro, Oklahoma; *d.* 9 April 2001 in Wilmington, North Carolina), Hall of Fame baseball player with the Pittsburgh Pirates who won the National League (NL) and World Series Most Valuable Player (MVP) award in 1979.

Stargell, of African-American and Seminole Indian descent, was born in 1940, although his autobiography lists the date as 7 March 1941. He was the only child of William Stargell and Gladys Vernell (Russell) Stargell, a homemaker. Stargell's teenage parents separated prior to his birth, and he did not meet his biological father until nearly twenty years later. Stargell's mother remarried in 1946, and, after living with a maternal aunt in Orlando, Florida, for several years, Stargell was reunited with his stepfather, mother, and sister in 1951. He graduated from Encinal High School in Alameda, California, in 1958, then attended Santa Rosa Junior College in California for one year.

Upon the insistence of George Reed, the Encinal coach, Robert Zuk, a West Coast scout for the Pittsburgh Pirates, came to scrutinize Stargell, visiting three times before making an offer. In 1959 Stargell agreed to terms with the Pirates organization and received a signing bonus of $1,500.00. While at Encinal, Stargell was a baseball teammate to Tommy Harper and Curt Motton, both of whom went on to have major league careers.

Assigned to San Angelo, Texas, in the Class D Sophomore League, Stargell played left field, batting .274 with eighty-seven runs batted in (RBI) and seven home runs. While playing for this Pirate farm club, Stargell faced racism for the first time in his life. The league, comprised of eight cities located in southeastern New Mexico and midwestern Texas, permitted no more than four nonwhites on any team roster, and segregation was practiced in matters of lodging and dining. Stargell later said, "Though I was deeply bothered by the racism in the Sophomore League, I always hid the hurt inside and never allowed it to escape."

During his initial professional season, Stargell met a gun-toting bigot outside a Plainview, Texas, ballpark who threatened, "if you play in that game tonight, I'll blow your brains out." Stargell recalled, "I was real scared. But by the

Willie Stargell. AP/WIDE WORLD PHOTOS

time the rest of the team got there, I decided that if I was gonna die, I was gonna die doing exactly what I wanted to do. I had to play ball."

On 14 May 1962 Stargell married Lois Evelyn Beard, and on 16 September he made his major league debut in a pinch-hitting role against the San Francisco Giants. On 8 May 1963 the six-foot, three-inch, 225-pound left-handed outfielder clubbed the first of his 475 career home runs in a 9–5 loss to the Chicago Cubs. During the next season he divided his play between the outfield and first base, batting 421 times and crushing twenty-one home runs, including the first home run ever hit at the newly built Shea Stadium in New York City.

In 1965 Stargell won the starting left field position and swatted twenty-seven home runs, netting the first of his five 100-plus RBI seasons. He also divorced, marrying his second wife, Dolores Parker, in the winter of 1966.

On 9 July 1967, in the bottom of the ninth inning, Stargell broke a 1–1 tie with the Cincinnati Reds by thumping a Jim Maloney pitch over the right field roof of Forbes Field in Pittsburgh. With its 457-foot right field line and

eighty-six-foot-high grand stands, the cavernous Forbes Field was not favorable to left-handed batters. Yet Stargell accomplished this remarkable feat six more times in his career. On 16 July 1969 he splashed a pitch by Montreal Expo Dan McGinn over the right field fence and into the municipal swimming pool at Jarry Park. On 5 August 1969 he hit the first home run completely out of Dodger Stadium, a 512-foot shot off Alan Foster (some accounts note 506 or 480 feet). He repeated the feat on 8 May 1973 with a 470-foot blast off Andy Messersmith.

In June 1970 the Pirates moved to Three Rivers Stadium, where the field's dimensions suited Stargell's power swing. Stargell hit home runs in all thirteen NL stadiums that year. The next season the seven-time All-Star led the NL with a career-high forty-eight home runs, batting .295 with 125 RBI. Off the field, he opened a fried chicken restaurant in Pittsburgh's Hill District. As a promotion, orders were free for anyone who was waiting in line when Stargell homered. The Pirates broadcaster Bob Prince began to call for Stargell to homer with the words, "Come on, Wilver. Let's spread some chicken on the Hill." In 1971 he had his best offensive year, but in post-season play he went 0–14 in the NL playoffs against the Giants, with a single RBI in the Pirates seven-game World Series victory over the favored Baltimore Orioles.

On 31 December 1972, after the Pirate superstar Roberto Clemente died in a plane crash, Stargell reluctantly became team captain. As he said, "There's a time in a man's life when he has to decide if he's going to be a man." Known as "Pops," Stargell was a dynamic leader, who awarded players with "Stargell Stars" for special accomplishments; his teammates responded by displaying them on their caps.

In 1979 Stargell adopted the Sister Sledge disco hit "We Are Family" as the Pirates unofficial team anthem. Known as "The Family," the 1979 Pirates won the World Series and, for the first time in history, two players shared NL MVP honors: Stargell and the St. Louis Cardinal Keith Hernandez.

On 6 September 1982 the Pirates retired Stargell's number "8" at Three Rivers Stadium before 38,000 fans. He hit a pinch single in a 6–1 Pirate triumph over the New York Mets. After his 1982 retirement, Stargell served as a coach in the Pirates and Atlanta Braves organizations. He divorced his second wife, but married again to Margaret Weller. On 12 January 1988 Stargell was elected into the National Baseball Hall of Fame, becoming only the seventeenth player to be elected in his first year of eligibility.

In February 1997 Stargell became an assistant to the Pirates general manager Cam Bonifay. He remained in this position until his death, which dampened the celebration surrounding the opening of the Pirates new stadium, PNC Park, in the spring of 2001. Plagued by a long history of high blood pressure and a kidney disorder, Stargell died of a stroke at New Hanover Regional Medical Center in Wilmington, North Carolina, and was buried at Oleander Memorial Gardens in Wilmington. He was survived by his wife and five children.

★

Stargell's autobiography is *Willie Stargell: An Autobiography* (1984). Information about Stargell is in David Pietrusza, Matthew Silverman, and Michael Gershman, eds., *Baseball: The Biographical Encyclopedia* (2000), John McCollister, *Tales from the Pirates Dugout* (2003), and Richard Peterson, ed., *The Pirates Reader* (2003). Obituaries are in the *New York Times, Pittsburgh Post-Gazette,* and *Washington Post* (all 10 Apr. 2001).

JOHN VORPERIAN

STASSEN, Harold Edward (*b.* 12 November 1907 in West Saint Paul, Minnesota; *d.* 4 March 2001 in Bloomington, Minnesota), Minnesota governor, university president, and adviser to President Dwight D. Eisenhower, best known for his nine failed campaigns for the Republican nomination for president of the United States between 1948 and 1988.

Harold E. Stassen, May 1963. BETTMANN/CORBIS

Stassen was the third of four sons born to William Andrew Stassen, a farmer, and Elsie Emma (Mueller) Stassen, a homemaker. He graduated from Humboldt High School in Saint Paul at age fourteen. He managed the family farm until he was old enough, at age sixteen, to enter the University of Minnesota, where he held every important student office and captained the rifle team to three national championships. He graduated with a B.A. in political science in 1927 and two years later received an L.L.B. from the university's law school. On 14 November 1929 he married Esther G. Glewwe, with whom he had a son and a daughter.

Stassen opened a law office with a classmate in South Saint Paul in 1929 and, within three years, had prospered enough to add four other attorneys to the firm. He was elected Dakota County attorney in 1930, a position he held until 1938, when he won the Minnesota governorship with a victory margin of almost 300,000 votes. Six feet, three inches tall, blue-eyed and ruddy complexioned, with what one reporter called "a wide, contagious smile," he radiated energy and integrity. At age thirty-one he was the youngest governor in the state's history.

Within a year Stassen pushed through landmark reforms, revamping the civil service system, reducing the state debt by 30 percent, and revising Minnesota's outdated labor laws. Easily reelected governor in 1940 and 1942, he resigned four months into his third term—as he had warned voters he would do—to go on active duty as a lieutenant commander in the U.S. Navy. He served as aide and flag secretary to Admiral William F. Halsey, commander of the south Pacific area and the U.S. Third Fleet, and was awarded the Legion of Merit for combat duty in the Pacific, notably in the battle of the Philippine Sea in 1944.

Given temporary leave, Stassen was one of eight U.S. delegates sent by President Franklin D. Roosevelt to the San Francisco Conference (April–June 1945) that created the United Nations (U.N.) A signer of the U.N. charter, he fought unsuccessfully to keep the veto power out of the Security Council, but secured the charter provision that allows member states to defend themselves should the U.N. fail to act because of that veto. He returned to active duty to oversee the evacuation of 13,000 U.S. prisoners of war from Japan to the United States, and was discharged from the navy on 15 November 1945 with the rank of captain.

Beginning in early 1946, Stassen made a serious run for the Republican presidential nomination. A nationally recognized figure among Republicans—he had delivered the keynote address at the party's 1940 national convention— he traveled extensively throughout the United States, including the solidly Democratic South, his campaign financed by friends and the proceeds of his own lectures and magazine articles. In the spring of 1947 Stassen visited sixteen countries overseas where, over a span of seventy-two days, he met with world leaders, including the Soviet leader Joseph Stalin and Pope Pius XII. Casting himself as a liberal Republican, he advocated internationalism in foreign affairs, and in domestic affairs he supported collective bargaining, tax reform, government assistance to relieve the postwar housing shortage, and vigilance against communist influence. He won four major primaries in 1948 but lost in Oregon and Ohio. Unable to secure an early ballot victory in the national convention, Stassen threw his support behind Thomas E. Dewey, who became the party's standard-bearer. This was the closest Stassen would come to the nomination in his nine presidential tries.

In September 1948 Stassen assumed the presidency of the University of Pennsylvania. Four years later he again sought the Republican nomination, entering the contest as the front-runner, only to fade in the early primaries. Realizing that Dwight D. Eisenhower had the best chance to win, Stassen withdrew to play a key role in the general's campaign. Following Eisenhower's victory over Adlai Stevenson, Stassen resigned his university post in 1952 and joined the new administration as a special assistant to the president with cabinet rank.

Under the Eisenhower administration, Stassen served as director of the Mutual Security Agency and the Foreign Operations Administration, each of which provided military or technical assistance to cold war allies. In 1955 he was appointed special assistant to the president for disarmament policy, in which capacity he formulated proposals that laid the groundwork for later successful efforts at arms reduction. Stassen left the cabinet briefly in 1956 to lead an unsuccessful effort to replace Vice President Richard M. Nixon as Eisenhower's running mate in the fall election. He returned to the administration as chief U.S. negotiator at the 1957 London arms control negotiations, which ended in a stalemate. His continuing opposition to Secretary of State John Foster Dulles's policy of brinksmanship led Stassen to resign from the cabinet on 18 February 1958.

Stassen settled in Philadelphia and opened a flourishing international law practice. He ran unsuccessfully for governor of Pennsylvania in 1958, for mayor of Philadelphia in 1959, and for governor again in 1966.

A deeply committed Baptist, Stassen was a lifelong activist in church affairs, helping to establish the National Council of Churches (1950), serving a term as president of the American Baptist Convention (1963) and representing the denomination on the U.S. Inter-religious Committee on Peace during the Vietnam War. He was widely respected for his legal talents and his efforts on behalf of international cooperation.

In sharp contrast to his reputation in the mid-twentieth century, Stassen became an object of ridicule in the final third of the century as he pursued a disastrous series of political campaigns, every one of them a failure. He said later that he ran so often because he felt obligated to give voice to liberal Republicanism in a party that after 1964 moved increasingly to the right. With the exception of 1972, he sought the GOP nomination in every presidential election year from 1964 to 1992. In addition, after he returned to Minnesota in the 1970s, he was defeated in races for

senator (1978), governor (1982), and representative (1986). Despite lampooning cartoons, Stassen entered each campaign with optimism and accepted each defeat with equanimity and grace.

Stassen died of natural causes in a retirement village nursing home four months after the death of his wife. He is buried in Acacia Cemetery in Mendota Heights, Minnesota.

In every respect but one, Stassen had a distinguished public career, making significant contributions to public policy as governor of Minnesota and as adviser to President Eisenhower, particularly in areas of international cooperation and disarmament. But it was not Stassen the liberal statesman that Americans would remember at his death. It was instead Stassen the quixotic candidate in pursuit of a presidential prize he would never win.

★

The Harold E. Stassen papers, portions of which are restricted until 2020, are in the Minnesota Historical Society, Saint Paul, Minnesota. His papers as president of the University of Pennsylvania are in Special Collections, Van Pelt Library, University of Pennsylvania, Philadelphia. His *Man Was Meant to Be Free: Selected Statements, 1940–1951* (1951), ed. by Amos J. Peaslee, was published for the 1952 presidential campaign. Stassen's contributions to U.S. arms control policy are described in H. W. Brands, Jr., *Cold Warriors: Eisenhower's Generation and American Foreign Policy* (1988), and Robert E. Matteson, *Harold Stassen: His Career, the Man, and the 1957 London Arms Control Negotiations* (1993). An obituary is in the *New York Times* (5 Mar. 2001). "Reminiscences of Harold Edward Stassen: Oral History" (1967) is in the Oral History Research Office, Butler Library, Columbia University, New York City. Another oral history record, of an interview conducted 26 June 1973, is in the Harry S Truman Library and Museum, Independence, Missouri.

ALLAN L. DAMON

STEIGER, Rodney Stephen ("Rod") (*b.* 14 April 1925 in Westhampton, New York; *d.* 9 July 2002 in Los Angeles, California), versatile actor best-known for his gripping portrayals of working-class characters, tough guys, and historical figures.

Steiger was born in what was then the rural eastern end of Long Island and was raised mostly in the Newark, New Jersey, area. His parents, Fredrick and Lorraine (Driver) Steiger, worked in vaudeville as a song-and-dance team, but both suffered from alcoholism, which led to the dissolution of the family when Steiger was in his teens. Living with neighbors, he attended high school for only a year before dropping out. When he was sixteen-and-a-half, he forced his mother to sign a paper so he could join the U.S. Navy.

Rod Steiger. THE KOBAL COLLECTION

Steiger served as a torpedo specialist aboard the destroyer USS *Taussig* in the Pacific for three years during World War II, seeing action at Iwo Jima and Okinawa. Upon his discharge, he returned to Newark. Admitted into the federal civil service under a special program for veterans, Steiger was assigned to janitorial and clerking duties at the Department of Dependents and Beneficiaries, a job he found frustrating and maddening. "It made me understand why postal workers kill each other every once in a while," he later remarked. In 1946 he joined a weekly drama group that had been organized for federal workers because he had heard it was a good way to meet women, which might explain his comment that his "motivation for performance was completely sexual. It had nothing to do with art whatsoever."

Nevertheless, Steiger found the acting exercises stimulating and used benefits from the GI Bill to take a drama workshop at the New School for Social Research in New York City. His teacher, the German theatrical producer and director Erwin Piscator, encouraged him to pursue a career as a performer. In 1947 Steiger successfully auditioned to study at the Actors Studio, where his classmates included such future luminaries as Marlon Brando, Eva Marie Saint, Karl Malden, and Elia Kazan, with whom he would later

work in the film *On the Waterfront* (1954). At the Actors Studio and in courses at the New York Theatre Wing, he learned "the Method," a theoretically based approach to performance in which the actor imagines and assumes the personality of a character as fully as possible. Steiger gradually began to take acting seriously, quitting his day job and moving to Manhattan. "I just fell in love with the whole thing," he confessed. "I used to carry a black bag filled with books on acting, stagecraft, makeup, directing, theater design, even books on fantasy. The others would make fun of me." In 1951 he appeared in his first Broadway production, Clifford Odets's *Night Music.*

Television programming was starting up in New York City during the early 1950s, creating a steady stream of opportunities for younger actors. Steiger began to get small roles in anthology drama series, such as *Lux Video Theatre, Danger,* and *Kraft Television Theatre.* In 1952 Fred Coe, the producer of the National Broadcasting Company's (NBC) *Goodyear-Philco Playhouse,* cast Steiger in his first lead in the teleplay "Raymond Schindler, Case One."

One year later, Steiger achieved instant fame in the title role in Paddy Chayefsky's "Marty," another *Goodyear-Philco* production. In his portrayal of a lonely, middle-aged bachelor living with his mother in the Bronx, Steiger made use of live television's dependence on close-ups to create a character that straddles pathos and empathy. "To the surprise of all of us, Marty touched the loneliness of the whole country in one hour," said Steiger, who received a Sylvania Award for his performance. He was offered the role in a Hollywood feature-film adaptation, but declined to sign the contract when the producers, Burt Lancaster and Harold Hecht, insisted it be part of a seven-picture deal. The role went instead to Ernest Borgnine.

Meanwhile, Steiger was able to capitalize on another Hollywood opportunity. In 1954 the director Elia Kazan cast him as the mobster Charlie ("The Gent") Malloy in *On the Waterfront.* The role included playing opposite Brando in the movie's memorable scene in which the latter bemoans his fate, saying "I could've been a contender." Steiger was nominated for an Academy Award as best supporting actor.

Armed with an Oscar nomination, Steiger was cast opposite Humphrey Bogart as a greedy boxing promoter in *The Harder They Fall* (1956), moving on to his first star billing in the western *Run of the Arrow* (1957). In 1959 he played the title role in *Al Capone,* the first of many biographical roles, which included Napoleon in *Waterloo* (1970), W. C. Fields in *W. C. Fields and Me* (1976), and Pontius Pilate in the television miniseries *Jesus of Nazareth* (1977).

Steiger was at the height of his powers during the 1960s. His performance in *The Pawnbroker* (1964) as Sol Nazerman, a Jewish holocaust survivor, can be counted among his most fully realized achievements onscreen. It won him a Silver Bear from the Berlin Festival and a British Academy Award for best foreign actor, as well as an Oscar nomination for best actor. In 1967 Steiger won the Oscar for best actor and a Golden Globe Award for *In the Heat of the Night,* in which he plays a bigoted southern sheriff forced to work with an urban African-American colleague played by Sidney Poitier. In *The Sergeant* (1968), a picture Steiger agreed to appear in for a fraction of his normal fee, he plays a homosexual army sergeant struggling to suppress his passion for a private, thereby becoming one of the first established stars in American film to portray a gay character. Other noteworthy onscreen appearances during the 1960s included the role of Edoardo Nottola in the Italian director Francesco Rosi's *Hands over the City* (1963), the role of Victor Komarovsky in *Doctor Zhivago* (1965), and the role of Willy Loman in Arthur Miller's *Death of a Salesman* for British television (1966).

Steiger married five times. His first marriage to Sally Gracie in 1952 was very brief, but the couple did not formally divorce until 1958. He married the actress Claire Bloom in 1959; they had one child, Anna Justine, who would become a ballet dancer. Steiger and Bloom divorced in 1969, but not before costarring together that year in the film *Three into Two Won't Go,* which concerned a couple whose marriage was dissolving. His third marriage in 1973 to Sherry Nelson ended in a 1979 divorce. A common-law marriage to Paula Ellis followed. It was his longest-lasting relationship, spanning a period from the late 1970s to 1997. The couple had one child. Steiger married Joan Benedict in 2000.

Although the stocky, rough-hewn Steiger was never a romantic lead, he nevertheless fell victim to what he called a culture that "worships youth," finding progressively fewer interesting roles to play in Hollywood as he neared fifty. He spent much of the 1970s in Europe, appearing in Italian, German, and British productions. Notable among these are Sergio Leone's spaghetti western *A Fistful of Dynamite* (1972) and *Last Days of Mussolini* (1974), in which he played the title role. He portrayed Mussolini again in *Lion of the Desert* (1980).

Disappointed by many of these projects, Steiger returned to Hollywood, where he worked prolifically in both feature films and television for the balance of his career, often in supporting roles with secondary billing. His performance as a Hasidic Jewish rabbi in *The Chosen* (1981), an adaptation of Chaim Potok's novel, stands out. In some of his later films, especially *Modern Vampires* (1998) and *The Kindred* (1986), Steiger managed to turn threadbare scripts into hilarious self-reflexive parodies, as he had done in *The Loved One* (1965).

Steiger and Benedict were living in the hills above Malibu, California, at the time of his death of pneumonia and kidney failure. His remains were cremated and his ashes buried at Forest Lawn Memorial Park in Hollywood Hills.

"I pride myself on being 60 percent virgin, 40 percent whore," was how Steiger sized up his career in Hollywood. "I've done films I didn't want to do to feed my family, but I believe I have done 10 percent more good work than crap." Asked how he managed to succeed with so little formal preparation, he replied, "One of the greatest foundations for creativity is the fear of failure. You're so afraid of failing, sometimes you do it better than you ever dreamed."

For Steiger, acting was a form of personal salvation. As a young man, it saved him from a life of monotony at a job in which he had no interest, and in middle age it became his chief weapon in a protracted battle with clinical depression. He believed that the seriousness with which he took his craft stigmatized him in a culture more interested in screen worship than drama, but he insisted upon it nonetheless.

★

Steiger did not write an autobiography and would not consent to cooperate with a biographer. Todd Hutchinson, *Rod Steiger: Memoirs of a Friendship* (2000), written by a long-time friend of the actor, is perhaps the closest portrait done of Steiger. A profile of Steiger appeared in the *New Yorker* (28 Oct. 1961) during his early stardom. For additional information about his life and career, see the interview in Mike Sagar, "What I've Learned: Rod Steiger," *Esquire* (Oct. 1998). An obituary is in the *New York Times* (10 July 2002). Oral histories with useful information include "Closeup on Rod Steiger: A Hollywood Star Discusses Drama Critics and Method Acting" (1975, audiotape and transcript), produced by the Center for Cassette Studies; and an interview with David Marc (1997, audiotape and transcript), in the oral history collections of the Center for the Study of Popular Television, Syracuse University Library, Syracuse, New York.

DAVID MARC

STERN, Isaac (*b.* 21 July 1920 in Kremenets, Russia [now Ukraine]; *d.* 22 September 2001 in Manhattan, New York City), renowned violinist who served as an important champion of classical music throughout the world and led the struggle to save New York's Carnegie Hall from destruction in 1960.

Stern was the eldest child of Solomon Stern, a housepainter whose passport gave his profession as artist-painter, and Clara Stern, a music student who had received a scholarship to study voice at the Saint Petersburg Conservatory. When Stern was ten months old, his parents, both of whom were Russian Jews, moved the family from their home on the Russian-Polish border. They traveled east through Siberia and crossed the Pacific to settle in San Francisco, following an uncle who had settled there previously.

Stern began to study piano with his mother at age six. Two years later he was inspired to study the violin because his childhood friend Nathan Koblick had taken up the instrument. Stern's parents noticed his natural talent and quick progression on the violin and enrolled him in the San Francisco Conservatory of Music with the financial support of Lutie Goldstein, a wealthy arts patron in San Francisco. Goldstein arranged for Stern and his mother to travel to New York City for six months, and there he studied with Louis Persinger, who also taught the famed violinist Yehudi Menuhin. Stern then returned to San Francisco where he took up his studies with Naoum Blinder, the concertmaster of the San Francisco Symphony. Blinder became his primary teacher and an important influence on his musical development.

In February 1935 Stern made his debut at the Veterans Auditorium in San Francisco, playing the Bach Double Violin Concerto with Blinder and a piano accompanist, and in March 1937 he performed the Brahms Violin Concerto with the San Francisco Symphony under the direction of Pierre Monteux. That concert led to his first tour and appearances throughout the Pacific Northwest. Financed once again by Goldstein, Stern made his New York debut at Town Hall in October 1937. The recital garnered mixed reviews, and he returned to San Francisco determined to focus on practicing with the intent of presenting a second and, he hoped, more successful Town Hall concert. Stern's February 1939 appearance at the venue was an unqualified success.

The impresario Sol Hurok took on the management of Stern's career soon thereafter and served as his manager until Hurok's death in 1974. Hurok presented Stern's Carnegie Hall debut on 8 January 1943, and one year later, on 12 January 1944, Stern performed again at Carnegie. He later credited this performance with the launch of his international career. In 1941 Stern began his long collaboration with the pianist Alexander Zakin. They performed and recorded together until 1973, and Stern considered Zakin one of his closest musical associates. During 1944 and 1945 Stern and Zakin performed for U.S. troops in the South Pacific, Iceland, and Greenland under the auspices of the United Service Organizations.

Stern's career took off upon his return to the United States. In 1945 he signed a contract with, and made his first recordings for, Columbia Records. Columbia and its related labels, CBS Masterworks and Sony Classical, recorded Stern until his death, issuing and reissuing numerous recordings of his performances of solo repertoire, chamber works, and works with orchestra. In 1946 Stern performed Édouard Lalo's *Symphonie Espagnole* at the Hollywood Bowl, under the baton of Leopold Stokowski. While he was

Isaac Stern. MR. HENRY GROSSMAN

in Hollywood, he came to the attention of Warner Bros. Studios, which engaged him to play the violin for John Garfield's performance as a violinist in the movie *Humoresque* (1946).

On 10 November 1949 Stern married the dancer Nora Kaye; the marriage ended in divorce after only a few months. On 17 August 1951 he married Vera Lindenblit, an American whom he had met in Israel earlier that year. The couple had three children before their marriage ended in divorce in 1995. On 3 November 1996 he married Linda Reynolds; they had no children.

In August 1948 Stern and Zakin toured Europe, presenting concerts in France, Italy, Norway, Sweden, and Switzerland. In reaction to the horrors of the Nazi regime, Stern was adamant about not performing in Germany and did not appear there until 1999. Stern and Zakin toured Japan, India, and the Philippines in the fall of 1953. In April 1956 they toured the Soviet Union, aided by Stern's friendship with the Russian violinist David Oistrakh, whom he had met in 1951.

In September 1949 Stern made his first visit to Israel, beginning a life-long connection with that nation. He traveled throughout the small country, presenting concerts in

Jerusalem, Tel Aviv, and Haifa, and returned to Israel on numerous occasions throughout his life, often traveling there on short notice to be present for important events in the country's history. He performed Mendelssohn's Violin Concerto with the Israel Philharmonic under the direction of Leonard Bernstein on Mount Scopus immediately after the 1967 Six-Day War, and also appeared there during the 1991 Persian Gulf War. In 1964 Stern became chairman of the America-Israel Cultural Foundation and in 1973 helped establish the Jerusalem Music Center.

In 1950 his fellow violinist Alexander (Sasha) Schneider invited Stern to attend the Casals Festival in Prades, France. This began his long connection with the cellist Pablo Casals, as well as his renewed dedication to the performance of chamber music. By the mid-1950s Stern was presenting more than 100 concerts each year. He suffered a mild heart attack in 1968, and although he stopped smoking and lost some weight, he did not substantially reduce his rather grueling performance schedule. In 1987 he underwent a triple bypass operation after falling ill during a tour of Israel.

Stern, who had felt a strong connection to Carnegie Hall since his debut performance there in 1943, became involved in the fight to save the famed space from demolition in late 1959. He organized the Citizens Committee to Save Carnegie Hall and enlisted the help of fellow artists, including Fritz Kreisler, Arthur Rubinstein, Van Cliburn, and Marian Anderson. He also engaged political figures and philanthropists in the successful campaign to rescue the hall and establish the Carnegie Hall Corporation. Stern became its first president, a position he held until his death. In 1996 Carnegie's main auditorium was named for Stern in recognition of his important role in the hall's history. He later wrote, "The struggle to save Carnegie Hall . . . taught me things about myself I had not known before: I could sway influential people through speech; I had the ability to stir crowds not only with music but also with words."

In 1965 President Lyndon B. Johnson appointed Stern a member of the first advisory group for the National Council on the Arts, which oversaw the establishment of the National Endowment for the Arts. Stern remained involved in efforts to promote government support of the arts throughout his lifetime. In the 1960s Stern began a new chamber music initiative with the pianist Eugene Istomin and the cellist Leonard Rose, with whom he had first performed in 1952. The Istomin-Stern-Rose Trio presented its formal debut in Israel in 1961, and the three performed and recorded numerous works together until Rose's death in 1984. Stern then established a new trio with the pianist Emmanuel Ax and the cellist Yo-Yo Ma.

In addition to his performances of the standard solo violin and chamber music repertoire, Stern had a strong commitment to the performance of new works. He championed Leonard Bernstein's *Serenade after Plato's Symposium,* for violin and orchestra (1954), and premiered the violin concerti of George Rocberg in 1975, Kryzystof Penderecki in 1977, Henri Dutilleux in 1985, and Peter Maxwell Davies in 1986. He presented the American premieres and made the first recordings of Béla Bartók's Violin Concerto no. 1 and Paul Hindemith's Violin Concerto.

In 1979 Stern became one of the first U.S. artists allowed to visit China, and he arranged to bring along a film crew to document the entire journey. *From Mao to Mozart* received the 1980 Academy Award for best documentary film. Committed to music education, Stern instituted a series of master classes and chamber music workshops at Carnegie Hall in the 1990s. He received numerous honors and awards, including the Kennedy Center Honors in 1984, a Lifetime Achievement Grammy Award in 1987, and an Emmy Award for outstanding individual classical music performance, also in 1987. In honor of his fiftieth anniversary with the company, in 1995 Sony Classical released a forty-four–disc collection of his recordings, *Isaac Stern: A Life in Music.* In September 2000 Carnegie Hall presented a special weekend-long celebration in honor of Stern's eightieth birthday. During his last years Stern suffered from arthritis and carpal tunnel syndrome, which curtailed his performance activities. He died of heart failure in a Manhattan hospital and is buried in Morningside Cemetery, Gaylordsville, Connecticut.

A natural musician and superb interpreter, Stern was known more for his rich tone and musicianship than for his flashy technique. He had perfect pitch and could learn new works relatively quickly. He was keenly aware of his technical shortcomings and worked tirelessly to perfect his performances. The fight to save Carnegie Hall threw him quickly into a role as public spokesperson for the arts, a role he appeared to take on as naturally as he took to violin performance. He had a profound influence on the classical music culture of the United States and the world.

★

Stern's archives are in private hands. Selected items from his personal collection, including his fine instruments and bows, were offered for auction in May 2003 by the Tarisio.com auction house and are documented in the auction catalog, *The Stern Collection: Important Instruments, Bows and Memorabilia from the Collection of the Late Isaac Stern* (2003). The Music Division of the New York Public Library houses four volumes of scrapbooks. Stern's autobiography, *My First 79 Years* (1999), written with Chaim Potok, provides detailed and candid insights into his long career. The July 1990 issue of the *Strad* was devoted to Stern in honor of his seventieth birthday. It includes Tully Potter, "Isaac Stern: A Profile," as well as a discography by Jean-Michel Molkhou. The April 2002 issue of the *Strad* was published as a tribute to Stern after his death. An obituary is in the *New York Times* (24 Sept.

2001). A video documentary, *Isaac Stern, A Life: A Biography in Music,* was written and directed by Lee R. Bobker and produced in 1993.

JANE GOTTLIEB

STONE, W(illiam) Clement   (*b.* 4 May 1902 in Chicago, Illinois; *d.* 4 September 2002 in Lake Forest, Illinois), insurance company executive, civic leader, philanthropist, and believer in positive thinking.

Stone was the only child of Louis Stone and Anna (Gunn) Stone, a dressmaker. His father died before he was three years old, leaving Stone and his mother impoverished as a result of his gambling losses. At age six Stone was selling newspapers on street corners to supplement his mother's meager income. His mother taught him the following prayer, which she claimed was based on a statement by President Abraham Lincoln, and insisted that he repeat it every morning and night: "May I be truly and highly esteemed by my fellow man, and may I be worthy of that esteem." At age thirteen Stone owned his own newsstand. When Stone was sixteen he dropped out of high school and moved with his mother to Detroit to open an insurance agency.

Stone went from office to office selling insurance policies for his mother's agency. He referred to his sales calls as "gold calls," and was soon making $100 a week. He spent his evenings reading Horatio Alger stories in which poor boys make good. In 1922, at age twenty, Stone moved back to Chicago and invested $100 in his own insurance agency, which was exclusively devoted to selling casualty and life insurance. His biggest seller was the "little giant," a six-month travel/accident policy that sold for $3.

At age sixteen Stone met Jessie Verna Tarson and vowed to marry her when he turned twenty-one. True to his word, they married on 16 June 1923. They had three children and remained married until her death seventy-nine years later. Stone eventually completed his high school education at the Young Men's Christian Association Central High School in Chicago. The balance of his formal education consisted of a few courses at the Detroit College of Law in 1920 (from which he received an honorary LL.D. in 1983) and two years (1930–1932) at Northwestern University in Evanston, Illinois.

A consummate salesman, Stone built his insurance agency by hiring people of limited education, such as truck drivers and store clerks, and having them memorize a sales pitch. As sales increased, Stone parlayed this business into an insurance empire by using other people's money to acquire a string of insurance agencies. By 1930 his companies had 1,000 agents across the United States selling insurance as representatives for large casualty companies. In 1982 all

W. Clement Stone, 1969. AP/WIDE WORLD PHOTOS

of his companies were merged into the Ryan Insurance Group, which was renamed the Aon Corporation in 1987.

Early on, Stone took an active role in promoting material wealth through positive thinking and in motivating himself and others. He frequently started meetings with the following pitch: "Stand up. Raise your arms. Repeat after me: I feel healthy! I feel happy! I feel terrific!" Among his publications were *Success Through a Positive Mental Attitude* (1960), with Napoleon Hill; *The Success System That Never Fails* (1962); and *The Other Side of the Mind* (1964), with Norma L. Browning. He also wrote several magazine articles, including "How to Grow Wealthy with Positive Thought," *Business Week* (3 July 1968), and "How to Motivate Yourself and Others," *Nations Business* (July 1968).

Stone acquired control of Hawthorn Books in 1967. Later that year he made a bid for a mass audience when he published *Success Unlimited,* a monthly magazine modeled upon *Reader's Digest.* Each issue consisted of a potpourri of personal rags-to-riches stories that promoted a Protestant work ethic. Stone made money in a variety of other ways. For example, he purchased three warehouses of Cuban cigars just before the Cuban revolution. In 1972 his personal fortune was estimated at $400 million.

Known for his pencil-thin moustache, polka-dot bow ties, and pinstripe trousers held up by suspenders, Stone was a fervent supporter of President Richard M. Nixon, whose comeback after losing the 1960 and 1962 presidential elections won his admiration. In 1967 Stone was linked to the publication of misleading information about the safety of charcoal-filtered cigarettes. The following year he reputedly played a role in some shady dealings, including financing a gang war on Chicago's South Side designed to keep African-American voters from the polls. In 1968 Stone gave an estimated $8 million to Nixon's campaigns, and his contributions earned him an influential role among Nixon's inner circle of friends, known as his "kitchen cabinet."

In 1970 Stone also made significant contributions to George H.W. Bush's failed Senate campaign. In 1972 he gave the Committee to Re-Elect the President (known by the acronym CREEP) more than $2 million toward Nixon's reelection. In the congressional debates following the Watergate break-in, Stone's campaign contributions were given as a reason for the institution of campaign spending limits. To his credit, in 1972 he established the A. W. Clement and Jessie V. Stone Foundation, which supports early childhood development and the prevention of child abuse, as well as providing scholarships.

Stone was awarded twenty honorary degrees. He died at age one hundred and is buried in Forest Lawn, Illinois.

★

There is no full-length biography of Stone. For information about his life and career, see "Stone Is New President of Hawthorn Books," *Publishers Weekly* 191 (24 Apr. 1967): 67; and "American Original," *Time* (7 Feb. 1969): 78. See also Dom Bonafede, "White House Report: President's Inner Circle of Friends Serves as Influential 'Kitchen Cabinet,'" *National Journal* (22 Jan. 1972); and Terry Savage, "W. Clement Stone to Mark His 100th," *Chicago Sun-Times* (2 May 2002). Obituaries are in the *Chicago Sun-Times* and *New York Times* (both 5 Sept. 2002).

KEITH MCCLELLAN

STRAND, Kaj Aage (*b.* 27 February 1907 in Hellerup, Denmark; *d.* 31 October 2000 in Washington, D.C.), astronomer specializing in positional astronomy who performed groundbreaking research in binary star systems and stellar distances, and who served as scientific director of the U.S. Naval Observatory from 1963 to 1977.

Born and educated just outside Copenhagen, Denmark, Strand graduated from the University of Copenhagen in 1931 with the equivalent of a master's degree in astronomy. He received his doctorate from Copenhagen in 1938 for his work in photographing double stars, which he completed while studying in Leiden, Netherlands, under the direction of the well-known positional astronomer Eijnar Hertzsprung.

Soon after receiving his doctorate, Strand moved to the United States and began a photographic double star program at Swarthmore College in Swarthmore, Pennsylvania, where he worked as a research assistant. While there, Strand first found small systematic variations in the orbits of a double star system known as 61 Cygni A and B. He concluded that these orbital variations were caused by a third body, unseen from Earth-bound telescopes, that was orbiting 61 Cygni A. Strand came back to this double star system many years later, using more data to calculate the mass, orbital period, and orbital distance of this still unseen body.

As did most of the scientifically trained young men of his time, Strand put his training to use for the U.S. armed forces during World War II, serving from 1942 to 1945. After serving as captain and chief navigator on test flights of B-29 bombers, Strand became head of the navigation department for the U.S. Army Air Force. In this position, he trained special aircrews, one of which flew the mission to drop the first atomic bomb.

After a brief return to Swarthmore College after the war, Strand became chairman of the astronomy department at Northwestern University in Evanston, Illinois, in 1946. At the same time, he was named visiting associate professor at the nearby Yerkes Observatory, operated by the University of Chicago. At Northwestern, Strand's responsibilities included planning the new computer center and serving as director of the university's Dearborn Observatory. It was at Yerkes, however, that Strand was able to do much of his research in the field of astrometrics, a relatively new branch of astronomy that dealt with the measurement of the positions and distances of celestial bodies. Working under the tutelage of Otto Struve, who had built the once-neglected Yerkes facility on the shores of Lake Geneva, Wisconsin, into an internationally respected research observatory, Strand headed the astrometrics program at Yerkes, directed graduate students, and continued to use the Yerkes telescopes for his own research.

Strand also played important roles in the national and international astronomical communities, particularly during two international astronomy conferences. The first, held in 1953 at Northwestern, provided renewed interest in the science of astrometry, and Strand played a pivotal role in organizing and carrying out various activities planned by the gathered scientists. Strand's proposals concerning the most effective methods for observing binary stars resulted in renewed efforts by specialists in astrometry worldwide. The second important conference, held at the University of Virginia in 1956, also provided Strand with a chance to interact with his international colleagues. At this meeting, the Cosmic Distance Seale Conference, Strand unveiled plans to study the parallaxes of faint stars using a large reflecting telescope, a significant alteration to the accepted practice of studying such phenomena with refracting telescopes.

In 1958, Strand left Northwestern and Yerkes to become head of the astrometry and astrophysics division of the U.S. Naval Observatory in Washington, D.C. The naval observatory had a long history as the official timekeeper and astronomical observatory of the United States. Strand immediately began a program of research based on his own specialty, photographic observations of double stars. In 1963 he became scientific director of the Naval Observatory, where he remained until his retirement in 1977. Under his leadership the Naval Observatory established its first station in the Southern Hemisphere, in El Leoncito, Argentina. Strand also spearheaded the design and construction of the sixty-one-inch astrometric telescope (now known as the Strand Astrometric Telescope) installed by the Naval Observatory in 1964 at its station in Flagstaff, Arizona. In the twenty-first century, this telescope continues to play a critical role in the determination of stellar distances.

After his retirement from the Naval Observatory in 1977, Strand worked as a consultant to various universities and government agencies, including NASA, the Office of Naval Research, the National Bureau of Standards, and the National Science Foundation. He received the Navy's Distinguished Civilian Service Award in 1973.

Strand married Ulla Nilson on 11 March 1943; they had one child. They divorced in December 1948, and Strand married Emilie Rashevksy on 10 June 1949. They also had one child.

Strand died at age ninety-three of cardiac arrest after suffering a stroke. His importance to astronomy through his research and leadership at the Naval Observatory will long be remembered.

★

Obituaries are in the *New York Times* and *Washington Post* (both 4 Nov. 2000), and the *Bulletin of the American Astronomical Society* 33, no. 4 (2001). An oral history interview with Strand is at the U.S. Naval Observatory Library, Washington, D.C.

W. TODD TIMMONS

STRATTON, William Grant (*b*. 26 February 1914 in Ingleside, Illinois; *d*. 2 March 2001 in Chicago, Illinois), U.S. congressman, state treasurer, and two-term governor of Illinois, the state's youngest chief executive in the twentieth century.

Born into a political tradition, Stratton was the son of William Joseph Stratton, the first director of the Illinois

William G. Stratton, June 1958. AP/WIDE WORLD PHOTOS

Department of Conservation and later Illinois secretary of state, and Zula (Van Wormer) Stratton, a teacher. "I was reared in an atmosphere of politics," the younger Stratton later recalled. "My ambition from the time I can first remember . . . was to be engaged in public life and affairs." During a trip to the Illinois state capitol, at the age of eight, he got to sit in the governor's chair for a half hour.

Attending public schools in Lake County, Stratton graduated from Gurnee High School in 1930. He studied political science at the University of Arizona at Tucson, where he was a member of Delta Chi fraternity, took part in intramural sports, and joined the Arizona National Guard. After graduating with a B.A. in 1934, he returned to Illinois and worked for the next five years as a salesman for the Northern Illinois Public Service Company, a subsidiary of Commonwealth Edison. On 4 September 1934 he married Marion Hook. They had two children and divorced in 1949. On 27 December 1950 he married Shirley Breckinridge; they had one child.

In 1940 Stratton became the youngest member of the U.S. House of Representatives when he was elected congressman-at-large for Illinois. Like most other Midwestern Republican congressmen of this era, he opposed U.S. involvement in World War II and compiled an isolationist voting record, voting against the Lend-Lease Bill of 1941, arming merchant ships, amendments to the neutrality act, and extending the draft.

Stratton, who never intended to spend a career in the House, was elected to a two-year term as Illinois state treasurer in 1942 and used this office to begin building a statewide political organization. In 1944 he tried for higher office but was defeated in the Republican primary for secretary of state. Stratton said years later that this defeat was the turning point in his career. "I lost but gained a lot of respect because I took on Gov. [Dwight] Green and his administration," he recalled. "That showed I could stand up to anyone in the party."

In 1945 Stratton enlisted in the U.S. Navy as a lieutenant and served in the South Pacific as a personnel officer. While still on active duty, he won the Republican nomination for congressman-at-large and ousted the Democrat Emily Taft Douglas in the 1946 general election.

On his return to Congress in April 1947, Stratton introduced legislation that would have allowed 400,000 displaced persons to immigrate into the United States over the next four years. The Stratton Bill was supported by the Citizens Committee on Displaced Persons (CCDP), which was headed by Earl G. Harrison, the dean of the University of Pennsylvania Law School. President Harry S. Truman also privately favored the bill. But the House Judiciary Committee would not send Stratton's legislation to the floor, and it never came to a vote.

Stratton voted against the Truman administration's 1947 Greek-Turkish aid bill, and in favor of the constitutional amendment limiting presidents to two terms and of legislation to increase farm aid and extend postwar rent controls.

For a second time, Stratton gave up his congressional seat to seek executive office in Illinois. In 1948 he won the Republican nomination for secretary of state but was defeated in the general election. Stratton made a comeback in 1950 when he recaptured the state treasurer's office.

In 1952 Stratton won the Republican nomination for governor after the early front-runner, the Cook County Board president William N. Erickson, was indicted in a ghost-payrolling scandal and quit the race. Stratton had expected to run against the Democratic governor, Adlai E. Stevenson, but Stevenson stepped down from the state ticket when he was drafted by the 1952 Democratic National Convention as their party's nominee for the presidency. Stratton easily won the general election over Lieutenant Governor Sherwood Dixon.

At the age of thirty-eight, Stratton was the youngest chief executive in Illinois in seventy years, and he became one of the state's more productive governors. In 1955 he pushed through the first reapportionment in over fifty years by making population the basis for house districts and allowing downstate counties to retain control of the state senate by using geography to draw districts. "Without redistricting, we would have been unable to meet the problems of the state," he said.

In the postwar boom of the 1950s, Stratton built more than 7,000 miles of new roads, including 187 miles of expressway in the Chicago area. He won approval for bond issues to construct the University of Illinois at Chicago and Southern Illinois University Edwardsville campuses and also expanded northern, eastern, and western Illinois universities. He developed a close working relationship with the Democratic mayor Richard J. Daley of Chicago, with whom he cooperated in building O'Hare International Airport, a lakefront convention center in Chicago, and other large-scale projects.

Calling Stratton Illinois' "first progressive governor," the four-term Illinois governor James R. Thompson noted that Stratton "modernized state government, modernized the state's road system, and understood the importance of Chicago and keeping a balance with the rest of the state."

Stratton appointed the first woman and the first African American to an Illinois gubernatorial cabinet. In 1953 he vetoed legislation that would have required a loyalty oath for state officials. Stratton wrote in his veto message that such an oath "would place upon all governmental units in the state a burden of administration which I feel is completely disproportionate to the dangers that may be involved." Stratton failed to win approval for his proposals to choose judges on a merit basis instead of by partisan elections and for his bill that would have created a fair employment practices commission.

In 1956 Stratton narrowly won reelection to a second term despite President Dwight D. Eisenhower's reelection landslide. He was politically hurt when it was disclosed that the Republican state auditor Orville Hodge had embezzled more than $1.5 million in state funds. Stratton demanded Hodge's resignation and forced him off the state ticket. Defeated for a third term in 1960 by the Democrat Otto Kerner, Stratton became vice president of the Chicago-based Canteen Corporation.

In 1964 Stratton was indicted on charges that he had evaded payment of over $40,000 in taxes on unreported income during his second term as governor. Stratton's lawyers argued that the Internal Revenue Service had incorrectly listed political expenditures as private spending from personal income. Stratton was acquitted in 1965 in what is regarded as a landmark case in campaign finance law. Illinois Senator Everett M. Dirksen, who testified in Stratton's defense, argued that a public official should have wide discretion in the expenditure of political contributions. "In this game, sometimes a curve ball comes your way," Stratton said after he was found not guilty. "If you can't hit a curve ball, you don't belong in the major leagues."

Stratton attempted to regain the governorship in 1968

but finished a distant third in the Republican primary, which was won by Richard B. Ogilvie. In 1991 Stratton served as cochair of Governor Jim Edgar's transition team, and in 1997 served with Senator Paul Simon as cochair of a task force that recommended the reform of Illinois campaign finance and disclosure laws. Some of these recommendations were enacted into law.

Stratton died of natural causes at Northwestern Memorial Hospital. He is buried in Rosehill Cemetery and Mausoleum in Chicago.

★

Stratton's papers are at the Illinois State Historical Library in Springfield. David Kenney, *A Political Passage: The Career of Stratton of Illinois* (1990), is a balanced and authoritative biography. See also the chapter about Stratton in Robert P. Hatton, *Mostly Good and Competent Men* (1988). An obituary is in the *Chicago Sun-Times* (4 Mar. 2001).

STEVE NEAL

STREET, George Levick, III (*b.* 27 July 1913 in Richmond, Virginia; *d.* 26 February 2000 in Andover, Massachusetts), U.S. Navy submarine commander who won the Medal of Honor for heroism during World War II.

The son of George Levick Street, Jr., a steel company executive, and Florence Prince, a homemaker, Street attended Saint Christopher's School in Richmond for eleven years and the Severn School, Severn Park, Maryland, for one year. He had three siblings. In 1931 he enlisted as a seamen, second class, in the U.S. Naval Reserve, and two years later he was admitted to the U.S. Naval Academy at Annapolis, Maryland, after earning a competitive appointment for one of the vacancies set aside each year for naval reservists. Street graduated in 1937 and became an ensign in the U.S. Navy.

After attending cruiser school, Street served on the cruiser *Concord* as junior gunnery officer from July 1937 to December 1938. Shifting to the battleship *Arkansas,* he served in the navigation and engineering department until he was sent to the submarine school at New London, Connecticut, in September 1940. He graduated in December 1940, ranking second in a class of forty. In January 1941 Street was assigned to the new submarine *Gar,* then in the final stages of outfitting at Groton, Connecticut. Following the *Gar*'s commissioning in April 1941, Street served during the next three years as the submarine's gunnery and torpedo officer, torpedo data computer officer, and executive officer and navigator while rising to the rank of lieutenant commander. During the first two years of World War II, Street participated in nine war patrols in the southwest Pacific and western Pacific patrol areas, receiving two silver

stars for assisting the *Gar*'s commanding officers in sinking Japanese ships.

From February to May 1944 Street held several shore posts in the Pacific theater, the most important as staff engineer for Submarine Division Sixty-One and as engineer of the submarine base at Midway Island, where he was in charge of refitting submarines between war patrols. Returning to the United States in the summer of 1944, Street assisted in the outfitting of the new submarine *Tirante* at Portsmouth, New Hampshire, and after attending the Prospective Commanding Officers School at New London, he assumed command of the *Tirante* when it was commissioned in November 1944.

During the next two months Street engaged in training exercises off Portsmouth and New London and then sailed to Pearl Harbor, Hawaii. Leaving on its first war patrol on 3 March 1945, the *Tirante* was assigned to the East China and Yellow Seas. On 25 March, Street sank the small tanker *Fuji Maru* in the approaches to Nagasaki on Kyushu Island. Three days later he sank the small cargo ship *Nase Maru*. Over the next two weeks the *Tirante* sank a lugger at the western end of the Inland Sea, a small freighter off the south coast of Korea, the 5,500-ton transport *Nikko Maru* off Kyushu, and an escort vessel off Kyushu, although postwar records do not confirm the sinkings of the freighter and the escort vessel.

On 13 April, Street received word that an "important" Japanese ship was in the small harbor on Quelpart Island, about 100 miles south of the Korean Peninsula. In the early hours of 14 April, Street boldly entered the heavily mined and shoal-obstructed harbor on the surface because of the shallow waters, hugging the shore and remaining undetected despite numerous Japanese patrol vessels and shore-based radar stations. Ably served by his experienced crew and making effective use of the *Tirante*'s powerful SJ radar, the target bearing transmitter, and the torpedo data computer to pinpoint his target, Street fired three torpedoes at the "important" ship, later identified as the 4,000-ton *Juzan Maru,* an ammunition ship, at a range of 2,300 yards. One torpedo hit the ship, destroying it in a blinding explosion that shot a mushroom of white flames nearly 2,000 feet into the air. Quickly, Street spotted two 900-ton frigates silhouetted against the flames of the burning ammunition ship and promptly sunk them with three torpedoes.

By then sighted and unable to dive because of the shallow waters, Street headed for deep water at full emergency speed along the coastline and then endured a depth charge attack from Japanese patrol vessels when he finally was able to submerge. With only one torpedo left, Street sailed for Midway, completing the patrol on 23 April. According to the Joint Army Navy Assessment Committee, he destroyed six ships totaling 12,621 tons, the seventh-best war patrol for an American submarine during the war. For his "gal-

499

lantry and intrepidity" in attacking the Japanese vessels at Quelpart, Street was awarded the Medal of Honor by President Harry S Truman at a White House ceremony on 5 October 1945. In addition, the *Tirante* was awarded a Presidential Unit Citation. Street took the *Tirante* on a second war patrol between 20 May and 19 July 1945, sinking two ships totaling 3,265 tons in the East China Sea, most notably a collier in Nagasaki harbor. For "extraordinary heroism" during this patrol, Street was awarded the Navy Cross.

During the next twenty years Street held a variety of shore and sea assignments, including tours in the Navy Department with the Office of Naval Research and the Office of the Chief of Naval Operations, a stint as fleet operations and training officer with the U.S. Atlantic Fleet, and command of a submarine, a destroyer escort, an attack transport, a submarine division, a submarine squadron, and a submarine group. He also attended the Armed Forces Staff College and the National War College, was a professor of naval science at the Massachusetts Institute of Technology, and worked with the Institute of Naval Studies at the Naval War College. Street retired from the navy in August 1966 with the rank of captain.

An unassuming commander who preferred to give credit for his accomplishments to the crew of the *Tirante,* Street was married to Mary Martha McKimmey. They had two children. He died at the Academy Manor Nursing Home in Andover, Massachusetts and is buried at Arlington National Cemetery. Street stands out as an inspiring leader, an able seaman, and one of the navy's most skillful and daring submarine commanders during World War II.

★

A biographical sketch summarizing Street's naval career is located in the U.S. Naval Academy Archives, Annapolis, Maryland. Street's exploits as commander of the *Tirante* are described in Clay Blair, Jr., *Silent Victory: The U.S. Submarine War Against Japan* (1975), and two books by Edward L. Beach, *Submarine!* (1952) and *Salt and Steel: Reflections of a Submariner* (1999). Beach served as executive officer of the *Tirante* during its first war patrol, and in his best-selling novel, *Run Silent, Run Deep* (1955), he draws upon his experiences while serving with Street. Obituaries are in the *Boston Herald* (2 Mar. 2000) and *New York Times* (5 Mar. 2000).

JOHN KENNEDY OHL

SULLIVAN, Leon Howard (*b.* 16 October 1922 in Charleston, West Virginia; *d.* 24 April 2001 in Scottsdale, Arizona), Baptist minister and social activist who developed economic self-help programs for African Americans in the 1960s and later led a campaign to end apartheid in South Africa.

Sullivan was the only child of Charles Sullivan, a movie theater janitor, and Helen (Trueheart) Sullivan, an elevator operator. He was raised by his grandmother, Carrie Sullivan, after his young parents separated. Growing up poor in a racist environment, Sullivan was spurred to social activism at an early age. He was convinced that the church had to play a leading role in addressing the discrimination that confronted African Americans. For that reason he opted to enter the ministry after graduating from high school. In 1942 Sullivan met the renowned New York City minister Adam Clayton Powell, Jr., who urged him to come to New York after finishing his college education.

In 1943 the gangly six-foot, five-inch Sullivan received a B.A. from West Virginia State University and followed Powell's call. He married Grace Banks in August 1945, shortly after his arrival in New York City. The couple had one son and two daughters. His work as assistant minister at Powell's prestigious Abyssinian Baptist Church in Harlem reinforced his long-held belief that black clergy and their congregations were the most important agents of change in the struggle for black freedom. Another mentor, the labor activist A. Philip Randolph, familiarized Sullivan with nonviolent protest techniques and community organizing.

In 1945 Sullivan and his wife moved to suburban South

Leon H. Sullivan, 1987. AP/WIDE WORLD PHOTOS

Orange, New Jersey, where he became the pastor of a small Baptist church. In the ensuing years he continued his education, studying theology at Union Theological Seminary and sociology at Columbia University in New York City. In 1947 he received an M.A. in religion from Columbia. In South Orange, he further developed his ideas on social activism. In 1950 Sullivan became the minister of Zion Baptist Church in Philadelphia, Pennsylvania, where he intended to implement these ideas. He first sought to expand economic opportunities for African Americans. In 1958 he initiated a successful boycott campaign against discriminatory employment practices in Philadelphia. Aided by other ministers, Sullivan's campaign forced hundreds of businesses to adopt a policy of fair employment by 1962.

Sullivan soon learned, however, that few African Americans had the skills that were necessary for the new jobs that opened up. To address this need, Sullivan founded the Opportunities Industrialization Center (OIC), a job-training center that taught specific job skills and attempted to instill the unemployed with a new sense of self-esteem. Proclaiming "We Help Ourselves," Sullivan started the first OIC program in an abandoned jailhouse in a poor section of Philadelphia in 1964. Within a few years there were successful OIC programs in almost 100 American cities. Sullivan later assisted in implementing the OIC concept in Latin America, Asia, and Africa. In addition, he developed investment schemes that allowed African Americans to generate new capital by pooling their money. Sullivan's innovative programs reflected his belief that black economic development could be accomplished only by integrating African Americans into the mainstream of American society. Accordingly, he countered the black militant battle cry "Burn, Baby, Burn" with the call "Build, Brother, Build."

Having developed close ties with the corporate world in the 1960s, he was invited to join the board of directors of General Motors (GM) in 1971, the first African American to hold such a position. During a trip to racially segregated South Africa in 1975, where he was arrested and humiliated by white police officers, he committed himself to fighting that country's oppressive system of apartheid. Two years later, after winning the support of several large American companies, such as GM and International Business Machines, he officially presented what came to be known as the Sullivan Principles, a code of conduct for American companies doing business in South Africa. In its original version, it set forth six principles: desegregation of all work facilities, equal and fair employment policies, equal wages, training programs to prepare blacks for promotion, an increase in the numbers of black managers and supervisors, and improvement of black workers' living conditions outside the workplace. In 1984 Sullivan added a seventh principle, which urged companies to eliminate all laws and customs that helped sustain apartheid.

By the early 1980s hundreds of American companies adhered to the Sullivan Principles. Although supported by many, the code of conduct was also subject to criticism. South African labor activists complained that Sullivan ignored the workers' right to collective bargaining. Others warned that his code would have an impact on the lives of relatively few blacks and might help perpetuate apartheid. By the mid-1980s even Sullivan had to admit that segregation and discrimination remained firmly entrenched in South African society. In 1985, therefore, Sullivan officially presented the South African regime with a two-year deadline to end apartheid, free the black activist Nelson Mandela, and grant blacks the right to vote. He threatened to urge American companies to withdraw from the country if the regime refused to comply.

By that time Sullivan's campaign had transformed many Americans into ardent opponents of apartheid. The passage of the Anti-Apartheid Act of 1986 reflected this changing mood and formalized Sullivan's principles into legislation. South Africa nonetheless remained defiant, and on 3 June 1987 Sullivan officially called for American companies to end all business relationships with South Africa. Within a year, seventy companies had announced that they would leave the country. Opposed by world opinion and confronted with the prospect of financial ruin, the system of apartheid began to crumble. By 1990 apartheid had collapsed, Mandela had been freed, and blacks had gained the right to vote.

Sullivan did not rest there. After retiring from his position as pastor of the Zion Baptist Church in 1988, he focused on his International Foundation for Education and Self-Help to introduce self-help methods to Africa's developing countries. In addition, he sought to strengthen relations between blacks in America and Africa. For that reason, and to help sub-Saharan countries obtain debt relief, he organized several summits, the first of which took place in 1991 in Abidjan, Ivory Coast. Toward the end of the 1990s he worked with the United Nations to implement the Global Sullivan Principles, an international code of ethical business conduct for multinational corporations. Sullivan died of leukemia at age seventy-eight. He is buried in Phoenix.

Sullivan was an exceptional fighter for human rights. His accomplishments were acknowledged by numerous awards, among them the Presidential Medal of Freedom and honorary degrees from more than fifty colleges and universities. While they were not without critics, the Sullivan Principles prepared the ground for a successful assault on the system of apartheid in South Africa. Sullivan's lifelong activism clearly reflected his conviction "that with faith and determination, there is no such thing as an impossible dream."

★

Sullivan's autobiography, *Moving Mountains: The Principles and Purposes of Leon Sullivan* (1998), provides a detailed account of both his life and his activist career. His other publications, *Build, Brother, Build* (1969) and *Alternatives to Despair* (1972), also contain useful biographical information. Obituaries are in the *New York Times* and *Washington Post* (both 26 Apr. 2001).

SIMON WENDT

SZULC, Tadeusz Witold ("Tad") (*b.* 25 July 1926 in Warsaw, Poland; *d.* 21 May 2001 in Washington, D.C.), journalist who broke the news about the Bay of Pigs invasion and an influential biographer of Pope John Paul II and the Cuban dictator Fidel Castro, among others.

Szulc was born in Warsaw, the only child of Seweryn Szulc and Janina (Baruch) Szulc. As a child he was sent to Le Rosey boarding school in Switzerland. In the mid-1930s, while he was there, his parents fled Poland for Brazil, fearing, as they were Jewish, persecution in the face of Adolph Hitler's Nazi regime in Germany, which was threatening to encroach on Poland. Szulc joined them in 1941, after spending a year in France, and from 1943 to 1945 he studied at the University of Brazil in Rio de Janeiro. He never graduated, instead joining the Associated Press bureau in Rio de Janeiro in 1945, then transferring to the United States in 1947. In 1949 he jumped to the rival United Press International, covering the recently formed United Nations in New York. That led to a job on the night rewrite desk at the *New York Times* in 1953—and, two years later, to his first overseas assignment, covering Southeast Asia. Szulc became naturalized as a U.S. citizen in 1954.

The assignment at the *Times* lasted less than a year. Soon Szulc was in Latin America, his favorite part of the world and the place where he wrote perhaps his most significant story. Using his connections with both U.S. and Cuban sources, Szulc broke the Bay of Pigs invasion story in April 1961. Not everything he reported appeared in the *Times;* in what is now a famous tale in journalistic and political circles, advisers to President John F. Kennedy begged *Times* editors not to publish Szulc's knowledge that an exile-led invasion of Cuba was imminent. The editors listened, and crucial parts of Szulc's reporting were left out of published accounts. The invasion, which took place on 17 April 1961, was a disaster, resulting in the death of 114, the capture of another 1,000, and international scorn for the Kennedy administration.

Szulc came under scrutiny from the Central Intelligence Agency, which considered him a possible hostile foreign agent. The failure of the *Times* to provide full coverage of the Kennedy administration's plans to overthrow the Cuban leader, Fidel Castro, remains an example of media compliance in the face of political pressure—pressure Kennedy said he later regretted placing on the newspaper. Szulc himself left Latin America within a year of the incident for the first of two stints at the *New York Times* Washington bureau.

Szulc covered Spain and Portugal for the *Times* from 1965 to 1968; his next stop was Eastern Europe, where he once again showed a reporter's talent for being in the right place as history happened. As Prague bureau chief, he returned from a family holiday in August 1968 on a hunch that Czechoslovakia's experiment in open government, the "Prague Spring," might soon come to an end. Five days after his return Soviet tanks rumbled into the city. "I would have hated myself forever had I been on Cape Cod at that time," he later said. For four months Szulc covered the Soviet repression of the once-promising democracy movement—until he was expelled from the country. One reason for his expulsion, Czech officials said, was that he showed too much interest in "secret military questions."

Returning to the *Times*'s Washington bureau, Szulc helped cover the Pentagon Papers scandal before leaving newspapers for good in 1972 to write freelance articles and books. Szulc wrote ten books while at the *Times,* most of them having to do with the countries and events he covered; *The Cuban Invasion* (1962), written with Karl E. Meyer, is a typical title. After leaving the *Times* he wrote ten more books about a wider range of topics and in different styles. In the dedication to *Then and Now: How the World Has Changed Since World War II* (1990), he explained that despite the terrible events he had witnessed as a reporter, including wars, concentration camps, and human rights violations, he was "still optimistic."

Compulsive Spy: The Strange Case of E. Howard Hunt (1974), and *Fidel: A Critical Portrait* (1986), drew both on Szulc's reporting skills and his personal impressions of his subjects. The latter book is one of his two most enduring works; the other is *Pope John Paul II: The Biography* (1995). This profile features lengthy interviews and is widely admired for its focus on the pope's pre-papacy years in Poland. Szulc used files from the Polish secret police and the Soviet Politburo to augment his research. The last book to appear in his lifetime, *To Kill the Pope* (2000), was one of his two novels. When he died, Szulc was investigating the scriptural tale of Abraham, the patriarch of the world's three major monotheistic religions.

Szulc maintained a stable family life during his years across the globe. He married Marianne Carr on 8 July 1948; they had a son and a daughter. "No girl or boy could ever have had a better, more loving, interesting, fun father," his daughter told the *Miami Herald* after his death. "He took us all over the world." Szulc died at his home at age seventy-four of liver and lung cancer, and his remains were cremated.

As a Polish immigrant, an international journalist, and an influential biographer, Szulc participated in, reported on, and, in one famous case, possibly shaped some of the twentieth century's most significant events. Fluent in six languages, he reported news stories from more than ninety countries. Throughout, he chain-smoked, wrote on a man-ual typewriter, and wrestled mightily with the world, which he considered his personal reporting beat.

★

There is no biography of Szulc. For more information about his life and work, see an interview about his relationship with Castro in *Publishers Weekly* (5 Dec. 1986), and a critique of his attitudes toward U.S. foreign policy in the *New Republic* (12 Dec. 1983). Obituaries are in the *New York Times* and *Washington Post* (both 22 May 2001).

ALAN BJERGA

T

TALMADGE, Herman Eugene (*b.* 9 August 1913 in McRae, Georgia; *d.* 21 March 2002 in Hampton, Georgia), Georgia governor and U.S. senator, whose career ended in disgrace in 1979 when he was denounced by the U.S. Senate for financial misconduct.

Talmadge grew up in rural Telfair County in southern Georgia. His father, Eugene Talmadge, was a farmer, lawyer, and Georgia governor, and his mother, Mattie (Thurmond) Talmadge, was a telegraph operator. Talmadge was the middle of three children and the only son. He attended public schools in McRae until his senior year, when the family moved to Atlanta. He graduated from Druid Hills High School in 1930.

Talmadge was an average student who was more interested in hunting and fishing than in school, but he excelled in history and debate. He entered the University of Georgia in Athens in the fall of 1931 and took advantage of a five-year course of study that allowed students to skip the baccalaureate degree and graduate with an LL.B. Out of a class of twenty-seven, he was one of only seven to pass the Georgia bar on the first attempt. He graduated in 1936, began work as a lawyer, and served on his father's political campaigns. In 1937 Talmadge married Kathryn Williamson, but the couple divorced in 1940. He married again in 1941, to Betty Shingler. They had two sons, Herman Eugene, Jr., and Robert.

Talmadge's legal career was put on hold in 1941 when he was commissioned as an ensign in the U.S. Navy. On his first assignment he was attached to the Naval Intelligence Division's cable censor's office in New York City, where he helped monitor incoming and outgoing cables for sensitive information. Bored with the work and tired of New York, Talmadge volunteered for combat duty and after training was assigned to the USS *Tryon,* a heavily armed hospital ship. He spent twenty-two months in the South Pacific transporting both fresh troops and casualties. After serving on the *Tryon,* Talmadge was transferred to the USS *Dauphin,* where he trained sailors for sea duty. In the summer of 1945 the *Dauphin* was preparing for the invasion of Japan when the atomic bombs were dropped on Hiroshima and Nagasaki.

With the war over, Talmadge, by then a lieutenant commander, returned home intent on pursuing a legal career, farming, and running his father's newspaper, the *Statesman.* In 1946 Eugene Talmadge won a record fourth term as governor of Georgia, but he died before he could take the oath of office, setting in motion one of the more bizarre events in political history. The controversy revolved around the outgoing governor, Ellis Arnall; the lieutenant governor elect, Melvin E. Thompson; and Talmadge, a write-in candidate. All three men claimed the office of governor. Before 1945 the Georgia General Assembly would simply have elected a new governor from the two runners-up, but the new post of lieutenant governor, created during the Arnall administration, was specifically intended for the case in

Herman E. Talmadge, October 1966. BETTMANN/CORBIS

which a governor died while in office. The problem was that Eugene Talmadge had died before he was actually sworn in as governor.

When the Georgia General Assembly convened in January 1947, their first order of business was to decide who should become the next governor. While waiting to vote, Thompson supporters served drinks laced with a sedative to Talmadge supporters in the hope that they would miss the vote, but the ploy was discovered, and the legislators were revived. In the meantime, the legislature determined that Talmadge had placed third in votes, not second. However, a box of uncounted ballots from his home county, all written in the same handwriting and bearing signatures of deceased persons, was "found" just in time to put Talmadge over the top.

Ignoring the new law concerning the role of the lieutenant governor, the Georgia General Assembly elected Talmadge governor, and he was sworn in at 2:00 A.M. on 15 January 1947. Arnall, however, refused to relinquish his office and labeled Talmadge a "pretender." That night Talmadge and his supporters changed the locks of the governor's office. On 18 January Arnall resigned in favor of Thompson, who was acting governor (as lieutenant governor elect) and pursued the case in court. Three days later, on 21 January, Talmadge proposed that both men resign and that the general assembly hold a special election; Thompson, however, refused. In March the Georgia Supreme Court ruled in favor of Thompson until a special election could be held in 1948. Talmadge decided not to pursue the case in court but defeated Thompson in the

special election. Talmadge also won the next election in 1950.

During his six years as governor of Georgia, Talmadge worked to improve Georgia's economic situation. A new sales tax, for example, allowed the improvement of roads, hospitals, and schools. He built more and better hospitals; helped the Medical College of Georgia in Augusta double the number of students; raised and equalized pay for white and black teachers; and helped make Georgia, formerly ranked forty-sixth in forestry, a leader in that industry.

Throughout his early political career, Talmadge remained a staunch segregationist. After the 1954 U.S. Supreme Court ruling in *Brown* v. *Board of Education,* which provided the basis for the subsequent desegregation of schools, he wrote *You and Segregation* (1955), which extolled the benefits of "separate but equal" facilities for African Americans. In November 1956 Talmadge defeated his former gubernatorial adversary Thompson, this time for a seat in the U.S. Senate. He held this position for twenty-four years, in the process becoming the fifth most-senior senator, as well as a powerful force in Washington. During his early years in the Senate, Talmadge was part of the coalition of southern senators who opposed civil rights legislation, but he eventually evolved into a strong proponent of economic development for all.

In 1957 Talmadge joined the Agriculture Committee and from 1971 to 1980 chaired the Committee on Agriculture, Nutrition, and Forestry. Talmadge advocated the Rural Development Act of 1973, championed industrial growth, and served on the Senate Select Committee on

Presidential Campaign Activities, which investigated the Watergate scandal. (This scandal involved a break-in at Democratic Party headquarters that eventually was determined to have been arranged by the White House, and led to the resignation of President Richard M. Nixon.)

Just as Talmadge was at the height of his power, personal problems and scandal ended his political career. His twenty-nine-year-old son, Robert, drowned at a Memorial Day celebration in 1975, and thereafter Talmadge began to have serious drinking problems. In 1977 his wife, Betty, divorced him, charging "cruel treatment and habitual intoxication." During the divorce proceedings, she reported finding a wad of cash stuffed in her husband's overcoat pocket.

Talmadge received treatment for alcohol abuse at a naval facility in 1979 and returned to Washington ready to work. Upon his return, however, the Senate Ethics Committee launched an investigation into his campaign and office finances. Betty Talmadge testified against him, elaborating on her previous accusations, and an aide, Daniel Minchew, was accused of diverting $37,000 in expense money and campaign contributions to a secret Washington bank account in Talmadge's name. Despite his protestations of a setup, Talmadge was denounced by his fellow senators for "reprehensible conduct." He narrowly lost the 1980 election to Mack Mattingly, the first Republican senator from Georgia since Reconstruction.

Talmadge returned to his farm and ham-curing business. In 1984 he married for the last time, to the much-younger Lynda Cowart Pierce. They had no children. Talmadge was in failing health throughout the 1990s, undergoing surgery for throat cancer in 1996 and open-heart surgery in 1997. He died at home and was buried in the family cemetery in Lovejoy, Georgia.

Talmadge was a popular and effective governor and senator. Late in his career, he mellowed on segregation, calling his earlier views on the subject a "mistake." He even earned a "man of the year" award in 1975 from Morris Brown College, a predominantly African-American school in Atlanta. His most significant contributions stemmed from his role as chairman of the Senate Agriculture Committee, which created price support programs for peanuts, cotton, wheat, and various other commodities.

★

Talmadge's papers are housed in the Richard B. Russell Library for Political Research and Studies at the University of Georgia in Athens. Talmadge's autobiography, written with Mark Royden Winchell, is *Talmadge: A Political Legacy, A Politician's Life: A Memoir* (1987). Obituaries are in the *Augusta Chronicle* (21 Mar. 2002) and *New York Times* (22 Mar. 2002).

LISA A. ENNIS

THOMAS, R. David ("Dave") (*b.* 2 July 1932 in Atlantic City, New Jersey; *d.* 8 January 2002 in Fort Lauderdale, Florida), fast-food entrepreneur who founded Wendy's Restaurants.

Thomas was born to a woman named Mollie from Camden, New Jersey, who gave him up for adoption when he was six weeks old. His adoptive parents, a young couple from Kalamazoo, Michigan, were Rex Thomas, a construction worker, and Auleva Thomas, a housewife. After Auleva died of rheumatic fever in 1937 when Thomas was five, Rex, who was working as an auto mechanic, moved to various towns in the Midwest and South, taking a variety of jobs. During this period, Thomas spent most of his summers with his adoptive grandmother, Minnie Sinclair. He described her as a compelling and uncompromising religious woman who gave him happiness and the one thing his father had not, a refuge from isolation.

Thomas, who estimated that his family moved at least twelve times, worked as a newspaper deliverer, golf caddy, bowling pin setter, grocery delivery clerk, and soda fountain counterman to help his adoptive father pay the bills and to escape his isolation. None of these jobs lasted very long, but his luck changed when, at age twelve, he got a job as

Dave Thomas, 1998. AP/WIDE WORLD PHOTOS

a counterman at Regas Restaurant in Knoxville, Tennessee. It was this job and his love of eating out with family that sowed the seeds of his interest in the food service industry. When his family relocated to Fort Wayne, Indiana, in 1947, Thomas found work at the Hobby House Restaurant, where he felt more at home than with his family. When his father moved yet again, Thomas remained in Fort Wayne and moved into the Young Men's Christian Association (YMCA), dropping out of school so that he could focus on his restaurant job. His career goals were temporarily delayed by his entry into the U.S. Army during the Korean War. Thomas was sent to Fort Benning, Georgia, in October 1950, where he attended the army's Cook and Baker's School.

Sent overseas to Frankfurt, Germany, Thomas made friends with the cook at the base, and, putting his restaurant skills to work, he impressed him and the commanding officer so much that they eventually made him manager of the enlisted men's club. Thomas served in the army for two and a half years, and by the time he was discharged he had achieved the rank of staff sergeant. Upon leaving the military, he returned to Fort Wayne and worked as a short-order cook at the Hobby House. There, in October 1953, he met Lorraine Buskirk, who worked as a waitress. She came from a similar family environment, and the two began to date. They married in April 1954 and continued to work at the Hobby House. When his boss, Phil Clauss, decided to open a second restaurant, he selected Thomas as the assistant manager.

In the mid-1950s Clauss began working with Harland Sanders (later known as Colonel Sanders). Thomas was taught how to prepare chicken using Sanders's recipe and how to sell it to customers. In the late 1950s Clauss bought four Kentucky Fried Chicken (KFC) restaurants in Columbus, Ohio. When they failed to make a profit, he offered to sell 45 percent of his ownership to Thomas if he was able to make them solvent. Thomas, who by then had a family of four children, with a fifth on the way, was determined to succeed. In January 1962 he moved to Columbus to look for a house and to begin work as manager of the restaurants. A few months later his family settled in Columbus, and after four years under his leadership, the four restaurants made a profit. Sanders became Thomas's mentor, and Thomas took advantage of the experience, learning everything he could from the fried chicken entrepreneur about the quickly evolving fast-food industry. Thomas helped create the famous revolving KFC bucket sign, and, according to Nancy Millman of the *Chicago Tribune,* he helped persuade Sanders to appear in his own commercials, the move that boosted profits for KFC and made Sanders a familiar face in the late 1960s and early 1970s. Having made his four franchise shops profitable, Thomas sold

them back to KFC in 1968. The sale made him a millionaire, and he took a position at the parent company.

Because of a business dispute with John Y. Brown, another executive, Thomas's stay at KFC headquarters was brief. Brown and Jack Massey had bought KFC from Sanders in the mid-1960s, prompting Thomas to take his money and to use part of it to start his own restaurant. When he was young, Thomas had dreamed of opening a hamburger restaurant. After complaining that he could not find a good hamburger in Columbus, he opened his first restaurant in an unused portion of a downtown Columbus building, which one of his friends used for prepping cars before moving them to showrooms.

The restaurant's specialty was fresh-cooked, made-to-order hamburgers, not burgers made from frozen meat patties. He served his freshly cooked hamburgers on a square bun and offered customers a variety of toppings. The original menu consisted of hamburgers, chili, french fries, soft drinks, and the Frosty Dairy Dessert. To make his restaurants even more inviting, Thomas created a relaxed, homey atmosphere with carpeting and Tiffany-style lamps over newsprint tabletops with bentwood chairs. As a final touch, Thomas used the face of a freckled, red-haired girl in ponytails as the logo for his new business. The image was the likeness of his eight-year-old daughter, Melinda Lou, nicknamed Wendy.

The first Wendy's Old-Fashioned Hamburgers restaurant opened in Columbus on 15 November 1969. Thomas's new enterprise began to make a profit within six weeks of its opening, and he expanded throughout the state. By 1973 Thomas was opening restaurants across the country. He negotiated with entire cities and geographic regions rather than selling single franchises to individual buyers. Wendy's Restaurants became a familiar sight in cities across the United States. In 1979 he received the Horatio Alger Award for his business efforts.

In 1982 Thomas decided to step aside and let his corporate office run the business. Serving as senior chairman, he invested in other smaller businesses. By 1986 sliding quality and business mistakes led Thomas to return to a leadership position in the company. He immediately began visiting restaurants and espousing his earnest, hardworking attitude, which he called "MBA" for "mop bucket attitude." As Wendy's began to turn around, Thomas became the restaurant's television spokesman. He made folksy, humorous commercials that stressed the difference between Wendy's and its leading competitors. The campaign worked, and by 2002 Wendy's was the number three food franchise in the country, with more than six thousand restaurants worldwide.

Thomas believed in giving back to the community and contributed to a variety of charitable organizations. He came to terms with his adoption and became an advocate for foster parent and adoption programs, establishing the Dave Thomas Foundation for Adoption, which provided employee benefits for people who adopted. He also published an autobiography and two additional books in which he explained his business philosophy. Thomas, a high school dropout, frequently spoke to teenagers and young adults, urging them to stay in school. To prove the benefits of an education, he earned his general equivalency diploma in 1993 from Coconut Creek High School in Fort Lauderdale, Florida. Thomas remained active and outgoing despite being diagnosed with cancer in the early 1990s. He died at home in Fort Lauderdale of liver cancer and is buried at Union Cemetery in Columbus.

★

Thomas's autobiography is *Dave's Way: A New Approach to Old-Fashioned Success* (1991). Dave Thomas, *Dave Says—Well Done!: The Common Guy's Guide to Everyday Success* (1994), written with Ron Beyma, also provides valuable background information. Important articles regarding milestones in Thomas's career include Linda Killian, "Hamburger Helper," *Forbes* (5 Aug. 1991): 106–107; Nancy Millman, "Huckster Honchos," *Chicago Tribune* (2 Mar. 1993) 5:1–2; and Marilyn Achiron and Julie Greenwalt, "Dave Thomas," *People Weekly* (2 Aug. 1993): 86–88. Obituaries are in the *New York Times, Washington Post,* and *USA Today* (all 9 Jan. 2002).

Brian B. Carpenter

THOMAS, Robert McG(ill), Jr. (*b.* 1940 in Shelbyville, Tennessee; *d.* 6 January 2000 in Rehoboth Beach, Delaware), *New York Times* journalist known for his obituaries of odd, infamous, and little-known New Yorkers.

Thomas was the son of Robert McGill Thomas, a hosiery manufacturer, and Jane (Carey Folk) Thomas, a teacher. He attended Yale University in New Haven, Connecticut, where he worked on the school newspaper. His college career was short-lived: as reported in his *New York Times* obituary, Thomas flunked out of Yale because he decided to "major in New York rather than anything academic." In 1959 Thomas started as a copy boy at the *New York Times,* where he worked for the next four decades.

Soon after taking a job at the *Times,* Thomas began to receive assignments that found him haunting police stations or manning the phones in an effort to cinch a last-minute story. Thomas earned a reputation as a stylish writer, albeit one who often carried his stories further than his editors thought warranted. During his tenure at the *Times,* Thomas covered a variety of beats, writing everything from police and crime stories to society news, from sports to financial commentary. Throughout the 1970s Thomas worked at the rewrite desk, honing the prose of fellow reporters.

In 1995 he received an assignment to write obituaries. It was in this position that Thomas, already regarded as a fine newspaperman, made his mark. His more than 650 funny, elegant, memorable, and often moving send-offs for New York's eccentric and unknown citizens quickly earned an eager following among readers, who each morning turned first to the "obits" page for the latest "McGs.," as his obituaries came to be called. Thomas's editor, Marvin Siegal, realized that he had found a genius of sorts, and made certain he assigned Thomas to write about the colorful, the forgotten, and the celebrities of the city.

Thomas's flair for writing obituaries earned him a certain freedom from the strictures of editorial policy at the *Times.* Instead of working in advance on his stories, Thomas could choose his subjects and write his articles until the daily edition was nearly ready to go to press. This procedure made for tight deadlines, but in his view, the tighter the better. One colleague remembered that editors commonly assigned Thomas a story late in the afternoon, knowing that he would have something ready to go to press by early evening.

While enjoying a great deal of editorial latitude, Thomas's obituaries followed a prescribed pattern. The lead sentence of every story summed up the life of the deceased person. Although Thomas included a wealth of information in brief essays, his description of the dead never seemed hurried. Thomas spent a great deal of time on the phone teasing out information about his subjects that not only humanized them but also celebrated their unusual lives rather than mourned their passing. Still, Thomas was not above skewering his subjects with horrible puns or ironic twists, which made his writing, and the figures about which he wrote, all the more memorable.

For Thomas no information was off-limits, and nothing was too odd or strange to include in his commemoration of the dead. The reader was also likely to learn unexpected facts. A case in point was his obituary for R. V. Patwardhan, a Manhattan Hindu priest who adapted the incendiary portion of his religion's wedding ritual to conform to New York fire laws. Whether he was writing about a Du Pont executive who, despairing of his staid, routine life, became a spy for the Manhattan Project; the "Mitten Lady," who spent all her time knitting mittens, hats, and scarves for poor children all over the world; or the man who invented Kitty Litter, Thomas always strove to capture the essence of a life lived, to allow the dead to stand up and walk one last time. Thomas died at his family's summer home of abdominal cancer. He was survived by his wife, Joan, two sons (he had three children), and two grandchildren.

In the five years that Thomas worked the obituary desk, he turned a mundane and dreary task into one that was filled with humor and insight into the human condition. He elevated obituary writing to a literary form. As Michael

T. Kaufman, the colleague who had the unenviable task of writing Thomas's own obituary, put it, Thomas "single-handedly humanized the paper."

★

There is little published information about Thomas. For biographical background, see Chris Calhoun, ed., *52 McGs.: The Best Obituaries from Legendary "New York Times" Writer Robert McG. Thomas, Jr.* (2001). Thomas's work also appears in Marvin Siegel, ed., *The Last Word: The "New York Times" Book of Obituaries and Farewells: A Celebration of Unusual Lives* (1997). See also Bruce Porter, "King of the Obits," *Columbia Journalism Review* 38, no. 3 (Sept. 1999): 11. Thomas's own obituary is in the *New York Times* (8 Jan. 2000).

MEG GREENE MALVASI

TIEN, Chang-Lin (*b.* 24 July 1935 in Wuhan, China; *d.* 29 October 2002 in Redwood City, California), eminent scholar in the thermal sciences; chancellor of the University of California, Berkeley (1990–1997); and the first Asian American to head a major research university in the United States.

Tien was the sixth of eight children born to Yun Chien Tien, a ranking treasury official and a banker, and Yun Di (Li) Tien, a homemaker. Growing up in Wuhan and Shanghai, China, during the war with Japan (1937–1945) and the civil war in the late 1940s, Tien had a childhood that was marked with volatile changes. Although his father managed to shield the family from devastation, first from the Japanese in 1938 and later from the Communist takeover in 1949, taking the family to Taiwan, the Tiens had brushes with hardship as well as periods of privileged life.

The family's newfound stability and prosperity in Taiwan was disrupted by the death of Tien's father from a heart attack in 1952. Drawing strength from their devoted mother and the family's spiritual heritage, the children succeeded in life. Tien excelled academically. Although Tien was only five feet, six inches tall, he played semiprofessional basketball at National Taiwan University and continued playing later for a military academy. Tien tutored Di-Hwa Liu, his first student, and the two fell in love.

In 1955 Tien graduated from National Taiwan University with a B.S. in mechanical engineering, and in 1956 came to the United States as a graduate student. He raced through two master's degrees (an M.M.E. from the University of Louisville in Kentucky in 1957, and an M.A. from Princeton University in New Jersey) and a Ph.D. in mechanical engineering from Princeton in 1959. On 25 July 1959 Tien married Liu, now a graduate of Taiwan's Dan Jiang University. Their honeymoon was a three-week cross-country trip to Tien's teaching position at the University of California (UC), Berkeley, where Tien would leave his

legacy as a professor, a scholar, and ultimately, a university chancellor.

Despite his accented English, Tien became a popular professor. At age twenty-six, he was the youngest recipient of the Distinguished Teaching Award. Tien never stopped teaching, even when he was working eighteen hours a day as chancellor. Tien's scientific achievements carved out new fields in the thermal sciences. The knowledge and technology were also applied in space shuttle projects, nuclear reactors, fire-retardant materials for high-rise buildings, and magnetic levitation trains in Japan.

Tien's many honors included becoming one of the youngest members of the National Academy of Engineering (NAE), which awarded him its highest honor, the NAE Founders Award (2001). He also received the Max Jakob Memorial Award, the highest international award in the field of heat transfer. Tien also held administrative posts as chair of the department of mechanical engineering (1974–1981), vice chancellor for research (1983–1985), and executive vice chancellor at UC Irvine (1988–1990). He returned to Berkeley as chancellor in July 1990.

The new chancellor faced looming state budget cuts and racial tension on the campus over an admissions policy that allegedly favored African-American and Hispanic applicants over white and Asian applicants. Tien was unfazed, setting four goals for his tenure: maintaining the excellence of Berkeley's faculty and its academic programs, strengthening undergraduate education, raising private funds, and achieving excellence through diversity.

On 25 August 1992, less than two months after Tien took office, a local activist with a history of mental illness attempted to assassinate Tien. She broke into the chancellor's residence with a machete, reaching the master bedroom suite and trapping the Tiens in a side bedroom on the same floor. The would-be assassin triggered the silent alarm, and the police soon arrived. She was shot and killed when she lunged at the police with the machete. The Tiens were being escorted out of the house, unharmed, when the shooting took place at 6:00 A.M. The Tiens responded to the incident with stoicism. When day broke, Tien was on campus, conducting business as usual.

Tien was a tireless and skillful fund-raiser. By the end of his tenure as chancellor, the campus had raised more than $975 million. In the process, he became an informal ambassador, meeting top leaders and business elites while building bridges between the United States and the Asian countries of the Pacific Rim.

A staunch advocate of affirmative action, Tien had first-hand experience with racial discrimination. Despite his objections, the University of California Board of Regents voted to eliminate affirmative action programs in July 1995. Tien responded by announcing the Berkeley Pledge, a campus initiative to help prepare public school students to meet

UC eligibility standards for admission. He personally contributed $10,000 to the pledge at the outset of the campaign.

Tien was a man of personal integrity and conscience. Newly arrived in the segregated South in 1956, he was told to sit with the whites in the front of the bus, while blacks sat in back. Tien did not take the bus again for an entire year. At the University of Louisville, a professor kept calling him "Chinaman." Tien insisted that he be called by his name. The professor did not bother to say his name, but he did stop using the derogatory term. In the 1960s, Tien applied for U.S. citizenship. An immigration officer said that Tien would have to wait 142 years for his turn. Tien did not despair. He said it only made him want to live longer. Tien became a citizen in 1969.

As a young faculty member at Berkeley in the early 1970s, Tien joined the Bao Diao Movement, denouncing Taiwan's government for its handling of the territory dispute with the Japanese government over the Diaoyu Islands. In June 1989 Tien sent a telegram to Chinese leaders condemning the Tiananmen Square massacre in Beijing and asking for the dismissal of the prime minister. When Dr. Wen Ho Li was jailed, without being convicted, for allegedly spying for the Chinese government, Tien publicly offered support. When the mood in the United States was against affirmative action and immigration, Tien penned a defense of both in the *New York Times* and *Los Angeles Times*. He feuded openly with the UC Board of Regents and the state governor, Pete Wilson, attempting to preserve affirmative action programs. He lost that battle but spearheaded a campus initiative to help prepare public school students to meet UC's eligibility standards for admission. In June 1997 he stepped down as chancellor.

In the post-chancellor years, Tien remained at Berkeley as the NEC Distinguished Professor of Engineering. He continued to teach and lecture at universities, and consulted on scientific projects. He also spoke out in support of affirmative action, and sat on a number of boards of Asian-American organizations and corporations. Tien was reportedly considered for the post of energy secretary in the administration of President Bill Clinton, but he was affected negatively by a campaign contributions scandal involving the Lippo Group, which made illegal contributions to the Clinton campaign, as well as a legal donation of $200,000 to Berkeley, when Tien was chancellor.

In September 2000 Tien was diagnosed with a brain tumor. He suffered a debilitating stroke during a test and never regained his health. Tien died at Kaiser Permanente Hospital in Redwood City, and is buried at Skylawn Memorial Park in San Mateo, California.

Tien's contribution to the thermal sciences was notable, as was his tenure as the first Asian-American chancellor of a major research university.

★

Information about Tien is in Denise K. Magner, "Asian American to Head a Major U.S. Research University," *Chronicle of Higher Education* (24 Oct. 1990); M. Shao, "He's Seen Our Future, And . . . ," *World Monitor* (July 1992); Chang-Lin Tien, "A View from Berkeley," *New York Times* (31 Mar. 1996); and Alethea Yip, "Time Out for Chancellor Tien," *Asian Week* (4–10 July 1997). Obituaries are in the *Los Angeles Times, New York Times,* and *San Francisco Chronicle* (all 31 Oct. 2002).

SHAOSHAN LI

TOBIN, James (*b.* 5 March 1918 in Champaign, Illinois; *d.* 11 March 2002 in New Haven, Connecticut), economist and winner of the Nobel Prize for economics in 1981.

Tobin was one of two children of Louis Michael Tobin and Margaret (Edgerton) Tobin. His father was a journalist by training, and publicity director for the University of Illinois Athletic Department. His mother was a social worker who, following a sixteen-year hiatus while raising her children, served as the director of the family service agency of Champaign-Urbana, Illinois.

Tobin attended public elementary schools in Champaign, but he went to high school at what was known as Uni-High, an affiliate of the University of Illinois College of Education. Although the school's mission was to provide practical training in teaching, its distinguishing features were its small size and outstanding teaching faculty, who produced many leaders in their future professions. Tobin won a competitive scholarship to Harvard University in Cambridge, Massachusetts, in 1935 and went on to graduate summa cum laude with an B.A. in economics in 1939. This honor led to a traveling fellowship that, because of the outbreak of World War II, he was unable to utilize. He remained at Harvard, earning an M.A. in economics in 1940.

Tobin worked in the Office of Price Administration and on the Civilian Supply and War Production Board before enlisting in the U.S. Navy in 1942. He underwent a three-month training period at Columbia University, during which he met Herman Wouk, the future author of *The Caine Mutiny.* Wouk incorporated into his story a figure, named Tobit, loosely modeled on Tobin. After training, Tobin was assigned to USS *Kearney,* a destroyer serving primarily in the Atlantic and Mediterranean theaters. On 14 September 1946 Tobin married Elizabeth Fay Ringo; they had three children.

In 1946 Tobin returned to Harvard, completing his Ph.D. in 1947 with a dissertation on "A Theoretical and Statistical Analysis of Consumer Saving." The paper, which foreshadowed much of his later research, made

James Tobin, December 1967. AP/WIDE WORLD PHOTOS

heavy use of statistical analysis. In 1950 Tobin joined the Yale Department of Economics, where he remained on the faculty for the rest of his career, retiring in 1988. In 1955 he also became the director of the Cowles Foundation, an endowed fund to underwrite economic research and publications. Tobin served as director from 1955 to 1961, and again from 1964 to 1965.

In 1961 President John F. Kennedy invited Tobin to serve on his Council of Economic Advisers. He served actively for a year and for several more years as a consultant. During his active service, Tobin contributed to the 1962 *Economic Report of the President*. This report advocated policies with which Tobin came to be closely associated, basically an expansion of the ideas of John Maynard Keynes, the dominant economic theorist of the twentieth century. The report advocated a policy directed at both price stability and full employment, and stressed the role of government in economic prosperity.

Tobin's research focused on macroeconomics, or the operation of the entire economic system. He modified the Keynesian theory of general employment by incorporating into it some of the microanalysis of the classical economists. In particular, Tobin argued that an individual investor would hold some of his assets in cash or in highly liquid investments, a decision he called "liquidity preference." The purpose was the avoidance of the risk associated with longer-term investments in stocks and bonds. By demonstrating that investors traded off risk against return in the way they allocated their assets, Tobin fundamentally modified economic thinking. This work on liquidity preference earned Tobin the Nobel Prize for economics in 1981.

Tobin also developed an idea called the "Q Concept," which was a way of valuing financial assets. "Q" was essentially a fraction, in which the numerator was the stock-market price multiplied by the number of shares outstanding and the denominator was the replacement cost of the assets the stock represented. If the "Q" value is more than 1 (as it usually is in prosperous times), then the market value exceeds the replacement cost of the assets. Thus, the "Q" value is an indicator of investors' faith in the future growth of the company. But if this faith in future growth is absent, there will be little investment in the stock, causing its market price to decline.

Tobin's views won wide acceptance among economists in the latter years of the twentieth century. In particular, the Federal Reserve Board appeared to adopt Tobin's position that the level of employment was just as important as the level of inflation, and its manipulation of credit policies was designed to achieve both objectives.

Tobin wrote numerous books and a vast number of articles, both professional and popular. His books include *National Economic Policy: Essays* (1966), *Welfare Programs: An Economic Appraisal* (1968), *The New Economics, One Decade Older* (1974), *Asset Accumulation and Economic Activity: Reflections on Contemporary Macroeconomic Theory* (1980), *Policies for Prosperity: Essays in a Keynesian Mode*

(1987), *Two Revolutions in Economic Policy: The First Economic Reports of Presidents Kennedy and Reagan* (1988), and *Full Employment and Growth: Further Essays in a Keynesian Mode* (1996). Tobin's books reflect his two primary interests, public policy in economics and analysis of investment behavior. His numerous articles were gathered together and published in four volumes between 1971 and 1996, under the title *Essays in Economics*.

In addition to the Nobel Prize, Tobin won many other honors. He received a public service award from the Connecticut Bar Association, and was a fellow of the American Academy of Arts and Sciences. In 1955 he received the John Bates Clark Bronze Medal of the American Economic Association. He was elected president of the American Econometric Association in 1958, vice president of the American Economic Association in 1964, and president of the American Economic Association in 1971. In 1988 Japan conferred on him the Grand Cordon of the Order of the Sacred Treasure. In 1989 he received the Centennial Medal of the Harvard Graduate School.

Tobin died at his home following a stroke. A memorial service was held for him at Yale's Battell Chapel on 27 April 2002.

★

There is no biography of Tobin. For details about his life, see the entry about him by Betty J. Blecha in *Nobel Laureates in Economics* (1989), Bernard S. Katz, ed. There is an extensive interview with Tobin by David Fettig in *The Region* (Dec. 1996). An obituary is in the *New York Times* (13 Mar. 2002).

NANCY M. GORDON

TOWNSEND, Lynn Alfred (*b.* 12 May 1919 in Flint, Michigan; *d.* 17 August 2000 in Farmington Hills, Michigan), president and chairman of Chrysler Corporation from 1961 to 1975.

Townsend was the son of Lynn A. Townsend and Georgia (Crandall) Townsend. The family moved to Los Angeles, where his father operated an automotive repair shop and his mother was a teacher. He attended school in Beverly Hills until his father died when Townsend was fourteen years old. (His mother had died when he was nine years old.) He then moved to Evansville, Indiana, to live with his father's brother, North I. Townsend, and graduated from Benjamin Bosse High School in 1935. He earned his B.A. from the University of Michigan in 1940 and married Ruth M. Laing on 14 September of the same year. By 1941 he had earned his M.B.A., and he and his wife had moved to Detroit, where he worked for the accounting firm Ernst and Ernst.

Shortly after the United States entered World War II,

Lynn A. Townsend, August 1964. GETTY IMAGES

Townsend joined the U.S. Navy and served as a disbursing officer on the aircraft carrier USS *Hornet* in the Pacific theater, earning the rank of lieutenant. By 1946 he had returned to Ernst and Ernst, but he soon followed George Bailey, one the firm's partners, when the latter formed his own company, which eventually became Touche, Ross, Bailey, and Smart. Townsend was made a partner in 1952. Between 1942 and 1951 the Townsends had three sons. By 1957 Townsend had left the firm to work for Chrysler as controller. His first action was to lay off seven thousand white-collar workers, bringing down the company deficit. The success of his fiscal policy propelled Townsend to vice president of international operations, then to administrative vice president, and, on 27 July 1961, to president of the corporation.

During his first year as president, Townsend turned Chrysler around from $5 million in losses to $11 million in net profits. He pushed for advancements in technology and overhauled the marketing program for car dealers with the motto "We intend to fix what's wrong, keep what's right, and move ahead." In the early 1960s Chrysler competed with General Motors and Ford Motor Company as one of the "Big Three" American car manufacturers. General Motors outsold Ford by two to one, leaving Chrysler at the bottom. Townsend merged Chrysler and Plymouth, closed plants, and offered car warranties. Caught in the high-stakes competition among the "Big Three," Townsend relied more on greater horsepower, more chrome, and longer, sleeker cars than on technological improvement. The companies were in a race to convince consumers that cars defined who they were. In 1963 Townsend was honored with the coveted Business Award of the Year by the University of Michigan, the Industrialist of the Year by the Society of Industrial Realtors, and the New York Financial Association's Man of the Year in Finance and Business award.

In 1964 Townsend recognized the growing competition from the foreign car market. He strengthened the relationship between Canadian and American automotive businesses, acknowledging the fact that North American production had shrunk from 75 percent of the global production of cars in 1953 to 47 percent in 1963. In order to remain competitive, Townsend eliminated duplication in large-scale manufacturing between Canada and America. He saw the need for a common North American market that eventually would include Mexico and other countries in the hemisphere, creating a "tariff-free" area similar to the one in Europe. With globalization in mind, Townsend bought the English company Rootes, the French Simca, and the Spanish Barreiros. He also established ties with the Mitsubishi Motors Corporation in Japan and with other companies in South America. With his keen interest in the navy, Townsend also nurtured Chrysler's marine line, and in 1965 the company won government contracts in space and defense worth $220 million. Townsend became chairman and chief executive officer of Chrysler Corporation in 1967.

Chrysler sales doubled in the American market in 1968. When he became president in 1961, Chrysler controlled 8 percent of the automotive market. By 1968 Townsend had increased that figure to 18 percent. But Townsend turned his attention away from a customer-oriented policy in an effort to please his stockholders, commenting that "all the public wants is its [stock] splits." His preoccupation with stocks left him vulnerable in terms of sales. The acquisition of foreign car companies proved to be unsuccessful. Townsend also threw aside the time-honored creed of following supply and demand, and he ordered an overproduction of cars as a way to impress stockholders. As a result, Chrysler built a surplus of 408,302 cars, all manufactured without orders from dealers. This, in turn, created poor public relations with dealers who were forced to buy cars they could not sell. In an effort to address the crisis of overproduction in 1969, Townsend formed the Chrysler Financial Corporation. Under this plan the overflow of cars sat in Detroit, waiting for orders from dealers that never came.

As the 1960s drew to a close, Townsend's troubles in-

creased. In 1970 Chrysler's debt was close to $800 million, and Chrysler had to raise millions from banks in order to avoid bankruptcy. Then the oil embargo in 1973–1974 created a crisis for all of the American car corporations that had been marketing gas-guzzling luxury cars. The stage was set for small, fuel-efficient cars to take over the market, and German and Japanese car manufacturers produced cars to meet that demand. Layoffs in American car manufacturing plants followed. To add to Chrysler's troubles, less money was available for research and development. In July 1975, at the age of fifty-six, Townsend resigned as chairman of the board, noting, "It is my opinion that a corporation of this size . . . should not be dominated by one person for a quarter of a century." He was succeeded by John Riccardo, who also could not turn the company around. That was accomplished in 1979, with an all-out American sales campaign initiated by Lee A. Iacocca, the former president of Ford who moved to Chrysler as chief executive officer.

During the early 1970s Townsend was the president of New Detroit Inc., which was dedicated to rebuilding the inner city, and he raised funds to establish an opera company in Detroit. Townsend also served as chairman of the National Alliance of Businessmen under President Richard Nixon. His philanthropic activities included acting as trustee of the Automotive Safety Foundation and the Children's Hospital of Michigan. He was a director of the Automobile Manufacturers Association.

Chrysler Corporation is now owned by the German company DaimlerChrysler A.G. Under Townsend's stewardship Chrysler went from near bankruptcy to profitability in 1961, but he was unable to repeat his success in the mid-1970s. He stepped down in time for a new generation of industrial titans to save the corporation from the ravages of recessions, oil embargoes, and foreign competition. Townsend died at Botsford Continuing Health Center in suburban Farmington Hills, Michigan, at age eighty-one.

★

David Halberstam, *The Reckoning* (1986), provides good insight into Townsend. Robert Sobel, *Car Wars: The Untold Story* (1984), discusses Townsend and compares him to Henry Ford II and to Ernst Breech and Alfred Sloan of General Motors. In a speech given to the Empire Club of Canada, "A Great Economic Opportunity: An Address by Lynn A. Townsend, President, Chrysler Corporation of America" (20 Feb. 1964), published in *The Empire Club of Canada Speeches* (1963–1964), Townsend addresses the Canadian-American automotive relationship. Additional information about Townsend is in *Current Biography* 25, no. 8 (Sept. 1966). Obituaries are in the *New York Times* (22 Aug. 2000), *Washington Post* (24 Aug. 2000), *Chicago Tribune* (23 Aug. 2000), and *Automotive News* (28 Aug. 2000).

JANE FRANCES AMLER

TREVOR, Claire (*b.* 8 March 1909 in Brooklyn, New York City; *d.* 8 April 2000 in Newport Beach, California), actress of stage, film, radio, and television, best known for her roles in *Stagecoach* (1939) and *Key Largo* (1948), the second of which won her an Academy Award for best supporting actress.

Trevor, who grew up in the Bensonhurst neighborhood of Brooklyn, was born Claire Wemlinger, the only child of Noel Wemlinger, a custom tailor who owned a shop on New York City's Fifth Avenue, and Betty (Morrison) Wemlinger, a homemaker. She adapted the name "Trevor" when working later on the stage, choosing the name from the telephone book in her agent's office. Both parents were immigrants, her father from France and her mother from Ireland. As a child, Trevor dreamed of being a ballerina, but her interest turned to acting when she became involved with church and school plays. In 1917, as an eight-year-old, she acted on stage in a revival of *The Blue Bird*. She graduated from Mamaroneck High School in suburban Larchmont, New York, and attended Columbia University for six months.

Trevor's father's business had suffered in the stock market crash of 1929, and after a brief stint at the American Academy of Dramatic Arts, she dropped out of school to supplement her family's income. For the next two years,

Claire Trevor (*left*) with her son, Charles Bren, 1964. AP/WIDE WORLD PHOTOS

she performed in community repertory theater productions in Michigan, St. Louis, and Long Island. She also acted in Vitaphone short subjects filmed in Brooklyn. Trevor's big break came when she starred in the hit Broadway play *Whistling in the Dark* (1932). Discovered by Twentieth Century–Fox, she was signed to a five-year contract, and moved to Hollywood.

In Trevor's first two feature films, *Life in the Raw* and *The Last Trail* (both 1933), she performed opposite George O'Brien, the brawny star of westerns. She went on to make several films for Fox, but she received greater notice when loaned out to Samuel Goldwyn in 1937 for *Dead End* with Humphrey Bogart. For her portrayal of an ailing prostitute in that film, she earned an Academy Award nomination. In 1938 Trevor concluded her contract with Fox, starring in *The Amazing Dr. Clitterhouse,* a black comedy with Bogart and Edward G. Robinson in which she played a faithless lover. Cast mostly in B movies during this period, she gained a reputation for bringing sympathy and vulnerability to characters of dubious morals. In John Ford's *Stagecoach* (1939), which gave her top billing opposite John Wayne, Trevor played the sympathetic prostitute Dallas, who is run out of town on the stagecoach, only to be redeemed by her kindness and generosity.

During the 1940s Trevor, often cast as the villainess, was a fixture of film noir, a genre popular in that era. In 1944 she was the conspiratorial killer in the Raymond Chandler thriller *Murder, My Sweet.* In *Born to Kill* (1947), Trevor played a desperate woman whose lust for wealth ensnares her in a partnership with a dangerous killer. In 1948 she assumed the part of Gaye Dawn in *Key Largo.* Her tragically compelling portrayal of the defeated alcoholic mistress of gangster Johnny Rocco, played by Robinson, earned her the Academy Award for best supporting actress. In 1951 Trevor became the scheming mother who loses the trust of her daughter, performed by Ida Lupino, in *Hard, Fast and Beautiful.* Three years later, she was nominated for another Oscar after starring opposite Wayne in *The High and the Mighty,* the classic airborne disaster film.

Appearing in several television dramas in the 1950s, Trevor was awarded an Emmy in 1956 for her performance in *Dodsworth,* an episode of the National Broadcasting Company's *Producers' Showcase,* in which she played the vain and unfaithful wife of the title character, portrayed by Fredric March. Trevor's career slowed after the 1950s, as she accepted only occasional film and television roles. Her last part was that of an aging schoolteacher in the 1987 television movie *Norman Rockwell's Breaking Home Ties.*

Devoted to family, Trevor never allowed her career to take precedence over her commitments to loved ones. In 1938 she married Clark Andrews, a director of *Big Town,* the radio show she starred in with Robinson. Divorced in 1942, Trevor married Cylos William Dunsmoore, a navy lieutenant, in 1943. The marriage, which ended in divorce in 1947, produced a son, Charles. After these two false starts, Trevor settled into a successful marriage with Milton Bren, a film producer who had two sons from a previous marriage. Married in 1948, they and their children formed a close-knit family in which Trevor raised Bren's sons as her own. Charles died in an airline collision over San Diego in 1978, and in 1979 Bren died of a brain tumor. Following these tragedies, Trevor returned to New York City to live in an apartment on Fifth Avenue.

Later Trevor moved to Newport Beach, California, where she kept a busy social schedule. Reflecting on her film career, she cherished her acting experiences while remaining modest about her success. After suffering from a respiratory ailment, Trevor died in a hospital near her home. Her ashes were scattered over the Pacific Ocean. She had donated money to help renovate the performing arts theater at the University of California, Irvine, in 1998, and after her death, her stepsons (both successful businessmen) contributed $7 million to the school in her memory. The Claire Trevor School of the Arts was named to honor her support of young people in their artistic endeavors.

Trevor played roles in a gripping and sensitive manner that often defied description and simple categorization. Her penetrating looks, steely eyes, and the sense of severity and yearning in her expressions were atypical for a leading lady. Her stark attractiveness and smoky voice made her the ideal actress to play the boozy moll, femme fatale, and underworld floozy. She enjoyed a host of leading roles but was also intent on bringing her well-honed talents to supporting roles. Hardworking rather than self-promoting, she brought depth and subtlety to leading, supporting, and character parts throughout her prolific career. Trevor appeared in nearly seventy films, working with many of Hollywood's greatest directors and leading men.

★

Trevor's papers are at the Claire Trevor School of the Arts at the University of California, Irvine. Published interviews with Trevor are found in Karen Burroughs Hannsberry, *Femme Noir: The Bad Girls of Film* (1998); William M. Drew, *At the Center of the Frame: Leading Ladies of the Twenties and Thirties* (1999); and Robert Porfirio, *Film Noir Reader 3: Interviews with Filmmakers of the Classic Noir Period* (2002). See also Alain Silver and Elizabeth Ward, *Film Noir* (1979), and Bruce Crowther, *Film Noir: Reflections in a Dark Mirror* (1988). Obituaries are in the *New York Times* (9 Apr. 2000) and *Los Angeles Times* (10 Apr. 2000).

JOHN ALLAN SIMMONS

TRIGÈRE, Pauline (*b.* 5 November 1908 in Paris, France; *d.* 13 February 2002 in Manhattan, New York City), designer of elegant fashions for women for more than fifty years, who was a major force in elevating the American fashion industry to prominence in the 1940s and for several decades thereafter.

The daughter of Russian-Jewish parents who had emigrated from Russia to France, Trigère was surrounded by tailors from infancy. Her father, Alexandre Triger (the "e" was added later, in the United States), created military uniforms for aristocrats in his native Russia; her mother, Cecile (Corine) Triger, was a dressmaker. Together they owned a tailoring business in Paris. As their shop and family apartment were in the same building, it was their daughter's job at an early age to pick up pins after she returned from school. Trigère, who created and sewed her first dress as a teenager, early on aspired to be a surgeon, a dream quashed by her father, who viewed that profession as unsuitable for his daughter. Her subsequent theatrical aspirations were similarly discouraged, although her flair for the dramatic came to serve her well in her fashion career.

Trigère's marriage to Lazar Radley (originally Radzinsky),

Pauline Trigère, 1994. MITCHELL GERBER/CORBIS

a Russian immigrant and tailor, in 1929 further solidified her ties to the garment trade. They formed a business in Paris, along with her brother, Robert, who handled sales. In 1937, with the threat looming of invasion by the German dictator Adolf Hitler and his troops, the Radleys and other family members, including their two young sons, left France bound for Chile. What was intended to be a brief stop in New York City became their final destination, as Trigère became entranced by the city. She was naturalized as a U.S. citizen in 1942.

Once more fashion beckoned. Trigère worked briefly as an assistant to the designer Travis Benton at the fashion house owned by the designer Hattie Carnegie. Ascertaining that Carnegie valued only male designers, Trigère left and formed a business again with her husband and brother. After a few years, Radley left Trigère and their children, thus dissolving the partnership; Trigère claimed in later years that her husband did not want a working wife. In 1942 she and her brother formed the House of Trigère with her first collection of eleven styles. Because of financial constraints, Robert Trigère traveled the country on a bus, showing the fashions from a suitcase. Fortunately, Pauline Trigère's talent was recognized by the owners of some of the most fashionable shops in America, including Nan Duskin in Philadelphia, Martha in New York City, and Hany Blum in Chicago. Within a few years her name became synonymous with elegance, and her clothes were worn by some of the most chic women in the world.

Eschewing sketches, except in the vaguest manner that only she could interpret, Trigère created her designs by draping and cutting fabric on her models in the manner of the French masters Jeanne Lanvin and Coco Chanel. Her tailoring was impeccable, and often her dresses had no discernible seams. She focused on dresses and coats, producing garments that were comfortable as well as stylish; ruffles and frills were not part of her design scheme. A trim woman, she wore her own designs exclusively and thus knew firsthand what was functional, particularly for women who traveled a great deal, as she did. Known for her "look"—dressed in black or red, sporting tinted glasses and a turtle pin—she distinguished between fashion and style, the latter being a completely individual and personal statement and the former being a look others try to impose. Her fashion advice to women was to buy the best clothes they could afford, starting with basics and adding as they could.

Trigère was among the first to use common fabrics, such as cotton and wool, in eveningwear. In the 1960s she introduced the jumpsuit. A woman of strong beliefs, often blunt and outspoken, she also was the first "name" designer to hire an African American to model her clothes. Trigère received her first Coty Award, a high honor in the fashion industry, in 1949. This award was followed by numerous other honors, including two more Coty Awards, the Silver Medal of the City of Paris in 1972, the Medal of Vermeil of the City of Paris in 1982, a Lifetime Achievement Award from the Council of Fashion Designers of America in 1993, and the French Legion of Honor in 2001.

Trigère acknowledged her diva-like personality. She ruled her little empire, taking part in every facet of her business, even after her son Jean-Pierre was named president. She had a streak of vanity, not disclosing her age until she held a birthday party for herself in 1998 to celebrate having attained ninety years. She was a yoga devotee, continuing to exercise until her death. Although she always retained a touch of her French accent, she was proudly American. She closed her ready-to-wear business in 1994 but continued to design accessories, such as scarves, ties, and jewelry, forming a company called P. T. Concepts; she also created fragrances. Unlike many other designers, she did not widely license her name. She frequently lectured at the Fashion Institute of Technology and Parsons School of Design in New York City, astonishing students with her deft way with scissors, cutting into expensive fabric and turning it into a beautiful garment in a matter of minutes.

Trigère was an accomplished hostess and cook. She entertained frequently at her Manhattan apartment and her South Salem, Connecticut, home, La Tortue, named after her signature turtle. She transformed La Tortue from a rundown country house into an estate of comfortable elegance. After she bought the property, she immersed herself in horticulture and surrounded her house with beautiful gardens. Trigère died in her sleep of natural causes in her Manhattan apartment. A viewing was held at Riverside Memorial Chapel. She had left instructions with her family that she wanted to be cremated wearing her usual bright red lipstick. When asked why it mattered, as no one would know, she responded, "I'll know."

With a career that spanned fifty years, Trigère exemplified the combination of talent, entrepreneurial spirit, and hard work valued highly by her adopted country. A designer of exquisite yet functional clothes for women, she set a high standard for tailoring and wearability. Her designs continue to be prized as vintage clothing.

★

Trigère did not write an autobiography, nor are there any biographies. A collection of Trigère's garments and designs are available for viewing in the June F. Mohler Fashion Library at Kent State University, Kent, Ohio. An extensive interview appears in Barbaralee Diamonstein, *Fashion: The Inside Story* (1985). Another interview appears in the *Westchester WAG* (Mar. 2000). Obituaries are in the *New York Times* (14 Feb. 2002) and *Washington Post* (15 Feb. 2002).

MYRNA W. MERRON

TROUT, Robert (*b.* 15 October 1909 [many sources indicate 1908] in Wake County, North Carolina; *d.* 14 November 2000 in Manhattan, New York City), pioneer broadcasting journalist in radio and television whose career spanned several decades and whose professionalism, polite demeanor, endurance, and ability to ad-lib while covering worldwide news events earned him the nickname the "Iron Man of Radio."

Born Robert Albert Blondheim, he took Trout, the last name of a friend, as his professional name in 1932. His father, Louis Blondheim, owned a shoe store; his mother, Juliette (Mabee) Blondheim, was a homemaker. Trout grew up in Washington, D.C., where his family moved when he was nine years old. After graduating from Central High School in 1927, he wandered throughout the country, working at a multitude of odd jobs, including soda jerk, taxicab driver, and merchant seaman.

One day in 1931, while working as a handyman for WJSV, a small independent radio station in Mount Vernon Hills, Virginia, Trout was asked to fill in for the regular news reporter. He performed so well that he became a regular announcer, thus beginning his long broadcasting career. The following year, the Columbia Broadcasting System (CBS) radio network bought the station and retained Trout, who moved to Washington, D.C, where he became

Robert Trout, 1952. BETTMANN/CORBIS

a staff reporter for the station, newly renamed WTOP. By 1933 he had been invited to New York by Edward R. Murrow, who was forming the network's news division, and Trout became one of nine reporters known as "Murrow's Boys," the elite of the American news corps. He covered President Franklin D. Roosevelt's inauguration in 1933 and later introduced the president's regular informal talks to the nation as "fireside chats," a phrase Trout was credited with having coined, although, in a later interview, he stated that it was his radio-station manager who had first used the expression.

In 1935 Trout was transferred to WABC, the CBS flagship station in New York City. In 1937 his prestige rose, owing to the fact that he was the only American broadcaster to cover the coronation of England's King George VI. On 13 March 1938 Trout went on the air to anchor the CBS half-hour *World News Roundup,* the first live radio newscast combining reports from distant world capitals, and most newscasters credit Trout with thereby creating the role of news anchor. In this position, he kept the United States posted throughout World War II and for years thereafter, covering presidential conventions, coronations, marriages, funerals, and natural disasters. On 4 July 1938 he married Catherine ("Kit") Crane of Toledo, Ohio; the couple had no children.

In October 1941 Trout replaced Edward R. Murrow in London as CBS European news chief, and from there he covered the London Blitz (German air raids). It was during this period that he cemented his reputation as a poised, eloquent narrator. His "We interrupt this program to bring you an important bulletin" caught the attention of every radio listener. On D day, 6 June 1944, Trout, who by then had returned to New York, was the first to broadcast news of the Allied invasion, remaining on the air for more than seven hours at a stretch. Fourteen months later, on 14 August 1945, he was the CBS announcer who officially notified the United States that the Japanese had surrendered and the war was over.

By 1947 Trout had his own daily program, *Robert Trout with the News Till Now.* The following year he left CBS to join the National Broadcasting Company (NBC), where from 1948 to 1951 he moderated a quiz show, *Who Said That?,* which became television's first panel show. He returned to CBS in 1952, covering the presidential conventions on radio for fifteen consecutive hours. During the 1950s Trout was the leading radio newsman for CBS, while other faces and names became more familiar owing to their exposure on CBS television, including Walter Cronkite and Eric Sevareid.

In 1964 Trout and Roger Mudd were made anchormen for CBS's televised coverage of the Democratic National Convention. Although the Trout-Mudd team did not diminish the ratings of NBC's crack team of Chet Huntley and David Brinkley, Trout earned praise for his smooth, polished delivery and his seemingly effortless ad-libs. The following year he left the daily evening television news program and became a special roving correspondent in Europe for CBS, working from his homes in Paris and Madrid. In 1974 Trout joined ABC as a special contributing correspondent. That year he and his wife settled in Madrid, where he lived until his wife died in 1994.

In 1994 Trout moved to the West Side of Manhattan. He retired from full-time reporting in 1996 but in his final years continued to work as a commentator, delivering oral essays on the National Public Radio program *All Things Considered*. During the last years of his life, he was bent over, suffering from osteoporosis. He died of congestive heart failure at Lenox Hill Hospital in New York City at the age of ninety-one.

Trout, whom the renowned television journalist Walter Cronkite called "one of the greatest broadcasters of all time," introduced to the world of broadcasting many of the techniques that would later make it one of the prime methods of communication. His rich baritone voice was recognizable to every American of the radio era. Television viewers soon became fond of his rich, eloquent delivery mixed with just the right amount of wit and sarcasm. Trout's trademarks were his pencil-thin mustache, which he grew early in his career to appear older, and his walking cane, which he used on his daily walks of at least one hundred blocks. Trout's six-foot, one-inch height and 160-pound frame gave him an aristocratic bearing that was complemented by his athleticism; he was a devoted walker and an ardent sailor. One of the ironies of his roving career was the fact that he hated to fly, traveling to his destination by car, train, or ship.

Trout's accomplishments as a journalist and broadcaster are numerous. He was the first to report live congressional hearings, to transmit from an airplane in flight, and to broadcast a daily news program. He almost single-handedly created the role of anchorman. Throughout his seven decades of broadcasting, he reported on two coronations, seventeen presidential campaigns, twenty-six elections, thirty-three political conventions, and four wars. In 1980 Trout received the George Foster Peabody Award for distinguished and meritorious public service.

★

Trout's papers and archives are in the Media History Archives of the Center for American History at the University of Texas at Austin. Arthur Unger, "Bob Trout's Roosevelt's Days," *Christian Science Monitor* (29 Jan. 1982), is an interview in which Trout relates that it was his station manager, not he, who coined the phrase "fireside chat." Charles Strum, "A Model Anchorman Can't Escape the Microphone," *New York Times* (12 Mar. 2000),

contains an interview with Trout, aged ninety, who gives his personal vision of the art of the broadcaster and some anecdotes of his career. Polly Ross Hughes, "A Voice of America," *Houston Chronicle* (9 Jan. 2000), is a lengthy article detailing Trout's career and describing the items he chose to place in his archives. Obituaries are in the *New York Times* and *Washington Post* (both 15 Nov. 2000). Extensive oral history interviews conducted in 1998, including tapes and transcriptions, are in the Steven H. Scheuer Collection at the Center for the Study of Popular Television, Syracuse University.

JOHN J. BYRNE

TUKEY, John W(ilder) (*b.* 16 June 1915 in New Bedford, Massachusetts; *d.* 26 July 2000 in New Brunswick, New Jersey), mathematician who coined the computer terms "software" and "bit" and pioneered the field of data analysis, which facilitated new applications of statistics to an extensive array of problems.

Tukey was the only child of Dr. Ralph H. Tukey, a Latin teacher in a private school, and Adah M. (Tasker) Tukey,

John W. Tukey. ALFRED EISENSTAEDT/TIME LIFE PICTURES/GETTY IMAGES

a private tutor. His parents, who had themselves been excellent students at Bates College, recognized their son's exceptional abilities and decided to educate him at home. His mother was his teacher, except in specialized subjects, for which he went to a school.

He entered Brown University in Providence, Rhode Island, earning a B.S. in 1936 and an M.S. in 1937, both in chemistry. He subsequently earned two degrees in mathematics from Princeton University in New Jersey, including a Ph.D. in 1939, at which time he was appointed instructor of mathematics at the university. Tukey's professional origin in theoretical mathematics (his dissertation was in topology) would prove helpful as his interests shifted to applied mathematics.

During World War II, Tukey worked on military research projects at Princeton's Fire Control Research Office and at the Frankfort Arsenal Fire Control Design Division. These facilities conducted research on weapons development. Meanwhile, he acquired an interest in statistics and began his lifelong commitment to government service. His affiliation with Samuel Wilks, a Princeton mathematics and statistics professor, as well as other mathematicians working on practical problems, was influential in stimulating an interest in the application of mathematics to statistical problems. In 1945 Wilks offered Tukey a position in statistics at the Princeton mathematics department. Five years later he was promoted to full professor at the relatively young age of thirty-five. As the field gained recognition as a discipline of its own, Princeton founded a department of statistics in 1966 with Tukey as its founding chair. The university professorship seemed inadequate to consume Tukey's professional energies, however, and he began in 1945 what would be a forty-year stint on the technical staff at American Telephone and Telegraph Bell Laboratories. On 19 July 1950 he married Elizabeth Louise Rapp; they had no children and remained together until her death in 1998.

Tukey is best known for his formulation of the Fast Fourier Transform and his pioneering research in the fields of exploratory data analysis and robust estimation. The Fast Fourier Transform, which Tukey described with collaborator J. W. Cooley in a 1965 paper published in *Mathematics of Computation,* is an algorithm that simplifies the calculation of complex mathematical problems in a wide range of science disciplines.

Just over a century old as a branch of mathematics when Tukey became familiar with the field, statistics was governed by formal rules that limited researchers in making the best use of their data. Scientists knew that their data often contained interesting insights, but traditional statistical methods were too restrictive to bring them to light. Such practitioners found a champion in Tukey, who reportedly said, "An approximate answer to the right question is worth a good deal more than an exact answer to the wrong question." This quote, and variations on it that appear in both his writing and that of others who attribute it to him, symbolizes his commitment to expanding statistical applications in service to science.

As Tukey's influence on applied statistics was reaching its peak during the 1960s and 1970s, practitioners were gaining access to ever more powerful computers. Tukey became a leading advocate for the use of computing to expand the range of statistical analyses. He recognized early the significance of the language that connects the electronic capabilities of computers—the hardware—to the problem solving of users. In fact, he invented the word "software" for this mediating language. He was fond of coining words, and although many of his invented words did not persist in common usage, he also coined the term "bit," as an abbreviation of "binary digit," for the basic unit of information in computing. Both bit and software have become standard in the terminology of computers. Further evidence of his diverse and continuing influence is the invention of stem-and-leaf diagrams to organize and graph data, a technique still commonly used in high school mathematics classes.

One of the earliest of Tukey's lifelong engagements with scientific and government commissions came in 1950 with his appointment to a National Research Council (NRC) committee evaluating the Kinsey report on human sexual behavior, which shocked many Americans by describing the country's sexual habits as far more diverse than had been thought. Although Kinsey vigorously defended his work, the NRC committee's conclusions were critical of the Kinsey report because of flawed sampling design in the research. During the presidencies of Kennedy, Johnson, Nixon, Ford, and Carter, Tukey served on various government commissions to investigate and advise on environmental pollution, most notably on air pollution. From 1975 to 1979 he chaired NRC committees that issued the earliest groundbreaking reports on the dangers of ultraviolet radiation resulting from depletion of atmospheric ozone. From 1963 to 1982 Tukey also chaired the Technical Advisory Committee of the National Assessment of Educational Progress (NAEP), a long-term project that continues as the national standard for benchmarking educational performance in kindergarten through high school. He later served the NAEP in an advisory capacity.

Tukey was a key expert witness in the court case against the 1990 federal census, brought by New York City and other municipalities, which alleged that urban populations had been undercounted. Many statisticians, including Tukey, believed that the accuracy of measuring urban populations could be improved by using statistical estimation methods. When the statistical projection of national election outcomes became commonplace beginning with the

1960 presidential election, Tukey began a twenty-year stretch as chief consultant to the National Broadcasting Company (NBC) television network, until such methods were replaced by exit polling in 1980.

Tukey received many awards and honors for his work, including his appointment as a foreign member of the Royal Society of London and membership in the prestigious National Academy of Sciences in 1961. He was active over many years as a member and chair of NRC special commissions. In 1973 he won the National Medal of Science. When asked in the 1990 federal census trial how many honorary degrees he had received, he responded, "About five . . . but it doesn't really matter."

Tukey sustained an active professional life after retirement from his professorship and from the technical staff at the Bell Laboratories. He died of a heart attack at the age of eighty-five.

A pioneer in the field of data analysis, which expanded the uses of applied statistics, Tukey consulted in many venues on the uses of statistics to address societal problems. His greatest impact was in devising data analysis methods and statistical applications to exploit the inherent value of data in various fields of research. In his words, researchers should seek "the approximately right, rather than the exactly wrong" conclusion from their research. He knew that some of the most interesting questions researchers pose do not lend themselves to precise answers, yet their importance makes it incumbent upon analysts to find the best possible answers. He derived satisfaction from finding ways to help practitioners who posed difficult questions, and he lived an exemplary life of service to government and society at large.

★

Tukey's book *Exploratory Data Analysis* (1977) made a new field of statistics accessible to a wider audience of researchers. The range of his work, encompassing more than 500 papers and reports, is compiled in the series *The Collected Works of John W. Tukey* (1998). Tukey gives an exposition of his views about the interrelationship between statistics and computing at a critical point in the development of both fields in "The Technical Tools of Statistics," *American Statistician* 19, no. 2 (Apr. 1965): 23–29. An obituary is in the *New York Times* (28 July 2000).

W. HUBERT KEEN

U-V

UNITAS, John Constantine ("Johnny")   (*b*. 7 May 1933 in Pittsburgh, Pennsylvania; *d*. 11 September 2002 in Timonium, Maryland), professional football player known as the "golden arm" whose "Cinderella story" career took him from the sandlots of Pittsburgh to acclaim as the greatest quarterback ever to play the game.

Both of Unitas's parents were of Lithuanian ancestry. His father, Leon Unitas, owned a small coal-delivery business. He died when Unitas was four years old. His mother, Helen Unitas, ran the business after her husband's death but was forced to work at other rather menial jobs, such as cleaning offices at night, to keep the family (three boys and two girls) together. She also worked in a bakery, sold insurance, and eventually went to night school to qualify as a bookkeeper and passed a civil service test. She worked for the city of Pittsburgh for many years.

As a youngster Unitas shoveled coal from people's backyards into cellar coal bins for seventy-five cents a ton. His early schooling was at Catholic parochial schools. He went to Saint Justin's, a small Catholic high school in Pittsburgh. Not eligible to play varsity football as a freshman, Unitas played mostly end and halfback in preseason practice before his sophomore year. The week before the opening game, the quarterback broke his ankle and Unitas was thrust into the starting position. Under a new head coach the next year, Unitas was still the quarterback, and by his senior season he was talented enough to earn All-City honors and gain honorable mention on *Scholastic* magazine's high school All-America team.

Like nearly every football-playing Catholic youth at the time, Unitas had his heart set on playing for the University of Notre Dame. He was given a tryout at the South Bend, Indiana, university in the spring of 1951, his senior year. The Notre Dame coaches liked what they saw of the young passer, but at six feet, one inch and 138 pounds (eventually he would play at 196 pounds), he was considered unable to take the pounding of big-time college football. Unitas also visited Indiana University in Bloomington and his hometown college, the University of Pittsburgh, but the verdict was the same—not heavy enough. A chance meeting between his high school coach, Max Carey, and John Dromo, an assistant at the University of Louisville in Louisville, Kentucky, proved fortuitous. Dromo said that Louisville "had the makings of a pretty good football team, if we could find a passer." Carey had Louisville's man. Dromo mentioned Unitas to the Louisville head coach Frank Camp, and Unitas was given an invitation to campus, a tryout, and a scholarship. As in high school, he was thrown into the starting lineup early in his first season as the result of an injury to the quarterback. Unitas and the Cardinals had a winning season, 5–4, but it was the last winning season for Unitas at Louisville. Despite the fact that the team went 7–19 during his last three seasons, Unitas compiled respectable numbers: 243 completions in 501 attempts for 2,984 yards and 27 touchdowns.

523

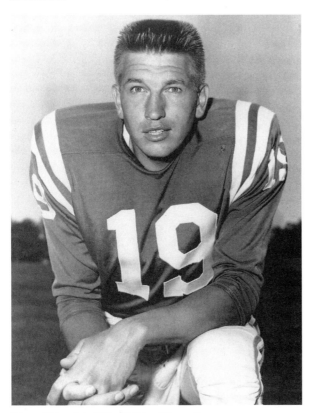

Johnny Unitas, July 1960. AP/WIDE WORLD PHOTOS

On 20 November 1954 Unitas married his high-school sweetheart, Dorothy Jean Hoelle. He graduated from Louisville in 1955 with a B.S. in education; that spring the Pittsburgh Steelers took Unitas in the National Football League (NFL) draft in the ninth round. He signed for $5,500 but had to make the team before he would draw any of the money. Working construction until it was time to report to training camp in New York, Unitas was ready to play. What happened to him in camp turned out to be the first chapter of his "Cinderella" story. Walt Kiesling, the Steelers' head coach, never gave him a chance to play in any of the team's five exhibition games. Unitas was waived and given the bus fare home. Dorothy was pregnant at the time, so he kept the $10 and hitchhiked home to Pittsburgh. It was back to the construction crew and a chance to play semiprofessional football.

Unitas played on the rock-strewn, hardscrabble sandlots in and around Pittsburgh for the Bloomfield Rams for $6 a game. That winter another chapter of the Cinderella story was written. Don Kellett, general manager of the Baltimore Colts, made an eighty-cent phone call, offering a tryout and a contract ($7,000) to Unitas for the 1956 season. George Shaw, the overall first choice in the 1955 draft, was Coach Weeb Ewbank's starting quarterback, but fate stepped in once more. Shaw was seriously injured in the fourth game

of the season (against the Chicago Bears), and once again Unitas found himself thrown into the breach. It was not all "Cinderella," though, as his first pass was intercepted and returned by the Bears for a touchdown. The Colts, ahead by a point when Unitas entered the game for Shaw, lost the game 58–27. The Colts finished 5–7 for the season, but a last-game victory over the Washington Redskins entrenched Unitas as quarterback.

The 1957 season got off to a great start. Unitas guided the team to seven victories in the first ten games, but two losses in the final games left the Colts in third place in the Western Division. The 1958 season would be different. The Colts breezed to nine wins in the first ten games. (Only a 24–21 loss to the New York Giants marred the slate when Unitas was sidelined by injury). Again the Colts lost two late road games, in this case to the Los Angeles Rams and the San Francisco 49ers, but their 9–3 mark won them the Western Conference crown.

The 1958 NFL championship game pitted the Colts against the Giants in a rematch of the regular season game. This game, later called the "greatest game ever played," saw the Colts get off to an early 14–3 lead. The Giants came back in the second half and led 17–14 late in the game. Unitas engineered a drive from the Colts 14-yard line to set up a field goal. Steve Myhra kicked it, and the game went into "sudden death" overtime, the first time a championship game was extended past regulation play. Players would later say that they thought the game would "just end in a tie and we'd be declared co-champions." Not so!

The Giants had the ball first but were forced to punt. Unitas, as he had done on the game-tying drive, moved the team flawlessly. He performed as he would during the rest of his storied career—passing when a run was expected and running when a pass was expected (like other quarterbacks of the time, Unitas called all his own plays). On the day, Unitas and end Raymond Berry connected twelve times for 173 yards—many of them on the game-tying and game-winning drives. Within field goal range in overtime, Unitas eschewed the kick and passed to Jim Mutcheller at the one-yard line, from where Alan Ameche bulled over the goal line for the winning score. A photograph, shot immediately after Ameche's score, speaks volumes of Unitas's workmanlike approach to his sport. It shows him, head down, simply walking off the field. The final score was Baltimore 23, Giants 17. When asked if it was foolish to risk an interception rather than kicking a short field goal, Unitas said, "You don't get intercepted when you know what you're doing."

The game has been called the "greatest" because of its riveting drama, the national television audience (50 million), and the awakening of Madison Avenue (New York City) advertising agencies to the promotional value of professional football. There were better-played games, but arguably none of greater significance.

In 1959 Unitas again led the Colts to the NFL championship, beating the Giants 31–16. His flattop crew cut and high-top black shoes had become identifying trademarks. Nationwide, youngsters (including the future New York Jets quarterback Joe Namath) wanted to wear his jersey number 19. He was professional football's brightest star. As Unitas piled up amazing statistics and burnished his legend, the Colts remained a contender for much of the 1960s. They were in the 1964 championship game but lost to the Cleveland Browns 27–0, and in 1965 they lost to the Green Bay Packers 13–10 in a playoff. In 1968 the Colts advanced to Super Bowl III. An arm injury reduced Unitas to a late-game appearance, where he tried to rally his team against the New York Jets, led by a hero-worshipping Namath. The Colts lost 16–7.

Unitas guided the Colts to high finishes in 1969 and 1970. In Super Bowl V in 1970, the Colts defeated the Dallas Cowboys for another championship, but Unitas was hurt midway through the game, and Earl Morrall was quarterbacking the team at the end of a 16–13 triumph. By 1971 Unitas—owing mainly to arm injuries—was splitting time with Morrall. In 1972 the Colts management benched Unitas at times in favor of the young Marty Domres. Sensing the end was near, Unitas accepted a trade to the San Diego Chargers and retired after playing the 1973 season. He was inducted into the Pro Football Hall of Fame in his first year of eligibility, 1979.

Unitas was first to amass 40,000 passing yards (40,239). He had the most lifetime attempts (5,186), most completions (2,830), most touchdown passes (290), and a still-standing record that is likely to remain in the books as long as professional football is played—forty-seven consecutive games (1956–1960) with at least one touchdown pass. He compiled this mark, which is sometimes compared to Joe DiMaggio's hitting safely in fifty-six consecutive baseball games, from 1956 to 1960. His closest challenger, Dan Marino of the Miami Dolphins, had only thirty.

Unfortunately, Unitas's post-playing career was not as bright as his on-field career. He was victimized by poor business advice and sometimes just victimized. A restaurant, the Golden Arm, failed, and other ventures did not pan out. Later on he regrouped and successfully operated Unitas Management Company. Through it all, Unitas remained "Mr. Colt" and, arguably, "Mr. Baltimore," always a vital part of the city. In June 1972, late in his career, he and his wife, Dorothy, with whom he had five children, divorced. Unitas and his second wife, Sandy Lemon, had three children.

Unitas, whose football-related injuries left his once magical right arm virtually useless, suffered a heart attack in 1993 and had triple-bypass surgery. He died at the age of sixty-nine after suffering a heart attack while exercising as part of his physical therapy. His body was cremated. His teammate John Mackey, a Pro Football Hall of Fame tight end, best described Unitas when he said, "It was like being in the huddle with God."

★

Unitas wrote an autobiography with Ed Fitzgerald, *Pro Quarterback: My Own Story* (1965). His career is discussed further in Murray Olderman, *Pro Quarterbacks* (1966), and Beau Riffenburgh and Dave Boss, *Great Ones* (1989). In *Sports Illustrated* (7 May 2001), William Nack discusses Unitas's post-playing days injuries. An obituary is in the *New York Times* (12 Sept. 2002).

JIM CAMPBELL

VANCE, Cyrus Roberts (*b.* 27 March 1917 in Clarksburg, West Virginia; *d.* 12 January 2002 in Manhattan, New York City), lawyer who served as secretary of the army (1962–1964), deputy secretary of defense (1964–1967), and secretary of state (1977–1980).

Vance was the second of two sons born to John Carl Vance, an insurance executive and landowner, and Amy (Roberts) Vance, a civic activist. The year after Vance was born, the family moved to suburban Bronxville, New York, but in 1922 Vance's father died suddenly of pneumonia. Raised by his mother, Vance found a role model and mentor in her eminent cousin John W. Davis, a leading New York lawyer, former U.S. ambassador to Great Britain, and a 1924 Democratic presidential nominee.

Athletic and intellectually able, from 1930 to 1935 Vance attended the Kent School, an Episcopalian school in Connecticut, which instilled in him both religious faith and a lifelong habit of personal responsibility. He spent college summers working at the Christian physician Wilfred Grenfell's mission in the town of Churchill Falls in Canada's Labrador region, where he acquired a strong commitment to community and governmental service and a sense of duty to the less fortunate. Entering Yale University in New Haven, Connecticut, in 1935, together with the future politician William Scranton, the future Peace Corps director R. Sargent Shriver, and the future government official William P. Bundy, Vance received a B.A. in economics in 1939. In 1942 he earned an LL.B. from Yale Law School, graduating with honors. Tall, rumpled, lanky, and personally unassuming, Vance became known for his excellent memory and outstanding athletic prowess in rowing, football, and hockey.

Upon graduation Vance immediately joined the U.S. Naval Reserve, serving as a destroyer gunnery officer in actions at Bougainville, Tarawa, Saipan, Guam, and the Philippines. Discharged in 1946 as a lieutenant, he spent a

Cyrus R. Vance, 1977. CORBIS

year with the Mead Corporation, was admitted to the New York bar in 1947, and promptly joined the elite law firm of Simpson, Thacher and Bartlett, where, except for periods of government service, he remained a partner from 1956 to 1998. On 15 February 1947 Vance married Grace Elsie Sloane; they had five children. A lifelong Democrat, Vance soon joined assorted New York civic groups, including the Council on Foreign Relations.

Vance's first government assignment came in 1957, as special counsel to the Senate Preparedness Investigating Subcommittee of the Senate Armed Services Committee, chaired by Lyndon B. Johnson, the majority leader. In 1961 Vance became general counsel to the Department of Defense, negotiating the release of prisoners from Cuba after the abortive 1961 Bay of Pigs invasion, implementing a major restructuring of departmental organization, and modernizing weapons and personnel systems. The low-key, hardworking Vance impressed Secretary of Defense Robert S. McNamara, who appointed him secretary of the army in 1962, in which capacity Vance advised President John F. Kennedy to deploy federal troops to handle the growing racial violence in the South.

From January 1964 until June 1967, when back problems forced his resignation, Vance was deputy secretary of

defense, serving primarily as a troubleshooter in efforts to resolve U.S. difficulties with Panama in 1964 and the Dominican Republic in 1965, and to mediate the 1967 civil war in Cyprus. Initially, Vance was a hawk on Vietnam, recommending bombing the North after the August 1964 Tonkin Gulf incident and the February 1965 communist attacks on U.S. advisers at Pleiku. However, by mid-1966 Vance was skeptical over the effectiveness of continued U.S. air and ground escalation, and he left office disillusioned with the U.S. commitment to Vietnam.

As one of the "Wise Men," or senior advisers to President Lyndon B. Johnson, after the communist Tet Offensive of January 1968, Vance recommended that the United States cease bombing and open peace negotiations. He then served as deputy to the chief negotiator, W. Averell Harriman, in the fruitless 1968 Paris peace talks. Appointed Johnson's personal representative during the July 1967 Detroit riots, Vance recommended the deployment of federal troops to suppress the growing violence in the city. In February 1968, after North Korea seized the USS *Pueblo,* Vance visited South Korea to reaffirm U.S. support for its government.

In 1971 Vance met the future president and fellow Trilateral Commission member Jimmy Carter, and served as a foreign policy adviser in Carter's 1976 presidential campaign. Carter's first presidential appointment was to make Vance secretary of state. Vance believed the international situation no longer fit the early cold war bipolar model and sought to adapt U.S. diplomacy to a more complicated and less schematic world, pragmatically dealing with individual problems one by one. He was popular with his State Department subordinates, but soon clashed with Carter's assertive national security adviser, the fiercely anti-Soviet Zbigniew Brzezinski.

Vance, an advocate of negotiation and compromise, was strongly committed to continuing the two previous administrations' policies of arms control and détente with the communist world. Against opposition from such hardliners as Washington Senator Henry M. Jackson, he fought successfully to win confirmation of his moderate nominee, Paul Warnke, as head of the Arms Control and Disarmament Agency. In 1979 Vance negotiated the second Strategic Arms Limitation Treaty (SALT II) with the Soviet Union, which imposed ceilings on the number of nuclear missiles and delivery vehicles, and banned the introduction of new missile and antimissile systems. Other major accomplishments included the negotiation of the 1977–1978 treaties returning the Panama Canal to Panamanian ownership and operation; the 1978 Camp David accords normalizing relations between Israel and Egypt; the full normalization in 1978 of U.S. relations with China; and the conclusion of a settlement in Rhodesia (Zimbabwe) that brought black majority rule in 1979. Vance also shared Carter's commitment to human rights.

On other issues, however, Brzezinski undercut Vance. This was especially the case after the Soviet invasion of Afghanistan in 1979 caused a dramatic cooling between the two superpowers, and Carter increasingly favored Brzezinski's advice over Vance's. In early 1980 Vance urged that either the president or he meet with their Soviet counterparts in an effort to resolve the Afghan crisis, but Carter refused. Vance's early hopes to normalize U.S. relations with Cuba also fell victim to the deteriorating U.S.-Soviet situation and to revelations that Cuban troops were deployed in Ethiopia. Over Vance's opposition and at Brzezinski's urging, Carter drastically increased U.S. aid to Ethiopia's hostile neighbor, Somalia, effectively fueling an ongoing military conflict. After Vietnam signed a treaty of friendship with the Soviet Union in November 1978, U.S. efforts to reopen relations with Vietnam also stalled.

In Iran, where growing popular discontent threatened the government's stability, Vance advised the autocratic Shah that introducing genuine reform was the best means to counter growing domestic unrest. In January 1979 the Shah fled, and a strongly anti-American fundamentalist Muslim regime took power. Ten months later, on 4 November 1979, Iranian students sacked the U.S. embassy in Teheran and took fifty-three Americans hostage. Vance believed that quiet diplomacy was the best means of freeing them, but Brzezinski disagreed, maintaining that the United States should mount a dramatic rescue as a major demonstration of its military strength. Carter, with the 1980 presidential election approaching, sought to improve his public standing. On 11 April 1980 the National Security Council met during Vance's absence and authorized a rescue mission, a decision Vance protested on his return. Vance submitted his resignation on 21 April, becoming only the third secretary of state to resign over a matter of principle. Three days later the rescue mission was aborted: three out of eight helicopters malfunctioned in the desert, with the loss of eight American lives.

Vance returned to his law practice and in 1983 published his memoirs, a characteristically restrained account of his time as secretary. He also chaired the Rockefeller Foundation, held various directorships, accepted assorted assignments on public commissions and public service boards, and accepted several further diplomatic assignments from the United Nations. Vance continued to support the resumption of dialogue and diplomatic relations between the United States and Iran. During the early 1990s he helped to mediate the Nagorno-Karabakh conflict between Azerbaijan and Armenia and a peaceful end to white rule in South Africa. And in collaboration with the former British foreign secretary David Owen, he also successfully negotiated a cease-fire in Croatia.

In his final years, Vance suffered from Alzheimer's disease. He died of pneumonia at Mount Sinai Medical Center in Manhattan, and is buried in Arlington National Cemetery in Arlington, Virginia.

Writing in the mid-1970s, the British journalist Godfrey Hodgson regarded Vance as the de facto head of the American establishment. Vance embodied the virtues and perhaps the weaknesses of the patrician twentieth-century U.S. foreign policy elite. "A lot of us," he once said, "were taught that we were very fortunate, . . . that we had the responsibility to return to the community some of the benefits and blessings we had, and that there was an obligation to participate in government service." Vance's abilities were particularly evident in matters demanding a talent for negotiation. As his post-1980 career demonstrated, Vance's greatest strength was as an effective problem-solver and troubleshooter. Although able to adapt pragmatically to changing international circumstances, Vance lacked the intellectual originality that might have enabled him to rise above the conventional prevailing wisdom and function as an outstanding, not just a competent, secretary of state.

★

Vance donated his personal papers to Yale University. Official records generated during his service in the Departments of Defense and State are located in the U.S. National Archives II, College Park, Maryland; the John Fitzgerald Kennedy Presidential Library in Boston; the Lyndon Baines Johnson Presidential Library, the University of Texas at Austin, Texas; and the Jimmy Carter Presidential Library in Atlanta. Vance wrote a memoir covering his years as secretary of state, *Hard Choices: Critical Years in America's Foreign Policy* (1983). The only full biography is David S. McLellan, *Cyrus Vance* (1985). There is a short biographical sketch in William Gardner Bell, *Secretaries of War and Secretaries of the Army: Portraits and Biographical Sketches* (2003). Useful works on the U.S. defense bureaucracy during the McNamara years include Carl W. Borklund, *Men of the Pentagon: From Forrestal to McNamara* (1966) and *The Department of Defense* (1968). Vance features prominently in the Carter administration memoirs, including Jimmy Carter, *Keeping Faith: Memoirs of a President* (1982); Hamilton Jordan, *Crisis: The Last Year of the Carter Presidency* (1982); and Zbigniew Brzezinski, *Power and Principle: Memoirs of the National Security Adviser, 1977–1981* (1985). Vance's role and contributions as secretary of state are discussed in Joshua Muravchik, *The Uncertain Crusade: Jimmy Carter and the Dilemmas of Human Rights Policy* (1986); William B. Quandt, *Camp David: Peacemaking and Politics* (1986); Gaddis Smith, *Morality, Reason, and Power: American Diplomacy in the Carter Years* (1986); Donald S. Spencer, *The Carter Implosion: Jimmy Carter and the Amateur Style of Diplomacy* (1988); Richard C. Thornton, *The Carter Years: Toward a New Global Order* (1991); David Skidmore, *Reversing Course: Carter's Foreign Policy, Domestic Politics, and the Failure of Reform* (1996); Robert A. Strong, *Working in the*

World: Jimmy Carter and the Making of American Foreign Policy (2000); and David Patrick Houghton, *U.S. Foreign Policy and the Iran Hostage Crisis* (2001). Vance's Yugoslav mediation efforts are described in James Gow, *Triumph of the Lack of Will: International Diplomacy and the Yugoslav War* (1994); David Owen, *Balkan Odyssey* (1995); Richard C. Holbrooke, *To End a War* (1998); and Saadia Touval, *Mediation in the Yugoslav Wars: The Critical Years, 1990–95* (2002). Primary source material on Vance's part in U.S. foreign policy during the 1960s is in the relevant volumes of the series *Foreign Relations of the United States;* Mike Gravel, ed., *The Pentagon Papers: The Defense Department History of United States Decisionmaking on Vietnam* (1971–1972); and George C. Herring, ed., *The Secret Diplomacy of the Vietnam War: the Negotiating Volumes of the Pentagon Papers* (1983). Informative summaries of Vance's contributions to the 1960s Democratic presidential administrations are in Nelson Lichtenstein, ed., *Political Profiles* (1976). Obituaries are in the *Washington Post* (13 Jan. 2002), and the (London) *Times* and *New York Times* (both 14 Jan. 2002). The John Fitzgerald Kennedy and Lyndon Baines Johnson Presidential Libraries each hold oral histories recorded by Vance.

PRISCILLA ROBERTS

VERDON, Gwyneth Evelyn ("Gwen") (*b.* 16 January 1925 in Culver City, California; *d.* 18 October 2000 in Woodstock, Vermont), dancer, actress, singer, choreographer, and dance educator who won four Tony Awards and was widely regarded as the best dancer ever to appear on the Broadway stage.

Verdon was born the younger of two children of the British expatriates Joseph William Verdon, an electrician at Metro-Goldwyn-Mayer (MGM), and Gertrude (Standring) Verdon, a former vaudeville dancer who ran a dance studio. As a toddler, Verdon suffered from rickets, a condition causing defective bone growth. As a result, she wore heavy corrective-therapy boots. Her mother nonetheless was determined that Verdon be a dancer and believed that dance would strengthen her daughter's legs, so the boots came off for dance lessons. Time would prove Verdon's mother right. By age three Verdon was dancing professionally, and by age six she was billed as Baby Alice, the "fastest little tapper in the world." At age fourteen, claiming she was twenty-two years old, she appeared in a nightclub as half of a comedy dance team, Verdon and DelValle. Verdon attended local schools and graduated from Los Angeles's Hamilton High. In 1942, at age seventeen, she eloped with James Henaghan, a reporter for the *Hollywood Reporter.* Later that year her son was born, but her marriage was soon over. Verdon and Henaghan divorced in 1947.

Leaving her son in the care of her parents, Verdon resumed her dance career. Strikingly beautiful, with flaming

Gwen Verdon, 1989. AP/WIDE WORLD PHOTOS

red hair, Verdon had a perfectly proportioned body and the physical coordination of an athlete. The rickets had left her pigeon-toed and knock-kneed, which only added to her appeal. She joined the Jack Cole Dancers, led by the Hollywood choreographer and dance coach Jack Cole. Cole was regarded as a guru by dancers; his groundbreaking choreography was unique, exotic, and openly erotic. Verdon thrived under Cole's choreography and became his assistant, alter ego, lead dancer, and model for his dance inspirations. She already had the style that would endear her to future audiences: she could appear sexy, vulnerable, and funny at the same time. Her voice had a loveable squeaky quality. As Cole's assistant, she served as an assistant choreographer, coaching Hollywood stars, including Jane Russell and Marilyn Monroe, how to move and sing in that same sexy style. She danced in movie musicals and was an assistant choreographer on the 1952 movie *Singin' in the Rain.*

In 1950 Verdon made her New York stage debut in a Cole variety revue called *Alive and Kicking.* The show closed after forty-six performances, and Verdon followed Cole back to Hollywood. In 1953 the New York stage producer Cy Feuer picked Verdon to be a featured dancer in his Broadway production of *Can-Can,* a Cole Porter musical comedy set in Paris. On opening night Verdon created an unforgettable sensation. Her fiery Apache dance at the end of the first act brought the audience to its feet. They did not stop applauding until Verdon, back in her dressing room, was brought out on stage to take more bows. Only then did the tumultuous applause end, and the show was allowed to go on. At age twenty-eight, Verdon was declared a star and won her first Tony Award.

Her next Broadway show was *Damn Yankees* (1955), for which she worked with the choreographer Bob Fosse. Their collaboration and the resulting sexually explosive choreography would make dance history. "I was a great dancer when Fosse got a hold of me," she would say, "but he developed and created me." "Fosse" she said "choreographs to the second joint of your little finger." His view was that everything she did made him look good; she was the greatest personification of his choreography. *Damn Yankees* was a hit, and once again Verdon, as the character Lola, brought down the house with her slinky rendition of "Whatever Lola Wants." The show ran for more than 1,000 performances and won Verdon her second Tony.

Damn Yankees was followed by *New Girl in Town* (1957), which established Verdon as an actress as well as a dancer and earned her a third Tony. In 1958 she starred in the film version of *Damn Yankees*. In 1959 she took the lead in a show designed and built around her, the musical *Redhead*. At her behest Fosse directed as well as choreographed the show. It was a personal triumph, running for more than a year and winning seven Tony Awards, including outstanding actress in a musical, which went to Verdon. Verdon also won a Grammy for her singing in the cast album.

On 3 April 1960 Verdon and Fosse were married and she announced her professional retirement. In 1963 the couple's daughter was born. In 1966 Verdon returned to the stage to star in another Fosse show, *Sweet Charity*. The show became something of a cult hit, running for six hundred performances even after a fatigued Verdon bowed out. In 1968, when a film version of *Sweet Charity* was made, Verdon lost out to a younger Shirley MacLaine but graciously coached MacLaine for the role.

In 1971 Fosse and Verdon legally separated, although they never divorced. Fosse was a notorious womanizer, but he and Verdon remained friends and continued working together. They collaborated on the 1975 musical *Chicago*, with Verdon in the role of Roxie Hart, a woman jailed, tried, and acquitted of murdering her lover. Some said that *Chicago* was Fosse's gift to Verdon. He directed and choreographed it, taking care that the other dancers did not upstage the fifty-two-year-old Verdon. *Chicago* won raves for its leads, including Verdon. *Chicago* would be Verdon's last Broadway show. The nightly grind was too much for her, and she was replaced by Ann Reinking.

Verdon worked as an assistant choreographer on Fosse's 1978 musical *Dancin'* and his 1979 film *All That Jazz*. In 1987 she and Fosse were working together on a revival of *Sweet Charity* when he suffered a fatal heart attack. After his death, she worked to preserve his legacy, serving as artistic adviser on *Fosse,* the 1999 Tony Award–winning Broadway musical that featured highlights of his career.

Throughout her career, Verdon appeared in films and television. Her screen credits include *The Cotton Club* (1984), *Cocoon* (1985), *Cocoon: The Reunion* (1988), and *Marvin's Room* (1996). Verdon died of natural causes in her sleep at the home of her daughter. On 19 October 2000, the evening after her death, the lights of Broadway were dimmed in memory of this beloved dancer and Broadway star.

★

Information about Verdon and her career is in Kevin Boyd Grubb, *Razzle Dazzle: The Life and Work of Bob Fosse* (1989), Margery Beddow, *Bob Fosse's Broadway* (1996), and Martin Gottfried, *All His Jazz: The Life and Death of Bob Fosse* (1998). Verdon's place in dance history is discussed by Larry Billman in *The International Encyclopedia of Dance,* vol. 6 (1998). Obituaries are in the *Chicago Tribune, Los Angeles Times, New York Times,* and *Washington Post* (all 19 Oct. 2001).

JULIANNE CICARELLI

VICENTE, Esteban (*b.* 20 January 1903 in Turégano, Spain; *d.* 10 January 2001 in Bridgehampton, New York), Spanish-born painter who was an original member of the first generation of the New York School of abstract expressionists.

Born in the Spanish province of Segovia, Vicente was the third of six children of Toribio Vicente Ruiz, a Spanish army officer and amateur painter from a military family, and Sofía Pérez y Álvarez, from an Asturian family in Valladolid. Vicente's father resigned from the army and moved the family to Madrid to raise and school his children. Vicente was educated in a Jesuit school, and his father exposed him to art at an early age through visits to the Prado museum. At age seventeen Vicente enrolled in a military school in the hope that he would follow the family tradition, but he left after three months to pursue a career in art. Setting out to be a sculptor in 1921, Vicente studied for three years at the Real Academia de Bellas Artes de San Fernando in Madrid. Soon after, he abandoned sculpture for the immediacy of painting. He held his first exhibition in 1928.

As a young painter, Vicente traveled to Paris to experience the modern art scene in 1929. From the start, he was accepted by a group of Spanish artists living in Paris, yet he struggled to support himself by retouching photographs and working on theater sets, with little choice but to paint at night. Gradually, he saw works by such artists as Paul

Esteban Vicente, November 1998. AFP/CORBIS

Cézanne, Pablo Picasso, Juan Gris, Henri Matisse, Raoul Dufy, and Max Ernst, many of which he knew from poor reproductions. Vicente eventually met the revered compatriot artist Picasso, whom he found engaging. After this meeting Vicente spent most of his time painting *à plein-air* landscapes (ones executed out of doors), which he exhibited between Paris and Barcelona. Despite being drawn to the art and culture of continental Europe, he was curious about America and had many American acquaintances abroad. In 1935 he married Esther Cherniakofsky Harac (also known as Estelle Charney), an American student who studied at the Sorbonne. The couple lived for a year on the island of Ibiza, where Vicente painted verdant landscapes reminiscent of Camille Pissarro's late works.

While en route to America in July 1936, the couple went to Madrid to say goodbye to Vicente's family, but three days after they arrived, the Spanish Civil War began. Intent on fighting on the side of the Loyalists, Vicente volunteered for the army, painting camouflage on mountainsides near Madrid. Later that same year, Vicente and his wife moved to the United States, settling in Greenwich Village, a neighborhood of Manhattan in New York City. He attained his first one-person exhibition at New York City's Kleeman Gallery in 1937. Ever sympathetic to the Republic of Spain during the Civil War, Vicente accepted the request of the

Spanish ambassador to the United States to serve as vice consul in the Philadelphia consulate until the end of the Spanish Civil War in 1939.

After his return to New York City, Vicente became an American citizen in 1941. The subsequent years were filled with profound personal and professional change. His only daughter died at the age of six. He divorced his first wife and soon remarried a poetess named Maria Teresa Babin (whom he divorced in 1961). Deliberately, Vicente began to explore and grow through painting, occasionally exhibiting during the decade of the forties. Vicente was inspired by European modernism, arriving at abstraction through a long period of dedicated experimentation. Toward the end of the decade, Vicente became friendly and conversant with numerous key modernist artists, including Willem de Kooning, Jackson Pollock, Mark Rothko, Franz Kline, and Barnett Newman, all of whom were instrumental in the formation of the New York School.

Perhaps the most defining moment in his career as an artist occurred in 1950, when Vicente was invited by the art historian Meyer Shapiro and the critic Clement Greenberg to show his work in the "Talent 1950" exhibition at the Sam Kootz Gallery. Sharing a studio on Tenth Street with de Kooning, Vicente found himself in the heart of the downtown New York City art scene. As an initiated member of "The Club," Vicente participated in lively discussions among critics and artists that shaped the principles of the New York School. The following year Vicente's work was shown at the "Ninth Street" exhibition, thus decidedly launching his career as a New York School abstract expressionist. Thereafter, he exhibited in numerous solo and group shows and was represented by such art dealers as Leo Castelli, Andre Emmerich, and the Berry-Hill Galleries. In the late 1950s he met Harriet Godfrey Peters, who became his third wife in 1961 and with whom he remained for forty years. They soon divided their time between New York City in the winter and Long Island, New York, in the summer.

A long-standing teacher of art, Vicente noted, "People make a mess of the world. It takes artists to put it in order." Vicente was a founder of the New York Studio School and taught at Black Mountain College, Boston University, New York University, Yale University, and Princeton University. His former students included Chuck Close, Janet Fish, Dorothea Rockburne, and Brice Marden. His most celebrated paintings are known for their striking, yet pleasing color contrasts of soft-edged blocks grouped, often overlapping, in a deliberate cubist structure. In the early 1970s he achieved luminosity in his paintings by using an airbrush. Vicente's oeuvre included collage, a forty-year-long pursuit he first chanced upon while he was in California in the late 1940s. Considered an aloof member of the downtown New York School painters, Vicente was one of its last surviving members. He followed an artistic course that transformed his paintings from colorful cubist works to glowing fields of color.

Seemingly noble in stature and demeanor, Vicente always dismissed being characterized as a Spanish-born painter, insisting that he was an American painter of Spanish heritage. Nonetheless, Spaniards recognized his contribution to art in 1987 by mounting a major retrospective exhibition in Madrid. Winning numerous honors and awards over his lifetime, Vicente received Spain's highest award, the Gold Medal for Fine Arts, from King Juan Carlos in 1991. He died of respiratory failure at the age of ninety-seven. Today, there is a street named in his honor in Turégano and a museum dedicated to his art in Segovia, where his ashes are interred.

★

Elizabeth Frank, *Esteban Vicente* (1995), is the definitive source about his life and art. Vicente is referred to throughout various books, including Thomas Hess, *Abstract Painting: Background and American Phase* (1951); Harold Rosenberg, *The Anxious Object: Art Today and Its Audience* (1964); and Irving Sandler, *The New York School: The Painters and Sculptors of the Fifties* (1978). To hear the artist in his words, consult the unpublished interviews (1980 and 1991) by Elizabeth Frank, manuscripts of which are at the Museum of Modern Art in New York City. See also an unpublished taped interview by Irving Sandler in the Smithsonian Archives of American Art (26 Aug. 1968). An obituary is in the *New York Times* (12 Jan. 2001).

LISA A. ELLIS

W

WADE, Henry Menasco (*b.* 11 November 1914 in Rockwall, Texas; *d.* 1 March 2001 in Dallas, Texas), Dallas County district attorney who gained national prominence while prosecuting Jack Ruby for the murder of Lee Harvey Oswald and as the defendant in the landmark *Roe* v. *Wade* abortion case.

Born on the family farm, Wade was one of eleven children—three girls and eight boys—born to Henry M. Wade, a teacher and lawyer who served as county attorney and county judge, and Lula Ellen (Michie) Wade, a teacher. The accomplishments of the elder Wade sometimes are mistakenly attributed to his son owing to their similar names. All of Wade's siblings graduated from college, and five of his brothers also went into law.

Wade attended Rockwall High School, where he excelled in athletics and was the quarterback of the football team of 1931. His football prowess won him an athletic scholarship to the University of Texas at Austin, in 1933, although part of his first-year college expenses were paid for by a bale of cotton that his father sold for $85. While at the University of Texas, he helped elect John Connally, the future Texas governor, to student body president and campaigned for Lyndon Johnson's bid to become a member of the U.S. House of Representatives. After earning his undergraduate degree, Wade attended the University of Texas School of Law, where he edited the *Texas Law Review,* graduating in 1938 with honors.

In 1939 Wade joined the Federal Bureau of Investigation,

becoming a special agent assigned to anti-espionage and working first along America's East Coast and later in South America. He enlisted in the U.S. Navy in 1943, during World War II, serving on the aircraft carriers USS *Hornet* and USS *Enterprise* during the invasion of Okinawa and the liberation of the Philippines. Wade married Gladys Yvonne Hillman on 10 January 1948; they had five children.

In 1947 Wade was hired as a counsel for the Dallas County district attorney's office, where he advanced to criminal prosecutor. In 1950 he was elected district attorney for Dallas County, and he took office in 1951. During the 1950s he earned a reputation for his keen, well-focused intelligence and vigorous prosecutions. Before retiring thirty-six years later, he would become one of the most successful prosecuting attorneys in the history of the United States. In 1956 he ran for the U.S. House of Representatives but lost.

On 22 November 1963 President John F. Kennedy and Wade's old friend, the Texas governor John Connally, were shot while traveling in a motorcade through downtown Dallas; Kennedy died soon after. This was the key event in Wade's career, the one that not only made him a nationally known figure but also established him as one of America's most important district attorneys. Wade was compiling evidence to prosecute Lee Harvey Oswald for the murder of Kennedy and a Dallas policeman when Jack Ruby, a strip club owner, shot Oswald to death. Wade later presented his evidence and conclusions concerning the Kennedy as-

Henry Wade, November 1973. BETTMANN/CORBIS

sassination to the Warren Commission. His testimony reflected his belief that he had an airtight case against Oswald as the lone assassin.

Wade chose to prosecute the case against Ruby, who was defended by the flamboyant Melvin Belli, who heaped contempt on Wade as a brainless hick who did not understand the law. Wade retaliated by mispronouncing Belli's name "Bell-ee" until the judge made him stop. Apparent during the trial was Wade's fine legal mind and his detailed knowledge of the law and the evidence of the case he was trying. On 14 March 1964 the jury for the trial deliberated for two hours and returned a verdict of guilty. In October 1966 the Texas Court of Criminal Appeals ordered a new trial, saying that there should have been a change of venue. Ruby died of lung cancer on 3 January 1967, before a new trial could begin.

The Ruby case was one of thirty death penalty trials that Wade prosecuted during his career; the death penalty was handed down in twenty-nine of those cases. As his career progressed into the 1980s, Wade's success at winning death penalties would become the subject of controversy. Death penalty opponents suggested that Wade was winning death penalty convictions on the basis of his legal skills rather than the evidence. Wade remained a staunch advocate of the death penalty.

In 1969 Norma McCorvey, a waitress, became pregnant with a child that she did not want to have. At the time Texas law allowed a woman to have an abortion only if her life was endangered by her pregnancy, which was not the case with McCorvey. The attorney Linda Coffee saw in McCorvey an excellent prospect for a constitutional challenge to the Texas law. She contacted the lawyer Sarah Weddington, who filed suit on McCorvey's behalf. Under the law in Texas, she had to file suit against the highest-ranking law enforcement officer who had responsibility for enforcing the abortion laws. Thus McCorvey, called Jane Roe to protect her identity, filed suit against Wade. Although Wade occasionally expressed his opposition to abortion on demand, he chose not to represent himself in the trial, having assistant district attorneys do so instead. Although McCorvey was forced to deliver her unwanted baby because of the length of the appeals process, *Roe* v. *Wade* resulted in the 21 January 1973 U.S. Supreme Court ruling that struck down antiabortion laws as unconstitutional intrusions on a woman's right to privacy.

Wade never lost a case he personally prosecuted, and his office had the highest conviction rate of any district attorney's office in the country. This caused concern in Dallas that he might be sending innocent people to prison on the basis of overly aggressive prosecutions. To Wade's credit, he was sensitive to the issue and occasionally petitioned for the release of wrongfully imprisoned people, such as Lenell Geter, who was sentenced to life in prison for a 1982 armed robbery that turned out to be a matter of mistaken identity. Wade supported his release in December 1983.

In 1987 Wade retired from the district attorney's office and joined the law firm of Geary, Porter, and Donovan. He died of complications from Parkinson's disease in a Dallas assisted-living facility. He is buried in the Meadow of Reflection in Hillcrest Memorial Park in Dallas. In his capacity as district attorney, Wade was respected for his honesty and good judgment and his even-handed and inclusive business practices. His immense capacity for learning, united with his fine mind and skill that was tempered by compassion, made him one of the greatest district attorneys in America's history.

★

Marian Faux, *Roe v. Wade: The Untold Story of the Landmark Supreme Court Decision that Made Abortion Legal* (1988), explains the details of the case. A memorial by Wade's family is in the *Dallas Morning News* (3 Mar. 2001). Obituaries are in the *New York Times* and *Washington Post* (both 2 Mar. 2001).

KIRK H. BEETZ

WALSTON, Ray (*b.* 2 November 1918 [some sources say 2 November 1924] in New Orleans, Louisiana [some sources say Laurel, Mississippi]; *d.* 1 January 2001 in Beverly Hills, California), character actor in theatre, film, and television who was best known for his performances in the Broadway and film versions of *Damn Yankees* and *South Pacific,* and the television series *My Favorite Martian* and *Picket Fences.*

The true date and place of Walston's birth are unknown. He once said, "I always juggled the places of my birth and the dates, so no one is ever sure." What is sure is that he was born Herman Walston in the South, but to add further confusion regarding his birth year, in a 1992 interview in *People Weekly,* he stated that he was born in 1914. His father, Harry Norman, was either an oilman, a lumberjack, or a night watchman for United Fruit. His mother was Mittie (Kimbrell) Walston, a homemaker. Walston had three siblings.

Growing up in New Orleans, Walston enjoyed going to shows put on by local companies. Because of financial constraints, Walston quit high school and went to work in a printing studio. When the print shop moved to Houston, he went with the job. There, he joined Margo Jones's Houston Community Players and made his stage debut in 1938 as Buddy in Maxwell Anderson's *High Tor.* The troupe performed twelve plays a year, and Walston sold tickets, acted, and learned his craft.

On 3 November 1943 he married the local actress Ruth Calvert, with whom he had one child. In 1943 Walston went to Cleveland and joined the Cleveland Playhouse, which he described as "the finest regional theater in America . . . a wonderful training ground." When Walston moved to New York City in 1945, he worked as a linotype operator for the *New York Herald Tribune* to pay the bills while he pursued his acting career.

Walston's Broadway debut, in 1945, was a walk-on part in the Maurice Evans production of *Hamlet.* Other parts followed, including the reporter Schwartz in a 1946 revival of Ben Hecht and Charles MacArthur's *The Front Page.* His portrayal of the traveling salesman, Mr. Kramer, in Tennessee Williams's *Summer and Smoke* (1948) earned Walston the Clarence Derwent Award as best supporting actor in 1949. He played the comic role of the telephone man in Garson Kanin's *The Rat Race* in 1949. A major break came in 1950, when he was cast as Seabee Luther Billis in the national company of Rogers and Hammerstein's *South Pacific.* He played the role for two years on tour and opened in the London production. Walston also played nonsinging roles in *Me and Juliet* (1953) and *House of Flowers* (1954).

Walston's most important role of the period was that of Mr. Applegate, the Devil, in *Damn Yankees* (1955). As Mr. Applegate, he was able to use his quirky looks, comic timing, and understated mischievousness to perfection, and for an actor who stated that he could neither sing nor dance, he did both with aplomb. His song "Those Were the Good Old Days" and his parody of "Whatever Lola Wants" were highlights in the show. For his performance, Walston won the Tony Award for best male musical comedy star.

Walston made his Hollywood film debut in *Kiss Them for Me* (1957) with Cary Grant. He reprised his roles in the film versions of *South Pacific* and *Damn Yankees,* both in 1958. Walston also appeared in several other films, including *Portrait in Black* (1960) with Lana Turner and *The Apartment* (1960) with Jack Lemmon. However, he later regretted his next major career decision. Because he needed the money, he starred as Uncle Martin on the television series *My Favorite Martian* (1963–1966). After the first season, he heard that Billy Wilder needed a replacement for Peter Sellers, who had had a heart attack, to star in *Kiss Me, Stupid* (1964). Walston got the part; it was his only starring role. However, the film was condemned by the Legion of Decency (which was formed by Catholic bishops in 1934 to combat immorality in films) and despised by the critics, and it became a box office disaster.

Once *My Favorite Martian* concluded, Walston found it difficult to get acting parts; too many people saw him as the weird, wisecracking alien with antennae. In a 1995 interview in *USA Today,* Walston stated his regrets about playing the role: "I didn't work in TV or film for three years after. Everyone thought of me as a Martian." As late as 1996, still identified as the Martian, he was asked to appear on a television news program with two of the world's most renowned scientists to discuss the possibility of life on Mars. Walston turned down the offer. In 1966 he went on the road, doing theatre in an attempt to divest himself of the image of Uncle Martin; he also appeared in

Ray Walston, in a still from *My Favorite Martian.* AP/WIDE WORLD PHOTOS

a number of films, including *Paint Your Wagon* (1969), *The Sting* (1973), and *Silver Streak* (1976). His portrayal of Mr. Hand in *Fast Times at Ridgemont High* (1982) is the classic stereotype of the prissy, slacker-hating schoolteacher. Between films and television appearances on such shows as *The Wild, Wild West* and *Night Court,* Walston kept busy.

In 1992 he played the farmhand Candy in the film adaptation of John Steinbeck's *Of Mice and Men,* but it was his work with the producer/writer David E. Kelley on the television series *L.A. Law* that brought him another award-winning role. Originally, the role of the no-nonsense judge Henry Bone on *Picket Fences,* in 1993, was supposed to last one episode, but Kelley was so impressed by Walston's performance that he made the judge a series regular. Viewers admired a character who could say what they could not. For example, as Judge Bone, his favorite comment at someone's stupidity in his courtroom was either "sit down" or "get out." Walston said, "It's the best part I've ever had." For this role, Walston received the Emmy for best supporting actor in a drama series in 1995 and 1996. The series ended in 1996. Never one to sit still, Walston was involved in the Los Angeles Actors Studio and continued to work in television. His final role was in the October 2000 season premiere of *Touched by an Angel,* playing a wealthy entrepreneur who disinherits his materialistic son to teach him a lesson. Walston died at home following a six-year struggle with lupus, and his body was cremated.

Walston was an actor who played a variety of roles in different venues. His best parts were those that enabled him to use his wry humor and cranky persona.

★

Walston's papers are in the Harry Ransom Humanities Research Center of the University of Texas at Austin. Interviews are by Mark Goodman, *People* (30 Nov. 1992), and Dina-Marie Kulzer, *Television Series Regulars of the Fifties and Sixties in Interview* (1992), which focuses on Walston's role in *My Favorite Martian.* An article, "Devil's Due," *Theatre Arts* (Apr. 1958), discusses his early career in the theatre. Jefferson Graham, "Walston Is a Good Judge of Character," *USA Today* (10 Mar. 1995), includes Walston's views on his role in *Picket Fences.* Obituaries are in the *Los Angeles Times* and *New York Times* (both 3 Jan. 2001).

MARCIA B. DINNEEN

WARFIELD, William Caesar (*b.* 20 January 1920 in West Helena, Arkansas; *d.* 25 August 2002 in Chicago, Illinois), concert bass baritone, actor, and educator who achieved fame for his rendition of "Ol' Man River" in *Show Boat* and his portrayal of Porgy in *Porgy and Bess.*

Warfield was the eldest of five sons (a sister died in infancy) of Robert Elza Warfield, a sharecropper, and Bertha (McCamery) Warfield, a homemaker. Shortly after Warfield's birth, his father received "the call" to the ministry. When Warfield was two the family moved to Saint Joseph, Missouri; three years later the family relocated to Rochester, New York, where his father became assistant pastor of Aenon Missionary Baptist Church. There Warfield made his public debut in a church pageant.

Both parents were musical, and at age nine Warfield began piano lessons, paying with the money he earned from washing cars. Throughout his schooling, to contribute to the household income, he held jobs ranging from a newspaper route, to working part time at a junkyard, to selling Cloverine Salve hair products. At Washington High School he sang in the chorus and took voice lessons from music teacher Elsa Miller. During his first recital in 1936, he sang "Deep River," by the African-American composer Harry T. Burleigh. The audience response was so positive that Warfield determined to pursue a career in music. However, he realized that it would be important to have a trade if he could not make a living as a concert singer. He studied at Mrs. Scott's Beauty Culture School and acquired a New York State License in Cosmetology and Beauty in 1937. This skill came in handy when he and his wife, the singer Leontyne Price, were touring Europe. Few salons there could style black hair, and Warfield was his wife's hairdresser.

In 1938 Warfield entered a competition sponsored by the National Music Educators League. After winning the local and regional contests, he entered the national contest, held in St. Louis. Registered as a competitor at the Jefferson Hotel, he became the hotel's first African-American guest. Warfield won first prize, a full music scholarship to a nationally recognized school of his choice. His choice was the Eastman School of Music in Rochester, New York, where he majored in voice and graduated with a B.A. in music in 1942. Shortly thereafter he was drafted into the U.S. Army. While in the army he experienced segregation and, despite his education, was relegated to "grunt work" because of his race. Fortunately his training in the German and Italian languages, acquired for his singing at Eastman, was discovered, and Warfield was moved to military intelligence at Camp Ritchie, Maryland.

After mustering out of the army in March 1946, he returned to Eastman to study for a M.A. so that he could teach music. School was interrupted when he auditioned for and won the lead in the national touring company of Harold Rome's Broadway hit *Call Me Mister.* In 1947, following the tour, Eastman enrolled under the GI Bill at the American Theatre Wing in New York City. There he studied with the voice coach Otto Herz and continued to develop his concert repertoire with the voice instructor Yves Tinayre. To pay the rent, Warfield worked at cocktail lounges and nightclubs, singing and accompanying himself

William Warfield. CORBIS

on the piano. His first acting job in an off-Broadway production was a bit part in *Set My People Free* (1947); he later created the role of Cal in the original Broadway cast of Marc Blitzsteins's opera *Regina* (1949).

When singing at the Club Norman in Toronto, Warfield had a stroke of luck. Walter Carr, a businessman, heard him sing and financed his Town Hall debut in New York City on 19 March 1950. The next morning, after rave reviews, Warfield was a star, and offers started pouring in. He accepted an engagement with the Australian Broadcasting Commission for an international tour, performing a variety of music—oratorio, opera, lieder, folk, and spiritual—in thirty-five concerts in three months. During the fall of 1950 Metro-Goldwyn-Mayer (MGM) was looking for a bass baritone to play the part of Joe in the film remake of *Show Boat*. Warfield, an admirer of Paul Robeson, who had played the part in the 1936 film, jumped at the chance. His recording of "Ol' Man River," completed on the first take, is part of Hollywood legend.

Another role with which Warfield became identified is Porgy from George Gershwin's musical *Porgy and Bess*. The production toured the United States in 1952; then, sponsored by the U.S. State Department, it traveled to a number of European capitals, finally opening in New York City in the fall of 1953. Playing the part of Bess was Leontyne

Price. On 31 August 1952, the day before the company was to sail for Europe, Warfield and Price were married at the Abyssinian Baptist Church in Harlem with the entire cast in attendance. Although Warfield and Price separated in 1958, they did not divorce until 1972. They had no children. Because of contract obligations, Warfield was unable to open on Broadway in the role of Porgy. He did perform the role in other productions; in 1961 he finally played Porgy on Broadway with the New York City Opera, and the role was a yearly event at the Volksoper in Vienna, Austria, from 1965 through 1972.

Warfield sang in churches and concert halls on six continents. He went on six U.S. State Department tours, more than any other American solo artist. In 1958 he traveled around the world twice. He sang on television shows such as the *Ed Sullivan Show,* the *Milton Berle Show,* the *Voice of Firestone,* and the *Bell Telephone Hour.* In October 1957 he played the straight dramatic role of De Lawd in the Hallmark Hall of Fame production of Marc Connelly's *Green Pastures.* Warfield won a Grammy award in 1984 for his narration of Aaron Copland's *A Lincoln Portrait.* Many of his recordings became classics, including the 1956 recording of Handel's *Messiah,* conducted by Leonard Bernstein, and the 1963 excerpts from *Porgy and Bess* with Price.

In 1975 Warfield joined the music faculty at the University of Illinois at Champaign-Urbana. He retired from his full-time position in 1990, but continued teaching as a visiting professor within the Illinois university system and at Northwestern University in Evanston, Illinois. He served as president of the National Association of Negro Musicians from 1985 to 1990 and was inducted into the American Classical Music Hall of Fame in 1999. During his teaching career he continued to perform on stage and in concert. As he told John von Rhein, music critic for the *Chicago Tribune,* "as long as this old voice holds out and I still enjoy it, I'll never stop singing." Warfield was scheduled to sing at Carnegie Hall in New York City in March 2003. However, he died the previous year at the Rehabilitation Institute of Chicago due to complications from a broken neck he suffered in a fall in July 2002. He is buried in Mount Hope Cemetery in Rochester.

Throughout Warfield's long career his voice could be heard in concert halls, on stage, and in churches. He displayed a wide repertoire and thrilled audiences with his deep, powerful, yet supple voice.

★

Warfield's papers are at the Amistad Research Center, Tulane University, New Orleans. His autobiography, *William Warfield: My Music and My Life* (1991), includes a variety of anecdotes as well as some reviews of his concerts. Articles include Gloster B. Current, "An Interview with William Warfield," *The Crisis* (Jan. 1985); and Abby Ellis, "William Warfield: Preserving Black Heritage," *Music Educator's Journal* (Oct. 1986). Also see John von Rhein's tribute to Warfield in the *Chicago Tribune* (26 Oct. 2000). Obituaries are in the *Los Angeles Times, New York Times,* and *Washington Post* (all 27 Aug. 2002).

MARCIA B. DINNEEN

WARNKE, Paul Culliton (*b.* 31 January 1920 in Webster, Massachusetts; *d.* 31 October 2001 in Washington, D.C.), lawyer and diplomat who opposed the Vietnam War as a Defense Department official in the Lyndon Baines Johnson administration and who advocated nuclear arms reduction as a strategic arms negotiator under President Jimmy Carter.

Born to Paul Martin and Lillian (Culliton) Warnke, Warnke grew up in Marlborough, Massachusetts, between Worcester and Boston. Warnke's New England upbringing led him to Yale University, where he earned his A.B. in 1941. Upon graduation he served five years in the U.S. Coast Guard during World War II in both the Atlantic and the Pacific. Following his war service, he used the GI Bill to attend Columbia University, where he earned his LL.B. in 1948, becoming editor of the *Columbia Law Review.* On 9 September 1948 he married Jean Farjeon Rowe; they had three sons and two daughters. In 1957 Warnke became a partner in the firm of Covington and Burling, specializing in trade and antitrust law.

Warnke entered the government in 1966 as general counsel in the Defense Department on the recommendation of Cyrus Vance, who had been working for President Lyndon B. Johnson as a deputy secretary of defense. His hard work resulted in a rapid rise to the third-highest position in the Defense Department. After one year he became assistant secretary of defense for international security affairs, a position in which he became one of Washington's leading "doves," opposed to the war in Vietnam. His reserved calm enhanced his intellectual approach to any task. One of Warnke's assignments during this brief period was to supervise the writing of the then secret history of the war, now known as *The Pentagon Papers.* Warnke also gained experience in nuclear arms negotiations during a visit to Washington, D.C., by Israeli Prime Minister Levi Eshkol in January 1968. Warnke argued against the Israeli negotiator, Ambassador Yitzak Rabin, over Israel's uncompromising reticence to sign the Nuclear Non-Proliferation Treaty.

When Richard M. Nixon became president in 1969, Warnke returned to private law practice and to his work for the Democratic National Committee, during which time he became increasingly vocal in his opposition to the war. In 1972 he drew the attention of the Democratic candidate for president, Senator George McGovern of South Dakota. McGovern's own position on the war matched that of Warnke, and he invited Warnke to lead his team of foreign policy advisers during the campaign. With the failure of the Democrats to win the election and then with the end of the war, Warnke focused again on his private law practice. He maintained his public voice against war, however, shifting his primary concern to the growing nuclear arms race. His position was expressed most eloquently in his 1975 *Foreign Policy* article, "Apes on a Treadmill," in which he recommended "reciprocal restraint." Initiated by

Paul C. Warnke, March 1977. BETTMANN/CORBIS

an American show of good faith in delaying nuclear weapons development, it would be possible to leave the treadmill of one superpower blindly following the other in nuclear arms production.

In 1977, as one of President Jimmy Carter's nominees to become part of his foreign policy team, Warnke drew heavy criticism for what was considered to be accommodation to the Soviet Union. This critique was based upon opposition to his ideas, such as those expressed in his *Foreign Policy* article; his antiwar position; and his association with the liberal George McGovern. Warnke's opponents reasoned that Warnke would not be able to stand up to hard-line Soviet negotiating. During the nomination hearings in Congress to consider his confirmation as director of the Arms Control and Disarmament Agency, Warnke confronted considerable criticism from his former colleague in the Defense Department, Paul Nitze, who testified that Warnke's approach to negotiating with the Russians would lead to a weaker United States. The debate between the "two Pauls," as they came to be known, over appropriate cold war policy limited the extent to which Warnke could follow through on his ideas of reciprocal restraint.

Nitze's concerns over Warnke's nomination were seconded by the senators Barry Goldwater, Strom Thurmond, Henry ("Scoop") Jackson, Sam Nunn, and Daniel Patrick Moynihan. Although Warnke's nomination was confirmed, the vote in the Senate did not achieve a two-thirds majority. In fact, a divided Congress therefore meant that the Strategic Arms Limitation Treaty (SALT) II, the negotiations for which had begun during the administration of Gerald Ford and which were successfully completed by Warnke as chief negotiator, would not be ratified. Later, although U.S. nuclear policy followed the treaty for nearly ten years, the administration of Ronald Reagan in 1986 decided that it was no longer bound by the treaty. Warnke completed the SALT II negotiations in 1978 and resigned, concerned that his presence might jeopardize further negotiations.

Warnke returned to private law practice but continued to write and speak on global issues, particularly on arms control and nuclear nonproliferation. Over the years, Warnke served as a trustee of Columbia University and Georgetown University, as chair of the District of Columbia Bar Association, and as a member of the Trilateral Commission. In 1995 he served on President Bill Clinton's Advisory Board on Arms Control and Non-Proliferation Policy. Although Warnke was beset in the 1990s by legal charges against him and his senior law partner, his former Defense Department colleague Clark Clifford, his legacy nevertheless remains that of an articulate champion of peace. Warnke suffered from kidney disease and died of a pulmonary embolism at his home in Washington, D.C., at the age of eighty-one.

Warnke was a "cold warrior" of a different sort. During the Vietnam War and then during the tense period of détente, he was a radical voice against war. His radicalism was as much due to his location as his position: he spoke from within the halls of the institutions of power. He went against the mainstream, which got him into trouble with his opponents and with most of the Washington establishment. Nonetheless, he succeeded in voicing an opinion that normally was heard only on America's streets or university campuses.

★

A relatively small collection of memoranda and other materials from the mid-1960s is located in the Manuscripts Collection at the Lyndon Baines Johnson Library in Austin, Texas. Warnke's contribution to the SALT II negotiations is discussed in David S. McLellan, *Cyrus Vance* (1985). A "Man in the News" piece on Warnke can be found in the *New York Times* (15 Aug. 1972). Additional information about Warnke is in Bill Keller, "The Lives They Lived: Paul Warnke, b. 1920," *New York Times Magazine* (30 Dec. 2001). Obituaries are in the *New York Times* and *Washington Post* (both 1 Nov. 2000).

BRIAN MCCORMACK

WASHBURN, Sherwood L(arned) (*b.* 26 November 1911 in Cambridge, Massachusetts; *d.* 16 April 2000 in Berkeley, California), anthropologist known as the father of modern primatology.

Washburn was the second of two sons born to Henry Bradford Washburn, a dean of the Episcopal Theological School in Cambridge, and Edith (Hall) Washburn. From an early age Washburn showed an interest in animal behavior and biology. He was particularly fascinated by skeletal remains, which he saw as providing clues to the living primate. While still in high school, he volunteered at the Harvard Museum of Comparative Zoology, gaining a working knowledge of comparative anatomy that would lay the foundation for future studies in evolutionary anthropology.

After graduating from Groton School in 1931, Washburn enrolled at Harvard University. Having never heard of the discipline, he stumbled into anthropology when he signed up for a course being taught by a family friend. The multidisciplinary approach appealed to him, and he abandoned his earlier plan to major in zoology. Graduating summa cum laude in 1935, he continued on toward his Ph.D. degree, which he earned in 1940.

In 1937, while still a graduate student, Washburn traveled to Thailand and Borneo as part of the Asiatic Primate Expedition led by Harold Coolidge, C. R. Carpenter, and Adolph Schultz. Washburn's assignment was dissecting primates—mostly gibbons—and preparing the skeletons for shipment back to the United States. Unlike his previous

Sherwood L. Washburn, January 1969. TED STRESHINSKY/CORBIS

in New York City. During his eight years at Columbia, he conducted numerous experiments with rats and pigs, seeking correlations to the evolution of skeletal growth in humans. Such studies earned him the derision of such mainstream anthropologists and anatomists as Franz Weidenreich, who asked, "But what have rats to do with anthropology?" His introduction of experimental methodology to physical anthropology was a bold departure from the descriptive techniques that had long dominated the field.

Washburn left Columbia for the University of Chicago in 1947, where he taught anthropology for eleven years and was chair of the department from 1952 to 1955. There he had hoped to expand his experimental work, but at the last moment the anatomy department withdrew its offer of laboratory space. A 1948 expedition to East Africa provided Washburn with another opportunity to collect primates and to expand his theories on the interrelationships between anatomy, function, and ecology.

In 1955 Washburn's primary focus shifted to primate behavior. After attending a conference in South Africa, he planned to go into the field to collect baboon specimens, as he had done in 1937 and 1948. This time, however, he became intrigued by a troop of habituated baboons living near his hotel in Victoria Falls. "Almost at once," he later recalled, "the animals ceased to be just baboons; they became personalities." Rather than capturing and dissecting them, Washburn subsequently spent an instructive month observing baboons in their natural habitat.

Ironically, during the 1937 Asiatic Primate Expedition, Washburn had expressed no interest in behavioral observations of living primates, believing more could be learned from their skeletal remains. By the late 1950s, however, he became the leading proponent of behavioral primatology. His writings demonstrated a link between the behavior of nonhuman primates and the evolution of human social behavior. As primate field studies proliferated during the 1950s and 1960s, Washburn's theories dominated the scene.

The pioneering primatologist hoped to divide his time between Berkeley, California, and Africa, but the discovery that his wife was suffering from Parkinson's disease and would be unable to accompany him into the field restricted his travels. From 1958 until his retirement in 1979, Washburn taught anthropology at the University of California, Berkeley, establishing one of the nation's most influential programs for the study of primatology and human evolution. He was chair of the department from 1961 to 1963. His lectures often resulted in standing ovations. Many of his graduate students went on to establish outstanding careers.

Washburn died of pneumonia at age eighty-eight. (His wife had predeceased him in 1985.) His contributions to anthropology extended far beyond his professorships. He organized several benchmark conferences and served as

experience in museum settings, the yearlong expedition allowed him to relate the animals' anatomical functions to their ecological context. He observed that the gibbon's anatomy was closer in form to that of humans than that of monkeys—a radical notion in those days since it was not yet known that apes are related more closely genetically to humans than to monkeys. He later remarked, "I was . . . holding fast to the belief that apes were close to humans in the evolutionary line. . . . Most of my colleagues had come to evolve into an anti-Darwinism that suggested they were not so close."

Later in his life the trend was toward conservation, with the killing of primates for their skeletal remains no longer accepted. In 1992 Washburn defended his earlier actions: "Taking animals in the field was an excellent way of getting a detailed understanding of what the animals were doing and how they were doing it." He conceded, however, that "those early studies have now been done, and we in the field of primate study should no longer need to take the lives of primates."

Washburn married Henrietta Faxon Pease on 10 September 1938. The couple had two sons. In 1939 he began teaching anatomy at Columbia University Medical School

president of the American Association of Physical Anthropologists (1951–1952) and the American Anthropological Association (1962). He earned nearly every honor bestowed by his field, including the Viking Fund Medal, the Huxley Memorial Medal, the Distinguished Service Award of the American Anthropological Association, and the Charles Darwin Lifetime Achievement Award. Although his writings never aimed at a mainstream readership, he was a frequent contributor to scientific journals and edited several volumes of essays.

Among Washburn's works are *Thinking About Race* (1946), *Social Life of Early Man* (1961), *Classification and Human Evolution* (1963), *The Study of Evolution* (1968), and (with Ruth Moore) *Ape into Human: A Study of Human Evolution* (2d. ed., 1980). Among Washburn's coedited works are *Perspectives on Human Evolution,* with Phyllis C. Jay (1968), and *Human Evolution: Biosocial Perspectives,* with Elizabeth R. McCown (1978).

Credited as the first to link the evolution of human behavior to the actions of monkeys and apes, Washburn's theories frequently pitted him against the anthropological establishment. His holistic approach—integrating anatomy, biology, behavior, and paleontology—changed the course of American anthropological study.

★

The Bancroft Library of the University of California, Berkeley, is home to the Sherwood L. Washburn Papers (1932–1996), including correspondence, research notes, lectures, field notes, and photographs relating to Washburn's career in physical anthropology. Washburn reflected on his professional development in an autobiographical essay entitled "Evolution of a Teacher," *Annual Review of Anthropology* 12 (1983): 1–24. A former student, Irven DeVore, questioned Washburn extensively about his upbringing, education, and career achievements in "An Interview with Sherwood Washburn," *Current Anthropology* 33 (Aug.–Oct. 1992): 411–423. An obituary is in the *New York Times* 33 (19 Apr. 2000).

Brenda Scott Royce

WASSERMAN, Lewis Robert ("Lew") (*b.* 22 March 1913 in Cleveland, Ohio; *d.* 3 June 2002 in Beverly Hills, California), chairman and chief executive officer of Music Corporation of America, the parent company of Universal Studios.

Wasserman was the son of Russian immigrants Isaac Wasserman, a restaurant owner, and Minnie Wasserman, a homemaker. Wasserman and his two brothers grew up amid the speakeasies and silent movie palaces of Cleveland. He worked from his early teens as a candy salesman and usher at night while attending public schools during the

Lew Wasserman. The Kobal Collection

day. Following high school graduation in 1930, Wasserman worked for Cleveland's infamous Mayfield Road gang, a Mob organization, operating a casino. He met Edith T. Beckerman, the only daughter of the Mob lawyer Henry Beckerman, and they married on 5 July 1936. They had one child. When the casino went bankrupt in 1936, the Wassermans moved to Chicago, where Wasserman became a talent agent for the Music Corporation of America (MCA).

Founded in 1924 by the Chicago ophthalmologist Jules Stein, MCA was by far the richest and most influential dance band agency in the world, with ties to both James C. Petrillo's American Federation of Musicians and Al Capone's skein of nightclubs, brothels, and gambling halls. When Stein moved his headquarters from Chicago to Beverly Hills in 1938, Wasserman rose quickly among the ranks in MCA's drive to monopolize motion picture, stage, and radio talent. Among Wasserman's earliest clients were Bette Davis, John Garfield, Jane Wyman, Betty Grable, and the future president Ronald Reagan. Wasserman cemented their lifelong friendship when he negotiated one of Hollywood's first million-dollar movie contracts on Reagan's behalf in 1941 with Warner Bros. Studios.

Wasserman spent scant time at home throughout the rest of the decade, devoting his energies instead to building

Stein's MCA into a talent powerhouse. He brokered a merger with the Broadway talent lord Leland Hayward, and in 1945 MCA absorbed two of its biggest competitors: the Hayward-Deverich Agency in Beverly Hills and the Leland Hayward Agency in New York City. In 1946 Stein named Wasserman MCA president.

Wasserman was one of the first people in Hollywood to own a television set. Foreseeing the potential influence of television, in the late 1940s he created Revue Productions, which produced most early television programs throughout the 1950s, including *General Electric Theater,* hosted by Reagan. As Screen Actors Guild (SAG) president, Reagan oversaw an MCA waiver of SAG bylaws, which prevented talent agencies from producing television shows or films while simultaneously representing the artists in those shows. The secret waiver gave MCA the advantage of selling stars at the same time that its Revue Productions arm hired them, but by the time the waiver came to light in 1960, Wasserman and his army of agents had secured MCA's position as the most powerful force in the entertainment industry.

During the 1950s, Wasserman also turned film stars into independent contractors. He made the actor Jimmy Stewart a millionaire with a single role in the Universal Pictures film *Winchester '73* (1950). By taking his salary in the form of profit participation instead of a paycheck, Stewart paved the way for actors, directors, producers, and writers to leverage their celebrity at the negotiating table. Similarly, Wasserman formed independent production companies for stars such as Jack Benny, Alfred Hitchcock, Errol Flynn, and dozens of other MCA clients, allowing them to minimize taxes while exploiting their star salaries and expanding their influence in movie production.

In 1962 a lengthy Department of Justice investigation into MCA's monopolistic practices resulted in a face-off between Wasserman and U.S. Attorney General Robert Kennedy. In order to avoid criminal and civil penalties for alleged antitrust violations, MCA divested itself of its talent agency at the same time that the company bought the struggling Universal Pictures and Decca Records. Literally overnight, MCA quit the talent business and created the largest entertainment assembly line in Hollywood. Building on its Revue library of detective shows, westerns, situation comedies, and specials, MCA and Wasserman transformed the moribund Universal Pictures into Universal Studios, the largest and busiest lot in Hollywood. A backstage motion picture studio tram tour hatched by Wasserman's brain trust became second only to Disneyland as Southern California's biggest tourist attraction.

Wasserman succeeded Stein as MCA chairman in 1973, expanding his role beyond Hollywood to Washington and all over the world. During this period MCA extended its influence to publishing (Putnam/Berkley), retail stores (Spencer Gifts), banking (Columbia Savings and Loan), and even Yosemite National Park, where MCA monopolized concessions. At its height, MCA had offices in forty-two countries. Wasserman became politically active, organizing large fund-raisers and contributing to the political campaigns of John F. Kennedy, Lyndon B. Johnson, Jimmy Carter, William J. ("Bill") Clinton, and of course Reagan.

Although much of MCA/Universal's output during Wasserman's rein was insignificant, the studio nurtured a host of producing talent that moved through the Universal television, music, and movie mill, among them Steven Spielberg, George Lucas, Ron Howard, Stephen Cannell, and Stephen Bochco. During Wasserman's tenure, the studio won an Academy Award for *The Sting* and Emmys for such enduring programs as *Columbo* and *The Rockford Files,* but Wasserman and his successor as MCA president, Sid Sheinberg, were more interested in profit than in art. Thus, MCA led Hollywood's negotiations to keep wages low and profit margins high, cutting costs at every turn. Sets, stars, and scripts were recycled so often that Universal became a butt of jokes about Hollywood homogeneity during the 1980s.

His nonstop quest to meld developing technology with his passion for profit continued to make Wasserman an innovator, just as he had been in the early days of television. In the early 1960s, he installed one of the earliest industrial computer systems at MCA headquarters, and in the late 1960s he acquired patents for digital and laser technology that would eventually make MCA the pioneer in developing compact disks (CDs) and digital video discs (DVDs). MCA locked Sony Corporation in an epic struggle to corner the early market on videocassette recording, ultimately winning the battle to make video home system (VHS) tapes standard in the United States but losing the war over MCA's right to prevent taping off of television in a lawsuit that went all the way to the U.S. Supreme Court.

Despite MCA's continued dominance through the 1970s and 1980s in television, popular music, and motion pictures with blockbusters such as *Jaws, Back to the Future,* and *E.T.,* Wasserman opted to sell MCA in 1990 to Matsushita Electric for a then-whopping price of $6.13 billion, of which Wasserman's share was more than $500 million. He and Sheinberg continued to manage MCA on Matsushita's behalf through 1995, but a falling-out with the Japanese over profligacy in the production of the costly MCA flop *Waterworld* (1995) ended in a surprise sale of MCA/Universal to the Canadian liquor company Seagram. Within weeks of the takeover, Seagram's chief executive officer, Edgar Bronfman, Jr., dismissed most of Wasserman's executive hierarchy, supplanted Wasserman in all but an advisory role, and slowly eased the eighty-two-year-old MCA patriarch out of the company. In 1998 Wasserman left the MCA headquarters building—renamed for him—for the last time.

Wasserman continued in his role as a major Democratic Party fund-raiser and contributor to Southern California institutions ranging from the University of California, Los Angeles (UCLA) to the Holocaust Museum, but he bowed out of the motion picture business. He died at age eighty-nine at his Beverly Hills estate, after an extended illness following a stroke. He is buried in Hillside Memorial Park in Culver City, California.

★

The Margaret Herrick Library of the Academy of Motion Picture Arts and Sciences in Beverly Hills has extensive files on both Wasserman and MCA/Universal, as do the Louis B. Mayer Library of the American Film Institute, the research libraries at UCLA and the University of Southern California (USC), and the Billy Rose Theatre Collection of the New York Public Library. Dennis McDougal, *The Last Mogul: Lew Wasserman, MCA, and the Hidden History of Hollywood* (1998), was the first full-length, fully annotated source for information about Wasserman's life and career. Other biographies include Connie Bruck, *When Hollywood Had a King: The Reign of Lew Wasserman, Who Leveraged Talent into Power and Influence* (2003), and Kathleen Sharp, *Mr. and Mrs. Hollywood: How Lew and Edie Wasserman Created a Global Entertainment Empire* (2003). Other than *The Last Mogul,* the most definitive works about MCA are Michael Pye, *Moguls: Inside the Business of Show Business* (1980); Dan Moldea, *Dark Victory: Ronald Reagan, MCA, and the Mob* (1986); and William Knoedelseder, *Stiffed: A True Story of MCA, the Music Business, and the Mafia* (1993). Obituaries are in the *Los Angeles Times, New York Times,* and *Washington Post* (all 4 June 2002).

DENNIS MCDOUGAL

WEAVER, Sylvester Laflin, Jr. ("Pat") (*b.* 21 December 1908 in Los Angeles, California; *d.* 15 March 2002 in Santa Barbara, California), advertising and broadcasting executive who led the National Broadcasting Company (NBC) into the television era with innovative programming ideas, including the creation of the *Today Show* (1952) and the *Tonight Show* (1954).

Weaver was raised in an affluent home in Los Angeles, one of four children of Sylvester Weaver, the proprietor of a roofing company, and Annabel (Dixon) Weaver, a homemaker. An older brother, Winstead, known by the stage name Doodles Weaver, had a successful career as a comedian in vaudeville, radio, and television. Weaver excelled as a student in Los Angeles public schools and entered Dartmouth College in 1926. A philosophy major with a keen interest in classical civilizations, he was elected to Phi Beta Kappa as a junior and received his B.A. magna cum

Sylvester ("Pat") Weaver, 1985. CORBIS

laude in 1930. Hoping to become a novelist, he spent a year working on short fiction as he traveled in Europe and North Africa.

Unable to sell any of his stories, Weaver returned to Los Angeles in 1931. With the help of his family, he found several jobs in advertising and broadcasting, settling on a position with the radio station KHJ. Like many future pioneers of the television industry, Weaver learned the commercial broadcasting business "on the job" in local radio, writing advertisement and entertainment copy and serving as announcer, actor, news reporter, advertising salesman, and in other capacities as needed. After just two years, he was promoted to program manager of KFRC in San Francisco, which, like KHJ, was owned by the Don Lee broadcasting organization. In later years he credited his radio experiences with making him a lifetime "information optimist" who believed that broadcasting could, as he wrote, "enrich the common man and make him an uncommon man."

Weaver moved to New York City in 1935 to work on the NBC radio musical-variety series *Evening in Paris,* overseeing content for the network and writing advertising copy for the show's sponsor, the United Cigar Company. In 1937 Young & Rubicam (Y&R), then the leading advertising agency in the broadcast field, hired Weaver to produce *Town Hall Tonight,* a CBS radio series that starred the satirist Fred Allen and was sponsored by the American Tobacco Company, one of the medium's biggest advertisers. When Y&R announced its intention to promote Weaver to head of its radio division at the end of the 1937–1938 broadcast season, George Washington Hill, head of American Tobacco, persuaded Weaver to leave Y&R instead. In an extraordinary move, Hill hired the twenty-nine-year-old Weaver as advertising manager, giving him full authority over radio strategy as well as production of the tobacco company's many radio programs.

Weaver enjoyed the prerogatives of a successful urban executive during what were otherwise the economic hard times of the late 1930s. Tall, athletic, erudite, and personable, he became a well-known figure in Manhattan society. An avid theatergoer and patron of the fine arts, he also enjoyed skiing and playing tennis. For a time he was considered among the city's most "eligible bachelors." On 23 January 1942 Weaver married Elizabeth Inglis (née Desiree Mary Hawkins), an English actor, and the couple had two children. Their daughter, Susan, known by the stage name Sigourney Weaver, became a highly successful screen actor.

An early and vocal opponent of fascism, Weaver took a leave of absence from American Tobacco in 1941 to accept a federal government appointment with the Office of Inter-American Affairs to produce antifascist radio programs for broadcast to Latin America. Following the U.S. entry into World War II, he was commissioned as a naval officer and served from 1942 to 1945, first aboard a submarine chaser in the Atlantic and then with the Armed Forces Radio Network in Hollywood.

When Weaver returned to American Tobacco after the war, he was shocked to find that his mentor, Hill, was dying of lung cancer and, furthermore, that Hill would not admit to it publicly. Nor would he stop, or even curtail, his habit of smoking three to four packs of cigarettes per day. "In the three years before the war, I took the Lucky Strike brand from [sales of] 32 million to 100 million packs a year," Weaver recalled in an oral history interview. "But I could tell that smoking was interfering with my health, and particularly my skiing. After Mr. Hill died, I stopped smoking and I left the company in 1947."

Weaver did not lack for offers. Although not yet forty, Weaver was by this time a consummate insider in the world of American broadcast advertising, having worked for major employers in three key elements of the industry: network broadcasting (NBC), Madison Avenue (Y&R), and the advertising division of a national sponsor (American Tobacco). He had also forged personal relationships with dozens of radio stars, including Fred Allen, Jack Benny,

and Kate Smith. As the broadcast advertising industry geared up for the implementation of plans for television service, he returned to Y&R in 1947 as vice president in charge of radio and television, with a seat on the agency's powerful executive committee. "Y&R had dominated radio advertising and I soon realized that my job was to maintain that status quo in television," he said. "But that's not what I wanted to do. I wanted to avoid the mistakes of radio and make television something better."

That opportunity came in 1949 when David Sarnoff of the Radio Corporation of America (RCA) offered Weaver a job overseeing the budding NBC television network. He eagerly accepted. Having spent some fifteen years performing relatively conventional duties with great success, Weaver re-emerged in his new job showing some of the creative energies of the idealist who had studied philosophy with hopes of becoming a novelist. As a *New Yorker* profile put it, while at NBC, Weaver became "not only the leading showman in television, but also its most unrelenting thinker and most vocal theorist."

A sampling of the programs that Weaver was responsible for conceptualizing, creating (in some cases by memoranda), or rehabilitating is impressive. *Today* and *Tonight* (developed from Weaver's 1950 late-night talk-variety show, *Broadway Open House*), as well as *Meet the Press* (which he saved from cancellation and redesigned), are the only series to have remained on the air continuously for more than a half-century. *Your Show of Shows* (1950–1954) is considered by many critics to have been the greatest realization of the art of television sketch comedy, as well as a creative watershed that would influence American television and film comedy for decades. *Home,* an afternoon show targeted for women, and *Wide, Wide World,* a cerebral video magazine, were early prototypes of contemporary "infotainment" programming. NBC "spectaculars" (as Weaver dubbed special prime-time programs meant for family entertainment) included *Peter Pan,* the first Broadway-style musical presented live on television, and Gian Carlo Menotti's *Amahl and the Night Visitors,* the first opera commissioned for television.

In terms of business innovation, Weaver was a champion of "spot advertising," which he preferred to "full sponsorship," the production system that television had inherited from radio. Under the old system, advertising agencies and their clients maintained hands-on control over the making of fully sponsored programs. This often resulted in heavy-handed commercialism that worked against the artistic development of the medium. For example, in weekly series sponsored by cigarette makers, criminals could never be shown smoking and police almost always were. Weaver preferred for the network to produce its own programming, independent of agency/sponsor control. Clients were then invited to preview completed programs and buy commercial spots.

Weaver's authority at NBC was expanded to include the radio network in 1952. As radio lost the mass audience for drama and variety entertainment to television, radio stations began dropping network shows in favor of local programs hosted by disc jockeys who played recorded music. Weaver created a new concept, "NBC Monitor," designed to revive network radio. Rather than traditional programs or series, Monitor presented a twenty-four-hour "magazine of the air," moving between hard news, soft news, comedy spots, consumer information, entertainment reviews, sports coverage, and so on. It was introduced as an experimental weekend service in 1955.

Almost from the day he arrived at NBC, Weaver found himself in conflict with his boss, Sarnoff. At the heart of the matter was a personality clash. Weaver was operating as a kind of impresario, asking for exorbitant budgets to sign stars and produce new programming. Sarnoff considered "show business" a vulgar undertaking and preferred to think of himself as an engineer working in the "communications business." As a result, he vetoed many of Weaver's attempts to sign or retain major stars, including Jackie Gleason, Red Skelton, and Jack Benny, all of whom were phenomenal successes on television for the rival Columbia Broadcasting System.

Moreover, Sarnoff, who had risen from a lowly telegraph operator to an imperial position of power at RCA, fully expected his son, Robert, to succeed him. In that regard, Weaver was a rival who became more unwanted with his every success. Unable to fire Weaver without embarrassing himself, Sarnoff "promoted" him four times in seven years. He finally succeeded in forcing Weaver to resign from the impressive-sounding—but largely ceremonial—post of vice-chairman of the board of RCA.

At forty-eight years of age, Weaver was wealthy and had made a lasting mark on the character of television, yet his efforts after leaving NBC in 1956 ranged from the unremarkable to the unsuccessful. From 1958 to 1963, he headed the powerful marketing firm of McCann-Erikson, but left, he said, "out of boredom." He then moved back to his native Los Angeles to start up Subscription TV, an early pay-television effort built around a combination of sports by day and fine arts by night. However, California broadcasting interests organized a ballot initiative proposing to make it illegal to charge money for television programming, although they knew full well that such a law would be struck down by the U.S. Supreme Court. The referendum, to no one's surprise, passed, and was indeed ruled unconstitutional. But it had its intended effect, as the three-year court battle bankrupted Weaver's fledgling company.

Weaver was active in many charities throughout his life,

serving as chair of the American Heart Association in the early 1960s and as president of the Muscular Dystrophy Association in the 1970s. He received the Peabody Award in 1956, as well as a special career achievement Emmy Award in 1967, and was elected to the Television Hall of Fame in 1985. He lived with his wife, Elizabeth, in Santa Barbara during his retirement, and died of pneumonia at age ninety-three.

★

Weaver's autobiography, written with Thomas W. Coffey, *The Best Seat in the House: The Golden Years in Radio and Television* (1994), is a straightforward narrative of his life, reaching emotional depth only in his resentment of Sarnoff for curtailing his career at NBC. The article, "'Operation Frontal Lobes' versus the Living Room Toy," in the critical anthology *Media, Culture and Society* (1967), offers an in-depth look at Weaver's efforts to produce high quality news, documentary, and arts programming at NBC. An obituary is in the *New York Times* (18 Mar. 2002). A two-hour videotaped interview and transcript are held by the Center for the Study of Popular Culture at Syracuse University Library in Syracuse, New York.

DAVID MARC

WEBER, Joseph (*b.* 17 May 1919 in Paterson, New Jersey; *d.* 30 September 2000 in Pittsburgh, Pennsylvania), physicist who described and built one of the first experiments designed to detect gravitational waves.

Weber was the youngest of four children born to Jacob Weber and Lena (Stein) Weber, who were both Lithuanian immigrants. Weber was a precocious child whose early readings included scientific books well beyond his years. He was educated in public schools in his hometown of Paterson before taking a competitive examination to gain entry to the U.S. Naval Academy.

After winning an appointment to the Naval Academy, Weber led his class in mathematics and engineering before receiving a B.S. in 1940. Weber was commissioned in the U.S. Navy, where he spent eight years serving at several posts. During World War II, aboard the aircraft carrier USS *Lexington,* he applied his mathematical talents to the business of navigation. Weber survived several close calls aboard the *Lexington,* the first being the ship's fortuitous exit from Pearl Harbor the day before the Japanese attack in December 1941, and the last being his rescue from the sinking carrier during the Battle of the Coral Sea in 1942. On 18 October 1942 Weber married his high school sweetheart, Anita Meinhart Straus; they had four sons. After Straus's death in 1971, Weber married Virginia Trimble, an astrophysicist, on 16 March 1972.

Weber commanded the submarine chaser *SC 690* and

participated in the first Sicilian landing in 1943. After the war Weber served in the navy's Bureau of Ships as head of the electronic design section. In this position Weber used his background in amateur radio and radar to specialize in electronic countermeasures.

After resigning his commission as a lieutenant commander in 1948, Weber became a professor of electrical engineering at the University of Maryland in Baltimore. At the same time Weber began graduate studies at the Catholic University of America in Washington, D.C., where he was awarded a Ph.D. in physics in 1951 for his research on the microwave inversion spectrum of ammonia. In the ensuing years Weber was an early pioneer in microwave spectroscopy and quantum electronics. In fact, his work on microwave emissions formed the foundation for the new field of quantum electronics. He was named a fellow at the Institute for Advanced Study in Princeton, New Jersey, for the 1955–1956 academic year and was able to concentrate on general relativity, a subject that would prove fruitful in his research many years later. Weber was then awarded a fellowship by the Institute of Radio Engineers for work that led to the development of the MASER (Microwave Amplification by the Stimulated Emission of Radiation). His insight that molecules in an energetic state might amplify coherent light was also fundamental to the later development of the laser. These ideas helped to guide research and inventions in twentieth-century optics.

Weber soon left the field of optics to pursue a new interest. Since his days at the Institute for Advanced Study, Weber had been thinking and writing about Albert Einstein's general theory of relativity and its prediction of the existence of gravitational waves. In 1961 Weber moved to the physics department of the University of Maryland and began investigating gravitational waves in earnest. Also in 1961, Weber published his book *General Relativity and Gravitational Radiation*. This began a new chapter in physics that would eventually lead to a cadre of physicists looking for the elusive gravitational wave.

Weber was among the earliest scientists to describe and then build a device to detect gravitational waves. After nearly a decade of experimentation, Weber published his results in 1969. In his paper, Weber described an experiment in which he claimed to have detected gravitational waves, using a massive aluminum cylinder as an antenna. These cylinders, now known as Weber bars, were designed to oscillate in the presence of gravitational waves, with this oscillation measured on a recorder similar to a seismograph. Although his results were called into question by other physicists, Weber's work influenced a generation of scientists who set out to build ever more sensitive machines to give more reliable results in the search for gravitational waves. Weber himself continued to carry out experiments designed to detect their presence.

Joseph Weber, November 1987. JAMES A. SUGAR/CORBIS

Weber's groundbreaking work on gravitational waves led to multinational projects to detect them. Projects in the United States, such as the Laser Interferometer Gravitational Wave Observatory (LIGO), and in Japan, as well as cooperative projects between the French and Italians and between the British and Germans, continue to search for gravitational waves. A cooperative project by NASA and the European Space Agency, the Laser Interferometer Space Antenna (LISA), in which such experiments would be conducted in space, was in the planning stages by 2003.

Although Weber spent most of his career at the University of Maryland, after 1973, when he became professor emeritus at Maryland, Weber split his time between Maryland and the University of California, Irvine. Weber also held Guggenheim, National Research Council, and Fulbright fellowships. He received the Scientific Achievement Award from the Washington Academy of Sciences, the Babson Award from the Gravity Research Foundation, and the Boris Pregel Prize from the New York Academy of Sciences. Weber was also elected to the Maryland Engineering Hall of Fame. In 2001 the American Astronomical

Society announced the establishment of the Joseph Weber Award for Astronomical Instrumentation in honor of Weber's contributions to astronomy. This award is given to individuals who have invented or significantly improved an instrument leading to advances in astronomy.

After a long life filled with major advances in physics and physical activity (he was known as an outdoor enthusiast who loved jogging, swimming, and rock climbing), Weber died in a Pittsburgh, Pennsylvania, hospital while being treated for non-Hodgkin's lymphoma.

★

Weber's papers are in the archives and manuscripts department of the University of Maryland library. Obituaries are in the *Washington Post* (8 Oct. 2000), *New York Times* (9 Oct. 2000), and *Physics Today* 54, no. 7 (July 2001).

W. TODD TIMMONS

WECHSLER, Herbert (*b.* 4 December 1909 in New York City; *d.* 26 April 2000 in New York City), attorney and legal educator who was noted for his writings and for his argument of a famous libel case.

Wechsler was one of two children of Samuel Wechsler, a lawyer, and Anna (Weisberger) Wechsler. His brother, James, later became a noted reporter for the *New York Post*. He enrolled at City College of New York at age sixteen, and earned a B.A. in French in 1928. His father talked the faculty out of hiring him as a French instructor, and Wechsler wound up at Columbia Law School in New York City, where his father wanted him to go. At Columbia he attained the coveted position of editor in chief of that school's *Law Review,* and earned an LL.B. in 1931.

In 1932 Wechsler served as law clerk to Harlan Fiske Stone of the U.S. Supreme Court, passed the bar examination, and on 29 May married Elzie Stix. A short period at a number of positions, including that of New York State assistant attorney general, led to a post with the U.S. Supreme Court Committee on the Rules of Criminal Procedure, on which he served from 1941 to 1945.

Wechsler also served during World War II in the Department of Justice War Division, overseeing interments of Japanese Americans on the West Coast. When the war ended he was assigned to assist the American judge and alternate at the Nuremberg war crimes trial for Nazi leaders. There was reportedly some tension between Wechsler and the military officials assigned to the tribunal, but he is believed to have written a large part of the judgment of the tribunal with respect to the charged conspiracy of the German leadership to engage in unlawful war combat under cover of war.

In 1945 Wechsler was named full professor at Columbia Law School, where he had been on the faculty since 1937.

Herbert Wechsler, September 1957. PETER STACKPOLE/TIME LIFE PICTURES/GETTY IMAGES

In 1953 he co-edited, with Henry M. Hart, Jr., the first edition of *The Federal Courts and the Federal System,* which became the standard textbook on the scope and power of federal judicial authority within the framework of the constitutional system. The U.S. Supreme Court justice Ruth Bader Ginsburg later stated that the book, annotated with Wechsler's comments, was the one to which she most often referred when considering her opinions.

Wechsler was a frequent critic of the "Warren Court" (the Supreme Court under the leadership of Chief Justice Earl Warren), which made a number of key changes in the area of civil rights and liberties. However, he was on the winning end of one of the Court's most celebrated decisions, in *New York Times* v. *Sullivan* (1967), perhaps the most significant decision in U.S. history on the issue of libel.

In *Sullivan,* the Court ruled unanimously that the *New York Times,* for which Wechsler served as legal counsel, could not be held responsible for defaming the character of a public official unless the newspaper acted with "reckless disregard" of the truth. Thus political figures could no longer readily threaten newspapers with expensive libel cases for publishing truthful statements about them. Traditionally, the Court has affirmed individuals' right to be free of incorrect statements about their conduct, but Wechsler persuaded the justices to concentrate on the misuse of libel laws for political purposes. He used the Alien and Sedition Acts, applied in the very early nineteenth century to suppress dissent, as a particularly reprehensible example of the conduct that he maintained the Court should control.

Wechsler sought rationality from the legal system. In his essay "Toward Neutral Principles of Constitutional Law," he argued that judges should base their decisions not on the pull of social or historical context, but on principles that seemed rational to them. In 1952 Wechsler became the reporter for the Model Penal Code, a project initiated by the American Law Institute (ALI) in an attempt to rationalize criminal law. Wechsler noted, for example, that many states had as many as eight different sentence lengths for some major crimes. With the Model Code, the ALI—an affiliation of legal scholars—sought to replace this hodgepodge with but four degrees of felonies carrying four possible sentence lengths. Wechsler also sought to redefine various crimes, such as larceny, which had come to have many different definitions or names in the various state statutes. Wechsler's efforts became law in many states, although the code's sentencing guidelines came under attack in later years for being insufficiently attentive to the effect of criminal actions on the victims, particularly in the case of violent crimes.

In 1963 Wechsler became director of the ALI, a position that enabled him to bring the same type of legal-concept reshaping to many different areas of the law, including property, torts, and judgments. The institute crafted "restatements of law" designed to represent the best thinking of not only what the law was, but also what it ought to be. Wechsler advised the institute to keep to a middle course, content neither to rigidly follow existing court opinions, nor to create entirely new areas of legal theory. Nevertheless, the restatements were critical in reforming several areas of law, particularly with respect to the liability of manufacturers for defects in their goods that injured consumers of the product. They also became teaching devices for law students, as they conveniently but accurately stated legal principles without the need to read through extensive court decisions.

Wechsler also served on the editorial board of the Uniform Commercial Code, enacted by virtually every state to uniformly govern transactions between businesses and between businesses and consumers. It has virtually replaced the previous common law with respect to commercial transactions within the United States.

Divorced from his first wife in 1957, Wechsler married Doris L. Klauber, also an attorney, on 13 April 1957. He had no children.

In addition to *The Federal Courts and the Federal System* (published in a 1973 second edition as *Hart and Wechsler's*

The Federal Courts and the Federal System), Wechsler's publications include *Criminal Law and Its Administration: Cases, Statutes, and Commentaries* (1940), with Jerome Michael; and *Principles, Politics and Fundamental Law* (1961), which presents Wechsler's view of federal constitutional rights. In 1969 he criticized some of the Warren Court's extensions of civil liberties in *The Nationalization of Civil Rights and Civil Liberties*. The most famous of his many articles, originally printed in the *Harvard Law Review* in 1959, was published as a monograph, *Toward Neutral Principles of Constitutional Law* (1960).

Wechsler achieved emeritus status at Columbia in 1978. He died in his home of undisclosed causes at the age of ninety.

★

There is no biography of Wechsler. Bradley R. Smith, *Reaching Judgment at Nuremberg* (1977), gives a glimpse of Wechsler's participation in the Nuremberg trials. The Sullivan case is treated in detail in Anthony Lewis, *Make No Law: The Sullivan Case and the First Amendment* (1991). An obituary is in the *New York Times* (28 Apr. 2000).

JOHN DAVID HEALY

WEINMEISTER, Arnold George ("Arnie") (*b.* 23 March 1923 in Rhein, Saskatchewan, Canada; *d.* 28 June 2000 in Seattle, Washington), the premier defensive tackle of his time, whose brief career was so brilliant that he was inducted into the Pro Football Hall of Fame in 1984.

The youngest of eight children born to the German immigrants John George Weinmeister, a carpenter, and Suzannah (Werner) Weinmeister, a homemaker, Weinmeister moved with his family first to Spokane, Washington, and later to Portland, Oregon, in 1924. Naturalized, along with his seven siblings, when his father earned U.S. citizenship, Weinmeister attended Jefferson High School in Portland, where he had his first taste of organized football. A "big, fast, versatile kid" in high school, he attracted the attention of many West Coast colleges. Weinmeister played tackle, end, and fullback as a scholastic athlete before accepting an athletic grant-in-aid to the University of Washington in Seattle in 1941. With the United States at war, Weinmeister dropped out of college after the Huskies' 1942 season and served four years in the army with an artillery battalion in the European theater of operations, rising to the rank of sergeant.

After the war Weinmeister returned to Washington and continued his collegiate playing career as both end and fullback. His reputation was based on size (six feet, four inches tall, weighing 235 pounds), speed, and controlled aggressiveness. During the 1946 season Weinmeister suffered a knee injury, and when he was able to return to the gridiron, he played tackle exclusively. He earned a solid reputation on the West Coast but did not garner major All-America mention. At the time, Ray Flaherty, a Pro Football Hall of Fame coach, called Weinmeister "the best-looking fullback prospect in the country."

Thanks to his military service, Weinmeister was eligible for the 1945 National Football League (NFL) player draft. He was chosen by the Brooklyn Dodgers in the seventeenth round as a "future," while still fighting in World War II. Weinmeister elected to return to college. After graduating, he signed with the New York Yankees, a member of the NFL-rival All-America Football Conference (AAFC), for the 1948 season. Weinmeister was an immediate star, earning accolades as "football's fastest lineman." He earned All-AAFC honors in both 1948 and 1949. When the AAFC merged with the NFL for the 1950 season, Weinmeister and his Yankees teammate Tom Landry were quickly claimed by the New York Giants.

As part of the defensive guru Steve Owen's miserly unit, Weinmeister further burnished his credentials. In four years with the Giants (1950–1953), he was named All-Pro four times and played in four Pro Bowls. His speed and intelligence were the talk of the league. The San Francisco 49ers coach Buck Shaw remarked at the time, "He is the outstanding tackle in the NFL. One man can't handle him." Weinmeister was so fast (even at 250 pounds) that Owen would pit him against rookie backs and receivers; when Weinmeister beat them in a footrace, the coach would say, "How do you expect to make the Giants when you get beaten by a fat, old tackle?" Despite his bulk, Weinmeister could keep up with most of the speedy halfbacks in the league. His speed and penetration were something new to defensive football, as was his lateral movement and sideline-to-sideline pursuit. Weinmeister was so sharp that the Giants Hall of Fame offensive tackle Roosevelt Brown commented, "I consider myself fortunate to have only had to play against him in practice. He was more than a handful!"

In the 1950s the Canadian Football League (CFL) made overtures to established NFL stars. A Canada native and All-Pro, Weinmeister was a prime target. After the 1953 season Weinmeister "jumped" to the British Columbia Lions of the CFL, where he played stellar football for two more seasons as a player-coach—for considerably more money than the Giants were willing to pay. Having left the Giants on less than amicable terms (the team sued to retain his services), Weinmeister became an eager and active proselytizer for the CFL. He almost persuaded the Giants' star player Frank Gifford to bolt to Canada.

Considered something of a "clubhouse lawyer," Weinmeister's post-playing job was a good fit. In 1956 he became a labor organizer for the International Brotherhood of

Arnie Weinmeister, 1948. AP/WIDE WORLD PHOTOS

Teamsters in the Seattle area. Eventually he rose to become director of the Western Conference of Teamsters, a thirteen-state organization with nearly half a million dues-paying members. In the late 1980s Weinmeister was the powerful union's second vice president. He was subsequently elected president of Teamsters Joint Council 28, which covered locals in Washington, Idaho, and Alaska. Before retiring in 1992, he also served as secretary-treasurer of Local 117 in Seattle.

The Justice Department filed a lawsuit in 1988 to remove the Teamsters' senior leadership, contending that a "devil's pact" existed between the union and organized crime. Together with more than a dozen other officials (mainly executive board members), Weinmeister was accused of failing to "root out corruption." Although he managed to retain his position, many others were forced out of office. In a 1988 deposition, Weinmeister declared that his knowledge of organized crime and its operatives was limited to what he "read in the papers and saw in *The Godfather* motion pictures."

Weinmeister died at age seventy-seven of congestive heart failure in a Seattle hospital. His remains were cremated. He had previously married JoAnn ("Joey") Bruns, with whom he had three sons and two daughters. A testimony to Weinmeister's stature as a football player is his inclusion in the Pro Football Hall of Fame after playing only four seasons in the NFL. His teammate Tom Landry said of his ability, "If you want to know where the football is, look for Arnie's number 73 [jersey]."

★

Although there exists no formal biography of Weinmeister, his career is discussed in the following works: Steve Owen, *My Kind of Football* (1952); Barry Gottehrer, *The Giants of New York: The History of Professional Football's Most Fabulous Dynasty* (1963); Murray Olderman, *The Defenders* (1973); and Gerald Eskenazi, *There Were Giants in Those Days* (1987). An obituary is in the *New York Times* (7 July 2000).

JIM CAMPBELL

WEISS, Paul (*b.* 19 May 1901 in Manhattan, New York City; *d.* 5 July 2002 in Washington, D.C.), speculative philosopher, founder of the *Review of Metaphysics* and the Metaphysical Society of America, coeditor of the Charles Sanders Peirce papers, and author of twenty-six books and at least 155 scholarly articles.

Weiss was the second of four sons in a poor Jewish immigrant family on the Lower East Side of Manhattan. His father, Samuel Weiss, was a Hungarian smith and boilermaker. His mother, Emma (Rothschild) Weiss, the daughter of a German butcher, was a house servant. The boys were given Hebrew names, Isaac, Peretz, Moses, and Abraham, later Americanized respectively to Irving, Paul, Milford, and Arthur.

Weiss was always an avid reader but drifted without focus through childhood, adolescence, and his early twenties. He was not inclined toward any of the vocations available in his working-class neighborhood, and did not know what he wanted to do. He enrolled at City College of New York, part-time at age twenty-one and full-time at twenty-two. There, motivated by the professor of philosophy Morris R. Cohen, Weiss gained a purpose for his life and a vision for his career. He received his B.S. cum laude and Phi Beta Kappa in 1927. Cohen wanted him to attend graduate school at Columbia University in New York City to learn from John Dewey, but Weiss chose to become the student of Alfred North Whitehead at Harvard University in Cambridge, Massachusetts.

Harvard disappointed Weiss. Its narrow, one-sided approach to philosophy emphasized logic and discounted the speculative tradition. Weiss felt that Whitehead, Etienne Gilson, and to some extent C. I. Lewis, were the lone exceptions to this bias. Charles Hartshorne, a 1923 Harvard Ph.D. and postdoctoral research fellow, was editing the gigantic trove of manuscripts that the widow of the famous logician Charles Sanders Peirce had sold to Harvard. Weiss

Paul Weiss, February 1962. AP/WIDE WORLD PHOTOS

joined him in 1927 as coeditor and continued the project alone after Hartshorne went to the University of Chicago in 1928. Weiss wrote his dissertation under Whitehead on the nature of philosophical systems, took his Ph.D. in 1929, and spent a year as a Sears Traveling Fellow in Berlin and Paris.

Weiss married his sweetheart from the Lower East Side, Victoria Brodkin, on 27 October 1928. They had two children. Victoria died of lung cancer on 31 December 1953, and Weiss never remarried.

Weiss returned from Europe in 1930, taught for one year at Radcliffe College and Harvard, then in 1931 went to Bryn Mawr College in Pennsylvania, where, mostly on the strength of his first book, *Reality* (1938), he became full professor of philosophy in 1940. Impressed by the intellectual quality of Bryn Mawr students but wanting a greater number of graduate students, he accepted an offer from Yale University in New Haven, Connecticut, where he taught from 1946 to 1969, becoming the first Jew allowed to teach undergraduates there. Weiss was the Sterling Professor of Philosophy at Yale from 1962 to 1969.

In 1947, perceiving a dearth in the philosophical periodical literature then dominated by logical and linguistic analysis, Weiss founded the *Review of Metaphysics,* which soon became the premier journal in its field. He edited it until 1964, when he passed the reins to one of his Yale students from the 1950s, Richard J. Bernstein. Also striving to foster greater cooperation among speculative philosophers, Weiss founded the Philosophy of Education Society in 1941 and the Metaphysical Society of America in 1947.

Out of a job in 1969 because of Yale's mandatory retirement rules, Weiss and his son Jonathan, a lawyer, became advocates against age discrimination. In 1970 Fordham University in the Bronx, New York, offered Weiss a prestigious teaching position, but quickly rescinded, citing his age. In 1971 he sued Fordham for age discrimination, but lost the case when the U.S. Supreme Court refused to hear his appeal. Thereafter Weiss seldom missed an opportunity to mention that many of the judges who decided against him were in their eighties. Meanwhile the Catholic University of America in Washington, D. C., appointed him Heffer Visiting Professor of Philosophy on an indefinite series of annual contracts. In 1992 the university did not want to retain Weiss, again on account of his age, but pressure from Weiss's son, then director of Legal Services for the Elderly in New York City, and the federal Equal Employment Opportunity Commission compelled Catholic University to apologize and present Weiss with a two-year contract. He retired voluntarily in 1994 but continued to write until his death at his home in Washington, D.C., at age 101.

Weiss's thought was less systematic than one might expect from a logician turned metaphysician. His writings show tremendous breadth but are sometimes criticized for lack of depth and even coherence or relevance. He was not afraid to be wrong or to change his mind in public. His thought was eclectic and provocative, and he was known as a gadfly. Other than Whitehead and Peirce, his most significant influences were Plato, Aristotle, Gottfried Wilhelm Leibniz, Immanuel Kant, Georg Wilhelm Friedrich Hegel, Ralph Waldo Emerson, Friedrich Nietzsche, and Edmund Husserl. Weiss considered Hegel's *Phenomenology of Spirit* the best philosophical book ever written. He believed that philosophical thought required disdain for authority, distrust of easy solutions, and a readiness to challenge the impossible. Among his favorite sayings was, "A philosopher should always look for trouble."

In his seven-decade teaching career, Weiss inspired countless students, many of whom became outstanding philosophers through his mentorship. Many former students who excelled in other fields, such as the political commentator William F. Buckley and the entertainer Dick Cavett, also acknowledged Weiss's positive impact. An exception might be President George W. Bush, as Weiss gave him a C as a Yale undergraduate and criticized his assertion that Jesus Christ was the world's greatest philosopher. Probably Weiss's closest philosophical disciple was his 1938 Bryn Mawr doctoral student Isabel Scribner Stearns, whose dissertation, "The Nature of the Individual," harmonized Weiss's thought with that of Whitehead, Peirce, Lewis, H. H. Price, and Grace DeLaguna. Teaching at Bryn Mawr until 1979, Stearns tirelessly promoted Weiss's works, especially *Nature and Man* (1947) and *Reality*.

★

Weiss's papers from 1916 to 1975 are in the Southern Illinois University Library Special Collections. An autobiography and comprehensive bibliography are in Lewis Edwin Hahn, ed., *The Philosophy of Paul Weiss* (1995). A detailed tribute appeared in the *Washington Post* (19 May 2001), Weiss's 100th birthday. Two festschrifts have appeared: Irwin C. Lieb, ed., *Experience, Existence, and the Good* (1961), and Thomas Krettek, ed., *Creativity and Common Sense* (1987). Obituaries are in the *Washington Post* (7 July 2002), *New York Times* (24 July 2002), and *Yale Bulletin and Calendar* (30 Aug. 2002).

ERIC V.D. LUFT

WEISSKOPF, Victor Frederick (*b.* 19 September 1908 in Vienna, Austria; *d.* 21 April 2002 in Newton, Massachusetts), physicist who helped to build the first atomic bomb and who later became an activist for nuclear arms control.

Weisskopf was the son of Emile Weisskopf and Martha (Gut) Weisskopf. Growing up in Vienna between the two World Wars, Weisskopf was exposed to a culture that valued art, music, and especially science. He married Ellen Tvede on 5 September 1934; they had two children. After the death of his first wife in 1989, he married Duscha Schmid in May 1991.

During Weisskopf's youth, quantum mechanics was revolutionizing the study of physics. Under the direction of the renowned physicist Eugene Wigner, the young Weisskopf became interested in the new problem arising in physics. After receiving his Ph.D. from the University of Göttingen in 1931, Weisskopf studied throughout Europe with some of the most important names in twentieth-century physics, including Erwin Schrödinger at the University of Berlin in Germany, Niels Bohr at the University of Copenhagen in Denmark, and Wolfgang Pauli at the University of Zurich in Switzerland. While in Zurich, Weisskopf and Pauli used the new quantum theory to predict the existence of a new particle. The pair discovered this particle, the meson, more than a decade after the prediction of its existence.

Weisskopf left Nazi-controlled Europe in 1937, escaping much of the persecution experienced by Jewish scientists and intellectuals under the rule of Adolf Hitler. After brief stops in the Soviet Union (where he was offered, and briefly considered accepting, a permanent academic position), Copenhagen, and Cambridge, England, Weisskopf landed in the United States. His first position was at the University of Rochester in New York, where he worked for six years.

Victor F. Weisskopf, February 1956. GJON MILI/TIME LIFE PICTURES/ GETTY IMAGES

Weisskopf then moved to the Los Alamos National Laboratory in New Mexico in 1943, the same year he became a naturalized United States citizen. At Los Alamos, Weisskopf began working on the Manhattan Project, helping to build the world's first atomic bomb. During his tenure at Los Alamos, Weisskopf served as the deputy director of the theoretical physics group.

Although Weisskopf, like many scientists at Los Alamos and throughout the country, had reservations about the possible use of such a terrible weapon, the fear that Hitler would obtain the bomb first spurred them on. Germany's program, led by Werner Heisenberg, was never as advanced as many in the United States feared; however, when a group of scientists, including Weisskopf, examined a Heisenberg drawing smuggled out of Europe, they concluded that the primitive design was a fake, planted to throw Allied intelligence off track. It was not until after the war that the Allies realized the drawing was not a fake; rather, the Germans had lagged far behind the group at Los Alamos in developing an atomic weapon.

After the war Weisskopf joined the Massachusetts Institute of Technology (MIT) in Boston in 1946 as a professor of physics, a position he held (with a leave of absence in the 1960s to work in Europe) until his retirement in

1974. In addition to making many important contributions to quantum physics and particle physics during his long career at MIT, Weisskopf served as head of the Department of Physics from 1967 to 1973 and founded the Center for Theoretical Physics at that institution. When he retired, a symposium was organized at MIT and attended by the top physicists in the world. A collection of essays, *Physics and Our World: A Symposium in Honor of Victor F. Weisskopf* (1976), resulted from these meetings.

Weisskopf maintained a long relationship with the European Center for Nuclear Research (CERN), arriving at the Geneva, Switzerland, institute first as a guest professor in 1957. CERN, which operates one of the world's largest particle accelerators, was a place where scientists from all over Europe came to perform groundbreaking experiments in elementary particle physics. From 1961 to 1965 Weisskopf served as the director general of the renowned institute. The first experiments involving neutrino beams occurred at CERN during Weisskopf's tenure.

Weisskopf received many honors, including numerous honorary degrees and the prestigious Planck Medal in 1956. He was president of the American Physical Society from 1960 to 1961 and president of the American Academy of Arts and Sciences from 1976 to 1979. Weisskopf published countless papers and several influential books, including *Theoretical Nuclear Physics* (1952), a textbook coauthored with John M. Blatt; *Knowledge and Wonder: The Natural World As Man Knows It* (1962); *Concepts of Particle Physics* (1984–1986), with Kurt Gottfried; *The Privilege of Being a Physicist* (1989); and *The Joy of Insight: Passions of a Physicist* (1991).

Weisskopf was widely known also as an activist involved with the peace movement and for his warnings about the dangers of nuclear war. Groups such as the Emergency Committee of Atomic Scientists and the Federation of Atomic Scientists (the latter cofounded by Weisskopf) were instrumental in defining the roles of scientists in the new world of atomic weapons. Robert Oppenheimer, the director of the Manhattan Project, was a victim of the "Red scare" hysteria that swept the nation after the end of World War II. Weisskopf and other scientists who rallied to Oppenheimer's side risked their careers to defend their belief in the dangers of escalated weapons development. The Emergency Committee, organized by the Princeton physicist Leo Szilard and chaired by Albert Einstein, conducted a heated attack on U.S. government plans to develop a thermonuclear, or hydrogen, bomb. Weisskopf also became involved with a group of scientists who met to discuss the increasing public consciousness of and international cooperation in atomic research. This group, known as Pugwash after a city in Nova Scotia, Canada, where the first meeting took place, continues to play an active role in the interaction between scientists and nuclear policy makers.

Weisskopf died of a heart attack at his home in Newton, Massachusetts, at the age of ninety-three. His work as a physicist and as an activist played foundational roles in twentieth-century physics.

★

Weisskopf's *The Joy of Insight: Passions of a Physicist* (1991) is semiautobiographical. For information about Weisskopf's role in the development of nuclear weapons, see Thomas Powers, *Heisenberg's War* (1993) and Richard Rhodes, *The Making of the Atomic Bomb* (1986). Obituaries are in the *New York Times* and *Washington Post* (both 25 Aug. 2002), and the *CERN Courier* 42, no. 5 (2003).

W. TODD TIMMONS

WELLS, Herman B. (*b.* 7 June 1902 in Jamestown, Indiana; *d.* 18 March 2000 in Bloomington, Indiana), president of Indiana University who presided over that institution's expansion and development into a respected research center.

The son of Joseph Granville Wells, a teacher and banker, and Anna Bernice (Harting) Wells, a housewife, Wells (whose middle name was the letter B) grew up in Jamestown and Lebanon, Indiana. After a year at the commerce college of the University of Illinois, he transferred to the business school of Indiana University in Bloomington. He graduated with a B.S. in 1924, enjoying association with his fellow students Hoagy Carmichael, the musician; Charles Halleck, the future U.S. congressman; and the newspaper owner Nelson Poynter.

After two years in a Lebanon bank, Wells returned to the university for a master's degree in economics, earning his A.M. in 1927. He then attended the University of Wisconsin to work on a doctorate but gave it up for a post with the Indiana Bankers Association. During the depression years he helped Governor Paul V. McNutt reorganize the state's banks. This led to appointment as dean of his alma mater's business school in 1935 and as university president in 1937.

The twenty-six years of Wells's presidency of Indiana University saw remarkable advances not merely in state appropriations but also in the quality of the faculty. A gregarious man and fifth-generation Hoosier (native of Indiana), he wielded much influence in the state legislature. He improved the university by seeking out young, promising scholars from around the country for faculty appointments, a tactic he had employed as dean of the business school. He also traveled to other campuses and asked department chairpersons about the availability of staff members, occasionally inviting the chairpersons themselves. He was careful in choosing deans and checked up on them in an enterprising way: a lifelong bachelor who enjoyed food and possessed a sizable girth, he accepted all faculty invi-

Herman B. Wells, 1959. AP/WIDE WORLD PHOTOS

tations for dinner, taking advantage of these opportunities to talk with his hosts about their academic problems.

In the years after World War II he vigorously defended academic freedom, no easy task in the case of the faculty member Alfred C. Kinsey, the controversial investigator of human sexuality. Seeking to make the university more international, Wells solicited government programs abroad, notably in Thailand, and welcomed foreign students to his predominantly Hoosier institution. He selected the dean of the university's school of music, who, in turn, built that division into one of the finest in the nation.

Wells was a member of the U.S. mission to Greece in 1947, an adviser on education and cultural affairs during the American occupation of Germany in 1947–1948, and a delegate to the twelfth session of the U.N. General Assembly in 1957. Upon retiring from the presidency in 1962, Wells became the university's first chancellor, a largely honorary position he held until his death at his home in Bloomington. He died from a heart ailment at age ninety-seven and is buried in Oddfellows Cemetery in Jamestown.

★

Wells's papers are in the university archives at Indiana University. His autobiography is *Being Lucky: Reminiscences and Reflections* (1980). Obituaries are in the *Bloomington Herald-Times, Chicago Sun-Times,* and *Indianapolis Star* (all 20 Mar. 2000), and the *New York Times* (21 Mar. 2000).

ROBERT H. FERRELL

WELLSTONE, Paul David (*b.* 21 July 1944 in Washington, D.C.; *d.* 25 October 2002 near Eveleth, Minnesota), college teacher and progressive Democrat from Minnesota who served as a U.S. senator from 1991 until his death in a plane crash in 2002.

Wellstone was the son of Russian immigrants Leon Wellstone, a former writer for the U.S. Information Service, and Minnie (Danishepsky) Wellstone, a worker in a junior high school cafeteria. Born in Washington, D.C., Wellstone grew up in suburban Arlington, Virginia. He did not excel at academic subjects but proved a remarkable lightweight wrestler, a skill that enabled him to enter the University of North Carolina in Chapel Hill (UNC). There he took interest in the civil rights movement. Completing his B.A. in 1965, he remained at UNC to work on a Ph.D. in political science, which he completed in 1969 with a dissertation on the roots of black militancy. While still an undergraduate, he married Sheila Ison on 24 August 1963.

With a growing family—they eventually had two sons and a daughter—the Wellstones had no time for the student activist movement so prominent during the 1960s. The family moved to Northfield, Minnesota, in 1969, where Wellstone obtained an appointment at Carleton College,

Paul D. Wellstone, March 2001. AP/WIDE WORLD PHOTOS

teaching courses in political science. There he flourished in and out of the classroom, attracting many students. He did not bother with the usual academic procedure, which involved dividing attention between teaching and the production of articles and books. The college denied him tenure, but protests of his students persuaded the authorities to revoke their decision, and he remained on the faculty until 1990. Wellstone's reputation as a progressive activist was on display during this period, as he took part in workers' strikes in and around Northfield and on two occasions was arrested.

Politics beckoned, and in 1982 Wellstone ran for state auditor and lost on the Democratic-Farmer-Labor ticket. In 1988 he was cochairman of the state committee supporting Jesse Jackson in the presidential primary, and in the November election cochairman of the committee to elect Michael S. Dukakis.

His prominence around the state led to his challenge of the incumbent Republican senator Rudy Boschwitz in 1990, an effort that at first seemed unlikely to succeed. However, Wellstone displayed the extraordinary electoral abilities that would bring him two Senate terms and nomination to a third. He ran a poor man's campaign, $1 million against his opponent's $7 million, but carefully used this financial disparity to his advantage. One of his former students made a tape for use on television and speeded it up, with the candidate explaining that he had to talk fast because he didn't have Boschwitz's extra $6 million. Wellstone toured the state in an old green school bus. In this first important contest, he showed the people-to-people electioneering that was his special talent. On the circuit he was down-to-earth, friendly, and interested in everyone. Audiences small and large responded to his shouted speeches in which he announced in a series of sentences all the groups that were not in favor of what his opponent favored. After the recital would come the summing up, "And we are going to win!" which raised a hearty cheer. To the surprise of many doubters, he won the Senate seat of his rival, with 50.4 percent of the vote. The exuberance of this campaign was well illustrated in a sign a supporter held up as the senator-elect and his family left for the nation's capital. It read, "Bye bye Boschwitz."

Wellstone ran successfully against Boschwitz again in 1996, and at the time of his death was in a hard-fought campaign against a former supporter, Norm Coleman, who had been mayor of Saint Paul, Minnesota, and shifted to the Republican Party. Coleman obtained the Senate seat after Wellstone's death by winning an election against the former U.S. vice president Walter Mondale.

The senator, having conducted a populist campaign in 1990 and winning on it, did not disappoint his supporters. During his eleven years in the Senate, Wellstone showed well what critics described as his foolish positions and what friends found endearing, if not altogether practical. His ebullience brought attention. He would bounce into a room, not merely walk in. Small in stature and balding, he smiled at everyone. Always he did what seemed right in his own eyes. His remarks about his new colleagues were rarely up to Senate standards of gentility. His most notable pronouncement at the beginning of his incumbency was in regard to the conservative Senator Jesse Helms of North Carolina, who, Wellstone said, "represents everything to me that is ugly and wrong and awful about politics." After this dismissal of Helms, so typical of Wellstone, the freshman senator made Helms's acquaintance and grew to like him. They even collaborated in legislation seeking to advance human rights in China.

As a legislator Wellstone did not shine, and perhaps his only triumph was in regard to his interest in helping individuals with Parkinson's disease, which both of his parents had suffered from. He attended Senate hearings that looked to increase support for research into Parkinson's, and the result was an extra $100 million appropriation. During the 2002 campaign he discovered that his own marked limp in walking was a symptom of multiple sclerosis. In the Senate he represented his own views rather than adhering to any party line, and his points of view were backed up by his supporters whatever the legislative result. It was said that he specialized in the losing end of 99–1 votes. None of this fazed him, for he was in the Minnesota tradition of independent-minded senators such as Mondale, Eugene McCarthy, and Hubert Humphrey.

In Minnesota, interest in foreign affairs never had been prominent, and Wellstone was a believer in allowing other nations to handle their own problems. His first Senate vote was against a resolution endorsing the 1991 Gulf War, sponsored by President George H. W. Bush. One of his last votes was to vote against the resolution authorizing military action against Iraq, an action favored by President George W. Bush. Friends in the Democratic Party, judging that popular sentiment was in favor of the push for war, advised him against the second vote, given his tight race against Coleman. In keeping with his independent streak, he refused to change his mind about the vote.

In his last months Wellstone was much bothered by what he deemed the failure of the Democratic Party to take anticapitalist positions and to oppose the Bush administration's agenda in both foreign and domestic affairs. As he wrote in his last political ad: "I don't represent the big oil companies, I don't represent the big pharmaceutical companies, I don't represent the Enrons of this world. But know what, they already have great representation in Washington. It's the rest of the people that need it." His supporters in his home state had been union workers, family farmers, peace activists, abortion rights campaigners, and racial and ethnic minorities. When he died, along with his wife and daughter, three campaign workers, and two pilots in an airplane crash near Eveleth, Minnesota, he was on his way in a snowstorm to attend the funeral of a humble supporter in northeastern Minnesota. A member of the Minnesota Democratic-Farmer-Labor Party, the long-time state party of reform, he never let his constituents forget his progressive commitment. He sometimes described himself as a member of the democratic wing of the Democratic Party.

He briefly considered running for the presidency in 2000. He was the first to organize an exploratory presidential committee for that election, doing so in 1998, and his was the first to close.

Testimony to his unforgettable personality was in evidence when newspaper headlines and radio and television reports announced his death. Former Republican senator Robert Dole of Kansas, with whom he seldom agreed, broke into tears when he described Wellstone as "a decent, genuine guy who had a different philosophy from almost everyone else in the Senate." The *New York Times* celebrated his record of fearless positions on controversial issues. The *Wall Street Journal* published an appreciation by an acknowledged conservative reporter under the heading, "Not a faker, just plain honest." Speaking to thousands of anti–Iraq War demonstrators in Washington, D.C., the day after Wellstone's death, the poet and rock star Patti Smith lamented his loss, adding, "He would not want us to give him a moment of silence." Wellstone would have liked what she said, for he was fond of organized labor's slogan, "Don't mourn, organize." Wellstone is buried in Lakewood Cemetery in Minneapolis.

★

Donald J. McGrath and Dane Smith, *Professor Wellstone Goes to Washington: The Inside Story of a Grassroots U.S. Senate Campaign* (1995), discusses Wellstone's first sizable effort in electioneering in 1990. Paul Wellstone, *The Conscience of a Liberal: Reclaiming the Compassionate Agenda* (2001), takes its stand against Senator Barry Goldwater's *The Conscience of a Conservative* (1960), though Wellstone admired Goldwater's outspokenness. Appraisals of Wellstone include Fred Barnes, "Paul Wellstone: Not a Faker, Just Plain Honest," *Wall Street Journal* (28 Oct. 2002); Gloria Borger, "Paul Wellstone: 1944–2002," *U.S. News and World Report* (4 Nov. 2002); and the *Nation* (18 Nov. 2002). Obituaries are in the *New York Times* and *Washington Post* (both 26 Oct. 2002).

ROBERT H. FERRELL

WELTY, Eudora Alice (*b.* 13 April 1909 in Jackson, Mississippi; *d.* 23 July 2001 in Jackson, Mississippi), renowned short-story writer, novelist, and photographer.

The daughter of Chestina Andrews Welty, a native West Virginian, and Christian Webb Welty, a native of Ohio,

Eudora Welty. AP/WIDE WORLD PHOTOS

Welty was born and reared in Mississippi with her two younger brothers. Her father rose through the ranks of the Lamar Life Insurance Company's home office in Jackson, becoming the company president in 1931. Her mother remained at home, though she had been a schoolteacher before marriage. The family was a close-knit one, and Welty's parents were devoted to each other and to their children. The nature of family life would become one of Welty's important fictional themes. She stressed the blessings of loving relationships, but she also acknowledged the difficulties inherent in them, in particular, the tensions between parents who seek to protect their children and children who are striving for independence. Welty attended public schools in Jackson, graduating at age sixteen from Jackson High School. Her parents thought her too young to attend a distant college, but they agreed that she might enroll at the Mississippi State College for Women in Columbus. There she studied for two years before entering the University of Wisconsin–Madison, where she majored in English and received her B.A. in 1929.

Upon graduating, Welty returned to Jackson for a year, writing occasional feature stories for a local newspaper. In September 1930 she and several friends from Jackson enrolled in Columbia University in New York City. Upon her father's insistence, Welty studied at the School of Business, although her true interests lay elsewhere. She attended lectures by noted scholars of literature and psychology, and she enjoyed her ready access to art museums and galleries, classical concerts, Broadway shows, and Harlem jazz venues. In September 1931, at the start of her second academic year at Columbia, Welty was called home. Her father was ill with leukemia and would not live through the autumn. At age twenty-two Welty witnessed the fragility of human life and recognized the urgency implicit in life's brevity. These would be central concerns in her fiction.

After working for a time at a Jackson radio station, Welty sought a more challenging position in New York City, but during the Great Depression such opportunities were limited. Instead, Welty remained in Jackson, working as a society columnist for the *Memphis Commercial Appeal;* then, for five months in 1936, as a junior publicity agent for the Works Progress Administration (WPA); and in 1939 as a photographer and writer at the Mississippi Advertising Commission. Quite apart from any job, Welty was active with her camera. Her father had been a photography enthusiast, and she followed in his footsteps. Early in the 1930s, having seen and disliked Doris Ulmann's sentimental photographs in *Roll, Jordan, Roll,* Welty hoped to publish a book containing snapshots of Mississippi's African-American community. Such a book did not come to pass for almost forty years, but in 1936 and 1937 two New York City galleries mounted exhibitions of Welty's photographs.

In 1936 she published her first short story, "Death of a Traveling Salesman," and over the next five years published nineteen other stories, seven in the *Southern Review,* edited by Cleanth Brooks and Robert Penn Warren. This fiction captured the attention of the writer Katherine Anne Porter, who tried to help Welty find a publishing house. Welty did not see book publication, however, until she obtained the services of the agent Diarmuid Russell, who managed to place two stories with the *Atlantic Monthly.* Russell and the editor John Woodburn next persuaded Doubleday to bring out a book by Welty. *A Curtain of Green* was published in 1941. The seventeen stories in this volume range from the comic to the tragic, from realistic portraits to surrealistic ones, and display Welty's wry wit, keen observation of detail, and sure rendering of dialect. Here Welty at times translated into fiction memories of people and places she had earlier photographed, and the volume's three stories focusing upon African-American characters exemplify the empathy that was present in her photos. The writer Toni Morrison later observed that Welty wrote "about black people in a way that few white men have ever been able to write. It's not patronizing, not romanticizing—it's the way they should be written about."

Before publishing her first story collection, Welty completed a novella, *The Robber Bridegroom* (1942), which partook of folklore, fairy tale, and Mississippi's legendary history. More than thirty years later, this long story was transformed by Alfred Uhry and Robert Waldman into a musical that ran on Broadway. A year after her novella appeared, Welty published a third book of fiction, *The Wide Net* (1943), which contained stories that were more darkly lyrical than those in her first volume. The World War II years, however, slowed Welty's production. Worry about John Robinson, the young man with whom she was romantically involved and who would remain her close friend even though they never married, about her brothers, and about other friends serving in the military left her with few words for fiction. Instead, she spent several months in 1944 working at the *New York Times Book Review*. During these difficult years she managed to write a short story, "Delta Cousins," which she sent to Robinson overseas. The story was never published, but it led Welty to write *Delta Wedding* (1946), a novel completed shortly after the war ended. Set in the Mississippi Delta during 1923, the book at first was criticized as a nostalgic portrait of the plantation South. Critical opinion has since counteracted such views, seeing in the novel, to use Albert Devlin's words, the "probing for a humane order."

The peacetime return of family and friends was exhilarating for Welty, but she found herself increasingly discouraged by the provincial mindset of many Mississippians and by the nature of Mississippi politics, especially the election of white supremacists such as Theodore Bilbo and John Rankin. In late 1946 Welty traveled to San Francisco, where she spent four months living near Robinson. In August 1947 Welty lectured at a writers' conference in Seattle and returned for ten weeks to San Francisco. Both her dissatisfaction with her home state and her enduring love of it took fictional form during these years, and her stories written during this period set the limitations of small-town southern life against its strengths. *The Golden Apples* (1949) is a book of seven interlocking stories that trace life in the fictional town of Morgana, Mississippi, from the turn of the century until the late 1940s. When Welty began writing the stories, however, she had no idea that they would be connected. Then, midway through the composition process, she realized that she was writing about a common cast of characters, that the characters of one story seemed to be younger or older versions of the characters in other stories, and she decided to create a book that was neither novel nor story collection. It is perhaps the greatest triumph of her distinguished career.

In 1949 Welty received her second Guggenheim Fellowship and traveled abroad, as she had been unable to do during the war years. She journeyed through Italy and France, making lengthy stays in Paris and Florence before going to England and Ireland, where she met and became a friend of the Anglo-Irish writer Elizabeth Bowen. Welty subsequently returned to Italy and, in June 1950, sailed home. She again traveled to England and Ireland in 1951, and she lectured at Cambridge University in 1954. Welty drew upon her European experiences in two stories, which she eventually grouped with "Circe," a story narrated by the witch-goddess, and four stories set in the American South. These stories often investigate the multiple ways that individuals can live and create meaning for themselves without being rooted in time and place. But before collecting them in *The Bride of the Innisfallen* (1955), Welty published *The Ponder Heart* (1954), a comic novella that was dramatized by Jerome Chodorov and Joseph Fields and became a Broadway hit in 1956.

After the pleasure of seeing her novella adapted for the stage, Welty encountered difficult personal times. Her brother Walter was stricken with a virulent form of arthritis, complications of which claimed his life in 1959. During this time, Welty's mother suffered from eye problems and later had a series of strokes, including one that took her life in January 1966. Additionally, in October 1965 Welty's brother Edward fell, broke his neck, and was hospitalized. In 1966, four days after his mother had died, Edward succumbed to a brain infection. Welty was bereft. She had been working on a massive novel since 1955, but the need to care for her mother, help Walter and his wife with their children, and provide support to Edward had prevented her from completing it.

She had difficulty turning back to the novel so long in progress. Instead, she wrote a novella that dealt with the experience of loss and grief and that incorporated a good bit of biographical information about her mother. "The Optimist's Daughter" was published in the *New Yorker* in 1969, by which time Welty was readying her lengthy comic novel for publication. In 1970 *Losing Battles* was finally in print. Set in the 1930s, it describes a family reunion and the conflict of a traditional Mississippi family with the forces of modernity. Welty's burst of creativity continued when she published her depression-era photographs under the title *One Time, One Place* (1971) and when she revised and expanded "The Optimist's Daughter" for book publication in 1972. *The Optimist's Daughter* received the Pulitzer Prize in 1973.

From the 1970s until her death, Welty's genius for friendship—a genius cherished by her family and old friends at home and by such literary friends as William Maxwell, William Jay Smith, Reynolds Price, and Mary Lou Aswell—continued to expand, and she came to number the writers Ross Macdonald and V. S. Pritchett among those she held closest. Three publishing triumphs came to Welty during these years. In 1980 she gathered her four books of short stories and two powerful *New Yorker* stories, written during and about the civil rights movement, into one volume, *The Collected Stories of Eudora Welty*. In 1983

Welty delivered three autobiographical lectures at Harvard University and then published them as *One Writer's Beginnings* (1984), the first best-seller in the history of Harvard University Press. In 1989 *Photographs,* an extensive collection of images taken in the 1930s and 1940s, received critical acclaim.

During her last three decades, Welty periodically worked at fiction but completed nothing to her own high standards, standards that made her a literary celebrity. She appeared on televised interviews, received the Presidential Medal of Freedom (1980) and the French Legion of Honor (1996), served as the subject of a British Broadcasting Corporation documentary, and became the first living writer to be published in the Library of America series. After a short illness, and as the result of cardiopulmonary failure, Welty died at age ninety-two in Jackson, her lifelong home, where she is buried.

Welty's achievements as a short-story writer, novelist, and photographer are profoundly significant. In her stories Welty used a wide variety of modes and styles, never falling into repetitive patterns and always developing innovative approaches to short fiction. Welty began each of her novels with the plan to write a short story, and the novels have the intricate structure, the detailed interplay of images, that characterize the shorter form. Still, her approach to the novel was different each time. She worked on *The Optimist's Daughter* and *Losing Battles* almost simultaneously in the late 1960s and succeeded in producing two major novels: one a taut contemporary narrative from a single point of view, walking a tightrope between irony and affirmation, and the other a large, sprawling narrative set in the past and recounted by many voices, boldly comic but also clear-eyed and hard-hitting.

Welty's focus on the inner lives of characters has long been recognized as complex and compelling, but in the twenty-first century scholars also have identified and discussed the political import of her fiction, notably its incisive commentary upon questions of race, poverty, gender, and community. A parallel concern with both inner and outer worlds is evident in Welty's photographs, which at once capture resilient individuals in revealing moments and document the racism and poverty that afflicted Mississippi.

These powerful photographs notwithstanding, Welty's most substantial contribution to American culture lies in her fiction. Her unflinching examination of crucial issues—love and death, hope and despair, dominance and subjection, tolerance and prejudice—her diverse and fully rendered characters, and her supple prose, be it fierce or mystical, colloquial or highly metaphoric, have influenced generations of writers in the United States and abroad. Welty, as Reynolds Price noted, ranks with the Russian writers Ivan Turgenev, Count Leo Tolstoy, and Anton Chekhov, her "peers for breadth and depth."

★

The Mississippi Department of Archives and History in Jackson, Mississippi, holds most of Welty's manuscripts, photographic negatives, and correspondence. The Harry Ransom Humanities Research Center at the University of Texas at Austin also houses important Welty manuscripts and correspondence. Welty's autobiography is *One Writer's Beginnings* (1984). She collected many of her book reviews, essays on the art of writing, and other essays in *The Eye of the Story* (1979). Michael Kreyling, *Author and Agent* (1991), details the long friendship and professional association of Welty and Diarmuid Russell. Ann Waldron, *Eudora: A Writer's Life* (1998), is an unauthorized biography of Welty. There are numerous book-length critical studies of Welty's fiction, including Ruth Vande Kieft, *Eudora Welty* (1962; rev. ed., 1987); Michael Kreyling, *Eudora Welty's Achievement of Order* (1980); Albert J. Devlin, *Eudora Welty's Chronicle: A Story of Mississippi Life* (1983); Gail L. Mortimer, *Daughter of the Swan: Love and Knowledge in Eudora Welty's Fiction* (1994); Ruth D. Weston, *Gothic Traditions and Narrative Techniques in the Fiction of Eudora Welty* (1994); and Suzanne Marrs, *One Writer's Imagination: The Fiction of Eudora Welty* (2002). Obituaries are in the *New York Times* and *Washington Post* (both 24 July 2001).

Suzanne Marrs

WHITE, Byron Raymond ("Whizzer") (*b.* 8 June 1917 in Fort Collins, Colorado; *d.* 15 April 2002 in Denver, Colorado), U.S. Supreme Court justice.

White was the second of two sons born to Alpha Albert White, who managed a branch office of a lumber company, and Maude (Burger) White, a homemaker. In 1920 the family moved to Wellington, Colorado. Neither of White's parents had graduated from high school, but they stressed education. White won a scholarship that the University of Colorado awarded to the valedictorian of every high school class in the state. A junior Phi Beta Kappa, he graduated from the University of Colorado in 1938 at the top of his class and won a Rhodes scholarship to Oxford University in England. He was also elected student body president and the most popular man on campus, and was the only candidate for the highest honor at graduation, "cane-bearer." But he was better known as an athlete.

White was All-Conference in football, basketball, and baseball. In football he became a legend. Switched to full-back for the 1935 season, he was a triple threat—to pass, run, or punt. He also played defense. In 1937 he was the leading scorer in the country and averaged 246 all-purpose yards gained per game, a national record that lasted for fifty-one years. At six feet, two inches tall, and weighing 190 pounds, he had the speed either to run around defenders or to run over them. "He was hard as iron all over,"

Byron R. White. THE LIBRARY OF CONGRESS

said an assistant coach. "He was just plain mean and ornery and tenacious. But he wasn't dirty." White also kept his job doing kitchen duty at a fraternity house.

Despite all the media attention, he carried himself with what one classmate called a "painfully genuine" modesty. This was difficult. "He's in the headlines more than Mr. Roosevelt," one journalist wrote. One reason was his nickname. In 1935, because of his speed, a Denver sportswriter referred to him as "a real whizzer." From then on, he was known as "Whizzer" White. White detested the nickname. Asked by a waitress in Washington, D.C., in 1961 if he was Whizzer White, he said, "I was."

In the fall of 1938 White postponed his Rhodes scholarship to play with the Pittsburgh Pirates (later Steelers) of the fledgling National Football League (NFL) for a record starting salary of $15,800, which he used to pay his way through law school. He led the league in rushing and was named rookie of the year, as well as a member of the All-NFL team; then he went to Oxford. In the spring of 1939 he met the future president John F. Kennedy in France and toured Munich with him that summer. White called Kennedy "the most fun-producing man I ever met."

White entered Yale Law School in New Haven, Con-

necticut, in the fall of 1939 and led his class that year. Potter Stewart, a classmate and later a colleague on the Supreme Court, seeing him studying in the library wearing steel-rimmed glasses during the week and reading about his football exploits on weekends, thought of White as "both Clark Kent and Superman." Traded to the Detroit Lions in 1940, he again led the NFL in rushing. Dubbed "the one-man football team" and praised for his defense as much as his offense, he was voted All-League. He played in 1941, but the lack of continuity in his legal education limited the courses he could take and denied him an opportunity for sustained reflection. White graduated from Yale in 1946.

As a naval intelligence officer in the South Pacific during World War II, White cowrote a report on the Japanese sinking of PT-109, the patrol boat that Kennedy commanded in the Solomon Islands. His report effectively cleared Kennedy. The two spent a month together at the same base, and developed a warm friendship.

On 15 June 1946 White married Marion Stearns, the daughter of the president of the University of Colorado; they had two children. She "softened his edges—or some of them," according to a friend.

In 1946 White turned down an offer to teach at Yale Law School. He wanted to serve as a law clerk to Supreme Court Justice William O. Douglas, but Douglas took only graduates of West Coast law schools and instead set up a clerkship for White with Chief Justice Fred M. Vinson. White moved to Denver after turning down offers from two leading Washington law firms when they would not meet his demand for a partnership after two years. Joining the small firm of Lewis, Grant, Newton, Davis and Henry, he was largely an office lawyer, negotiating real estate and business deals. His memoranda were exhaustive, as White almost physically attacked the library, giving new meaning to the phrase "hit the books." He was not in court much; when he was, he was effective rather than eloquent. Scornful of theory, his approach was rooted in the facts of a case.

"I want to establish my practice, contribute to the community, and keep my name out of the goddam newspapers," White told a friend. But fame accompanied him wherever he went. He escaped it by dry fly fishing, a lifelong passion, and he was active in numerous civic causes. He rejected numerous offers to run for office and was a neighborhood organizer for the Democratic Party. In 1959 White organized the Colorado Committee for Kennedy, and after Kennedy won the Democratic nomination in 1960, he became codirector of the nationwide Citizens for Kennedy. He hit it off so well with Robert Kennedy, the candidate's brother and campaign manager, that Robert wanted to make him chairman of the Democratic National Committee. White wished to return to Denver after Kennedy's victory, but at his brother's direction Robert, designated the new attorney general, offered him the position of deputy attorney general. His bond with Robert having become too strong to say no, White accepted.

Working outward from contemporaries at Yale, White chose nearly all of the assistant attorneys general. He spent five days in Alabama in May 1961, successfully leading a contingent of more than 500 National Guardsmen to protect "Freedom Riders" seeking to integrate interstate buses. He was in charge of selecting all federal judges. With the attorney general often at the White House, White ran the Justice Department far more than most deputy attorneys general. His "healthy skepticism" and "probing questioning of premises" provided a sounding board for department lawyers, and his decisions were instrumental in giving the Kennedy administration's Justice Department a lasting reputation as one of the best in history.

On 6 March 1962, Supreme Court Justice Charles E. Whittaker, mentally and physically exhausted, entered the hospital. On 16 March he retired, effective 1 April. The Kennedy administration considered several candidates, most notably the federal court of appeals judge William H. Hastie, who would have been the first African American on the Court, but John Kennedy really had only one person in mind from the beginning. White was a friend he knew well, admired enormously, and trusted. White was nonplussed. "Why would the president want to do something like that?" he asked Robert Kennedy. "I guess they want to put me out to pasture early," he told a friend. White "was not very enthusiastic, really," Robert Kennedy later noted. But in White's words, he also "wanted to get out of the political front lines" because of an ulcer condition that had hospitalized him three times in the past year. (The ailment also limited the Whites' social life because, as his wife said, most Washington hostesses "do not serve Cream of Wheat for a dinner diet.") "I never wanted to be a judge," White later admitted, "I said to the president I would give it a try." The Senate confirmed him without a roll call on 11 April 1962.

The Court was on the verge of the greatest expansion of the rights of individuals and criminal defendants in history. White largely disagreed with this development. "The trouble with these liberals up here," he told a friend, "is that they think they have all the answers to social problems like crime and race, and what's worse, they're putting them into the Constitution." He accorded a strong presumption of validity to the actions of Congress and the executive branch. One of the Constitution's main goals, White believed, was to consolidate national power to cope with national problems, and the Court's role was simply "to decide cases."

White decided cases on the narrowest grounds possible and avoided sweeping pronouncements. "The point is there," he said. "It doesn't need any window dressing." He was suspicious of intellectuals, and his opinions marshaled past decisions and arguments, marching forward relentlessly. Imbued with his impatience to conclude an argument, his writing was frequently ambiguous by design, and free of theory or rhetorical flourishes. They plowed through problems rather than running around them. "He wrote a lot like he played," observed a friend. "Not pretty, not graceful, but he got the job done and didn't leave anything standing in his wake."

On the bench, the gravelly voiced White was a tough interrogator who insisted on a direct answer or swiveled in his chair to turn his back on a floundering lawyer who did not grasp his hint of help or whose argument he did not like. Off the bench, in public, his brusque manner made many uncomfortable. Privately, White could be caring and had a talent for whimsy that included riding a unicycle indoors. He worked hard to keep this compassionate side from any public view. He was "at his best when things were the worst," said a clerk White called daily when the clerk was hospitalized with cancer.

White was one of the first to arrive at Robert Kennedy's house after President Kennedy was assassinated in November 1963, and walked with him, his arm around Robert's shoulders. Robert Kennedy's assassination in 1968 led White to question whether he was "in the best place to make the best contribution" to society. In the 1970s he toyed with the idea of leaving the Supreme Court to return to Colorado to practice law, only to drop it when President Jimmy Carter was not reelected in 1980.

White dissented in *Roe* v. *Wade* in 1973, calling it "the only illegitimate decision the Court rendered during my tenure. In every other case, there was something in the Constitution you could point to for support. There, nothing." White's claim that "for no reason at all" a woman is entitled to an abortion struck many as insensitive even though he said that if he had been a legislator, he would have been pro-choice. He did not consider *Roe* a binding precedent. In 1986 White upheld for the Court a Georgia law that made private, consensual homosexual sex a crime. "To argue that the Constitution's right to privacy includes such conduct is at best facetious," he wrote.

Starting in the 1970s, White became central to the Court's functioning. He felt "most comfortable" with more conservative colleagues. Memoranda analyzing cases were his most valuable contributions to the Court as an institution. In this capacity as a pure legal analyst, he was clear, crisp, and forceful. He dissented in the 1976 campaign finance case, *Buckley* v. *Valeo,* arguing that Congress could limit both contributions to and spending on candidates. "Judges have an exaggerated view of their role in our polity," he said afterwards. "It can't be . . . : 'The First Amendment, therefore . . . Congress has the authority. . . .'" He dissented from the Court's 1983 decision to invalidate the legislative veto, the practice under which one house of Congress nullified regulations. His 1984 opinion for the Court permitted prosecutors for the first time to use evidence that was obtained illegally but in "good faith."

When Chief Justice William H. Rehnquist in open court noted White's thirtieth anniversary on the bench in 1992 and turned to him, White replied, "you may hold your applause." By then he had started to reflect on his career on the Court as he never before had done. One area was freedom of the press. White had intensely disliked the press since 1938, when New York sportswriters had scrutinized him intently at the National Invitational Tournament, established largely because of the clamor they had raised to watch him play basketball. "It was their job," he said later. "But I didn't like it, even so." He regretted hastily joining the Court's landmark 1964 opinion, *New York Times* v. *Sullivan,* expanding the protection against libel as applied to public figures, he said. And "I wish I had been more consistent in the employment discrimination area." In 1979 White joined the Court's upholding of a voluntary program that set aside half the positions in an in-plant training program for minorities. But by 1987 he argued that this decision should be overruled. His fears that affirmative action would degenerate into academic admissions and employment decisions driven by race had become apparent, he said. "You can't take an innocent man's job away. You can't call that a remedy."

White retired from the Court in 1993, his tenure longer than all but eight other justices in the Court's history. The physical competitiveness remained. Into his sixties, he played basketball with law clerks in "the highest court in the land," on the Court's top floor, throwing elbows with abandon. He died of complications from pneumonia, and is buried at Saint John's Episcopal Cathedral in Denver.

Individualism was White's defining trait. "No one knows what Byron is thinking," one justice noted. "If he disagreed with you," said another, "you had to endure the frozen glare." Political currents did not affect White. "I don't have a doctrinal legacy," White admitted after his retirement, "I shouldn't." What he left was a legacy of public service of "iron integrity and rigid probity."

★

For information about White's life and career, see Victor S. Navasky, *Kennedy Justice* (1971); James F. Simon, *In His Own Image: The Supreme Court in Richard Nixon's America* (1973); Arthur M. Schlesinger, Jr., *Robert Kennedy and His Times* (1978); Ken Gormley, *Archibald Cox: Conscience of a Nation* (1997); Dennis J. Hutchinson, *The Man Who Once Was Whizzer White: A Portrait of Justice Byron R. White* (1998); and David G. Savage, *Turning Right: The Making of the Rehnquist Supreme Court* (1992). See also Dennis J. Hutchinson, "'So Much for History,'" *Legal Times* (22 Apr. 2002). Obituaries are in the *Denver Post, Los Angeles Times, New York Times,* and *Washington Post* (all 16 Apr. 2002).

ROGER K. NEWMAN

WHYTE, William Foote   (*b.* 11 June 1914 in Springfield, Massachusetts; *d.* 16 July 2000 in Ithaca, New York), sociologist whose *Street Corner Society* (1943) established the method of "participatory action research."

Whyte was the only child of John Whyte, a professor of German, and Caroline (Van Sickle) Whyte, a homemaker. As a child he moved with his family throughout the New York City area, including the Bronx and Caldwell, New Jersey, before finally settling in Bronxville, an affluent suburb. Whyte was an inquisitive child, and a creative writer and researcher. At the age of sixteen, while still in high school, he worked for the *Bronxville Press* and wrote numerous articles on the community's public schools. During the early 1930s Whyte traveled with his father to Germany, where he witnessed firsthand the demagoguery and fanaticism of the new Nazi regime.

Whyte enrolled at Swarthmore College near Philadelphia in 1932, and through Quaker contacts he was able to witness urban slum life firsthand as an undergraduate. Inner-city life would remain an interest throughout his early career. After earning a B.A. in economics in 1936, Whyte became a junior fellow at Harvard University in Cambridge, Massachusetts, but years later, in *Participant, Observer: An Autobiography* (1994), he would reveal his disdain for Harvard's environment and what he regarded as its lack of commitment to apply academic study to useful social ends.

In 1937 Whyte moved in with the Orlandi family in Boston's North End, and this relationship allowed him an entrée into the gangs of this urban slum. While working on his Ph.D. in sociology, which he earned from the University of Chicago in 1943, he established the methodology for participatory action research that became the basis for *Street Corner Society.*

On 29 May 1938 Whyte married Kathleen King, an old friend. They had three boys and two girls during the years from 1940 to 1953. Their middle child, Bruce, died at age five in 1951. In 1943 Whyte was struck down with polio, a condition that directed the next phase of his life. He was offered a position at Harvard to teach army veterans, but because of the polio he was unable to accept. He underwent experimental rehabilitation treatments at Massachusetts General Hospital in Boston, then spent a year with his family at the Georgia Warm Springs Foundation, where he recovered some of the use of his legs. (During this time, polio's most famous victim, President Franklin D. Roosevelt, also received treatment at Warm Springs.)

Able to walk with the aid of braces, crutches, and canes, Whyte joined the faculty of the University of Chicago in 1944. He published *Human Relations in the Restaurant Industry* (1948), the same year he took a position at the new University School of Industrial and Labor Relations at Cornell University in Ithaca, New York, where he remained until his retirement in 1979.

Street Corner Society, originally published by the University of Chicago Press in 1943, received little attention until it was published again in 1950. It became the icon of participatory action research, and achieved extraordinary notoriety for an academic work. Reissued in 1953, 1955, 1981, and 1993, it was translated into Japanese, Chinese, German, Spanish, French, and Italian, and sold more than a quarter of a million copies. Considered a classic in sociology today, it is still used as an introduction to the study of organizational forms in the inner city.

Whyte studied with Kurt Lewin's disciples at the National Training Laboratory in Bethel, Maine, and spent sabbatical years (1954–1955) in Maracaibo, Venezuela, where he became sensitized to life in a dictatorship. He did fieldwork in Arvida, Quebec, and spent another sabbatical year (1961–1962) in Peru on a Fulbright fellowship. There he performed research, cosponsored by the National Institute of Mental Health, for a study entitled "Human Problems of Industrial Development."

Whyte continued his academic social research for nearly twenty years after his retirement. In 1981 he served as president of the American Sociological Association (ASA), and lobbied for the cause of applied sociology—that is, the belief that the solution of practical problems can advance sociological thinking. The ASA established the William Foote Whyte Award for significant contributions to the practice of sociology in 1996.

In 1984 Whyte articulated his methodology in *Learning from the Field: A Guide from Experience,* written with his wife, Kathleen. The Whytes collaborated again on *Making Mondragon: The Growth of the Worker Cooperative Complex* (1988), which discusses the social history of Basque workers in Spain who fought Francisco Franco's dictatorship and established a successful cooperative. After retiring and suffering a stroke in 1990, Whyte published *Participant, Observer.*

Creative Problem Solving in the Field: Reflections on a Career (1997), Whyte's final publication, helps locate the man in his research. In the book, he articulates explanations for the importance of applied sociology and its methods. Over the course of his career, Whyte's work appeared in the most prestigious journals of social science, including the *American Journal of Sociology, American Anthropologist, American Ethnologist, Industrial Relations,* and *Annals of the American Academy of Political and Social Science.* Although he always wanted to write fiction, Whyte never fulfilled that dream.

Whyte was a tall—six feet, three inches—energetic man who did not allow polio to get the better of him. Although he was not able to drive for long distances, he did travel far and wide. For the last several years of his life, he

and his wife lived in Kendal, an Ithaca retirement community. He died at the age of eighty-six at Tompkins County Hospital. He was cremated, and his ashes scattered over Cayuga Lake in New York.

Whyte believed that researchers could maintain necessary scientific distance from their work while being fully immersed in the social settings they are researching. His twenty books revealed his broad interests and participant research (interaction between the researcher and the group he is studying) methodologies. He examined Oklahoma oil fields while on a short appointment at the University of Oklahoma in 1942, as well as observing Stouffer's dining rooms, rural Peruvian villages, and the Mondragon cooperative complex in Spain.

Dubbed the "storytelling sociologist" by peers, who believed that his work violated the rules of scientific research, Whyte considered himself to be a social anthropologist. He was a specialist in organizational behavior who gained renown as an expert on employee-owned firms, and through his extensive work in employee and industrial relations, Whyte brought the world of work into the consciousness of academia. His emphasis on social action revealed his belief that social science should be put to practical use, and should never be exclusively academic.

★

The best source of information on Whyte is his own *Participant, Observer: An Autobiography* (1994). See also his *Learning from the Field: A Guide from Experience* (1984), with Kathleen King Whyte, and *Creative Problem Solving in the Field: Reflections on a Career* (1997). An obituary is in the *New York Times* (20 July 2000).

GOLDIE SATT-ARROW

WIEBE, Robert Huddleston (*b.* 22 April 1930 in Amarillo, Texas; *d.* 10 December 2000 in Evanston, Illinois), leading scholar of U.S. history, particularly during the Gilded Age and the Progressive Era.

Wiebe was the second of two children of Richard Wiebe, a research chemist, and Jean (Huddleston) Wiebe, a homemaker and later a social worker. While Wiebe was still an infant, his family moved to Peoria, Illinois, where he attended Peoria High School. After high school he studied at Carleton College in Northfield, Minnesota, where he was a member of Phi Beta Kappa. He received a B.A. magna cum laude in 1951. In August 1952 Wiebe married Allene Davis, a truant officer for the Rochester, New York, board of education and later a mental health administrator; they had three sons.

From 1954 to 1956 he served in the United States Army, attaining the rank of private first class, and spent six months in Berlin, Germany. In 1957 he was awarded a Ph.D. from the University of Rochester. In 1957–1958 he was instructor in the department of humanities at Michigan State University in East Lansing, and from 1958 to 1960 he held the same position, teaching history, at Columbia University in New York City. From 1960 until his retirement in 1997, he taught at Northwestern University in Evanston, Illinois, moving up the ranks from assistant to full professor. In 1972–1973 he was visiting professor at Harvard University in Cambridge, Massachusetts, and in 1984–1985 he was Pitt Professor of American History and Institutions at Cambridge University in England.

Wiebe's first book, *Businessmen and Reform: A Study of the Progressive Movement* (1962), was based on his doctoral thesis. It showed how businessmen took the lead in the period 1900–1916 in demanding such reforms as a strengthened Interstate Commerce Commission, a Federal Reserve system, and a Federal Trade Commission. Wiebe described how business, never a monolithic entity, divided into bitterly hostile factions competing for economic and political power. At the same time, it usually could unite on such matters as opposition to trade unions, to public welfare services, and to vehicles to advance direct democracy. By the 1920s the very groups that the new federal regulatory agencies sought to control had captured the enforcement mechanism; indeed, they were the group that ultimately benefited most from the progressive movement.

Wiebe's best-known work remains *The Search for Order, 1877–1920* (1967), a volume in the Making of America series, edited by David Donald. Introducing phrasing that would later become commonplace, Wiebe began by describing the United States in the Gilded Age as being composed of autonomous "island communities," where most individuals lived in small personal centers. Because of revolutions in such fields as transportation, finance, and technology, however, the United States became a "distended society," "a society without a core" afflicted by a general splintering process. Finally, a "new middle class," composed primarily of urban professionals and modernizing business leaders, imposed a bureaucratic direction upon such anarchy.

In 1975 Wiebe produced *The Segmented Society: An Historical Preface to the Meaning of America.* In this book Wiebe divides U.S. history into three distinct social systems, each corresponding to a specific century. In the eighteenth century, communities dealt with each other and with distant authorities through the colonial elites. The nineteenth century was marked by fragmentation, a system of "isolated lanes where Americans, singly and in groups, dashed like rows of racers towards their goals." The twentieth century saw the decay of family culture, rampant consumerism, and greatly increased inequality.

In 1995 Wiebe extended such investigations, publishing *Self-Rule: A Cultural History of American Democracy.* Again he divided U.S. history into three periods, albeit somewhat different ones. From 1820 to 1890, a broad middle class emerged—it was the Americans who virtually conceived of a functioning democracy. During the period 1890 to 1920 the nation subdivided into a national class of highly educated elites, which created centralized hierarchies composed of bureaucratic managers; a local middle class, possessing an older, more tradition-directed ethos; and a sinking lower class. Third was the period 1920 to the present (1995), when the state itself replaced an essentially discarded public. Only by pulling down "the large structures," Wiebe maintained, could "ordinary citizens . . . move in and participate."

In the meantime, Wiebe offered a more detailed work, *The Opening of American Society: From the Adoption of the Constitution to the Eve of Disunion* (1984). Here Wiebe contends that, in actuality, the United States was created twice. It was first founded by a "gentry minority," a social, economic, and political elite that sought to fashion a government from the top down. Despite their uncommon learning and sagacity, this group could not prevent the nation's second founding, in which, by the 1820s, the hierarchical social order was cast aside. A "revolution in choices" enabled white American men to participate in a new more egalitarian social order.

Wiebe's last book, published posthumously, was *Who We Are: A History of Popular Nationalism* (2002). An effort at comparative history, the work examines many countries to see how nationalism as an entity interplays with democracy and socialism. Contrary to many observers, Wiebe saw nationalism as under siege by both tribal warlords and religious fundamentalists. Wiebe was coeditor with Grady McWhiney of *Historical Vistas: Readings in United States History* (1963) and coauthor with Bernard Bailyn (and others) of *The Great Republic: A History of the American People* (1985), a leading survey of U.S. history. Wiebe and Davis divorced in about 1997, after which he married Penelope Whiteside, a nurse. Wiebe died of a stroke, and his ashes were scattered in the Shakespeare Garden at Northwestern.

During his career Wiebe received numerous grants and fellowships, including those from the Social Science Research Council (1956–1957, 1964–1965), the Institute for Advanced Study at Princeton (1969–1970), the National Endowment for the Humanities (1976–1977), and the Guggenheim Foundation (1981–1982). Wiebe was one of the most influential figures in the writing of U.S. history, one whose interpretations recast the fundamental understanding of the Gilded Age and Progressive Era. He was revered not only as a scholar but also as an excellent classroom teacher, whose lectures manifested enthusiasm, passion, and knowledge. An activist, Wiebe was a vocal advocate for civil rights and an opponent of the Vietnam War.

Late in his life, he joined the intergenerational activist group the Gray Panthers. In all his works Wiebe wrestled with a fundamental issue: how knowledge of the past can best illuminate the conditions needed to sustain a viable democracy.

★

Wiebe's papers are at Northwestern University, Evanston, Illinois. For a major scholarly treatment of his earlier work, see Frederick Robert Lynch, "The Social Bases of Historical Interpretation: A Study of the Progressive Era" (Ph.D. thesis, University of California at Riverside, 1972). An effort to put Wiebe's best-known work in the context of modernization theory is Kenneth Cmiel, "Destiny and Amnesia: The Vision of Modernity in Robert Wiebe's *The Search for Order," Reviews in American History* 21, no. 2 (June 1993): 352–368. Obituaries are in the *Chicago Sun-Times* (13 Dec. 2000) and *New York Times* (26 Dec. 2000).

JUSTUS D. DOENECKE

WIGGINS, James Russell ("Russ") (*b.* 4 December 1903 in Luverne, Minnesota; *d.* 19 November 2000 in Brooklin, Maine), newspaper editor who was instrumental in transforming the *Washington Post* into a premier national paper during the 1950s and 1960s.

Wiggins was born on a farm in the rural southwestern corner of Minnesota. His parents, James Wiggins and Edith (Binford) Wiggins, were farmers. As a child Wiggins was an avid reader who spent long hours at the public library. Although he never attended college, he would later impress colleagues with his self-acquired erudition. Wiggins began his lifelong career in journalism as editor of his high school paper.

In 1922, while still in high school, Wiggins took a part-time position at the *Rock County Star,* a local newspaper. On 8 February 1923, a week after graduating, he married his high-school girlfriend, Mabel E. Preston, with whom he had two sons and two daughters. Their sixty-seven-year marriage lasted until Mabel's death in 1990. Upon graduation from high school, Wiggins was immediately hired as a full-time reporter at the *Rock County Star.* In 1925, at age twenty-two, he secured a $10,000 loan to purchase the paper, which he renamed the *Luverne Star* and presided over for the next five years. In 1930 Wiggins became an editorial writer with the *Dispatch-Pioneer Press* in Saint Paul, Minnesota. He left Saint Paul in 1933 to serve as the paper's Washington correspondent, and returned in 1938 to take the managing editor post.

During World War II Wiggins served in North Africa and Italy as an air combat intelligence officer for the U.S. Army Air Forces from 1943 to 1945 and attained the rank of major. In 1945 Wiggins returned as editor of the

J. Russell Wiggins, September 1968. WALLY McNAMEE/CORBIS

Dispatch-Pioneer Press, but in 1946 he took a new position at the *New York Times* as assistant to the publisher, Arthur Hays Sulzberger. After only a year in New York, Wiggins left to work as managing editor at the *Washington Post,* a position personally offered to him by the publisher Philip Graham, with whom Wiggins served in the Army Air Forces. When Wiggins arrived in 1947, the *Post* was one of four newspapers in the nation's capital and only the third ranked in terms of circulation. Although it was respected for its editorial column, the understaffed and under-resourced paper consisted largely of newswire stories and national syndications. Under Wiggins's editorial leadership, the paper emerged as one of the nation's foremost independent news outlets.

A staunch advocate for the freedom and integrity of the press, Wiggins introduced new standards of probity and professional responsibility at the *Washington Post.* He warned his staff against the perils of the "Jehovah complex," by which reporters mistook their newsgathering obligation for omniscience. To banish any semblance of bias, he demanded that his journalists refuse favors such as free tickets and lodging offered by sports teams, theaters, and other event sponsors, as well as any outside employment that might pose a conflict of interest. He even banned coffee from the pressroom, an act that reflected the occasional excesses of his fastidiousness. In addition to enforcing a strict boundary between the paper and special interests, Wiggins also displayed his integrity in refusing to report an individual's identity as African American unless this was essential to the story. Likewise, he declined to publish news that would compromise national security interests, as when he withheld his knowledge of U.S. spy-plane flights over the Soviet Union during the 1950s.

Wiggins's defense of journalistic independence made him a target of Senator Joseph McCarthy's anticommunist crusade. In 1953 McCarthy condemned Wiggins for his role in an American Society of Newspaper Editors inquiry into the alleged communist sympathies of a *New York Post* columnist. Wiggins served as chair of the inquiry and issued a minority report asserting that a free press meant that journalists should not be obligated to justify their opinions to the government. Wiggins stood firm, and McCarthy relented. In 1956 Wiggins published *Freedom or Secrecy,* in which he defended the freedom of the press and criticized what he perceived to be an insidious proliferation of closed and increasingly secretive legislative, executive, and military committees responsible for government decision-making.

Wiggins was promoted to executive editor of the *Washington Post* in 1955 and served simultaneously as executive vice president of the Washington Post Company from 1960 to 1968, heading both the news and editorial departments at the paper. During the Vietnam War, Wiggins adamantly supported the foreign policy of President Lyndon B. Johnson and resisted a growing tide of opposition at the paper. In editorials he affirmed the importance of U.S. military engagement in Southeast Asia as necessary to stem communist expansion. He single-handedly presented this view as the editorial judgment of the *Washington Post* until he left the paper in 1968, at which time the paper promptly turned antiwar.

In September 1968, shortly before his planned retirement on his sixty-fifth birthday, Wiggins accepted an offer from Johnson to serve as the U.S. ambassador to the United Nations. Because Johnson had declined to run for reelection, Wiggins's appointment by the lame-duck administration was essentially a token of appreciation for his support of the president. Wiggins was criticized by some for compromising his own journalistic standards in taking the U.N. position, though he had closed out his Washington newspaper career before doing so. Others objected to his lack of diplomatic credentials, but his friend the author E. B. White publicly defended him. Wiggins served as U.N. ambassador for only four months, a term that ended on 20 January 1969, with the inauguration of Richard M. Nixon as president.

In 1969 Wiggins moved to Maine to serve as editor and publisher of the *Ellsworth American,* a weekly paper he had purchased in 1966. Although he eventually sold the paper in 1989, he remained its editor until his death in 2000. He brought the same skills and journalistic principles to the much smaller paper that had earned him distinction at what by then had become one of the nation's preeminent dailies, the *Washington Post.* During the thirty years that he presided over the *Ellsworth American,* he transformed it into a respected regional paper and more than tripled its circulation. Wiggins continued to write editorials and light verse for the paper until his death from congestive heart failure at age ninety-six. He is buried at Rural Cemetery in Sedgwick, Maine.

Wiggins was widely respected for his integrity, seriousness, and high-minded sense of purpose, all qualities that he imputed to the *Washington Post* as editor during the paper's postwar rise to national prominence. His insistence on journalistic ethics and his belief that the public is "entitled to at least one clean shot at the facts"—which stood in contrast to the fad for subjective journalism during the 1960s—reflected his faith in the civic duty of independent, objective news reporting. An energetic and collegial man who was widely read in history, law, and politics and was an amateur Thomas Jefferson scholar, he embodied an appealing blend of self-taught sophistication and naive righteousness that, while at times perceived as morally simplistic and heavy-handed, was commendable for its steadfastness. Although his support for the Vietnam War and, to a lesser extent, his U.N. appointment caused some to doubt the consistency of his principles, his commitment to professional journalism and freedom of the press earned him broad admiration. He was awarded ten honorary degrees and served as president of the American Society of Newspaper Editors and the American Antiquarian Society and on the board of directors of the National Press Club.

★

Discussion of Wiggins's role at the *Washington Post* is contained in Tom Kelly, *The Imperial Post: The Meyers, the Grahams, and the Paper that Rules Washington* (1983), and Chalmers M. Roberts, *In the Shadow of Power: The Story of the "Washington Post"* (1989). Wiggins's *Freedom or Secrecy* is reviewed in Erwin D. Canham, "Shutters Are Closed," *New York Times* (11 Nov. 1956), and Robert K. Carr, "Short Shrift for Privacy," *New Republic* (19 Nov. 1956). Obituaries are in the *Washington Post* (20 Nov. 2000) and *New York Times* (21 Nov. 2000).

JOSH LAUER

WILDER, Billy (*b.* 22 June 1906 in Sucha Beskidzka, Galicia, Austria-Hungary; *d.* 27 March 2002 in Los Angeles, California), motion-picture director, screenwriter, and producer.

Wilder, the second son of Max Wilder and Eugenia (Dittler) Wilder, was born in a small town southwest of Kraków

Billy Wilder, November 2000. REUTERS NEWMEDIA INC./CORBIS

eager for a change, he traveled to Berlin with the American bandleader Paul Whiteman and decided to stay. The only work Wilder could find at first was as a gigolo, escorting women around a dance floor for pay. He wrote about his experiences for the newspaper *Berliner Zeitung am Mittag,* where his articles earned him notice among Berlin's journalism elite, who helped him find more writing assignments.

In 1929 Wilder wrote the scripts for *Der Teufelsreporter* ("The Daredevil Reporter"), his first screen credit, and *Menschen am Sonntag* (shown in the United States under the name *People on Sunday*), a so-called cross-section film, or documentary-style fiction film about the lives of ordinary people in Berlin. The second of these films, made with Robert Siodmak, Curt Siodmak, and Fred Zinnemann, among others, was an enormous success, and by 1931 Wilder was working steadily as a screenwriter for Ufa, the preeminent German film studio, and other smaller companies. His screenplays from this period include *Der Mann, der seinen Mörder sucht* ("The Man Who Sought His Own Murderer," 1931), *Emil und die Detektive* ("Emil and the Detectives," 1931), *Scampolo, ein Kind der Strasse* ("Scampolo, a Child of the Streets,"1932; released in New York under the title *Ein Mädel der Strasse,* "A Girl of the Street"), and *Was Frauen träumen* ("What Women Dream," 1933).

In March 1933, two months after Adolf Hitler became Germany's chancellor, Wilder fled to Paris. While living in a small room in the Ansonia Hotel, where the actor Peter Lorre and the musician Friedrich Holländer were also lodging, Wilder directed his first film, *Mauvaise graine* ("Bad Seed," 1934), an intermittently comical drama about car thieves. By that time he had learned French. The experience of directing *Mauvaise graine* was so harrowing to Wilder that he declared he would never direct another film.

For Wilder, Paris was a way station. His goal was Hollywood, where he moved in 1934 on the promise of obtaining work. He knew very little English when he emigrated and learned the language, he later claimed, by listening to the radio and dating many women. After co-writing such films as *Music in the Air* (1934), starring Gloria Swanson, for the Fox Film Company, Wilder landed at Paramount Pictures, where in 1938 the restless, energetic immigrant began working with his first longstanding writing partner, the patrician Charles Brackett, on the Ernst Lubitsch screwball comedy *Bluebeard's Eighth Wife* (1938). It was the beginning of one of Hollywood's most successful collaborations. Their later works include *Midnight* (1939) for Mitchell Leisen, *Ninotchka* (1939) for Lubitsch, *Hold Back the Dawn* (1941) for Leisen, and *Ball of Fire* (1941) for Howard Hawks. On 20 December 1936 Wilder married Judith Frances Coppicus; the couple had two children and divorced in 1947.

Wilder returned to directing with *The Major and the*

in what is now Poland. His parents named him Samuel, but his mother, a homemaker, having become enthralled with Buffalo Bill's Wild West Show on a visit to New York as a young girl, soon began calling him Billy (or "Billie," as it was spelled at the time), and the nickname stuck. The Wilders, who were Jewish, moved often, owing to Max Wilder's unsuccessful business ventures, which included snack bars in train stations and a hotel in Kraków. Eventually they settled in Vienna, the sophisticated if stuffy capital of Austria-Hungary (and of Austria alone after 1918), where Wilder attended high school. He was an indifferent student, bored by formal learning, and he nearly flunked French; it seemed that Wilder had little facility with foreign languages.

Wilder's parents wanted him to become a lawyer, and after graduating from high school in 1924, he told them that he had matriculated at the University of Vienna. In fact, he did no such thing, but rather took a job with two tabloid newspapers, *Die Stunde* and *Die Bühne.* Working at first as a crossword-puzzle editor, Wilder moved on to reporting—sports, theater, music, and cinema. By 1926,

Minor (1942), from a script by Wilder and Brackett. The duo also made the espionage drama *Five Graves to Cairo* (1943), with Brackett producing. In 1944 Wilder and Brackett parted company briefly so that Wilder could co-write and direct the film noir *Double Indemnity.* Brackett found the material too vulgar and refused to have anything to do with it, so Wilder chose the American mystery writer Raymond Chandler as his collaborator. *Double Indemnity,* starring Fred MacMurray and Barbara Stanwyck, was a hit, but Wilder and Chandler detested each other and never worked together again. Wilder teamed with Brackett again for *The Lost Weekend* (1945), a groundbreaking study of an alcoholic writer that won Wilder his first Academy Awards, for best director and best picture. Shortly after World War II ended in 1945, Wilder worked for several months with the U.S. Army in Germany, where he discovered that his mother and grandmother had been killed in the Holocaust. On 30 June 1949 Wilder married Audrey Young; they had no children.

Wilder and Brackett followed *The Lost Weekend* with *A Foreign Affair* (1947), a comedy set in bombed-out Berlin; *The Emperor Waltz* (1948), a lavish Technicolor musical set in Austria and starring Bing Crosby and Joan Fontaine; and their masterpiece, *Sunset Boulevard* (1950), the story of a has-been silent film star, played by Gloria Swanson, and her relationship with a younger screenwriter, William Holden. During the writing of *Sunset Boulevard,* Wilder announced to Brackett that he wanted to break up the collaboration. Brackett was devastated.

Wilder went on to co-write a number of films: the bitter *Ace in the Hole* (also called *The Big Carnival,* 1951), about a down-and-out newspaper reporter exploiting a mining disaster; *Stalag 17,* a comedy set in a Nazi prisoner-of-war camp; the romantic *Sabrina* (1954), with Audrey Hepburn, William Holden, and Humphrey Bogart; and the threat-of-adultery comedy *The Seven Year Itch* (1955), starring Tom Ewell and Marilyn Monroe. (Wilder had a love hate relationship with Monroe: he loved her screen chemistry but found her taxing to work with.)

By the mid-1950s Wilder was one of the most commercially successful filmmakers and screenwriters in the world. His worldview was unusually bitter for Hollywood, and his characters often were as cynical and hard-edged as he was, although frequently with the same underlying romanticism and wit. In 1957 Wilder began working on screenplays with I. A. L. Diamond, a quiet but forceful man whose ironic sensibilities matched his own. Their first collaboration, *Love in the Afternoon* (1957), starred Gary Cooper and Audrey Hepburn. With only one exception—the commercially unsuccessful *Spirit of St. Louis* (1958), in which James Stewart played Charles Lindbergh—Wilder never wrote with any other screenwriter again. At this time Wilder also began a long and fruitful business relationship with the

Mirisch Company, an independent production firm that combined low overheads with a strong personal and financial commitment to dynamic, talented filmmakers such as Wilder.

Some Like It Hot (1959), Wilder's next film, was one of his most successful efforts. The third-biggest moneymaker of the year, it told the story of two musicians, played by Jack Lemmon and Tony Curtis, who are forced to dress in drag and join an otherwise all-girl band in order to escape death at the hands and guns of the Mafia. Monroe also starred. *Some Like It Hot* was both of its time and ahead of its time and now is widely considered one of the best film comedies ever made. Wilder followed it with *The Apartment* (1960), which won five Academy Awards: for best picture, best director (Wilder), best original screenplay (Wilder and Diamond), best art direction–set direction (Alexander Trauner and Edward G. Boyle), and best editing (Daniel Mandell). The story of a placekick accountant (Lemmon) who is promoted by his insurance company boss, not because of his talent, but because of his willingness to provide the boss access to his apartment for adulterous trysts, *The Apartment* resonated with audiences because of its bleak, but comical look at American corporate life.

Wilder's subsequent films continued to mix wit and acidity in equal measure. *One, Two, Three* (1961) is a cold war comedy set in divided Berlin. *Irma la Douce* (1963), his most commercially successful film, is the story of a Parisian prostitute. *Kiss Me, Stupid* (1964), a particularly vulgar adultery comedy, was condemned by the Legion of Decency. *The Fortune Cookie* (1966) concerns insurance fraud. In 1970 Wilder released his most cherished and personal film, *The Private Life of Sherlock Holmes,* but it fared poorly at the box office. He went on to make *Avanti!* (1972), a sweet-tempered adultery comedy; a remake of *The Front Page* (1974), starring Jack Lemmon and Walter Matthau; and the quirky *Fedora* (1978), which returned him to the themes of *Sunset Boulevard.* The acrid *Buddy Buddy* (1981), starring Lemmon and Matthau, was his final film, although he continued to spend most days in his office working on script ideas until shortly before his death.

A prodigious art collector, Wilder owned important works by Pablo Picasso, Balthus, Alberto Giacometti, Ernst Ludwig Kirchner, David Hockney, Paul Klee, and Fernando Botero, among many others. He sold only a portion of his holdings in 1989 at auction for $32.6 million. Apart from his Academy Awards for *The Lost Weekend* and *The Apartment,* Wilder's honors included the Academy's Thalberg Award; the National Medal of Arts; the Grand National Prize and the Golden Order, First Class, both from the Republic of Austria; the American Film Institute Life Achievement Award; an honorary Golden Bear from the Berlin Film Festival; and the first Lifetime Achievement

Award in Screenwriting from PEN, an international organization of poets, playwrights, and novelists. Wilder died of pneumonia and is buried at Pierce Brothers Westwood Memorial Park in Los Angeles.

Wilder's cinematic legacy is his harsh wit, his meticulous filmmaking craft, and his extraordinary success as an independent writer/producer/director in command of a coherent artistic vision.

★

Biographies of Wilder include Kevin Lally, *Wilder Times* (1996); Ed Sikov, *On Sunset Boulevard: The Life and Times of Billy Wilder* (1998); Cameron Crowe, *Conversations with Wilder* (1999); and Charlotte Chandler, *Nobody's Perfect: Billy Wilder. A Personal Biography* (2002). An obituary is in the *New York Times* (29 Mar. 2002).

ED SIKOV

WILHELM, (James) Hoyt (*b.* 26 July 1923 [some sources say 1922] in Huntersville, North Carolina; *d.* 23 August 2002 in Sarasota, Florida), first relief pitcher and first knuckleball pitcher elected to the National Baseball Hall of Fame.

Wilhelm was born in a small town in either 1922 or 1923. During his baseball career, he gave 1923 as his date of birth, and that is the one listed in the Hall of Fame, but his widow, Peggy (with whom he had three children), said he had been born in 1922. Baseball players commonly claim to be a year or two younger than they actually are. When Wilhelm was in the eighth grade, he saw a newspaper picture of Washington Senators pitcher Emil "Dutch" Leonard, who was the most successful knuckleball pitcher in baseball. The picture showed the way Leonard gripped the pitch, so Wilhelm practiced throwing a tennis ball with that grip.

Wilhelm's minor-league career was interrupted by U.S. Army service in World War II, during which he won a Purple Heart in the Battle of the Bulge. Returning to organized baseball after the war, Wilhelm had two twenty-game-winning seasons in the minor leagues but found that many teams were wary of him because of his favorite pitch.

The knuckleball was invented in the nineteenth century by a pitcher known as "Toad" Ramsey. By holding the ball with his knuckles instead of his fingers, a pitcher can throw it with little or no spin. A ball pitched that way causes turbulence as it moves toward the batter and thus moves unpredictably. This makes it difficult to hit if it is thrown properly, but the approach has drawbacks. If the ball does not cause enough turbulence, it is simply a slow, easy-to-hit pitch. Even when it is thrown correctly it may miss the strike zone, and it is difficult to catch.

Wilhelm threw nothing but knuckleballs, and he remained in the minor leagues until he was officially twenty-

Hoyt Wilhelm, March 1956. AP/WIDE WORLD PHOTOS

eight years old—an age at which most successful players have been in the majors for several years. In 1952 the New York Giants decided to take a chance on him. On his first time at bat he hit a home run—an unusual feat, especially for a pitcher. More remarkably, it was the only home run of his major league career.

This was a time when relief pitching was becoming increasingly important. The assumption had been that starters should finish most of their games, and if the starter had to be taken out, his replacement would be someone not good enough to be in the starting rotation. In the late 1940s, however, relief specialists such as Joe Page and Jim Konstanty pitched fifty or more games and helped their team to the pennant.

Wilhelm fitted right into that approach. In his rookie season he pitched in seventy-one games, all in relief, winding up with an impressive record of fifteen wins and three losses with a league-leading earned run average (ERA) of 2.43; he finished fourth in the voting for the National League Most Valuable Player. For the next four years he remained with the Giants, averaging about sixty appearances a year.

Wilhelm was already somewhat elderly by baseball standards, but it was not then generally realized that throwing the knuckleball puts less strain on the arm than throwing other pitches, so a knuckleballer can last longer than other pitchers. The Giants thought he was through and traded him to the St. Louis Cardinals in 1957; the Cardinals soon sold him to the Cleveland Indians. In 1958 the Cleveland manager Bobby Bragan used Wilhelm in a starting role for the first time in his major league career, but he did not distinguish himself, and he was placed on waivers late in the season.

The Baltimore Orioles picked him up, and on 20 September 1958 Wilhelm started against the New York Yankees. It was a cold, drizzly day, and—more important for a knuckleballer—there was little wind. Wilhelm pitched a no-hitter, winning 1–0. In 1959 he was in the starting rotation, and his record was 15–11, but the team's catchers committed a record forty-nine passed balls. After the season his manager, the innovative Paul Richards, designed a larger glove for catchers to use when Wilhelm was pitching.

Wilhelm improved with age. The starting experiment ended with one game in 1961, and he returned to the bullpen. In 1963 he was traded to the Chicago White Sox, and in every year from 1964 through 1968 his ERA was below 2.00. In 1968 he appeared in a career-high seventy-two games. In 1969 he was selected in the expansion draft by the Kansas City Royals, then traded to the California Angels. Late in the 1969 season his old manager, Paul Richards, then the general manager of the Atlanta Braves, purchased him, and Wilhelm helped the team to its first divisional title with two wins and two saves. He remained in major league baseball into the 1972 season, then retired to work as a pitching coach in the Yankee organization.

Wilhelm pitched in 1,070 games, more than any player before him. (He has since been passed by Jesse Orosco and Dennis Eckersley.) In 1985 he was voted into the National Baseball Hall of Fame, both the first relief specialist and the first knuckleball pitcher to be so honored, although others have followed him. He died of diabetes and heart failure at the age of eighty, and was buried in Palms Memorial Park, Sarasota, Florida.

In several ways Wilhelm was a pivotal figure in the history of pitching. There had never been a comparable knuckleballer before him, although in later years Phil Niekro also reached the Hall of Fame with that pitch. Wilhelm was also a major transitional figure in the development of the relief pitcher to the point where every team needs a closer. He also demonstrated that a pitcher can keep playing into his late forties if he takes care of himself.

★

Danny Peary, ed., *Cult Baseball Players* (1990), includes a chapter on Wilhelm by Peter Baida. He is discussed in Donald Honig, *The Greatest Pitchers of All Time* (1988), and in Bill James,

The New Bill James Historical Baseball Abstract (2001). Obituaries are in the *New York Times* and *Washington Post* (both 26 Aug. 2002).

ARTHUR D. HLAVATY

WILLIAMS, Hosea Lorenzo (*b.* 5 January 1926 in Attapulgus, Georgia; *d.* 16 November 2000 in Atlanta, Georgia), civil rights leader and politician who first came to prominence for his work in Savannah, Georgia, and who remained a controversial and outspoken figure throughout a long political career.

Williams was born the illegitimate son of blind parents. His teenage mother had met his father, a broom maker, at a school for the blind in Macon, Georgia. After the early death of his mother, Williams was raised by his grandparents, Turner and Lela Williams, on a farm in the southwest Georgia town of Attapulgus. Early on, Williams was exposed to the region's pervasive racism. At age fourteen, for example, a lynch mob threatened to kill him for befriending a white girl. Shortly thereafter, he left his impoverished home, working at odd jobs for several years.

After the United States entered World War II, Williams was accepted into the U.S. Army despite his rheumatic heart and served in Europe as the staff sergeant of an all-black unit. During the war he miraculously survived a German mortar attack that killed his entire platoon. Severely wounded, Williams spent thirteen months in a British hospital. Upon his return to the United States, Williams, still in his uniform, was beaten bloody by a mob of white southerners for drinking from a segregated water fountain at a bus station in Americus, Georgia. His experience of such blatant injustice, after he had been fighting against racist Nazi Germany, would prompt him later to join the National Association for the Advancement of Colored People (NAACP).

Initially, Williams had no intention of becoming a civil rights activist. At age twenty-three he completed his high school education and then earned a B.S. from Morris Brown College in Atlanta. After receiving an M.S. in chemistry from Atlanta University, he went to work as a high school teacher. In 1953 he secured a job as a research chemist with the U.S. Department of Agriculture in Savannah. His well-paid position afforded Williams and his wife, Juanita Terry, a comfortable middle-class life. He hoped that his prestigious position ultimately would enable him to escape segregation and discrimination, but reality soon caught up with him.

One key event that spurred Williams to civil rights activism occurred in early 1960, when his two young sons (he also had three daughters) asked why they could not order

Hosea Williams. AP/WIDE WORLD PHOTOS

a soda at a segregated lunch counter. Shortly thereafter, he assisted in organizing the first sit-ins against segregation in Savannah. By that time he had become vice president of the Savannah chapter of the NAACP. In addition, he led the Savannah-based Chatham County Crusade for Voters and the Southeastern Georgia Crusade for Voters, which successfully added thousands of blacks to the voter registration rolls. Much of these organizations' success stemmed from Williams's forceful leadership and his rousing oratory.

In 1962 the ambitious Williams ran for a position on the national board of the NAACP, but the organization's leadership, in particular, executive secretary Roy Wilkins, was critical both of his militancy and of his family background (especially the fact that his parents had not been married) and rejected his candidacy. Frustrated by this setback, he began to build close ties with the Southern Christian Leadership Conference (SCLC) and its president, King. Williams had long been fascinated by King and his resolute leadership, which he favored over the quiet lobbying of Wilkins. After affiliating his voter registration organizations with the SCLC, Williams severed his ties with the NAACP.

Still employed as a chemist, Williams organized Savannah's first nonviolent protest marches against segregation in the summer of 1963. Almost daily he rushed downtown during his lunch break to mobilize new demonstrators. Thousands heeded his call, joining their leader in confrontational night marches, a tactical innovation that Williams introduced. He was a staunch believer in the power of nonviolent direct action and rigidly enforced nonviolence. At almost every meeting he called upon black teenagers to

come forward and give up their knives and similar weapons. His forceful leadership in Savannah produced some of the largest and most assertive demonstrations of the 1960s. Mobilizing as many as three thousand marchers a night, Williams was able to put considerable pressure on the city government and local businessmen. When authorities arrested him for his activism, he ran the local movement from his jail cell. That summer he spent more than two months in custody, longer than any other black civil rights leader. In the end, white city officials and businessmen yielded to the local movement's pressure, initiating the desegregation of Savannah toward the end of 1963. By that time Williams had taken a year's leave of absence from his job and was working as a full-time organizer.

In 1964 Williams joined the staff of the SCLC. That same year, he organized voter registration drives throughout the South and served as a field worker in Saint Augustine, Florida, where local activists adopted his night-march tactic. In 1965 Williams helped organize the SCLC's protest campaign for federal voting rights legislation in Selma, Alabama. On 7 March 1965 Williams and John Lewis of the Student Nonviolent Coordinating Committee (SNCC) were leading a column of marchers across the Edmund Pettus Bridge toward Selma when local police and mounted state troopers stopped them with tear gas and clubs. Later that day millions of American television viewers were shocked to see white police officers beat Williams and Lewis unconscious, while the two activists' fellow marchers were brutally forced to the ground. Considered the climax of the civil rights movement, this incident and the subsequent protest march from Selma to Montgomery are credited with spurring the passage of the Voting Rights Act of 1965.

After the Selma campaign, Williams organized the SCLC's Summer and Community Organization and Political Education (SCOPE) program, intended to bring hundreds of white volunteers to the South to register large numbers of black voters. In 1966 Williams and other field workers initiated a similar campaign in Chicago, but the SCOPE project was not successful. Despite generous funding, few new voters were registered, a fact that frustrated white volunteers and angered local black leaders. Within the SCLC many believed that Williams was responsible for this failure. His egocentric personality alienated many of the people whom he supervised, and some openly questioned his administrative abilities. Despite this criticism, Williams became the head of the SCLC's field staff in 1967. By that time Williams had become one of King's closest aides. When King was assassinated on 4 April 1968 in Memphis, Tennessee, Williams stood just below the balcony of the Gaston Motel, where a sniper's bullet hit the SCLC's young president. After King's death, Williams co-organized and supervised the SCLC's Poor People's Campaign in Washington, D.C., which called attention to the plight of America's poor and protested against economic injustice. After the Washington project, which was the SCLC's last major campaign, Williams became the organization's executive director, a position that he resigned in 1971.

After the decline of the civil rights movement, Williams continued his activism for the disadvantaged. In 1970, for example, he initiated annual holiday dinners for the poor in Atlanta. Each year for the next three decades, these dinners fed tens of thousands of destitute and homeless people. As the 1970s progressed, Williams's interests increasingly revolved around politics. In 1970 he ran unsuccessfully for the Georgia General Assembly as a Republican, and in 1974, switching to the Democratic Party, he won a seat. In 1977, despite the burden of his political office, he returned to his old position of executive director of the SCLC but was ousted by the organization's board of directors two years later. The board justified its action by stating that Williams was preoccupied with Atlanta affairs and had neglected the SCLC's national projects. In the 1980s Williams continued to focus on his political career. Resigning his seat in the Georgia General Assembly in 1984, he ran as a Republican for the United States Senate but was overwhelmingly defeated by his Democratic opponent, Wyche Fowler. One year later he was elected to the Atlanta City Council.

In 1987 Williams again demonstrated his skills as a civil rights leader, organizing a protest campaign against racial discrimination in traditionally white Forsyth County, Georgia. When he entered the county with a small column of marchers, members of the Ku Klux Klan pelted the demonstrators with rocks. Shortly thereafter, Williams returned with some twenty thousand protestors, focusing nationwide attention on the Klan's racism and the discriminatory practices in Forsyth County.

In 1989 Williams made another run for higher office, unsuccessfully campaigning as a Republican for the position of mayor of Atlanta. From 1990 to 1994 he served on the county commission of DeKalb County, at the heart of metropolitan Atlanta. His departure from the county commission in 1994 marked the conclusion of his political career, and from the mid-1990s onward he devoted his attention to the careers of his children. After the death of one son in 1998 and his wife in August 2000, Williams himself succumbed to cancer in an Atlanta hospital and was buried in Atlanta.

Throughout his life, Williams proved a controversial figure. In the 1960s he put his career and personal safety on the line to defend ideas that are commonly accepted today but were incendiary at the time. Even after the main battles of the civil rights movement had been fought and won, he continued to raise hackles, often within the very community from which he had first emerged into national prominence. For example, his affinity for the Republican Party in the 1970s and 1980s, including his endorsement of Ronald Reagan's presidential campaign in 1980, puzzled many and angered others. Still, Williams remains one of the most inspiring figures of the civil rights era. Jailed more than one hundred times during his activist career, he proved that forceful leadership and the determination to remain on the front lines of the struggle could successfully mobilize people to effect social change.

★

David Garrow, *Bearing the Cross: Martin Luther King and the Southern Christian Leadership Conference* (1986), and Adam Fairclough, *To Redeem the Soul of America: The Southern Christian Leadership Conference and Martin Luther King, Jr.* (1987), chronicle parts of Williams's activist career in the 1960s. Howell Raines, *My Soul Is Rested: Movement Days in the Deep South Remembered* (1977), and Donald L. Grant, *The Way It Was in the South: The Black Experience in Georgia* (1993), provide additional biographical information. An obituary is in the *New York Times* (17 Nov. 2000). The Hosea Williams Oral History Collection is housed at the Martin Luther King Center in Atlanta.

SIMON WENDT

WILLIAMS, Theodore Samuel ("Ted") (*b.* 30 August 1918 in San Diego, California; *d.* 5 July 2002 in Inverness, Florida), professional baseball player widely regarded as the game's greatest hitter and remembered as the last man to bat over .400.

Williams's birth certificate shows his name as Teddy, but Williams always insisted on Theodore. Still, he later earned the nickname "Teddy Ballgame." He was the elder of two sons of Samuel Steward Williams and May (Venzer) Williams, who had arrived in San Diego three years earlier from Hawaii, where they had met and married. Williams's father, of Welsh and English extraction, claimed to have served in Theodore Roosevelt's cavalry unit. For a time he ran a small photography shop above a restaurant. When the business failed, he found work as an inspector of prisons for the state of California, a position that required being away from home. He was also an alcoholic, so he was often an absent parent. Williams's mother, of Mexican and French extraction, was a devoted soldier in the Salvation Army. As a youngster, Williams, to his everlasting embarrassment, was often forced to accompany her as she solicited donations for her cause. Williams's brother, born in 1920, as well as being frail and often ailing, was a troubled child. So Williams was a lonely soul, mostly on his own.

From his earliest days Williams's mind was fixed on hitting a baseball better than anybody else. He spent his after-school and vacation time at a playground near his home on Utah Street, into which the family moved in 1924. There he honed his skill as a batsman with friends who helped him play pickup games or simply pitched to him endlessly. The countless practice swings Williams took as

Ted Williams, 1950. BETTMANN/CORBIS

he drove imaginary home runs into imaginary bleachers became so habitual, that as a big-leaguer he once knocked a sleeping roommate to the floor in the middle of the night when he swung and accidentally smashed a bedpost to smithereens.

At Hoover High School in San Diego, where legend has it that he always carried his glove and bat, he pitched and played the outfield. When he was a senior he hit an overwhelming .583. Skipping further schooling, in 1936 Williams joined the San Diego Padres of the Pacific Coast League for $150 a month, his parents signing the contract because he was still under age. In 1937, his first full season, in 138 games Williams hit .291, including twenty-nine home runs. The following year he was discovered by Eddie Collins, the Boston Red Sox general manager, who had come West to look over a couple of Williams's teammates. Shortly afterward, the Red Sox exercised an option for Williams's services, paying $25,000 and two players.

In 1938 the Red Sox brought their prize rookie to spring training in Florida. Now nineteen years old, Williams felt ready for the Big Show. When a sportswriter accompanying him said casually, "Wait until you see Foxx hit"—referring to the renowned Sox slugger Jimmie Foxx—Williams retorted, "Wait until Foxx sees me hit!" But after only a week, Williams was sent down to Boston's farm team, the Minneapolis Millers in the American Association. He proceeded to burn up the league, winning the triple crown by hitting .366, walloping forty-three homers, and driving in 142 runs.

On 20 April 1939 Williams made his major league debut at Yankee Stadium in New York City, playing right field. Although he struck out the first time he batted, he later smacked a double—the first of the 2,654 hits (including 521 home runs) he would amass in his spectacular career. The following Sunday at Fenway Park in Boston he drove a ball into the right field bleachers, a place previously reached by only a handful of hitters, including Babe Ruth. By midseason Williams had slammed six homers there. On 4 May, playing against the Tigers in Detroit, he hit a massive four-bagger over the roof of Briggs Stadium—the first player ever to do so. When the year was over, Williams was without question the outstanding rookie. He had compiled a .327 average, struck thirty-one home runs, and driven in a league-leading 145 runs. In 1940 his selection for the American League (AL) All-Star team seemed automatic; he eventually received this honor eighteen times. Williams was a good outfielder, but not a great one, and the Sox moved him from right field to left so he would not have to fight the sun on fly balls.

Lanky and skinnier than some of his fellow power hitters, Williams became an idol of millions as the "Splendid Splinter," although he never shook off another nickname, "the Kid." To many fans also he was "the Thumper." He batted left-handed, but he could not explain why except that that was the way he first began to hit. He did everything else right-handed. Standing six feet, three inches tall, and weighing only 150 pounds when he came to the big leagues, the gawky youth was blessed with perfect eyesight as well as powerful wrists and forearms. Moreover, he took onto the playing field an obsession to outshine all competitors—as well as the confidence that he could. His matchless smooth swing, slightly uppercut to compensate for the pitcher's stance on a mound, was a thing of beauty, and teammates and rivals fixed their eyes on him with envy and admiration whenever he stepped up to the plate. His dour, even grouchy, public personality seemed to convey a sense that concentration on his craft was his sole concern. In truth, his seeming rudeness and sometimes-insolent manner may have compensated for the feeling of personal inferiority he carried from an unorthodox upbringing.

Williams was the toast of Beantown, but the love affair did not last. At odds with the newsmen who covered the team, his thin skin feeling every critical remark, he tangled not only with media people but also with teammates and often with the paying customers, even spitting at them and sometimes hurling his bat toward the stands. After his rookie year he refused to acknowledge the cheers of the crowd by tipping his cap, a scorning of the fans that became a trademark. But he had a generous side, too. He worked tirelessly for the Jimmy Fund of the Children's Cancer Foundation (now the Dana-Farber Cancer Institute) and raised millions of dollars for it, as well as making countless unannounced visits to the bedside of ailing youngsters. Many a parent learned at discharge time that "Mr. Williams has taken care of your bill."

The year 1941 provided what is now regarded as baseball's most wondrous season, witnessing two matchless dramas: Joe DiMaggio's fifty-six–game hitting streak and Williams's triumphant effort to hit .400. His ninth-inning, two-out, three-run homer in the All-Star game in Detroit in July provided the American League a 7–5 victory and earned him hero status. But the capstone of his year lay ahead. Williams had been tooling along over .400 for most of the season when his hitting began to tail off. A close student of opposing pitchers, he was now facing rookies, called up by their teams from the minor leagues, whose stuff he was unfamiliar with. On 27 September his average stood at .3995, technically .400. The Red Sox manager, Joe Cronin, offered to allow him to sit out the Sunday doubleheader that would complete the schedule. Williams would have none of it. He wanted nothing more in the world than to go into the record books with a .400 average—but, as he later said, "I figure a man's a .400 hitter or he isn't." That afternoon in the first game he drove out four hits, raising his average to .404. He could have bagged the second game, for he was well aware that if he went 0 for 5 in

it his average would again fall to .3995. Undaunted, he went for the brass ring, and the two hits he stroked—making six for the day—gave him a lofty .406 average, which no player since has come close to matching.

When Pearl Harbor was attacked on 7 December 1941, pulling the United States into World War II, Williams, unlike some other stars, including Bob Feller and Joe DiMaggio, did not immediately get into uniform. Draft-deferred because he was the sole support of his mother, he played the 1942 season, winning the triple crown (he would win it again in 1947), hitting .356, driving out thirty-six home runs, and batting in 137 runs. At the end of the year he enlisted as a naval airman. He earned his wings and became a flight instructor, but the war ended before he could see action. Upon returning to baseball in 1946, he showed his skill was undiminished, hitting .342 and including thirty-eight home runs. Having enlisted in the U.S. Marine Air Reserve, he was called back into service during the Korean War, and completed thirty-nine missions as a fighter pilot in 1952–1953, surviving a near-fatal crash. On a few occasions he flew alongside John Glenn, the pioneer astronaut.

Williams led his league in batting six times—remarkably, at the age of thirty-nine in 1957 with a .388 average, and again the following year, when he hit .320. His lifetime average of .344 tied him for third place on the all-time list with Tris Speaker after Ty Cobb (.367) and Roger Hornsby (.358). His lifetime on-base percentage of .483 is unmatched. In 1946 and 1949 he was named the AL Most Valuable Player. (Joe DiMaggio edged him out in 1941.) He ended his playing days in 1960, hitting a home run in his last trip to the plate. He was inducted into the National Baseball Hall of Fame in 1966. One can only guess what his lifetime statistics would have been had he not lost baseball years while in military uniform. Williams was aware that his numbers had also been hurt by the "Williams shift" originated in 1946 by Lou Boudreau, the youthful player-manager of the Cleveland Indians. Williams, a pull hitter, would find himself facing four infielders between first and second base, and the center fielder stationed in right field.

Persuaded to become the manager of the Washington Senators, Williams worked with the chronically losing franchise from 1969 to 1971. In 1969 he led the Senators to their first winning season in eighteen years and was named AL Manager of the Year. He managed the Texas Rangers in 1972.

In retirement Williams enjoyed deep-sea fishing in Florida, making his home in Hernando, and in many places around the world. He was inducted into the Fresh Water Fisherman's Hall of Fame. He was also a sports consultant for Sears, Roebuck and Company. But he continued to keep in touch with baseball, offering instruction and advice as called upon. On the fiftieth anniversary of his .406 year in

1991, he was honored at Fenway Park, where, in a bravura moment, he drew a cap from his pocket, placed it on his head, and lifted it in response to the fans. By then his number "9" had been retired by the Sox, a new tunnel under Boston Harbor bore his name, and the Ted Williams Museum and Hitters Hall of Fame in Hernando was a tourist attraction.

Williams was married three times: in 1944 to Doris Soule, with whom he had a daughter; in 1961 to Lee Howard; and in 1968 to Dolores Wettach, with whom he had a son and a daughter. All the unions ended in divorce. Williams suffered several strokes in the 1990s; when his heart began to fail, he had a pacemaker installed, and in 2001 he underwent open-heart surgery. At the end he suffered cardiac arrest and died in Citrus Memorial Hospital.

His children became embroiled in an angry dispute over their father's remains. His daughter, Bobby-Jo Ferrell, insisted her father had always spoken of his wish to be cremated and that the ashes should be scattered over the Florida Keys, where he had had so much enjoyment as a fisherman. Her half-brother, John Henry, also claiming to be heeding his father's wishes and citing a note showing Williams wished at his death "to be put in bio-stasis," had the body shipped to a cryogenic laboratory in Arizona, aiming eventually to obtain DNA that could clone the slugger. Before the year was over, however, Ferrell gave up her fight, citing prohibitive legal costs. Her decision came after a circuit court judge gave permission to immediately distribute the corpus of the trust of $645,000 that Williams had established for his children in 1986.

Williams remains a folk hero to those who saw him play and to aspiring young people who know his achievements on the diamond may well be the apex of baseball greatness.

★

Williams's unusually candid autobiography, written with John Underwood, is *My Turn at Bat: The Story of My Life* (1988). John Underwood and Ted Williams, *Ted Williams Fishing "the Big Three"—Tarpon, Bonefish, and Atlantic Salmon* (1982), showcases Williams's "other life." An eloquent hagiography accompanied by excellent photographs is Richard Ben Cramer, *Ted Williams: The Season of the Kid* (1991). A segment of this book, including new material, is in Cramer's *What Do You Think of Ted Williams Now?: A Remembrance* (2002). On William's glory year, see John Holway, *Last .400 Hitter: The Anatomy of a .400 Season* (1992). An outstanding treatment of Williams's career is Edward Linn, *Hitter: The Life and Turmoils of Ted Williams* (1993). But the best account is Michael Seidel, *Ted Williams: A Baseball Life* (2003). The latest appreciation is in David Halberstam, *Teammates: A Portrait of a Friendship* (2003). A valuable retrospective work is Lawrence Baldassaro, ed., *Ted Williams: Reflections on a Splendid Life* (2003), which complements Baldassaro's earlier, *Ted Williams Reader* (1991). Two encomiums are Dick Johnson, ed., text by

Glenn Stout, *Ted Williams: A Portrait in Words and Pictures* (1991), and Jim Prime and Bill Nowlin, *Ted Williams: A Tribute* (1997). Obituaries are in the *Boston Globe* and *New York Times* (both 6 July 2002).

HENRY F. GRAFF

WILSON, Robert R(athbun) (*b.* 4 March 1914 in Frontier, Wyoming; *d.* 16 January 2000 in Ithaca, New York), physicist, architect, sculptor, and environmentalist best known for his design and direction of the Department of Energy's Fermi National Accelerator Laboratory (Fermilab).

Wilson and his sister were the children of Platt Elvin Wilson, a politician, and Edith Rathbun Wilson. His parents divorced when he was eight years old, and he attended seven elementary schools in four states. Summers provided some sense of stability on relatives' Wyoming cattle ranches. He later applied life lessons learned there to physics, recalling that "we could do anything in the blacksmith shop." In his youth Wilson read Sinclair Lewis's novel *Arrowsmith,* identifying himself with the lonely protagonist, a young scientist. At age seventeen he paid twenty-five cents for a small book on scientific instruments, which inspired

Robert R. Wilson, April 1955. AP/WIDE WORLD PHOTOS

both his 1929 invention of a little accelerator he called a "gaseous discharge tube" and his 1931 invention of a vacuum device.

After graduating from high school in 1932, Wilson enrolled at the University of California, Berkeley. He decided to major in physics after seeing the flashing generators in the physics laboratory. Wilson recalled, "It just seemed like a heaven." As a junior Wilson conducted research under the supervision of Ernest O. Lawrence, director of the university's radiation laboratory and inventor of the cyclotron, a high-energy particle accelerator. During his senior year Wilson published a significant article in *Physical Review* dealing with the time lag for sparks in the field of gaseous discharge. He received his B.A. in 1936.

Wilson continued graduate study under Lawrence's direction, spending nearly all his waking hours in the radiation laboratory. He published two major papers in the field of physics, one experimentally verifying the first theoretical analysis of how protons move in stable cyclotron orbits within magnetic fields and the other expounding the theory of the cyclotron. He also invented a vacuum seal for improving the cyclotron, now referred to as the "Wilson seal." He earned his Ph.D. in 1940.

That same year, on 20 August, he married Jane Inez Scheyer. They had three sons in the course of their fifty-nine-year marriage. Near the end of 1940, Wilson joined the uranium project as instructor at Princeton University, serving in that capacity until 1942. He collaborated with the Italian physicist Enrico Fermi in the preliminary development of the production of a chain reaction. At Princeton he discovered how U-238 (uranium with 238 isotopes) could be split to form U-235 (uranium with 235 isotopes), which is basic to nuclear fission. In 1943 the scientist J. Robert Oppenheimer recruited Wilson as the youngest Cyclotron Group leader for the Manhattan Project, a top-secret endeavor led by the U.S. Army Code of Engineers to ensure that the United States would develop an atomic weapon before its World War II foe Germany. The project was based at the Los Alamos National Laboratory in New Mexico. On 16 July 1945 Wilson's division recorded nuclear measurements of the first atomic bomb, which was detonated at Trinity, New Mexico. Shocked and appalled by the destruction caused by the "Trinity Test," Wilson later told Richard Feynman, a physicist and colleague who was also present, that he could not join in the celebration of the test's success. Wilson vowed to pursue civilian control of atomic energy following the war.

While he was an associate professor at Harvard University (1946–1947), Wilson designed the 150 MeV cyclotron and wrote about the potential of proton therapy for cancer radiation treatment. During his twenty years as director of Cornell University's Laboratory for Nuclear Studies (1947–1967), Wilson oversaw the construction of four successively more powerful energetic electron synchrotrons (which permit particles to travel in a circular orbit at elevated speeds), culminating in the 12 GeV Cornell synchrotron. He also created a device for energy measurement called the quantameter, thereby adding the term "quanta" to the physics lexicon.

Wilson's contributions to physics waned by the 1960s, and he seriously considered pursuing his avocation—sculpture—on a full-time basis. At age fifty he was appointed professor of physics at the Enrico Fermi Institute of Nuclear Studies of the University of Chicago (1967–1976), as well as designer and director at the Fermi National Accelerator Laboratory (Fermilab) (1967–1978), thus combining the two loves of his life: science and art.

Wilson's architectural inspiration for his design of the twin towers of Fermilab was the Saint-Pierre Cathedral in Beauvais, France. The accelerator laboratory, known as Wilson Hall, replicates the cathedral's 250-foot height. The facility and its sculpture were first situated on farmland near Batavia, Illinois. As a result of Wilson's environmental efforts, the grounds are now a prairie teeming with wildlife. Beneath the pastoral four-mile earth berm ring lies a proton machine capable of producing massive electron voltage.

Under Wilson's directorship, the particle accelerator at Fermilab increased its energy after 1972, making it the most powerful particle accelerator in the world. At an energy level of 2 TeV, it mimics the creation of the universe. An apt symbol of physics, its flash utilizes four to five hundred billion electron volts, enabling the detection of minute particles, or fields of force, of the proton—the b-quark or bottom quark (in 1977) and the top quark (in 1995). With the discovery of the bottom quark and measurement of quark charges, a new theory termed "quantum chromodynamics" emerged to explain nuclear structure. The Large Hadron Collider accelerator at the laboratory of the European Organization for Nuclear Research (CERN) in Geneva, Switzerland, was scheduled to supersede the energy production of Fermilab by 2006.

Wilson resigned from the directorship of Fermilab in 1978 to become Peter B. Ritzma Professor of Physics at the University of Chicago (1978–1980). He held the title of Michael Pupin Professor of Physics at Columbia University (1980–1983) until his retirement. After suffering from the effects of a stroke for several years, Wilson died at age eighty-five at his home in Ithaca, New York. A memorial service was held on 28 April 2000, with the deposition of his ashes in the nineteenth-century Pioneer Cemetery on the Fermilab site.

During his forty-year career in particle physics, Wilson received numerous honors, including the Elliott Cresson Medal from the Franklin Institute (1964), the National Medal of Science (1973), and the Enrico Fermi Award from the United States Department of Energy (1984). In 1996 he was recognized by CERN for his pioneering work in cancer research. He helped organize the Association of Los Alamos Scientists and the Federation of Atomic Scientists (now known as the Federation of American Scientists), serving as the latter's chairman in 1946 and again in 1963. He was a member of the scientific research society Sigma Xi and the American Academy of Arts and Sciences. Named a fellow in the American Physical Society, he served as its president in 1985. He also served as chairman of the board of sponsors for the *Bulletin of the Atomic Scientists* from 1982 to 1993.

The best journal articles by Wilson are "A Review of *Brighter Than a Thousand Suns: A Personal History of the Atomic Scientists,* by Robert Jungk," *Scientific American* (December 1958): 145–148; "My Fight Against Team Research," *Daedalus* 99 (fall 1970): 1076–1087; "Niels Bohr and the Young Scientists," *Bulletin of the Atomic Scientists* 41, no. 8 (August 1985): 23–26; and "Hiroshima: The Scientists' Social and Political Reaction," *Proceedings of the American Philosophical Society* 140, no. 3 (1996): 350–357. Wilson and Raphael Littauer's *Accelerators: Machines of Nuclear Physics* (1960) is a general study on particle accelerators.

Wilson was both reserved and outspoken. His wife described him as shy, introverted, "a lone wolf," but throughout his career Wilson often exhibited boldness. At Fermilab he demanded quality research combined with thrift, which occasionally resulted in displays of anger. Wilson's most memorable statement was addressed to Senator John Pastore in 1969 while appearing before the Congressional Joint Committee on Atomic Energy. Explaining the importance of research in high-energy physics to national defense, Wilson stated, "It has nothing to do directly with defending our country except to make it worth defending."

★

The Robert R. Wilson papers are located at the Cornell University Library. Jane Wilson's edited volume *All in Our Time: The Reminiscences of Twelve Nuclear Pioneers* (1975) devotes a chapter to Wilson's years at Los Alamos. Philip J. Hilts, *Scientific Temperaments: Three Lives in Contemporary Science* (1982), contains an in-depth biographical sketch of Wilson. Mary Palevsky, *Atomic Fragments: A Daughter's Questions* (2000), provides insights into Wilson's relationship with Oppenheimer. Francis George Gosling, *The Manhattan Project: Making the Atomic Bomb* (1994), clearly explains chain reactions. Gerard Piel, *The Age of Science: What Scientists Learned in the 20th Century* (2001), quotes Wilson in the course of presenting a succinct history of the cyclotron. Pertinent journal articles about Wilson include "Medal of Science Goes to Three Physicists," *Physics Today* (Dec. 1973); "Robert R. Wilson Resigns in Protest," *Science News* (18 Feb. 1978); and "DOE Fermi Award to Vendryes and Wilson," *Physics Today* (Jan. 1985). Obituaries are in *Cornell News* (17 Jan. 2000); *Nature* (23 Mar. 2000); *Bulletin of Atomic Scientists* (Mar.–Apr. 2000); *Fermi National Accelerator Laboratory, Press Pass* (28 Apr. 2000); and the *New York Times* (18 Jan. 2000).

SANDRA REDMOND PETERS

WOODCOCK, Leonard Freel (*b.* 15 February 1911 in Providence, Rhode Island; *d.* 16 January 2001 in Ann Arbor, Michigan), a highly skilled labor negotiator who was president of the United Auto Workers and an American statesman who became the first U.S. ambassador to China.

Woodcock was the only son of Ernest Woodcock and Margaret (Freel) Woodcock. His father was a skilled machinist and a staunch trade unionist, and his mother a homemaker. When Woodcock was three years old, his father was given an assignment to install machinery at a factory in Germany, where the Woodcock family moved in 1913. When World War I began, Leonard and his mother moved to England, but his father, a British subject, was interned in Germany for the duration of the war. The family reunited in England after the war, and for the next eight years Leonard attended Saint Wilford's and the Northampton town and county schools.

The Woodcocks moved to Detroit in 1926, and Woodcock attended classes at the College of the City of Detroit (now Wayne State University) and the Walsh Institute of Accounting. Forced to drop out of school as a result of the depression, Woodcock in 1933 took a job as a machine assembler at Detroit Gear and Machine Company. The low wages, poor working conditions, and lack of respect on the part of management for the workforce had a profound effect on Woodcock. He became a charter member of a federal local union affiliated with the American Federation of Labor and, following in his father's footsteps, began a lifelong commitment to the labor movement.

After a bout of tuberculosis in 1936 forced him to leave his job and recuperate, in 1939 Woodcock began work as an organizer for the Wayne County (Michigan) Congress of Industrial Organizations. He married his first wife, Loula A. Martin, on 28 May 1941. That marriage lasted for more than twenty-five years and produced three children before ending in divorce in 1962. His career in the United Automobile Workers (UAW) began in 1940 when he accepted a position as a staff representative for UAW local unions in western Michigan. Woodcock had great success as an organizer, beginning with the General Motors (GM) Fisher Body plant in Grand Rapids, Michigan, its last non-union plant. Moreover, he developed a loyal following among western Michigan UAW members. In 1944 Woodcock went to work as a production worker at Continental Aviation and Engineering's plant in Muskegan, Michigan,

Leonard Woodcock, May 1970. BETTMANN/CORBIS

thus transferring his UAW membership to Local 113 in the union's Region 1-D.

During this period Woodcock became a close ally of the labor leader Walter P. Reuther and a member of the Reuther Caucus, which was considered to be on the UAW's political right-wing—although many in the caucus, including Reuther and Woodcock, were former socialists. When Reuther was elected president of the UAW in 1946, Woodcock became his first administrative assistant. He left that position in 1947 and returned to work at the Continental plant in Grand Rapids. That same year Woodcock was elected director of UAW Region 1-D and became a member of the union's executive board. He also served as director of the UAW's agricultural and aerospace departments until 1955.

In 1955 Woodcock was appointed director of the UAW's GM department, the largest in the union. That same year he also became a UAW vice president. By 1958 Woodcock was a national negotiator and spokesman for the UAW, bargaining with the largest automotive company in the world during a recession. He helped achieve a landmark contract that gave UAW local unions the right to negotiate supplements to the national contract. In another significant bargaining agreement with GM, in 1961 Woodcock negotiated the first contract clause that prohibited discriminatory employment practices.

By the 1960s Woodcock had earned a national reputation as a tough, shrewd, and highly successful negotiator. "If we can't do that well [in negotiations]," he stated, "we can't unite our people on other questions." Tall and lanky, Woodcock's conservative appearance often was likened to

that of a university professor—which, ironically, he would become late in his career. Although Woodcock was cool, analytical, and well prepared and viewed as a labor intellectual, he also was a tough, intense negotiator who possessed a "magnificent temper." Both union members and company executives found him to be honest.

In 1970 Woodcock became UAW president following Reuther's death in a plane crash. For many years Reuther had groomed Woodcock to succeed him, but since he was only three years younger than Reuther, Woodcock could remain president for only a short time based on the unwritten protocol that union members should retire at age sixty-five. Hence Reuther began to groom Douglas Fraser as his successor. Reuther's sudden death gave Woodcock an opportunity to campaign for the presidency of the UAW. The battle between Woodcock and Fraser was intense. When a poll of the UAW executive board showed a single-vote lead for Woodcock, Fraser, not wishing to create dissension within the union, threw his support behind Woodcock, who became president in 1970.

Woodcock's first major task as UAW president was to lead the union in 1970 bargaining sessions with GM. This round of negotiations was marked by frustration and anger, since each side considered this labor contract crucial to their future. UAW members were angry over working conditions, while GM believed that the union was making unwarranted demands. Early negotiations failed, and on 14 September 1970 Woodcock led GM workers on a strike that would last sixty-seven days and prove costly for both sides. GM lost important production and sales, and the UAW's finances were seriously depleted, forcing it to borrow $25 million from the International Brotherhood of Teamsters. In the end, however, the UAW signed a contract that restored cost of living increases without a cap and implemented a "30 and out" retirement plan that allowed workers to retire after thirty years of service regardless of their age. Although Woodcock regretted the strident anti-GM statements he had made during the early part of the strike, he emerged with a path-breaking contract and gained national recognition. For the remainder of his UAW presidency, Woodcock successfully enhanced wages, pensions, and health and safety benefits for UAW members.

Woodcock also developed political influence during his career. Always active in local, state, and national Democratic Party affairs, Woodcock was a delegate to Democratic National Conventions from 1952 to 1968 and was a significant force in the Michigan Democratic Party. In 1972 he supported the antiwar presidential candidacy of Senator George McGovern, and later he was an early supporter of Jimmy Carter's presidential campaign. In line with Reuther's philosophy that the labor movement should be in the forefront of the fight for social justice, during the 1960s Woodcock made the UAW a leader in promoting national issues involving civil rights (he marched with the civil rights leader Martin Luther King, Jr.), education, health care, and social justice.

In 1977, a few weeks before Woodcock's retirement from the UAW, the newly elected president Jimmy Carter asked him to head a delegation to Vietnam and Laos to determine the fate of missing American servicemen. Woodcock returned with the remains of twenty-two soldiers, laying the groundwork for reconciliation between Vietnam and the United States. Impressed with his negotiating skills, Carter asked him to head a mission to establish diplomatic relations with China. Woodcock personally led the primary negotiations with the Chinese leader Deng Xiaoping. On 1 January 1979 the United States established full diplomatic relations with China, with Woodcock named as the first U.S. ambassador to the world's most populous nation, a position he held until 1981. Until his death he remained involved in U.S.-China relations, continuously seeking to improve understanding between the two nations. While he was stationed in China, Woodcock met Sharon Tuohy, a nurse who opened the medical unit for the American Liaison Office. Woodcock married her there on 14 April 1978. They had no children.

After successful careers in labor and foreign relations, Woodcock began his final career in 1982 as an adjunct professor of political science at the University of Michigan. This was not his first experience at a university: from 1959 to 1970 he had served as a member of the board of governors at Wayne State University in Detroit, the only elected public office he ever held. Woodcock died of pulmonary complications at his home in Ann Arbor at age eighty-nine. His ashes were scattered over Lake Michigan.

The former UAW president Douglas Fraser summarized Woodcock's achievement as follows by noting, "He served our union well and our country well. He was an excellent example of what a labor leader should be." Indeed, few leaders were as well respected for their accomplishments in the labor movement, and no other labor leader made such an impact on international relations and world peace.

★

The best sources for Woodcock's career in the UAW are the Leonard Woodcock and UAW archival collections, containing two oral interviews and various UAW publications and clippings, housed in the Archives of Labor and Urban Affairs, Walter P. Reuther Library, Wayne State University, Detroit, Michigan. A full-length biography of Woodcock has yet to be written. Although brief, the best biographical sketch is Gilbert Gall, "Leonard Woodcock," *The Encyclopedia of American Business History and Biography: The Automobile Industry, 1920–1980,* ed. by George S. May (1989). The Gerald R. Ford Presidential Library in Ann Arbor, Michigan, houses the records of the United States–China Business Council, which contains information on Woodcock's work in China. William Serrin, *The Company and the Union: The "Civilized Relationship" of the General Motors Corporation and the United Automobile Workers* (1973), a journalistic account of Woodcock's actions during the 1970 GM strike, presents a somewhat biased portrait of Woodcock as UAW president. Patrick Tyler, *A Great Wall: Six Presidents and China* (1999), discusses Woodcock's diplomatic work. Obituaries are in the *Detroit Free Press, Los Angeles Times, New York Times,* and *Washington Post* (all 18 Jan. 2001).

MICHAEL O. SMITH

Y-Z

YARMOLINSKY, Adam (*b*. 17 November 1922 in New York City; *d*. 5 January 2000 in Washington, D.C.), attorney, writer, and social activist noted for the positions he held during the administrations of Presidents John F. Kennedy and Lyndon B. Johnson.

Yarmolinsky was the elder of two sons born to the distinguished Slavonic scholars Avrahm Yarmolinsky and Babette (Deutsch) Yarmolinsky. Avrahm, a Jewish immigrant from Ukraine, was a librarian and a Fëdor Dostoevski scholar whose translations of Russian works earned him the Townsend Harris Medal for "his contribution to a highly specialized field of knowledge." The New York native Babette was a Columbia professor and a writer of poetry and fiction whose many accolades included a *Nation* Poetry Prize. Avrahm and Babette also collaborated on translations of works by the writers Aleksandr Pushkin and Aleksandr Blok.

Both of Yarmolinsky's parents were political leftists who supported numerous liberal causes. As a junior at the prestigious Fieldston School in the Bronx in New York City, Yarmolinsky himself attended meetings of the Young Communists but never joined, owing to what he considered their logical shortcomings. After Fieldston, he entered Harvard University in Cambridge, Massachusetts, where he became active in leftist political organizations and served as editor of the *Harvard Crimson*. He enlisted in the U.S. Army Air Forces immediately upon his graduation in 1943

with a B.A., earning the rank of sergeant by the time of his marriage on 24 March 1945 to Harriet Leslie Rypins, an early childhood education specialist. They later had a daughter and three sons.

After his 1946 discharge, Yarmolinsky attended Yale Law School, graduating with an LL.B. in 1948 and earning admission to the New York state bar in 1949. His clerkship with Chief Judge Charles E. Clark of the U.S. Court of Appeals, New York (Second District), led to a clerkship with the U.S. Supreme Court justice Stanley F. Reed, after which he entered private practice with a Washington, D.C., firm. During the late 1950s he involved himself increasingly with liberal causes, becoming active with several disarmament societies and serving as director of the Fund for the Republic before joining the presidential campaign of Senator John F. Kennedy.

Kennedy recognized Yarmolinsky's brilliance and saw him as an excellent liaison to the New York liberal intellectual community. Yarmolinsky began recruiting bright Easterners for work in the Kennedy campaign and continued as a "talent scout" for positions in the administration after Kennedy's election. For his efforts, Yarmolinsky was rewarded with the position of special assistant to Secretary of Defense Robert S. McNamara.

Although he was almost forty years old, Yarmolinsky quickly became billed as "the brightest of McNamara's whiz kids." In spite of his own military service during World War II, Yarmolinsky could scarcely have been more

Adam Yarmolinsky, October 1965. AP/WIDE WORLD PHOTOS

different from most of the Pentagon officials. He was a diminutive man (five feet, four inches tall) of very obvious Semitic and Slavic ancestry, and the columnists Rowland Evans and Robert Novak described him as "looking like the anarchist bomb thrower in old political cartoons." The New York Jewish intellectual was unpopular with the conservative Christian power structure of the early 1960s Pentagon. Yarmolinsky himself confessed to a tendency toward arrogance, and his enemies dubbed him the "Cardinal Richelieu of the Pentagon" for his heavy-handedness.

Yarmolinsky's most important work in the Defense Department included his efforts to further integrate the armed forces. He lobbied for closing bases in communities that were still segregated (a potentially devastating blow to the economies of many pre-integration southern cities), the immediate closing of off-base segregated facilities, and the use of the dormant facilities for the occupational training of impoverished and minority youth. Although the measures McNamara adapted were less extreme, Yarmolinsky's radicalism forced southern politicians to comply with federal orders, earning him lifelong political enemies in the process.

Yarmolinsky's other contributions as special assistant secretary of defense included the overseeing, through his handpicked assistants, of new computerization, centralized data, and experimental management systems. Although he was an ardent opponent of nuclear testing, he also worked

to increase public awareness of and funding for fallout shelters and became one of the earliest and most vocal opponents of U.S. military involvement in Vietnam.

After Kennedy's assassination in November 1963 and the inauguration of Lyndon B. Johnson as president, Yarmolinsky was reassigned to domestic issues as deputy director (under Kennedy's brother-in-law, Sargent Shriver) of the Anti-Poverty Task Force. He became the primary author of the program's legislation and was designated as first choice for director of the Office of Economic Opportunity. But a group of southern congressmen refused to vote for the legislation that would assure Yarmolinsky a position of influence. Disliked for his work in desegregation and for his general liberalism, Yarmolinsky was described as a "race mongrelizer" by one North Carolina representative and was demonized in speeches throughout the South. It eventually became clear to Johnson that the antipoverty program would not pass as long as Yarmolinsky was employed by the administration. Shriver himself told Yarmolinsky, "We've just thrown you to the wolves, and this is the worst day of my life."

Denied any form of consolation position, the embittered Yarmolinsky returned to Harvard as a professor of urban law in 1966. He then had a successful career in academia that led to a number of posts at the Universities of Massachusetts and Maryland and Georgetown University. Some of his academic writings formed the basis of *The Military Establishment* (1971), a best-seller that was part political science and part memoir. Militant in his detestation of nuclear research, he returned briefly to political life as President Jimmy Carter's counselor to the United States Arms Control and Disarmament Agency from 1977 to 1979.

His marriage to Harriet Rypins ended in divorce after thirty-six years, after which Yarmolinsky married Jane Cox Vonnegut (ex-wife of the novelist Kurt Vonnegut) in 1984. After her death in 1986, Yarmolinsky married Sarah Ames Ellis in 1990. He continued to write articles, editorials, and books for the remaining years of his life, the most notable including *Paradoxes of Power* (1983) and *Rethinking Liberal Education* (1996). He spent his final years in Washington and died at Georgetown University Hospital from complications caused by leukemia treatment.

★

Yarmolinsky's most notable book was *The Military Establishment: Its Impacts on American Society* (1971), which, while primarily a psycho-political overview of the role of the American military, does contain reminiscences of his career as special assistant to Robert McNamara. Robert Dallek, *Flawed Giant: Lyndon Johnson and His Times, 1961–1973* (1998), provides some detail on the "political decapitation" of Yarmolinsky in order to pass the Anti-Poverty Act. A scholarly article that discusses Yarmolinsky's role in desegregating the army is Peter Karsten, "The New American Military: A Map of the Territory, Explored and Unexplored," *American Quarterly* 36, no. 3 (1984): 389–418. Obituaries are in the *New York Times* and *Washington Post* (both 7 Jan. 2000).

JON DARBY

YATES, Sidney Richard (*b.* 27 August 1909 in Chicago, Illinois, *d.* 5 October 2000 in Washington, D.C.), U.S. congressman from Illinois for nearly half a century, and a strong defender of government support for the arts and environmental protection.

Yates, who grew up on the North Side of Chicago, was the youngest of six children of the Lithuanian immigrants Louis Yates, a teamster, and Ida (Siegel) Yates. He attended the Nettlehorst elementary school and graduated with honors from Lake View High School in 1927, where he excelled in basketball and made the All-City team. Yates graduated with a B.A. from the University of Chicago in 1931; there he starred as a guard on the basketball team and earned All–Big Ten recognition.

After graduating from the University of Chicago Law School with a J.D. in 1933, Yates began practicing law. In 1935 he married Adeline Holleb, whom he had met while both were students at the university. They had one son.

Yates's father-in-law was A. Paul Holleb, who had served as an assistant Cook County (Illinois) state's attorney and was president of the Twenty-fourth Ward Regular Democratic Organization on the city's West Side. This connection helped Yates get started in politics. From 1935 through 1937 he served as assistant attorney for the Illinois state bank receiver and from 1937 to 1940 was assistant attorney general attached to the Illinois Commerce Commission. In his first run for elective office, Yates challenged an incumbent member of the Chicago City Council in 1939 and was defeated by a lopsided margin. After this insurgency failed, he reconciled with the regular Democratic organization.

Yates enlisted in the U.S. Navy in 1944 and served in Washington as a lawyer for the Bureau of Ships. After his discharge in 1946 with the rank of lieutenant, he returned to Chicago with political ambitions. In an upset victory, Yates won his first congressional term in 1948, narrowly defeating the first-term Republican incumbent, Robert Twyman, from the North Side's Ninth District. The liberal Yates would represent this district for all but two years of the next half-century, consistently supporting civil rights, organized labor, social welfare programs, affordable housing, and consumer rights. "I tell constituents I owe them my judgment, as well as my honesty," he once told the *Chicago Tribune*. Early in his tenure he alienated House

Sidney R. Yates, October 1962. ART RICKERBY/TIME LIFE PICTURES/GETTY IMAGES

Speaker Sam Rayburn of Texas by voting against deregulation of the oil industry. "They wanted to fix their own rates. Rayburn represented the oil and gas people. I joined the other liberal Democrats," he recalled. "I don't know if Rayburn ever forgave me."

But Yates developed a good relationship with Representative Thomas O'Brien, the leader of the Chicago delegation and one of Rayburn's closest allies. Through O'Brien's sponsorship, he was appointed as a freshman to a slot on the powerful appropriations committee. There he obtained federal funding for the construction of new federal buildings in Chicago, expressways and highways, aid to cultural institutions and higher education, and appropriations to protect the Lake Michigan shoreline and dredge the Calumet River to make it navigable for international shipping.

Yates took on the navy in 1953, when the controversial Captain Hyman Rickover was passed over for promotion to rear admiral and about to be forced into retirement. Yates felt Rickover was being unfairly treated because of his prickly personality, and that the nation could not afford to lose his leadership at a critical time in the development of the atomic submarine. After Yates intervened, Secretary of the Navy Robert B. Anderson ordered Rickover's promotion. Rickover credited Yates with allowing him to finish the construction of the *Nautilus,* the first nuclear submarine. "When the road was rough," Rickover later wrote Yates, "you gave help when help was needed."

In 1962 Yates gave up his congressional seat to run for the U.S. Senate against the Republican incumbent, Everett M. Dirksen, who as minority leader enjoyed a close working relationship with President John F. Kennedy. During the Cuban Missile Crisis, Kennedy undercut Yates by openly consulting with Dirksen. The administration gave Yates nominal support. Even so, Yates gave Dirksen a surprisingly close race and received 47 percent of the vote. As a consolation prize, in 1963 Kennedy appointed Yates as the U.S. representative to the United Nations Trusteeship Council, a position he held for more than a year.

Yates made a political comeback in 1964, and recaptured his old congressional seat. This was the only time during Mayor Richard J. Daley's long tenure as Cook County Democratic chairman that he gave a second chance to a defeated member of the city's congressional delegation. Daley made this exception because Yates had been effective in delivering federal aid for Chicago projects.

On his return to the House, Yates had to give up fourteen years of seniority but regained a slot on the appropriations committee. He supported President Lyndon B. Johnson's Great Society programs but became a critic of the Vietnam War. Following the defeat of Emanuel Celler of New York in 1972, Yates, as the senior Jewish member of Congress, became the leader of a group known unofficially as the Jewish caucus. In this role he helped obtain increased funding for the state of Israel, worked on behalf of Soviet Jews, and sponsored legislation for the construction of the Holocaust Museum in Washington.

From 1975 through 1994 Yates chaired the Interior Subcommittee of the appropriations committee, and used this position to help expand both the wilderness areas and the national park system, protect endangered species, and oppose efforts by the administrations of Ronald W. Reagan and George H. W. Bush to open federally owned land for private development.

Yates, who sponsored the legislation that created the National Endowment for the Arts in 1965, became the nation's foremost champion of public cultural funding. "I've always wanted Washington to be the artistic capital of the country, as well as the political capital," he said in 1998 after the National Symphony Orchestra performed in his honor. Yates pushed for the establishment of the John F. Kennedy Center for the Performing Acts, which was dedicated in 1971, and for increased support for cultural institutions throughout the United States. During the Reagan and Bush administrations, Yates thwarted efforts by conservatives to eliminate public funding for the arts. "No public official battled harder or more successfully to support cultural and artistic life," President William J. ("Bill" Clinton said of Yates. "Everyone who knew Sid will miss his warmth, urbanity and dedication to his country."

Following his retirement from Congress in 1999, Yates lived in Washington, D.C. He died at age ninety-one of kidney failure and complications of pneumonia at Sibley Hospital. He is buried in Memorial Park Cemetery in Skokie, Illinois.

★

Yates's papers are at the Harry S. Truman Presidential Library in Independence, Missouri, and at the Chicago Historical Society. There is no biography. Profiles include William Hines, "The Winner," *Chicago Sun-Times Magazine* (3 Oct. 1976); Ruth Dean, "Sidney Yates—Monitoring the Arts' Money," *Washington Star* (10 Sept. 1979); Michael Killian, "Genteel Giant," *Chicago Tribune* (19 Apr. 1993); and Faye Fiore, "Sidney Yates: On 50 Years of Fighting for Arts Funding for America," *Los Angeles Times* (14 Sept. 1997). See also Philip D. Duncan and Christine D. Lawrence, *Congressional Quarterly's Politics in America 1996: The 104th Congress.* Obituaries are in the *Chicago Sun-Times* (6 Oct. 2000) and *New York Times* (8 Oct. 2000).

STEVE NEAL

YOUNG, Loretta (*b.* 6 January 1913 in Salt Lake City, Utah; *d.* 12 August 2000 in Los Angeles, California), one of the only actresses to make a successful transition from silent films to sound, and later from the movies to a dramatic television series; also the first actress to win both an Academy Award as best actress and an Emmy Award for best actress in a continuing series.

Born with the given names Gretchen Michaela, Young was one of four children born to John Earle Young, an auditor for the Denver, Rio Grande, and Western Railroad, and Gladys (Royal) Young. Her father abandoned the family when Young was about four years old, whereupon her mother took the children to Los Angeles to live with her sister. With financial help from a parish priest, Gladys opened a boardinghouse, and later became an interior designer whose clients included many Hollywood stars.

In addition to her two older sisters, Polly Ann and Elizabeth, and a younger brother, John Royal Young, Young had a half-sister, Georgiana, born after her mother's marriage to George Belzer in 1923.

After briefly attending a Catholic girls' school in the Los Angeles area, Young dropped out to pursue an acting career. She had made her first film appearance at the age of four, as a fairy in *The Primrose Ring* (1918), and in the next year she was an extra in *The Only Way*. At age fourteen she responded to a telephone casting call for her sister, Polly Ann, who was unavailable at the time. Young subsequently signed a contract with First National Studios for a part in *Naughty but Nice* (1927), which resulted in her first leading role, opposite Lon Chaney in *Laugh, Clown, Laugh* (1928). While working for First National, Young changed her first name to Loretta at the suggestion of Mervyn Leroy, the director of *Naughty but Nice*, and Colleen Moore, her costar.

Loretta Young with her Academy Award for *The Farmer's Daughter,* March 1948. AP/WIDE WORLD PHOTOS

On 26 January 1930, two weeks after her seventeenth birthday, Young married Grant Withers, her costar in *The Second-Floor Mystery* (1930). The marriage was annulled the following year. In 1935 Cecil B. DeMille directed her in *The Crusades*. She then appeared with her three sisters in *The Story of Alexander Graham Bell* (1939). For her memorable performance as the Swedish maid in *The Farmer's Daughter* (1948), Young won the Academy Award for best actress over Rosalind Russell, Joan Crawford, Susan Hayward, and Dorothy McGuire.

Young had a high-profile romance with Spencer Tracy while working on *Man's Castle* (1933) and admitted to having a crush on Orson Welles, who played her husband in *The Stranger* (1946). During the filming of *The Call of the Wild* (1935), Young had an affair with her thirty-four-year-old costar, Clark Gable, which resulted in the birth of a baby girl. Knowing that having a child born out of wedlock would ruin her career, Young left for London to conceal her pregnancy, then secretly returned to the United States to give birth to her daughter, Judy.

On 31 July 1940 Young married Tom Lewis, with whom she had two sons, Christopher and Peter. She continued to play lead roles opposite Hollywood's most popular male stars, including Cary Grant and David Niven in *The Bishop's Wife* (1947), William Holden and Robert Mitchum in *Rachel and the Stranger* (1948), and Gable in *Key to the City* (1950).

In 1955 Young and Lewis formed Lewislor Enterprises, which produced the television series *The Loretta Young Show* (originally *Letters to Loretta*). The show presented different dramatic stories and casts each week; Young starred in half of the sketches, playing everything from nuns to housewives. The eight-season series conveyed inspirational, moral messages about family, community, and personal convictions, ending each week with a quotation from the Bible or a few lines of poetry. Her entrance through a door with a full-skirted designer dress whirling around her became Young's trademark. She paved the way for other actresses who soon followed her into dramatic television series, including Jane Wyman, June Allyson, and Barbara Stanwyck. John Forsythe, a costar with Young in *It Happens Every Thursday* (1953), said Young knew herself exceptionally well: "When she moved to TV, she was brave enough to say, 'To hell with what other people think, I'm going to do what I do best.'"

In 1961 Young cooperated with Helen Ferguson on *The Things I Had to Learn,* a philosophical study of her life, success, and faith. She and Lewis divorced in 1969 after twenty-nine years of marriage.

In addition to her films and television series, Young starred in two made-for-television movies: *Christmas Eve* (1966) and *Lady in the Corner* (1989). Also in 1989, she appeared on stage in *An Evening with Loretta Young*. In the final years of her life, Young worked with Joan Wester Anderson, providing her with information for Anderson's *Forever Young* (2000), a biography that illustrated Young's faith and dedication to the Catholic Church and its various charities.

In 1993, at the age of eighty, Young married Jean Louis, a Hollywood fashion designer. Louis passed away in 1997, and three years later Young died of ovarian cancer at the home of her sister, Georgiana, and Georgiana's husband, the actor Ricardo Montalban. Young's ashes were placed in the grave of her mother at Holy Cross Cemetery in Culver City, California.

Young was an elegant, shapely beauty, well known for her rosy complexion, large liquid eyes, full lips, prominent cheekbones, and a strong fashion sense. Unlike other stars who succeeded only in silent pictures, she made a smooth transition from her bit parts in "the flickers" to sound because her voice matched her face. Young opened the path for other women in the field of acting and production. She created a prime-time dramatic series when other actresses had succeeded only in comedies, and was, along with Lucille Ball, one of the few women of her era who controlled her own television series. The actress Pat Crowley, who appeared on *The Loretta Young Show,* said Young was "an amazing pioneer who could stand up to any man as a producer, yet she had the incredible facility of being the most feminine human being there ever was."

A devout Catholic with passionate religious beliefs, Young refused roles that she considered objectionable, including drunks, cold-blooded killers, and women of loose morals. She depicted femininity and beauty while opting to play strong-willed heroines. Marlo Thomas, an actress and Young's godchild, said of her, "She was a rare breed in Hollywood, a Catholic who wore her moral spirit on her shoulder and never compromised her principles." While portraying a nun in the film *Come to the Stable* (1949), Young brought a "swear box" to the set and insisted that anyone who used God's name in vain contribute a quarter to the box. The funds collected were to be given to Saint Anne's Maternity Home, one of her favorite charities. During her lifetime she performed numerous acts of charity, including visits to soldiers in hospitals during World War II, and financially supported and promoted hospitals and adoption agencies for unmarried mothers.

★

Biographies of Young include Joe Morella and Edward Z. Epstein, *Loretta Young: An Extraordinary Life* (1986), and Joan Wester Anderson, *Forever Young* (2000). Judy Lewis, *Uncommon Knowledge* (1994), provides the unique perspective of Young and Gable's daughter. An obituary is in the *New York Times* (13 Aug. 2000).

CONSTANCE C. McGRIFF

ZUCKERT, Eugene Martin (*b.* 9 November 1911 in New York City; *d.* 5 June 2000 in Washington, D.C.), secretary of the U.S. Air Force and cofounder of Project HOPE.

Zuckert, the first child of Harry M. Zuckert, a successful lawyer, and Eugenie Adrienne (Pincoffs) Zuckert, a homemaker, was reared in the New York City area, where his father was a successful lawyer. Moving successively to Washington Heights, New Rochelle, Pelham Heights, and Pelham, the Zuckerts eventually settled in Scarsdale, New York. Zuckert attended the public elementary and high schools of suburban New York until his father, who had become weary of his son's less-than-distinguished academic performance, opted to send him to the Salisbury School, an all boys' Episcopal school in rural Connecticut.

Zuckert's academic performance improved, and he gained entrance to Yale University in New Haven, Connecticut, earning a B.A. in English in 1933. He then entered the combined Yale Law School–Harvard Business School course sponsored by Professor William O. Douglas, who later became a U.S. Supreme Court justice. Zuckert received his LL.B. from Yale in 1937. He married Kathleen Barns on 25 June 1938; the couple had two children.

In 1940, after a three-year stint as an attorney for the U.S. Securities and Exchange Commission, Zuckert be-

Eugene M. Zuckert, 1947. AP/WIDE WORLD PHOTOS

584

came an instructor in government and business relations at the Harvard Graduate School of Business Administration at Cambridge, Massachusetts, where he advanced to professor and then to assistant dean. He also served as a special consultant to the commanding general of the U.S. Army Air Forces (AAF) in developing statistical controls, and as an instructor in the AAF Statistical Control School at Harvard, which trained more than 3,000 air force officers. He also served at various AAF bases in the United States on special assignments for the commanding general of the AAF.

In 1944 Zuckert entered the U.S. Navy as a lieutenant (junior grade), and worked in the Office of the Chief of Naval Operations, where he was assigned to the navy's inventory control program. In September 1945, he was released from the navy to become the executive assistant to the administrator of the Surplus Property Administration (SPA) under W. Stuart Symington. When Symington became the assistant secretary of war for air in February 1946, Zuckert became his special assistant. Following the death of his first wife in January 1945, he married Barbara E. Jackman on 5 May 1945. They had one child and remained together until Barbara's death in 1985.

With the passage of the National Security Act in 1947 and Symington's subsequent appointment as the first secretary of the U.S. Air Force (USAF), the thirty-five-year-old Zuckert took the oath as assistant secretary of the air force. His principal duties were in the field of management. He helped institute Symington's program of "Management Control Through Cost Control," which sought to place the USAF on a businesslike basis, utilizing accepted industrial practices as a yardstick for establishing air force procedures.

The accomplishment that gave Zuckert the most professional satisfaction stemmed from President Harry S. Truman's 1948 directive requiring the armed services to abolish segregation. Working with Lieutenant General Idwal H. Edwards, head of Air Force personnel, Zuckert oversaw implementation of the integration program. Zuckert also served as the air force member of an interservice committee created by Secretary of Defense James Forrestal to develop a Uniform Code of Military Justice (UCMJ) for the Department of Defense.

Continuing as assistant secretary after Thomas K. Finletter succeeded Symington as secretary, Zuckert was charged with the difficult job of dealing with civilian components, including the reserves and the Air Force National Guard. As Finletter concentrated more on larger issues, such as the North Atlantic Treaty Organization (NATO) and the development of nuclear weapons, Zuckert dealt with the daily operations of the office.

When he left the air force in February 1952 to join the Atomic Energy Commission (AEC), Zuckert left behind an air force cost-control system that had established a new high point in sound business administration within the military establishment. After a two-year stay at the AEC, he went into private law practice, joining an old friend, Coates Lear, in what was primarily an aviation law practice. During the 1950s, Zuckert held numerous positions on boards of various companies. He directed the People-to-People Health Foundation and in 1958 helped to found a nonprofit organization that operated the Health Opportunities for People Everywhere (HOPE) ship, the world's first peacetime hospital ship, as part of President Eisenhower's People-to-People Program. Zuckert served as chairman of its medical training and relief organizations board from 1967 to 1981.

In December 1960, Robert McNamara, President-elect John F. Kennedy's designated secretary of defense, recommended to Kennedy that Zuckert be appointed air force secretary. Zuckert was nominated and confirmed in January 1961. With his nearly six years of air force experience, he had perhaps better preparation for and more knowledge about the office and its organization than any person appointed to that post. During his service as secretary, he witnessed the shifting of decision-making powers from the military departments to the Office of the Secretary of Defense, a process ongoing during the 1950s, but culminating under McNamara. Zuckert was also involved in controversies associated with the Vietnam War. Both he and the air force chief of staff General Thomas D. White opposed the administration's decision to cut the B-70 bomber program, although Zuckert later admitted that he erred in promoting the bomber because of its increasing vulnerability to enemy defenses.

The Tactical Fighter Experimental (TFX) aircraft was a tactical fighter-bomber designed and built for both the air force and the navy. In negotiations over the development of this weapon, Zuckert supported the administration, which wanted the plane, against the air force, which did not. In so doing, he strained his relationship with the air force and lost a measure of the confidence it had placed in him. When the Skybolt missile program was canceled in December 1962, Zuckert and the air staff were allied, as they had been during the B-70 debate, against the secretary of defense and the administration. Zuckert often found himself the "man in the middle," at times supporting the air force against the secretary of defense and the administration. Both the air force and the secretary of defense agreed on one of Zuckert's ideas, Project Forecast. This study, initiated in March 1963, was prompted by Zuckert's observation that the air force ought to look at the technologies that would have some bearing on future aerospace military operations.

Shortly after Zuckert left office in September 1965, the air force instituted the Eugene M. Zuckert Management Award, given each year to a general officer or high-level civilian for "outstanding management performance."

After several months as an attorney in private practice, Zuckert joined Scoutt and Rasenberger, the successor to the aviation law firm he had left in 1961. Until 1988, when he retired, Zuckert practiced law, did consulting, and was active in pursuing his long-held interest in corporate governance. Over the years, he served as a director of several small technology companies. In 1967 he became a member of the board of Washington Gas Light and Martin Marietta Corporation. Following the death of his second wife in 1985, Zuckert married Harriet Zimmerly in June 1986.

Zuckert died of pneumonia at the age of eighty-eight after a long illness. A funeral service was held for him on 8 June 2000 at St. Margaret's Episcopal Church in Washington, D.C. His body was cremated.

★

Zuckert's papers as Secretary of the Air Force are maintained at the National Archives in College Park, Maryland, and in an additional microfilm collection held at the Air Force Historical Research Agency at Maxwell Air Force Base, Alabama. In his later years, he prepared and privately published memoirs titled *Recollections*. His article "The Service Secretary: Has He a Useful Role?," *Foreign Affairs* (Apr. 1966), is a fine commentary on his air force secretariat career. Another source is George M. Watson, Jr., *The Office of the Secretary of the Air Force, 1947–1965* (1993). Zuckert's 1997 "History as Biography" speech, published in Rebecca H. Cameron and Barbara Wittig, eds., *Golden Legacy, Boundless Future: Essays on the United States Air Force and the Rise of Aerospace Power: Proceedings of a Symposium Held on May 28–29, 1997 at the Double Tree Hotel, Crystal City, Virginia* (2000), gives an overview of his fifty years of service to the air force. George M. Watson, Jr., "Eugene M. Zuckert: The Man in the Middle," *Airpower Historian* (summer 1989), is another informative source. An obituary is in the *New York Times* (7 June 2000).

GEORGE M. WATSON, JR.

ZUMWALT, Elmo Russell, Jr. ("Bud") (*b.* 29 November 1920 in San Francisco, California; *d.* 2 January 2000 in Durham, North Carolina), admiral in the U.S. Navy who served as chief of naval operations and commander of naval forces during the Vietnam War.

Zumwalt was one of four children born to Elmo Zumwalt, Sr., and Frances Zumwalt, both physicians. He was raised in the San Joaquin Valley town of Tulare, an agricultural community where he attended school. Although his parents were doctors and thus financially stable, the Great Depression ensured that Zumwalt and his family did not live in luxury. Throughout these lean years, Zumwalt's father taught him humility, kindness, and compassion by not charging, or by accepting other forms of payments, such as eggs or vegetables, for services rendered to the destitute residents of Tulare.

Elmo R. Zumwalt, Jr., August 1970. CORBIS/SYGMA

During this time, Zumwalt experienced his first traumatic loss when his brother died from tubercular meningitis. This incident, combined with encouragement from his parents, pushed him to earn good grades so that he, too, could become a physician. Before he began high school, Zumwalt's mother was diagnosed with cancer, which eventually caused her death. Nearing high school graduation, Zumwalt pondered where he would obtain a higher education. Growing global unrest, his father's stories about serving in the U.S. Army Medical Corps during World War I, and the near-exhaustion of the family funds to combat his mother's illness steered Zumwalt toward a service academy. As an army veteran, his father advocated West Point, but the enticement of life at sea persuaded Zumwalt to apply to the U.S. Naval Academy at Annapolis, Maryland, where he was accepted.

After graduating as valedictorian of his Tulare High School Class in 1938, in 1939 Zumwalt began his first year at the Academy as part of the class of 1943. He excelled in public speaking and graduated cum laude, although his education was not intellectually stimulating, and he compared the Academy to a trade school more than a university. World conflict soon altered his last year in Annapolis, and the academically unfulfilled Zumwalt was elated to learn that his class would skip their fourth year and go directly to sea in June 1942.

During World War II, Zumwalt served as a junior surface warfare officer on board destroyers in the Pacific theater. He participated in the battles of Savo Island and Surigao Strait, and took part in the U.S. invasions of Attu, Kiska, Tinian, Peleliu, Palau, Saipan, Lingayen, and Balikpapan. Immediately following the war, Zumwalt assisted in clearing Japanese mines from the Yangtze and Hwangpoo rivers. While there he met and married Mouza Coutelais du Roche, the daughter of Russian and French parents, on 22 October 1945. Zumwalt and Mouza had four children, including a son, Elmo Zumwalt III, who served as a naval officer during Vietnam and who died in 1988 of cancer attributed to his exposure to the toxic herbicide Agent Orange during the war.

Between 1946 and 1949, while at sea and at shore postings, Zumwalt contemplated leaving the navy and attending either medical or law school. A chance meeting with General George C. Marshall in 1949, however, decided Zumwalt's future. Marshall, after listening to Zumwalt's concerns about the postwar navy, persuaded him to remain in the service. This led to his participation in the Korean War aboard the battleship *Wisconsin.*

From 1952 to 1962 Zumwalt attended the U.S. Naval War College in Newport, Rhode Island; worked at the Bureau of Naval Personnel (BuPers); skippered the destroyer USS *Arnold J. Isbell* and the navy's first guided missile frigate, the USS *Dewey;* and completed a tour at the National War College. While attending the latter, Zumwalt researched, wrote, and presented the thesis "The Problem of the Next Succession in the U.S.S.R" to the faculty and student body. Zumwalt's insightful paper was directed to Paul H. Nitze, the assistant secretary of defense for International Security Affairs (ISA), who, after investigating Zumwalt's record, offered him a job. Despite the objections of his BuPers detailer, who believed the position was not prestigious enough for career advancement, Zumwalt accepted the assignment. At ISA, Zumwalt's knowledge of political-military affairs in the upper echelons of the U.S. government prepared him for both administrative and operational duties in the navy. In addition, he developed a close working and personal relationship with Nitze, which resulted in an early promotion to rear admiral in 1965.

That July, Zumwalt assumed command of Cruiser Division Seven, but the next year, at the behest of Nitze and Admiral David L. McDonald, the chief of naval operations (CNO), he returned to Washington, D.C., to head the navy's Division of Systems Analysis. For the next two years Zumwalt strove to replace the navy's obsolescent fleet in order to provide a better naval deterrent to Soviet power. Zumwalt spearheaded three studies that later transformed the navy into a viable blue water force to match the Soviets. The first, known as the Major Fleet Escort Study, led to the construction of the *Spruance*-class destroyer, while the

second, the Surface Missile Study, ultimately created the Harpoon antiship missile. Zumwalt's contribution to the STRAT-X study, the final report, resulted in the building of the *Trident* nuclear submarine and its ballistic missile system. Following these successful tours in Washington, Zumwalt was promoted to vice-admiral and ordered to war-torn Southeast Asia.

In 1968 Zumwalt arrived in South Vietnam and assumed command of all in-country naval components. Prior to his arrival, the inshore, or riverine, navy conducted independent or combined operations with the U.S. Army along South Vietnam's major rivers to thwart communist logistics and movement. Zumwalt determined that the enemy had shifted its focus to South Vietnam's smaller inland waterways to avoid U.S. naval forces. With this awareness, he established SEALORDS (Southeast Asia Lake, Ocean, River, Delta Strategy), which utilized the entire "brown water navy" to interdict the enemy on South Vietnam's smaller rivers and tributaries. His bold concept placed naval forces along interdiction barriers from the Cambodian border to the South China Sea, which assisted in the overall pacification of South Vietnam's southernmost provinces, or IV Corps Tactical Zone.

Despite the success of SEALORDS, the election of President Richard M. Nixon triggered a new policy of complete withdrawal for U.S. armed forces in South Vietnam, labeled "Vietnamization" by the Nixon administration. Zumwalt's program for untangling all inshore and coastal naval elements by 1970 was ACTOV (Accelerated Turnover to the Vietnamese). In early 1969 Zumwalt presented his aggressive ACTOV outline to Secretary of Defense Melvin Laird, who was visiting South Vietnam. Unbeknownst to Zumwalt, this briefing earmarked him for the navy's top post the next year.

In 1970 Zumwalt was selected over many senior officers for promotion to full admiral, becoming at age forty-nine the youngest Chief of Naval Operations (CNO) in U.S. naval history. Immediately, he prioritized his goals in the Project Sixty study, which guided the navy under his watch. With indefatigable energy, he set out to finish what he had started as head of the Division of System Analysis: the development of a U.S. maritime force that could check Soviet naval power. This resulted in the creation of Zumwalt's new vision for the fleet, dubbed the "high-low mix." Disputed by many in the navy as flawed strategic thinking, Zumwalt's plan called for the construction of moderate to low-priced ships with correspondingly cheaper technology and weapons systems to balance the high-end ships, such as carriers and ballistic missile submarines. He believed this would enable the navy to deploy larger numbers of low-end ships into sea control missions rather than a few high-end vessels. Zumwalt's efforts resulted in the *Oliver Hazard Perry*–class frigate.

Although Zumwalt advocated the high-low program, he also wanted to increase the lethality of the surface navy, which eventually culminated in the adoption of the Harpoon and Tomahawk cruise missiles. Yet the most controversial of his programs focused on people. Concerned about the enlistment and retention of naval personnel, Zumwalt began altering how the navy addressed these issues. In "Z-Grams," which were dispatched immediately to the fleet, he changed naval customs and regulations, such as hair length, to demonstrate his willingness to adjust entrenched tradition to make navy life more palatable. Continuing in his reforming efforts, Zumwalt also championed more roles for women and minorities. When he retired from the navy in 1974, he had established the core elements necessary for the modern U.S. Navy.

With expertise in leadership and research from years of naval service, Zumwalt became president of American Medical Buildings, and later served as director for a number of companies, such as Gifford Hill and Company and Transway. He also ran for the U.S. Senate and served as governor of the American Stock Exchange. Zumwalt received honorary degrees from Texas Tech University in Lubbock, Texas, Villanova University in Pennsylvania, the University of North Carolina at Chapel Hill, Central Michigan University in Mount Pleasant, and Michigan Technological University in Houghton. In addition to his involvement in the corporate world, he continually fought for veterans' rights, primarily those associated with service-related cancers, such as that responsible for his own son's illness and death. In honor of Zumwalt's involvement in veterans' affairs in peacetime, combined with thirty-five years of duty in the navy, President William J. ("Bill") Clinton awarded him the Presidential Medal of Freedom in 1998.

Zumwalt died at Duke University Medical Center in Durham, North Carolina, as a result of complications from surgery to remove a chest tumor. He is buried in the Naval Academy cemetery in Annapolis.

★

The majority of Zumwalt's papers are housed in the Naval Historical Center's Operational Archives at the Washington Navy Yard in Washington, D.C. Autobiographical information is available in Zumwalt, *On Watch: A Memoir* (1976). *My Father, My Son* (1986), written by Zumwalt and his son Elmo Zumwalt III, discusses the latter's struggle with cancer. Information about Zumwalt is available in Robert William Love, Jr., ed., *The Chiefs of Naval Operations* (1980); James C. Bradford, ed., *Quarterdeck and Bridge: Two Centuries of American Naval Leaders* (1997); and R. Blake Dunnavent, *Brown Water Warfare: The U.S. Navy in Riverine Warfare and the Emergence of a Tactical Doctrine, 1775–1970* (2003). See also Leslie Julian Cullen, "Brown Water Admiral: Elmo R. Zumwalt Jr. and United States Naval Forces, Vietnam, 1968–1970," Ph.D. dissertation, Texas Tech University, 1998. Obituaries are in the *New York Times* and *Washington Post* (both 3 Jan. 2000).

R. BLAKE DUNNAVENT

DIRECTORY OF CONTRIBUTORS

AGNEW, BRAD
Northeastern State University
    Albert, Carl B.
    Ambrose, Stephen E.
ALLEN, HOWARD
Brooklyn College of the City University of New York
    (Retired)
    Pais, Abraham
ALLENBAUGH, MARK H.
George Washington University (Adjunct)
    McVeigh, Timothy
AMLER, JANE FRANCES
Manhattanville College
    Townsend, Lynn A.
ATON, RUSTY D.
    Nomellini, Leo
AURAND, HAROLD W., JR.
Pennsylvania State University, Schuylkill Campus
    Groza, Lou
BALKEN, ROBERT D.
Southwest Missouri State University
    Fairbanks, Douglas, Jr.
BALTAKE, JOE
Sacramento Bee film critic
    Lemmon, John Uhler, III ("Jack")
BANDY, LEE
    Spence, Floyd D.
BARBEAU, ART
West Liberty State College
    Quinn, Anthony
BECK, SHEILA
Queensborough Community College
    Canby, Vincent
BEEKMAN, SCOTT M.
Ohio University
    Henderson, Joseph A. ("Joe")
BEETZ, KIRK H.
Author and Educator
    Atherton, Alfred L., Jr.
    Balaban, Elmer
    Beckwith, Byron De La
    Fannin, Paul J.

    Harsanyi, John C.
    Kleindienst, Richard G.
    Price, Cecil R.
    Wade, Henry
BERLAGE, GAI INGHAM
Iona College
    Dancer, Faye
BJERGA, ALAN
    Brown, J. Carter
    Kiam, Victor
    MacArthur, Jean Faircloth
    Pucinski, Roman C.
    Szulc, Tad
BLOOM, ALAN
Valparaiso University
    Schaap, Richard Jay ("Dick")
BOSKY, BERNADETTE LYNN
Freelance Writer and Instructor
    Hanna, William
BOYLES, MARY
University of North Carolina at Pembroke (Emeritus)
    Brown, Dee
BRILEY, RON
Sandia Preparatory School, Albuquerque, N. Mex.
    Budge, Don
BRITTON, KATHARINE FISHER
Freelance Writer, Norwich, Vt.
    Epstein, Julius J.
BUSTER, ALAN
Harvard-Westlake School, Los Angeles
    Sothern, Ann
BYRNE, JOHN J.
Bronx Community College
    Trout, Robert
CAMPBELL, JIM
Bucknell University (Retired)
    Albert, Frank Culling ("Frankie")
    Fears, Thomas Jesse ("Tom")
    Hayes, Robert Lee ("Bob")
    Landry, Thomas Wade ("Tom")
    McKay, John

Rote, Kyle
Unitas, John Constantine ("Johnny")
Weinmeister, Arnold George ("Arnie")

CANNON, DONALD J.
St. Peters College and John Jay College of Criminal Justice of the City University of New York
Feehan, William

CARDOSO, JACK J.
Professor Emeritus, State University of New York College, Buffalo
Nash, Gerald

CARDOSO, ROSEMARIE S.
Artist and Retired Art Educator
Marcus, Stanley

CARPENTER, BRIAN B.
Texas A&M University Libraries
Thomas, Rex David ("Dave")

CASTAÑEDA, JAMES AGUSTÍN
Rice University
Lemons, A. E. ("Abe")

CHABORA, ROBERT J.
Concordia College
Fitch, James Marston

CHAVEZ, PABLO L.
Attorney at Law
Gunther, Gerald

CHAVEZ, REBECCA BILL
United States Naval Academy
Gunther, Gerald

CHEN, JEFFREY H.
Cambridge University Press
Hay, Henry, Jr. ("Harry")

CICARELLI, JAMES
Roosevelt University
Miller, Merton H.

CICARELLI, JULIANNE
Freelance Writer, Arlington Heights, Ill.
Verdon, Gwen

COCHRAN, CHARLES L.
United States Naval Academy
Gonzalez, Henry B.
Helms, Richard

COLBERT, THOMAS BURNELL
Marshalltown Community College
Foerstner, George

CONE, TEMPLE
Wake Forest University
Koch, Kenneth

COOKSEY, GLORIA
Freelance Writer, Chicago
Dertouzos, Michael L.
Elias, Peter
Fariña, Mimi

Friedman, Herbert
Martin, Donald Edward ("Don")

CRAWFORD, DESSA
Delaware County Community College
Evans, Dale

CRAWFORD, SCOTT A. G. M.
Eastern Illinois University
Petty, Lee
Saddler, Joseph ("Sandy")

CROUSE, TIM MARTIN
MTV2
Aaliyah

CROWTHER-HEYCK, HUNTER
University of Oklahoma, Norman
Simon, Herbert A.

DAMON, ALLAN L.
Horace Greeley High School (retired), Chappaqua, N.Y.
Lindbergh, Anne Morrow
Pusey, Nathan M.
Smith, Howard K.
Stassen, Harold E.

DARBY, JON
Maas, Peter
Yarmolinsky, Adam

DARR, JEN
Ritts, Herb

DAVIDMAN, RICHARD L.
Downtown Financial Network, New York City
Alger, David

DAVIDSON, ABRAHAM A.
Tyler School of Art, Temple University
Gillespie, Gregory
Lawrence, Jacob

DAVIDSON, KEAY
Science Writer, San Francisco Chronicle
Rawls, John
Salmon, Wesley C.

DINNEEN, MARCIA B.
Bridgewater State College
Farrell, Eileen
Walston, Ray
Warfield, William

DOENECKE, JUSTUS D.
New College of Florida
McIntire, Carl
Wiebe, Robert H.

DORINSON, JOSEPH
Long Island University, Brooklyn Campus, and St. Francis College of Brooklyn
Berle, Milton

DROBNICKI, JOHN A.
York College, City University of New York
Hibbler, Albert George ("Al")

DUNNAVENT, BLAKE
Louisiana State University, Shreveport
   Zumwalt, Elmo R., Jr.
DUZINKIEWICZ, JANUSZ
Purdue University North Central
   Karski, Jan
EDELMAN, ROBERT
University at Albany, State University of New York
   Matthau, Walter
ELLIS, LISA A.
Baruch College of the City University of New York
   Vicente, Esteban
ENDERS, ERIC
Historian, Cooperstown, N.Y.
   Black, Joseph, Jr. ("Joe")
ENNIS, LISA A.
Austin Peay State University
   Talmadge, Herman E.
FAIR, JOHN D.
Georgia College and State University
   Coverdell, Paul
FERRARA, ADI R.
Freelance Writer, Bellevue, Wash.
   Neel, James V.
FERRELL, ROBERT H.
Indiana University
   Wells, Herman B.
   Wellstone, Paul D.
FINNEGAN, JOHN R., SR.
University of Minnesota
   Ridder, Bernard H., Jr.
FITZPATRICK, JANE BRODSKY
Stephen B. Luce Library, State University of New York
      Maritime College
   Boland, Edward P.
   McLean, Malcom P.
   Moakley, J. Joseph ("Joe")
FLANNERY, MAURA
St. John's University, New York
   Bloch, Konrad E.
FLYNN, JOSEPH G.
Distinguished Service Professor Emeritus, State University of
      New York College of Technology, Alfred
   Gardner, John W.
   Rosenberg, William
FRANCIS, BILL
National Baseball Hall of Fame
   Lemon, Robert Granville ("Bob")
FRICK, LISA
Freelance Writer, Columbia, Mo.
   Loeb, Nackey Scripps
   Pearl, Daniel ("Danny")

FRIED, RONALD K.
Television Producer and Writer, New York City
   Futch, Eddie
FRIGUGLIETTI, JAMES
Montana State University, Billings
   Palmer, R. R.
FRISBIE, MARGERY
   Egan, John J.
FRISCH, PAUL A.
Our Lady of the Lake University, San Antonio, Tex.
   Chapman, Leonard F., Jr.
   Rivero, Horacio ("Rivets")
GAAR, GILLIAN G.
Freelance Writer, Seattle, Wash.
   Donahue, Troy
GARGAN, WILLIAM M.
Brooklyn College of the City University of New York
   Kesey, Kenneth Elton ("Ken")
GATES, JONATHAN A.
Nyack College
   Gilbreth, Frank, Jr.
GENTILE, RICHARD H.
Freelance Writer and Editor, South Easton, Mass.
   Boudreau, Louis ("Lou")
   Francis, Arlene
GIETSCHIER, STEVEN P.
The Sporting News
   Buck, John Francis ("Jack")
   Slaughter, Enos ("Country")
GOLWAY, TERRY
Author
   Judge, Mychal
GOODBODY, JOAN
Michigan Technological University
   Howe, Harold, II
   Jovanovich, William
GOODFOX, JULIA
University of Kansas
   Ripley, S(idney) Dillon, II
GOODHAND, GLEN R.
Society for International Hockey Research
   Abel, Sidney Gerald ("Sid")
GORDON, NANCY M.
Independent Scholar, Amherst, Mass.
   Dallin, Alexander
   McIntosh, Millicent Carey
   Tobin, James
GOTTLIEB, JANE
The Juilliard School
   Stern, Isaac
GRAFF, HENRY F.
Professor Emeritus, Columbia University
   Williams, Theodore Samuel ("Ted")

GREENBERG, DAVID
Yale University
Graham, Katharine
HARMOND, RICHARD P.
St. John's University, New York
Lord, Walter
HARPEL-BURKE, PAM
Hofstra University
Greenberg, Joseph H.
HARRISON, HELEN A.
The New York Times, and Pollock-Krasner House and Study Center
Rivers, Larry
HASENFUS, WILLIAM A.
Community College of Rhode Island, Bridgewater State College
Pastore, John O.
HASKINS, JAMES
University of Florida
Hampton, Lionel
HEALY, JOHN DAVID
Drew University
Rogers, William P.
Wechsler, Herbert
HLAVATY, ARTHUR D.
Freelance Writer and Editor, Yonkers, N.Y.
Cannon, Howard W.
Davis, James Houston ("Jimmie")
Nozick, Robert
Wilhelm, Hoyt
HODGES, GRAHAM GAO RUSSELL
Colgate University
Case, Everett N.
HOOGENBOOM, LYNN
The New York Times News Service
Benson, Mildred Wirt
Landers, Ann (Esther Friedman Lederer)
HORGAN, JOHN
Shannon, Claude E.
HORN, BARBARA LEE
St. John's University, New York
Merrick, David
HOUSE, ROB
Tidewater Community College
Phillips, William
HOWLETT, CHARLES F.
Adelphi University
Hart, Leon
IVERSON, STEPHANIE DAY
Bonnie Cashin Collection, Charles E. Young Research Library, University of California, Los Angeles
Cashin, Bonnie

JALENAK, NATALIE B.
Abram, Morris B.
Schindler, Alexander M.
JEWETT, ANDREW
Yale University
Ginzberg, Eli
JONES, DAVID
Baseball Historian
Mathews, Edwin Lee ("Eddie")
KASHATUS, WILLIAM C.
Philadelphia Daily News
Gray, Pete
KEEN, W. HUBERT
System Administration, State University of New York
Tukey, John W.
KEOGAN, WILLIAM L.
St. Johns University, New York
Phillips, John
KINKELA, DAVID
New York University
Sawhill, John C.
KINYATTI, NJOKI-WA-
York College Library, City University of New York
Gibson, William F.
Jackson, George
LAIRD, KIM
Library of Michigan
Cleage, Albert B.
LAKIN, PAMELA ARMSTRONG
Research Services Libraries, Alfred University
Claiborne, Craig
LANKEVICH, GEORGE J.
Professor Emeritus of History, City University of New York
Lindsay, John V.
O'Connor, John Joseph
LAUER, JOSH
Annenberg School for Communication, University of Pennsylvania
Annenberg, Walter H
Wiggins, J. Russell
LI, SHAOSHAN
New York City Department of Education
Tien, Chang-Lin
LITTLE, KIMBERLY
Ohio University
Lovelace, Linda
LOBRUTTO, VINCENT
School of Visual Arts, New York City
Hill, George Roy
LOZA, STEVEN
University of California, Los Angeles
Puente, Ernest Anthony, Jr. ("Tito")

LUFT, ERIC V. D.
State University of New York Upstate Medical University
Masters, William H.
Weiss, Paul

McCLAY, WILFRED M.
Riesman, David

McCLELLAN, KEITH
Historian and Writer
Stone, W. Clement

McCORMACK, BRIAN
Arizona State University
Warnke, Paul C.

MACDONALD, GINA
Nicholls State University
Ludlum, Robert

McDOUGAL, DENNIS
California State University, Long Beach
Wasserman, Lewis Robert ("Lew")

McELWAINE, JAMES
*Purchase College of the State University of
    New York*
Lee, Peggy
Lewis, John
Lomax, Alan

McGRIFF, CONSTANCE C.
Southwest Missouri State University
Young, Loretta

McLEAN, MICHAEL
Freelance Writer, New York City
Hooker, John Lee

McQUEEN, LEE
Owner, Mighty Literati Bookshop
Brown, Claude
Jordan, June

MALONE, ELOISE F.
United States Naval Academy
Casey, Robert P.
Le Clercq, Tanaquil

MALONEY, WENDY HALL
*Brooklyn College of the City University of
    New York*
Ash, Mary Kay
Connor, John T.
Rudin, Lewis ("Lew")

MALVASI, MEG GREENE
Midlothian, Va.
Biggers, John
Rutherford, Margaret Russell
Thomas, Robert McG., Jr.

MAMIYA, LAWRENCE H.
Vassar College
Lincoln, C. Eric

MARC, DAVID
Syracuse University
Allen, Stephen Valentine Patrick William ("Steve")
De Cordova, Frederick Timmons ("Fred")
Glickman, Martin Irving ("Marty")
Hearn, Francis ("Chick")
Hearst, Randolph A.
O'Connor, Carroll
Steiger, Rodney Stephen ("Rod")
Weaver, Sylvester ("Pat")

MARKHAM, REED
California State Polytechnic University, Pomona (Emeritus)
Dixon, Julian C.
Levi, Edward H.
Nason, John W.

MARKLEY, PATRICIA L.
Siena College
Borge, Victor

MARKOE, LAUREN
Washington Reporter and The State
Potok, Chaim

MARRS, SUZANNE
Welty Foundation Scholar-in-Residence, Millsaps College
Welty, Eudora

MECKNA, MICHAEL
Texas Christian University
Como, Pierino Ronald ("Perry")

MERRON, MYRNA W.
Trigère, Pauline

MEYER, FRED
The New York Times
Jam Master Jay (Jason Mizell)

MILLER, MICHAEL C.
Eifler, Carl F.

MOORE, WILLIAM HOWARD
University of Wyoming
Bonanno, Joseph ("Joe Bananas")
Gotti, John

MORALES-VÁZQUEZ, RUBIL
Bergen Community College
O'Farrill, Arturo ("Chico")

MORAN, DOROTHY L.
Freelance Writer, Brooklyn, N.Y.
Lamarr, Hedy

MORAN, JOHN
Queens Borough Public Library, New York
Hall, Gus

MORGAN, BILL
Writer, Editor, and Freelance Archivist
Corso, Gregory

MUFSON, DANIEL
Brooklyn College of the City University of New York
Robards, Jason

MURRAY, PAUL T.
Siena College
  Davis, Benjamin O., Jr.
MYERS, R. DAVID
The College of Santa Fe
  Reuss, Henry S.
NAGEL, M. C.
Freelance Writer
  Cram, Donald J.
  Shull, Clifford G.
NEAL, STEVE
Chicago Sun-Times
  Daniel, Clifton
  Neuberger, Maurine Brown
  Stratton, William G.
  Yates, Sidney R.
NELSON, MURRY R.
Pennsylvania State University
  Hannum, Alex
NEUMANN, CARYN E.
The Ohio State University
  Rhodes, James A.
NEWMAN, ROGER K.
New York University
  Greene, Harold H.
  White, Byron R. ("Whizzer")
NIELSEN, FRED
University of Nebraska at Omaha
  Curtis, Carl T.
  Hillegass, Clifton K.
OHL, JOHN KENNEDY
Mesa Community College
  Sitter, Carl L.
  Street, George L., III
O'KEEFE, KEVIN
Stetson University
  Oakes, John B.
ORMSBY, RITA
  Maple, John E. ("Jack")
PETECHUK, DAVID
Freelance Writer
  Abbott, Jack Henry
  Fahey, John
  Feshbach, Herman
  Hunter, Kim
PETERS, SANDRA REDMOND
Independent Scholar
  Wilson, Robert R.
PHARR, ANN E.
National Academy of Public Administration
  Pierce, Samuel R., Jr.

POLNER, MURRAY
Freelance Writer
  Berrigan, Philip
PORTER, DAVID L.
William Penn University
  Cranston, Alan
  Luisetti, Angelo Enrico ("Hank")
PRESTON, ANDREW
University of Victoria, British Columbia, Canada
  Bundy, William P.
PRONO, LUCA
Independent Scholar
  Greer, Jane
RECIO, MARIA
Journalist, Washington, D.C.
  Dana, Charles A., Jr.
REYNOLDS, CLARK G.
Distinguished Professor Emeritus, College of Charleston, South Carolina
  Brown, Lester Raymond ("Les")
  Hinton, Milton John ("Milt")
  Nicholas, Harold
RICHARDSON, KIM
Freelance Writer, Salt Lake City, Utah
  Rostow, Eugene V.
RITCHIE, DONALD A.
United States Senate Historical Office
  Block, Herbert L. ("Herblock")
  Mansfield, Michael Joseph ("Mike")
ROBERTS, PRISCILLA
University of Hong Kong
  Vance, Cyrus R.
ROBERTS, RANDY
Purdue University
  Arledge, Roone
ROCCO, JOHN
State University of New York, Maritime College
  Kramer, Stanley
  Ramone, Joey
ROSENDAHL, SARAH JANE
Southwest Missouri State University
  Lardner, Ring, Jr.
ROTHENBERG, DAVID
  Cohen, Alexander H.
ROYCE, BRENDA SCOTT
Freelance Writer and Editor
  Washburn, Sherwood L.
SATT-ARROW, GOLDIE
Brooklyn College of the City University of New York
  Whyte, William F.

SAVAGE, STEVEN P.
Eastern Kentucky University
  Jones, Horace Allyn ("Jimmy")
SENNETT, TED
Author, Closter, N.J.
  Coca, Imogene
  McGuire, Dorothy
SHERMER, MICHAEL
Skeptic
  Gould, Stephen Jay
SHERWIN, MARTIN J.
Tufts University
  Callaway, Ely
  Jones, Robert Trent, Sr.
  Snead, Samuel Jackson ("Sam")
SHOR, RACHEL
Queens Borough Public Library, New York City
  Lewis, Flora
SIKOV, ED
Haverford College
  Wilder, Samuel ("Billy")
SIMMONS, JOHN ALLAN
  Trevor, Claire
SINGH, ANNMARIE
Hofstra University
  Cantwell, Mary
SMALLWOOD, JAMES M.
Professor Emeritus, Oklahoma State University
  Evans, Rowland, Jr.
SMITH, JAMES F.
Pennsylvania State University
  Atkins, Chester Burton ("Chet")
SMITH, MICHAEL
Walter Reuther Library, Wayne State University
  Woodcock, Leonard
SMITH, PATRICK S.
Freelance Writer, Pittsburgh, Penn.
  Donovan, Carolyn Gertrude Amelia ("Carrie")
  Handler, Ruth
  Knowles, John
  Kriendler, H. Peter
SMITH, WHITNEY
The Indianapolis Star
  Hovhaness, Alan
SPATT, HARTLEY S.
State University of New York, Maritime College
  Brooks, Gwendolyn
  Cocke, John
  Hewlett, William R.
  Kamen, Martin D.
  Shapiro, Karl

STEEN, IVAN D.
*University at Albany, State University of
  New York*
  Logue, Edward J.
STERTZ, STEPHEN A.
Montclair State University
  Simon, William E.
STRICKLIN, DAVID
Lyon College
  Jennings, Waylon
SUMNER, JIM L.
North Carolina Museum of History
  Earnhardt, (Ralph) Dale
SUSSER, MARGALIT
Queens Borough Public Library System
  Gerstenberg, Richard
  Kemper, James S., Jr.
TAMBORRINO, VICTORIA
St. John's University, New York
  Goodman, Louis S.
TASSINARI, EDWARD J.
State University of New York, Maritime College
  Jack, Beau
  Lane, Richard ("Dick"; "Night Train")
THOMPSON, MARIE L.
Freelance Writer
  Horstmann, Dorothy M.
  Kennedy, Florynce ("Flo")
  Reel, A. Frank
  Scott, Roland B.
THOMPSON-FEUERHERD, JENNIFER
New York Institute of Technology
  Sagan, Ginetta
THORNTON, JOYCE K.
Texas A&M University Libraries
  Rowan, Carl T.
THORSEN, CONNIE
St. John's University, New York
  Horwich, Frances R.
TIMMONS, REBECCA
  Blass, William Ralph ("Bill")
  Dillard, William T.
  Gennaro, Peter
  Marriott, Alice Sheets
TIMMONS, W. TODD
University of Arkansas
  Gilruth, Robert R.
  Piore, Emanuel R.
  Strand, Kaj Aage
  Weber, Joseph
  Weisskopf, Victor F.

TOMASINO, ADRIANA C.
Ph.D. Candidate, City University of
New York
Mink, Patsy T.
Richards, Faith ("Bucky")
VANDOREN, SANDRA SHAFFER
Adler, Lawrence Cecil ("Larry")
Greco, José
VELLANI, ROBERT
University of Houston
Coburn, James
Stanley, Kim
VORPERIAN, JOHN
Attorney, White Plains, N.Y.
Stargell, Wilver Dornel ("Willie")
WASHBURN, MARK
The Charlotte Observer
Ketcham, Henry King ("Hank")
Reber, Grote
Schulz, Charles M.
WATSON, GEORGE M., JR.
Air Force History Support Office
Zuckert, Eugene M.
WATSON, MARY ANN
Eastern Michigan University
Barnouw, Erik
Frankenheimer, John
WEDGE, ELEANOR F.
Freelance Writer and Editor
Baskin, Leonard
Broun, Heywood Hale

WEISBLAT, LEIGH BULLARD
Independent Art Historian, New York City
Segal, George
WEISBLAT, TINKY "DAKOTA"
Independent Journalist and Singer,
Hawley, Mass.
Clooney, Rosemary
Green, Adolph
WELTMAN, BURTON
William Paterson University
Adler, Mortimer J.
WENDT, SIMON
JFK Institute for North American Studies,
Free University of Berlin
Sullivan, Leon H.
Williams, Hosea
WISE, STEVEN
Sueltenfuss Library, Our Lady of the
Lake University
Black, Charles L., Jr.
XIAO, JUDY
College of Staten Island, City University of
New York
Kingman, Dong
YAGODA, BEN
University of Delaware
Kael, Pauline
Maxwell, William
YOUNG, HOPE E.
York College, City University of New York
Dana, Charles A., Jr.
Parton, James

OCCUPATIONS INDEX, VOLUMES 1–6 and THEMATIC VOLUMES

See also the Alphabetical List of Subjects beginning on p. 681. Note that the Sports and 1960s thematic series each comprise two volumes. Thus, for example, a citation for "1960s-2" means that the subject is found in Volume 2 of the 1960s thematic set.

	Volume		*Volume*
Acting Teacher		Baxter, Anne	1
Adler, Stella	3	Beatty, (Henry) Warren	1960s-1
Donahue, Troy	6	Beck, Julian	1, 1960s-1
Meisner, Sanford	5	Bellamy, Ralph Rexford	3
Stanley, Kim	6	Belushi, John	1
Strasberg, Lee	1	Bennett, Joan	2
Actor		Bergman, Ingrid	1
Aaliyah (Aaliyah Dana Haughton)	6	Berle, Milton	6
Ace, Goodman	1	Blaine, Vivian	4
Adler, Luther	1	Blanc, Mel(vin) Jerome	2
Adler, Stella	3	Bolger, Ray(mond) Wallace	2
Albertson, Jack	1	Booth, Shirley	3
Allen, Woody	1960s-1	Bridges, Lloyd Vernet, Jr.	5
Allison, Fran(ces)	2	Brooks, (Mary) Louise	1
Ameche, Don	3	Broun, Heywood Hale ("Woodie")	6
Anderson, Judith	3	Brown, James Nathaniel ("Jim")	1960s-1
Andrews, (Carver) Dana	3	Brynner, Yul	1
Andrews, Julie	1960s-1	Bubbles, John William	2
Arden, Eve	2	Burnett, Carol	1960s-1
Arnaz, Desi	2	Burns, George	4
Arthur, Jean	3	Burr, Raymond William Stacy	3
Astaire, Adele Marie	1	Cagney, James Francis, Jr.	2
Astaire, Fred	2	Candy, John Franklin	4
Astor, Mary	2	Canutt, Enos Edward ("Yakima")	2
Autry, (Orvon) Gene	5	Carmichael, Howard Hoagland	
Avalon, Frankie, and Annette Joanne		("Hoagy")	1
Funicello	1960s-1	Carnovsky, Morris	3
Axton, Hoyt Wayne	5	Carradine, John	2
Backus, James Gilmore ("Jim")	2	Carroll, Diahann	1960s-1
Bailey, Pearl Mae	2	Checker, Chubby	1960s-1
Baker, Carroll	1960s-1	Childress, Alvin	2
Ball, Lucille Désirée	2	Clooney, Rosemary	6
Bancroft, Anne	1960s-1	Coburn, James	6
Bartholomew, Frederick Llewellyn		Coca, Imogene	6
("Freddie")	3	Colbert, Claudette	4

	Volume		Volume
Actor (*continued*)		Gish, Lillian Diana	3
Connors, Kevin Joseph Aloysius		Gleason, Herbert John ("Jackie")	2
("Chuck")	3	Goddard, Paulette	2
Coogan, John Leslie, Jr. ("Jackie")	1	Gordon, Ruth	1
Cotten, Joseph Cheshire	4	Gordone, Charles	4
Crabbe, Clarence Linden ("Buster")	1	Gosden, Freeman Fisher	1
Crawford, (William) Broderick	2	Goulding, Ray(mond) Walter	2
Crisp, Quentin	5	Grant, Cary	2
Crothers, Benjamin Sherman		Greene, Lorne	2
("Scatman")	2	Greer, Jane	6
Daniels, William Boone ("Billy")	2	Guthrie, Arlo Davy	1960s-1
Davis, Bette	2	Hackman, Eugene Alden ("Gene")	1960s-1
Davis, Raiford Chatman ("Ossie")	1960s-1	Hamilton, Margaret	1
Davis, Sammy, Jr.	2, 1960s-1	Harris, (Wanga) Phillip ("Phil")	4
Day, Dennis	2	Hartman, Phil(ip) Edward	5
Day, Doris	1960s-1	Hayes, Helen	3
Dee, Ruby	1960s-1	Hayworth, Rita	2
Dennis, Sandra Dale ("Sandy")	3	Hemingway, Margaux	4
Dewhurst, Colleen	3	Hepburn, Audrey Kathleen	3, 1960s-1
Diamond, Selma	1	Heston, Charlton	1960s-1
Dietrich, Marlene	3	Hoffman, Dustin Lee	1960s-1
Divine, (Harris Glenn Milstead)	2	Holden, William	1
Donahue, Troy	6	Hope, Leslie Townes ("Bob")	1960s-1
Douglas, Melvyn	1	Hopper, Dennis	1960s-1
Drake, Alfred	3	Houseman, John	2
Duke, Anna Marie ("Patty")	1960s-1	Hudson, Rock	1, 1960s-1
Dullea, Keir	1960s-1	Hunter, Kim	6
Dunaway, (Dorothy) Faye	1960s-1	Huston, John Marcellus	2, 1960s-1
Dunne, Irene Marie	2	Ives, Burl Icle Ivanhoe	4
Eastwood, Clinton, Jr. ("Clint")	1960s-1	Jessel, George Albert ("Georgie")	1
Evans, Dale	6	Johnson, Rafer Lewis	1960s-1
Ewell, Tom	4	Jones, James Earl	1960s-1
Fairbanks, Douglas Elton, Jr.	6	Julia, Raul Rafael Carlos	4
Farley, Chris(topher) Crosby	5	Kahn, Madeline Gail	5
Farrow, Mia	1960s-1	Kaufman, Andrew G. ("Andy")	1
Faye, Alice	5	Kaye, Danny	2
Ferrer, José	3	Keeler, Ruby	3
Fetchit, Stepin	1	Kelly, Eugene Curran ("Gene")	4
Fidler, James Marion ("Jimmy")	2	Kelly, Grace Patricia ("Princess Grace")	1
Fonda, Henry Jaynes	1, 1960s-1	Kiley, Richard Paul	5
Fonda, Jane Seymour	1960s-1	Knight, Ted	2
Fonda, Peter Seymour	1960s-1	Lamarr, Hedy	6
Fontanne, Lynn	1	Lamour, Dorothy	4
Francis, Arlene	6	Lancaster, Burt(on) Stephen	4
Furness, Elizabeth Mary ("Betty")	4	Lanchester, Elsa	2
Gabor, Eva	4	Landon, Michael	3
Garbo, Greta	2	Lawford, Peter Sydney Vaughn	1
Gardner, Ava Lavinia	2	Lee, Peggy	6
Garland, Judy	1960s-1	Le Gallienne, Eva	3
Garson, Greer	4	Lemmon, John Uhler, III ("Jack")	6, 1960s-1
Gaynor, Janet	1	Lenya, Lotte	1
Gilford, Jack	2	Lewis, Jerry	1960s-1

	Volume		*Volume*
Livingstone, Mary	1	Picon, Molly	3
Lodge, John Davis	1	Pidgeon, Walter	1
Lovelace, Linda Susan	6	Poitier, Sidney	1960s-2
Loy, Myrna	3	Powell, William Horatio	1
Ludlam, Charles	2	Presley, Elvis Aron	1960s-2
Ludlum, Robert	6	Preston, Robert	2
Lupino, Ida	4	Price, Vincent Leonard, Jr.	3
McCrea, Joel Albert	2	Pryor, Richard Franklin Lenox Thomas	1960s-2
McDowall, Roderick Andrew Anthony		Questel, Mae	5
Jude ("Roddy")	5	Quinn, Anthony Rudolph Oaxaca	6, 1960s-2
McGuire, Dorothy Hackett	6	Radner, Gilda	2
MacLaine, Shirley	1960s-2	Ray, Aldo	3
MacMurray, Fred(erick) Martin	3	Raye, Martha	4
McQueen, Steve	1960s-2	Reagan, Ronald Wilson	1960s-2
McQueen, Thelma ("Butterfly")	4	Redford, (Charles) Robert, Jr.	1960s-2
MacRae, Gordon	2	Reed, Donna	2
Markham, Dewey ("Pigmeat")	1	Remick, Lee Ann	3
Marshall, E(dda) G(unnar)	5	Rickles, Donald Jay ("Don")	1960s-2
Martin, Dean	4	Rigby, Cathy	1960s-2
Martin, Mary Virginia	2	Ritt, Martin	2
Marvin, Lee	2	Robards, Jason Nelson, Jr.	6, 1960s-2
Massey, Raymond Hart	1	Rogers, Charles ("Buddy")	5
Matthau, Walter	6, 1960s-2	Rogers, Ginger	4
Mature, Victor John	5	Rogers, Roy	5
May, Elaine	1960s-2	Roland, Gilbert	4
Meadows, Audrey	4	Romero, Cesar	4
Meeker, Ralph	2	Ross, Diana Earle	1960s-2
Meredith, (Oliver) Burgess	5	Rowan, Dan Hale	2
Merman, Ethel	1	Sainte-Marie, Buffy	1960s-2
Milland, Ray	2	Savalas, Aristoteles ("Telly")	4
Mitchum, Robert Charles Durman	5	Schlamme, Martha Haftel	1
Monroe, Marilyn	1960s-2	Scott, (George) Randolph	2
Montgomery, Elizabeth	4	Scott, George C(ampbell)	5, 1960s-2
Montgomery, Robert	1	Scourby, Alexander	1
Moore, Jack Carlton ("Clayton")	5	Shakur, Tupac Amaru	4
Moore, Mary Tyler	1960s-2	Shearer, (Edith) Norma	1
Moreno, Rita	1960s-2	Shore, Dinah	4
Murphy, George Lloyd	3	Sidney, Sylvia	5
Negri, Pola	2	Sillman, Leonard Dexter	1
Nelson, Eric Hilliard ("Rick")	1	Silvers, Phil	1
Nelson, Harriet Hilliard	4	Sinatra, Francis Albert ("Frank")	5
Newhart, George Robert ("Bob")	1960s-2	Skelton, Richard Bernard ("Red")	5
Newman, Paul Arthur	1960s-2	Sothern, Ann	6
Nicholas, Harold Lloyd	6	Stanley, Kim	6
Nicholson, Jack	1960s-2	Stanwyck, Barbara	2
O'Brien, William Joseph, Jr. ("Pat")	1	Steiger, Rodney Stephen ("Rod")	6, 1960s-2
O'Connor, Carroll	6	Stewart, James Maitland ("Jimmy")	5
O'Sullivan, Maureen	5	Strasberg, Lee	1
Page, Geraldine	2	Strasberg, Susan Elizabeth	5
Peppard, George	4	Streisand, Barbra	1960s-2
Perkins, Anthony	3	Strode, Woodrow Wilson Woolwine	
Phoenix, River Jude	3	("Woody")	4

	Volume
Actor (*continued*)	
Swanson, Gloria	1
Tandy, Jessica	4
Thomas, Danny	3
Thomas, Marlo	1960s-2
Tierney, Gene Eliza	3
Tillstrom, Burr	1
Trevor, Claire	6
Turner, Lana	4
Vallee, Hubert Prior ("Rudy")	2
Van Dyke, Richard Wayne ("Dick")	1960s-2
Verdon, Gwyneth Evelyn ("Gwen")	6
Voight, Jon	1960s-2
Walston, Ray	6
Warfield, William Caesar	6
Webb, John Randolph ("Jack")	1
Weissmuller, John Peter ("Johnny")	1
Welch, Raquel	1960s-2
Welles, Orson	1
Wolfman Jack (Robert Weston Smith)	4
Wood, Natalie	1, 1960s-2
Woodward, Joanne Gignilliat	1960s-2
Young, Loretta	6
Young, Robert George	5
Actuary	
Jacoby, Oswald ("Ozzie")	1
Admiral. *See* **Naval Officer.**	
Agent	
Bernays, Edward L.	4
Broccoli, Albert Romolo ("Cubby")	4
Fidler, James Marion ("Jimmie")	2
Hecht, Harold	1
Lazar, Irving Paul ("Swifty")	3
Orr, Robert Gordon ("Bobby")	Sports-2
Parker, Thomas Andrew ("Colonel")	5
Rote, Kyle, Jr.	Sports-2
Stein, Julian Caesar ("Jules")	1
Susskind, David Howard	2, 1960s-2
Wasserman, Lewis Robert ("Lew")	6
Agronomist	
Redenbacher, Orville	4
Air Force Officer	
Blanchard, Felix Anthony, Jr. ("Doc")	Sports-1
Boyington, Gregory ("Pappy")	2
Clay, Lucius DuBignon, Jr.	4
Davis, Benjamin O(liver), Jr.	6
Doolittle, James Harold	3
Eaker, Ira Clarence	2
Grisson, Virgil Ivan ("Gus")	1960s-1
Holloway, Bruce Keener	5
Howard, James Howell	4
Johnson, Leon William	5
Lansdale, Edward Geary	1960s-1

	Volume
LeMay, Curtis Emerson	2, 1960s-1
Norstad, Lauris	2
Quesada, Elwood Richard ("Pete")	3
Ryan, John D.	1
Slayton, Donald Kent ("Deke")	3
Smith, Joseph	3
Stewart, James Maitland ("Jimmy")	5
Twining, Nathan Farragut	1
Zuckert, Eugene Martin	6
Anatomist	
Corner, George Washington	1
Sperry, Roger Wolcott	4
Washburn, Sherwood L(arned)	6
Animal Rights Activist	
Amory, Cleveland ("Clip")	5
McCartney, Linda Louise Eastman	5
Animator	
Freleng, Isadore ("Friz")	4
Hannah, John Frederick ("Jack")	4
Lantz, Walter	4
Anthropologist	
Castaneda, Carlos César Salvador Arana	5, 1960s-1
Coon, Carleton Stevens	1
Davis, (William) Allison	1
Drake, (John Gibbs) St. Clair	2
Greenberg, Joseph H(arold)	6
Lewis, Oscar	1960s-1
Montagu, Ashley	5
Primus, Pearl Eileen	4
Red Thunder Cloud (Cromwell Ashbie Hawkins West)	4
Tax, Sol	4
Washburn, Sherwood L(arned)	6
Architect	
Breuer, Marcel	1
Bunshaft, Gordon	2
Butts, Alfred Mosher	3
Fitch, James Marston	6
Fuller, R(ichard) Buckminster	1
Goodman, Percival	2
Graham, John	3
Johnson, Philip Cortelyou	1960s-1
Jones, Robert Trent, Sr.	6
Kahn, Louis Isidore	1960s-1
Mies van der Rohe, Ludwig	1960s-2
Owings, Nathaniel Alexander	1
Pei, I(eoh) M(ing)	1960s-2
Rudolph, Paul Marvin	5
Saarinen, Eero	1960s-2
Sert, José Luis	1
Stone, Edward Durell	1960s-2
Venturi, Robert	1960s-2
Weese, Harry Mohr	5

	Volume
Wilson, Robert R(athbun)	6
Wright, Olgivanna Lloyd	1
Yamasaki, Minoru	2

Army Officer

Abrams, Creighton William, Jr.	1960s-1
Bradley, Omar Nelson	1
Calley, William Lewis, Jr.	1960s-1
Chase, William Curtis	2
Clark, Mark Wayne	1
Clay, Lucius Du Bignon, Jr.	4
Clay, Lucius Dubignon, Sr.	1960s-1
Collins, J(oseph) Lawton ("Lightning Joe")	2
Doolittle, James Harold	3
Eaker, Ira Clarence	2
Eifler, Carl Frederick	6
Fish, Hamilton	3
Gavin, James Maurice	2, 1960s-1
Gruenther, Alfred Maximilian	1
Hobby, Oveta Culp	4
Holloway, Bruce Keener	5
Howard, James Howell	4
Johnson, Leon William	5
LeMay, Curtis Emerson	1960s-1
Lemnitzer, Lyman Louis	2
Norstad, Lauris	2
Quesada, Elwood Richard ("Pete")	3
Reeder, Russell Potter, Jr. ("Red")	5
Ridgway, Matthew Bunker	3
Robinson, Roscoe, Jr.	3
Ryan, John Dale	1
Smith, Joseph	3
Smith, Ralph Corbett	5
Taylor, Maxwell Davenport	2, 1960s-2
Twining, Nathan Farragut	1
Urban, Matt Louis	4
Van Fleet, James Alward	3
Vann, John Paul	1960s-2
Walker, Edwin Anderson	3
Walt, Lewis William	2
Wedemeyer, Albert Coady	2
Westmoreland, William Childs	1960s-2
Wheeler, Earle Gilmore	1960s-2
Zwicker, Ralph Wise	3

Art Collector

Annenberg, Walter Hubert	6
de Menil, Dominique Schlumberger	5
Getty, Jean Paul	1960s-1
Hammer, Armand	2, 1960s-1
Hirshhorn, Joseph Herman	1
Janis, Sidney	2
Marcus, Stanley	6
Mellon, Paul	5

	Volume
Paley, William Samuel	2
Phillips, Marjorie Acker	1
Ray, Gordon Norton	2
Rockefeller, John Davison, III	1960s-2
Sackler, Arthur Mitchell	2
Simon, Norton Winfred	3
Whitney, Betsey Maria Cushing	5
Whitney, John Hay	1

Art Critic

Ashbery, John Lawrence	1960s-1
Canaday, John Edwin	1
de Kooning, Elaine Marie Catherine	2
Greenberg, Clement	4
Sweeney, James Johnson	2

Art Dealer

Castelli, Leo	5
De Nagy, Tibor	3
Janis, Sidney	2
Parsons, Elizabeth Pierson ("Betty")	1
Kraus, Hans Peter	2

Art Director (Magazine)

Liberman, Alexander Semeonovitch	5

Art Historian

Geldzahler, Henry	4
Newhall, Beaumont	3
Schapiro, Meyer	4

Artist (Animator)

Freleng, Isadore ("Friz")	4
Hannah, John Frederick ("Jack")	4
Lantz, Walter	4

Artist (Avant-Garde)

Cage, John Milton, Jr.	3, 1960s-1
Dine, James ("Jim")	1960s-1
Grooms, Charles Rogers ("Red")	1960s-1
Hansen, Al(fred) Earl	4
Kienholz, Edward Ralph	4
Lichtenstein, Roy	5, 1960s-1
Nevelson, Louise	2, 1960s-2
Noguchi, Isamu	2
O'Keeffe, Georgia Totto	2
Paik, Nam June	1960s-2
Rivers, Larry	6, 1960s-2
Warhol, Andy	2, 1960s-2

Artist (Ceramist)

Arneson, Robert Carston	3
Wood, Beatrice	5

Artist (Graphic Designer)

Kalman, Tibor	5
Rand, Paul	4

Artist (Painter)

Basquiat, Jean-Michel	2
Bearden, Romare Howard	2
Benn, Ben	1

	Volume
Artist (Painter) (*continued*)	
Biggers, John Thomas	6
Blume, Peter	3
Cadmus, Paul	5
de Kooning, Elaine Marie Catherine	2
de Kooning, Willem	5, 1960s-1
Diebenkorn, Richard Clifford	3
Dine, James ("Jim")	1960s-1
Dzubas, Friedel Alfred	4
Ernst, Hans-Ulrich ("Jimmy")	1
Fasanella, Raphaele ("Ralph")	5
Francis, Sam(uel) Lewis	4
Gillespie, Gregory Joseph	6
Graves, Nancy Stevenson	4
Hannah, John Frederick ("Jack")	4
Haring, Keith Allen	2
Hopper, Edward	1960s-1
Indiana, Robert	1960s-1
Johns, Jasper	1960s-1
Kane, Robert ("Bob")	5
Kent, Corita	2
Kingman, Dong	6
Krasner, Lee	1
Lawrence, Jacob Armstead	6
Lerner, Nathan Bernard	5
Lichtenstein, Roy	5, 1960s-1
Mitchell, Joan	3
Motherwell, Robert	3
Okada, Kenzo	1
O'Keeffe, Georgia Totto	2
Oldenburg, Claes Thure	1960s-2
Phillips, Marjorie Acker	1
Pousette-Dart, Richard Warren	3
Rauschenberg, Robert	1960s-2
Rexroth, Kenneth Charles Marion	1
Rivers, Larry	6, 1960s-2
Rosenquist, James Albert	1960s-2
Roszak, Theodore	1, 1960s-2
Rothko, Mark	1960s-2
Segal, George	6, 1960s-2
Sloane, Eric	1
Soyer, Raphael	2
Stella, Frank Philip	1960s-2
Vargas, Alberto ("Varga")	1
Vicente, Esteban	6
Walker, Edward Patrick ("Mickey"; "The Toy Bulldog")	1
Warhol, Andy	2, 1960s-2
Wojnarowicz, David Michael	3
Artist (Printmaker)	
Biggers, John Thomas	6
Baskin, Leonard	6
Lawrence, Jacob Armstead	6

	Volume
Artist (Sculptor)	
Alferez, Enrique ("Rique")	5
Arneson, Robert Carston	3
Baskin, Leonard	6
Biggers, John Thomas	6
Burke, Selma Hortense	4
de Kooning, Willem	5, 1960s-1
Graves, Nancy Stevenson	4
Grooms, Charles Rogers ("Red")	1960s-1
Hanson, Duane Elwood	4
Johns, Jasper	1960s-1
Judd, Donald Clarence	4
Kienholz, Edward Ralph	4
Lichtenstein, Roy	5, 1960s-1
Marisol (Marisol Escobar)	1960s-2
Morris, Robert	1960s-2
Nevelson, Louise	2, 1960s-2
Noguchi, Isamu	2
Oldenburg, Claes Thure	1960s-2
Parsons, Elizabeth Pierson ("Betty")	1
Rivers, Larry	6, 1960s-2
Roszak, Theodore	1, 1960s-2
Segal, George	6, 1960s-2
Smith, David Roland	1960s-2
Warhol, Andy	2
Arts Administrator	
Barr, Alfred Hamilton, Jr.	1
Bing, Franz Josef Rudolf	5
Brown, J(ohn) Carter	6
Burden, William Armistead Moale	1
Clurman, Richard Michael	4
Hanks, Nancy	1
Kirstein, Lincoln	4
Lindsay, John Vliet	6
Papp, Joseph	3, 1960s-2
Schuller, Gunther Alexander	1960s-2
Schuman, William Howard	3
Serkin, Rudolf	3
Sills, Beverly	1960s-2
Sweeney, James Johnson	2
Astronaut	
Armstrong, Neil Alden	1960s-1
Carpenter, (Malcolm) Scott	1960s-1
Glenn, John Herschel, Jr.	1960s-1
Grissom, Virgil Ivan ("Gus")	1960s-1
Irwin, James Benson	3
McAuliffe, (Sharon) Christa	2
McNair, Ron(ald) Erwin	2
Schirra, Walter Marty, Jr. ("Wally")	1960s-2
Shepard, Alan Bartlett, Jr.	5, 1960s-2
Slayton, Donald Kent ("Deke")	3
White, Edward Higgins, II	1960s-2

Volume

Astronomer

Friedman, Herbert 6

Reber, Grote 6

Sagan, Carl Edward 4

Strand, Kaj Aage 6

Tombaugh, Clyde William 5

Astrophysicist

Chandrasekhar, Subrahmanyan
("Chandra") 4

Fowler, William Alfred 4

Friedman, Herbert 6

Sagan, Carl Edward 4

Von Braun, Wernher 1960s-2

Athlete (Auto Racing)

Andretti, (Gabriele) Mario Sports-1

Bernstein, Kenneth Dale ("Kenny") Sports-1

Earnhardt, (Ralph) Dale 6, Sports-1

Foyt, A(nthony) J(oseph), Jr. Sports-1

France, William Henry Getty, Sr.
("Bill") Sports-1

Garlits, Don(ald) Sports-1

Gordon, Jeff Sports-1

Gurney, Dan(iel) Sexton Sports-1

Johnson, Robert Glenn, Jr. ("Junior") Sports-1

Muldowney, Shirley Roque Sports-2

Oldfield, Berna Eli ("Barney") Sports-2

Parsons, Johnnie 1

Penske, Roger S. Sports-2

Petty, Lee Arnold 6

Petty, Richard Lee Sports-2

Unser, Al(fred), Jr. Sports-2

Unser, Al(fred), Sr. Sports-2

Athlete (Baseball)

Aaron, Henry Louis ("Hank") 1960s-1,
Sports-1

Alexander, Grover Cleveland Sports-1

Alston, Walter Emmons 1

Anderson, George Lee ("Sparky") Sports-1

Anson, Adrian Constantine ("Cap,"
"Pop") Sports-1

Appling, Lucius Benjamin, Jr. ("Luke") 3

Ashburn, Don Richard ("Richie") 5

Averill, Howard Earl ("Rock") 1

Banks, Ernest ("Ernie") Sports-1

Bell, James Thomas ("Cool Papa") 3, Sports-1

Bench, Johnny Lee Sports-1

Berra, Lawrence Peter ("Yogi") Sports-1

Black, Joseph, Jr. ("Joe") 6

Bonds, Barry Lamar Sports-1

Boudreau, Louis ("Lou") 6

Brett, George Howard Sports-1

Brock, Lou(is Clark) Sports-1

Brown, Mordecai Peter Centennial Sports-1

Volume

Bunning, James Paul David ("Jim") Sports-1

Campanella, Roy 3, Sports-1

Carew, Rod(ney) Cline Sports-1

Carlton, Steven Norman Sports-1

Cartwright, Alexander Joy, Jr. Sports-1

Chadwick, Henry Sports-1

Chandler, Albert Benjamin ("Happy") Sports-1

Charleston, Oscar McKinley ("Charlie") Sports-1

Chesbro, John Dwight ("Jack") Sports-1

Clemens, (William) Roger Sports-1

Clemente, Roberto Walker 1960s-1,
Sports-1

Cobb, Ty(rus) Raymond Sports-1

Cochrane, Gordon Stanley ("Mickey") Sports-1

Collins, Edward Trowbridge ("Eddie") Sports-1

Comiskey, Charles Albert Sports-1

Conigliaro, Anthony Richard ("Tony") 2

Conlan, John Bertrand ("Jocko") 2

Connors, Kevin Joseph Aloysius
("Chuck") 3

Coveleski, Stanley Anthony ("Covey") 1

Cronin, Joseph Edward 1

Dancer, Faye Katherine 6

Dandridge, Raymond Emmett
("Squatty") 4, Sports-1

Day, Leon 4

Dean, Jay Hanna ("Dizzy") Sports-1

Dean, Paul ("Daffy") 1

Dickey, William Malcolm ("Bill") 4, Sports-1

DiMaggio, Joseph Paul ("Joe") 5, Sports-1

Doby, Lawrence Eugene ("Larry") Sports-1

Drysdale, Donald Scott ("Don") 3, 1960s-1,
Sports-1

Durocher, Leo Ernest 3, Sports-1

Ewing, William ("Buck") Sports-1

Feller, Robert William Andrew ("Bob") Sports-1

Fingers, Roland Glen ("Rollie") Sports-1

Flood, Curt(is) Charles 5, Sports-1

Ford, Edward Charles ("Whitey") Sports-1

Foster, Andrew ("Rube") Sports-1

Fox, Jacob Nelson ("Nellie") Sports-1

Foxx, James Emory ("Jimmie") Sports-1

Frick, Ford Christopher Sports-1

Frisch, Frank Francis ("Frankie") Sports-1

Garciaparra, (Anthony) Nomar Sports-1

Gehrig, (Henry) Lou(is) Sports-1

Gehringer, Charles Leonard ("Charlie") 3, Sports-1

Giamatti, A(ngelo) Bartlett ("Bart") Sports-1

Gibson, Josh(ua) Sports-1

Gibson, Pack Robert ("Bob") Sports-1

Gomez, Vernon Louis ("Lefty") Sports-1

Gray, Peter Wyshner ("Pete") 6

Greenberg, Henry Benjamin ("Hank") 2, Sports-1

	Volume		*Volume*
Athlete (Baseball) (*continued*)		McLain, Dennis Dale ("Denny")	Sports-2
Griffey, (George) Ken(neth), Jr.	Sports-1	MacPhail, Leland Stanford, Sr. ("Larry")	
Griffith, Clark Calvin	Sports-1		Sports-2
Grimes, Burleigh Arland	1	Maddux, Greg(ory) Alan	Sports-2
Grove, Robert Moses ("Lefty")	Sports-1	Mantle, Mickey Charles	4, 1960s-2,
Gwynn, Anthony Keith ("Tony")	Sports-1		Sports-2
Henderson, Rickey	Sports-1	Marichal, Juan Antonio	Sports-2
Herman, Floyd Caves ("Babe")	2	Maris, Roger Eugene	1, 1960s-2,
Herman, William Jennings ("Billy")	3		Sports-2
Hornsby, Rogers ("Rajah")	Sports-1	Martin, Alfred Manuel, Jr. ("Billy")	2
Hoyt, Waite Charles ("Schoolboy")	1	Martinez, Pedro Jaime	Sports-2
Hubbard, (Robert) Cal	Sports-1	Mathews, Edwin Lee ("Eddie")	6
Hubbell, Carl Owen	2, Sports-1	Mathewson, Christopher ("Christy")	Sports-2
Huggins, Miller James	Sports-1	Mays, William Howard, Jr. ("Willie")	1960s-2,
Hunter, James Augustus ("Catfish";			Sports-2
"Jim")	5, Sports-1	Miller, Marvin Julian	Sports-2
Jackson, Joseph Jefferson Wofford		Mize, John Robert ("Johnny")	3
("Shoeless Joe")	Sports-1	Morgan, Joe Leonard	Sports-2
Jackson, Reginald Martinez ("Reggie")	Sports-1	Musial, Stanley Frank ("Stan the Man")	Sports-2
Jackson, Travis Calvin ("Stonewall")	2	Newhouser, Harold ("Prince Hal")	5
Jeter, Derek Sanderson	Sports-1	Ott, Mel(vin) Thomas	Sports-2
Johnson, Randall David ("Randy")	Sports-1	Paige, Leroy Robert ("Satchel")	1, Sports-2
Johnson, Walter Perry ("The Big Train")		Palmer, James Alvin ("Jim")	Sports-2
	Sports-1	Piazza, Michael Joseph ("Mike")	Sports-2
Johnson, William Julius ("Judy")	2, Sports-1	Pride, Charles Frank ("Charley")	1960s-2
Kaline, Al(bert) William	Sports-1	Radbourn, Charles Gardner	Sports-2
Keeler, William Henry	Sports-1	Reese, Harold Henry ("Pee Wee")	5, Sports-2
Kelly, George Lange ("Highpockets")	1	Reynolds, Allie Pierce	4
Kelly, Michael Joseph ("King")	Sports-1	Richards, Paul Rapier	2
Killebrew, Harmon Clayton, Jr.	1960s-1,	Rickey, Branch Wesley	Sports-2
	Sports-1	Ripken, Cal(vin) Edward, Jr.	Sports-2
Kiner, Ralph McPherran	Sports-1	Roberts, Robin Evan	Sports-2
Klem, William Joseph ("Bill")	Sports-1	Robinson, Brooks Calbert, Jr.	Sports-2
Kluszewski, Theodore Bernard ("Ted";		Robinson, Frank, Jr.	1960s-2,
"Big Klu")	2		Sports-2
Koufax, Sanford ("Sandy")	1960s-1,	Robinson, Jack Roosevelt ("Jackie")	Sports-2
	Sports-1	Rodriguez, Alex Emmanuel	Sports-2
Lajoie, Nap(oleon)	Sports-2	Rose, Pete ("Charley Hustle")	Sports-2
Landis, Kenesaw Mountain	Sports-2	Roush, Edd J.	2
Lemon, Robert Granville ("Bob")	6	Ruffing, Charles Herbert ("Red")	2
Leonard, Walter Fenner ("Buck")	5, Sports-2	Ruppert, Jacob	Sports-2
Lindstrom, Frederick Charles, Jr.		Ruth, George Herman ("Babe")	Sports-2
("Lindy")	1	Ryan, (Lynn) Nolan, Jr.	Sports-2
Lloyd, John Henry ("Pop")	Sports-2	Sanders, Deion Luwynn	Sports-2
Lyons, Theodore Amar ("Ted")	2	Schacht, Al(exander)	1
McCarthy, Joseph Vincent ("Joe")	Sports-2	Schmidt, Michael Jack ("Mike")	Sports-2
McCormick, Frank Andrew	1	Seaver, George Thomas ("Tom")	1960s-2,
McCovey, Willie Lee	1960s-2,		Sports-2
	Sports-2	Simmons, Al(oysius) Harry	Sports-2
McGraw, John Joseph	Sports-2	Sisler, George Harold	Sports-2
McGwire, Mark David	Sports-2	Slaughter, Enos Bradsher ("Country")	6
Mack, Connie	Sports-2	Smith, Osborne Earl ("Ozzie")	Sports-2

	Volume
Snider, Edwin Donald ("Duke")	Sports-2
Sosa, Samuel Peralta ("Sammy")	Sports-2
Spahn, Warren Edward	Sports-2
Spalding, Albert Goodwill ("A.G.")	Sports-2
Speaker, Tris(tram) E.	Sports-2
Stargell, Wilver Dornel ("Willie")	6
Steinbrenner, George Michael, III	Sports-2
Stengel, Charles Dillon ("Casey")	Sports-2
Stratton, Monty Franklin Pierce	1
Tatum, Reece ("Goose")	Sports-2
Terry, William Harold ("Bill")	2, Sports-2
Thorpe, James Francis ("Jim")	Sports-2
Torre, Joseph Paul ("Joe")	Sports-2
Traynor, Harold Joseph ("Pie")	Sports-2
Veeck, William Louis, Jr. ("Bill")	2, Sports-2
Waddell, George Edward ("Rube")	Sports-2
Wagner, John Peter ("Honus")	Sports-2
Walker, Fred ("Dixie")	1
Walker, Moses Fleetwood ("Fleet")	Sports-2
Walsh, Ed(ward) Augustine	Sports-2
Waner, Lloyd James ("Little Poison")	1
Ward, John Montgomery	Sports-2
Wells, Willie James	Sports-2
Wilhelm, (James) Hoyt	6
Williams, Theodore Samuel ("Ted")	6, Sports-2
Wilson, Lewis Robert ("Hack")	Sports-2
Winfield, David Mark ("Dave")	Sports-2
Wright, William Henry ("Harry")	Sports-2
Wynn, Early, Jr. ("Gus")	5
Yastrzemski, Carl Michael, Jr.	1960s-2, Sports-2
Young, Denton True ("Cy")	Sports-2

Athlete (Basketball)

Abdul-Jabbar, Kareem	Sports-1
Allen, Forrest Clare ("Phog")	Sports-1
Archibald, Nathaniel ("Nate"; "Tiny")	Sports-1
Arizin, Paul Joseph	Sports-1
Auerbach, Arnold ("Red")	Sports-1
Barkley, Charles Wade	Sports-1
Barry, Richard Francis, III ("Rick")	Sports-1
Baylor, Elgin	Sports-1
Beckman, John	Sports-1
Berenson Abbott, Senda	Sports-1
Bing, David ("Dave")	Sports-1
Bird, Larry Joe	Sports-1
Blazejowski, Carol Ann	Sports-1
Bradley, William Warren ("Bill")	1960s-1
Bryant, Kobe	Sports-1
Carter, Vincent Lamar, Jr. ("Vince")	Sports-1
Chamberlain, Wilton Norman ("Wilt")	5, 1960s-1, Sports-1
Clifton, Nat(haniel) ("Sweetwater")	2

	Volume
Connors, Kevin Joseph Aloysius ("Chuck")	3
Cooper, Charles Henry ("Chuck")	1
Cooper, Cynthia	Sports-1
Cousy, Robert ("Bob")	Sports-1
Cunningham, William John ("Billy")	Sports-1
Donovan, Anne	Sports-1
Drexler, Clyde	Sports-1
Duncan, Timothy Theodore	Sports-1
Edwards, Teresa	Sports-1
Erving, Julius Winfield, II ("Dr. J.")	Sports-1
Ewing, Patrick Aloysius	Sports-1
Forte, Fulvio Chester, Jr. ("Chet")	4
Frazier, Walt, II ("Clyde")	Sports-1
Fulks, Joseph Franklin ("Joe")	Sports-1
Gaines, Clarence Edward, Sr. ("Bighouse")	Sports-1
Gates, William ("Pop")	5
Hannum, Alex	6
Haskins, Donald Lee	Sports-1
Havlicek, John Joseph	Sports-1
Hawkins, Cornelius L. ("Connie")	Sports-1
Hayes, Elvin Ernest	Sports-1
Haynes, Marques Oreole	Sports-1
Holdsclaw, Chamique Shaunta	Sports-1
Holman, Nathan ("Nat")	4, Sports-1
Holzman, William ("Red")	5
Iba, Henry Payne ("Hank")	Sports-1
Iverson, Allen Ezail	Sports-1
Jackson, Philip Douglas ("Phil")	Sports-1
Johnson, Earvin, Jr. ("Magic")	Sports-1
Jones, K. C.	Sports-1
Jordan, Michael Jeffrey ("Air")	Sports-1
Knight, Robert Montgomery ("Bob")	Sports-1
Krzyzewski, Michael William ("Mike")	Sports-1
Kurland, Robert ("Bob")	Sports-1
Lapchick, Joseph Bohomiel ("Joe")	Sports-2
Lemon, Meadow George ("Meadowlark")	Sports-2
Leslie, Lisa DeShaun	Sports-2
Lieberman-Cline, Nancy	Sports-2
Lobo, Rebecca Rose	Sports-2
Luisetti, Angelo Enrico ("Hank")	6, Sports-2
Malone, Karl Anthony	Sports-2
Malone, Moses Eugene	Sports-2
Maravich, Peter Press ("Pistol Pete")	2, Sports-2
Meyers, Ann Elizabeth	Sports-2
Mikan, George Lawrence, Jr.	Sports-2
Miller, Cheryl DeAnn	Sports-2
Miller, Reginald Wayne ("Reggie")	Sports-2
Monroe, Earl Vernon, Jr. ("the Pearl")	Sports-2
Mourning, Alonzo Harding, Jr.	Sports-2

Volume

Athlete (Basketball) (*continued*)

Murphy, Calvin Jerome	Sports-2
Naismith, James	Sports-2
Newell, Pete(r)	Sports-2
Olajuwon, Hakeem Abdul	Sports-2
O'Neal, Shaq(uille) Rashaun	Sports-2
Pettit, Robert E. Lee, Jr. ("Bob")	Sports-2
Pippen, Scottie	Sports-2
Pollard, James Clifford ("Jim")	Sports-2
Reed, Willis, Jr.	Sports-2
Riley, Pat(rick) James	Sports-2
Ripley, Elmer Horton	1
Robertson, Oscar Palmer	Sports-2
Robinson, David Maurice	Sports-2
Rupp, Adolph Frederick	Sports-2
Russell, William Felton ("Bill")	1960s-2, Sports-2
Schayes, Adolph ("Dolph")	Sports-2
Smith, Dean Edwards	Sports-2
Staley, Dawn	Sports-2
Stern, David	Sports-2
Stockton, John Houston	Sports-2
Summitt, Pat(ricia) Head	Sports-2
Swoopes, Sheryl Denise	Sports-2
Tatum, Reece ("Goose")	Sports-2
Thomas, Isiah Lord, III	Sports-2
Thompson, David O'Neal	Sports-2
Thompson, John Robert, Jr.	Sports-2
Walton, William Theodore, III ("Bill")	Sports-2
Weatherspoon, Teresa	Sports-2
West, Jerry Alan	Sports-2
Wilkens, Leonard Randolph ("Lenny")	Sports-2
Woodard, Lynette	Sports-2
Wooden, John Robert	Sports-2
Worthy, James Ager	Sports-2

Athlete (Bowling)

Carter, Don(ald) James	Sports-1
Nagy, Steve	Sports-2
Varipapa, Andrew ("Andy")	1, Sports-2
Weber, Pete	Sports-2

Athlete (Boxing)

Ali, Muhammad (Cassius Clay)	1960s-1, Sports-1
Armstrong, Henry Jackson, Jr.	Sports-1
Conn, William David, Jr. ("Billy")	3, Sports-1
Corbett, James John	Sports-1
D'Amato, Constantine ("Cus")	Sports-1
Dempsey, William Harrison ("Jack")	1, Sports-1
Dundee, Angelo	Sports-1
Frazier, Joseph William ("Joe")	1960s-1, Sports-1
Futch, Eddie	6

Volume

Graham, William Patrick ("Billy")	3
Graziano, Rocky	2, Sports-1
Greb, Edward Henry ("Harry")	Sports-1
Griffith, Emile Alphonse	Sports-1
Hagler, Marvin Nathaniel	Sports-1
Hearns, Thomas	Sports-1
Jack, Beau	6
Jeffries, James Jackson	Sports-1
Johnson, John Arthur ("Jack")	Sports-1
Ketchel, Stanley	Sports-1
King, Don(ald)	Sports-1
LaMotta, Jake	Sports-2
Leonard, Benny	Sports-2
Leonard, Ray Charles ("Sugar Ray")	Sports-2
Liston, Charles ("Sonny")	1960s-1, Sports-2
Louis, Joseph ("Joe")	1, Sports-2
Marciano, Rocky	Sports-2
Moore, Archibald Lee ("Archie")	5, Sports-2
Patterson, Floyd	1960s-2, Sports-2
Pep, Willie	Sports-2
Rickard, George Lewis ("Tex")	Sports-2
Robinson, Ray ("Sugar Ray")	2, Sports-2
Saddler, Joseph ("Sandy")	6
Sharkey, Jack	4
Sullivan, John Lawrence	Sports-2
Tunney, James Joseph ("Gene")	Sports-2
Tyson, Michael Gerard ("Mike"; "Iron Mike")	Sports-2
Walcott, "Jersey Joe"	4
Walker, Edward Patrick ("Mickey")	1, Sports-2
Zale, Tony	5, Sports-2

Athlete (Cricket)

Wright, William Henry ("Harry")	Sports-2

Athlete (Cycling)

Armstrong, Lance	Sports-1
LeMond, Greg(ory) James	Sports-2
Taylor, Marshall Walter ("Major")	Sports-2

Athlete (Figure Skating)

Albright, Tenley Emma	Sports-1
Boitano, Brian Anthony	Sports-1
Button, Richard Totten ("Dick")	Sports-1
Fleming, Peggy Gale	1960s-1, Sports-1
Hamill, Dorothy Stuart	Sports-1
Hamilton, Scott Scovell	Sports-1
Heiss Jenkins, Carol Elizabeth	Sports-1
Henie, Sonja	Sports-1
Jenkins, David Wilkinson	Sports-1
Jenkins, Hayes Alan	Sports-1

	Volume
Kwan, Michelle Wing	Sports-1
Yamaguchi, Kristi Tsuya	Sports-2
Athlete (Football)	
Aikman, Troy Kenneth	Sports-1
Albert, Frank Culling ("Frankie")	6
Allen, Marcus LeMarr	Sports-1
Alworth, Lance Dwight	Sports-1
Baker, Hobart Amory Hare ("Hobey")	Sports-1
Battles, Clifford Franklin ("Gyp")	1
Baugh, Samuel Adrian ("Sammy")	Sports-1
Bednarik, Charles Philip ("Chuck")	Sports-1
Bell, DeBenneville ("Bert")	Sports-1
Berry, Raymond Emmett	Sports-1
Blaik, Earl Henry ("Red")	Sports-1
Blanchard, Felix Anthony, Jr. ("Doc")	Sports-1
Blanda, George Frederick	Sports-1
Bowden, Robert Cleckler ("Bobby")	Sports-1
Bradshaw, Terry Paxton	Sports-1
Brown, James Nathaniel ("Jim")	1960s-1,
	Sports-1
Brown, Paul Eugene	Sports-1
Bryant, Paul William ("Bear")	Sports-1
Buchanan, Junious ("Buck")	Sports-1
Butkus, Richard Marvin ("Dick")	Sports-1
Camp, Walter Chauncey	Sports-1
Campbell, Earl Christian	Sports-1
Campbell, Milton Gray ("Milt")	Sports-1
Carter, Cris D.	Sports-1
Conerly, Charles Albert ("Charlie"), Jr.	4
Crisler, Herbert Orin ("Fritz")	1
Davis, Al(len)	Sports-1
Davis, Glenn Woodward ("Junior")	Sports-1
Dickerson, Eric Demetric	Sports-1
Ditka, Mike	Sports-1
Dodd, Robert Lee ("Bobby")	2
Dorsett, Anthony Drew ("Tony")	Sports-1
Elway, John Albert	Sports-1
Engle, Charles Albert ("Rip")	1
Ewbank, Wilbur Charles ("Weeb")	Sports-1
Favre, Brett Lorenzo	Sports-1
Fears, Thomas Jesse ("Tom")	6, Sports-1
Fish, Hamilton	3
Friedman, Benjamin ("Benny")	1
Gibbs, Joe Jackson	Sports-1
Gifford, Frank Newton	Sports-1
Gillman, Sid(ney)	Sports-1
Graham, Otto Everett, Jr.	Sports-1
Grange, Harold Edward ("Red")	3, Sports-1
Greene, Charles Edward ("Mean Joe")	Sports-1
Gregg, (Alvis) Forrest	Sports-1
Groza, Louis Roy ("Lou")	6, Sports-1
Halas, George Stanley	Sports-1

	Volume
Hannah, John Allen	Sports-1
Harmon, Thomas Dudley ("Tom")	2, Sports-1
Harris, Franco	Sports-1
Hart, Leon	6
Hayes, Robert Lee ("Bob")	6
Hayes, Wayne Woodrow ("Woody")	Sports-1
Heffelfinger, William Walter ("Pudge")	Sports-1
Hein, Mel(vin) John	Sports-1
Heisman, John William ("Johnny")	Sports-1
Hirsch, Elroy Leon ("Crazylegs")	Sports-1
Hornung, Paul Vernon	Sports-1
Hubbard, (Robert) Cal	Sports-1
Hunt, Lamar	Sports-1
Hutson, Don(ald) Montgomery	5, Sports-1
Jones, David ("Deacon")	Sports-1
Jones, Jerral Wayne ("Jerry")	Sports-1
Kinard, Frank Manning ("Bruiser")	1
Lambeau, Earl Louis ("Curly")	Sports-2
Lambert, John Harold ("Jack")	Sports-2
Landry, Thomas Wade ("Tom")	6, Sports-2
Lane, Richard ("Dick"; "Night Train")	6, Sports-2
Lanier, Willie E.	Sports-2
Largent, Steve	Sports-2
Layne, Robert Lawrence ("Bobby")	2, Sports-2
Leahy, Francis William ("Frank")	Sports-2
Lillard, Joseph ("Joe")	Sports-2
Lilly, Robert Lewis ("Bob")	Sports-2
Lombardi, Vincent Thomas ("Vince")	Sports-2
Lott, Ronald Mandel ("Ronnie")	Sports-2
Luckman, Sid(ney)	5, Sports-2
Lujack, John Christopher, Jr. ("Johnny")	Sports-2
McElhenny, Hugh Edward, Jr.	Sports-2
McNally, John Victor ("Johnny Blood")	1, Sports-2
Marchetti, Gino John	Sports-2
Marino, Daniel Constantine, Jr.	
("Dan")	Sports-2
Marshall, George Preston	Sports-2
Matson, Oliver Genoa, II ("Ollie")	Sports-2
Maynard, Don(ald) Rogers	Sports-2
Mitchell, Robert Cornelius, Sr.	
("Bobby")	Sports-2
Montana, Joseph Clifford ("Joe")	Sports-2
Motley, Marion	5, Sports-2
Nagurski, Bronislau ("Bronko")	2, Sports-2
Namath, Joseph William ("Joe")	1960s-2,
	Sports-2
Nevers, Ernest Alonzo ("Ernie")	Sports-2
Nitschke, Ray(mond) Ernest	5, Sports-2
Noll, Charles Henry ("Chuck")	Sports-2
Nomellini, Leo Joseph	6
Olsen, Merlin Jay	Sports-2
Osborne, Thomas William ("Tom")	Sports-2

	Volume
Athlete (Football) (*continued*)	
Page, Alan Cedric	Sports-2
Parcells, Duane Charles ("Bill")	Sports-2
Parker, James Thomas ("Jim")	Sports-2
Paterno, Joseph Vincent ("Joe")	Sports-2
Payton, Walter Jerry	5, Sports-2
Peabody, Endicott ("Chub")	5
Pollard, Frederick Douglass ("Fritz")	2, Sports-2
Rice, Jerry Lee	Sports-2
Ringo, James Stephen ("Jim")	Sports-2
Robinson, Edward Gay ("Eddie")	Sports-2
Robustelli, Andrew ("Andy")	Sports-2
Rockne, Knute Kenneth	Sports-2
Rooney, Arthur Joseph ("Art"), Sr.	Sports-2
Rote, (William) Kyle, Sr.	6
Rozelle, Alvin Ray ("Pete")	Sports-2
Sanders, Barry	Sports-2
Sanders, Deion Luwynn	Sports-2
Sayers, Gale Eugene	Sports-2
Schmidt, Joseph Paul ("Joe")	Sports-2
Selmon, Lee Roy	Sports-2
Shula, Don(ald) Francis	Sports-2
Simpson, Orenthal James ("O. J.")	Sports-2
Smith, Emmitt James, III	Sports-2
Stagg, Amos Alonzo, Sr.	Sports-2
Starr, Bryan Bartlett ("Bart")	Sports-2
Staubach, Roger Thomas	Sports-2
Strode, Woodrow Wilson Woolwine ("Woody")	4
Tarkenton, Fran(cis) Asbury	Sports-2
Taylor, Lawrence Julius ("LT")	Sports-2
Thorpe, James Francis ("Jim")	Sports-2
Tittle, Y(elberton) A(braham), Jr.	Sports-2
Trippi, Charles Louis ("Charley")	Sports-2
Turner, Clyde Douglas ("Bulldog")	5, Sports-2
Unitas, John Constantine ("Johnny")	6, 1960s-2, Sports-2
Upshaw, Eugene Thurman, Jr. ("Gene")	Sports-2
Van Brocklin, Norm(an) Mack	1, Sports-2
Van Buren, Stephen Wood ("Steve")	Sports-2
Walker, (Ewell) Doak, Jr.	5, Sports-2
Walsh, William ("Bill")	Sports-2
Warner, Glenn Scobey ("Pop")	Sports-2
Waterfield, Robert Staton ("Bob")	1, Sports-2
Weinmeister, Arnold George ("Arnie")	6
White, Byron Raymond	6
White, Reginald Howard ("Reggie")	Sports-2
Wilkinson, Charles Burnham ("Bud")	Sports-2
Winslow, Kellen Boswell	Sports-2
Young, Claude, Jr. ("Buddy")	1
Young, Jon Steven ("Steve")	Sports-2

	Volume
Zuppke, Robert Carl ("Bob")	Sports-2
Athlete (Golf)	
Armour, Thomas Dickson ("Tommy")	Sports-1
Berg, Patricia Jane ("Patty")	Sports-1
Demaret, James Newton ("Jimmy")	1
Didrikson Zaharias, Mildred Ella ("Babe")	Sports-1
Gibson, Althea	Sports-1
Hagen, Walter C.	Sports-1
Hogan, William Benjamin ("Ben")	5, Sports-1
Inkster, Juli Simpson	Sports-1
Jones, Robert Tyre, Jr. ("Bobby")	Sports-1
Lopez, Nancy Marie	Sports-2
Middlecoff, (Emmett) Cary ("Doc")	5
Nelson, (John) Byron, Jr.	Sports-2
Nicklaus, Jack William	1960s-2, Sports-2
Ouimet, Francis DeSales	Sports-2
Palmer, Arnold Daniel ("Arnie")	Sports-2
Sarazen, Gene	5, Sports-2
Snead, Samuel Jackson ("Sam")	6, Sports-2
Stewart, (William) Payne	5
Suggs, (Mae) Louise	Sports-2
Trevino, Lee Buck	Sports-2
Vare, Glenna Collett	2
Vines, Henry Ellsworth, Jr. ("Elly")	Sports-2
Watson, Thomas Sturges ("Tom")	Sports-2
Woods, Eldrick ("Tiger")	Sports-2
Athlete (Gymnastics)	
Conner, Bart	Sports-1
Karolyi, Béla	Sports-1
Miller, Shannon Lee	Sports-2
Retton, Mary Lou	Sports-2
Rigby, Cathy	1960s-2, Sports-2
Athlete (Hockey)	
Abel, Sidney Gerald ("Sid")	6, Sports-1
Baker, Hobart Amory Hare ("Hobey")	Sports-1
Bossy, Michael Dean ("Mike")	Sports-1
Boucher, Frank Xavier	Sports-1
Brimsek, Francis Charles ("Frank")	5, Sports-1
Brooks, Herb(ert) P.	Sports-1
Chelios, Chris ("Chel")	Sports-1
Clarke, Robert Earle ("Bobby")	Sports-1
Delvecchio, Alex Peter ("Fats")	Sports-1
Esposito, Phil(ip) Anthony	Sports-1
Gretzky, Wayne Douglas ("The Great One")	Sports-1
Hall, Glenn Henry	Sports-1
Howe, Gordon ("Gordie")	Sports-1
Hull, Brett	Sports-1
Hull, Robert Marvin, Jr. ("Bobby")	Sports-1

	Volume
Jagr, Jaromir	Sports-1
Leetch, Brian	Sports-2
Lemieux, Mario	Sports-2
Lindsay, Robert Blake Theodore ("Ted")	Sports-2
Mikita, Stan	Sports-2
Mullen, Joseph ("Joey")	Sports-2
Orr, Robert Gordon ("Bobby")	1960s-2,
	Sports-2
Parent, Bernard Marcel ("Bernie")	Sports-2
Patrick, (Curtis) Lester	Sports-2
Potvin, Denis Charles	Sports-2
Sawchuk, Terrance Gordon ("Terry")	Sports-2
Schmidt, Milt(on) Conrad	Sports-2
Shore, Edward William ("Eddie")	1, Sports-2

Athlete (Horse Racing)

Arcaro, George Edward ("Eddie")	5, Sports-1
Cordero, Angel Tomas, Jr.	Sports-1
Fitzsimmons, James Edward ("Sunny Jim")	Sports-1
Hartack, William J. ("Bill")	Sports-1
Haughton, William Robert ("Billy")	2
Jacobs, Hirsch	Sports-1
Krone, Julieanne Louise ("Julie")	Sports-1
Longden, John Eric ("Johnny")	Sports-2
Pincay, Laffit Alegando, Jr.	Sports-2
Sande, Earl	Sports-2
Shoemaker, William Lee ("Bill")	1960s-2,
	Sports-2
Sloan, James Forman ("Tod")	Sports-2
Stephens, Woodford Cefis ("Woody")	Sports-2

Athlete (Polo)

Hitchcock, Thomas, Jr. ("Tommy")	Sports-1

Athlete (Rodeo)

Canutt, Enos Edward ("Yakima")	2

Athlete (Rowing)

Kelly, John Brendan, Sr. ("Jack")	Sports-1

Athlete (Sailing)

Conner, Dennis W.	Sports-1
Hart, Marion Rice	2
Jobson, Gary	Sports-1
Mosbacher, Emil, Jr. ("Bus")	Sports-2
Shields, Cornelius	1

Athlete (Skiing)

Fraser, Gretchen Claudia	Sports-1
Johnson, William D. ("Bill")	Sports-1
Kidd, William Winston ("Billy")	Sports-1
Mahre, Phil(ip)	Sports-2
Street, Picabo	Sports-2

Athlete (Soccer)

Akers, Michelle Anne	Sports-1
Hamm, Mariel Margaret ("Mia")	Sports-1
Lalas, Alexi	Sports-2
Lilly, Kristine Marie	Sports-2

	Volume
Meola, Tony	Sports-2
Rote, Kyle, Jr.	Sports-2

Athlete (Speed Skating)

Blair, Bonnie	Sports-1
Heiden, Eric Arthur	Sports-1
Jansen, Dan	Sports-1

Athlete (Surfing)

Kahanamoku, Duke	Sports-1

Athlete (Swimming and Diving)

Babashoff, Shirley	Sports-1
Biondi, Matt(hew)	Sports-1
Bleibtrey, Ethelda	Sports-1
Chadwick, Florence May	4, Sports-1
Counsilman, James Edward ("Doc")	Sports-1
Crabbe, Clarence Linden ("Buster")	1, Sports-1
De Varona, Donna	1960s-1,
	Sports-1
Ederle, Gertrude Caroline ("Trudy")	Sports-1
Evans, Janet	Sports-1
Kahanamoku, Duke	Sports-1
Kiphuth, Robert John Herman ("Bob")	Sports-1
Louganis, Greg(ory) Efthimios	Sports-2
McCormick, Pat(ricia) Joan	Sports-2
Nyad, Diana	Sports-2
Sanders, Summer Elisabeth	Sports-2
Schollander, Don(ald) Arthur	Sports-2
Spitz, Mark Andrew	Sports-2
Weissmuller, Peter John ("Johnny")	1, Sports-2

Athlete (Tennis)

Agassi, Andre Kirk	Sports-1
Ashe, Arthur Robert, Jr.	3, 1960s-1,
	Sports-1
Betz, Pauline May	Sports-1
Budge, John Donald ("Don")	6, Sports-1
Connolly, Maureen Catherine ("Little Mo")	Sports-1
Connors, James Scott ("Jimmy")	Sports-1
Davenport, Lindsay	Sports-1
Evert, Christine Marie ("Chris")	Sports-1
Gibson, Althea	Sports-1
Gonzales, Richard Alonzo ("Pancho")	4, Sports-1
Jacobs, Helen Hull	5, Sports-1
King, Billie Jean Moffitt	1960s-1,
	Sports-1
Kramer, John Albert ("Jack")	Sports-1
McEnroe, John Patrick, Jr.	Sports-2
Marble, Alice	2, Sports-2
Navratilova, Martina	Sports-2
Riggs, Robert Larimore ("Bobby")	4, Sports-2
Sampras, Pete	Sports-2
Tilden, William Tatem, Jr. ("Bill")	Sports-2
Trabert, Marion Anthony ("Tony")	Sports-2

	Volume
Athlete (Tennis) (*continued*)	
Vines, Henry Ellsworth, Jr. ("Elly")	Sports-2
Williams, Venus Ebone Starr	Sports-2
Wills (Moody), Helen Newington	5, Sports-2
Athlete (Track and Field)	
Ashford, Evelyn	Sports-1
Beamon, Robert Alfred ("Bob")	Sports-1
Boston, Ralph	Sports-1
Calhoun, Lee Quency	Sports-1
Campbell, Milton Gray ("Milt")	Sports-1
Connolly, Harold V. ("Hal")	Sports-1
Cunningham, Glenn V.	2, Sports-1
Didrikson Zaharias, Mildred Ella ("Babe")	Sports-1
Dillard, Harrison	Sports-1
Ewell, Henry Norwood ("Barney")	Sports-1
Fixx, James Fuller	1
Fosbury, Richard Douglas ("Dick")	Sports-1
Glickman, Martin Irving ("Marty")	6
Griffith Joyner, Florence Delorez ("Flo Jo")	5, Sports-1
Hayes, Robert Lee ("Bob")	6, Sports-1
Jenner, (William) Bruce	Sports-1
Johnson, Michael	Sports-1
Johnson, Rafer Lewis	1960s-1, Sports-1
Jones, Marion Lois	Sports-1
Joyner-Kersee, Jacqueline ("Jackie")	Sports-1
Lewis, Frederick Carlton ("Carl")	Sports-2
Liquori, Martin William, Jr. ("Marty")	Sports-2
Mathias, Robert Bruce ("Bob")	Sports-2
Matson, James Randel ("Randy")	Sports-2
Metcalfe, Ralph Horace	Sports-2
Moses, Ed(win) Corley	Sports-2
O'Brien, (William) Parry, Jr.	Sports-2
Oerter, Al(fred) Adolph, Jr.	Sports-2
Owens, James Cleveland ("Jesse")	Sports-2
Prefontaine, Steve Roland ("Pre")	Sports-2
Richards, Robert Eugene ("Bob")	Sports-2
Rodgers, William Henry ("Bill")	Sports-2
Rudolph, Wilma Glodean	4, 1960s-2, Sports-2
Ryun, James Ronald ("Jim")	1960s-2, Sports-2
Shorter, Frank Charles	Sports-2
Thorpe, James Francis ("Jim")	Sports-2
Tyus, Wyomia	Sports-2
Warmerdam, Cornelius Anthony ("Dutch")	Sports-2
Whitfield, Mal(vin) Greston	Sports-2
Athlete (Volleyball)	
Chamberlain, Wilt(on) Norman	Sports-1
Kiraly, Karch	Sports-1

	Volume
Athlete (Weightlifting)	
Anderson, Paul Edward	Sports-1
Davis, John Henry	Sports-1
Kono, Tommy Tamio	Sports-1
Athlete (Wrestling)	
Blatnick, Jeff(rey)	Sports-1
Gable, Dan(iel)	Sports-1
Gotch, Frank Alvin	Sports-1
Nomellini, Leo Joseph	6
Schultz, David Lesky ("Dave")	4
Smith, John William	Sports-2
Author (Children's Literature)	
Adams, Harriet Stratemeyer	1
Bee, Clair Francis	1
Benson, Mildred Wirt	6
Geisel, Theodor Seuss (Dr. Seuss)	3
Giovanni, Nikki	1960s-1
Horwich, Frances Rappaport ("Miss Frances")	6
Jacobs, Helen Hull	5, Sports-1
Jordan, June	6
Kesey, Kenneth Elton ("Ken")	6
Petry, Ann Lane	5
Reeder, Russell Potter, Jr. ("Red")	5
Scarry, Richard McClure	4
Sendak, Maurice Bernard	1960s-2
Silverstein, Shel(don) Allan	5
Singer, Isaac Bashevis	3, 1960s-2
Thompson, Kay	5
Author (Comic Book and Strip)	
Siegel, Jerome ("Jerry")	1
Author (Cookbook)	
Chen, Joyce	4
Beard, James Andrew	1
Nearing, Helen Knothe	4
Author (Drama)	
Abbott, George Francis	4
Albee, Edward Franklin, III	1960s-1
Ashman, Howard Elliot	3
Auden, W(ystan) H(ugh)	1960s-1
Baldwin, James Arthur	1960s-1
Beck, Julian	1, 1960s-1
Bellow, Saul	1960s-1
Berlin, Irving	2
Burrows, Abe	1
Canby, Vincent	6
Chase, Mary Coyle	1
Chayefsky, Sidney Aaron ("Paddy")	1, 1960s-1
Childress, Alice Herndon	4
Corso, Gregory Nunzio	6
Davis, Raiford Chatman ("Ossie")	1960s-1
Garson, Barbara	1960s-1

	Volume
Gershwin, Ira	1
Goodrich, Frances	1
Gordon, Ruth	1
Gordone, Charles	4, 1960s-1
Hansberry, Lorraine Vivian	1960s-1
Harburg, Edgar Yipsel ("Yip")	1
Heller, Joseph	1960s-1
Hellman, Lillian Florence	1
Herlihy, James Leo	1960s-1
Isherwood, Christopher William	2
Jones, Everett LeRoy (Amiri Baraka; "LeRoi")	1960s-1
Kanin, Garson	5
Kerr, Walter Francis	4
Koch, Kenneth Jay	6
Lardner, Ringgold Wilmer ("Ring")	Sports-2
Larson, Jonathan	4
Lerner, Alan Jay	2
Levin, Meyer	1
Logan, Joshua Lockwood, III	2
Loos, Anita	1
Lowell, Robert Traill Spence IV ("Cal")	1960s-1
Luce, Clare Boothe	2
Ludlam, Charles	2
McCullers, Carson	1960s-2
MacLeish, Archibald	1
McNally, Terrence	1960s-2
Maltz, Albert	1
Mannes, Marya	2
May, Elaine	1960s-2
Merriam, Eve	3
Merrill, James Ingram	4
Miller, Arthur Asher	1960s-2
Oates, Joyce Carol	1960s-2
Piñero, Miguel	2
Rosten, Norman	4
Ryskind, Morrie	1
Sackler, Howard Oliver	1960s-2
Saroyan, William	1
Schuyler, James Marcus	3
Shaw, Irwin Gilbert	1
Shulman, Max	2
Sillman, Leonard Dexter	1
Silverstein, Shel(don) Allan	5
Simon, (Marvin) Neil	1960s-2
Taylor, Peter Hillsman	4
Terry, Megan	1960s-2
Vidal, Gore	1960s-2
Warren, Robert Penn	2
Williams, Thomas Lanier, III ("Tennessee")	1
Willson, (Robert Reiniger) Meredith	1

	Volume
Author (Fiction)	
Abbey, Edward Paul	2
Adams, Harriet Stratemeyer	1
Algren, Nelson	1
Armour, Richard Willard	2
Asimov, Isaac	3
Baker, Carlos Heard	2
Baldwin, James Arthur	2, 1960s-1
Bancroft, Mary	5
Barnes, Djuna Chappell	1
Barth, John Simmons	1960s-1
Barthelme, Donald, Jr.	2
Bee, Clair Francis	1
Bellow, Saul	1960s-1
Berberova, Nina Nikolaevna	3
Bloch, Robert Albert	4
Bowles, Paul Frederic(k)	5
Boyle, Katherine ("Kay")	3
Boylston, Helen Dore	1
Bradbury, Ray	1960s-1
Brautigan, Richard	1
Brooks, Richard	3
Brown, Claude	6, 1960s-1
Brown, Dee Alexander	6
Bukowski, Charles	4
Burke, Kenneth Duva	3
Burroughs, William S(eward)	5, 1960s-1
Caldwell, (Janet Miriam) Taylor	1
Caldwell, Erskine Preston	2
Canby, Vincent	6
Capote, Truman Garcia	1, 1960s-1
Carver, Raymond Clevie	2
Castaneda, Carlos César Salvador Arana	5, 1960s-1
Cheever, John	1
Childress, Alice Herndon	4
Clampitt, Amy Kathleen	4
Clarke, John Henrik	5
Clavell, James duMaresq	4
Condon, Richard Thomas	4
Connell, Evan Shelby, Jr.	1960s-1
De Vries, Peter	3
Dick, Philip K(indred)	1, 1960s-1
Dickey, James Lafayette	5
Dorris, Michael Anthony	5
Douglas, Marjory Stoneman	5
Drury, Allen Stuart	5
Dubus, Andre Jules	5
Ehrlichman, John Daniel	5
Elkin, Stanley Lawrence	4
Ellison, Ralph Waldo	4
Ephron, Nora Louise	1960s-1
Exley, Frederick Earl	3

	Volume		*Volume*
Author (Fiction) (*continued*)		McCullers, Carson	1960s-2
Fariña, Richard George	1960s-1	MacDonald, John Dann	2
Finney, Walter Braden ("Jack")	4	Macdonald, Ross	1
Foote, Shelby Dade, Jr.	1960s-1	MacInnes, Helen Clark	1
Fuller, Samuel Michael	5	McMurtry, Larry Jeff	1960s-2
Gaddis, William	5	Mailer, Norman Kingsley	1960s-2
Gann, Ernest Kellogg	3	Malamud, Bernard	2
Gardner, John Champlin, Jr.	1	Maltz, Albert	1
Geisel, Theodor S. ("Dr. Seuss")	3	Mannes, Marya	2
Gellhorn, Martha Ellis	5	Maxwell, William Keepers, Jr.	6
Gill, Brendan	5	Merrill, James Ingram	4
Goodman, Paul	1960s-1	Michener, James Albert	5
Guthrie, Alfred Bertram, Jr.	3	Momaday, N(avarre) Scott	1960s-2
Haley, Alexander Murray Palmer		Monette, Paul Landry	4
("Alex")	3, 1960s-1	Morris, William Weaks ("Willie")	5
Halper, Albert	1	Nabokov, Vladimir	1960s-2
Heinlein, Robert Anson	2	Nemerov, Howard	3
Heinz, Wilfred Charles ("Bill")	Sports-1	Nin, Anaïs	1960s-2
Heller, Joseph	5, 1960s-1	Oates, Joyce Carol	1960s-2
Herlihy, James Leo	1960s-1	O'Connor, Flannery	1960s-2
Hersey, John Richard	3	Paredes, Américo	5
Highsmith, (Mary) Patricia	4	Percy, Walker	2, 1960s-2
Himes, Chester Bomar	1	Petry, Ann Lane	5
Hobson, Laura Kean Zametkin	2	Plath, Sylvia	1960s-2
Holmes, John Clellon	2	Porter, Katherine Anne	1960s-2
Hornberger, H(iester) Richard, Jr.		Potok, Chaim Tzvi	6
(Richard Hooker)	5	Powers, J(ames) F(arl)	5
Hubbard, L(afayette) Ron(ald)	2	Puzo, Mario	5, 1960s-2
Huie, William Bradford	2	Pynchon, Thomas Ruggles, Jr.	1960s-2
Huncke, Herbert Edwin	4	Rand, Ayn	1, 1960s-2
Isherwood, Christopher William	2	Reeder, Russell Potter, Jr. ("Red")	5
Jackson, J(ohn) B(rinckerhoff)	4	Robbins, Harold	5
Jacobs, Helen Hull	5	Rosten, Leo Calvin	5
Jordan, June	6	Rosten, Norman	4
Jovanovich, William Ilija ("Bill")	6	Roszak, Theodore	1, 1960s-2
Kanin, Garson	5	Roth, Henry	4
Kaufman, Bel	1960s-1	Roth, Philip Milton	1960s-2
Kesey, Kenneth Elton ("Ken")	6, 1960s-1	Runyon, Damon	Sports-2
Knowles, John	6	St. Johns, Adela Rogers	2
Koch, Kenneth Jay	6	Salinger, J(erome) D(avid)	1960s-2
Kosinski, Jerzy Nikodem	3, 1960s-1	Saroyan, William	1
L'Amour, Louis	2	Sarton, May	4
Landon, Margaret Dorothea Mortenson	3	Scarry, Richard McClure	4
Lardner, Ringgold Wilmer ("Ring")	Sports-2	Schuyler, James Marcus	3
Lardner, Ringgold Wilmer, Jr. ("Ring")	6	Selby, Hubert, Jr.	1960s-2
Lee, (Nelle) Harper	1960s-1	Sendak, Maurice Bernard	1960s-2
Levin, Meyer	1	Shaara, Michael Joseph, Jr.	2
Lincoln, C(harles) Eric	6	Shaw, Irwin Gilbert	1
Loos, Anita	1	Shulman, Max	2
Ludlum, Robert	6	Silverstein, Shel(don) Allan	5
Maas, Peter Guttrich	6	Singer, Isaac Bashevis	3, 1960s-2
McCarthy, Mary Therese	2, 1960s-2	Skinner, B(urrhus) F(rederic)	2

	Volume
Sontag, Susan	1960s-2
Southern, Terry Marion, Jr.	4, 1960s-2
Stegner, Wallace Earle	3
Stein, Aaron Marc	1
Steinbeck, John Ernst	1960s-2
Stone, Irving	2
Sturgeon, Theodore	1
Styron, William Clark, Jr.	1960s-2
Taylor, Peter Hillsman	4
Thompson, Kay	5
Trilling, Lionel	1960s-2
Updike, John Hoyer	1960s-2
Vidal, Gore	1960s-2
Vonnegut, Kurt, Jr.	1960s-2
Wallace, Irving	2
Warren, Robert Penn	2
Welty, Eudora Alice	6
Wescott, Glenway	2
West, Dorothy	5
West, (Mary) Jessamyn	1
White, E(lwyn) B(rooks)	1
Williams, Sherley Anne	5
Williams, Thomas Lanier, III ("Tennessee")	1
Wolfe, Thomas Kennerly, Jr. ("Tom")	1960s-2
Yates, Richard Walden	3
Yerby, Frank Garvin	3
Zelazny, Roger Joseph	4

Author (Nonfiction)

Abbey, Edward Paul	2
Abbott, Jack Henry	6
Ace, Goodman	1
Ackley, H(ugh) Gardner	5
Adams. Walter	5
Adler, Lawrence Cecil ("Larry")	6
Adler, Mortimer J(erome)	6
Allen, Forrest Clare ("Phog")	Sports-1
Allen, Stephen Valentine Patrick William ("Steve")	6, 1960s-1
Ambrose, Stephen Edward	6
Amory, Cleveland ("Clip")	5
Anson, Adrian Constantine ("Cap"; "Pop")	Sports-1
Arendt, Hannah	1960s-1
Armour, Richard Willard	2
Armour, Thomas Dickson ("Tommy")	Sports-1
Arrington, Leonard James	5
Ashe, Arthur Robert, Jr.	1960s-1
Ashmore, Harry Scott	5
Ashmore, Harry Scott, and William Calhoun ("Bill") Baggs	1960s-1
Asimov, Isaac	3

	Volume
Atkinson, (Justin) Brooks	1
Attwood, William Hollingsworth	2
Bailey, Thomas A.	1
Bailyn, Bernard	1960s-1
Bainton, Roland Herbert	1
Baker, Carlos Heard	2
Baldwin, Hanson Weightman	3
Baldwin, James Arthur	2, 1960s-1
Barber, Walter Lanier ("Red")	3
Barnes, Djuna Chappell	1
Barnett, A(rthur) Doak	5
Barnouw, Erik	6
Barr, Stringfellow	1
Barrett, William Christopher	3
Barzun, Jacques Martin	1960s-1
Bate, Walter Jackson	5, 1960s-1
Beard, James Andrew	1
Bee, Clair Francis	1
Bell, Daniel	1960s-1
Belli, Melvin Mouron	4
Berberova, Nina Nikolaevna	3
Bettelheim, Bruno	2
Bettmann, Otto Ludwig	5
Betz, Pauline May	Sports-1
Billington, Ray Allen	1
Bishop, James Alonzo ("Jim")	2
Black, Charles Lund, Jr.	6
Bloch, Konrad Emil	6
Bloom, Allan David	3
Bloom, Benjamin Samuel	5
Bombeck, Erma Louise Fiste	4
Boulding, Kenneth Ewart	1960s-1
Boyer, Ernest LeRoy, Sr.	4
Boyington, Gregory ("Pappy")	2
Boyle, Katherine ("Kay")	3
Bradley, Omar Nelson	1
Brodie, Fawn McKay	1
Brooks, Cleanth	4
Brooks, (Mary) Louise	1
Brown, Dee Alexander	6
Brown, Helen Gurley	1960s-1
Brown, Raymond Edward	5
Brozen, Yale	5
Buckley, William Frank, Jr.	1960s-1
Bundy, McGeorge	4, 1960s-2
Bundy, William Putnam	6
Burke, Kenneth Duva	3
Buscaglia, Felice Leonardo ("Leo")	5
Button, Richard Totten ("Dick")	Sports-1
Byers, Walter	Sports-1
Byrnes, Robert Francis	5
Cage, John Milton, Jr.	1960s-1

	Volume		*Volume*
Author (Nonfiction) (*continued*)		Dichter, Ernest	3
Calderone, Mary Steichen	5	Dixon, Jeane Lydia	5
Calvin. Melvin	5	Dmytryk, Edward	5
Campbell, Joseph John	2, 1960s-1	Dolgun, Alexander Michael	2
Canaday, John Edwin	1	Dorris, Michael Anthony	5
Cantwell, Mary Lee	6	Douglas, Marjory Stoneman	5
Capote, Truman	1, 1960s-1	Drake, (John Gibbs) St. Clair	2
Carmichael, Stokely (Kwame Touré;		Drucker, Peter Ferdinand	1960s-1
Kwame Turé)	1960s-1	Drury, Allen Stuart	5
Carson, Rachel Louise	1960s-1	Dubus, Andre Jules	5
Castañeda, Carlos Cesar Salvador Arana	5, 1960s-1	Dubos, René Jules	1
Chall, Jeanne Sternlicht	1960s-1	Durant, Will(iam) James and Ariel	
Chamberlain, John Rensselaer	4	Durant	1
Chamberlain, Wilt(on) Norman	5, Sports-1	Edel, (Joseph) Leon	5
Chase, Stuart	1	Ehrlichman, John Daniel	5
Childs, Marquis William	2	Eliade, Mircea	2
Chomsky, (Avram) Noam	1960s-1	Elkin, Stanley Lawrence	4
Ciardi, John Anthony	2	Ellis, John Tracy	3
Claiborne, Craig Raymond	6	Ellison, Ralph Waldo	4
Clark, Kenneth Bancroft	1960s-1	Engel, A. Lehman	1
Clarke, John Henrik	5	Ephron, Nora Louise	1960s-1
Cleaver, (Leroy) Eldridge	5, 1960s-1	Erikson, Erik Homburger	4
Cochran, Thomas Childs	5	Espy, Willard Richard ("Wede")	5
Commager, Henry Steele	5	Evans, Dale	6
Connell, Evan Shelby, Jr.	1960s-1	Evans, Rowland, Jr. ("Rowly")	6
Coon, Carleton Stevens	1	Exner, Judith Campbell	5
Corner, George Washington	1	Fadiman, Clifton Paul	5
Cousins, Norman	2, 1960s-1	Fairbank, John King	3
Cowley, (David) Malcolm	2	Fall, Bernard B.	1960s-1
Cox, Harvey Gallagher, Jr.	1960s-1	Farmer, James Leonard, Jr.	5, 1960s-1
Cremin, Lawrence A(rthur)	1960s-1	Faulk, John Henry	2
Crisp, Quentin	5	Feather, Leonard Geoffrey	4
Crowther, (Francis) Bosley, Jr.	1	Fehrenbacher, Don Edward	5
Cunliffe, Marcus Falkner	2	Fenwick, Millicent Hammond	3
Curti, Merle Eugene	4	Feshbach, Herman	6
Dabney, Virginius	4	Festinger, Leon	3
Dallin, Alexander	6	Feyerabend, Paul Karl	4
Dangerfield, George	2	Feynman, Richard Phillips	1960s-1
Daniels, Jonathan Worth	1	Fielding, Temple Hornaday	1
Davis, David Brion	1960s-1	Fine, Reuben	3
Dawidowicz, Lucy Schildkret	2	Finkelstein, Louis	3
Delany, Annie Elizabeth ("Bessie")	4	Fish, Hamilton	3
Delany, Sarah Louise ("Sadie")	5	Fisher, M(ary) F(rances) K(ennedy)	3
Della Femina, Jerry	1960s-1	Fitch, James Marston	6
Dellinger, David	1960s-1	Fixx, James Fuller	1
Deloria, Vine, Jr.	1960s-1	Flesch, Rudolf Franz	2
de Man, Paul	1	Fletcher, Joseph Francis, III	3
de Mille, Agnes George	3	Flood, Curt(is) Charles	5, Sports-1
Deming, W(illiam) Edwards	3	Foner, Philip Sheldon	4
Denby, Edwin Orr	1	Foote, Shelby Dade, Jr.	1960s-1
Dertouzos, Michael Leonidas	6	Forbes, Malcolm Stevenson	2
Deutsch, Helene Rosenbach	1	Fossey, Dian	1, 1960s-1

	Volume		Volume
Franklin, John Hope	1960s-1	Hartdegen, Stephen Joseph	2
Frazier, Walt, II ("Clyde")	Sports-1	Hartz, Louis	2
Fredericks, Carlton	2	Hayakawa, S(amuel) I(chiye)	3, 1960s-1
Freund, Paul Abraham	3	Hayden, Thomas Emmett ("Tom")	1960s-1
Friedan, Betty Naomi	1960s-1	Hayek, Friedrich August von	3
Friedman, Milton	1960s-1	Hazlitt, Henry Stuart	3
Friedrich, Carl Joachim	1	Hearst, William Randolph, Jr.	3
Friendly, Fred W.	5	Heinz, Wilfred Charles ("Bill")	Sports-1
Fuller, R(ichard) Buckminster, Jr.	1	Heller, Joseph	5, 1960s-1
Galbraith, John Kenneth	1960s-1	Heller, Walter Wolfgang	1960s-1
Gallup, George Horace	1	Hellman, Lillian Florence	1
Gann, Ernest Kellogg	3	Hemingway, Mary Welsh	2
Gardner, John Champlin, Jr.	1	Hentoff, Nathan Irving ("Nat")	1960s-1
Gardner, John William	6, 1960s-1	Herrnstein, Richard Julius	4
Garrison, Earling Carothers ("Jim")	3, 1960s-1	Hersey, John Richard	3
Gavin, James Maurice	2	Hersh, Seymour M.	1960s-1
Gay, Peter ("Jack")	1960s-1	Hexter, J. H. ("Jack")	4
Gellhorn, Martha Ellis	5	Hicks, Granville	1
Gellhorn, Walter	4	Higginbotham, A(loysius) Leon, Jr.	5
Genovese, Eugene Dominick	1960s-1	Hillcourt, William ("Green Bar Bill")	3
Giamatti, A(ngelo) Bartlett ("Bart")	2, Sports-1	Hilsman, Roger	1960s-1
Gibson, Pack Robert ("Bob")	Sports-1	Hirsch, Eric Donald, Jr.	1960s-1
Gilbert, Felix	3	Hoffer, Eric	1
Gilbreth, Frank Bunker, Jr.	6	Hoffman, Abbott Howard ("Abbie";	
Gill, Brendan	5	"Barry Freed")	2, 1960s-2
Ginzberg, Eli	6	Hofstadter, Richard	1960s-1
Goffman, Erving Manual	1	Hogan, William Benjamin ("Ben")	5, Sports-1
Golden, Harry	1	Holt, John Caldwell	1, 1960s-1
Goldman, Eric Frederick	2	Hook, Sidney	2
Goldwater, Barry Morris	5, 1960s-1	Horwich, Frances Rappaport ("Miss	
Goodman, Louis Sanford	6	Frances")	6
Goodman, Paul	1960s-1	Houseman, John	2
Goren, Charles Henry	3	Hoving, Walter	2
Gould, Stephen Jay	6	Howe, Irving	1960s-1
Gowdy, Curt(is)	Sports-1	Hubbard, L(afayette) Ron(ald)	2
Graham, Sheilah	2	Hughes, Emmet John	1
Graham, Virginia	5	Hughes, H(enry) Stuart	5
Graziano, Rocky	2, Sports-1	Huie, William Bradford	2
Greenberg, Clement	4	Huncke, Herbert Edwin	5
Greenberg, Joseph H(arold)	6	Hutchinson, G(eorge) Evelyn	3
Grizzard, Lewis McDonald, Jr.	4	Illich, Ivan	1960s-1
Grosvenor, Melville Bell	1	Isherwood, Christopher William	2
Gunther, Gerald	6	Jackson, J(ohn) B(rinckerhoff)	4
Guthrie, Alfred Bertram, Jr.	3	Jacobs, Helen Hull	5
Halberstam, David	1960s-1	Jacobs, Jane	1960s-1
Haley, Alex(ander) Murray Palmer	3	Jacoby, James Oswald ("Jim")	3
Hall, Gus	6	Jacoby, Oswald ("Ozzie")	1
Hargis, Billy James	1960s-1	Janeway, Eliot	3
Harrington, (Edward) Michael	1960s-1	Janowitz, Morris	2
Harris, Sydney Justin	2	Jenner, (William) Bruce	Sports-1
Harsanyi, John C.	6	Jessel, George Albert ("Georgie")	1
Hart, Marion Rice	2	Johnson, Haynes Bonner	1960s-1

	Volume		*Volume*
Author (Nonfiction) (*continued*)		Lichine, Alexis	2
Jones, Robert Reynolds, Jr. ("Bob")	5	Lilienthal, David Eli	1
Jordan, June	6	Lincoln, C(harles) Eric	6
Jovanovich, William Ilija ("Bill")	6	Lindbergh, Anne (Spencer) Morrow	6
Kael, Pauline	6	Link, Arthur Stanley	5
Kahn, Herman Bernard	1, 1960s-1	Liquori, Martin William, Jr. ("Marty")	Sports-1
Kanin, Garson	5	Logan, Rayford Whittingham	1
Kardiner, Abram	1	Lord, Walter	6
Karnow, Stanley	1960s-1	Lorde, Audre Geraldine	3
Karski, Jan	6	Lovelace, Linda Susan	6
Kazin, Alfred	5	Lubell, Samuel	2
Kempton, (James) Murray	5	Lukas, J(ay) Anthony	5
Kendrick, Alexander	3	Lynd, Helen Merrell	1
Kennan, George Frost	1960s-1	Lynes, (Joseph) Russell, Jr.	3
Keppel, Francis	2	Maas, Peter Guttrich	6
Kerr, Walter Francis	4	McCarthy, Eugene Joseph	1960s-2
Kieran, John Francis	1	McCarthy, Mary Therese	2, 1960s-2
Killian, James Rhyne, Jr.	2	Macdonald, Dwight	1, 1960s-2
Kirk, Grayson Louis	5, 1960s-1	McGee, Gale William	3
Kirk, Russell Amos	4	McGill, Ralph Emerson	1960s-2
Kirstein, Lincoln	4	McGinniss, Joseph ("Joe")	1960s-2
Kissinger, Henry Alfred	1960s-1	MacLaine, Shirley	1960s-2
Kohl, Herbert R.	1960s-1	McLuhan, (Herbert) Marshall	1960s-2
Koopmans, Tjalling Charles	1	McNamara, Robert Strange	1960s-2
Kozol, Jonathan	1960s-1	Mailer, Norman Kingsley	1960s-2
Kramer, John Albert ("Jack")	Sports-1	Maleska, Eugene Thomas	3
Kristeller, Paul Oskar	5	Malone, Dumas	2
Kuhn, Thomas Samuel	4	Manchester, William Raymond	1960s-2
Kunstler, William Moses	1960s-1	Mannes, Marya	2
Kuralt, Charles Bishop	5	Marcus, Stanley	6
Kurland, Philip B.	4	Marcuse, Herbert	1960s-2
Kutner, Luis	3	Martin, John Bartlow	1960s-2
Kuznets, Simon Smith	1	Masters, William Howell	6
Ladd, George Eldon	1	Masters, William Howell, and Virginia	
Lamont, Corliss	4	Eshelman Johnson	1960s-2
Langer, Susanne Katherina	1	May, Rollo Reece	4
Lardner, Ringgold Wilmer ("Ring")	Sports-2	Mays, Benjamin Elijah	1
Larson, (Lewis) Arthur	3	Means, Gardiner Coit	2
Lasch, (Robert) Christopher	4, 1960s-1	Menninger, Karl Augustus	2
Lash, Joseph P.	2	Merriam, Eve	3
Lattimore, Owen	2	Merrill, James Ingram	4
Leary, Timothy Francis	4, 1960s-1	Meyendorff, John	3
Le Gallienne, Eva	3	Michener, James Albert	5
Leinsdorf, Erich	3	Middleton, Drew	2
Lekachman, Robert	2	Milgram, Stanley	1
Lelyveld, Arthur Joseph	4	Miller, William Mosely	2
Leontief, Wassily	5	Mills, C(harles) Wright	1960s-2
Lerner, Max	3	Mitchell, Joseph Quincy	4
Levin, Meyer	1	Mitford, Jessica ("Decca")	4
Lewis, (Joseph) Anthony	1960s-1	Mizener, Arthur Moore	2
Lewis, Flora	6	Monette, Paul Landry	4
Lewis, Oscar	1960s-1	Monroe, Marion	1
Lewis, Shari	5	Montagu, Ashley	5

	Volume		*Volume*
Moos, Malcolm Charles	1	Ray, Dixy Lee	4
Morison, Elting Elmore	4	Reeder, Russell Potter, Jr. ("Red")	5
Morris, Richard Brandon	2	Reel, A(dolf) Frank	6
Morris, William Weaks ("Willie")	5	Regnery, Henry	4
Moynihan, Daniel Patrick	1960s-2	Reischauer, Edwin Oldfather	2, 1960s-2
Mumford, Lewis Charles	2	Reshevsky, Samuel Herman	3
Murray, Anna Pauline ("Pauli")	1	Reston, James Barrett	4
Nader, Ralph	1960s-2	Rickover, Hyman George	2
Nagel, Ernest	1, 1960s-2	Riesman, David, Jr.	6
Nash, Gerald David	6	Ripley, S(idney) Dillon, II	6
Nason, John William	6	Roberts, Oral	1960s-2
Nearing, Helen Knothe	4	Rock, John Charles	1
Nearing, Scott	1	Rockefeller, David	1960s-2
Nef, John Ulric	2	Rockefeller, John Davison, III	1960s-2
Nemerov, Howard	3	Rome, Esther Rachel Seidman	4
Neustadt, Richard Elliott	1960s-2	Roosevelt, James	3
Newhall, Beaumont	3	Rosten, Leo Calvin	5
Niebuhr, Reinhold	1960s-2	Rosten, Norman	4
Niel, Cornelis Bernardus van	1	Rostow, Eugene Victor Debs	6
Nin, Anaïs	1960s-2	Rostow, Walter Whitman ("Walt")	1960s-2
Nisbet, Robert Alexander	4	Roszak, Theodore	1, 1960s-2
Nixon, Richard Milhous	4, 1960s-2	Rothwax, Harold J(ay)	5
Nizer, Louis	1960s-2	Rowan, Carl T(homas)	6
Nozick, Robert	6	Royko, Mike	5
Oates, Joyce Carol	1960s-2	Rubin, Jerry Clyde	4, 1960s-2
O'Connor, John Joseph	6	Sachar, Abram Leon	3
O'Hair, Madalyn Murray	4, 1960s-2	Sagan, Carl Edward	4
Packard, Vance Oakley	4	St. Johns, Adela Rogers	2
Padover, Saul Kussiel	1	Salisbury, Harrison Evans	3, 1960s-2
Pais, Abraham	6	Salk, Lee	3
Paredes, Américo	5	Salmon, Wesley C(harles)	6
Parks, Gordon, Sr.	1960s-2	Samora, Julian	1960s-2
Peale, Norman Vincent	3, 1960s-2	Samuelson, Paul Anthony	1960s-2
Penick, Harvey Morrison	4	Sarton, May	4
Perkins, Dexter	1	Schapiro, Meyer	4
Peter, Laurence Johnston	2, 1960s-2	Schell, Jonathan Edward	1960s-2
Peterson, Roger Tory	4	Schlafly, Phyllis Stewart	1960s-2
Philbrick, Herbert Arthur	3	Schlesinger, Arthur Meier, Jr.	1960s-2
Phillips, Kevin Price	1960s-2	Schoenbrun, David Franz	2
Pike, James Albert, Jr.	1960s-2	Schuller, Gunther Alexander	1960s-2
Podhoretz, Norman Harold	1960s-2	Schultz, Theodore William	5
Pogue, Forrest Carlisle	4	Scott, Austin Wakeman	1
Ponnamperuma, Cyril Andrew	4	Seale, Robert George ("Bobby")	1960s-2
Pool, Ithiel de Sola	1	Seldes, George Henry	4
Porter, Sylvia Field	3	Selznick, Irene Mayer	2
Potok, Chaim Tzvi	6	Sevareid, (Arnold) Eric	3
Pritikin, Nathan	1	Shannon, William Vincent	2
Puller, Lewis Burwell, Jr.	4	Sheed, Francis Joseph ("Frank")	1
Purcell, Edward Mills	5	Sheehan, Cornelius Mahoney ("Neil")	1960s-2
Quarles, Benjamin Arthur	4	Shils, Edward Albert	4
Rafferty, Maxwell Lewis, Jr. ("Max")	1, 1960s-2	Shilts, Randy Martin	4
Rand, Ayn	1, 1960s-2	Shirer, William Lawrence	3
Rawls, John Bordley	6	Shook, Karel Francis Antony	1

Volume   *Volume*

Author (Nonfiction) (*continued*)

Shulman, Max	2
Simon, Herbert A(lexander)	6
Simon, William E(dward)	6
Skinner, B(urrhus) F(rederic)	2
Sloane, Eric	1
Slonimsky, Nicolas (Nikolai Leonidovich)	4
Smith, Henry Nash	2
Smith, Howard K(ingsbury)	6
Smith, (Charles) Page (Ward)	4
Snead, Samuel Jackson ("Sam")	6
Sorensen, Theodore Chaikin ("Ted")	1960s-2
Spock, Benjamin McLane ("Dr. Spock")	5
Stegner, Wallace Earle	3
Stein, Herbert	1960s-2
Stone, I. F.	1960s-2
Stone, Irving	2
Stone, Lawrence	5
Stone, W(illiam) Clement	6
Stuart, Jesse Hilton	1
Sullivan, Walter Seager, Jr.	4
Sulzberger, Cyrus Leo	3
Swanberg, W(illiam) A(ndrew)	3
Szulc, Tadeusz Witold ("Tad")	6
Taylor, Harold Alexander	3
Taylor, Maxwell Davenport	2, 1960s-2
Taylor, Peter Hillsman	4
Taylor, Telford	5
Terry, Walter	1
Thomas, Lewis	3
Thomas, Lowell Jackson	1
Thompson, Hunter S(tockton)	1960s-2
Tobin, James	6
Trapp, Maria von	2
Trilling, Diana Rubin	4
Trilling, Lionel	1960s-2
Tsongas, Paul Efthemios	5
Tuchman, Barbara Wertheim	2
Udall, Morris King	5
Veeck, William Louis, Jr. ("Bill")	2
Venturi, Robert	1960s-2
Vernon, Raymond	5
Wallace, Irving	2
Ward, John William	1
Washburn, Sherwood L(arned)	6
Watson, James Dewey	1960s-2
Weaver, Robert Clifton	5, 1960s-2
Wechsler, Herbert	6
Weil, André	5
Weiss, Paul	6
Weisskopf, Victor Frederick	6
Welch, Robert Henry Winborne, Jr.	1
Wellek, René Maria Eduard	4, 1960s-2
West, (Mary) Jessamyn	1
White, E(lwyn) B(rooks)	1
White, Theodore Harold	1960s-2
Whitehead, Don(ald) Ford	1
Whyte, William Foote	6
Whyte, William Hollingsworth, Jr.	5
Wiebe, Robert H(uddleston)	6
Wildavsky, Aaron Bernard	3
Williams, William Appleman	1960s-2
Wills, Garry	1960s-2
Wojnarowicz, David Michael	3
Wolfe, Thomas Kennerly, Jr. ("Tom")	1960s-2
Wood, Beatrice	5
Wood, Evelyn Nielsen	4
Woodward, Comer Vann	1960s-2
Wright, Olgivanna Lloyd	1
Yarmolinsky, Adam	6

Author (Poetry)

Armour, Richard Willard	2
Ashbery, John Lawrence	1960s-1
Auden, W(ystan) H(ugh)	1960s-1
Baker, Carlos Heard	2
Berryman, John Allyn	1960s-1
Bishop, Elizabeth	1960s-1
Bowles, Paul Frederic(k)	5
Boyle, Katherine ("Kay")	3
Brautigan, Richard	1
Brodsky, Joseph	4
Brooks, Gwendolyn Elizabeth	6, 1960s-1
Bukowski, Charles	4
Carver, Raymond Clevie	2
Ciardi, John Anthony	2
Clampitt, Amy Kathleen	4
Corso, Gregory Nunzio	6
Cowley, (David) Malcolm	2
Denby, Edwin Orr	1
Dickey, James Lafayette	5
Duncan, Robert	2
Engle, Paul Hamilton	3
Espy, Willard Richard ("Wede")	5
Everson, William Oliver (Brother Antoninus)	4
Fitzgerald, Robert Stuart	1
Ginsberg, (Irwin) Allen	5, 1960s-1
Giovanni, Nikki	1960s-1
Goodman, Paul	1960s-1
Guthrie, Alfred Bertram, Jr.	3
Holmes, John Clellon	2

	Volume
Jones, Everett LeRoy (Amiri Baraka; "LeRoi")	1960s-1
Jordan, June	6
Koch, Kenneth Jay	6
Laughlin, James	5
Levertov, Denise	5
Lorde, Audre Geraldine	3
Lowell, Robert Traill Spence IV ("Cal")	1960s-1
MacLeish, Archibald	1
Merriam, Eve	3
Merrill, James Ingram	4
Monette, Paul Landry	4
Nabokov, Vladimir	1960s-2
Nemerov, Howard	3
Oates, Joyce Carol	1960s-2
Oppen, George	1
Plath, Sylvia	1960s-2
Rexroth, Kenneth Charles Marion	1
Rice, Helen Steiner	1
Rich, Adrienne Cecile	1960s-2
Riding, Laura	3
Rosten, Norman	4
Sarton, May	4
Schuyler, James Marcus	3
Sexton, Anne	1960s-2
Shapiro, Karl Jay	6, 1960s-2
Silverstein, Shel(don) Allan	5
Stuart, Jesse Hilton	1
Updike, John Hoyer	1960s-2
Warren, Robert Penn	2
Williams, Sherley Anne	5
Williams, William Carlos	1960s-2

Author (Radio and Television)

	Volume
Ace, Goodman	1
Allen, Stephen Valentine Patrick William ("Steve")	6, 1960s-1
Allen, Woody	1960s-1
Barnouw, Erik	6
Bloch, Robert Albert	4
Cavett, Richard Alva ("Dick")	1960s-1
Chayefsky, Sidney Aaron ("Paddy")	1, 1960s-1
Diamond, Selma	1
Funt, Allen	5
Gosden, Freeman Fisher	1
Goulding, Ray(mond) Walter	2
Herlihy, James Leo	1960s-1
Hill, George Roy	6
Moore, Garry	3
Peckinpah, David Samuel ("Sam")	1, 1960s-2
Pryor, Richard Franklin Lenox Thomas	1960s-2
Roddenberry, Eugene Wesley ("Gene")	1960s-2
Serling, Rodman Edward ("Rod")	1960s-2

	Volume
Shulman, Max	2
Simon, (Marvin) Neil	1960s-2
Vidal, Gore	1960s-2
Webb, John Randolph ("Jack")	1

Author (Science Fiction)

	Volume
Asimov, Isaac	3
Bradbury, Ray	1960s-1
Dick, Philip Kindred	1, 1960s-1
Heinlein, Robert Anson	2
Hubbard, L(afayette) Ron(ald)	2
Roddenberry, Eugene Wesley ("Gene")	3, 1960s-2
Sturgeon, Theodore	1
Zelazny, Roger Joseph	4

Author (Screenplays)

	Volume
Abbott, George Francis	4
Bloch, Robert Albert	4
Bradbury, Ray	1960s-1
Brooks, Richard	3
Bukowski, Charles	4
Capote, Truman Garcia	1, 1960s-1
Capra, Frank	3
Chayefsky, Sidney Aaron ("Paddy")	1, 1960s-1
Clavell, James duMaresq	4
Condon, Richard Thomas	4
Ephron, Nora Louise	1960s-1
Epstein, Julius J. ("Julie")	6
Foreman, Carl	1
Fuller, Samuel Michael	5
Gann, Ernest Kellogg	3
Geisel, Theodor Seuss ("Dr. Seuss")	3
Goodrich, Frances	1
Gordon, Ruth	1
Green, Adolph	6
Guthrie, A(lfred) B(ertram), Jr.	3
Heller, Joseph	1960s-1
Hellman, Lillian	1
Huston, John Marcellus	1960s-1
Kanin, Garson	5
Kesey, Kenneth Elton ("Ken")	6
Kubrick, Stanley	1960s-1
Lardner, Ringgold Wilmer, Jr. ("Ring")	6
Lerner, Alan Jay	2
Lewis, Jerry	1960s-1
Loos, (Corinne) Anita	1
Lorentz, Pare	3
Lupino, Ida	4
McMurtry, Larry Jeff	1960s-2
Mailer, Norman Kingsley	1960s-2
Maltz, Albert	1
Mankiewicz, Joseph Leo	3
May, Elaine	1960s-2
Meredith, (Oliver) Burgess	5

Volume

Author (Screenplays) *(continued)*

Nabokov, Vladimir	1960s-2
Nicholson, Jack	1960s-2
Pakula, Alan Jay	5
Peckinpah, David Samuel ("Sam")	1, 1960s-2
Pryor, Richard Franklin Lenox Thomas	1960s-2
Puzo, Mario	5, 1960s-2
Roach, Harold Eugene ("Hal")	3
Roddenberry, Eugene Wesley ("Gene")	3
Rosten, Leo Calvin	5
Rosten, Norman	4
Ryskind, Morrie	1
Sackler, Howard Oliver	1960s-2
St. Johns, Adela Rogers	2
Salt, Waldo	2
Saroyan, William	1
Serling, Rodman Edward ("Rod")	1960s-2
Shaw, Irwin Gilbert	1
Simon, (Marvin) Neil	1960s-2
Skolsky, Sidney	1
Southern, Terry Marion, Jr.	4, 1960s-2
Vidal, Gore	1960s-2
Vidor, King Wallis	1
Wallace, Irving	2
Webb, John Randolph ("Jack")	1
Welles, Orson	1
Wilder, Samuel ("Billy")	6
Williams, Thomas Lanier, III ("Tennessee")	1

Author (Translation)

Auden, W(ystan) H(ugh)	1960s-1
Bancroft, Mary	5
Bowles, Paul Frederic(k)	5
Fadiman, Clifton Paul	5
Fitzgerald, Robert Stuart	1
Hartdegen, Stephen Joseph	2
Howe, Irving	3
Isherwood, Christopher William	2
Levin, Meyer	1
Singer, Isaac Bashevis	1960s-2

Aviator

Boyington, Gregory ("Pappy")	2
Carl, Marion Eugene	5
Corrigan, Douglas ("Wrong-Way Corrigan")	4
Doolittle, James Harold	3
Gann, Ernest Kellogg	3
Hart, Marion Rice	2
Howard, James Howell	4
Johnson, Leon William	5
Johnson, Robert Samuel	5

Volume

Johnston, Alvin Melvin ("Tex")	5
Lindbergh, Anne (Spencer) Morrow	6
Quesada, Elwood Richard ("Pete")	3
Richards, Faith Buchner ("Bucky")	6

Banker. *See* **Business Executive (Banking and Financial Services Industry).**

Baseball Manager. *See* **Sports Manager (Baseball).**

Baseball Player. *See* **Athlete (Baseball).**

Basketball Player. *See* **Athlete (Basketball).**

Biochemist

Anfinsen, Christian Boehmer	4
Beadle, George Wells ("Beets")	2
Bloch, Konrad Emil	6, 1960s-1
Cori, Carl Ferdinand	1
Doisy, Edward Adelbert	2
Elion, Gertrude Belle ("Trudy")	5
Hershey, Alfred Day	5, 1960s-1
Hitchings, George Herbert, Jr.	5
Holley, Robert William	3, 1960s-1
Kamen, Martin D(avid)	6
Khorana, Har Gobind	1960s-1
Lipmann, Fritz Albert	2
MacCorquodale, Donald William ("Mac")	2
Moore, Stanford	1
Nathans, Daniel	5
Niel, Cornelis Bernardus van	1
Nirenberg, Marshall Warren	1960s-2
Northrop, John Howard	2
Pauling, Linus Carl	1960s-2
Rodbell, Martin	5
Sabin, Albert Bruce	1960s-2
Szent-Györgyi, Albert (von Nagyrapolt)	2
Wald, George David	1960s-2

Biologist

Anfinsen, Christian Boehmer	4
Beadle, George Wells ("Beets")	2
Bunting-Smith, Mary Alice Ingraham ("Polly")	5
Carson, Rachel Louise	1960s-1
Claude, Albert	1
Cournand, André Frederic	2
Delbrück, Max Ludwig Henning	1, 1960s-1
Dubos, René Jules	1
Friend, Charlotte	2
Hall, Theodore Alvin	5
Hammond, E(dward) Cuyler	2
Hartline, Haldan Keffer	1, 1960s-1
Holley, Robert William	3
Kamen, Martin D(avid)	6

	Volume
Niel, Cornelis Bernardus van	1
Pauling, Linus Carl	1960s-2
Ripley, S(idney) Dillon, II	6
Sabin, Albert Bruce	3
Sepkoski, J(oseph) John, Jr.	5
Stern, Curt	1
Thomas, Lewis	3
Wald, George David	5
Watson, James Dewey	1960s-2
Weiss, Paul Alfred	2

Bishop. *See* **Clergy.**

Boxer. *See* **Athlete (Boxing).**

Business Executive (Accounting)

Townsend, Lynn Alfred	6

Business Executive (Advertising Industry)

Bernbach, William	1
Bowles, Chester Bliss ("Chet")	2
Della Femina, Jerry	1960s-1
Dichter, Ernest	3
Foote, Emerson	3
Haldeman, H(arry) R(obbins) ("Bob")	3, 1960s-1
Hughes, Harold Everett	4
Husted, Marjorie Child	2
Odell, Allan Gilbert	4
Ogilvy, David Mackenzie	5
Sackler, Arthur Mitchell	2
Stevens, Brooks	4
Weaver, Sylvester Laflin, Jr. ("Pat")	6

Business Executive (Arts)

Brown, J(ohn) Carter	6
Kirstein, Lincoln	4

Business Executive (Automobile Industry)

Albert, Frank Culling ("Frankie")	6
Donner, Frederic Garrett	2
Ford, Henry, II ("Hank the Deuce")	2
Gerstenberg, Richard Charles	6
Luisetti, Angelo Enrico ("Hank")	6, Sports
McNamara, Robert Strange	1960s-2
Romney, George Wilcken	4
Townsend, Lynn Alfred	6, 1960s-2

Business Executive (Aerospace and Defense)

Adams, Charles Francis	5
Douglas, Donald Wills	1
Geneen, Harold Sydney	5, 1960s-1
Grumman, Leroy Randle ("Roy")	1
Haughton, Daniel Jeremiah	2
Johnson, Clarence Edward ("Kelly")	2
Johnston, Alvin Melvin ("Tex")	5
Kappel, Frederick Russell	4
Little, Royal	2

	Volume
McCone, John Alex	3
Northrop, John Knudsen ("Jack")	1

Business Executive (Airlines)

Beebe, William Thomas	1
Chalk, (Oscar) Roy	4
Hitchcock, Thomas, Jr. ("Tommy")	Sports-1
Mackey, Joseph Creighton	1
Mitchell, John James, Jr.	1
Smith, C(yrus) R(owlett)	2
Trippe, Juan Terry	1

Business Executive (Banking and Financial Services Industry)

Alger, David Dewey	6
Batten, William Milford	5
Bernhard, Arnold	2
Bishop, Hazel Gladys	5
Black, Eugene Robert	3
Black, Fischer Sheffey	4
Case, Everett Needham	6
Clay, Lucius Dubignon, Sr.	1960s-1
Cornfeld, Bernard ("Bernie")	4
De Nagy, Tibor	3
Evans, Thomas Mellon	5
Johnson, Edward Crosby, 2d	1
Little, Royal	2
Lovett, Robert Abercrombie	2
Mansfield, Michael Joseph ("Mike")	6
Martin, William McChesney, Jr.	5, 1960s-2
Mitchell, John James, Jr.	1
Morgan, Henry Sturgis ("Harry")	1
Nomellini, Leo Joseph	6
Pierce, Samuel Riley, Jr.	6
Price, T(homas) Rowe, Jr.	1
Rockefeller, David	1960s-2
Sawhill, John Crittenden	6
Shields, Cornelius	1
Simon, William E(dward)	6
Snyder, John Wesley	1
Weinberg, Harry	2

Business Executive (Beverage Industry)

Callaway, Ely Reeves, Jr.	6

Business Executive (Broadcast Industry)

Arledge, Roone Pinckney, Jr.	6, Sports-1
Balaban, Elmer	6
Forte, Fulvio Chester, Jr. ("Chet")	4
Goldenson, Leonard Harry	5
Hagerty, James Campbell	1
Hewitt, Don S.	1960s-1
Paley, William Samuel	2
Reel, A(dolf) Frank	6
Robertson, Marion Gordon ("Pat")	1960s-2

	Volume
Business Executive (Broadcast Industry) (*continued*)	
Ross, Steven Jay	3
Shepley, James Robinson	2
Tartikoff, Brandon	5
Weaver, Sylvester Laflin, Jr. ("Pat")	6
Wood, Robert Dennis	2
Business Executive (Chemical Industry)	
Connor, John Thomas ("Jack")	6
Grace, J(oseph) Peter, Jr.	4
Mason, (William) Birny J., Jr.	5
Plough, Abe	1
Swanson, Robert Arthur	5
Business Executive (Clothing Industry)	
Erteszek, Olga Bertram	2
Fredericks, Sara	2
Haas, Walter A., Jr., and Peter E. Haas, Sr.	1960s-1
Haggar, Joseph Marion	2
Marcus, Stanley	6
Simpson, Adele Smithline	4
Trigère, Pauline	6
Business Executive (Communications Industry)	
Clurman, Richard Michael	4
Geneen, Harold Sydney	5, 1960s-1
Hearst, Randolph Apperson	6
Henson, Paul Harry	5
Johnson, Rafer Lewis	1960s-1
Kappel, Frederick Russell	4
McGowan, William George	3
Business Executive (Computer Industry)	
Cocke, John	6
Hewlett, William Redington ("Bill")	6
Hewlett, William Redington ("Bill"), and David Packard	1960s-1
Noyce, Robert Norton	2, 1960s-2
Piore, Emanuel Ruben ("Mannie")	6
Wang, An	2, 1960s-2
Watson, Thomas John, Jr.	3, 1960s-2
Business Executive (Construction Industry)	
Bechtel, Stephen Davison, Sr.	2
Brown, George Rufus	1
Crown, Henry	2
Mas Canosa, Jorge	5
Volpe, John Anthony	4
Business Executive (Cosmetics and Personal Care Industry)	
Ash, Mary Kay	6, 1960s-1
Bishop, Hazel Gladys	5
Factor, Max, Jr.	4
Kiam, Victor Kermit, II	6
Sassoon, Vidal	1960s-1
Business Executive (Courier Industry)	
Casey, James E.	1

	Volume
Business Executive (Direct Sales)	
Ash, Mary Kay	6, 1960s-1
DeVos, Richard Marvin, and Jay Van Andel	1960s-1
Business Executive (Electrical and Electronics)	
Case, Everett Needham	6
Business Executive (Entertainment Industry)	
Acuff, Roy Claxton	3
Arnaz, Desi	2
Asch, Moses ("Moe")	2
Aubrey, James Thomas, Jr.	1960s-1
Autry, (Orvon) Gene	5
Balaban, Elmer	6
Ball, Lucille Désirée	2
Brown, Helen Gurley	1960s-1
Cohen, Alexander H(enry)	6
Davis, Martin S.	5
Dietz, Howard	1
Ellington, Mercer Kennedy	4
Fahey, John	6
Feld, Irvin	1
Goldenson, Leonard Harry	5
Goodson, Mark	3
Gordy, Berry, Jr.	1960s-1
Grucci, Felix James, Sr.	3
Hammond, John Henry, Jr.	2
Hecht, Harold	1
Hefner, Hugh Marston	1960s-1
Jackson, George Anthony	6
Jacobs, Bernard B.	4
Jaffe, Leo	5
Jones, Quincy Delight, Jr.	1960s-1
Knott, Walter	1
Krim, Arthur B.	4
Lancaster, Burt(on) Stephen	4
Lantz, Walter	4
Laughlin, James	5
Levine, Joseph Edward	2
Monroe, Earl Vernon, Jr.	Sports-2
Murray, Kathryn Hazel	5
North, John Ringling	1
Paley, William Samuel	2
Roach, Harold Eugene ("Hal")	3
Ruby, John ("Jack")	1960s-2
Sackler, Howard Oliver	1960s-2
Spector, Philip Harvey ("Phil")	1960s-2
Steel, Dawn Leslie	5
Stein, Julian Caesar ("Jules")	1
Tartikoff, Brandon	5
Wallis, Harold Brent ("Hal")	2
Wasserman, Lewis Robert ("Lew")	6
Wilson, Flip	5
Wood, Robert Dennis	2

Volume

Business Executive (Entrepreneur)

DeVos, Richard Marvin, and Jay Van
Andel — 1960s-1

Fisher, Avery Robert — 4

Gardner, Edward George — 1960s-1

Grace, J(oseph) Peter, Jr. — 4

Kroc, Raymond Albert ("Ray") — 1, 1960s-1

McLean, Malcom Purcell — 6

Rosenberg, William ("Bill") — 6

Sassoon, Vidal — 1960s-2

Thomas, Rex David ("Dave") — 6, 1960s-2

Vernon, Lillian — 1960s-2

Business Executive (Food Industry)

Austin, John Paul — 1

Black, William — 1

Bunker, Ellsworth — 1, 1960s-1

Busch, August Anheuser, Jr. ("Gussie") — 2

Carvel, Thomas Andrew — 2

Chen, Joyce — 4

Cohen, N(ehemiah) M(yer) — 1

Gallo, Julio Robert — 3

Goizueta, Roberto Crispulo — 5

Heinz, Henry John, II ("Jack") — 2

Husted, Marjorie Child — 2

Knott, Walter — 1

Kroc, Raymond Albert ("Ray") — 1, 1960s-1

Lay, Herman W. — 1

Lewis, Reginald Francis — 3

Lichine, Alexis — 2

Mack, Walter Staunton, Jr. — 2

Magowan, Robert Anderson — 1

Maris, Roger Eugene — 1, 1960s-2, Sports-2

Marriott, J(ohn) Willard — 1

Mars, Forrest Edward, Sr. — 5

Morton, Thruston Ballard — 1

Parks, Henry Green, Jr. — 2

Pillsbury, Philip — 1

Redenbacher, Orville — 4

Rosenberg, William ("Bill") — 6

Samuels, Howard Joseph — 1

Sanders, Harlan David ("Colonel") — 1960s-2

Simon, Norton Winfred — 3

Smucker, Paul Highnam — 5

Thomas, Rex David ("Dave") — 6, 1960s-2

Woodruff, Robert Winship — 1

Business Executive (Food Services)

Rosenberg, William ("Bill") — 6

Business Executive (Franchise Industry)

Carvel, Thomas Andrew — 2

Kroc, Ray(mond) Albert — 1, 1960s-1

Marchetti, Gino John — Sports-2

Murray Arthur — 3

Murray, Kathryn Hazel — 5

Rosenberg, William ("Bill") — 6

Sanders, Harlan David ("Colonel") — 1960s-2

Thomas, Rex David ("Dave") — 6, 1960s-2

Business Executive (Greeting Card Industry)

Hall, Joyce Clyde — 1

Business Executive (Hotel Industry)

Bates, Clayton ("Peg Leg") — 5

Johnson, Wallace Edward — 2

Marriott, Alice Sheets — 6

Marriott, J(ohn) Willard — 1

Pritzker, A(bram) N(icholas) — 2

Pritzker, Jay Arthur — 5

Business Executive (Insurance Industry)

Groza, Louis Roy ("Lou") — 6

Kemper, James Scott — 1

Kemper, James Scott, Jr. — 6

Kennedy, William Jesse, Jr. — 1

Roosevelt, James — 4

Stone, W(illiam) Clement — 6

Business Executive (Manufacturing Industry)

Adams, Charles Francis — 5

Baldrige, (Howard) Malcolm — 2

Blough, Roger Miles — 1, 1960s-1

Callaway, Ely Reeves, Jr. — 6

Castro, Bernard — 3

Clay, Lucius Dubignon, Sr. — 1960s-1

Donner, Frederic Garrett — 2

Foerstner, George Christian — 6

Ford, Henry, II ("Hank the Deuce") — 2

Fuller, S. B. — 2

Handler, Ruth — 6

Hart, Leon — 6

Houghton, Arthur Amory, Jr. — 2

Jarvis, Howard Arnold — 2

Ling, James Joseph — 1960s-1

Ludwig, Daniel Keith — 3

Spanel, Abram Nathaniel — 1

Tandy, Charles David — 1960s-2

Tupper, Earl Silas — 1

Wilson, Joseph Chamberlain — 1960s-2

Zamboni, Frank Joseph, Jr. — 2

Business Executive (Mining Industry)

Crown, Henry — 2

Hirshhorn, Joseph Herman — 1

Business Executive (Music Industry)

Asch, Moses ("Moe") — 2

Ellington, Mercer Kennedy — 4

Fisher, Avery Robert — 4

Gordy, Berry, Jr. — 1960s-1

Graham, Bill — 3

Hammond, John Henry, Jr. — 2

Jackson, George Anthony — 6

Volume

Business Executive (Music Industry) (*continued*)

Jones, Quincy Delight, Jr.   1960s-1
Mayfield, Curtis Lee   5
Sackler, Howard Oliver   1960s-2
Spector, Philip Harvey ("Phil")   1960s-2

Business Executive (Nonprofit)

Bundy, McGeorge   4
Case, Everett Needham   6
Cohen, Audrey C.   4
Fariña, Margarita Baez ("Mimi")   6
Gardner, John William   6, 1960s-1
Gerstenberg, Richard Charles   6
Gibson, William Frank   6
Hay, Henry, Jr. ("Harry")   6
Nader, Ralph   1960s-2
Pusey, Nathan Marsh   6
Ray, Gordon Norton   2
Ripley, S(idney) Dillon, II   6
Rudin, Lewis ("Lew")   6
Rusk, (David) Dean   1960s-2
Sagan, Ginetta Teresa Moroni   6
Sawhill, John Crittenden   6
Shriver, Eunice Mary Kennedy   1960s-2
Simon, William E(dward)   6
Sullivan, Leon Howard   6
Townsend, Lynn Alfred   6
Warne, Colston Estey   2
Williams, Hosea Lorenzo   6
Ylvisaker, Paul Norman   3

Business Executive (Petroleum Industry)

Bradshaw, Thornton Frederick ("Brad")   2
Brown, George Rufus   1
Doolittle, James Harold   3
Fannin, Paul Jones   6
Getty, Jean Paul   1960s-1
Hammer, Armand   2, 1960s-1
Hunt, H(aroldson) L(afayette), Jr.   1960s-1
Jones, Jerral Wayne ("Jerry")   Sports-1
Keeler, William Wayne   2
Landon, Alf(red) Mossman   2
McCarthy, Glenn Herbert   2
Pauley, Edwin Wendell   1
Tavoulareas, William Peter   4

Business Executive (Pharmaceutical Industry)

Connor, John Thomas ("Jack")   6
Hammer, Armand   2, 1960s-1
Hitchings, George Herbert, Jr.   5
Johnson, D(aniel) Mead   3
Kauffman, Ewing Marion   3
Plough, Abe   1
Searle, John Gideon ("Jack")   1960s-2
Swanson, Robert Arthur   5

Volume

Business Executive (Physical Fitness Industry)

Carter, Cris D.   Sports-1
Tanny, Victor Anthony ("Vic")   1

Business Executive (Political Research Industry)

Collbohm, Franklin Rudolph   2

Business Executive (Public Relations)

Bernays, Edward L.   4
O'Brien, Lawrence Francis ("Larry")   1960s-2
Rosenberg, Anna Marie Lederer   1

Business Executive (Publishing)

Annenberg, Walter Hubert   6
Attwood, William Hollingsworth   2
Ballantine, Ian Keith   4
Berlin, Richard Emmett   2
Bingham, (George) Barry, Sr.   2
Boni, Albert   1
Brett, George Platt, Jr.   1
Cerf, Bennett Albert   1960s-1
Chalk, (Oscar) Roy   4
Chandler, Dorothy Buffum   5
Cowles, Gardner, Jr. ("Mike")   1
Dedmon, Emmett   1
Delacorte, George Thomas, Jr.   3
Forbes, Malcolm Stevenson   2
Fuller, S. B.   2
Gilbreth, Frank Bunker, Jr.   6
Graham, Katharine Meyer   6
Hearst, William Randolph, Jr.   3
Hefner, Hugh Marston   1960s-1
Hillegass, Clifton Keith   6
Hobby, Oveta Culp   4
Ingersoll, Ralph McAllister   1
Johnson, Robert Edward   4
Jovanovich, William Ilija ("Bill")   6
Kennedy, John Fitzgerald, Jr.   5
Klopfer, Donald Simon   2
Knight, John Shively   1
Knopf, Alfred Abraham   1
Laughlin, James   5
Loeb, Nackey Scripps   6
Loeb, William   1
McCormick, Kenneth Dale   5
Mayfield, Curtis Lee   5
Maynard, Robert Clyve   3
Minow, Newton Norman   1960s-2
Parton, James   6
Pope, Generoso Paul, Jr.   2
Praeger, Frederick Amos   4
Regnery, Henry   4
Reston, James Barrett   4
Ridder, Bernard Herman, Jr. ("Bernie")   6
Ridder, Eric   4

	Volume
Rodale, Robert	2
Sackler, Arthur Mitchell	2
Schiff, Dorothy	2
Scribner, Charles, Jr.	4
Sheed, Francis Joseph ("Frank")	1
Shepley, James Robinson	2
Shimkin, Leon	2
Wallace, (William Roy) DeWitt, and Lila (Bell) Acheson	1
Washington, Chester Lloyd, Jr. ("Chet")	1
Whitney, John Hay	1
Wiggins, James Russell ("Russ")	6

Business Executive (Real Estate Industry)

Cafaro, William Michael	5
Chalk, (Oscar) Roy	4
Crown, Henry	2
Cranston, Alan MacGregor	6
DeBartolo, Edward John, Sr.	4
Dixon, Jeane Lydia	5
Forbes, Malcolm Stevenson	2
Helmsley, Henry Brakmann ("Harry")	5
Klutznick, Philip M.	5
Levitt, William Jaird ("Bill")	4
Rockefeller, Nelson Aldrich	1960s-2
Rose, Frederick Phineas	5
Rouse, James Wilson	4
Rubell, Steve	2
Rudin, Lewis ("Lew")	6
Starr, Bryan Bartlett ("Bart")	Sports-2
Trump, Frederick Christ	5
Uris, Harold David	1

Business Executive (Retail Industry)

Batten, William Milford	5
Bauer, Eddie	2
Cohen, N(ehemiah) M(yer)	1
Cunningham, Harry Blair	1960s-1
Daché, Marie-Louise ("Lilly")	2
Dillard, William Thomas, Sr.	6
Fredericks, Sara	2
Goldwater, Barry Morris	5, 1960s-1
Grace, J(oseph) Peter, Jr.	4
Hall, Joyce Clyde	1
Hoving, Walter	2
Lazarus, Ralph	2
Magnin, Cyril	2
Marcus, Stanley	6
Steloff, (Ida) Frances	2
Tandy, Charles David	1960s-2
Walton, Samuel Moore ("Sam")	3, 1960s-2

Business Executive (Shipbuilding)

| Ludwig, Daniel Keith | 3 |
| Steinbrenner, George Michael, III | Sports-2 |

	Volume
Business Executive (Sporting Goods)	
Bauer, Eddie	2
Bowerman, William Jay ("Bill")	5
Callaway, Ely Reeves, Jr.	6
Hogan, William Benjamin ("Ben")	5, Sports-1
Snelling, Richard Arkwright	3
Spalding, Albert Goodwill ("A. G.")	Sports-2

Business Executive (Sports). *See* **Sports Executive.**

Business Executive (Steel Industry)

Bing, David ("Dave")	Sports-1
Block, Joseph Leopold	3
Blough, Roger Miles	1, 1960s-1
McCone, John Alex	3

Business Executive (Technology)

Ash, Roy Lawrence	1960s-1
Packard, David	4
Perot, H(enry) Ross	1960s-2
Watson, Thomas John, Jr.	1960s-2

Business Executive (Tobacco Industry)

| Stokes, Colin | 1 |

Business Executive (Tourism Industry)

| Laughlin, James | 5 |
| Luisetti, Angelo Enrico ("Hank") | 6, Sports |

Business Executive (Toy and Game Industry)

Grucci, Felix James, Sr. ("Pops")	3
Handler, Ruth	6
Hassenfeld, Merrill Lloyd	1960s-1
Hassenfeld, Stephen David	2

Business Executive (Transportation Industry)

Black, Joseph, Jr. ("Joe")	6
Casey, James E.	1
Chalk, (Oscar) Roy	4
Grace, J(oseph) Peter, Jr.	4
Harriman, William Averell	1960s-1
Hughes, Harold Everett	4
Ludwig, Daniel Keith	3
McLean, Malcom Purcell	6
Penske, Roger S.	Sports-2

Cardinal. *See* **Clergy (Roman Catholic).**

Cardiologist

Gruentzig, Andreas Roland	1
Harken, Dwight Emary	3
Taussig, Helen Brooke	2
Zoll, Paul Maurice	5

Cartoonist

Addams, Charles Samuel	2
Block, Herbert Lawrence ("Herblock")	6
Buell, Marjorie Lyman Henderson ("Marge")	3
Caniff, Milton Arthur	2
Conrad, Paul	1960s-1
Crumb, Robert	1960s-1

	Volume
Cartoonist (*continued*)	
Geisel, Theodor Seuss (Dr. Seuss)	3
Gould, Chester	1
Kane, Robert ("Bob")	5
Ketcham, Henry King ("Hank")	6
Kurtzman, Harvey	3
Martin, Donald Edward ("Don")	6
Mauldin, William Henry ("Bill")	1960s-2
Oliphant, Patrick Bruce ("Pat")	1960s-2
Schulz, Charles M(onroe)	6
Shuster, Joseph E.	3
Siegel, Jerome ("Jerry")	4
Silverstein, Shel(don) Allan	5
Steinberg, Saul	5
Vargas, Alberto ("Varga")	1
Chef	
Beard, James Andrew	1
Chen, Joyce	4
Chemist	
Anfinsen, Christian Boehmer	4
Bloch, Konrad E(mil)	1960s-1
Calvin, Melvin	5, 1960s-1
Cram, Donald James	6
Elion, Gertrude Belle ("Trudy")	5
Factor, Max, Jr.	4
Flory, Paul John	1
Giauque, William Francis	1
Heidelberger, Michael	3
Hill, Julian Werner	4
Kamen, Martin D(avid)	6
Kistiakowsky, George Bogdan	1
Libby, Willard Frank	1960s-1
Mark, Herman Francis	3
Mulliken, Robert Sanderson	2, 1960s-2
Noyce, Robert Norton	1960s-2
Onsager, Lars	1960s-2
Pauling, Linus Carl	4, 1960s-2
Pedersen, Charles John	2
Ponnamperuma, Cyril Andrew	4
Seaborg, Glenn Theodore	5, 1960s-2
Swanson, Robert Arthur	5
Urey, Harold Clayton	1
Williams, Hosea Lorenzo	6
Woodward, Robert Burns	1960s-2
Chess Expert	
Fine, Reuben	3
Fischer, Robert James ("Bobby")	1960s-1
Reshevsky, Samuel Herman	3
Choreographer	
Ailey, Alvin	2, 1960s-1
Balanchine, George	1, 1960s-1

	Volume
Bennett, Michael	2
Champion, Gower	1960s-1
Cunningham, Mercier Phillip ("Merce")	1960s-1
Danilova, Alexandra Dionysievna ("Choura")	5
de Mille, Agnes George	3
Fosse, Robert Louis ("Bob")	2
Gennaro, Peter	6
Graham, Martha	3
Greco, Costanzo ("José")	6
Hawkins, Frederick ("Erick")	4
Holm, Hanya	3
Joffrey, Robert	2, 1960s-1
Kelly, Eugene Curran ("Gene")	4
Nikolais, Alwin Theodore ("Nik")	3, 1960s-2
Page, Ruth Marian	3
Primus, Pearl Eileen	4
Robbins, Jerome	5, 1960s-2
Shook, Karel Francis Antony	1
Tudor, Antony	2
Verdon, Gwyneth Evelyn ("Gwen")	6
Circus Executive	
Feld, Irvin	1
North, John Ringling	1
Civic Worker	
Boyer, Ernest LeRoy, Sr.	4
Chandler, Dorothy Buffum	5
Cohen, Audrey C.	4
Duke, Angier Biddle	4
Frick, Helen Clay	1
Furness, Elizabeth Mary ("Betty")	4
Ginsberg, Mitchell Irving	4
Hale, Clara McBride ("Mother")	3
Horton, Mildred Helen McAfee	4
Hughes, Harold Everett	4
Johnson, Rachel Harris	1
McNamara, Margaret Craig	1, 1960s-2
McQueen, Thelma ("Butterfly")	4
Rouse, James Wilson	4
Rudolph, Wilma Glodean	4
Shriver, Eunice Mary Kennedy	1960s-2
Civil Liberties Advocate	
Abzug, Bella Savitzky	5
Baldwin, Roger Nash	1
Boudin, Leonard B.	2
Fortas, Abraham ("Abe")	1, 1960s-1
Hay, Henry, Jr. ("Harry")	6
Hefner, Hugh Marston	1960s-1
Kennedy, Florynce Rae ("Flo")	6
Kunstler, William Moses	4, 1960s-1
Lamont, Corliss	4

Civil Rights Activist

	Volume
Abernathy, Ralph David	2
Abram, Morris Berthold	6
Baez, Joan Chandos	1960s-1
Baker, Ella Josephine	2
Baldwin, Roger Nash	1
Banks, Dennis J.	1960s-1
Bates, Daisy Lee Gatson	5
Berrigan, Philip Francis	6
Blackwell, Randolph Talmadge	1
Bond, (Horace) Julian	1960s-1
Boudin, Leonard B.	2
Brown, Hubert Gerold ("H. Rap")	1960s-1
Brown, James Nathaniel ("Jim")	1960s-1
Carmichael, Stokely (Kwame Touré; Kwame Turé)	5, 1960s-1
Chaney, James Earl, Andrew Goodman, and Michael Henry Schwerner	1960s-1
Chávez, César Estrada	1960s-1
Chisholm, Shirley Anita	1960s-1
Cleaver, Eldridge	1960s-1
Cunningham, Mercier Phillip ("Merce")	1960s-1
Davis, Angela Yvonne	1960s-1
Dee, Ruby	1960s-1
Delany, Annie Elizabeth ("Bessie")	4
Deloria, Vine, Jr.	1960s-1
Diggs, Charles Coles, Jr.	5
Dohrn, Bernardine Rae	1960s-1
Egan, John Joseph ("Jack")	6
Evers, Medgar Wylie	1960s-1
Farmer, James Leonard, Jr.	5, 1960s-1
Garcia, Hector Perez	4
Gibson, William Frank	6
Golden, Harry	1
Gordone, Charles	1960s-1
Groppi, James Edmund	1, 1960s-1
Hansberry, Lorraine Vivian	1960s-1
Harris, Patricia Roberts Fitzgerald	1
Hatcher, Richard Gordon	1960s-1
Hayden, Thomas Emmett ("Tom")	1960s-1
Hays, Lee	1
Henry, Aaron Edd Jackson	5
Hentoff, Nathan Irving ("Nat")	1960s-1
Heston, Charlton	1960s-1
Higginbotham, A(loysius) Leon, Jr.	5
Holland, Jerome Heartwell ("Brud")	1
Huie, William Bradford	2
Jackson, Jesse Louis	1960s-1
Kahane, Meir	2
Kelman, Wolfe	2
Kennedy, Florynce Rae ("Flo")	6

	Volume
King, Martin Luther, Jr.	1960s-1
King, Martin Luther, Sr. ("Daddy King")	1
Kuhn, Margaret Eliza ("Maggie")	4
Kunstler, William Moses	4
Lamont, Corliss	4
Lelyveld, Arthur Joseph	4
Lewis, John Robert	1960s-1
McCree, Wade Hampton, Jr.	2
McKissick, Floyd B.	3
Malcolm X (Malik El-Shabazz)	1960s-2
Marshall, Thurgood	3
Mays, Benjamin Elijah	1
Meredith, J(ames) H(oward)	1960s-2
Moses, Robert Parris	1960s-2
Muhammad, Elijah	1960s-2
Murray, Anna Pauline ("Pauli")	1
Nabrit, James Madison, Jr.	5
Newton, Huey Percy	1960s-2
Perlmutter, Nathan	2
Pierce, Samuel Riley, Jr.	6
Prinz, Joachim	2
Rauh, Joseph Louis, Jr.	3
Rustin, Bayard Taylor	2, 1960s-2
Sagan, Ginetta Teresa Moroni	6
Scott, Hazel Dorothy	1
Seale, Robert George ("Bobby")	1960s-2
Shabazz, Betty Jean	5
Shilts, Randy Martin	4
Snyder, Mitch(ell) Darryl	2
Sullivan, Leon Howard	6
Taylor, Telford	5
Washington, Chester Lloyd, Jr. ("Chet")	1
Washington, Harold	2
Wheeler, Raymond Milner	1
White, Ryan	2
Wilkins, Roy	1, 1960s-2
Williams, Hosea Lorenzo	6
Young, Andrew Jackson, Jr.	1960s-2

Clergy (Baptist)

Abernathy, Ralph David	2
Cox, Harvey Gallagher, Jr.	1960s-1
Jackson, Jesse Louis	1960s-1
King, Martin Luther, Jr.	1960s-1
King, Martin Luther, Sr. ("Daddy King")	1
Ladd, George Eldon	1
Mays, Benjamin Elijah	
Powell, Adam Clayton, Jr.	1960s-2
Robertson, Marion Gordon ("Pat")	1960s-2
Sullivan, Leon Howard	6

	Volume
Clergy (Christian Church)	
Hargis, Billy James	1960s-1
Clergy (Church of God)	
Armstrong, Herbert W.	2
Clergy (Church of the Brethren)	
Richards, Robert Eugene ("Bob")	Sports-2
Clergy (Congregationalist)	
Bainton, Roland Herbert	1
Cleage, Albert Buford, Jr.	6
Young, Andrew Jackson, Jr.	1960s-2
Clergy (Conservative Judaism)	
Kelman, Wolfe	2
Clergy (Dutch Reformed)	
Chino, Wendell	5
Peale, Norman Vincent	3
Clergy (Eastern Orthodox)	
Meyendorff, John	3
Clergy (Episcopalian)	
Allin, John Maury	5
Fletcher, Joseph Francis, III	3
Murray, Anna Pauline ("Pauli")	1
Pike, James Albert, Jr.	1960s-2
Stokes, Anson Phelps, Jr.	2
Clergy (Evangelical Synod of North America)	
Niebuhr, Reinhold	1960s-2
Clergy (Jewish)	
Baron, Salo Wittmayer	2
Finkelstein, Louis	3
Kahane, Meir	2, 1960s-1
Kelman, Wolfe	2
Lelyveld, Arthur Joseph	4
Prinz, Joachim	2
Schindler, Alexander Moshe	6
Schneerson, Menachem Mendel	4
Soloveitchik, Joseph Baer	3
Clergy (Lutheran)	
Preus, Jacob Aall Ottesen, Jr. ("Jake")	4
Clergy (Methodist)	
Lord, John Wesley	2
Mueller, Reuben Herbert	1
Peale, Norman Vincent	1960s-2
Roberts, Oral	1960s-2
Clergy (Mormon)	
Kimball, Spencer Woolley	1
Clergy (Pentecostal)	
Roberts, Oral	1960s-2
Clergy (Presbyterian)	
Blake, Eugene Carson	1
Coffin, William Sloane, Jr.	1960s-1
McIntire, Carl Curtis	6
Naismith, James	Sports-2

	Volume
Clergy (Roman Catholic)	
Bernardin, Joseph Louis	4
Berrigan, Daniel Joseph, and Philip Francis Berrigan	1960s-1
Berrigan, Philip Francis	6
Brown, Raymond Edward	5
Campion, Donald Richard	2
Carberry, John Joseph	5
Cody, John Patrick	1
Cooke, Terence James	1
Egan, John Joseph ("Jack")	6
Ellis, John Tracy	3
Groppi, James Edmund	1, 1960s-1
Hartdegen, Stephen Joseph	2
Healy, Timothy Stafford	3
Hesburgh, Theodore Martin	1960s-1
Illich, Ivan	1960s-1
Judge, Mychal Fallon	6
Krol, John Joseph	4
Manning, Timothy	2
Medeiros, Humberto Sousa	1
O'Connor, John Joseph	6
Perry, Harold Robert	3
Coach. *See* **Sports Coach.**	
Comedian (*See also* **Actor**)	
Allen, Stephen Valentine Patrick William ("Steve")	6, 1960s-1
Allen, Woody	1960s-1
Backus, James Gilmore ("Jim")	2
Ball, Lucille Désirée	2
Belushi, John	
Berle, Milton	6
Bruce, Lenny	1960s-1
Burnett, Carol	1960s-1
Burns, George	4
Candy, John Franklin	4
Carson, John William ("Johnny")	1960s-1
Cavett, Richard Alva ("Dick")	1960s-1
Coca, Imogene	6
Diller, Phyllis Ada	1960s-1
Farley, Chris(topher) Crosby	5
Foxx, Redd	3
Gilford, Jack	2
Gleason, Herbert John ("Jackie")	2
Gobel, George Leslie	3
Goulding, Ray(mond) Walter	2
Gregory, Richard Claxton ("Dick")	1960s-1
Harris, (Wanga) Phillip ("Phil")	4
Hartman, Phil(ip) Edward	5
Hope, Leslie Townes ("Bob")	1960s-1
Jessel, George Albert ("Georgie")	1

	Volume
Kaufman, Andrew Geoffrey ("Andy")	1
Kaye, Danny	2
Kirby, George	4
LaMotta, Jake	Sports-1
Lee, Pinky	3
Lewis, Jerry	1960s-1
Markham, Dewey ("Pigmeat")	1
Martin, Dean	1960s-2
Matthau, Walter	1960s-2
May, Elaine	1960s-2
Meader, (Abbott) Vaughn	1960s-2
Newhart, George Robert ("Bob")	1960s-2
Nichols, Mike	1960s-2
Pearl, Minnie (Sarah Ophelia Colley Cannon)	4
Picon, Molly	3
Pryor, Richard Franklin Lenox Thomas	1960s-2
Radner, Gilda	2
Raye, Martha	4
Rickles, Donald Jay ("Don")	1960s-2
Rowan, Dan Hale	2
Schacht, Al(exander)	1
Silvers, Phil	1
Skelton, Richard Bernard ("Red")	5
Smothers, Thomas ("Tom"), and Richard ("Dick") Smothers	1960s-2
Sothern, Ann	6
Thomas, Danny	3
Van Dyke, Richard Wayne ("Dick")	1960s-2
Walker, Nancy	3
Wilson, Flip	5
Youngman, Henny	5

Communications Theorist

Pool, Ithiel de Sola	1

Composer (Avant-garde)

Cage, John Milton, Jr.	3, 1960s-1
Feldman, Morton	2
Hansen, Al(fred) Earl	4
Hovhaness, Alan	6
Paik, Nam June	1960s-2
Schuller, Gunther Alexander	1960s-2
Slonimsky, Nicolas (Nikolai Leonidovich)	4
Ussachevsky, Vladimir	2

Composer (Blues)

Hunter, Alberta	1
Waters, Muddy	1

Composer (Classical)

Bacon, Ernst	2
Barber, Samuel	1
Bennett, Robert Russell	1
Bernstein, Leonard	2

	Volume
Bowles, Paul Frederic(k)	5
Copland, Aaron	2
Feldman, Morton	2
Gould, Morton	4
Hanson, Howard Harold	1
Harkness, Rebekah West	1, 1960s-1
Hovhaness, Alan	6
Kay, Ulysses Simpson	4
Luening, Otto Clarence	4
Moross, Jerome	1
Persichetti, Vincent Ludwig	2
Robinson, Earl	3
Rózsa, Miklós	4
Schuller, Gunther Alexander	1960s-2
Schuman, William Howard	3
Sessions, Roger Huntington	1, 1960s-2
Talma, Louise Juliette	4
Thompson, (Ira) Randall	1
Thomson, Virgil Garnett	2
Ussachevsky, Vladimir	2
Watts, John Everett	1
Weiner, Lazar	1
Wright, Olgivanna Lloyd	1

Composer (Film)

Adler, Lawrence Cecil ("Larry")	6
Arlen, Harold	2
Bennett, Robert Russell	1
Berlin, Irving	2
Bernstein, Leonard	2
Carmichael, Howard Hoagland ("Hoagy")	1
Copland, Aaron	2
Fain, Sammy	2
Gould, Morton	4
Jenkins, Gordon Hill	1
Jones, Quincy Delight, Jr.	1960s-1
Kaye, Sylvia Fine	3
Lane, Burton	5
Lewis, John Aaron	6
Loewe, Frederick	2
Mancini, Henry Nicola	4, 1960s-2
Moross, Jerome	1
Nilsson, Harry Edward, II	4
Parks, Gordon, Sr.	1960s-2
Riddle, Nelson Smock, Jr.	1
Robinson, Earl	3
Rózsa, Miklós	4
Schwartz, Arthur	1
Silverstein, Shel(don) Allan	5
Styne, Jule	4
Thompson, Kay	5
Thomson, Virgil Garnett	2

	Volume
Composer (Film) (*continued*)	
Van Heusen, James ("Jimmy")	2
Warren, Harry	1
Willson, (Robert Reiniger) Meredith	1
Composer (Gospel)	
Dorsey, Thomas Andrew	3
Composer (Jazz)	
Brubeck, David Warren ("Dave")	1960s-1
Calloway, Cab	4
Cherry, Don(ald) Eugene	4
Coltrane, John William	1960s-1
Davis, Miles Dewey, III	3, 1960s-1
Ellington, Mercer Kennedy	4
Evans, Gil	2
Farmer, Art(hur) Stewart	5
Feather, Leonard Geoffrey	4
Blake, James Hubert ("Eubie")	1
Lewis, John Aaron	6
MacDermot, (Arthur Terence) Galt	1960s-2
Monk, Thelonious Sphere	1, 1960s-2
Mulligan, Gerald Joseph ("Gerry")	4
O'Farrill, Arturo ("Chico")	6
Puente, Ernest Anthony, Jr. ("Tito")	6
Sun Ra (Herman Blount)	3
Williams, Mary Lou	1
Composer (Liturgical)	
Weiner, Lazar	1
Composer (Musical Theater)	
Bennett, Robert Russell	1
Berlin, Irving	2
Bernstein, Leonard	2
Blake, James Hubert ("Eubie")	1
Bowles, Paul Frederic(k)	5
Engel, A. Lehman	1
Fain, Sammy	2
Gould, Morton	4
Kaye, Sylvia Fine	3
Lane, Burton	5
Larson, Jonathan	4
Loewe, Frederick	2
MacDermot, (Arthur Terence) Galt	1960s-2
Miller, Roger Dean	3
Moross, Jerome	1
Rado, James, and Gerome Ragni	1960s-2
Schwartz, Arthur	1
Sondheim, Stephen Joshua	1960s-2
Styne, Jule	4
Warren, Harry	1
Willson, (Robert Reiniger) Meredith	1
Composer (Popular)	
Arlen, Harold	2
Calloway, Cab	4

	Volume
Carmichael, Howard Hoagland ("Hoagy")	1
Fain, Sammy	2
Gleason, Herbert John ("Jackie")	2
Jenkins, Gordon Hill	1
Jones, Quincy Delight, Jr.	1960s-1
Kaye, Sylvia Fine	3
Loewe, Frederick	2
Mancini, Henry Nicola	1960s-2
Marks, John D. ("Johnny")	1
Martin, Freddy	1
Nilsson, Harry Edward, II	4
Riddle, Nelson Smock, Jr.	1
Schwartz, Arthur	1
Styne, Jule	4
Van Heusen, James ("Jimmy")	2
Warren, Harry	1
Willson, (Robert Reiniger) Meredith	1
Composer (Radio and Television)	
Bennett, Robert Russell	1
Gleason, Herbert John ("Jackie")	2
Gould, Morton	4
Jenkins, Gordon Hill	1
Jones, Quincy Delight, Jr.	1960s-1
Mancini, Henry Nicola	4, 1960s-2
Riddle, Nelson Smock, Jr.	1
Computer Scientist	
Atanasoff, John Vincent	4
Church, Alonzo	4
Cocke, John	6
Cray, Seymour Roger	4
Dertouzos, Michael Leonidas	6
Eckert, J(ohn Adam) Presper, Jr.	4
Elias, Peter	6
Hopper, Grace Brewster Murray	3
Kemeny, John George	3
Licklider, J(oseph) C(arl) R(obnett)	2
Molnar, Charles Edwin	4
Newell, Allen	3
Noyce, Robert Norton	2, 1960s-2
Piore, Emanuel Ruben ("Mannie")	6
Postel, Jonathan Bruce	5
Simon, Herbert A(lexander)	6
Stibitz, George Robert	4
Tukey, John W(ilder)	6
Wang, An	2
Conductor. *See* **Musician (Conductor).**	
Congressman/woman. *See* **Politician (United States Representative).**	
Consultant (Public Relations)	
Bernays, Edward L.	4

	Volume
Consumer Advocate	
Furness, Elizabeth Mary ("Betty")	4
Nader, Ralph	1960s-2
Peterson, Esther	5
Warne, Colston Estey	2
Cook. *See* **Chef.**	
Costume Designer	
Cashin, Bonnie Jeanne	6
Head, Edith	1
Crime Figure (Murderer)	
Beckwith, Byron De La, Jr. ("Delay")	6
Bundy, Theodore Robert ("Ted")	2
Abbott, Jack Henry	6
Dahmer, Jeffrey Lionel	4
Gacy, John Wayne, Jr.	4
McVeigh, Timothy James	6
Manson, Charles Milles	1960s-2
Oswald, Lee Harvey	1960s-2
Price, Cecil Ray	6
Ray, James Earl	5, 1960s-2
Ruby, John ("Jack")	1960s-2
Salvi, John C., III	4
Sirhan, Sirhan Bishara	1960s-2
Speck, Richard Benjamin	3
Crime Figure (Organized Crime)	
Accardo, Anthony ("Big Tuna")	3
Giancana, Salvatore ("Sam")	1960s-1
Gotti, John Joseph	6
Bonanno, Joseph ("Joe Bananas")	6
Lansky, Meyer	1
Marcello, Carlos	3
Patriarca, Raymond	1
Provenzano, Anthony ("Tony Pro")	2
Trafficante, Santo, Jr.	2
Cult Leader	
Applewhite, Marshall Herff, Jr. ("Herff"; "Do")	5
Koresh, David	3
Cultural Critic	
Barrett, William Christopher	3
Elkin, Stanley Lawrence	4
Goodman, Paul	1960s-1
Jackson, J(ohn) B(rinckerhoff)	4
Jacobs, Jane	1960s-1
Kirk, Russell Amos	4
Lasch, Christopher	4
Lerner, Max	3
Lynes, (Joseph) Russell, Jr.	3
Macdonald, Dwight	1, 1960s-2
McLuhan, (Herbert) Marshall	1960s-2
Mills, C(harles) Wright	1960s-2
Mitford, Jessica ("Decca")	4

	Volume
Mumford, Lewis Charles	2
Packard, Vance Oakley	4
Patterson, Louise Alone Thompson	5
Roszak, Theodore	1, 1960s-2
Sontag, Susan	1960s-2
Trilling, Diana Rubin	4
Whyte, William Hollingsworth, Jr.	5
Wills, Garry	1960s-2
Cytologist	
Stern, Curt	1
Dance Instructor	
Ailey, Alvin	2, 1960s-1
Balanchine, George	1, 1960s-1
Danilova, Alexandra Dionysievna ("Choura")	5
Gennaro, Peter	6
Graham, Martha	3
Greco, Costanzo ("José")	6
Holm, Hanya	3
Joffrey, Robert	2, 1960s-1
Kelly, Eugene Curran ("Gene")	4
Le Clercq, Tanaquil ("Tanny")	6
Murray, Arthur	3
Murray, Kathryn Hazel	5
Primus, Pearl Eileen	4
Shook, Karel Francis Antony	1
Verdon, Gwyneth Evelyn ("Gwen")	6
Dancer	
Ailey, Alvin	2, 1960s-1
Astaire, Adele Marie	1
Astaire, Fred	2
Balanchine, George	1, 1960s-1
Bates, Clayton ("Peg Leg")	5
Bennett, Michael	2
Bolger, Ray(mond) Wallace	2
Bruhn, Erik Belton Evers	2
Bubbles, John William	2
Cagney, James	2
Champion, Gower	1960s-1
Chase, Lucia Hosmer	2
Coles, Charles ("Honi")	3
Cunningham, Mercier Phillip ("Merce")	1960s-1
Danilova, Alexandra Dionysievna ("Choura")	5
Davis, Sammy, Jr.	2
de Mille, Agnes George	3
Denby, Edwin Orr	1
Farrell, Suzanne	1960s-1
Fosse, Robert Louis ("Bob")	2
Gennaro, Peter	6
Graham, Martha	3
Greco, Costanzo ("José")	6

	Volume
Dancer (*continued*)	
Hawkins, Frederick ("Erick")	4
Hayworth, Rita	2
Holm, Hanya	3
Joffrey, Robert	1960s-1
Keeler, Ruby	3
Kelly, Eugene Curran ("Gene")	4
Le Clercq, Tanaquil ("Tanny")	6
MacLaine, Shirley	1960s-2
Moreno, Rita	1960s-2
Murphy, George Lloyd	3
Murray, Arthur	3
Nicholas, Harold Lloyd	6
Nikolais, Alwin Theodore	3
Page, Ruth Marian	3
Powell, Eleanor Torrey ("Ellie")	1
Primus, Pearl Eileen	4
Robbins, Jerome	5
Rogers, Ginger	4
Rutherford, Maude Russell	6
Shook, Karel Francis Antony	1
Tudor, Antony	2
Verdon, Gwyneth Evelyn ("Gwen")	6
Villella, Edward Joseph	1960s-2
Dentist	
Delany, Annie Elizabeth ("Bessie")	4
Perpich, Rudolph George ("Rudy")	4
Designer (Furniture)	
Breuer, Marcel	1
Eames, Ray	2
Designer (Industrial)	
Lerner, Nathan Bernard	5
Loewy, Raymond Fernand	2
Stevens, Brooks	4
Designer (Interior)	
Neumann, Vera Salaff ("Vera")	3
Parish, Dorothy May Kinnicutt ("Sister")	4
Designer (Textile)	
Neumann, Vera Salaff ("Vera")	3
Diplomat	
Anderson, (Helen) Eugenie Moore	5
Anderson, George Whelan, Jr.	3
Annenberg, Walter Hubert	6
Armour, Norman	1
Atherton, Alfred Leroy, Jr. ("Roy")	6
Attwood, William Hollingsworth	2
Bohlen, Charles Eustis ("Chip")	1960s-1
Bowles, Chester Bliss ("Chet")	2, 1960s-1
Brewster, Kingman, Jr.	2
Bruce, David Kirkpatrick Este	1960s-1
Bunker, Ellsworth	1, 1960s-1

	Volume
Burden, William Armistead Moale	1
Clay, Lucius Dubignon, Sr.	1960s-1
Clubb, O(liver) Edmund, II	2
Colby, William Egan	4
Cooper, John Sherman	3
Cousins, Norman	1960s-1
Davies, John Paton, Jr.	5
Dean, Arthur Hobson	2
Duke, Angier Biddle	4
Dulles, Allen Welsh	1960s-1
Eisenhower, Milton Stover	1
Ferguson, Homer Samuel	1
Galbraith, John Kenneth	1960s-1
Gates, Thomas Sovereign, Jr.	1
Gavin, James Maurice	2, 1960s-1
Goldberg, Arthur Joseph	2
Habib, Philip Charles	3
Harriman, Pamela Beryl Digby Churchill Hayward	5
Harriman, William Averell	1960s-1
Harris, Patricia Roberts Fitzgerald	1
Helms, Richard McGarrah	6
Hickerson, John Dewey	2
Hildreth, Horace Augustus	2
Hilsman, Roger	1960s-1
Holland, Jerome Heartwell ("Brud")	1
Jessup, Philip Caryl	2
Keeny, Spurgeon Milton ("Sam")	2
Kemper, James Scott	1
Kennan, George Frost	1960s-1
Kissinger, Henry Alfred	1960s-1
Kohler, Foy David	1960s-1
Labouisse, Henry Richardson	2
Lansdale, Edward Geary	2
Lattimore, Owen	2
LeMay, Curtis Emerson	2
Lodge, Henry Cabot, Jr.	1, 1960s-1
Lodge, John Davis	1
Luce, Clare Boothe	2
McCloy, John Jay	2
McGee, Gale William	3
Mansfield, Michael Joseph ("Mike")	6
Martin, John Bartlow	2, 1960s-2
Moynihan, Daniel Patrick	1960s-2
Reischauer, Edwin Oldfather	2, 1960s-2
Richardson, Elliot Lee	5
Riddleberger, James Williams	1
Rivero, Horacio, Jr.	6
Scali, John Alfred	4
Shannon, William Vincent	2
Shriver, (Robert) Sargent, Jr.	1960s-2
Stevenson, Adlai Ewing	1960s-2

	Volume		Volume
Stoessel, Walter John, Jr.	2	Mamoulian, Rouben Zachary	2
Taylor, Maxwell Davenport	1960s-2	Mankiewicz, Joseph Leo	3
Thompson, Llewellyn E., Jr.		May, Elaine	1960s-2
("Tommy")	1960s-2	Meredith, (Oliver) Burgess	5
Tree, Mary Endicott Peabody FitzGerald		Milland, Ray	2
("Marietta")	3	Minnelli, Vincente	2
Vance, Cyrus Roberts	6, 1960s-2	Montgomery, Robert	1
Volpe, John Anthony	4	Nichols, Mike	1960s-2
Wagner, Robert Ferdinand	3	Pakula, Alan Jay	5
Warnke, Paul Culliton	6	Parks, Gordon, Sr.	1960s-2
Watson, Thomas John, Jr.	3	Peckinpah, David Samuel ("Sam")	1, 1960s-2
Whitney, John Hay	1	Penn, Arthur Hiller	1960s-2
Williams, G(erhard) Mennen	2	Poitier, Sidney	1960s-2
Woodcock, Leonard Freel	6	Preminger, Otto Ludwig	2
Yost, Charles Woodruff	1	Redford, (Charles) Robert, Jr.	1960s-2
Young, Andrew Jackson, Jr.	1960s-2	Ritt, Martin	2
Director (Film)		Roach, Harold Eugene ("Hal")	3
Abbott, George Francis	4	Robbins, Jerome	5
Allen, Woody	1960s-1	Schaffner, Franklin James	2
Beatty, (Henry) Warren	1960s-1	Scott, George C(ampbell)	1960s-2
Brooks, Richard	3	Siegel, Don	3
Canutt, Enos Edward ("Yakima")	2	Sirk, Douglas	2
Capra, Frank	3	Steiner, Ralph	2
Carnovsky, Morris	3	Streisand, Barbra	1960s-2
Clavell, James duMaresq	4	Sturges, John	3
Cukor, George	1	Vidor, King Wallis	1
Dmytryk, Edward	5	Warhol, Andy	2, 1960s-2
Eames, Ray	2	Webb, John Randolph ("Jack")	1
Eastwood, Clinton, Jr. ("Clint")	1960s-1	Welles, Orson	1
Ephron, Nora Louise	1960s-1	Wilder, Samuel ("Billy")	6
Ferrer, José	3	Wiseman, Frederick	1960s-2
Foreman, Carl	1	Wyler, William	1
Fosse, Robert Louis ("Bob")	2	Zinnemann, Alfred ("Fred")	5
Frankenheimer, John Michael	6, 1960s-1	**Director (Stage)**	
Freleng, Isadore ("Friz")	4	Abbott, George Francis	4
Fuller, Samuel Michael	5	Adler, Stella	3
Hannah, John Frederick ("Jack")	4	Ashman, Howard Elliot	3
Henson, James Maury ("Jim")	2	Beck, Julian	1, 1960s-1
Hill, George Roy	6	Bennett, Michael	2
Hitchcock, Alfred Joseph	1960s-1	Burrows, Abe	1
Hopper, Dennis	1960s-1	Carnovsky, Morris	3
Huston, John Marcellus	2, 1960s-1	Champion, Gower	1960s-1
Kanin, Garson	5	De Cordova, Frederick Timmins	
Kelly, Eugene Curran ("Gene")	4	("Fred")	6
Kramer, Stanley Earl	6	de Mille, Agnes George	3
Kubrick, Stanley	5, 1960s-1	Drake, Alfred	3
LeRoy, Mervyn	2	Ferrer, José	3
Lewis, Jerry	1960s-1	Fosse, Robert Louis ("Bob")	2
Logan, Joshua Lockwood, III	2	Gordone, Charles	4, 1960s-1
Lorentz, Pare	3	Hill, George Roy	6
Lumet, Sidney	1960s-1	Houseman, John	2
Lupino, Ida	4	Kanin, Garson	5

	Volume
Director (Stage) (*continued*)	
Le Gallienne, Eva	3
Logan, Joshua Lockwood, III	2
Ludlam, Charles	2
Mamoulian, Rouben Zachary	2
Meisner, Sanford	5
Meredith, (Oliver) Burgess	5
Montgomery, Robert	1
Nichols, Mike	1960s-2
O'Horgan, Thomas ("Tom")	1960s-2
Papp, Joseph	3, 1960s-2
Penn, Arthur Hiller	1960s-2
Perkins, Anthony	3
Preminger, Otto Ludwig	2
Quintero, José Benjamin	5
Robbins, Jerome	5, 1960s-2
Schechner, Richard	1960s-2
Schneider, Alan	1
Sillman, Leonard Dexter	1
Strasberg, Lee	1
Welles, Orson	1
Director (Television)	
De Cordova, Frederick Timmins ("Fred")	6
Forte, Fulvio Chester, Jr. ("Chet")	4
Frankenheimer, John Michael	6, 1960s-1
Hewitt, Don S.	1960s-1
Hill, George Roy	6
Hitchcock, Alfred Joseph	1960s-1
Landon, Michael	3
Leonard, Sheldon	5, 1960s-1
Liebman, Max	1
Lumet, Sidney	1960s-1
Lupino, Ida	4
Montgomery, Robert	1
Peckinpah, David Samuel ("Sam")	1, 1960s-2
Penn, Arthur Hiller	1960s-2
Ritt, Martin	2
Ritts, Herbert, Jr. ("Herb")	6
Schaffner, Franklin James	2
Siegel, Don	3
Walker, Nancy	3
Webb, John Randolph ("Jack")	1
Doctor. *See* **Physician.**	
Dramatist. *See* **Author (Drama).**	
Ecologist	
Hutchinson, G(eorge) Evelyn	3
Ripley, S(idney) Dillon, II	6
Economist	
Ackley, H(ugh) Gardner	5
Adams, Walter	5
Arrington, Leonard James	5
Baker, George Pierce	4

	Volume
Blaisdell, Thomas Charles, Jr.	2
Boulding, Kenneth Ewart	1960s-1
Brozen, Yale	5
Burns, Arthur Frank	2, 1960s-1
Chase, Stuart	1
Cherne, Leo	5
De Nagy, Tibor	3
Drucker, Peter Ferdinand	1960s-1
Friedman, Milton	1960s-1
Galbraith, John Kenneth	1960s-1
Ginzberg, Eli	6
Harsanyi, John C.	6
Hayek, Friedrich August von	3
Hazlitt, Henry Stuart	3
Heller, Walter Wolfgang	
Henderson, Leon	2
Hoyt, Homer	1
Janeway, Eliot	3
Kerr, Clark	1960s-1
Keyserling, Leon Hirsch	2
Koopmans, Tjalling Charles	1
Kuznets, Simon Smith	1
Lancaster, Kelvin John	5
Lekachman, Robert	2
Leontief, Wassily	5
Means, Gardiner Coit	2
Miller, Marvin Julian	Sports-2
Miller, Merton Howard	6
Mitchell, (John) Broadus	2
Nearing, Scott	1
Nef, John Ulric	2
Rostow, Eugene Victor Debs	6
Rostow, Walter Whitman ("Walt")	1960s-2
Samuelson, Paul Anthony	1960s-2
Schultz, Theodore William	5
Shultz, George Pratt	1960s-2
Snyder, John Wesley	1
Stein, Herbert	5, 1960s-2
Tobin, James	6
Vernon, Raymond	5
Wallis, W(ilson) Allen	5
Warne, Colston Estey	2
Weaver, Robert Clifton	5
Wharton, Clifton Reginald, Jr.	1960s-2
Editor (Books)	
Adler, Mortimer J(erome)	6
Clampitt, Amy Kathleen	4
Fadiman, Clifton Paul	5
Flexner, Stuart Berg	2
Hartdegen, Stephen Joseph	2
Hitchcock, Alfred Joseph	1960s-1
Link, Arthur Stanley	5
Lord, Walter	6

Volume

McCormick, Kenneth Dale — 5
Onassis, Jacqueline Lee Kennedy
 ("Jackie") — 4, 1960s-2
Parton, James — 6
Swanberg, W(illiam) A(ndrew) — 3
Trilling, Diana Rubin — 4
Weiss, Paul — 6

Editor (Comic Books)
Siegel, Jerome ("Jerry") — 4

Editor (Crossword Puzzles)
Farrar, Margaret Petherbridge — 1
Maleska, Eugene Thomas — 3

Editor (Magazines)
Attwood, William Hollingsworth — 2
Bell, Daniel — 1960s-1
Bloch, Konrad Emil — 6
Brown, Helen Gurley — 1960s-1
Buckley, William Frank, Jr. — 1960s-1
Bundy, William Putnam — 6
Campion, Donald Richard — 2
Cantwell, Mary Lee — 6
Chamberlain, John Rensselaer — 4
Connell, Evan Shelby, Jr. — 1960s-1
Cousins, Norman — 2
Cowley, (David) Malcolm — 2
Dellinger, David — 1960s-1
Donovan, Carolyn Gertrude Amelia
 ("Carrie") — 6
Donovan, Hedley Williams — 2
Feshbach, Herman — 6
Fixx, James Fuller — 1
Gill, Brendan — 5
Goodman, Paul — 1960s-1
Grosvenor, Melville Bell — 1
Hazlitt, Henry Stuart — 3
Hefner, Hugh Marston — 1960s-1
Howe, Irving — 3
Ingersoll, Ralph McAllister — 1
Jackson, J(ohn) B(rinckerhoff) — 4
Johnson, Eleanor Murdock — 2
Johnson, Robert Edward — 4
Kalman, Tibor — 5
Kennedy, John Fitzgerald, Jr. — 5
Killian, James Rhyne, Jr. — 2
Kirk, Russell Amos — 4
Knowles, John — 6
Kurland, Philip B. — 4
Levin, Meyer — 1
Liberman, Alexander Semeonovitch — 5
Luce, Clare Boothe — 2
Lynes, (Joseph) Russell, Jr. — 3
Macdonald, Dwight — 1, 1960s-2
Maxwell, William Keepers, Jr. — 6

Volume

Morris, William Weaks ("Willie") — 5
Nash, Gerald David — 6
Phillips, Kevin Price — 1960s-2
Phillips, William — 6
Podhoretz, Norman Harold — 1960s-2
Potok, Chaim Tzvi — 6
Schechner, Richard — 1960s-2
Schindler, Alexander Moshe — 6
Shapiro, Karl Jay — 6, 1960s-2
Shawn, William — 3
Shils, Edward Albert — 4
Singer, Isaac Bashevis — 3, 1960s-2
Steinem, Gloria Marie — 1960s-2
Stone, I. F. — 1960s-2
Tilberis, Elizabeth Jane Kelly ("Liz") — 5
Vreeland, Diana — 2, 1960s-2
Warhol, Andy — 1960s-2
Weiss, Paul — 6
West, Dorothy — 5
Whitney, Ruth Reinke — 5

Editor (Newspapers)
Ashmore, Harry Scott — 5
Ashmore, Harry Scott, and William
 Calhoun ("Bill") Baggs — 1960s-1
Bingham, George (Barry), Sr. — 2
Browne, Malcolm Wilde — 1960s-1
Canham, Erwin Dain — 1
Cantwell, Mary Lee — 6
Catledge, Turner — 1
Cowles, Gardner, Jr. ("Mike") — 1
Daniel, (Elbert) Clifton, Jr. — 6
Daniels, Jonathan Worth — 1
Dedmon, Emmett — 1
Deford, Frank — Sports-1
Donovan, Carolyn Gertrude Amelia
 ("Carrie") — 6
Gates, John — 3
Greenfield, Mary Ellen ("Meg") — 5
Gruening, Ernest — 1960s-1
Hearst, William Randolph, Jr. — 3
Hobby, Oveta Culp — 4
Kahane, Meir — 1960s-1
Knight, John Shively — 1
McGill, Ralph Emerson — 1960s-2
Maynard, Robert Clyve — 3
Oakes, John Bertram — 6
Pope, Generoso Paul, Jr. — 2
Pope, James Soule, Sr. — 1
Reston, James Barrett ("Scotty") — 4, 1960s-2
Salisbury, Harrison Evans — 3, 1960s-2
Shapiro, Karl Jay — 1960s-2
Sheppard, Eugenia — 1
Smith, Hazel Brannon — 1960s-2

	Volume
Editor (Newspapers) (*continued*)	
Sutton, Carol	1
Washington, Chester Lloyd, Jr. ("Chet")	1
Wechsler, James Arthur	1
Wiggins, James Russell ("Russ")	6
Educational Reformer	
Fannin, Paul Jones	6
Howe, Harold, II ("Doc")	6
Adler, Mortimer J(erome)	6
Educator	
Ackley, H(ugh) Gardner	5
Adams, Walter	5
Albion, Robert G.	1
Alvarez, Luis Walter	2, 1960s-1
Ambrose, Stephen Edward	6
Anderson, Carl David, Jr.	3
Anfinsen, Christian Boehmer	4
Arbus, Diane	1960s-1
Archibald, Nathaniel ("Nate"; "Tiny")	Sports-1
Arendt, Hannah	1960s-1
Armour, Richard Willard	2
Arrington, Leonard James	5
Aserinsky, Eugene	5
Asimov, Isaac	3
Atanasoff, John Vincent	4
Bailey, Thomas A.	1
Bailyn, Bernard	1960s-1
Bainton, Roland Herbert	1
Baker, Carlos Heard	2
Baker, George Pierce	4
Bardeen, John	3
Barnett, A(rthur) Doak	5
Barnett, Marguerite Ross	3
Barnouw, Erik	6
Baron, Salo Wittmayer	2
Barr, Stringfellow	1
Barrett, William Christopher	3
Barth, John Simmons	1960s-1
Barzun, Jacques Martin	1960s-1
Baskin, Leonard	6
Bate, Walter Jackson	5, 1960s-1
Beadle, George Wells ("Beets")	2
Bell, Daniel	1960s-1
Bell, Terrel Howard	4
Berberova, Nina Nikolaevna	3
Berenson Abbott, Senda	Sports-1
Bernard, Anna Jones	1
Biggers, John Thomas	6
Billington, Ray Allen	1
Bishop, Hazel Gladys	5
Black, Fischer Sheffey	4
Black, Joseph, Jr. ("Joe")	6
Bloch, Felix	1
Bloch, Konrad Emil	6, 1960s-1
Bloom, Allan David	3
Bloom, Benjamin Samuel	5
Boulding, Kenneth Ewart	1960s-1
Boyer, Ernest LeRoy, Sr.	4
Boyle, Katherine ("Kay")	3
Branscomb, (Bennett) Harvie	5
Breuer, Marcel	1
Brewster, Kingman, Jr.	2, 1960s-1
Brodie, Fawn McKay	1
Brodsky, Joseph (Iosif or Josip Alexandrovich)	4
Brooks, Cleanth	4
Brown, Raymond Edward	5
Brozen, Yale	5
Bundy, McGeorge	4, 1960s-1
Bunting-Smith, Mary Alice Ingraham ("Polly")	5
Burke, Kenneth Duva	3
Burns, Arthur Frank	2, 1960s-1
Buscaglia, Felice Leonardo ("Leo")	5
Byrnes, Robert Francis	5
Calvin, Melvin	5, 1960s-1
Campbell, Joseph John	2, 1960s-1
Carnovsky, Morris	3
Chall, Jeanne Sternlicht	1960s-1
Chandrasekhar, Subrahmanyan ("Chandra")	4
Chomsky, (Avram) Noam	1960s-1
Church, Alonzo	4
Clampitt, Amy	4
Clark, Kenneth Bancroft	1960s-1
Clark, Mark Wayne	1
Clarke, John Henrik	5
Cochran, Thomas Childs	5
Cohen, Audrey C.	4
Coleman, James Samuel	4, 1960s-1
Collins, John Frederick	4
Commager, Henry Steele	5
Cooley, Denton Arthur	1960s-1
Cooper, Irving Spencer	1
Cori, Carl Ferdinand	1
Cormack, Allan MacLeod	5
Corner, George Washington	1
Cox, Harvey Gallagher, Jr.	1960s-1
Cram, Donald James	6
Cremin, Lawrence A(rthur)	2, 1960s-1
Cunliffe, Marcus Falkner	2
Curti, Merle Eugene	4
Dallin, Alexander	6
Dangerfield, George	2

	Volume
Davis, Angela Yvonne	1960s-1
Davis (William) Allison	1
Dawidowicz, Lucy Schildkret	2
de Kooning, Elaine Marie Catherine	2
Delany, Sarah Louise ("Sadie")	5
de Man, Paul	1
Dickey, James Lafayette	5
Dickey, John Sloan	3
Dirac, Paul Adrien Maurice	1
Dmytryk, Edward	5
Doisy, Edward Adelbert	2
Dorris, Michael Anthony	5
Drake, (John Gibbs) St. Clair	2
Dubos, René Jules	1
Edel, (Joseph) Leon	5
Eisenhower, Milton Stover	1
Eliade, Mircea	2
Elias, Peter	6
Elkin, Stanley Lawrence	4
Ellis, John Tracy	3
Ellmann, Richard David	2
Engel, A. Lehman	1
Engle, Paul Hamilton	3
Erikson, Erik Homburger	4
Fairbank, John King	3
Fall, Bernard B.	1960s-1
Farmer, James Leonard, Jr.	1960s-1
Farrell, Eileen Frances	6
Fehrenbacher, Don Edward	5
Feshbach, Herman	6
Festinger, Leon	2
Feyerabend, Paul Karl	4
Feynman, Richard Phillips	1960s-1
Finkelstein, Louis	3
Flesch, Rudolf Franz	2
Fletcher, Harvey	1
Fletcher, Joseph Francis, III	3
Foner, Philip Sheldon	4
Fowler, William Alfred	4
Franklin, John Hope	1960s-1
Freund, Paul Abraham	3
Friedman, Herbert	6
Friedman, Milton	1960s-1
Friedrich, Carl Joachim	1
Friendly, Fred W.	5
Fulbright, J(ames) William	4, 1960s-1
Galarza, Ernesto, Jr.	1
Gallup, George Horace	1
Gardner, John Champlin, Jr.	1
Gardner, John William	6, 1960s-1
Gay, Peter ("Jack")	1960s-1
Gellhorn, Walter	4

	Volume
Genovese, Eugene Dominick	1960s-1
Giamatti, A(ngelo) Bartlett ("Bart")	2
Gilbert, Felix	3
Ginsberg, (Irwin) Allen	5, 1960s-1
Ginsberg, Mitchell Irving	4
Ginzberg, Eli	6
Goeppert-Mayer, Maria	1960s-1
Goffman, Erving Manual	1
Goldman, Eric Frederick	2
Goodman, Louis Sanford	6
Gordone, Charles	4
Gould, Samuel Brookner	5
Gould, Stephen Jay	6
Graham, Martha	3
Greco, Costanzo ("José")	6
Green, Edith Starrett	2
Greenberg, Joseph H(arold)	6
Griswold, Erwin Nathaniel	4
Gunther, Gerald	6
Hannah, John Frederick ("Jack")	4
Hanson, Howard Harold	1
Harken, Dwight Emary	3
Harrington, (Edward) Michael	2
Harris, Patricia Roberts Fitzgerald	1
Harsanyi, John C.	6
Hartdegen, Stephen Joseph	2
Hartz, Louis	2
Hathaway, Starke Rosecrans	1
Hayakawa, S(amuel) I(chiye)	1960s-1
Hayek, Friedrich August von	3
Healy, Timothy Stafford	3
Heidelberger, Michael	3
Heiden, Eric Arthur	Sports-1
Herrnstein, Richard Julius	4
Hersey, John Richard	3
Hershey, Alfred Day	5, 1960s-1
Hexter, J. H. ("Jack")	4
Hicks, Granville	1
Hilsman, Roger	1960s-1
Hirsch, Eric Donald, Jr.	1960s-1
Hitchings, George Herbert, Jr.	5
Hoffmann, Banesh	2
Hofstadter, Richard	1960s-1
Hofstadter, Robert	2, 1960s-1
Holland, Jerome Heartwell ("Brud")	1
Holley, Robert William	3, 1960s-1
Holt, John Caldwell	1, 1960s-1
Hook, Sidney	2
Hooker, Evelyn Gentry	4
Horton, Mildred Helen McAfee	4
Horwich, Frances Rappaport ("Miss Frances")	6

	Volume		*Volume*
Educator (*continued*)		Leary, Timothy Francis	1960s-1
Howe, Harold, II ("Doc")	6	Lekachman, Robert	2
Howe, Irving	1960s-1	Leontief, Wassily	5
Huggins, Charles Brenton	5	Lerner, Max	3
Hughes, Emmet John	1	Levertov, Denise	5
Hughes, H(enry) Stuart	5	Levi, Edward H(irsch)	6
Humphry, (Ann) Wickett	3	Lewis, Oscar	1960s-1
Hutchinson, G(eorge) Evelyn	3	Libby, Willard Frank	1960s-1
Jackson, J(ohn) B(rinckerhoff)	4	Lillehei, C(larence) Walton ("Walt")	5
Janowitz, Morris	2	Lincoln, C(harles) Eric	6
Jensen, Arthur Robert	1960s-1	Link, Arthur Stanley	5
Johnson, Eleanor Murdock	2	Logan, Rayford Whittingham	1
Jones, Robert Reynolds, Jr. ("Bob")	5	Lorde, Audre Geraldine	3
Jordan, Barbara Charline	4	Lowenstein, Allard Kenneth	1960s-1
Jordan, June	6	Luening, Otto Clarence	4
Karski, Jan	6	Luria, Salvador Edward	1960s-1
Kaufman, Bel	1960s-1	Lynd, Helen Merrell	1
Kay, Ulysses Simpson	4	McAuliffe, (Sharon) Christa	2
Kazin, Alfred	5	McCarthy, Eugene Joseph	1960s-2
Kemeny, John George	3	McClintock, Barbara	3
Kendall, Henry Way	5	McGee, Gale William	3
Keppel, Francis	2	McGill, William James	5
Kerr, Clark	1960s-1	McIntosh, Millicent Carey	6
Kerr, Walter Francis	4	MacLeish, Archibald	1
Killian, James Rhyne, Jr.	2	McMillan Edwin Mattison	3
Kingman, Dong	6	McMurtry, Larry Jeff	1960s-2
Kiphuth, Robert John Herman ("Bob")	Sports-1	McNamara, Margaret Craig	1, 1960s-2
Kirk, Grayson Louis	5, 1960s-1	Maleska, Eugene Thomas	3
Kirk, Russell Amos	4	Malone, Dumas	2
Kissinger, Henry Alfred	1960s-1	Mann, Jonathan Max	5
Kistiakowsky, George Bogdan	1	Mansfield, Michael Joseph ("Mike")	6
Kline, Nathan Schellenberg	1	Marcuse, Herbert	1960s-2
Knowles, John	6	Mark, Herman Francis	3
Koch, Kenneth Jay	6	Marston, Robert Quarles	5
Kohl, Herbert R.	1960s-1	May, Rollo Reece	4
Kohlberg, Lawrence	2	Mays, Benjamin Elijah	1
Koontz, Elizabeth Duncan ("Libby")	1960s-1	Merriam, Eve	3
Koopmans, Tjalling Charles	1	Meyendorff, John	3
Kozol, Jonathan	1960s-1	Milgram, Stanley	1
Kristeller, Paul Oskar	5	Miller, Merton Howard	6
Kuhn, Thomas Samuel	4	Mitchell, (John) Broadus	2
Kunstler, William Moses	4	Molnar, Charles Edwin	4
Kurland, Philip B.	4	Momaday, N(avarre) Scott	1960s-2
Kuznets, Simon Smith	1	Monroe, Marion	1
Ladd, George Eldon	1	Montagu, Ashley	5
Lamont, Corliss	4	Moos, Malcolm Charles	1
Lancaster, Kelvin John	5	Morison, Elting Elmore	4
Langer, Susanne Katherina	1	Morris, Richard Brandon	2
Larson, (Lewis) Arthur	3	Moses, Robert Parris	1960s-2
Lasch, (Robert) Christopher	1960s-1	Moynihan, Daniel Patrick	1960s-2
Lattimore, Owen	2	Mulliken, Robert Sanderson	2, 1960s-2
Lawrence, Jacob Armstead	6	Murphy, Joseph Samson	5

	Volume		Volume
Murray, Arthur	3	Revelle, Roger Randall Dougan	3
Nabrit, James Madison, Jr.	5	Rich, Adrienne Cecile	1960s-2
Nagel, Ernest	1, 1960s-2	Riesman, David, Jr.	6
Nash, Gerald David	6	Rogers, Carl Ransom	2
Nason, John William	6	Rostow, Eugene Victor Debs	6
Nathans, Daniel	5	Rostow, Walter Whitman ("Walt")	1960s-2
Nef, John Ulric	2	Roszak, Theodore	1, 1960s-2
Nemerov, Howard	3	Rothwax, Harold J(ay)	5
Neuberger, Maurine Brown	6	Rudolph, Paul Marvin	5
Neustadt, Richard Elliott	1960s-2	Rudolph, Wilma Glodean	4, 1960s-2,
Newell, Allen	3		Sports-2
Newhall, Beaumont	3	Sabin, Albert Bruce	3, 1960s-2
Neyman, Jerzy	1	Sachar, Abram Leon	3
Niebuhr, Reinhold	1960s-2	Sagan, Carl Edward	4
Niel, Cornelis Bernardus van	1	Salk, Lee	3
Nisbet, Robert Alexander	4	Salmon, Wesley C(harles)	6
Nozick, Robert	6	Samora, Julian	1960s-2
Oates, Joyce Carol	1960s-2	Sanford, (James) Terry	5
O'Connor, Carroll	6	Sarton, May	4
Onsager, Lars	1960s-2	Schapiro, Meyer	4
Padover, Saul Kussiel	1	Schawlow, Arthur Leonard	5
Pais, Abraham	6	Schechner, Richard	1960s-2
Palmer, R(obert) R(oswell)	6	Schlesinger, Arthur Meier, Jr.	1960s-2
Paredes, Américo	5	Schultz, Theodore William	5
Parsons, James Benton	3	Schuman, William Howard	3
Pauling, Linus Carl	4, 1960s-2	Schwinger, Julian Seymour	1960s-2
Pendleton, Clarence Mclane, Jr.	2	Scott, Austin Wakeman	1
Perkins, Dexter	1	Scott, Roland Boyd	6
Perkins, James Alfred	5, 1960s-2	Seaborg, Glenn Theodore	5, 1960s-2
Persichetti, Vincent Ludwig	2	Sepkoski, J(oseph) John, Jr.	5
Peter, Laurence Johnston	1960s-2	Sessions, Roger Huntington	1, 1960s-2
Phillips, William	6	Shabazz, Betty Jean	5
Pike, James Albert, Jr.	1960s-2	Shanker, Albert ("Al")	5, 1960s-2
Pogue, Forrest Carlisle	4	Shannon, Claude Elwood	6
Ponnamperuma, Cyril Andrew	4	Shapiro, Karl Jay	6, 1960s-2
Pool, Ithiel de Sola	1	Shils, Edward Albert	4
Powers, J(ames) F(arl)	5	Shull, Clifford Glenwood	6
Preus, Jacob Aall Ottesen, Jr. ("Jake")	4	Shultz, George Pratt	1960s-2
Primrose, William	1	Simon, Herbert A(lexander)	6
Primus, Pearl Eileen	4	Simpson, Alan	5
Purcell, Edward Mills	5	Siskind, Aaron	3
Pusey, Nathan Marsh	6, 1960s-2	Skinner, B(urrhus) F(rederick)	2
Quarles, Benjamin Arthur	4	Smith, Henry Nash	2
Rafferty, Maxwell Lewis, Jr. ("Max")	1, 1960s-2	Smith, (Charles) Page (Ward)	4
Rainey, Homer Price	1	Soloveitchik, Joseph Baer	3
Randolph, Jennings	5	Sperry, Roger Wolcott	4
Rawls, John Bordley	6	Stegner, Wallace Earle	3
Ray, Dixy Lee	4	Stein, Herbert	5, 1960s-2
Ray, Gordon Norton	2	Sterling, J(ohn) E(wart) Wallace	1
Reeder, Russell Potter, Jr. ("Red")	5	Stibitz, George Robert	4
Reines, Frederick	5	Stone, Lawrence	5
Reischauer, Edwin Oldfather	1960s-2	Strand, Kaj Aage	6

	Volume		Volume
Educator (*continued*)		Yarmolinsky, Adam	6
Strasberg, Lee	1	Yates, Richard Walden	3
Street, George Levick, III	6	Yerby, Frank Garvin	3
Stuart, Jesse Hilton	1	Ylvisaker, Paul Norman	3
Suomi, Verner Edward	4	Zacharias, Jerrold Reinach	2
Talma, Louise Juliette	4	Zuckert, Eugene Martin	6
Tarski, Alfred	1	**Endocrinologist**	
Tax, Sol	4	Corner, George Washington	1
Taylor, Harold Alexander	3	Rodbell, Martin	5
Taylor, Telford	5	**Engineer (Audio)**	
Temin, Howard Martin	4	Asch, Moses ("Moe")	2
Thomas, Lewis	3	Fletcher, Harvey	1
Thompson, (Ira) Randall	1	Wiesner, Jerome Bert	4, 1960s-2
Tien, Chang-Lin	6	**Engineer (Aviation)**	
Tobin, James	6	Collbohm, Franklin Rudolph	2
Tower, John Goodwin	3	Doolittle, James Harold	3
Trilling, Lionel	1960s-2	Douglas, Donald Wills	1
Vernon, Raymond	5	Gilruth, Robert Rowe	6
Vicente, Esteban	6	Grumman, Leroy Randle ("Roy")	1
Voorhis, Horace Jeremiah ("Jerry")	1	Johnson, Clarence Leonard ("Kelly")	2
Wald, George David	5, 1960s-2	Johnston, Alvin Melvin ("Tex")	5
Wallis, W(ilson) Allen	5	Link, Edwin Albert	1
Ward, John William	1	Northrop, John Knudsen ("Jack")	1
Warfield, William Caesar	6	Slayton, Donald Kent ("Deke")	3
Waring, Fred(eric) Malcolm	1	**Engineer (Chemical)**	
Warne, Colston Estey	2	Dessauer, John Hans	3
Washburn, Sherwood L(arned)	6	Mason, (William) Birny J., Jr.	5
Watson, James Dewey	1960s-2	Wigner, Eugene Paul	4, 1960s-2
Weaver, Robert Clifton	5	Wyeth, Nathaniel Convers	2
Weber, Joseph	6	**Engineer (Civil)**	
Wechsler, Herbert	6	Philbrick, Herbert Arthur	3
Weil, André	5	Rose, Frederick Phineas	5
Weiss, Paul	6	Turner, Francis Cutler ("Frank")	5
Weisskopf, Victor Frederick	6	**Engineer (Communications)**	
Wellek, René Maria Eduard	4, 1960s-2	Noyce, Robert Norton	2, 1960s-2
Wellstone, Paul David	6	Zworykin, Vladimir Kosma	1
Whyte, William Foote	6	**Engineer (Construction)**	
Wiebe, Robert H(uddleston)	6	McCone, John Alex	3
Wiesner, Jerome Bert	1960s-2	Volpe, John Anthony	4
Wigner, Eugene Paul	4, 1960s-2	**Engineer (Electrical)**	
Wildavsky, Aaron Bernard	3	Atanasoff, John Vincent	4
Williams, Sherley Anne	5	Brattain, Walter Houser	2
Williams, William Appleman	1960s-2	Cray, Seymour Roger	4
Wills, Garry	1960s-2	Dertouzos, Michael Leonidas	6
Wilson, Logan	2	Eckert, J(ohn Adam) Presper, Jr.	4
Wilson, Robert R(athbun)	6	Elias, Peter	6
Wood, Evelyn Nielsen	4	Fletcher, Harvey	1
Woodcock, Leonard Freel	6	Henson, Paul Harry	5
Woodward, C(omer) Vann	5, 1960s-2	Hewlett, William Redington ("Bill")	6
Woodward, Robert Burns	1960s-2	Hewlett, William Redington ("Bill"),	
Wright, Olgivanna Lloyd	1	and David Packard	1960s-1
Wu, Chien-Shiung	5	Molnar, Charles Edwin	4

	Volume
Packard, David	4
Reber, Grote	6
Shannon, Claude Elwood	6
Wang, An	2
Weber, Joseph	6
Wiesner, Jerome Bert	4, 1960s-2
Zworykin, Vladimir Kosma	1

Engineer (Mechanical)
Tien, Chang-Lin	6

Engineer (Nuclear)
Rickover, Hyman George	2
Ulam, Stanislaw Marcin	1

Engineer (Rocket Science)
Debus, Kurt Heinrich	1

Engineer
Fuller, R(ichard) Buckminster	1
Rose, Frederick Phineas	5
Stibitz, George Robert	4
Townes, Charles Hard	1960s-2
Turner, Francis Cutler ("Frank")	5
Von Braun, Wernher	1960s-2
Wang, An	1960s-2
Wiesner, Jerome Bert	1960s-2

Environmentalist
Abbey, Edward Paul	2
Adams, Ansel Easton	1
Denver, John	5
Douglas, Marjory Stoneman	5
Dubos, René Jules	1
Fuller, R(ichard) Buckminster	1
Holden, William	1
Hutchinson, G(eorge) Evelyn	3
Kieran, John Francis	1
McCall, Thomas William Lawson	1
Nearing, Scott	1
Owings, Nathaniel Alexander	1
Perkins, (Richard) Marlin	2
Revelle, Roger Randall Dougan	3
Stegner, Wallace Earle	3

Epidemiologist
Hammond, E(dward) Cuyler	2
Horstmann, Dorothy Millicent	6
Mann, Jonathan Max	5

Espionage Agent
Angleton, James Jesus	2
Bancroft, Mary	5
Casey, William Joseph	2
Eifler, Carl Frederick	6
Hall, Theodore Alvin	5
Hiss, Alger	4
Karski, Jan	6
Lansdale, Edward Geary	2, 1960s-1

	Volume
Marble, Alice	Sports-2
Powers, Francis Gary	1960s-2

Ethnologist
Red Thunder Cloud (Cromwell Ashbie Hawkins West)	4
Tax, Sol	4

Ethnologist
Lomax, Alan	6

Evangelist
McIntire, Carl Curtis	6

Farmer
Aiken, George David	1, 1960s-1
Nearing, Helen Knothe	4

Fashion Designer
Blass, William Ralph ("Bill")	6, 1960s-1
Cashin, Bonnie Jeanne	6
Daché, Marie-Louise ("Lilly")	2
Ellis, Perry Edwin	2
Erteszek, Olga Bertram	2
Fogarty, Anne Whitney	1960s-1
Fredericks, Sara	2
Gernreich, Rudolph ("Rudi")	1, 1960s-1
Halston,	2, 1960s-1
Head, Edith	1
Klein, Anne	1960s-1
Klein, Calvin	1960s-1
Lauren, Ralph	1960s-1
Maxwell, Vera Huppé	4
Neumann, Vera Salaff ("Vera")	3
Parnis, Sarah Rosen ("Mollie")	3
Simpson, Adele Smithline	4
Trigère, Pauline	6

Fashion Model
Hemingway, Margaux	4

Feminist
Abzug, Bella Savitzky	5, 1960s-1
Barnes, Djuna Chappell	1
Collins, Judy	1960s-1
De Varona, Donna	1960s-1, Sports-1
Fonda, Jane Seymour	1960s-1
Friedan, Betty Naomi	1960s-1
Lorde, Audre	3
King, Billie Jean Moffitt	1960s-1, Sports-1
Merriam, Eve	3
Murray, Anna Pauline ("Pauli")	1
Peterson, Esther	5
Rich, Adrienne Cecile	1960s-2
Steinem, Gloria Marie	1960s-2
Terry, Megan	1960s-2
Thomas, Marlo	1960s-2

	Volume
Film Director. *See* Director (Film).	
Film Producer. *See* Producer (Film).	
Financier. *See* Business Executive (Banking and Financial Services Industry).	
First Lady	
Johnson, Claudia Alta Taylor ("Lady Bird")	1960s-1
Nixon, Pat(ricia)	3
Onassis, Jacqueline Lee Kennedy ("Jackie")	4, 1960s-2
Truman, Bess Wallace	1
Football Player. *See* **Athlete (Football).**	
Futurologist	
Kahn, Herman Bernard	1, 1960s-1
Gambler	
Scarne, John	1
Snyder, Jimmy ("Jimmy the Greek")	4
Games Expert (Billiards)	
Minnesota Fats (Rudolph Walter Wanderone, Jr.)	4
Mosconi, William Joseph ("Willie")	3
Games Expert (Card Games)	
Scarne, John	1
Games Expert (Contract Bridge)	
Goren, Charles Henry	3
Jacoby, James Oswald ("Jim")	3
Jacoby, Oswald ("Ozzie")	1
Geneticist	
Beadle, George Wells ("Beets")	2
Bunting-Smith, Mary Alice Ingraham ("Polly")	5
Delbrück, Max Ludwig Henning	1, 1960s-1
Hershey, Alfred Day	1960s-1
Luria, Salvador Edward	1960s-1
McClintock, Barbara	3
Neel, James Van Gundia	6
Shockley, William Bradford	2
Snell, George Davis	4
Stern, Curt	1
Wright, Sewall	2
Geographer	
Grosvenor, Melville Bell	1
Jackson, J(ohn) B(rinckerhoff)	4
Geophysicist	
Urey, Harold Clayton	1
Golf Course Architect	
Jones, Robert Trent, Sr.	6
Golfer. *See* **Athlete (Golf).**	
Government Official (Cabinet)	
Anderson, Robert Bernerd	2
Aspin, Les(lie), Jr.	4
Baldrige, (Howard) Malcolm	2

	Volume
Bell, Terrel Howard	4
Benson, Ezra Taft	4
Brannan, Charles Franklin	3
Brown, Ron(ald) Harmon	4
Brownell, Herbert, Jr.	4
Celebrezze, Anthony Joseph	5
Clark, (William) Ramsey	1960s-1
Clifford, Clark McAdams	5, 1960s-1
Cohen, Wilbur Joseph	2
Connally, John Bowden, Jr.	3
Connor, John Thomas ("Jack")	6
Finch, Robert Hutchinson	4
Gardner, John William	6, 1960s-1
Gates, Thomas Sovereign, Jr.	1
Goldberg, Arthur Joseph	2
Harriman, William Averell	2, 1960s-1
Harris, Patricia Roberts Fitzgerald	1
Hobby, Oveta Culp	4
Katzenbach, Nicholas De Belleville	1960s-1
Kennedy, Robert Francis	1960s-1
Kissinger, Henry Alfred	1960s-1
Kleindienst, Richard G.	6
Klutznick, Philip M.	5
Levi, Edward H(irsch)	6
Lovett, Robert Abercrombie	2
McNamara, Robert Strange	1960s-2
Mitchell, John Newton	2, 1960s-2
Muskie, Edmund Sixtus	4, 1960s-2
O'Brien, Lawrence Francis, Jr. ("Larry")	2, 1960s-2
Pierce, Samuel Riley, Jr.	6
Ribicoff, Abraham Alexander	5
Richardson, Elliot Lee	5
Rogers, William Pierce	6
Romney, George Wilcken	4
Rusk, (David) Dean	4, 1960s-2
Shultz, George Pratt	1960s-2
Simon, William E(dward)	6
Smith, William French	2
Snyder, John Wesley	1
Stans, Maurice Hubert	5
Vance, Cyrus Roberts	6, 1960s-2
Volpe, John Anthony	4
Weaver, Robert Clifton	5, 1960s-2
Government Official (Other Federal)	
Ackley, H(ugh) Gardner	5
Albright, Horace Marden	2
Angleton, James Jesus	2
Ash, Roy Lawrence	1960s-1
Atherton, Alfred Leroy, Jr. ("Roy")	6
Ball, George Wildman	4, 1960s-1
Bane, Frank B.	1
Blaisdell, Thomas Charles, Jr.	2

	Volume		*Volume*
Bowles, Chester Bliss ("Chet")	2, 1960s-1	Lewis, John Robert	1960s-1
Bundy, McGeorge	4, 1960s-1	Licklider, J(oseph) C(arl) R(obnett)	2
Burch, (Roy) Dean	3	Lilienthal, David Eli	1
Burns, Arthur Frank	2, 1960s-1	Lindsay, John Vliet	6
Casey, William Joseph	2	McCloy, John Jay	2
Chafee, John Hubbard	5	McCone, John Alex	3
Chancellor, John William	4	MacLeish, Archibald	1
Chapman, Leonard Fielding, Jr.	6	Marshall, Thurgood	3, 1960s-2
Cohen, Benjamin Victor	1	Martin, William McChesney, Jr.	5, 1960s-2
Cohn, Roy Marcus	2	Means, Gardiner Coit	2
Colby, William Egan	4	Miller, William Mosely	2
Corcoran, Thomas Gardiner	1	Minow, Newton Norman	1960s-2
Coverdell, Paul Douglas	6	Mosbacher, Emil, Jr. ("Bus")	Sports-2
Daly, John Charles, Jr.	3	Moynihan, Daniel Patrick	1960s-2
Daniel, Price Marion	2	Murphy, Joseph Samson	5
Daniels, Jonathan Worth	1	Murrow, Edward Roscoe	1960s-2
Dickey, John Sloan	3	Myer, Dillon Seymour	1
DiSalle, Michael Vincent	1	Nabrit, James Madison, Jr.	5
Dolgun, Alexander Michael	2	Pendleton, Clarence Mclane, Jr.	2
Duke, Angier Biddle	4	Perkins, James Alfred	5, 1960s-2
Dulles, Allen Welsh	1960s-1	Peterson, Esther	5
Eisenhower, Milton Stover	1	Piore, Emanuel Ruben ("Mannie")	6
Farmer, James Leonard, Jr.	5, 1960s-1	Prichard, Edward Fretwell, Jr.	1
Fortas, Abraham ("Abe")	1, 1960s-1	Quesada, Elwood Richard, Jr. ("Pete")	3
Foster, Vincent William, Jr.	3	Raborn, William Francis, Jr. ("Red")	2
Garrity, W(endell) Arthur, Jr.	5	Ray, Dixy Lee	4
Gilpatric, Roswell Leavitt	4	Reuss, Henry Schoellkopf	6
Griswold, Erwin Nathaniel	4	Rogers, William Pierce	6
Gruening, Ernest	1960s-1	Rosenberg, Anna Marie Lederer	1
Hagerty, James Campbell	1	Rostow, Eugene Victor Debs	6
Hanks, Nancy	1	Rostow, Walter Whitman ("Walt")	1960s-2
Hays, (Lawrence) Brooks	1	Rowan, Carl T(homas)	6
Heller, Walter Wolfgang	2	Russell, Charles Hinton	2
Helms, Richard McGarrah	6	Sawhill, John Crittenden	6
Henderson, Leon	2	Seaborg, Glenn Theodore	5
Hesburgh, Theodore Martin	1960s-1	Shriver, (Robert) Sargent, Jr.	1960s-2
Hilsman, Roger	1960s-1	Stein, Herbert	5, 1960s-2
Hiss, Alger	4	Symington, (William) Stuart, III	2
Hoover, John Edgar	1960s-1	Terry, Luther Leonidas	1
Howe, Harold, II ("Doc")	6	Tukey, John W(ilder)	6
Hoyt, Homer	1	Turner, Francis Cutler ("Frank")	5
Jaworski, Leon	1	Vance, Cyrus Roberts	6, 1960s-2
Johnson, Frank Minis, Jr.	5	Vann, John Paul	1960s-2
Kaufman, Irving Robert	3	Vernon, Raymond	5
Kelsey, Frances Kathleen Oldham	1960s-1	Warnke, Paul Culliton	6
Kennan, George Frost	1960s-1	Webb, James Edwin	3
Keppel, Francis	2	Wharton, Clifton Reginald, Jr.	1960s-2
Killian, James Rhyne, Jr.	2	Wiesner, Jerome Bert	4, 1960s-2
Kistiakowsky, George Bogdan	1	Williams, G(erhard) Mennen	2
Koontz, Elizabeth Duncan	2, 1960s-2	Wyzanski, Charles Edward, Jr.	2
Labouisse, Henry Richardson	2	Yarmolinsky, Adam	6
Lansdale, Edward Geary	2, 1960s-1	Zuckert, Eugene Martin	6

	Volume
Government Official (State, County, Municipal)	
Bird, Rose Elizabeth	5
Brooke, Edward William, III	1960s-1
Connor, Theophilus Eugene ("Bull")	1960s-1
Davis, James Houston ("Jimmie")	6
Feehan, William M.	6
Furness, Elizabeth Mary ("Betty")	4
Garrrison, Earling Carothers ("Jim")	3, 1960s-1
Geldzahler, Henry	4
Ginsberg, Mitchell Irving	4
Gore, Albert Arnold, Sr.	5
Javits, Jacob Koppel	2
Kelly, John Brendan, Sr. ("Jack")	Sports-1
Klutznick, Philip M.	5
Logue, Edward Joseph	6
Maple, John Edward ("Jack")	6
Moses, Robert	1
O'Dwyer, (Peter) Paul	5
Page, Alan Cedric	Sports-2
Powell, Lewis Franklin, Jr.	5
Price, Cecil Ray	6
Pucinski, Roman Gordon	6
Rafferty, Maxwell Lewis, Jr. ("Max")	1, 1960s-2
Rhodes, James Allen ("Jim")	6
Richardson, Elliot Lee	5
Rizzo, Frank Lazzaro	3
Samuels, Howard Joseph ("Howie the Horse")	1
Scott, Hugh Doggett, Jr.	4
Sitter, Carl Leonard	6
Stratton, William Grant	6
Unruh, Jesse Marvin	2
Wade, Henry Menasco	6
Ylvisaker, Paul Norman	3
Governor. *See* **Politician (Governor).**	
Guitarist. *See* **Musician.**	
Graphic Designer	
Fisher, Avery Robert	4
Kalman, Tibor	5
Rand, Paul	4
Hair Stylist	
Sassoon, Vidal	1960s-2
Historian	
Albion, Robert G.	1
Ambrose, Stephen Edward	6
Arrington, Leonard James	5
Bailey, Thomas A.	1
Bailyn, Bernard	1960s-1
Bainton, Roland Herbert	1
Barnouw, Erik	6
Baron, Salo Wittmayer	2
Barr, Stringfellow	1

	Volume
Barzun, Jacques Martin	1960s-1
Bettmann, Otto Ludwig	5
Billington, Ray Allen	1
Brodie, Fawn McKay	1
Brown, Dee Alexander	6
Butterfield, Lyman Henry	1
Byrnes, Robert Francis	5
Clarke, John Henrik	5
Cochran, Thomas Childs	5
Commager, Henry Steele	5
Corner, George Washington	1
Cremin, Lawrence A(rthur)	2, 1960s-1
Cunliffe, Marcus Falkner	2
Curti, Merle Eugene	4
Dabney, Virginius	4
Dallin, Alexander	6
Dangerfield, George	2
Davis, David Brion	1960s-1
Dawidowicz, Lucy Schildkret	2
Deloria, Vine, Jr.	1960s-1
Durant, Will(iam) James, and Ariel Durant	1
Eliade, Mircea	2
Ellis, John Tracy	3
Fairbank, John King	3
Fehrenbacher, Don Edward	5
Foner, Philip Sheldon	4
Foote, Shelby Dade, Jr.	1960s-1
Franklin, John Hope	1960s-1
Gay, Peter ("Jack")	1960s-1
Genovese, Eugene Dominick	1960s-1
Gilbert, Felix	3
Goldman, Eric Frederick	2
Hartz, Louis	2
Hexter, J. H. ("Jack")	4
Hofstadter, Richard	1960s-1
Howe, Irving	3
Hughes, H(enry) Stuart	5
Kennan, George Frost	1960s-1
Kuhn, Thomas Samuel	4
Lasch, (Robert) Christopher	4, 1960s-1
Lattimore, Owen	2
Link, Arthur Stanley	5
Logan, Rayford Whittingham	1
Lord, Walter	6
Lynes, (Joseph) Russell, Jr.	3
Malone, Dumas	2
Manchester, William Raymond	1960s-2
Mitchell, (John) Broadus	2
Moos, Malcolm Charles	1
Morison, Elting Elmore	4
Morris, Richard Brandon	2

	Volume
Nash, Gerald David	6
Nef, John Ulric	2
Nisbet, Robert Alexander	4
Padover, Saul Kussiel	1
Pais, Abraham	6
Palmer, R(obert) R(oswell)	6
Perkins, Dexter	1
Pogue, Forrest Carlisle	4
Pusey, Nathan Marsh	6, 1960s-2
Quarles, Benjamin Arthur	4
Reischauer, Edwin Oldfather	2
Rostow, Walter Whitman ("Walt")	1960s-2
Sachar, Abram Leon	3
Salisbury, Harrison Evans	3
Schlesinger, Arthur Meier, Jr.	1960s-2
Schoenbrun, David Franz	2
Shirer, William Lawrence	3
Simpson, Alan	5
Smith, Henry Nash	2
Smith, (Charles) Page (Ward)	4
Sterling, J(ohn) E(wart) Wallace	1
Stone, Lawrence	5
Tuchman, Barbara Wertheim	2
Ward, John William	1
Wellek, René Maria Eduard	4
White, Theodore Harold ("Teddy")	2, 1960s-2
Wiebe, Robert H(uddleston)	6
Williams, William Appleman	2, 1960s-2
Wills, Garry	1960s-2
Woodward, C(omer) Vann	5, 1960s-2

Horse Trainer

Stephens, Woodford Cefis ("Woody")	5

Horticulturist

Aiken, George David	1, 1960s-1

Humorist

Ace, Goodman	1
Allen, Woody	1960s-1
Armour, Richard Willard	2
Bombeck, Erma Louise Fiste	4
Burrows, Abe	1
De Vries, Peter	3
Faulk, John Henry	2
Golden, Harry	1
Grizzard, Lewis McDonald, Jr.	4
Kurtzman, Harvey	3
Morgan, Henry	4
Shulman, Max	2
White, E(lwyn) B(rooks)	1

Illustrator

Geisel, Theodor Seuss ("Dr. Seuss")	3
Peterson, Roger Tory	4
Rand, Paul	4

	Volume
Scarry, Richard McClure	4
Sendak, Maurice Bernard	1960s-2

Immunologist

Snell, George Davis	4

Intelligence Official

Angleton, James Jesus	2
Aspin, Les(lie), Jr.	4
Bundy, William Putnam	6
Casey, William Joseph	2
Colby, William Egan	4
Dulles, Allen Welsh	1960s-1
Helms, Richard McGarrah	6
Hoover, John Edgar	1960s-1
Karski, Jan	6
Lansdale, Edward Geary	2, 1960s-1
McCone, John Alex	3
Powers, Francis Gary ("Frank")	1960s-2
Raborn, William Francis, Jr. ("Red")	2

Inventor

Alvarez, Luis Walter	2, 1960s-1
Atanasoff, John Vincent	4
Bardeen, John	3
Bauer, Eddie	2
Bowerman, William Jay ("Bill")	5
Brattain, Walter Houser	2
Butts, Alfred Mosher	3
Carvel, Thomas Andrew	2
Castro, Bernard	3
Cooper, Irving Spencer	1
Cormack, Allan MacLeod	5
Cray, Seymour Roger	4
DeBakey, Michael Ellis	1960s-1
Eames, Ray	2
Eckert, J(ohn Adam) Presper, Jr.	4
Elion, Gertrude Belle ("Trudy")	5
Factor, Max, Jr.	4
Fender, Clarence Leonidas ("Leo")	3
Fletcher, Harvey	1
Fuller, R(ichard) Buckminster	1
Glaser, Donald Arthur	1960s-1
Hewlett, William Redington ("Bill")	6
Hewlett, William Redington ("Bill"), and David Packard	1960s-1
Hill, Julian Werner	4
Hopper, Grace Brewster Murray	3
Kemeny, John George	3
Land, Edwin Herbert	3
Link, Edwin Albert	1
Margulies, Lazar	1
Miller, Carl S.	2
Noyce, Robert Norton	2
Olin, John Merrill	1

	Volume
Inventor (*continued*)	
Packard, David	4
Postel, Jonathan Bruce	5
Pritikin, Nathan	1
Rock, John Charles	1
Ryan, John William ("Jack")	3
Salk, Jonas Edward	4
Schawlow, Arthur Leonard	5
Shockley, William Bradford	2
Spanel, Abram Nathaniel	1
Stibitz, George Robert	4
Suomi, Verner Edward	4
Tupper, Earl Silas	1
Wang, An	1960s-2
Waring, Fred(eric) Malcolm	1
Wyeth, Nathaniel Convers	2
Zamboni, Frank Joseph, Jr.	2
Zworykin, Vladimir Kosma	1
Journalist (Book Critic)	
Broyard, Anatole Paul	2
Chamberlain, John Rensselaer	4
Fadiman, Clifton Paul	
Trilling, Diana Rubin	4
Journalist (Broadcast)	
Barber, Walter Lanier ("Red")	3
Bergman, Jules Verne	2
Chancellor, John William	4
Collingwood, Charles Cummings	1
Cosell, Howard	4
Cronkite, Walter Leland, Jr.	1960s-1
Daly, John Charles, Jr.	3
De Varona, Donna	1960s-1
Dickerson, Nancy	5, 1960s-1
Diggs, Charles Coles, Jr.	5
Edwards, Douglas	2
Frederick, Pauline	2
Friendly, Fred W.	5
Garroway, David Cunningham	1
Gillars, Mildred Elizabeth Sisk ("Axis Sally")	2
Goode, Malvin Russell ("Mal")	4, 1960s-1
Huntley, Chester Robert ("Chet"), and David McClure Brinkley	1960s-1
Kendrick, Alexander	3
Kuralt, Charles Bishop	5
McCall, Thomas William Lawson	1
Murrow, Edward Roscoe	1960s-2
Rather, Daniel Irvin ("Dan")	1960s-2
Reasoner, Harry	3
Reynolds, Frank	1
Rountree, Martha	5
Salant, Richard S.	3
	Volume
Savitch, Jessica Beth	1
Scali, John Alfred	4
Schaap, Richard Jay ("Dick")	6
Schoenbrun, David Franz	2
Sevareid, (Arnold) Eric	3
Shilts, Randy Martin	4
Shirer, William Lawrence	3
Smith, Howard K(ingsbury)	6
Stokes, Carl Burton	4, 1960s-2
Swayze, John Cameron	4
Thomas, Lowell Jackson	1
Trout, Robert	6
Wallace, Mike	1960s-2
Journalist (Dance Critic)	
Denby, Edwin Orr	1
Kirstein, Lincoln	4
Terry, Walter	1
Journalist (Drama Critic)	
Atkinson, (Justin) Brooks	1
Canby, Vincent	6
Gill, Brendan	5
Kerr, Walter Francis	4
Knowles, John	6
McCarthy, Mary Therese	2, 1960s-2
Journalist (Fashion Columnist)	
Donovan, Carolyn Gertrude Amelia ("Carrie")	6
Sheppard, Eugenia	1
Vreeland, Diana	2, 1960s-2
Journalist (Film Critic)	
Canby, Vincent	6
Crowther, (Francis) Bosley, Jr.	1
Fidler, James Marion ("Jimmy")	2
Kael, Pauline	6
Lorentz, Pare	3
Macdonald, Dwight	1, 1960s-2
Siskel, Eugene Kal ("Gene")	5
Journalist (Foreign Correspondent)	
Lewis, Flora	6
Szulc, Tadeusz Witold ("Tad")	6
Journalist (Gossip Columnist)	
Fidler, James Marion ("Jimmy")	2
Graham, Sheilah	2
Skolsky, Sidney	1
Sullivan, Edward Vincent ("Ed")	1960s-2
Wilson, Earl	2
Journalist (Magazines)	
Ace, Goodman	1
Amory, Cleveland ("Clip")	5
Bancroft, Mary	5
Buckley, William Frank, Jr.	1960s-1
Chamberlain, John Rensselaer	4

	Volume
Clurman, Richard Michael	4
Cousins, Norman	1960s-1
Cowles, Gardner ("Mike")	1
Deford, Frank	Sports-1
Ephron, Nora Louise	1960s-1
Feather, Leonard Geoffrey	4
Fitch, James Marston	6
Fuller, Samuel Michael	5
Garson, Barbara	1960s-1
Gellhorn, Martha Ellis	5
Gill, Brendan	5
Greenfield, Mary Ellen ("Meg")	5
Gruening, Ernest	1960s-1
Halberstam, David	1960s-1
Haley, Alexander Murray Palmer ("Alex")	1960s-1
Hazlitt, Henry Stuart	3
Hemingway, Mary Welsh	2
Hentoff, Nathan Irving ("Nat")	1960s-1
Hersey, John Richard	3
Hersh, Seymour M.	1960s-1
Hobson, Laura Kean Zametkin	2
Howe, Irving	1960s-1
Hughes, Emmet John	1
Huie, William Bradford	2
Ingersoll, Ralph McAllister	1
Johnson, Robert Edward	4
Karnow, Stanley	1960s-1
Kempton, (James) Murray	5
Kraft, Joseph	2
Lerner, Max	3
Lippmann, Walter	1960s-1
Luce, Clare Boothe	2
Lynes, (Joseph) Russell, Jr.	3
Maas, Peter Guttrich	6
McCarthy, Mary Therese	2,1960s-2
Macdonald, Dwight	1, 1960s-2
McGinnis, Joseph ("Joe")	1960s-2
Mailer, Norman Kingsley	1960s-2
Mannes, Marya	2
Martin, John Bartlow	2, 1960s-2
Mitchell, Joseph Quincy	4
Mohr, Charles Henry	2
Murray, James Patrick ("Jim")	5
Packard, Vance Oakley	4
Parks, Gordon, Sr.	1960s-2
Phillips, William	6
Porter, Sylvia Field	3
Ryskind, Morrie	1
Samuelson, Paul Anthony	1960s-2
Schaap, Richard Jay ("Dick")	6
Schell, Jonathan Edward	1960s-2

	Volume
Shepley, James Robinson	2
Sontag, Susan	1960s-2
Southern, Terry Marion, Jr.	4
Stein, Aaron Marc	1
Steinem, Gloria Marie	1960s-2
Stone, I. F.	1960s-2
Strout, Richard Lee	2
Thompson, Hunter S(tockton)	1960s-2
Trilling, Diana Rubin	4
Updike, John Hoyer	1960s-2
Vreeland, Diana	2, 1960s-2
Whitaker, Rogers E(rnest) M(alcolm) ("E. M. Frimbo")	1
White, Theodore Harold ("Teddy")	2, 1960s-2
Whitney, Ruth Reinke	5
Whyte, William Hollingsworth	5
Wolfe, Thomas Kennerly, Jr.	1960s-2

Journalist (Music Critic)

Feather, Leonard Geoffrey	4
Slonimsky, Nicolas (Nikolai Leonidovich)	4
Thomson, Virgil Garnett	2

Journalist (Newspaper)

Alsop, Joseph Wright, V	2, 1960s-1
Amory, Cleveland ("Clip")	5
Ashmore, Harry Scott	5
Atkinson, (Justin) Brooks	1
Attwood, William Hollingsworth	2
Baldwin, Hanson Weightman	3
Bancroft, Mary	5
Barnes, Djuna Chappell	1
Benson, Mildred Wirt	6
Bigart, Homer William	3
Bingham, (George) Barry, Sr.	2
Bishop, James Alonzo ("Jim")	2
Bombeck, Erma Louise Fiste	4
Browne, Malcolm Wilde	1960s-1
Broyard, Anatole Paul	2
Buckley, William Frank, Jr.	1960s-1
Caen, Herb Eugene	5
Canham, Erwin Dain	1
Catledge, Turner	1
Chamberlain, John Rensselaer	4
Chase, Mary Coyle	1
Childs, Marquis William	2
Claiborne, Craig Raymond	6
Cowles, Gardner, Jr. ("Mike")	1
Cronkite, Walter Leland, Jr.	1960s-1
Crowther, (Francis) Bosley, Jr.	1
Dabney, Virginius	4
Daniel, (Elbert) Clifton, Jr.	6
Daniels, Jonathan Worth	1

Volume

Journalist (Newspaper) (*continued*)

Dedmon, Emmett	1
Denby, Edwin Orr	1
Douglas, Marjory Stoneman	5
Drury, Allen Stuart	5
Ephron, Nora Louise	1960s-1
Evans, Rowland, Jr. ("Rowly")	6
Fidler, James Marion ("Jimmie")	2
Frick, Ford Christopher	Sports-1
Garson, Barbara	1960s-1
Gates, John	3
Gellhorn, Martha Ellis	5
Gilbreth, Frank Bunker, Jr.	6
Goode, Malvin Russell ("Mal")	4, 1960s-1
Graham, Katharine Meyer	6
Graham, Sheilah	2
Greenfield, Mary Ellen ("Meg")	5
Grizzard, Lewis McDonald, Jr.	4
Gruening, Ernest	1960s-1
Guthrie, A(lfred) B(ertram), Jr.	3
Hagerty, James Campbell	1
Halberstam, David	1960s-1
Harris, Sydney Justin	2
Hazlitt, Henry Stuart	3
Hearst, William Randolph, Jr.	3
Heinz, Wilfred Charles ("Bill")	Sports-1
Hemingway, Mary Welsh	2
Hersh, Seymour M.	1960s-1
Hobson, Laura Kean Zametkin	2
Huie, William Bradford	2
Ingersoll, Ralph McAllister	1
Irish, Edward Simmons, Sr. ("Ned")	1
Janeway, Eliot	3
Johnson, Haynes Bonner	1960s-1
Johnson, Robert Edward	4
Karnow, Stanley	1960s-1
Kempton, (James) Murray	5
Kendrick, Alexander	3
Kerr, Walter Francis	4
Kieran, John Francis	1
Knight, John Shively	1
Kraft, Joseph	2
Kuralt, Charles Bishop	5
Landers, Ann (Esther Friedman Lederer)	6
Lardner, Ringgold Wilmer ("Ring")	Sports-2
Lash, Joseph P.	2
Lerner, Max	3
Levin, Meyer	1
Lewis, (Joseph) Anthony	1960s-1
Lippmann, Walter	1960s-1
Lodge, Henry Cabot, Jr.	1, 1960s-1
Lubell, Samuel	2

Volume

Lukas, J(ay) Anthony	5
McGill, Ralph Emerson	1960s-2
McGinniss, Joseph ("Joe")	1960s-2
Manchester, William Raymond	1960s-2
Mannes, Marya	2
Martin, John Bartlow	2
Maynard, Robert Clyve	3
Middleton, Drew	2
Mohr, Charles Henry	2
Murray, James Patrick ("Jim")	5, Sports-2
Oakes, John Bertram	6
Parton, James	6
Pearl, Daniel ("Danny")	6
Pope, James Soule, Sr.	1
Porter, Sylvia Field	3
Povich, Shirley Lewis	5
Pucinski, Roman Gordon	6
Randolph, Jennings	5
Reasoner, Harry	3
Reston, James Barrett ("Scotty")	4, 1960s-2
Rice, Grantland	Sports-2
Riesel, Victor	4
Rountree, Martha	5
Rowan, Carl T(homas)	6
Royko, Mike	5
Runyon, Damon	Sports-2
Ryskind, Morrie	1
St. Johns, Adela Rogers	2
Salisbury, Harrison Evans	3, 1960s-2
Schaap, Richard Jay ("Dick")	6
Schell, Jonathan Edward	1960s-2
Seldes, George Henry	4
Sevareid, (Arnold) Eric	3
Shannon, William Vincent	2
Sheehan, Cornelius Mahoney ("Neil")	1960s-2
Shepley, James Robinson	2
Sheppard, Eugenia Benbow	1
Shilts, Randy Martin	4
Shirer, William Lawrence	3
Siskel, Eugene Kal ("Gene")	5
Skolsky, Sidney	1
Slonimsky, Nicolas (Nikolai Leonidovich)	4
Smith, Howard K(ingsbury)	6
Smith, Walter Wellesley ("Red")	1, 1960s-2, Sports-2
Stein, Aaron Marc	1
Stone, I(sidor) F(einstein) ("Izzy")	2
Strout, Richard Lee	2
Sullivan, Edward Vincent ("Ed")	1960s-2
Sullivan, Walter Seager, Jr.	4
Sulzberger, Cyrus Leo	3

	Volume
Sutton, Carol	1
Swayze, John Cameron	4
Szulc, Tadeusz Witold ("Tad")	6
Terry, Walter	1
Thomas, Lowell Jackson	1
Thomas, Robert McG(ill), Jr.	6
Thomson, Virgil Garnett	2
Washington, Chester Lloyd, Jr. ("Chet")	1
Wechsler, James Arthur	1
Welty, Eudora Alice	6
White, Theodore Harold	1960s-2
Whitehead, Don(ald) Ford	1
Wiggins, James Russell ("Russ")	6
Wilson, Earl	2
Wolfe, Thomas Kennerly, Jr. ("Tom")	1960s-2

Journalist (Photographer)
Eisenstaedt, Alfred	4

Journalist (Political Commentator)
Buckley, William Frank, Jr.	1960s-1
Chancellor, John William	4
Dabney, Virginius	4
Davies, John Paton, Jr.	5
Evans, Rowland, Jr. ("Rowly")	6
Janeway, Eliot	3
Kirk, Russell Amos	4
Lerner, Max	3
Maynard, Robert Clyve	3
Mitford, Jessica ("Decca")	4
Reston, James Barrett	4
Riesel, Victor	4
Scali, John Alfred	4

Journalist (Sportswriter)
Broun, Heywood Hale ("Woodie")	6
Chadwick, Henry	Sports-1
Deford, Frank	Sports-1
Frick, Ford Christopher	Sports-1
Heinz, Wilfred Charles ("Bill")	Sports-1
Irish, Edward Simmons, Sr. ("Ned")	1
Kieran, John Francis	1
Lardner, Ringgold Wilmer ("Ring")	Sports-2
Murray, James Patrick ("Jim")	5, Sports-2
Povich, Shirley Lewis	5, Sports-2
Rice, Grantland	Sports-2
Runyon, Damon	Sports-2
Schaap, Richard Jay ("Dick")	6
Smith, Walter Wellesley ("Red")	1, 1960s-2, Sports-2
Whitaker, Rogers E(rnest) M(alcolm) ("E. M. Frimbo")	1

Journalist (Television Critic)
Amory, Cleveland ("Clip")	5

Jurist
	Volume
Baldwin, Raymond Earl	2
Bird, Rose Elizabeth	5
Brown, John R.	3
Burger, Warren Earl	4, 1960s-1
Celebrezze, Anthony Joseph	5
Coleman, J(ames) P(lemon)	3
Daniel, Price Marion	2
Ervin, Samuel James, Jr.	1
Ferguson, Homer Samuel	1
Fortas, Abraham ("Abe")	1, 1960s-1
Friendly, Henry Jacob	2
Gabel, Hortense Wittstein	2
Garrison, Earling Carothers ("Jim")	3, 1960s-1
Garrity, W(endell) Arthur, Jr.	5
Goldberg, Arthur Joseph	2
Greene, Harold Herman	6
Haynsworth, Clement Furman, Jr.	2, 1960s-1
Higginbotham, A(loysius) Leon, Jr.	5
Hoffman, Julius Jennings	1960s-1
Hofheinz, Roy Mark	1
Jessup, Philip Caryl	2
Johnson, Frank Minis, Jr.	5
Kaufman, Irving Robert	3
Kerner, Otto, Jr.	1960s-1
Landis, Kenesaw Mountain	Sports-2
Lausche, Frank John	2
McCree, Wade Hampton, Jr.	2
Marshall, Thurgood	3, 1960s-2
Matthews, Burnita Shelton	2
Medina, Harold Raymond	2
Mills, Wilbur Daigh	3
Page, Alan Cedric	Sports-2
Parsons, James Benton	3
Powell, Lewis Franklin, Jr.	5
Ribicoff, Abraham Alexander	5
Rothwax, Harold J(ay)	5
Sirica, John Joseph	3
Smith, William French	2
Stewart, Potter	1
Wallace, George Corley	5
White, Byron Raymond	6
Wisdom, John Minor	5
Wyzanski, Charles Edward, Jr.	2
Yarborough, Ralph Webster	4

Labor Leader
Abel, I(orwith) W(ilbur) ("Abe")	2
Beck, David	3
Bellamy, Ralph Rexford	3
Boyle, William Anthony ("Tony")	1
Bridges, Harry	2
Chaikin, Sol (Chick)	3

	Volume		Volume
Labor Leader (*continued*)		Bird, Rose Elizabeth	5
Chávez, César Estrada	3, 1960s-1	Blackmun, Harry Andrew	5
Curran, Joseph Edwin	1	Blough, Roger Miles	1, 1960s-1
de Mille, Agnes George	3	Boudin, Leonard B.	2
Dubinsky, David	1	Bradley, Thomas ("Tom")	5
Fasanella, Raphaele ("Ralph")	5	Brannan, Charles Franklin	3
Fitzsimmons, Frank Edward	1	Brennan, William J., Jr.	5, 1960s-1
Galarza, Ernesto, Jr.	1	Brewster, Kingman, Jr.	2, 1960s-1
Gleason, Thomas William ("Teddy")	3	Brooke, Edward William, III	1960s-1
Heston, Charlton	1960s-1	Brown, Edmund Gerald ("Pat")	4
Hoffa, James Riddle ("Jimmy")	1960s-1	Brown, John R.	3
Kirkland, (Joseph) Lane	5	Brown, Ron(ald) Harmon	4
Koontz, Elizabeth Duncan	2	Brownell, Herbert, Jr.	4
Korshak, Sidney Roy	4	Burch, (Roy) Dean	3
Lovestone, Jay	2	Burdick, Quentin Northrop	3
McBride, Lloyd	1	Burger, Warren Earl	4
Miller, Arnold Ray	1	Cannon, Howard Walter	6
Miller, Marvin Julian	Sports-2	Casey, Robert Patrick ("Spike")	6
Montgomery, Robert	1	Casey, William Joseph	2
Murphy, George Lloyd	3	Celebrezze, Anthony Joseph	5
Peterson, Esther	5	Celler, Emanuel	1
Petrillo, James Caesar	1	Chalk, (Oscar) Roy	4
Presser, Jackie	2	Chandler, Albert Benjamin ("Happy")	3
Provenzano, Anthony ("Tony Pro")	2	Cherne, Leo	5
Quill, Michael Joseph ("Mike")	1960s-2	Clark, Joseph Sill, Jr.	2
Reagan, Ronald Wilson	1960s-2	Clark, (William) Ramsey	1960s-1
Reuther, Walter Philip	1960s-2	Clifford, Clark McAdams	5, 1960s-1
Riesel, Victor	4	Cohen, Benjamin Victor	1
Shanker, Albert ("Al")	5, 1960s-2	Cohn, Roy Marcus	2
Upshaw, Eugene Thurman, Jr.		Colby, William Egan	4
("Gene")	Sports-2	Coleman, J(ames) P(lemon)	3
Van Arsdale, Harry, Jr.	2	Collins, John Frederick	4
Ward, John Montgomery	Sports-2	Collins, (Thomas) LeRoy	3
Weinmeister, Arnold George ("Arnie")	6	Connally, John Bowden, Jr.	3
Williams, Roy Lee	2	Connor, John Thomas ("Jack")	6
Woodcock, Leonard Freel	6	Cooper, John Sherman	3
Wurf, Jerome	1	Corcoran, Thomas Gardiner	1
Lawyer		Cosell, Howard	4, Sports-1
Abram, Morris Berthold	6	Cotton, Norris Henry	2
Abzug, Bella	5, 1960s-1	Curtis, Carl Thomas	6
Agnew, Spiro Theodore	4, 1960s-1	Daniel, Price Marion	2
Albert, Carl Bert	6	Dean, Arthur Hobson	2
Alioto, Joseph Lawrence	5	Dickey, John Sloan	3
Allott, Gordon Llewellyn	2	DiSalle, Michael Vincent	1
Anderson, Robert Bernerd	2	Dixon, Julian C.	6
Austin, John Paul	1	Dulles, Allen Welsh	1960s-1
Baldwin, Raymond Earl	2	Ehrlichman, John Daniel	5
Ball, George Wildman	4	Ervin, Samuel James, Jr.	1
Barnett, Ross Robert	1960s-1	Ferguson, Homer Samuel	1
Belli, Melvin Mouron	4	Fortas, Abraham ("Abe")	1, 1960s-1
Berman, Emile Zola	1	Foster, Vincent William, Jr.	3
Bernard, Anna Jones	1	Freund, Paul Abraham	3
Bible, Alan Harvey	2	Friendly, Henry Jacob	2

	Volume		*Volume*
Fulbright, J(ames) William	4, 1960s-1	Matsunaga, Spark Masayuki ("Sparkie")	2
Furcolo, (John) Foster	4	Matthews, Burnita Shelton	2
Gabel, Hortense Wittstein	2	Medina, Harold Raymond	2
Garrison, Earling Carothers ("Jim")	3, 1960s-1	Meyner, Robert Baumle	2
Garrity, W(endell) Arthur, Jr.	5	Mikan, George Lawrence, Jr.	Sports-2
Gellhorn, Walter	4	Mink, Patsy Matsu Takemoto	6
Gilpatric, Roswell Leavitt	4	Minow, Newton Norman	1960s-2
Goldberg, Arthur Joseph	2	Mitchell, John Newton	1960s-2
Greene, Harold Herman	6	Murray, Anna Pauline ("Pauli")	1
Griswold, Erwin Nathaniel	4	Muskie, Edmund Sixtus	4, 1960s-2
Gunther, Gerald	6	Nabrit, James Madison, Jr.	5
Halleck, Charles Abraham	2	Nader, Ralph	1960s-2
Harris, Patricia Roberts Fitzgerald	1	Nixon, Richard Milhous	4
Haynsworth, Clement Furman, Jr.	2	Nizer, Louis	4, 1960s-2
Higginbotham, A(loysius) Leon, Jr.	5	O'Dwyer, (Peter) Paul	5
Hiss, Alger	4	Ogilvie, Richard Buell	2
Hofheinz, Roy Mark	1	Page, Alan Cedric	Sports-2
Hunter, Howard William	4	Parsons, James Benton	3
Jackson, Henry Martin ("Scoop")	1, 1960s-1	Pastore, John Orlando	6
Jacobs, Bernard B.	4	Peabody, Endicott ("Chub")	5
Javits, Jacob Koppel	2	Perlmutter, Nathan	2
Jaworski, Leon	1	Pierce, Samuel Riley, Jr.	6
Jenkins, Hayes Alan	Sports-1	Pike, James Albert, Jr.	1960s-2
Jessup, Philip Caryl	2	Powell, Lewis Franklin, Jr.	5
Johnson, Edward Crosby 2d	1	Prichard, Edward Fretwell, Jr.	1
Johnson, Frank Minis, Jr.	5	Puller, Lewis Burwell, Jr.	4
Johnson, Paul Burney	1	Rauh, Joseph Louis, Jr.	3
Jones, Robert Tyre, Jr. ("Bobby")	Sports-1	Reel, A(dolf) Frank	6
Jordan, Barbara Charline	4	Ribicoff, Abraham Alexander	5
Katzenbach, Nicholas de Belleville	1960s-1	Richardson, Elliot Lee	5
Kaufman, Irving Robert	3	Rickey, Branch Wesley	Sports-2
Kennedy, Florynce Rae ("Flo")	6	Rogers, William Pierce	6
Kennedy, John Fitzgerald, Jr.	5	Rostow, Eugene Victor Debs	6
Kleindienst, Richard G.	6	Rothwax, Harold J(ay)	5
Klutznick, Philip M.	5	Russell, Richard Brevard, Jr. ("Dick")	1960s-2
Korshak, Sidney Roy	4	Salant, Richard S.	3
Krim, Arthur B.	4	Scott, Austin Wakeman	1
Kunstler, William Moses	4, 1960s-1	Seasongood, Murray	1
Kurland, Philip B.	4	Seymour, Whitney North	1
Kutner, Luis	3	Shivers, (Robert) Allan	1
Landis, Kenesaw Mountain	Sports-2	Sirica, John Joseph	3
Lausche, Frank John	2	Smith, William French	2
Lazar, Irving Paul ("Swifty")	3	Stassen, Harold Edward	6
Lewis, Reginald Francis	3	Stern, David	Sports-2
Lilienthal, David Eli	1	Stewart, Potter	1
Liman, Arthur Lawrence	5	Stokes, Carl Burton	1960s-2
Lindsay, John Vliet	6	Taylor, Peter Hillsman	4
Lodge, John Davis	1	Taylor, Telford	5
McCloy, John Jay	2, 1960s-2	Tsongas, Paul Efthemios	5
McCree, Wade Hampton, Jr.	2	Udall, Morris King	5
McKissick, Floyd B.	3	Vance, Cyrus Roberts	6, 1960s-2
MacLeish, Archibald	1	Wade, Henry Menasco	6
Marshall, Thurgood	3	Wagner, Robert Ferdinand	3

	Volume
Lawyer (*continued*)	
Wallace, George Corley	5, 1960s-2
Ward, John Montgomery	Sports-2
Warnke, Paul Culliton	6
Wechsler, Herbert	6
White, Byron Raymond	6
Whitten, Jamie Lloyd	4
Wilentz, David Theodore	2
Williams, Edward Bennett	2
Wisdom, John Minor	5
Wylie, Chalmers Pangburn	5
Wyzanski, Charles Edward, Jr.	2
Yarborough, Ralph Webster	4
Yarmolinsky, Adam	6
Yates, Sidney Richard	6
Young, Jon Steven ("Steve")	Sports-2
Young, Stephen M.	1
Legal Scholar	
Black, Charles Lund, Jr.	6
Freund, Paul Abraham	3
Gellhorn, Walter	4
Griswold, Erwin Nathaniel	4
Gunther, Gerald	6
Jessup, Philip Caryl	2
Kurland, Philip B.	4
Larson, (Lewis) Arthur	3
Levi, Edward H(irsch)	6
Scott, Austin Wakeman	1
Wechsler, Herbert	6
Legislator, State. *See* **Politician (State Legislator).**	
Librarian	
Bettmann, Otto Ludwig	5
Brown, Dee Alexander	6
Mumford, Lawrence Quincy	1
Wright, Louis Booker	1
Librettist	
Abbott, George Francis	4
Ashman, Howard Elliot	3
Auden, W(ystan) H(ugh)	1960s-1
Harburg, Edgar Yipsel ("Yip")	1
Larson, Jonathan	4
Lerner, Alan Jay	2
Rado, James, and Gerome Ragni	1960s-2
Ryskind, Morrie	1
Sessions, Roger Huntington	1, 1960s-2
Willson, (Robert Reiniger) Meredith	1
Linguist	
Chomsky, (Avram) Noam	1960s-1
Greenberg, Joseph H(arold)	6
Literary Critic	
Baker, Carlos Heard	2
Brooks, Cleanth	4

	Volume
Burke, Kenneth Duva	3
Campbell, Joseph	2
Ciardi, John Anthony	2
Cowley, (David) Malcolm	2
de Man, Paul	1
Edel, (Joseph) Leon	5
Ellmann, Richard David	2
Fadiman, Clifton Paul	5
Gardner, John Champlin, Jr.	1
Hicks, Granville	1
Howe, Irving	3, 1960s-1
Kazin, Alfred	5
Kosinski, Jerzy Nikodem	3
McCarthy, Mary Therese	1960s-2
Macdonald, Dwight	1, 1960s-2
Mizener, Arthur Moore	2
Nemerov, Howard	3
Podhoretz, Norman Harold	1960s-2
Riding, Laura	3
Sontag, Susan	1960s-2
Trilling, Diana Rubin	4
Trilling, Lionel	1960s-2
Warren, Robert Penn	2
Wellek, René Maria Eduard	4, 1960s-2
Williams, Sherley Anne	5
Lyricist	
Ashman, Howard Elliot	3
Berlin, Irving	2
Caesar, Irving	4
Cahn, Sammy	3
Dietz, Howard	1
Gershwin, Ira	1
Green, Adolph	6
Harburg, Edgar Yipsel ("Yip")	1
Kaye, Sylvia Fine	3
Larson, Jonathan	4
Lerner, Alan Jay	2
Mercer, John Herndon ("Johnny")	1960s-2
Miller, Roger Dean	3
Rado, James, and Gerome Ragni	1960s-2
Sondheim, Stephen	1960s-2
Willson, (Robert Reiniger) Meredith	1
Madam	
Stanford, Sally	1
Magician	
Scarne, John	1
Management Theorist	
Deming, W(illiam) Edwards	3
Drucker, Peter Ferdinand	1960s-1
Marine Corps Officer	
Boyington, Gregory ("Pappy")	2
Carl, Marion Eugene	5

	Volume
Chapman, Leonard Fielding, Jr.	6
Day, James Lewis	5
Glenn, John Herschel, Jr.	1960s-1
Krulak, Victor Harold	1960s-1
Lee, William Andrew	5
Puller, Lewis Burwell, Jr.	4
Shoup, David Monroe	1, 1960s-2
Sitter, Carl Leonard	6
Walt, Lewis William	2

Maritime Worker
Hoffer, Eric	1

Mathematician
Atanasoff, John Vincent	4
Chandrasekhar, Subrahmanyan ("Chandra")	4
Church, Alonzo	4
Harsanyi, John C.	6
Hoffmann, Banesh	2
Hopper, Grace Brewster Murray	3
Kahn, Herman Bernard	1, 1960s-1
Kemeny, John George	3
Neyman, Jerzy	1
Robinson, Julia Bowman	1
Shannon, Claude Elwood	6
Tarski, Alfred	1
Tukey, John W(ilder)	6
Ulam, Stanislaw Marcin	1
Weil, André	5

Mayor. *See* **Politician (Mayor).**

Media Theorist
McLuhan, (Herbert) Marshall	1960s-2

Medical Administrator
Thomas, Lewis	3

Meteorologist
Charney, Jule Gregory	1
Fitch, James Marston	6
Sloane, Eric	1
Suomi, Verner Edward	4

Microbiologist
Bunting-Smith, Mary Alice Ingraham ("Polly")	5
Dubos, René Jules	1
Friend, Charlotte	2
Luria, Salvador Edward	3
Nathans, Daniel	5
Niel, Cornelis Bernardus van	1

Military Officer. *See* **Air Force Officer, Army Officer, Naval Officer.**

Minister. *See* **Clergy.**

Missionary
Judd, Walter Henry	4

	Volume
Motion Picture Actor, Director, Producer, etc. *See* **Actor, Director, Producer, etc.**	

Mountaineer
Lowe, Steward Alexander ("Alex")	5

Museum Curator
Geldzahler, Henry	4

Museum Director
Barr, Alfred Hamilton, Jr.	1
Sweeney, James Johnson	2

Museum Founder
Burden, William Armistead Moale	1
Getty, J(ean) Paul	1960s-1
Hirshhorn, Joseph Herman	1
Phillips, Marjorie Acker	1

Museum President
Burden, William	1

Music Promoter
Graham, Bill	3
Hammond, John Henry, Jr.	2

Musical Arranger
Bennett, Robert Russell	1
Brown, Lester Raymond ("Les")	6
Dixon, Willie James	3
Evans, Gil	2
Fahey, John	6
Jenkins, Gordon Hill	1
Jones, Quincy Delight, Jr.	1960s-1
Mancini, Henry Nicola	4, 1960s-2
Mulligan, Gerald Joseph ("Gerry")	4
O'Farrill, Arturo ("Chico")	6
Riddle, Nelson Smock, Jr.	1
Tormé, Mel(vin) Howard	5
Vaughn, Richard Smith ("Billy")	3
Webb, James Layne ("Jimmy")	1960s-2
Williams, Mary Lou	1

Musician (Big Band)
Arnaz, Desi	2
Basie, William James ("Count")	1
Bauzá, Mario	3
Blakey, Arthur ("Art"; Abdullah Ibn Buhaina)	2
Brown, Lester Raymond ("Les")	6
Calloway, Cab	4
Cugat, Xavier	2
Daniels, William Boone ("Billy")	2
Day, Doris	1960s-1
Eckstine, William Clarence ("Billy")	3
Elgart, Les(ter) Elliot	4
Ellington, Mercer Kennedy	4
Fitzgerald, Ella Jane	4
Forrest, Helen	5

	Volume
Musician (Big Band) (*continued*)	
Getz, Stan(ley)	3
Gleason, Herbert John ("Jackie")	2
Goodman, Benjamin David ("Benny")	2
Hampton, Lionel	6
Harris, (Wanga) Phillip ("Phil")	4
Hawkins, Erskine Ramsay	3
Herman, Woody	2
Hines, Earl Kenneth ("Fatha")	1
Hirt, Alois Maxwell ("Al")	5
James, Harry Haag	1
Jones, Quincy Delight, Jr.	1960s-1
Kaye, Sammy	2
Machito, (Frank Raúl Grillo)	1
McPartland, James Dugald ("Jimmy")	3
McRae, Carmen Mercedes	4
Mancini, Henry Nicola	4, 1960s-2
Martin, Freddy	1
Mulligan, Gerald Joseph ("Gerry")	4
Norvo, Joseph Kenneth ("Red")	5
Rich, Bernard ("Buddy")	2
Riddle, Nelson Smock, Jr.	1
Rogers, Charles ("Buddy")	5
Sinatra, Francis Albert ("Frank")	5
Stacy, Jess Alexandria	4
Vallee, Hubert Prior ("Rudy")	2
Vaughan, Sarah Lois	2
Vaughn, Richard Smith ("Billy")	3
Waring, Fred(eric) Malcolm	1
Welk, Lawrence LeRoy	3
Wilson, Theodore Shaw ("Teddy")	2
Musician (Blues)	
Dixon, Willie James	3
Dorsey, Thomas Andrew	3
Hooker, John Lee	6
Hopkins, Sam ("Lightnin'")	1
Hunter, Alberta	1
King, B. B.	1960s-1
Turner, Joseph Vernon ("Big Joe")	1
Wallace, Sippie	2
Waters, Muddy	1
Williams, Joe	5
Musician (Cabaret)	
Bailey, Pearl Mae	2
Bricktop, (Ada Smith)	1
Carroll, Diahann	1960s-1
Daniels, William Boone ("Billy")	2
Davis, Sammy, Jr.	2
Eckstine, William Clarence ("Billy")	3
Green, Adolph	6
Hunter, Alberta	1
Martin, Dean	4
Mercer, Mabel	1

	Volume
Schlamme, Martha Haftel	1
Scott, Hazel Dorothy	1
Sherwood, Roberta	5
Thompson, Kay	5
Vaughan, Sarah Lois	2
Musician (Classical)	
Abravanel, Maurice	3
Anderson, Marian	3
Arrau, Claudio	3
Bacon, Ernst	2
Bennett, Robert Russell	1
Bernstein, Leonard	2
Bolet, Jorge	2
Borge, Victor	6
Brico, Antonia Louisa	2
Bumbry, Grace	1960s-1
Byrd, Charlie Lee	5
DeGaetani, Jan	2
Dorati, Antal	2
Elgart, Les(ter) Elliot	4
Engel, A. Lehman	1
Gleason, Herbert John ("Jackie")	2
Gould, Morton	4
Hanson, Howard Harold	1
Heifetz, Jascha	2
Horowitz, Vladimir	2
Jenkins, Gordon Hill	1
Kamen, Martin D(avid)	6
Kirsten, Dorothy	3
Leinsdorf, Erich	3
Lenya, Lotte	1
Liberace, Wladziu Valentino	2
Luening, Otto Clarence	4
McCracken, James Eugene	2
Mancini, Henry Nicola	4, 1960s-2
Martin, Freddy	1
Menuhin, Yehudi	5
Milanov, Zinka	2
Milstein, Nathan	3
Ormandy, Eugene	1
Peerce, Jan	1
Ponselle, Rosa Melba	1
Primrose, William	1
Riddle, Nelson Smock, Jr.	1
Robinson, Earl	3
Rubinstein, Arthur	1
Schlamme, Martha Haftel	1
Schuller, Gunther Arthur	1960s-2
Serkin, Rudolf	3
Shaw, Robert Lawson	5
Sills, Beverly	1960s-2
Slonimsky, Nicolas (Nikolai Leonidovich)	4

	Volume
Smith, Kathryn Elizabeth ("Kate")	2
Solti, Georg	5
Steber, Eleanor	2
Stern, Isaac	6
Trapp, Maria von	2
Tully, Alice Bigelow	3
Vaughn, Richard Smith ("Billy")	3
Wallenstein, Alfred Franz	1
Watts, André	1960s-2
Welk, Lawrence LeRoy	3
Zimbalist, Efrem Alexandrovich	1

Musician (Conductor)

Abravanel, Maurice	3
Arnaz, Desi	2
Basie, William James ("Count")	1
Bennett, Robert Russell	1
Bernstein, Leonard	2
Blakey, Arthur ("Art"; Abdullah Ibn Buhaina)	2
Brico, Antonia Louisa	2
Brown, Lester Raymond ("Les")	6
Calloway, Cab	4
Cugat, Xavier	2
Dorati, Antal	2
Elgart, Les(ter) Elliot	4
Ellington, Mercer Kennedy	4
Gleason, Herbert John ("Jackie")	2
Goodman, Benjamin David ("Benny")	2
Gould, Morton	4
Hampton, Lionel	6
Hanson, Howard Harold	1
Herman, Woody	2
Hines, Earl Kenneth ("Fatha")	1
Hirt, Alois Maxwell ("Al")	5
James, Harry Haag	1
Kaye, Sammy	2
Leinsdorf, Erich	3
Machito (Frank Raúl Grillo)	1
Mancini, Henry Nicola	4, 1960s-2
Martin, Freddy	1
Menuhin, Yehudi	5
Mulligan, Gerald Joseph ("Gerry")	4
Norvo, Joseph Kenneth ("Red")	5
Ormandy, Eugene	1
Rich, Bernard ("Buddy")	2
Riddle, Nelson Smock, Jr.	1
Schuller, Gunther Arthur	1960s-2
Slonimsky, Nicolas (Nikolai Leonidovich)	4
Solti, Georg	5
Waring, Fred(eric) Malcolm	1
Weiner, Lazar	1
Willson, (Robert Reiniger) Meredith	1

Musician (Country)

	Volume
Acuff, Roy Claxton	3
Atkins, Chester Burton ("Chet")	6
Autry, (Orvon) Gene	5
Cash, John R. ("Johnny")	1960s-1
Cline, Patsy	1960s-1
Ford, Ernest Jennings ("Tennessee Ernie")	3
Haggard, Merle Ronald	1960s-1
Jennings, Waylon Arnold	6
Miller, Roger Dean	3
Monroe, William Smith ("Bill")	4
Pearl, Minnie (Sarah Ophelia Colley Cannon)	4
Pride, Charles Frank ("Charley")	1960s-2
Rich, Charles Allan ("Charlie")	4
Robbins, Marty	1
Rogers, Roy	5
Snow, Clarence Eugene ("Hank")	5
Tubb, Ernest Dale	1
Twitty, Conway	3
Wynette, Tammy	5, 1960s-2

Musician (Folk)

Axton, Hoyt Wayne	5
Baez, Joan Chandos	1960s-1
Chapin, Harry Forster	1
Collins, Judy	1960s-1
Crosby, Stills, and Nash	1960s-1
Denver, John	5
Dylan, Bob	1960s-1
Fariña, Margarita Baez ("Mimi")	6
Fariña, Richard George	1960s-1
Guthrie, Arlo Davy	1960s-1
Hays, Lee	1
Ives, Burl Icle Ivanhoe	4
Ochs, Philip David	1960s-2
Odetta	1960s-2
Peter, Paul and Mary	1960s-2
Phillips, John Edmund Andrew	6, 1960s-2
Sainte-Marie, Buffy	1960s-2
Schlamme, Martha Haftel	1
Seeger, Peter R. ("Pete")	1960s-2
Simon and Garfunkel	1960s-2
Smothers, Thomas ("Tom"), and Richard ("Dick") Smothers	1960s-2

Musician (Gospel)

Dorsey, Thomas Andrew	3
Ford, Ernest Jennings ("Tennessee Ernie")	3

Musician (Jazz)

Baker, Chesney Henry ("Chet")	2
Barrett, Emma ("Sweet Emma")	1
Basie, William James ("Count")	1

Volume

Musician (Jazz) (*continued*)

Bauzá, Mario	3
Bennett, Tony	1960s-1
Blake, James Hubert ("Eubie")	1
Blakey, Arthur ("Art"; Abdullah Ibn Buhaina)	2
Brown, Lester Raymond ("Les")	6
Brubeck, David Warren ("Dave")	1960s-1
Byrd, Charlie Lee	5
Calloway, Cab	4
Carter, Betty	5
Cherry, Don(ald) Eugene	4
Clarke, Kenny ("Klook")	1
Cole, William R. ("Cozy")	1
Coltrane, John William	1960s-1
Cugat, Xavier	2
Daniels, William Boone ("Billy")	2
Davis, Miles Dewey, III	3, 1960s-1
Davison, William Edward ("Wild Bill")	2
Eckstine, William Clarence ("Billy")	3
Eldridge, (David) Roy ("Little Jazz")	2
Ellington, Mercer Kennedy	4
Evans, Gil	2
Farmer, Art(hur) Stewart	5
Feather, Leonard Geoffrey	4
Fitzgerald, Ella Jane	4
Forrest, Helen	5
Getz, Stan(ley)	3
Gillespie, John Birks ("Dizzy")	3
Goodman, Benjamin David ("Benny")	2
Gordon, Dexter Keith	2
Greer, William Alexander ("Sonny")	1
Hampton, Lionel	6
Henderson, Joseph A. ("Joe")	6
Herman, Woody	2
Hibbler, Albert George ("Al")	6
Hines, Earl Kenneth ("Fatha")	1
Hinton, Milton John ("Milt")	6
Hirt, Alois Maxwell ("Al")	5
Jackson, Walter Milton ("Milt"; "Bags")	5
James, Harry Haag	1
Jones, Quincy Delight, Jr.	1960s-1
Kaye, Sammy	2
Kirby, George	4
Lee, Peggy	6
Lewis, John Aaron	6
Machito (Frank Raúl Grillo)	1
McPartland, James Dugald ("Jimmy")	3
McRae, Carmen Mercedes	4
Manne, Sheldon ("Shelly")	1
Monk, Thelonious Sphere	1, 1960s-2
Mulligan, Gerald Joseph ("Gerry")	4

Volume

Norvo, Joseph Kenneth ("Red")	5
O'Farrill, Arturo ("Chico")	6
Palmieri, Carlos Manuel, Jr. ("Charlie")	2
Puente, Ernest Anthony, Jr. ("Tito")	6
Rich, Bernard ("Buddy")	2
Rivers, Larry	6
Rutherford, Maude Russell	6
Scott, Hazel Dorothy	1
Stacy, Jess Alexandria	4
Stewart, Leroy Elliott ("Slam")	2
Sun Ra (Herman Blount)	3
Tormé, Mel(vin) Howard	5
Valentine, Kid Thomas	2
Vaughan, Sarah Lois	2
Wallace, Sippie	2
Williams, Joe	5
Williams, Mary Lou	1
Wilson, Theodore Shaw ("Teddy")	2

Musician (Latin)

Arnaz, Desi	2
Bauzá, Mario	3
Cugat, Xavier	2
Machito (Frank Raúl Grillo)	1
O'Farrill, Arturo ("Chico")	6
Palmieri, Carlos Manuel, Jr. ("Charlie")	2
Puente, Ernest Anthony, Jr. ("Tito")	6
Selena (Selena Quintanilla Pérez)	4

Musician (Liturgical)

Weiner, Lazar	1

Musician (Musical Theater)

Adler, Lawrence Cecil ("Larry")	6
Andrews, Julie	1960s-1
Bailey, Pearl Mae	2
Blaine, Vivian	4
Calloway, Cab	4
Carroll, Diahann	1960s-1
Davis, Sammy, Jr.	2, 1960s-1
Drake, Alfred	3
Engel, A. Lehman	1
Kiley, Richard Paul	5
Lenya, Lotte	1
Martin, Mary Virginia	2
Meadows, Audrey	4
Merman, Ethel	1
Sothern, Ann	6
Streisand, Barbra	1960s-2
Tracy, Arthur	5
Warfield, William Caesar	6

Musician (Opera Singer)

Bumbry, Grace	1960s-1
Farrell, Eileen Frances	6

	Volume		*Volume*
Sills, Beverly	1960s-2	Ray, John Alvin ("Johnnie")	2
Warfield, William Caesar	6	Robinson, William, Jr. ("Smokey")	1960s-2
Musician (Popular)		Ronstadt, Linda	1960s-2
Aaliyah (Aaliyah Dana Haughton)	6	Ruffin, Davis Eli ("David")	3, 1960s-2
Andrews, Maxene Angelyn	4	Selena (Selena Quintanilla Pérez)	4
Arnaz, Desi	2	Shakur, Tupac Amaru	4
Avalon, Frankie, and Annette Joanne		Shore, Dinah	4, 1960s-2
Funicello	1960s-2	Sinatra, Francis Albert ("Frank")	5
Axton, Hoyt Wayne	5	Sonny and Cher	1960s-2
Bennett, Tony	1960s-1	Streisand, Barbra	1960s-2
Bono, Salvatore Phillip ("Sonny")	5	Tormé, Mel(vin) Howard	5
Borge, Victor	6	Tracy, Arthur	5
Byrd, Charlie Lee	5	Vallee, Hubert Prior ("Rudy")	2
Calloway, Cab	4	Vaughan, Sarah Lois	2
Carpenter, Karen	1	Vaughn, Richard Smith ("Billy")	3
Checker, Chubby	1960s-1	Walker, Junior	4
Clooney, Rosemary	6	Waring, Fred(eric) Malcolm	1
Como, Pierino Ronald ("Perry")	6	Warwick, Dionne	1960s-2
Crosby, Stills, and Nash	1960s-1	Welk, Lawrence LeRoy	3
Davis, James Houston ("Jimmie")	6	Wells, Mary Esther	3
Davis, Sammy, Jr.	2, 1960s-1	Wilson, Brian Douglas	1960s-2
Day, Dennis	2	Wilson, Carl Dean	5
Day, Doris	1960s-1	Wonder, Stevie	1960s-2
Denver, John	5	**Musician (Rap)**	
Dion	1960s-1	Jam Master Jay (Jason William Mizell)	6
Downey, Morton	1	Notorious B.I.G. ("Biggie Smalls")	5
Eckstine, William Clarence ("Billy")	3	Shakur, Tupac Amaru	4
Evans, Dale	6	**Musician (Rhythm and Blues)**	
Fahey, John	6	Aaliyah (Aaliyah Dana Haughton)	6
Farrell, Eileen Frances	6	Brown, James Joe, Jr.	1960s-1
Fitzgerald, Ella Jane	4	Fitzgerald, Ella Jane	4
Forrest, Helen	5	Franklin, Aretha Louise	1960s-1
Franklin, Aretha Louise	1960s-1	Gaye, Marvin Pentz, Jr.	1, 1960s-1
Garcia, Jerome John ("Jerry")	4	Kendricks, Eddie James	3
Garland, Judy	1960s-1	Mayfield, Curtis Lee	5
Gaye, Marvin Pentz, Jr.	1, 1960s-1	Pickett, Wilson, Jr.	1960s-2
Gleason, Herbert John ("Jackie")	2	Ramone, Joey	6
Gobel, George Leslie	3	Redding, Otis	1960s-2
Harris, (Wanga) Phillip ("Phil")	4	Robinson, William, Jr. ("Smokey")	1960s-2
Hibbler, Albert George ("Al")	6	Ross, Diana Earle	1960s-2
Jenkins, Gordon Hill	1	Ruffin, Davis Eli ("David")	3, 1960s-2
Kaye, Sammy	2	Turner, Ike, and Tina Turner	1960s-2
Kendricks, Eddie James	3	Walker, Junior	4
Lamour, Dorothy	4	Warwick, Dionne	1960s-2
Lewis, Jerry	1960s-1	Wells, Mary Esther	3
Lee, Peggy	6	Wonder, Stevie	1960s-2
Liberace, Wladziu Valentino	2	**Musician (Rock)**	
Martin, Dean	4, 1960s-2	Axton, Hoyt Wayne	5
Martin, Freddy	1	Bono, Salvatore Phillip ("Sonny")	5
Meadows, Audrey	4	Carpenter, Karen	1
Mercer, Mabel	1	Checker, Chubby	1960s-1
Phillips, John Edmund Andrew	6	Clayton-Thomas, David	1960s-1

	Volume
Musician (Rock) (*continued*)	
Cobain, Kurt Donald	4
Dion	1960s-1
Fogerty, John Cameron	1960s-1
Garcia, Jerome John ("Jerry")	4, 1960s-1
Haley, William John Clifton, Jr. ("Bill")	1
Hendrix, James Marshall ("Jimmy"; "Maurice James"; "Jimi")	1960s-1
Joplin, Janis Lyn	1960s-1
McCartney, Linda Louise Eastman	5
Morrison, James Douglas ("Jim")	1960s-2
Nelson, Eric Hilliard ("Rick")	1
Orbison, Roy Kelton	2, 1960s-2
Perkins, Carl Lee	5
Phillips, John Edmund Andrew	1960s-2
Presley, Elvis Aron	1960s-2
Ronstadt, Linda	1960s-2
Slick, Grace Wing	1960s-2
Sonny and Cher	1960s-2
Spector, Philip Harvey ("Phil")	1960s-2
Turner, Izear Luster ("Ike"), and Tina Turner	1960s-2
Twitty, Conway	3
Vaughan, Stevie Ray	2
Warwick, Dionne	1960s-2
Wilson, Brian Douglas	1960s-2
Wilson, Carl Dean	5
Zappa, Francis Vincent ("Frank")	3, 1960s-2
Musicologist	
Lomax, Alan	6
Schuller, Gunther Alexander	1960s-2
Schwann, William Joseph	5
Slonimsky, Nicolas (Nikolai Leonidovich)	4
Tiny Tim (Herbert Butros Khaury)	4
Mythologist	
Campbell, Joseph John	2, 1960s-1
Narrator	
Cotten, Joseph Cheshire	4
Greene, Lorne	2
Heston, Charlton	1960s-1
Jones, James Earl	1960s-1
Kiley, Richard Paul	5
Scourby, Alexander	1
Webb, John Randolph ("Jack")	1
NASA Administrator	
Armstrong, Neil Alden	1960s-1
Debus, Kurt Heinrich	1
Hagen, John Peter	2
Killian, James Rhyne, Jr.	2
Webb, James Edwin	3

	Volume
Native American Leader	
Banks, Dennis J.	1960s-1
Belvin, Harry J. W.	2
Chino, Wendell	5
Deloria, Vine, Jr.	1960s-1
Keeler, William Wayne	2
Naval Officer	
Anderson, George Whelan, Jr.	3
Boorda, Jeremy Michael ("Mike")	4
Burke, Arleigh Albert	4
Carney, Robert Bostwick	2
Hancock, Joy Bright	2
Hopper, Grace Brewster Murray	3
Jacobs, Helen Hull	5, Sports-1
McCain, John Sidney, Jr.	1, 1960s-2
Raborn, William Francis, Jr. ("Red")	2
Rickover, Hyman George	2
Riggs, Ralph Smith	1
Rivero, Horacio, Jr.	6
Shepard, Alan Bartlett, Jr.	5, 1960s-2
Street, George Levick, III	6
Struble, Arthur D.	1
Zumwalt, Elmo Russell, Jr. ("Bud")	6
Nephrologist	
Merrill, John Putnam	1
Neurologist	
Geschwind, Norman	1
Neuroscientist	
Hartline, Haldan Keffer	1, 1960s-1
Sperry, Roger Wolcott	4
Nightclub Owner	
Bricktop (Ada Smith)	1
Manne, Sheldon ("Shelly")	1
Rubell, Steve	2
Ruby, John ("Jack")	1960s-2
Nurse	
Bleibtrey, Ethelda	Sports-1
Boylston, Helen Dore	1
Nutritionist	
Fredericks, Carlton	2
Husted, Marjorie Child	2
Pritikin, Nathan	1
Obstetrician/Gynecologist	
Margulies, Lazar	1
Masters, William Howell	6, 1960s-2
Rock, John Charles	1
Oceanographer	
Revelle, Roger Randall Dougan	3
Oncologist	
Huggins, Charles Brenton	5, 1960s-1
Temin, Howard Martin	4

Volume

Opthamologist
Stein, Julian Caesar ("Jules")   1
Ornithologist
Ripley, S(idney) Dillon, II   6
Painter. *See* **Artist (Painter).**
Paleontologist
Gould, Stephen Jay   6
Sepkoski, J(oseph) John, Jr.   5
Pathologist
Percy, Walker   2, 1960s-2
Rous, (Francis) Peyton   1960s-2
Peace Activist
Abzug, Bella   5, 1960s-1
Ashmore, Harry Scott   5
Ashmore, Harry Scott, and William
    Calhoun ("Bill") Baggs   1960s-1
Baez, Joan Chandos   1960s-1
Berrigan, Philip Francis   6
Berrigan, Daniel Joseph, and Philip
    Francis Berrigan   1960s-1
Boulding, Kenneth Ewart   1960s-1
Boyle, Katherine ("Kay")   3
Church, Frank Forrester   1
Coffin, William Sloane, Jr.   1960s-1
Cousins, Norman   2, 1960s-1
Dellinger, David   1960s-1
Fonda, Jane   1960s-1
Fulbright, J(ames) William   4, 1960s-1
Garson, Barbara   1960s-1
Gruening, Ernest   1960s-1
Hoffman, Abbott Howard ("Abbie";
    "Barry Freed")   2, 1960s-1
Hughes, H(enry) Stuart   5
Kennedy, Robert Francis   1960s-1
Kent, Corita   2
King, Martin Luther, Jr.   1960s-1
Lamont, Corliss   4
Levertov, Denise   5
Lowell, Robert Traill Spence, IV   1960s-1
Lowenstein, Allard Kenneth   1960s-1
Macdonald, Dwight   1, 1960s-2
McCarthy, Eugene Joseph   1960s-2
McGovern, George Stanley   1960s-2
Morse, Wayne Lyman   1960s-2
Nearing, Scott   1
Pauling, Linus Carl   4, 1960s-2
Rubin, Jerry Clyde   4, 1960s-2
Seeger, Peter R. ("Pete")   1960s-2
Spock, Benjamin McLane ("Dr. Spock")   5
Terry, Megan   1960s-2
Wald, George David   5, 1960s-2
Weisskopf, Victor Frederick   6

Volume

Pediatrician
Horstmann, Dorothy Millicent   6
Scott, Roland Boyd   6
Spock, Benjamin McLane
    ("Dr. Spock")   5
Williams, William Carlos   1960s-2
Pharmacist
Henry, Aaron Edd Jackson   5
Pharmacologist
Goodman, Louis Sanford   6
Kelsey, Frances Kathleen Oldham   1960s-1
Philanthropist
Annenberg, Walter Hubert   6
Ash, Mary Kay   6, 1960s-1
Black, William   1
Bradshaw, Thornton Frederick ("Brad")   2
Brown, George Rufus   1
Casey, James E.   1
Castro, Bernard   3
Chandler, Dorothy Buffum   5
Chase, Lucia Hosmer   2
Crown, Henry   2
Dana, Charles Anderson, Jr.   6
DeBartolo, Edward John, Sr.   4
Delacorte, George Thomas, Jr.   3
de Menil, Dominique Schlumberger   5
Duke, Doris   3
Fisher, Avery Robert   4
Frick, Helen Clay   1
Garson, Greer   4
Goodson, Mark   3
Hammer, Armand   2, 1960s-1
Harkness, Rebekah West   1, 1960s-1
Heinz, Henry John, II ("Jack")   2
Hirshhorn, Joseph Herman   1
Houghton, Arthur Amory, Jr.   2
Jaffe, Leo   5
Kauffman, Ewing Marion   3
Kaye, Sylvia Fine   3
Kemper, James Scott   1
Kirstein, Lincoln   4
Kroc, Ray(mond) Albert   1, 1960s-1
Lasker, Mary Woodward   4
Luce, Clare Boothe   2
McCarty, Oseola ("Kelli")   5
McNamara, Margaret Craig   1, 1960s-2
Marriott, Alice Sheets   6
Marriott, J(ohn) Willard   1
Mellon, Paul   5
Mott, Stewart Rawlings   1960s-2
Olin, John Merrill   1
Paley, William Samuel   2

Volume

Philanthropist (*continued*)

Parnis, Sarah Rosen ("Mollie") — 3
Phillips, Marjorie Acker — 1
Plough, Abe — 1
Pritzker, A(bram) N(icholas) — 2
Pritzker, Jay Arthur — 5
Rockefeller, David — 1960s-2
Rockefeller, John Davison, III — 1960s-2
Rose, Frederick Phineas — 5
Sackler, Arthur Mitchell — 2
Spanel, Abram Nathaniel — 1
Stein, Julian Caesar ("Jules") — 1
Stokes, Colin — 1
Stone, W(illiam) Clement — 6
Sulzberger, Iphigene Bertha Ochs — 2
Thomas, Danny — 3
Tully, Alice Bigelow — 3
Uris, Harold David — 1
Vanderbilt, William Henry — 1
Wallace, (William Roy) DeWitt, and Lila
   (Bell) Acheson Wallace — 1
Whitney, Betsey Maria Cushing — 5
Whitney, John Hay — 1
Woodruff, Robert Winship — 1

Philosopher

Adler, Mortimer J(erome) — 6
Arendt, Hannah — 1960s-1
Barrett, William Christopher — 3
Bloom, Allan David — 3
Boulding, Kenneth Ewart — 1960s-1
Chomsky, (Avram) Noam — 1960s-1
Church, Alonzo — 4
Feyerabend, Paul Karl — 4
Friedrich, Carl Joachim — 1
Harsanyi, John C. — 6
Hoffer, Eric — 1
Hook, Sidney — 2
Kirk, Russell Amos — 4
Kristeller, Paul Oskar — 5
Kuhn, Thomas Samuel — 4
Lamont, Corliss — 4
Langer, Susanne Katherina — 1
Marcuse, Herbert — 1960s-2
May, Rollo Reece — 4
Nagel, Ernest — 1, 1960s-2
Nisbet, Robert Alexander — 4
Nozick, Robert — 6
Rand, Ayn — 1, 1960s-2
Rawls, John Bordley — 6
Salmon, Wesley C(harles) — 6
Tarski, Alfred — 1
Weiss, Paul — 6

Volume

Photographer

Abbott, Berenice — 3
Adams, Ansel Easton — 1
Arbus, Diane — 1960s-1
Cadmus, Paul — 5
Eisenstaedt, Alfred — 4
Feininger, Andreas Bernhard Lyonel — 5
Hinton, Milton John ("Milt") — 6
Horst, Horst Paul — 5
Kertész, André (Andor) — 1
Lerner, Nathan Bernard — 5
Liberman, Alexander Semeonovitch — 5
McCartney, Linda Louise Eastman — 5
McDowall, Roderick Andrew Anthony
   Jude ("Roddy") — 5
Mapplethorpe, Robert — 2
Newhall, Beaumont — 3
Parks, Gordon, Sr. — 1960s-2
Ritts, Herbert, Jr. ("Herb") — 6
Siskind, Aaron — 3
Steiner, Ralph — 2
VanDerZee, James Augustus Joseph — 1
Welty, Eudora Alice — 6
Winogrand, Garry — 1
Wojnarowicz, David Michael — 3

Photojournalist

Eisenstaedt, Alfred — 4
Onassis, Jacqueline Lee Bouvier — 4
Parks, Gordon, Sr. — 1960s-2

Physician

Albright, Tenley Emma — Sports-1
Calderone, Mary Steichen — 5
Cooley, Denton Arthur — 1960s-1
Cooper, Irving Spencer — 1
Corner, George Washington — 1
Cournand, André Frederic — 2
DeBakey, Michael Ellis — 1960s-1
Garcia, Hector Perez — 4
Geschwind, Norman — 1
Gruentzig, Andreas Roland — 1
Harken, Dwight Emary — 3
Hartline, Haldan Keffer — 1, 1960s-1
Heiden, Eric Arthur — Sports-1
Hornberger, H(iester) Richard, Jr.
   (Richard Hooker) — 5
Huggins, Charles Brenton — 5, 1960s-1
Jenkins, David Wilkinson — Sports-1
Judd, Walter Henry — 4
Kelsey, Frances Kathleen Oldham — 1960s-1
Lillehei, C(larence) Walton ("Walt") — 5
Luria, Salvador Edward — 3, 1960s-1
Margulies, Lazar — 1

	Volume
Masters, William Howell	1960s-2
Merrill, John Putnam	1
Moore, Francis Daniels, and Thomas Earl Starzl	1960s-2
Nathans, Daniel	5
Ochsner, (Edward William) Alton	1
Percy, Walker	2, 1960s-2
Rock, John Charles	1
Rous, (Francis) Peyton	1960s-2
Rusk, Howard Archibald	2
Sabin, Albert Bruce	3, 1960s-2
Salk, Jonas Edward	4
Spock, Benjamin McLane	5
Stein, Julian Caesar ("Jules")	1
Taussig, Helen Brooke	2
Terry, Luther Leonidas	1
Thomas, Lewis	3
Wheeler, Raymond Milner	1
White, Jack Edward, Sr.	2
Wiliams, William Carlos	1960s-2
Zoll, Paul Maurice	5

Physicist (Acoustician)

| Fletcher, Harvey | 1 |

Physicist (Astrophysicist)

Chandrasekhar, Subrahmanyan ("Chandra")	4
Fowler, William Alfred	4
Von Braun, Wernher	1960s-2

Physicist

Alvarez, Luis Walter	2, 1960s-1
Anderson, Carl David, Jr.	3
Bardeen, John	3
Békésy, Georg von ("György")	1960s-1
Bloch, Felix	1
Bradbury, Norris Edwin	5
Brattain, Walter Houser	2
Chandrasekhar, Subrahmanyan ("Chandra")	4
Cormack, Allan MacLeod	5
Dirac, Paul Adrien Maurice	1
Feshbach, Herman	6
Feynman, Richard Phillips	2, 1960s-1
Fletcher, Harvey	1
Fowler, William Alfred	4
Gell-Mann, Murray	1960s-1
Glaser, Donald Arthur	1960s-1
Goeppert-Mayer, Maria	1960s-1
Hagen, John Peter	2
Hall, Theodore Alvin	5
Hoffmann, Banesh	2
Hofstadter, Robert	2, 1960s-1
Kahn, Herman Bernard	1, 1960s-1

	Volume
Kendall, Henry Way	5
Kuhn, Thomas Samuel	4
Kusch, Polykarp	3
Libby, Leona Woods Marshall	2
Livingston, M(ilton) Stanley	2
McMillan, Edwin Mattison	3
McNair, Ron(ald) Erwin	2
Mulliken, Robert Sanderson	1960s-2
Pais, Abraham	6
Piore, Emanuel Ruben ("Mannie")	6
Purcell, Edward Mills	5
Rabi, I(sidor) I(saac)	2
Rainwater, (Leo) James	2
Reines, Frederick	5
Schawlow, Arthur Leonard	5
Schwinger, Julian Seymour	4, 1960s-2
Seaborg, Glenn Theodore	5
Segrè, Emilio Gino	2
Shockley, William Bradford	2
Shull, Clifford Glenwood	6
Townes, Charles Hard	1960s-2
Ulam, Stanislaw Marcin	1
Urey, Harold Clayton	1
Weber, Joseph	6
Weisskopf, Victor Frederick	6
Wigner, Eugene Paul	4, 1960s-2
Wilson, Robert R(athbun)	6
Wu, Chien-Shiung [Jianshiung]	5
Zacharias, Jerrold Reinach	2

Physiologist

| Aserinsky, Eugene | 5 |
| Hartline, Haldan Keffer | 1, 1960s-1 |

Pianist. *See* **Musician.**

Playwright. *See* **Author (Drama).**

Poet. *See* **Author (Poetry).**

Police Officer

Bradley, Thomas ("Tom")	5
Eifler, Carl Frederick	6
Maple, John Edward ("Jack")	6
Rizzo, Frank Lazzaro	3

Political Activist

Abzug, Bella	5, 1960s-1
Amory, Cleveland ("Clip")	5
Baez, Joan Chandos	1960s-1
Baker, Ella Josephine	2
Banks, Dennis J.	1960s-1
Berrigan, Philip Francis	6
Berrigan, Daniel Joseph, and Philip Francis Berrigan	1960s-1
Bowman, Thea Bertha ("Sister Thea")	2
Boyle, Katherine ("Kay")	3
Bradshaw, Thornton Frederick ("Brad")	2

Volume

Political Activist (*continued*)

Brown, Hubert Gerold ("H. Rap") 1960s-1

Buckley, William Frank, Jr. 1960s-1

Carmichael, Stokely (Kwame Touré, Kwame Turé) 1960s-1

Chase, Stuart 1

Chomsky, (Avram) Noam 1960s-1

Cleaver, (Leroy) Eldridge 5, 1960s-1

Coffin, William Sloane, Jr. 1960s-1

Collins, Judy 1960s-1

Commager, Henry Steele 5

Davis, Angela Yvonne 1960s-1

Dellinger, David 1960s-1

de Menil, Dominique Schlumberger 5

Dohrn, Bernardine Rae 1960s-1

Faulk, John Henry 2

Fonda, Jane Seymour 1960s-1

Friedan, Betty Naomi 1960s-1

Garson, Barbara 1960s-1

Gates, John 3

Genovese, Eugene Dominick 1960s-1

Ginsberg, Allen 1960s-1

Gregory, Richard Claxton ("Dick") 1960s-1

Hale, Clara McBride ("Mother Hale") 3

Hansberry, Lorraine Vivian 1960s-1

Hargis, Billy James 1960s-1

Harriman, Pamela Beryl Digby Churchill Hayward 5

Harrington, (Edward) Michael 2

Hayden, Thomas Emmett ("Tom") 1960s-1

Hays, Lee 1

Hellman, Lillian Florence 1

Heston, Charlton 1960s-1

Hicks, Granville 1

Hoffman, Abbott Howard ("Abbie"; "Barry Freed") 2, 1960s-1

Hook, Sidney 2

Howe, Irving 3

Hughes, H(enry) Stuart 5

Humphry, (Ann) Wickett 3

Hunt, H(aroldson) L(afayette) 1960s-1

Husted, Marjorie Child 2

Jackson, Jesse Louis 1960s-1

Jarvis, Howard Arnold 2

Jones, Everett LeRoy (Amiri Baraka, "LeRoi") 1960s-1

Kahane, Meir 2

Kemper, James Scott 1

Kent, Corita 2

King, Martin Luther, Jr. 1960s-1

King, Martin Luther, Sr. ("Daddy King") 1

Kuhn, Margaret Eliza ("Maggie") 4

Kutner, Luis 3

Volume

Lash, Joseph P. 2

Lekachman, Robert 2

Loeb, William 1

Lord, John Wesley 2

Lorde, Audre Geraldine 3

Lovestone, Jay 2

Lowenstein, Allard Kenneth 1960s-1

McCartney, Linda Louise Eastman 5

Macdonald, Dwight 1, 1960s-2

MacLaine, Shirley 1960s-2

Mailer, Norman Kingsley 1960s-2

Malcolm X (Malik El-Shabazz) 1960s-2

Mas Canosa, Jorge 5

Mott, Stewart Rawlings 1960s-2

Mueller, Reuben Herbert 1

Muhammad, Elijah 1960s-2

Murray, Anna Pauline ("Pauli") 1

Nader, Ralph 1960s-2

Nearing, Helen Knothe 4

Nearing, Scott 1

Newton, Huey Percy 2, 1960s-2

Ochs, Philip David ("Phil") 1960s-2

O'Dwyer, (Peter) Paul 5

Olin, John Merrill 1

Patterson, Louise Alone Thompson 5

Pauling, Linus Carl 4

Perlmutter, Nathan 2

Peterson, Esther 5

Philbrick, Herbert Arthur 3

Rafferty, Maxwell Louis, Jr. ("Max") 1, 1960s-2

Rauh, Joseph Louis, Jr. 3

Robertson, Marion Gordon ("Pat") 1960s-2

Robinson, Earl 3

Rome, Esther Rachel Seidman 4

Roosevelt, James 3

Rubin, Jerry Clyde 4, 1960s-2

Rustin, Bayard Taylor 2, 1960s-2

Samuels, Howard Joseph ("Howie the Horse") 1

Savio, Mario 4, 1960s-2

Schlafly, Phyllis Stewart 1960s-2

Seale, Robert George ("Bobby") 1960s-2

Seasongood, Murray 1

Seeger, Peter R. ("Pete") 1960s-2

Shilts, Randy Martin 4

Snyder, Mitch(ell) Darryl 2

Spock, Benjamin McLane ("Dr. Spock") 5

Steinem, Gloria Marie 1960s-2

Taylor, Peter Hillsman 4

Tree, Mary Endicott Peabody FitzGerald ("Marietta") 3

Vidal, Gore 1960s-2

	Volume
Wald, George David	5
Wechsler, James Arthur	1
Welch, Robert Henry Winborne, Jr.	1
Wojnarowicz, David Michael	3
Young, Coleman Alexander	5

Political Adviser

Adams, (Llewellyn) Sherman	2
Atwater, Harvey Leroy ("Lee")	3
Ball, George Wildman	1960s-1
Blaisdell, Thomas Charles, Jr.	2
Bliss, Ray Charles	1
Brown, Ron(ald) Harmon	4
Brownell, Herbert, Jr.	4
Bundy, McGeorge	1960s-1
Burch, (Roy) Dean	3
Burns, Arthur Frank	2
Casey, William Joseph	2
Clifford, Clark McAdams	5, 1960s-1
Cohn, Roy Marcus	2
Dean, Arthur Hobson	2
Ehrlichman, John Daniel	5, 1960s-1
Galbraith, John Kenneth	1960s-1
Gavin, James Maurice	2, 1960s-1
Goldman, Eric Frederick	2
Green, Edith Starrett	2
Haldeman, H(arry) R(obbins) ("Bob")	1960s-1
Harlow, Bryce Nathaniel	2
Harriman, W(illiam) Averell	2
Heller, Walter Wolfgang	1960s-1
Hilsman, Roger	1960s-1
Hughes, Emmet John	1
Jordan, Barbara Charline	4
Kahn, Herman Bernard	1, 1960s-1
Keeny, Spurgeon Milton ("Sam")	2
Kennedy, Robert Francis	1960s-1
Keyserling, Leon Hirsch	2
Kleindienst, Richard G.	6
Lodge, Henry Cabot, Jr.	1, 1960s-1
Logue, Edward Joseph	6
Lowenstein, Allard Kenneth	1960s-1
McCloy, John Jay	1960s-2
Martin, John Bartlow	2, 1960s-2
Minow, Newton Norman	1960s-2
Mitchell, John Newton	1960s-2
O'Brien, Lawrence Francis ("Larry"), Jr.	1960s-2
Phillips, Kevin Price	1960s-2
Revelle, Roger Randall Dougan	3
Rostow, Walter Whitman ("Walt")	1960s-2
Samuelson, Paul Anthony	1960s-2
Schlesinger, Arthur Meier, Jr.	1960s-2
Shriver, (Robert) Sargent, Jr.	1960s-2
Smith, William French	2

	Volume
Sorensen, Theodore Chaikin ("Ted")	1960s-2
Stein, Herbert	1960s-2
Taylor, Maxwell Davenport	1960s-2
Thompson, Llewellyn E., Jr. ("Tommy")	1960s-2
Wallis, W(ilson) Allen	5
Wiesner, Jerome Bert	1960s-2

Political Scientist

Barnett, Marguerite Ross	3
Bloom, Allan	3
Dallin, Alexander	6
Fall, Bernard B.	1960s-1
Friedrich, Carl Joachim	1
Gay, Peter ("Jack")	1960s-1
Harrington, (Edward) Michael	1960s-1
Hartz, Louis	2
Hook, Sidney	2
Kissinger, Henry Alfred	1960s-1
Lubell, Samuel	2
Moos, Malcolm Charles	1
Neustadt, Richard Elliott	1960s-2
Padover, Saul Kussiel	1
Perkins, James Alfred	5, 1960s-2
Pool, Ithiel de Sola	1
Simon, Herbert A(lexander)	6
Voorhis, Horace Jeremiah ("Jerry")	1
Wildavsky, Aaron Bernard	3

Politician (Governor)

Adams, (Llewellyn) Sherman	2
Agnew, Spiro Theodore	1960s-1
Aiken, George David	1, 1960s-1
Arnall, Ellis Gibbs	3
Baldwin, Raymond Earl	2
Barnett, Ross Robert	2, 1960s-1
Benson, Elmer Austin	1
Blanton, (Leonard) Ray	4
Bowles, Chester Bliss ("Chet")	2, 1960s-1
Bricker, John William	2
Brown, Edmund Gerald ("Pat")	4
Casey, Robert Patrick ("Spike")	6
Chafee, John Hubbard	5
Chandler, Albert Benjamin ("Happy")	3
Chiles, Lawton Mainor, Jr.	5
Clements, Earle C.	1
Coleman, J(ames) P(lemon)	3
Collins, (Thomas) LeRoy	3
Connally, John Bowden, Jr.	3
Daniel, Price Marion	2
Davis, James Houston ("Jimmie")	6
DiSalle, Michael Vincent	1
Fannin, Paul Jones	6
Faubus, Orval Eugene	4
Folsom, James	2

	Volume
Politician (Governor) (*continued*)	
Furcolo, (John) Foster	4
Grasso, Ella Rosa Giovanna Oliva Tambussi	1
Harriman, William Averell	2, 1960s-1
Hildreth, Horace Augustus	2
Hughes, Harold Everett	4
Johnson, Paul Burney	1
Jordan, Leonard Beck ("Len")	1
Kerner, Otto, Jr.	1960s-1
Landon, Alf(red) Mossman	2
Lausche, Frank John	2
Lee, J(oseph) Bracken ("Brack")	4
Lodge, John Davis	1
McCall, Thomas William Lawson	1
Meyner, Robert Baumle	2
Muskie, Edmund Sixtus	1960s-2
Ogilvie, Richard Buell	2
Pastore, John Orlando	6
Peabody, Endicott ("Chub")	5
Perpich, Rudolph George ("Rudy")	4
Ray, Dixy Lee	4
Reagan, Ronald Wilson	1960s-2
Rhodes, James Allen ("Jim")	6
Ribicoff, Abraham Alexander	5
Rockefeller, Nelson Aldrich	1960s-2
Romney, George Wilcken	4
Russell, Charles Hinton	2
Sanford, (James) Terry	5
Shivers, (Robert) Allan	1
Snelling, Richard Arkwright	3
Stassen, Harold Edward	6
Stevenson, Adlai Ewing	1960s-2
Stratton, William Grant	6
Talmadge, Herman Eugene	6
Vanderbilt, William Henry	1
Volpe, John Anthony	4
Wallace, George Corley, Jr.	5, 1960s-2
Warren, Earl	1960s-2
Williams, G(erhard) Mennen	2
Williams, John Bell	1
Politician (Mayor)	
Alioto, Joseph Lawrence	5
Bono, Salvatore Phillip ("Sonny")	5
Bradley, Thomas ("Tom")	5
Brown, George Edward, Jr.	5
Celebrezze, Anthony Joseph	5
Clark, Joseph Sill, Jr.	2
Collins, John Frederick	4
Corning, Erastus, 2d	1
Daley, Richard Joseph, Sr.	1960s-1

	Volume
DiSalle, Michael Vincent	1
Eastwood, Clinton, Jr. ("Clint")	1960s-1
Hatcher, Richard Gordon	1960s-1
Hays, Wayne Levere	2
Hofheinz, Roy Mark	1
Humphrey, Hubert Horatio, Jr.	1960s-1
Lee, J(oseph) Bracken ("Brack")	4
Lindsay, John Vliet	6, 1960s-1
Loeb, Henry, III	3
Rhodes, James Allen ("Jim")	6
Rizzo, Frank Lazzaro	3
Seasongood, Murray	1
Stanford, Sally	1
Stokes, Carl Burton	4, 1960s-2
Wagner, Robert Ferdinand	3
Washington, Harold	2
Yorty, Samuel William	5
Young, Andrew Jackson, Jr.	1960s-2
Young, Coleman Alexander	5
Politician (Party Leader)	
Atwater, Harvey Leroy ("Lee")	3
Bernard, Anna Jones	1
Bliss, Ray Charles	1
Brown, Ron(ald) Harmon	4
Brownell, Herbert, Jr.	4
Burch, (Roy) Dean	3
Daley, Richard Joseph	1960s-1
Gates, John	3
Hall, Gus	6
Jackson, Henry Martin ("Scoop")	1, 1960s-1
Kahane, Meir	1960s-1
Kuhn, Margaret Eliza ("Maggie")	4
Lovestone, Jay	2
Morton, Thruston Ballard	1
O'Brien, Lawrence Francis, Jr. ("Larry")	2, 1960s-2
Scott, Hugh Doggett, Jr.	4
Wilentz, David Theodore	2
Yarborough, Ralph Webster	4
Politician (President of the United States)	
Johnson, Lyndon Baines	1960s-1
Kennedy, John Fitzgerald	1960s-1
Nixon, Richard Milhous	4, 1960s-2
Reagan, Ronald Wilson	1960s-2
Politician (Presidential Candidate)	
Bradley, William Warren ("Bill")	1960s-1
Bricker, John William	2
Chisholm, Shirley Anita	1960s-1
Church, Frank Forrester	1
Connally, John Bowden, Jr.	3
Cranston, Alan MacGregor	6
Glenn, John Herschel, Jr.	1960s-1

	Volume
Goldwater, Barry Morris	5, 1960s-1
Hall, Gus	6
Harriman, William Averell	2
Humphrey, Hubert Horatio, Jr.	1960s-1
Jackson, Henry Martin ("Scoop")	1, 1960s-1
Jackson, Jesse Louis	1960s-1
Kennedy, Robert Francis	1960s-1
Landon, Alf(red) Mossman	2
Lindsay, John Vliet	1960s-1
McCarthy, Eugene Joseph	1960s-2
McGovern, George Stanley	1960s-2
Mills, Wilbur Daigh	3
Muskie, Edmund Sixtus	4
Nader, Ralph	1960s-2
Perot, H(enry) Ross	1960s-2
Rockefeller, Nelson Aldrich	1960s-2
Romney, George Wilcken	4
Russell, Richard Brevard, Jr. ("Dick")	1960s-2
Smith, Margaret Chase	4
Spock, Benjamin McLane ("Dr. Spock")	5
Stassen, Harold Edward	6
Stevenson, Adlai Ewing	1960s-2
Symington, (William) Stuart, III	2
Tsongas, Paul Efthemios	5
Udall, Morris King	5
Wallace, George Corley, Jr.	5, 1960s-2
Yorty, Samuel William	5

Politician (State Legislator)

Adams, (Llewellyn) Sherman	2
Aiken, George David	1, 1960s-1
Arnall, Ellis Gibbs	3
Boland, Edward Patrick	6
Bond, (Horace) Julian	1960s-1
Brown, George Edward, Jr.	5
Brownell, Herbert, Jr.	4
Bruce, David Kirkpatrick Este	1960s-1
Casey, Robert Patrick ("Spike")	6
Celebrezze, Anthony Joseph	5
Chafee, John Hubbard	5
Chiles, Lawton Mainor, Jr.	5
Collins, John Frederick	4
Collins, (Thomas) LeRoy	3
Cotton, Norris Henry	2
Daniel, Price Marion	2
Diggs, Charles Cole, Jr.	5
Dixon, Julian C.	6
Ervin, Samuel James, Jr.	1
Fascell, Dante Bruno	5
Fenwick, Millicent Hammond	3
Fish, Hamilton	3
Forbes, Malcolm Stevenson	2

	Volume
Gonzalez, Henry Barbosa	6
Grasso, Ella Rosa Giovanna Oliva Tambussi	1
Hayden, Thomas Emmett ("Tom")	1960s-1
Hays, Wayne Levere	2
Henry, Aaron Edd Jackson	5
Hildreth, Horace Augustus	2
Jordan, Barbara Charline	4
Lodge, Henry Cabot, Jr.	1, 1960s-1
Matsunaga, Spark Masayuki ("Sparkie")	2
Meyner, Robert Baumle	2
Mink, Patsy Matsu Takemoto	6
Moakley, John Joseph ("Joe")	6
Muskie, Edmund Sixtus	4, 1960s-1
Neuberger, Maurine Brown	6
O'Neill, Thomas Philip, Jr. ("Tip")	4
Pastore, John Orlando	6
Perpich, Rudolph George ("Rudy")	4
Ribicoff, Abraham Alexander	5
Ruppert, Jacob	Sports-2
Russell, Richard Brevard, Jr. ("Dick")	1960s-2
Shivers, (Robert) Allan	1
Spence, Floyd D(avidson)	6
Stennis, John Cornelius	4
Stokes, Carl Burton	1960s-2
Taft, Robert, Jr.	3
Unruh, Jesse Marvin	2
Vinson, Carl	1
Wagner, Robert Ferdinand	3
Wallace, George Corley	5, 1960s-2
Washington, Harold	2
Yorty, Samuel William	5
Young, Coleman Alexander	5

Politician (United States Representative)

Abzug, Bella	5, 1960s-1
Albert, Carl Bert	6
Arends, Leslie Cornelius	1
Aspin, Les(lie), Jr.	4
Bingham, Jonathan Brewster ("Jack")	2
Blanton, (Leonard) Ray	4
Boland, Edward Patrick	6
Bono, Salvatore Phillip ("Sonny")	5
Bowles, Chester Bliss ("Chet")	2
Brown, George Edward, Jr.	5
Bunning, James Paul David ("Jim")	Sports-1
Burdick, Quentin Northrop	3
Burton, Phillip	1
Case, Clifford Philip	1
Celler, Emanuel	1
Chisholm, Shirley Anita	1960s-1
Clements, Earle Chester	1
Cotton, Norris Henry	2

	Volume
Politician (United States Representative) (*continued*)	
Curtis, Carl Thomas	6
Diggs, Charles Coles, Jr.	5
Dirksen, Everett McKinley	1960s-1
Dixon, Julian C.	6
Ervin, Samuel James, Jr.	1
Fascell, Dante Bruno	5
Fenwick, Millicent Hammond	3
Fish, Hamilton	3
Fulbright, J(ames) William	4, 1960s-1
Furcolo, (John) Foster	4
Gonzalez, Henry Barbosa	6
Gore, Albert Arnold, Sr.	5
Grasso, Ella Rosa Giovanna Oliva	
Tambussi	1
Green, Edith Starrett	2
Halleck, Charles Abraham	2
Hays, (Lawrence) Brooks	1
Hays, Wayne Levere	2
Heinz, Henry John, III	3
Hill, (Joseph) Lister	1
Hruska, Roman Lee	5
Jackson, Henry Martin ("Scoop")	1, 1960s-1
Javits, Jacob Koppel	2
Johnson, Lyndon Baines	1960s-1
Jordan, Barbara Charline	4
Judd, Walter Henry	4
Largent, Steve	Sports-2
Lewis, John Robert	1960s-1
Lindsay, John Vliet	6, 1960s-1
Lodge, John Davis	1
Lowenstein, Allard Kenneth	1960s-1
Luce, Clare Boothe	2
McCarthy, Eugene Joseph	1960s-2
McGovern, George Stanley	1960s-2
Madden, Ray John	2
Magnuson, Warren Grant	2
Mansfield, Michael Joseph ("Mike")	6
Mathias, Robert Bruce ("Bob")	Sports-2
Matsunaga, Spark Masayuki ("Sparkie")	2
Metcalfe, Ralph Horace	Sports-2
Mills, Wilbur Daigh	3
Mink, Patsy Matsu Takemoto	6
Moakley, John Joseph ("Joe")	6
Morton, Thruston Ballard	1
Nixon, Richard Milhous	1960s-2
O'Neill, Thomas Philip, Jr. ("Tip")	4
Osborne, Thomas William ("Tom")	Sports-2
Passman, Otto Ernest	2
Pepper, Claude Denson	2
Powell, Adam Clayton, Jr.	1960s-2
Pucinski, Roman Gordon	6
Randolph, Jennings	5

	Volume
Reuss, Henry Schoellkopf	6
Ribicoff, Abraham Alexander	5
Roosevelt, James	3
Ryun, James Ronald ("Jim")	1960s-2
Scott, Hugh Doggett, Jr.	4
Smith, Margaret Chase	4
Sparkman, John Jackson	1
Spence, Floyd D(avidson)	6
Staggers, Harley Orrin	3
Stratton, William Grant	6
Taft, Robert, Jr.	3
Tsongas, Paul Efthemios	5
Udall, Morris King	5
Ullman, Al(bert) Conrad	2
Velde, Harold Himmel	1
Vinson, Carl	1
Voorhis, Horace Jeremiah ("Jerry")	1
Washington, Harold	2
Whitten, Jamie Lloyd	4
Williams, John Bell	1
Wylie, Chalmers Pangburn	5
Yates, Sidney Richard	6
Yorty, Samuel William	5
Young, Andrew Jackson, Jr.	1960s-2
Young, Stephen M.	1
Politician (United States Senator)	
Aiken, George David	1, 1960s-1
Allott, Gordon Llewellyn	2
Baldwin, Raymond Earl	2
Benson, Elmer Austin	1
Bible, Alan Harvey	2
Bradley, William Warren ("Bill")	1960s-1
Bricker, John William	2
Brooke, Edward William, III	1960s-1
Bunning, James Paul David ("Jim")	Sports-1
Burdick, Quentin Northrop	3
Cannon, Howard Walter	6
Case, Clifford P.	1
Chafee, John Hubbard	5
Chandler, Albert Benjamin ("Happy")	3
Chiles, Lawton Mainor, Jr.	5
Church, Frank Forrester	1
Clark, Joseph Sill, Jr.	2
Clements, Earle C.	1
Cooper, John Sherman	3
Cotton, Norris Henry	2
Coverdell, Paul Douglas	6
Cranston, Alan MacGregor	6
Curtis, Carl Thomas	6
Daniel, Price Marion	2
Dirksen, Everett McKinley	1960s-1
Eastland, James Oliver	2
Ervin, Samuel James, Jr.	1

	Volume
Fannin, Paul Jones	6
Ferguson, Homer Samuel	1
Fulbright, J(ames) William	4, 1960s-1
Glenn, John Herschel, Jr.	1960s-1
Goldwater, Barry Morris	5, 1960s-1
Gore, Albert Arnold, Sr.	5
Gruening, Ernest	1960s-1
Hayakawa, S(amuel) I(chiye)	3, 1960s-1
Heinz, Henry John, III	3
Hill, (Joseph) Lister	1
Hruska, Roman Lee	5
Hughes, Harold Everett	4
Humphrey, Hubert Horatio, Jr.	1960s-1
Jackson, Henry Martin ("Scoop")	1, 1960s-1
Javits, Jacob Koppel	2
Jenner, William Ezra	1
Johnson, Lyndon Baines	1960s-1
Jordan, Barbara Charline	4
Jordan, Leonard Beck ("Len")	1
Kennedy, Edward Moore ("Ted")	1960s-1
Kennedy, John Fitzgerald	1960s-1
Kennedy, Robert Francis	1960s-1
Lausche, Frank John	2
Lodge, Henry Cabot, Jr.	1, 1960s-1
McCarthy, Eugene Joseph	1960s-2
McGee, Gale William	3
McGovern, George Stanley	1960s-2
Magnuson, Warren Grant	2
Mansfield, Michael Joseph ("Mike")	6
Matsunaga, Spark Masayuki ("Sparkie")	2
Mink, Patsy Matsu Takemoto	6
Morse, Wayne Lyman	1960s-2
Morton, Thruston Ballard	1
Moynihan, Daniel Patrick	1960s-2
Murphy, George Lloyd	3
Muskie, Edmund Sixtus	4, 1960s-2
Neuberger, Maurine Brown	6
Nixon, Richard Milhous	4, 1960s-2
Pastore, John Orlando	6
Pepper, Claude Denson	2
Randolph, Jennings	5
Ribicoff, Abraham Alexander	5
Russell, Richard Brevard, Jr. ("Dick")	1960s-2
Sanford, (James) Terry	5
Scott, Hugh Doggett, Jr.	4
Smith, Margaret Chase	4
Sparkman, John Jackson	1
Stennis, John Cornelius	4
Symington, (William) Stuart, III	2
Taft, Robert, Jr.	3
Talmadge, Herman Eugene	6
Taylor, Glen Hearst	1
Tower, John Goodwin	3

	Volume
Tsongas, Paul Efthemios	5
Wellstone, Paul David	6
Williams, John James	2
Yarborough, Ralph Webster	4
Young, Stephen M.	1

Politician (Vice President of the United States)

Agnew, Spiro Theodore	4, 1960s-1
Humphrey, Hubert Horatio, Jr.	1960s-1
Johnson, Lyndon Baines	1960s-1
Nixon, Richard Milhous	4, 1960s-2
Rockefeller, Nelson Aldrich	1960s-2

Politician (Vice-Presidential Candidate)

Bricker, John William	2
LeMay, Curtis Emerson	2, 1960s-1
Lodge, Henry Cabot, Jr.	1, 1960s-1
Muskie, Edmund Sixtus	4
Peabody, Endicott ("Chub")	5
Shriver, (Robert) Sargent, Jr.	1960s-2
Sparkman, John Jackson	1
Taylor, Glen Hearst	1
Warren, Earl	1960s-2

Preacher. *See* **Clergy.**

President of the United States. *See* **Politician (President of the United States).**

Presidential Adviser

Ackley, H(ugh) Gardner	5
Adams, (Llewellyn) Sherman	2
Anderson, Robert Bernerd	2
Ash, Roy Lawrence	1960s-1
Atwater, Harvey Leroy ("Lee")	3
Brownell, Herbert, Jr.	4
Bundy, McGeorge	4, 1960s-1
Burns, Arthur Frank	2, 1960s-1
Celebrezze, Anthony Joseph	5
Cherne, Leo	5
Clifford, Clark McAdams	5, 1960s-1
Cohen, Benjamin Victor	1
Connally, John Bowden, Jr.	3
Corcoran, Thomas Gardiner	1
Daniel, Price Marion	2
Daniels, Jonathan Worth	1
Dean, Arthur Hobson	2
Ehrlichman, John Daniel	5, 1960s-1
Eisenhower, Milton Stover	1
Finch, Robert Hutchinson	4
Fortas, Abraham ("Abe")	1, 1960s-1
Foster, Vincent William, Jr.	3
Galbraith, John Kenneth	1960s-1
Goldman, Eric Frederick	2
Hagerty, James Campbell	1
Haldeman, H(arry) R(obbins)	3, 1960s-1
Harlow, Bryce Nathaniel	2
Harriman, William Averell	2, 1960s-1

	Volume
Presidential Adviser (*continued*)	
Heller, Walter Wolfgang	2
Henderson, Leon	2
Hughes, Emmet John	1
Janeway, Eliot	3
Kennedy, Robert Francis	1960s-1
Keyserling, Leon Hirsch	2
Killian, James Rhyne, Jr.	2
Kissinger, Henry Alfred	1960s-1
Kistiakowsky, George Bogdan	1
Krim, Arthur B.	4
Larson, (Lewis) Arthur	3
MacLeish, Archibald	1
McNamara, Robert Strange	1960s-2
Mitchell, John Newton	2
Montgomery, Robert	1
Moos, Malcolm Charles	1
Moynihan, Daniel Patrick	1960s-2
Neustadt, Richard Elliott	1960s-2
O'Brien, Lawrence Francis, Jr. ("Larry")	2, 1960s-2
Pauley, Edwin Wendell	1
Prichard, Edward Fretwell, Jr.	1
Ribicoff, Abraham Alexander	5
Rostow, Walter Whitman ("Walt")	1960s-2
Samuelson, Paul Anthony	1960s-2
Scali, John Alfred	4
Schlesinger, Arthur Meier, Jr.	1960s-2
Smith, William French	2
Snyder, John Wesley	1
Sorensen, Theodore Chaikin ("Ted")	1960s-2
Stassen, Harold Edward	6
Stein, Herbert	5, 1960s-2
Taylor, Maxwell Davenport	2, 1960s-2
Vance, Cyrus Roberts	6, 1960s-2
Wallis, W(ilson) Allen	5
Weaver, Robert Clifton	5
Wiesner, Jerome Bert	4
Presidential Secretary	
Tully, Grace	1
Priest. *See* **Clergy.**	
Primatologist	
Fossey, Dian	1, 1960s-1
Washburn, Sherwood L(arned)	6
Printer	
Everson, William Oliver (Brother Antoninus)	4
Prison Guard	
Davis, John Henry	Sports-2
Producer (Film)	
Beatty, (Henry) Warren	1960s-1
Berman, Pandro Samuel	4
Broccoli, Albert Romolo ("Cubby")	4
Capra, Frank	3

	Volume
Clavell, James duMaresq	4
Fonda, Henry Jaynes	1, 1960s-1
Fonda, Peter Seymour	1960s-1
Foreman, Carl	1
Freleng, Isadore ("Friz")	4
Hecht, Harold	1
Henson, James Maury ("Jim")	2
Houseman, John	2
Jackson, George Anthony	6
Kanin, Garson	5
Kaye, Sylvia Fine	3
Kramer, Stanley Earl	6
Kubrick, Stanley	5, 1960s-1
Lancaster, Burt(on) Stephen	4
Lemmon, John Uhler, III ("Jack")	6
LeRoy, Mervyn	2
Levine, Joseph Edward	2
Lupino, Ida	4
Mankiewicz, Joseph Leo	3
Merrick, David	6
Pakula, Alan Jay	5
Parks, Gordon, Sr.	1960s-2
Pasternak, Joseph Herman ("Joe")	3
Preminger, Otto Ludwig	2
Quinn, Anthony Rudolph Oaxaca	6
Redford, (Charles) Robert, Jr.	1960s-2
Ritt, Martin	2
Roach, Harold Eugene ("Hal")	3
Roddenberry, Eugene Wesley ("Gene")	3
Siegel, Don	3
Skolsky, Sidney	1
Spiegel, Sam(uel)	1
Steel, Dawn Leslie	5
Susskind, David Howard	2, 1960s-2
Wallis, Harold Brent ("Hal")	2
Welles, Orson	1
Wilder, Samuel ("Billy")	6
Wiseman, Frederick	1960s-2
Wyler, William	1
Producer (Radio and Television)	
Arnaz, Desi	2
Arledge, Roone Pinckney, Jr.	6
Aubrey, James Thomas, Jr.	1960s-1
Autry, (Orvon) Gene	5
Ball, Lucille Désirée	2
Bartholomew, Frederick Llewellyn ("Freddie")	3
Cohen, Alexander H(enry)	6
Cooney, Joan Ganz	1960s-1
De Cordova, Frederick Timmins ("Fred")	6
Friendly, Fred W.	5
Funt, Allen	5
Goodson, Mark	3

Volume

Hanna, William Denby ("Bill") — 6
Hewitt, Don S. — 1960s-1
Jackson, George Anthony — 6
James, Dennis — 5
Landon, Michael — 3
Leonard, Sheldon — 5, 1960s-1
Liebman, Max — 1
Montgomery, Robert — 1
Roach, Harold Eugene ("Hal") — 3
Roddenberry, Eugene Wesley ("Gene") — 3, 1960s-2
Rountree, Martha — 5
Serling, Rodman Edward ("Rod") — 1960s-2
Siegel, Don — 3
Susskind, David Howard — 2, 1960s-2
Tartikoff, Brandon — 5
Thomas, Danny — 3
Wasserman, Lewis Robert ("Lew") — 6
Weaver, Sylvester Laflin, Jr. ("Pat") — 6
Webb, John Randolph ("Jack") — 1

Producer (Recordings)

Atkins, Chester Burton ("Chet") — 6
Dixon, Willie James — 3
Gordy, Berry, Jr. — 1960s-1
Hammond, John Henry, Jr. — 2
Jackson, George Anthony — 6
Notorious B.I.G. ("Biggie Smalls") — 5
Robinson, William, Jr. ("Smokey") — 1960s-2
Sackler, Howard Oliver — 1960s-2
Spector, Philip Harvey ("Phil") — 1960s-2
Warhol, Andy — 1960s-2
Wilson, Carl Dean — 5
Zappa, Francis Vincent ("Frank") — 1960s-2

Producer (Stage)

Abbott, George Francis — 4
Cohen, Alexander H(enry) — 6
Crawford, Cheryl — 2
Ferrer, José — 3
Houseman, John — 2
Jessel, George Albert ("Georgie") — 1
Kanin, Garson — 5
Le Gallienne, Eva — 3
Logan, Joshua Lockwood, III — 2
Ludlum, Robert — 6
Merrick, David — 6
Papp, Joseph — 3, 1960s-2
Schechner, Richard — 1960s-2
Selznick, Irene Mayer — 2
Sillman, Leonard Dexter — 1
Stewart, Ellen — 1960s-2
Styne, Jule — 4
Welles, Orson — 1

Professor. *See* **Educator.**

Volume

Psychiatrist

Bender, Lauretta — 2
Fine, Reuben — 3
Kline, Nathan Schellenberg — 1
Menninger, Karl Augustus — 2
Sackler, Arthur Mitchell — 2

Psychic

Dixon, Jeane Lydia — 5

Psychoanalyst

Bettelheim, Bruno — 2
Deutsch, Helene Rosenbach — 1
Erikson, Erik Homburger — 4
Kardiner, Abram — 1

Psychologist

Bender, Lauretta — 2
Bettelheim, Bruno — 2
Chall, Jeanne Sternlicht — 1960s-1
Clark, Kenneth Bancroft — 1960s-1
Clark, Mamie Phipps — 1
Davis, (William) Allison — 1
Dichter, Ernest — 3
Festinger, Leon — 2
Gardner, John William — 6, 1960s-1
Hathaway, Starke Rosencrans — 1
Herrnstein, Richard Julius — 4
Hooker, Evelyn Gentry — 4
Jensen, Arthur Robert — 1960s-1
Kohlberg, Lawrence — 2
Leary, Timothy Francis — 4
McGill, William James — 5
Milgram, Stanley — 1
Monroe, Marion — 1
Rogers, Carl Ransom — 2
Salk, Lee — 3
Skinner, B(urrhus) F(rederic) — 2
Wechsler, David — 1

Psychotherapist

May, Rollo Reece — 4
Perls, Laura — 2

Public Relations Executive. *See* **Business Executive (Public Relations).**

Public Opinion Researcher

Gallup, George Horace — 1
Lubell, Samuel — 2

Publisher (Books)

Ballantine, Ian Keith — 4
Boni, Albert — 1
Brett, George Platt, Jr. — 1
Cerf, Bennett Albert — 1960s-1
Delacorte, George Thomas, Jr. — 3
Espy, Willard Richard ("Wede") — 5
Hillegass, Clifton Keith — 6

	Volume
Publisher (Books) (*continued*)	
Jovanovich, William Ilija ("Bill")	6
Klopfer, Donald Simon	2
Knopf, Alfred Abraham	1
Laughlin, James	5
McCormick, Kenneth Dale	5
Praeger, Frederick Amos	4
Regnery, Henry	4
Schwann, William Joseph	5
Scribner, Charles, Jr.	4
Sheed, Francis Joseph ("Frank")	1
Shimkin, Leon	2
Wallace, (William Roy) DeWitt, and Lila (Bell) Acheson Wallace	1
Publisher (Catalog)	
Schwann, William Joseph	5
Publisher (Magazines)	
Berlin, Richard Emmett	2
Cowles, Gardner ("Mike")	1
Forbes, Malcolm Stevenson	2
Gaines, William Maxwell	3
Hearst, William Randolph, Jr.	3
Ingersoll, Ralph McAllister	1
Johnson, Robert Edward	4
Kennedy, John Fitzgerald, Jr.	5
Parton, James	6
Rodale, Robert	2
Shepley, James Robinson	1
Steinem, Gloria Marie	1960s-2
Wallace, (William Roy) DeWitt, and Lila (Bell) Acheson Wallace	1
Publisher (Newsletters)	
Cherne, Leo	5
Schlafly, Phyllis Stewart	1960s-2
Stone, I. F.	2, 1960s-2
Publisher (Newspapers)	
Annenberg, Walter Hubert	6
Attwood, William Hollingsworth	2
Bates, Daisy Lee Gatson	5
Berlin, Richard Emmett	2
Bingham, (George) Barry, Sr.	2
Dedmon, Emmett	1
Gilbreth, Frank Bunker, Jr.	6
Golden, Harry	1
Graham, Katharine Meyer	6
Hearst, William Randolph, Jr.	3
Hobby, Oveta Culp	4
Ingersoll, Ralph McAllister	1
Knight, John Shively	1
Loeb, William	1
Loeb, Nackey Scripps	6

	Volume
Maynard, Robert Clyve	3
McGill, Ralph Emerson	1960s-2
Pope, Generoso Paul, Jr.	2
Ridder, Bernard Herman, Jr. ("Bernie")	6
Ridder, Eric	4
Sackler, Arthur Mitchell	2
Schiff, Dorothy	2
Smith, Hazel Brannon	1960s-2
Washington, Chester Lloyd, Jr. ("Chet")	1
Whitney, John Hay	1
Puppeteer	
Baird, William Britton ("Bil")	2
Henson, James Maury ("Jim")	2
Lewis, Shari	5
Smith, Robert Emil ("Buffalo Bob")	5
Tillstrom, Burr	1
Rabbi. *See* **Clergy.**	
Radio Personality	
Ace, Goodman	1
Allen, Mel(vin)	4
Allen, Stephen Valentine Patrick William ("Steve")	6, 1960s-1
Ameche, Don	3
Backus, James Gilmore ("Jim")	2
Buck, John Francis ("Jack")	6
Burns, George	5
Conover, Willis Clark, Jr.	4
Cosell, Howard	4
Day, Dennis	2
Fadiman, Clifton Paul	5
Faulk, John Henry	2
Fidler, James Marion ("Jimmy")	2
Francis, Arlene	6
Frederick, Pauline	2
Fredericks, Carlton	2
Garroway, David Cunningham	1
Gillars, Mildred Elizabeth Sisk ("Axis Sally")	2
Godfrey, Arthur (Morton)	1
Goulding, Ray(mond) Walter	2
Gray, Barry	4
Harmon, Thomas Dudley	2
Kaufman, Murray ("Murray the K")	1
Kieran, John Francis	1
Livingstone, Mary	1
Lomax, Alan	6
McNeill, Don(ald) Thomas	4
Moore, Garry	3
Morgan, Henry (Lerner von Ost)	4
Nelson, Eric Hilliard ("Rick")	1
Nelson, Harriet Hilliard	4

	Volume
Parks, Bert	3
Rowan, Carl T(homas)	6
Skolsky, Sidney	1
Smith, Kathryn Elizabeth ("Kate")	2
Smith, Robert Emil ("Buffalo Bob")	5
Swayze, John Cameron	4
Thomas, Lowell Jackson	1
Tracy, Arthur	5
Trout, Robert	6
Wallace, Mike	1960s-2
Williams, William B.	2
Wolfman Jack (Robert Weston Smith)	4, 1960s-2

Relief Administrator
| Keeny, Spurgeon Milton ("Sam") | 2 |

Religious Leader (Church of Scientology)
| Hubbard, L(afayette) Ron(ald) | 2 |

Religious Leader (Eastern Orthodox)
| Meyendorff, John | 3 |

Religious Leader (Episcopalian)
| Pike, James Albert, Jr. | 1960s-2 |
| Stokes, Anson Phelps, Jr. | 2 |

Religious Leader (Jewish)
Kelman, Wolfe	2
Lelyveld, Arthur Joseph	4
Potok, Chaim Tzvi	6
Prinz, Joachim	2
Schneerson, Menachem Mendel	4
Soloveitchik, Joseph Baer	3

Religious Leader (Lutheran)
| Preus, Jacob Aall Ottesen, Jr. ("Jake") | 4 |

Religious Leader (Mormon)
Arrington, Leonard James	5
Benson, Ezra Taft	4
Hunter, Howard William	4
Kimball, Spencer Woolley	1

Religious Leader (Nation of Islam)
| Cleage, Albert Buford, Jr. | 6 |
| Muhammad, Elijah | 1960s-2 |

Religious Leader (Presbyterian)
| Blake, Eugene Carson | 1 |

Religious Leader (Roman Catholic)
Bernardin, Joseph Louis	4
Bowman, Thea Bertha ("Sister Thea")	2
Cody, John Patrick	1
Cooke, Terence James	1
Krol, John Joseph	4
Manning, Timothy	2
Medeiros, Humberto Sousa	1
O'Connor, John Joseph	6
Perry, Harold Robert	3
Sheed, Francis Joseph ("Frank")	1

	Volume
Religious Leader (See also Clergy)	
Abernathy, Ralph David	2
Applewhite, Marshall Herff, Jr. ("Herff"; "Do")	5
Armstrong, Herbert W.	2
Bowman, Thea Bertha ("Sister Thea")	2
Hargis, Billy James	1960s-1
Hubbard, L(afayette) Ron(ald)	2
Kelman, Wolfe	2
Koresh, David	3
Meyendorff, John	3
Perlmutter, Nathan	2
Soloveitchik, Joseph Baer	3

Religious Leader (Shaker)
| Lindsay, Goldie Ina Ruby ("Eldress Bertha") | 2 |
| Soule, Gertrude May | 2 |

Religious Leader (Southern Baptist)
| Hays, (Lawrence) Brooks | 1 |
| King, Martin Luther, Sr. ("Daddy King") | 1 |

Religious Leader (United Methodist)
Armstrong, Herbert W.	2
Lord, John Wesley	2
Mueller, Reuben Herbert	1

Religious Leader (Worldwide Church of God)
| Armstrong, Herbert W. | 2 |

Religious Scholar
Bainton, Roland Herbert	1
Baron, Salo Wittmayer	2
Branscomb, (Bennett) Harvie	5
Brown Raymond Edward	5
Campbell, Joseph	2
Eliade, Mircea	2
Ellis, John Tracy	3
Finkelstein, Louis	3
Hartdegen, Stephen Joseph	2
Ladd, George Eldon	1
Lincoln, C(harles) Eric	6

Representative, United States. See Politician (United States Representative).

Restaurateur
Chen, Joyce	4
Dempsey, William Harrison ("Jack")	1
Fears, Thomas Jesse ("Tom")	6
Kriendler, H. Peter ("Pete")	6
Kroc, Ray(mond) Albert	1, 1960s-1
Marchetti, Gino John	Sports-2
Marriott, Alice Sheets	6
Marriott, J(ohn) Willard ("Bill")	1

	Volume
Restaurateur (*continued*)	
Sanders, Harland David ("Colonel")	1960s-2
Schacht, Al(exander)	1
Stanford, Sally	1
Thomas, Rex David ("Dave")	6, 1960s-2
Rocket Scientist	
Debus, Kurt Heinrich	1
Gilruth, Robert Rowe	6
Von Braun, Wernher	1960s-2
Rock Star. *See* **Musician (Rock).**	
Runner. *See* **Athlete (Track and Field).**	
Scientific Administrator	
Bradbury, Norris Edwin	5
Hagen, John Peter	2
Hershey, Alfred Day	5, 1960s-1
Luria, Salvador Edward	3, 1960s-1
Salk, Jonas Edward	4
Townes, Charles Hard	1960s-2
Scientist. *See* **individual fields.**	
Screenwriter. *See* **Author (Screenplays).**	
Sculptor. *See* **Artist (Sculptor).**	
Seismologist	
Richter, Charles Francis	1
Semanticist	
Hayakawa, S(amuel) I(chiye)	3, 1960s-1
Senator, United States. *See* **Politician (United States Senator).**	
Sex Researcher	
Masters, William Howell	6
Masters, William Howell, and Virginia Eshelman Johnson	1960s-1
Singer. *See* **Musician.**	
Socialite	
Duke, Doris	3
Harkness, Rebekah West	1, 1960s-1
Harriman, Pamela Beryl Digby Churchill Hayward	5
Hemingway, Margaux	4
Tree, Mary Endicott Peabody FitzGerald ("Marietta")	3
Tully, Alice Bigelow	3
Whitney, Betsey Maria Cushing	5
Windsor, Wallis Warfield (Simpson), Duchess of	2
Sociologist	
Bell, Daniel	1960s-1
Coleman, James Samuel	4, 1960s-1
Drake, (John Gibbs) St. Clair	2
Goffman, Erving Manual	1
Janowitz, Morris	2

	Volume
Kohlberg, Lawrence	2
Lynd, Helen Merrell	1
Mills, C(harles) Wright	1960s-2
Mumford, Lewis Charles	2
Peter, Laurence Johnston	2
Riesman, David, Jr.	6
Rosten, Leo Calvin	5
Samora, Julian	1960s-2
Shils, Edward Albert	4
Whyte, William Foote	6
Wilson, Logan	2
Soldier (*See also* **Army Officer**)	
Calley, William Laws, Jr.	1960s-1
Keeny, Spurgeon Milton ("Sam")	2
Kelly, Charles E. ("Commando")	1
Urban, Matt Louis	4
Songwriter (*See also* **Musician**)	
Allen, Stephen Valentine Patrick William ("Steve")	6, 1960s-1
Arlen, Harold	2
Ashman, Howard Elliot	3
Autry, (Orvon) Gene	5
Axton, Hoyt Wayne	5
Baez, Joan Chandos	1960s-1
Berlin, Irving	2
Blake, James Hubert ("Eubie")	1
Bono, Salvatore Phillip ("Sonny")	5, 1960s-1
Caesar, Irving	4
Cahn, Sammy	3
Calloway, Cab	4
Carmichael, Howard Hoagland ("Hoagy")	1
Carter, Betty	5
Cash, John R. ("Johnny")	1960s-1
Chapin, Harry Forster	1
Clayton-Thomas, David	1960s-1
Collins, Judy	1960s-1
Crosby, Stills, and Nash	1960s-2
Denver, John	5
Dietz, Howard	1
Dorsey, Thomas Andrew	3
Dylan, Bob	1960s-1
Evans, Dale	6
Fain, Sammy	2
Fariña, Richard George	1960s-1
Fogerty, John Cameron	1960s-1
Garcia, Jerry	4
Gaye, Marvin Pentz, Jr.	1, 1960s-1
Gershwin, Ira	1
Gordy, Berry, Jr.	1960s-1
Guthrie, Arlo Davy	1960s-1
Haggard, Merle Ronald	1960s-1

	Volume
Harburg, Edgar Yipsel ("Yip")	1
Harkness, Rebekah West	1, 1960s-1
Hays, Lee	1
Hendrix, James Marshall ("Jimi"; "Jimmy"; "Maurice James")	1960s-1
Hooker, John Lee	6
Hopkins, Sam ("Lightnin'")	1
Hunter, Alberta	1
Jenkins, Gordon Hill	1
Jennings, Waylon Arnold	6
Kaye, Sylvia Fine	3
Lane, Burton	5
Larson, Jonathan	4
Lee, Peggy	6
Lerner, Alan Jay	2
Lincoln, C(harles) Eric	6
Loewe, Frederick	2
MacDermot, (Arthur Terence) Galt	1960s-2
Mancini, Henry Nicola	4, 1960s-2
Marks, John D. ("Johnny")	1
Mayfield, Curtis Lee	5
Mercer, John Herndon ("Johnny")	1960s-2
Miller, Roger Dean	3
Monroe, William Smith ("Bill")	4
Morrison, James Douglas ("Jim")	1960s-2
Nilsson, Harry Edward, II	4
Ochs, Philip David ("Phil")	1960s-2
Orbison, Roy Kelton	2, 1960s-2
Perkins, Carl Lee	5
Peter, Paul and Mary	1960s-2
Phillips, John Edmund Andrew	6, 1960s-2
Rado, James, and Gerome Ragni	1960s-2
Ramone, Joey	6
Ray, John Alvin ("Johnnie")	2
Rich, Charles Allan ("Charlie")	4
Robbins, Marty	1
Robinson, William, Jr. ("Smokey")	1960s-2
Sainte-Marie, Buffy	1960s-2
Schwartz, Arthur	1
Seeger, Peter R. ("Pete")	1960s-2
Silverstein, Shel(don) Allan	5
Simon and Garfunkel	1960s-2
Slick, Grace Wing	1960s-2
Snow, Clarence Eugene ("Hank")	5
Sonny and Cher	1960s-2
Spector, Philip Harvey ("Phil")	1960s-2
Streisand, Barbra	1960s-2
Styne, Jule	4
Tiny Tim (Herbert Butros Khaury)	4
Tormé, Mel(vin) Howard	5
Tubb, Ernest Dale	1
Van Heusen, James ("Jimmy")	2

	Volume
Warren, Harry	1
Waters, Muddy	1
Webb, James Layne ("Jimmy")	1960s-2
Willson, (Robert Reiniger) Meredith	1
Wilson, Brian Douglas	1960s-2
Wilson, Carl Dean	5
Wonder, Stevie	1960s-2

Sports Administrator

Brundage, Avery	Sports-1
Byers, Walter	Sports-1

Sports Broadcaster/Commentator

Abel, Sidney Gerald ("Sid")	6, Sports-1
Albert, Frank Culling ("Frankie")	6
Allen, Marcus LeMarr	Sports-1
Allen, Mel(vin)	4
Ashburn, Don Richard ("Richie")	5
Barber, Walter Lanier ("Red")	Sports-1
Barkley, Charles Wade	Sports-1
Barry, Richard Francis, III ("Rick")	Sports-1
Boudreau, Louis ("Lou")	6
Bradshaw, Terry Paxton	Sports-1
Brickhouse, John Beasley ("Jack")	5, Sports-1
Buck, John Francis ("Jack")	6
Butkus, Richard Marvin ("Dick")	Sports-1
Button, Richard Totten ("Dick")	Sports-1
Caray, Harry Christopher	5, Sports-1
Conigliaro, Anthony Richard ("Tony")	2
Cosell, Howard	4, Sports-1
Costas, Robert Quinlan ("Bob")	Sports-1
Cousy, Robert ("Bob")	Sports-1
Cunningham, William John ("Billy")	Sports-1
Dean, Jay Hanna ("Dizzy")	Sports-1
Deford, Frank	Sports-1
Demaret, James Newton ("Jimmy")	1
De Varona, Donna	1960s-1, Sports-1
Dickerson, Eric Demetric	Sports-1
Ditka, Mike	Sports-1
Drysdale, Don(ald) Scott	3, 1960s-1, Sports-1
Durocher, Leo Ernest	3, Sports-1
Evert, Christine Marie ("Chris")	Sports-1
Fleming, Peggy Gale	1960s-1, Sports-1
Frazier, Walt, II ("Clyde")	Sports-1
Frick, Ford Christopher	Sports-1
Frisch, Frank Francis	Sports-1
Gifford, Frank Newton	Sports-1
Glickman, Martin Irving ("Marty")	6, Sports-1
Gowdy, Curt(is)	Sports-1
Grange, Harold Edward ("Red")	3, Sports-1
Harmon, Thomas Dudley ("Tom")	2, Sports-1

	Volume
Sports Broadcaster/Commentator (*continued*)	
Hearn, Francis Dayle ("Chick")	6
Hoyt, Waite Charles ("Schoolboy")	1
Jenner, (William) Bruce	Sports-1
Jones, David ("Deacon")	Sports-1
Kaline, Al(bert) William	Sports-1
Kiner, Ralph McPherran	Sports-1
Koufax, Sanford ("Sandy")	1960s-1,
	Sports-1
Kramer, John Albert ("Jack")	Sports-1
Leonard, Ray Charles ("Sugar Ray")	Sports-2
Liquori, Martin William, Jr. ("Marty")	Sports-2
Lujack, John Christopher, Jr. ("Johnny")	Sports-2
McCormick, Frank Andrew	1
McEnroe, John Patrick, Jr.	Sports-2
McKay, James McManus ("Jim")	Sports-2
McNamee, Graham	Sports-2
Madden, John Earl	Sports-2
Meyers, Ann Elizabeth	Sports-2
Middlecoff, (Emmett) Cary ("Doc")	5
Morgan, Joe Leonard	Sports-2
Nelson, (John) Byron	Sports-2
Olsen, Merlin Jay	Sports-2
Ott, Mel(vin) Thomas	Sports-2
Palmer, James Alvin ("Jim")	Sports-2
Reese, Harold Henry ("Pee Wee")	5, Sports-2
Rigby, Cathy	1960s-2,
	Sports-2
Rote, (William) Kyle, Sr.	6
Russell, William Felton ("Bill")	1960s-2,
	Sports-2
Sanders, Summer Elizabeth	Sports-2
Sarazen, Gene	5, Sports-2
Scully, Vin(cent) Edward	1960s-2,
	Sports-2
Seaver, George Thomas ("Tom")	Sports-2
Shorter, Frank Charles	Sports-2
Snider, Edwin Donald ("Duke")	Sports-2
Snyder, James ("Jimmy the Greek")	4, Sports-2
Stern, William ("Bill")	Sports-2
Thomas, Isiah Lord, III	Sports-2
Trabert, Marion Anthony ("Tony")	Sports-2
Traynor, Harold Joseph ("Pie")	Sports-2
Unitas, John Constantine ("Johnny")	Sports-2
Valvano, James Thomas ("Jim")	3
Walton, William Theodore, III ("Bill")	Sports-2
Wilkinson, Charles Burnham ("Bud")	4, Sports-2
Sports Coach (Baseball)	
Alston, Walter Emmons	1
Dickey, William Malcolm ("Bill")	4
Grimes, Burleigh Arland	1

	Volume
Herman, William Jennings ("Billy")	3
Kelly, George Lange ("Highpockets")	1
Mathews, Edwin Lee ("Eddie")	6
Reese, Harold Henry ("Pee Wee")	5
Schacht, Al(exander)	1
Slaughter, Enos Bradsher ("Country")	6
Stargell, Wilver Dornel ("Willie")	6
Sports Coach (Basketball)	
Allen, Forrest Clare ("Phog")	Sports-1
Archibald, Nathaniel ("Nate"; "Tiny")	Sports-1
Auerbach, Arnold ("Red")	Sports-1
Baylor, Elgin	Sports-1
Bee, Clair Francis	1
Bird, Larry Joe	Sports-1
Cousy, Robert ("Bob")	Sports-1
Cunningham, William John ("Billy")	Sports-1
Donovan, Anne Theresa	Sports-1
Drexler, Clyde	Sports-1
Gaines, Clarence ("Bighouse")	Sports-1
Gates, William ("Pop")	5
Hannum, Alex	6
Haskins, Donald Lee	Sports-1
Holman, Nathan ("Nat")	4
Holzman, William ("Red")	5
Iba, (Payne) Henry ("Hank")	3
Jackson, Philip Douglas ("Phil")	Sports-1
Johnson, Earvin, Jr. ("Magic")	Sports-1
Jones, K. C.	Sports-1
Knight, Robert Montgomery ("Bob")	Sports-1
Krzyzewski, Michael William ("Mike")	Sports-1
Lapchick, Joseph Bohomiel ("Joe")	Sports-2
Lemons, A. E. ("Abe")	6
Lieberman-Cline, Nancy	Sports-2
Luisetti, Angelo Enrico ("Hank")	6, Sports-2
McGuire, Francis Joseph ("Frank")	4
Miller, Cheryl DeAnn	Sports-2
Newell, Peter ("Pete")	Sports-2
Pollard, James Clifford ("Jim")	Sports-2
Reed, Willis, Jr.	Sports-2
Riley, Pat(rick) James	Sports-2
Ripley, Elmer Horton	1
Rupp, Adolph Frederick	Sports-2
Russell, William Felton ("Bill")	1960s-2
Schayes, Adolph ("Dolph")	Sports-2
Smith, Dean Edwards	Sports-2
Staley, Dawn	Sports-2
Summitt, Pat(ricia) Head	Sports-2
Thomas, Isiah Lord, III	Sports-2
Thompson, John Robert, Jr.	Sports-2
Valvano, James Thomas ("Jim")	3
West, Jerry Alan	Sports-2

Volume

Wilkens, Leonard Randolph ("Lenny") Sports-2
Wooden, John Robert 1960s-2, Sports-2

Sports Coach (Figure Skating)
Heiss Jenkins, Carol Elizabeth Sports-1
Sports Coach (Football)
Albert, Frank Culling ("Frankie") 6
Allen, George Herbert 2
Battles, Clifford Franklin ("Gyp") 1
Baugh, Samuel Adrian ("Sammy") Sports-1
Berry, Raymond Emmett Sports-1
Blaik, Earl Henry ("Red") 2, Sports-1
Blanchard, Felix Anthony, Jr. ("Doc") Sports-1
Bowden, Robert Cleckler ("Bobby") Sports-1
Brown, Paul Eugene ("P. B.") 3
Bryant, Paul William ("Bear") 1
Camp, Walter Chauncey Sports-1
Crisler, Herbert Orin ("Fritz") 1
Daugherty, Hugh ("Duffy") 2
Davis, Al(len) Sports-1
Ditka, Mike Sports-1
Dodd, Robert Lee ("Bobby") 2
Engle, Charles Albert ("Rip") 1
Ewbank, Wilbur Charles ("Weeb") 5
Fears, Thomas Jesse ("Tom") 6, Sports-1
Friedman, Benjamin ("Benny") 1
Gaines, Clarence Edward, Sr.
  ("Bighouse") Sports-1
Gibbs, Joe Jackson Sports-1
Gillman, Sid(ney) Sports-1
Graham, Otto Everett, Jr. Sports-1
Gregg, (Alvis) Forrest Sports-1
Groza, Louis Roy ("Lou") 6
Halas, George 1
Hayes, Wayne Woodrow ("Woody") 2
Heffelfinger, William Walter ("Pudge") Sports-1
Hein, Mel(vin) John Sports-1
Heisman, John William ("Johnny") Sports-1
Kinard, Frank Manning ("Bruiser") 1
Lambeau, Earl Louis ("Curly") Sports-2
Landry, Thomas Wade ("Tom") 6, Sports-2
Lane, Richard ("Dick"; "Night Train") 6, Sports-2
Leahy, Francis William ("Frank") Sports-2
Lombardi, Vincent Thomas ("Vince") 1960s-1
McKay, John Harvey 6
McNally, John Victor ("Johnny Blood") 1, Sports-2
Madden, John Earl Sports-2
Noll, Charles Henry ("Chuck") Sports-2
Osborne, Thomas William ("Tom") Sports-2
Parcells, Duane Charles ("Bill") Sports-2
Paterno, Joseph Vincent ("Joe") Sports-2
Pollard, Frederick Douglass ("Fritz") 2

Volume

Robinson, Edward Gay ("Eddie") Sports-2
Rockne, Knute Kenneth Sports-2
Schwartzwalder, Floyd Burdette ("Ben") 3
Shula, Don(ald) Francis Sports-2
Stagg, Amos Alonzo, Sr. Sports-2
Starr, Bryan Bartlett ("Bart") Sports-2
Thorpe, James Francis ("Jim") Sports-2
Turner, Clyde Douglas ("Bulldog") 5, Sports-2
Van Brocklin, Norm(an) ("The
  Dutchman") 1
Walsh, William ("Bill") Sports-2
Warner, Glenn Scobey ("Pop") Sports-2
Waterfield, Robert Staton
  ("Bob"; "Rifle") 1
Wilkinson, Charles Burnham ("Bud") 4
Zuppke, Robert Carl ("Bob") Sports-2
Sports Coach (Golf)
Penick, Harvey Morrison 4
Sports Coach (Gymnastics)
Conner, Bart Sports-1
Karolyi, Béla Sports-1
Sports Coach (Hockey)
Abel, Sidney Gerald ("Sid") 6, Sports-1
Boucher, Frank Xavier Sports-1
Brooks, Herb(ert) P. Sports-1
Delvecchio, Alex Peter ("Fats") Sports-1
Esposito, Phil(ip) Anthony Sports-1
Patrick, (Curtis) Lester Sports-2
Schmidt, Milt(on) Conrad Sports-2
Shore, Edward William ("Eddie") 1, Sports-2
Sports Coach (Skiing)
Kidd, William Winston ("Billy") Sports-1
Sports Coach (Swimming)
Counsilman, James Edward ("Doc") Sports-1
Kiphuth, Robert John Herman ("Bob") Sports-1
Nyad, Diana Sports-2
Sports Coach (Tennis)
Budge, John Donald ("Don") 6
Marble, Alice Sports-2
Sports Coach (Track and Field)
Bowerman, William Jay ("Bill") 5
Elliot, James Francis ("Jumbo") 1
Warmerdam, Cornelius Anthony
  ("Dutch") Sports-2
Sports Coach (Weightlifting)
Kono, Tommy Tamio Sports-1
Sports Coach (Wrestling)
Gable, Dan(iel) Sports-1
Smith, John William Sports-2
Sports Executive (Auto Racing)
Earnhardt, (Ralph) Dale 6, Sports-1
France, William Henry Getty, Sr. 3, Sports-1

	Volume
Sports Executive (Auto Racing) (*continued*)	
Gibbs, Joe Jackson	Sports-1
Gurney, Dan(iel) Sexton	Sports-1
Penske, Roger S.	Sports-2
Sports Executive (Baseball)	
Aaron, Henry Louis ("Hank")	1960s-1, Sports-1
Autry, (Orvon) Gene	5
Brett, George Howard	Sports-1
Busch, August Anheuser, Jr. ("Gussie")	2
Carpenter, Robert Ruliph Morgan, Jr.	2
Chandler, Albert Benjamin ("Happy")	3
Collins, Edward Trowbridge ("Eddie")	Sports-1
Comiskey, Charles Albert	Sports-1
Cronin, Joseph Edward	1
Finley, Charles Oscar ("Charlie")	4
Foster, Andrew ("Rube")	Sports-1
Frick, Ford Christopher	Sports-1
Gehringer, Charles Leonard ("Charlie")	3, Sports-1
Giamatti, A(ngelo) Bartlett ("Bart")	2
Greenberg, Henry Benjamin ("Hank")	2, Sports-1
Griffith, Calvin Robertson	5
Griffith, Clark Calvin	Sports-1
Hofheinz, Roy Mark	1
Hubbard, (Robert) Cal	Sports-1
Hubbell, Carl Owen	2, Sports-1
Kauffman, Ewing Marion	3
Kiner, Ralph McPherran	Sports-1
Kroc, Ray(mond) Albert	1, 1960s-1
Landis, Kenesaw Mountain	Sports-2
Lane, Frank Charles	1
Lemon, Robert Granville ("Bob")	6
Mack, Connie	Sports-2
MacPhail, Leland Stanford, Sr. ("Larry")	Sports-2
Martin, Alfred Manuel, Jr. ("Billy")	2
Mathewson, Christopher ("Christy")	Sports-2
Richards, Paul Rapier	2
Rickey, Branch Wesley	Sports-2
Robinson, Frank, Jr.	1960s-2
Ruppert, Jacob	Sports-2
Steinbrenner, George Michael, III	Sports-2
Stoneham, Horace	2
Veeck, William Louis, Jr. ("Bill")	2, Sports-2
Williams, Edward Bennett	2
Wright, William Henry ("Harry")	Sports-2
Sports Executive (Basketball)	
Auerbach, Arnold ("Red")	Sports-1
Baylor, Elgin	Sports-1
Blazejowski, Carol Ann	Sports-1
Cunningham, William John ("Billy")	Sports-1
Hannum, Alex	6
Irish, Edward Simmons, Sr. ("Ned")	1
Jordan, Michael Jeffrey ("Air")	Sports-1

	Volume
Lieberman-Cline, Nancy	Sports-2
Mikan, George Lawrence, Jr.	Sports-2
Monroe, Earl Vernon, Jr.	Sports-2
Newell, Peter ("Pete")	Sports-2
O'Brien, Lawrence Francis, Jr. ("Larry")	2, 1960s-2
Reed, Willis, Jr.	Sports-2
Schayes, Adolph ("Dolph")	Sports-2
Stern, David	Sports-2
Thomas, Isiah Lord, III	Sports-2
West, Jerry Alan	Sports-2
Sports Executive (Football)	
Bell, DeBenneville ("Bert")	Sports-1
Brown, Paul Eugene ("P. B.")	3
Davis, Al(len)	Sports-1
DeBartolo, Edward John, Sr.	4
Graham, Otto Everett, Jr.	Sports-1
Halas, George	1, Sports-1
Hein, Mel(vin) John	Sports-1
Hirsch, Elroy Leon ("Crazylegs")	Sports-1
Hunt, Lamar	Sports-1
Jones, Jerral Wayne ("Jerry")	Sports-1
Lane, Richard ("Dick"; "Night Train")	6, Sports-2
Lombardi, Vincent Thomas ("Vince")	1960s-1
Marshall, George Preston	1960s-2, Sports-2
Mitchell, Robert Cornelius, Sr. ("Bobby")	Sports-2
Murchison, Clint(on) Williams, Jr.	2
Parcells, Duane Charles ("Bill")	Sports-2
Rooney, Arthur Joseph	2, Sports-2
Rozelle, Alvin Roy ("Pete")	4, 1960s-2, Sports-2
Starr, Bryan Bartlett ("Bart")	Sports-2
Thorpe, James Francis ("Jim")	Sports-2
Van Brocklin, Norm(an) Mack	Sports-2
Walsh, William ("Bill")	Sports-2
Williams, Edward Bennett	2
Young, Claude, Jr. ("Buddy")	1
Sports Executive (Hockey)	
Clarke, Robert Earle ("Bobby")	Sports-1
Delvecchio, Alex Peter ("Fats")	Sports-1
Esposito, Phil(ip) Anthony	Sports-1
Lemieux, Mario	Sports-2
Patrick, (Curtis) Lester	Sports-2
Schmidt, Milt(on) Conrad	Sports-2
Shore, Edward William ("Eddie")	1, Sports-2
Sports Executive (Soccer)	
Hunt, Lamar	Sports-1
Sports Executive (Tennis)	
Hunt, Lamar	Sports-1
King, Billie Jean Moffitt	1960s-1
Kramer, John Albert ("Jack")	Sports-1
Sports Executive (Volleyball)	
Chamberlain, Wilt(on) Norman	Sports-1

	Volume
Sports Manager (Baseball)	
Alston, Walter Emmons	1
Anderson, George Lee ("Sparky")	Sports-1
Anson, Adrian Constantine ("Cap," "Pop")	Sports-1
Appling, Lucius Benjamin, Jr. ("Luke")	3
Bell, James Thomas ("Cool Papa")	3, Sports-1
Berra, Lawrence Peter ("Yogi")	Sports-1
Boudreau, Louis ("Lou")	6
Bunning, James Paul David ("Jim")	Sports-1
Charleston, Oscar McKinley ("Charlie")	Sports-1
Cobb, Ty(rus) Raymond	Sports-1
Cochrane, Gordon Stanley ("Mickey")	Sports-1
Collins, Edward Trowbridge ("Eddie")	Sports-1
Comiskey, Charles Albert	Sports-1
Cronin, Joseph Edward	1
Dickey, William Malcolm ("Bill")	4
Durocher, Leo Ernest	3
Ewing, William ("Buck")	Sports-1
Foster, Andrew ("Rube")	Sports-1
Frisch, Frank Francis ("Frankie")	Sports-1
Griffith, Clark Calvin	Sports-1
Grimes, Burleigh Arland	1
Herman, William Jennings ("Billy")	3
Hornsby, Rogers ("Rajah")	Sports-1
Huggins, Miller James	Sports-1
Johnson, Walter Perry ("The Big Train")	Sports-1
Kelly, Michael Joseph ("King")	Sports-1
Lajoie, Nap(oleon)	Sports-2
Lemon, Robert Granville ("Bob")	6
Lindstrom, Frederick Charles, Jr. ("Lindy")	1
Lloyd, John Henry ("Pop")	Sports-2
Lyons, Theodore Amar ("Ted")	2
Mack, Connie	Sports-2
Martin, Alfred Manuel, Jr. ("Billy")	2
Mathewson, Christopher ("Christy")	Sports-2
McCarthy, Joseph Vincent ("Joe")	Sports-2
McGraw, John Joseph	Sports-2
Ott, Mel(vin) Thomas	Sports-2
Richards, Paul Rapier	2
Rickey, Branch Wesley	Sports-2
Robinson, Frank, Jr.	1960s-2
Rose, Peter Edward ("Pete")	Sports-2
Sisler, George Harold	Sports-2
Spahn, Warren Edward	Sports-2
Spalding, Albert Goodwill ("A. G.")	Sports-2
Speaker, Tris(tram) E.	Sports-2
Stengel, Charles Dillon ("Casey")	Sports-2
Terry, William Harold ("Memphis Bill")	2, Sports-2
Torre, Joseph Paul ("Joe")	Sports-2
Traynor, Harold Joseph ("Pie")	Sports-2

	Volume
Ward, John Montgomery	Sports-2
Wells, Willie James	Sports-2
Williams, Theodore Samuel ("Ted")	Sports-2
Wright, William Henry ("Harry")	Sports-2
Sports Official (Baseball Umpire)	
Conlan, John Bertrand ("Jocko")	2
Sports Promoter (Football)	
Rooney, Arthur Joseph	2
Sports Trainer (Boxing)	
Arcel, Ray	4
D'Amato, Constantine ("Cus")	1, Sports-1
Dundee, Angelo	Sports-1
Futch, Eddie	6
Jack, Beau	6
Saddler, Joseph ("Sandy")	6
Sports Trainer (Horse Racing)	
Fitzsimmons, James Edward ("Sunny Jim")	Sports-1
Jacobs, Hirsch	Sports-1
Jones, Horace Allyn ("Jimmy")	6
Shoemaker, William Lee ("Bill")	Sports-2
Stephens, Woodford Cefis ("Woody")	5, Sports-2
Sportswriter. *See* **Journalist (Sportswriter).**	
Spy. *See* **Espionage Agent.**	
Statistician	
Deming, W. Edwards	3
Gallup, George Horace	1
Jacoby, Oswald ("Ozzie")	1
Kuznets, Simon Smith	1
Neyman, Jerzy	1
Stunt Man	
Canutt, Enos Edward ("Yakima")	2
Supreme Court Justice	
Blackmun, Harry Andrew	5
Brennan, William Joseph, Jr.	5, 1960s-1
Burger, Warren Earl	4, 1960s-1
Fortas, Abraham ("Abe")	1, 1960s-1
Goldberg, Arthur Joseph	2
Marshall, Thurgood	3, 1960s-2
Powell, Lewis Franklin, Jr.	5
Stewart, Potter	1
Warren, Earl	1960s-2
White, Byron Raymond	6
Surgeon	
Albright, Tenley Emma	Sports-1
Cooley, Denton Arthur	1960s-1
DeBakey, Michael Ellis	1960s-1
Hornberger, H(iester) Richard, Jr. (Richard Hooker)	5
Huggins, Charles Brenton	5, 1960s-1
Judd, Walter Henry	4
Lillehei, C(larence) Walton ("Walt")	5

	Volume
Surgeon (*continued*)	
Merrill, John Putnam	1
Moore, Francis Daniels, and Thomas Earl Starzl	1960s-2
Ochsner, (Edward William) Alton	1
Stein, Julian Caesar ("Jules")	1
White, Jack Edward, Sr.	2
Swimmer. *See* **Athlete (Swimming).**	
Teacher. *See* **Educator.**	
Television Personality	
Allen, Stephen Valentine Patrick William ("Steve")	6, 1960s-1
Allison, Fran(ces)	2
Arnaz, Desi	2
Ball, Lucille Désirée	2
Belushi, John	1
Berle, Milton	6
Bombeck, Erma Louise Fiste	4
Bono, Salvatore Phillip ("Sonny")	5, 1960s-2
Borge, Victor	6
Broun, Heywood Hale ("Woodie")	6
Buckley, William Frank, Jr.	1960s-1
Burnett, Carol	1960s-1
Carson, John William ("Johnny")	1960s-1
Cavett, Richard Alva ("Dick")	1960s-1
Cerf, Bennett Albert	1960s-1
Clooney, Rosemary	6
Coca, Imogene	6
Como, Pierino Ronald ("Perry")	6
Cosell, Howard	4, Sports-1
Cronkite, Walter Leland, Jr.	1960s-1
Daly, John Charles, Jr.	3
Day, Dennis	2
Day, Doris	1960s-1
Diller, Phyllis Ada	1960s-1
Evans, Dale	6
Evans, Rowland, Jr. ("Rowly")	6
Farley, Chris(topher) Crosby	5
Ford, Ernest Jennings ("Tennessee Ernie")	3
Foxx, Redd	3
Francis, Arlene	6
Frederick, Pauline	2
Funt, Allen	5
Furness, Elizabeth Mary ("Betty")	4
Garland, Judy	1960s-1
Garroway, David Cunningham	1
Gleason, Herbert John ("Jackie")	2
Gobel, George Leslie	3
Godfrey, Arthur (Morton)	1
Graham, Virginia	5
Graziano, Rocky	2

	Volume
Hartman, Phil(ip) Edward	5
Hobson, Laura Kean Zametkin	2
Hope, Leslie Townes ("Bob")	1960s-1
Horwich, Frances Rappaport ("Miss Frances")	6
Huntley, Chester Robert ("Chet"), and David McClure Brinkley	1960s-1
James, Dennis	5
Kaufman, Andrew Geoffrey ("Andy")	1
Kirby, George	4
Kuralt, Charles Bishop	5
Lee, Pinky	3
Lewis, Shari	5
Liberace, Wladziu Valentino	2
Livingstone, Mary	1
Martin, Dean	1960s-2
Meadows, Audrey	4
Moore, Garry	3, 1960s-2
Moore, Mary Tyler	1960s-2
Morgan, Henry (Lerner von Ost)	4
Murray, Arthur	3
Murray, Kathryn Hazel	5
Murrow, Edward Roscoe	1960s-2
Newhart, George Robert ("Bob")	1960s-2
Parks, Bert	3
Perkins, (Richard) Marlin	2
Puente, Ernest Anthony, Jr. ("Tito")	6
Radner, Gilda	2
Rather, Daniel Irvin ("Dan")	1960s-2
Raye, Martha	4
Reagan, Ronald Wilson	1960s-2
Rickles, Donald Jay ("Don")	1960s-2
Robertson, Marion Gordon ("Pat")	1960s-2
Rowan, Dan Hale	2
Sagan, Carl Edward	4
Shore, Dinah	1960s-2
Silvers, Phil	1
Siskel, Eugene Kal ("Gene")	5
Skelton, Richard Bernard ("Red")	5
Smith, Kathryn Elizabeth ("Kate")	2
Smith, Robert Emil ("Buffalo Bob")	5
Smothers, Thomas ("Tom"), and Richard ("Dick") Smothers	1960s-2
Snyder, Jimmy ("Jimmy the Greek")	4
Sonny and Cher	1960s-2
Streisand, Barbra	1960s-2
Sullivan, Edward Vincent ("Ed")	1960s-2
Susskind, David Howard	2, 1960s-2
Swayze, John Cameron	4
Thomas, Danny	3
Thomas, Marlo	1960s-2
Tiny Tim (Herbert Butros Khaury)	4

	Volume		Volume
Trout, Robert	6	Hesburgh, Theodore Martin	1960s-1
Van Dyke, Richard Wayne ("Dick")	1960s-2	Holland, Jerome Heartwell ("Brud")	1
Vidal, Gore	1960s-2	Horton, Mildred Helen McAfee	4
Walker, Nancy	3	Kemeny, John George	3
Wallace, Mike	1960s-2	Kerr, Clark	1960s-1
Warwick, Dionne	1960s-2	Killian, James Rhyne, Jr.	2
Welk, Lawrence LeRoy	3	Kirk, Grayson Louis	5, 1960s-1
Wilson, Flip	5	Levi, Edward H(irsch)	6
Wolfman Jack (Robert Weston Smith)	4, 1960s-2	McGill, William James	5

Theologian

		McIntosh, Millicent Carey	6
Branscomb, (Bennett) Harvie	5	Marston, Robert Quarles	5
Cox, Harvey Gallagher, Jr.	1960s-1	Mays, Benjamin Elijah	1
Eliade, Mircea	2	Moos, Malcolm Charles	1
Fletcher, Joseph Francis, III	3	Murphy, Joseph Samson	5
Illich, Ivan	1960s-1	Nabrit, James Madison, Jr.	5
Ladd, George Eldon	1	Nason, John William	6
Mays, Benjamin Elijah	1	Perkins, James Alfred	5, 1960s-2
Meyendorff, John	3	Pusey, Nathan Marsh	6, 1960s-2
Murray, Anna Pauline ("Pauli")	1	Rainey, Homer Price	1
Niebuhr, Reinhold	1960s-2	Sachar, Abram Leon	3

Translator. *See* **Author (Translator).**

		Sanford, (James) Terry	5

Union Official. *See* **Labor Leader.**

		Sawhill, John Crittenden	6

University Administrator

		Schuller, Gunther Alexander	1960s-2
Baker, George Pierce	4	Schuman, William Howard	3
Bundy, McGeorge	4, 1960s-1	Seaborg, Glenn Theodore	5, 1960s-2
Ginsberg, Mitchell Irving	4	Simpson, Alan	5
Griswold, Erwin Nathaniel	4	Stassen, Harold Edward	6
Jones, Robert Reynolds, Jr. ("Bob")	5	Sterling, J(ohn) E(wart) Wallace	1
Levi, Edward H(irsch)	6	Taylor, Harold Alexander	3
McIntosh, Millicent Carey	6	Thomas, Lewis	3
Smith, (Charles) Page (Ward)	4	Townes, Charles Hard	1960s-2
Tien, Chang-Lin	6	Wallis, W(ilson) Allen	5

University President

		Ward, John William	1
Abram, Morris Berthold	6	Weaver, Robert Clifton	5, 1960s-2
Barnett, Marguerite Ross	3	Wells, Herman B.	6
Barr, (Frank) Stringfellow	1	Wharton, Clifton Reginald, Jr.	1960s-2
Beadle, George Wells ("Beets")	2	Wiesner, Jerome Bert	4, 1960s-2
Boyer, Ernest LeRoy, Sr.	4	Wilson, Logan	2
Branscomb, (Bennett) Harvie	5		

Urban Planner

Brewster, Kingman, Jr.	2, 1960s-1	Collins, John Frederick	4
Bunting-Smith, Mary Alice Ingraham		Goodman, Percival	2
("Polly")	5	Hoyt, Homer	1
Case, Everett Needham	6	Jacobs, Jane	1960s-1
Clark, Mark Wayne	1	Logue, Edward Joseph	6
Cremin, Lawrence Arthur	2, 1960s-1	McKissick, Floyd B.	3
Dickey, John Sloan	3	Moses, Robert	1
Eisenhower, Milton Stover	1	Mumford, Lewis Charles	2
Fulbright, J(ohn) William	4, 1960s-1	Owings, Nathaniel Alexander	1
Giamatti, A(ngelo) Bartlett ("Bart")	2, Sports-1	Rouse, James Wilson	4
Gould, Samuel Brookner	5	Sert, José Luis	1
Hayakawa, S(amuel) I(chiye)	3, 1960s-1	Whyte, William Hollingsworth, Jr.	5
Healy, Timothy Stafford	3	Ylvisaker, Paul Norman	3

	Volume
United Nations Official	
Keeny, Spurgeon Milton ("Sam")	2
Mann, Jonathan Max	5
Vice President of the United States. *See* **Politician (Vice President of the United States).**	
Violinist. *See* **Musician.**	
Virologist	
Horstmann, Dorothy Millicent	6
Sabin, Albert Bruce	1960s-2
Salk, Jonas Edward	4
Temin, Howard Martin	4
Writer. *See* **Author.**	
Yachtsman	
Conner, Dennis W.	Sports-1

	Volume
Hart, Marion Rice	2
Jobson, Gary	Sports-1
Morgan, Henry Sturgis ("Harry")	1
Mosbacher, Emil, Jr. ("Bus")	Sports-2
Shields, Cornelius	1
Zoologist	
Carson, Rachel Louise	1960-1
Fossey, Dian	1, 1960s-1
Neel, James Van Gundia	6
Perkins, (Richard) Marlin	2
Ray, Dixy Lee	4
Snell, George Davis	4
Sperry, Roger Wolcott	4
Stern, Curt	1

ALPHABETICAL LIST OF SUBJECTS, VOLUMES 1–6
and THEMATIC VOLUMES

See also the Occupations Index beginning on p. 597. Note that the Sports and 1960s thematic series each comprise two volumes.
Thus, for example, a citation for "1960s-2" means that the subject is found in Volume 2 of the 1960s thematic set.

Subject	Volume	Subject	Volume
Aaliyah (Aaliyah Dana Haughton)	6	Agnew, Spiro Theodore	4, 1960s-1
Aaron, Henry Louis ("Hank")	1960s-1, Sports-1	Aiken, George David	1, 1960s-1
Abbey, Edward Paul	2	Aikman, Troy Kenneth	Sports-1
Abbott, Berenice	3	Ailey, Alvin	2, 1960s-1
Abbott, George Francis	4	Akers, Michelle Anne	Sports-1
Abbott, Senda Berenson. *See* Berenson Abbott, Senda.		Al-Amin, Jamil Abdullah. *See* Brown, Hubert Gerold.	
Abdul-Jabbar, Kareem	Sports-1	Albee, Edward Franklin, III	1960s-1
Abel, I(orwith) W(ilbur) ("Abe")	2	Albert, Carl Bert	6
Abel, Sidney Gerald ("Sid")	6, Sports-1	Albert, Frank Culling ("Frankie")	6
Abernathy, Ralph David	2	Albertson, Jack	1
Abram, Morris Berthold	6	Albion, Robert Greenhalgh	1
Abrams, Creighton William, Jr.	1960s-1	Albright, Horace Marden	2
Abravanel, Maurice	3	Albright, Tenley Emma	Sports-1
Abzug, Bella	5, 1960s-1	Alexander, Grover Cleveland	Sports-1
Accardo, Tony ("Big Tuna")	3	Alferez, Enrique ("Rique")	5
Ace, Goodman	1	Alger, David Dewey	6
Ackley, H(ugh) Gardner	5	Algren, Nelson	1
Acuff, Roy Claxton	3	Ali, Muhammad (Cassius Clay)	1960s-1, Sports-1
Adams, Ansel Easton	1	Alioto, Joseph Lawrence	5
Adams, Charles Francis	5	Allen, Forrest Clare ("Phog")	Sports-1
Adams, Harriet Stratemeyer	1	Allen, George Herbert	2
Adams, (Llewellyn) Sherman	2	Allen, Marcus LeMarr	Sports-1
Adams, Walter	5	Allen, Mel(vin)	4
Addams, Charles Samuel	2	Allen, Stephen Valentine Patrick William ("Steve")	6, 1960s-1
Addie, Pauline May Betz. *See* Betz, Pauline May.		Allen, Woody	1960s-1
Adler, Lawrence Cecil ("Larry")	6	Allin, John Maury	5
Adler, Luther	1	Allison, Fran(ces)	2
Adler, Mortimer J(erome)	6	Allott, Gordon Llewellyn	2
Adler, Stella	3	Alsop, Joseph Wright, V	2, 1960–1
Agassi, Andre Kirk	Sports-1	Alston, Walter Emmons	1

Subject	Volume
Alvarez, Luis Walter	2, 1960s-1
Alworth, Lance Dwight	Sports-1
Ambrose, Stephen Edward	6
Ameche, Don	3
Amory, Cleveland ("Clip")	5
Andel, Jay Van. *See* DeVos, Richard Marvin, and Jay Van Andel.	
Anderson, Carl David, Jr.	3
Anderson, (Helen) Eugenie Moore	5
Anderson, George Lee ("Sparky")	Sports-1
Anderson, George Whelan, Jr.	3
Anderson, Judith	3
Anderson, Marian	3
Anderson, Paul Edward	Sports-1
Anderson, Robert Bernerd	2
Andretti, (Gabriele) Mario	Sports-1
Andrews, (Carver) Dana	3
Andrews, Julie	1960s-1
Andrews, Maxene Angelyn	4
Anfinsen, Christian Boehmer	4
Angleton, James Jesus	2
Annenberg, Walter Hubert	6
Anson, Adrian Constantine ("Cap," "Pop")	Sports-1
Antoninus, Brother. *See* Everson, William Oliver.	
Applewhite, Marshall Herff, Jr. ("Herff"; "Do")	5
Appling, Lucius Benjamin, Jr. ("Luke")	3
Arbus, Diane	1960s-1
Arcaro, George Edward ("Eddie")	5, Sports-1
Arcel, Ray	4
Archibald, Nathaniel ("Nate"; "Tiny")	Sports-1
Arden, Eve	2
Arends, Leslie Cornelius	1
Arendt, Hannah	1960s-1
Arizin, Paul Joseph	Sports-1
Arledge, Roone Pinckney, Jr.	6, Sports-1
Arlen, Harold	2
Armour, Norman	1
Armour, Richard Willard	2
Armour, Thomas Dickson ("Tommy")	Sports-1
Armstrong, Henry Jackson, Jr.	Sports-1
Armstrong, Herbert W.	2
Armstrong, Lance	Sports-1
Armstrong, Neil Alden	1960s-1
Arnall, Ellis Gibbs	3
Arnaz, Desi	2
Arneson, Robert Carston	3
Arrau, Claudio	3
Arrington, Leonard James	5
Arthur, Jean	3
Asch, Moses ("Moe")	2
Aserinsky, Eugene	5
Ash, Mary Kay	6, 1960s-1
Ash, Roy Lawrence	1960s-1
Ashbery, John Lawrence	1960s-1
Ashburn, Don Richard ("Richie")	5
Ashe, Arthur Robert, Jr.	3, 1960s-1, Sports-1
Ashford, Evelyn	Sports-1
Ashman, Howard Elliot	3
Ashmore, Harry Scott	5
Ashmore, Harry Scott, and William Calhoun ("Bill") Baggs	1960s-1
Asimov, Isaac	3
Aspin, Les(lie), Jr.	4
Astaire, Adele Marie	1
Astaire, Fred	2
Astor, Mary	2
Atanasoff, John Vincent	4
Atherton, Alfred Leroy, Jr. ("Roy")	6
Atkins, Chester Burton ("Chet")	6
Atkinson, (Justin) Brooks	1
Attwood, William Hollingsworth	2
Atwater, Harvey Leroy ("Lee")	3
Aubrey, James Thomas, Jr.	1960s-1
Auden, W(ystan) H(ugh)	1960s-1
Auerbach, Arnold ("Red")	Sports-1
Austin, John Paul	1
Autry, (Orvon) Gene	5
Avalon, Frankie, and Annette Joanne Funicello	1960s-1
Averill, Howard Earl ("Rock")	1
Axis Sally. *See* Gillars, Mildred Elizabeth Sisk.	
Axton, Hoyt Wayne	5
Babashoff, Shirley	Sports-1
Backus, James Gilmore ("Jim")	2
Bacon, Ernst	2
Baez, Joan Chandos	1960s-1
Baggs, William Calhoun. *See* Ashmore, Harry Scott, and William Calhoun ("Bill") Baggs.	
Bailey, Pearl Mae	2
Bailey, Thomas Andrew	1
Bailyn, Bernard	1960s-1
Bainton, Roland Herbert	1
Baird, William Britton ("Bil")	2
Baker, Carlos Heard	2
Baker, Carroll	1960s-1
Baker, Chesney Henry ("Chet")	2

Subject	Volume	Subject	Volume
Baker, Ella Josephine	2	Baxter, Anne	1
Baker, George Pierce	4	Baylor, Elgin	Sports-1
Baker, Hobart Amory Hare ("Hobey")	Sports-1	Beadle, George Wells ("Beets")	2
Balaban, Elmer	6	Beamon, Robert Alfred ("Bob")	Sports-1
Balanchine, George	1, 1960s-1	Beard, James Andrew	1
Baldrige, (Howard) Malcolm	2	Bearden, Romare Howard	2
Baldwin, Hanson Weightman	3	Beatty, (Henry) Warren	1960s-1
Baldwin, James Arthur	2, 1960s-1	Bechtel, Stephen Davison, Sr.	2
Baldwin, Raymond Earl	2	Beck, David	3
Baldwin, Roger Nash	1	Beck, Julian	1, 1960s-1
Ball, George Wildman	4, 1960s-1	Beckman, John	Sports-1
Ball, Lucille Désirée	2	Beckwith, Byron De La, Jr. ("Delay")	6
Ballantine, Ian Keith	4	Bednarik, Charles Philip ("Chuck")	Sports-1
Bancroft, Anne	1960s-1	Bee, Clair Francis	1
Bancroft, Mary	5	Beebe, William Thomas	1
Bane, Frank B.	1	Békésy, Georg von (György)	1960s-1
Banks, Dennis J.	1960s-1	Bell, Daniel	1960s-1
Banks, Ernest ("Ernie")	Sports-1	Bell, DeBenneville ("Bert")	Sports-1
Baraka, Amiri. *See* Jones, Everett LeRoy.		Bell, James Thomas ("Cool Papa")	3, Sports-1
		Bell, Terrel Howard	4
Barber, Samuel Osborne, II	1	Bellamy, Ralph Rexford	3
Barber, Walter Lanier ("Red")	3, Sports-1	Belli, Melvin Mouron	4
Bardeen, John	3	Bellow, Saul	1960s-1
Barkley, Charles Wade	Sports-1	Belushi, John	1
Barnes, Djuna Chappell	1	Belvin, Harry J. W.	2
Barnett, A(rthur) Doak	5	Bench, Johnny Lee	Sports-1
Barnett, Marguerite Ross	3	Bender, Lauretta	2
Barnett, Ross Robert	2, 1960s-1	Benn, Ben	1
Barnouw, Erik	6	Bennett, Joan	2
Baron, Salo Wittmayer	2	Bennett, Michael	2
Barr, Alfred Hamilton, Jr.	1	Bennett, Robert Russell	1
Barr, (Frank) Stringfellow	1	Bennett, Tony	1960s-1
Barrett, Emma ("Sweet Emma")	1	Benson, Elmer Austin	1
Barrett, William Christopher	3	Benson, Ezra Taft	4
Barry, Richard Francis, III ("Rick")	Sports-1	Benson, Mildred Wirt	6
Barth, John Simmons	1960s-1	Berberova, Nina Nikolaevna	3
Barthelme, Donald, Jr.	2	Berenson Abbott, Senda	Sports-1
Bartholomew, Frederick Llewellyn ("Freddie")	3	Berg, Patricia Jane ("Patty")	Sports-1
Barzun, Jacques Martin	1960s-1	Bergman, Ingrid	1
Basie, William James ("Count")	1	Bergman, Jules Verne	2
Baskin, Leonard	6	Berle, Milton	6
Basquiat, Jean-Michel	2	Berlin, Irving	2
Bate, Walter Jackson	5, 1960s-1	Berlin, Richard Emmett	2
Bates, Clayton ("Peg Leg")	5	Berman, Emile Zola	1
Bates, Daisy Lee Gatson	5	Berman, Pandro Samuel	4
Batten, William Milford	5	Bernard, Anna Jones	1
Battles, Clifford Franklin ("Gyp")	1	Bernardin, Joseph Louis	4
Bauer, Eddie	2	Bernays, Edward L.	4
Baugh, Samuel Adrian ("Sammy")	Sports-1	Bernbach, William	1
Bauzá, Mario	3	Bernhard, Arnold	2
		Bernstein, Kenneth Dale ("Kenny")	Sports-1

Subject	Volume
Bernstein, Leonard	2
Berra, Lawrence Peter ("Yogi")	Sports-1
Berrigan, Daniel Joseph, and Philip Francis Berrigan	1960s-1
Berrigan, Philip Francis	6, 1960s-1
Berry, Raymond Emmett	Sports-1
Berryman, John Allyn	1960s-1
Bettelheim, Bruno	2
Bettmann, Otto Ludwig	5
Betz, Pauline May	Sports-1
Bible, Alan Harvey	2
Bigart, Homer William	3
Biggers, John Thomas	6
Biggie Smalls. See Notorious B.I.G.	
Billington, Ray Allen	1
Bing, David ("Dave")	Sports-1
Bing, Franz Josef Rudolf	5
Bingham, (George) Barry, Sr.	2
Bingham, Jonathan Brewster ("Jack")	2
Biondi, Matt(hew)	Sports-1
Bird, Larry Joe	Sports-1
Bird, Rose Elizabeth	5
Bishop, Elizabeth	1960s-1
Bishop, Hazel Gladys	5
Bishop, James Alonzo ("Jim")	2
Black, Charles Lund, Jr.	6
Black, Eugene Robert	3
Black, Fischer Sheffey	4
Black, Joseph, Jr. ("Joe")	6
Black, William	1
Blackmun, Harry Andrew	5
Blackwell, Randolph Talmadge	1
Blaik, Earl Henry ("Red")	2, Sports-1
Blaine, Vivian	4
Blair, Bonnie	Sports-1
Blaisdell, Thomas Charles, Jr.	2
Blake, Eugene Carson	1
Blake, James Hubert ("Eubie")	1
Blakey, Arthur (Abdullah Ibn Buhaina; "Art")	2
Blanc, Mel(vin) Jerome	2
Blanchard, Felix Anthony, Jr. ("Doc")	Sports-1
Blanda, George Frederick	Sports-1
Blanton, (Leonard) Ray	4
Blass, William Ralph ("Bill")	6, 1960s-1
Blatnick, Jeff(rey)	Sports-1
Blazejowski, Carol Ann	Sports-1
Bleibtrey, Ethelda	Sports-1
Bliss, Ray Charles	1
Bloch, Felix	1
Bloch, Konrad Emil	6, 1960s-1

Subject	Volume
Bloch, Robert Albert	4
Block, Herbert Lawrence ("Herblock")	6, 1960s-1
Block, Joseph Leopold	3
Blood, Johnny. See McNally, John Victor.	
Bloom, Allan David	3
Bloom, Benjamin Samuel	5
Blough, Roger Miles	1, 1960s-1
Blume, Peter	3
Bohlen, Charles Eustis ("Chip")	1960s-1
Boitano, Brian Anthony	Sports-1
Boland, Edward Patrick	6
Bolet, Jorge	2
Bolger, Ray(mond) Wallace	2
Bombeck, Erma Louise Fiste	4
Bonanno, Joseph (Joe Bananas)	6
Bond, (Horace) Julian	1960s-1
Bonds, Barry Lamar	Sports-1
Boni, Albert	1
Bono, Salvatore Phillip ("Sonny"). See also Sonny and Cher.	5
Boorda, Jeremy Michael ("Mike")	4
Booth, Shirley	3
Boreman, Linda. See Lovelace, Linda Susan.	
Borge, Victor	6
Bossy, Michael Dean ("Mike")	Sports-1
Boston, Ralph	Sports-1
Boucher, Frank Xavier	Sports-1
Boudin, Leonard B.	2
Boudreau, Louis ("Lou")	6
Boulding, Kenneth Ewart	1960s-1
Bowden, Robert Cleckler ("Bobby")	Sports-1
Bowerman, William Jay ("Bill")	5
Bowles, Chester Bliss ("Chet")	2, 1960s-1
Bowles, Paul Frederic(k)	5
Bowman, Thea Bertha ("Sister Thea")	2
Boyer, Ernest LeRoy, Sr.	4
Boyington, Gregory ("Pappy")	2
Boyle, Katherine ("Kay")	3
Boyle, William Anthony ("Tony")	1
Boylston, Helen Dore	1
Bradbury, Norris Edwin	5
Bradbury, Ray	1960s-1
Bradley, Omar Nelson	1
Bradley, Thomas ("Tom")	5
Bradley, William Warren ("Bill")	1960s-1
Bradshaw, Terry Paxton	Sports-1
Bradshaw, Thornton Frederick ("Brad")	2
Brannan, Charles Franklin	3

Subject	Volume
Branscomb, (Bennett) Harvie	5
Brattain, Walter Houser	2
Brautigan, Richard	1
Brennan, William Joseph, Jr.	5, 1960s-1
Brett, George Howard	Sports-1
Brett, George Platt, Jr.	1
Breuer, Marcel	1
Brewster, Kingman, Jr.	2, 1960s-1
Bricker, John William	2
Brickhouse, John Beasley ("Jack")	5, Sports-1
Bricktop, (Ada Smith)	1
Brico, Antonia Louisa	2
Bridges, Harry	2
Bridges, Lloyd Vernet, Jr.	5
Brimsek, Francis Charles ("Frank")	5, Sports-1
Brinkley, David. *See* Huntley, Chester Robert ("Chet"), and David McClure Brinkley.	
Broccoli, Albert Romolo ("Cubby")	4
Brock, Lou(is Clark)	Sports-1
Brodie, Fawn McKay	1
Brodsky, Joseph (Iosif or Josip Alexandrovich)	4
Brooke, Edward William, III	1960s-1
Brooks, Cleanth	4
Brooks, Gwendolyn Elizabeth	6, 1960s-1
Brooks, Herb(ert) P.	Sports-1
Brooks, (Mary) Louise	1
Brooks, Richard	3
Broun, Heywood Hale ("Woodie")	6
Brown, Claude	6, 1960s-1
Brown, Dee Alexander	6
Brown, Edmund Gerald ("Pat")	4
Brown, George Edward, Jr.	5
Brown, George Rufus	1
Brown, Helen Gurley	1960s-1
Brown, Hubert Gerold ("H. Rap")	1960s-1
Brown, J(ohn) Carter	6
Brown, James Joe, Jr.	1960s-1
Brown, James Nathaniel ("Jim")	1960s-1, Sports-1
Brown, John R.	3
Brown, Lester Raymond ("Les")	6
Brown, Mordecai Peter Centennial	Sports-1
Brown, Paul Eugene ("P. B.")	3, Sports-1
Brown, Raymond Edward	5
Brown, Ron(ald) Harmon	4
Browne, Malcolm Wilde	1960s-1
Brownell, Herbert, Jr.	4
Broyard, Anatole Paul	2
Brozen, Yale	5
Brubeck, David Warren ("Dave")	1960s-1
Bruce, David Kirkpatrick Este	1960s-1
Bruce, Lenny	1960s-1
Bruhn, Erik Belton Evers	2
Brundage, Avery	Sports-1
Bryant, Kobe	Sports-1
Bryant, Paul William ("Bear")	1, Sports-1
Brynner, Yul	1
Bubbles, John William	2
Buchanan, Junious ("Buck")	Sports-1
Buck, John Francis ("Jack")	6
Buckley, William F(rank), Jr.	1960s-1
Budge, John Donald ("Don")	6, Sports-1
Buell, Marjorie Lyman Henderson ("Marge")	3
Buhaina, Abdullah Ibn. *See* Blakey, Arthur.	
Bukowski, Charles	4
Bumbry, Grace	1960s-1
Bundy, McGeorge	4, 1960s-1
Bundy, Theodore Robert ("Ted")	2
Bundy, William Putnam	6
Bunker, Ellsworth	1, 1960s-1
Bunning, James Paul David ("Jim")	Sports-1
Bunshaft, Gordon	2
Bunting-Smith, Mary Alice Ingraham ("Polly")	5
Burch, (Roy) Dean	3
Burden, William Armistead Moale	1
Burdick, Quentin Northrop	3
Burger, Warren Earl	4, 1960s-1
Burke, Arleigh Albert	4
Burke, Kenneth Duva	3
Burke, Selma Hortense	4
Burnett, Carol	1960s-1
Burns, Arthur Frank	2, 1960s-1
Burns, George	4
Burr, Raymond William Stacy	3
Burroughs, William S(eward)	5, 1960s-1
Burrows, Abe	1
Burton, Phillip	1
Buscaglia, Felice Leonardo ("Leo")	5
Busch, August Anheuser, Jr. ("Gussie")	2
Butkus, Richard Marvin ("Dick")	Sports-1
Butterfield, Lyman Henry	1
Button, Richard Totten ("Dick")	Sports-1
Butts, Alfred Mosher	3
Byers, Walter	Sports-1
Byrd, Charlie Lee	5
Byrnes, Robert Francis	5
Cadmus, Pauldefined.	5
Caen, Herb Eugene	5

Subject	Volume
Caesar, Irving	4
Cafaro, William Michael	5
Cage, John Milton, Jr.	3, 1960s-1
Cagney, James Francis, Jr.	2
Cahn, Sammy	3
Calderone, Mary Steichen	5
Caldwell, Erskine Preston	2
Caldwell, (Janet Miriam) Taylor	1
Calhoun, Lee Quency	Sports-1
Callaway, Ely Reeves, Jr.	6
Calley, William Laws, Jr.	1960s-1
Calloway, Cab	4
Calvin, Melvin	5, 1960s-1
Camp, Walter Chauncey	Sports-1
Campanella, Roy	3, Sports-1
Campbell, Earl Christian	Sports-1
Campbell, Joseph John	2, 1960s-1
Campbell, Milton Gray ("Milt")	Sports-1
Campion, Donald Richard	2
Canaday, John Edwin	1
Canby, Vincent	6
Candy, John Franklin	4
Canham, Erwin Dain	1
Caniff, Milton Arthur	2
Cannon, Howard Walter	6
Cannon, Sarah Ophelia Colley. *See* Pearl, Minnie	.
Cantwell, Mary Lee	6
Canutt, Enos Edward ("Yakima")	2
Capote, Truman Garcia	1, 1960s-1
Capra, Frank	3
Caray, Harry Christopher	5, Sports-1
Carberry, John Joseph	5
Carew, Rod(ney) Cline	Sports-1
Carl, Marion Eugene	5
Carlton, Steven Norman	Sports-1
Carmichael, Howard Hoagland ("Hoagy")	1
Carmichael, Stokely (Kwame Touré, Kwame Turé)	5, 1960s-1
Carney, Robert Bostwick	2
Carnovsky, Morris	3
Carpenter, Karen	1
Carpenter, Robert Ruliph Morgan, Jr.	2
Carpenter, (Malcolm) Scott	1960s-1
Carradine, John	2
Carroll, Diahann	1960s-1
Carson, John William ("Johnny")	1960s-1
Carson, Rachel Louise	1960s-1
Carter, Betty	5
Carter, Cris D.	Sports-1
Carter, Don(ald) James	Sports-1
Carter, Vincent Lamar, Jr. ("Vince")	Sports-1
Cartwright, Alexander Joy, Jr.	Sports-1
Carvel, Thomas Andrewdefined.	2
Carver, Raymond Clevie	2
Case, Clifford Phillip	1
Case, Everett Needham	6
Casey, James E.	1
Casey, Robert Patrick ("Spike")	6
Casey, William Joseph	2
Cash, John R. ("Johnny")	1960s-1
Cashin, Bonnie Jeanne	6
Castaneda, Carlos César Salvador Arana	5, 1960s-1
Castelli, Leo	5
Castro, Bernard	3
Catledge, Turner	1
Cavett, Richard Alva ("Dick")	1960s-1
Celebrezze, Anthony Joseph	5
Celler, Emanuel	1
Cerf, Bennett Albert	1960s-1
Chadwick, Florence May	4, Sports-1
Chadwick, Henry	Sports-1
Chafee, John Hubbard	5
Chaikin, Sol (Chick)	3
Chalk, (Oscar) Roy	4
Chall, Jeanne Sternlicht	1960s-1
Chamberlain, John Rensselaer	4
Chamberlain, Wilton Norman ("Wilt")	5, 1960s-1, Sports-1
Champion, Gower	1960s-1
Chancellor, John William	4
Chandler, Albert Benjamin ("Happy")	3, Sports-1
Chandler, Dorothy Buffum	5
Chandrasekhar, Subrahmanyan ("Chandra")	4
Chaney, James Earl, Andrew Goodman, and Michael Henry Schwerner	1960s-1
Chapin, Harry Forster	1
Chapman, Leonard Fielding, Jr.	6
Charleston, Oscar McKinley ("Charlie")	Sports-1
Charney, Jule Gregory	1
Chase, Lucia Hosmer	2
Chase, Mary Coyle	1
Chase, Stuart	1
Chase, William Curtis	2
Chávez, César Estrada	3, 1960s-1
Chayefsky, Sidney Aaron ("Paddy")	1, 1960s-1
Checker, Chubby	1960s-1

Subject	Volume
Cheever, John William	1
Chelios, Chris ("Chel")	Sports-1
Chen, Joyce	4
Cher. *See* Sonny and Cher.	
Cherne, Leo	5
Cherry, Don(ald) Eugene	4
Chesbro, John Dwight ("Jack")	Sports-1
Childress, Alice Herndon	4
Childress, Alvin	2
Childs, Marquis William	2
Chiles, Lawton Mainor, Jr.	5
Chino, Wendell	5
Chisholm, Shirley Anita	1960s-1
Chomsky, (Avram) Noam	1960s-1
Church, Alonzo	4
Church, Frank Forrester	1
Ciardi, John Anthony	2
Claiborne, Craig Raymond	6
Clampitt, Amy Kathleen	4
Clark, Joseph Sill, Jr.	2
Clark, Kenneth Bancroft	1960s-1
Clark, Mamie Phipps	1
Clark, Mark Wayne	1
Clark, (William) Ramsey	1960s-1
Clarke, John Henrik	5
Clarke, Kenny ("Klook")	1
Clarke, Robert Earle ("Bobby")	Sports-1
Claude, Albert	1
Clavell, James duMaresq	4
Clay, Cassius. *See* Ali, Muhammad.	
Clay, Lucius DuBignon, Jr.	4
Clay, Lucius DuBignon, Sr.	1960s-1
Clayton-Thomas, David	1960s-1
Cleage, Albert Buford, Jr.	6
Cleaver, (Leroy) Eldridge	5, 1960s-1
Clemens, (William) Roger	Sports-1
Clemente, Roberto Walker	1960s-1, Sports-1
Clements, Earle Chester	1
Clifford, Clark McAdams	5, 1960s-1
Clifton, Nat(haniel) ("Sweetwater")	2
Cline, Patsy	1960s-1
Clooney, Rosemary	6
Clubb, O(liver) Edmund, II	2
Clurman, Richard Michael	4
Cobain, Kurt Donald	4
Cobb, Ty(rus) Raymond	Sports-1
Coburn, James	6
Coca, Imogene	6
Cochran, Thomas Childs	5
Cochrane, Gordon Stanley ("Mickey")	Sports-1
Cocke, John	6

Subject	Volume
Cody, John Patrick	1
Coffin, William Sloane, Jr.	1960s-1
Cohen, Alexander H(enry)	6
Cohen, Audrey C.	4
Cohen, Benjamin Victor	1
Cohen, N(ehemiah) M(yer)	1
Cohen, Wilbur Joseph	2
Cohn, Roy Marcus	2
Colbert, Claudette	4
Colby, William Egan	4
Cole, William Randolph ("Cozy")	1
Coleman, J(ames) P(lemon)	3
Coleman, James Samuel	4, 1960s-1
Coles, Charles ("Honi")	3
Collbohm, Franklin Rudolph	2
Collingwood, Charles Cummings	1
Collins, Edward Trowbridge ("Eddie")	Sports-1
Collins, J(oseph) Lawton ("Lightning Joe")	2
Collins, John Frederick	4
Collins, Judy	1960s-1
Collins, (Thomas) LeRoy	3
Coltrane, John William	1960s-1
Comiskey, Charles Albert	Sports-1
Commager, Henry Steele	5
Como, Pierino Ronald ("Perry")	6
Condon, Richard Thomas	4
Conerly, Charles Albert ("Charlie"), Jr.	4
Conigliaro, Anthony Richard ("Tony")	2
Conlan, John Bertrand ("Jocko")	2
Conn, William David, Jr. ("Billy")	3, Sports-1
Connally, John Bowden, Jr.	3
Connell, Evan S(helby), Jr.	1960s-1
Conner, Bart	Sports-1
Conner, Dennis W.	Sports-1
Connolly, Harold V ("Hal")	Sports-1
Connolly, Maureen Catherine ("Little Mo")	Sports-1
Connor, John Thomas ("Jack")	6
Connor, Theophilus Eugene ("Bull")	1960s-1
Connors, James Scott ("Jimmy")	Sports-1
Connors, Kevin Joseph Aloysius ("Chuck")	3
Conover, Willis Clark, Jr.	4
Conrad, Paul	1960s-1
Coogan, John Leslie, Jr. ("Jackie")	1
Cooke, Terence James	1
Cooley, Denton Arthur	1960s-1
Coon, Carleton Stevens	1
Cooney, Joan Ganz	1960s-1
Cooper, Charles Henry ("Chuck")	1

Subject	Volume
Cooper, Cynthia	Sports-1
Cooper, Irving Spencer	1
Cooper, John Sherman	3
Copland, Aaron	2
Corbett, James John	Sports-1
Corcoran, Thomas Gardiner	1
Cordero, Angel Tomas, Jr.	Sports-1
Cori, Carl Ferdinand	1
Cormack, Allan MacLeod	5
Corner, George Washington	1
Cornfeld, Bernard ("Bernie")	4
Corning, Erastus, 2d	1
Corrigan, Douglas ("Wrong-Way Corrigan")	4
Corso, Gregory Nunzio	6
Cosell, Howard	4, Sports-1
Costas, Robert Quinlan ("Bob")	Sports-1
Cotten, Joseph Cheshire	4
Cotton, Norris Henry	2
Counsilman, James Edward ("Doc")	Sports-1
Cournand, André Frederic	2
Cousins, Norman	2, 1960s-1
Cousy, Robert ("Bob")	Sports-1
Coveleski, Stanley Anthony ("Covey")	1
Coverdell, Paul Douglas	6
Cowles, Gardner, Jr. ("Mike")	1
Cowley, (David) Malcolm	2
Cox, Harvey Gallagher, Jr.	1960s-1
Crabbe, Clarence Linden ("Buster")	1, Sports-1
Cram, Donald James	6
Cranston, Alan MacGregor	6
Crawford, (William) Broderick	2
Crawford, Cheryl	2
Cray, Seymour Roger	4
Cremin, Lawrence A(rthur)	2, 1960s-1
Crisler, Herbert Orin ("Fritz")	1
Crisp, Quentin	5
Cronin, Joseph Edward	1
Cronkite, Walter Leland, Jr.	1960s-1
Crosby, Stills, and Nash	1960s-1
Crothers, Benjamin Sherman ("Scatman")	2
Crown, Henry	2
Crowther, (Francis) Bosley, Jr.	1
Crumb, Robert	1960s-1
Cugat, Xavier	2
Cukor, George Dewey	1
Cunliffe, Marcus Falkner	2
Cunningham, Glenn V.	2, Sports-1
Cunningham, Harry Blair	1960s-1
Cunningham, Mercier Philip ("Merce")	1960s-1
Cunningham, William John ("Billy")	Sports-1
Curran, Joseph Edwin	1
Curti, Merle Eugene	4
Curtis, Carl Thomas	6
Dabney, Virginius	4
Daché, Marie-Louise ("Lilly")	2
Dahmer, Jeffrey Lionel	4
Daley, Richard Joseph	1960s-1
Dallin, Alexander	6
Daly, John Charles, Jr.	3
D'Amato, Constantine ("Cus")	1, Sports-1
Dana, Charles Anderson, Jr.	6
Dancer, Faye Katherine	6
Dandridge, Raymond Emmett ("Squatty")	4, Sports-1
Dangerfield, George	2
Daniel, (Elbert) Clifton, Jr.	6
Daniel, Price Marion	2
Daniels, Jonathan Worth	1
Daniels, William Boone ("Billy")	2
Danilova, Alexandra Dionysievna ("Choura")	5
Daugherty, Hugh ("Duffy")	2
Davenport, Lindsay	Sports-1
Davies, John Paton, Jr.	5
Davis, Al(len)	Sports-1
Davis, (William) Allison	1
Davis, Angela Yvonne	1960s-1
Davis, Benjamin O(liver), Jr.	6
Davis, Bette	2
Davis, David Brion	1960s-1
Davis, Glenn Woodward ("Junior")	Sports-1
Davis, James Houston ("Jimmie")	6
Davis, John Henry	Sports-1
Davis, Martin S.	5
Davis, Miles Dewey, III	3, 1960s-1
Davis, Raiford Chatman ("Ossie")	1960s-1
Davis, Sammy, Jr.	2, 1960s-1
Davison, William Edward ("Wild Bill")	2
Dawidowicz, Lucy Schildkret	2
Day, Dennis	2
Day, Doris	1960s-1
Day, James Lewis	5
Day, Leon	4
Dean, Arthur Hobson	2
Dean, Jay Hanna ("Dizzy")	Sports-1
Dean, Paul ("Daffy")	1

Subject	Volume
DeBakey, Michael Ellis	1960s-1
DeBartolo, Edward John, Sr.	4
Debus, Kurt Heinrich	1
De Cordova, Frederick Timmins ("Fred")	6
Dedmon, Emmett	1
Dee, Ruby	1960s-1
Deford, Frank	Sports-1
DeGaetani, Jan	2
de Kooning, Elaine Marie Catherine	2
de Kooning, Willem	5, 1960s-1
Delacorte, George Thomas, Jr.	3
Delany, Annie Elizabeth ("Bessie")	4
Delany, Sarah Louise ("Sadie")	5
Delbrück, Max Ludwig Henning	1, 1960s-1
Della Femina, Jerry	1960s-1
Dellinger, David	1960s-1
Deloria, Vine, Jr.	1960s-1
Delvecchio, Alex Peter ("Fats")	Sports-1
de Man, Paul	1
Demara, Ferdinand Waldo, Jr. ("Fred")	1
Demaret, James Newton ("Jimmy")	1
de Menil, Dominique Schlumberger	5
de Mille, Agnes George	3
Deming, W(illiam) Edwards	3
Dempsey, William Harrison ("Jack")	1, Sports-1
De Nagy, Tibor	3
Denby, Edwin Orr	1
Dennis, Sandra Dale ("Sandy")	3
Denver, John	5
Dertouzos, Michael Leonidas	6
Dessauer, John Hans	3
Deutsch, Helene Rosenbach	1
De Varona, Donna	1960s-1, Sports-1
DeVos, Richard Marvin, and Jay Van Andel	1960s-1
De Vries, Peter	3
Dewhurst, Colleen	3
Diamond, Selma	1
Dichter, Ernest	3
Dick, Philip K(indred)	1, 1960s-1
Dickerson, Eric Demetric	Sports-1
Dickerson, Nancy	5, 1960s-1
Dickey, James Lafayette	5
Dickey, John Sloan	3
Dickey, William Malcolm ("Bill")	4, Sports-1
Didrikson Zaharias, Mildred Ella ("Babe")	Sports-1
Diebenkorn, Richard Clifford	3
Dietrich, Marlene	3

Subject	Volume
Dietz, Howard	1
Diggs, Charles Coles, Jr.	5
Dillard, Harrison	Sports-1
Dillard, William Thomas, Sr.	6
Diller, Phyllis Ada	1960s-1
DiMaggio, Joseph Paul ("Joe"; "The Yankee Clipper")	5, Sports-1
Dine, James ("Jim")	1960s-1
Dion	1960s-1
Dirac, Paul Adrien Maurice	1
Dirksen, Everett McKinley	1960s-1
DiSalle, Michael Vincent	1
Ditka, Mike	Sports-1
Divine, (Harris Glenn Milstead)	2
Dixon, Jeane Lydia	5
Dixon, Julian C.	6
Dixon, Willie James	3
Dmytryk, Edwarddefined.	5
Doby, Lawrence Eugene ("Larry")	Sports-1
Dodd, Robert Lee ("Bobby")	2
Dohrn, Bernardine Rae	1960s-1
Doisy, Edward Adelbert	2
Dolgun, Alexander Michael	2
Donahue, Troy	6
Donner, Frederic Garrett	2
Donovan, Anne	Sports-1
Donovan, Carolyn Gertrude Amelia ("Carrie")	6
Donovan, Hedley Williams	2
Doolittle, James Harold	3
Dorati, Antal	2
Dorris, Michael Anthony	5
Dorsett, Anthony Drew ("Tony")	Sports-1
Dorsey, Thomas Andrew	3
Douglas, Donald Wills	1
Douglas, Marjory Stoneman	5
Douglas, Melvyn	1
Downey, Morton	1
Dr. Seuss. See Geisel, Theodor S.	
Drake, Alfred	3
Drake, (John Gibbs) St. Clair	2
Drexler, Clyde	Sports-1
Drucker, Peter Ferdinand	1960s-1
Drury, Allen Stuart	5
Drysdale, Donald Scott ("Don")	3, 1960s-1, Sports-1
Dubinsky, David	1
Dubos, René Jules	1
Dubus, Andre Jules	5
Duke, Angier Biddle	4

Subject	Volume
Duke, Anna Marie ("Patty")	1960s-1
Duke, Doris	3
Dullea, Keir	1960s-1
Dulles, Allen Welsh	1960s-1
Dunaway, (Dorothy) Faye	1960s-1
Duncan, Robert	2
Duncan, Timothy Theodore	Sports-1
Dundee, Angelo	Sports-1
Dunne, Irene Marie	2
Durant, Will(iam) James, and Ariel Durant	1
Durocher, Leo Ernest	3, Sports-1
Dylan, Bob	1960s-1
Dzubas, Friedel Alfred	4
Eaker, Ira Clarence	2
Eamcs, Ray	2
Earnhardt, (Ralph) Dale	6, Sports-1
Eastland, James Oliver	2
Eastwood, Clinton, Jr. ("Clint")	1960s-1
Eckert, J(ohn Adam) Presper, Jr.	4
Eckstine, William Clarence ("Billy")	3
Edel, (Joseph) Leon	5
Ederle, Gertrude Caroline ("Trudy")	Sports-1
Edwards, Douglas	2
Edwards, Teresa	Sports-1
Egan, John Joseph ("Jack")	6
Ehrlichman, John Daniel	5, 1960s-1
Eifler, Carl Frederick	6
Eisenhower, Milton Stoverdefined.	1
Eisenstaedt, Alfred	4
Eldridge, (David) Roy ("Little Jazz")	2
Elgart, Les(ter) Elliot	4
Eliade, Mircea	2
Elias, Peter	6
Elion, Gertrude Belle ("Trudy")	5
Elkin, Stanley Lawrence	4
Ellington, Mercer Kennedy	4
Elliott, James Francis ("Jumbo")	1
Ellis, John Tracy	3
Ellis, Perry Edwin	2
Ellison, Ralph Waldo	4
Ellmann, Richard David	2
Elway, John Albert	Sports-1
Enders, John Franklin	1
Engel, A. Lehman	1
Engle, Charles Albert ("Rip")	1
Engle, Paul Hamilton	3
Ephron, Nora Louise	1960s-1
Epstein, Julius J. ("Julie")	6
Erikson, Erik Homburger	4
Ernst, Hans-Ulrich ("Jimmy")	1
Erteszek, Olga Bertram	2
Ervin, Samuel James, Jr.	1
Erving, Julius Winfield, II ("Dr. J.")	Sports-1
Esposito, Phil(ip) Anthony	Sports-1
Espy, Willard Richard ("Wede")	5
Evans, Dale	6
Evans, Gil	2
Evans, Janet	Sports-1
Evans, Rowland, Jr. ("Rowly")	6
Evans, Thomas Mellon	5
Evers, Medgar Wylie	1960s-1
Everson, William Oliver (Brother Antoninus)	4
Evert, Christine Marie ("Chris")	Sports-1
Ewbank, Wilbur Charles ("Weeb")	5, Sports-1
Ewell, Henry Norwood ("Barney")	Sports-1
Ewell, Tom	4
Ewing, Patrick Aloysius	Sports-1
Ewing, William ("Buck")	Sports-1
Exley, Frederick Earl	3
Exner, Judith Campbell	5
Factor, Max, Jr.	4
Fadiman, Clifton Paul	5
Fahey, John	6
Fain, Sammy	2
Fairbank, John King	3
Fairbanks, Douglas Elton, Jr.	6
Fall, Bernard B.	1960s-1
Fannin, Paul Jones	6
Fariña, Margarita Baez ("Mimi")	6
Fariña, Richard George	1960s-1
Farley, Chris(topher) Crosby	5
Farmer, Art(hur) Stewart	5
Farmer, James Leonard, Jr.	5, 1960s-1
Farrar, Margaret Petherbridge	1
Farrell, Eileen Frances	6
Farrell, Suzanne	1960s-1
Farrow, Mia	1960s-1
Fasanella, Raphaele ("Ralph")	5
Fascell, Dante Bruno	5
Faubus, Orval Eugene	4
Faulk, John Henry	2
Favre, Brett Lorenzo	Sports-1
Faye, Alice	5
Fears, Thomas Jesse ("Tom")	6, Sports-1
Feather, Leonard Geoffrey	4
Feehan, William M.	6
Fehrenbacher, Don Edward	5
Feininger, Andreas Bernhard Lyonel	5
Feld, Irvin	1
Feldman, Morton	2

Subject	Volume
Feller, Robert William Andrew ("Bob")	Sports-1
Fender, Clarence Leonidas ("Leo")	3
Fenwick, Millicent Hammond	3
Ferguson, Homer Samuel	1
Ferrer, José	3
Feshbach, Herman	6
Festinger, Leon	2
Fetchit, Stepin	1
Feyerabend, Paul Karl	4
Feynman, Richard Phillips	2, 1960s-1
Fidler, James Marion ("Jimmie")	2
Fielding, Temple Hornaday	1
Finch, Robert Hutchinson	4
Fine, Reuben	3
Fingers, Roland Glen ("Rollie")	Sports-1
Finkelstein, Louis	3
Finley, Charles Oscar ("Charlie")	4
Finney, Walter Braden ("Jack")	4
Fischer, Robert James ("Bobby")	1960s-1
Fish, Hamilton	3
Fisher, Avery Robert	4
Fisher, M(ary) F(rances) K(ennedy)	3
Fitch, James Marston	6
Fitzgerald, Ella Jane	4
Fitzgerald, Robert Stuart	1
Fitzsimmons, Frank Edward	1
Fitzsimmons, James Edward ("Sunny Jim")	Sports-1
Fixx, James Fuller	1
Fleming, Peggy Gale	1960s-1, Sports-1
Flesch, Rudolf Franzdefined.	2
Fletcher, Harvey	1
Fletcher, Joseph Francis, III	3
Flexner, Stuart Berg	2
Flood, Curt(is) Charles	5, Sports-1
Flory, Paul John	1
Foerstner, George Christian	6
Fogarty, Anne Whitney	1960s-1
Fogerty, John Cameron	1960s-1
Folsom, James Elisha ("Big Jim")	2
Fonda, Henry Jaynes	1, 1960s-1
Fonda, Jane Seymour	1960s-1
Fonda, Peter Seymour	1960s-1
Foner, Philip Sheldon	4
Fontanne, Lynn	1
Foote, Emerson	3
Foote, Shelby Dade, Jr.	1960s-1
Forbes, Malcolm Stevenson	2
Ford, Edward Charles ("Whitey")	Sports-1
Ford, Ernest Jennings ("Tennessee Ernie")	3
Ford, Henry, II ("Hank the Deuce")	2
Foreman, Carl	1
Forrest, Helen	5
Fortas, Abraham ("Abe")	1, 1960s-1
Forte, Fulvio Chester, Jr. ("Chet")	4
Fosbury, Richard Douglas ("Dick")	Sports-1
Fosse, Robert Louis ("Bob")	2
Fossey, Dian	1, 1960s-1
Foster, Andrew ("Rube")	Sports-1
Foster, Vincent William, Jr.	3
Fowler, William Alfred	4
Fox, Jacob Nelson ("Nellie")	Sports-1
Foxx, James Emory ("Jimmie")	Sports-1
Foxx, Redd	3
Foyt, A(nthony) J(oseph), Jr.	Sports-1
France, William Henry Getty, Sr. ("Bill")	3, Sports-1
Francis, Arlene	6
Francis, Sam(uel) Lewis	4
Frankenheimer, John Michael	6, 1960s-1
Franklin, Aretha Louise	1960s-1
Franklin, John Hope	1960s-1
Fraser, Gretchen Claudia	Sports-1
Frazier, Joseph William ("Joe")	1960s-1, Sports-1
Frazier, Walt, II ("Clyde")	Sports-1
Frederick, Pauline	2
Fredericks, Carlton	2
Fredericks, Sara	2
Freleng, Isadore ("Friz")	4
Freund, Paul Abraham	3
Frick, Ford Christopher	Sports-1
Frick, Helen Clay	1
Friedan, Betty Naomi	1960s-1
Friedman, Benjamin ("Benny")	1
Friedman, Herbert	6
Friedman, Milton	1960s-1
Friedrich, Carl Joachim	1
Friend, Charlotte	2
Friendly, Fred W.	5
Friendly, Henry Jacob	2
Frisch, Frank Francis ("Frankie")	Sports-1
Frowick, Roy Halston. See Halston.	
Fulbright, J(ames) William	4, 1960s-1
Fulks, Joseph Franklin ("Joe")	Sports-1
Fuller, R(ichard) Buckminster	1
Fuller, S. B.	2
Fuller, Samuel Michael	5
Funicello, Annette. See Avalon, Frankie, and Annette Joanne Funicello.	
Funt, Allen	5

Subject	Volume
Furcolo, (John) Foster	4
Furness, Elizabeth Mary ("Betty")	4
Futch, Eddie	6
Gabel, Hortense Wittstein	2
Gable, Dan(iel)	Sports-1
Gabor, Eva	4
Gacy, John Wayne, Jr.	4
Gaddis, William	5
Gaines, Clarence Edward, Sr. ("Bighouse")	Sports-1
Gaines, William Maxwell	3
Galarza, Ernesto, Jr.	1
Galbraith, John Kenneth	1960s-1
Gallo, Julio Robert	3
Gallup, George Horace	1
Gann, Ernest Kellogg	3
Ganz Cooney, Joan. *See* Cooney, Joan Ganz.	
Garbo, Greta	2
Garcia, Hector Perez	4
Garcia, Jerome John ("Jerry")	4, 1960s-1
Garciaparra, (Anthony) Nomar	Sports-1
Gardner, Ava Lavinia	2
Gardner, Edward George	1960s-1
Gardner, John Champlin, Jr.	1
Gardner, John William	6, 1960s-1
Garfunkel, Art. *See* Simon and Garfunkel.	
Garland, Judy	1960s-1
Garlits, Don(ald)	Sports-1
Garrison, Earling Carothers ("Jim")	3, 1960s-1
Garrity, W(endell) Arthur, Jr.	5
Garroway, David Cunningham	1
Garson, Barbara	1960s-1
Garson, Greer	4
Gates, John	3
Gates, Thomas Sovereign, Jr.	1
Gates, William ("Pop")	5
Gavin, James Maurice	2, 1960s-1
Gay, Peter ("Jack")	1960s-1
Gaye, Marvin Pentz, Jr.	1, 1960s-1
Gaynor, Janet	1
Gehrig, (Henry) Lou(is)	Sports-1
Gehringer, Charles Leonard ("Charlie")	3, Sports-1
Geisel, Theodor Seuss ("Dr. Seuss")	3
Geldzahler, Henry	4
Gellhorn, Martha Ellis	5
Gellhorn, Walter	4
Gell-Mann, Murray	1960s-1
Geneen, Harold Sydney	5, 1960s-1

Subject	Volume
Gennaro, Peter	6
Genovese, Catherine ("Kitty")	1960s-1
Genovese, Eugene Dominick	1960s-1
Gernreich, Rudolph ("Rudi")	1, 1960s-1
Gershwin, Ira	1
Gerstenberg, Richard Charles	6
Geschwind, Norman	1
Getty, J(ean) Paul	1960s-1
Getz, Stan(ley)	3
Giamatti, A(ngelo) Bartlett ("Bart")	2, Sports-1
Giancana, Salvatore ("Sam")	1960s-1
Giauque, William Francis	1
Gibbs, Joe Jackson	Sports-1
Gibson, Althea	Sports-1
Gibson, Josh(ua)	Sports-1
Gibson, Pack Robert ("Bob")	Sports-1
Gibson, William Frank	6
Gifford, Frank Newton	Sports-1
Gilbert, Felix	3
Gilbreth, Frank Bunker, Jr.	6
Gilford, Jack	2
Gill, Brendan	5
Gillars, Mildred Elizabeth Sisk ("Axis Sally")	2
Gillespie, Gregory Joseph	6
Gillespie, John Birks ("Dizzy")	3
Gillman, Sid(ney)	Sports-1
Gilpatric, Roswell Leavitt	4
Gilruth, Robert Rowe	6
Ginsberg, (Irwin) Allen	5, 1960s-1
Ginsberg, Mitchell Irving	4
Ginzberg, Eli	6
Giovanni, Nikki	1960s-1
Gish, Lillian Diana	3
Glaser, Donald Arthur	1960s-1
Gleason, Herbert John ("Jackie")	2
Gleason, Thomas William ("Teddy")	3
Glenn, John Herschel, Jr.	1960s-1
Glickman, Martin Irving ("Marty")	6, Sports-1
Gobel, George Leslie	3
Goddard, Paulette	2
Godfrey, Arthur Michael	1
Goeppert-Mayer, Maria	1960s-1
Goffman, Erving Manual	1
Goizueta, Roberto Crispulo	5
Goldberg, Arthur Joseph	2
Golden, Harry Lewis	1
Goldenson, Leonard Harry	5
Goldman, Eric Frederick	2
Goldwater, Barry Morris	5, 1960s-1
Gomez, Vernon Louis ("Lefty")	Sports-1

Subject	Volume
Gonzales, Richard Alonzo ("Pancho")	4, Sports-1
Gonzalez, Henry Barbosa	6
Goode, Malvin Russell ("Mal")	4, 1960s-1
Goodman, Andrew. *See* Chaney, James Earl, Andrew Goodman, and Michael Henry Schwerner.	
Goodman, Benjamin David ("Benny")	2
Goodman, Louis Sanford	6
Goodman, Paul	1960s-1
Goodman, Percival	2
Goodrich, Frances	1
Goodson, Mark	3
Gordon, Dexter Keith	2
Gordon, Jeff	Sports-1
Gordon, Ruth	1
Gordone, Charles	4, 1960s-1
Gordy, Berry, Jr.	1960s-1
Gore, Albert Arnold, Sr.	5
Goren, Charles Henry	3
Gosden, Freeman Fisher	1
Gotch, Frank Alvin	Sports-1
Gotti, John Joseph	6
Gould, Chester	1
Gould, Morton	4
Gould, Samuel Brookner	5
Gould, Stephen Jay	6
Goulding, Ray(mond) Walter	2
Gowdy, Curt(is)	Sports-1
Grace, J(oseph) Peter, Jr.	4
Grace, Princess, of Monaco. *See* Kelly, Grace.	
Graham, Bill	3
Graham, John	3
Graham, Katharine Meyer	6
Graham, Martha	3
Graham, Otto Everett, Jr.	Sports-1
Graham, Sheilah	2
Graham, Virginia	5
Graham, William Patrick ("Billy")	3
Grange, Harold Edward ("Red")	3, Sports-1
Grant, Cary	2
Grasso, Ella Rosa Giovanna Oliva Tambussi	1
Graves, Nancy Stevenson	4
Gray, Barry	4
Gray, Peter Wyshner ("Pete")	6
Graziano, Rocky	2, Sports-1
Greb, Edward Henry ("Harry")	Sports-1
Greco, Costanzo ("José")	6
Green, Adolph	6
Green, Edith Starrett	2

Subject	Volume
Greenberg, Clement	4
Greenberg, Henry Benjamin ("Hank")	2, Sports-1
Greenberg, Joseph H(arold)	6
Greene, Charles Edward ("Mean Joe")	Sports-1
Greene, Harold Herman	6
Greene, Lorne	2
Greenfield, Mary Ellen ("Meg")	5
Greer, Jane	6
Greer, William Alexander ("Sonny")	1
Gregg, (Alvis) Forrest	Sports-1
Gregory, Richard Claxton ("Dick")	1960s-1
Gretzky, Wayne Douglas ("The Great One")	Sports-1
Griffey, (George) Ken(neth), Jr.	Sports-1
Griffith Joyner, Florence Delorez ("Flo Jo")	5, Sports-1
Griffith, Calvin Robertson	5
Griffith, Clark Calvin	Sports-1
Griffith, Emile Alphonse	Sports-1
Grillo, Frank Raúl. *See* Machito.	
Grimes, Burleigh Arland	1
Grissom, Virgil Ivan ("Gus")	1960s-1
Griswold, Erwin Nathaniel	4
Grizzard, Lewis McDonald, Jr.	4
Grooms, Charles Rogers ("Red")	1960s-1
Groppi, James Edmund	1, 1960s-1
Grosvenor, Melville Bell	1
Grove, Robert Moses ("Lefty")	Sports-1
Groza, Louis Roy ("Lou")	6, Sports-1
Grucci, Felix James, Sr. ("Pops")	3
Gruening, Ernest	1960s-1
Gruenther, Alfred Maximilian	1
Gruentzig, Andreas Roland	1
Grumman, Leroy Randle ("Roy")	1
Gunther, Gerald	6
Gurney, Dan(iel) Sexton	Sports-1
Guthrie, A(lfred) B(ertram), Jr.	3
Guthrie, Arlo Davy	1960s-1
Gwynn, Anthony Keith ("Tony")	Sports-1
Haas, Walter A., Jr., and Peter E. Haas., Sr.	1960s-1
Habib, Philip Charles	3
Hackman, Eugene Alden ("Gene")	1960s-1
Hagen, John Peter	2
Hagen, Walter C.	Sports-1
Hagerty, James Campbell	1
Haggar, Joseph Marion	2
Haggard, Merle Ronald	1960s-1
Hagler, Marvin Nathaniel	Sports-1
Halas, George Stanley	1, Sports-1
Halberstam, David	1960s-1

Subject	Volume
Haldeman, H(arry) R(obbins) ("Bob")	3, 1960s-1
Hale, Clara McBride ("Mother Hale")	3
Haley, Alexander Murray Palmer ("Alex")	3, 1960s-1
Haley, William John, Jr. ("Bill")	1
Hall, Glenn Henry	Sports-1
Hall, Gus	6
Hall, Joyce Clyde	1
Hall, Theodore Alvin	5
Halleck, Charles Abraham	2
Halper, Albert	1
Halston	2, 1960s-1
Hamill, Dorothy Stuart	Sports-1
Hamilton, Margaret	1
Hamilton, Scott Scovell	Sports-1
Hamm, Mariel Margaret ("Mia")	Sports-1
Hammer, Armand	2, 1960s-1
Hammond, E(dward) Cuyler	2
Hammond, John Henry, Jr.	2
Hampton, Lionel	6
Hancock, Joy Bright	2
Handler, Ruth	6
Hanks, Nancy	1
Hanna, William Denby ("Bill")	6
Hannah, John Allen	Sports-1
Hannah, John Frederick ("Jack")	4
Hannum, Alex	6
Hansberry, Lorraine Vivian	1960s-1
Hansen, Al(fred) Earl	4
Hanson, Duane Elwood	4
Hanson, Howard Harold	1
Harburg, Edgar Yipsel ("Yip")	1
Hargis, Billy James	1960s-1
Haring, Keith Allen	2
Harken, Dwight Emary	3
Harkness, Rebekah West	1, 1960s-1
Harlow, Bryce Nathaniel	2
Harmon, Thomas Dudley ("Tom")	2, Sports-1
Harriman, Pamela Beryl Digby Churchill Hayward	5
Harriman, William Averell	2, 1960s-1
Harrington, (Edward) Michael	2, 1960s-1
Harris, Franco	Sports-1
Harris, Patricia Roberts Fitzgerald	1
Harris, (Wanga) Phillip ("Phil")	4
Harris, Sydney Justin	2
Harsanyi, John C.	6
Hart, Leon	6
Hart, Marion Rice	2
Hartack, William J. ("Bill")	Sports-1
Hartdegen, Stephen Joseph	2

Subject	Volume
Hartline, Haldan Keffer	1, 1960s-1
Hartman, Phil(ip) Edward	5
Hartz, Louis	2
Haskins, Donald Lee	Sports-1
Hassenfeld, Merrill Lloyd	1960s-1
Hassenfeld, Stephen David	2
Hatcher, Richard Gordon	1960s-1
Hathaway, Starke Rosecrans	1
Haughton, Daniel Jeremiah	2
Haughton, William Robert ("Billy")	2
Havlicek, John Joseph	Sports-1
Hawkins, Cornelius L. ("Connie")	Sports-1
Hawkins, Erskine Ramsaydefined.	3
Hawkins, Frederick ("Erick")	4
Hay, Henry, Jr. ("Harry")	6
Hayakawa, S(amuel) I(chiye)	3, 1960s-1
Hayden, Thomas Emmett ("Tom")	1960s-1
Hayek, Friedrich August von	3
Hayes, Elvin Ernest	Sports-1
Hayes, Helen	3
Hayes, Robert Lee ("Bob")	6, Sports-1
Hayes, Wayne Woodrow ("Woody")	2, Sports-1
Haynes, Marques Oreole	Sports-1
Haynsworth, Clement Furman, Jr.	2, 1960s-1
Hays, (Lawrence) Brooks	1
Hays, Lee Elhardt	1
Hays, Wayne Levere	2
Hayworth, Rita	2
Hazlitt, Henry Stuart	3
Head, Edith	1
Healy, Timothy Stafford	3
Hearn, Francis Dayle (Chick)	6
Hearns, Thomas	Sports-1
Hearst, Randolph Apperson	6
Hearst, William Randolph, Jr.	3
Hecht, Harold	1
Heffelfinger, William Walter ("Pudge")	Sports-1
Hefner, Hugh Marston	1960s-1
Heidelberger, Michael	3
Heiden, Eric Arthur	Sports-1
Heifetz, Jascha	2
Hein, Mel(vin) John	Sports-1
Heinlein, Robert Anson	2
Heinz, Henry John, II ("Jack")	2
Heinz, Henry John, III	3
Heinz, Wilfred Charles ("Bill")	Sports-1
Heisman, John William ("Johnny")	Sports-1
Heiss Jenkins, Carol Elizabeth	Sports-1
Heller, Joseph	5, 1960s-1
Heller, Walter Wolfgang	2, 1960s-1
Hellman, Lillian Florence	1

Subject	Volume	Subject	Volume
Helms, Richard McGarrah	6	Hiss, Alger	4
Helmsley, Henry Brakmann ("Harry")	5	Hitchcock, Alfred Joseph	1960s-1
Hemingway, Margaux	4	Hitchcock, Thomas, Jr. ("Tommy")	Sports-1
Hemingway, Mary Welsh	2	Hitchings, George Herbert, Jr.	5
Henderson, Joseph A. ("Joe")	6	Hobby, Oveta Culp	4
Henderson, Leon	2	Hobson, Laura Kean Zametkin	2
Henderson, Rickey	Sports-1	Hoffa, James Riddle ("Jimmy")	1960s-1
Hendrix, James Marshall ("Jimmy"; "Maurice James"; "Jimi")	1960s-1	Hoffer, Eric	1
		Hoffman, Abbott Howard ("Abbie"; "Barry Freed")	2, 1960s-1
Henie, Sonja	Sports-1	Hoffman, Dustin Lee	1960s-1
Henry, Aaron Edd Jackson	5	Hoffman, Julius Jennings	1960s-1
Henson, James Maury ("Jim")	2	Hoffmann, Banesh	2
Henson, Paul Harrydefined.	5	Hofheinz, Roy Mark	1
Hentoff, Nathan Irving ("Nat")	1960s-1	Hofstadter, Richard	1960s-1
Hepburn, Audrey	3, 1960s-1	Hofstadter, Robert	2, 1960s-1
"Herblock." See Block, Herbert Lawrence.		Hogan, William Benjamin ("Ben")	5, Sports-1
Herlihy, James Leo	1960s-1	Holden, William	1
Herman, Floyd Caves ("Babe")	2	Holdsclaw, Chamique Shaunta	Sports-1
Herman, William Jennings ("Billy")	3	Holland, Jerome Heartwell ("Brud")	1
Herman, Woody	2	Holley, Robert William	3, 1960s-1
Herrnstein, Richard Julius	4	Holloway, Bruce Keener	5
Hersey, John Richard	3	Holm, Hanya	3
Hersh, Seymour M.	1960s-1	Holman, Nathan ("Nat")	4, Sports-1
Hershey, Alfred Day	5, 1960s-1	Holmes, John Clellon	2
Hesburgh, Theodore Martin	1960s-1	Holt, John Caldwell	1, 1960s-1
Heston, Charlton	1960s-1	Holzman, William ("Red")	5
Hewitt, Don S.	1960s-1	Hook, Sidney	2
Hewlett, William Redington ("Bill")	6, 1960s-1	Hooker, Evelyn Gentry	4
Hewlett, William Redington ("Bill"), and David Packard	1960s-1	Hooker, John Lee	6
		Hoover, John Edgar	1960s-1
Hexter, J. H. ("Jack")	4	Hope, Leslie Townes ("Bob")	1960s-1
Hibbler, Albert George ("Al")	6	Hopkins, Sam ("Lightnin'")	1
Hickerson, John Dewey	2	Hopper, Dennis	1960s-1
Hicks, Granville	1	Hopper, Edward	1960s-1
Higginbotham, A(loysius) Leon, Jr.	5	Hopper, Grace Brewster Murray	3
Highsmith, (Mary) Patricia	4	Hornberger, H(iester) Richard, Jr. (Richard Hooker)	5
Hildreth, Horace Augustus	2		
Hill, George Roy	6	Hornsby, Rogers ("Rajah")	Sports-1
Hill, Julian Werner	4	Hornung, Paul Vernon	Sports-1
Hill, (Joseph) Lister	1	Horowitz, Vladimir	2
Hillcourt, William ("Green Bar Bill")	3	Horst, Horst Paul	5
Hillegass, Clifton Keith	6	Horstmann, Dorothy Millicent	6
Hilsman, Roger	1960s-1	Horton, Mildred Helen McAfee	4
Himes, Chester Bomar	1	Horwich, Frances Rappaport ("Miss Frances")	6
Hines, Earl Kenneth ("Fatha")	1		
Hinton, Milton John ("Milt")	6	Haughton, Aaliyah Dana. See Aaliyah.	
Hirsch, Elroy Leon ("Crazylegs")	Sports-1	Houghton, Arthur Amory, Jr.	2
Hirsch, Eric Donald, Jr.	1960s-1	Houseman, John	2
Hirshhorn, Joseph Herman	1	Hovhaness, Alan	6
Hirt, Alois Maxwell ("Al")	5	Hoving, Walter	2

Subject	Volume	Subject	Volume
Howard, James Howell	4	Jackson, Philip Douglas ("Phil")	Sports-1
Howe, Gordon ("Gordie")	Sports-1	Jackson, Reginald Martinez ("Reggie")	Sports-1
Howe, Harold, II ("Doc")	6	Jackson, Travis Calvin ("Stonewall")	2
Howe, Irving	3, 1960s-1	Jackson, Walter Milton ("Milt"; "Bags")	5
Hoyt, Homer	1	Jacobs, Bernard B.	4
Hoyt, Waite Charles ("Schoolboy")	1	Jacobs, Helen Hull	5, Sports-1
Hruska, Roman Lee	5	Jacobs, Hirsch	Sports-1
Hubbard, (Robert) Cal	Sports-1	Jacobs, Jane	1960s-1
Hubbard, L(afayette) Ron(ald)	2	Jacoby, James Oswald ("Jim")	3
Hubbell, Carl Owen	2, Sports-1	Jacoby, Oswald (Ozzie)	1
Hudson, Rock	1, 1960s-1	Jaffe, Leo	5
Huggins, Charles Brenton	5, 1960s-1	Jagr, Jaromir	Sports-1
Huggins, Miller James	Sports-1	Jam Master Jay (Jason William Mizell)	6
Hughes, Emmet John	1	James, Dennis	5
Hughes, H(enry) Stuart	5	James, Harry Haag	1
Hughes, Harold Everett	4	Janeway, Eliot	3
Huie, William Bradford	2	Janis, Sidney	2
Hull, Brett	Sports-1	Janowitz, Morris	2
Hull, Robert Marvin, Jr. ("Bobby")	Sports-1	Jansen, Dan	Sports-1
Humphrey, Hubert Horatio, Jr.	1960s-1	Jarvis, Howard Arnold	2
Humphry, (Ann) Wickett	3	Javits, Jacob Koppel	2
Huncke, Herbert Edwin	4	Jaworski, Leon	1
Hunt, H(aroldson) L(afayette), Jr.	1960s-1	Jeffries, James Jackson	Sports-1
Hunt, Lamar	Sports-1	Jenkins, Carol Elizabeth Heiss. *See*	
Hunter, Alberta	1	Heiss Jenkins, Carol Elizabeth.	
Hunter, Howard William	4	Jenkins, David Wilkinson	Sports-1
Hunter, James Augustus ("Catfish";		Jenkins, Gordon Hill	1
"Jim")	5, Sports-1	Jenkins, Hayes Alan	Sports-1
Hunter, Kim	6	Jenner, (William) Bruce	Sports-1
Huntley, Chester Robert ("Chet"), and		Jenner, William Ezra	1
David McClure Brinkley	1960s-1	Jennings, Waylon Arnold	6
Husted, Marjorie Child	2	Jensen, Arthur Robert	1960s-1
Huston, John Marcellus	2, 1960s-1	Jessel, George Albert ("Georgie")	1
Hutchinson, G(eorge) Evelyn	3	Jessup, Philip Caryl	2
Hutson, Don(ald) Montgomery	5, Sports-1	Jeter, Derek Sanderson	Sports-1
Iba, Henry Payne ("Hank")	3, Sports-1	Jimmy the Greek. *See* Snyder, James.	
Illich, Ivan	1960s-1	Jobson, Gary	Sports-1
Indiana, Robert	1960s-1	Joffrey, Robert	2, 1960s-1
Ingersoll, Ralph McAllister	1	Johns, Jasper	1960s-1
Inkster, Juli Simpson	Sports-1	Johnson, Clarence Leonard ("Kelly")	2
Irish, Edward Simmons, Sr. ("Ned")	1	Johnson, Claudia Alta Taylor ("Lady	
Irwin, James Benson	3	Bird")	1960s-1
Isherwood, Christopher William	2	Johnson, D(aniel) Mead	3
Iverson, Allen Ezail	Sports-1	Johnson, Earvin, Jr. ("Magic")	Sports-1
Ives, Burl Icle Ivanhoe	4	Johnson, Edward Crosby, II	1
Jack, Beau	6	Johnson, Eleanor Murdock	2
Jackson, George Anthony	6	Johnson, Frank Minis, Jr.	5
Jackson, Henry Martin ("Scoop")	1, 1960s-1	Johnson, Haynes Bonner	1960s-1
Jackson, J(ohn) B(rinckerhoff)	4	Johnson, John Arthur ("Jack")	Sports-1
Jackson, Jesse Louis	1960s-1	Johnson, Leon William	5
Jackson, Joseph Jefferson Wofford		Johnson, Lyndon Baines	1960s-1
("Shoeless Joe")	Sports-1	Johnson, Michael	Sports-1

Subject	Volume	Subject	Volume
Johnson, Paul Burney, Jr.	1	Kamen, Martin D(avid)	6
Johnson, Philip Cortelyou	1960s-1	Kane, Robert ("Bob")	5
Johnson, Rachel Harris	1	Kanin, Garson	5
Johnson, Rafer Lewis	1960s-1, Sports-1	Kappel, Frederick Russell	4
Johnson, Randall David ("Randy")	Sports-1	Kardiner, Abram	1
Johnson, Robert Edward	4	Karnow, Stanley	1960s-1
Johnson, Robert Glenn, Jr. ("Junior")	Sports-1	Karolyi, Béla	Sports-1
Johnson, Robert Samuel	5	Karski, Jan	6
Johnson, Virginia. See Masters, William		Katz, Lillian. See Vernon, Lillian.	
Howell, and Virginia Eshelman		Katzenbach, Nicholas de Belleville	1960s-1
Johnson.		Kauffman, Ewing Marion	3
Johnson, Wallace Edwards	2	Kaufman, Andrew Geoffrey ("Andy")	1
Johnson, Walter Perry ("The Big		Kaufman, Bel	1960s-1
Train")	Sports-1	Kaufman, Irving Robert	3
Johnson, William D. ("Bill")	Sports-1	Kaufman, Murray ("Murray the K")	1
Johnson, William Julius ("Judy")	2, Sports-1	Kay, Ulysses Simpson	4
Johnston, Alvin Melvin ("Tex")	5	Kaye, Danny	2
Jones, David ("Deacon")	Sports-1	Kaye, Sammy	2
Jones, Everett LeRoy (Amiri		Kaye, Sylvia Fine	3
Baraka,"LeRoi")	1960s-1	Kazin, Alfred	5
Jones, Horace Allyn ("Jimmy")	6	Keeler, Ruby	3
Jones, James Earl	1960s-1	Keeler, William Henry	Sports-1
Jones, Jerral Wayne ("Jerry")	Sports-1	Keeler, William Wayne	2
Jones, K. C.	Sports-1	Keeny, Spurgeon Milton ("Sam")	2
Jones, Marion Lois	Sports-1	Kelly, Charles E. ("Commando")	1
Jones, Quincy Delight, Jr.	1960s-1	Kelly, Eugene Curran ("Gene")	4
Jones, Robert Reynolds, Jr. ("Bob")	5	Kelly, George Lange ("Highpockets")	1
Jones, Robert Trent, Sr.	6	Kelly, Grace Patricia (Princess Grace)	1
Jones, Robert Tyre, Jr. ("Bobby")	Sports-1	Kelly, John Brendan, Sr. ("Jack")	Sports-1
Joplin, Janis Lyn	1960s-1	Kelly, Michael Joseph ("King")	Sports-1
Jordan, Barbara Charline	4	Kelman, Wolfe	2
Jordan, June	6	Kelsey, Frances Kathleen Oldham	1960s-1
Jordan, Leonard Beck ("Len")	1	Kemeny, John George	3
Jordan, Michael Jeffrey ("Air")	Sports-1	Kemper, James Scott	1
Jorgensen, Christine	2	Kemper, James Scott, Jr.	6
Jovanovich, William Ilija ("Bill")	6	Kempton, (James) Murray	5
Joyner, Florence Delorez Griffith ("Flo		Kendall, Henry Way	5
Jo"). See Griffith Joyner, Florence		Kendrick, Alexander	3
Delorez ("Flo Jo").		Kendricks, Eddie James	3
Joyner-Kersee, Jacqueline ("Jackie")	Sports-1	Kennan, George Frost	1960s-1
Judd, Donald Clarence	4	Kennedy, Edward Moore ("Ted")	1960s-1
Judd, Walter Henry	4	Kennedy, Florynce Rae ("Flo")	6
Judge, Mychal Fallon	6	Kennedy, John Fitzgerald	1960s-1
Julia, Raul Rafael Carlos	4	Kennedy, John Fitzgerald, Jr.	5
Kael, Pauline	6	Kennedy, Robert Francis	1960s-1
Kahanamoku, Duke	Sports-1	Kennedy, Rose Elizabeth Fitzgerald	4
Kahane, Meir	2, 1960s-1	Kennedy, William Jesse, Jr.	1
Kahn, Herman Bernard	1, 1960s-1	Kent, Corita	2
Kahn, Louis Isidore	1960s-1	Keppel, Francis	2
Kahn, Madeline Gail	5	Kerner, Otto, Jr.	1960s-1
Kaline, Al(bert) William	Sports-1	Kerr, Clark	1960s-1
Kalman, Tibor	5	Kerr, Walter Francis	4

Subject	Volume	Subject	Volume
Kertész, André (Andor)	1	Kohlberg, Lawrence	2
Kesey, Kenneth Elton ("Ken")	6, 1960s-1	Kohler, Foy David	1960s-1
Ketcham, Henry King ("Hank")	6	Kono, Tommy Tamio	Sports-1
Ketchel, Stanley	Sports-1	Koontz, Elizabeth Duncan ("Libby")	2, 1960s-1
Keyserling, Leon Hirsch	2	Koopmans, Tjalling Charles	1
Khaury, Herbert Butros. *See* Tiny Tim.		Koresh, David	3
Khorana, Har Gobind	1960s-1	Korshak, Sidney Roy	4
Kiam, Victor Kermit, II	6	Kosinski, Jerzy Nikodem	3, 1960s-1
Kidd, William Winston ("Billy")	Sports-1	Koufax, Sanford ("Sandy")	1960s-1, Sports-1
Kienholz, Edward Ralph	4	Kozol, Jonathan	1960s-1
Kieran, John Francis	1	Kraft, Joseph	2
Kiley, Richard Paul	5	Kramer, John Albert ("Jack")	Sports-1
Killebrew, Harmon Clayton, Jr.	1960s-1, Sports-1	Kramer, Stanley Earl	6
Killian, James Rhyne, Jr.	2	Krasner, Lee	1
Kimball, Spencer Woolley	1	Kraus, Hans Peter	2
Kinard, Frank Manning ("Bruiser")	1	Kriendler, H. Peter ("Pete")	6
Kiner, Ralph McPherran	Sports-1	Krim, Arthur B.	4
King, B. B.	1960s-1	Kristeller, Paul Oskar	5
King, Billie Jean Moffitt	1960s-1, Sports-1	Kroc, Raymond Albert ("Ray")	1, 1960s-1
King, Don(ald)	Sports-1	Krol, John Joseph	4
King, Martin Luther, Jr.	1960s-1	Krone, Julieanne Louise ("Julie")	Sports-1
King, Martin Luther, Sr. ("Daddy King")	1	Krulak, Victor Harold	1960s-1
Kingman, Dong	6	Krzyzewski, Michael William ("Mike")	Sports-1
Kiphuth, Robert John Herman ("Bob")	Sports-1	Kubrick, Stanley	5, 1960s-1
Kiraly, Karch	Sports-1	Kuhn, Margaret Eliza ("Maggie")	4
Kirby, George	4	Kuhn, Thomas Samuel	4
Kirk, Grayson Louis	5, 1960s-1	Kunstler, William Moses	4, 1960s-1
Kirk, Russell Amos	4	Kuralt, Charles Bishop	5
Kirkland, (Joseph) Lane	5	Kurland, Philip B.	4
Kirstein, Lincoln	4	Kurland, Robert ("Bob")	Sports-1
Kirsten, Dorothy	3	Kurtzman, Harvey	3
Kissinger, Henry Alfred	1960s-1	Kusch, Polykarp	3
Kistiakowsky, George Bogdan	1	Kutner, Luis	3
Klein, Anne	1960s-1	Kuznets, Simon Smith	1
Klein, Calvin	1960s-1	Kwan, Michelle Wing	Sports-1
Kleindienst, Richard G.	6	Labouisse, Henry Richardson	2
Klem, William Joseph ("Bill")	Sports-1	Ladd, George Eldon	1
Kline, Nathan Schellenberg	1	Lajoie, Nap(oleon)	Sports-2
Klopfer, Donald Simon	2	Lake, Harriete. *See* Sothern, Ann.	
Kluszewski, Theodore Bernard ("Ted"; "Big Klu")	2	Lalas, Alexi	Sports-2
Klutznick, Philip M.	5	Lamarr, Hedy	6
Knight, John Shively	1	Lambeau, Earl Louis ("Curly")	Sports-2
Knight, Robert Montgomery ("Bob")	Sports-1	Lambert, John Harold ("Jack")	Sports-2
Knight, Ted	2	Lamont, Corliss	4
Knopf, Alfred Abraham	1	LaMotta, Jake	Sports-2
Knott, Walter	1	Lamour, Dorothy	4
Knowles, John	6	L'Amour, Louis	2
Koch, Kenneth Jay	6	Lancaster, Burt(on) Stephen	4
Kohl, Herbert R.	1960s-1	Lancaster, Kelvin John	5
		Lanchester, Elsa	2
		Land, Edwin Herbert	3

Subject	Volume
Landers, Ann (Esther Friedman Lederer)	6
Landis, Kenesaw Mountain	Sports-2
Landon, Alf(red) Mossman	2
Landon, Margaret Dorothea Mortenson	3
Landon, Michael	3
Landry, Thomas Wade ("Tom")	6, Sports-2
Lane, Burton	5
Lane, Frank Charles	1
Lane, Richard ("Dick"; "Night Train")	6, Sports-2
Langer, Susanne Katherina	1
Lanier, Willie E.	Sports-2
Lansdale, Edward Geary	2, 1960s-1
Lansky, Meyer	1
Lantz, Walter	4
Lapchick, Joseph Bohomiel ("Joe")	Sports-2
Lardner, Ringgold Wilmer, Jr. ("Ring")	6, Sports-2
Largent, Steve	Sports-2
Larson, (Lewis) Arthur	3
Larson, Jonathan	4
Lasch, (Robert) Christopher	4, 1960s-1
Lash, Joseph P.	2
Lasker, Mary Woodward	4
Lattimore, Owen	2
Laughlin, James	5
Lauren, Ralph	1960s-1
Lausche, Frank John	2
Lawford, Peter Sydney Vaughn	1
Lawrence, Jacob Armstead	6
Lay, Herman W.	1
Layne, Robert Lawrence, Sr. ("Bobby")	2, Sports-2
Lazar, Irving Paul ("Swifty")	3
Lazarus, Ralph	2
Leahy, Francis William ("Frank")	Sports-2
Leary, Timothy Francis	4, 1960s-1
Lebow, Fred	4
Le Clercq, Tanaquil ("Tanny")	6
Lee, (Nelle) Harper	1960s-1
Lee, J(oseph) Bracken ("Brack")	4
Lee, Peggy	6
Lee, Pinky	3
Lee, William Andrew	5
Leetch, Brian	Sports-2
Le Gallienne, Eva	3
Leinsdorf, Erich	3
Lekachman, Robert	2
Lelyveld, Arthur Joseph	4
LeMay, Curtis Emerson	2, 1960s-1
Lemieux, Mario	Sports-2
Lemmon, John Uhler, III ("Jack")	6, 1960s-1
Lemnitzer, Lyman Louis	2
Lemon, Meadow George ("Meadowlark")	Sports-2
Lemon, Robert Granville ("Bob")	6
LeMond, Greg(ory) James	Sports-2
Lemons, A. E. ("Abe")	6
Lenya, Lotte	1
Leonard, Benny	Sports-2
Leonard, Ray Charles ("Sugar Ray")	Sports-2
Leonard, Sheldon	5, 1960s-1
Leonard, Walter Fenner ("Buck")	5, Sports-2
Leontief, Wassily	5
Lerner, Alan Jay	2
Lerner, Max	3
Lerner, Nathan Bernard	5
LeRoy, Mervyn	2
Leslie, Lisa DeShaun	Sports-2
Levertov, Denise	5
Levi, Edward H(irsch)	6
Levin, Meyer	1
Levine, Joseph Edward	2
Levitt, William Jaird	4
Lewis, (Joseph) Anthony	1960s-1
Lewis, Flora	6
Lewis, Frederick Carlton ("Carl")	Sports-2
Lewis, Jerry	1960s-1
Lewis, John Aaron	6
Lewis, John Robert	1960s-1
Lewis, Oscar	1960s-1
Lewis, Reginald Francis	3
Lewis, Shari	5
Libby, Leona Woods Marshall	2
Libby, Willard Frank	1960s-1
Liberace, Wladziu Valentino	2
Liberman, Alexander Semeonovitch	5
Lichine, Alexis	2
Lichtenstein, Roy	5, 1960s-1
Licklider, J(oseph) C(arl) R(obnett)	2
Lieberman-Cline, Nancy	Sports-2
Liebman, Max	1
Lilienthal, David Eli	1
Lillard, Joseph ("Joe")	Sports-2
Lillehei, C(larence) Walton ("Walt")	5
Lilly, Kristine Marie	Sports-2
Lilly, Robert Lewis ("Bob")	Sports-2
Liman, Arthur Lawrence	5
Lincoln, C(harles) Eric	6
Lindbergh, Anne (Spencer) Morrow	6
Lindsay, Goldie Ina Ruby ("Eldress Bertha")	2
Lindsay, John Vliet	6, 1960s-1

Subject	Volume
Lindsay, Robert Blake Theodore ("Ted")	Sports-2
Lindstrom, Frederick Charles, Jr. ("Lindy")	1
Ling, James Joseph	1960s-1
Link, Arthur Stanley	5
Link, Edwin Albert	1
Lipmann, Fritz Albert	2
Lippmann, Walter	1960s-1
Liquori, Martin William, Jr. ("Marty")	Sports-2
Liston, Charles ("Sonny")	1960s-1, Sports-2
Little, Royal	2
Livingston, M(ilton) Stanley	2
Livingstone, Mary	1
Lloyd, Christine Marie ("Chris") Evert. *See* Evert, Christine Marie ("Chris").	
Lloyd, John Henry ("Pop")	Sports-2
Lobo, Rebecca Rose	Sports-2
Lodge, Henry Cabot, Jr.	1, 1960s-1
Lodge, John Davis	1
Loeb, Henry, III	3
Loeb, Nackey Scripps	6
Loeb, William	1
Loewe, Frederick	2
Loewy, Raymond Fernand	2
Logan, Joshua Lockwood, III	2
Logan, Rayford Whittingham	1
Logue, Edward Joseph	6
Lomax, Alan	6
Lombardi, Vincent Thomas ("Vince")	1960s-1, Sports-2
Longden, John Eric ("Johnny")	Sports-2
Loos, (Corinne) Anita	1
Lopez, Nancy Marie	Sports-2
Lord, John Wesley	2
Lord, Walter	6
Lorde, Audre Geraldine	3
Lorentz, Pare	3
Lott, Ronald Mandel ("Ronnie")	Sports-2
Louganis, Greg(ory) Efthimios	Sports-2
Louis, Joseph ("Joe")	1, Sports-2
Lovelace, Linda Susan	6
Lovestone, Jay	2
Lovett, Robert Abercrombie	2
Lowe, Stewart Alexander ("Alex")	5
Lowell, Robert Traill Spence, IV ("Cal")	1960s-1
Lowenstein, Allard Kenneth	1960s-1
Loy, Myrna	3
Lubell, Samuel	2
Luce, Clare Boothe	2

Subject	Volume
Luckman, Sid(ney)	5, Sports-2
Ludlam, Charles	2
Ludlum, Robert	6
Ludwig, Daniel Keith	3
Luening, Otto Clarence	4
Luisetti, Angelo Enrico ("Hank")	6, Sports-2
Lujack, John Christopher, Jr. ("Johnny")	Sports-2
Lukas, J(ay) Anthony	5
Lumet, Sidney	1960s-1
Lupino, Ida	4
Luria, Salvador Edward	3, 1960s-1
Lynd, Helen Merrell	1
Lynes, (Joseph) Russell, Jr.	3
Lyons, Theodore Amar ("Ted")	2
Maas, Peter Guttrich	6
MacArthur, Jean Marie Faircloth	6
McAuliffe, (Sharon) Christa	2
McBride, Lloyd	1
McCain, John Sidney, Jr.	1, 1960s-2
McCall, Thomas William Lawson	1
McCarthy, Eugene Joseph	1960s-2
McCarthy, Glenn Herbert	2
McCarthy, Joseph Vincent ("Joe")	Sports-2
McCarthy, Mary Therese	2, 1960s-2
McCartney, Linda Louise Eastman	5
McCarty, Oseola ("Kelli")	5
McClintock, Barbara	3
McCloy, John Jay	2, 1960s-2
McCone, John Alex	3
McCormick, Frank Andrew ("Buck")	1
McCormick, Kenneth Dale	5
McCormick, Pat(ricia) Joan	Sports-2
MacCorquodale, Donald William ("Mac")	2
McCovey, Willie Lee	1960s-2, Sports-2
McCracken, James Eugene	2
McCrea, Joel Albert	2
McCree, Wade Hampton, Jr.	2
McCullers, Carson	1960s-2
MacDermot, (Arthur Terence) Galt	1960s-2
Macdonald, Dwight	1, 1960s-2
MacDonald, John Dann	2
Macdonald, Ross	1
McDowall, Roderick Andrew Anthony Jude ("Roddy")	5
McElhenny, Hugh Edward, Jr.	Sports-2
McEnroe, John Patrick, Jr.	Sports-2
McGee, Gale William	3
McGill, Ralph Emerson	1960s-2
McGill, William James	5

Subject	Volume
McGillicuddy, Cornelius. *See* Mack, Connie.	
McGinniss, Joseph ("Joe")	1960s-2
McGovern, George Stanley	1960s-2
McGowan, William George	3
McGraw, John Joseph	Sports-2
McGuire, Dorothy Hackett	6
McGuire, Francis Joseph ("Frank")	4
McGwire, Mark David	Sports-2
Machito, (Frank Raúl Grillo)	1
MacInnes, Helen Clark	1
McIntire, Carl Curtis	6
McIntosh, Millicent Carey	6
Mack, Connie	Sports-2
Mack, Walter Staunton, Jr.	2
McKay, James McManus ("Jim")	Sports-2
McKay, John Harvey	6
Mackey, Joseph Creighton	1
McKissick, Floyd B.	3
McLain, Dennis Dale ("Denny")	Sports-2
MacLaine, Shirley	1960s-2
McLean, Malcom Purcell	6
MacLeish, Archibald	1
McLuhan, (Herbert) Marshall	1960s-2
McMillan, Edwin Mattison	3
MacMurray, Fred(erick) Martin	3
McMurtry, Larry Jeff	1960s-2
McNair, Ron(ald) Erwin	2
McNally, John Victor ("Johnny Blood")	1, Sports-2
McNally, Terrence	1960s-2
McNamara, Margaret McKinstry Craig	1, 1960s-2
McNamara, Robert Strange	1960s-2
McNamee, Graham	Sports-2
McNeill, Don(ald) Thomas	4
McPartland, James Dugald ("Jimmy")	3
MacPhail, Leland Stanford, Sr. ("Larry")	Sports-2
McQueen, Steve	1960s-2
McQueen, Thelma ("Butterfly")	4
McRae, Carmen Mercedes	4
MacRae, (Albert) Gordon	2
McVeigh, Timothy James	6
Madden, John Earl	Sports-2
Madden, Ray John	2
Maddux, Greg(ory) Alan	Sports-2
Magnin, Cyril	2
Magnuson, Warren Grant	2
Magowan, Robert Anderson	1
Mahre, Phil(ip)	Sports-2
Mailer, Norman Kingsley	1960s-2
Malamud, Bernard	2

Subject	Volume
Malcolm X (Malik El-Shabazz)	1960s-2
Maleska, Eugene Thomas	3
Malone, Dumas	2
Malone, Karl Anthony	Sports-2
Malone, Moses Eugene	Sports-2
Maltz, Albert	1
Mamoulian, Rouben Zachary	2
Manchester, William Raymond	1960s-2
Mancini, Henry Nicola	4, 1960s-2
Mankiewicz, Joseph Leo	3
Mann, Jonathan Max	5
Manne, Sheldon ("Shelly")	1
Mannes, Marya	2
Manning, Timothy	2
Mansfield, Michael Joseph ("Mike")	6
Manson, Charles Milles	1960s-2
Mantle, Mickey Charles	4, 1960s-2, Sports-2
Maple, John Edward (Jack)	6
Mapplethorpe, Robert	2
Maravich, Peter Press ("Pete")	2, Sports-2
Marble, Alice	2, Sports-2
Marcello, Carlos	3
Marchetti, Gino John	Sports-2
Marciano, Rocky	Sports-2
Marcus, Stanley	6
Marcuse, Herbert	1960s-2
Margulies, Lazar	1
Marichal, Juan Antonio	Sports-2
Marino, Daniel Constantine, Jr. ("Dan")	Sports-2
Maris, Roger Eugene	1, 1960s-2, Sports-2
Marisol (Marisol Escobar)	1960s-2
Mark, Herman Francis	3
Markham, Dewey ("Pigmeat")	1
Marks, John D. ("Johnny")	1
Marriott, Alice Sheets	6
Marriott, J(ohn) Willard	1
Mars, Forrest Edward, Sr.	5
Marshall, E(dda) G(unnar)	5
Marshall, George Preston	Sports-2
Marshall, Thurgood	3, 1960s-2
Marston, Robert Quarles	5
Martin, Alfred Manuel, Jr. ("Billy")	2
Martin, Dean	4, 1960s-2
Martin, Donald Edward ("Don")	6
Martin, Freddy	1
Martin, John Bartlow	2, 1960s-2
Martin, Mary Virginia	2
Martin, William McChesney, Jr.	5, 1960s-2

Subject	Volume	Subject	Volume
Martinez, Pedro Jaime	Sports-2	Meyendorff, John	3
Marvin, Lee	2	Meyers, Ann Elizabeth	Sports-2
Mas Canosa, Jorge	5	Meyner, Robert Baumle	2
Mason, (William) Birny J., Jr.	5	Michener, James Albert	5
Massey, Raymond Hart	1	Middlecoff, (Emmett) Cary ("Doc")	5
Masters, William Howell	6, 1960s-2	Middleton, Drew	2
Masters, William Howell, and Virginia Eshelman Johnson	1960s-2	Mies van der Rohe, Ludwig	1960s-2
Mathews, Edwin Lee ("Eddie")	6	Mikan, George Lawrence, Jr.	Sports-2
Mathewson, Christopher ("Christy")	Sports-2	Mikita, Stan	Sports-2
Mathias, Robert Bruce ("Bob")	Sports-2	Milanov, Zinka	2
Matson, James Randel ("Randy")	Sports-2	Milgram, Stanley	1
Matson, Oliver Genoa, II ("Ollie")	Sports-2	Milland, Ray	2
Matsunaga, Spark Masayuki ("Sparkie")	2	Millar, Kenneth. See Macdonald, Ross.	
Matthau, Walter	6, 1960s-2	Miller, Arnold Ray	1
Matthews, Burnita Shelton	2	Miller, Arthur Asher	1960s-2
Mature, Victor John	5	Miller, Carl S.	2
Mauldin, William Henry ("Bill")	1960s-2	Miller, Cheryl DeAnn	Sports-2
Maxwell, Vera Huppé	4	Miller, Marvin Julian	Sports-2
Maxwell, William Keepers, Jr.	6	Miller, Merton Howard	6
May, Elaine	1960s-2	Miller, Reginald Wayne ("Reggie")	Sports-2
May, Rollo Reece	4	Miller, Roger Dean	3
Mayer, Maria Goeppert. See Goeppert-Mayer, Maria.		Miller, Shannon Lee	Sports-2
Mayfield, Curtis Lee	5	Miller, William Mosely	2
Maynard, Don(ald) Rogers	Sports-2	Mills, C(harles) Wright	1960s-2
Maynard, Robert Clyve	3	Mills, Wilbur Daigh	3
Mays, Benjamin Elijah	1	Milstein, Nathan	3
Mays, William Howard, Jr. ("Willie")	1960s-2, Sports-2	Mink, Patsy Matsu Takemoto	6
Meader, (Abbott) Vaughn	1960s-2	Minnelli, Vincente	2
Meadows, Audrey	4	Minnesota Fats (Rudolf Walter Wanderone, Jr.)	4
Means, Gardiner Coit	2	Minow, Newton Norman	1960s-2
Medeiros, Humberto Sousa	1	Mitchell, (John) Broadus	2
Medina, Harold Raymond	2	Mitchell, Joan	3
Meeker, Ralph	2	Mitchell, John James, Jr.	1
Meisner, Sanford	5	Mitchell, John Newton	2, 1960s-2
Mellon, Paul	5	Mitchell, Joseph Quincy	4
Menninger, Karl Augustus	2	Mitchell, Robert Cornelius, Sr. ("Bobby")	Sports-2
Menuhin, Yehudi	5	Mitchum, Robert Charles Durman	5
Meola, Tony	Sports-2	Mitford, Jessica ("Decca")	4
Mercer, John Herndon ("Johnny")	1960s-2	Mize, John Robert ("Johnny")	3
Mercer, Mabel	1	Mizell, Jason William. See Jam Master Jay.	
Meredith, (Oliver) Burgess	5	Mizener, Arthur Moore	2
Meredith, J(ames) H(oward)	1960s-2	Moakley, John Joseph (Joe)	6
Merman, Ethel	1	Mohr, Charles Henry	2
Merriam, Eve	3	Molnar, Charles Edwin	4
Merrick, David	6	Momaday, N(avarre) Scott	1960s-2
Merrill, James Ingram	4	Monette, Paul Landry	4
Merrill, John Putnam	1	Monk, Thelonious Sphere	1, 1960s-2
Metcalfe, Ralph Horace	Sports-2	Monroe, Earl Vernon, Jr	Sports-2

Subject	Volume	Subject	Volume
Monroe, Marilyn	1960s-2	Murphy, Calvin Jerome	Sports-2
Monroe, Marion	1	Murphy, George Lloyd	3
Monroe, Rose Leigh Will	5	Murphy, Joseph Samson	5
Monroe, William Smith ("Bill")	4	Murray, Anna Pauline ("Pauli")	1
Montagu, Ashley	5	Murray, Arthur	3
Montana, Joseph Clifford, Jr. ("Joe")	Sports-2	Murray, James Patrick ("Jim")	5, Sports-2
Montgomery, Elizabeth	4	Murray, Kathryn Hazel	5
Montgomery, Robert	1	Murrow, Edward Roscoe	1960s-2
Moody, Helen Wills. *See* Wills (Moody), Helen Newington.		Musial, Stanley Frank ("Stan the Man")	Sports-2
Moore, Archibald Lee ("Archie")	5, Sports-2	Muskie, Edmund Sixtus	4, 1960s-2
Moore, Francis Daniels, and Thomas Earl Starzl	1960s-2	Myer, Dillon Seymour	1
		Nabokov, Vladimir	1960s-2
Moore, Garry	3, 1960s-2	Nabrit, James Madison, Jr.	5
Moore, Jack Carlton ("Clayton")	5	Nader, Ralph	1960s-2
Moore, Mary Tyler	1960s-2	Nagel, Ernest	1, 1960s-2
Moore, Stanford	1	Nagurski, Bronislau ("Bronko")	2, Sports-2
Moos, Malcolm Charles	1	Nagy, Steve	Sports-2
Moreno, Rita	1960s-2	Naismith, James	Sports-2
Morgan, Henry (Lerner von Ost)	4	Namath, Joseph William ("Joe")	1960s-2, Sports-2
Morgan, Henry Sturgis ("Harry")	1	Nash, Gerald David	6
Morgan, Joe Leonard	Sports-2	Nash, Graham. *See* Crosby, Stills, and Nash.	
Morganfield, McKinley. *See* Waters, Muddy.		Nason, John William	6
Morison, Elting Elmore	4	Nathans, Daniel	5
Moross, Jerome	1	Navratilova, Martina	Sports-2
Morris, Richard Brandon	2	Nearing, Helen Knothe	4
Morris, Robert	1960s-2	Nearing, Scott	1
Morris, William Weaks ("Willie")	5	Neel, James Van Gundia	6
Morrison, James Douglas ("Jim")	1960s-2	Nef, John Ulric	2
Morse, Wayne Lyman	1960s-2	Negri, Pola	2
Morton, Thruston Ballard	1	Nelson, (John) Byron, Jr.	Sports-2
Mosbacher, Emil, Jr. ("Bus")	Sports-2	Nelson, Eric Hilliard ("Rick")	1
Mosconi, William Joseph ("Willie")	3	Nelson, Harriet Hilliard	4
Moses, Edwin Corley	Sports-2	Nemerov, Howard	3
Moses, Robert	1	Neuberger, Maurine Brown	6
Moses, Robert Parris	1960s-2	Neumann, Vera Salaff ("Vera")	3
Motherwell, Robert	3	Neustadt, Richard Elliott	1960s-2
Motley, Marion	5, Sports-2	Nevelson, Louise	2, 1960s-2
Mott, Stewart Rawlings	1960s-2	Nevers, Ernest Alonzo ("Ernie")	Sports-2
Mourning, Alonzo Harding, Jr.	Sports-2	Newell, Allen	3
Moynihan, Daniel Patrick	1960s-2	Newell, Peter ("Pete")	Sports-2
Mueller, Reuben Herbert	1	Newhall, Beaumont	3
Muhammad, Elijah	1960s-2	Newhart, George Robert ("Bob")	1960s-2
Muldowney, Shirley Roque	Sports-2	Newhouser, Harold ("Prince Hal")	5
Mullen, Joseph ("Joey")	Sports-2	Newman, Paul Arthur	1960s-2
Mulligan, Gerald Joseph ("Gerry")	4	Newton, Huey Percy	2, 1960s-2
Mulliken, Robert Sanderson	2, 1960s-2	Neyman, Jerzy	1
Mumford, Lawrence Quincy	1	Nicholas, Harold Lloyd	6
Mumford, Lewis Charles	2	Nichols, Mike	1960s-2
Murchison, Clint(on) Williams, Jr.	2	Nicholson, Jack	1960s-2

Subject	Volume
Nicklaus, Jack William	1960s-2, Sports-2
Niebuhr, Reinhold	1960s-2
Niel, Cornelis Bernardus van	1
Nikolais, Alwin Theodore ("Nik")	3, 1960s-2
Nilsson, Harry Edward, III	4
Nin, Anaïs	1960s-2
Nirenberg, Marshall Warren	1960s-2
Nisbet, Robert Alexander	4
Nitschke, Ray(mond) Ernest	5, Sports-2
Nixon, Pat(ricia)	3
Nixon, Richard Milhous	4, 1960s-2
Nizer, Louis	4, 1960s-2
Noguchi, Isamu	2
Noll, Charles Henry ("Chuck")	Sports-2
Nomellini, Leo Joseph	6
Norris, Clarence	2
Norstad, Lauris	2
North, John Ringling	1
Northrop, John Howard	2
Northrop, John Knudsen ("Jack")	1
Norvo, Joseph Kenneth ("Red")	5
Notorious B.I.G. ("Biggie Smalls")	5
Noyce, Robert Norton	2, 1960s-2
Nozick, Robert	6
Nyad, Diana	Sports-2
Oakes, John Bertram	6
Oates, Joyce Carol	1960s-2
O'Brien, Lawrence Francis, Jr. ("Larry")	2, 1960s-2
O'Brien, (William) Parry, Jr.	Sports-2
O'Brien, William Joseph, Jr. ("Pat")	1
Ochs, Philip David	1960s-2
Ochsner, (Edward William) Alton	1
O'Connor, Carroll	6
O'Connor, Flannery	1960s-2
O'Connor, John Joseph	6
Odell, Allan Gilbert	4
Odetta	1960s-2
O'Dwyer, (Peter) Paul	5
Oerter, Al(fred) Adolph, Jr.	Sports-2
O'Farrill, Arturo ("Chico")	6
Ogilvie, Richard Buell	2
Ogilvy, David Mackenzie	5
O'Hair, Madalyn Murray	4, 1960s-2
O'Horgan, Thomas ("Tom")	1960s-2
Okada, Kenzo	1
O'Keeffe, Georgia Totto	2
Olajuwon, Hakeem Abdul	Sports-2
Oldenburg, Claes Thure	1960s-2
Oldfield, Berna Eli ("Barney")	Sports-2
Olin, John Merrill	1

Subject	Volume
Oliphant, Patrick Bruce ("Pat")	1960s-2
Olsen, Merlin Jay	Sports-2
Onassis, Jacqueline Lee Kennedy ("Jackie")	4, 1960s-2
O'Neal, Shaq(uille) Rashaun	Sports-2
O'Neill, Thomas Philip, Jr. ("Tip")	4
Onsager, Lars	1960s-2
Oppen, George	1
Orbison, Roy Kelton	2, 1960s-2
Ormandy, Eugene	1
Orr, Robert Gordon ("Bobby")	1960s-2, Sports-2
Osborne, Thomas William ("Tom")	Sports-2
O'Sullivan, Maureen	5
Oswald, Lee Harvey	1960s-2
Ott, Mel(vin) Thomas	Sports-2
Ouimet, Francis DeSales	Sports-2
Owens, James Cleveland ("Jesse")	Sports-2
Owings, Nathaniel Alexander	1
Packard, David. *See also* Hewlett, William Redington, and David Packard.	4
Packard, Vance Oakley	4
Padover, Saul Kussiel	1
Page, Alan Cedric	Sports-2
Page, Geraldine	2
Page, Ruth Marian	3
Paige, Leroy Robert ("Satchel")	1, Sports-2
Paik, Nam June	1960s-2
Pais, Abraham	6
Pakula, Alan Jay	5
Paley, William Samuel	2
Palmer, Arnold Daniel ("Arnie")	Sports-2
Palmer, James Alvin ("Jim")	Sports-2
Palmer, R(obert) R(oswell)	6
Palmieri, Carlos Manuel, Jr. ("Charlie")	2
Papp, Joseph	3, 1960s-2
Parcells, Duane Charles ("Bill")	Sports-2
Paredes, Américo	5
Parent, Bernard Marcel ("Bernie")	Sports-2
Parish, Dorothy May Kinnicutt ("Sister Parish")	4
Parker, James Thomas ("Jim")	Sports-2
Parker, Thomas Andrew ("Colonel")	5
Parks, Bert	3
Parks, Gordon, Sr.	1960s-2
Parks, Henry Green, Jr.	2
Parnis, Sarah Rosen ("Mollie")	3
Parsons, Elizabeth Pierson ("Betty")	1
Parsons, James Benton	3
Parsons, Johnnie	1

Subject	Volume	Subject	Volume
Parton, James	6	Phillips, Kevin Price	1960s-2
Passman, Otto Ernest	2	Phillips, Marjorie Acker	1
Pasternak, Joseph Herman ("Joe")	3	Phillips, William	6
Pastore, John Orlando	6	Phoenix, River Jude	3
Paterno, Joseph Vincent ("Joe")	Sports-2	Piazza, Michael Joseph ("Mike")	Sports-2
Patriarca, Raymond	1	Pickett, Wilson, Jr.	1960s-2
Patrick, (Curtis) Lester	Sports-2	Picon, Molly	3
Patterson, Floyd	1960s-2, Sports-2	Pidgeon, Walter	1
Patterson, Louise Alone Thompson	5	Pierce, Samuel Riley, Jr.	6
Pauley, Edwin Wendell	1	Pike, James Albert, Jr.	1960s-2
Pauling, Linus Carl	4, 1960s-2	Pillsbury, Philip Winston	1
Payton, Walter Jerry	5, Sports-2	Pincay, Laffit Alegando, Jr.	Sports-2
Peabody, Endicott ("Chub")	5	Piñero, Miguel	2
Peale, Norman Vincent	3, 1960s-2	Piore, Emanuel Ruben ("Mannie")	6
Pearl, Daniel ("Danny")	6	Pippen, Scottie	Sports-2
Pearl, Minnie	4	Plath, Sylvia	1960s-2
Peckinpah, David Samuel ("Sam")	1, 1960s-2	Plough, Abe	1
Pedersen, Charles John	2	Podhoretz, Norman Harold	1960s-2
Peerce, Jan	1	Pogue, Forrest Carlisle	4
Pei, I(eoh) M(ing)	1960s-2	Poitier, Sidney	1960s-2
Pendleton, Clarence Mclane, Jr.	2	Pollard, Frederick Douglass ("Fritz")	2, Sports-2
Penick, Harvey Morrison	4	Pollard, James Clifford ("Jim")	Sports-2
Penn, Arthur Hiller	1960s-2	Ponnamperuma, Cyril Andrew	4
Penske, Roger S.	Sports-2	Ponselle, Rosa Melba	1
Pep, Willie	Sports-2	Pool, Ithiel de Sola	1
Peppard, George	4	Pope, Generoso Paul, Jr.	2
Pepper, Claude Denson	2	Pope, James Soule, Sr.	1
Percy, Walker	2, 1960s-2	Porter, Katherine Anne	1960s-2
Perkins, Anthony	3	Porter, Sylvia Field	3
Perkins, Carl Lee	5	Postel, Jonathan Bruce	5
Perkins, Dexter	1	Potok, Chaim Tzvi	6
Perkins, James Alfred	5, 1960s-2	Potvin, Denis Charles	Sports-2
Perkins, (Richard) Marlin	2	Pousette-Dart, Richard Warren	3
Perlmutter, Nathan	2	Povich, Shirley Lewis	5, Sports-2
Perls, Laura	2	Powell, Adam Clayton, Jr.	1960s-2
Perot, H(enry) Ross	1960s-2	Powell, Eleanor Torrey ("Ellie")	1
Perpich, Rudolph George ("Rudy")	4	Powell, Lewis Franklin, Jr.	5
Perry, Harold Robert	3	Powell, William Horatio	1
Perry, Lincoln. See Fetchit, Stepin.		Powers, Francis Gary ("Frank")	1960s-2
Persichetti, Vincent Ludwig	2	Powers, J(ames) F(arl)	5
Peter, Laurence Johnston	2, 1960s-2	Praeger, Frederick Amos	4
Peter, Paul and Mary	1960s-2	Prefontaine, Steve Roland	Sports-2
Peterson, Esther	5	Preminger, Otto Ludwig	2
Peterson, Roger Tory	4	Presley, Elvis Aron	1960s-2
Petrillo, James Caesar	1	Presser, Jackie	2
Petry, Ann Lane	5	Preston, Robert	2
Pettit, Robert E. Lee, Jr. ("Bob")	Sports-2	Preus, Jacob Aall Ottesen, Jr. ("Jake")	4
Petty, Lee Arnold	6	Price, Cecil Ray	6
Petty, Richard Lee	Sports-2	Price, T(homas) Rowe, Jr.	1
Philbrick, Herbert Arthur	3	Price, Vincent Leonard, Jr.	3
Phillips, John Edmund Andrew	6, 1960s-2	Prichard, Edward Fretwell, Jr.	1

Subject	Volume	Subject	Volume
Pride, Charles Frank ("Charley")	1960s-2	Reber, Grote	6
Primrose, William	1	Red Thunder Cloud	4
Primus, Pearl Eileen	4	Redding, Otis	1960s-2
Prinz, Joachim	2	Redenbacher, Orville	4
Pritikin, Nathan	1	Redford, (Charles) Robert, Jr.	1960s-2
Pritzker, A(bram) N(icholas)	2	Reed, Donna	2
Pritzker, Jay Arthur	5	Reed, Willis, Jr.	Sports-2
Provenzano, Anthony ("Tony Pro")	2	Reeder, Russell Potter, Jr. ("Red")	5
Pryor, Richard Franklin Lenox Thomas	1960s-2	Reel, A(dolf) Frank	6
Pucinski, Roman Gordon	6	Reese, Harold Henry ("Pee Wee")	5, Sports-2
Puente, Ernest Anthony, Jr. ("Tito")	6	Regnery, Henry	4
Puller, Lewis Burwell, Jr.	4	Reines, Frederick	5
Purcell, Edward Mills	5	Reischauer, Edwin Oldfather	2, 1960s-2
Pusey, Nathan Marsh	6, 1960s-2	Remick, Lee Ann	3
Puzo, Mario	5, 1960s-2	Reshevsky, Samuel Herman	3
Pynchon, Thomas Ruggles, Jr.	1960s-2	Reston, James Barrett ("Scotty")	4, 1960s-2
Quarles, Benjamin Arthur	4	Retton, Mary Lou	Sports-2
Quesada, Elwood Richard ("Pete")	3	Reuss, Henry Schoellkopf	6
Questel, Mae	5	Reuther, Walter Philip	1960s-2
Quill, Michael Joseph ("Mike")	1960s-2	Revelle, Roger Randall Dougan	3
Quinlan, Karen Ann	1	Rexroth, Kenneth Charles Marion	1
Quinn, Anthony Rudolph Oaxaca	6, 1960s-2	Reynolds, Allie Pierce	4
Quintanilla Pérez, Selena. *See* Selena.		Reynolds, Frank	1
Quintero, José Benjamin	5	Rhodes, James Allen ("Jim")	6
Rabi, I(sidor) I(saac)	2	Ribicoff, Abraham Alexander	5
Raborn, William Francis, Jr. ("Red")	2	Rice, Grantland	Sports-2
Radbourn, Charles Gardner		Rice, Helen Steiner	1
("Charley"; "Old Hoss")	Sports-2	Rice, Jerry Lee	Sports-2
Radner, Gilda	2	Rich, Adrienne Cecile	1960s-2
Rado, James, and Gerome Ragni	1960s-2	Rich, Bernard ("Buddy")	2
Rafferty, Maxwell Lewis, Jr. ("Max")	1, 1960s-2	Rich, Charles Allan ("Charlie")	4
Ragni, Gerome. *See* Rado, James, and		Richards, Faith Buchner (Bucky)	6
Gerome Ragni.		Richards, Paul Rapier	2
Rainey, Homer Price	1	Richards, Robert Eugene ("Bob")	Sports-2
Rainwater, (Leo) James	2	Richardson, Elliot Lee	5
Ramone, Joey	6	Richter, Charles Francis	1
Rand, Ayn	1, 1960s-2	Rickard, George Lewis ("Tex")	Sports-2
Rand, Paul	4	Rickey, Branch Wesley	Sports-2
Randolph, Jennings	5	Rickles, Donald Jay ("Don")	1960s-2
Rather, Daniel Irvin ("Dan")	1960s-2	Rickover, Hyman George	2
Rauh, Joseph Louis, Jr.	3	Ridder, Bernard Herman, Jr. ("Bernie")	6
Rauschenberg, Robert	1960s-2	Ridder, Eric	4
Rawls, John Bordley	6	Riddle, Nelson Smock, Jr.	1
Ray, Aldo	3	Riddleberger, James Williams	1
Ray, Dixy Lee	4	Ridgway, Matthew Bunker	3
Ray, Gordon Norton	2	Riding, Laura	3
Ray, James Earl	5, 1960s-2	Riesel, Victor	4
Ray, John Alvin ("Johnnie")	2	Riesman, David, Jr.	6
Raye, Martha	4	Rigby, Cathy	1960s-2, Sports-2
Reagan, Ronald Wilson	1960s-2	Riggs, Ralph Smith	1
Reasoner, Harry	3	Riggs, Robert Larimore ("Bobby")	4, Sports-2

Subject	Volume
Riley, Pat(rick) James	Sports-2
Ringo, James Stephen ("Jim")	Sports-2
Ripken, Cal(vin) Edward, Jr.	Sports-2
Ripley, Elmer Horton	1
Ripley, S(idney) Dillon, II	6
Ritt, Martin	2
Ritts, Herbert, Jr. ("Herb")	6
Rivero, Horacio, Jr.	6
Rivers, Larry	6, 1960s-2
Rizzo, Frank Lazzaro	3
Roach, Harold Eugene ("Hal")	3
Robards, Jason Nelson, Jr.	6, 1960s-2
Robbins, Harold	5
Robbins, Jerome	5, 1960s-2
Robbins, Marty	1
Roberts, Oral	1960s-2
Roberts, Robin Evan	Sports-2
Robertson, Marion Gordon ("Pat")	1960s-2
Robertson, Oscar Palmer	Sports-2
Robinson, Brooks Calbert, Jr.	Sports-2
Robinson, David Maurice	Sports-2
Robinson, Earl	3
Robinson, Edward Gay ("Eddie")	Sports-2
Robinson, Frank, Jr.	1960s-2, Sports-2
Robinson, Jack Roosevelt ("Jackie")	Sports-2
Robinson, Julia Bowman	1
Robinson, Ray ("Sugar Ray")	2, Sports-2
Robinson, Roscoe, Jr.	3
Robinson, William, Jr. ("Smokey")	1960s-2
Robustelli, Andrew ("Andy")	Sports-2
Rock, John Charles	1
Rockefeller, David	1960s-2
Rockefeller, John Davison, III	1960s-2
Rockefeller, Nelson Aldrich	1960s-2
Rockne, Knute Kenneth	Sports-2
Rodale, Robert	2
Rodbell, Martin	5
Roddenberry, Eugene Wesley ("Gene")	3, 1960s-2
Rodgers, William Henry ("Bill")	Sports-2
Rodriguez, Alex Emmanuel	Sports-2
Rogers, Carl Ransom	2
Rogers, Charles ("Buddy")	5
Rogers, Ginger	4
Rogers, Roy	5
Rogers, William Pierce	6
Roland, Gilbert	4
Rome, Esther Rachel Seidman	4
Romero, Cesar	4
Romney, George Wilcken	4
Ronstadt, Linda	1960s-2
Rooney, Arthur Joseph, Sr. ("Art")	2, Sports-2

Subject	Volume
Roosevelt, James	3
Rose, Frederick Phineas	5
Rose, Peter Edward ("Pete")	Sports-2
Rosenberg, Anna Marie Lederer	1
Rosenberg, William ("Bill")	6
Rosenquist, James Albert	1960s-2
Rosie the Riveter. *See* Monroe, Rose Leigh Will.	
Ross, Diana Earle	1960s-2
Ross, Steven Jay	3
Rosten, Leo Calvin	5
Rosten, Norman	4
Rostow, Eugene Victor Debs	6
Rostow, Walter Whitman ("Walt")	1960s-2
Roszak, Theodore	1, 1960s-2
Rote, Kyle, Jr.	Sports-2
Rote, (William) Kyle, Sr.	6
Roth, Henry	4
Roth, Philip Milton	1960s-2
Rothko, Mark	1960s-2
Rothwax, Harold J(ay)	5
Rountree, Martha	5
Rous, (Francis) Peyton	1960s-2
Rouse, James Wilson	4
Roush, Edd J.	2
Rowan, Carl T(homas)	6
Rowan, Dan Hale	2
Royko, Mike	5
Rozelle, Alvin Ray ("Pete")	4, 1960s-2, Sports-2
Rózsa, Miklós	4
Rubell, Steve	2
Rubin, Jerry Clyde	4, 1960s-2
Rubinstein, Arthur	1
Ruby, John ("Jack")	1960s-2
Rudin, Lewis ("Lew")	6
Rudolph, Paul Marvin	5
Rudolph, Wilma Glodean	4, 1960s-2, Sports-2
Ruffin, Davis Eli ("David")	3, 1960s-2
Ruffing, Charles Herbert ("Red")	2
Runyon, Damon	Sports-2
Rupp, Adolph Frederick	Sports-2
Ruppert, Jacob	Sports-2
Rusk, (David) Dean	4, 1960s-2
Rusk, Howard Archibald	2
Russell, Charles Hinton	2
Russell, Richard Brevard, Jr. ("Dick")	1960s-2
Russell, William Felton ("Bill")	1960s-2, Sports-2
Rustin, Bayard Taylor	2, 1960s-2
Ruth, George Herman ("Babe")	Sports-2

Subject	Volume
Rutherford, Maude Russell	6
Ryan, John Dale	1
Ryan, John William ("Jack")	3
Ryan, (Lynn) Nolan, Jr.	Sports-2
Ryskind, Morrie	1
Ryun, James Ronald ("Jim")	1960s-2, Sports-2
Saarinen, Eero	1960s-2
Sabin, Albert Bruce	3, 1960s-2
Sachar, Abram Leon	3
Sackler, Arthur Mitchell	2
Sackler, Howard Oliver	1960s-2
Saddler, Joseph ("Sandy")	6
Sagan, Carl Edward	4
Sagan, Ginetta Teresa Moroni	6
St. Johns, Adela Rogers	2
Sainte-Marie, Buffy	1960s-2
Salant, Richard S.	3
Salinger, J(erome) D(avid)	1960s-2
Salisbury, Harrison Evans	3, 1960s-2
Salk, Jonas Edward	4
Salk, Lee	3
Salmon, Wesley C(harles)	6
Salt, Waldo	2
Salvi, John C., III	4
Samora, Julian	1960s-2
Sampras, Peter ("Pete")	Sports-2
Samuels, Howard Joseph ("Howie the Horse")	1
Samuelson, Paul Anthony	1960s-2
Sande, Earl	Sports-2
Sanders, Barry	Sports-2
Sanders, Deion Luwynn	Sports-2
Sanders, Harlan David ("Colonel")	1960s-2
Sanders, Summer Elisabeth	Sports-2
Sanford, (James) Terry	5
Sarazen, Gene	5, Sports-2
Saroyan, William	1
Sarton, May	4
Sassoon, Vidal	1960s-2
Savalas, Aristoteles ("Telly")	4
Savio, Mario	4, 1960s-2
Savitch, Jessica Beth	1
Sawchuk, Terrance Gordon ("Terry")	Sports-2
Sawhill, John Crittenden	6
Sayers, Gale Eugene	Sports-2
Scali, John Alfred	4
Scarne, John	1
Scarry, Richard McClure	4
Schaap, Richard Jay ("Dick")	6
Schacht, Al(exander)	1
Schaffner, Franklin James	2

Subject	Volume
Schapiro, Meyer	4
Schawlow, Arthur Leonard	5
Schayes, Adolph ("Dolph")	Sports-2
Schechner, Richard	1960s-2
Schell, Jonathan Edward	1960s-2
Schiff, Dorothy	2
Schindler, Alexander Moshe	6
Schirra, Walter Marty, Jr. ("Wally")	1960s-2
Schlafly, Phyllis Stewart	1960s-2
Schlamme, Martha Haftel	1
Schlesinger, Arthur Meier, Jr.	1960s-2
Schmidt, Joseph Paul ("Joe")	Sports-2
Schmidt, Michael Jack ("Mike")	Sports-2
Schmidt, Milt(on) Conrad	Sports-2
Schneerson, Menachem Mendel	4
Schneider, Alan	1
Schoenbrun, David Franz	2
Schollander, Don(ald) Arthur	Sports-2
Schuller, Gunther Alexander	1960s-2
Schultz, David Lesky ("Dave")	4
Schultz, Theodore William	5
Schulz, Charles M(onroe)	6
Schuman, William Howard	3
Schuyler, James Marcus	3
Schwann, William Joseph	5
Schwartz, Arthur	1
Schwartzwalder, Floyd Burdette ("Ben")	3
Schwerner, Michael Henry. See Chaney, James Earl, Andrew Goodman, and Michael Henry Schwerner.	
Schwinger, Julian Seymour	4, 1960s-2
Scott, Austin Wakeman	1
Scott, George C(ampbell)	5, 1960s-2
Scott, Hazel Dorothy	1
Scott, Hugh Doggett, Jr.	4
Scott, (George) Randolph	2
Scott, Roland Boyd	6
Scourby, Alexander	1
Scribner, Charles, Jr.	4
Scully, Vin(cent) Edward	Sports-2
Seaborg, Glenn Theodore	5, 1960s-2
Seale, Robert George ("Bobby")	1960s-2
Searle, John Gideon ("Jack")	1960s-2
Seasongood, Murray	1
Seaver, George Thomas ("Tom")	1960s-2, Sports-2
Seeger, Peter R. ("Pete")	1960s-2
Segal, George	6, 1960s-2
Segrè, Emilio Gino	2
Selby, Hubert, Jr.	1960s-2

Subject	Volume
Seldes, George Henry	4
Selena	4
Selmon, Lee Roy	Sports-2
Selznick, Irene Mayer	2
Sendak, Maurice Bernard	1960s-2
Sepkoski, J(oseph) John, Jr.	5
Serkin, Rudolf	3
Serling, Rodman Edward ("Rod")	1960s-2
Sert, José Luis	1
Sessions, Roger Huntington	1, 1960s-2
Seuss, Dr., *See* Geisel, Theodor S.	
Sevareid, (Arnold) Eric	3
Sexton, Anne	1960s-2
Seymour, Whitney North	1
Shaara, Michael Joseph, Jr.	2
Shabazz, Betty Jean	5
Shakur, Tupac Amaru	4
Shanker, Albert ("Al")	5, 1960s-2
Shannon, Claude Elwood	6
Shannon, William Vincent	2
Shapiro, Karl Jay	6, 1960s-2
Sharkey, Jack	4
Shaw, Irwin Gilbert	1
Shaw, Robert Lawson	5
Shawn, William	3
Shearer, (Edith) Norma	1
Sheed, Francis Joseph ("Frank")	1
Sheehan, Cornelius Mahoney ("Neil")	1960s-2
Shepard, Alan Bartlett, Jr.	1960s-2, 5
Shepley, James Robinson	2
Sheppard, Eugenia Benbow	1
Sherwood, Roberta	5
Shields, Cornelius	1
Shils, Edward Albert	4
Shilts, Randy Martin	4
Shimkin, Leon	2
Shirer, William Lawrence	3
Shivers, (Robert) Allan	1
Shockley, William Bradford	2
Shoemaker, William Lee ("Bill")	1960s-2, Sports-2
Shook, Karel Francis Antony	1
Shore, Dinah	4, 1960s-2
Shore, Edward William ("Eddie")	1, Sports-2
Shorter, Frank Charles	Sports-2
Shoup, David Monroe	1, 1960s-2
Shriver, Eunice Mary Kennedy	1960s-2
Shriver, (Robert) Sargent, Jr.	1960s-2
Shula, Don(ald) Francis	Sports-2
Shull, Clifford Glenwood	6
Shulman, Max	2
Shultz, George Pratt	1960s-2
Shuster, Joseph E.	3
Sidney, Sylvia	5
Siegel, Don	3
Siegel, Jerome ("Jerry")	4
Sillman, Leonard Dexter	1
Sills, Beverly	1960s-2
Silvers, Phil	1
Silverstein, Shel(don) Allan	5
Simmons, Al(oysius) Harry	Sports-2
Simon, Herbert A(lexander)	6
Simon, (Marvin) Neil	1960s-2
Simon, Norton Winfred	3
Simon, Paul, and Art Garfunkel	1960s-2
Simon, William E(dward)	6
Simpson, Adele Smithline	4
Simpson, Alan	5
Simpson, Orenthal James ("O. J.")	Sports-2
Simpson, Wallis Warfield. *See* Windsor, Wallis Warfield (Simpson), Duchess of.	
Sinatra, Francis Albert ("Frank")	5
Singer, Isaac Bashevis	3, 1960s-2
Sirhan, Sirhan Bishara	1960s-2
Sirica, John Joseph	3
Sirk, Douglas	2
Sisk, Mildred Elizabeth. *See* Gillars, Mildred Elizabeth Sisk ("Axis Sally").	
Siskel, Eugene Kal ("Gene")	5
Siskind, Aaron	3
Sisler, George Harold	Sports-2
Sitter, Carl Leonard	6
Skelton, Richard Bernard ("Red")	5
Skinner, B(urrhus) F(rederic)	2
Skolsky, Sidney	1
Slaughter, Enos Bradsher (Country)	6
Slayton, Donald Kent ("Deke")	3
Slick, Grace Wing	1960s-2
Sloan, James Forman ("Tod")	Sports-2
Sloane, Eric	1
Slonimsky, Nicolas (Nikolai Leonidovich)	4
Smith, Ada Beatrice Queen Victoria Louisa Virginia. *See* Bricktop.	
Smith, C(yrus) R(owlett)	2
Smith, David Roland	1960s-2
Smith, Dean Edwards	Sports-2
Smith, Emmitt James, III	Sports-2
Smith, Hazel Brannon	1960s-2
Smith, Henry Nash	2
Smith, Howard K(ingsbury)	6

Subject	Volume
Smith, John William	Sports-2
Smith, Joseph	3
Smith, Kathryn Elizabeth ("Kate")	2
Smith, Margaret Chase	4
Smith, Osborne Earl ("Ozzie")	Sports-2
Smith, (Charles) Page (Ward)	4
Smith, Ralph Corbett	5
Smith, Robert Emil ("Buffalo Bob")	5
Smith, Robert Weston. *See* Wolfman Jack.	
Smith, Walter Wellesley ("Red")	1, 1960s-2, Sports-2
Smith, William French	2
Smothers, Thomas ("Tom"), and Richard ("Dick") Smothers	
Smucker, Paul Highnam	5
Snead, Samuel Jackson ("Sam")	6, Sports-2
Snell, George Davis	4
Snelling, Richard Arkwright	3
Snider, Edwin Donald ("Duke")	Sports-2
Snow, Clarence Eugene ("Hank")	5
Snyder, James ("Jimmy the Greek")	4, Sports-2
Snyder, John Wesley	1
Snyder, Mitch(ell) Darryl	2
Soloveitchik, Joseph Baer	3
Solti, Georg	5
Sondheim, Stephen Joshua	1960s-2
Sonny and Cher	1960s-2
Sontag, Susan	1960s-2
Sorensen, Theodore Chaikin ("Ted")	1960s-2
Sosa, Samuel Peralta ("Sammy")	Sports-2
Sothern, Ann	6
Soule, Gertrude May	2
Southern, Terry Marion, Jr.	4, 1960s-2
Soyer, Raphael	2
Spahn, Warren Edward	Sports-2
Spalding, Albert Goodwill ("A.G.")	Sports-2
Spanel, Abram Nathaniel	1
Sparkman, John Jackson	1
Speaker, Tris(tram) E.	Sports-2
Speck, Richard Benjamin	3
Spector, Philip Harvey ("Phil")	1960s-2
Spence, Floyd D(avidson)	6
Sperry, Roger Wolcott	4
Spiegel, Sam(uel)	1
Spitz, Mark Andrew	Sports-2
Spock, Benjamin McLane ("Dr. Spock")	5
Stacy, Jess Alexandria	4
Stagg, Amos Alonzo, Sr.	Sports-2
Staggers, Harley Orrin	3
Staley, Dawn	Sports-2

Subject	Volume
Stanford, Sally	1
Stanley, Kim	6
Stans, Maurice Hubert	5
Stanwyck, Barbara	2
Stargell, Wilver Dornel ("Willie")	6
Starr, Bryan Bartlett ("Bart")	Sports-2
Starzl, Thomas. *See* Moore, Francis Daniels, and Thomas Earl Starzl.	
Stassen, Harold Edward	6
Staubach, Roger Thomas	Sports-2
Steber, Eleanor	2
Steel, Dawn Leslie	5
Stegner, Wallace Earle	3
Steiger, Rodney Stephen ("Rod")	6, 1960s-2
Stein, Aaron Marc	1
Stein, Herbert	5, 1960s-2
Stein, Julian Caesar ("Jules")	1
Steinbeck, John Ernst	1960s-2
Steinberg, Saul	5
Steinbrenner, George Michael, III	Sports-2
Steinem, Gloria Marie	1960s-2
Steiner, Ralph	2
Stella, Frank Philip	1960s-2
Steloff, (Ida) Frances	2
Stengel, Charles Dillon ("Casey")	Sports-2
Stennis, John Cornelius	4
Stephens, Woodford Cefis ("Woody")	5, Sports-2
Sterling, J(ohn) E(wart) Wallace	1
Stern, Curt	1
Stern, David	Sports-2
Stern, Isaac	6
Stern, William ("Bill")	Sports-2
Stevens, Brooks	4
Stevenson, Adlai Ewing	1960s-2
Stewart, Ellen	1960s-2
Stewart, James Maitland ("Jimmy")	5
Stewart, Leroy Elliott ("Slam")	2
Stewart, (William) Payne	5
Stewart, Potter	1
Stibitz, George Robert	4
Stills, Stephen. *See* Crosby, Stills, and Nash.	
Stockton, John Houston	Sports-2
Stoessel, Walter John, Jr.	2
Stokes, Anson Phelps, Jr.	2
Stokes, Carl Burton	4, 1960s-2
Stokes, Colin	1
Stone, Edward Durell	1960s-2
Stone, I. F.	2, 1960s-2
Stone, Irving	2
Stone, Lawrence	5
Stone, W(illiam) Clement	6

Subject	Volume
Stoneham, Horace Charles	2
Stookey, Paul. *See* Peter, Paul and Mary.	
Strand, Kaj Aage	6
Strasberg, Lee	1
Strasberg, Susan Elizabeth	5
Stratton, Monty Franklin Pierce ("Gander")	1
Stratton, William Grant	6
Street, George Levick, III	6
Street, Picabo	Sports-2
Streisand, Barbra	1960s-2
Strode, Woodrow Wilson Woolwine ("Woody")	4
Strout, Richard Lee	2
Struble, Arthur Dewey	1
Stuart, Jesse Hilton	1
Sturgeon, Theodore	1
Sturges, John	3
Styne, Jule	4
Styron, William Clark, Jr.	1960s-2
Sublett, John William. *See* Bubbles, John William.	
Suggs, (Mae) Louise	Sports-2
Sullivan, Edward Vincent ("Ed")	1960s-2
Sullivan, John Lawrence	Sports-2
Sullivan, Leon Howard	6
Sullivan, Walter Seager, Jr.	4
Sulzberger, Cyrus Leo	3
Sulzberger, Iphigene Bertha Ochs	2
Summitt, Pat(ricia) Head	Sports-2
Sun Ra	3
Suomi, Verner Edward	4
Susskind, David Howard	2, 1960s-2
Sutton, Carol	1
Swanberg, W(illiam) A(ndrew)	3
Swanson, Gloria	1
Swanson, Robert Arthur	5
Swayze, John Cameron	4
Sweeney, James Johnson	2
Swoopes, Sheryl Denise	Sports-2
Symington, (William) Stuart, III	2
Szent-Györgyi, Albert (von Nagyrapolt)	2
Szulc, Tadeusz Witold ("Tad")	6
Taft, Robert, Jr.	3
Talma, Louise Juliette	4
Talmadge, Herman Eugene	6
Tandy, Charles David	1960s-2
Tandy, Jessica	4
Tanny, Victor Anthony ("Vic")	1
Tarkenton, Fran(cis) Asbury	Sports-2

Subject	Volume
Tarski, Alfred	1
Tartikoff, Brandon	5
Tatum, Reece ("Goose")	Sports-2
Taussig, Helen Brooke	2
Tavoulareas, William Peter	4
Tax, Sol	4
Taylor, Glen Hearst	1
Taylor, Harold Alexander	3
Taylor, Lawrence Julius ("LT")	Sports-2
Taylor, Marshall Walter ("Major")	Sports-2
Taylor, Maxwell Davenport	2, 1960s-2
Taylor, Peter Hillsman	4
Taylor, Telford	5
Temin, Howard Martin	4
Terry, Luther Leonidas	1
Terry, Megan	1960s-2
Terry, Walter	1
Terry, William Harold ("Bill")	2, Sports-2
Thomas, Danny	3
Thomas, David R. ("Dave"). *See* Thomas, Rex David ("Dave")	
Thomas, Isiah Lord, III	Sports-2
Thomas, Lewis	3
Thomas, Lowell Jackson	1
Thomas, Marlo	1960s-2
Thomas, Rex David ("Dave")	6, 1960s-2
Thomas, Robert McG(ill), Jr.	6
Thompson, David O'Neal	Sports-2
Thompson, Hunter S(tockton)	1960s-2
Thompson, John Robert, Jr.	Sports-2
Thompson, Kay	5
Thompson, Llewellyn E., Jr. ("Tommy")	1960s-2
Thompson, (Ira) Randall	1
Thomson, Virgil Garnett	2
Thorpe, James Francis ("Jim")	Sports-2
Tien, Chang-Lin	6
Tierney, Gene Eliza	3
Tilberis, Elizabeth Jane Kelly ("Liz")	5
Tilden, William Tatem, Jr. ("Bill")	Sports-2
Tillstrom, Burr	1
Tiny Tim (Herbert Butros Khaury)	4
Tittle, Y(elberton) A(braham), Jr.	Sports-2
Tobin, James	6
Tombaugh, Clyde William	5
Tormé, Mel(vin) Howard	5
Torre, Joseph Paul ("Joe")	Sports-2
Touré, Kwame. *See* Carmichael, Stokely.	
Tower, John Goodwin	3
Townes, Charles Hard	1960s-2
Townsend, Lynn Alfred	6, 1960s-2

Subject	Volume
Trabert, Marion Anthony ("Tony")	Sports-2
Tracy, Arthur	5
Trafficante, Santo, Jr.	2
Trapp, Maria von	2
Travers, Mary. *See* Peter, Paul and Mary.	
Traynor, Harold Joseph ("Pie")	Sports-2
Tree, Mary Endicott Peabody FitzGerald ("Marietta")	3
Trevino, Lee Buck	Sports-2
Trevor, Claire	6
Trigère, Pauline	6
Trilling, Diana Rubin	4
Trilling, Lionel	1960s-2
Trippe, Juan Terry	1
Trippi, Charles Louis ("Charley")	Sports-2
Trout, Robert	6
Truman, Bess Wallace	1
Trump, Frederick Christ	5
Tsongas, Paul Efthemios	5
Tubb, Ernest Dale	1
Tuchman, Barbara Wertheim	2
Tudor, Antony	2
Tukey, John W(ilder)	6
Tully, Alice Bigelow	3
Tully, Grace	1
Tunney, James Joseph ("Gene")	Sports-2
Tupper, Earl Silas	1
Turé, Kwame. *See* Carmichael, Stokely.	
Turner, Clyde Douglas ("Bulldog")	5, Sports-2
Turner, Francis Cutler ("Frank")	5
Turner, Ike and Tina	1960s-2
Turner, Joseph Vernon ("Big Joe")	1
Turner, Lana	4
Turner, Tina. *See* Turner, Ike and Tina.	
Twining, Nathan Farragut	1
Twitty, Conway	3
Tyson, Michael Gerard ("Mike"; "Iron Mike")	Sports-2
Tyus, Wyomia	Sports-2
Udall, Morris King	5
Ulam, Stanislaw Marcin	1
Ullman, Al(bert) Conrad	2
Unitas, John Constantine ("Johnny")	6, 1960s-2, Sports-2,
Unruh, Jesse Marvin	2
Unser, Al(fred), Jr.	Sports-2
Unser, Al(fred), Sr.	Sports-2
Updike, John Hoyer	1960s-2
Upshaw, Eugene Thurman, Jr. ("Gene")	Sports-2
Urban, Matt Louis	4
Urey, Harold Clayton	1
Uris, Harold David	1
Ussachevsky, Vladimir Alexis	2
Valentine, Thomas ("Kid")	2
Vallee, Hubert Prior ("Rudy")	2
Valvano, James Thomas ("Jim")	3
Van Andel, Jay. *See* DeVos, Richard Marvin, and Jay Van Andel.	
Van Arsdale, Harry, Jr.	2
Van Brocklin, Norm(an) Mack ("The Dutchman")	1, Sports-2
Van Buren, Stephen Wood ("Steve")	Sports-2
Vance, Cyrus Roberts	6, 1960s-2
Vanderbilt, William Henry	1
VanDerZee, James Augustus Joseph	1
Van Dyke, Richard Wayne ("Dick")	1960s-2
Van Fleet, James Alward	3
Van Heusen, James ("Jimmy")	2
Van Niel, Cornelis Bernardus. *See* Niel, Cornelis Bernardus Van.	
Vann, John Paul	1960s-2
Vare, Glenna Collett	2
Vargas, Alberto ("Varga")	1
Varipapa, Andrew ("Andy")	1, Sports-2
Vaughan, Sarah Lois	2
Vaughan, Stevie Ray	2
Vaughn, Richard Smith ("Billy")	3
Veeck, William Louis, Jr. ("Bill")	2, Sports-2
Velde, Harold Himmel	1
Venturi, Robert	1960s-2
Vera. *See* Neumann, Vera Salaff.	3
Verdon, Gwyneth Evelyn ("Gwen")	6
Vernon, Lillian	1960s-2
Vernon, Raymond	5
Vicente, Esteban	6
Vidal, Gore	1960s-2
Vidor, King Wallis	1
Villella, Edward Joseph	1960s-2
Vines, Henry Ellsworth, Jr. ("Elly")	Sports-2
Vinson, Carl	1
Voight, Jon	1960s-2
Volpe, John Anthony	4
Von Békésy, Georg. *See* Békésy, Georg von.	
Von Braun, Wernher	1960s-2
Vonnegut, Kurt, Jr.	1960s-2
von Trapp, Maria. *See* Trapp, Maria von.	
Voorhis, Horace Jeremiah ("Jerry")	1
Vreeland, Diana	2, 1960s-2

Subject	Volume
Waddell, George Edward ("Rube")	Sports-2
Wade, Henry Menasco	6
Wagner, John Peter ("Honus")	Sports-2
Wagner, Robert Ferdinand	3
Walcott, "Jersey Joe"	4
Wald, George David	5, 1960s-2
Walker, (Ewell) Doak, Jr.	5, Sports-2
Walker, Edward Patrick ("Mickey")	1, Sports-2
Walker, Edwin Anderson	3
Walker, Fred ("Dixie")	1
Walker, Junior	4
Walker, Moses Fleetwood ("Fleet")	Sports-2
Walker, Nancy	3
Walker, Roberto Clemente. *See* Clemente, Roberto Walker.	
Wallace, Christopher George Latore. *See* Notorious B.I.G.	
Wallace, (William Roy) DeWitt, and Lila (Bell) Acheson Wallace	1
Wallace, George Corley, Jr.	5, 1960s-2
Wallace, Irving	2
Wallace, Mike	1960s-2
Wallace, Sippie	2
Wallenstein, Alfred Franz	1
Wallis, Harold Brent ("Hal")	2
Wallis, W(ilson) Allen	5
Walsh, Ed(ward) Augustine	Sports-2
Walsh, William ("Bill")	Sports-2
Walston, Ray	6
Walt, Lewis William	2
Walton, Samuel Moore ("Sam")	3, 1960s-2
Walton, William Theodore, III ("Bill")	Sports-2
Wanderone, Rudolf. *See* Minnesota Fats.	
Waner, Lloyd James ("Little Poison")	1
Wang, An	2, 1960s-2
Ward, John Montgomery	Sports-2
Ward, John William	1
Warfield, William Caesar	6
Warhol, Andy	2, 1960s-2
Waring, Fred(eric) Malcolm	1
Warmerdam, Cornelius Anthony ("Dutch")	Sports-2
Warne, Colston Estey	2
Warner, Glenn Scobey ("Pop")	Sports-2
Warnke, Paul Culliton	6
Warren, Earl	1960s-2
Warren, Harry	1
Warren, Robert Penn	2
Warwick, Dionne	1960s-2
Washburn, Sherwood L(arned)	6

Subject	Volume
Washington, Chester Lloyd, Jr. ("Chet")	1
Washington, Harold	2
Wasserman, Lewis Robert ("Lew")	6
Waterfield, Robert Staton ("Bob")	1, Sports-2
Waters, Muddy	1
Watson, James Dewey	1960s-2
Watson, Thomas John, Jr.	3, 1960s-2
Watson, Thomas Sturges ("Tom")	Sports-2
Watts, André	1960s-2
Watts, John Everett	1
Weatherspoon, Teresa	Sports-2
Weaver, Robert Clifton	5, 1960s-2
Weaver, Sylvester Laflin, Jr. (Pat)	6
Webb, James Edwin	3
Webb, James Layne ("Jimmy")	1960s-2
Webb, John Randolph ("Jack")	1
Weber, Joseph	6
Weber, Pete	Sports-2
Wechsler, David	1
Wechsler, Herbert	6
Wechsler, James Arthur	1
Wedemeyer, Albert Coady	2
Weese, Harry Mohr	5
Weil, André	5
Weinberg, Harry	2
Weiner, Lazar	1
Weinmeister, Arnold George ("Arnie")	6
Weiss, Paul	6
Weiss, Paul Alfred	2
Weisskopf, Victor Frederick	6
Weissmuller, Peter John ("Johnny")	1, Sports-2
Welch, Raquel	1960s-2
Welch, Robert Henry Winborne, Jr.	1
Welk, Lawrence LeRoy	3
Wellek, René Maria Eduard	4, 1960s-2
Welles, Orson	1
Wells, Herman B.	6
Wells, Mary Esther	3
Wells, Willie James	Sports-2
Wellstone, Paul David	6
Welty, Eudora Alice	6
Wescott, Glenway	2
West, Cromwell Ashbie Hawkins. *See* Red Thunder Cloud.	
West, Dorothy	5
West, Jerry Alan	Sports-2
West, (Mary) Jessamyn	1
Westmoreland, William Childs	1960s-2
Wharton, Clifton Reginald, Jr.	1960s-2
Wheeler, Earle Gilmore	1960s-2

Subject	Volume
Wheeler, Raymond Milner	1
Whitaker, Rogers E(rnest) M(alcolm) ("E. M. Frimbo")	1
White, Byron Raymond	6
White, E(lwyn) B(rooks)	1
White, Edward Higgins, II	1960s-2
White, Jack Edward, Sr.	2
White, Reginald Howard ("Reggie")	Sports-2
White, Ryan	2
White, Theodore Harold ("Teddy")	2, 1960s-2
Whitehead, Don(ald) Ford	1
Whitfield, Mal(vin) Greston	Sports-2
Whitney, Betsey Maria Cushing	5
Whitney, John Hay	1
Whitney, Ruth Reinke	5
Whitten, Jamie Lloyd	4
Whyte, William Foote	6
Whyte, William Hollingsworth, Jr.	5
Wiebe, Robert H(uddleston)	6
Wiesner, Jerome Bert	4, 1960s-2
Wiggins, James Russell ("Russ")	6
Wigner, Eugene Paul	4, 1960s-2
Wildavsky, Aaron Bernard	3
Wilder, Samuel ("Billy")	6
Wilentz, David Theodore	2
Wilhelm, (James) Hoyt	6
Wilkens, Leonard Randolph ("Lenny")	Sports-2
Wilkins, Roy	1, 1960s-2
Wilkinson, Charles Burnham ("Bud")	4, Sports-2
Williams, Edward Bennett	2
Williams, G(erhard) Mennen	2
Williams, Hosea Lorenzo	6
Williams, Joe	5
Williams, John Bell	1
Williams, John James	2
Williams, Mary Lou	1
Williams, Roy Lee	2
Williams, Sherley Anne	5
Williams, Theodore Samuel ("Ted")	6, Sports-2
Williams, Thomas Lanier, III ("Tennessee")	1
Williams, Venus Ebone Starr	Sports-2
Williams, William Appleman	2, 1960s-2
Williams, William B.	2
Williams, William Carlos	1960s-2
Wills, Garry	1960s-2
Wills (Moody), Helen Newington	5, Sports-2
Willson, (Robert Reiniger) Meredith	1
Wilson, Brian Douglas	1960s-2
Wilson, Carl Dean	5
Wilson, Earl	2
Wilson, Flip	5
Wilson, Joseph Chamberlain	1960s-2
Wilson, Lewis Robert ("Hack")	Sports-2
Wilson, Logan	2
Wilson, Robert R(athbun)	6
Wilson, Theodore Shaw ("Teddy")	2
Windsor, Wallis Warfield (Simpson), Duchess of	2
Winfield, David Mark ("Dave")	Sports-2
Winogrand, Garry	1
Winslow, Kellen Boswell	Sports-2
Wisdom, John Minor	5
Wiseman, Frederick	1960s-2
Wojnarowicz, David Michael	3
Wolfe, Thomas Kennerly, Jr. ("Tom")	1960s-2
Wolfman Jack (Robert Weston Smith)	4, 1960s-2
Wonder, Stevie	1960s-2
Wood, Beatrice	5
Wood, Evelyn Nielsen	4
Wood, Natalie	1, 1960s-2
Wood, Robert Dennis	2
Woodard, Lynette	Sports-2
Woodcock, Leonard Freel	6
Wooden, John Robert	1960s-2, Sports-2
Woodruff, Robert Winship	1
Woods, Eldrick ("Tiger")	Sports-2
Woodward, C(omer) Vann	5, 1960s-2
Woodward, Joanne Gignilliat	1960s-2
Woodward, Robert Burns	1960s-2
Worthy, James Ager	Sports-2
Wright, Louis Booker	1
Wright, Olgivanna Lloyd	1
Wright, Sewall	2
Wright, William Henry ("Harry")	Sports-2
Wu, Chien-Shiung [Jianshiung]	5
Wurf, Jerome	1
Wyeth, Nathaniel Convers	2
Wyler, William ("Willi")	1
Wylie, Chalmers Pangburn	5
Wynette, Tammy	5, 1960s-2
Wynn, Early, Jr. ("Gus")	5
Wyzanski, Charles Edward, Jr.	2
Yamaguchi, Kristi Tsuya	Sports-2
Yamasaki, Minoru	2
Yarborough, Ralph Webster	4
Yarmolinsky, Adam	6
Yarrow, Peter. *See* Peter, Paul and Mary.	
Yastrzemski, Carl Michael, Jr.	1960s-2, Sports-2
Yates, Richard Walden	3

Subject	Volume	Subject	Volume
Yates, Sidney Richard	6	Zaharias, Mildred ("Babe") Didrikson.	
Yerby, Frank Garvin	3	*See* Didrikson Zaharias, Mildred	
Ylvisaker, Paul Norman	3	Ella ("Babe").	
Yorty, Samuel William	5	Zale, Tony	5, Sports-2
Yost, Charles Woodruff	1	Zamboni, Frank Joseph, Jr.	2
Young, Andrew Jackson, Jr.	1960s-2	Zappa, Francis Vincent ("Frank")	3, 1960s-2
Young, Claude, Jr. ("Buddy")	1	Zelazny, Roger Joseph	4
Young, Coleman Alexander	5	Zimbalist, Efrem Alexandrovich	1
Young, Denton True ("Cy")	Sports-2	Zinnemann, Alfred ("Fred")	5
Young, Jon Steven ("Steve")	Sports-2	Zoll, Paul Maurice	5
Young, Loretta	6	Zuckert, Eugene Martin	6
Young, Robert George	5	Zumwalt, Elmo Russell, Jr. ("Bud")	6
Young, Stephen Marvin	1	Zuppke, Robert Carl ("Bob")	Sports-2
Youngman, Henny	5	Zwicker, Ralph Wise	3
Zacharias, Jerrold Reinach	2	Zworykin, Vladimir Kosma	1

ISBN 0-684-31292-1

90000